Irlande
Englande
Denmarke
Lowe Countries
Germanie
France
Spaigne
Italie
Barbarie
Africa
Guinea
Ilandes of Cape Verde
Equinoctiall Lyne
Brasill

THE SAFEGUARD OF THE SEA

Also by N. A. M. Rodger

THE WOODEN WORLD: AN ANATOMY OF THE GEORGIAN NAVY

THE SAFEGUARD OF THE SEA

A Naval History of Britain

660–1649

N. A. M. RODGER

W. W. Norton & Company
New York London

The publishers and author gratefully acknowledge the Society for Nautical Research and the Navy Records Society for their help and assistance with the publication of this volume.

First American edition 1998
Published by arrangement with HarperCollins Publishers, Ltd.

Originally published in England under the title *The Safeguard of the Sea: A Naval History of Britain, Volume One, 660–1649*

Printed in the United States of America

The text of this book is composed in Postscript Linotype Minion
Manufacturing by The Maple-Vail Book Manufacturing Group
Maps by Gerald and Pat Fleuss

Library of Congress Cataloging-in Publication Data

Rodger, N. A. M., 1949–
The safeguard of the sea : a naval history of Britain, 660–1649 / N.A.M. Rodger.
p. cm.
Includes bibliographical references and index.
Contents: v. 1. 660–1649
ISBN 0-393-04579-X
1. Great Britain—History, Naval. I. Title.
DA70.R56 1998
359'.00941—dc21 97-52403
CIP

W. W. Norton & Company, Inc., 500 Fifth Avenue, New York, N.Y. 10110
http://www.wwnorton.com

W. W. Norton & Company Ltd., 10 Coptic Street, London WC1A 1PU

2 3 4 5 6 7 8 9 0

FOR SUSAN

Τὸ δὲ τῆς θαλάσσης ἐπιστήμονας γενέσθαι οὐ ῥᾳδίως αὐτοῖς προσγενήσεται. οὐδὲ γὰρ ὑμεῖς, μελετῶντης αὐτὸ εὐθὺς ἀπὸ τῶν Μηδικῶν, ἐξείργασθέ πω . . . τὸ δὲ ναυτικὸν τέχνης ἐστιν, ὥσπερ καὶ ἄλλο τι, καὶ οὐκ ἐνδέχεται, ὅταν τύχῃ, ἐκ παρέργου μελετᾶσθαι, ἀλλὰ μᾶλλον μηδὲν ἐκείνῳ πάρεργον ἄλλο γίγνεσθαι.

As for naval skills, they [the Spartans] will not find them easy to acquire. You yourselves have scarcely mastered them, having worked at them ever since the Persian war . . . Seamanship is an art like any other; it is not something which can be picked up in one's spare time, indeed, it leaves no leisure for anything else.

Pericles addresses the Athenians
Thucydides, *History of the War between Athens and Sparta* I, 142.

CONTENTS

MAPS

ENDPAPER: 'The Famous West Indian Voyage', engraving by Baptista Boazio, published to accompany the *Summary and True Discourse* describing the West Indian expedition of 1584–5.

ILLUSTRATIONS

Unless marked otherwise all illustrations are held in copyright by the National Maritime Museum, Greenwich.

ILLUSTRATIONS IN TEXT

FOREWORD

We have it on weighty authority that 'great abilities are not requisite for an historian; for in historical composition, all the greatest powers of the human mind are quiescent. He has facts ready to his hand; so there is no exercise of invention. Imagination is not required in any high degree; only about as much as is used in the lower kinds of poetry. Some penetration, accuracy, and colouring will fit a man for the task, if he can give the application which is necessary.'[1] For that, as Dr Johnson well knew, even the least talented writer needs a patron. This book is the first fruit of a generous act of joint patronage by the National Maritime Museum, the Society for Nautical Research and the Navy Records Society, which together decided to apply a legacy from that eminent maritime historian, the late Dr R. C. Anderson, to support the writing of a new naval history of Britain. To the Councils of the two Societies and to the Trustees of the Museum, which also named me as its Anderson Fellow for the duration of the project, I am profoundly grateful. Without them I could not have undertaken the work, and whatever usefulness it may prove to possess, is owing to their support. I owe an especial debt of gratitude to Admiral of the Fleet Lord Lewin, formerly Chairman of the Trustees of the Museum, and to Dr R. J. B. Knight, its Deputy Director, who played a large part in setting up the arrangement. I must also thank the numerous colleagues in the Library and elsewhere in the Museum who supported the project in various ways.

I owe an additional debt of gratitude to the Museum, and to Mr Christopher Grey in particular, for obtaining the illustrations. The maps were prepared with the help of grants from the British Academy, the Marc Fitch Fund and the Scouloudi Foundation, to all of which I express my sincere thanks. Many others, friends, colleagues and strangers, have helped me. For references, advice, copies of manuscripts, help with translation and sundry offices of friendship I thank Dr Alex Hildred and Mr C. T. C. Dobbs of the Mary Rose Trust, Mr Richard Barker, Dr Martin Brett, Dr Jan Glete, Dr Poul Holm, Dr Gillian Hutchinson, Captain Niels Probst, Mr David Proctor, Dr H. M. Scott, and my brothers Messrs A. D. A. and J. H. S. Rodger. Dr Anne Crawford, Dr Julia Crick, Professor John Gillingham,

Dr Elizabeth Hallam, Professor P. D. A. Harvey, Professor David Loades, Dr Susan Rose and Dr Andrew Thrush were generous enough to read parts of the manuscript and give me their comments. Professor Geoffrey Parker undertook the heroic labour of reading the whole, at high speed and short notice, putting me under an additional obligation to add to the many I already owe him. The authors of the numerous unpublished theses listed in the bibliography (or in some cases the respective university libraries) kindly gave me leave to cite them.

Above all I owe more than I can express in words to my wife, to whom the book is dedicated, who bore so much of the load of the writing, and the writer.

N.A.M.R.
The Feast of St Arsenius the Great, 1996

A NOTE ON CONVENTIONS

DATES

For most of the period covered by this book, the countries of Europe kept a common calendar, but took the start of the year from a great variety of different dates in different circumstances. The English civil calendar dated the New Year from Lady Day (25 March). By the sixteenth century the Julian calendar had drifted away from astronomical reality, and in 1582 Pope Gregory XIII promulgated a reformed calendar, which eliminated ten days (5–14 October 1582), and took the New Year as 1 January. England, Scotland and some other non-Catholic countries refused to adopt it, and thereafter English 'Old Style' dates were always ten days (eleven days from 1700) behind continental 'New Style', until Britain finally accepted the Gregorian calendar in 1752. Over the same period British dates between 1 January and 24 March in each year were nominally one year behind those on the Continent. In this book all dates after 1582 are Old Style unless otherwise indicated, but the year is taken to begin on 1 January throughout.

NAMES

Established surnames were not common in England until late in the Middle Ages, nor in much of Wales, Scotland and Ireland until much later. In a polyglot age names were freely translated from one language to another. In all cases spelling only became more or less settled in the sixteenth and seventeenth centuries. I have used the standard modern forms of identifiable medieval surnames and place names, giving the Christian names in English for English people, and likewise for other nations.

I have treated ship names the same way, using modern English forms for English ships, and so on. I have however left in French some names – notably the ever-popular *Grace Dieu* – which were seldom or never translated. Note that some Elizabethan warship names circulated in two forms: *Lion/Golden Lion*, *Bear/White Bear*, *Elizabeth Bonaventure/Bonventure*; *Elizabeth*

Jonas/ Elizabeth; *Garland/Guardland*; *Merlin/Merlion*; *Convertine/Convertive*; *Repulse/Due Repulse*: I have used the first of each of these pairs.

TONNAGE

The 'tonnage' of ships is a reflection of the dominant position of the wine trade in Western Europe, and of the cask as a container in many other trades. It was originally a measure of the ship's cargo capacity in tuns; that is, in actual casks each containing (according to the modern standards) 252 gallons wine measure. By the fifteenth century tonnage was already being arrived at 'by estimation', and in the sixteenth, rules were developed for calculating tonnage or 'burthen' by multiplying the ship's principal internal dimensions. More than one rule existed, there were many variations between countries, and many figures were clearly reached by rough estimate or guesswork, so tonnage figures are not to be taken as exact. The essential point for the reader to understand is that all ship's tonnage measures used in the period covered by this book were (and most of those used today still are) measures of internal capacity or volume, not weights. Indeed the avoirdupois ton weight was used in early modern England for only two articles in common circulation: bells and guns. In other contexts references to 'tons' are generally either to ship tonnage, or to the tun cask.

Sixteenth- and seventeenth-century Englishmen shipping dry cargoes (not packed in cask) expressed the 'tons and tonnage' or 'deadweight' stowage of the ship by adding a proportion (normally one-third) to her burthen to allow for the 'dead' space which could not be filled by a cargo shipped in cask. The resulting figure notionally represented a carrying capacity in tons weight, but since it was still derived from a volume calculation, and the actual weight of a given volume of any particular cargo varied greatly across the range of commodities which might be shipped by sea, it is most realistic to regard deadweight as a measure of capacity, like the tonnage burthen from which it derived. True deadweight tonnage, taken from the actual weight of the cargo as loaded, was not then used, and is a useful measure only in the context of ships which trade in a single commodity (oil tankers being the obvious modern example).

The only system of ship tonnage which directly expresses the weight of the ship is displacement tonnage, which calls for mathematical techniques not widely used before the nineteenth century. It calculates the weight of water displaced by the underwater body of the ship, and hence (by Archimedes' rule) the weight of the ship herself. It is only useful for warships (with no weight of cargo to distort the calculation), and only then if their state of loading is exactly defined, but it is the most precise measure for technical purposes and is sometimes calculated retrospectively for the study of warships of the past. As a guide, the displacement (in long tons) of an Elizabethan or Jacobean warship, fully stored for a cruise, might be at least double her burthen. Note that any attempt to calculate the proportion of a ship's 'weight' taken up by, say, her armament, is only meaningful if the weight of guns is compared with the displacement (i.e. weight) of the ship; using burthen (i.e. volume) is seriously misleading.

In this book ships' tonnage is given in tons burthen unless otherwise indicated, and the spelling 'tun' is used for the cask.

WEIGHTS AND MEASURES

Unless otherwise indicated, the weights, measures and currencies in this book are the current or recent British standards. The following may be unfamiliar:

bolt (of canvas): a length variously given as 32–35 yards.

cable: a length, usually of 120 fathoms.

ell (usually of cloth): a length of 3ft 9ins (the English ell), or 2ft 3ins (the Flemish ell, also widely used in England).

fathom: a length of 6ft.

hide: an Anglo-Saxon land measure, the area of land sufficient to support one family.

knot: a measure of speed, one nautical mile an hour.

last: a measure; the English Ordnance Board last of powder was 24 barrels each of 100lbs net.

league: a distance, three miles. The mile itself varied from country to country; at sea the league was reckoned as one-twentieth of a degree of longitude, the value of which was disputed in the 16th–17th centuries.

livre [tournois]: the principal money of account in France. Like the pound sterling it was divided into twenty shillings (*sous*) each of twelve pence (*deniers*). Its value varied, but was always considerably less than sterling.

mark: An English money of account, 13s 4d.

quarter: 1. A dry measure, eight bushels or 64 gallons. 2. A weight, a quarter hundred, equal to two stone or 28lbs avoirdupois.

quintal: A weight, a short hundredweight of five score pounds, in English usually referring to foreign (e.g. French or Spanish) weights.

tun: A cask containing two butts or pipes, four hogsheads or eight barrels.

The capacity of the barrel varied from time to time and liquid to liquid; the beer barrel contained 36 gallons.

Note that these definitions apply to the contexts occurring in this book; most of these have many other possible values for other commodities in other circumstances or periods.

QUOTATIONS

English quotations in the text are given modern English spelling, capitalization, and if necessary punctuation. Unambiguous abbreviations and contractions have been silently expanded. English and Scots from the fifteenth century onward have been treated as modern English, with difficult words glossed as necessary, but Anglo-Saxon is taken as a foreign language. Editorial omissions are indicated thus . . ., additions [thus] and the original wording [*thus*]; other words in italic are emphasized in the original. Quotations from other languages are translated in the text (by the author unless otherwise indicated), with the original wording given in the note. Where no original wording is given, the quotation has been taken already translated from the source cited.

INTRODUCTION

In the dark days towards the end of the century, men looked back with longing to their grandfathers' time, to a lost age of imperial and naval greatness sixty years before, 'when no fleet was ever heard of except of our own people who held this land'.[1] The phrase, and the sentiment, has perhaps a certain modern resonance, but it is not quite a modern author from which it comes. It is in fact from the *Life of St Swithin* by Ælfric of Eynsham, a book written approximately a thousand years ago. Looking back on the reign of King Edgar, as the clouds gathered over Æthelred II, it must have seemed sadly obvious that England's brief period as a great naval power was past beyond recall, as another, greater, empire rose to dominate the northern world.

Ælfric was probably not the first, and certainly not the last English historian to look back with nostalgia, and forward with melancholy satisfaction to a future of inevitable national decline. He was not to know that the impressive but brief dominance of Æthelstan and Edgar was only the first of a series of overseas empires. It was followed by a similar growth of sea power in the following century, cut short by the Norman Conquest and replaced by a series of continental military empires. The transatlantic colonies lost in a fit of absence of mind in the 1770s may have been the 'First British Empire', as historians call them, but they were the third or fourth English empire.

These things would be better known if they had been more often studied. It is now a century since the first and last complete *History of the Royal Navy* was published by Sir William Laird Clowes;[2] and perhaps if a subject is of any importance in national history, it deserves to be looked at at least once in every hundred years. We now know many things which were not known in the 1890s, and we have questions to ask which were not then thought important, or not thought of at all. Laird Clowes and his contemporaries, who included the great figures who founded the serious study of naval history and still largely dominate it today – Sir Julian Corbett, Sir John Laughton, Rear-Admiral Alfred T. Mahan – were practical men writing history in the service of policy. Their object was to understand the past in order to guide the future of the Royal Navy (or in Mahan's case, the United

States Navy). Implicitly, their naval history was the history of sea power and empire, for in their day it was empire which made nations great, and navies which made empires. Explicitly, naval history was the history of navies; of the Royal Navy, for these English-speaking historians. The Service of their own day was the sum and epitome of sea power, and they neither wanted nor needed to distinguish the institution from the function, the Navy from naval warfare.

This gave rise to a paradox, for Laird Clowes, capable historian as he was, well knew and made perfectly clear that the Royal Navy, as an organization, could not be traced back before the sixteenth century. Yet his *History of the Royal Navy* begins before the Roman Conquest of Britain. What is avowedly the history of a national institution, the Royal Navy, begins nearly two thousand years before the Navy formally existed, and a good thousand before the country (leaving aside for the moment the question of what country he meant). This was not just an oddity of that period and that author, for the latest history of the Royal Navy[3] does much the same on a more modest scale, beginning in the eighth century AD. The editor feels no need to explain or excuse the discrepancy of eight centuries between his title and his contents. This must be because the word 'navy' is being used in more than one sense. At times it means, as it commonly means in modern English, the fighting service with which we are familiar, but at other times it is used much more loosely, to embrace all and every means of making war at sea.[4] If the word has such a breadth of meaning, we may fairly say that wherever and whenever men used the sea for warfare, the Navy or a navy must necessarily have been their instrument – even if it did not yet exist. But it is surely unhelpful to stretch the meaning of words so far. The common sense of the word as we use it today refers in this context to a permanent fighting service made up of ships designed for war, manned by professionals and supported by an administrative and technical infrastructure.

A navy in this sense is only one possible method of making war at sea, and by some way the most difficult and the most recent. There have in the past been, and to some extent still are, many other ways of generating sea power. Without exhausting the possibilities, we may distinguish seven well-known methods. Simplest and least effective of all was to have no warships and no permanent organization, but to requisition merchant shipping as necessary. This was the method of most medieval kings of England, but even then it was obsolete and ineffectual. Pre-Conquest England, like the Scandinavian countries, raised a national fleet by laying an obligation on every district to build and man a warship. These 'ship-muster' systems mobilized fleets of hundreds of warships for limited periods of service, at no direct cost to the government and with no central organization. Warships could equally be furnished by feudal obligation, as was done in Norman Sicily and the Highlands of Scotland. In the Mediterranean for much of the Middle Ages, warships were mainly built and operated by entrepreneurs who chartered their private squadrons to whomever could pay for them, or contracted to build and operate squadrons to order. The Genoese and Ragusans were noted specialists in this business, and the fleets of sixteenth-century Spain were mainly built up of such squadrons, provided to order by both Spanish and foreign contractors. Another system was to create fleets supported by local or particular tax revenue, so that the 'navies' protected particular areas or constituencies rather than serving national purposes. Such local navies formed an important part of Spanish sea power, and raised the Dutch to be the leading naval power of the world. Finally we have to consider private naval warfare, conducted for personal rather than national advantage within a legal context ('reprisals' or privateering) and outside it (piracy).

All these methods of making war at sea demanded less of the wealth and organization of the state than a modern standing national navy, and it is not surprising that only one medieval state, Venice, long possessed anything clearly identifiable as a navy in this sense. We shall see that no state in the British Isles attained this level of sophistication before the sixteenth century, and no history of the Royal Navy, in any exact sense of the words, could legitimately begin much before then. This book, which does, is not an institutional history of the Royal Navy, but a history of naval warfare as an aspect of national history. All and any methods of fighting at sea, or using the sea for warlike purposes, are its concern. It is interested in all connections between national and naval history, and seeks to make each known to the other. As has been well said:

> Naval history is a microcosm of national history; it is not a subject with its own particular technique, but an application of different subjects, each with their own technique, to a particular field. It has its own economic and constitutional history, its own legal problems and its own relations with diplomacy and politics. If national history may be compared to a cake, the different layers of which are different aspects of national life, then naval history is not a layer but a slice of that cake.[5]

The object of this book is to cut the naval slice of national history. Its subject is the slow and erratic process by which the peoples of the British Isles learnt – and then for long periods forgot – about the 'Safeguard of the Sea', as the fifteenth-century phrase had it, meaning the use of the sea for national defence, and the defence of those who used the sea.

What this means in practice is that the book is conceived as consisting of four main 'layers': policy, strategy and naval operations; finance, administration and logistics, including all sorts of technical and industrial support; social history; and the material elements of sea power, ships and weapons. Chapters or parts of chapters are devoted to each of these in turn, and it would be possible to read only those parts of the book describing, say, actual operations at sea. But this would be a mistake, and not only because the book would have to be many times its size to deal with operations in any detail. Here there is a summary of the most important naval campaigns and operations, but for detailed narratives the reader must look elsewhere. Appendix I gives a chronology of war at sea which can be used as a means of reference supporting the main text, but the aim of the book as a whole is to give an overview of naval history as part of national history, to supply the background as well as the foreground of naval warfare. Its object is not to divide but to unite, to write a history whose parts can only be understood in the context of the whole. Part of its underlying argument is that national and naval history need one another. Many naval historians much more talented than the present author have failed their readers by isolating their subject, and many national historians have distorted their studies by failing to appreciate the influence of sea power on their history. If this book persuades others to make connections, it will have served one of its most important purposes.

'National' history, of course, is an ambiguous term, and a 'Naval History of Britain' which begins in the seventh century has to explain what it means by Britain. My meaning is simply the British Isles as a whole, but not any particular nation or state of our own day. English-speaking historians have quite rightly become more sensitive than they used to be to the existence of Scottish, Welsh and Irish national histories running parallel to English history and interacting with it. 'Britain' is not a perfect word for this purpose, but 'Britain and Ireland' would be both cumbersome and misleading, implying an equality of treatment which is not possible. Ireland and the Irish figure often in this book, but Irish naval history, in the sense of the history of Irish fleets, is largely a history of what might have been rather than what actually happened. What is really needed is a word to express a history covering the whole British Isles in which the principal actors are English and Scots. This is a 'British' naval history not with reference to the modern state of Great Britain, nor to the Welsh imperialism of Queen Elizabeth's magician Dr

John Dee (who coined the phrase 'British Empire'), but because it tries to give due weight to sea power as an element of the history of every part of the British Isles. It begins with the sea power of Dalriada, not of England, and it argues that in the Middle Ages at least, it was Scotland as much as England whose national destiny was shaped by war at sea. War at sea lost England her independence and gained Scotland hers. As the largest and wealthiest state in the British Isles, England inevitably came to dominate this most expensive and demanding of all warlike activities, and from the mid-sixteenth century this is increasingly a naval history of England, but it tries not to be a crudely anglocentric history.

In any case it is in the nature of the history of the sea that it links many nations, and there is no true naval or maritime history which is not an international history. Whether in peaceful trade or warlike attack, the sea unites more than it divides. Even if it were possible to treat England, or the British Isles, as a single, homogenous, united nation, it would still be impossible to write its naval history without reference to the histories of the other nations, near and far, with which the sea has connected it. This is not a comparative history in the formal sense of one giving equal weight to the histories of two or more countries, but it is a history which attempts to make international comparisons, to illuminate the naval history of these islands by reference to the naval history of other countries.

All this is largely based on printed sources, as it must be in a work on this scale. As far as time and opportunity allowed, I have tried to fill some of the most obvious gaps in our knowledge (particularly of medieval naval warfare) with a limited amount of primary research, but the book is very largely a work of synthesis, deriving its strength from the work of others. At the same time it develops some ideas which have arisen from considering a thousand years of naval history as a whole. It is not surprising that they are not the ideas, still so influential today, by which Laird Clowes and his contemporaries traced the inexorable rise of the Royal Navy. This is not a history of the Royal Navy and it is not a history of inexorable rise – indeed, it is a history of failure at least as much as of success. Looking back over a thousand years in which seaborne empires rose and fell like billows, it may perhaps inspire the reflection that history is not a one-way street, that neither success nor failure must inevitably continue, and that people who so often make mistakes may also correct them. There are few if any moments over the thousand years which this volume covers when a discerning contemporary would have had strong reason to imagine that a world empire based on sea power would one day be ruled from the British Isles. Only towards the end of our period can hindsight discern the foundations of future naval supremacy being laid. This is not the pre-history of Nelson's Navy or Victoria's Empire. Later volumes will deal with them. It is sufficient for this one to show that naval warfare profoundly affected the lives of these islands over a thousand years, and shaped their subsequent history down to this day.

ONE

The Three Seas

660–899; Ships 660–1066

The peoples and polities of the British Isles in the Dark Ages were linked not by the accident of dwelling in the same part of the world, but by the seas and rivers which provided their surest and swiftest means of travel. Kept apart by history, language and religion; sundered by moor and mountain, fen and forest; repeatedly divided by dynastic rivalry; these little nations were joined to one another, and to the world beyond, by the three seas. In the British Isles three worlds met and collided: the Christian, romanized Celtic world of the west; the Christian, romanized Germanic world of the south, and the pagan, unromanized Scandinavian world of the east. To each world belonged a sea, and a common culture, which provided the essential connection when all other connections were wanting.

In the west the Irish Sea was the highway and forum of the Celtic world, connecting the many kingdoms of the Irish of Ireland (the 'Scots', in the terminology of the day) with their kinsmen of Dalriada on the west coast of Scotland. In the same way, it connected the Britons of Wales and Cornwall with their emigrant sons in Brittany, and with their cousins the Britons of Strathclyde, Galloway and Cumbria. The sea opened the Celts to the advancing English where the estuaries of the Dee and the Severn brought the Irish Sea into the English Midlands. By sea the Celtic peoples carried on their extensive trade with western France, by sea their scholars and missionaries voyaged to spread the Christian faith and classical learning throughout Western Europe and beyond, and by sea their saints set sail to settle the remote isles to the north and west beyond the limits of the known world.[1] The northern English kingdoms of Deira and Bernicia, the constituent parts of what became Northumbria, were converted largely by Irish missionaries coming from the great island monastery of Iona in Dalriada, and so belonged in part to the Celtic world.

In the south the English Channel, the 'Narrow Sea', carried from the Franks to the English the learning and faith inherited from the late Roman

Empire. By this route Saint Augustine came from Rome to convert the Kentish king to Christianity. From the south by many channels came the luxuries and the ideas of the late classical world to set before the new Christians of England the material goods, the spiritual values and the techniques of government to which they aspired. The English kingdoms which established themselves during the seventh and eighth centuries were all more or less consciously influenced by the examples of Rome and Rome's successors. The southern states of Kent, Wessex and East Anglia, which were converted mainly by missionaries from the south and adhered to the church government of the Latin world, were especially closely linked to the dominant culture.[2]

To the east the sea was broadest but in some ways the connections were closest of all. Across the North Sea the Angles and Saxons had come from their homelands in what are now north Germany and southern Denmark, and even after they became Christian they did not cease to look eastward to the lands of their origin, and to the peoples with whom they were so closely linked by language, culture and trade. It is easy today to forget that the English were Northmen just as much as the Vikings, sharing their gods and legends, sharing languages still near enough to be more or less mutually intelligible, sharing traditions of kingship and the ordering of society, sharing not least a common style of shipbuilding and a common maritime tradition; a world in which a warship was a natural present for a king.[3]

In the British Isles, and especially in England, the three worlds met, overlapped, mingled and clashed. In particular the English kingdoms of Northumbria in the north and Mercia in the Midlands, where Latin and Celtic Christianity met, faced east, west, north and south, at times at war and at times allied with Scots and Britons, with English and Vikings. The three seas which united the three worlds were the natural channels of war as well as trade; it was by sea that the representatives of the three worlds came to confront one another. What they seldom if ever did was to fight one another actually at sea. To intercept an enemy in the open sea calls for ships spread far away in a sophisticated scouting system which does not seem to have been attempted until the sixteenth century. It would in any case have been futile when no battle could be fought in the open sea. No missile weapons existed in northern waters capable of sinking a ship, nor was it possible to fit rams to the ships of the Northmen. All fighting was hand-to-hand, and naval battles could only take place where ships could come alongside one another. To attempt this in a seaway is almost a guarantee of being stove in and sunk. Most of the naval battles of which we have any

The British Isles in the Dark Ages
SHETLANDS
ORKNEYS
WESTERN ISLES
NORTH ATLANTIC OCEAN
SCOTLAND
IONA
DAL RIADA
STRATH CLYDE
NORTH SEA
ANTRIM
GALLOWAY
NORTHUMBRIA
BERNICIA
IRELAND
ISLE OF MAN
CUMBRIA
IRISH SEA
DEIRA
York
ENGLAND
Dublin
ANGLESEY
R. Dee
Wexford
WALES
MERCIA
EAST ANGLIA
Offa's Dyke
R. Severn
WESSEX
CORNWALL
KENT
Sandwich
STRAITS OF DOVER
Boulogne
ENGLISH CHANNEL
BRITTANY
FRANKISH EMPIRE

detailed knowledge, fought before the introduction of heavy guns, occurred in sheltered, inshore waters where the combatants could grapple and fight it out at close quarters. Only in coastal waters, moreover, was scouting possible and communication sufficiently easy to give any warning of the presence of the enemy.[4]

In this sense it can be said that 'true naval warfare did not exist',[5] if by 'true' one means autonomous, unconnected with war on land. No absolute 'command of the sea' was possible, for neither side in war could deny the use of the sea to an enemy. The sea was always a debatable space, available to whoever possessed a sea-coast and cared to use it. All naval operations were essentially combined operations. Ships were the means of transport which carried an attacking force swiftly and secretly to its target, with almost no possibility of detection or evasion. The gift of sea power was surprise, tactical and strategic. In this way ships were the natural partners of horses, for both were the means by which armies gained mobility. Both were instruments which multiplied the fighting value of even the smallest forces, allowing them to outflank and avoid, to surprise and overpower, to retreat and escape according to the requirements of the moment. This was true not only on and near the coast, but far inland. The ships of the day with their shallow draught could penetrate scores, sometimes hundreds of miles inland up even quite small rivers. The Swedish Vikings pushed up the great rivers of Russia, over the portages and down to the Black Sea to establish a lively commercial and cultural link with the Byzantine Empire, and in the process to found trading posts which grew into the original states of Russia. The early princes of Kiev and Novgorod were as much part of the Viking world as the settlers of Greenland, and the most land-locked of empires grew from the sea power of the Northmen. In Western Europe the major ports, almost all of them on rivers, were both harbours and gateways to the interior.[6]

The best answer to seaborne attack was a combination of fixed defences and ships. It was impossible to build or garrison fortresses to cover an entire coastline, but it was possible to fortify places which commanded the entrances to, and crossings of, rivers in such a way as to hinder a naval force from penetrating inland. A defending naval force could be held at a convenient location, ready to move as soon as an attack was detected, conveying men as rapidly as possible to the point under attack. Such a defensive reaction might land troops in the rear of the attackers, burning their ships and cutting off their retreat. It might intercept them moving along the coast and fight them afloat. It might blockade the mouth of a river and prevent escape. In any event it provided the defenders with the same mobility and flexibility as it offered the attackers, even though it could not deprive them of the initiative.[7]

This was the strategy adopted by the late Roman builders of the 'Saxon Shore' forts, erected in the third century on both sides of the Straits of Dover facing eastward, towards the raids of the Saxon pirates from across the North Sea. A base at Boulogne supported the naval forçe which provided the essential mobility to the defence. The siting of the forts makes it clear that only in the actual Straits was it possible to patrol with any prospect of intercepting the Saxon ships.[8] No attempt was or could have been made to meet them in the open sea.

These Saxon pirates were presumably among the ancestors of the Saxons, Angles and Jutes[9] who crossed the North Sea in the fifth century to settle in England. We know almost nothing for certain of the circumstances of their first coming, not even if it was warlike or peaceful, and by the time we can discern something of the English fighting the Britons and pushing westwards in the sixth and seventh centuries, they had long ceased to be seaborne attackers and become settled inhabitants of the island. It is almost certain that by then all the peoples inhabiting the British Isles were familiar with the sea and the use of sail.[10] We know they traded and travelled by sea, we know they often fought one another, and it would be remarkable if they never used ships in warfare when there were such great advantages to be gained by doing so. We have one isolated but remarkable piece of evidence, the document known as the *Senchus Fer n-Alban*, which seems to show that by the mid-seventh century Dalriada had a comprehensive ship-levy system, which obliged groups of households to provide and man a warship each; in theory 177 ships each manned by 14 men, a total of 2,478 men levied from 1,770 households. The same document gives a bare mention of the the earliest known naval battle around the British Isles, in the year 719 in the course of civil war between rival parties in Dalriada.[11] It is likely, however, that this was no more than an incident in what was already a long tradition of war at sea. The text refers also to no fewer than eight Dalriadan naval expeditions between 568 and 733, and we know that the Picts (the people then inhabiting the Highlands of Scotland) were also active in the same waters.[12] A people settled on both sides of the North Channel, in Antrim and the Western Isles, obviously had particular need of ships, but it would be surprising if one of the poorer and remoter kingdoms of the British Isles were the only one to have reached this level of sophistication, especially as we know that the Irish, Picts and Britons had naval traditions going back to Roman times,[13] and it was just at this time that missionaries from the great island monastery of Iona were spreading the fame of Dalriada throughout Western Europe. Further, it has been argued that systems of levying men and taxes on units of a hundred households, which are found from very early times among Irish, Welsh, Scots and English, are all based on Roman practice.[14] If the Scots of Dalriada could use such a system for naval purposes, there is no reason why the others should not have done so as well.

It is moreover quite likely that the *Senchus Fer n-Alban* represents the Dalriadan reaction to English naval aggression. In the early seventh century the expanding English kingdom of Northumbria reached the Irish Sea and occupied much of Lowland Scotland. King Edwin (616–33) conquered both Anglesey and the Isle of Man, which he cannot have done without using ships.[15] In 684 his successor King Ecgfrith mounted a large raid into Ireland.[16] This was probably connected with his wars against the Picts and the Irish of Dalriada, in which he met his death the following year when he was defeated by the Picts at an unidentified place in Scotland called *Nechtansmere*. This is the last we hear of Northumbrian naval activity, and indeed of Northumbria as a great power among the English kingdoms, but it is most unlikely that nothing at all happened at sea around the British Isles in the course of the next century, though our sources tell us nothing.

We may therefore guess that what on existing evidence looks like the establishment of navies and naval organization by Anglo-Saxon kings in the eight and ninth centuries, was in fact the borrowing or reform of systems which already existed. What seems to be clear is that the organization of a navy was associated with important developments in the power and complexity of the state. His great dyke, one of the largest engineering works ever undertaken in Europe, still stands as a testimony to the power of King Offa of Mercia (757–96), and it has recently been argued that throughout his kingdom he built interlinked fortifications to provide defence in depth.[17] These fortifications, and the strategy which went with them, were closely connected with the growing practice of granting land (initially to religious houses, later to secular landowners) in perpetuity by written charters modelled on Roman law. This 'bookland' was charged with what came to be called the *trimoda necessitas*, the 'threefold obligation' to provide men to serve in the army, to build and maintain fortifications, and to build and maintain bridges.[18] At the same time Offa was issuing an extremely sophisticated coinage, which fostered the economy of his kingdom and helped him to tax it.[19] The effect was to increase his wealth and power, and to strengthen and codify his right to call on his people's service.

Offa's defences were directed primarily against the Welsh, but his rule reached to the North Sea at a time when Danish raids were already beginning, and it is quite possible that he had ships as part of his defensive system.[20] Offa's Dyke itself, whose two ends rest on the sea, would have been vulnerable without ships on either flank.[21] We know that Mercia took part in extensive seaborne trade. Offa must have been familiar with ships, it would be odd if he never perceived their military potential, and it is at least possible that in his reign naval duties were already included in military service. When the 'threefold obligation' was laid on church lands in his sub-kingdom of Kent in 792 it was specifically to resist attacks from the sea;[22] and in 851, only fifty years after Offa's death (by which time Kent was ruled by Wessex), a Kentish naval force won a sea battle at Sandwich.[23]

By this time the English in their turn had become the defenders against seaborne Viking attacks from the eastward, no doubt very similar to those their own ancestors had mounted against the Romano-Britons five hundred years before. More accurately, the Viking attacks came from two directions. Norwegians made some raids against Northumbria, but their main thrust was westward to the Orkneys and Shetlands, which they settled, and thence south down the Irish Sea. They absorbed the Western Isles and made incursions into Ireland, founding the coastal trading cities of Dublin and Wexford. From these bases they intervened in the warfare and politics of the Irish kings, the Welsh princes and the English. They also moved on both south and north, to raid the western parts of France and to settle Iceland. These western Vikings became in many respects integrated into the Celtic world. They participated in its warfare and politics, they intermarried with its royal families, and many of them adopted its languages and customs. The Isle of Man and the Western Isles were the heart of this mingled culture, but settlers with distinctive Norse-Gaelic names can be traced in parts of Galloway, Cumbria and Wales, and for a time the Norwegians were able to erect a Viking kingdom in York on the ruins of English Northumbria.[24] The eastern Vikings were predominantly Danes, who crossed the North Sea direct, or by coasting along the Frisian islands, to attack eastern and southern England. Eventually their successes allowed them to settle thickly in parts of eastern and midland England, and for a while to establish their own Danish kings, until the victories of King Alfred's successors reduced them to English rule.

The Viking raids on England began in 789, when three Norwegian ships landed at Portland, killing the local official who took them for peaceful merchants. In 793 the great island monastery of Lindisfarne, Iona's most important daughter house, was sacked by Viking raiders, an event which sent a tremor throughout Christian Europe.[25] 'It is nearly 350 years that we

The Viking Invasions
ATLANTIC OCEAN
HEBRIDES
CAITH-NESS
IONA
LINDISFARNE
NORTH SEA
NORTHUMBRIA
CUMBERLAND
ISLE OF MAN
LEINSTER
Dublin
ANGLESEY
Tadcaster
York
Riccall
R. Humber
R. Dee
Lincoln
FRISIA
Warwick
MERCIA
Hereford
EAST ANGLIA
Isle of Ely
R. Severn
Malmesbury
Bedford
R. Stour
BRISTOL CHANNEL
R. Thames
R. Lea
Maldon
London
WANTSUM CHANNEL
ISLE OF THANET
Carhampton
SOMERSET
DEVON
Winchester
Sittingbourne
Weald
Canterbury
CORNWALL
Exeter
WESSEX
KENT
Sandwich
Hingston Down
SUSSEX
Romney Marsh
Southampton
PORTLAND
Swanage
ISLE OF WIGHT
FLANDERS
ENGLISH CHANNEL
NORMANDY
FRANKISH EMPIRE

and our fathers have inhabited this most lovely land', wrote the English scholar Alcuin from Charlemagne's court, 'and never before has such terror appeared in Britain as we have now suffered from a pagan race, nor was it thought that such an inroad from the sea could be made.'[26] The English were quickly to learn how easily it could. In 836 King Egbert of Wessex was defeated by a Viking force of 35 ships which landed at Carhampton in Somerset.[27] Since Carhampton is on the Bristol Channel, the attackers were probably Norwegians who had come down the Irish Sea. Two years later the same or another Viking force joined forces with the Cornish to attack Wessex, and were defeated by Egbert in a battle at Hingston Down on the border of Devon and Cornwall.[28] In 840 the men of Wessex were again defeated by Vikings at Portland, but won a victory over 33 'shiploads' of raiders at Southampton.[29] From this date the raids become almost continuous, not only on England but throughout Western Europe. Louis the Pious, emperor of the Franks, who had organized effective naval defences, died in that year, and the Vikings began to penetrate up the great rivers. In 841 Rouen was sacked, and Nantes followed in 842. In 845 Paris bought them off with 7,000lbs of silver; in 851 they wintered in the Seine for the first time.[30] That same winter Viking forces first wintered in England, on the Isle of Thanet, and 350 ships stormed London and Canterbury, but King Æthelstan of Kent fought on shipboard at Sandwich, took nine ships and put the rest to flight.[31] This action, no doubt fought inshore in the harbour or roadstead in the usual northern fashion, is the first English 'naval battle' of which we have explicit mention, though it is not likely to have been the first ever fought. In 860 a 'great ship-army' stormed Winchester, though it was later defeated.[32]

Until this point the Viking raids, though frequent and extremely destructive, had apparently not seriously affected the fabric of the Anglo-Saxon kingdoms. With the arrival in 865 of what the English simply called 'the great army', this began to change. It was a force much larger than before, under the leadership of men of royal rank, determined not only on plunder but on conquest. Under them the Danes overran much of eastern and northern England, extinguishing the kingdom of East Anglia, conquering Northumbria and reducing Mercia to a rump state.[33] When the 22-year-old Alfred succeeded to the throne of Wessex in 871, it was the only one of the ancient English kingdoms still substantially intact, and on him fell the burden of resisting the Danes for nearly thirty years. The military history of his reign is a succession of desperate battles and of prolonged chases after a highly mobile enemy. In 878 a surprise attack by the Danish leader Guthrum very nearly finished Wessex. This is the period when Alfred was driven to take refuge in the Somerset marshes. He recovered and won victories over Guthrum, who accepted baptism, made peace and withdrew to East Anglia. In 886 Alfred captured London and restored it to Mercia. His daughter Æthelflaed had married Ealdorman Æthelred, the last member of the Mercian royal house, and Mercia was now a dependency of Wessex.[34]

During the first twenty years of his reign (871–99) Alfred was almost continually at war, but almost all that warfare was on land. His naval activity seems to have been on a small scale. In 875 he put to sea with a 'fleet' (*sciphere*), fought seven enemy ships, took one and drove the others off.[35] In 882 he fought four enemy ships and captured them all, two of them with no survivors. In 885 a squadron not commanded by the king in person was sent after Danish ships escaping from a defeat in Kent. They intercepted and took sixteen enemy ships at the mouth of the Stour in Essex, but were then themselves defeated by a larger Danish squadron.[36] These were minor actions set against the hundreds of ships of the Danish forces.[37] They suggest that the navy available to Alfred was insufficient to attempt more than snapping up stragglers. When large bodies of Danes moved by sea, the English did not interfere. In 877, for example, part of the Danish army moved westward to Exeter, which they occupied, while the fleet moved along the coast in parallel. At Swanage 120 ships, we are told, were wrecked.[38] Alfred's army pursued the Danes on horseback and caught them in Exeter, but could do no better then make a truce allowing them to depart.[39] Had the English had a substantial fleet this would have been an excellent opportunity to trap the bulk of the Danish army, but so long as the Danes had unobstructed use of the sea, they could leave Exeter whenever they chose and a blockade on the land side was pointless.

In the late 880s and early 890s Alfred enjoyed a brief respite from large-scale warfare, which he employed in establishing a new system of fortifications. Faced with prolonged and repeated incursions by forces moving fast both by sea and on horseback as occasion demanded,[40] he developed a system of defence in depth which depended upon the combination of fixed defences, good communications and mobile forces ready to react to attack – the same basic combination as the Saxon Shore forts of five centuries before. Alfred's fortresses, the *burhs*, were substantial settlements with heavy earthwork and timber ramparts. It has been calculated that as much as one-fifth of the entire population of England may have been drawn on to provide their garrisons.[41] They were linked by good roads, and sited to command the major rivers and bridges. At key crossings 'double-burhs', linked by a bridge, denied the enemy passage either along or across the river. In addition to the garrisons of the *burhs*, Alfred maintained an army of men wealthy enough to ride to war, and built a fleet to move around the coasts as necessary. Ships and horses went together to provide the essential mobility to tackle a mobile enemy. *Burhs* too strong to be taken by even a large raiding force severely limited its freedom of movement, while Alfred's army could move swiftly to intercept or cut off the invader. It is probable that Alfred was not the inventor of this strategic system. In essence it provides a defence in depth against attacks by fast-moving forces whether by land or sea, and it appears that in all respects except, possibly, ships, it followed the system employed a century before by Offa of Mercia; it also resembles the defences developed by Alfred's contemporary, the Frankish emperor Charles the Bald.

In 892 another 'great army', recoiling from a reverse in Flanders, crossed the Channel in 200 ships and landed in Kent. The invaders stormed an unfinished *burh*, and encamped at Appledore on the edge of Romney Marsh. Meanwhile a second fleet of 80 ships came up the Thames and dug in at Milton Regis, near Sittingbourne. Alfred's reponse was a brilliant land campaign conducted from the forest of the Weald. From there, between the two enemy forces, he harassed them and watched their movements, and when they retreated towards their ships laden with booty, he seized the chance to strike.[42]

What he did not do was attempt any naval action. A fleet at London would have been perfectly placed to take the Milton group of Vikings in the rear, between two fires: we may fairly conclude that Alfred did not have a fleet at London. Much the same is suggested by a campaign in 895, when a Danish fleet sailed up the Thames and the River Lea, where they encamped, and repelled an attempt by the garrison of London to dislodge them. Alfred arrived with the main army and occupied the lower reaches of the river, where he built a double-burh to trap the Danes. They were obliged to abandon their ships and flee overland, pursued by Alfred's mounted army, while the London garrison emerged to seize the ships.[43] It was a successful campaign – but the fact that the Danes were able to sail up the Thames, that they were willing to sail up the Lea without fear for their retreat, and that in the end Alfred sent no ships to intercept their escape, indicates that there was no substantial English fleet to oppose them.

It is at this stage, facing a renewed crisis, and evidently conscious of the critical disadvantage of lack of sea power, that Alfred turned his attention to his fleet.[44] According to the *Anglo-Saxon Chronicle*, in 896 he built a force of large warships of a new design to oppose the Viking attacks.[45] It is for this that Alfred was traditionally described as the founder of the British Navy. Clearly the writer of the Chronicle (possibly representing the king's own views) judged that he had done something important, but it is difficult for us to tell how original it was. In 896 he had been twenty-five years on the throne of Wessex, during which time he had fought at sea on several occasions. As he is described as personally commanding a squadron in 875, he may have inherited a navy from his predecessors – it is worth noting that the Kentish ships which fought at Sandwich in 851 were commanded by his elder brother.[46] Moreover we are told only that Alfred fought at sea in ships, latterly in warships of his own design. We do not know how many he had, and we know nothing at all of what organization lay behind them.

To appreciate what was, or may have been different about Alfred's new ships we need to look at warship design in the Viking age. In English and all the northern languages, warships were clearly distinguished from other types, and there is no doubt that the distinction existed at least as early as the eighth century and probably much earlier. In Norway a ship-house has been excavated, presumably built for a warship, which is variously dated to the second and the beginning of the sixth century.[47] It was big enough for a ship over eighty feet long and fifteen wide. The obvious characteristic of warships was evidently that they were long in proportion to their beam; 'longship' is one of the commonest terms for them both in English and in the Scandinavian languages,[48] and 'snake' is another.[49] A great many other words are used, but we are in many cases ill-informed of the exact distinctions they imply, especially as most of them come from Norse poetry written down in the twelfth and thirteenth centuries, and it is doubtful how much can be applied to earlier periods and other countries. Moreover the alliterative verse of the Northmen called for a huge vocabulary of poetic synonyms, which is no help to the historian in search of precise terminology.[50] Our general knowledge of northern shipbuilding during the early Middle Ages has been vastly expanded by archaeology in the last thirty years, but it is unfortunate that the only general survey of the subject available until recently was written before all this evidence became available, and leans heavily on the Gokstad and Oseberg ships.[51] These two remarkable survivals have exercised a fascination over generations of scholars, and are still very often cited as models for the ships of the Viking age. They are, however, of the same size and type, buried within a few years and a few miles of one another, and there is no reason to assume that they represent anything more than mid-ninth century examples of one type, the *karfi*, from one district of southern

Norway.[52] Indeed, it is argued that they are unusual even for their type and period in being in the nature of 'royal yachts', with many archaic and ostentatious features not typical of ordinary working craft.[53] It is unlikely that they resembled Norwegian warships, still less English warships.

Unfortunately the archaeologists' discoveries as yet include only a single undoubted warship, the 'Skuldelev 2' wreck. This was a longship of about the year 1060, possibly built in Dublin, of which only a quarter survives.[54] Our knowledge of shipbuilding in general has much improved, but this remains a perilously narrow basis on which to generalize about English warships over several centuries. It is not even certain that they were all in the 'Viking' tradition of double-ended, clinker-built ships, though the Sutton Hoo ship of about 625 certainly is. We now know that there were at least three other major shipbuilding traditions in northern waters, and although they would be less suitable for building long, narrow, oared vessels, we cannot exclude them altogether.[55] The likelihood is, however, that all English warships, with the possible exception of King Alfred's, corresponded more or less to the 'Viking' type.

Ships of all sorts built in the Viking tradition were measured by 'rooms' or thwarts.[56] The 'room' is equivalent to the modern English shipwright's 'room and space', a section of the hull defined by two adjacent sets of frames and the beams spanning them. By convention only the full-size rooms were counted, ignoring the smaller spaces created by the cant frames in the bows

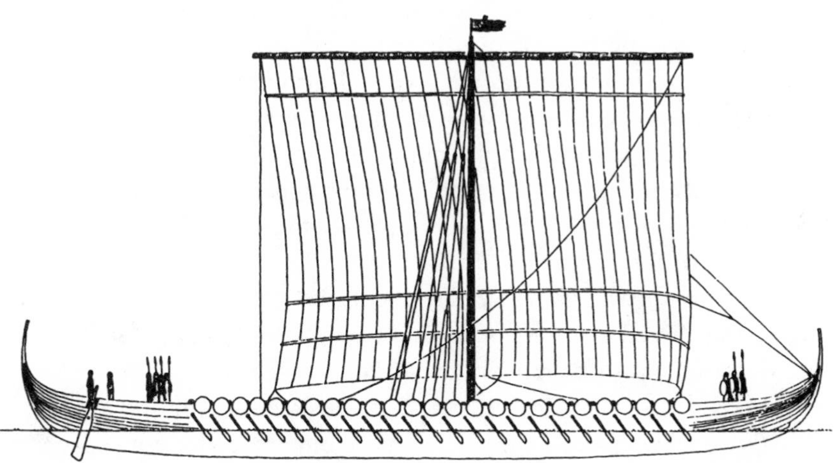

A reconstruction of 'Skuldelev 2,' a longship of about twenty-five rooms, part of which was recovered from the bed of Roskilde Fiord. This ship, which was built about 1060, possibly in Dublin, remains our best guide to the appearance of Viking warships.

and stern. In undecked ships like the Sutton Hoo ship the rowers sat on thwarts spanning the frames, and the number of rooms was necessarily the same as the number of pairs of oars.[57] In such a case a 'twenty-thwarter'[58] was equivalent to a ship of twenty rooms, and literary sources give the impression that this continued to be the case throughout the Viking age.[59] Archaeological evidence introduces some uncertainty,[60] but at the moment it still looks reasonable to assume that English warships would have had one pair of oars for each room.

It appears that among the Vikings, ships of less than twenty rooms (or at least 75 feet long) were not usually counted as warships, at least in the twelfth century.[61] That is not to say that smaller ships never went to war; *karfar*, in particular, seem to have been often used by Norwegian fleets when it was necessary to portage ships overland,[62] while the *knarr*, the typical merchantman of the Viking age, is also mentioned as taking part in battles.[63] On our present information, however, it is reasonable to assume that the regular fleets raised by Scandinavian kings of the eleventh century, and very likely earlier, would have been made up of longships, probably little if at all smaller than twenty rooms each, nor bigger than twenty-five. The verses of King Cnut's court poets celebrate the length of his warships as a symbol of his power.[64] In the later Norwegian fleet organization, of which we are relatively well-informed, almost all the ships were of twenty or twenty-five rooms, the type usually called 'snakes'.[65] Ships of thirty rooms and upwards, often called *drekkar*, 'dragons', are celebrated in the sagas as most unusual, indeed as famous and heroic. The earliest was possibly the ship of unstated size owned by King Harald Fairhair of Norway in the eighth century. The first whose size we know was King Olav Trygvåson's thirty-room *Tranin* ('Crane'), built in 995. By far the most famous was his later ship the *Ormrinn Langi* ('Long Serpent') of thirty-four rooms, built in 999. We know for certain of only six ships as large as thirty rooms afloat in the eleventh century, the largest being King Harald Hardrada's thirty-five-room ship built in 1061–2 as a copy of the *Ormrinn Langi*.[66]

With this as background we may offer some tentative conclusions about English warships. The nature of naval warfare, typically in coastal and often inland waters, placed a premium on shallow draught and the ability to use oars as well as sail. The English were certainly familiar with the use of sail, but oars would be essential for getting in and out of harbour, for penetrating up rivers, and for going into action. Since all fighting was hand-to-hand, we can assume that each ship carried as many warriors as she conveniently could. This has to be stressed, for much discussion of the subject is vitiated by the common and quite unfounded assumption that the number of men in the crew must be equal to the number of oars.[67] That is most unlikely to be true, except perhaps in small boats, for sea-going ships would be at least half-empty at this rate, while the biggest ships could scarcely move under oars with only one man to each. The Dalriadan ship-muster of the seventh century was supposedly based on seven-room ships with fourteen men each,[68] but this was much smaller than any warship likely to have been used by either Viking or English fleets. Norwegian evidence from the eleventh to the thirteenth centuries gives us ratios of between three and eight men to an oar, the highest figures in the biggest ships.[69] One complication is introduced by the evidence of the Bayeux Tapestry, which shows the English ships – presumably warships, from the rows of shields hung along their gunwales – which carried Harold Godwinson to Normandy and back in 1065.[70] These ships are shown with oar-ports fore and aft but not amidships, though the Norman ships have a full row of oar-ports.[71] We know this to have been characteristic of *knarrar* with their small crews and hold amidships,[72] but there seems no logical reason why a warship should forego the maximum possible number of oars, even if she did not often need them all; possibly Harold's ship, evidently small enough to beach easily, was in the nature of a yacht, with a cabin amidships.

From this we may return to King Alfred. The *Anglo-Saxon Chronicle* tells us that:

> King Alfred had long ships built to oppose the [Danish] warships [*lang scipu ongen ða aescas*]. They were almost twice as long as the others. Some had 60 oars, some more. They were both swifter and steadier and also higher than the others. They were built neither on the Frisian nor the Danish pattern, but as it seemed to him himself that they could be most useful.[73]

We may well believe that Alfred was the originator of the design, for his many talents included a familiarity with both carpentry and seafaring.[74] Unfortunately we know almost nothing of what is meant by the Frisian and Danish patterns. The Danish ships were presumably warships;[75] the Frisians were known as merchants, and their ships might have been of several types all of which had the relatively deep draught and high freeboard of the cargo-carrier.[76] This makes sense of the description, for big ships with deep hulls would have been more stable and higher out of the water, and both would be crucial advantages in hand-to-hand fighting. They might also have been faster, if their hulls were reasonably fine, and they had enough men pulling their oars.[77] If they really had sixty oars – thirty rooms – and more, these were among the biggest ships ever built in northern waters during the Middle Ages. They would certainly have been almost twice as long overall as ships of twenty rooms or so, much higher out of the water, with crews at least twice or thrice as large. They should be compared with the thirty-four-room *Ormrinn Langi*, built a century later, which is said to have been 145 feet long on the keel and to have had two complete watches of four men to an oar, making 544 men in addition to the rest of the crew.[78] These were formidable capital ships; like Alfred's *burhs*, they represent a massive application of money and manpower, and we may think of these huge ships, as perhaps he did, as floating fortresses, their great size intended to outweigh the larger numbers of the Danish ships. Whether such big ships were well-chosen for English coastal waters is another question; all the other ships of this size ever built in the northern lands were intended for the deep waters of Norway.

Great size certainly had disadvantages, which are illustrated by the *Anglo-Saxon Chronicle*'s account of an action in 896. It is almost unique among our sources in giving sufficient detail to reveal tactics in battle. A Danish squadron of six ships raided the Isle of Wight, then sailed westward along the coast and entered an unnamed estuary. Alfred sent nine of his new ships in pursuit, and they arrived off the estuary, where they found three Danish ships on watch, while the other three were beached upriver with their men ashore plundering. The English attacked the three guardships and captured two of them, while the third escaped with only five men left alive on board because the English ships grounded on the ebb tide. They grounded, moreover, three on the same side of the river as the other Danish ships, and six on the opposite bank. Seizing their opportunity, the Danish crews came down the riverbank and attacked the three English ships. In the ensuing battle 120 Danes were killed for the loss of 62 English – perhaps an indicator of the degree to which the larger English ship's crews outnumbered the Danes. Meanwhile the tide had turned, and began to refloat the Danish vessels before the bigger English ships. The surviving Danes were able to retreat to their ships and escape, but they were so few and so badly wounded that two ships were driven ashore on the coast of Sussex and their men taken. One ship alone returned to East Anglia.[79]

This bloody little fight was doubtless typical of much naval warfare of the time, and it illustrates the disadvantages as well as the advantages of building very big warships to operate in the shallow tidal waters of southern England. How successful they were overall it is impossible to say. The *Anglo-*

Saxon Chronicle mentions no further naval action in Alfred's reign, and his great ships disappear from history as suddenly as they appeared.[80] What organization, if any, lay behind them; in what sense Alfred may be said to have have had, or founded, a navy, we cannot tell. All that can be said is that he brought an original mind to bear on the problems of naval warfare, which themselves were familiar to every leader of his day. In Alfred's world no king could survive or flourish who did not understand ships and the sea.

TWO

The First English Empires

900–1066

In every age states of varying size and constitution and at every level of development have found naval warfare to be one of their most formidable and expensive tasks. Ships have always been large, costly and complicated, and warships much more costly and complicated than any others. Scholars are nowadays inclined to emphasize the power, wealth and sophistication of the Anglo-Saxon kingdoms, and there is no more striking illustration of this than the advanced and elaborate administrative structures of the early English navy. Our evidence for the means by which fleets were raised and sustained, however, is meagre and fragmentary; we are often obliged to proceed by inference and to guess at what may lie hidden beneath the silence of our sources. We know nothing of what organization lay behind Alfred's ships, but in the century after his death we can begin to discern an English (or at least Wessex) national fleet with something like a permanent structure.

Alfred's campaigns against the Danes were continued by his son Edward the Elder (899–924) and his daughter Æthelflaed, 'Lady of the Mercians' – certainly one of the most capable generals of her age. In Edward's reign his sovereignty was acknowledged by the Danish leaders in the Danelaw (the areas of Danish settlement in East Anglia and the East Midlands), by Northumbria, the King of Scots (meaning the 'Scots' in what is now Highland Scotland, conquered from the Picts), the Britons of Strathclyde and various Welsh princes. In 910 Edward trapped a Danish force with the help of a fleet of a hundred ships, the first English fleet of any size known to have existed.[1] We may infer that this fleet was responsible for applying the pressure which also persuaded the Scots and the Britons to submit, since both were far out of reach of the land forces of Wessex. In the reign of Æthelstan (927–39) it was certainly sea power which sustained his authority over much of the British Isles and beyond. In 934 he led a large expedition up the East Coast into Scotland. In this case the army reached as far north as Aberdeenshire, and the fleet went further, to Caithness – a voyage which indicates that English warships were in the hands of capable seamen.[2] The fleet and army moving in parallel was to be the invariable pattern of English campaigns in Scotland. The roads north were too few and poor to support the communications of any considerable army, and a fleet was essential to carry supplies. Three years later Æthelstan defeated a dangerous challenge from the Norse and Scots at the battle of *Brunanburh*, whose location has not been fixed.[3] It is certain that the attack came from the sea (in 615 ships, according to a late authority) and was defeated on land. Unfortunately the general references to Vikings, combined with the ambiguity of the word 'Scots', leaves us uncertain whether this was the Scots and the Dublin Vikings (with or without Irish help) landing on the west coast, which seems the most likely, or the Scots and the Northumbrian Vikings on the east coast.[4]

However and wherever Æthelstan won his victory, it clearly had consequences in establishing England as a power of consequence well beyond the British Isles. He was accepted as overlord by the Welsh princes,[5] and his daughter married the son of the Saxon king Henry the Fowler, on whose behalf the English fleet intervened in continental diplomacy.[6] Other daughters married into the royal houses of the Franks and of Burgundy, and the English fleet helped to restore both Louis IV of the Franks and Duke Richard of Brittany to their thrones by ravaging the coast, or threatening to do so.[7] King Harald Fairhair of Norway cultivated Æthelstan's favour and sent his son Håkon to be brought up at the English court.[8]

It is only with Edgar (959–75), however, that we can catch a glimpse of a developed naval administration, and once again it is associated with changes in government which strengthened the power of the king. Under Edgar's patronage Saint Dunstan and others were engaged in thorough reforms of monastic and church administration. These reforms involved strengthening the hands of the reforming bishops and abbots – and in the process strengthening the king who backed them – at the expense of various ecclesiastical and secular vested interests. It is in this connection that we find the institution, apparently new, of the 'ship-soke'. The evidence is mostly late, fragmentary and disputed, but what it seems to show is the establishment, initially from the estates of bishops and abbots associated with the reformers, of units of three 'hundreds' obliged to provide and man a ship each.[9] (The 'hundred' was a subdivision of the county for purposes of taxation and military service, in principle an area of one hundred 'hides', each hide being enough land to support one household.) It seems that throughout the country, or at least the midland and southern shires where the rule of the house of Wessex was secure, every five hides had to find and feed one man for the army or navy.[10]

In the ship-sokes it appears that the landowner himself provided the ship, and the three hundreds yielded the sixty men to man her. These sixty men served by land or sea as required, and the same officer led them into battle in either case. At some point, if not in Edgar's reign then later in the same century, the obligation to find and man warships was extended to secular landowners and to the counties. In 1005 Archbishop Ælfric of Canterbury bequeathed a warship each to the men of Kent and Wiltshire, presumably to help them fulfil their naval obligations, and about the same time the prominent Cambridgeshire landowner Ælfhelm of Wratting left a warship to Ramsey Abbey.[11] Laws from the end of the century lay down penalties for damaging one of 'the people's warships'.[12] There are many references during the first part of Æthelred II's reign (978–1016) which show what appears to be this fleet, levied from the country at large.[13] How big it was we cannot exactly tell, though if Edgar obtained one ship each from the bishops and abbots of his day he would have had about thirty. Late tradition claimed that he had a fleet of 3,600 ships; the figure is fantastic in itself, but it may be significant that it is a multiple of sixty. If 'ships' in this case were a slip for 'men', we might have a fleet of sixty ships, each with sixty men, which is easily within the resources and requirements of Edgar's kingdom. Late traditions tell us that every year he mobilized his fleet to cruise around the British Isles, and conquered Dublin.[14] We have several independent accounts of the curious ceremony which took place soon after his coronation, when he cruised with his fleet from the Severn round to the Dee, where he was rowed in state by the rulers of North and South Wales, Man, the Hebrides, Strathclyde and Galloway, while he took the helm.[15] To take the helm was to take command, for in all the northern countries the steersman was the captain of the ship. The symbolism is unmistakable: princes from around the shores of the Irish Sea submitted to the sea power of the English king.[16] Edgar, like Æthelstan, adopted imperial titles to emphasize his overlordship, and this was how he was still remembered two centuries later: 'he held the land as an emperor . . . He alone ruled over all the kings, and over the Scots and the Welsh. Never since Arthur had any king such power.'[17]

At the end of the tenth century Æthelred II (978–1016), teased in his own day as *unræd* (ill-advised, unwise),[18] and pilloried by mistranslation as 'unready', worked to recreate the naval and military strength of his ancestors. In 992 Æthelred ordered 'all the ships that were any use' to assemble at London,[19] a phrase which might indicate that the naval organization of Edgar had been allowed to decay. Æthelred rebuilt Alfred's boroughs with heavier defences, and used the threat of naval attack to force Duke Robert of Normandy to expel Viking raiders from his ports.[20] Æthelred's Irish Sea expedition in the year 1000, when the fleet ravaged the Isle of Man while the king with his army attacked Cumberland,[21] is recognizably an exercise of English naval power for traditional purposes, probably to forestall any league between the western Vikings and their Danish cousins.

This was necessary because in Æthelred's reign the Danes renewed their attacks on an even heavier scale than Alfred had faced a century before. The initial attacks were no more than irritants: seven ships attacked Southampton in 980, three ships landed at Portland in 982. There may have been a major English victory in East Anglia in 988, and the 991 campaign has been interpreted as a desperate last throw by the Danes.[22] If so the Danish victory at the battle of Maldon was a turning-point. That year a fleet of 93 ships attacking the south-east was bought off with a payment of £10,000, and the following year the same fleet received £16,000 from London in spite of having failed to capture it.[23] These enormous sums of money must have made the most effective possible advertisement of England's wealth and vulnerability. They also indicate naval weakness: it is most likely that Ealdorman Brythnoth accepted battle at Maldon even though he was outnumbered, lest a mobile enemy take to their ships and strike somewhere else where there was no army prepared to receive them;[24] London undoubtedly submitted to the threat of naval blockade stopping its trade. In either case a powerful English fleet would have transformed the strategic calculation. The *Anglo-Saxon Chronicle*'s account of the year 1001, with Danish forces raiding at will and neither fleet nor army daring to oppose them, confirms that the English fleet still existed; it was simply not big enough.[25] In 1008 Æthelred ordered that 'ships should be built unremittingly all over England, namely a warship from 310 hides and a helmet and corselet from eight hides'. Presumably this meant that not just some but all hundreds were to be formed into three-hundred ship-sokes (one manuscript reads '300 hides' rather than 310), each charged not only with the ship and her crew but with armour for thirty-seven or so men.[26] Domesday Book allows us to estimate the total hidage of England in 1066 at 70–80,000, which if the whole were assessed for naval service at one ship for every three hundreds would yield a fleet of between 230 and 270 ships, and we know that Æthelred had substantially more than 100 in 1009.[27]

The new naval programme evidently came too late. When the new fleet assembled at Sandwich in 1009, one Wulfnoth rebelled with twenty ships, the force of eighty ships sent after him was wrecked, and the fleet broke up in confusion.[28] Early in August a fresh Danish fleet under the formidable Thorkell the Tall landed in Kent, was bought off, and departed to ravage Hampshire and Sussex. Æthelred was not yet beaten, and he was able to divide his enemies by buying the services of the fleets of Thorkell and Olav Tryggvason.[29] Our view of English resistance has been greatly coloured by the tone adopted by the *Anglo-Saxon Chronicle*, which is gloomy, hostile to the king, and written with hindsight soon after his death. In fact it seems that under his leadership English resistance was vigorous and reasonably successful in the first part of his reign, but was progressively undermined by the unprecedented scale of the attacks and by internal disunity. Æthelred's fundamental problem was that the English were themselves divided. It has been plausibly argued that the strong government of King Edgar and the religious and civil reforms of his reign (including his naval reforms) had made many enemies, especially in Mercia, some of whom regarded a king of Denmark as no greater evil than a king of Wessex, and much further away.[30] It has also been suggested that Æthelred was rejected by many of his subjects as an unjust king who did not deserve their allegiance.[31] At all events, by 1013 King Swein Forkbeard of Denmark was acknowledged as King of England. When he died in February 1014 Æthelred was able to return from exile and re-establish his rule, and when he in turn died in April 1016 his son Edmund Ironside renewed the war. Had Edmund lived he might have succeeded, for he seems to have been a better leader, perhaps a better king, than his father, but his death after a reign of seven months left King Cnut of Denmark undisputed ruler of England.

It seems very probable that if Æthelred had had a stronger fleet earlier in his reign, it might have been a critical advantage against the Danish fleets. In the conditions of the time, seaborne attackers were bound to have enormous advantages, and in his reign he faced the regular forces of the kings of Denmark in unprecedented strength,[32] but it was never a foregone conclusion that England should be conquered. It can be argued that the fundamental factors were political and dynastic rather than military: a king better able to unite the English might have won through even without a powerful fleet, while if Edmund Ironside had had an adult heir, or Swein Forkbeard had lacked one, it might have been an English rather than a Danish king who offered the weary English the best possibilty of peace and stable government. When Cnut died in 1035 his sons Harald Harefoot and Harthacnut succeeded in turn, each dying without heirs and leaving the way open for Æthelred's son Edward 'the Confessor' (who had been not more than fourteen when his half-brother Edmund Ironside died, and had grown up in exile in Normandy) to become king in 1042. Thus the Danish empire broke up and an English king regained the throne of England.

The reign of Edward the Confessor (1042–66) was the golden age of the Anglo-Saxon navy, or at least the age of which we are best informed. For the first time sufficient evidence survives to allow us to understand its manning and organization in some detail. Almost all the men serving afloat of which we have any clear evidence in Anglo-Saxon times were soldiers of the *fyrd*, the national army raised by the shires. It used to be argued that the *fyrd* was originally a mass levy embracing every man who could bear arms, a peasant army of huge size but poor equipment, to which was later added a smaller, more professional force often referred to by historians as the 'select *fyrd*'. Recent research has virtually abolished the idea of a mass peasant army, at least in any period of which we have accurate knowledge.[33] It seems that at least as far back as Alfred and probably further, the *fyrd* was a semi-professional force made up of men of some social standing, small landowners who could afford proper weapons and equipment, including a sword, mail shirt and helmet, and a horse to ride to war – all of which were expensive – and the time for thorough training in their use.[34] Such a force was still a national levy in the sense that its men were contributed by the shires rather than retained at the king's wages, but it was a far smaller and more formidable force than a peasant levy. In addition the king could call upon the paid retainers of his household, his personal guard of warriors.

It is clear from all our Anglo-Saxon sources that the *fyrd* could serve by sea, when it was called a *scipfyrd*.[35] In references to the Danish invaders English writers often refer to them as consisting of so many 'shipfulls' of men,[36] and it looks as though on both sides the ship was the tactical unit of military organization, and the steersman the officer who commanded both ship and men.[37] This raises some awkward problems about the composition of ships' companies. There is no difficulty in supposing that soldiers could be as effective in hand-to-hand fighting afloat as they would be ashore, and it is perfectly possible that regular training every year would accustom them to handling oars; though rowing, especially in a seaway, is not as easy as it looks to the landsman. What is very difficult to believe is that men who were in ordinary life small landowners from inland shires were also experienced seamen. Yet the known passages of English fleets, the implication of all our evidence that they were regarded as able to reach into any northern waters, must indicate that they were handled by men thoroughly familiar with ships and the sea. The whole culture of the northern world was permeated with a sense of the sea, but this cannot possibly mean that skill in shiphandling and pilotage, knowledge of winds and tides, shoals and seamarks, were available by instinct to men who had no professional reason to acquire them.[38] In some cases we know not only where English ship-sokes lay, but from which villages the men were recruited. About the year 1000 both the Bishop of Sherborne's ship and the Bishop of London's drew their men largely from inland villages, though both bishops' estates bordered the sea.[39] It is very unlikely that many seamen lived in these villages, or if they did that they belonged to the class of substantial men from whom the *fyrd* was recruited. Eadric the Steersman who commanded the Bishop of Worcester's ship in 1066 came from Offerton, north-east of Worcester. In the same county Thorkell 'King Edward's steersman' held land in Pershore, while Eadric and Wulfeah, also described as King Edward's steersmen, came from Bradeston in Norfolk and Great Barford in Bedfordshire respectively.[40] These are all within reach of navigable rivers, but they are scarcely the obvious places to learn the skills needed to command a ship at sea.

Possibly some of each crew were small landowners who had somehow acquired specialist knowledge of the sea, but it is difficult to see how, in those cases where we know where they came from. More likely they (or their paid substitutes) were not in fact the whole ship's company, but the military part of it. As the later English fleets were based at London, a major commercial port where there were many seafarers, the ships could have found seamen there. In that case we should imagine the shires paying to have their ships built and laid up at London by means of the tax called the *scipscot*,[41] sending their *fyrd* men there whenever they were called upon for a *scipfyrd*, and also paying for some number of seamen to handle the ship under the steersman's orders. There are faint traces of evidence which might point to such a division of function. Alfred's great ships had Frisians as well as Englishmen in their crews, and Edgar employed Scandinavians, possibly in his ships.[42] In both cases one might guess that the foreigners were valued for their skills as seamen. Domesday Book, describing the situation at the end of Edward the Confessor's reign in 1066, records the obligation of Lewes to pay 20 shillings 'to those in charge of the arms' aboard ship whenever the king sent ships to guard the sea in his absence.[43] Perhaps 'those in charge of the arms' were the soldiers as distinct from the sailors, and guard of the sea in the king's absence refers to patrol or coastguard service, not with the main fleet. It is conceivable that the seaports may have had an obligation to furnish seamen for the fleet. Domesday Book does not much interest itself in matters beyond land ownership and tax revenue, and omits several of the largest ports altogether, so it would not necessarily record the fact.

Moreover there are hints that some inland boroughs were also responsible for finding seamen. Warwick sent some of its burgesses to join the army by land, but when the fleet went to sea it provided four *batsueins*, or £4 to pay for them. Malmesbury had to provide 20 shillings to feed the king's *buzecarls*.[44] The English word 'boat-swains' certainly refers to seamen, and the Danish *buzecarls* probably does so.[45]

If English ships were manned by a mixture of soldiers and sailors, it would help to explain what is otherwise a puzzling discrepancy between the size of the ships, insofar as we can guess it, and the size of the unit of men which they embarked. In the eleventh century English ships appear to have continued to carry about sixty men, though Earl Godwin gave Harthacnut a splendid ship manned by eighty chosen warriors with gilt armour.[46] Sixty men would be a full crew for a ship of only fifteen rooms or so – very small for a warship, especially by comparison with Alfred's ships of thirty rooms and more. Moreover the English may still have been building ships that large, for about the year 1008 Bishop Ælfwold of Crediton had a ship with 64 oars.[47] Admittedly this may mean equipped with so many oars, including an unknown proportion of spares, rather than actually rowing 32 a side, but it would be difficult to imagine her as small as fifteen rooms. The Danish ships of Cnut's fleet probably had crews of at least eighty on average.[48]

It is in the eleventh century that our evidence allows us for the first time to catch glimpses of other aspects of naval administration, perhaps already ancient. We gather that when they served afloat as when they formed part of the army ashore, the men levied from the shires were also fed at their expense for two months. If forces were needed for longer, they served by rotation, and if the fleet were needed for a long campaign, it had to return to base to exchange crews.[49] The English naval base was always London, where presumably most if not all the ships were laid up for the winter.[50] In the Scandinavian countries, especially Norway with its harsh winter, warships were kept in permanent ship-houses,[51] and it is not beyond possibility that somewhere, probably upstream of London Bridge, there were English ship-houses of the same type.[52] It would certainly make sense to protect an expensive warship from the inevitable decay attending winters hauled up on the open beach. We know that English ships were capable of beaching, but there are references to anchoring, and to men pulling out to their ships in small boats, which suggest that they were too large to beach comfortably.[53] By the eleventh century major ports, including London and Sandwich, had built quays at which ships could go alongside,[54] but probably these were reserved for ships with cargo to unload, and one would expect the characteristic requirement of the warship to be a ship-house. Every ship had a mast and sail, and English fleets evidently had no difficulty in sailing anywhere they needed to in northern waters. We know of several passages made by English fleets which suggest some capacity to hold a course on a wind, as Viking ships could by the ninth century at least.[55]

There are hints of some sort of coastal patrol maintained by selected ships while the main fleet was not at sea, and of a coast-watching organization with a system of beacons to carry swift warning of attack.[56] When the fleet was mobilized, it sailed from London to assemble at a strategic location, usually Sandwich. This excellent harbour gave easy access not only into the Channel and the North Sea, but also northward up the east coast through the Wantsum Channel between the Isle of Thanet and the mainland. As an alternative when the threat was from the west, the fleet sometimes assembled at the Isle of Wight.[57] Æthelred's law of 1008 required the fleet to assemble by Easter every year,[58] and in Edward the Confessor's reign the king himself regularly gathered part or all of his fleet at Sandwich for what appears to have been annual manoeuvres.[59]

On a report of raiders to the westward in 1048, Earl Godwin commanded a fleet of 44 ships; his sons Harald and Tosti each commanded one of the king's ships, and the rest of the fleet was made up of 42 'provincial ships'.[60] When part of this fleet was sent home it was described as the ships from Mercia, which implies that the fleet, like the army, was organized on a shire basis.[61] The distinction between the king's ships and the people's applies because by 1048 there were two distinct naval organizations in England. After Æthelred's death and the final triumph of King Cnut, a regular Danish fleet of forty ships was maintained at the English taxpayer's expense. The very large taxes levied to pay it provide some of the best evidence of the wealth and efficient government of eleventh-century England.[62] These foreign, mercenary ships' companies constituted a sort of standing army supporting the Danish king. After his death his son Harthacnut (1040–2) increased the force to not less than 94 ships,[63] supported by unprecedentedly heavy taxes. Edward the Confessor paid them off in stages, disposing of the last in 1051. He has been accused, by historians thinking of what happened in 1066, of weakening the kingdom's defences, but Edward had much more to fear from Denmark than from his friends the Normans who had no fleet, and Danish ships were not the best insurance against a Danish attack.[64] Moreover the abolition of the unpopular 'army-tax' which had supported the Danish ships, was accompanied by a sharp increase in the weight of the silver penny, which had the effect of increasing the real rate of ordinary taxation, so that Edward was as wealthy as before.[65]

Besides the *scipfyrd*, the Danish mercenaries, and whatever ships the English kings owned of their own, there may have been a fourth naval force in late Anglo-Saxon England. At (or possibly before) the time Edward the Confessor paid off the last of his Danish ships in 1051, he acquired in return for the grant of various privileges the right to annual ship-service from several ports in Kent.[66] These ports later formed the corporate body known as the Cinque Ports, although their communal organization cannot be traced earlier than the thirteenth century.[67] Dover and Sandwich each provided twenty ships for a fortnight, with crews of twenty-one men, and Fordwich, Romney, possibly Hythe and Hastings, probably served on a similar basis.[68] It is not clear what use Edward wished to make of ships with twenty-one men each for a fortnight a year. The period is too short for most military purposes, and twenty-one men far too few to man even the smallest warship. Conceivably these coastal boroughs (and some others such as Maldon[69]), provided seamen and ships which then embarked a 'shipfull' of sixty soldiers each for war service. More likely the Kentish ports were to provide small vessels to form a permanent scouting force, one or two at a time always on patrol in the Narrow Seas. They would have been well placed to watch the Flanders shore, where Earl Godwin was then waiting his opportunity; and we are informed that in the following year, 'King Edward had forty small boats manned which lay at Sandwich in order that they might keep watch for Earl Godwin who was at Bruges'.[70]

The English navy was not only powerful in itself, but seems to have inspired imitation. The Scandinavian monarchs of the twelfth and thirteenth centuries raised large fleets by a ship-muster system, the *leidang*, whose origins are disputed but which may have been modelled, or re-modelled, on the English example.[71] It first appears in Norway under Håkon the Good (935–61), Æthelstan's foster-son, who introduced many English-inspired governmental changes,[72] while in Denmark it has been suggested that Cnut the Great's taxation system, and by inference his methods of mustering forces, were copied from English practice.[73] It should also be noted that in the Western Isles, and possibly also in Orkney and Shetland, the Norwegians took over the existing ship-muster, probably before they had a developed system of their own, so that the Norwegian *leidang* may conceivably be derived from the precedent of Dalriada.[74] It is equally possible that all these systems are older than our evidence allows us to tell, and derive from common roots in late Roman organization.

In many ways, however, England was marked by Danish rule, and notably so in naval matters. Not only did Edward, as we have seen, retain a Danish fleet in English pay for some years, but his reign marks the high point of English naval activity in the early Middle Ages. The English fleet had never been more active. It had been used by Cnut against his enemies in Norway and Sweden,[75] and its assistance was sought by foreign monarchs.[76] No other English king, Edgar perhaps excepted, used his fleet so often, or commanded it so frequently in person. Edward used it as Æthelstan and Edgar had done before him to secure the submission of the Celtic rulers to the north and west.[77] In 1045 he gathered the largest fleet ever seen in England in response to a threat of invasion from King Magnus of Norway. Two years later, and again in 1048, King Swein Estrithson of Denmark asked for the help of fifty English ships against Norway. In 1049 Edward once more assembled a large fleet at Sandwich in support of the German Emperor Henry III's campaign against Count Baldwin of Flanders.[78] For most of Edward's reign the west and north – specifically the Norwegians and their potential allies in Ireland, Scotland and Wales – were probably the major external threat to England. In Scandinavia Norway was again in the ascendant over Denmark, and King Harald Hardrada ('the Ruthless') had claims on the English throne. The Welsh prince Gruffydd ap Llywellyn was one of the few Welsh rulers to achieve something like political unity, at least in North Wales, and he was the only one who is known to have had a fleet. Moreover his ally the exiled Mercian Earl Ælfgar had ships both of his own and from the Dublin Vikings.[79] In Ireland the power of Diarmait mac Maíl na mBó of Leinster was similarly dominant.[80] The combination of strong Celtic rulers with sea power and Norwegian allies represented real danger to England. In 1049 a Norse-Irish fleet said to include 36 'kings' came up the Severn to ravage.[81] In 1054 an English naval and military expedition to Scotland attempted without success to eject King Macbeth in favour of the English candidate Malcolm Canmore.[82] In 1055 Gruffydd and Earl Ælfgar attacked and burnt Hereford (on which occasion Earl Ralph 'the Timid', King Edward's Norman nephew, distinguished himself by leading the retreat).[83] In 1056 and 1057 Earl Harold Godwinson campaigned on land against Gruffydd with no conspicuous success. Both Gruffydd and Ælfgar were involved in the great expedition of 1058 organized by King Harald's son Magnus.[84] We know virtually nothing about this, except that it was successful in forcing the temporary restoration of Ælfgar to his earldom.[85] The English achieved nothing against Gruffydd until 1063, when Earl Harold first attacked Rhuddlan after Christmas, burning his ships, then at the end of May sailed with a fleet from Bristol and came round Wales, while his brother Tosti advanced by land along the north coast. (This is one of several known passages by English fleets, involving sharp alterations of course, which suggest that they were able to beat into the wind.) The combination forced the Welsh to submit, and presently Gruffydd was killed in a palace revolution. His successors sent King Edward his head and his ship's figurehead, and promised to obey 'by sea and land'.[86] Once again it had been demonstrated that only sea power deployed in the Irish Sea could counter the Norwegian and Celtic threat to England.

No other English king, Edgar perhaps excepted, used his fleet so often, or commanded it so frequently in person, as Edward the Confessor. In no other reign was it so common, indeed almost universal, for the great men of the kingdom, the ealdormen, earls and bishops, to serve at sea.[87] They are described as 'steersmen', as 'steering' their ships, and the words seem to be meant literally.[88] All this looks much more like a Danish tradition than an English one. Among the magnates none were more often afloat than Earl Godwin and his sons. Godwin (probably son of the Wulfnoth who led the 1009 mutiny) was a creation of Danish rule, a kinsman by marriage of King Cnut, who gave his sons conspicuously Danish names like Harold, Swein and Tosti. Endowed by Cnut with the former royal estates of Wessex, the source of much of the English kings' wealth and power, he represented for King Edward the Danish empire's most dangerous legacy.[89]

The political history of Edward's reign revolves around his attempts to escape from Godwin's tutelage, in part by promoting an alliance with Normandy to counterbalance Denmark. It was at sea that Godwin played out his struggle to control the English crown, in the fashion familiar to the Scandinavian world. The complex origins of the crisis need not be laid out in detail here. Edward hated Godwin personally for having murdered his brother Alfred in 1035, and had every motive of state to free himself from his over-mighty subject.[90] Duke William of Normandy, with whose father Edward had grown up in exile, began his struggle to win control of his whole duchy (including the Channel coast) at the battle of Val-ès-Dunes in 1047, and was presently in a position to give Edward support – in return, it seems probable, for a promise of the throne when the childless Edward should die.[91] The crisis came to a head in 1051, soon after Edward had paid off the last of his Danish fleet. Godwin may have seen this as his opportunity; two years earlier his son Swein had treacherously murdered Earl Beorn Estrithson, who has been identified as the commander of this fleet, so perhaps he had more than one reason to be glad to see the king's personal guard reduced.

Initially Godwin overplayed his hand and was driven into exile. Edward installed some of his Norman friends in key positions, and Duke William came to England to be recognized as his successor.[92] In 1052, however, Godwin's sons Harold and Leofwine led a successful raid on Devon and Somerset from their exile in Ireland, while their father crossed from Flanders to Sussex, the heart of his earldom and his estates. There many men, including the seamen of Hastings and the Kentish ports, came over to him. He eluded the ships which the king had stationed at Sandwich to watch for him, and which then returned to London. Off the Isle of Wight, Godwin met his sons coming up Channel, and together they moved to Sandwich and came up the Thames. At Southwark Godwin's army met them and the ships passed through London Bridge, preparing to encircle the king's fleet and army on the northern bank. At this juncture civil war was only averted by the reluctance of both armies to fight their fellow-countrymen. The result was a nominal reconciliation.[93] When Godwin died soon afterwards and was succeeded by his son Harold, the political issue, and with it the dynastic issue of who should succeed the childless king, was still unsettled.

THREE

The Partition of Britain

1066–1204

When Harold Godwinson seized the throne on the death of King Edward in January 1066, England gained a king with more experience of war at sea than any of his predecessors (Edgar possibly excepted), or any successor before James II. It also gained a king with virtually no blood connections with the English royal house, and shaky pretensions to legitimacy; one undoubtedly resented by many of the old English nobility and too strongly associated with Danish rule. He could command loyalty only so long as he could provide good government and avert the evils of civil war and foreign invasion, of which Englishmen had such bitter experience. As ruler of a strong and wealthy kingdom Harold had many advantages, but the diplomatic situation in 1066 was menacing. King Harald of Norway still cherished his claim on the throne. So did Duke William of Normandy, to whom the late king had forced Harold to swear allegiance, probably in 1065. This weakened his position abroad, where he could plausibly be presented as a perjured oath-breaker whom no Christian could honestly support. In the north Malcolm Canmore, King of Scots since 1058, was becoming steadily less friendly and more ambitious. Harold's brother Tosti had been deposed as Earl of Northumbria in 1065 by a revolt led by the old nobility. Edward had been obliged to accept; Harold may have come to an agreement with the new earl Morcar, and he certainly made an enemy of his brother. On the Continent the King of France, normally a reliable counterweight to Normandy, was a small child under the guardianship of Duke William's father-in-law Baldwin V, Count of Flanders, and the whole Channel coast from Ushant to the Rhine mouths was in the hands of Duke William or rulers friendly to him.[1]

It is arguable that Harold's actions in 1066 were driven as much by political as military priorities. England was a powerful state, but all recent history showed that it was less than united. Many people had reason to resent his usurpation, and only speedy and complete victory would guarantee loyalty. Speed was always a valuable asset in warfare, but in Harold's case he had political as well as military reasons to settle the issue quickly. It is clear that he regarded Duke William as the main threat. All through the summer the king lay with the English fleet at the Isle of Wight, as the Norman forces slowly assembled across the Channel.[2] At some point Harold took the English fleet to sea for a spoiling attack, of which unfortunately we know nothing but that it took place.[3] In September the Norwegian fleet entered the Humber and sailed up the Ouse to Riccal, where they left their ships and advanced on York. At Gate Fulford outside the city on 20 September they defeated the local forces and entered the city. It looks as though the people of York submitted readily enough, though the Norwegian army was accompanied by the same Tosti whom they had recently ejected as earl. Harold reacted at once. Marching rapidly north, he crossed the Wharfe at Tadcaster with the help of English ships which had retreated upriver, passed through York without stopping, and took the Norwegians by surprise on the other side of the city. The battle at Stamford Bridge on 25 September was one of the epic struggles of northern history, ending in the death of Harald Hardrada – a man literally as well as metaphorically larger than life – and most of his army with him.

On Michaelmas Day, four days after Harold's great victory, Duke William landed in Sussex. We do not know how much Harold knew in advance of Harald Hardrada's preparations, but there is reason to believe that William was informed about them.[4] It is the only obvious reason why he should have undertaken his invasion. Certainly he believed his cause was just and God would favour him, but he was a shrewd and experienced general, not given to risking the uncertainties of battle unless they were unavoidable, and he must have been aware of the extreme dangers of cross-Channel invasion. His barons certainly were:

> They remarked that Harold was blessed with great treasures wherewith he might win the support of dukes and powerful kings; that he had a great fleet and highly skilled sailors who had long experience of the dangers and hazards of sea-warfare; and that in wealth and military strength his country was many times richer than Normandy. Who could hope, they said, that the Norman ships would be ready in time, or that sufficient oarsmen would be found within a year?[5]

It was true that the Vikings had shown that seaborne attack virtually guaranteed surprise, but William's situation was different. Although his father Duke Robert is thought to have planned an expedition to England in 1035, aimed at expelling Cnut in favour of Robert's protégé Edward, the deaths of both duke and king had ended the project,[6] and William apparently had no fleet at all in 1066. The Bayeux Tapestry and other sources show us a fleet under construction from scratch; it is difficult to believe that a force of at least 700 ships could have been built so quickly, and it is perhaps more likely that many of the ships and crews were found among William's Flemish allies.[7] It is certain that the preparation of the expedition took many months, and cannot have been concealed from the English. For the first time in English history, it was possible to predict exactly where the invasion was coming from, and roughly where and when it would arrive.

This exposed the Normans to great danger. It was by no means unlikely that they would have to make an opposed landing, and almost certain that they would be opposed soon after landing, probably by strong forces. The English fleet had a good chance of intercepting the invaders on the coast, and excellent prospects of catching them in the rear soon after landing. What was worse, from the Norman point of view, their method of warfare emphasized the use of cavalry, whereas the English were accustomed to ride to battle, but to fight on foot. English soldiers could and would fight effectively on shipboard, or on the beach, but Norman knights, the armoured cavalrymen who formed the core of William's army, would lose their peculiar advantage without their horses.

The problem was more than simply that of providing transports for some thousands of horses and their forage.[8] Horses are badly affected by the confinement and motion of a ship at sea, and at best require some time to recover from a voyage.[9] Moreover Norman warhorses were highly-trained and expensive animals which had to be fresh for battle, so they were normally led rather than ridden. A Norman army was not fully mobile unless every knight had a minimum of four horses: a warhorse, a riding horse for himself, another for his squire who led the warhorse, and a packhorse to carry his armour and baggage.[10] It is usually suggested that William had an army of about 7,000, including 2–3,000 knights.[11] Fully equipped, they would have needed 8–12,000 horses, and more if any proportion of the infantry and archers were mounted. A fleet of between 700 and 1,000 ships cannot possibly have carried so many horses, which meant that the army was effectively immobilized until it could collect enough horses in England. In that rich country horses were common, and in the past Danish invaders had often gathered horses on landing, but the Norman army could not leave its bridgehead until it had collected a great many of them. The odds were heavily against the Normans being allowed an unopposed crossing plus a lengthy period of recuperation before battle. The only chance was that the Norwegians would draw off the defence for long enough.

Even this took no account of the English fleet, which by itself was sufficient to make the attempt unacceptably hazardous. Its weakness was the necessity of returning to base every two months for fresh men and supplies. By September the English ships had probably performed two two-month tours of duty, and on the 8th they were obliged to sail for London again in search of provisions.[12] Four days later William, who had been ready for a month, sailed from his assembly port of Dives.[13] The contemporary Norman historians, reluctant to present their hero as a man who avoided battle, labour to explain his prolonged wait as caused by foul winds, but it is stretching coincidence very far to believe that the elusive wind served just as the English fleet and army were obliged to withdraw.[14] Much of the discussion of this point among historians seems to assume that Norman ships had the sailing qualities of a rubber dinghy, capable only of drifting before the wind, but the ships on the Bayeux Tapestry carry the standard 'Viking' rig, including shrouds, forestay and backstay, and there is no reason to doubt that they could at least reach across the wind if not beat into it.[15] Even the most clumsy and leewardly horse-transport could surely have made good a course at least six points either side of downwind, which is to say that any wind from ENE to WNW would have allowed them to clear the Bay of the Seine and fetch some part of the south coast of England.

It is possible that William always intended to land near Hastings, where Edward the Confessor had endowed the Norman abbey of Fécamp with estates and the Duke had accurate local intelligence.[16] When he sailed his course was directly for Hastings, and there is no doubt that it was not from choice that he took refuge up the coast in the port of St Valéry-sur-Somme. The wind evidently veered north-westerly and blew up, driving some ships ashore and the rest into port.[17] This was a crisis for the expedition: supplies were running short, morale was sinking, the Somme estuary was impossible to clear on a westerly wind, and with every day the return of the English fleet and army grew nearer. They remained there for a fortnight, and now undoubtedly Duke William really did watch the church weathervane with anxiety.[18] On 27 September the wind backed, and on the evening tide the fleet put to sea.[19]

The Norman fleet landed first at Pevensey, which was separated from Hastings by two wide estuaries, and the fact that the Normans immediately moved there is the strongest evidence that it was their original target.[20] In the eleventh century the inlets of Brede and Bulverhythe made Hastings a peninsula which provided secure flanks for the bridgehead – secure, that is to say, against land attack.[21] It is probable that one of Harold's reasons for the much-criticized speed with which he marched south, without waiting to gather the resources of a rich and populous kingdom, was to seal the neck of the peninsula before the Norman army acquired the horses, and consequently the mobility, which they would need to break out.[22] Moreover a mounted army needed grass for fodder, and by the end of October the grass would stop growing. Having landed so late in the campaigning season, William had to move fast if he was going to move at all, and Harold had to move fast to stop him. It is also probable that he intended to catch the Normans between two fires, for several sources tell us that the English fleet, presumably re-victualled and re-manned, had sailed again from London.[23] It was too late to intercept the Normans at sea, but there was every opportunity to land in the Norman rear, and William had invested much labour and some substantial fraction of his force in fortifications which must have been inspired by just this possibility. [24] A joint attack from front and rear offered Harold excellent hopes, and they would be thrown away if the Normans were allowed to escape. Harold therefore halted his army on the neck of the peninsula, where no doubt he intended to remain until the fleet arrived. Presumably Duke William realized his peril; in any case he had much to risk and little to gain by delay once the English army was within his reach, and he hastened to force an action before his situation grew any worse. The event of that action, close-fought and doubtful to the last, was decided by the death of Harold.[25] His claim on the loyalties of Englishmen had always been that he alone could provide stability and good government; after his death there was no generally acceptable English candidate who could carry on the fight with any prospects of success. The young prince Edgar Ætheling was briefly chosen by the surviving English leaders, but failed to rally sufficient support.

William was now the obvious heir of King Edward, as he had always claimed to be. It is striking how quickly the English accepted him as their king, and how loyally they served him, with few exceptions. The history of his reign and his descendants' reigns for two centuries is a continuous series of rebellions and civil wars, but it was seldom the English who led them. It was the Norman baronage which represented the threat to stability, as the strong unitary state of Anglo-Saxon England was replaced by a feudal system which provided every great man with independent military power and jurisdiction.

The fleet had been one of the most potent symbols of England's power, and it seems to have been one of the first to wither. In 1068 Harold's sons raided Somerset in ships from Dublin, as he himself had done eighteen years before, and the next year they landed in north Devon. This time they were defeated, but no attempt was made to assert English power and eliminate the threat by sending ships into the Irish Sea.[26] The result was a vacuum of naval power which was swiftly filled by the Dublin Vikings, the Irish and the Norwegians. In the eleventh and twelfth centuries the fleets of the Irish Vikings were at their most formidable, and in the same period Irish kings were building fleets in the Viking style. Much of this naval warfare was on the inland waters and around the coasts of Ireland itself, but the ships were equally available for operations anywhere in the Irish Sea. Between 1075 and his final success in 1099 the exiled Welsh prince Gruffydd ap Cynan of Gwynedd (son of a Norse-Irish mother and born in Dublin) raised no fewer than five fleets in Dublin to regain power, and other Welsh princes did the same.[27] With no risk of English fleets appearing, the Irish Sea was now open to anyone with ships and the ambition to use them.

Among them were some members of the Norman baronage, more adaptable than their king. They had early acquired a foothold at Pembroke, and in the 1090s briefly overran much of North and South Wales, but Pembroke never had secure communication with England by land, and its lords had to keep up a squadron of ships for their own security. Pembroke was in effect a semi-independent island, like others in the Irish Sea, and its rulers had to adapt to the local way of warfare. They also had to learn the dangers of operating within reach of powerful fleets. In 1094 Welsh counter-attacks drove the Normans out of most of Wales. In 1098 Hugh the Fat of Avranches, Earl of Chester, was campaigning in North Wales against Gruffydd ap Cynan, who as usual relied on the support of a hired Viking fleet from Dublin. The Normans had reached Anglesey when Gruffydd's ships abandoned him, and he was forced to flee to Dublin. At that moment, however, the fleet of King Magnus Barelegs of Norway, cruising in the Irish Sea to assert his authority over Man and the Isles, entered the Menai Straits. In the ensuing skirmish, Hugh de Montgomery, Earl of Shrewsbury, was killed by a Norwegian arrow, and the Norman forces abandoned their campaign.[28] Though Chester later recovered Anglesey for a while, and in the south Pembroke held out, with no English fleet in the Irish Sea most of Wales passed out of the Norman sphere of control for a generation or more.

On the east coast William I was helpless in the face of serious Danish threats. In 1069 King Swein entered the Humber with 240 ships in support of a Northumbrian rebellion, stormed York castle and massacred the garrison.

The Norman & Angevin Empires
NORTH SEA
Dublin
Waterford
York
R. Humber
GWYNEDD
Kenilworth
Pembroke
Bristol
R. Thames
London
Sandwich
Dover
Portsmouth
Dartmouth
ISLE OF WIGHT
ENGLISH CHANNEL
FLANDERS
NORTH ATLANTIC OCEAN
GUERNSEY
SARK
JERSEY
St. Malo
Caen
Rouen
R. Seine
Château Gaillard
Paris
BRITTANY
NORMANDY
MAINE
Nantes
ANJOU
POITOU
ILE D'OLÉRON
La Rochelle
Tonnay
R. Charente
BAY OF BISCAY
Gironde
Blaye
Bourg
Bordeaux
R. Dordogne
R. Garonne
GASCONY
Bayonne
St. Jean-de-Luz

William recaptured the city and exacted a fearful revenge on the northern counties, but was unable to touch the Danish fleet, which lay all winter 'between the Ouse and the Trent'. William chased them from Yorkshire to Lincolnshire and back, experiencing much trouble in crossing the broad rivers without ships to help, while the Danes avoided him at their leisure and in 1070 moved south to lie in the Thames until William bought them off. He was the last English king to pay Danegeld. In 1075 they raided York and again escaped untouched.[29] No attempt was made to oppose any of these fleets by sea, though their position, beached or anchored and stationary for long periods, would have invited naval counter-attack had any ships been available. In 1085 King Cnut IV of Denmark gathered the greatest fleet ever seen in Denmark to invade England, inspiring in William something little short of panic. He hired mercenary troops from all over Europe to garrison every threatened point, and laid waste the coastal districts in a 'scorched earth' policy to deny them to the invader. In the event Cnut's murder cut short the operation, but there is no doubt that had it taken place the Danes would have enjoyed the strategic initiative and unfettered freedom of movement.[30]

References to the English navy after the Conquest are so few that it has been claimed that the *scipfyrd* was never mustered again after 1066, and that all naval services mentioned later in the eleventh century were performed by the Kentish ports.[31] The evidence is slender and ambiguous: the ships blockading English rebels in the Isle of Ely in 1071 are referred to in one source as a *scipfyrd*, which formerly meant the national fleet levied on the shires, and in another as *butsecarls*, which might perhaps refer to the men of the Kentish ports.[32] What seems to be certain is that the old English ship-muster system, and the great fleet it had supported, declined swiftly under the Norman kings. By the time Domesday Book was compiled in 1086 its organization seems to have largely disappeared.[33] The last occasion when it, or part of it, may have been at sea was the 1091 campaign against Scotland. We do not know what happened to the Norman invasion fleet after 1066, though at some date between 1066 and 1086 William bought a ship from a Lincoln man.[34]

William's only 'naval' successes were against enemies with few or no ships. The 1071 Ely blockade was one example,[35] and during Odo of Bayeux's 1088 rebellion William II was able to blockade Pevensey Castle by sea and intercept help coming from Normandy.[36] Both Williams also used fleets to provide the essential logistic support without which no English army could penetrate into Scotland. In 1072 a large-scale raid penetrated as far as the

Tay and forced King Malcolm to submit temporarily, but he continued to profit by the weakness and disorder of Norman England. By 1080 Cumbria was lost to England, Northumberland disputed, and the effective frontier was on the Tyne.[37] In 1091 William II mounted another expedition, but he started late, many of the ships were wrecked in a September gale, and as a natural consequence many of the cavalrymen, we are told, died of cold and hunger. Eventually the army reached the Forth and obliged Malcolm to make another tactical submission, but the only lasting English gain was the reconquest of Cumberland the following year.[38]

If William I had placed any value on sea power, he might have incorporated it into the feudal system. There was no intrinsic reason why feudal obligations should not have been discharged by naval service; they were in Norman Sicily,[39] possibly in Normandy itself,[40] and when feudalism was adopted in Scotland it easily assumed the galley-service of the Western Isles.[41] A little sea service was in fact performed under feudal tenure in England,[42] and more could have been. Moreover the Norman kings were wealthy and employed a substantial paid army,[43] but they did not spend their money on warships. If they failed to provide for a naval component of their new military system, it was from choice rather than necessity.

What they had to set up was a royal ferry service to carry the king and his court to and from Normandy. This royal transport service operated from Southampton, with sailings sometimes from Portchester or Bosham, to Barfleur and other Norman ports.[44] William I probably crossed the Channel seventeen times between 1066 and 1087, William II five times between 1096 and 1100, Henry I sixteen times between 1106 and 1135. We know of about fifty royal crossings in the eighty years after the Conquest, besides others by messengers and important dignitaries.[45] Between 1154 and 1189, according to the chroniclers, Henry II crossed the Channel certainly twenty-six, and probably twenty-eight times. Four of these crossings were on the Dover–Wissant route, when the king had occasion to visit Flanders, and one (in January 1188) was from Dieppe to Winchelsea. All the others were between Southampton or Portchester and Barfleur, Cherbourg, or another of the Côtentin ports.[46] In the late twelfth century a small group of Southampton shipmasters and owners like Ralph Calf (*Vitulus*), Samson Wascelin, William son of Stephen Mariner, Herbert Geldewin, Ralph Testard, Osbert Brochard and Berengar of Hampton[47] regularly supplemented the king's *esnecca*, or provided her with an escort when she carried treasure. Ralph Calf's ship seems to have been the normal relief when she was unavailable.[48] Under Richard I, Alan Trenchemer ('Plough-the-sea') her master was often charged with wide responsibilities. He repaired ships and purchased stores,[49] he built new ships and fitted them out,[50] he recruited and paid their men,[51] he commanded squadrons from 1196,[52] and in 1203 he led the Norman fleet at the battle of Les Andelys.[53]

In the twelfth century naval operations in northern waters remained largely a matter of transport. In 1101 Duke Robert Curthose of Normandy assembled a large invasion fleet to reclaim England from his younger brother Henry I, and many of the ships Henry gathered went over to the Normans, but this contest was temporarily compromised without fighting, and the war which eventually settled the succession was fought in Normandy.[54] The reign of King Stephen (1135–54) was troubled by civil war which left little scope to present English power beyond the kingdom, while the Angevin empire of Henry II (1154–89) occupied most of his attention on the Continent. Stephen did assemble a fleet in 1136 to tackle the piracy of Baldwin de Redvers in the Isle of Wight, but this seems to have been about the limit of his reach at sea, and when King Eric the Lamb of Denmark raided the east coast in 1138 nothing could be done to stop him.[55]

In the west the lords of Pembroke continued to play a semi-independent role in the politics of the Irish Sea. In 1102 Arnulf de Montgomery of Pembroke rebelled against Henry I and allied with the Irish king Muirchertach O'Brian (1086–1119), who controlled the fleets of Dublin and Waterford.[56] Such a combination was a serious threat to a Norman king with no fleet, and though Arnulf was eventually obliged to retreat to Ireland, Henry I had no answer to the Norse-Irish fleets. Henry II conducted a campaign in Wales in 1157 which tells us something of his attitude to sea power. Initially the king advanced from Chester and attempted to outflank the Welsh defensive works at Basingwerk by penetrating inland. He was ambushed in the forest and was lucky to escape with his life, though the Welsh were still obliged to withdraw. Meanwhile a squadron of ships sailed north from Pembroke and made a landing at Moelfre on Anglesey, but the indisciplined troops plundering ashore were attacked and suffered heavy losses. Compared to the 1063 campaign of Tosti and Harold Godwinson, this was a disorganized and ramshackle offensive, though in the end English military pressure achieved some gains. Henry's folly in attempting the forests of North Wales when the Welsh defences could have been easily and safely outflanked by sea is especially revealing.[57] When he again campaigned in Wales in 1165 he tried advancing into the central mountains, and hired a Viking squadron from Dublin to raid the coasts of Gwynedd. The army presently found itself stranded on the Berwyn Mountains, wet and starving, and was obliged to retreat with nothing gained. The full extent of English sea power in these campaigns was to carry supplies up the Severn from Worcester to Shrewsbury,[58] and to supply coastal fortresses like Neath.[59] Contemporaries were well aware of Wales's vulnerability to naval blockade, but Henry II was unable to exploit it.[60]

Henry's most important seaborne offensive was his expedition to Ireland in 1171, inspired by the acquisitions of Richard 'Strongbow' FitzGilbert, dispossessed lord of Pembroke. Frustrated in his ambitions in Wales, FitzGilbert escaped altogether from English royal control and began to establish what threatened to become an independent Norman-Irish state, complete with fleet. This was not entirely a Norman or English 'invasion' of Ireland. It can equally be seen as a sign of the absorption of the Normans of South Wales into the Irish Sea world. Son-in-law and successor of Diarmait MacMurchada of Leinster, Strongbow became a powerful Irish prince against whom his rival Rory O'Connor of Connaught, the High King, needed the help of Henry II, as well as the ships of Man and the Western Isles, to back his authority. Henry, for his part, might well have been unable to cross the Irish Sea if O'Connor's fleets had not been available to cover the crossing.[61] Another English adventurer, John de Courcy, married the daughter of King Godfrey of Man and carved out a lordship for himself in Ulster. From one perspective, it was an extension of Norman or English power, but it was equally a Manx triumph over an old enemy, which won the Manx fleet a new base in Carlingford Lough.[62]

At the same time circumstances were greatly improving the opportunities of the English kings to interfere in the Celtic world. The more advanced economy, the growing wealth, power and population of England (especially the southern counties), were undoubtedly putting social and economic pressure on much of South Wales, eastern Ireland and Lowland Scotland. Irishmen of the time complained loudly about English settlers occupying their best lands and subverting their laws and customs. These settlers were not engaged in royal military operations or officially-organized colonizing expeditions, but they naturally looked to England for protection, and they made it possible for the Anglo-Norman baronage and Anglo-Norman kings to increase their political power. Though nothing like an invasion in any military sense took place, over time there was a real transfer of effective control over wide areas.

This is the background to Henry II's intervention in 1171. With long preparation and great expense a substantial force was conveyed to Dublin, and Henry was rewarded with the title of overlord, but his growing power

The Irish Sea
NORTH CHANNEL
ULSTER
CUMBRIA
ISLE OF MAN
Carlingford Lough
Lancaster
LEINSTER
IRISH SEA
Dublin
ANGLESEY
Moelfre
MENAI STRAIT
Penmaenmawr
Rhuddlan
Liverpool
Beaumaris
Conway
Basingwerk
Chester
R. Dee
Denbigh
Caernarfon
Snowdonia
GWYNEDD
Harlech
Berwyn Mountains
BARDSEY
Pwllheli
Criccieth
Shrewsbury
MUNSTER
ST GEORGE'S CHANNEL
Llanbadarn
Waterford
Worcester
Cardigan
R. Severn
PEMBROKESHIRE
Haverford
Carmarthen
Kidwelly
Chepstow
Neath
Newport
Milford Haven
Tenby
Cardiff
Bristol
BRISTOL CHANNEL
LUNDY
Barnstaple
Bridgewater

was less the result of a naval operation than a function of the growing economic and demographic weight of Englishmen and Normans in Ireland. There is a clear contrast with the situation two hundred years before. Then English kings had used naval power in the Irish Sea to put pressure on Celtic rulers who would otherwise have been outside the English sphere of influence. By the twelfth century the wealth and population of England were so much greater than those of the Celtic realms that they could be converted into political power in the nearer parts of the Celtic world even without significant naval strength – so long as no hostile fleet appeared to disrupt English communications across the Irish Sea. But it is important to note that the power of Henry II was a different sort of power, with quite different effects, to the power of Æthelstan or Edgar. Their sea power applied a coercive force to the existing rulers without disrupting the social order of the Celtic world. For those who accepted this discreet overlordship, English sea power was a conservative force, tending to back their rule and support the existing social and political order. Henry's opportunity was based on a completely different situation; the widespread colonization of parts of Ireland by incomers who called themselves English (though many of them actually spoke French), and perceived themselves as bringing an advanced economy and a superior civilization to a barbarous and despicable people. A pattern was then established which was to endure.[63] We cannot say that things would have been different if Henry II had had powerful fleets, for the economic and demographic pressures behind English expansion would no doubt have been the same, but we might say that Irish and Welsh princes who were paid-up members of an English maritime empire would have had some reason to expect protection from their overlord against just the sort of pressures which were wrecking Irish society in the twelfth century. They might have enjoyed the same sort of relationship with English power as medieval Gascony did: its economy closely and productively linked to England, but its social system not essentially affected by English overlordship. As barbarians dwelling beyond the frontiers, the Irish had no such protection.

The first English naval operations in the Mediterranean occurred during the First Crusade, though no English ships are known to have participated in actual sea fighting. About 30 vessels, apparently merchantmen, commanded by the same Edgar Ætheling who had briefly been king of England in 1066, captured coastal fortresses in Syria in 1097 and played an important role in supplying the crusader army besieging Antioch.[64] After the battle of Ramleh

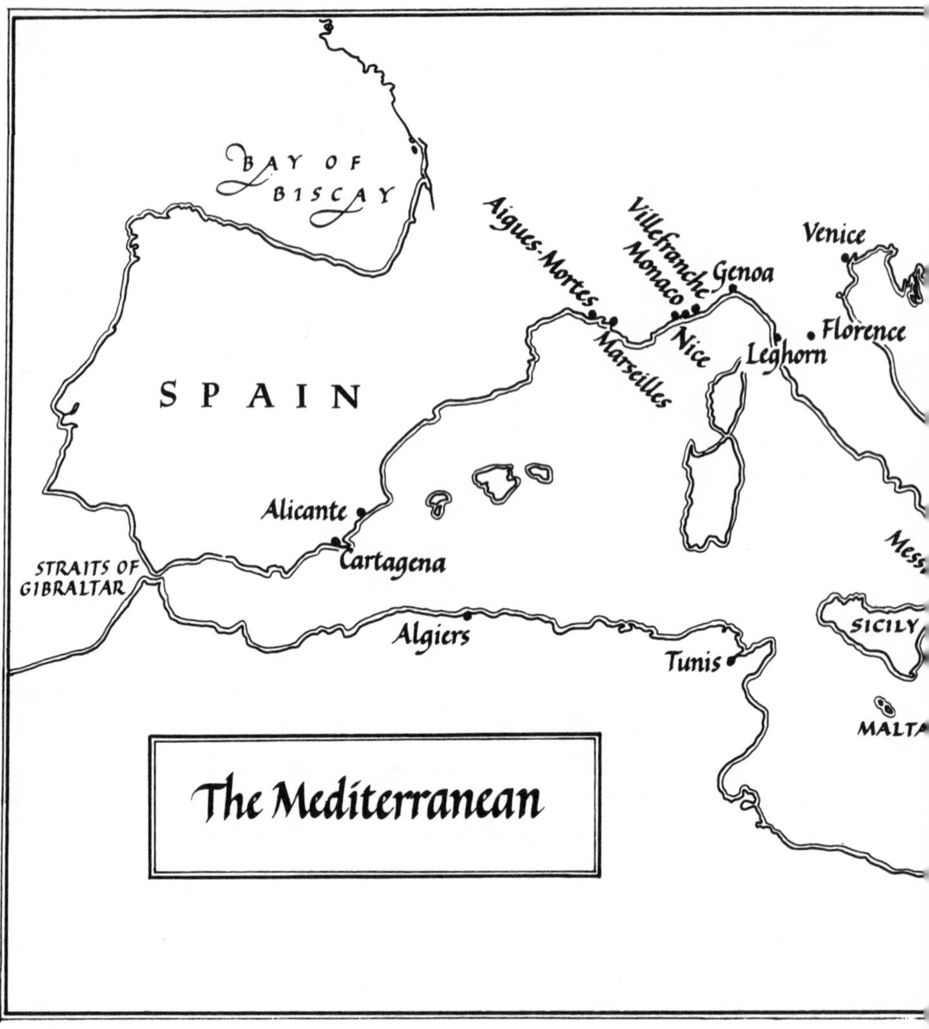

in 1102 King Baldwin I of Jerusalem was rescued by an English ship whose master was one Godric (possibly the future hermit Saint Godric of Finchale), who carried him from Arsuf to Jaffa.[65] These English ships, like a Flemish squadron and the Norwegian fleet of King Sigurd the Pilgrim, were able to enter the Mediterranean because Muslim sea power was weak between 1090 and 1107. What they could not do was return against the continual westerly wind and current in the Straits of Gibraltar. After 1107 the restoration of Almoravid power in Spain closed the Straits to eastbound Christian shipping as well.[66] The varying fortunes of Almoravid and Almohad power in Spain

and North Africa during the twelfth century gave some opportunities to Christian fleets to enter the Mediterranean, as they did in 1189 and 1190, but in neither case did they return to the Atlantic.[67] The mixed force of English, Normans, Flemings and Germans which in 1147 sailed from Dartmouth in 167 ships to take Lisbon from the infidel probably represents the furthest south an English expedition of the time could reach and return.[68]

Richard I (1189–99) sailed on the Third Crusade in 1190 from Marseilles, and much of his shipping seems to have been chartered locally, but a substantial English fleet (110 ships according to one account) sailed from Dartmouth.[69] His fleet as it sailed from Messina in April 1191 is given as 13 dromons (large warships of Byzantine design), 150 busses (a type of merchantman), and 53 galleys.[70] Off Beirut in June the king himself with some of his galleys encountered a large Turkish ship. Her size (she had three masts) and force, which excited the hyperbole of the English chroniclers, gave her every advantage over the attacking galleys, whose attempts to board were repelled, but in the end she was sunk – according to various writers by ramming, by the Saracen commander scuttling her with an axe, or by a little boy swimming underneath her with an auger and drilling a hole in the bottom.[71] Here, as so often with medieval chroniclers' accounts of naval battles, we are in the realm of literary fancies rather than factual information. The ram had long been abandoned in the Mediterranean and was never used in northern waters, but writers with a classical education knew how these things ought to be done, even if they did not understand how they actually were.

Richard I is the first post-Conquest English king who showed an appreciation of sea power – not initially northern sea power but the ships of the Italian states. As commander of the Third Crusade he twice came within sight of his goal, Jerusalem, but prudently refused to undertake major operations far from the sea, on which his army depended completely for its supplies. Though he failed to recapture Jerusalem, he conquered Cyprus and retook Acre (which in enemy hands posed a serious threat to sea communications), leaving a crusader state securely established along the coast, with Cyprus as its economic hinterland.[72] Thus the best Christian general of his age learnt the importance of the sea, at least when his lines of communication lay across it.

The strategic situation of Normandy in relation to England mirrored in miniature that of the crusader states (*Oultremer* or 'Oversea' as they were called) in relation to the rest of Christendom. Richard I returned from his crusade in 1194 to find Philip Augustus of France pushing towards the Channel coast by both diplomatic and military means.[73] Though our evidence is fragmentary, it looks as though Richard's response was to build a substantial squadron of what were possibly light galleys (seventy *cursoria* or 'runners' according to one source),[74] and to establish a naval strategic axis and supply route stretching from his new castle of Château Gaillard on the Norman frontier, down the Seine and across the Channel to the new town of Portsmouth, which he took into his own hands and on which he spent much money.[75] His clear strategic vision, evidently based on his experience in the Mediterranean, and his bold tactical handling of forces by land and sea were successful in foiling the French advance.

After the Norman Conquest the only English ships mentioned in our sources which might have been warships are of the type usually referred to as a *snacc* or *esnecca*. The word is related to the Norse *snekkjar*, 'snakes',[76] and the ships were evidently of the general 'Viking' type, with oars, used in entering and leaving port, and a sail, but it is difficult to say more. The *White Ship*, which was wrecked off Barfleur in 1120 with the loss of the king's son and many others, is said to have had 300 people aboard, of whom 50 were oarsmen.[77] Henry II's *esnecca* appears to have had a crew of 58 plus her steersman, and sailed on her last voyage to the Mediterranean in 1189 with 59.[78] The *enekes* which accompanied her on Richard I's crusade were described by contemporaries as smaller and swifter than Mediterranean types, but still big enough to carry horses, as such ships certainly did across the Channel.[79] Richard I's *esnecca* was replaced by a 'longship',[80] which possibly indicates a change of type, but other *esneccas* are mentioned as late as 1300, when the Cinque Ports fleet included two,[81] and it is most likely that only the name had changed. Certainly the king's three 'longships' in 1196 had crews of sixty each, so they were much the same size as their predecessors.[82] They were seaworthy vessels, capable of a voyage to Spain, though the references to 'tilts' or tents suggest that they had no permanent shelter.[83] Though men-at-arms might be embarked when ships carried money,[84] the only members of the ship's own company mentioned in the documents continue to be the sailors and the steersman[85] in command.

It is clear that the Norman and Angevin kings remained fully aware of the value of sea power in one sense; they were thoroughly familar with the use of the seas and rivers to transport men and goods, and no substantial army moved far without a train of ships and boats. Their empire depended heavily on seaborne trade, and a large part of their revenues came from customs receipts.[86] What they seem to have forgotten (with the brief but significant exception of Richard I between 1194 and his death in 1199) was the application of ships for directly military purposes. Ships were no longer used to move troops rapidly, but supplies slowly. They were used as auxiliaries to essentially land-based campaigns, not as weapons of war in their own right. Ships remained an essential component of military operations over any distance, but they were no longer the key to rapid mobility. As a natural result the speed of advance of Norman armies was only a fraction of that of English or Danish armies two centuries before, and their military reach was limited to those parts with which they had good land communications, which did not include Scotland, Wales or Ireland. The 1171 expedition showed that even in eastern Ireland where English economic and political influence was considerable, it was only possible for the king and his army to appear with great expense and effort.

It looks as though this change was associated with the abandonment of the naval organization of the Anglo-Saxons. Warships of the same general type continued to be built in small numbers, and all around England the rulers of Celtic and Norse states continued to profit from the exercise of sea power, but the Norman and Angevin kings were no longer able to do the same. Without the seagoing fleets available to the Anglo-Saxon kings, the Normans and Angevins exercised an authority limited to the reach of their armies. Though they were rulers of a substantial part of continental Europe, and enjoyed an economic and political weight far greater than that of their Anglo-Saxon predecessors, their authority in the British Isles was in important respects sharply restricted by comparison with that of Æthelstan or Edgar.

Nothing is pre-ordained in history, and there was no logical reason why England, the meeting place of the three cultures, should not have been absorbed by any one of them, or partitioned between them. In geographical terms, York is well placed to be a national capital of Britain, and if Æthelstan had lost the battle of Brunanburh, the Viking kingdom of York with its mixture of Norse, Celtic and English elements might have made a logical centre for a strong island kingdom. It would have been equally plausible at any period between the seventh century and the twelfth or even later to imagine a Norse-Celtic maritime empire, ruled from Dublin or Man and holding sway on both sides of the Irish Sea, perhaps with a land frontier in England with the Danish North Sea empire.[87] Though Gruffydd ap Llywellyn in the mid-eleventh century is the only Welsh prince known to have had a fleet of his own,[88] the ships of the Irish Vikings were always available to the highest bidder,[89] and there is no reason why a strong ruler should not have built an Irish Sea empire on the available sea power. That England should first be united and then survive as a unitary kingdom in the face of attacks from both east and west in the ninth century, that it should re-emerge as a single state on the break-up of Cnut's empire in the mid-eleventh century, were not inevitable facts, but the consequences of dynastic and military factors in which the sea played a very large part. So too was England's sudden and unexpected conquest from the south in 1066, which linked the country to the Continent in a Norman, later Angevin empire which lasted for a century and a half. By harnessing England's wealth and power to French politics, this had the effect of ensuring the survival and independence of the Irish, Welsh and Scots states, and of leaving the Northern and Western Isles as Norwegian colonies, when in all probability they would otherwise have fallen, or remained, under indirect English control.

It is a striking paradox that the Norman Conquest, made possible by an impressive fleet, caused the rapid collapse of English sea power. Where English kings of the mid-tenth century had circumnavigated the British Isles and secured the submission of all the rulers around the Irish Sea, the early Normans exercised only feeble and intermittent power over the nearer parts of the Celtic world, and were reduced to buying off Danish fleets which they had no means of fighting. We are not accustomed to thinking of William the Conqueror as a weak king, nor Æthelred 'the Unready' as a strong one, yet that is exactly the contrast suggested by their respective handling of sea power. It has been powerfully argued that the Norman Conquest replaced a strong unitary state with a weak and divided one, full of over-mighty subjects among whom every invader could find friends.[90] It certainly replaced a strong fleet with nothing at all to defend against seaborne attack. If Denmark and Norway had not declined into civil war and impotence in the late eleventh century, it is perfectly possible that the Norman Conquest would have proved only a brief interlude for England between the first and second Danish empires. In the Irish Sea the Dublin Vikings raided England and interfered in the wars of the Welsh princes. At intervals the kings of Norway sent fleets to assert their shaky authority over Man and the Western Isles. In the face of these threats the Normans abandoned the initiative and fell back on fixed defences. They had no answer to the flexibility and speed conferred by sea power, and no effective means of projecting their power to the northward and westward. The Norman Conquest led in effect to the partition of the British Isles which had almost been united under English rule in the previous century.

FOUR

The Fall of the House of Anjou

Operations 1204–1266; Administration 1204–1216

During the years 1203 and 1204 King Philip Augustus of France conquered Normandy, Maine, Poitou and Anjou. Both geographically and psychologically they were the heart of the Angevin empire; Anjou was the original territory of the royal house, Normandy the richest province, where most of the English nobility had come from and many still owned estates. Their loss left the English empire sharply reduced in power and influence, and made France a new and formidable enemy with a sea-coast along the Channel.

The strategic position of the English lands was now quite different. Instead of a unitary empire, divided only by the width of the Channel, and facing allies, dependencies and potential enemies across land frontiers, King John's dominions were now divided into two widely separated parts, England and Gascony, connected only by the long and dangerous voyage down Channel, round the cape of Brittany, and down into the Bay of Biscay. With its reefs and tide-races, lying open to the western ocean, the coast of Brittany was one of the most dangerous navigations in Europe. 'No one passes the Raz without fear or harm', as the Breton proverb had it.[1] Moreover with the limited ability of medieval ships to navigate out of sight of land or to beat to windward, a fair wind westerly down Channel was unlikely to serve for a south-easterly course towards Bordeaux, nor vice versa. This meant that large fleets of ships often lay for long periods off Le Conquet in the 'Trade' (the English name for the northern channel out of Brest Roads), or under St Matthew's Point, waiting for a fair wind.[2] This was an obvious place to intercept such ships, and a frequent scene of naval battles. Brest was the Suez of the medieval English empire, the hinge of the long imperial sea route.[3]

The campaigns which broke up the Angevin empire were fought largely on land, but the key to the French success in conquering Normandy was the siege and capture of Château Gaillard, standing above the River Seine where it crosses the frontier of Normandy. Had the Anglo-Norman relief force broken through the besiegers, Normandy would have been saved, at least for the moment. In fact the poorly co-ordinated attacks of the land forces under William the Marshal and the naval squadron under Alan Trenchemer were repulsed.[4] Thus it was in part a naval battle, though fought far inland up the Seine, which determined the fate of Normandy.

The immediate sequel to the French conquests was a war of raiding up and down the Channel, with a particular struggle for the Channel Isles, the last unconquered fragment of the Duchy of Normandy.[5] In this warfare a prominent part was played by the pirate Eustace 'the Monk', based on Sark in English service from not later than 1205 until 1215, and thereafter on the side of the baronial rebels and the French.[6] Meanwhile Poitou was restored to King John in 1206 by internal rebellion, and from then until his last fruitless expedition of 1214, a continuous naval effort was required to maintain communications with La Rochelle.[7]

John's strategy was to use Poitou as his base of operations for an attack on France in conjunction with his allies in Flanders. They were heavily defeated at the battle of Bouvines in 1214, but even if that battle had been more fortunate, John's strategy was misconceived. Poitou was one of the poorest and most disorderly provinces – 'the soft underbelly of the Angevin empire'[8] – and the Poitevins were disliked by Normans and Gascons alike. The English nobility, who would have fought eagerly to recover their lands in Normandy, were reluctant to be involved in Poitou.[9] John's fundamental fault, to be repeated by numerous English kings over the next three centuries, was to think of his ships simply as a means of transport connecting two friendly ports, rather than a strategic instrument in themselves. Instead of a long voyage to start his attack from an unpromising point remote from the enemy, John could have exploited the flexibility of sea power, landed on the Norman coast, and campaigned where the French had most to lose and he had most to gain.

His mistake was misuse rather than neglect of his fleet, for his was the most impressive English squadron (of which we have detailed knowledge) since the Conquest. By 1211 he had more than fifty vessels, including twenty galleys, in service. A document of 1206 lists fifty galleys, divided into four squadrons distributed around England,[10] but by 1212 the bulk of the fleet was concentrated at Portsmouth.[11] Traditionally John has been regarded as the creator of this fleet, but it seems more likely that he had inherited it from Richard I. It happens that the written evidence of the workings of the English government becomes much more plentiful at John's accession, which

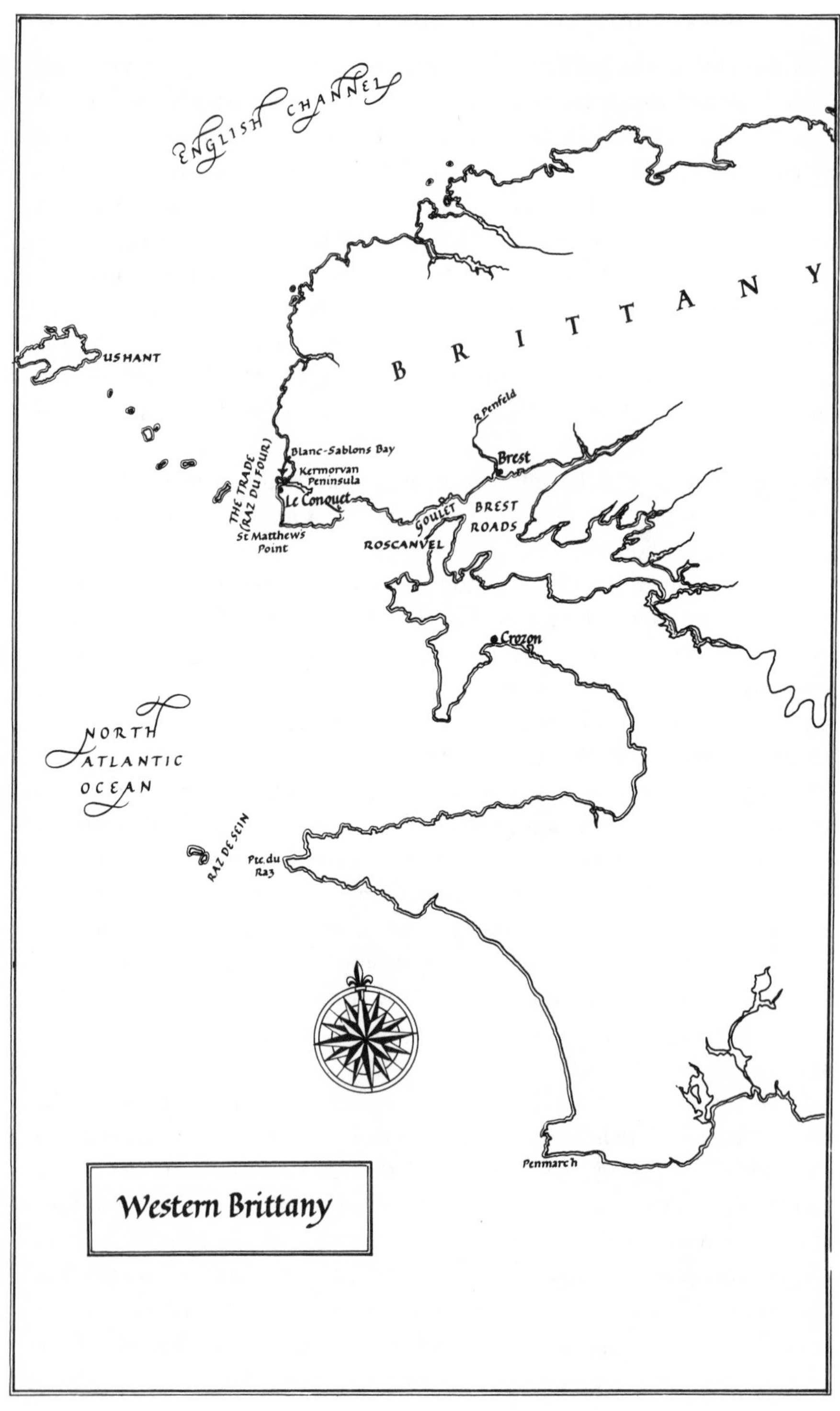

Western Brittany

can easily give the false impression that he was a more bureaucratic, efficient or 'modern' king than his brother.[12] In any case, even if King John built the fleet, he had very little idea how to use it.

This fleet did not have anything like a permanent administrative structure. John entrusted much of its management to two officials already much involved in collecting a new tax on French goods, Reginald of Cornhill, a London merchant whose father had been involved in naval administration under Henry II,[13] and William of Wrotham, Archdeacon of Taunton, a senior royal clerk.[14] Of these Wrotham came to be the dominant figure, with the title of 'Keeper of the King's Ports and Galleys'. He was also in charge of the royal stannaries (tin mines) in Devon and Cornwall, from which he derived an income which went directly to support the fleet. As an administrator his authority was extensive: he built, repaired, victualled and paid ships, expending very large sums.[15] In 1212, at the height of the naval preparations, Wrotham accounted for two years' revenue, totalling £6,912 8s 10d. Almost all of it was spent on the king's ships, and there may have been more from other sources.[16] He had subordinates in several ports, and was involved in all aspects of management of the king's ships except commanding them at sea.[17]

At Portsmouth King John built a substantial harbour which was probably a wet dock or basin with a lock, allowing galleys to lie in shelter, afloat at all states of the tide. It is certainly referred to as a 'lock' (*exclusa*), with the implication of water excluded or impounded. It had an 'enclosure' (*inclaustrum*) walled with stone, and also a perimeter wall: possibly they were the same, but a stone perimeter wall would have been an extraordinary luxury, not enjoyed by many castles then. As far as other evidence goes Portsmouth did not get so much as a fence 'to keep out beasts and hogs' until 1624,[18] and the best explanation is that the stone 'enclosure' was the basin itself.[19] This would have been an advanced piece of engineering for the time; no other enclosed basin is known to have existed so early, though there was a tidal stone dock built at Hartlepool in 1213, and others on the Thames in the fourteenth and fifteenth centuries.[20]

Access to the sea, and King John's unpopularity, gave Philip Augustus of France the opportunity to carry the war to England. Detested by many of his barons and excommunicated by the Church (partly because of the very heavy taxation he laid on both to pay for his rearmament programme), John was vulnerable. Philip had a large fleet and army assembled by 1213, when King John's submission to the Pope temporarily strengthened his position. France, however, had other opportunities. The marriage of King

Philip's son to the daughter of the Count of Boulogne had brought Calais as her dowry, giving France an opening towards the North Sea, and pointing King Philip's ambitions towards Flanders.[21] Flanders and England were not necessarily alternatives, for both commerce and geography made the control of Flanders a promising preliminary to attacking England. So the French forces moved into Flanders in 1213, the fleet proceeding along the coast in support of the army. King John is said to have decided to attempt to intercept a French invasion at sea,[22] and sent his fleet under William Longsword, Earl of Salisbury, to interfere with the French invasion. If so the orders cannot have been very precise, for when Salisbury found the French fleet in the port of Damme, he was so surprised that he could not immediately identify the enemy.[23] As the troops were elsewhere he had little difficulty in destroying the ships at anchor, but a landing the next day was driven off. Philip Augustus, however, disgusted by the poor performance of his seamen and apparently doubting their loyalty (they were almost all Normans and Poitevins), completed Salisbury's work by burning the remaining ships drawn up on the beaches. The battle of Damme was a tactical success for the English fleet, damaging French naval resources, making any invasion impossible for that year and encouraging John's Flemish allies, but it had no decisive effect on the French invasion of Flanders.[24] The issue of that campaign, and with it John's hopes of regaining Normandy, were settled by the French victory at Bouvines in 1214.

Meanwhile in England the outbreak of civil war gave the French new opportunities. The large fleet which King John had assembled should have made it possible for him to isolate the baronial rebels from outside help, but in practice, like Philip Augustus, he neither trusted his fleet nor appreciated how best to use it. Moreover the Cinque Ports were early recruits to the rebels, giving them easy communications with Calais, and John's fleet was badly damaged by a storm in May 1216. In this way the barons were joined in 1215 and 1216 by French forces under the Dauphin Louis.[25]

On the death of King John in 1216, the French and their allies controlled more than half the country. The new king Henry III was only nine years old, his government was bankrupt, and his father's fleet had disintegrated.[26] John's revenue had been about £35,000 a year; Henry III's in the early years of his reign was about £8,000.[27] The regent, however, was William the Marshal, one of the great figures of the Middle Ages, a leader with all the capacity to inspire loyalty which John had lacked. Over the winter of 1216–17 the Cinque Ports began to return to their allegiance, and ships were brought from Ireland. In May 1217 an English squadron under Philip d'Aubigny forced back a convoy bringing supplies to the French army besieging Dover Castle.[28]

The French tried again, and the English squadron, this time under Hubert de Burgh, met them at sea on 24 August. The chronicler Matthew Paris, who had his information (many years later) from de Burgh himself, gives a detailed and reasonably coherent account of this battle.[29] Though Paris was evidently out of his depth with nautical terms,[30] it is one of the few medieval sea battles which we can reconstruct with some confidence. The French squadron, which was the larger, sailed from Calais, probably for London (which was in rebel hands), certainly running up the Kentish coast before a south-westerly wind. It appears that the first English ships to put to sea (possibly from Dover) were daunted by the strength of the enemy, but a renewed attempt was made when de Burgh appeared to take command. As the French passed along the coast the English sailed from Sandwich, initially close-hauled to pass astern of the French. Eustace the Monk, the French commander, interpreted this as an attempt to avoid battle and attack Calais (which was well fortified) while they were absent. In fact de Burgh's object was to gain the weather gage; as soon as he was astern and to windward of the French, the English ships bore up and attacked. It looks as though the French squadron was straggling, and Eustace's ship, heavily laden with a trebuchet, was certainly astern of the rest. Thus the English were able to defeat and capture most of the enemy fleet in detail. This battle was fought at sea under sail, but probably in the sheltered waters of the Downs, or even further north off Ramsgate, rather than off Dover, the name conventionally given to it.[31] Fought under way, in an age when naval battles were usually stationary, it displays a precocious grasp of naval tactics by Hubert de Burgh which was hardly equalled by any other English admiral before the sixteenth century. It is one of the most decisive medieval naval battles in northern waters, for it effectively ended the French attempt to conquer England by exploiting civil war, and gave Henry III's government the time to rebuild its authority at home.

Forced to concentrate most of its remaining resources on suppressing revolt in England, Henry III's government was however unable to mount any effective resistance to France on the Continent. The death of Philip Augustus in 1223 seemed to open the possibility of recovery in France, but just as men and ships were summoned to Portsmouth, the rebellion of Fawkes de Breauté forced the king to concentrate on the siege of Bedford. In Ireland Hugh de Lacy was also in rebellion, in alliance with the Welsh prince Llywelyn ap Iorwerth, and the Earl of Pembroke, with substantial

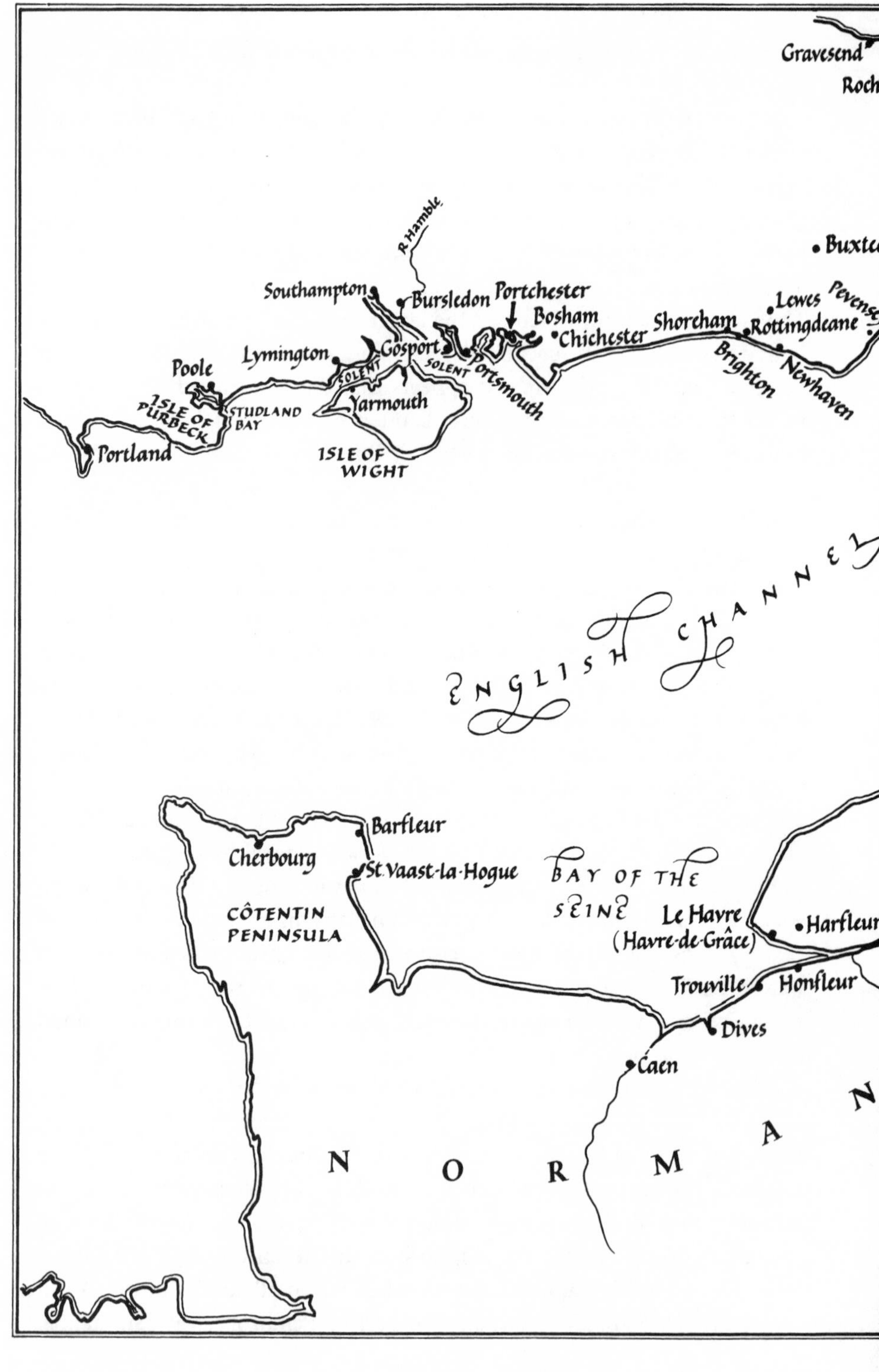

Gravesend
Roch
R. Hamble
Buxte
Southampton
Bursledon
Portchester
Bosham
Chichester
Shoreham
Lewes
Rottingdeane
Pevens
Brighton
Newhaven
Lymington
Gosport
SOLENT
SOLENT
Portsmouth
Poole
ISLE OF PURBECK
STUDLAND BAY
Yarmouth
Portland
ISLE OF WIGHT
ENGLISH CHANNEL
Barfleur
Cherbourg
St. Vaast-la-Hogue
BAY OF THE SEINE
CÔTENTIN PENINSULA
Le Havre
(Havre-de-Grâce)
Harfleur
Trouville
Honfleur
Dives
Caen
NORMAN

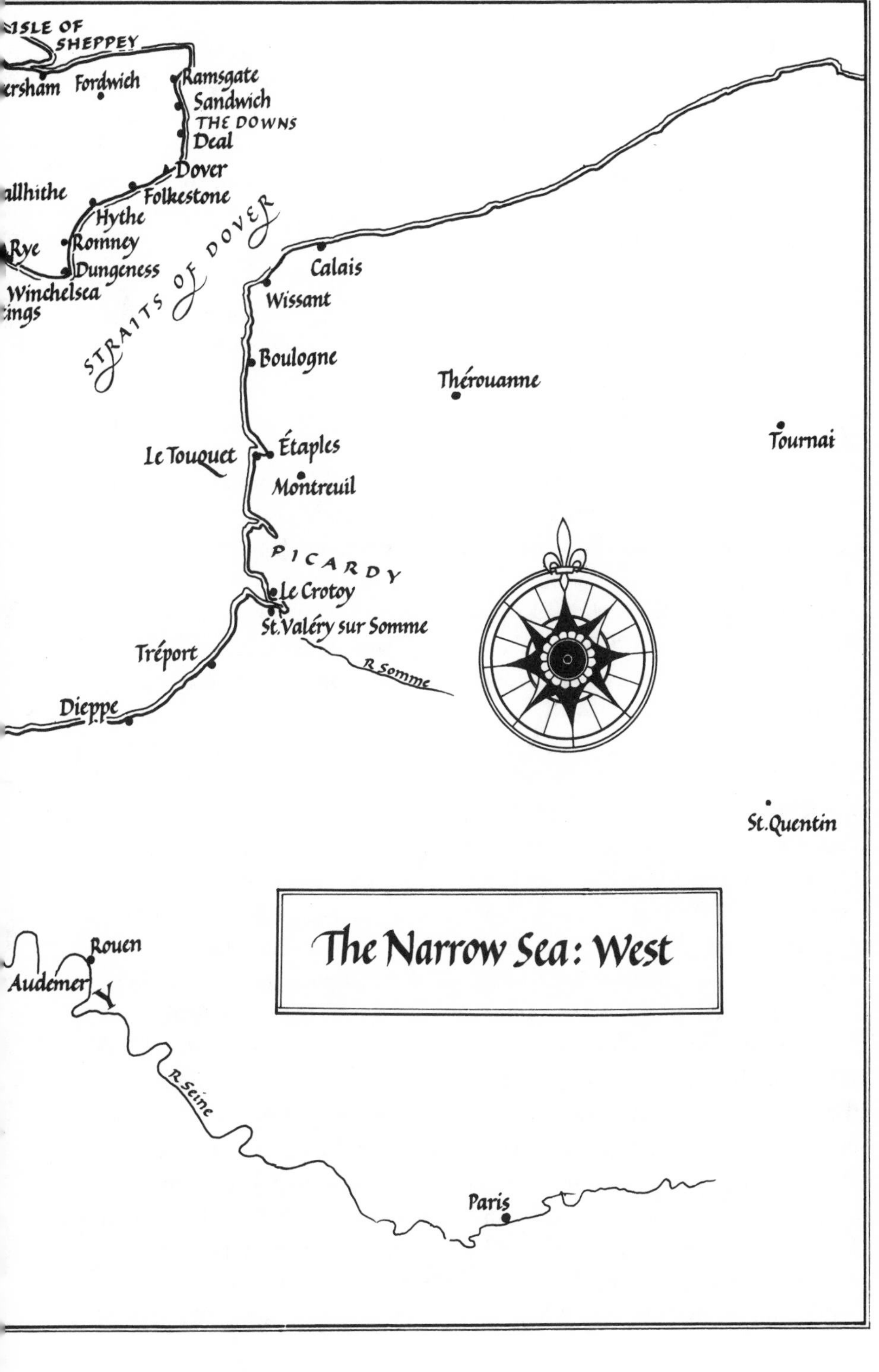

ISLE OF SHEPPEY
Fordwich
Ramsgate
Sandwich
THE DOWNS
Deal
Dover
Folkestone
Hythe
Romney
Rye
Dungeness
Winchelsea
STRAITS OF DOVER
Calais
Wissant
Boulogne
Thérouanne
Tournai
Le Touquet
Étaples
Montreuil
PICARDY
Le Crotoy
St.Valéry sur Somme
R.Somme
Tréport
Dieppe
St.Quentin
The Narrow Sea: West
Rouen
Audemer
Y
R.Seine
Paris

naval support, was fighting on both sides of the Irish Sea against them. Meanwhile Louis VIII was free to overrun Poitou and capture La Rochelle.[32] Where before they had been virtually landlocked, the French now had two sea coasts, both of which faced the English sea-route to Gascony. From now on all Anglo-French wars necessarily had a naval dimension, for the sea, which did something to protect England herself, made the Anglo-Gascon connection highly vulnerable.[33]

Not until 1225 did an expedition under the king's brother sail for Gascony, followed by reinforcements the next year. With the French now established directly on the flank of the sea-route to Bordeaux, such a campaign required substantial naval activity.[34] It succeeded in expelling the invaders from Gascony, but Bordeaux was hopelessly remote as a base for recapturing Poitou, let alone Normandy. The 1230 campaign was unsuccessful for the same reasons. Though the English army actually landed at St Malo in Brittany, within striking distance of Normandy (and some of the Norman ports actively helped the expedition by sending ships), they then marched in the opposite direction into Poitou. The collapse of this effort seems to have marked the point at which the English nobles abandoned hope of regaining their continental lands. The only gain was the capture of the island of Oléron, guarding one of the narrowest points on the inshore shipping route to Bordeaux.[35]

This campaign was followed in 1233 by the rebellion of Richard Marshal, Earl of Pembroke, in South Wales (the only part of Wales where the English had a significant foothold). His fleet, based on Chepstow, cut off the royal castles in South Wales until some of Henry III's ships managed to break the blockade. When Richard's ally Hubert de Burgh was rescued in dramatic circumstances from royal custody, Marshal's galleys took him off by night from the banks of the Severn, just ahead of his pursuers. The king summoned ships from as far away as Bordeaux, and eventually Pembroke was obliged to retreat to Ireland, but the campaign demonstrated how difficult it was for an English king to intervene in these parts without a large fleet.[36]

Henry III's final campaign in Poitou was stimulated by a rebellion against the French in 1241. All the reasons which had operated to prevent success before were present in greater strength than ever. By the time the king had assembled his forces, without help from his barons, the rebellion had been suppressed. Henry found himself invading Poitou from the south, in the face of a victorious French army and with negligible local support on either side of the frontier. Initially he had to concentrate most of his ships to protect the bridge over the Charente at Tonnay, across which he escaped with difficulty after his defeat by the French. The Gascons were interested only in attacking their commercial rival, La Rochelle, but the winter blockade of that port mounted by the Bayonne galleys, based on Oléron, was ineffectual. English galleys based on Dover and the Channel Isles were ordered to raid the coast of Normandy, but their main achievement was to escort the king home in 1243 from his futile expedition.[37]

Even if Henry III had had a more intelligent grand strategy, it must be doubtful if his financial and military base in England was ever strong enough to support his ambitions on the Continent. By the 1220s he had about £15,000 a year with which to fight Louis VIII of France, whose income was about £65,000 in English money.[38] Re-issuing Magna Carta in 1225 gained Henry a tax yielding £40,000 with which to finance another campaign,[39] but the 1242 campaign in Poitou, fought without the support of the English barons, cost about £80,000, of which at least £15,000, by then half a year's revenue, was still owing at the end.[40]

Henry III returned to Gascony once more, in 1253–4, and his passage generated substantial naval activity, but the object this time was to suppress disorder in Gascony rather than to wage war against France.[41] At home he was involved in fruitless campaigns in Wales in 1244, 1256 and 1257, which served only to demonstrate that indifferent troops, insufficient supplies and unimaginative strategy were not the way to succeed against a determined enemy at home in difficult country.[42]

No king who consistently failed in war found it easy to maintain his authority, especially one who tried to wage war without the consent of the great men of the kingdom. The terms of the Provisions of Oxford in June 1258 effectively placed the king under the control of the great barons led by Simon de Montfort, Earl of Leicester. Two years later, fortified by a papal bull absolving him from his oaths, Henry III dismissed the baronial officials and resumed control of his government. In April 1263 de Montfort returned from France to lead another baronial movement, and the king submitted in July after the barons had occupied London. In April 1264 Henry III resorted to open war, and on 14 May he was captured by de Montfort at the battle of Lewes. Just over a year later, on 4 August 1265, de Montfort was defeated and killed at the battle of Evesham by royalist forces led by the king's eldest son Prince Edward. With the surrender of Kenilworth Castle on 14 December the Barons' War was over. Throughout this turbulent time de Montfort (an even greater landowner in France than in England) derived great advantages from being able to move freely across the Channel. Once again, the Cinque Ports took the side of the rebels, allowing the barons easy access to the

Continent, and excluding both the forces which the queen had raised in Flanders, and the papal legate bearing the excommunication of the rebels. The ports were rewarded with permission for unlimited piracy, and they held out even after the collapse of the baronial cause. Sandwich, Hastings and Winchelsea were stormed in the spring of 1266, but only the feeblest attempt was made to punish the Cinque Ports afterwards, and that provoked them into burning Portsmouth.[43]

In strategic terms, the theme of the thirteenth century might be summed up as 'France's drive for the sea'. Hitherto almost landlocked, France acquired a Channel coast with the conquest of Normandy in 1204, an Atlantic coast at Poitou in 1224, and the beginnings of a Mediterranean naval presence with the foundation of the port of Aigues-Mortes in 1240.[44] The new territories made France the dominant military power in western Europe, and the collapse of the Angevin empire left England sharply reduced in strength and consequence. Moreover the remaining English empire in Gascony was at the end of a long and dangerous sea route, and England had little or no naval strength to protect it.

FIVE

Ships of War

Ships 1066–1455

Though our knowledge of medieval ship design has been extended by archaeology in recent years, it remains largely dependent on written records. The documents are abundant, but they were mostly the work of chroniclers and administrators who were not familiar with the nautical world, had no incentive to be especially accurate, and were writing in a language (Latin) with a more limited technical vocabulary than English or French, the dominant written languages among seafarers around the British Isles. For these reasons it is often difficult to extract reliable information about the design, construction and handling of ships in peace or war. The ships themselves are called by a great many different names;[1] it is evident that over time some names fell out of use and were replaced by others, but much harder to say what exactly the names indicated. In some cases names seem to have changed when the type described did not; in others the same name continued in use over a long period but changed its meaning, perhaps more than once. In a polyglot world in which Latin, French and English terms were freely mixed, we cannot always be sure which words in the different languages were equivalents of one another.

For all these reasons medieval ship design has to be discussed with caution, but the broad outlines of the subject are clear enough. First it is necessary to distinguish the dominant traditions of shipbuilding in Europe. In the ancient Mediterranean, both warships and merchantmen were 'shell-built', meaning that their principal hull strength lay in the same outer shell which excluded the water. This hull was made of timbers mortised to one another in such a way as to produce a remarkably light and strong structure, but one requiring very skilled construction and wasting much timber. The method was progressively superseded in late classical and early medieval times by a radically different tradition, skeleton-first or frame construction. Here the strength of the hull lay in a skeleton of heavy timbers, usually in the form of ribs erected on a keel, which was then covered with a light skin of planking, fitted edge to edge (carvel-built) with caulking to make it watertight. This combination of frame and carvel building was considerably more economical in timber and shipbuilding skills, and it seems to have become general for all types of ship in the Mediterranean by the eleventh century.[2]

The commonest rigs in the Mediterranean employed the lateen sail, a large triangular sail hoisted on a long running yard, one end of which was made fast to the deck forward of the mast. Lateen rig spreads a very large area of canvas, and the tall sail, laced to a yard at its 'leading edge', works well to windward. Its disadvantage is that it has to be passed around the mast when going about, which calls for a numerous and skilled crew. Moreover the large sail area, difficult to reduce in a hurry, and the heavy spar aloft are adapted to light and dependable winds – which are unusual in the Mediterranean in winter and in the Atlantic at all seasons. In any but the most expert hands lateen rig was a menace in heavy weather or squalls, especially to any vessel with low freeboard.[3]

In northern waters, both lateen rig and skeleton-building remained unknown until near the end of the Middle Ages. Here there were several shell-building traditions, of which the most important were the 'Viking' clinker (or clench) construction and the cog type. In clinker building, the hull was built up by overlapping strakes of planking riveted together, working upwards and outwards from a heavy keel. Light frames or ribs were inserted for stiffening only after the hull proper was well advanced.[4] Originally all clinker-built vessels were double-ended, but from the late twelfth century the design was adapted to carry a stern rudder, which differentiated the straight sternpost from the curved stem.[5] Clinker-building was relatively expensive, calling for skilled shipwrights and a lot of iron to make the rivets, but it produced a very strong hull. It was also capable of building very large ships; the clinker-built warships and merchantmen of thirteenth-century Norway were among the largest wooden ships ever seen,[6] and in the early fifteenth century Henry V built ships of over a thousand tons with triple-skinned clinker construction. In economic terms, clinker-building suffered badly in the fifteenth century from rising wage costs, the increasing price of iron, and the spread of the water-powered sawmill. Good clinker-building used expensive clove-board, split radially from a tree (preferably oak). The availability of cheap sawn softwood planks, and a lower requirement for skilled labour generally, gave a considerable economic advantage to carvel construction.[7]

The cog developed in the twelfth and thirteenth century into the dominant cargo vessel of northern waters. Like the clinker-built hull, it was essentially shell-built, but with a flat bottom formed of heavy timbers, on which clinker sides were built, the whole later strengthened by the insertion of frames and of 'through-beams', which spanned the whole hull and projected through it on both sides. The result was a strong, heavy hull, broad and high in proportion to length, able to carry a large cargo and sit upright on the mud at low water. With sawn planks rather than cloveboard, and nails rather than rivets, it was cheaper to build than the merchantmen of the 'Viking' tradition. The cog, with her deep hull and high freeboard, was best adapted to unload at a quay, and the rise of the cog goes in parallel with the building of quays at all the major ports of northern Europe.[8] The cog was a cargo-carrier, but her high freeboard gave her a great advantage in battle in an age when all sea fighting was hand-to-hand. Moreover her deep, heavy hull provided ample stability to allow the building of fighting 'castles' fore and aft, and the fitting of a 'topcastle' at the masthead. Castles, which may have been an English invention, were originally light stages erected temporarily on all sorts of ships, but by the fourteenth century were becoming permanent structures built onto the hull proper.[9]

In addition to the cog, another common merchant-ship type in northern waters was the hulk. This was clinker-built but without a keel, so that the sheer of the strakes coming together at bow and stern produced a characteristic banana-shaped form, quite different from the straight keel and curved stems of the Viking tradition.[10] In the fifteenth century the hulk tended to merge with the cog form to become the ancestor of the sixteenth-century Baltic merchantman called the 'hulk'.[11]

Until the fifteenth century, all northern ships were rigged very similarly, with a single mast and a square sail. In English ships the sail seems to have been taunt by comparison with either Viking or modern sails, and before the fifteenth century both sail and yard were hoisted from the deck.[12] With the whole sail area in a single sail both mast and yard had to be robust, and in the later Middle Ages the larger ships had 'made' masts several feet in diameter, able to support the great weight of sail, yard and topcastle. The mast of the galley *Philippa* of 1337 was probably 100ft or more in height from the deck, and the Winchelsea galley of the same year little if at all shorter.[13] The mainmast of Henry V's *Grace Dieu* was about 200ft high and seven feet in diameter at the deck.[14] The *Grace Dieu* of Hull, built in 1473, used not less than seventeen sticks to make her three masts, probably almost all for the mainmast.[15] The *Regent* of 1488 had a mainmast whose core was a stick 114ft high and 10ft 6ins in circumference at the base, with four filling pieces each 72ft long.[16] To hoist sail and yard even in a small ship was beyond unaided manpower; windlasses appear among ships' fittings from the twelfth century, and capstans in the fourteenth.[17]

The single square sail was a powerful rig, and off the wind must have driven a fine hull very fast, but it had serious limitations. Ships had been able to beat to windward for many centuries by 1204, and all seagoing ships seem to have been fitted with the spar known in English as a 'loof' to boom out the weather tack.[18] This was supplemented from at least the twelfth century by the bowline, and eventually the combination of bowline (to haul the leach forward) and tack (to haul it down) replaced the cumbersome loof altogether.[19] Nevertheless the performance of a large, especially a taunt, square sail to windward will always be limited by the difficulty of controlling the weather leach (the 'leading edge' in aerodynamic terms), and medieval sails seem from illustrations to have been cut with a very full bunt, when for best performance to windward they should have been cut as flat as possible.[20] Moreover the fine, shallow hull of the oared warship was leewardly, and the deeper hull of the cog was no better, to judge from the replica of the Bremen cog which has been tried at sea.[21] A well-designed quarter rudder can act as a centre-board, but the replacement of quarter by stern rudders on English galleys in the thirteenth century will have removed this benefit.[22]

In any circumstances, and in any design of ship, moreover, a single-masted rig is unhandy. For the purposes of manoeuvre, a ship may be compared to a weather-vane, pivoting about her centre of resistance. With a square sail set on a single mast, necessarily on or very near the centre of resistance, the only force available to turn the ship is the weak effect of the rudder.[23] Oared vessels probably used some oars to push the ship's head round when tacking, but merchantmen must have been unhandy, especially in confined waters.[24] This explains the very long delays while ships waited for a fair wind: the range of points of sailing available to them in the open sea was probably not greatly inferior to that of square-rigged vessels of the seventeenth or even eighteenth centuries, and there are clear references to ships sailing close-hauled.[25] However, the ability to work ships in confined waters must have been limited, condemning them to lie imprisoned in harbour for want of a leading wind out, on many occasions when there was a fair wind in the offing for their intended passage.

The unhandiness of single-masted ships was one among several circumstances which made galleys so important in medieval naval warfare. Oared vessels, like sailing ships, divided into the Mediterranean skeleton-built types and the northern shell-first tradition. In the Mediterranean the galley appears to have been perfected by the Byzantine navy not later than the tenth century. It was distinguished from the classical building tradition by its light skeleton construction, with oars on a single level rowed over an outrigger framework (the *apostis*), and a light spur above the water in place of a ram below.[26] This last point needs to be emphasized: writers throughout the Middle Ages, persuaded by the literature of the ancient world that oared warships must have rams, continued to refer to rams and describe ramming actions which existed only in their imaginations.[27] Some do so still,[28] but the medieval galley owed its very name to its above-water spur,[29] and was capable, at most, of crippling an opponent by smashing her *apostis*. This is only one of the many misconceptions which hang about the galley and oared warships in general. Human muscle-power is an extremely inefficient method of moving so large a body as a ship; it has been calculated that sixteenth-century galleys developed less than twenty horsepower at most, to move a hull of about 170 tons.[30] The galley was capable of high speed only for very short periods: the best theoretically possible is about ten knots, but it is most unlikely that medieval or Renaissance galleys exceeded six or seven.[31] Usually galleys sailed, and under either oars or sail a speed of two and a half or three knots sustained over twenty-four hours was a record-breaking performance.[32] In a moment of crisis in 1509, a squadron of Venetian merchant galleys made a famous non-stop passage of thirty-one days from Southampton to Otranto at an average speed of over three knots, but war galleys could not have stayed at sea so long.[33] With their large crews and narrow, shallow hulls they could not be stored for cruises of more than a fortnight or so, and under oars might need water every few days. They were a short-range weapon; with a radius of action under 500 miles in ideal conditions, in practice usually much less, they needed to be based near their scene of operations.[34] Moreover their low freeboard made galleys very vulnerable to heavy weather; even in the Mediterranean they seldom operated far from land, or in wintertime.[35]

In the Mediterranean, as in the northern world, galleys were outmatched in hand-to-hand fighting by sailing vessels with their high freeboard.[36] Galleys could only fight ships in unusual circumstances. In a flat calm they might risk attacking ships at sea, but even a light breeze would put them in danger.[37] Galley fleets could and sometimes did fight one another, but their peculiar advantage lay in amphibious warfare. Shallow draught and free movement under oars allowed them to penetrate harbours and estuaries, making them the ideal instrument of the coastal raid. Medieval oarsmen were not slaves but free men and trained soldiers, so every galley represented a substantial force of infantry and archers, delivered with speed and surprise to any point where there was water to float her. Thirteenth-century galleys with one man to an oar carried about 145 men for a 120-oared galley; the bigger galleys of the fifteenth century had 200 or more.[38] In this way the Mediterranean galley of the Middle Ages was a counterpart to the Viking longship. Moreover the galley, being faster under sail, and if need be under oars, than a pure sailing vessel, was the obvious choice for scouting and carrying messages in fair weather.[39]

Larger galleys were developed in the late thirteenth century for carrying passengers and cargo in those trades where goods of high value could pay for high speed. The 'great galley' was the medieval equivalent of the air freighter. It was developed originally to allow trade through the Straits of Gibraltar, where a few days creeping along the coast under oars in the teeth of the westerly wind and current created a navigational and commercial opportunity which justified the expense of trading with an oared vessel with her large crew and small hold.[40] The oarsmen of the great galley, moreover, like those of the light galley, were available to fight. Trading in dangerous waters, the great galley could defend herself without the expense of convoy escorts.[41] The first great galleys were sent on a commercial voyage to Flanders and England by the Genoese in 1277, and from 1298 they made annual voyages to the north.[42] Soon after the Venetians entered the same trade,[43] while by the early fifteenth century Florentine merchant galleys were also making the annual voyage up the Channel.[44] The great galley also had military potential, and Henry V briefly had one – the only Mediterranean galley to be owned by any medieval English king.[45]

The galley proper was a Mediterranean type. Though often used in English waters, it was only built in the north by the French, at the Clos des Gallées at Rouen, during the fourteenth century; briefly by the Burgundians in the fifteenth century; and on the Atlantic coast possibly at Bayonne and St Jean-de-Luz.[46] The native type, or types, of oared warship were of different construction. Unfortunately the Mediterranean term was widely adopted in the north, obscuring the great differences between the true galley and the local 'galleys'. In England the change comes early in King John's reign.[47] It seems clear, however, that these English 'galleys' were and continued to be throughout the twelfth and thirteenth centuries recognizable descendants of the 'Viking' type.[48] Certainly those built in east (though not south) coast ports were built by shipwrights using Norse words for the different timbers, and the quantities of rivets clearly indicate clinker-building.[49] When an English ship visited Bergen in 1247 carrying a papal legate to crown King Håkon IV, the Norwegians marvelled at her luxurious fittings (which included cabins), but classified the ship herself without comment as a 25-room *snekkja*, evidently of the type with which they were familiar.[50] Since the galleys built in 1294 had oars of two different lengths, they were probably pulled by oarsmen sitting in staggered rows.[51]

In England this type was superseded in the early fourteenth century by the balinger. This was also clinker-built, developed originally in the Bay of Biscay for the Basque whale fishery (whence the name), and came to England from Bayonne.[52] Speed must have been essential for the original balingers to chase the whales, but we do not know how balingers differed from the older type, except that it was about the 1290s that the stern rudder (the 'Bayonne rudder', as it was called in the Mediterranean) was adopted by English galleys, initially in conjunction with the older quarter rudders.[53] English galleys at least as late as the *Phillipa* of 1337 had stemheads fore and aft in the Viking style.[54] English balingers of the fourteenth and fifteenth centuries could be substantial vessels as large as 50 tons, able to carry a useful cargo. Related to the balinger was the barge, at first mentioned as a clinker-built, oared vessel smaller than the galley, but by the fifteenth century often larger than the balinger.[55]

These northern oared vessels evidently shared many of the general characteristics of the true galley, but in time, if not originally, they approached nearer to the sailing vessel. There were a significant number of English balingers and barges in ordinary trade (especially in the fifteenth century, when 'ordinary trade' so often meant piracy[56]), and even in wartime English oared vessels of all periods often put to sea with too few men to allow even one to an oar, which shows that oar power was generally an auxiliary to sail.[57] As early as 1281 Edward I's two 'big galleys' in the Welsh war had only 50 men each, which was not a full complement unless they were in fact very small,[58] and there are similar figures for galleys and barges later in his reign.[59]

The pure 'Viking' type of warship survived longest in the West Highlands and parts of Ireland, where the Lords of the Isles and other chiefs maintained large fleets of them throughout the Middle Ages. There the ship-muster system directly inherited from seventh-century Dalriada continued to furnish the means of rapid movement in the essentially amphibious warfare of the Irish Sea. The Highland 'galleys', with their smaller cousins the lymphads and birlins, carried into the sixteenth and even seventeenth centuries the naval traditions of the Viking world. Though adapted to use the stern rudder, these galleys were in other respects unchanged examples of a building tradition which was by then more than a thousand years old.[60]

Because oared warships were so valuable in war, especially in coastal warfare, and because there were few of them in the merchant fleet, they were usually the first choice of English kings wanting to build their own ships. They were particularly the priority of kings planning warfare on the Continent. King John built at least twenty galleys; Henry III possibly more than 33 galleys and barges between his accession and 1257.[61] Edward I, having fought three Welsh wars and the opening campaigns in Scotland entirely with requisitioned shipping, ordered twenty large galleys in 1294 when war with France broke out, though only eight are known to have been completed.[62] He followed this programme with further orders in 1298 and 1303.[63] Edward II built no galleys, and Edward III none until the Hundred Years War broke out, when at least seventeen galleys, barges and smaller oared vessels were built between 1336 and 1356. In the face of the naval disasters of the 1370s no fewer than 70 barges and 32 balingers were ordered in five years.[64] But the crown's capacity to pay for all these vessels had gone, if it had ever existed, and they were built at the expense of the towns.[65] The ambitious programme of 1401 to build 36 balingers and 18 barges, again at the towns' expense, aroused widespread protest and was not completed.[66]

Meanwhile the design of sailing ships had undergone important developments in the Mediterranean in the fourteenth century, as local shipwrights adopted and adapted the northern cog. Converted to skeleton-building, the cog grew into the Mediterranean cocha, known in the north as a carrack, and this in turn grew into the great ships which in the fifteenth century dominated the bulk trades out of the Mediterranean ports.[67] Some of these big carracks, whose very high freeboard gave them a great advantage in battle, found their way into northern waters, and it must have been they – perhaps specifically the Genoese *Santa Maria & Santa Brigida* taken by English pirates in Milford Haven in 1409[68] – which inspired Henry V to build, in the quite different clinker tradition, even bigger ships of his own.

Whereas his predecessors for three centuries had concentrated their spasmodic building efforts on galleys and balingers, usually at their subjects' expense and almost always for local defence,[69] Henry V spent his own revenues on building very big ships. Though his fleet included at least fifteen balingers and barges,[70] his efforts centred on a group of great carracks. The *Trinity Royal* of about 500 tons was rebuilt in 1413.[71] The *Jesus*, completed at Smallhythe in 1416, was of about 1,000 tons.[72] She was followed by the prize *Santa Clara* of about 750 tons, rebuilt in a dock at Southampton as the *Holy Ghost of the Tower*.[73] Possibly in the same dock the *Grace Dieu* was built between 1416 and 1418.[74] She is recorded as being 1,400 tons burthen, a figure which would never have been believed had not enough of her wreck survived (in the River Hamble at Bursledon, where she was accidentally burnt in 1439) to allow us to calculate that she was if anything bigger than that. Her displacement has been estimated as 2,750 tons at 21ft 4ins draught; she was nearly as big as the *Victory* of 1759.[75] Another ship almost as large was building for Henry V at Bayonne in 1419, though she was probably not finished.[76] It used to be argued that the *Grace Dieu* was a failure which never went to sea, but we now know that she had a successful cruise in 1420.[77] There is no reason to suppose that her triple-skinned clinker construction was unequal to the strain of so large a hull.[78]

To drive well under oars or sail galleys had long, fine, shallow and light hulls, which had to stand high stresses in a seaway. By comparison with the heavy, compact hull of a cog, a galley was expensive to build and maintain, with a short working life.[79] Since the light hull deteriorated rapidly if left afloat, and still more rapidly at tidal moorings which dried out at low water, it was necessary to build costly docks or covered slips on which the galleys could be housed when out of commission.[80] The Portsmouth dock built by King John did not last long, being dismantled in 1253.[81] It may have been too expensive to maintain, but more likely it was no longer useful in the changed strategic situation. Henry III's galleys were not concentrated but dispersed to places within range of their likely areas of operations. The force maintained at Portsmouth had dwindled to two galleys by 1233, when they were transferred to Bristol to deal with Pembroke's rebellion.[82] In place of the dockyard Henry III established a number of covered slips or galley-houses. A house for two galleys was built at Winchelsea in 1237,[83] and that at Rye extended to take seven galleys in 1243, when at least two galleys were moved there to be laid up.[84] Other galley-houses may have been built at Bristol, Chester and Dunwich.[85] They, like the galleys they housed, do not seem to have survived to the end of his reign. Orders to cover (or house-over) galleys at Rye and Winchelsea in 1259 and 1260 suggest that the galley-houses were then no longer serviceable.[86]

Like warships themselves, the docks and slips necessary to support them were among the most costly and sophisticated possessions of any medieval monarch. The impoverished government of Henry III, struggling to sustain its authority and avert civil war, was in no condition to maintain such things. Nor, in the event, was any other English monarch until the fifteenth century. The galleys built by Edward I and Edward III were maintained by the towns which built them – how is not clear, though a galley-house was made at Fordwich in 1373.[87] Throughout the fourteenth century the only royal

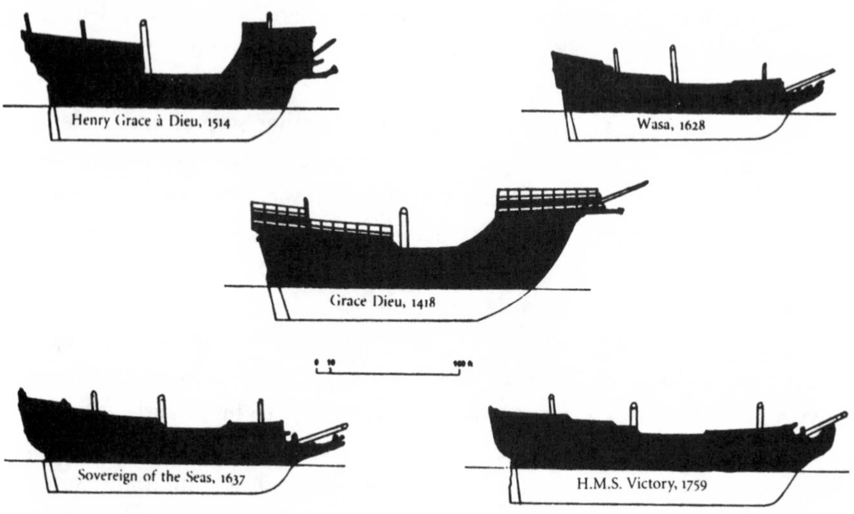

The (conjectural) profile of the *Grace Dieu* of 1418, compared with the *Henry Grace à Dieu* of 1514, the *Wasa* of 1628, the *Sovereign of the Seas* of 1637, and the *Victory* of 1759, gives an idea of her size.

establishment having any naval function was the Tower, the principal depot of military stores. It had a stone quay,[88] and the king's ships took on stores and arms there, but it had nothing to do with their maintenance.[89] When repairs were called for, they were beached wherever happened to be most convenient, and in winter they were laid up on the mudflats (*les Wozes*) at Greenwich, with a master and one or two seamen aboard each as shipkeepers.[90] Not until Henry V chose Southampton as a base suitable for the reconquest of Normandy was there another attempt to establish a naval base in England. There in 1420 William Soper, Clerk of the King's Ships, built a stone building 126ft long, incorporating stores and a forge, which was probably the first stone naval building ever put up in England.[91] Southampton was supplemented by the Hamble, where Soper built other stores (including a masthouse 140ft long and 14ft wide), and where three of Henry's four great carracks were later laid up.[92]

Henry V's big ships were built and laid up in 'docks',[93] which were evidently much what in later ages were called mud docks. These varied in sophistication: at its simplest, a mud dock was just a place to beach the ship at high water spring tides, after which a fence or hedge would be put up to protect her. When ships were built in dock, or if they were taken in for a major refit or rebuilding, an excavation would be made in the shore into or out of which the ship could be floated down a channel dug for the purpose. Such docks needed a watertight dockhead, which had to be broken through to get the ship out – a laborious process, but not an impossibly difficult one when unskilled labour was cheap, if the ship was to spend a long period in dock. A mud dock of this sort might need timbering to support its sides.[94]

From here it is only a short step to the dock rebuilt at Portsmouth in 1496, which is commonly, but quite wrongly, referred to as the first dry dock. It was not new, having been built in 1492,[95] and it differed from the more sophisticated mud docks, if at all, only in having a timbered dock head, with outer and inner coffer dams enclosing a filling of earth. The dock head still had to be dug out to release a ship, and it was only used for long stays.[96] It had a pump to help empty it, but pumps had long been in use aboard ship[97] and may not have been a novelty for a dock. If a true dry dock is a permanent structure with gates or a caisson to allow ships to be worked straight in and out on any high tide, this was not a dry dock, and it is probably only the survival (and printing) of the rebuilding accounts which makes it seem that it differed in any respect from its predecessors. Medieval docks were for processes involving a long stay. They were not designed for routine maintenance, which took place on the beach at low water for most ships, though a diver was employed for underwater work on Henry V's big ships.[98]

The limitations of the old single-masted rig were broken in the space of little more than a generation by the development in the fifteenth century of the three-masted square rig, the ancestor of the modern 'ship' rig.[99] Several of Henry V's ships had two masts (possibly copied from the Genoese carracks taken in 1416 and 1417), but with most of the sail area on a single mast amidships, one further mast was not a perfect solution to the difficulties of handling a big ship.[100] What was needed, it was soon realized, was three masts, and the standard rig came to set square sails on fore and main masts, with a lateen mizzen. The main mast continued to carry most of the canvas to drive the ship, but sail could be spread forward and aft to balance the ship on any point of sailing and, by unbalancing the rig, to force her rapidly onto another course. In particular it became much easier to tack, by taking in canvas forward so that the sail set on the mizzen would force the ship's head up into the wind, then backing the headsails to blow the ship's head off onto the new tack. In this and other ways very large ships could now be handled in conditions when even small ships had hitherto been helpless, conferring an enormous advantage in both economic and military terms.[101] At the same time footropes were developed, so that yards could be left standing and sails clewed up to them by men working aloft.[102] This greatly reduced the work of the ship and the number of men required, and it permitted the big square sails to be subdivided into a course and a topsail, providing better performance to windward and needing fewer men, at the price of a small reduction in performance off the wind.[103] After divided sails came divided masts;[104] the combination of lower mast and topmast was cheaper, lighter and safer than the huge single masts of the carracks.

Meanwhile a much smaller type called the caravel had developed on the Atlantic coasts of Spain and Portugal. This was initially a two- or three-masted, lateen-rigged and skeleton-built vessel, fast and handy, used for war, fishing and local trade.[105] As it developed in size it came to be rigged with a combination of square and lateen rig on two, three or more masts. The type seems to have been developed in this form in Brittany in the 1430s or 1440s, and from there it spread rapidly throughout northern Europe. At the same time it was carried into the Mediterranean by Catalan and Sicilian owners.[106] The new rig, applied to a fine hull, made a fast and handy ship ideal for war, trade and piracy. The caravel, or carvel, introduced carvel-building into England, though the attraction of the type lay not simply in the lie of the planking, but in the combination of cheap frame construction, using the new sawn deals, with a highly efficient rig. As a result the size of the average merchantman seems to have fallen, for a small, fast and cheaply-built vessel could now do more, and earn more, than bigger and clumsier vessels. The shipping slump of the late fifteenth century hastened the decline of the carrack.[107] They continued to be valued as 'capital ships' well into the sixteenth century,[108] but in the long run they represented a 'dead-end' in warship design. In place of the huge ships of Henry V, unmatched in size by any British man-of-war for nearly three hundred years after, the warships of the late Tudor age were to be developed from the quite small but fast and handy ships descended from the caravel.

SIX

The Northern Wars

Operations 1266–1336

Ever since the Conquest the kings of England had turned their strategic gaze southward, and conceived of ships as an auxiliary means of transport, necessary to carry the troops to and from the Continent where important wars were fought. On the infrequent occasions when they had attempted to intervene in the north and west, they had found it difficult or impossible to bring effective military strength to bear and were easily and swiftly drawn back to campaigning in France, where they felt at home. Though Henry III had given his eldest son an English rather than a Norman name, there is no reason to think that when Edward I succeeded to the throne in 1272 he differed in outlook from his father and ancestors. He was an effective leader in war who embodied the kingly virtues which the age expected, but he was no more an original strategist than they had been.

But the Norse-Celtic world had not disappeared for two hundred years because the kings of England were looking in the opposite direction, and the retreat of English sea power from the Irish Sea effectively restored its autonomy. The Welsh, who never developed naval power of their own in the Middle Ages, understood the importance of overseas links. As early as 1212 Llywelyn ap Iorwerth of Gwynedd concluded a treaty with France.[1] In his age Wales was still at home in a polyglot Irish Sea world to which the English kings did not really belong. His contemporary Alan, Lord of Galloway (died 1234), was head of one of the larger fractions of the Celtic world, but he witnessed Magna Carta as an English baron, his mother came of an Anglo-Norman family settled in Scotland, his brother-in-law was Constable of Chester, his father-in-law Earl of Huntingdon in England and of Lennox in Scotland. Lord of Lauderdale and Constable of Scotland, Alan was the greatest warrior of his day, with a large army and two hundred ships. His kinsman John the Scot, next Earl of Huntingdon, heir to the earldom of Chester, cousin of the King of Scots, was married to Llywelyn's daughter Helen, while her sister Gwenllian married William Lacy, half-brother of the

Anglo-Norman Earl of Ulster and grandson of Rory O'Connor, High King of Ireland.[2] A generation later Llywelyn ap Gruffydd maintained links both with Scotland and with Brian O'Neill, High King of Ireland, and is said to have had galleys of his own.[3] Their world lay about the shores of the Irish Sea, and was bound together by ships. The kings of England were largely excluded from direct participation in it, and when they intervened, they did so in the most costly and inefficient manner possible.

The fleets of the Vikings, eclipsed in the twelfth century by prolonged warfare within and among the Scandinavian kingdoms, enjoyed a revival from the 1180s and were once again capable of intervention in the British Isles. In the thirteenth century Norwegian kings were building some of the largest warships ever constructed of timber, culminating in the great *Kristsúðin* of 37 rooms, 260ft long, built at Bergen for King Håkon Håkonsson in 1262–3.[4] This king with his great ships, unequalled in the northern world, was a direct threat to both England and Scotland. In 1257 he provided Castile with naval technical assistance.[5] In 1262 he was negotiating with Aed O'Connor of Connaught for an alliance against the English, and he was also supported by Man and the Hebrides.[6] The next year his fleet, led by the *Kristsúðin*, entered the Irish Sea and attacked Scotland, but at the Battle of Largs the Norwegians were defeated by King Alexander III of Scots, and in the ensuing peace Man and the Hebrides were ceded to Scotland.

Though it is doubtful if the English fully realized it, this campaign had an immediate and powerful effect on the strategic relationship between England and the Celtic world, especially Wales. For two hundred years the intermittent cruises of Norwegian fleets, and the declining forces of the Irish and the Dublin Vikings (last active in Wales in 1144)[7] had represented the only major sea power in the Irish Sea, which was insufficient to interfere with the growth of English trade and influence in Ireland and South Wales. The rise of Norwegian naval strength in the thirteenth century threatened England's control of South Wales and eastern Ireland at its most vulnerable point. The departure of the Norwegians in 1265 left Scotland the dominant naval power in the northern Irish Sea. In 1275 Alexander III crushed a Manx revolt with a fleet of 90 galleys belonging to Alexander MacDougall of Lorne, Alan MacRuairi of Garmoran and other chiefs of the Isles.[8] In the southern Irish Sea, however, there was a naval vacuum in which the English were free to operate without fear of interference so long as they did not trench on Scottish interests. The consequences for the Welsh princes were especially serious, for their chances of independence from England depended largely on friendly, or at least neutral sea power at their backs.[9] If English fleets dominated those waters, as they had done before the Norman Conquest, the Welsh princes had no means of real independence. If the resources of Ireland and Scotland were available, however (to say nothing of those of France, Brittany and Castile), the situation was transformed. This applied not only to the Welsh princes but also to the Norman barons of South Wales. For centuries the English had found frontal attack across Offa's Dyke a profitless exercise, but the three coasts of Wales were always open to attack by sea. Now it was possible even for England with its vestigial naval resources to intervene in West and North Wales in a way it had not been able to do regularly since 1066.

In 1277 Edward I invaded North Wales, centre of the power of the Welsh prince Llewelyn ap Gruffydd. He established an ample supply depot at Chester, with a fleet of supply ships to bring victuals from Ireland as well as England to the army, before advancing slowly along the coast of North Wales. Eighteen out of twenty large ships (later followed by seven more) came from the Cinque Ports. He appreciated the importance of Anglesey, not simply as an advance position in the rear of the Welsh, but as the source of the grain which fed Snowdonia, and the seaborne force which was sent to occupy the island included 360 reapers to get in the harvest. Edward was rewarded for his methodical advance by the gain of substantial territories, but it must have become clear that for all his preparations, a summer campaign, with the fleet sent home at the end of September, would never suffice to conquer Wales.[10]

The second Welsh war of 1282 was on a more ambitious scale. The Cinque Ports alone provided forty ships, and two of the king's galleys came from Ireland. The basic strategy remained the same cautious advance along the north coast of Wales. Again Anglesey was occupied by a seaborne force, but this time its objectives were more ambitious. Fourteen small ships were bought to support a pontoon bridge across the Menai Strait in order to attack the Welsh in the rear. Unfortunately for Edward the scheme misfired. On 6 November, when the king had got no further than Denbigh, Luke de Tany, the commander of the force, attacked prematurely and was heavily defeated. In the retreat de Tany was killed and the bridge broken. Though Llywelyn was killed in mid-Wales on 11 December, the king's campaign continued in the north throughout the winter, sustained by large quantities of supplies from Ireland, Gascony and elsewhere. With the capture of Llywelyn's brother Dafydd in April, Welsh resistance finally collapsed.[11] The war demonstrated the successful, if unimaginative, application of overwhelming force; logistics were the key to victory, and ships the key to logistics, but the

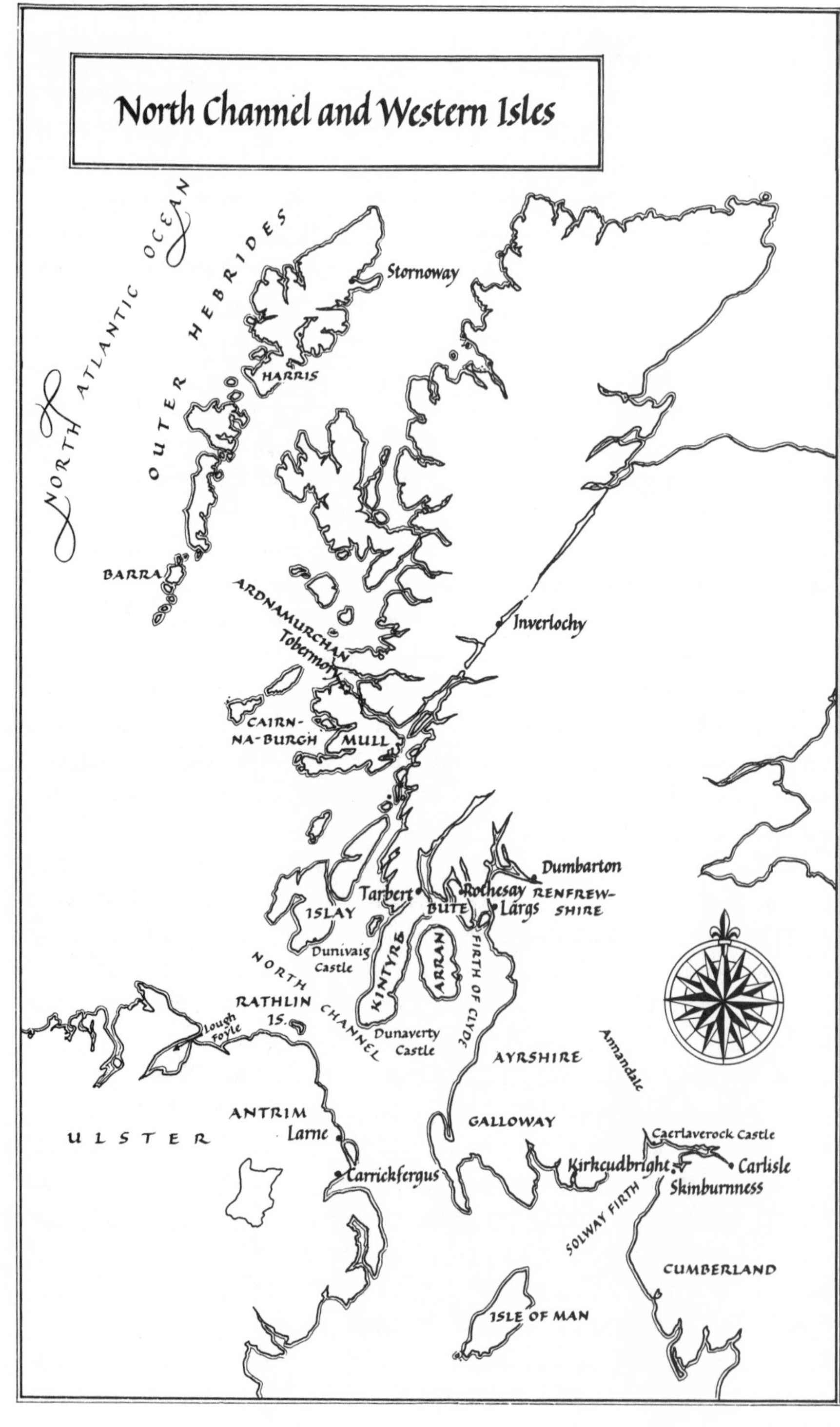
North Channel and Western Isles
NORTH ATLANTIC OCEAN
OUTER HEBRIDES
Stornoway
HARRIS
BARRA
ARDNAMURCHAN
Tobermory
Inverlochy
CAIRN-NA-BURGH
MULL
Dumbarton
Tarbert
Rothesay
RENFREW-SHIRE
ISLAY
BUTE
Largs
Dunivaig Castle
KINTYRE
ARRAN
FIRTH OF CLYDE
NORTH CHANNEL
RATHLIN IS.
Lough Foyle
Dunaverty Castle
AYRSHIRE
Annandale
ANTRIM
Larne
ULSTER
GALLOWAY
Caerlaverock Castle
Kirkcudbright
Carlisle
Skinburnness
Carrickfergus
SOLWAY FIRTH
CUMBERLAND
ISLE OF MAN

campaign was only possible because there was no hostile fleet in the Irish Sea, and Edward's new castle-building programme showed how little he really understood sea power.

There is no better example of the English medieval military mind at work than Edward I's great fortresses, built around North Wales at the end of the second Welsh war. There they still stand as masterpieces of military engineering,[12] and eloquent witnesses to the Maginot mentality. Certainly they all had harbours, which demonstrates a foolhardy confidence that no enemy ships could intervene to frustrate their resupply by sea – but if Edward I had had any real conception of the flexibility conferred by sea power, he would never have built them. A castle filled many roles, as a symbol of power, a residence and administrative centre, but its military function was, in the modern jargon, as a 'force-multiplier'. High initial investment bought long-term economy by allowing a small force of cavalry to dominate a wide district. If an enemy appeared, a well-supplied castle could be defended for months by a small garrison, and the difficulties of feeding an army, stationary for a long period, were such that the besiegers were as likely to be starved out as the garrison.[13]

Little of this applied in Wales, where small cavalry forces were very vulnerable and large bodies of infantry were needed to campaign among the forests and mountains. Since small garrisons were impotent and the Welsh were indifferent to siegecraft, the new castles did not even serve to tie down the enemy. Many of them, moreover, were built in quite the wrong places; the West Coast castles of Harlech, Criccieth and Llanbadarn were as far away as they could well be from points of strategic importance.[14] Only Conwy could clearly be justified, as commanding the important position of Penmaenmawr which otherwised blocked all advance along the north coast, as well situated to be the English capital of North Wales, and as relatively easily supplied from Chester and Dublin. The value of the others was more symbolic or political than military.

The Welsh rebellion of 1294 revealed the true worth of these symbols. It has been remarked that the existence of the castles made sea power 'more important';[15] what this means is that most of the naval and military strength urgently needed for the recapture of English Gascony had to be diverted in a desperate and only partly successful attempt to save the king's white elephants from slaughter; the entire overseas empire was put at risk to preserve garrisons of 26 men in Harlech and 30 in Criccieth.[16] Caernarfon was taken by the rebels in 1294 with heavy loss of life, and heavier loss of prestige.[17] Edward I himself was forced to set off on another campaign in North Wales.

He spent most of the winter besieged in Conwy, short of food because all the ships were committed to relieving more exposed fortresses like Harlech and Criccieth. In January he was ambushed on a rash raid into the Lleyn Peninsula, losing his baggage train. In April no fewer than 140 ships were assembled for a landing on Anglesey, an even larger effort than the same operation had called for in the first two Welsh wars; the existing castles (Beaumaris was not yet begun) were no help at all.[18]. By June 1295 the king had completed a circuit of most of Wales and was back in Conwy.

Very little of this would have been necessary if there had been no expensive and vulnerable symbols of royal prestige at risk. A Welsh rebellion in itself posed little threat to England, could easily have been contained and starved out by small naval and military forces, and need not have taken priority over the larger and more urgent concerns of Gascony.[19] The campaign had cost over £55,000,[20] besides at least £80,000 spent in building the castles.[21] A small part of this money would have provided a fleet capable of landing and supporting English troops on any point of the Welsh coast where they were actually needed, and of interfering with foreign assistance to Wales. Edward I was lucky that there was no enemy fleet in the Irish Sea to demonstrate the fundamental vulnerability of English control in Wales.

Meanwhile a more serious crisis had been developing overseas. A scuffle between Norman seamen and those of Bayonne and the Cinque Ports in 1292 was followed by a Norman raid on the Gironde. Then on 15 May 1293 a major sea battle took place in the Trade between Norman ships and a combined fleet from Gascony, Ireland and the Cinque Ports.[22] How it was provoked and who was chiefly to blame are questions still difficult to disentangle from the claims and counter-claims of those involved, but its consequences were soon clear enough. Not content with victory at sea, the Gascons went on to attack their ancient rival La Rochelle, causing heavy loss and damage. This was a diplomatic disaster for Edward, because as Duke of Aquitaine he could be, and was, cited before the Parisian courts to answer for allowing his Gascon subjects to fight those of his feudal lord the King of France. It would have been far less embarrassing had the affair been between two sovereign nations on an equal footing, so English diplomats claimed that the kings of England 'time out of mind had been in peaceable possession of the sovereign lordship of the English sea and the islands therein'.[23] The doctrine of English 'sovereignty of the sea' was an imaginative attempt to extract the dispute from a legal context in which the King of France had all the advantages, and reclassify it as an internal disorder within English jurisdiction.[24] This 'peaceable possession' was a legal fiction, unconnected with practical control. The harsh reality, according to the islanders of Jersey and Guernsey in 1331, was that they were 'oppressed, ruined and imperilled, surrounded by the great sea, on the marches of every nation'.[25] The sea was a lawless domain beyond the borders of civilized society, and a seaport was 'a real frontier town', as Yarmouth put it in 1385.[26]

Though 'sovereignty of the sea' had nothing to do with command or control of the sea in the modern sense, it was potentially important, for in the Middle Ages legal jurisdiction was the most immediate and potent symbol of royal authority, and an important source of revenue. Had the kings of England been able to make good the claim by restraining and punishing indiscriminate piracy they might have made real diplomatic and political capital from it. Unfortunately they hardly ever could, and the empty boast was a source of embarrassment and expense. It was difficult to claim sovereignty and yet avoid all responsibility, so Edward III was driven to pay large sums in compensation for piracy by the subjects he had been unable to control.[27] In practice the claim to 'sovereignty of the sea' was only put forward officially at irregular intervals in particularly favourable circumstances. It was more often quoted by litigants, foreign monarchs[28] or domestic opponents seeking to exploit the kings' embarrassment. Thus in 1320 some Flemish victims of English piracy reminded Edward II that 'he is lord of the sea and the said robbery was committed at sea in his jurisdiction';[29] much later historians cited this as an acknowledgement of medieval English sea power,[30] but it was actually an exploitation of English diplomatic embarrassment.

The immediate consequence of the 1293 dispute was the French occupation of Gascony, supposedly 'temporarily', until the affair could be resolved. The economic value of England's remaining continental province was enormous. After the loss of Poitou, the English abandoned the white wines of that territory in favour of the light red wines ('clarets') from the country around Bordeaux.[31] The wine trade grew in importance until by the early fourteenth century over 80,000 tuns a year were being exported, and at least a thousand ships a year cleared the Gironde.[32] The duty levied on wine exported through Bordeaux became equal to, sometimes greater than, the customs revenue of the whole kingdom of England, while Bordeaux itself was the largest and richest city of the English empire.[33] In 1324 Gascony's net contribution to the English exchequer was £13,000.[34] The growth of the wine-producing areas, however, coupled with loss of territory to France, made it impossible for Gascony to feed itself. By the fourteenth century English Gascony depended largely on grain, fish and other commodities imported from England,[35] so that interruption of the regular convoys threatened famine in Gascony as well as financial disaster for the English crown.[36] The greatest seaport of Gascony was the wealthy and loyal city of Bayonne, whose shipowners handled much of the wine trade and contributed largely to English naval strength.[37] Gascony and the Bordeaux trade, the ships they maintained and the skills they required, were the foundation of English mercantile and naval strength in the Middle Ages.

Edward I was not naive enough to imagine that he would get all this back without fighting, and he immediately set about assembling the ships and men for a major expedition.[38] The king's plan was the same which had failed his father and grandfather; to stand on the defensive in Gascony and concentrate on an offensive alliance in Flanders. England's staple export was raw wool, and to a lesser extent semi-finished cloth, sent to the great industrial cities of Flanders where the most advanced textile industry of Europe was concentrated. Antwerp on the Scheldt, and the ports of Damme and Sluys on the Swyn, the estuary which led up to Bruges, were the nearest and commonest of all ports of call for English shipping. Close economic ties had long formed the foundation of alliances between Flanders and England against France, and successive English kings, learning by experience the cost and difficulty of long-range war from Gascony, dreamed of attacking France from the north.[39] For much of the Middle Ages, however, the Low Countries were divided among a large number of small states, and the assembling of a working coalition among them, and setting it in motion against the formidable defences of France, repeatedly proved to be a costly and futile undertaking.[40]

In this case the small forces which could be spared from Wales all went to Gascony. The first ships sailed in October 1294, passing up the Gironde and the Garonne past Bordeaux, capturing Bourg, Blaye and other riverside towns on the way; disembarking their horses after seventeen weeks at sea,[41] they marched overland and retook Bayonne, which welcomed the relieving force at once. At Easter 1295, however, a large French army invaded; with few English troops available, the burden of the war fell largely on local forces raised by the towns and petty nobility of Gascony, which (unlike the city of Bordeaux) remained loyal to the English connection. The 1295 expedition of the king's brother Edmund Crouchback, Earl of Lancaster, achieved little, and Lancaster himself died in June.[42] If there was one man who saved English Gascony it was Barrau de Sescas, 'Captain and Admiral' of Bayonne. Bayonne's ships and money were the key to the defence of English Gascony; they fought the convoys from England through the French blockade of the Gironde to the besieged fortresses of Bourg and Blaye, allowing them to

The Bay of Biscay

hold out until the truce of 1297.[43] We have much information about these operations, down to the lading of ships like the *Plenty* of Winchelsea, Robert Kingston master, which carried from the Thames to Bourg a cargo including 385 quarters of corn, 20 tons of wheat, 3 springalds, 48 crossbows, and ammunition amounting to 52,000 crossbow bolts and 500 springald bolts.[44]

In the Channel the French were working hard on their new naval base the Clos des Gallées at Rouen, built between 1284 and 1293,[45] apparently after the model of the Castilian naval base at Seville. Here a force of craftsmen imported at great expense from the Mediterranean constructed and maintained Genoese-style galleys, manned by crews brought up from Marseilles every spring. These galleys were built and preserved in permanent galley-houses, though it is unclear whether they were launched straight into the river or into a basin. There were certainly locks giving access to channels, perhaps leading into a basin. A separate force of local shipwrights built clinker-built barges, presumably similar to English barges of the time. Besides about 30 galley-houses, there were also extensive workshops, stores, barracks and a parade-ground.[46] In 1295 the French Mediterranean galley squadron came up the Channel, raided the Channel Isles, burnt part of Dover, and attacked Winchelsea and Hythe with less success.[47] The same year, Eric VI of Norway promised to send twenty longships and a hundred round ships with 50,000 men to support a French invasion of England.[48] These threats inspired the English galley-building programme of 1294–5.[49]

Meanwhile Edward devoted most of his energies, and the promise of about £250,000 (of which about £165,000 was actually paid), to his projected coalition in Flanders. Finally in 1297 the alliance seemed to be ready – but so were the French. They invaded Flanders in June, while Edward did not sail until 24 August, with an army of only 895 horse and 8,000 foot embarked in 273 ships. Before they had even landed, the 73 ships from the Cinque Ports and the 59 from Yarmouth had fought a pitched battle which left at least seventeen ships sunk.[50] This expedition cost about £50,000,[51] but it was soon obvious that the military and diplomatic situation in Flanders was all but hopeless, and Edward was glad to conclude a truce in October 1297, followed by peace in June 1299. Between 1294 and 1298 the king spent about £750,000 on his wars, at least £250,000 of it in the first eighteen months.[52] Naval wages alone cost £12,852 6s 1d in 1295, £18,278 11s 6d in 1296, but only £1,519 15s in 1297, when no major fleet sailed to Gascony.[53] In three years (1294–7) a single tax on wool extracted at least £110,000 from an economy in which there was probably only about a million pounds in circulation.[54] It is no wonder that the result was a domestic crisis as the king tried and failed to impose taxes without parliamentary consent. Meanwhile the French remained in occupation of Bordeaux, and five years of war had yielded almost nothing.[55]

The English position on the Continent was retrieved, but not by any military or diplomatic efforts of Edward's. In May 1302 the Flemings revolted against French occupation and massacred the garrison of Bruges, and on 11 July King Philip the Fair was heavily defeated by a Flemish army at Courtrai. All Europe was shocked that armoured knights, who had dominated war and society for hundreds of years, should be routed by a force of townsmen and peasants. The disaster caused an abrupt collapse of French prestige, followed in 1303 by the revolt of Bordeaux and the restoration of Gascony to Edward I by the Treaty of Paris. The French mounted another campaign into Flanders in 1304, during which their fleet under the command of the Genoese admiral Rainier Grimaldi won a great battle against the Flemish and Zealander ships blockading Zierickzee.[56] Grimaldi's fleet was made up of French, Hollander, Genoese and Castilian ships, and briefly included English ships as well, as Edward was by this time an ally of France.[57]

In order to explain this diplomatic reversal, it is necessary to go back to the 1290s. Alexander III of Scots died in 1286, when the kingdom passed to his infant granddaughter the Norwegian princess Margaret. She died in 1290 on her passage to Scotland, leaving no obvious heir to the throne. This was Edward I's opportunity; claiming to be feudal overlord of Scotland, he arbitrated between various claimants, and in 1292 awarded the throne to John Balliol. Presumably Edward hoped for a loyal client; by 1295 when the Scots formally allied with France, it was clear that he had not succeeded. In 1296 the king invaded Scotland to enforce his claim to overlordship. The Scots were defeated in a skirmish at Dunbar, Balliol proved to be lacking in the qualities of a king and a general, and by the autumn he had abdicated and left Edward apparently in full control of the kingdom. Scotland was subjected to the same ruthless demands for men and money to support the continental war as England, leading to growing resistance by clergy and barons in both kingdoms. In August 1297 the king sailed for Flanders with the political situation sliding into crisis.[58]

This was the context of the Scottish rebellion led by Sir William Wallace in May 1297. Edward was unable to turn his attention to Scotland until the following year, and then he found things much more difficult than his experience two years before might have led him to expect. The English army was ambushed at Stirling Bridge when its commander the Earl of Warenne overslept, and Wallace's forces raided into Northumberland before Edward could react. Eventually he defeated the main Scots army at Falkirk, but a campaign marked throughout by logistical difficulties turned to near disaster when supplies failed to arrive from Ireland and the English army had to retreat through Annandale to Carlisle. In Scotland, as in Wales, English armies could deploy and exploit their military superiority only by relying heavily on ships for supplies.[59]

Absorbed in political crisis at home and negotiation with France abroad, Edward attempted nothing in Scotland in the summer of 1299, and his hopes of a winter campaign in November collapsed when the English barons failed to appear. The result was the fall of the key fortress of Stirling Castle, which dominated movement across the Forth–Clyde line – Scotland this side, and Scotland beyond 'the Scottish Sea', as medieval English geographers called it.[60] In 1300 a substantial English campaign was organized on the west coast, with thirty ships from the Cinque Ports and a larger number from elsewhere shipping supplies from Ireland to the assembly port of Skinburnness (on the English shore of the Solway Firth) and thence across to the army besieging Caerlaverock Castle in Galloway. The capture of this castle was the only gain of the campaign.[61] In 1301 English armies advanced from both Berwick and Carlisle, and succeeded in taking some Scottish castles, but the Scottish army avoided battle and no decisive result was obtained. More than eighty ships were summoned to support this campaign, and the number present was considerably greater: 74 (including 46 Irish ships) on the west coast alone. In this year for the first time English ships operated in the Western Isles, though under Scottish command, for these were the home waters of their allies the MacRuaris of Garmoran.[62] In January 1302, probably under French pressure, Edward agreed to a truce until November.[63]

After their disaster in Flanders, the French were in no condition to sustain far-away allies; in fact they became notionally allies of England. With his rear secure Edward was able in 1303 to mount the biggest English campaign in Scotland yet. The main army advanced up the east coast, crossing the Forth by means of prefabricated assault bridges shipped from Lynn in a convoy of 29 ships with two escorts.[64] This army advanced as far north as Brechin, and Edward himself wintered at Dunfermline. On the west coast the Earl of Ulster led an army of 3,500 men in 173 ships from Ireland to the Clyde, where they captured Rothesay Castle. By the summer of 1304 almost all the Scottish magnates had capitulated, though Wallace was still at large. The surrender of Stirling Castle on 20 July completed the English conquest of Scotland.[65] The campaign had laid an immense burden on English shipping

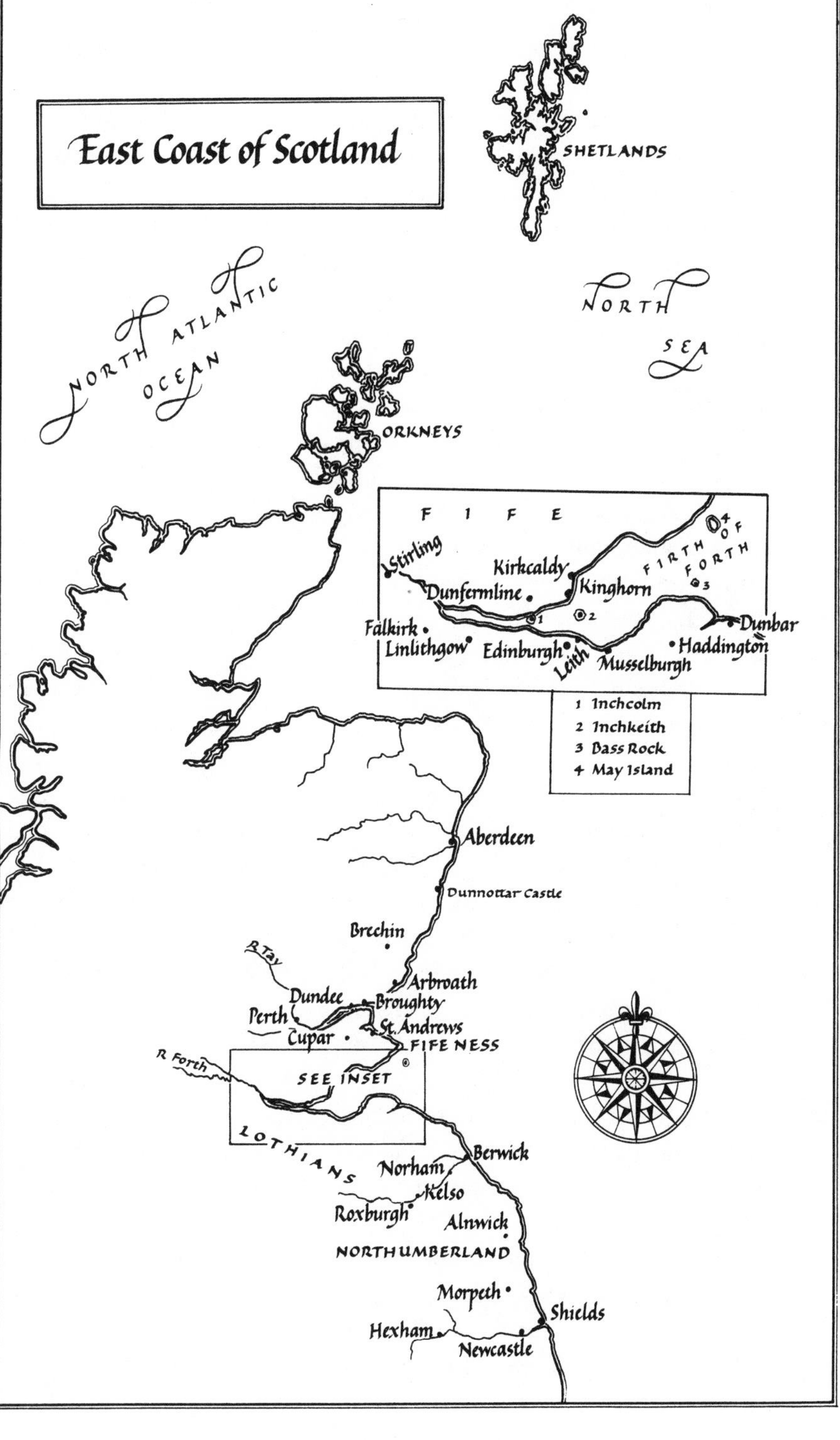
East Coast of Scotland
SHETLANDS
NORTH ATLANTIC
OCEAN
NORTH
SEA
ORKNEYS
FIFE
Stirling
Kirkcaldy
FIRTH OF FORTH
Dunfermline
Kinghorn
Falkirk
Linlithgow
Edinburgh
Leith
Musselburgh
Haddington
Dunbar
1 Inchcolm
2 Inchkeith
3 Bass Rock
4 May Island
Aberdeen
Dunnottar Castle
Brechin
R Tay
Arbroath
Dundee
Broughty
Perth
St. Andrews
Cupar
FIFE NESS
R Forth
SEE INSET
LOTHIANS
Berwick
Norham
Kelso
Roxburgh
Alnwick
NORTHUMBERLAND
Morpeth
Shields
Hexham
Newcastle

and aroused widespread complaint and resistance, but at the end it seemed to have achieved decisive victory.[66]

In fact the English government in Scotland lasted less than two years. In February 1306 a Scottish rebellion broke out under the leadership of Robert Bruce, Earl of Carrick, and once again Edward found himself sending large armies into Scotland. By this time he must have been aware how much his operations depended on seaborne supplies, but he probably did not appreciate the danger that exposed him to. The 1303 treaty with France, which secured both the return of Gascony and the expulsion of Scots from France, was a diplomatic triumph bought at a price: the expulsion of Flemings from England. The Flemings and Scots were brought together, providing Scotland with powerful naval assistance in the North Sea. In the west Bruce's connections in the Hebrides included Angus the Young, the Lord of the Isles, whose galleys were a powerful addition of strength to the rebel cause, allowing men and supplies to be carried to and from Ireland (from which the Isles imported food) and presenting a standing peril to English armies in Scotland. In these waters only Bruce's enemies the MacDougalls of Argyll, lords of Lorne, now supported the English cause. The confident English assumption that supplies would always come in by sea whatever else went wrong, already falsified in Wales, was about to bring disaster in Scotland as well.[67]

The war moved to the sea almost at once. Defeated on land, Bruce took refuge in the Isles in the summer of 1306. English ships under the command of Sir John Botetourt and the Scots admiral John of Menteith besieged and captured Dunaverty Castle in Kintyre in September, believing Bruce to be there. In fact he was hiding on Rathlin Island off the Antrim coast, part of the lands of the Bissets of the Glens. That winter a squadron under the command of Hugh Bisset and Eoin MacDougall of Lorne patrolled the North Channel to prevent Irish supplies reaching the Western Isles; Bisset had a history of equivocal relations with the Scots in previous commands, and was later a close ally of Bruce, so it is not unlikely that he was playing a double game and knew more of what was going on in his lands than he admitted. Certainly Bruce returned to Scotland unscathed, and defeated English forces in Ayrshire in May 1307.[68]

Two months later, advancing northward once again, Edward I died. His son Edward II campaigned only briefly, and his withdrawal gave Bruce valuable time to establish his rule. In January 1308 Edward married Isabella, daughter of King Philip the Fair of France, cementing both the Anglo-French and (as a natural reaction) the Scots-Flemish alliances. The new king inherited his father's unpopularity with few of his talents; neither his character nor his policy earned him respect in England. During 1308 Bruce continued to extend his authority in Scotland and before the end of the year he was raiding northern England. Edward II was forced to accept a baronial reform commission (the Lords Ordainers) in May 1310, and in August 1311 to banish his favourite Piers Gaveston. His ineffectual campaign in Scotland that summer, followed by a Scots raid into Northumberland, did nothing to strengthen his position. In June 1312 Gaveston, who had returned to England, was murdered by the Earls of Lancaster and Warwick. All this while the English continued to lose ground in Scotland. In 1312 Bruce raided Hexham and Durham, while Sir James Douglas raided Hartlepool. Linlithgow Castle surrendered, followed by Perth, Roxburgh and Edinburgh early in 1313.[69]

Edward badly needed to restore his authority in England and Scotland. The two were closely linked, for defeat abroad and weakness at home fed upon one another. The most important remaining English position in Scotland, Stirling Castle, had agreed to surrender unless relieved by Midsummer's Day 1314. To save it, and himself, Edward led what was possibly the biggest English army ever into Scotland. On Midsummer's Day itself, at Bannockburn within five miles of Stirling, he suffered a calamitous defeat. It is conventional to regard this as the turning-point of the Scottish War of Independence, but in reality its effects were political more than military. Robert Bruce gained enormously in loyalty and authority, and Edward lost them in proportion. The military significance of Bannockburn, like Courtrai twelve years before and the Swiss victory at Morgarten in 1315, was to herald the rise of infantry and archers to dominate the battlefield. It did not in itself decide the war, for in strictly military terms English resources continued to be vastly greater than Scots even after the battle. It is not necessary to follow literally the chronicle called the *Scottichronicon*, which claims that the Scottish tactics at Bannockburn had been learnt from naval warfare,[70] to realize that the decisive changes in the Anglo-Scottish war were taking place at sea, not on land. The failure of seaborne supplies forced the surrender of Perth and brought Stirling to terms. Scottish and Flemish ships were active on the east coast of England, after Bannockburn English ships on the east coast had to be convoyed, and in 1318 a Scottish naval blockade made possible the capture of Berwick.[71]

In the Irish Sea Scots ships took the Isle of Man in 1313. Though it was retaken in 1314, nothing could be done to prevent Robert Bruce's brother Edward invading Ireland the following year. For a time it looked as though

English rule would be speedily extinguished, and in 1317 Man was again taken by Scottish ships, but Bruce's death in battle in 1318 checked the Scottish advance. Both Ireland and the Irish Sea, however, remained throughout the lifetime of Robert Bruce (who visited Ireland in 1328, shortly before his death) a contested area in which King Robert counted for as much or more than King Edward. Genoese galleys had to be chartered in 1316 to run supplies through to the beleaguered garrison of Carlisle, and the coasts of Wales were continually warned of Scottish landings, though in the event none took place.[72]

The personal authority of Edward II never recovered after Bannockburn, and the political history of the rest of his reign is of cold war verging on civil war between the king, his few supporters, and many of the great magnates, while others tried in vain to reconcile them. This was no foundation for effective military operations. Once only, in 1319, something like a full English army assembled to try to recapture Berwick, but the main Scottish army moved south well inland and sharply defeated the local Yorkshire levies in Swaledale, whereupon the English army broke up as the northern earls hastened south to protect their lands. In 1322 the political crisis came to a head with an armed confrontation between the king's forces and the Earl of Lancaster's at Boroughbridge. Edward emerged triumphant, but not for long. His new favourites the two Despencers, father and son, were no more popular than Gaveston had been, and the unconcealed piracy of Sir Hugh Despencer the younger was particularly damaging. Neither they nor the king had any answer to the Scots. When the truce expired in 1322 Scots forces raided at will in northern England. The king himself was almost captured near Byland in Yorkshire, and all over the north country men spoke openly of the necessity of making terms with the dominant power of the north. Edward II attempted a counter-raid into the Lothians, but what ships the English could collect were fully occupied resisting Flemish attacks on the shipping and fishing fleets of East Anglia, so for want of supplies his army starved and he soon had to withdraw.[73] In 1323 a truce of thirteen years between England and Scotland was agreed, though Edward still could not bring himself to recognize Bruce as King of Scots.

In 1325 Queen Isabella went to Paris on a diplomatic mission to reconcile her husband and her father over the Gascon question. In this she succeeded, and it was agreed that the young prince Edward, heir to the throne, should receive the Duchy of Aquitaine. He travelled to France for his investiture that autumn, and he did not return. The queen, now openly estranged from her husband and with the prince in her hands, became the centre of opposition to Edward. She raised troops and ships with the help of William II, Count of Hainault, Holland and Zealand, to whose daughter Philippa the young prince was betrothed. Edward's government made desperate attempts to muster a fleet, even summoning the galleys of Bayonne, but when the queen and her force sailed from Dordrecht in September 1326 they met no opposition.[74] The sequel was the deposition and subsequent murder of Edward II, and his replacement by a government of the queen and her lover Edmund Mortimer, ruling in the name of the fourteen-year-old Edward III. In 1328 the new regime made peace with Scotland on terms dictated by Robert Bruce.

This 'shameful peace' was one of the many reasons why the queen and her lover were soon as unpopular as Edward II had been. In October 1330 the young king seized power. Already he displayed all the conventional military virtues which his father had so obviously lacked, and he was anxious to establish his reputation by erasing the disgrace of the Scottish wars. It was a good moment to try, for Robert I had died in 1329 leaving the kingdom of Scots to the five-year-old David II. Moreover Edward Balliol, son of Edward I's hapless candidate for the throne, was available, and possessed many of the kingly qualities his father had lacked. With Edward's connivance, Balliol's small force of exiles and malcontents, the 'Disinherited', sailed from the Humber in 1332. They forced a landing at Kinghorn in Fife, and against all expectations, defeated the main Scots army near Perth on 11 August. In September Balliol was crowned as King of Scots, and in November he acknowledged Edward III as his overlord and agreed to cede the greater part of Lowland Scotland to England. With this act Balliol's chances of making good his authority disappeared, and by the spring he had been driven out of Scotland. Edward III now showed his hand. The English army besieged Berwick, and on 19 July 1333, at Halidon Hill outside the town, he heavily defeated the Scottish relieving army, using the new tactics of dismounted infantry and archers standing in a defensive position. English ships blockaded Berwick, brought in supplies for the besiegers, and in the final assault (delivered at high water) came alongside the walls. At the same time in the Irish Sea English ships again occupied the Isle of Man. By the summer of 1334 Balliol was King of Scots once more, David II was in exile in France, and all the Lowlands as far as the Forth–Clyde line (Galloway excepted) had been handed over to England.[75]

But the Bruce cause was still alive in the west, and the galleys of the Western Isles were still available to bring troops across the Clyde and raise Ayrshire and Renfrewshire against Balliol and the English. Edward III gathered his army at Newcastle in November 1334 to retrieve the situation, but he soon found winter campaigning impossible, and the English army did not enter Scotland in force until the summer of 1335, when they marched from Carlisle up to the Clyde and thence east to meet supply ships in the Forth and the Tay.[76] In 1336 the English army penetrated as far as Perth, aiming for Aberdeen, the only major port on the east coast by which the Scots could still receive help from overseas. This offensive was preceded by a small seaborne force under Sir Thomas Rosslyn sent up the coast to seize an advance base. They succeeded in taking the ruined Dunottar Castle fifteen miles south of Aberdeen, though Rosslyn was mortally wounded in the landing.[77] (This was an interesting example of a successful medieval 'assault landing'.) The Scots, however, remained active at sea throughout this period. East Anglia was raided during the abortive winter campaign of 1334; in 1335 and 1336 Edward III issued urgent orders to prepare naval and coastal defences against an anticipated Scots invasion; and in 1336 Scots ships were active in the Channel, raiding the Channel Isles and taking prizes off the Isle of Wight.[78] In 1338 Edward III was forced to charter two Genoese galleys to strengthen English forces in the North Sea, and in 1339 all shipping going to Scotland was put under convoy.[79] In spite of the brief triumph of Balliol and the English party in Scotland, the first essential for English dominance in Scotland remained safe use of the waters on both coasts, and that was as uncertain as ever.

SEVEN

Edward III at Sea

Operations 1336–1360

By this time the English war with Scotland had become subsumed in a larger struggle with France. Queen Isabella's diplomatic settlement of 1325 ended the brief 'war of St Sardos', but it did not resolve the underlying tension over Gascony, nor did an English attack on Norman shipping in May 1326 and a raid on Cherbourg in September.[1] French support for Scotland added another element of dispute, and the death of Charles IV of France in 1328, leaving his nephew Edward III with a plausible claim to be his heir, contributed the last. Even so, the war did not come at once. Queen Isabella naturally did not desire it, and the young Edward III was initially preoccupied with his Scottish campaigns.

By sea as by land the first part of the Hundred Years War saw the deployment of new and devastating weapons and tactics, overthrowing established forces and ideas – only at sea it was the English who were the victims of innovation. Raiding, the deliberate destruction of resources, lay at the heart of medieval strategy. Sometimes derided by modern writers as 'aimless',[2] it was carefully and ruthlessly calculated. 'War without fire,' Henry V said, was 'no better than sausages without mustard': in a war of attrition, victory went to the side which could waste the enemy's economic resources while preserving his own means of making war.[3] This was truest of all in naval war, then as in every age the most costly and capital-intensive way of warfare. Ships were extremely valuable; they incorporated a large fraction of the medieval economy's scarce liquid capital in a very vulnerable form. Though it was difficult to intercept them on the open sea, it was easy to find their home ports. Even if the ships themselves were absent, the destruction of the towns ruined the merchants and their trade. Coastal raids were very effective and relatively easy to mount with galleys, and there was no sure defence against them. Some ports lay so far up rivers and inlets as to be difficult for even galleys to attack, but many were exposed, few were fortified, and even fortifications were vulnerable to surprise. Beacons gave warning of attack,[4] but seldom until it actually took place, and the raiders might stay ashore as long as twenty-four hours before any concentration of troops could be brought against them. The costly 'home guard' scheme of 1339 laid a heavy burden on the inhabitants of the maritime counties, sharply reduced the recruiting area of the English field army, and gave real security only against raiders who were stupid enough to give long warning of their coming.[5] Defensive patrols were sometimes attempted,[6] but the chances of catching raiders this way were poor, even in an age when most navigation was along the coast. Barrages of piles and chains were erected to protect ports,[7] but to no great effect.

Though England suffered little from the enemy by comparison with France, on whose soil the Hundred Years War was fought, the damage done by coastal attacks was political and psychological as much as physical, and they acted at least as powerfully as royal exactions in causing the decline of English shipping.[8] Ravaging the enemy's territory was the classic way to provoke him into a rash attack, often employed by Edward III against the French;[9] it offered the defender the choice of risking battle on the enemy's terms, or accepting the reputation of a coward and a weakling. The English had enjoyed substantial immunity from attack during most of the thirteenth century chiefly because their enemies were too poor or too unenterprising to use the sea. In the fourteenth they faced naval attack first from Scotland, then from France, Genoa, Castile and Monaco; all of them with more powerful fleets and more intelligent strategic ideas than England possessed.

Medieval writers were perfectly capable of sophisticated strategy. In the Mediterranean world, especially, theorists turned powerful minds to that perennial subject of dreams, the recovery of the Holy Land. The crusader states had always depended on sea power, and only sea power could restore them.[10] The Franciscan missionary Brother William Adam, writing about 1300, proposed to ruin Arab trade and cut off the Near East from India by stationing a Christian galley squadron in the Indian Ocean – a sound strategy, and not as far beyond the limits of the possible as one might think, for in his day (nearly two hundred years before the Portuguese first rounded the Cape of Good Hope) Genoese merchants had already penetrated the Indian Ocean trade routes.[11] The strategic relationship of France and Scotland as allies against England was commented on by contemporaries on both sides. The English knight Sir Thomas Grey, writing as a prisoner in Scotland in the 1350s, describes the Franco-Scots policy of raiding across the border 'in the semblance of an invasion in order to force the said king of England to retreat from France to rescue his country'.[12] But nothing like naval strategic thinking emerges in England in the fourteenth century. It was England's enemies who thought about war at sea, and put their thoughts into action.

Of the Mediterranean powers, Genoa played the largest part in the northern wars. Not only was it the most powerful of the Italian city-states at sea (Venice perhaps excepted), but its violent internal politics ensured a steady supply of exiled noblemen with galleys at their command, anxious to earn their living in the wars. Prominent among them were the Grimaldis, driven into exile and forced to settle on the remote rock of Monaco in the farthest corner of Genoese territory, whence their galleys put to sea to intervene (usually in alliance with France) in the Channel and the North Sea.[13] At times the French hired both Grimaldi galleys (of the Guelf faction), and the Dorias (who belonged to their enemies the Ghibellines), though it was necessary to keep the two squadrons well apart.[14] The Genoese supplied the initial technical help to establish the Aragonese and French galley fleets, and they contributed senior officers to most of the galley squadrons of Europe.[15] Aragon in turn was the source of the technical expertise on which the Castilian and Portuguese galley squadrons were based,[16] and it was the Aragonese galleys under their great commander Roger of Lauria which defeated the French invasion of 1284–5.[17] In 1295 the Aragonese fleet and its commander were offered to France for the English wars, though in the event they never came north.[18]

Though poor, militarily backward, and absorbed in the reconquest of the peninsula from the Arabs, Castile was a maritime power of the first importance, and for much of the fourteenth century the dominant naval power on the Atlantic coast of Europe.[19] Seville fell to the Castilians in 1249, and four years later they began to build a galley squadron there in imitation of the Moorish galleys which had for so long controlled the Straits of Gibraltar.[20] In the fourteenth century this little force (never more than twenty galleys), exercised an influence out of all proportion to its size. In the same period the Castilians' rivals the Portuguese also put galley squadrons to sea which sometimes intervened in northern waters.[21]

The French began the fighting with naval activity in support of Scotland. The Clos des Gallées at Rouen was hard at work building up a galley fleet; by 1336 there were eight large and five smaller galleys at Rouen and La Rochelle together, plus twelve in the Mediterranean which were transferred north. Further galleys were chartered from Genoa, but English agents persuaded the Genoese government to arrest and destroy them (paying 6,000 marks to satisfy claims against English pirates, notably the late Sir Hugh Despencer). In August the French galleys put to sea, taking prizes off the

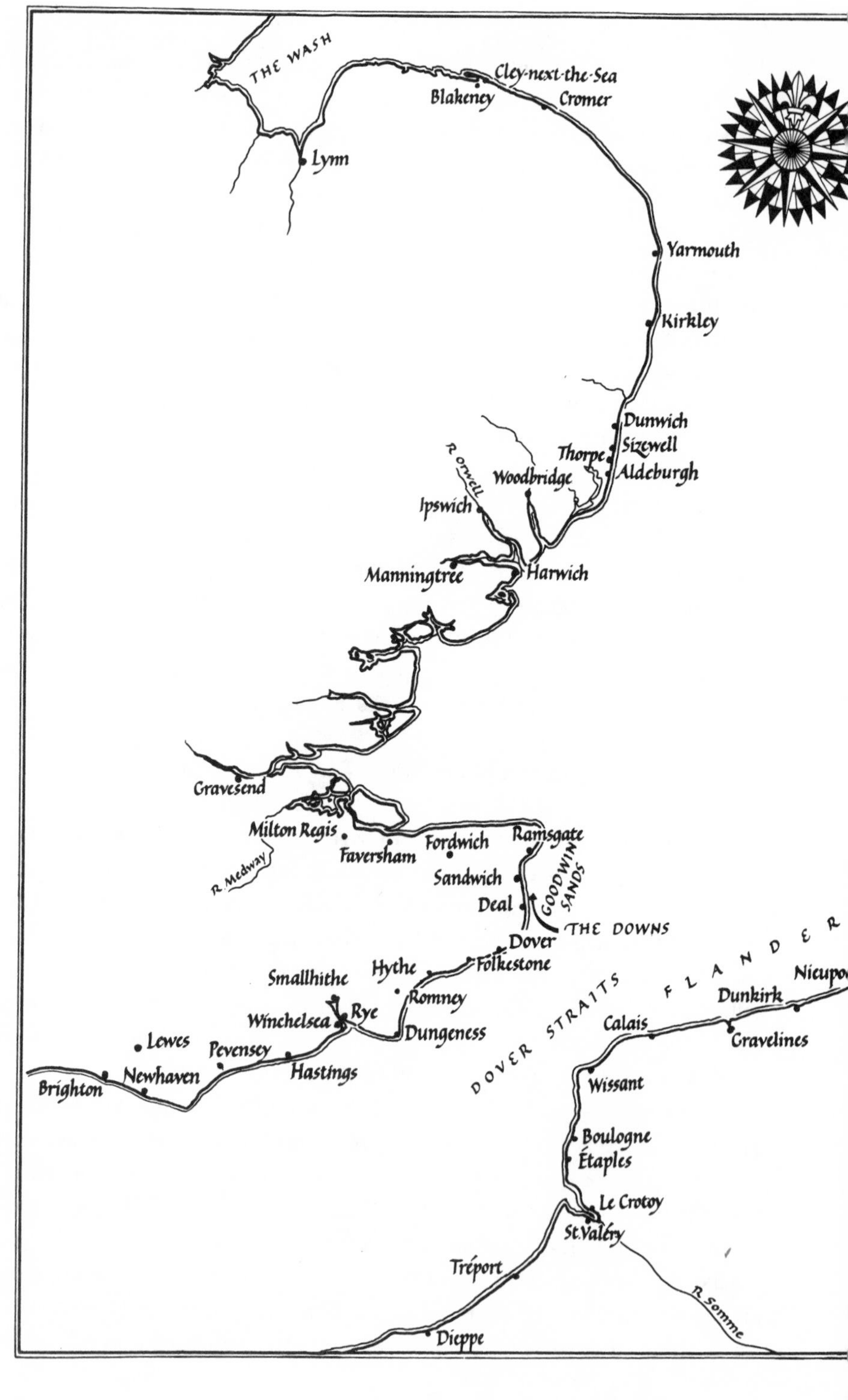
THE WASH
Cley-next-the-Sea
Blakeney
Cromer
Lynn
Yarmouth
Kirkley
Dunwich
Sizewell
Thorpe
Aldeburgh
Woodbridge
R. Orwell
Ipswich
Manningtree
Harwich
Gravesend
Milton Regis
Faversham
Fordwich
Ramsgate
R. Medway
Sandwich
Deal
GOODWIN SANDS
THE DOWNS
Dover
Folkestone
Hythe
Smallhithe
Romney
Winchelsea
Rye
Dungeness
Lewes
Pevensey
Hastings
Newhaven
Brighton
DOVER STRAITS
FLANDER
Calais
Dunkirk
Gravelines
Wissant
Boulogne
Étaples
Le Crotoy
St. Valéry
Tréport
R. Somme
Dieppe

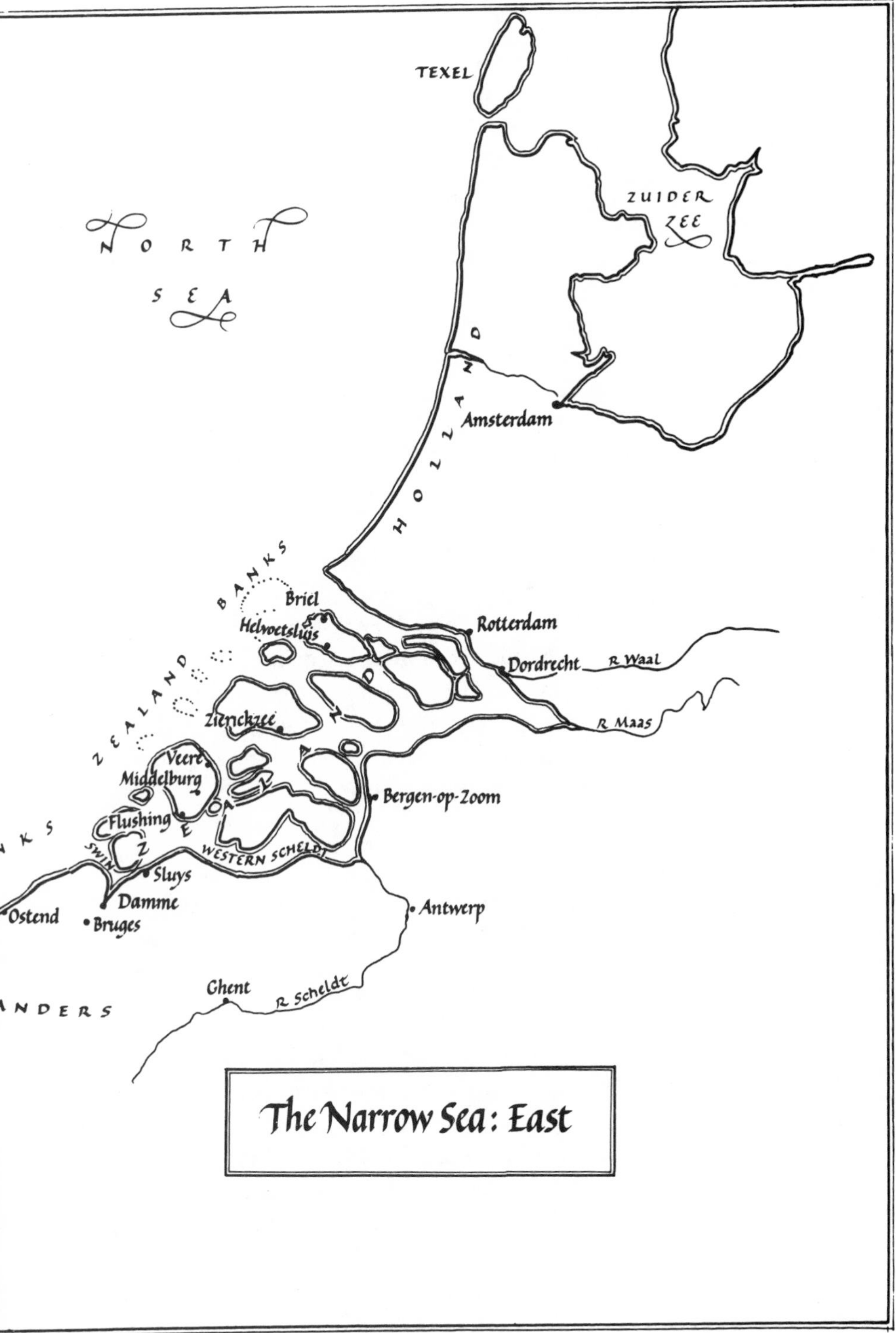

The Narrow Sea: East

Isle of Wight and the Suffolk coast, and adding to English fears of invasion. Though a fleet of requisitioned merchantmen finally gathered in the Downs in October, there was no effective English resistance to a squadron of galleys. Philip VI's ambitious plans for a fleet to carry assistance to Scotland were frustrated by lack of money rather than English opposition.[22]

In 1338 the French naval campaign was resumed. On 24 March the French galleys burnt Portsmouth and moved on to raid Jersey. Meanwhile no fewer than twenty Genoese galleys under Ayton Doria were on their passage north to reinforce the French campaign, later followed by a further seventeen Grimaldi galleys from Monaco. In the Bay of Biscay a Castilian galley squadron based on La Rochelle took two ships out of an English convoy off the Gironde on 23 August. In September the Genoese took Guernsey. They arrived in the Channel too late to stop Edward III crossing to Flanders, but his lines of communication were cut behind him and he himself remained in Flanders until February 1340. Five English ships, including the king's own biggest ships the *Cog Edward* and the *Christopher*, were taken in Arnemuiden harbour. Then on 5 October the Franco-Genoese galleys captured and burnt Southampton, by far the most important English seaport to have been attacked in living memory. By the end of the year many coastal areas were devastated, and England was in a state of panic.[23] No naval force existed which was capable of opposing a powerful force of galleys, and the coast defence system was useless against a fast-moving enemy.[24] In October 1338 the king warned that the enemy galleys would soon be back:

> Intending to proceed from port to port and place to place along the coast, wherever ships may be found, to sink, burn and destroy the shipping of the kingdom; and then to attack, occupy, plunder and burn the ports and other towns on the sea or its inlets, perpetrating every evil that man can work.[25]

He was right. In March 1339 Carlo Grimaldi sailed with his own 17 galleys, about 35 Norman barges and the prize *Christopher*, later joined by five more galleys. Aboard was a force of 8,000 men. This was by medieval standards a large army, joined to the mobility of a professional fleet. No king of England since the Conquest had deployed such a weapon, and Edward had no answer to it. Grimaldi's squadron failed to capture Jersey, reinforced Guernsey, then took a convoy round to La Rochelle before entering the Gironde and capturing Bourg and Blaye. At the same time Doria took the rival Genoese force into the North Sea, where they attacked Harwich but were driven off. In May they were in the Solent, whence they swept along the south coast and round into the Bristol

Channel. Hastings was completely destroyed, and ships sheltering at Plymouth were taken, though the town itself resisted assault. At this time Philip VI was seriously planning another Norman conquest, and there seemed to be very little to stand in his way. In northern waters Scottish barges attacked the shipping bringing supplies to isolated castles. In July Sir William Douglas and the French privateer Hugh Hautpol closed the Tay and starved the English garrisons of Cupar and Perth into surrender.[26]

Eventually the ponderous machinery of English naval organization began to get some ships to sea. In April Lord Morley, admiral of the northern fleet, sailed with a convoy of 63 ships for Flanders. On the Flanders coast they met an enemy convoy escorted by Genoese galleys and chased them into the port of Sluys, taking many prizes. As usual, however, the English were undisciplined and piratical, plundering neutral Flemings and Spaniards, causing immense damage to Edward's efforts to construct an anti-French coalition. Returning to the Orwell, Morley's ships fell out over their booty and part of the fleet deserted. Nevertheless it was Morley who achieved the first English naval success of the war. In July the Franco-Genoese squadrons attempted a raid on the Cinque Ports, but were driven off from Sandwich and caught off Rye by Morley's fleet, escaping with difficulty. By this time the men of Doria's squadron were discontented, for want of pay among other reasons. When their representatives sent to petition Philip VI were arrested, the squadron mutinied and sailed for home, taking two of Grimaldi's galleys with them. In September the rest of the Franco-Genoese galley force moved to Sluys, intending to raid the English herring fishery off Yarmouth, but when they put to sea on 2 October they were dispersed by an autumn gale. By the end of the year Grimaldi had returned to Monaco and the remaining Italian galleys were beached, which allowed Morley to raid the French coast in retaliation. It also had an unexpected result, for in September 1339 Doria's returning galleymen led a populist revolution in Genoa which ejected both the noble factions of the Guelfs and Ghibellines, and installed a popular government under the Doge Simon Boccanegra. This directly affected the war in the north by breaking France's existing diplomatic links with Genoa, and allowing Niccolò Usodimare, a Genoese officer in Edward III's service as Vice-Admiral of Gascony, to acquire the galleys which Philip VI had chartered for the new campaigning season. Meanwhile in January 1340 the Cinque Ports had information from a prize that eighteen galleys were lying at Boulogne with only shipkeepers aboard. Favoured by fog, they attacked and burnt them all, with twenty-four merchantmen and much of the lower town.[27]

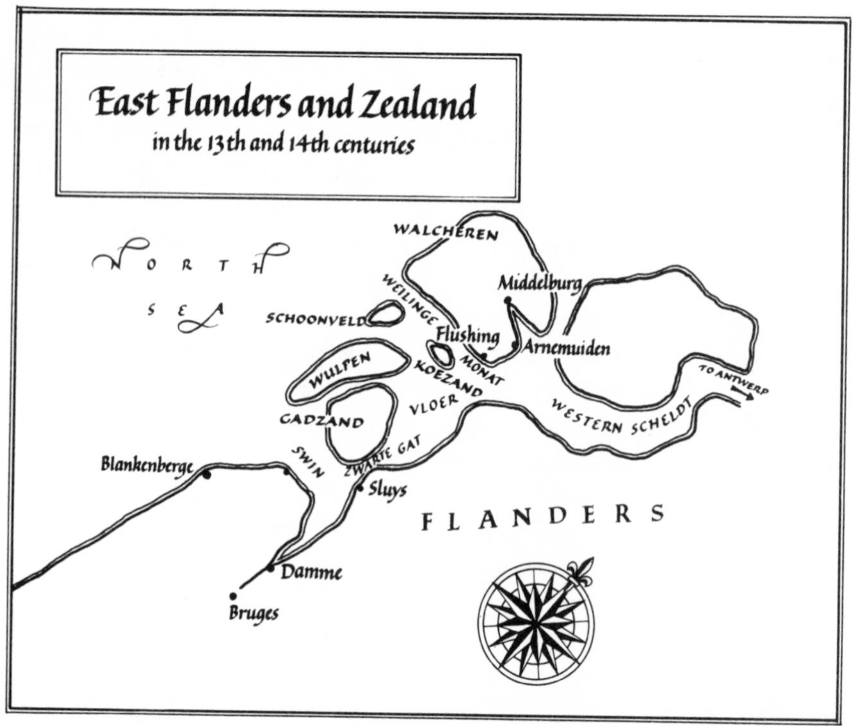

Philip VI was left with a total of only four French and two Genoese galleys in 1340, plus 22 barges – insufficient to prevent English raids on Dieppe in January, and Le Tréport in May. It was also too little to interfere directly with Edward III's return to England in February and his subsequent voyage to Flanders. The English king, an outstanding example of the conventional military and kingly virtues, had no more strategic imagination than any of his predecessors, and was just as wedded as his grandfather had been to an expensive and unwieldy continental coalition. The French were well informed of his plans, and on 26 May their fleet sailed to occupy the seaports of Flanders in support of Philip's invading army. Edward did not get away from the Orwell until 22 June, even then without his whole force. On the afternoon of the 23rd his ships made the Flanders coast and sighted the French fleet anchored in the Swyn off Sluys.[28]

Both sides spent the next twenty-four hours preparing for battle. As usual with medieval naval battles, the narratives are confused and contradictory, but a plausible reconstruction of the action can be attempted.[29] The main channel of the Swyn ran inland, roughly south-eastwards, from the North Sea coast to Sluys, and thence south-westward up to Damme, the port for Bruges. Sluys could also be reached from the western Scheldt, behind the island of Cadzand which the French had occupied.[30] The English did not attack at once from the seaward, but worked up the coast to gain the advantage of wind and tide on the 24th; since, as all accounts agree, the sun was behind them that morning, they must have approached Sluys from the Scheldt rather than the North Sea. The French admirals rejected the advice of the Genoese commander Pietro Barbavera to get to sea and attack the English under way. Instead they anchored their fleet, chained together in three lines, to make a solid and impenetrable formation.[31] This was a traditional galley or longship tactic,[32] serving to make the naval battlefield as much like a battlefield ashore as possible, but of course it removed any possibility of manoeuvre and resigned the initiative to the enemy. Several accounts, moreover, state that the French shifted their position, and weakened their cohesion, shortly before the English attacked; possibly it was not until dawn on the 24th that they realized that the English were attacking from the east, in the rear of a fleet facing north-west towards the open sea. The French had 202 ships, 6 galleys and 22 barges against 120 to 160 English ships, but by abandoning the possibility of manoeuvre they nullified their greater numbers and allowed themselves to be defeated in detail by a fleet which was much the stronger in archers and soldiers. Barbavera's galleys, which he had refused to moor, escaped with most of the barges. Virtually all the remainder were taken, and there were few if any prisoners. The French lost 190 ships and 16–18,000 men, including both their admirals.[33]

The crushing victory of Sluys, fought on the exact anniversary of Bannockburn, established the prestige of the young Edward III at home and abroad. In France it devastated the Norman ports and destroyed French hopes of mounting any sort of invasion. What it did not do, in spite of Edward's revival of the claim to 'sovereignty of the seas',[34] was to confer command of the sea on the English. No such command was possible against an enemy who still had access to the sea and the means to exploit it. Moreover Philip VI's means were much greater than Edward III's, and he was not wasting them on an expensive and fruitless continental coalition. Though Edward had won a great victory, he had not touched the main French army, and it soon proved that he was no nearer setting his allies in effective motion. Tactical errors and bad luck had cost the French dearly, but their appreciation of the uses of naval power remained more intelligent than Edward III's, and they still had the core of a professional naval force which he lacked.[35]

A month after Sluys the French had a squadron of three galleys, seven barges and some chartered Spanish merchantmen at sea, running supplies to Scotland and attacking English ships. On 26 July they took thirty ships out of a wool convoy. In August they landed on the Isle of Wight, raided Portland, burnt Teignmouth and unsuccessfully attacked Plymouth. The English southern fleet had to be mobilized to support the siege of Castle Cornet in Guernsey. In 1341 French, Castilian and Portuguese galleys cruised in the Bay of Biscay to interrupt communications with Gascony.[36]

By this time the continental war had been halted by a truce, but at the same time the French and British became embroiled on opposite sides in the Breton War of Succession (1341–62), so that over much of the next eleven years the Hundred Years War was in effect fought by proxy in Brittany.[37] Like Egypt in the nineteenth century, Brittany was for England a state which it was vital to influence, if not control, because of its position athwart the main imperial sea route.[38] The Bretons, combining a land frontier with France with extensive property in England (for the Dukes of Brittany were also Earls of Richmond), could play off the rivals against one another to ensure their independence. The dukes also derived a substantial part of their income from organizing convoys and levying what amounted to protection money from passing shipping.[39]

The English should have enjoyed a great advantage in a country remote from central France and easily accessible by sea, but in practice English fleets were so slow to gather, and so unreliable when they were set in motion, that the French almost always had moved first. Moreover they had not only the remaining galleys of their own and the Genoese, but also the unofficial support of Castile, which contributed another galley squadron, and the combined force had excellent bases available at La Rochelle and Guernsey. In the opening phase of the war in 1342 the French captured the English claimant John de Montfort, leaving his countess holding only a few castles. In spite of her desperate need, English help came extremely slowly. In April Sir Walter Mauny with a small squadron caught some French and Genoese galleys in the Quimperlé river with their men ashore raiding and burnt them all. From there he went on to relieve the countess's castle of Hennebont. In August a French squadron of three galleys and 29 ships of various sizes, commanded by Ayton Doria and the Castilian admiral Luis de la Cerda, fought an English force of 46 ships off Guernsey. By this time the countess was reduced to a single castle, Brest, where she was besieged by the French and blockaded by Genoese galleys. At the last moment the Earl of Northampton arrived with 1,350 men in 140 ships, escorted by the galleys of Bayonne. The Genoese galleys were surprised and eleven were caught and burnt. Northampton's force was small, but the French were obliged to evacuate western Brittany. Edward III and the Earl of Warwick were supposed to follow

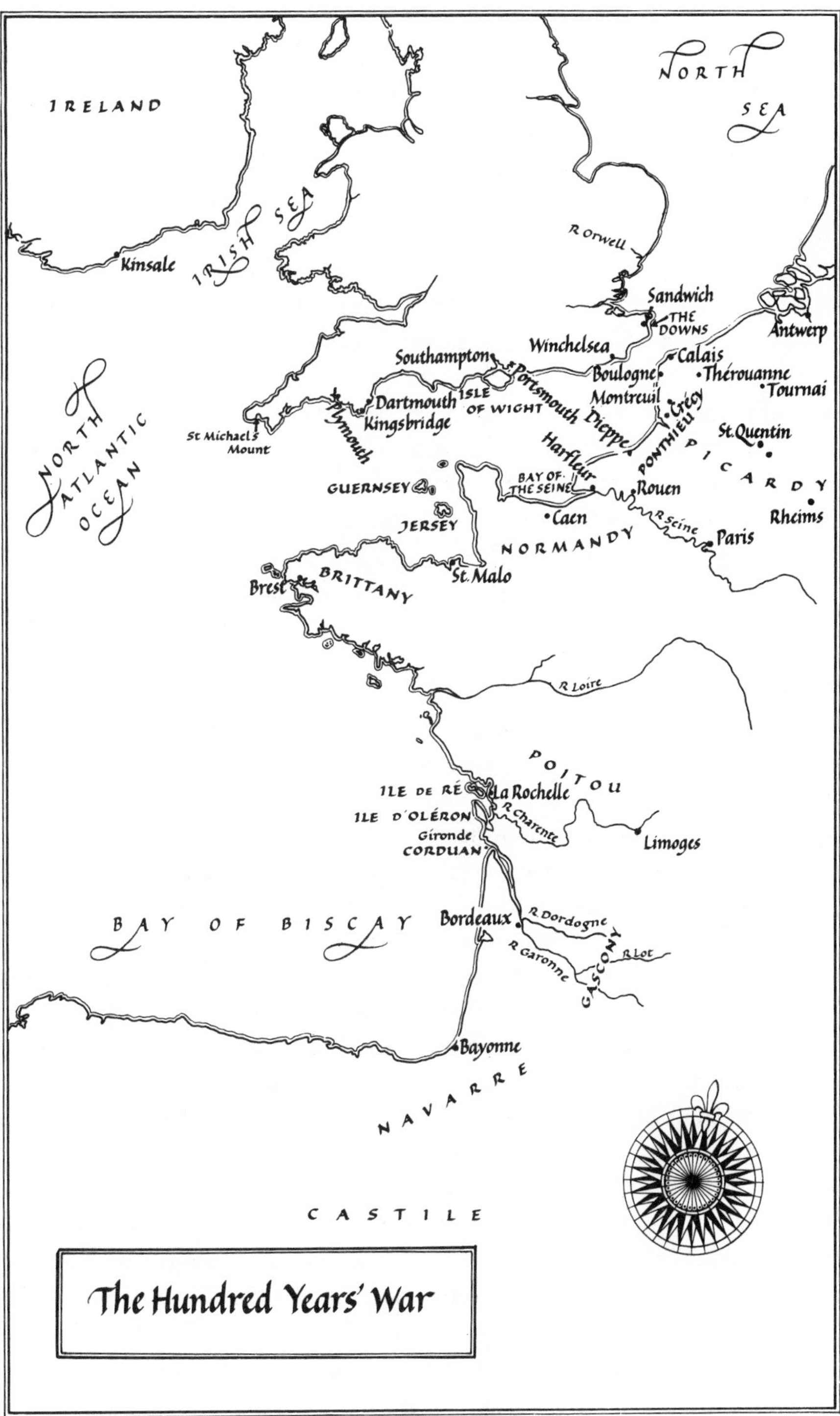
IRELAND
NORTH SEA
IRISH SEA
R Orwell
Kinsale
Sandwich
THE DOWNS
Antwerp
Winchelsea
Calais
Southampton
Boulogne
Thérouanne
Tournai
Portsmouth
ISLE OF WIGHT
Montreuil
Dartmouth
Kingsbridge
Dieppe
Crécy
Plymouth
St Michael's Mount
NORTH ATLANTIC OCEAN
Harfleur
PONTHIEU
St. Quentin
PICARDY
BAY OF THE SEINE
Rouen
GUERNSEY
Caen
Rheims
R Seine
Paris
JERSEY
NORMANDY
St. Malo
Brest
BRITTANY
R Loire
POITOU
ILE DE RÉ
La Rochelle
ILE D'OLÉRON
R Charente
Gironde
CORDUAN
Limoges
BAY OF BISCAY
Bordeaux
R Dordogne
R Garonne
GASCONY
R Lot
Bayonne
NAVARRE
CASTILE
The Hundred Years' War

in September with a much larger army, but so many ships deserted that much of the army had to be left behind. After three weeeks of gales, the king finally reached Brittany on 26 October, and early the next month began his march on Vannes. Much of his remaining fleet slipped away after the landing; the rest sailed along the south coast in parallel with the army. In the Bay of Bourgneuf they attacked the Castilian galley squadron and were beaten; soon after they failed to take Vannes by *coup de main*, where their commander Robert d'Artois was mortally wounded. By the time Edward arrived with the army, Vannes was thoroughly alert, and the king had to settle down to a winter siege. Most of his remaining ships deserted, few supplies or reinforcements arrived, and in the face of a superior French relieving army Edward was lucky to conclude a truce until September 1346. From this first phase of the Breton war the English gained the fortress of Brest, critically situated for their communications with Gascony and the south coast of Brittany. This fortress (in English hands 1342–62 and 1372–97) safeguarded English shipping to Gascony for over half a century.[40] Moreover in the summer of 1345 the Bayonne galleys retook Guernsey. For their part the French burnt Portsmouth in August 1342, shortly after Northampton had sailed, while in the north the Scots retook both Stirling and Roxburgh over the winter of 1341–2.[41]

The continental war resumed with the expiry of the Anglo-French truce in 1346. This time Edward III did not rely on a coalition in Flanders, but summoned the largest fleet ever known in England to carry a great army overseas. His original intention may have been to land in Brittany, had the Earl of Lancaster's small army there managed to take a port on the north coast, but by April or May he was planning to take his army to the far southern frontier of Gascony where a French army was besieging Aiguillon. He finally sailed from Portsmouth on 28 June, heading westward down the Solent, but he had got no further than Yarmouth when the fleet anchored to wait for stragglers, and by the time they had caught up the wind was foul. When the king changed his mind is uncertain; it may not have been until after he finally sailed on 11 July, with the wind still unfavourable for a voyage down Channel. Had he reached Gascony he could not have won a decisive victory in the Garonne valley, and he risked disaster by committing his army to a country dependent on imported food, for Carlo Grimaldi, acting for Philip VI, had assembled a fleet of not less than 32 galleys from Monaco, Nice and Genoa, all but two of them of 60 oars and 200 men or more. So formidable a force might very well have blockaded the Gironde and imprisoned Edward and his army, starving and far away from the centre of events, if the king had pursued his intended strategy.[42]

Instead the English landed without opposition on the beach to the south of St Vaast-la-Hougue on 12 July. Grimaldi's galleys were still south of La Rochelle, and the French armies were unprepared for a campaign in Normandy. By accident rather than design, Edward had achieved complete strategic surprise, and delivered his army into the heart of the French position, where they would find it extremely hard to avoid the risk of battle. Whether or not Edward fully realized it and really sought a decisive victory,[43] his troops had mastered the new tactics learned in the hard school of the Scottish wars, and were ready to deploy them against an old-fashioned army of heavy cavalry. First, he was able to achieve a major naval success. As the English army marched south to besiege and capture Caen, the fleet moved along the coast of Normandy systematically destroying the ports and shipping. More than a hundred ships were burnt, sixty-one of them 'warships' with castles fitted. These must have been the ships newly built to replace those lost at Sluys; without them there was no possibility of backing Grimaldi's galleys with a major landing force.[44]

Edward's subsequent march through Normandy and Picardy led to the battle of Crécy on 26 August, when the English archers and infantry inflicted a crushing defeat on the main French army. This opened the way for the English to besiege Calais over the winter of 1346–7. The place was surrounded by wide marshes and impossible to assault directly, so the siege turned essentially on naval blockade and logistics. The French were in no condition to attack the besieging army itself, but devoted their efforts to bringing in supplies by sea. Grimaldi's galleys took 25 ships out of the blockading fleet on 17 September while Edward watched from the dunes, but they were were paid off in November, and a fleet of 200 ships offered by Alfonso XI of Castile and his admiral Egidio Boccanegra (brother of the Doge of Genoa) did not arrive in time in 1347. Nevertheless by strenuous efforts over the winter the French assembled a force of 13 galleys and barges (including one last Genoese galley), 25 ships and 60 smaller vessels at Boulogne. In March and April they forced convoys through to Calais, but on 25 June the English fleet under the earls of Northampton and Pembroke raided Boulogne and Le Crotoy, destroying a convoy assembling there, and in July another attempt was intercepted and scattered. Calais surrendered on 4 August, and on 28 September France and England agreed a truce.[45]

With David II of Scots an English prisoner after the battle of Neville's Cross in 1346, Edward III had temporarily driven both his enemies out of the war. There was no peace at sea, however, for Castile was now an ally of France, and the ports of northern Spain were traditional enemies of the

Gascons. In 1349 a Castilian fleet was formed to attack English communications with Gascony, and the next year it sailed to Flanders with cargoes of Spanish wool, taking some English prizes on the way. The English determined to intercept it on its return. Interception was the most difficult of all medieval naval operations, but intelligence from Flanders was good, and the distances were very short. Edward III and his son the Black Prince lay with their ships at Winchelsea. On 29 August 1350 they sighted the enemy running down Channel. There were 47 Castilian ships under the command of Carlos de la Cerda, larger than the English ships and prepared for action, but apparently not well concentrated. According to Froissart's vivid (though probably romanticized) account, the king ordered Robert Passelow, the master of the *Cog Thomas*, to 'steer for that ship for I want to joust with her'. The result was a collision in which his ship was damaged and began to sink. Luckily the king's ship managed to grapple and board another Castilian before she sank. The same happened to the Prince of Wales's ship, which was rescued in a sinking condition by the Earl of Derby's – a near disaster which illustrates why medieval sea battles were fought in sheltered waters. The battle of Winchelsea (or 'Les Espagnols sur Mer') is presented by the chroniclers as a famous victory, but it is probable that there were other, perhaps many other sea battles as important, which the chroniclers ignored because no kings and princes were involved. Though the English took a number of prizes, it was in truth only a partial success, which left the Castilian fleet still formidable. The outbreak of the Castilian civil war, not English sea power, kept their ships from northern waters for twenty years.[46]

Nevertheless the 1350s was the most peaceful decade for English shipping in the fourteenth century. Major fleets were summoned in several years to carry armies to Calais, Gascony and Scotland, and shipping to Gascony was ordered to sail under convoy in 1353, but there appears to have been no serious fighting at sea.[47] It was not until 1360, just before the Treaty of Brétigny brought the Hundred Years War temporarily to a close, that the English were reminded again of the danger of French raids. On 15 March a force assembled to try to liberate King John II, a prisoner in England since the battle of Poitiers in 1356, captured and burnt Winchelsea. The raid caused a sensation. The English were especially alarmed that the raiders had spent 24 hours ashore before re-embarking unmolested, and that they had come with horses, prepared for a campaign.[48] In response the government went so far as to order all ships to be 'hauled out of the water far enough from the sea to make them safe'.[49]

This absurd instruction vividly evokes the sense of helpless panic which French raids aroused, even at the high point of English military fortunes. It highlights the extraordinary contrast between the English armies, everywhere triumphant on the Continent, and the abject failure of English naval defence. The reason was mainly that the English kings had no permanent squadron of professional warships comparable to the galleys of France, Castile, Genoa, Monaco or Portugal. Such a standing force was ready to take the initiative or respond to threats with a speed which no requisitioned fleet could possibly match. With the sea effectively open to all, the side which could mount its raid or expedition before the other had excellent possibilities of forestalling or disrupting the enemy's projects. For this reason even a small squadron of the king's own ships was of immense value, for they could be made available when he wanted them, long before the ponderous fleets of requisitioned merchantmen could be assembled.

The importance of striking the first blow was doubled by the difficulty of mounting an effective defence without timely information of the enemy. The importance of intelligence was well understood: all nations employed spies and sent out scouting vessels.[50] Calais and Flanders were centres of English espionage, and in 1387 the town clerk of Ghent was an English agent.[51] In England French and later Burgundian agents were active, particularly gathering information with which to plan raids,[52] and when important movements were planned embargoes on shipping or overseas correspondence might be ordered to prevent intelligence reaching the enemy.[53] But in spite of this effort the information usually arrived too late to be useful. Thus in 1326 Edward II reproved his admirals for negligent reconnaissance: 'he presumes that John [Sturmy] causes the transactions on the sea coasts in parts beyond sea to be spied upon too slackly'.[54] Usually intelligence was useful at a tactical level, if at all.[55] Edward III sailed for Flanders in 1340 having only just learned that a French fleet was there before him; he sent out boats to make a reconnaissance the day before they met, but neither side had long warning and the battle of Sluys was essentially an accident.[56] Often intelligence, even local and urgent, arrived too late. The French burnt Portsmouth in 1338 in spite of two months' warning.[57] The same year the *Christopher* and the *Cog Edward* were surprised in port by the French galleys in spite of warnings which came too late.[58]

The intelligence problem was one major reason why sea battles were uncommon. The chances of locating an enemy at sea were extremely small, and if one was encountered it was scarcely possible to bring the ships alongside one another to fight in a seaway. Normally all fighting took place inshore, if not in harbour, and it was possible for one or both sides to be aided and resupplied from the shore during the action.[59] It was sometimes possible to intercept an enemy on a coastal passage, when it was known well in advance where he must pass, or a squadron tied down by a siege might remain stationary for long enough for a counterattack to be developed; but at sea, as on land, battles often occurred, unplanned and undesired, because forces blundered into one another by accident.[60] The prudent medieval commander avoided battles because they were unacceptably chancy. The weaker side risked catastrophe; the stronger had surer means of bring his strength to bear.[61] A commander might be forced to fight to avoid certain disaster, or he might choose to fight to exploit secret advantages or tactical surprise, but it did not happen often. Even a crushing victory at sea was not usually decisive. A triumph like Sluys was worth many successful raids, but no amount of destruction would deny the enemy the use of the sea so long as he had access to it and some economic resources for shipbuilding. To a great extent this has always been true of naval warfare, but it was especially true in the Middle Ages when it was so difficult to control or intercept movement across the open sea.

The most characteristic form of naval activity, and the one which most often led to fighting, was the sailing of convoys. In its simplest form, a convoy was just a body of merchantmen sailing in company for mutual protection, electing one of their number as 'admiral' to take command – an arrangement which did not involve the crown, left no trace in the records, and is very probably as old as seaborne commerce itself.[62] Corporate bodies of merchants were often responsible: escorts for some convoys to Bordeaux, for example, were provided by the Bayonne Shipowners' Society.[63] The first 'convoys' known to have been organized by English kings date from Henry II and III's reigns, and consisted of a body of shipping assembled to accompany a ship or ships carrying money to the king's forces in Poitou or Gascony.[64] Victuallers and supply ships were convoyed in the thirteenth century, especially in the Irish Sea where Scottish ships were most active.[65] Trade protection became progressively more prominent as the war at sea turned against England during the fourteenth century, increasing the threat and in the process increasing the political influence of the merchant community. Convoys of the modern type, with escorts provided by the state to protect merchant ships, had long been known in the Mediterranean,[66] and were adopted in England early in the fourteenth century – chiefly, it seems, against Scottish attacks. The development was gradual rather than sudden, and when all merchantmen were armed and defensible, the distinction between 'convoy' and 'escort' had more to do with the crown becoming involved in the organization than with an actual change in practice. Almost as soon as English admirals were established at the beginning of the fourteenth century they started to receive orders to protect trade in terms which imply or directly state that they were to assemble convoys.[67] By 1339, when a parliamentary resolution deplored the losses suffered by ships 'running' from convoy,[68] convoys to Gascony had become routine,[69] and in dangerous years from the 1350s, convoy to and from Bordeaux and Flanders was made compulsory for all ships.[70] Even the short passage to Calais called for them.[71] In such a situation mutual defence was regarded as a duty, even a legal obligation. When the *Christopher* of Hull was taken by the Castilians in 1395 out of a Bordeaux convoy, the rest of which fled rather than support their commodore, the courts obliged the other ships to pay her owner compensation.[72]

Medieval naval activity often involved cruising, but the term has to be used with caution, for it is a relatively precise modern concept, and the language used by contemporaries did not usually attempt to specify how a squadron was to be employed once it had been assembled. Most patrolling, like most navigation of all sorts, was along the coast, seldom out of sight of land. Often it was in the nature of scouting; in the English case, usually to give warning of attack.[73] This seems to have been the main function of the English galleys of the fourteenth century, dispersed around the coasts in ones and twos.

The range of activities which might be undertaken by a medieval English ship on a war cruise may be illustrated by a single example. On 8 June 1337 the *Grace Dieu* of Lynn, John of Weasenham master and owner, sailed from her home port with a ship's company of 48 seamen, 40 archers and 39 men-at-arms, under orders to intercept Flemish ships reported to be loading supplies at Sluys for Scotland. The *Grace Dieu* proceeded northward up the coast, meeting no Flemings, until she reached the Tay, where she searched unsuccessfully for a Scots captain who had taken many English supply ships. She then returned to London and berthed at Tower Quay, where she took on stores and lay until the end of September waiting for Edward III's intended voyage to the Continent. When this was cancelled the *Grace Dieu* sailed in company with the king's ship *All Hallows Cog* and others to search for French ships reported in the Channel. The squadron sailed as far as St Matthews, then returned to Guernsey where they remained until Christmas. They then cruised for a while in search of English ships exporting wool illegally; evidently with success, for the *Grace Dieu* was next sent to Bordeaux laden with a considerable quantity of wool confiscated at sea, directed to the Seneschal of Bordeaux. (Since the wool would fetch a high price, this was an indirect method of sending him money.) She returned from Bordeaux in company with three ships belonging to the Earl of Salisbury, attacking and burning several French villages on passage, and bringing into Southampton a prize laden with 240 tuns of wine from Poitou. Thence they were ordered to the Orwell to await the Earl of Northampton's passage to Antwerp. Having landed him, the *Grace Dieu* and another ship cruised along the Flanders coast as far as Calais and then returned to Harwich, where she was paid off on 15 August 1338, after fourteen months' service.[74]

Weasenham's failure to intercept the Flemish ships sailing to Scotland shows the difficulty of such a mission in medieval conditions. The enemy could be expected to proceed along the coast, though the fact is usually assumed rather than expressed in sailing orders.[75] This should have made interception relatively easy, but it seems to have been most unusual for such an operation to succeed, if only because it took so long to receive and act on intelligence. Weasenham's orders were dated 10 March, and he sailed three months later;[76] a normal delay, with a natural result. The admiral concerned was rebuked for his negligence in allowing supplies to reach Scotland, but it is hard to see what more he could have done without a standing force available for quick reaction.[77] In 1315 Edward II declared that he had concentrated his ships against the Scots, 'to attack our said enemies and break up the invasion':[78] the invasion was presumably the Scots attack on Ireland, which might in principle have been 'broken up' by a sufficient and timely naval force, but in practice it was virtually impossible for English kings to concentrate ships in a remote, or indeed nearby, area without very long notice. For want of a professional fleet they were for ever three months behind the enemy.

EIGHT

Decline and Fall

Operations 1360–1410

The Treaty of Brétigny halted the Hundred Years War in France, but the French and English continued to fight by proxy elsewhere. The war in Brittany was finally ended in September 1364, when the English defeated and killed the French claimant Charles de Blois and captured the French general Bertrand du Guesclin. The following year, however, a new front was opened when the French intervened in the Castilian civil war, backing Henry of Trastámara against his brother Pedro the Cruel, with the object of gaining control of the Castilian fleet. In 1367 Edward III's eldest son the Black Prince invaded Castile on behalf of Pedro, defeated Henry and again captured du Guesclin (who had meanwhile been ransomed) at the battle of Nájera. But after his withdrawal fresh revolts broke out against Pedro the Cruel, who was finally defeated and killed in March 1369. Henry had already signed a secret treaty with France offering naval assistance. Initially he was fully occupied with the much stronger Portuguese fleet, but in 1371 he made peace with Portugal and was free to help the French. In that year Edward III's fourth son John of Gaunt, Duke of Lancaster, married Pedro the Cruel's daughter and assumed the title of King of Castile – but the Castilian galleys remained firmly in the hands of King Henry.[1] Meanwhile King Valdemar II of Denmark offered France an invasion force of 12,000 men (for 600,000 florins) in 1363, and in 1369 the offer was repeated. In 1366 his fleet actually raided East Anglia, and the next year Denmark concluded an alliance with Scotland which was plainly aimed against England.[2]

Thus the war began again with a dangerous accession of naval strength against England. The English response to these new and formidable naval threats was to impose compulsory archery practice and ban football;[3] an admirable measure, but no substitute for a navy. In September 1369, soon after the war restarted, French raiders burnt Portsmouth again. Two months later a squadron commanded by the exiled Welsh soldier of fortune Owain Llawgoch ap Thomas ap Rhodri ('Owen of the Red Hand'), great-nephew of Llewelyn ap Iorwerth, sailed from Harfleur to land in Wales, but was scattered by a storm. In 1370, as the English government struggled with reluctant shipowners to raise shipping for two major expeditions, the French raided Gosport, and Rainier Grimaldi with four galleys appeared in the Channel, taking a ship out of an English convoy.[4] Edward III responded with hysterical warnings that the French intended 'to destroy the realm of England and all the English tongue'.[5]

In the spring of 1372 a squadron of twelve Castilian galleys commanded by Fernán Ruiz Cabeza de Vaca and Ruiz Díaz de Rojas [6] entered the Bay of Biscay. At La Rochelle on 23 June they intercepted a small English force carrying the Earl of Pembroke to take command in Poitou (English once more since 1360). Though Pembroke was carrying £20,000 in gold his squadron was small and unprepared. It seems to have been at anchor in or off the harbour of La Rochelle, and the confused accounts of the action suggest that the tide played a critical part; possibly the English ships were aground at low water, with enough water to float the attacking galleys and allow them to pick their targets off one by one. Most of the English ships were burnt; Pembroke and the gold were taken. This disaster was redoubled when a second Castilian force under Díaz de Rojas combined with a French squadron under Owain ap Thomas (which had just raided Guernsey) to blockade La Rochelle.[7]

Edward III was forced to abandon his intended expedition, which was converted into a force to relieve La Rochelle. It sailed at the end of August, but could make no progress against headwinds, and was abandoned in early October, by which time it was known that La Rochelle had surrendered on 15 August.[8] A week later Owain's galleys moved up the Charente by night and in a surprise attack captured the Captal de Buch, the most celebrated of the Gascon generals.[9] The effect of these disasters in England was to stimulate naval activity. A barge building programme was set on foot, Genoese galleys were chartered, and in 1373 and 1374 the Earl of Salisbury commanded strong fleets cruising in the Channel, with no known effect beyond relieving the garrison of Brest and burning St Malo. In 1375 a truce was negotiated with France and Castile, though Lancaster on his way to Bruges to negotiate it captured Grimaldi. That summer the Castilian galleys under the new Admiral of Castile, Fernán Sánchez de Tovar, ignoring the truce, took 37 ships out of an English convoy loading salt in the Bay of Bourgneuf. The losses were valued at £18,000, possibly the heaviest single loss suffered by England at sea in the fourteenth century.[10]

By now Edward III was in his dotage, his country exhausted by ceaseless war and troubled by growing unrest. In France Charles V and his energetic Admiral Jean de Vienne (appointed in 1373), with the less well-known deputy Etienne du Moustier (Vice Admiral of France 1359–84) had developed the Clos de Gallées and its galley squadron to a new level of efficiency.[11] The Castilian galleys under Sánchez de Tovar still provided the professional core of the allied fleet, though for political reasons Vienne took overall command, and they were supplemented by Rainier Grimaldi's galleys. When the truce expired Vienne's squadron was ready. On 24 June 1377 (three days after Edward III died) the combined French, Castilian, Monegasque and Portuguese force sailed for a cruise during which they destroyed Rye, Rottingdean, Lewes, Folkestone, Portsmouth, Dartmouth and Plymouth. In August they returned to ransom the Isle of Wight and burn Poole and Hastings, though they were repulsed from the walled towns of Southampton, Dover and Winchelsea. In July barges from Boulogne attacked the Yarmouth herring fishery.[12]

Apart from desperate measures of coastal defence there was no English response until October, when Boulogne was raided by ships from Calais and the Earl of Buckingham sailed from London in an attempt to intercept a Castilian convoy reported to be at Sluys ready to sail for home. His fleet was dispersed by gales and mutiny, but a part of it under Sir Thomas Percy did take twenty-two Castilian prizes.[13] In January Buckingham relieved Brest, and in the summer a larger fleet under Lancaster sailed to take over Cherbourg, one of the Norman fortresses offered by England's ally Charles II of Navarre,[14] which he was unable to defend. While he was present, Lancaster was able to blockade the Seine, as well as attempting without success to attack St Malo and relieve the besieged Navarrese garrison of Pont Audemer.[15] The Castilian galleys made no attempt to attack his large fleet directly, but as soon as he went home they returned to dominate the Channel. The Earl of Arundel's squadron was defeated as it left Cherbourg, the port was blockaded, and a squadron under Sir Peter Courtenay which tried to escape was captured. In August the Castilian galleys raided Cornwall, burning coastal towns and levying tribute.[16]

The following year the Castilian galleys intervened in Brittany against the Anglo-Breton armies. They successfully prevented Sir Hugh Calverley landing troops at St Servan, but were caught at a disadvantage trying to support land operations at the mouth of the Loire.[17] In December a long-delayed expedition to Brittany sailing under Sir John Arundel was destroyed by storms, and Arundel himself was drowned when his ship was wrecked on the coast of Ireland.[18]

In 1380 Jean de Vienne captured Jersey and Guernsey, while the Castilians, with only one French galley in company, burnt Winchelsea and Gravesend and threatened London. In July Buckingham took an army to campaign in Brittany, but the direct crossing now seemed too dangerous, so he sailed to Calais and marched overland. In the same year English ships took some French and Castilian merchantmen in the port of Kinsale, but it was a small compensation.[19] Though English fleets, when once assembled for major operations, had more to fear from the weather than the enemy, it was clear to all observers that England had no answer to the mobility, readiness and professional skills of the Castilian squadron. Squadrons of balingers were ordered to be built in 1373 and 1378,[20] but they were never concentrated as a striking force, and could never have effectively deterred a skilful enemy. Nor could the king's own ships. From about forty ships early in Edward III's reign, the royal squadron had fallen to five when he died, of which the last were sold by 1380.[21]

In strictly military terms English operations in France continued to inflict damage out of all proportion to a few coastal raids, but those raids struck the seafaring and shipowning community, upon whose prosperity and co-operation English naval strength depended, and they struck it hard. Coastal areas were ravaged and deserted; flourishing seaports like Melcombe in Dorset were reduced to an obscurity from which they never recovered.[22] One of the few unqualified English naval successes of the decade was the action of the London merchant John Philpot, in a squadron equipped without permission at his own expense, in capturing the Scottish captain Andrew Mercer[23] – a pointed contrast to the repeated failures of the great men about the young king Richard II, notably his uncle John of Gaunt. The political damage caused to the government by its inability to defend the coasts, in a country accustomed to victory, unused to devastation at home and less and less willing to pay the high cost of the war, was very great. Immediate relief came not from any English efforts, naval or otherwise, but from the death in September 1380 of Charles V of France. His successor Charles VI also had to face opposition to the war, had less understanding of sea power, and consequently less appreciation of the Castilian alliance. From this date the efficiency of the French galleys began to decline. At the same time the Portuguese (with English help) attacked Castile and forced the withdrawal of the Castilian galleys to face a naval threat in home waters – though their victory over the larger Portuguese fleet at Saltes on 17 June 1381 negated most of the effects of English intervention and left the ships which had transported the Earl of Cambridge's army blockaded in Lisbon for six months.[24]

A series of truces combined with political turmoil in both France and England kept the war at a relatively low level in the early 1380s. During this period the French planned for a decisive stroke. The Franco-Scots alliance was renewed in 1383, and Jean de Vienne planned to lead a French expedition to Scotland. He would invade from the north, while the main French army under Olivier de Clisson, Constable of France, would land simultaneously in Kent. It was a formidable threat to a distracted and enfeebled enemy. An English squadron having been blown off the coast, Vienne sailed to Scotland without interruption, landing at Leith on 1 June, one month after the expiry of the last truce. The Franco-Scots force raided as far south as Morpeth, but meanwhile the French plan miscarried in the south. The men of Ghent rebelled against French occupation, and the invasion fleet was diverted to recapture the port of Damme from the rebels. An English force under the Bishop of Norwich was sent to support the Flemings, but Cabeza de Vaca with a squadron of Castilian galleys delayed his crossing until it was too late. Meanwhile Richard II took the main English army into Scotland, where he burnt Edinburgh but achieved nothing else; the Scots, to Vienne's disgust, avoided battle.[25]

The following year the French renewed their attempts on a much bigger scale. Hoping to profit from the absence of John of Gaunt with much of the English army in Portugal, the French assembled in Sluys an invasion force of 50–60,000 men and between 900 and 1,200 ships from all the Channel ports – from every port between Seville and Prussia, according to the chronicler Froissart. The elaborate preparations included the building of a prefabricated fortress twenty feet high and several miles long, transported in 72 ships, to defend the bridgehead. In England the threat inspired panic and political crisis, with ships and troops assembled and then dispersed, unpaid. Only internal disunity of purpose and continuing unrest in Flanders prevented the French force from sailing.[26]

In 1387 the indefatigable Vienne assembled yet another invasion fleet at Harfleur. He defeated an English squadron off Dieppe and captured its commander. Once again, however, the invasion plan went awry when Clisson its commander was imprisoned by his enemy the Duke of Brittany.[27] Meanwhile in March the Earl of Arundel intercepted a Flemish-Castilian convoy in the Straits of Dover (a rare instance of the timely exploitation of intelligence, gained by interrogating the crew of a captured French scout). In this action Arundel worked to windward to get the weather gage before pursuing the enemy over two days and chasing him into the Swyn. He took at least 70 prizes laden with 19,000 tuns of wine, which he distributed to the people, gaining great popularity.[28] Once more naval events directly affected politics, for the next year Arundel was one of the 'Lords Appellant' who took control of the government from Richard II.

In 1389 a general truce was agreed, and from mutual distraction and exhaustion the war at sea declined to a low level. Henry III of Castile (1390–1406) preferred the profits of peaceful trade in Flanders to French subsidies.[29] In England there was growing political turmoil. Failure to protect the kingdom from naval attack in the 1370s and 1380s contributed powerfully to the sense that Edward III in his dotage, and Richard II in his youth, were failing in that most basic of all the obligations of the medieval king, 'good government', of which the core was defence against enemies abroad, and the dispensing of equitable justice at home. Twenty years before, the Commons remarked pointedly in 1372, 'every nation acknowledged and named our lord king of the sea';[30] once again the empty claim to 'sovereignty of the sea' had come back to haunt the king. Disasters at sea, especially coastal raids by the enemy, were a public demonstration of failure, especially when combined with inequitable burdens laid on shipowners.[31] So naval failure, 'want of good government at sea',[32] contributed substantially to the public fury which led to the Peasants' Revolt in 1381, and the deposition and murder of Richard II in 1399.

The new king Henry IV was fully occupied with rebellion at home, war with Scotland, and above all with the Welsh revolt led by Owain Glyndŵr. Appreciating that the sea was the strategic key to Wales, and profiting from the international situation, Glyndŵr obtained naval help. In 1401 Scottish ships, possibly galleys from the Isles, patrolled the Menai Strait and helped the rebels take Conwy. In 1403 Breton ships assisted at the sieges of Glamorgan and Kidwelly, and blockaded Caernarfon and Beaumaris. A formal Franco-Welsh alliance was concluded in July 1404, and Glyndŵr supplied detailed infomation on the ports and geography of Wales. In the spring of 1404 Criccieth, Harlech and Llanbadarn, blockaded by French ships, all surrendered, though at the last moment Beaumaris was relieved by ships from Ireland. In August a French and Breton fleet of at least 120 ships from Brest arrived in Milford Haven.[33] (It is possible that an English raid that spring may have been intended to frustrate this expedition.) The Franco-Welsh army then took Carmarthen and advanced nearly to Worcester, while their fleet followed up the Bristol Channel, suffering losses while supporting the siege of Tenby when they were attacked by English ships under Lord Berkeley and the Poole pirate Harry Pay. The same force also intercepted French reinforcements in 1406, and the French had difficulty gathering enough ships to take off their army after its defeat that spring. Nevertheless the sea was open to enemy ships throughout Glyndŵr's rebellion, with the result that the English castles in Wales were a worse liability than ever. It took nearly ten years of campaigning to restore English rule to Wales, by mutual exhaustion rather than military victory. Glyndŵr was never captured, and died in his bed.[34]

During these years Henry IV pursued a cautious policy towards France, and the war at sea continued chiefly in the form of piracy, more or less officially tolerated on all sides. Many French pirates operated under the Scottish flag. A Castilian squadron patrolled the Channel to protect trade, though some of the galleys under Pero Niño indulged in unauthorized piracy and attacked West Country ports.[35] As the unofficial war grew in intensity there were more coastal raids. In 1403 a force of French and Bretons attacked Plymouth by night and burnt it. Dartmouth, Plymouth and Bristol retaliated, taking a total of eighty prizes off the coast of Brittany and burning St Matthews. Just before Christmas a French force landed in the Isle of Wight, but were driven off. In 1404 they returned, with no more success, and in April a Breton force attacked Dartmouth. There they made the fatal mistake of showing themselves in the offing for several days before landing, losing the advantage of surprise essential to a successful raid. The Dartmouth men were ready, and the Bretons were driven off with heavy losses, including their commander.[36]

It is always a mistake to look at medieval naval warfare with the modern distinction between warships and merchantmen too much in mind. Not only were the two hardly distinct in design, but 'peaceful trade' was almost a contradiction in terms. The sea was widely regarded as lying beyond laws, treaties and truces; even in peacetime foreign ships were always in danger, and in wartime the distinction between enemies and neutrals was difficult to observe on the rare occasions when English seamen tried. Medieval jurists agreed that there was such a thing as piracy, but in practice outright piracy and peaceable commerce were separated, not by any clear legal distinction, but by a very wide area of debatable ground and questionable practices. Even in peacetime, there was not much peace at sea. Unprovoked attacks were common, torture was often used to extract information, and prisoners were usually drowned unless they were worth a ransom. The crown's relationship with this violence was ambiguous. It was a normal part of seafaring life, inseparable from the other activities of the merchant fleet on which English kings had to draw for most of their naval resources, and it developed the hardy and warlike seamen so useful in wartime. On the other hand attacks on allies and powerful neutrals repeatedly disrupted English foreign policy. In England, public opinion generally regarded all foreigners as fair game, but kings could not afford to do so. In practice strong kings with effective fleets did not want or need piracy and suppressed it ruthlessly. Weak kings with few or no naval resources of their own were obliged to tolerate piracy because they could not eliminate it, and it was the only naval power available.[37]

Piracies were often committed by ships in royal service, and sometimes by the king's own ships, while they in turn were the victims of other English pirates.[38] In 1314 a Gascon merchant shipped wine to England in the ship owned by John Perbroun, a future admiral then in the king's service. They were robbed by the Cinque Ports fleet commanded by a recent admiral, Gervase Alard.[39] Edward III had to pay 8,000 marks in compensation for a Genoese ship taken by his father's favourite Sir Hugh Le Despencer.[40] His attempts to construct a coalition of Flemish allies in 1338–9 were not helped by his own ships plundering Flemings and Spaniards, causing huge diplomatic damage and obliging him to pay £23,000 in compensation.[41] In 1341 he had to pay a further £20,000 for a ship taken by East Anglian pirates – who were then pardoned in return for serving in the king's fleet.[42] It was common for pirates to be pardoned in return for serving the crown, so that what was supposed to be a universal obligation easily became a universal excuse.[43] In May 1386 Richard II had to borrow £900 against Aragonese claims arising from English piracy; two months later ten Genoese ships were taken by a fleet commanded by both the king's admirals, the Warden of the Cinque Ports and the Controller of the Royal Household.[44] The Duke of Burgundy confiscated English ships and goods to the value of £10,000 in Sluys in 1403 in response to the activities of Devon and Cornish pirates; they were not much involved in the wool trade to Flanders and could view the stroke with indifference, but Henry IV could not.[45]

Piracy was the mark of a weak government unable to defend its subjects or restrain their attacks. Under Henry IV, it was the policy of a king whose own subjects could not always cross from the Isle of Wight to Lymington without being captured.[46] He was not completely impotent, and to an extent controlled piracy as an instrument of foreign policy, applying pressure just short of open war, when he wanted to, and against the countries he chose.[47] The king still had some means of asserting and defending the national interests against lawless violence, and England was not altogether undefended – but after seventy years of fighting a war overseas with no proper navy, that was the best that could be claimed.

1. The Norman fleet crossing the Channel in 1066, from the Bayeux Tapestry. The ship on the right with the dragon heads and the lantern at the masthead is presumably Duke William's ship the *Mora*. The men are out of scale, but the height of the ships' gunwales against the horses' necks gives some idea of their size.

2. Disembarking horses in 1066, from the Bayeux Tapestry.

3. Disembarking horses in 1967: this is the *Imme Gram*, a copy of the tenth-century Ladby ship built by Danish Boy Scouts. Seagoing horse-transports would certainly have been bigger than this.

4. *Left* The seal of Ipswich, of 1200, is the first clear picture of a ship with a stern rudder. Note the early forms of the castles, perhaps temporary structures, certainly added after construction.

5. *Below* The early fourteenth-century seal of Winchelsea, showing a Viking style ship with light castles. The ship is about to sail: the trumpeters in the aftercastle announce her departure, the men at the windlass aft are weighing anchor, while the ship's boy swarms up the backstay to the yard.

6. Cogs in action, from an early fourteenth-century manuscript. The men are out of scale but the details are otherwise fairly accurate. The aftercastle is now integrated into the structure of the ship.

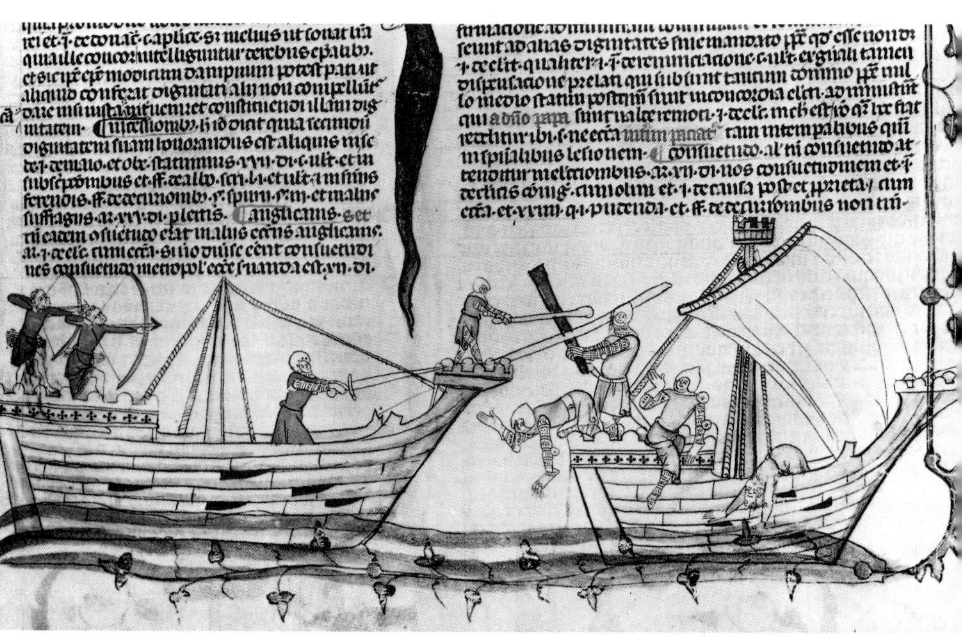

7. A modern replica of the Bremen cog of about 1360, under (rather modest) sail. Compare the men on the aftercastle with those in the fourteenth-century cogs for a true sense of scale. She has no forecastle or topcastle fitted.

8. *Left* Seal of the Duke of Exeter as Lord Admiral of England, 1412-1426.

9. *Below* Seal of the Earl of Huntingdon as deputy to the Duke of Bedford, Lord Admiral 1427-1435. Both seals show big clinker-built ships of the last single-masted generation. Note their sails bearing the king's arms.

10. The fourteenth-century lighthouse of St. Catherine's, Isle of Wight.

11. A carved pew-end of about 1415 from St.Nicholas's church, Kings Lynn, showing an early two-master. This was the rig of several of Henry V's big ships. The thickness of the mainmast is not exaggerated.

12. Early fifteenth-century two-masted Mediterranean carracks, from a retable from St.Ursula's church, Reixach, near Barcelona. Note the boys going aloft up the backstays and crawling out along the yards.

13. *Right* A three-masted Flemish carrack, probably drawn by the engraver William à Crucis in 1468. Note the loading port, and the small guns mounted beneath the aftercastle.

14 and 15. Two views of a four-masted ship from the 'Warwick Roll,' illustrating the life of Richard Beauchamp, Earl of Warwick (died 1439) with ships drawn from the artist's own day. The dating of the manuscript is not certain, but it was probably illustrated in the 1490s, and shows either the *Regent* or *Sovereign.*

Here shewes howe kyng henry the vj.te made Erle Richard his
lieutenant of ffraunce and Normandye
25
225

16. The Portuguese carrack *Santa Caterina do Monte Sinai* painted by an unknown artist off Villefranche in 1521; the same ship is shown four times from different angles. Portuguese carracks of this type were the targets of English attacks in the 1590s. On the right are Mediterranean galleys under oars and sail.

17. An engraving (clearer than the original, which is now very dark) of the painting known as *The Embarkation of Henry VIII for the Field of the Cloth of Gold, 1520*, done by an unknown artist about 1545. Allowing for somewhat exaggerated proportions, it gives a good impression of Henry VIII's bigger ships - none of which were in fact present on the occasion, as they drew too much water to get into Dover Harbour. Note how their sterns are turned towards the viewer, showing off their biggest guns at the sternports.

NINE

The Chief Support of the Kingdom

Administration 1216–1420

The concept of a navy as a permanent fighting service did not exist in the northern world in the Middle Ages. In the Mediterranean a clear distinction was understood between galleys, predominantly used for war and in Venice maintained on a permanent footing, and the 'round' ships which carried most trade. In the British Isles both the concept and the organization of a fighting sea service were much less distinct. No words any longer existed in any of the local languages which clearly distinguished warships from merchantmen, or described an established fighting service. In this sense there was no English or Scots navy during the Middle Ages. The French word 'navy' was in common use, but it referred to a body of shipping at large. Depending on the context, it might mean the whole merchant fleet of the country, or all the ships participating in a single trade, or those forming a particular convoy or squadron. The 'navy of the next vintage'[1] meant the shipping sailing to Bordeaux for the next year's wine, and when the House of Commons in 1415 invoked 'the Navy . . . the chief support of the well-being, earnings and prosperity of your kingdom',[2] they were referring to the merchant fleet, though Henry V, almost alone among medieval English kings, actually had something like a Royal Navy in the modern sense.

Even when people referred to 'the king's ships', they did not necessarily mean that the ships belonged to the crown or were in any sense in regular royal service. Ships might be called 'king's ships' which actually belonged to the king, or in which he held shares, but they were equally or more likely to be privately-owned ships chartered for royal service or arrested to serve without payment.[3] For a time in the fourteenth century the suffix 'of Westminster', later 'of the Tower',[4] was attached to the king's ships, almost in the manner of the modern 'H.M.S.', but 'ship of the Tower' soon came to be used as one of several phrases for a 'warship' (in the sense of a merchant ship fitted for war),[5] and ceased to distinguish the king's own ships with any precision. Even when ships were built at the king's command, it is often unclear who was considered to own them. Sometimes the Exchequer actually paid for them directly, or indirectly allowed the cost to be offset against the tax revenue owed by the towns which had built the ships, or compensated them in some other way (Winchester's charter of privileges was renewed without charge in 1378 'because they made a balinger').[6] At other times towns were ordered to build ships at their own expense, in which case they might be considered as owning them or promised that they would revert to private ownership after a period of royal service.[7] The king's own ships, differing little from ordinary merchantmen in design, were available to carry cargo if not needed for war. Often they went to Bordeaux to fetch wine for the royal household, and they sometimes exported wool to Flanders on the royal account.[8] For all these reasons it is difficult, and to some extent futile, to distinguish between 'merchant ships' and 'king's ships' in the Middle Ages.

It is a mistake, moreover, to concentrate too much on the king's own ships, for the vast majority of the ships on English royal service in the Middle Ages did not belong to the crown, but were merchant ships taken up for compulsory service at the king's order. In the summer of 1338, for example, out of 361 ships in royal service, only 14 belonged to the king.[9] This was not an exceptionally large fleet. The Poitou expedition of 1230 sailed in a fleet of 288 ships.[10] The 1297 expedition required 305 ships with more than 6,000 seamen to carry a force of about 9,000 men the short distance to Flanders.[11] In 1342 at least 440 ships were needed, some for several voyages, to carry troops to Brittany.[12] At least 750 ships were employed to carry Edward III to Normandy in 1346 – and the king had planned for a fleet and army twice the size.[13] The following year another fleet just as large was needed to support the siege of Calais.[14]

Law and custom sanctioned a general duty laid on all subjects to serve the king in time of war, and no distinction was made between the knight who served with his horse and his sword, and the merchant who served with his ship. In practice the shipowner was in a uniquely unfavourable position. The knight was obliged to serve in return for the land he held, under the feudal system, and his income from that land did not cease when he went to war. When paid military service replaced feudalism in the thirteenth century, the knight received a wage proportionate, in principle, to his rank and the expense of his equipment. His horse, which was his most expensive possession, was carefully valued, and full compensation paid if the animal died on service. Throughout this period the shipowner, by contrast, sacrificed his livelihood for as long as his ship was in royal service, and very seldom received any compensation if she were lost or damaged. His obligation was not even limited to war service, for ships could be arrested for non-warlike purposes as well.[15] The underlying attitude seems to have been that the merchant, being a wealthy man, could and should make greater sacrifices than others.

Certainly shipowners were in a sense wealthy, for a seagoing ship was probably the most expensive single piece of capital investment in the medieval money economy. It was an extremely risky investment, however, for the perils of the sea were numerous, and marine insurance still unknown in the northern world (though developing in the Mediterranean in the later Middle Ages). Those who had the capital and chose to risk it at sea could hope for very high returns on a successful voyage. Figures are hard to find, but it has been calculated that in the mid-thirteenth century Genoese shipowners were earning a return on capital of at least 150 per cent per annum, and a contemporary Venetian merchant 110 per cent.[16] About 1300 the freight of wine from Bordeaux to Southampton was about 10s a tun and in the 1320s it had fallen to 6s or 8s, but in the calamitous 1380s it rose above 20s, and was as high again at several periods in the next century.[17] It is difficult to assess building costs, but they can hardly have been higher than £1 a ton,[18] on which basis Southampton ships in the dangerous years of the late fourteenth century could pay back their initial cost in two or three voyages[19] to Gascony, that is, in a year or less[20] – if they survived, and if the king left them free to carry freight.

The system in the thirteenth and fourteenth centuries was for a royal order to be issued for all merchant ships to be embargoed (forbidden to sail until further notice), ordered to return from abroad, arrested for unspecified service, or arrested with orders to be at a named port by a particular day.[21] Very often the order was directed to particular sectors of the coastline, especially if more than one fleet was to be assembled at once, and usually it specified that only ships (not necessarily English ships alone[22]) over a given size were to be taken up. In the twelfth century this size was often specified in terms of capacity to carry horses; eight, in one of the earliest orders, of 1206,[23] though fifteen to twenty horses was the usual figure by the 1240s.[24] About this time the requirement began to be expressed in tonnage, and an order of 1254 implies that sixteen horses about equalled 70 tons.[25] In the fourteenth century the orders often referred to 'warships',[26] which seems to have meant merchantmen particularly suited to warfare from their size or design, possibly because they had permanent castles fitted. Thus in 1335 Simon of Geltoft was ordered to take up 'six warships among the largest and strongest' to be found between Liverpool and Skinburnness on the Solway Firth.[27] Five years later another order called for ships of not less than one hundred tons.[28] In the fifteenth century orders often specified ships within a certain tonnage range, excluding the largest as well as the smallest,[29] perhaps because the biggest ships were limited to too few ports to be useful for transport purposes.

When time and foresight admitted, a survey of the available shipping might be organized. As early as 1214 Bristol was asked for a list of all ships of at least eighty tons belonging to the port.[30] In the spring of 1297 orders were issued for every county and seaport to send up lists of all their ships over forty tons, with their owners' and masters' names.[31] There were other surveys in 1315,[32] 1352–3,[33] and as part of the unusually strenuous efforts of 1370, when ships as small as twelve tons were taken up.[34] Some of these lists have survived, but it is not always possible to tell if they represent all the ships belonging to each place, or all that were in port at the date of the return. Occasionally such surveys even recorded the number of seamen available.[35] Invariably the ships were ordinary merchantmen, and not much is normally recorded about them except their size. The traditional 'Viking' type was certainly common, with hulks mentioned, and cogs were increasingly common in the fourteenth century.[36]

The actual work of arresting shipping was supervised by royal officials travelling from port to port along an assigned stretch of coast, choosing ships that satisfied the required conditions, seeing them properly fitted, manned and armed, and sailing them to their muster ports.[37] They had to see castles built on those ships not already fitted with them, and supply the ubiquitous brows and hurdles, for embarking horses and making stalls to secure them at sea.[38] Brows seem to have been used not only when ships lay at quays, but also when they lay at anchor and the horses were brought alongside in lighters.[39] In some cases we can infer from the dimensions of the brows that wheeled transport was being embarked as well.[40] In this work they would demand the co-operation of the local authorities. The officials were either royal clerks, usually from the Exchequer, or other royal officers like sergeants-at-arms, and they might be accompanied by nautical experts to help with surveying and assessing shipping.[41] In the fourteenth century the admirals' clerks and deputies were often responsible.[42] It was possible for ships to be arrested at sea. In 1345, for example, the *Trinity* of Southampton, Thomas Warner master and owner, was boarded by the royal clerk John of Wettenhall as she came up the Solent, inward bound from Bordeaux with a cargo of 94 tuns of wine. She was brought into Southampton where her cargo was discharged and handed over to the shippers' agents. She was then loaded with men-at-arms, archers and horses, and sailed as part of the Earl of Northampton's expedition to Brittany.[43]

On this occasion the business seems to have gone smoothly, but the practical difficulties of this work in medieval conditions were great and, even if all worked with good will, innumerable delays could and frequently would prevent all the ships reaching their assigned ports by the due date. The dates were often unrealistically close when they were first named, and frequently had to be put back.[44] The expedition which eventually carried Edward III to Normandy before the battle of Crécy began when an order was issued on 28 August 1345 for all ships of thirty tons or more to be at Portsmouth by the Octave of Michaelmas – less than six weeks away. By the end of October the assembly date had drifted to mid-February 1346, subsequently amended to mid-Lent (19 March), and then to Palm Sunday.[45] The fleet finally sailed more than three months after that, on 11 July – nearly eleven months after the first orders went out. Even when they reached their assembly port it was not unusual for ships to wait for three to six months before they sailed,[46] during which period the owners were expected to feed and pay their crews. Sometimes their supplies were exhausted before they sailed.[47] In 1404 Nicholas Bygge, master of the barge *Trinity* of Brixham, petitioned the crown explaining that he and his sixteen men had been under arrest for seven weeks without pay; he had pawned all her gear to pay them, and would very soon be ruined. A generous sovereign allowed him to visit his home port in search of supplies, but no money was offered.[48] Very rarely was anything like demurrage paid, and usually only to Gascons, who were treated better than Englishmen, or to foreigners.[49] When operations began, the crown took the men into pay, but it still paid nothing for the ships.[50] Whatever obligation it did assume was generally paid long in arrears,[51] and not always in full. The only mitigation of this burden was that in many cases the local authority agreed to find the ship, and paid the owner and crew[52] – but this only transferred the load from one individual shipowner to the town as a whole, which was of limited use if many or all the ships of the port were taken into service at once. On condition that all the inhabitants contributed to support their ships, the seaports were exempted from some special taxes imposed to pay for the war in 1295 and 1300.[53]

If ships were lost on the king's service the owners could not normally expect any compensation. The *Dieu Garde* of Bristol was taken up for the 1344 Brittany expedition and lost with her cargo; her owners were then fined £60 for deserting from the king's fleet. On learning the facts Edward III remitted the fine, but there was no suggestion of paying for ship or cargo.[54] Only occasionally were lucky and patient sufferers rewarded by some allowance, usually not at the king's expense. In 1296 and 1297 some confiscated ships were given away to shipowners who had lost ships in the king's service,[55] and the owner of a vessel scuttled as a blockship during the siege of Calais in 1347 was granted a confiscated pirate ship.[56] In the winter of 1295 to 1296 eleven Dunwich ships served on the expedition to Gascony, including thirteen weeks without wages, and four of them were lost. The men of Dunwich petitioned for recompense, and Edward I ordered an enquiry into their claims. Twenty-three years later the report was produced, valuing the lost ships at £200, and the unpaid wages at £1220 10s. Seven years later still, in 1327, the new government of the boy-king Edward III (actually controlled by his mother Queen Isabella), ordered the sum to be allowed against the town's tax obligations.[57] Almost certainly the men of Dunwich owed their good fortune to the queen's urgent need to buy support.[58] Apparently only one other shipowner in the fourteenth century received compensation for a ship lost in royal service; Robert de Paris of London, in consideration of his exceptional services, was given a prize cog in 1387 to replace his fine new barge.[59]

Very occasionally a fortunate shipmaster received some compensation for damage sustained in the king's service. A Southampton cog was paid for a lost anchor in 1242,[60] in 1340 Edward III paid £5 for the damaged mast of the *Nichola* of Hull,[61] in 1352 a shipowner was allowed to import some wine duty-free to recoup his losses,[62] and in 1352 some merchants who had had ground tackle stolen were permitted to export wheat duty-free.[63] Once, good service at sea was rewarded by the remission of debts due to the crown.[64]

The burdens of naval service were heavy enough in the thirteenth century, and as warfare in both France and Scotland intensified in the fourteenth, both Edward II and III tried to reduce the cost of the war at sea by transferring naval costs from the Exchequer to shipowners, or anyone else who could be found. Attempts were made to classify smaller and smaller places, further and further from the sea, as 'ports' liable for naval service.[65] From the 1290s ships were sometimes arrested to serve for three or four months at their owners' expense before reverting to the king's wages.[66] In 1326 Edward II ordered the wages of long-delayed ships paid, not by himself, but by those citizens of the seaports who were not otherwise contributing to the fleet.[67] In 1337 Edward III demanded entirely unpaid service, with no suggestion that the crown would pay any wages at all.[68] Seven great ships of Hull served for thirteen weeks without pay in the southern fleet, and had no sooner been released than they were arrested for the northern fleet, 'to the great impoverishment of the town'. In this case the crown was obliged to pardon £118 13s 4d in taxes owed by the town.[69] In the next year coastal towns were taxed to pay for the fleet.[70] In 1339 London was persuaded to send a force of 440 men to sea at their own expense.[71] In 1340, having asked parliamentary advice, the king induced western ports to find seventy ships of a hundred tons as far as possible at their own expense.[72]

This was possible at a time of high patriotic sentiment, with a popular young king and a successful war. But long before the high point of English military fortunes in 1360, the naval effort was meeting increasing resistance. Faced with heavy loss if not actual ruin in the king's service, many shipowners and local authorities did not co-operate in the process of assembling a fleet. At first they would plead excuses, well or ill founded: all their ships were too old, perhaps, or too small, or in royal service already, or away on voyages.[73] This last was not always a coincidence: in 1281, for example, Thomas of Gargrave was sent to a group of south coast ports with orders to arrest every ship of forty tons or more. At Shoreham he found nine out of the ten of that size belonging to the port; by the time he had worked his way along the coast to Southampton there were only two in port and thirty away.[74] Evidently the shipowners of Southampton had heard he was coming. By this date evasion of royal service was already common;[75] in the fourteenth century resistance became more open,[76] and officials sent to arrest ships were liable to be assaulted.[77] When Robert of Burghersh arrived in Winchelsea sometime late in Edward I's reign, he was met by 'a great outcry of the townspeople who say that they suffer such hardships that they can do the king no service'; they complained of the king's unpaid debts, of tallies (assignments on tax revenue) which 'broke without yielding writ or allowance or anything else of value . . . they are extremely upset'.[78] So were the many other towns whose ships failed to answer the summons to serve in the Scots war.[79] In 1335 a ship was fitting out for war service at Blakeney when persons unknown attacked the king's men and sawed through her timbers to make her unseaworthy.[80] Ships arrested in Welsh ports in 1336 refused to sail without advance wages, which had to be paid, though 'such wages were not paid to those about to set out for the defence of the realm in the time of the king or his progenitors, and all are compelled as a duty to the defence of the realm against foreign invasion'.[81] Later that year John of Norwich commanding the northern fleet was given £100 to distribute among his men, doubtless to forestall similar trouble.[82] In the same admiralty in 1338 Hartlepool denied having any ships over thirty tons ('but I proved that answer false'), the bailiff of Ravenser refused to co-operate, at Hull eight ships were arrested but escaped at once, at Whitby another eight were immobilized by mutiny.[83] In 1342 there was a successful mutiny among ships assembled at Southampton to carry Sir Walter Mauny's expedition to Brittany, refusing to load until they were paid.[84] Later that year the king found himself and his army stranded in Brittany and in great danger because no fewer than 278 ships of the fleet had sailed home without permission;[85] when shipmasters would not obey the king in person, it is not surprising that admirals found it difficult to secure obedience.[86]

A steadily increasing burden laid on merchant shipping led naturally to a declining merchant fleet.[87] Yarmouth, for instance, probably had about 65 ships of a hundred tons or more in the wine trade alone in the early years of the fourteenth century. In forty individual years of that century the crown demanded ships from the port; an average of thirty or more a year between 1335 and 1340.[88] Between 1340 and 1346 forty Yarmouth ships were lost at sea and five taken by the enemy; by 1348 they claimed to have only 24 large ships left.[89] The town was declining for other reasons and is probably not typical, but it seems very probable that most ports had suffered from the war. About 1400 it was claimed that in fifteen years the number of 'warships' (meaning defensible merchantmen) in England had fallen from 150 to 25,[90] and it is notable that a substantial part of Henry V's 1416 invasion fleet was made up of Dutch and Flemish ships.[91]

By the late fourteenth century neither the authority of the crown nor the resources of the shipowners could sustain the old system any longer. The only effective answer to its difficulties was a great deal of money, sufficient to support a proper navy, or at least to pay the shipowners and their men enough to keep up an adequate merchant fleet. This was Parliament's opportunity. Because naval warfare was both a highly technical and a highly expensive business, calling for expertise and money which few English kings could deploy, they were obliged to turn to the commons, increasingly to the House of Commons, for assistance.[92] In the thirteenth century the crown was already summoning representatives of the seaports (particularly at this period the Cinque Ports and Bayonne[93]) to advise the royal council on naval affairs. The full council was hardly distinguished from Parliament, and the assemblies of merchants or seaport deputies fed into the growth of the House of Commons, and particularly to its urban, mercantile part.[94] Quasi-parliamentary assemblies of seaport representatives were summoned to advise on naval affairs in 1326,[95] 1337,[96] 1341,[97] 1342,[98] 1344,[99] 1347,[100] 1369,[101] 1373,[102] and 1374.[103] Long the natural source of expertise and advice on maritime affairs, the

Commons began to take the lead in articulating maritime grievances,[104] particularly the decline of the merchant fleet, which they attributed to long delays under arrest.[105]

From complaint it was a short step to action. The customs duties known as 'tunnage and poundage' were first levied in 1347 to support a fleet of 120 ships for the siege of Calais. From their original level of 1s a tun on imported wines, 2s on a sack of wool, and 6d a pound on other goods imported or exported, they were increased to 3s a tun and 1s a pound in 1425.[106] The Commons not only voted the money, but specified how many ships, with how many men, it was to pay for, and insisted that the monies were paid directly to the admiral responsible to ensure that none of it was diverted to other objects.[107] But in spite of all these precautions it never provided sufficient ships for long enough to make a real difference.[108] As the authority of government weakened so did its powers of coercion, and it was obliged to make concessions to shipowners. As early as 1340 a few towns like Dartmouth were receiving valuable privileges in return for quite moderate offers of service.[109] By 1370 the crown itself was paying ships' crews at least some advance wages from the date of sailing from their home port.[110] In 1375 the Commons asked that ships be paid from the day of arrest, and for an allowance to the owners for wear and tear.[111] In 1380 they were granted for an experimental period of a year an allowance of 3s 4d a ton for every three months from arrival at the assembly port. In 1385 they demanded the restoration of this grant, but were allowed only 2s a ton,[112] and when they asked again the following year they appear to have received nothing.[113] This payment was an allowance for wear and tear, not a payment for charter; if 20s a ton was the freight rate for a voyage from Bordeaux to England in the 1380s, a round trip of three months or so at most,[114] then 2s a quarter was about one-tenth of what the ship could theoretically earn (though in practice few ships traded all the year round). Not until the 1480s was it normal for the crown to pay commercial freights (in this case a shilling a ton a month)[115] for merchant ships taken up for an expedition.[116]

One further source of English medieval sea power remains to be discussed; the Cinque Ports. They are usually given a place of honour in medieval history, as the main component of English naval power, but it is not at all clear that they ever deserved it. In principle their charters obliged them to provide 57 ships, each with a crew of 21 men, for a fortnight each. There is no evidence that they ever did so, and no period in their history (except possibly the 1050s) in which we know of a real naval requirement for a large number of small ships serving for very short periods. In practice the Cinque

Ports' due service was always commuted for a smaller number of larger ships, and by the fourteenth century it was unusual for them to serve unpaid even for a fortnight. Their period of greatest importance was the thirteenth century, when they contributed the majority of the ships involved in the two Welsh wars, and were often drawn on by the crown for advice, expertise and manpower, occasionally acting almost as a primitive naval staff. Even then, however, they were for administrative purposes hardly distinguished from other ports, and by the fourteenth century there was very little from the naval point of view to mark them out them from other ports of similar size.[117]

Bayonne, the enemy and sometimes target of the Cinque Ports, was the port whose naval contributions, professional skills and unwavering loyalty really justified the privileges it received.[118] Next in value to the crown was perhaps Yarmouth, against which the Ports waged a private war for a century.[119] They also shared with the Franco-Genoese forces the distinction of having burnt Portsmouth[120] and attacked Southampton, where they destroyed seventeen ships in 1321.[121] It can be argued that the Cinque Ports' significance, and their privileges, derived less from their naval value than from their strategic position facing across the Narrow Seas to Flanders, making their loyalty valuable to any government facing a foreign threat. Their repeated disloyalty, their willingness to be be bought by enemies at home and abroad, was demonstrated particularly during the baronial revolts against King John and Henry III; it was worth successive sovereigns trying to buy their support, but it was not primarily naval service that they were buying.[122]

England went to war in the 1330s with a national income of £18,000 to £33,000 a year, or at best a third of that of France (400–600,000 *livres*).[123] In addition the kings of England received about £13,000 net from Gascon revenues.[124] In 1339 Edward III had to borrow £20,000 to charter ships.[125] Between 1368 and 1381 naval warfare absorbed about 23 per cent of total spending on the war, or £246,050.[126] This was the cost of a third-class system which provided few or no specialized warships, only fleets of reluctant merchantmen levied with endless difficulty and delay. The expense of real men-of-war with professional officers and men was vastly higher. Benedetto Zaccaria, Admiral of Castile, proposed to Philip the Fair in 1297 a scheme for naval war against England. He required a fleet of four galleys, 20 transports and 24 other ships, manned by 400 knights, 400 foot-soldiers and 4,800 seamen, costing 63,800 *livres* (about £12,600)[127] for four months. With this force he offered to raid the English coast, and if possible seize a seaport as a base.[128] In 1404 another French invasion plan was estimated to cost 1,212,500 *livres*.[129] In 1336 the French reckoned a Mediterranean-type galley of 60 oars cost 800 *livres* to build at Rouen (for a working life of three years), and 3,555 *livres* to keep in service for a year, not counting the cost of the dockyard.[130] In English terms the running cost of one galley was £760 a year; at this rate to build and maintain a squadron of twenty galleys for three years would have cost Edward III about £50,000, or more than half his total revenues. It is hardly surprising that English kings could seldom, and French kings only intermittently, afford a proper navy. Twenty Castilian galleys for the summer of 1380 cost France over 50,000 *livres*.[131] Only four times in the fourteenth century did English kings charter Mediterranean galleys. Five Genoese galleys obtained by Edward II in 1316 as part of his efforts to regain control of the Irish Sea from the Scots cost 250 marks each a month, or £3,750 for the four and a half months projected.[132] In 1338 two Genoese galleys were chartered at the same rate.[133] Ten Genoese galleys and a smaller vessel taken for five months in 1373, in the aftermath of the disaster of La Rochelle, cost £9,550 (about 270 marks a month each).[134] Finally in 1386 ten Portuguese galleys were acquired at 1,200 *livres* (about 220 marks sterling) a month each.[135] Hired or owned, even the smallest professional navy was beyond the pocket of an English king for more than a few months.

So the hunt for expedients continued. What was wanted was someone else to pay what neither the crown, nor the shipowners, nor the taxpayers could sustain. Prize money was one answer. From the earliest times the king had claimed a large share in all prizes, and the whole of any taken by ships in his service.[136] Granting some or all of this to the captors was an obvious way to encourage them, and King John was already doing it.[137] In 1242 Henry III granted a half share to ships of Oléron and Bayonne,[138] and in 1294 the Oléron men were allowed the whole value.[139] Edward II in 1319 was the first king to give his whole share to English ships.[140] By the fourteenth century prizes taken by ships in the king's service were usually divided one quarter to the king, one quarter to the owners, and half to the captors; ships not in royal service kept the whole value of the prize less a tenth due to the admiral.[141] On several occasions in the fourteenth century the king's quarter share in prizes taken by the Cinque Ports was allowed to the captors.[142] The 1380 scheme granted a quarter of the value of each prize in addition to 3s 4d a quarter.[143] In 1400 all ships serving with the expedition against Scotland were allowed the whole value of their prizes,[144] and by the 1440s this became a standard inducement,[145] the prizes being divided between the owners (one-third), the masters (one-sixth) and the crews (half).[146] The problem with prize money was that it could be had more easily out of royal service. Implicitly, the king was bidding for support from shipowners by encouraging piracy, and medieval shipmasters needed very little encouragement. Thus the decline of English sea power was accompanied by the rise of English piracy.[147] From the 1290s at latest,[148] English piracy was sanctioned or encouraged by the issue of royal licences, usually referred to by modern writers as 'letters of marque'. These were more accurately letters of reprisal, authorizing those who had suffered from foreign piracy in peacetime, and failed to find redress in foreign courts, to recompense themselves by force. In principle they were limited to the actual value of the losses, to be taken from ships of the country if not the port which had committed the original attack. In practice the distinctions were easily and often forgotten, and reprisals almost always provoked counter-reprisals.[149]

All these ceaseless efforts to raise fleets and raise money called for considerable administrative effort, but the growth of anything like specialized naval administration was slow and haphazard. Usually naval affairs were transacted by the same small group of royal clerks in the Exchequer and Chancery who dealt with all sorts of government business. Under Henry III the king's ships were the responsibility of no particular person, but were treated as an aspect of royal administration among others. Both the king and de Montfort appointed local officials called 'Keepers of the Sea',[150] who were particularly responsible for levying merchant shipping, but there was nothing that could be called a settled system, and the Keepers were not much concerned with the king's own ships.[151] The galleys laid up in different ports were entrusted to local officials, and whenever they were needed for operations a specific order had to be issued to hand them over to whoever was to command.[152]

In the fourteenth century the growing responsibilities of English admirals called for clerks to handle their records and correspondence. These admirals' clerks provided a useful element of continuity and experience, and from them (not, as is sometimes asserted,[153] from William of Wrotham over a century before) grew the office of Clerk of the King's Ships, of which the first holders were Matthew Torksey, Thomas of Snettisham, and William Clewar, who were active in the years between 1336 and 1363.[154] Some Clerks of the King's Ships exercised wide responsibilities, but they had no monopoly of naval administration, much of which continued to be transacted by other officials. Torksey, for example, was responsible for some repairs to the king's ships, but others were undertaken by the ships' masters, accounting directly for money which had not passed through his hands.[155] Moreover it was not unusual for more than one official styled 'Clerk of the King's Ships' to be active at once.

Several English kings found it advantageous to by-pass the cumbersome formality of Exchequer accounting procedures, especially in wartime, by setting up flexible and relatively informal financial departments within the royal household, under their immediate eye. These departments were controlled by the use of private royal seals. The Chamber served this function under Henry II,[156] and under King John and Henry III the Wardrobe developed in the same way.[157] Besides its financial duties, the Wardrobe had departments responsible for storing clothes, furniture and arms. By the fourteenth century they had developed into the Great Wardrobe, which not only stored arms and armour, for delivery to troops and ships, but employed many artificers to make and repair them. Later the function of store passed to the Privy Wardrobe of the Tower, which by the mid-fourteenth century was an independent ordnance department of considerable size.[158] Its stocks in 1360, for example, included 15,365 bows and 23,643 sheaves of arrows, and it was already manufacturing guns and powder.[159] Meanwhile in the 1330s the Chamber with its Griffon Seal returned to prominence as a financial department heavily involved in the wars.[160] The relationship of these departments to each other and to the Clerks of Ships was close and complex. Torksey, for example, rendered his accounts to the Receiver of the Chamber, not the Exchequer.[161] John Hatfield moved from being Clerk of Ships (*c.*1370–7) to be Keeper of the Privy Wardrobe (1378–81), but he is also described as 'Clerk of Array of the King's Ships and Barges', which seems to combine parts of the two offices.[162] ('To array' was to gather and equip a military or naval force.)

These semi-private royal financial departments could be used to evade baronial or parliamentary control, and they were always a target of opposition, which associated them with royal tyranny and particularly with the misappropriation of money voted for specific purposes such as the defence of trade. Hence when kings were obliged to bow to popular discontent, the Exchequer was usually restored to primacy. The Wardrobe as a financial department was under attack in Edward II's time, which was why Edward III built up the Chamber to replace it. As parliamentary taxation became essential to support the war, the Exchequer was restored to authority.[163] Parliament appointed financial controllers called Treasurers at War, who took over from royal administrators when major operations were undertaken.[164]

At the end of the fourteenth century the office of Clerk of the King's

Ships almost disappeared from view, not just because there were hardly any king's ships, but because the governments of Richard II and Henry IV were in no position to sustain instruments of private administration like the Wardrobe or Chamber. John Elmeshale was appointed in 1394[165] and John Chamberleyn in 1399,[166] but not much trace of their activities survives.[167] John Elmeton succeeded in 1406 with wider powers than his predecessors[168] (doubtless marking the change as Prince Henry began to involve himself in naval affairs), and John Starlyng followed in 1409.[169] The rise of Henry V's fleet was accompanied by a revival of the office. His Clerk of Ships William Catton took on much of the responsibility for the maintenance of the king's own ships, though he was by no means the only official involved.[170] Unlike his predecessors in Edward III's time, he was not much involved with mustering fleets of merchantmen, and when the king's ships went to sea he handed over responsibility for them to the Treasurers at War. When Catton retired in 1420 he was succeeded by the Southampton merchant and Collector of Customs William Soper, already much involved in building Henry V's new ships.[171] Soper was the first Clerk of the King's Ships not to be a 'clerk' in the literal sense of a clergyman and civil servant.[172]

Medieval England was a great military power with a sophisticated machinery of government, but her naval administration, at best improvised and for long periods missing altogether, pointed to a grave weakness: the lack of any reliable means of putting a force of warships at the disposal of the crown. Only Richard I and Henry V of all the kings of England can be said to have understood the problem and attempted to remedy it. It is no coincidence that they were by far the most successful in war.

TEN

Captains and Admirals

Social History 1204–1455

The outbreak of naval war with France in 1293, in the middle of his Scottish campaigns, forced Edward I to tighten up his naval administration. He needed to raise and organize much larger fleets than had been called for hitherto, and he urgently needed to bring them under tighter control. Indiscriminate violence, particularly by the Cinque Ports, had precipitated the war, and the king's authority had to be brought to bear. In these circumstances Sir William Leyburn was in 1294 appointed 'Captain of the Sailors and Mariners of the Realm'.[1] 'Captain' was the ordinary military term for a middle-ranking general officer, such as might command a division of the army or a smaller detached force. Leyburn was an experienced soldier, and the title of 'Captain' was used in the same sense at sea as ashore (the only exception being the four 'captains of seamen' who assisted Gervase Alard as Admiral of the Southern Fleet in 1300, paid 1s a day, half the admiral's pay and twice that of a master[2]). The following year Leyburn was joined by a colleague, Sir John de Botetort (previously referred to as 'under-captain of certain sailors and mariners of the king'[3]), and for the first time they were described as 'Admirals', as was Barrau de Sescas the new commander of the Bayonne fleet.[4]

The word 'admiral', which is of Arabic origin, was one of several naval words imported from the sophisticated world of the Mediterranean.[5] There it meant a fleet commander, but as applied in England it indicated a position which was more administrative than operational. English admirals were essentially responsible for assembling fleets, almost entirely from impressed merchantmen, and establishing good order and military discipline in the king's name.[6] Leyburn's orders in 1295 were to 'gather all the ships and seamen from every one of our ports, allowing no straggling, in a single place which you shall judge suitable for the defence of our kingdom and the defeat of the enemy fleet'.[7] He was not ordered to defeat the enemy himself. Admirals often went to sea with their fleets, but as these fleets were not usually expected to fight battles, they were not primarily fleet commanders in the modern sense. Nor were they the sole authority in naval administration. In 1370 a fleet assembled at Rye and Winchelsea to carry the army of Sir Robert Knolles to France. Lord Latymer, Steward of the King's Household, went down to superintend the embarkation with a substantial staff of senior officers and officials, among them Lord Neville, the Admiral of the Northern Fleet.[8] As an admiral Neville was expected to take an important part, but not to bear sole responsibility.

The best of medieval fleet organization was not directed at the rare and unpredictable circumstances of fleet action, but at the common problems of handling scores or hundreds of ships in company. The Anglo-Flemish agreements of 1286 and 1297 provided for recognition signals and identification papers by which allied ships might know one another,[9] and the proposed Anglo-Flemish agreement of 1403 provided for Flemish ships to wear the arms of their home ports painted on their bows.[10] Medieval ships were always liberally provided with flags, besides being painted in bright colours;[11] the galley built at Ipswich in 1304 had an initial outfit of eleven ensigns.[12] Especially if in royal service, they often used the king's arms rather than a national flag.[13] From the fourteenth century at latest kings and admirals wore the royal arms painted or embroidered on their sails,[14] and with the big sails of the day they must have been recognizable at a great distance. This is the implication of an incident in 1316 when the Bayonne ship *St James* was attacked by Scots and Flemings, who had killed all but three of the crew when the English admiral Sir John Botetort appeared on the horizon. The attackers identified him at once and fled, while the *St James* hoisted the English royal standard and was rescued.[15] Pendants or 'streamers', especially red ones, were regarded as signals of warlike intent, and the Cinque Ports men excused their action in 1293 by claiming that the Normans wore 'banners of red silk each two ells broad and 30 long called "bausans", what the English call "streamers", which among seamen everywhere signify war to the death'.[16] By the mid-fourteenth century both French and English fleets had simple signals and standing orders designed to keep the ships together, though in bad weather some dispersal was inevitable.[17] By day the admiral wore his flag, and at night he carried distinguishing masthead lights.[18] In all navies there was a particular flag to summon a council of war,[19] and English orders mention another to indicate 'enemy in sight'.[20]

This sort of organization was most essential for overseas expeditions, when very large fleets might sail together, but it was also needed for coastal campaigns when ships accompanied and supplied the army marching along the shore. This was the usual pattern of English warfare against Scotland and Wales. Because the troops went by land – above all the horses with their extravagant demands on shipping space – many fewer ships were needed, and in a regular stream delivering supplies to forward ports rather than in a single large fleet. When castles were captured they had to be supplied by sea, for even when English armies were successful the roads were seldom safe except for large forces.[21] If a coastal campaign developed into a siege, ships were essential both to blockade the besieged fortress and to supply the besiegers.[22] In such a case a seaborne relieving expedition might provoke a naval battle, as it did at Calais in 1347. Siege and blockade often involved naval warfare inland along navigable waters. The whole southern campaign of 1346 turned on the siege of the Gascon town of Aiguillon, at the confluence of the Lot and the Garonne, where both sides were completely dependent on the rivers for the means of supply and attack.[23] When the French besieged Bourg, north of Bordeaux, in 1407, their supplies came, not overland from their rear but by sea from La Rochelle and up the Gironde, and they had to abandon the siege in a hurry when the Bordelais captured one of their convoys in the estuary.[24] These operations took place on large rivers still navigable today, but many others depended on much smaller waterways. When the French besieged the Navarrese garrison of Pont-Audemer in Normandy in 1378, Rainier Grimaldi with four of his galleys lay in the River Risle and repelled all English attempts to relieve their allies.[25] Even the Risle is deep and wide compared with the Warwickshire Avon at Kenilworth, scene of substantial naval activity during the siege of 1266.[26]

Even if an admiral sailed on an expedition, the overall commander of the force was the same afloat as ashore; the king, or at least a nobleman of higher rank than an admiral. In 1374, for example, Sir Philip Courtenay was 'Admiral of the Fleet of the King's Ships in the South and West' which carried the expedition of the Earl of Cambridge to Brittany. Courtenay was a senior officer, paid as a knight-banneret, with a retinue of his own troops,[27] but there was no question of his outranking the king's son. English medieval admirals did not very often fight at sea, and were present at sea battles, if at all, only in a subordinate capacity. Officers of their rank and experience, however, often commanded detached forces on land, and several of Edward III's admirals (notably Sir Walter Mauny) had an outstanding record as generals in the field.[28] It has been calculated that about half of Edward III's prominent captains served afloat as well as ashore.[29]

The only other occasions on which the title 'captain' was used at sea was when Mediterranean galleys imported the quite different terminology of the south. There a 'captain' was a commodore commanding a squadron of galleys, or a convoy of great galleys. Individual galleys were commanded by a 'patron', usually a merchant in peacetime, often a soldier in wartime, who took overall command but was not expected to be a seaman. Either a 'pilot', or one or more 'comitres' or boatswains, were responsible for actual navigation. Possibly when King John in 1205 sent two galleys to Yarmouth, ordering the townsmen to find 'two masters to command them and two others to take overall charge of them',[30] he was thinking of Mediterranean practice, and on the rare occasions when a king of England could afford to employ Mediterranean galleys, they naturally used their usual ranks. Thus in 1338 Giovanni Doria and Niccolò Blanco were the patrons of two Genoese galleys in Edward III's service,[31] and in 1372 Piero de Campofregoso (brother of the Doge of Genoa) was appointed Captain of the (Genoese) Galleys.[32]

The early English admirals were usually knights or barons, with some merchants and shipowners, especially from the Cinque Ports. Almost at once their responsibilities began to be divided on a geographical basis into 'fleets' or 'admiralties', which were really stretches of coast for which the admiral was responsible. As a rule the Northern Fleet ran from the Thames to the Scottish border at Berwick, and the Southern (often confusingly called 'Western') Fleet from the Thames round to Bristol. If operations were called for in the Irish Sea a Western Fleet was organized, usually from Bristol to Carlisle, sometimes with West Country and Irish ports as well. The object of the division was primarily administrative: it kept an admiral's charge within practicable bounds, and made it easier to assemble expeditions to Scotland (on either coast), Gascony, Brittany and Flanders as necessary. It also separated the bitter enemies of Yarmouth and the Cinque Ports, though even so admirals had to be ordered to keep them apart as far as possible.[33]

From the mid-fourteenth century the rank of admirals began to rise; the first earls (Suffolk and Salisbury) were appointed in 1337, though many admirals up to the end of the century were still only knights.[34] Smaller squadrons might be commanded by an admiral, a knight or other officer of suitable rank, or by a senior master, but the status and rank of all squadron commanders tended to rise with that of the admirals. Thus in 1295 the Yorkshire knight Sir Osbert of Spaldington was sent 'up the coast to the northward' with four ships, three galleys and a barge.[35] Knights might also agree to serve by sea on the staff of an admiral or commander, and the wording of their contracts, stipulating that they would remain in the senior officer's personal retinue, seems to be designed to ensure that they were not embarrassed by having to serve in a private ship under a master.[36] The senior officers of convoys were appointed in the same way as those of any other squadron, and their rank reflected the importance of the ships they were in charge of. An ordinary wine convoy to Gascony in the fourteenth century called for an officer of knight's rank, such as Sir Thomas Coke, appointed in 1352 and invested with full powers 'according to maritime law'.[37] In 1373, after the disaster of La Rochelle the previous year, an unusually strong convoy with not less than twenty escorts sailed for Bordeaux under the command of both the admirals, Sir William Nevill and Sir Philip Courtenay.[38]

Admirals were responsible for recruiting men as well as ships. About 1370, for example, John Neville, Admiral of the North, was instructed to order John Hankin, sergeant-at-arms, to arrest all ships of twenty tons or more between the Thames and Boston and have them at Lynn within ten days, then to levy all ships over sixty tons to go on the king's service, 'according to the custom of the sea', and provide them with seamen 'for equipping the said ships'.[39] The system was not tidy, however; admirals were by their office (if not necessarily by their personal experience) specialists in naval administration, but they did not monopolize it, and similar orders issued directly from the crown.[40] Hankin had his orders from his admiral, but at the same time his colleague John Hale, together with William Hawley the Mayor of Dartmouth and others, received a direct order from the king, not passing through the hands of Lord Brian the Admiral of the Western Fleet, to find some of the most capable seamen in Devon 'to man urgently three barges which are ordered to Dartmouth'.[41] Moreover much of the admirals' recruitment effort was made not as admirals but as generals. The usual method of forming English armies in the fourteenth and fifteenth centuries was by the assembling of 'indentured retinues': noblemen and gentlemen who were more or less professional soldiers undertook by a contract (the indenture) to raise a specified number of men (the retinue) and serve for a given time, receiving from the crown their wages and victualling allowance in instalments.[42] Detachments were recruited for sea service by this means from the 1370s.[43] There was no great difference between admirals and 'captains' ashore; even if they were not actually the same officers, squadron commanders were chosen and appointed in the same way as officers of equivalent rank in the army. Men like Lord Clifford, who indented to serve in 1416 with four knights, 195 men-at-arms and 400 archers,[44] or Sir Hugh Courtenay in 1419 with his retinue of three knights, 380 men-at-arms and 780 archers,[45] might equally have served on land in command of a force of that size, and often did so. Since the sea commanders, whether or not styled 'admirals', were the same officers who commanded troops ashore, and their retinues were equally amphibious, the same system of service by indenture was easily adopted for whole fleets.

As well as establishing the first admirals in the 1290s, Edward I also re-instituted the old title of Keeper of the Coast (or Keeper of the Sea) to superintend local defence.[46] The 1339 'Sea Guard', a coastal militia raised from all districts within eighteen miles of the coast, was likewise entrusted to Keepers or Wardens for each county.[47] A Keeper's duties were closely related to those of an admiral, and they were sometimes discharged by the same person (Botetort in 1295 was Keeper of the Coast of Norfolk as well as Admiral).[48] By the 1380s coast defence was generally added to the admirals' responsibilities,[49] or in practice to those of their subordinates and local assistants the Vice-Admirals, usually one to each coastal county.[50]

Victualling was usually the responsibility of royal clerks, but not necessarily the Clerks of Ships.[51] The feeding of very large fleets assembled for overseas expeditions presented an enormous problem. It was possible to have a population larger than the largest towns in England gathered for an uncertain period, often in a remote place, before sailing for an equally uncertain period of service.[52] The quantities of provisions required were formidable.[53] The single (admittedly large) merchantman *Anthony* of Hull, sailing on a trading voyage to Bordeaux in 1459, took in six months' stores, including ten tuns of salt meat, five tuns of flour and biscuit, thirteen tuns of salt fish, twenty tuns of water and thirty tuns of 'drink or beverage' (probably wine).[54] Many English fleets included hundreds of such ships, with troops to feed as well as the crews. In order to generate a supply, the king might attempt to distort the market. When the fleet assembled in the Orwell in 1370, markets throughout East Anglia as far as Hertfordshire were forbidden to sell foodstuffs until it sailed, except at places within 36 miles of the fleet.[55] Ordinary consumers were presumably expected to go hungry, but when the University of Cambridge and the city of London began to feel the pinch this order had to be hastily cancelled.[56] Victuallers often exploited the royal right of purveyance, by which the royal household was entitled to pre-empt the market at a fixed price, to buy in the far larger quantities needed for a fleet or army.[57]

The foodstuffs in common consumption in the Middle Ages were not very numerous, and those which could be preserved for use at sea were fewer. Wheat, barley and flour (often pea or bean meal rather than wheat flour) were bought to make bread, usually in the form of biscuit.[58] It has been calculated that biscuit constituted up to 70 per cent of the sailor's diet.[59] Oats were probably for the horses; cheese undoubtedly for the men. Beer, cider[60] and wine were supplied to drink. Meat was usually purchased in the form of livestock, sometimes as carcasses; oxen, bullocks, calves, sheep, hogs and piglets, hens and capons are mentioned. The animals were butchered and salted, rather than taken to sea on the hoof,[61] but only ham and bacon was commonly supplied in a preserved form. Salt meat in cask was certainly usual in the fifteenth century,[62] and possibly earlier. Fish, usually salted and in cask, was a prominent item of diet. Fruit and vegetables seem to have been unknown, except the ubiquitous peas and beans, staple of the peasant's diet.[63] Some leeks and onions, together with spices, dried fruit and gingerbread were supplied to a ship in 1290, but she was sailing to bring home a Norwegian princess; they were certainly not for the consumption of the common seamen.[64] The astonishing quantities of mustard included among the victuals of fifteenth-century Burgundian fleets do not figure in English accounts.[65]

There is seldom sufficient evidence about the men who ate these victuals to allow us to catch more than a glimpse of them as flesh and blood, and we know far too little about the routine of their daily lives at sea and in port, but it is nevertheless possible to distinguish in the thirteenth and fourteenth centuries a growing range and diversity of ranks and duties aboard ship, to perceive something of the internal organization of a ship's company, to see how men were recruited to serve at sea and how much they were paid.

At the beginning of the thirteenth century, English and other northern ships still appear, as they did before the Norman Conquest, to have had simply a number of seamen and a single officer, the steersman in command. Very occasionally a ship on important royal business was allowed two masters.[66] Sometimes we hear of crossbowmen or other soldiers embarked to strengthen the defence, as for instance when the king's ship carried money to pay troops in Normandy, Poitou or Gascony, but the documents give the impression that the ship's company consisted of an undifferentiated body of seamen. They continue to do so for much of the thirteenth century, with no difference except that the old English title of 'steersman' gives way to the modern 'master'.[67] The master of a ship in the Middle Ages was in almost all circumstances of peace or war in sole command of his ship, and it was common for the masters of merchantmen also to be their owners. When troops were embarked, the senior military officer did not normally outrank the master. In formal documents such as press warrants the master's name almost invariably stands before that of the senior officer of troops. Even John Arnold, a royal sergeant-at-arms and an officer of the king's household, did not take rank over John Mayhew, the master of Richard II's ship the *Trinity of the Tower*.[68] When military expeditions sailed, always under the command of the king, a prince or other nobleman of rank appropriate to so great a charge, they would naturally take overall command, but otherwise an individual master was normally subordinate only to an admiral, or to an officer appointed to command a fleet or squadron.

Seven ships seems to have been the smallest force ever commanded by a captain,[69] and smaller squadrons were often in charge of a master. From Henry II's time,[70] and probably earlier, the king himself employed one or more masters, more or less permanently, to command his own ships. Such men, sometimes called 'the king's mariners',[71] were often trusted with wider responsibilities, both at sea and in port. Throughout the Middle Ages it was common for masters of the king's ships to impress seamen, to act as their own paymasters, victuallers and accountants, to refit or repair their own ships, and to buy or build others for the king.[72] Richard Marchant commanded two galleys stationed in the Channel Isles in 1294.[73] Thomas Springet was entrusted with a diplomatic mission in 1326, being sent to Brittany to rescue one of the king's ships which had gone aground and another which had been arrested.[74] John Getour, one of Edward III's masters, was in command of a squadron of three barges in 1338.[75]

The royal sea service was sufficiently established to run in families. Thomas fitz Stephen who commanded the *White Ship* when she was wrecked on the Quilleboeuf rock off Barfleur in 1120, drowning Henry I's eldest son, was the son of Stephen fitz Airard, master of William I's ship the *Mora* in 1066.[76] Henry III's great ship in 1226 had no fewer than six masters, listed almost as though they were a corps of royal mariners.[77] Of these six Stephen Calf (*le Vel*) was doubtless another generation of the family which had produced four royal shipmasters in the 1170s.[78] In the fourteenth century other families were prominent in Edward III's service. At the battle of Sluys in 1340 Simon Springet was master of the king's ship *Portjoy* and Alexander Springet of the pinnace *Margaret*, while Thomas Springet had been master of the *Cog Edward*, captured the previous year, and another Thomas commanded the galley of Lynn.[79] In the same fleet John Loveryk was master of the *Edmund* (or *Esmond*), William Loveryk senior of the *Swallow*, and William Loveryk junior of the *Cog John*, to which he had lately turned over from the *Trinity of the Tower*.[80]

Ship's officers under the master begin to be mentioned in the thirteenth century, beginning with the constable.[81] A constable was a junior army officer, and aboard ships constables were appointed only in wartime. Sometimes they were evidently in command of detachments of troops embarked for naval service, but they also figure aboard ships with no soldiers. They were paid the same as the master, but invariably ranked after him. Their functions were clearly military, in a general sense, and the number of them was roughly in proportion to the size of the ship's company, but we cannot tell exactly what were their duties. In the English fleet operating around Wales in 1281–2 each ship had ten to twenty men-at-arms embarked, usually with a constable in command, but the king's two 'big galleys' had 48 men and two constables each. This squadron also had four 'principal constables' (at double the normal wages), who appear to have been in overall charge of the troops embarked.[82] There are hints that the companies of these ships, and perhaps others at this time, may have been organized in units of twenty men with a 'vintenar' in command, following the contemporary military practice.[83] The galley built at Southampton in 1294 had a master and three constables for a crew of 120.[84] In the Cinque Ports fleet of 1327, every ship had a master and a constable, but there were no troops aboard, and it is clear from the constables' names that they came from the same group of families (notably the Cundys and Loveryks of Sandwich, the Baddings, Brokers and Ambroses of Winchelsea) which supplied the masters and the ships.[85] Mates or master's mates are not mentioned by that name until the fifteenth century,[86] but from at latest the 1370s press warrants and similar documents often name one or two 'mariners' after the master, who are clearly ship's officers.[87]

Clerks or pursers appear aboard bigger ships by the fourteenth century.[88] The York galley sailed on her maiden voyage in 1295 with a clerk, Richard of Doncaster,[89] who is possibly the first English naval 'supply officer' whose name we know. Some of the first clerks mentioned were royal clerks embarked as part of the staff for a major expedition,[90] but others seem to have been permanent officers of particular ships, responsible for victualling and paying their crews. Edward III's biggest ships the *Christopher*, *Cog Thomas* and *Cog Edward* all had clerks of their own;[91] Thomas of Snettisham began as clerk of the *Christopher* before being promoted to be Clerk of the King's Ships.[92]

Big ships, particularly king's ships, also carried master carpenters by the fourteenth century. Henry Hellward, who built the York galley in 1294–5, sailed as her carpenter on her first voyage; an unusually early case, and an unusually small vessel to bear a carpenter.[93] Probably he took a voyage to see how his galley would behave at sea; three years later he was again ashore building a new barge.[94] In 1340 the *Christopher* and the *Cog Thomas* both had carpenters.[95] Such men had something of the same relationship of trust as the 'king's mariners', and might be given powers, for example to press carpenters or shipwrights for royal service.[96]

The troops embarked aboard ship were usually a mixture of infantry or dismounted cavalry with archers. Bows were valuable at sea, where the enemy was necessarily massed on deck, a concentrated target with little cover. There was limited space, however, to deploy the archers, for which reason the standard proportion of archers to men-at-arms was two to one at sea, instead of three to one for land service.[97] It was normal for ships intended as 'warships' (as distinct from transports) to be double-manned, which sometimes meant taking on a contingent of soldiers, sometimes just twice as many seamen. When all fighting was at close quarters, the more numerous crew would usually have the advantage, and in that violent age it could be assumed that all merchant seamen would be familiar with handling weapons. Nevertheless they were not a match for professional soldiers. One of the keys to the English victory at Sluys was that Edward III's fleet, transporting an expeditionary force, carried many thousands of knights, archers and infantrymen, while the French had only 150 men-at-arms and 500 crossbowmen amongst 19,000 men.[98] Galleys had room for only a small military detachment of infantry and crossbowmen, significantly known in Mediterranean practice as 'boarders'.[99] The Bayonnais authorities advised Edward I in 1276 that a galley of 120 oars needed eight comitres and 25 soldiers.[100]

Of the ordinary seamen of English ships at war in the Middle Ages we can say very little. One man to every three or four tons was regarded as a sufficient crew for transports to Gascony in the fourteenth century.[101] They were usually recruited by their masters, a process leaving no trace in official records except when the masters of the king's ships, and less often other masters or local authorities, were issued with warrants to press seamen.[102] It appears that impressment usually happened ashore rather than aboard ship, though in 1360 the *Rood Cog* of Newcastle was immobilized in the Thames by impressment of her men and was unable to sail with the royal fleet;[103] while in 1398 John Mayhew, master of the *Trinity of the Tower*, was authorized to press 55 men for her forthcoming voyage to Gascony, taking no more than two or three from any one ship.[104] Normally the men were taken up for service with their ships, and whatever compulsion might have been called for operated at a local level.[105] Thus in 1347 various men of Strood and Gillingham received advance wages to man the Rochester ship *Plenty* and then failed to appear, while the authorities of Strood were assessed to find a number of men and refused to do so.[106] Actual desertion is mentioned only rarely.[107] Though we hear of resistance to impressment by seamen themselves, it was primarily shipowners and local authorities on whom the burden of service was directly laid, and who led the opposition to it. The recruitment of troops often involved very similar difficulties.[108] Impressment was an ordinary application of royal prerogative powers, and not at all (as the jurists of later centuries argued) something applicable only to seamen. Shipwrights and carpenters were impressed to build or repair the king's ships,[109] and even private ships;[110] ropemakers to make rope;[111] pilots when the king's ships went overseas;[112] fishermen to provide fish for the royal household;[113] masons and labourers to build cathedrals;[114] even glaziers were impressed to repair the windows of the royal chapel.[115]

Boys appear among the seamen from the fourteenth century.[116] They were not very numerous; about one for every eight seamen aboard Edward III's big ships the *Christopher*, *Cog Edward* and *Cog Thomas*.[117] Even in the 1470s a ship like the carvel *Edward* had only one, 'Roger, the child of the ship'.[118] The *Packer Howard*, another of Lord Howard's ships, also had only one, though his flagship the *Mary Howard* had several 'children' among her complement of 400.[119] The boys are particularly mentioned as working aloft; though it is not easy to see how a few boys could possibly have handled a big sail, especially from the awkward and precarious position of sitting astride the yard.[120] One function they could have performed is suggested by the sea trials of the replica Hansa cog: with yard and sail lowered it has to be stowed fore and aft, so that in making sail it is necessary to clear one yardarm of the shrouds. Before the development of ratlines allowed men to climb the shrouds, only a person astride the yardarm could easily do this; the smaller the person the better, as his weight had to be hoisted with the yard.[121] Pictures of medieval ships making sail, of which there are many on the seals of seaport towns, often show a boy on each yardarm as the yard is hoisted.[122]

Discipline at sea seems to have been relaxed, according to the Laws of Oléron. This code of maritime law is now thought to have been compiled in the thirteenth century under English royal authority, initially to govern the Gascon trade which passed by the island of Oléron.[123] A law code is in its nature evidence for what people thought ought to happen rather than what actually did, but the Laws of Oléron certainly were accepted as current law among English seamen and in English courts,[124] and must have borne some relation to reality. A master was forbidden to punish his men (at least physically), but had to bring them before the admiral for judgement.[125] 'If the master strike any of his shipmates, he should stand the first blow whether with the fist or the flat of the hand, but if the seaman suffer more he may defend himself'.[126] One cannot help wondering how easily in practice an aggrieved seaman could invoke this law, but some cases survive of masters prosecuted under it.[127] It seems to have been part of an attitude by which the men were in many respects partners in the running of the ship, whose consent was required in matters both of business and navigation, and who might be held partly responsible if ship or cargo were lost or spoilt as a result of a decision in which they had shared.[128] The master was expected to act as judge and peacemaker among his men, punishing mildly if at all, with the support of the whole company, for example by 'sending a man to Coventry'.[129] The Laws prescribe that a sick man was to be landed and cared for at the ship's expense, with one of the boys left to look after him, or a woman engaged as nurse.[130] Another maritime law code, the Catalan *Consolato del Mare*, insists that the seaman has an absolute right to his wages, though the owners have to sell the ship 'to the last nail' to pay them.[131]

Numerous seamen's churches and chapels – several of them built or beautified from the profits of piracy[132] – testify to the seafarer's faith, and there is one reference to an English squadron going to sea with a chaplain.[133] This does not contradict the evidence of an English confessor's manual which describes the seaman as subject to every kind of vice, with a 'wife' in every port.[134]

ELEVEN

The End of the Empire

Operations 1410–1455; Administration 1420–1455

Throughout Henry IV's reign his kingdom was preoccupied by rebellions in England and Wales, attacks from Scotland and (in Gascony) France. Little was done to rebuild the naval strength which was the only means of carrying the war to any of these enemies. What was achieved was the work of the young Prince Henry. Even before he became king, the future Henry V was already acquiring ships of his own, and in his short reign he built up the most impressive royal fleet owned by any English medieval king. From two ships in 1410, when he took control of the royal council, it increased to six ships at his accession in 1413, and 34 by 1417:[1] 140 per cent growth a year in numbers, and considerably more in tonnage terms. Henry's ships were not a transport force but a battle fleet, and they were employed not to convey armies to Flanders or Gascony for yet another futile peripheral campaign, but to destroy French sea power in the Channel and open the way for decisive victory.[2]

Henry V's first expedition (much of it carried in Dutch ships for want of English ones) sailed from Southampton in August 1415 and landed him in Normandy with little naval opposition. There his first priority was to capture the port of Harfleur as a base of operations. This was the only achievement of the first campaign, and it must have been obvious that the real issue would turn on French attempts to retake it in 1416. For that campaign the French engaged a force of 600 Genoese crossbowmen aboard eight galleys and eight carracks, which were based on the new harbour of Honfleur, across the Seine from Harfleur and perfectly situated to blockade it. From there they put to sea to raid the Isle of Wight and cruise off Portsmouth, while the English fleet gathered at Southampton. Finally the Duke of Bedford got to sea, and on 15 August 1416 he met the Franco-Genoese fleet in a great battle off Harfleur. The English had only four carracks against eight, which put them at a great disadvantage, but they probably had more troops: over 7,000, two-thirds of them archers. Bedford won a complete victory, capturing three of the Genoese carracks. A fourth was wrecked trying to escape.[3]

This victory lifted the siege of Harfleur and opened the way for the invasion of Normandy. The next year on 25 July the Earl of Huntingdon, his fleet reinforced by the prizes, won another victory in the Bay of the Seine in which he took four more Genoese carracks, together with the French admiral and a quarter's pay for the French fleet.[4] Probably these two victories damaged French naval power nearly as much as Sluys and the 1346 campaign had done. The difference this time was that they were followed up. Henry began his Norman campaign in 1417, and by January 1419, when Rouen fell, the entire duchy was in English hands after over two hundred years of French occupation. During these years the English fleet was busy patrolling the Channel ('skimming the sea' in the contemporary phrase),[5] escorting convoys and blockading ports still in French hands. By 1419 they had very little left to do. With no sea-coast left on the Channel, French sea power in northern waters was eliminated, and under the terms of the Treaty of Troyes of 1420, Henry V was heir to the throne of France.[6]

The remaining naval threat to England came from a revival of the Franco-Castilian alliance. By a treaty in June 1419 Castile undertook to send a fleet of 40 ships of 500 tons with 4,000 men. Henry V's intelligence was excellent; he was able to warn of the possibility of a Castilian attack on Southampton four months before the treaty was signed, he sent scouts as far away as La Rochelle to give warning of the expected Castilian fleet, and a Bayonne balinger took a prize which carried a copy of the Franco-Castilian treaty from which he learned that Castilian ships were to sail to Scotland. But even good intelligence well in advance did not guarantee interception. He ordered ships into the Irish Sea, but they made no contact with the Spanish squadron carrying more than 6,000 Scottish troops to France, while on 30 December 1419 near La Rochelle a Franco-Castilian squadron under Alfons Sarrias defeated an English convoy to Gascony. Henry's fleet, powerful though it was, does not appear to have operated outside the Channel. The naval threat in the Bay was removed by a coup d'état in July 1420 which reversed Castilian foreign policy, not by English action at sea.[7]

Henry V developed the practice of seakeeping by contract, based on the established system of recruitment by indentured retinue. The king would undertake to provide ships, sometimes of specified size and type, while the commander would agree, not only to find his retinue, but to 'keep' or 'safeguard' the sea for a particular period. The successful fleets of 1415 to 1420 were organized by this method. Its weakness was the inadequacy of a legal contract as an operational order, and the difficulty of binding anyone to perform something as vaguely defined as 'keeping the sea'. Henry, however, was a brilliant strategist and a careful planner;[8] in his reign fleet commanders received explicit and realistic instructions. Sir Hugh Courtenay's 1419 indenture, for example, contained detailed operational orders: he was to cruise between Dieppe and Cherbourg, paying particular attention to the blockade of the Seine. If an enemy squadron came out he was to pursue them, leaving at least one ship and two balingers on station to keep up the blockade.[9]

Henry V can justly be regarded as the first English king since Richard I who understood the use of sea power as a primary weapon of war. Dogged frontal assault over long distances and impossible terrain, the strategy of the three Edwards against both Wales and Scotland, succeeded only against Wales, the smallest, weakest and most divided nation in Europe, and even then only because of the fortuitous absence of foreign fleets in the Irish Sea. Campaigning on the Continent, successive English kings displayed a fatal determination to start from friendly territory, either Flanders or Gascony, however far it lay from the centres of French power or the sources of English supply. In the long term England's only hope against a much richer and stronger power was to use the mobility conferred by the sea to gain the strategic initiative, then exploit superior weapons and tactics by forcing decisive battle. The least likely way to achieve this was by raiding the remote borders of France.[10] The Battle of Poitiers in 1356 was the only major English victory gained by an expedition starting overland from friendly territory. It was landing directly in Normandy which led to Crécy in 1346 and Agincourt in 1415, and in the former case Edward III had not intended to sail to Normandy if the wind had served for Gascony.[11] Only Henry V deliberately built up a fleet to strike directly at the heart of the enemy's position by invading Normandy, and he was rewarded not just by the reconquest of the Angevin empire, but by France's virtual extinction as a northern sea power as she lost her entire Channel coast.[12]

In the medieval context this was still the only way to achieve anything like command of the sea. Though by the fifteenth century patrolling and scouting were increasingly used and it was becoming possible to dominate confined sea areas for limited periods of time, the sea in general remained a debatable space outside any man's control, impossible to deny to an enemy who possessed ships and cared to use them.[13] Moreover Henry's fleet, sophisticated though it was by English standards, remained a part-time and short-range force,[14] its small ships often widely dispersed. The Council in 1415 proposed to dispose twelve ships and balingers in three squadrons covering sections of the coast from Plymouth to Berwick: the force was too small and scattered to do more than observe the enemy and deter minor raids.[15]

At the time it did not seem to matter. When Henry V died in 1422, after less than ten years on the throne, England appeared to have achieved complete triumph. Much of France was partitioned between the English and their Burgundian allies, and there was no enemy naval force to justify keeping up the great and costly fleet which he had built up. The Council which ruled on behalf of the infant Henry VI, led by Bedford and his other uncles, decided to sell of most of the ships, retaining only the four biggest carracks in reserve. At first there was no reason to think this policy mistaken, but soon things began to go wrong. When Charles VI died in October 1422, two months after Henry V, his son claimed the throne instead of resigning it to Henry VI under the terms of the Treaty of Troyes. The war therefore continued, and in 1435 England's fortunes turned sharply for the worse when the Burgundians changed sides. The Dukes of Burgundy were rulers of most of what is now eastern France and the Low Countries, powerful and strategically placed to affect the war. That autumn the French captured Dieppe, followed by other Channel ports. Now there were both French and Burgundian ships in the Channel to threaten England's trade and shores, and there was almost no royal fleet to counter them.[16] The worst period was between 1435 and 1439, when a truce with Burgundy was agreed.

Henry VI's government had neither the money, nor the resolution, nor the strategic sense to revive English sea power. In 1433 Lord Cromwell, Treasurer of England, estimated that the king's income was just under £27,000 a year, expenditure nearly £57,000, and the accumulated debt already £165,000. 'Custody and repair of the king's ships' was allowed £100 a year.[17] The situation was probably not quite as bad as Cromwell's figures suggested: according to modern calculations Henry VI had an income of about £50,000 a year in the 1440s, but it was falling rapidly as territory was lost, lands and offices sold, and revenues mortgaged.[18] The consequence of public fury and government incapacity was a series of experiments with private squadrons. One form was seakeeping by licence, in which unpaid squadrons organized by noblemen or merchant syndicates undertook to 'keep the sea' under admirals of their own choice in return for all the profits except the shares due to the Lord Admiral. Though there were some fourteenth-century precedents[19] this was first tried on a large scale in 1436,[20] but the disadvantages of what amounted to state-sponsored piracy were soon obvious[21] and by

1440 the indenture method was again employed to raise a fleet sent to relieve Harfleur.[22]

Alternatively, fleets might be organized by parliamentary initiative, financed by tunnage and poundage, whose proceeds were paid directly to the admirals without passing through the Exchequer. Weak and distrusted, the government of Henry VI was now forced to accept defence at sea being removed completely from its control. The first official scheme of this nature had been in 1406, when the merchants undertook to keep the seas against all enemies 'except royal fleets'.[23] It collapsed almost at once.[24] In 1442 the Commons sponsored a much more ambitious scheme, planned in detail including the names of every ship which was to take part, but it only lasted six months.[25] It was the same with the plan of 1454 backed by the Commons, the Duke of York and other noblemen.[26] A similar scheme for local defence, organized by the Irish government in 1454 and paid for by a levy on merchants and fishermen, seems to have worked better,[27] but English government found that neither tunnage and poundage nor the profits of piracy could yield enough to provide an efficient fleet.

The worst consequence of the neglect of the royal fleet under Henry VI was the dispersal of the corps of 28 masters whom Henry V had retained at a regular annual salary of from five to ten marks, according to the size of their ships.[28] Men like these of long service and experience, whom one may perhaps call the first corps of regular sea officers, qualified to command a ship or a squadron or to handle considerable administrative responsibilities, were the real basis of royal naval power. Not shipowners or merchants or great magnates, they were professional seamen belonging to the king alone. Ships could be acquired relatively easily, but their experience and loyalty could not be improvised.

English piracy, suppressed by Henry V with a ruthlessness and thoroughness unequalled by any medieval English king,[29] revived rapidly after his death, and the pirates were quick to adopt the new carvels.[30] In the fifteenth century English pirates, especially from the West Country, were savage and successful. Men like the elder and younger John Hawley of Dartmouth, Henry Pay of Poole, William Long of Rye, Richard Spicer of Plymouth, Thomas Gill of Kingsbridge and Mark Mixtow of Fowey were known and feared throughout the ports of Europe.[31] At home they enjoyed the backing of all the prominent men of their counties. It was idle to investigate piracy by means of royal officials, justices and jurymen most of whom were themselves pirates, receivers or investors in pirate ventures.[32] Thus some hapless Breton merchants offered in 1432,

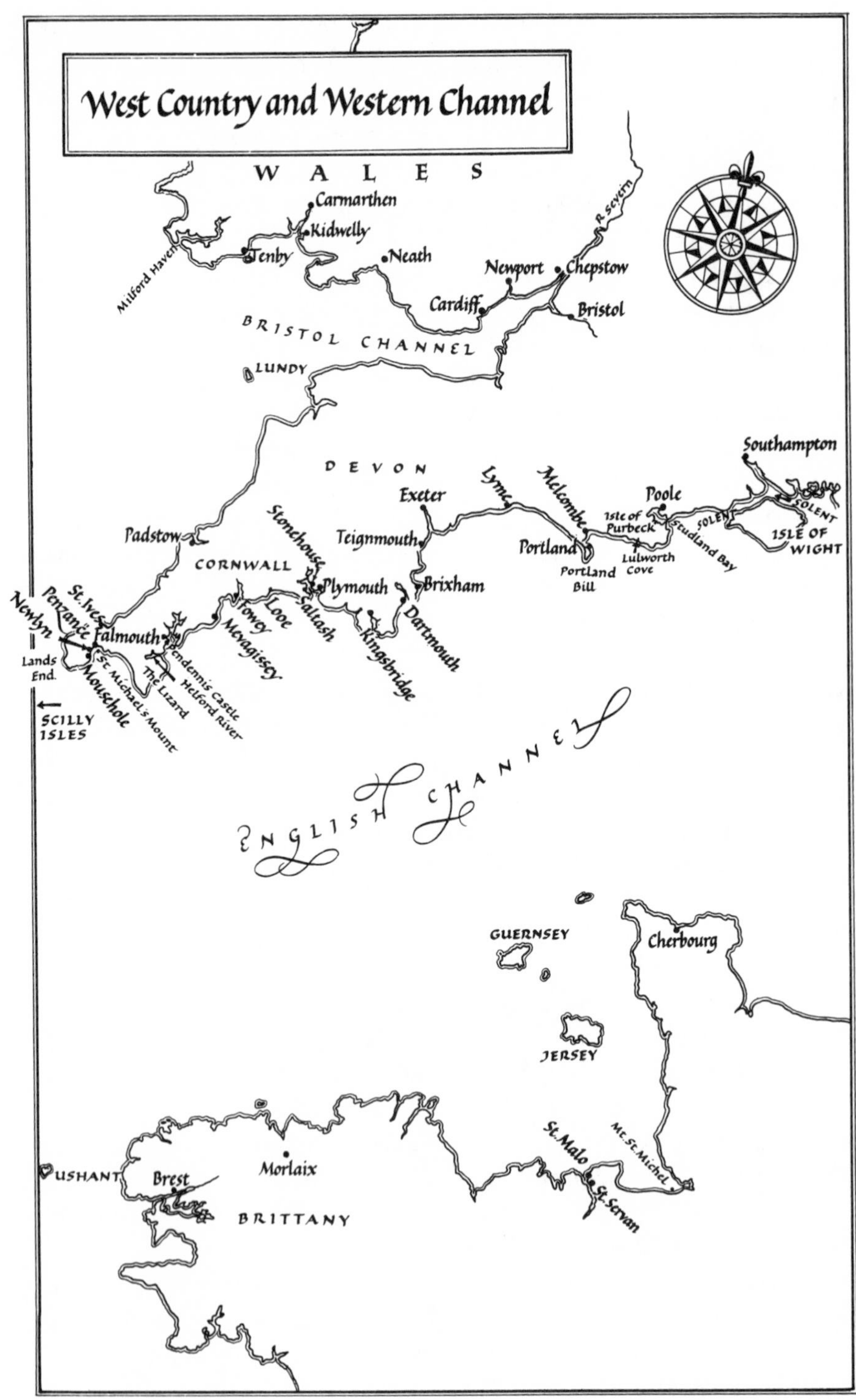

West Country and Western Channel
WALES
Carmarthen
Kidwelly
Milford Haven
Tenby
Neath
Newport
Chepstow
R. Severn
Cardiff
Bristol
BRISTOL CHANNEL
LUNDY
DEVON
Southampton
Exeter
Lyme
Melcombe
Poole
Isle of Purbeck
SOLENT
ISLE OF WIGHT
Studland Bay
Lulworth Cove
Portland
Portland Bill
Teignmouth
Stonehouse
Padstow
CORNWALL
Plymouth
Brixham
St. Ives
Penzance
Newlyn
Falmouth
Fowey
Looe
Saltash
Dartmouth
Kingsbridge
Mevagissey
Lands End
St. Michael's Mount
Mousehole
The Lizard
Pendennis Castle
Helford River
SCILLY ISLES
ENGLISH CHANNEL
GUERNSEY
Cherbourg
JERSEY
St. Malo
Mt. St. Michel
St. Servan
USHANT
Brest
Morlaix
BRITTANY

> To show the Chancellor how well protected the wrongdoers on the sea-coasts of Devonshire were: when they had taken any vessel or goods or merchandise of the king's friends, they sent at once for the deputy of the admiral of England and induced him to empanel a jury of 24 or 12 men who were for the most part the relatives and friends of the same wrongdoers and the victualers and owners. They gave their verdict that vessels, goods and merchandise taken from the king's friends belonged to the king's enemies, and then the wrongdoers caused the deputy to be in league with them, and to enrol and record the verdict so given, by giving him half the goods and merchandise for his trouble.[33]

The notorious pirate barge the *Mackerel* of Fowey belonged to Henry VI's Admiral of England the Duke of Exeter.[34]

As Admiral, Exeter was connected with piracy officially as well as unofficially. An admiral's disciplinary authority had always implied judicial powers, though they are not explicitly mentioned in a commission until 1360.[35] Besides military discipline, admirals had come to exercise a civil jurisdiction in disputes involving prizes,[36] shipping and maritime affairs, especially where the suit involved foreigners. In these matters the Admiralty Courts (the Admirals' courts, in other words), acting by civil or Roman law, were able to take over cases which had hitherto been dealt with, very inadequately, by the common law courts. Until the sixteenth century they had no criminal jurisdiction, and piracy cases came before them, if at all, only in the form of civil suits for damages.[37] Nevertheless commercial litigation was frequent, and for the court very profitable. The income the admirals drew from their courts, together with their share of prizes, was certainly one of the main reasons for the creation early in the fifteenth century of the title of Admiral of England, Ireland and Aquitaine. This divided the practical military and naval duty from what had become an extremely lucrative office, and attached the office to a person of suitable rank; in the first case the Earl of Dorset, Henry V's uncle, in 1408,[38] followed in 1426 by the Duke of Bedford, Henry VI's uncle and guardian. Bedford was himself the victor of the battle of Harfleur, and Admirals did not cease to command at sea, but from this date they tended to be rather too exalted to attend to administrative detail. They had, however, a direct financial interest in the profits of piracy and in the litigation which flowed from disorder at sea. It was not the best way to encourage the suppression of piracy, even if Henry VI's government had had the will and means to do so.

Piracy embroiled England in quarrels with the very foreign powers whose alliance she badly needed against France. The list of enemies needlessly created by English pirates included Brittany, Aragon, Castile and Denmark.[39] There were especially severe diplomatic consequences from Robert Winnington's capture of the Hansa salt convoy returning from the Bay of Bourgneuf in 1449. He used the old excuse of their failing to ackowledge England's 'sovereignty' of the Narrow Seas: 'I came aboard the admiral and bade them strike in the name of the King of England, and they bade me shit in the name of the King of England'. By this time the loose alliance of German-speaking seaport cities known as the Hansa had risen to dominate the Baltic grain and fish trades, together with many of the carrying trades of Western Europe, including some Bordeaux wine, and much of the salt exported from the Bay of Bourgneuf near La Rochelle.[40] They were powerful and dangerous rivals, not to be lightly offended even by kings who were much stronger at sea than Henry VI. The incident led to the immediate seizure of all English property in the Hansa towns, and helped to provoke a damaging war.[41] As the military situation in France rapidly worsened, the debilitated English merchant fleet was called upon for efforts which it could not sustain. In the year of final disaster, 1453, when the French overran Gascony, the Gironde was blockaded by a strong force of ships from La Rochelle, Brittany and Castile.[42]

Repeated disasters made naval affairs an even more intensely political issue than they had been in the previous century.[43] The Duke of Suffolk was impeached (and later murdered) in 1450 because, among other reasons, he was held responsible for 'the defence of this your realm, and the safe keeping of the sea, not had nor kept, to over great impoverishing and hurt of this your realm'.[44] This is the context of the parliamentary resolutions of 1382[45] and 1463,[46] which have been called the first 'Navigation Acts', attempting (without much success) to reserve English trade to English ships. Under Henry VI men could not help contrasting the great fleet his father had built up and the security his victories had brought them, with their own miserable condition exposed to continual attack.[47] (In 1450 Sir Henry Stradling was even captured by a Breton pirate out of a ferry-boat across the Severn.)[48] The contrast was both painful and thought-provoking, and for the first time in England it provoked some public discussion of naval strategy.

In this context Englishmen spoke most often of the 'safeguard' or 'safe keeping' of the sea, by which they meant the protection of the country and its seaborne trade from attack; 'the safety of intercourse of merchandises to great enriching of this land, and also for the defence of the enemies'.[49] They had no thought that it would be possible to deny the sea itself to the enemy, only that English ships and coasts should be defended against the inevitable attacks. Preparedness was the key to defence, and the best minds of the age turned to organization as the most accessible aspect of strategy. Much could be achieved if only a fleet could be got to sea before the enemy's; how it was to be achieved was not much studied. In 1435 Sir John Fastolf urged the protection of the wool trade to Flanders:

> that the sea may be kept mightily, as well for the king's worship and the realm's, as for the salvation of the merchandise and of the navy of England and of Normandy . . . and that the said navy make sharp war and keep the course of merchandise as much as they can or may from Sluys.[50]

The same approach appears in the Commons scheme of 1442:

> the least purveyance that can be made for the worship of the King our Sovereign Lord, and welfare and defence of this realm of England, is for to have upon the sea continually, for the seasons of the year from Candlemas to Martinmas, eight ships . . .'[51]

'Though we have not alway war upon the sea,', wrote Sir John Fortescue in the 1470s,

> yet it shall be necessary that the king have alway some fleet upon the sea, for the repressing of rovers, saving of our merchants, our fishers, and the dwellers upon our coasts; and that the king keep alway some great and mighty vessels, for the breaking of an army when any shall be made again him upon the sea; for than it shall be too late to do make [*sic*] such vessels.[52]

The emphasis throughout was on the readiness of the force rather than its exact employment. In the same vein Henry VI in 1452 proposed,

> to occupy the sea in such wise as we shall more have the rule and the governance therof, and withstand the malicious purpose of all our adversaries and enemies.[53]

But 'occupying', like 'keeping' the sea, was a generality which did not imply exclusive control, and was not linked to any particular strategy to carry it into effect. 'It is thought here', wrote the Governor of Calais in 1483, 'that the king should have a navy upon the sea to show himself as a king, to rule and keep his streams betwixt this and Dover'.[54] A fleet was a symbol of majesty, but contemporaries were not so clear how to make it an instrument of practical control, even in the very near waters they were thinking of.

One thing they did appreciate was the importance of concentration.

Though in practice English ships, especially English galleys, were often distributed in small units 'for the welfare, surety and safeguard of the coasts thereabouts',[55] reflecting poor communications and the short range of oared vessels, the necessity of concentration in the face of major threats had always been understood. English fleets had been ordered to concentrate against threatened invasion from France for centuries.[56] In 1454 the Duke of York urged Parliament,

> that substantial provision be made in all haste possible for the keeping of the sea, to the intent that all your navy [*navire*] be ready togethers, and of power, for to assemble in such place as is most convenable for the assembling of them, for to break the puissance of the navy of the said adversary, before their assembling.[57]

Here again, however, there was no indication what to do once the fleets were assembled; the practical application of theory still did not go beyond such fourteenth-century platitudes as 'bridling the king's enemies',[58] or the generous imprecision of orders to 'hasten to sea to find, chase, take and destroy the said galleys in whatever way may seem best, with God's help'.[59]

The best-thought-out English naval strategy was advanced by the anonymous author of the *Libel of English Policy*, a political poem of the late 1430s, which advocated making war against Burgundy by blockading the Straits of Dover, with the double aim of safeguarding communications with Calais (then under Burgundian attack) and stopping the commerce of the cities of Flanders which were both the most important and the most reluctant supporters of the Burgundian war-effort:

> Cherish merchandise, keep the Admiralty,
> That we be masters of the Narrow Sea.[60]

The Narrow Sea was the limit of the writer's ambition, but he had an intelligent grasp of the potential of sea power on a small scale.[61] An economic blockade such as he proposed had been successfully applied in 1338, and there is no reason why it should not have worked again.[62] Unfortunately his proposal was directly opposed to the policy of Henry VI's government, and it called for naval resources which probably could not have been found.

TWELVE

Change and Decay

1456–1509

Having lost all her overseas possessions except Calais and parts of Ireland, with the king insane and the government paralysed, England was now on the verge of civil war. As always, the side with access to the sea enjoyed access to foreign help and denied it to their enemies. In this case the sea was especially important because of the pivotal role played by the English garrison and squadron of Calais. The Earl of Warwick became Captain of Calais in 1456, and soon showed himself a skilful and unscrupulous exponent of sea power, building his squadron on the revenue of the Wool Staple and the plunder of unrestrained piracy. In May 1458 he took six prizes out of a Castilian fleet. They at least were enemies, which the Hansa and Genoese, whom he plundered soon afterwards, were not. All this was extremely popular in England, where people cared nothing for legality or diplomatic consequences, and saw only an English commander whose bold deeds did something to restore battered national self-esteem: the 'Earl of Warwick, having a strong and a mighty navy, kept the straight sea'. The Lancastrian government presented a miserable contrast. In August 1457 there was an outcry when a French squadron under Pierre de Brézé sacked Sandwich and departed unscathed. Warwick 'had what the government should have had, a fleet, and did what the government should have done, kept the sea. Their failure in this aspect of good government was thus one of the direct reasons for their downfall'.[1]

The crisis came in 1460. In May Warwick's squadron met the Lancastrian fleet under the Duke of Exeter at sea in the Channel, and Exeter ran away. The next month Warwick raided Sandwich, where the royal fleet lay, and captured the entire force. The royal commanders, Lord Rivers and Sir Anthony Woodville, were taken in their beds. The Kentish ports, following their tradition, had long been disaffected, and Warwick had little difficulty occupying Sandwich. With that as his base he led the campaign which culminated in the battle of Northampton the following year, when Warwick the naval kingmaker installed Edward IV on the throne.[2]

He remained at Calais as the naval commander and strong man of the new regime. Besides operating directly against the Lancastrians, he deterred the French from intervening on their side. After a French squadron took Mont Orgeuil castle in Jersey in 1461, he raided Le Conquet and the Ile de Ré in the next year. This had the intended effect, and Louis XI agreed a truce until 1468. By then Warwick and Edward IV were drifting apart. An expensive and futile expedition was sent to assist Brittany against France, but failed to sail until after they had made peace. Warwick meanwhile was embroiled in war against the Hansa, and was at sea again early in 1469. In July he landed again at Sandwich to 'petition' the king. Now openly acting on the Lancastrian side, he briefly captured Edward IV but soon had to flee to his ships. Refused entry to Calais, he cruised the Channel for some time, taking a Flemish convoy in the Straits, and was pursued by Edward IV's admiral Lord Howard into Honfleur (to the embarrassment of Louis XI). There he was blockaded by English and Burgundian ships, until a gale in September 1470 scattered Edward IV's fleet and permitted Warwick and Queen Margaret to invade England again. In spite of an intelligent naval defence and the large fleet provided by his Burgundian allies, Edward IV found, as other English kings had done, that in the conditions of the day naval patrols could provide no absolute security. A month later Henry VI was restored to power, the second king installed by Warwick and his ships.[3]

Edward IV took refuge in Flanders, where he had no difficulty in collecting support from the enraged victims of Warwick's piracy, which had achieved the remarkable feat of uniting in a common purpose Bretons, Hansards, French and Burgundians. In March 1471 Edward returned aboard a fleet of Burgundian and Hansard ships, and on 14 April Warwick was killed at the battle of Barnet. Though the ships of the Cinque Ports made an attack on London in May (one of the earliest examples of a bombardment by naval guns), all the Lancastrian forces were defeated or dispersed by the summer, and Warwick's fleet had surrendered.[4] Back on his throne, Edward IV showed a shrewd appreciation of the importance of ships, which had both gained and lost him his kingdom. He had already built, or encouraged the building of, the first English royal carvel the *Edward*, 'sumptuously made and plen[tifu]lly furnished' by John Spens of Dunwich in 1464, though she actually belonged at least in part to the king's admiral Lord Howard.[5] He also began to build up a cadre of trusted masters as Henry V had done.[6] William Featherstone, for example, transferred from the service of the Earl of Warwick. In 1473–4 he was master of the *Caricon* and senior officer of a squadron of three ships blockading the Lancastrian garrison of St Michael's Mount. He was not only the operational commander but the administrator and paymaster of his force.[7] In 1480, as master of the *Falcon*, he was trusted to command a convoy of wool ships from Boston to Calais, and to convey the king's sister the Duchess of Burgundy.[8] Nevertheless Edward kept only a few of Warwick's old fleet, and worked for peace rather than victory at sea. Negotiations were opened to end the war with the Hansa which Winnington and Warwick had provoked, and in 1474 a treaty was signed, though the price of peace was £25,000 in compensation to the victims of English piracy and the effective abandonment of English trade to the Baltic.[9] Burgundy also became an ally. All this opened the way for the 1475 expedition to France, which crossed with no naval interruption, thanks to diplomatic as well as naval preparations.[10] In 1481 an expedition against Scotland was supported by two fleets: Lord Howard on the east coast and Sir Thomas Fulford on the west. The next year smaller forces supported the Duke of Gloucester's campaign in Scotland. None of these had any outstanding success, beyond their basic function of keeping the English army supplied, and in 1482 Scots ships were active in the Irish Sea and the Channel.[11] When Richard III succeeded his brother in 1483 he continued the same policy, keeping small squadrons patrolling against Brittany, France and Scotland, but avoiding major naval commitments. In 1484, when another expedition went north, his ships won an action against Scots ships in the North Sea.[12]

The modest and cautious naval policies of Edward IV and Richard III were certainly realistic and matched to England's weakness, but they carried risks. Both of them suffered considerably from their inability to suppress piracy: in December 1474 Edward IV had to pay 11,000 crowns to shipowners of the Spanish Basque ports;[13] by 1476, when the Breton alliance was crucial to his foreign policy, the outstanding claims of Breton merchants against England amounted to at least 50,000 crowns;[14] and Richard III had to meet further claims.[15] In medieval conditions no fleet, however large, could altogether command the sea, but with the rapidly improving rig and hull design of late fifteenth-century ships, patrol and blockade were becoming more effective. Uneasy upon their thrones, with rivals in exile abroad, these kings understood the importance of keeping foreign powers friendly, and of watching and intercepting seaborne invasions, but did not have enough ships to do so effectively. Early in 1485 Richard III began urgently to build up his fleet, but he was too late.[16] On 1 August Henry Tudor, Earl of Richmond, sailed from Harfleur with a small force, meeting no opposition on his passage to Milford Haven. Three weeks later Richard III was dead on Bosworth Field, and Henry VII was king of England.

The new monarch was just as cautious in foreign policy as his predecessors, and less aware of the uses of the sea. Early in his reign he built the large carracks *Regent* and *Sovereign*, possibly in imitation of the Breton flagship the *Colombe* which had impressed him when he was in exile there;[17] but though he maintained, and occasionally used, a handful of large ships, English naval activity remained at a low ebb, and no ships interfered with the invasion of England from Ireland by the pretender Lambert Simnel in 1487. Henry sent ships to help rebels against James III of Scots in 1489, but they were heavily defeated by the Scottish commander Sir Andrew Wood.[18] Henry's greatest concern was the expanding power of France, and in particular the marriage of Charles VIII with Duchess Anne of Brittany in December 1491, which gave France access to ports to windward of the south coast of England. It was this which almost certainly inspired the revival of interest in Portsmouth as a naval base.[19] Endeavouring to counter the menace of French expansion, Henry VII repeated in 1492 Edward IV's strategy of 1475, with the identical result: an army of 14,000 or more was carried to France to fight alongside continental allies, but when they failed to take the field, the king allowed himself to be bought off with an expensive indemnity. There was no fighting at sea, and the majority of the transports had to be chartered in Holland and Zealand for want of English ships.[20] Soon afterwards the French threat was effectively diverted by Charles VIII's invasion of Italy in 1494, where the French remained deeply engaged for most of the following sixty-five years. Henry's biggest naval operation was possibly the 1497 expedition to Scotland, retaliation for James IV's raid into Northumberland the previous winter, but though the ships certainly reached the Forth very little is known about the campaign.[21] Throughout his reign Henry VII maintained both his navy and his naval activity at a low ebb. Insofar as he was aware of the importance of the sea, his vision extended no further than that of any medieval English king – up the coast to Scotland, and across the Narrow Seas to France and Flanders, and even there he never interfered with the pretenders Lambert Simnel and Perkin Warbeck in their movements between Flanders, Ireland, Scotland and England.[22] Meanwhile shipbuilding for the crown in England almost ceased. Henry V's *Grace Dieu* was the last ship built for an English king for nearly half a century. Only six ships of all sorts are known to have been built for the crown in the eighty-seven years from the accession of Henry VI in 1422 to the death of Henry VII in 1509.[23]

Throughout the fifteenth century the routine naval activities continued on a diminished scale. Convoy was still the automatic response to any threat against shipping. It was adopted by Henry V against the Franco-Genoese fleet in 1416 and 1417,[24] and it was used for the Bordeaux trade as long as Gascony remained in English hands and indeed long after.[25] Edward IV, who was twice helped to the throne with the support of the Londoners, was particularly attentive to their trade, and provided regular convoys.[26] In 1475, for example, the 'carrack called the king's ship' with 200 men, and the *Burnet* with 50, escorted a convoy from London to Calais. Two 'feeder' convoys joined them on passage; one from Sandwich under escort of the *Mary Bodrugan*, and another from Ipswich escorted by the *Good Grace* of Woodbridge.[27] The Company of Merchant Venturers ran convoys to Zealand and the Baltic.[28] In 1481 a fishery protection squadron was created (possibly following Burgundian practice)[29] to guard the East Anglian fishermen against Scottish raids,[30] while Richard III instituted convoys for the Iceland trade, which was carried on in the teeth of the disapproval of the king of Denmark and the attacks of Hamburg privateers.[31] It is at this period that the English language developed its first words relating to convoy: to 'waft' and a 'wafter'. The 1484 Iceland fleet was informed that William Combershall, captain of the *Elizabeth*, was appointed 'your conveyer and wafter to such place or places as he shall think convenient', and that they were, 'to be ordered and guided by him and in no wise to depart from him unto such time as the whole fleet of you shall come together and meet with other of our army now being upon the sea'.[32]

The fact that the crown became involved in organizing convoys did not mean that it was either willing or able to pay for them. It had always been normal for convoy escorts to be directly or indirectly paid for by the shipowners who benefited from them. In 1373 a special duty was levied on imported wine to pay for the powerful convoys organized on the Bordeaux route after the disaster of La Rochelle,[33] and convoy commanders were sometimes given explicit powers to compel shipowners to pay for their services.[34] More often private agreements sufficed, like that which Lord Howard made in 1469 with shipowners of Dunwich, Cromer, Sizewell, Eston, Thorpe, Aldeburgh and Cley-next-the-Sea, undertaking to escort their shipping with his new carvel the *Edward*.[35] Convoys were first provided at the crown's expense in 1473, when Edward IV provided escorts for the wool ships to Calais as a means of repaying his debts to the merchants of the Staple.[36] Richard III in 1484 was the first English king to provide free convoy escorts, when he refunded the Mercers' Company £349 15s which they had paid to the king's ships which had taken a convoy to Flanders,[37] and Henry VII did the same occasionally.[38]

Under Edward IV and Henry VII the raising and organizing of particular fleets and squadrons was usually entrusted to particular officers by indenture,[39] or to the nominees of Parliament in the case of the parliamentary fleets keeping the seas by licence. These officers were given most or all the powers of an admiral over their fleets, but styled 'Captains' or 'Lieutenants'. Thus Thomas Wentworth was appointed in December 1483 to be 'principal leader and Captain of our . . . fleet and army set unto the sea to recounter the fleet of our enemies of Brittany'.[40] Edward IV's admiral Lord Howard not only contracted to serve the king, but himself issued indentures to subordinates who recruited for his ships.[41] In 1481 he

> indented with the King my Sovereign Lord to do him service upon the sea, and to be his lieutenant and captain in the same voyage, with 3,000 men, landmen and mariners, well and sufficiently arrayed for the war, for the term of sixteen weeks, toward the parts of Scotland, or such places as it shall please his Highness to command me.[42]

Howard then made similar agreements with men like Lord Cobham, who undertook to serve with his ships the *George Cobham* and the *Mary* of Lynn, with a retinue of 105 mariners and 115 soldiers. Similarly, Sir Harry Wentworth undertook to bring 160 seamen and 190 soldiers to serve in the king's ship *Anthony*, 'if she may be ready, and else in such ships as it shall please the King or the said Lord Howard to appoint him'.[43]

William Soper had no active successor as Clerk of the King's Ships, for there were no king's ships left when he retired in 1442, and no clerk dealt with raising fleets of merchantmen. His nominal successor Richard Clevedon, a courtier and shipowner, had little to do but sell off old stores,[44] and for Peter Bowman (appointed 1464) the post was a sinecure.[45] Under Edward IV the Exchequer and the Privy Seal which controlled it were pushed aside again by the Chamber and the Signet, through which most military and naval expenditure passed,[46] and an effective Clerk of Ships reappeared on the outbreak of the Scottish war in 1480. Thomas Rogers, a former purser and master of king's ships, was the first seaman ever to hold the office, and his appointment can be held to mark the re-establishment of a standing force of king's ships.[47] Rogers exercised wide responsibilities, being trusted, for example, with a 'blank cheque' to rebuild the *Mary Ashe* in 1483.[48] By this date he, unlike his predecessors, was in sole charge of the repair and maintenance of the king's ships, though he still shared responsibility for paying them with their masters. With powers to take up shipping, sell prizes and appoint masters and pursers; with money allowed him for 'all things necessary for the safeguard and sure keeping our said ships, and for wages and victual of mariners attending upon the same', he came nearer to being an embryonic unified naval department than any of his predecessors since Wrotham.[49]

Under Henry VII the office, like the navy itself, was nominally continued but practically neglected. Rogers's successor Thomas Combershall, also an old master, was an insubstantial figure, not responsible for shipbuilding or paying ships.[50] He had no budget, but had to apply for payment of every petty expense.[51] He was succeeded by Robert Brigandine, a senior royal clerk who undoubtedly discharged the duties by deputy and regarded the job as no more than an addition to his salary, and who did not get closely involved in the 1497 expedition to Scotland.[52] In this period administration, like command, was largely contracted out. As late as 1486 the Earl of Oxford acted as paymaster of his own fleet, and admirals sometimes victualled their squadrons as private contractors.[53] Lord Howard commanded the fleet against Scotland in 1481, but he also victualled the squadron of twenty-three ships with 1,200 men for sixteen weeks at 12½d a man a week.[54] (Under Henry VII the figure was 12d, rising to 14d near the end of the reign.[55]) More often it seems that victualling was entrusted to contractors with suitable experience; the 1484 expedition was victualled by Richard Forthey, who as Marshal of the Hall had to feed the royal household, and the Faversham merchant John Eltherbek.[56]

Edward IV, the 'merchant king', used the sea for profitable trade more than than war. His Admiral Lord Howard was a substantial shipowner himself, as were many of his contemporaries.[57] In Devon the Courtenays, Earls of Devon, were involved in many of the local trades, including the pilgrim traffic and piracy.[58] Henry VII carried this policy farther than any of his predecessors, 'bareboat' chartering his biggest ships to merchants trading into the Mediterranean who manned and fitted the ships themselves, and received for their payment commercial favours in addition to the use of the ships.[59] In the same period James IV of Scots was trading with his ships.[60] The logic of doing so was obvious; maintaining wooden ships has always been a costly business (Henry VII's big ships cost £8 a month simply in wages to shipkeepers), and they were likely to be better maintained if they were also earning their living (though the *Sovereign* was handed back in poor condition in 1507 after a trading voyage to the Mediterranean).[61] Moreover the business could be highly profitable; it has been calculated that Henry could earn the building cost of a big carrack in three or four voyages.[62]

The hidden cost of chartering out the king's ships was the dispersal once more of the 'king's mariners', just at the time when the growing size of the ships and the complexity of their internal organization was making experience more valuable than ever. Until this time the title of 'captain' was confined to admirals and squadron commanders of equivalent rank; in other words it was used in the same sense at sea as on land. The title 'captain' first came into use at sea in its modern sense in the late fifteenth century. It was not, as is usually stated, the style of the army officer who took command of the ship in wartime, outranking the master;[63] rather it was a new style for the master himself, reflecting the fact that, with wartime companies of seven hundred or more,[64] the big carracks of Henry VII were approaching the size of force proper for a captain's command. The first master to be given the title officially was possibly William Combershall, commanding the *Elizabeth* in 1484,[65] while in 1489 the *Sovereign* had both a captain and a master.[66]

The pursers of the king's ships in the fifteenth century, the successors of the earlier ship's clerks, often accounted independently for considerable sums spent victualling and paying their men,[67] and sometimes received press warrants;[68] though impressment seems not to have been often needed for the smaller fleets of the period, and indentured retinues, originally a method of recruiting soldiers alone, were sometimes composed of a mixture of soldiers and seamen.[69] At the same period large merchant ships in the Bordeaux trade had pursers, who kept accounts, paid the men, signed contracts together with the master or supercargo, and sometimes acted as ship's husband.[70] By the late fifteenth century big ships had a steward as well as the purser.[71] Quartermasters appear in the 1470s, evidently officers of some trust who might handle considerable sums of money.[72] The *Sovereign* in 1496 had nineteen officers (for 146 men and two boys), including (in descending order of pay) master, purser, boatswain, gunner, quartermasters, steward and cook; and both boatswain and quartermasters had mates.[73] These last, plus the coxswain, are almost the first identifiable as what we would call petty officers, though the Guernsey seaman Periot Lorielx was described as 'steersman of the king's ship' in 1405.[74]

By the late fifteenth century ships on war service were likely to have one or two master gunners. In the 1470s, to judge from Lord Howard's accounts, English gunners like Harry Thompson and Nicholas Armourer were serving alongside foreign experts like Jan van Delft and Hans van Brussel,[75] and in the 1490s the *Sovereign* had a master gunner and forty ordinary gunners out of a wartime complement of at least 700.[76]

The fifteenth century was perhaps the height of heraldic activity, when indentured retinues were often clothed in the colours of their leader's arms, and seamen also were sometimes provided with uniforms. Dinham's squadron in the Straits of Dover in 1475 had red and white jackets, and in Henry VII's ships the men were issued with uniform jackets.[77] In the Burgundian fleet of 1477 the officers wore tabards bearing the arms of the respective towns which had fitted out their ships, and uniforms appear about the same time in French ships.[78]

Trumpeters were carried aboard ship from at latest the fourteenth century, to convey signals and attest the dignity of great men.[79] In the 1470s Lord Howard had five trumpeters and seven drummers.[80] This was part of the state of a great and wealthy man, who went to sea with luxuries including feather beds, tapestry, table linen, a small library, and 'a pissing basin of silver'.[81] Common seamen certainly did not live in this style, but we know only a little of their daily lives. They must have had hot food, since many of the foodstuffs taken to sea were inedible without cooking, and the fact is confirmed by references to firewood among ship's stores, and to the brick fire-hearths in some, probably most ships.[82] A curious provision of the Laws of Oléron states that in Breton ships the men were to have one hot meal a day with wine, but in Norman ships, two meals with water.[83]

The Iceland convoys of the 1480s were probably the first occasion English warships had undertaken regular operations across the open ocean. Most medieval navigation was essentially coastal pilotage; highly skilled, but largely helpless if long out of sight of land.[84] Chaucer himself was familiar with the use of the astrolabe, by which latitude can be determined, but his Dartmouth shipman (probably modelled on the elder John Hawley) is presented as a coastal pilot rather than a deep-sea navigator:

> But of his craft to reckon well his tides,
> His streams, and his dangers him besides,
> His harbouring [herberwe], and his moon, his lodemenage,
> There was none such from Hull to Carthage.
> Hardy he was and wise to undertake;
> With many a tempest had his beard been shake.
> He knew all the havens, as they were,
> From Gotland to the Cape of Finisterre,
> And every creek in Brittany and in Spain.[85]

He would know the creeks especially well because that was where pirates like him lay in wait for their victims. Such pilots could make short passages out of sight of land, from one good landfall to another, steering by the sun or (preferably) a star, but they had no method of plotting a position.[86] To steer clear of the dangers of the land was only seamanlike prudence, and in fair weather ships navigated by 'caping' from one seamark to another: for example from the lighthouse of Corduan at the mouth of the Gironde to the headland of Penmarc'h outside Brest, or from Ushant to the Isle of Wight, where a lighthouse built in 1314 still stands on St Catherine's Point.[87] These were passages of no more than thirty-six hours with a fair wind, and could be made safely in clear weather.[88] The Castilian galleys of Chaucer's day already used charts, took soundings and tried to keep their reckoning at sea (though it is fair to add that they referred to dead reckoning as navigation *de fantasía*).[89] Only in Henry V's reign did even the biggest English ships begin to acquire such equipment.[90] Cruising in the open sea became progressively more feasible as rig and navigation improved in the fifteenth century. The *Libel of English Policy* refers to ships in the rapidly-developing Iceland trade as having adopted the magnetic compass within the past twelve years, or sometime in the 1420s, but the Hansa and other northern seafarers had been using it for many years before that date.[91] There is no evidence that any English seamen knew how to observe their latitude even in the late fifteenth century, and all their navigation out of sight of land had to depend on the uncertainties of dead reckoning, but their knowledge (and with it the length of the sailing season) was gradually improving.[92]

The armament of English ships in Henry V's time remained essentially the same as it had been throughout the Middle Ages. All fighting was hand-to-hand, using standard infantry weapons, with the addition of spears or lances, with 'gads' (iron darts) and heavy stones for throwing down from the topcastle.[93] Soft soap to make the enemy's decks slippery was a real threat to men-at-arms in armour so heavy that they could not easily get up if they fell over. Caltraps might also be tossed on to the enemy's decks, and quick-lime thrown from the windward position to blind the defenders at the moment of assault.[94] Crossbows were much used, including the springald, a heavy crossbow on a fixed mounting.[95] The Southampton galley of 1294 carried 60 crossbows each with 100 bolts, plus 120 lances, 100 halberds and 240 javelins, for a company of 120 men.[96] When the longbow was adopted by the army, it was naturally used at sea as well.

Guns fitted into the same pattern. The late Middle Ages knew the use of heavy guns, bombards, for siege warfare, and there are examples both of siege engines and bombards being fired at ships from fortresses,[97] but the great majority of guns in use ashore, and all those at sea, were light weapons firing a shot of no more than a pound or two. They were anti-personnel weapons, like the bow, and posed no threat to the structure of a ship. As early as 1338 the king's ship *All Hallows Cog* was equipped with 'a certain iron instrument for firing quarrels and lead pellets with powder, for the defence of the ship', but from its cost it must have been very small, and the few surviving guns of this period are barely a foot long.[98] Guns were being manufactured in the Tower of London no later than 1345, and were mounted on the defences of several castles (including Calais) by 1370.[99] The fleet of Lübeck at the battle of the Sound in 1362 carried a total of six guns, one of which fired the shot which killed Prince Christopher of Denmark.[100] By the reigns of Henry V and Henry VI guns were a common part of a big ship's armament, but still not a major part.[101] Even in Henry VII's reign, when big ships like the *Regent* and *Sovereign* mounted hundreds of 'serpentines' and other small guns in their upperworks, the longbow remained the dominant weapon.[102] When Sir Robert Clifford took over as Master of the Ordnance in 1496, his total stock was only 63 guns of all sorts and 406 barrels of powder, compared with 9,253 bows and 27,804 sheaves of arrows.[103] Between 1481 and about 1510 the town of Dartmouth built three forts commanding the harbour mouth which were possibly the first purpose-built coastal artillery fortifications in England, but it is clear from the design of the embrasures that they mounted only small breech-loaders.[104] Such guns would have been effective against galleys with their exposed rowing benches (which was no doubt the threat the Dartmouth men had principally in mind), but they were soon to be outclassed. Drawings from the 1480s and 1490s show carracks with small bombards mounted in the waist,[105] while in the 1490s Portuguese ships were already mounting heavy guns,[106] and the seal of Maximilian of Burgundy in 1493 shows a ship with a complete gundeck and six small guns a side.[107] Moreover in the last years of Henry VII there was a cautious but noteworthy increase in the size of the guns aboard his biggest ships.[108]

Meanwhile the real gunnery revolution at sea had occurred elsewhere. The Burgundian galleys built at Antwerp between 1446 and 1449 were armed with guns of four-inch calibre.[109] By the 1470s the Mediterranean galley fleets, beginning with the Venetians, were mounting a single large gun on a fixed mounting right forward in the eyes of the vessel.[110] These were heavy guns, capable of sinking ships, at least half a century before sailing ships mounted anything comparable. They brought about a revolution in Mediterranean naval warfare, but for the moment it did not affect the English.

THIRTEEN

Departed Dreams

Operations 1509–1523

When Henry VII died in 1509, England had enjoyed more peace and stability in twenty years than it had known for a century. Henry had fought off his dynastic rivals and left the kingdom in undisputed succession to his son. He left it peaceable, more or less united, with the royal finances in good order. These were considerable achievements to set against the anarchy of the Wars of the Roses, but they came nowhere near recovering England's lost glories. Gone was the great military power of western Europe, the England of Edward III and Henry V, which had bestrode its narrow world like a colossus. The new king, Henry VIII, was determined to revive those days. Young, handsome, statuesque, with a good mind and a good education, he seemed to embody in everyone's eyes (especially his own) all the virtues of the perfect Renaissance prince. Honour, reputation – all that defined and ennobled a king – were to be won on the field of battle. Handsome as the young monarch looked in his gilt armour at the tilting ground, it was not enough. He longed to take the centre of the only European stage which mattered, to lead his army to victory and reclaim the inheritance of Henry V. Public opinion greatly approved, his father had left him a good deal of money, and there was nothing to stop him indulging his ambition.[1]

The international situation in the early sixteenth century gave him easy opportunity to try, but much less chance to succeed than Henry V had had a century before. Western Europe was already dominated by the rivalry of two great powers, France and the Holy Roman Empire (neither Holy nor Roman, to echo Voltaire's jibe, but still very much an empire, ruling most of Germany, much of the Low Countries and Italy). Geography as well as history gave Henry no real choice of enemy; he had to fight France, to make good his claims on the French throne and because there was no other enemy English forces could hope to reach. This in turn dictated his ally, the Emperor, France's enemy and ruler of the Low Countries to which England was still economically tied. The two great powers were locked in the struggle for control of Italy which had begin in 1494 and was to go on intermittently until 1559. There was always scope for a second front in the north, and the Emperor was unlikely to refuse an ally. In these circumstances Henry VIII was easily persuaded in November 1511 to join the 'Holy League', whose nominal leader was Pope Julius II. Henry's price was a golden rose, some barrels of wine and one hundred Parmesan cheeses; for these he undertook an unlimited expenditure of English blood and treasure. His allies, his father-in-law King Ferdinand II of Aragon, the Emperor Maximilian, Venice and the Pope, were happy to give the young prince some easy glory and military experience, at his expense and to their profit.[2]

In 1512, the first year of the war, the main English army under the Marquis of Dorset was transported to northern Spain to campaign with King Ferdinand. Henry thought they were going to reconquer Gascony; in fact they spent an idle and drunken summer on the French frontier guarding Ferdinand's flank while he conquered Navarre, and returned in October sickly and mutinous.[3] But there was never any question of where Henry VIII was to gain his personal laurels. He was to invade northern France at the head of his army, and triumph as his ancestors had done. Henry's new minister Thomas Wolsey organized the invasion force of 25,000 men at the head of which the king marched out of Calais in June 1513. His allies left him to do the fighting, but the army was large enough to win him at least a show of glory. A French attempt to relieve the besieged fortress of Thérouanne was deflected in a cavalry skirmish known as the Battle of the Spurs, instantly magnified to a victory equal to Agincourt. Thérouanne, and later the more important city of Tournai, were taken, and in the autumn Henry went home with the satisfaction of a successful campaign and a small addition to the fragmentary remains of the English empire. Since by then all his allies had withdrawn or were withdrawing from the war, it was all that could be achieved.[4]

Historians have tended to credit Henry VIII with an instinctive appreciation of the importance of sea power and a precocious determination to build up a great navy. There is very little evidence that he had any such ideas when he came to the throne, or any realization of the part Henry V's ships had played in making Agincourt possible. In order to operate overseas it was practically necessary to increase the small fleet he had inherited, and Henry bought a number of big ships, mainly from abroad.[5] He also built two large ships, the *Peter Pomegranate* and the *Mary Rose*. Beyond this he might not have gone without the stimulus of an unexpected rival.

There were three sources of naval power in the British Isles in the early sixteenth century, and to set Henry VIII's ships in context we need to look beyond the usual anglocentric naval history. In Scotland there were two naval traditions, as there were two political traditions; closely related, often closely allied, but nevertheless distinct. The kings of Scots, whose kingdom's political and economic centre of gravity lay on the east coast, participated in the common maritime culture of northern Europe. As far as we are informed, Scottish ships there did not differ from English or Flemish ships. New designs and fashions from elsewhere in Europe were early and easily adopted by Scottish shipowners, including the king. James II had a carvel by 1449, and the Bishop of Aberdeen owned one in 1457.[6] In the same year Bishop Kennedy of St Andrew's owned a barge of 500 tons, among the largest merchantmen afloat.[7] In Scotland, as in England, naval activity for much of the fifteenth century consisted largely of piracy tolerated or encouraged by the crown, and captains like Andrew Barton and Sir Andrew Wood enjoyed wide fame at home and notoriety abroad.[8]

In the West Highlands and islands, on the other hand, the naval architecture of the Viking age, and the still older naval organization of Dalriada, survived and flourished. The galley fleets maintained by the MacDonald Lords of the Isles and their followers were the principal strength by which they maintained their semi-independent state, granting charters in royal style for service 'in war and peace on sea and land ... against ... any mortal male or female whatsoever' (not excepting the King of Scots their nominal overlord), and intervening at will in the wars of Scotland, Ireland and England.[9] The relations of the Lords of the Isles with the kings, first of Norway and then of Scots, had long been ambiguous. From playing off Norway against Scotland, they moved after 1266 to playing off Scotland against England. Moreover in the fifteenth century the Lords expanded their rule to include most of mainland Highland Scotland, provoking new political tensions. In the late fifteenth century the two trends worked to bring about a crisis in relations between the Kings of Scots and the Lords of the Isles. In 1462 John II of the Isles concluded the secret Treaty of Ardtornish with Edward IV. When this became known he bought his peace with Scotland, and the confirmation of his Lordship, at the price of most of his mainland territories. By this act he lost much of his authority at home, and his discontented heir Angus Og ('the Young') led his galleys on raids which made trouble between his father and the king.[10]

The trouble came to a head in 1481, when the fleets of father and son met to parley in the Sound of Mull. John had the galleys of the MacLeods

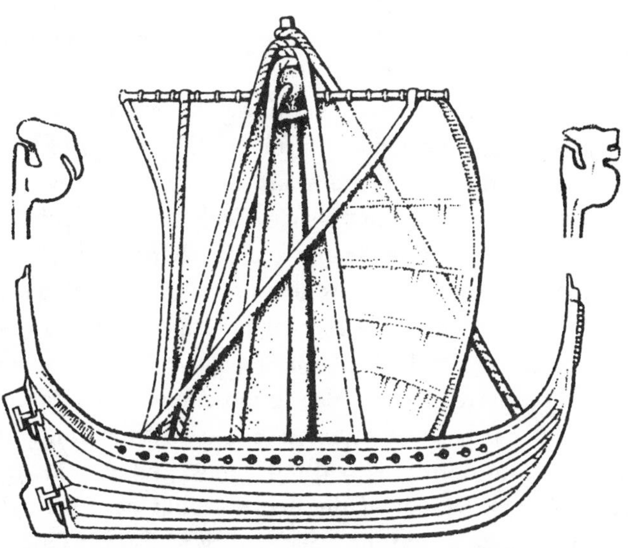

Viking seapower survived in the Western Isles centuries after it disappeared from Scandinavia. This is the seventeen-room galley of Alexander *Crotach* Macleod of Dunvegan (died 1528), from his tomb in Rodel Kirk, Harris. The exceptional quality of this stone carving reveals many details, including the halyard rove through a sheave set in the masthead, the shrouds set up over the masthead, the design of the rudder irons, and the slit cut in the oarports to allow the oar-blades to be shipped. The elaborate stemhead with its 'wings' or lands carved from the solid by the 'stemsmith' or master shipwright to receive the butts of the planking, was characteristic of Viking naval architecture.

of Lewis and Harris, the MacLeans of Duart and the MacNeills of Barra; Angus was backed by the two earls, John Stewart of Atholl and Colin Campbell of Argyll. The negotiations finished in the battle of Bloody Bay, at which Angus gained a complete victory. Henceforth he was the effective head of his kin, and his father an impotent pensioner of the King of Scots. The final struggle between them started in 1493. It was of necessity a naval struggle, for in the Isles there was no other kind of warfare. In 1494 James IV began to build up a royal fleet based at Tarbert on the Mull of Kintyre, with a shipbuilding yard at Dumbarton. His first move was to take the nearby castle of Dunaverty, belonging to the MacDonalds of Islay. The king's ships were not out of sight before the MacDonalds had retaken it and hanged the royal governor from the walls. It was not a promising beginning to the assertion of the crown's authority. The following summer James IV in his ship the *Flower*, commanded by Sir Andrew Wood, cruised through the Isles and established his headquarters at Mingarry Castle in Ardnamurchan. He was briefly back in 1498, with no greater effect than before. Neither the fleets nor the castles of the Lords and their supporters were vulnerable to occasional visits by the king's ships.[11]

But James IV of Scots shared one of the characteristic enthusiasms of the Renaissance prince; heavy guns. In spite of the poverty of his kingdom, he built up a powerful artillery train and maintained a royal foundry in Edinburgh Castle.[12] When the final struggle with Donald Dubh MacDonald ('the Black'), son of Angus the Young and last Lord of the Isles, came in 1504, the king embarked some of his heavy guns in Woods's squadron and with their help bombarded the castles of the islesmen into submission. With the fall of Torquil MacLeod's castle of Stornoway in 1506, followed soon after by Donald's capture, the struggle was more or less over. From the naval point of view, what is particularly interesting is that the king's heavy guns were not merely transported by sea, but almost certainly mounted to be fired from shipboard. Several of the castles would have been difficult to batter from the landward, and the isolated rock fortress of Cairn-na-Burgh in the Treshnish Isles, bombarded in 1504, over a mile from the nearest land, could only have been fired on by ships.[13]

It is very unlikely that anyone in England, certainly not Henry VII, appreciated the naval significance of mounting heavy guns on shipboard, and far from certain that his small fleet would have been capable of operating in the remote and dangerous waters of the Western Isles. Yet it is not fanciful to suggest that this obscure campaign, not anything done by English ships, marks the real end of medieval naval warfare in northern waters and the first hesitant beginnings in the British Isles of what was eventually to become an entirely new style of sea fighting. Poor though his kingdom was, James IV of Scots continued to build up his navy and his powerful artillery train. His ship the *Margaret* of 6–700 tons, built at Leith in 1504–7, cost a quarter of a year's revenue; what we know of her size and design, together with the coincidence of name, suggest she may have been the 'elder sister' of the English *Mary Rose* of 1509.[14] In 1506 James began a still bigger ship, the *Michael*, and as she neared completion in 1511–12 Henry VIII received a series of admiring reports from his ambassador in Edinburgh which left no doubt how much bigger and more powerful she was than anything in the English navy. The *Michael* was not just big (about 1,000 tons), she was revolutionary in design. Unlike the ships Henry had inherited from his father, unlike the carracks and other merchantmen he was buying to expand his fleet, possibly even unlike the new *Peter Pomegranate* and *Mary Rose*, the Scottish ship was more than a carrier of troops with small arms and light guns. She was designed from the first to carry a main armament of heavy artillery: twelve guns on each side, and three bronze 'basilisks', two aft and one forward, all cast especially for the ship by Robert Borthwick, the king's 'Master Melter' in Edinburgh Castle, and each needing six waggons to carry it down to the shore.[15]

The powerful Scottish fleet was not just a prick to Henry's tender vanity, but a dangerous complication to his strategic situation in 1512. In making war on France, Henry was necessarily attacking Brittany, linked to France by Duchess Anne's marriage to Charles VIII in 1491. Though the available French fleet was not large, the Breton navy was formidable, and perfectly placed to cut Henry's links with King Ferdinand. If James IV should take France's part, there was the prospect of a combined Breton-Scots-French fleet dominating the Channel. At the same time the Danish fleet was growing very rapidly, with Scottish assistance which included the transfer of at least three ships between 1507 and 1509. As an ally both of Scotland and the Hansa, capable at any moment of shutting off English Baltic trade, Denmark was an additional naval threat which Henry had to keep carefully in mind.[16] It was not yet certain that Scotland would fight England; quite apart from the obvious risks of war against so powerful a neighbour, James IV, as the husband of Henry's elder sister, had hopes of the English throne if Henry (still childless after three years of marriage) should fail to produce an heir. There had been several incidents of hostility, notably in June 1511 when the Lord Admiral of England, Sir Edward Howard, escorting a convoy to Zealand, accidentally encountered and killed the Scottish pirate Andrew Barton,[17] but still James hesitated. Finally Louis XII gained him with an offer of 50,000 *livres* to equip the Scottish fleet, and a galley squadron to co-operate with it, providing James would invade England as soon as Henry attacked France.[18]

Meanwhile the 1512 campaign proceeded without Scottish participation. Under the terms of the alliance, Spain was responsible for naval operations in the Bay of Biscay while England guarded the Channel. After an initial cruise in April, the English fleet under Howard escorted the transports carrying Dorset's army as far as Brest in early June. While Dorset continued south under Spanish escort, the English fleet under Howard remained in the 'Trade', once more the pivotal point of English naval strategy as it had been for so long in the days of the Gascon empire, and raided the coast of Brittany. In July he returned to Portsmouth for supplies and reinforcements, and there King Henry

> made a great banquet to all the captains, and every one sware to another ever to defend, aid and comfort one another without failing, and this they promised before the King, which committed them to God; and so with great noise of minstrelsy they took their ships, which were 25 in number of great burden, and well furnished of all things.[19]

When Howard returned to Brest on 10 August, he found that the French had at length assembled a fleet – or, rather, two ill co-ordinated fleets, French and Breton. The French admiral chose to withdraw, but the Breton flagship the *Cordelière* remained to fight. After some exchange of gunfire, the *Regent* came alongside and they fought hand to hand until the Breton caught fire; before the *Regent* could cast off both ships were destroyed with enormous loss of life. Howard remained in control of the local waters until he returned to England at the end of August. He had conducted a successful campaign of the traditional kind, harrying the enemy's coast, destroying his shipping and keeping open the sea lanes to the southward, as his predecessors had done for centuries. That autumn the English organized the usual winter patrols, apparently unaware that they were about to be rudely introduced to an entirely new way of waging war at sea.[20]

Louis XII had been advised that a fleet 'would do him marvellous service, and give the king of England something to think about.'[21] To that end he had ordered from the Mediterranean the galley squadron commanded by his most experienced sea officer, Prégent de Bidoux. He arrived in Brittany at the end of October with six galleys. Winter weather frustrated his hopes of an immediate assault on Plymouth or Falmouth, and he was still in port when Howard, newly appointed Lord Admiral of England, arrived off Brest in April. The main French fleet took refuge in the Penfeld River at Brest, while Prégent was cut off on the north coast. Howard once more had the initiative, but his supplies were precarious and he could not afford to wait for the situation to develop. His first plan for an assault on Brest was abandoned when one of his ships was wrecked. A few days later Prégent and his galleys arrived, forced their way through the English fleet which was lying in the Trade, and took up a position in Blanc-Sablons Bay. These galleys carried heavy guns, probably the first the English had ever met at sea, which sank one English ship outright and left another in a sinking condition.[22] It is hard to convey to a modern reader the terror induced by these 'basilisks', in men for whom guns had hitherto been a noisier kind of crossbow: 'Never man saw men in greater fear than all the masters and mariners be of the galleys, insomuch that in a manner they had as lief go into Purgatory as to the Trade.'[23]

Both psychologically and practically Prégent's arrival transformed the situation. Howard was now caught between two fleets, his men badly shaken. His first thought was to land guns on the opposite side of the Kermorvan peninsula, haul them across to bombard the galleys in the rear and force them out of their position. It would certainly have been the best course, and was recommended by his senior officers, but it called for time and steady nerves, and Howard evidently decided he had too little of either. He had always believed 'that never did seaman good that was not resolute to a degree of madness', and at that moment arrived an ill-timed exhortation from the king which seemed to imply that the fleet was shirking battle.[24] Howard decided to retrieve the situation with a bold frontal attack on the galleys. They were moored in a classic defensive position, stern-on to the shore in a small bay, their guns covering the entrance with batteries on either side to flank them. Howard attacked with all the oared vessels in the English fleet, and himself led the party which leapt aboard Prégent's galley, but before they could be reinforced his barge was cut free and fell away. The last his men saw of him he was 'waving with his hands and crying to the galley, "Come aboard again! Come aboard again!" And when my lord saw the galley could not come to him again . . . he saw him take his whistle from about his neck, and wrap it together, and hurled it into the sea, and thus he lost the sight of my said Lord Admiral.'[25] Demoralized, starving and leaderless, the English fleet was back in Plymouth on 30 April to report the death of their admiral.[26]

His brother Lord Thomas Howard was appointed Lord Admiral in turn, and reached Plymouth in May. His efforts to get the fleet to sea again were frustrated by the acute difficulty of victualling a large force in so remote a part of England, and in June Henry decided to abandon the naval campaign in Brittany. The fleet returned to the Narrow Seas to cover the king's invasion of France, which the French made no attempt to counter. Prégent's galleys were disabled by sickness for much of the summer, and Howard correctly estimated that the rest would take no initiative without the stimulus of Scottish assistance.[27] The English had been worrying all year about the Scottish fleet, and in July a strong squadron took station in the Straits of Dover in anticipation of James IV's declaration of war, which came on 11 August. The English precautions were useless, however, for the Earl of Arran, commanding the Scottish fleet, sailed round the north of Scotland, attacked Carrickfergus, and reached Brest early in September, where Prégent's galleys were once more operational, and a fleet was assembled which was intended to cut off Henry's return to England. Perhaps it might have done, but for the October gale which dispersed the allied fleet, and the news that James IV had been defeated and killed at the battle of Flodden by an English army commanded by the Earl of Surrey. Scotland was now knocked out of the war, her new king James V only one year old. The *Michael*, which the Scottish government could not afford to maintain, was sold to France to replace the lost *Cordelière*, and the rest of the fleet returned to Scotland.[28]

In 1514 both French and English prepared for new efforts at sea. In April Prégent de Bidoux, whose galleys had wintered at Dieppe, raided the obscure fishing village of Brighton. Henry put substantial forces to sea, but the French avoided any direct challenge, and the English achieved nothing beyond burning some Breton villages in retaliation for Brighton. By the summer the war had ended, from mutual exhaustion as much as any achievement. That autumn Prégent and his galleys returned to the Mediterranean where they were urgently needed, and Henry's favourite sister Mary (after whom the *Mary Rose* had been named) married Louis XII to seal the peace.[29]

The war of 1512–14 was of some importance for the rise of English naval power, but it is difficult to accept the traditional view that Henry VIII began it, or even ended it, with a real understanding of the uses of sea power. His sea commanders, the Howard brothers, were bold and determined, and the French admirals timid or feeble – Prégent de Bidoux always excepted. Had Henry had a real naval strategy, he might with these advantages have used his fleet to land his army somewhere unexpected and gain a decisive victory. As it was, he gained Thérouanne ('an ungracious doghole'),[30] and the fleet burnt a number of Breton villages. James IV, if anyone, had a real strategy, though his plans for joint action by Scotland, France, Denmark and the McDonnells in Ireland were highly ambitious and in the event fell to pieces. He too spoiled his prospects (and lost his life) by an invasion unco-ordinated with his fleet.[31]

All the English campaigns were marked by administrative collapse. Surrey's army was virtually starving when it fought at Flodden, and was extremely lucky to defeat a superior enemy.[32] Moreover in two years of war Henry had spent at least £922,000 (against an ordinary annual income of less than £150,000).[33] All that his father had saved had gone. His more intelligent servants drew the moral that England could no longer play at being a great power.[34] The king, however, was not prepared to think in those terms, and the international situation offered just as many temptations as before to a young man in search of glory. On the last day of 1514 old King Louis XII died; danced to death, it was said, by his vivacious young English wife. His successor Francis I was a warlike young monarch in the mould of Henry himself, and with much greater resources to lend force to his ambition. By the end of 1515 he had restarted the war, won great victories in Italy, and restored French domination in Scottish politics. Henry was intensely jealous, and watched Francis's progress with suspicious eye.[35]

So England remained at peace, but a watchful peace, especially towards France and Scotland. In January 1515 an English squadron sailed to Scotland, for purposes which are unclear, and the Scottish navy continued to worry the English.[36] Throughout the short peace, the French fleet remained active. In 1517 Francis I founded the new naval port of Franciscopolis, popularly Havre de Grâce (the modern Le Havre, known to the English of the day as 'Newhaven'). It was not difficult to guess what enemy it must be intended against, and in 1520 Francis ordered a survey of Norman shipping, undoubtedly with a view to using it. The grand negotiation that year with Henry VIII, known as the Field of the Cloth of Gold, was a theatre for competitive display rather than an occasion for real reconciliation. In October 1521 the French besieged and took the Spanish frontier fortress of Fuentarrabia, the *Michael* leading the blockading squadron.[37] In view of the tension, it is noteworthy that Henry, like his father, continued to charter his ships to merchants trading abroad, which was how the *Christ* was taken by Barbary pirates in the Mediterranean in 1515.[38]

This does not look like the action of a king with a profound understanding of sea power. In fact Henry was soon preparing to go to war again with exactly the same strategy as before. The death of the Emperor Maximilian in 1519, and the election as his successor of his grandson Charles V, already King of Spain and Duke of Burgundy, had created a Habsburg superpower which encircled and menaced France. War between them was likely – but England was in the happy and unusual position of not being threatened by either, nor forced to join in their quarrels. The first theatre of their warfare was bound to be far away in northern Italy, while for Charles V sea communications between Spain and Flanders were essential to his empire. England being perfectly placed either to guard or to cut them, both superpowers would bid high for English friendship, and Henry had an ideal opportunity to preserve a profitable neutrality balanced between them. Instead he agreed by secret treaty with Charles V to make joint war against France. His object was not only to win himself glory, but to solve the looming English succession crisis. Still without a male heir after thirteen years of marriage to Catherine of Aragon, he was hoping to betroth his five-year-old daughter Mary to Charles V in order to gain England a secure, if not independent future as part of the Habsburg empire. The Emperor, who visited England in person that summer, knew just how to play on Henry's fears and ambitions without making any inconvenient promises.[39]

In May 1522, therefore, England declared war on France. The first activity was by sea. The Earl of Surrey[40] planned to attack Havre de Grâce in June, was frustrated by victualling failures, and had to be contented with burning Morlaix on 1 July. Brest proved too strong to attack, and by the end of July Surrey had returned. The fleet returned later under the Vice-Admiral, Sir William FitzWilliam, and remained off Brittany until October, latterly in conjunction with Spanish ships, but achieved nothing more.[41] Meanwhile in August Surrey marched out of Calais with an army of 15,000 men. Unaided by the Imperial armies, which were already deeply engaged in Italy, he achieved nothing.[42]

War against France naturally meant war against Scotland, and in the north English ships took the initiative. In May a squadron under William Sabyn appeared off the Firth of Forth, attacked Leith and bombarded Kinghorn and the Bass Rock. The Scottish defences, however, prevented him from doing more, and about the 20th four French ships arrived with reinforcements. A bold plan to invade Scotland with 25,000 men carrying eight days' victuals, to rendezvous at the Firth of Forth with English ships carrying supplies, had to be abandoned as impossible in view of the usual logistical weaknesses.[43] The following year both English and Scottish ships were at sea again. The Scots mounted a blockade of the Humber, and the English commander Sir Henry Sherburn attempted to watch the East Coast, himself lying off Flamborough Head while Captain Christopher Coe and a small squadron lay 'two kennings in the sea' off Holy Island, until storms dispersed them. On 11 June Sherburn was killed attempting to stop a French ship on passage to Leith. Coe took over command, and succeeded in taking at least seven ships bound for Scotland, but Scottish ships had successes also, including the recapture of the *Jennet Purwyn* (one of Andrew Barton's ships, originally taken in 1511). On the border the only campaigning of 1523 was a raid by Surrey's army which burned the abbey of Kelso.[44]

In the Channel the main English squadron under FitzWilliam kept up communications with Calais and watched to prevent the Scottish regent the Duke of Albany, who was in France, returning to Scotland to reignite the war on that front. In August FitzWilliam attacked and looted the suburbs of the small port of Le Tréport, returning to land his plunder. This gave Albany his chance to sail, and having eluded Sir Anthony Poyntz's squadron in the Irish Sea, he landed at Kirkcudbright on 21 September with 3,000 French troops. Fortunately for the English, the Scots were reluctant to campaign so late in the year.[45]

Meanwhile in France the grand plan of the alliance was unfolding as the Duke of Suffolk's army advanced from Calais. The Emperor and his Regent in the Netherlands, Margaret of Austria, wanted the English army to penetrate as far into France as possible. Initially Henry planned to concentrate on something more useful to England, the siege of Boulogne, but presently he was diverted by the treason of the Duke of Bourbon, which promised to open eastern France to the advancing English and Imperial armies. Beguiled by the prospect of dividing France with the Emperor, Henry ordered Suffolk to march on Paris. But not for the first or last time, the Imperial armies failed to make an effective contribution; Bourbon's rebellion misfired and by November there was no money left to keep Suffolk's army in the field even if the weather had permitted. Suffolk did well to get within fifty miles of Paris, and to retrieve his army without disaster, but that was the best that could be said of the campaign. Two years of war had cost nearly £400,000, £325,000 of it raised by forced loans. Cardinal Wolsey's demand to Parliament for the extraordinary sum of £800,000 was met by a 'marvellous obstinate silence'; what money he did obtain came far too late to save either the campaign or the war.[46]

During 1524 the English did very little, by land or sea, and before the end of the year they were negotiating for peace. By the time Charles V won his great victory at Pavia on 24 February 1525, shattering the French army and capturing Francis I, it was too late for Henry to pretend that he had contributed anything to the triumph. It was equally too late to make yet another demand on the English taxpayer, the so-called 'Amicable Grant', which was most unamicably rejected that summer amid scenes threatening civil war. To complete Henry's bitterness, Charles V not only rejected all proposals of continuing the war, but repudiated his offer to marry the nine-year-old Princess Mary in favour of Isabella of Portugal, who was twenty-two and richly dowered.[47]

For England it may be said that the Middle Ages ended in the mud of October 1523 when Suffolk's army abandoned its march on Paris. This was the last campaign of the Hundred Years War, the last occasion when an English army attempted to uphold the ambitions of Henry V and Edward III, the last expression of vanished greatness. For centuries English power had been defined in military terms and expressed above all by campaigning against France. In the humiliation of failure on the Continent and rejection by the Emperor, it must have been clear to perceptive Englishmen, perhaps even to King Henry himself, that all this was gone for ever. A shrunken, post-imperial England faced an uncertain and vulnerable future on the margins of a Europe now dominated by the great powers.

FOURTEEN

Precarious Isolation

Operations 1523–1550

Until 1525, Henry VIII had done nothing by land or sea which Henry V had not done a great deal better. It has long been customary to proclaim him as the architect of a new, modern navy, in fact as the real founder of the Royal Navy.[1] He had indeed acquired many more ships than his father, and the example of the French and Scottish navies had already stimulated some English experiments in warship design. Almost everything, however, which English sea power had done and not done in the first part of his reign was as deeply traditional as his foreign policy, and if medieval naval warfare were more familiar people would recognize the usual business of convoy escort, coastal raids and local patrols which had been going on for centuries. In 1511 Henry was urged to abandon ideas of continental conquest:

> The natural situation of islands seems not to consort with conquests of that kind. England alone is a just empire. Or, when we would enlarge ourselves, let it be that way we can, and to which it seems the eternal Providence hath destined us, which is by the sea.[2]

This was not what the king wanted to hear. His grand strategy was just the same as Edward III's had been, and it called for ships strictly as ancillaries to an invasion of France in conjunction with allies in the Low Countries. If the ships were not needed to cover the passage of an army to a friendly port, they could always burn some villages in Brittany. The limits of English naval operations were effectively the Channel as far as Brest, the east coast as far as the Firth of Forth, and the southern part of the Irish Sea. Even within that limited area, the haphazard administration and chaotic victualling of the English navy sharply limited the duration and effectiveness of its operations. The use of sea power as a strategic instrument in its own right, or as the servant and agent of foreign trade or overseas expansion, were quite beyond Henry's comprehension.

It was in the period after 1525, and especially in the closing years of

Henry's reign and the uncertain time which followed his death in 1547, that England's attitude to naval power began to change. How much Henry himself had to do with the changes is unclear; he certainly had no sudden revelation of future greatness founded upon sea power, but his domestic and foreign policy drove England into an increasingly lonely and dangerous situation, and he, his ministers and successors invested increasing amounts of thought and money in what seemed to be their best defence. In the first part of his reign Henry had pursued an offensive strategy in which his ships had only an auxiliary role. The bankruptcy of that strategy, and the country's increasing peril and isolation, forced England down the road which Scotland had already taken – towards naval strength as the essential defence of a weak and unstable country threatened by powerful enemies who could only come by sea.

The engine which propelled Henry VIII and his ministers into ever deeper water was the succession question. Infuriated by Charles V's breach of faith, desperate to provide himself with an heir, Henry began to investigate the possibilities of divorcing Queen Catherine. The king swiftly persuaded his own conscience that he was justified, but as an orthodox Catholic as well as a long-standing supporter of the Pope's authority he had to get a papal dispensation. It did not seem unlikely that Clement VII would grant one, for the peace of a kingdom and its people were considerations which might legitimately sway a papal conscience – so long as it was free to sway. In 1527 Clement VII was by no means free; he was the virtual prisoner of Imperial armies – and Charles V would not sacrifice his aunt Catherine, especially as that might free Henry to marry a French princess.

So Henry's policy depended on the success of French armies in Italy in releasing the pope. It was a risky policy, involving a declaration of war in 1528 against the Emperor, alongside France, which redoubled the unpopularity of Henry's chief minister Cardinal Wolsey. Even so it might have worked, for Pope Clement was on the verge of granting the divorce in the summer of 1528 when the Genoese fleet under its great admiral Andrea Doria changed sides, cutting off the French army in Italy, where it was presently forced to surrender. By 1529 Henry's hopes of a divorce had evaporated, and he himself was infatuated with Anne Boleyn and determined to marry her. She moreover was a supporter of the religious views which were everywhere arousing opposition to papal authority, and which in England were especially identified with hatred of Cardinal Wolsey. Thus the stage was set for the breach with Rome, the attack on the Pope's English revenues and jurisdiction, and the assertion of royal supremacy over the English church.[3]

We need not follow the detail of English politics during the 1530s. Wrapped in its domestic concerns, the kingdom effectively withdrew from great-power politics. Charles V was too preoccupied elsewhere, above all with the terrifying advance of the Turks on land in Central Europe and at sea in the Mediterranean, to defend his aunt's position, and Henry was able to seek his own solutions to the succession crisis. Self-restraint had never been his leading virtue, and the discovery that he could flout with impunity the authority of the universal Church, the public opinion of Christendom and the personal interests of the Emperor, encouraged the king to further extremes. In the short term Henry gained much power, by the dissolution of the lesser monasteries in 1536 he gained much money, the crushing of the northern rebellion known as the Pilgrimage of Grace the same year confirmed his authority, and finally in 1537 his third queen Jane Seymour bore him a male heir. So long as France and the Empire remained at loggerheads all this carried no immediate penalty, but in the long run Henry was moving his country into a position of isolation. Though the king himself lived and died more or less a Catholic, he had already prepared the country for Protestantism, with all that that implied for relations with the great powers of Catholic Europe, and for the unity of a kingdom most of whose people were certainly not yet much attracted to the foreign religious fashions of an urban middle class. Henry's legacy was a permanent threat to the legitimacy of every English sovereign, symbolized by the position of Cardinal Pole, exiled leader of the English loyal to Rome, but also grandson of Edward IV's brother the Duke of Clarence and representative of the Yorkist line. In the future, moreover, the Catholics might look for support where the Yorkists had, in Ireland, the country which England had never managed to control, and whose southern and western coasts were too remote for the English navy to patrol. Scotland, too, was still Catholic, and closely tied to France. England had always been unstable; the price of the breach with Rome was permanent instability and weakness.[4]

The first portent of trouble was a brief crisis in 1539, when France and the Empire were at peace, and a fleet of sixty ships from the Low Countries on passage to Spain passed through English waters. In response Henry mobilized a force of almost 150 ships. In the new, more threatening situation which followed the breach with Rome there was an increasing realization that, in the words of the 1540 Navigation Act, 'the Navy or multitude of ships of this Realm [is] a great defence and surety in time of war, as well for offence and defence'.[5] The king began spending heavily on coastal defences of modern design, mounting large numbers of heavy guns.[6] It has been calculated that in the nine years

1539–47 Henry spent an average of 29 per cent of his ordinary revenue on fortifications.[7] Sir John Russell and a commission of 'sad and expert men' were sent to 'view and search all of the ports and dangers on the coasts where any meet or convenient landing place might be supposed'.[8] Several of the king's biggest ships had already been rebuilt with heavier armament. All this was paid for by the dissolution of the greater monasteries.[9]

This crisis passed, and by 1542 France and the Empire were at war again. Henry used the opportunity to tackle the threats within the British Isles which his own policies had exacerbated. Relations with Scotland were seldom easy during these years, and at sea mutual piracy was normal. The records give the impression that the Scots had much the better of this. Their ships kept the east coast under a virtual blockade for long periods, and were quite able to cruise in the English Channel, while for the English it was an achievement to get a squadron as far as the North Channel in 1540.[10] The only English warship which attempted to penetrate further north in this period was the new *Mary Willoughby*, sent into the Western Isles in the spring of 1533 in an endeavour to punish the piracies of the 'wild Scots'. It would be good to know more about this confrontation – the new Renaissance technology of the sailing ship and the heavy gun, versus the surviving representatives of Norse sea power. Unfortunately we know nothing but the result: the *Mary Willoughby* was captured by the galleys of Hector Maclean of Duart and joined the Scottish navy, where she enjoyed a busy and successful career for the next fifteen years.[11] In the following year the *Mary Walsingham* of Yarmouth, commanded by the future English admiral William Woodhouse, was similarly taken by Highland galleys while fishing off the Shetlands.[12]

These and other such incidents inspired the Duke of Norfolk's 1542 raid into Scotland, an operation which disintegrated after six days because English victualling arrangements were quite incapable of supporting any further advance.[13] Meanwhile the English vice-admiral John Cary sailed north with eight ships, but while he was windbound at Holy Island sixteen French ships passed by on their way to the Forth. Eventually the English squadron returned to port having achieved nothing except to have 'killed certain persons'. The king would have been happier if 'such a costly and notable enterprise had been more displeasant to the enemies'. Cary was left with a small squadron to blockade Scottish commerce and fisheries over the winter.[14] Meanwhile, however, the English achieved an unlooked-for triumph when the Scots were heavily defeated at Solway Moss. A few weeks later James V died, leaving Scotland yet again to the rule of a baby, the one-week-old Mary.

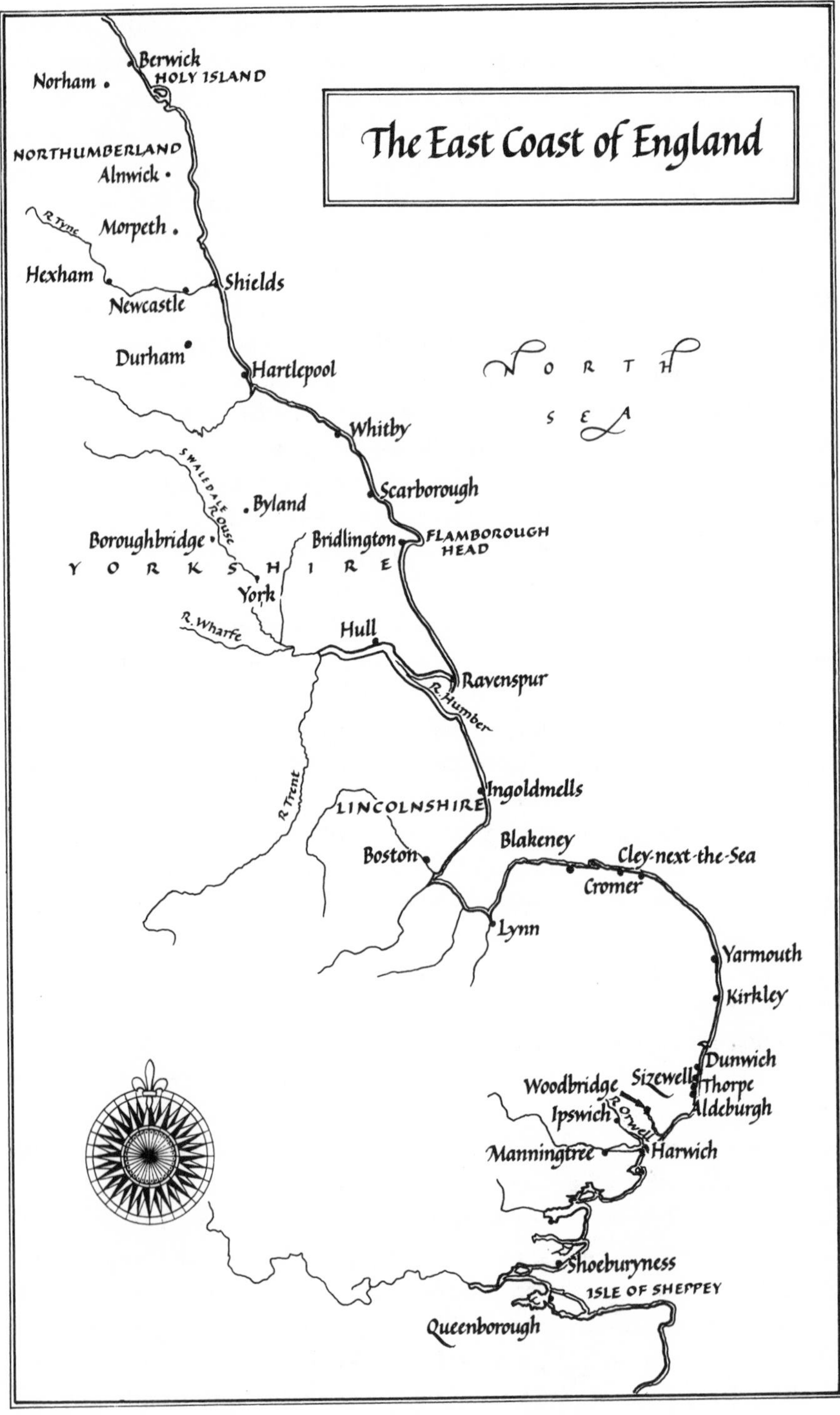

The East Coast of England
Berwick
HOLY ISLAND
Norham
NORTHUMBERLAND
Alnwick
R. Tyne
Morpeth
Hexham
Shields
Newcastle
Durham
Hartlepool
NORTH
SEA
Whitby
SWALEDALE
R. Ouse
Byland
Scarborough
Boroughbridge
Bridlington
FLAMBOROUGH HEAD
YORKSHIRE
York
R. Wharfe
Hull
Ravenspur
R. Humber
R. Trent
Ingoldmells
LINCOLNSHIRE
Boston
Blakeney
Cley-next-the-Sea
Cromer
Lynn
Yarmouth
Kirkley
Dunwich
Woodbridge
Sizewell
Thorpe
Aldeburgh
Ipswich
R. Orwell
Manningtree
Harwich
Shoeburyness
ISLE OF SHEPPEY
Queenborough

The English now had an unparalleled opportunity, especially as most of the Scottish ships were away in the Bay of Biscay trying to intercept the English convoy from Bordeaux. In January English ships were ordered to intercept French and Scottish ships reported to be sailing from Veere and Dieppe. Sir Francis Bryan did get to sea on 2 February, after intense difficulty cutting his ships through twelve feet of ice in the Tyne, but retreated rapidly back into port on learning that twenty-one Scottish ships (in fact the *Mary Willoughby* and *Salamander* returning with nineteen English prizes) had been sighted off Holy Island. Early in March the English made a further attempt to establish a blockade when William Woodhouse with the *Sweepstake* and three other ships sailed from Newcastle 'to keep the North Seas between the Humber and Berwick'. Woodhouse was notably more successful than earlier English sea commanders; he was at sea between March and August, taking a number of prizes and forcing back the French squadron which attempted to return from the Forth in July. Meanwhile, however, Henry VIII was throwing away his opportunities with the same political ineptitude by which English kings had so often revived Scottish independence at its last extremity. A friendly but discreet interest in the welfare of Scotland's orphan queen (a potential future wife for Henry's heir Prince Edward) might in time have nourished an effective English protectorate; Henry's brutal and undisguised lust for conquest merely succeeded in uniting all Scotland against him, and throwing the country back into the French camp. Though Woodhouse effectively isolated Scotland on the east coast, French assistance arrived at Dumbarton on the Clyde; by September England and Scotland were at peace, and the English representative the Earl of Arran had been forced to terms with his opponents, led by Cardinal Beaton, the head of the Scottish church.[15]

Infuriated by this reverse, Henry ordered the Earl of Hertford to invade Lowland Scotland in the spring of 1544 on a mission of destruction. Hertford and Suffolk failed to convince the king of the folly of an approach which would solve none of the military difficulties of conquering Scotland, while putting a political solution yet further out of reach. From the professional point of view, however, the invasion demonstrated intelligent planning and a logistical capacity which had been notably lacking in Henry's previous campaigns. Only a small cavalry force marched overland, while transports chartered from Dutch and Baltic ports carried a force of 12–15,000 men from Newcastle to the Forth, where they landed near Leith on 3 May. Hertford took several Scottish ships and burnt Leith and Edinburgh (except the castle, which held out). The foreign merchantmen then declined to serve any longer, so he returned overland by a forced march, destroying every town and village in his path, and just getting into Berwick before his food ran out.[16]

This, however, was only a preliminary to Henry's grand design. Heedless of the bitter experience of two previous wars, he agreed with the Emperor Charles V to strike at the root of the Franco-Scottish alliance by a joint invasion of France in 1544. As by now Henry might have anticipated, the emperor remained in the war just long enough to profit by English efforts before making a separate peace and leaving his allies to make the best of the war by themselves. The English land campaign was as usual disorganized and ill-supplied, and Norfolk was lucky to extricate his army from the siege of Montreuil, but the siege and naval blockade of Boulogne between 19 July and 14 September was successful and Henry once again won easy glory with a costly and irrelevant conquest. It was very soon clear that the supply of Boulogne was a going to be a heavy charge on English naval resources, and in November Sir Thomas Seymour's attempt to convoy stores thither and attack French warships reported in various ports was completely dispersed by gales.[17]

In December 1544 Henry issued a proclamation allowing his subjects unrestricted private warfare at sea, with no legal safeguards. Naturally they at once extended their range of targets from the French to any neutral shipping which offered, notably the rich and tempting traffic between Spain and Flanders. As his subjects suffered from English piracy, Charles V became rapidly more hostile towards his recent ally. Many of the privateering operations were backed by courtiers and others close to the king.[18] The most egregious capture came on 1 March 1545, when the wealthy Southampton merchant Robert Reneger took the Spanish *San Salvador* off Cape St Vincent, homeward bound from Hispaniola with a cargo including treasure officially valued at nearly 20,000 ducats. Reneger enjoyed protection in high places, and Spanish diplomacy badly bungled the affair, putting Spain legally in the wrong by imposing reprisals without recourse to the remedies prescribed by Anglo-Spanish treaties. The upshot was that peaceful trade between the two countries was damaged; many innocent English merchants suffered from Spanish seizures and learned to dislike Spanish officials as much as English pirates; while the pirates themselves, and those with a mind to imitate them, looked with new and greedy eyes on the wealth and vulnerability of the seaborne trade which bound together the far-flung Spanish empire.[19]

English piracy, which had so often imperilled the country before, was making an enemy of the Empire just as a French fleet of unprecedented size prepared to invade England. By June 1545 Francis I had gathered in the Seine a fleet of 150 ships and 25 galleys under the command of Claude d'Annebault, the Admiral of France, backed by over 50,000 men at Havre de Grâce. An English spoiling attack failed to have any effect, and on 12 July the great fleet sailed, watched by the king. The accidental loss of the flagship *Philippe*, which caught fire, and the grounding of the *Grande Maitresse* to which d'Annebault shifted his flag, somewhat spoiled the occasion, but did not much reduce the threat to England.[20] The French made the Sussex coast on 18 July, when the galleys launched a raid on the hamlet of Brighton.[21] Next day they entered the Solent, while the English fleet under Lord Lisle (heavily outnumbered with only about eighty ships) retreated into Portsmouth harbour. The stage was now set for a great naval battle to decide the fate of England, and d'Annebault's galleys were the most potent weapon to exploit the possibilities of confined water and shoals. The difficulty on both sides was to find effective tactical methods of integrating ships and galleys, heavy guns and small arms. The French drew up their fleet as an army in three divisions, and advanced with the galleys skirmishing like cavalry in front. Then the wind got up, allowing the English ships to sally out and forcing the galleys to withdraw in haste. What English sources we have, including the 'Cowdray engraving' which shows this stage of the action, suggest that Henry's big ships the *Henry Grace à Dieu* and the *Mary Rose* led the advance, but French accounts stress the contribution of the small 'rowbarges' which formed the bulk of the English oared warships. Late in the day the *Mary Rose*, going about on to the other tack, was caught by a flaw of wind, filled through her open gunports, and sank with the loss of almost all on board. Apart from this dramatic disaster, the day was indecisive and disappointing for both sides. French troops were landed on the Isle of Wight in an endeavour to draw the English fleet out again, but they were driven off by the local militia, and the English fleet remained safe in harbour.[22] Unable to force either a landing or a battle, increasingly sickly and lacking supplies to lie indefinitely in the Solent, d'Annebault was forced to sail on the 22nd. Lord Lisle followed him with the English fleet, now reinforced by ships which had been guarding the western Channel, and they met briefly off Shoreham on 15 August. Lisle's fleet was also organized in three lines, and seems to have been handled competently, but only the oared vessels on each side were seriously engaged. On 2 September Lisle landed near Tréport and burnt it, but his fleet was already affected by the plague, which soon disabled it altogether and forced him back to Portsmouth.[23] Over that winter, some of the French galleys remained in commission, based on Etaples, to support the siege of Boulogne. On 18 May 1546 eight of these galleys skirmished with four English ships and four pinnaces, with the capture of one of the French galleys. It was the last action of the war at sea; by June England and France were at peace.[24]

In Scotland there was little fighting in 1545. French ships landed 3,500 men at Dumbarton in July. At about the same time Donald the Black, last Lord of the Isles, invaded Ireland with 180 galleys in an attempt to recover his lordship.[25] Henry VIII's ships were fully occupied facing the French, and in any case he did not regard himself as having any obligation to protect English merchantmen from Scottish cruisers. When the men of Newcastle-on-Tyne complained, they were bluntly informed that 'it were over burdensome that the king should set ships to defend all parts of the realm and keep the Narrow Seas withal.'[26] It was the business of shipowners to protect themselves; it ill became the majesty of a king to concern himself with such sordid details. By 1546, though England was still at war with Scotland, Henry's means of prosecuting it were exhausted. Two years of war, plus the preparations of 1538–42 and the defence of Boulogne, had cost at least £2,135,000, of which £265,000 was for the Navy. To find this he had sold two-thirds of the newly-acquired monastic lands, heavily debased the coinage and borrowed deeply on the Antwerp money market at up to 14 per cent interest.[27] Breaking with Rome had radically weakened England's international position, and Henry's encouragement of English piracy had gone far to make real a potential alliance of the great powers, but at least the dissolution of the monasteries had briefly given the king a permanent income which could have rendered him independent of Parliament. He might have left future English sovereigns very much more powerful at home than they had ever been before. Instead he threw it away on futile dreams of glory and revenge. When Henry died on 28 January 1547 he left his nine-year-old son Edward a weakened, divided and exposed kingdom, with debts of £75,000 and an unresolved war with Scotland.[28]

The effective ruler of England was Edward VI's uncle, that experienced soldier Edward Seymour, Earl of Hertford and (in February) Duke of Somerset. Somerset genuinely desired peace with Scotland, but Henry VIII's brutality had shut off any possibility of reconciliation. Moreover Francis I of France died on 31 March, and his successor Henry II was more interested in the north than Italy, opening the real risk that if England did not act first, the French would effectively annex Scotland. So Somerset found himself obliged to keep up the war. On 7 March a Scottish squadron carrying help from France to Mary of Guise, the Queen Regent of Scotland, was captured off Yarmouth. On 29 May an opportunity opened for the English when a small band of Scottish Protestant fanatics broke into St Andrews Castle and murdered Cardinal Beaton. St Andrews is by the sea, the Scottish Protestants perforce looked to England for support, and the way was open for English ships to reinforce the bridgehead. Unfortunately it was equally open to the French. Late in June twenty-two French galleys under Leone Strozzi (a member of a noble Florentine family in the service of Catherine de' Medici, the Florentine-born Queen of France) sailed for St Andrews. On 30 July, after a fortnight's bombardment, the castle surrendered and Strozzi returned in triumph to France. Though an English squadron lay at Holy Island, Somerset dared not provoke another war with France by attacking Strozzi at the moment when the Emperor was equally threatening, and the result was a complete triumph for the French party in Scotland. The Scottish Protestants, never numerous, were now entirely identified as the party of Bloody Somerset and English dominion.[29]

Hoping to retrieve the situation before French control of Scotland could become irreversible, Somerset invaded Scotland on 4 September. The campaign was much better managed than its predecessors, and with an English fleet of sixty ships keeping close touch with the army and supplying it as it marched up the coast, Somerset arrived at Musselburgh on 9 September. There the way was barred by a larger Scottish army, strongly entrenched, but with that genius for snatching defeat from the jaws of victory which James IV and James V had shown before them, the Scottish commanders next day abandoned their position and descended to attack the English, who completely defeated them with the help of ships' guns bombarding the flank of the Scottish army. The disastrous battle of Pinkie Cleuch once again left Lowland Scotland open to the English, but as usual the English had no means of translating victory into conquest. English logistics, adequate so far, were incapable of supplying a field army at so great a distance for long, and by the end of September the English were back at Berwick. They had had a successful campaign, including the recapture of the *Mary Willoughby*, but were no nearer controlling Scotland than ever.[30]

Somerset hoped, as Edward III had hoped, to exercise at least a measure of control by leaving English garrisons in selected fortresses. In September troops occupied the islands of Inchcolm and Inchkeith in the Firth of Forth and Broughty Castle at the mouth of the Tay. In December the English occupied Dundee and Arbroath, and in April 1548, 4,500 men were installed in Haddington Castle in East Lothian, midway between Edinburgh and Dunbar. In addition several towns and castles along the border were garrisoned. This was certainly a more intelligent policy than Somerset himself, at King Henry's orders, had carried out in 1544, but it was not intelligent enough. Devastation by English troops, even devastation accompanied by the distribution of bibles, curiously failed to win Scottish hearts and minds; nor did the activities of the English squadron under Thomas Wyndham in the Firth of Forth, who looked forward with satisfaction to leaving 'neither town nor village nor fisher boat unburnt from Fifeness to Colmsinch'.[31] Even those in favour of Somerset's project for a future marriage of the boy King Edward and the girl Queen Mary, leading eventually to a peaceful union of the two crowns, rejected this 'rough wooing'. Moreover the English garrisons depended absolutely on uninterrupted seaborne supplies.[32]

Even if there had been no opposition, it is doubtful if English ships would have capable of keeping up communications so far north over the winter, and much of the squadron was immobilized at Shields in December for want of money and victuals. The garrisons began to fall almost at once. Dundee was abandoned by the end of January 1548, followed by Inchcolm in March and Inchkeith, taken by the French in July. By May the main English fleet under Lord Clinton was in the Tyne, ready to impose a new blockade of the Forth, but he entirely failed to prevent the arrival on 18 June of a French squadron of three warships, sixteen galleys, and transports carrying 6,000 troops. Piero Strozzi with his galleys sank the English ship *Pansy* and bombarded Broughty Castle. The French now dominated Scotland, and the English garrisons were quite impotent. To rub that in, the Franco-Scottish agreement by which Queen Mary was betrothed to the Dauphin of France, with the two crowns to be united in due course, was signed at Haddington on 7 July, within sight of the English soldiers. In August Clinton burnt some French transports in the Forth, but the galleys forced their way past him in September and returned to France with the loss of one of their number.[33]

As usual the Irish Sea was effectively open all this time, allowing French ships to land further supplies at Dumbarton in January 1548, accompanied by the Earl of Kildare with proposals for a Scottish-Irish alliance. By the same route Queen Mary of Scots left her kingdom in July to voyage to France aboard the French galley *Réale*, which had made the passage northabout from Leith.[34]

By 1549 Somerset's political position as Lord Protector and effective regent of England was looking increasingly insecure, not least because of the war, but this only made it more essential for him to achieve some sort of victory in Scotland. In the spring troops were ordered to assemble at Berwick, and squadrons gathered both in the North Sea and the Irish Sea. Wyndham revictualled Broughty Castle in April, and continued to cruise off the Tay.

Plague broke out in the garrison of Haddington, and on 14 August the survivors abandoned the castle. Broughty held out until the following February, when the starving survivors were evacuated. Meanwhile the English army achieved little beyond border raids, and the political situation in England continued to deteriorate.[35] Encouraged by English weakness, Henry II of France declared war in August, and at once besieged Boulogne. At the same time a squadron of fourteen galleys with transports sailed from Havre de Grâce for the Channel Isles, where on 27 July they seized and fortified the Isle of Sark. Another galley squadron under Leone Strozzi also attacked the Channel Isles in August, but was defeated by an English force under William Winter, when one of the galleys was captured.[36]

By this time England was in a state approaching civil war. Somerset's religious policy, including the imposition by force of the new Book of Common Prayer, aroused widespread rebellions which joined other disturbances springing from economic and social grievances. They were barely repressed by the German and Italian mercenaries hired to prosecute the war in Scotland. Somerset's dictatorship had brought the country disaster at home and abroad, and in October 1549 he was overthrown. The Privy Council, now led by the Earl of Warwick, at once opened negotiations for peace, which was concluded in March 1550. Its terms represented an almost complete defeat for England. Boulogne was to be sold back to France for 400,000 crowns. Any remaining English troops in Scotland were to be evacuated forthwith. Nothing was said about Mary's approaching marriage, so that in effect Scotland was confirmed as a future province of France.[37]

It is difficult to describe the foreign policy and grand strategy of Henry VIII and Somerset as anything short of a disaster. Perhaps the young king had to have his chance to prove that he was no reincarnation of Henry V, that the Hundred Years War was really over, and that England's days as a great military power were long gone. By the peace of 1525 it was clear that England was a shrunken, post-imperial power, but at least her marginal position, protected by the sea, and her natural links with the great imperial and maritime power of the Empire, gave her solid prospects of preserving a peaceful independence in an age when other second-class countries were being rapidly absorbed by the new great powers. Dynastic failure, and Henry's breach with Rome, dangerously undermined that hope, and to complete the tale of folly, his brutal aggression towards Scotland converted a delicate but potentially hopeful political situation into a diplomatic and military disaster. Somerset's chances of retrieving the situation were perhaps never good, but such as they were, he threw them away.

At the peace of 1550, England was not only isolated, but militarily exhausted. The wars of the 1540s had cost £3,200,000, of which £1,300,000 had gone on the defence of Boulogne, a million on operations in Scotland, and half a million on the Navy.[38] All this had achieved less than nothing. The country was isolated, exposed, dependent on coast defences which were already obsolete and falling to pieces, and on a navy which could only with difficulty mount operations as far away as Lowland Scotland. William Winter, the ablest of the younger sea commanders, successfully took a small squadron into the Firth of Forth in the winter of 1551 and damaged the French fleet then lying there – but that fleet of 160 sail far exceeded anything available to English admirals.[39] By this time English warships were unable to force foreigners to salute the English flag in English waters.[40]

At the same time Henry II of France was determined to build up a powerful navy, 'considering that one of the main things worthy of our greatness is to be strong and well-armed at sea'.[41] His plan of 1547 led to the building of a fleet of large ships and light galleys in the Channel, with forty galleys in the Mediterranean, ready to come north if needed.[42] Somerset continued to tolerate, if not encourage the piracy which Henry VIII had let loose in the 1540s. The targets were Scottish and French shipping, but as usual the English took advantage of the war to plunder anyone they could find, and as usual the result was to isolate the country when it most needed friends, and in particular to antagonize the Emperor.[43]

Moreover the wars had badly damaged the English economy, which in the early 1550s fell into a serious depression. The huge volume of former monastic land sold to finance the war absorbed great quantities of capital which might otherwise have financed trade or industry. The debasement of the coinage fed inflation whose destructive social effects reinforced popular unrest generated by Somerset's Protestant policies. An artificial boom fed by devalued money encouraged unscrupulous landlords to turn arable land into sheep pasture, depriving many of the peasantry of their livelihood. Economically this reinforced England's dependence on the export of cloth to Flanders. Financially England was little more than an appendix to the Antwerp money market to which she owed so much. As a result, she had less and less opportunity to take an independent line against the Emperor as sovereign of Flanders. Other English overseas trades, especially that to Spain, had been damaged by the wars. Among other consequences there was a decline in English merchant shipping, much of which now consisted of small ships trading across the narrow seas to Antwerp, whence 'one hoy will bring as much in one year as ten merchants' ships were wont to bring from the other places in two years'; and a further decline in the very small number of English seamen who knew anything about deep-sea navigation.[44]

England remained overwhelmingly an agricultural country, with a single, not very advanced industry, cloth-weaving. Virtually everything Henry VIII needed for his wars had to be imported. Cordage, pitch, tar and masts for ships came from the Baltic, where the trade was controlled by the Hansa and could at any moment be cut off by Scotland's ally Denmark – with whom Henry was obliged to keep friendly, 'considering that the most part of things for the equipage of ships cometh either out of his country or must pass by his country'.[45] Canvas for sails came from Brittany, Spain and the Low Countries. Iron for forging guns came from the Basque country, copper for bronze guns from central Europe, the guns themselves from Liège or Flanders. Anchors were forged in Flanders. Armour and small arms of all sorts, swords and hand guns, were largely or entirely imported, mainly from Italy and the Low Countries. Saltpetre for gunpowder was unknown in England. Even the longbow, most English of weapons, was made from bow-staves imported from Switzerland and Poland. Soldiers were hired from Italy and Germany, while grain to feed them was imported from Danzig and Holland. Every article needed for modern war had to be obtained abroad, and paid for by the reckless dissipation of capital.[46] Perhaps the wars against France and Scotland which Henry VIII initiated and his successors continued were morally and politically justifiable, though neither case is very easy to argue, but it seems beyond doubt that they represented a drain on English national resources which could not possibly be maintained and which threatened economic and political crisis.

FIFTEEN

The Flower of England's Garland

Operations 1550–1572

By the peace of 1550 Warwick bought time to repair some of the damage which had been done to England at home and abroad. To do so, however, he would have had to be a conciliator, prepared to share power at home and to compromise abroad. Perhaps his position as an aristocratic *parvenu*, son of one of Henry VII's most hated ministers, made it difficult for him to work with the great noblemen of ancient families who served with him on the Privy Council. The path of reconciliation, at home and abroad, led back towards Rome. Only with some accommodation of the religious question could the mass of Englishmen be quieted and diplomatic isolation avoided. Instead Warwick chose the extreme Protestant policy, and steered the opinions of Edward VI (now aged twelve) the same way. The result was a sharp decline in relations with the Emperor, who took the part of Edward's Catholic elder sister Princess Mary. There was little doubt that most of the people did the same. Warwick was driven to an alliance with France in July 1551, on terms which seemed to make England an appendix to French foreign policy and threatened to lead presently to a disastrous war with the Emperor. At home Warwick, who became Duke of Northumberland in October, depended largely on a small group of Protestant supporters whose private armies were supplemented by foreign mercenaries. In January 1552 the Duke of Somerset, leader of the more moderate and conciliatory magnates, was executed. To satisfy his followers, Northumberland forced through ever more strongly Protestant and unpopular laws. Even those who approved of the measures themselves were unhappy at seeing them imposed by a corrupt dictatorship to buttress its power. The country became ever more divided by the most divisive of all issues. Moreover Northumberland's clique expected more tangible rewards; the government's financial difficulties, inherited from the wars, were worsened by extensive gifts of crown land to the favoured few. Meanwhile the economy and the cloth trade continued in crisis.[1]

In this period a small number of merchants and noblemen, many of them strongly Protestant in sympathy and linked to Northumberland's regime, began to explore the possibilities of trade and plunder in distant waters where the Emperor did not control the markets. Some, like Robert Reneger, Thomas Wyndham and William Hawkins, began to invest in piracy in the eastern Atlantic and in trade with Morocco and West Africa. This group was particularly drawn from the West Country. Others, mainly in London, hoped to break into the wealth of the Orient by a North-East or North-West Passage around Asia or America. The first English expedition set out in search of a North-East Passage, and incidentally of shivering populations in need of English broadcloth, in May 1553, and two years later the Muscovy Company was founded.[2]

By then Northumberland's regime was in crisis. Having alienated the Emperor beyond reconciliation, without buying any real commitment from France, a friendless and divided England faced in the autumn of 1552 a real possibility of a French invasion in overwhelming force. In the event the French were distracted elsewhere, but it was Northumberland's last piece of luck. The young king was now evidently dying, and the heir was the Catholic Princess Mary. Desperate to avoid the gulf which opened before him when Edward died on 6 July 1553, Northumberland mounted a coup d'état to install on the throne Lady Jane Grey (a great-granddaughter of Henry VII) and her husband, his own son Lord Guildford Dudley. It was the last throw of a hated regime: almost the whole country rose spontaneously to vindicate Princess Mary's rights. Within a fortnight she was queen, and Northumberland (together with his unfortunate son and daughter-in-law) on the way to the scaffold.[3]

Probably the speed of this reaction saved England from a French invasion, for it was much in Henry II's interest to maintain Northumberland as a client with no other friend to turn to. As it was, Queen Mary's accession abruptly returned England to its traditional position as a Catholic country and a natural ally of the Emperor. She knew how difficult it would be to keep it there. She needed the help of the Emperor abroad and of a husband at home to survive in the man's world of sixteenth-century politics. Above all she needed an heir if she were not to be succeeded by her Protestant half-sister Elizabeth, Anne Boleyn's child – and in 1553 Mary was already thirty-seven. These considerations led her to marry Charles V's widowed son Prince Philip, shortly to become Philip II of Spain when the old Emperor abdicated and divided his vast dominions. This marriage was unpopular almost everywhere. Philip himself undertook it with distaste, purely out of a sense of duty, conscious of the importance of an English alliance to the security of an empire dependent on seaborne communications up and down the Channel. The majority of the English, Catholic just as much as Protestant, hated and feared the prospect that England would in due course be swallowed up by a Spanish empire, just as Scotland had been by the French. Mary's headstrong attempts to restore the Catholic Church naturally made her unpopular with Protestants (to say nothing of arousing the misgivings of Philip II and the Pope), but it was the Spanish Match which really upset the people. Within six months of coming to the throne almost universally popular, Mary was nearly overthrown by Wyatt's rebellion.[4]

Nevertheless the marriage went ahead. Substantial fleets from England and Flanders escorted Philip from Spain to England in July. He remained in England just over a year, sailing to Flanders in August 1555 disgusted by his obvious unpopularity among the English and their continued refusal to grant him the powers of a king. By this time it was evident that Mary was not pregnant, as she had for some time supposed. Philip's intention remained to draw England into war with France, but the majority of the Council and Parliament were violently opposed. In January 1557 France and Spain were at war again, but England remained neutral, even when Philip returned in March to present his case in person. Several of those involved in Wyatt's rebellion who had escaped capture had established themselves as Channel pirates under French protection, helping to worsen relations between the two countries and assisting Philip's efforts to bring them to war.[5] Even so he might have failed, had not a group of Protestant exiles from France, led by Thomas Stafford, seized Scarborough Castle at the end of April. As a military operation this was a joke, but Henry II's folly in openly supporting it made it impossible for the English to stand out any longer against the war.[6]

The first naval operation of the war was the thoroughly traditional one of escorting an army to the Continent to campaign alongside the Spaniards.[7] There was no major French fleet operational, though there was a skirmish off Dieppe on 22 June. In conjunction with the Flemish fleet, English ships sacked the village of Cherbourg, and covered Spanish ships bringing money to pay the troops in Flanders. Philip II left England with the army on 5 July, never to return. As usual, the English army failed to cover itself with glory, arriving too late to participate in the crushing victory of St Quentin. The troops came home in October, while the main English fleet under Sir William Woodhouse cruised in the Channel. A smaller force under Sir John Clere was sent to meet the homeward-bound Iceland fishing fleet off Orkney, where Clere was unwise enough to make a landing on 12 August. He met unexpected resistance and was drowned with three of his captains in trying to escape. By September most of the ships had been paid off for the winter.[8]

Philip was happy at the progress made by his army, and could look forward to the next campaigning season with optimism. Neither he nor the English regarded the French army as any longer a threat, and intelligence failed to discover until too late the preparations for a surprise assault on Calais. The fortress was by no means neglected, and the usual winter garrison of 1,500 should have been adequate, but the outer defences were abandoned almost at once when the Duke of Guise's army attacked on 1 January 1558. Crossing the frozen marshes, the French captured the Rysbank Fort, which closed the harbour and allowed them to bombard the castle into surrender on the 7th. Though the outlying fortress of Guines held out another fortnight, the campaign was effectively over in a week, before any help could be sent either from England or from adjoining Spanish territory. The disaster was not the fault of lack of naval protection. There was a small English squadron mounting the usual winter patrol. Woodhouse was ordered to sea with reinforcements on 31 December and arrived on 3 January – a remarkable performance for midwinter. Flemish ships under the Spanish admiral Luis de Carvajal also attempted to succour the castle, but once the Rysbank had surrendered in forty-eight hours there was nothing more anyone could do. Further attempts were frustrated by winter storms and an influenza epidemic. For the French, a bold gamble had been amply rewarded. In England it was the only thing wanting to make Queen Mary, her husband and his war still more unpopular. Whatever its intrinsic value, Calais was the last relic of England's lost empire, the last bulwark against the unwelcome truth that her days of greatness were gone for ever.[9]

In the summer of 1558 a force of English ships under Captain John Malen achieved an unexpected success. On 13 July French troops from Calais attempted to repeat their triumph by surprising Dunkirk. The Spanish army were actually fighting them on the beach when Malen's ships appeared and opened fire on the French from the seaward, contributing to a complete victory. Malen was rewarded with the title of Vice-Admiral of the Narrow Seas.[10] The main fleet's operations under Lord Clinton, the Lord Admiral, were less successful. He landed 7,000 men near Brest at the end of July, but they were driven off by the Breton peasantry, the Flemish contingent of his fleet sailed home, and the fleet was disabled by influenza. He was back in Portsmouth on 5 August with nothing achieved but the burning of the village of Le Conquet, and fog combined with sickness frustrated a later attempt to land on the coast of Normandy.[11]

Meanwhile the position of France's satellite Scotland was menacing, and the English worked hard to refortify Berwick lest it go the way of Calais. A squadron of twenty ships under William Winter cruised to prevent French ships reported to be about to sail from Havre de Grâce for Scotland, while Sir Thomas Cotton took nine more to Dublin to assist the Lord Deputy, the Earl of Sussex. There he embarked troops for an expedition against the MacDonalds of the Isles, whose operations in Ireland have already been mentioned. However Cotton got no further than the Clyde, where landings were made on Kintyre and Arran, and much damage caused. Even in these relatively safe waters, his big ships were a liability, and he was encouraged to return by sickness and storms.[12] Bv then peace negotiations had already begun, and on 17 November Queen Mary died.

Philip's brief and unhappy reign as 'king-consort' of England has often been seen as a turning-point in her naval development. Once Queen Mary's reign was associated with neglect of the Navy and the consequent loss of Calais. More recently, Philip has been seen as the real architect of the force which defeated him in 1588.[13] Both views seem to be exaggerated. The Navy had not in fact been much neglected by Northumberland's government, short of money though it was, nor was naval weakness the cause of the loss of Calais. A survey of 1552 lists twenty-four of the king's ships 'in good case to serve, so they may be grounded and caulked once a year to keep them tight.' Seven more 'must be docked and new dubbed to search their trenails and ironwork', three 'be already dry-docked to be new made', and nine (including five rowbarges) were 'thought meet to be sold', or 'not worth the keeping.'[14] Considering the rate at which wooden ships decay, this was a creditable picture. Philip II and his father were certainly conscious of the value to them of English naval support – apart from the facts of geography it was the main asset that Philip obtained by his marriage – but it is difficult to find evidence of his detailed knowledge or involvement. In August 1555, soon after he had left England, he rebuked the Privy Council when they made difficulties about providing an escort for his father's projected voyage down Channel to Spain, but the episode reveals more of the poor relations between Philip and the Council than his supposed attention to England's naval strength.[15] His remark that 'the defence of the kingdom of England consists in having ships always ready and in good order to safeguard against invasion' was not a blinding insight, while his protest that vessels damaged in a gale should lie in Portsmouth ready to put to sea, rather than go into the Thames for repair, suggests some remoteness from the practicalities of naval operations.[16] Important changes in English naval administration did occur during Mary's reign, but they were not her husband's work.

In the long term one of the most significant developments of these years was a matter of politics and public opinion in which Philip's part was entirely involuntary. Northumberland's aggressively Protestant regime involved itself in piracy, much of it against Spain and the Empire, and trading expeditions which breached the monopolies claimed by Spain and Portugal. Already there was a distinct identification between committed Protestantism, piracy, naval service, and experimental trade into distant waters. These activities involved different groups of people, but there was a considerable overlap between them, and some people were involved in all four. In Queen Mary's reign these connections were strengthened. The supporters of Wyatt's rebellion included William Winter, the ablest of the younger generation of naval commanders, who spent many months in the Tower. When the war broke out in 1557 Queen Mary was able to use it as a means of reconciliation with many of her opponents, including Protestants and rebels. Winter was restored to naval command, while Peter Killigrew, one of the pirates who had operated out of French ports, was given command of one of the Queen's ships. In that year, as in 1544, privateering was permitted by general proclamation, with the natural result of encouraging piracy, in which, as before, many great men about the court were involved. Philip's refusal to allow the English any entry into the trade monopolies of Spain, and his support for those of Portugal and the Hansa, added a further strand to the identification of anti-Spanish sentiment with Protestantism and overseas adventures.[17] The result was that Queen Elizabeth inherited from her sister a situation in which naval and maritime aggression were becoming identified with a heady combination of patriotism, Protestantism and private profit.

She also inherited a throne weaker, and a country yet more divided, than ever before. 'Our sweet Lady Elizabeth . . . a jolly liberal dame and nothing so unthankful as her sister',[18] was highly popular at her accession; but so had Mary been. For a generation the crown had been more or less the prisoner of aristocratic factions, the religious issue was unsettled and the treasury empty. Abroad the situation was menacing. England was exposed to the ambitions of France and Spain alike; 'a bone between two dogs'. The peace of Cateau-Cambrésis, signed in 1559, marked the end of more than sixty years of warfare for the control of northern Italy, and opened the possibility that the great powers might make northern Europe the next theatre of their rivalry. Because the cohesion of the Spanish empire depended on sea communications between Spain and Flanders, England and English sea power were prizes of high value to both superpowers. Economically, England remained dependent on the cloth trade with Flanders. Militarily, she was still trapped between France and Scotland. On 10 July Henry II of France died and was succeeded by his son Francis II, husband of Mary Queen of Scots, who (as legitimate great-granddaughter of Henry VII) took in addition the title of Queen of England. Scotland was now united with France just as certainly as Brittany had been by the marriage of the last duchess in 1491. Elizabeth herself, daughter of Anne Boleyn, was in the eyes of much of Europe illegitimate in four ways: as a bastard, a heretic, a usurper and a woman. Only by marrying and producing a son could she assure her kingdom of any long-term stability, but by marriage she would forfeit her independence. The example of her elder sister's husband was not encouraging – and yet, how could England expect to survive without the protection of a great power? There was probably not one Englishman, regardless of his opinions on other matters, who could see any advantage in the queen remaining unmarried and condemning the kingdom, in all likelihood, to weakness in her lifetime and civil war at her death.[19]

In this frailty and perplexity, England's only certain defence was the sea and her ships: 'Bend your force, credit, and device to maintain and increase your navy by all the means you can possible,' the Secretary of State was advised in 1560, 'for in this time, considering all circumstances, it is the flower of England's garland . . . your best and best cheap defence and most redoubted of your enemies and doubtful friends.'[20] Only with naval power was it possible to keep the French and Spanish threat at arm's length. Only by control of the Narrow Seas could England apply pressure on Spain; only by restraining communications between France and Scotland could she hinder Scotland's absorption into the realm of France. For the queen herself, her ships were her personal defence in a dangerous world which offered no other security. For some of her more Protestant subjects in particular, ships were the defence of their religion, and the means to make their fortunes. For the vast majority of Englishmen, naval strength was not yet a central concern. For every pirate or adventurer with an interest in overseas voyaging, there were a thousand dependent on the cloth trade and interested only in peace with Spain. For every committed Protestant worrying about Catholic conspiracies, there were probably a hundred puzzled, indifferent or conservative spirits who only wanted an end to controversy, and would happily have found it in some more or less nominal reconciliation with Rome. But the queen herself, and a large proportion of those to whom she looked for support, had strong reasons to keep up naval strength. The reasons were almost exclusively political and defensive. Even if Elizabeth and her naval men had foreseen the possibility of an overseas empire and extensive long-distance trade, such ambitions were far beyond their reach. Survival was her priority, over many years when the odds seemed to be heavily against it, and the queen's ships were designed and maintained almost exclusively for this purpose. Hers was a navy intended, not to found the British Empire, but to defend the country by dominating the Channel and the North Sea. We shall see that the design of the queen's ships and the administration of her navy were precocious achievements which left the great powers well behind, but its objectives were limited and defensive.[21]

In Scotland (still ruled by Mary of Guise, James V's French widow) the French were establishing control of their new province, and it was urgent for the English to frustrate them. Though France and England were at peace, and the peace treaty had confirmed France's right to garrison Scotland, Elizabeth felt she could not idly watch the French crush the rebellion of the Protestant 'Lords of Congregation'. In December 1559 William Winter was sent north with thirty-four ships and instructions to cut French communications as though on his own initiative:

> Although the Queen's Majesty hath so many occasions directly given by the French to show hostility, yet . . . for this occasion show none as in the Queen's Majesty's name . . . and so, as if of his own head, do that enterprise he shall see most hurtful to the French.[22]

This delicate task he executed with great skill, in the worst winter season, and he was helped by the gales which wrecked all but two ships of a French relief expedition from Havre de Grâce. In January he was allowed to intervene openly, entering the Firth of Forth and cutting off the French army operating in Fife. The troops had to abandon their guns and retreat to Leith by Stirling, while Winter captured two galleys. In February another French force was dispersed by storms, and reports of growing political disorder in France emboldened Elizabeth to send an army into Scotland. Together with the Scottish rebels, the English besieged Leith, but their assault on 8 May ('marvellously ill handled' in the Duke of Norfolk's opinion) was a costly failure, and it was Winter's blockade (and the death of the dowager queen on 11 June) which forced the French to negotiate. By July both France and England had agreed to withdraw their troops from Scotland, while Mary Queen of Scots formally abandoned her claim on the English throne. Winter then shipped the French garrison home, ending a campaign whose success was entirely due to his ability, and to a new-found efficiency in English naval administration in supporting him in distant waters throughout the winter. After the campaign there were many critics of the performance of English troops, 'but of Mr Winter all men speak so well that I need not mention him,' as Sir William Cecil the Secretary of State put it.[23]

The possession of an efficient navy, and a measure of good luck, had allowed Queen Elizabeth to neutralize the most dangerous threat to her position. Her luck continued, for on 5 December 1560 Francis II died, and in the following year his widowed and still childless queen returned to Scotland aboard a French galley. By this stroke of fortune the dynastic union of France and Scotland was dissolved. The new king of France, Charles IX, was ten years old, and effective power was in the hands of the dowager queen, Catherine de' Medici. With growing religious and political turmoil, France was sliding towards civil war. In June 1562 the leaders of the Huguenots (the French Protestants) offered Elizabeth the port of Havre de Grâce in return for her assistance against their Catholic enemies. She leapt at the chance to acquire a pledge which might be exchanged for Calais. A squadron under Sir William Woodhouse cruised in the Channel keeping communications open, in September a treaty with the rebels was signed, and in October the English garrison occupied 'Newhaven' and Dieppe. The Huguenots thought they had gained an essential reinforcement for their field army, and were disenchanted when Elizabeth refused to allow her troops out of the town. As a result the Huguenots were defeated, and Rouen besieged. A small squadron of English ships was pushed up the Seine in support of Huguenot troops trying to relieve the city. The supplies got through, with the loss of the small galley *Brigandine* forcing the besiegers' boom, but Rouen surrendered on 25 October (when the *Flower de Luce* was captured), and the Huguenots blamed the queen. Dieppe was abandoned as untenable in November, and throughout an extremely bad winter Warwick's garrison in Havre de Grâce was maintained with great difficulty. In April 1563 John Malen was drowned returning from Havre when the *Greyhound* was wrecked on Rye Bar.[24]

Meanwhile the parties in the French civil war signed a peace in March, and combined to drive out the English. The English Navy did its best to keep Havre open, and in July Lord Clinton the Lord Admiral was at sea with twenty-three ships, the largest English fleet in the queen's reign up to 1588. Gales, however, blew him into the North Sea, and on 28 July Warwick surrendered. In due course peace was restored, and of course the English did not get Calais back. The expedition had cost £246,380 and achieved almost no gain, apart from showing that sustained operations in winter, even seventy miles from Portsmouth, were approaching the limit of what an English fleet could support.[25] Henceforward Elizabeth was more cautious about committing her precious ships and men overseas. Though there were a few skirmishes elsewhere at sea, including one near La Rochelle on 28 September, the undeclared war was formally over by April 1564.[26]

This campaign marked the first extensive issue of letters of reprisal, in this case by Warwick and the Huguenot leader Condé, which provided a flimsy legal cover for piracy by English, French and other pirates against merchant shipping of all countries. The established connections between Protestantism and piracy grew stronger, while Queen Elizabeth was unable to dissociate herself from the activities of those on whom she and her Navy depended. Elizabethan local government was entirely in the hands of unpaid nobility and gentry, and it was extremely difficult for the crown to prevent them breaking the law if they chose to do so. In practice virtually no attempt was made to touch figures like the elder Sir Walter Ralegh, Vice-Admiral of Devon and an active pirate; or Sir Edward Horsey, Captain of the Isle of Wight, patron of pirates of all nations, who made the island the great market and fair of all Channel pirates. On the contrary, in 1563 the queen issued another proclamation permitting general privateering. The result was, as it had so often been in the past, to do English diplomacy much damage, and to make enemies when friends were badly needed.[27]

Here we need to pause a moment to define some terms. It is usual and convenient to talk of Elizabethan 'privateering', but the word is strictly anachronistic, for it was only coined in the seventeenth century to describe a legal status which was just then emerging from obscurity. In sixteenth-century England there were only two ways in law by which ships owned by private citizens might capture other ships for profit. One was a general proclamation, which in principle limited captures to the ships of a named enemy in wartime, but provided no means of enforcing its terms. The other was the much older 'letter of reprisal', deriving from medieval marcher law (whence the term *lettre de mark*), under which a merchant, traveller or shipowner who had been robbed in the territory or by the subjects of a foreign prince in time of peace, and had been unable to obtain justice in the courts of that country, was authorized by a court (the Admiralty Court in the case of reprisals by sea) to recoup his losses, up to a specified sum, by seizing the property of persons belonging to the town or country concerned.[28] This letter of reprisal, originally (and still in French) known as a 'letter of marque', was entirely different from the 'letter of marque' of the late seventeenth or eighteenth century, a licence issued by an Admiralty Court in time of war, under legal safeguards, empowering a privately-owned ship to cruise against the shipping of a named enemy, and to sell her prizes only after they had been condemned as enemy property by such a court. This, the classic form of privateering, could by definition be practised only in wartime, while in theory letters of reprisal could be issued only in peacetime. In sixteenth-century practice, however, 'peace' might very often mean undeclared war; civil wars and rebellions provided numerous authorities, desperate or unscrupulous, willing to issue letters with no questions asked; reprisals usually provoked counter-reprisals; and English Lords Admiral were notoriously ready to turn a blind eye towards any activity from which they were entitled to ten per cent of the proceeds.

The same was true in Scotland, and with the same results, as a proclamation of 1525 recognized:

> Our Sovereign Lord and Lords of Council are sickerly informed that an certain [number] of his lieges; masters, owners and mariners of ships [dwell]ing in Leith is to depart in warfare, and by their robberies and spoils made upon friends, they have caused our Sovereign Lord and his lieges to have many enemies whilks were friends before, and presuppones that they shall do siclike in time to come . . .[29]

In Scotland, moreover, a letter of reprisal was heritable property which might remain in force for generations: in 1561 Captain Patrick Blackader was taking Portuguese prizes by virtue of a letter originally granted in 1476.[30] Further confusion existed in the Mediterranean, where the North African 'Regencies' and the Christian powers maintained more or less permanent warfare of which the capture of slaves was a principal object. In the Americas, beyond the 'lines of amity',[31] all foreign ships were excluded by Spanish and Portuguese law, so that even if an English ship intended peaceful trade she had perforce to come armed and ready to fight – from which it was a short step to the cry of 'no peace beyond the line', for if the Spaniards regarded smuggling, interloping and piracy as all one, why should foreigners distinguish them?

All this is very relevant to English and Scottish naval history over the next twenty years, during which there was a rising tide of unofficial hostilities at sea. Though England remained at peace with Spain throughout the 1570s, the activities of English pirates and adventurers steadily undermined good relations, and as usual the queen's own connections with them remained ambiguous. On the one hand the cloth trade, though increasingly dispersed and disrupted, still connected England to Antwerp, and there was a growing trade with Spain herself, especially to the Basque Country (from which iron and fine merino wool was imported), and to Sanlúcar de Barrameda in Andalusia, a port belonging to the Duke of Medina Sidonia, who levied lower customs duties than the king and especially favoured English merchants.[32] On the other hand English pirates (and their Huguenot friends) in the Channel naturally fell upon the richest shipping, much of which was Spanish or Flemish. In the Spanish Netherlands a new governor, the Duke of Alba, arrived in 1567 with a powerful army and a repressive policy intended to enforce religious and political authority. Though both Alba and Philip II continued to profess friendship, the English government was bound to view with anxiety the presence of the finest field army in the world, only a day's sail away in Flanders, 'the very counterscarp of England'.[33]

Meanwhile English West Country merchants, with technical assistance from their Huguenot friends, were penetrating the Portuguese and Spanish empires. The elder William Hawkins (who died in 1554) had pioneered the Brazil and Guinea trades in Henry VIII's time. His younger son John started trading to Spain and the Canaries, and soon developed his father's interests. Between 1562 and 1568 he made four voyages, three of which he led himself, which opened a lucrative trade selling to the Spaniards in the West Indies slaves whom he had previously acquired from the Portuguese by piracy on the coast of West Africa. This of course broke the Spanish monopoly, but English traders were not always unwelcome to Spanish settlements away from the major ports, which were poorly served by official shipping. On Hawkins's fourth voyage, his backers included the queen herself, whose investment consisted of the large ship *Jesus of Lubeck*. Unfortunately for Hawkins, the *Jesus* was old and in poor condition. By the time they came to leave the Caribbean she was leaking so badly that 'living fish did swim upon the ballast', and Hawkins took refuge in the port of San Juan de Ulúa for repairs. Next day the new Viceroy of New Spain arrived to find the English in control of the port. The result was a brief, tense truce, but of course the Viceroy could not leave an illegal trader in possession of the port and did not regard himself as bound by a promise made at gunpoint. Presently he attacked, and there followed a battle in the harbour in which several Spanish and English ships were sunk. Hawkins himself got away in the *Minion*, and so did the pinnace *Judith*, commanded by his young cousin Francis Drake, but they lost many of their companions, and returned with a fixed hatred of the 'treacherous' Spaniards.[34]

The incident of San Juan de Ulúa, in which one of the queen's own ships had been involved, naturally did not improve Anglo-Spanish relations, but by the time Hawkins returned to England in January 1569 a major diplomatic crisis was in progress anyway. French civil war broke out again between 1568 and 1570, giving new opportunities for English ships to intervene. La Rochelle was the base of a Huguenot 'state' navy as well as numerous privateers, whose prizes helped to finance the war effort ashore. They operated out of English ports, especially Plymouth, received much support from English merchants, and in return many English pirates cruised with French letters of reprisal, issued by the Huguenot leader Henry of Navarre in his capacity of Admiral of Guienne. Queen Elizabeth covertly supported these activities, and lent the Huguenots money. Sir Arthur Champernowne, Vice-Admiral of Devon, was instructed to co-ordinate support, and he in turn involved the brothers William and John Hawkins of Plymouth. Naturally they did not confine themselves to French targets. In February 1569 Captain Philip Budockshide of the *New Bark* (jointly owned by Champernowne and the Hawkins brothers) took ten Spanish ships in Plymouth Harbour itself. Queen Elizabeth was not easily embarrassed, but this went too far and she began to grow cooler towards the Huguenots and their friends, even arresting the pirate Martin Frobisher. When the Norman Jacques de Sores took two rich Venetian prizes in December the Huguenots were expelled from English ports – but of course it was much too late for the queen to pretend that she had had no part in the business. At the same time her own ships and seamen were supplying the French rebels. When Sir William Winter escorted the annual wine convoy to Bordeaux in December 1568, he sent ammunition into La Rochelle in passing; the next year John Hawkins with another squadron relieved the city, returning with cargoes of wine, prize goods and church bells.[35]

Meanwhile, in November 1568, Huguenot privateers had chased into Plymouth some Spanish ships carrying money (£85,000 in English terms) to pay Alba's troops. There were too many pirates in and around Plymouth for this to be a safe place, so naturally it was the queen's duty to take the money into safe-keeping. Then it was discovered (possibly indeed pointed out to her by the Genoese banker Benedetto Spinola in London), that the money was a loan from the Genoese banks who financed the whole Spanish imperial system, and remained their property until delivered. This gave Elizabeth her opening to borrow the money herself. The Spaniards of course took this as another hostile gesture, but once again incompetent diplomacy betrayed them. Arresting English ships and goods, without recourse to the remedies provided by treaty, put them in the wrong and justified English seizures in reply.[36]

A year later the Earls of Northumberland and Westmorland rebelled, with the encouragement (as the English government knew) of the Spanish ambassador and the help (as they naturally but wrongly anticipated) of the Duke of Alba. The rebellion was barely suppressed when, in July 1570, news of a large Spanish fleet assembling at Antwerp prompted a partial mobilization of the queen's ships, and an alert of all coastal defences.[37] At the same time the Spanish ambassador was deeply involved in another conspiracy (the 'Ridolfi Plot') to murder Elizabeth and replace her with Mary Queen of Scots, now a refugee and effective prisoner in England. The plot was known to the English government, which of course connected it with the fleet at Antwerp.[38] In fact the fleet was only to escort Princess Anne of Austria to Spain to marry Philip II (his fourth wife), but in the circumstances it was well to be careful. This crisis caused the cancellation of a plan by John Hawkins to mount a private expedition, with royal backing, to attack the Spanish *flota* or annual convoy with bullion from the West Indies.[39] In the end the quarrel was patched up in 1574; English merchants were compensated from Spanish seizures, Genoese bankers were in due course paid back by Elizabeth – but Spanish and Flemish merchants never recovered their losses, and one critical weakness of the Spanish empire at sea was made very obvious.

SIXTEEN

The Galley and the Galleon

Ships 1509–1602

Henry VIII inherited from his father a small fleet dominated by the two big carracks *Regent* and *Sovereign*. Though they carried a numerous armament, most of the guns were small and, as far as we know, none of them were mounted below the waist. Soon after his accession, in 1509–10, the *Sovereign* was rebuilt. Though the details are uncertain, it looks as though she may have been converted from clinker to carvel construction, with the insertion of additional frames and riders to strengthen the hull. Possibly this was to carry an internal deck strong enough to support heavy guns, and very likely it was the example of James IV's new ships which suggested it.[1] It was almost certainly the threat of the Scottish navy which inspired Henry to build his new big ships the *Mary Rose*, *Peter Pomegranate* and *Henry Grace à Dieu* (popularly known as the *Great Harry*). Most of the expansion of the English fleet, however, did not involve any departures in design. The new big ships *Gabriel Royal*, *Katherine Fortileza*, *Maria de Loreto*, *John Baptist*, *Great Nicholas*, *Christ*, *Mary James*, *Mary George*, *Great Elizabeth* and *Spaniard* were all former merchantmen, many of them built abroad.[2] Their strength lay in their size, for men still thought in terms of hand-to-hand fighting, and the bigger the ship the more powerful and magnificent she seemed. The *Henry Grace à Dieu* was a symbol of Henry's prestige just as the *Michael* had been James IV's, and the 1,500-ton *Grand François* of 1521, 'the most triumphant thing that ever mariner saw', was meant to be for Francis I. This imposing edifice with a crew of 2,000, equipped with a chapel, a tennis court and a windmill, unfortunately proved to be just what a Venetian visitor predicted: 'so magnificent that it looks as though she will be incapable of putting to sea.'[3]

It is customary among historians to begin at about this point the story of how the naval genius of the English invented a new type of warship, the broadside-armed sailing ship, which in due course was to sweep away the obsolete carrack and galley and establish a dominance of the oceans of the world which endured for more than three centuries. With the rise of the broadside-armed warship is always linked the development of the line of battle, which has been discerned in embryo as far back as the fifteenth century, and identified with confidence during the sixteenth. This simple picture of how English naval genius mastered backward, Catholic southern Europe has been modified somewhat in recent years by the suggestion that in some respects the Portuguese may have been the real pioneers, but it remains otherwise the orthodox picture. There is a sense in which it is true. The English warships of Queen Elizabeth's reign (though not Henry VIII's big carracks) were the lineal ancestors of the ships of the line of the eighteenth century, and they did mount the majority of their armament on the broadside. In every other respect this simple tale of the origin of the ship of the line is a misunderstanding.[4]

To understand how warship design really developed we have to put ourselves into the minds of contemporaries. By the early sixteenth century naval men were throughly familiar with guns. Light pieces had been carried at sea for more than 150 years, and carracks had been mounting bombards in the waist for more than a generation. Fitting gun decks and shifting the heavy guns lower in the hull made it possible to increase the weight of armament without endangering the stability of the ship. What it did not involve was any change in established fighting tactics. We have a number of naval manuals written about the turn of the fifteenth and sixteenth centuries (notably Philip of Cleves's *Instruction de toutes manieres de guerroyer*), which make it clear how contemporaries expected to fight a naval battle.[5] The first essential was to get to windward of the enemy, which in a strange ship was a clear statement of hostility and in a friend was a grave discourtesy. Having gained the weather gage, the attacker bore up and ran down, firing arrows and small guns as he approached, and rounded to to run alongside the enemy. At this point the bombards in the waist were fired, at a range of a few feet, and, under cover of their prodigious concussion and smoke, the boarders scrambled across. More than half the combustion products of black powder are solid, and its high burning speed produces a blast effect sufficient to stun or even kill at close range;[6] these were more certainly effective than the shot itself. (When Sir Kenelm Digby fought the Venetians off Scanderoon in 1628, it is recorded that the gunfire shattered crockery in the town, and cracked the eggs of the English consul's carrier pigeons.)[7] If the enemy's decks were not cleared as the attacker drew alongside, or if he seemed to be much the stronger in men, it was recommended to fire all the available weapons without grappling and withdraw, perhaps to try again. Usually, however, ships ran alongside to fight it out, as the *Regent* and *Cordelière* did in Brest Water in 1512.

The slow growth in the number and size of heavy guns which big ships could take to sea involved no real modification to these tactics. The big guns of the early sixteenth century were almost all breech-loaders built up barrel-fashion with iron staves, sometimes forged together, always bound by iron hoops shrunk on to them. Guns of this sort could be very large. The biggest, often called basilisks, were sometimes twenty feet long or more and weighed upwards of five tons. Their construction, however, was not capable of resisting very great pressures, and their detachable breech chambers (in which the powder was loaded) were simply wedged in place against the rear of the heavy wooden bed or sledge on which the gun was mounted. Such guns fired either 'dice' or 'hail' shot against men, or stone shot against ships. Stone is much less dense than iron, so that a stone shot of large calibre could be fired at low velocity by a small charge. The fighting range was extremely short, but at short range the 'smashing' effect of a large shot flying slowly could do substantial damage to a ship's hull. The combination of a small charge, permitting a lightly-built gun but firing a large stone shot, was and remained a formidable one at close range, and continued to form an important part of ships' armament throughout the sixteenth century. It was gradually replaced in English, and later in foreign ships, as the high labour cost of making stone shot priced it out of a market increasingly dominated by cheap cast iron, but in the early part of Henry VIII's reign that was all in the future.[8]

Carrying heavy guns to sea made it possible to fire more effectively without actually grappling and boarding, but it made no essential difference to naval tactics. Except in very unusual circumstances, boarding remained the only decisive form of action. Heavy guns contributed effectively to successful boarding, but because of their fixed broadside mountings, and their extremely short range, they were usually fired only just before the moment of contact. Apart from the gun deck, there seems to have been only one significant structural development in the bigger warships. About the beginning of the century, northern shipwrights adopted from the Mediterranean the flat transom stern, and almost at once they began to cut in the stern a pair of gun ports, either side of the rudder low down near the waterline. Here, in the flat right aft on the lowest deck which soon became known as the gunroom, a pair of long heavy guns were mounted.[9] Philip of Cleves recommends

> On each side of the rudder there should be a cast [bronze] or [wrought] iron cannon, mounted suitably for this position. They should have port [lids] which can be hoisted with lines at will, so that they can fire the pieces whenever the weather permits.[10]

According to tradition, the gunport was invented about 1501 by a Breton shipwright called Descharges – a plausible date, though a suspiciously apt name, considering that the gunport was presumably adapted from the loading ports which had been used for centuries.[11] It is probable, though not certain, that these 'stern chasers' were the first really large guns to be taken to sea in sailing ships, and that broadside guns below decks followed soon after. Illustrations give the impression that the broadside guns spread from aft, and that initially the decks, at least of many ships, followed the considerable sheer of the hulls, dipping too close to the waterline amidships to permit a continuous line of ports. The *Mary Rose* was rebuilt in 1527 and again in 1536, when substantial diagonal riders were added in her hold, presumably to support heavy guns.[12] She may have had a gun deck earlier, but by 1536 at the latest it was certainly possible for a big ship to have a continuous gun deck with no extreme sheer, carrying the ports three or four feet clear of the water,[13] though ships continued to be built with considerable sheer, and also camber, on their gun decks; when the *Ark Royal* was bought for the Crown in 1587 she had her 'her upper overlop in the waist . . . taken up and brought to less cambering for the better use of the ordnance.'[14] Well into the seventeenth century in some ships the internal deck or decks were evidently set on more than one level, with 'falls' or steps to avoid cutting gunports through the wales which were essential to the structural strength of the hull.[15] It was clearly only in the gun room that really long guns could be mounted (the *Henry Grace à Dieu*'s two stern-chasers were forged iron breech-loaders respectively 20ft 6in and 22ft long without their breech chambers[16]), and it is noteworthy that pictures of northern warships between about 1500 and 1560 (but neither earlier nor later) usually portray them from aft, prominently displaying the sternports as though they were their principal military feature. Moreover, when a ship's armament is listed according to its disposition (which was not often) it is usually the stern-chasers which are mentioned first, as though they were regarded as the main armament.[17]

These heavy guns firing aft did not modify the traditional boarding tactics of a naval battle. The real gunnery revolution in sixteenth-century warship design had already come from an entirely different direction. By the beginning of the century all the major galley fleets were armed with heavy artillery. Galleys mounted a single large gun on a fixed mounting right forward in the eyes of the vessel. Initially these were iron breech-loaders of the basilisk type, but by the early years of the century Mediterranean galleys were already re-arming with the more formidable bronze muzzle-loaders which could stand much higher firing pressures, and fire either stone or the heavier iron shot over long ranges. The Venetians, with the best guns and gunners in the world, were prepared to open fire at up to five hundred yards.[18] Muzzle-loaders with heavy charges led galleys to adopt sliding carriages in order to absorb the shock of the recoil without shaking a flimsy hull to pieces. Later the single heavy gun came to be flanked by two, and eventually four lighter guns.[19]

Carrying heavy weights right forward in a slender and lightly-built hull involved severe penalties. It made galleys even worse seaboats than before, with a fatal tendency to dig their bows into the slightest head sea (for which reason the gun was often stowed amidships on passage). It made them much heavier, forcing the adoption of a different rowing arrangement needing more but less skilled oarsmen, which in turn led first the Spaniards and then the other galley fleets to use convicts or slaves to pull the oars. But none of these disadvantages counted for much against the brute fact that the galley had successfully entered the artillery age at least a generation before the sailing ship. Moreover it was the galley, not the ship, which had solved the critical tactical problem of the age. Because the galley's gun fired forward, it could be used in the attack, at a point and at a range at which the ship was still completely impotent. A galley fleet could attack with heavy guns in the standard line-abreast formation – almost the universal tactic at sea as on land – while sailing ships in the same formation could fire nothing but small arms. Galleys, for so many centuries fatally vulnerable to the high sides of the ships, could now stand off and sink them with impunity. The result was that carracks rapidly disappeared from the war fleets of the Mediterranean.[20]

How much the English knew about these developments is not clear, but they certainly found out all about them on the disastrous afternoon of 22 April 1513, when Prégent de Bidoux's galleys forced their way through Sir Edward Howard's fleet. It must have become clear then if it had not been before that the navies of the northern world faced a very grave and apparently insoluble problem: how to match the heavy gun-armed galley. One answer of course was to build oared vessels for themselves, which as we shall see Henry VIII did, but the galley's serious limitations of range and seaworthiness meant that this alone could not be a satisfactory response. The challenge was to arm a sailing ship to match the galley. It was not an abstract question of how best to arm a ship in theory, but a very concrete matter of how to imitate the only known method of mounting heavy guns offensively, on a fixed mounting in the eyes of the ship. Even if any other solution had presented itself, it was not easy to see how heavy guns could be used against galleys unless they could fire forward, for it was hardly plausible to imagine the ship sailing into action sideways or astern. Yet the construction of sailing ships in general, and in particular of the carracks with their lofty 'forestages' which had dominated northern naval warfare for a century, seemed to make it difficult or impossible to mount heavy guns firing forward. The only possibility was the arrangement recommended by Philip of Cleves and actually adopted by the *Mary Rose*; mounting a pair of heavy guns on the first level of the aftercastle firing forward on arcs just clearing the forecastle on either side.[21] This achieved some degree of ahead fire, but there was a large blind arc right ahead. Moreover contemporaries placed great stress on the need to mount a heavy gun low if it was to hit the enemy on or about the waterline. These ahead-firing guns could hit another big ship on the approach, while heavy guns in the gunroom were useful for shore bombardment at least, and protected the vulnerable stern from galley attack (which may have been the original idea), but neither they nor broadside mountings provided any direct answer to the gun-armed galley. Traditional tactics were very well against a sailing ship which waited to be attacked, but they offered no hope of pinning down a galley squadron. The galley had the initiative, the range and the fire-power, and, at least in inshore waters where most naval battles had always taken place, it was hard to see how a ship, however heavily armed, could possibly bring her advantage at close-quarters to bear.[22]

From another point of view the dilemma was not unlike that which faced naval architects in the 1830s. A new propulsion system was available (the ship rig in one case, the paddle steamer in the other) which was so much more powerful and effective than its predecessor that it was inconceivable that it should not be used for war, but it seemed to be incompatible with a serious armament. This was the problem which faced English naval men at the start of the sixteenth century, and which they did not solve until almost a century after the galley had first taken heavy guns to sea. What they were trying to do was not to develop the broadside armament, but to supersede it; to design a sailing ship with a powerful ahead-firing armament which could beat the galley at her own game.

There is little or no evidence that Henry VIII had any original ideas to offer on this problem, apart from the conventional interest of the Renaissance prince in heavy guns, fortifications and galleys.[23] Three small (but fully-rigged) galleys were built in 1512, and in 1515 they were followed by the *Great*

Galley, which in her original form carried a full bank of oars on a burthen of 800 tons. The king appeared for her launch dressed 'galley-fashion' in cloth of gold with an admiral's whistle, which at least demonstrated enthusiasm, if not expertise.[24] For the most part the English fleet continued to consist of a handful of big carracks and a larger number of smaller carvels and other vessels – much the size and composition of the fleet with which Henry had gone to war in 1512. It was the threatening international situation of the late 1530s which led to new building and new ideas. In 1536 the *Mary Rose* and the *Peter Pomegranate* were rebuilt, soon followed by the *Great Galley*, the *Great Harry* and several smaller ships. We know the *Mary Rose*, and may guess the others likewise, emerged from reconstruction with a complete gun deck, if they had not had one before. Guns were still scarce and costly, and when she sank in 1545 she was carrying a heterogenous armament mixing forged iron breech-loaders and bronze muzzle-loaders. A list of 1540 gives the *Mary Rose* eight heavy guns (demi-culverin and above) out of a total of 81, and the *Great Galley* seven out of 74; with the *Great Harry* disarmed in reserve these were the most heavily-armed ships in the fleet.[25] In simple weight of fire they could easily have matched any galley unwise enough to come close abeam. Unfortunately this was of limited use in practice. In the Cowdray engraving which provides our best evidence for the Spithead action, the *Henry Grace à Dieu* is advancing towards the French galleys firing a gun from her foremost broadside port, apparently canted round as far forward as possible. The *Mary Rose* foundered while going about to try to bring her other broadside to bear. In spite of the rapid and impressive growth in the artillery power of big English ships, they still had no effective answer to the French galleys, at least in the inshore waters where naval fighting usually occurred.

Meanwhile, however, new designs were making their appearance. There seem to have been three main approaches, or rather sizes, and all three involved using oars. The smallest English oared vessels were the rowbarges, allegedly designed and certainly supported by Henry VIII in person, which were undecked vessels of only twenty tons or so. English experts dismissed them as 'little and open and too weak', and they were cast off as soon as the king died, from which one might conclude that they were too small to be of any value against galleys.[26] The French, however, were very impressed by them, so much so the word 'roberge' or 'ramberge' entered the French language as a synonym for a warship of the newest and most formidable design, and was still being applied in that sense over a century later to ships utterly unlike the original rowbarges.[27] Moreover French sources also credit the rowbarge with an interesting technical innovation: a main armament of two guns, mounted galley-style side by side on sliding carriages so rigged that the recoil of one gun ran out the other. Unfortunately there seems to be no English evidence that this ingenious system actually existed.[28]

Henry VIII also built one true galley in the Mediterranean style, the *Galley Subtle* of 1543, and his ministers embraced with enthusiasm the new fashion for galley slaves. A proclamation of 1544 (the same year convicts were first ordered to the galleys in France) ordered that 'ruffians, vagabonds, masterless men, common players and evil-disposed persons', to be found 'at the Bank and suchlike naughty places where they much haunt and in manner lie nightly', were to be sent to the galleys.[30] Acts of 1548 and 1593 provided for criminals to be sentenced to the galleys, and the idea of using Scots prisoners of war was also canvassed. But in practice all these hopeful projects foundered, and English galleys seem usually to have been manned by free men. Queen Elizabeth later owned a galley named the *Bonavoglia*, the Italian word for a volunteer oarsman; no sense of irony obstructed Sir John Hawkins's 1589 proposal to man her with slaves, but it proved impossible in practice.[31]

At the other end of the scale of size the new ships included the 'galleasses' *Grand Maitresse* and *Anne Gallant*, both built in 1545, which were large ships of three or four hundred tons but with a complete bank of oars.[32] When Lisle's fleet met the French off Shoreham in 1545 these two led the 'wing' of oared vessels which skirmished with the French galleys.

> The *Mistress*, the *Ann Gallant* and the *Greyhound* with all your Highness's shallops and rowing pieces did their parts well, but especially the *Mistress* and the *Ann Gallant* did so handle the galleys, as well with their sides as with their prows, that your great-ships in a manner had little to do.[33]

They seem to have abandoned their oars very quickly, and it would be natural to conclude that such large ships could not be moved effectively under oars.[34] Perhaps it had never been intended that they should. Oars had never been a very effective propulsion system, and no sailor would have chosen them in preference to rig except for inshore work in a flat calm, but in addition to a full rig they offered the priceless advantage of manoeuvrability. A warship with oars could wind to present her main armament to the enemy, wherever it was mounted. Perhaps the most likely explanation for the rapid abandonment of this line of development is that in the meanwhile Henry's shipwrights had found a much more promising design.

The entire royal fleet, as it was in 1545–6, was painted in loving detail by the Flemish Ordnance official Antonius Anthoniszoon, known in England as 'Anthony Anthony'.[35] In the 'Anthony Roll' we can see a fleet full of experimental designs, many of them tending towards long and low ships, galley-like and equipped with oars as well as sail. In 1546, immediately after the Spithead and Shoreham actions, four new 'galleasses' were built, the *Antelope* and *Hart* of 300 tons, and the rather smaller *Bull* and *Tiger*. They were described soon after their completion as 'fast wingers', and were probably meant to counter the galley 'wings' of the French fleet. These ships were completely flush-decked and almost without sheer, with one deck above their bank of oars, carrying guns on the broadside, and a ship's transom stern with the usual heavy stern-chasers. Most importantly, their bows were clearly adapted from those of a galley, with the same prominent spur or beakhead, and the same heavy bow-chaser firing over it. These ships were notable for their 'exceeding nimbleness in sailing and swiftness of course', and having been rebuilt without oars, they went on to long and successful careers in the Elizabethan Navy.[36] (It is possible that these ships, rather than the English rowbarges, were the exemplar of the French 'roberges', which were 200 tons instead of 20.)

It looks as though these galleasses, like the larger *Grand Mistress* and *Anne Gallant*, were intended to fit into the awkward tactical situation of a sailing fleet with a 'wing' of galleys. In the event the English never again attempted this difficult if not unworkable arrangement, but in a different way the new galleasses pointed towards a much more satisfactory answer to the threat of the galley. They were probably the immediate origin in English service of a type which developed more or less simultaneously around the middle of the century in England, Scotland, Portugal, France, Denmark and elsewhere; the galleon. The looseness with which this name was used in the sixteenth century is exceeded only by the promiscuity with which modern authors apply it to almost anything afloat, but it does seem to have had a fairly precise meaning, similar in most languages,[37] in the years between about 1540 and 1570, though the English tended to use it more of foreign warships than of their own. The essence of the galleon was, crudely, that she combined the forepart of a galley with the afterpart of a ship, giving the characteristic crescent shape of high stern and low forecastle. The hull was considerably longer in relation to beam than was customary in sailing ships, and the bow design (the 'galleon nose very little' of one English ship in the 1540s)[38] was adapted from the galley. Two heavy chase guns were mounted under the low forecastle (corresponding to the *arrumbada* or fighting platform which in Spanish galleys covered the guns), firing either side of the galley spur or beakhead, on or through which the bowsprit was stepped. In the bigger ships two more heavy chase guns on the gun deck below fired from ports either side of the stem. Thus after more than half a century of effort, northern shipwrights finally arrived at a satisfactory solution to their problem: a fast and handy sailing ship with a powerful ahead-firing armament, combining the power and seaworthiness of sail with the military qualities of the galley.[39]

In these same critical years of the 1540s during which warship design was evolving so fast, English naval capability was being strengthened by developments in gunfounding. At the beginning of Henry's reign, as we have seen, England had been virtually without advanced industry of any kind, and obliged to import everything necessary for modern war. Scotland under James IV was ten years ahead in the crucial new technology of bronze gunfounding.[40] 'New technology' is in fact a misnomer, for bronze gunfounding was essentially an adaptation of the ancient art of the bellfounder, using the same metal (a copper-tin alloy, misleadingly referred to by contemporaries as 'brass'). The metal was scarce and expensive (for which reason church bells were a strategic commodity of great value), but the casting was relatively straightforward. The guns so produced were costly and beautiful, often elaborately decorated. Each was an individual with its own dimensions, weight and name, for the mould had to be broken after every casting. They were pre-eminent among the status symbols of the Renaissance prince, but even the wealthiest could not afford many of them.[41]

Henry of course was not the wealthiest prince, and all the copper for bronze guns had to be imported. So, initially, were the guns themselves, and the French and Italian experts to teach the English gunfounding. By 1529 the first English gunfounders, John and Robert Owen, were casting bronze guns for the crown. On one of their pieces, recovered with the *Mary Rose*, they proudly describe themselves as 'brethren, born in the City of London, the sons of an English'.[42] By 1550 hardly any bronze guns were still imported, though the copper to make them was discovered in England (in small quantities) only in Queen Elizabeth's reign.[43] In all this England was following wealthier and more advanced countries. In the early 1540s, however, something original and very important started. With the conscious patronage and support of the crown, the established iron industry in the Weald of Kent and Sussex was encouraged to experiment with gunfounding in iron. The first iron muzzle-loaders were cast at Buxted in 1543 by a team composed of the French gunfounder Pierre Baude, the king's 'gunstone maker' William Levett, and the local ironmaster Ralph Hogg (or Hodge).[44]

Iron was in many respects an unsuitable material for cast (as opposed to forged) guns. It melts at considerably higher temperatures than bronze, and it is much harder to achieve a consistent casting with no hidden flaws. Iron is about one-fifth heavier than bronze, and the bore of the gun is subject to corrosion by the explosion of powder, whose combustion products include about 2 per cent sulphuric acid. Moreover an overcharged bronze gun will bulge and then split, whereas an iron gun will fail catastrophically, exploding without warning.[45] In an age when there was no possible means of calculating the pressures and stresses generated in firing a gun except by trial and error, gunners were acutely aware of the difference. But iron had one overrriding advantage, especially for the English: the metal was plentiful in England, and it cost between one-tenth and one-fifth of the price of bronze.[46] In a period of rapid inflation, the price of cast iron guns fell from £10–12 a ton in 1565–70, to £8–9 in 1600.[47]

Over about thirty years, the iron gunfounding industry was carefully nursed by the Ordnance Board, which supplied foreign expertise and distributed favourable contracts among a small group of leading founders. By 1573, Ralph Hogg could estimate that there were seven furnaces casting 3–400 tons of guns and shot every year, and this was only a specialized part of a much larger industry in a period of explosive growth. In 1520 there was one active blast furnace in the Weald. In 1548 there were 53 furnaces, forges and bloomeries at work, and by 1574 there were 52 furnaces and 58 forges.[48] The result by the Elizabethan age was that in England alone of all Europe, small and medium-sized battery guns were available cheaply and in quantity. The largest cannon were not satisfactorily cast in iron until the next century, but already the English had entered an era in which battery guns had ceased to be the status symbol of the powerful, and became a workaday commodity within the pocket of any pirate or privateer. From importing almost all their heavy guns, the English had moved in a generation to regulating the export of a weapon of which they were virtually the only manufacturers.[49]

It is difficult to exaggerate the importance of this precocious industrial and technical growth, but easy to misconstrue it. The Navy Royal was still armed largely in bronze until right at the end of Elizabeth's reign, and the Ordnance Board continued to spend more money on the numerous forged iron guns (by the mid-century almost all small-calibre breech-loaders)[50] than on cast muzzle-loaders either of brass or iron. In the five years from 1553 to 1558 it spent £3,707 5s 6d on forged guns and only £164 4s 8d on cast iron.[51] Between 1568 and 1582 it bought 2,427 guns: 1,703 forged iron, 937 brass, and 417 cast iron.[52] Moreover the English superiority in heavy guns at sea is frequently misunderstood. For many years historians have debated whether the Spanish or English fleets in 1588 were armed predominantly with heavy, short-range guns, or with lighter guns of longer range, and many deductions have been made (in some cases from very slender evidence) about the fighting tactics of each side.[53] Much of this debate has been, and often still is based on the false assumption that long guns meant long range.

By the later sixteenth century there were broadly three families of muzzle-loading guns, cast either in bronze or iron in a range of sizes. Periers or stone guns were short, light, usually chambered pieces designed to fire stone shot with small charges. Their effective range was probably not more than musket shot (say one hundred yards). Cannon were heavier guns of medium length, able to withstand higher powder pressures, and firing either iron or stone shot. Culverins were the longest and heaviest guns of all, with the greatest weight of metal in proportion to their calibre (for which reason they were not cast in the largest calibres).[54] This greater length, however, did not give them a greater range than cannon. Given similar shot, range is dictated by muzzle velocity, and the muzzle velocity (about 2,000 feet per second in theory; 1,200–1,400 in practice) was set by the properties of black powder, which burns very rapidly and expands to its maximum volume before a shot has travelled ten feet. In practical sixteenth-century conditions no ballistic advantage could be gained by increasing the length of any gun beyond about ten feet. Though sixteenth-century gunnery manuals contain fanciful tables purporting to give maximum ranges of a mile or more for the bigger cannon and culverins, in reality the properties of black powder limited them all to much less.[55]

What is more, the maximum range which was ballistically possible greatly exceeded the distance at which it was worth fighting, for smooth-bore guns were inherently inaccurate. Even with the utmost effort to impose standard calibres (something in which the English seem to have been in advance of other nations[56]) it remained extremely difficult to cast guns to identical bores when each mould had to be made anew, so it was very difficult to fit the shot to the gun. Since bronze guns might remain usable for a century or more, there were many obsolete calibres in service. Moreover stone shot cannot at any reasonable cost be made absolutely smooth and round, while iron shot is liable to rust and swell. It was therefore usual to allow a 'windage' or gap between shot and gun of 10–12 per cent of the bore, which reduced the propulsive effect of the powder charge, and allowed the shot to 'ballot', or rebound from side to side of the barrel, so that the line of flight was not parallel with the line of the bore. Firing the gun by linstock (a length of slowmatch attached to a short staff), which was the universal method, introduced a short interval between the gunner deciding to fire, and the charge actually igniting. Since a ship at sea would be moving in several dimensions during this time, this meant further uncertainty in aim. For all these reasons, effective fighting range was very short. Firing at 'point-blank' (about 350 to 400 yards for the larger size of cannon and culverin) at a moving target like another ship was a matter of 'marvellous uncertainty', and if by chance one did hit, the energy of the shot would be largely spent at such a range.[57] 'How much the nearer, so much the better' was Sir Richard Hawkins's maxim;[58] 'he that shooteth far off at sea had as good not shoot at all', in the words of Sir William Monson, another late-Elizabethan admiral.[59] Fighting outside musket-shot was futile:

> Our enemy, playing upon us with their ordnance, made our gunners fall to it ere we were at musket shot, and no nearer could I bring them, though I had no hope to take any of them but by boarding. Here we popped away powder and shot to no purpose, for most of our gunners would hardly have stricken [St] Paul's steeple had it stood there . . .[60]

Yet the English clearly preferred culverin types to cannon. The typical heavy gun of Elizabethan warships, royal or private, was the demi-culverin (approximately 9pdr). Though it was possible to cast a cannon of the same calibre – shorter, cheaper and lighter, with the same ballistic performance – they did not often choose to do so. This was perfectly rational, for the culverin had real advantages. The heavier the gun, the greater the damping of the recoil force, which was important if the guns were made fast before firing and not allowed to run in on the recoil.[61] The heavier the metal of the gun in proportion to the charge, the greater the security against failure. Especially if the guns were to be fired frequently, and therefore most at risk of erosion and corrosion, the culverin had a greater margin of safety. Moreover the longer the gun, cast muzzle-upwards as was English foundry practice, the greater the 'head' of molten metal, the greater the casting pressure at the breech, and the less the risk of flaws at the point of greatest strain when the gun was fired.[62] The culverin was heavy and expensive (especially in bronze), but it would always be the practical gunner's choice for hard work and long service. The English chose it because in their style of warfare they expected to fire their heavy guns much more often than other people; and their choice was wise, for their guns did last. At the time of her loss in 1707, Sir Cloudesley Shovell's flagship the *Association* had a gun aboard cast in 1604; and when a British squadron captured the French West African fort of Goree in 1758 they found among its armament a fine bronze culverin, still serviceable, inscribed 'Thomas Pitt made this piece, 1582'.[63]

Strength and reliability became all the more important with the adoption of corned in place of serpentine powder. The older serpentine powder had all the disadvantages of a chemical mixture (not compound) whose constituents were liable to separate in storage, and whose key ingredient, saltpetre, is hygroscopic and extremely liable to decay in the presence of moisture. Even if the gunner managed to keep his powder dry (never easy in a seagoing ship) and remixed it before making up his cartridges, serpentine powder remained delicate and temperamental. Rammed too hard into the gun, it was liable to explode prematurely; not hard enough, and it might not explode at all, or not effectually. Corned powder underwent an additional stage of manufacturing by which small lumps or 'corns' of powder were glazed. The glaze protected the powder from decomposition or separation, and promoted slower and more regular burning. The result was a powder both more powerful and more reliable. Corned powder was initially confined to small arms, but in the early 1580s the English Navy Royal adopted it for great guns.[64] The more powerful charges naturally made culverins all the more attractive. In the long run, however, as English gunfounders continually improved their techniques, the great weight and length of culverins became unnecessary. By the 1590s English culverins were becoming shorter and lighter, and the evolution in the seventeenth century of a new style of fighting at sea was accompanied by the development of new types of gun adapted to the new tactics.

The key material elements of English naval strength in the Elizabethan age were the galleon hull with a powerful and flexible ship rig, and a heavy armament of cast bronze or iron muzzle-loaders. For contemporaries, as we have seen, the crucial technical achievement was to have combined sailing rig with a powerful battery of bow-chasers. However they handled their ships in action, whatever enemies they faced, it was always the galley which they regarded as their most dangerous enemy. Throughout the Elizabethan naval war against Spain, Spanish officers never ceased to call for galleys as their most effective naval weapon in coastal waters,[65] and English officers never ceased to warn against hazarding warships within reach of galleys. As late as 1602 Sir Henry Leveson and Sir William Monson cut out a Portuguese carrack from Cezimbra Roads – 'a precedent which has been seldom seen or heard of,' Monson claimed, 'for ships to be the destroyers of galleys'[66] – in direct disobedience of the Lord Admiral's orders not to risk the queen's ships within range of the Spanish galleys.[67] Well into the 1630s, retired officers like the former pirate and admiral Sir Henry Mainwaring were still insisting that 'a man-of-war pretends to fight most with his prow'.[68] Drake's *Golden Hind* in 1574 mounted four bow chasers and seven guns a side.[69] The *Elizabeth Bonaventure*, his flagship in the West Indies in 1585, is said to have carried no fewer than six culverins in the bow and four in the stern.[70] In 1590 the Spaniards were advised by an English exile that to match the English they would have to build ships with six bow and six stern chasers, though the *Warspite* of 1595 is given with only four of each.[71] All of these ships fitted Mainwaring's recommendation: 'Her chase and bow must be well contrived to shoot as many pieces right forward, and bowing, as may be (for those pieces come to be most used in fight)'.[72] Other writers proposed that, 'Bows and chases be so contrived that out of them as many guns as possibly may be, may shoot right forwards, and bowing (as the sea word is)';[73] again, 'her bow and chase so galley-like contrived, should bear as many ordnances as with conveniency she could, for that always cometh most to fight . . . neither should her gunroom be unprovided . . .'[74].

This emphasis on bow-chasers was not specifically English, but was a characteristic of the galleon everywhere.[75] The long hull with its low bow and galley beakhead distinguished the galleons of every nation. Nevertheless, English ships did have distinctive qualities. They carried a notably heavy armament of heavy guns. The smaller private men-of-war, in particular, profited from the availability of cheap iron guns to carry batteries capable of overwhelming much larger ships. Whereas Spanish warships were in most cases really armed merchantmen, designed to defend themselves while carrying useful cargoes over the long imperial sea routes,[76] English galleons were more or less pure men-of-war, whose fine underwater lines made them fast, handy and weatherly. As a result they lacked stowage; they were ill-fitted to carry bulk cargoes, or indeed to stow victuals and water to carry large forces over any long distance. The Spaniards comforted themselves with the reflection that 'the English eat so much that their ships are completely laden with victuals on the outward voyage, and even on a homeward passage of any length they can only carry half a cargo';[77] they were right in effect, even if they mistook the cause, for on long voyages English warships were invariably forced to stop at intervals in search of food and water. Queen Elizabeth's ships were essentially a short-range, defensive force, not designed or adapted for long-range cruising. The similar private men-of-war which her subjects used to attack Spanish trade were better fitted for predatory warfare than for peaceful trade; for stealing the products of other people's colonial empires, rather than developing one themselves.[78]

This was true of men-of-war of all sizes. Up to the 1560s the English still built small galley types for inshore work, such as the four brigantines built to support the English garrison of Rouen in 1562, but the development of the galleon seems to have been paralleled by that of the pinnace. Pinnaces might be large ships' boats, or small seagoing galleons, or an intermediate class which could be taken to pieces for long passages. When Drake sailed for his famous voyage round the world in 1577, he carried 'three dainty pinnaces, made in Plymouth, taken asunder all in pieces and stowed aboard, to be set up as occasion served'.[79] Like galleons, pinnaces were fast, weatherly, and carried a heavy armament for their size. They were indispensable for scouting, cruising and piracy, either operating on their own or in conjunction with bigger ships.[80]

In some respects English ships may have been technically in advance of their time, for we have some reason to believe that by the 1580s English shipwrights were developing techniques of design on paper. This was a development pregnant with consequences for the future. It made it possible for a shipwright to design a ship without being present to build her himself. The private warship *Galleon Leicester*, similar if not identical to the queen's *Revenge*, was built in 1578 on the Hamble to plans provided by the queen's leading shipwright Matthew Baker; 'the galleon was moulded by M. Baker and framed by John Ady'. She may have been the first large ship ever built in this way.[81] Paper designs also made possible the idea of ships being built in a class, all to the same plans. Most importantly, it made progressive improvements in design possible, as designers could learn from the work of their colleagues and predecessors.[82] We know that Baker was studying and developing the hull-form of the *Tiger* in the 1590s, forty-five years after she had been built.[83] The English may have been ahead of other nations in these skills, or at least ahead of all but the Portuguese, though it is hard to be sure when shipwrights kept such essential skills secret. Those in a position to judge were certainly proud of their work, and Baker (who 'for his skill and surpassing grounded knowledge for the building of ships advantageable to all purpose, hath not in any nation his equal') was compared in his day to Vitruvius and Dürer.[84]

Elizabethan Englishmen celebrated the 'strength, assurance, nimbleness, and swiftness of sailing'[85] of their ships in language which easily persuaded later historians that technical superiority sprang naturally from the English character:

> Our navy is such as wanteth neither goodly, great, nor beautiful ships who of mould are so clean beneath, or proportion so fine above, of sail so swift, the ports, fights, coins in them so well devised, with the

> ordnance so well placed, that none of any other region may seem comparable unto them.[86]

If so it was because of their situation rather than any innate technical genius. Any ship represents a balance of different qualities; superiority in one has to be bought by sacrificing others. Lacking any major long-distance trade, the English had no need of the carrying capacity the Spanish needed, and could afford to sacrifice it to make a more effective, more specialized man-of-war. Moreover the distinctive English design technique of 'whole-moulding' naturally produced fast and weatherly hulls.[87] But Spanish shipwrights could do the same when they had incentive: on the Pacific coast of South America, where wind and current set northerly thoughout the year and two-way traffic could only be kept up by beating to windward, the shipyards of Guayaquil built outstandingly weatherly galleons – as Richard Hawkins discovered to his cost, when they caught and captured his *Dainty* in 1592.[88] Meeting a squadron of Spanish galleons off Corunna in 1602, English ships fired a few shots and danced away 'teasingly';[89] but five years before and a hundred miles south Sir Walter Ralegh had the opposite experience: 'the caravels of Lisbon and of the parts thereabouts would daily come swarming about us like butterflies, so near that we might cast a stone into some of them, and yet we could never catch one of them, so yare and nimble they are.'[90]

The outstanding qualities of Elizabethan men-of-war, their speed, handiness and heavy armament, were not the result of ineffable national superiority, but of the intelligent exploitation of England's unique situation. In most respects poor, weak and marginal to the Europe of superpowers which was emerging in the sixteenth century, she depended absolutely on effective naval defence, and developed pure sailing men-of-war in an age when the galley was still the specialized warship *par excellence*. The English came late to naval warfare, late to oceanic voyaging, late to gunfounding, and late to carrying heavy guns to sea. They were able to profit from the hard-won experience of Scotland, Denmark, Portugal, Spain, Genoa, Flanders, France and other nations which had preceded them in one aspect or another, to develop a synthesis which in its day, in its circumstances, and within its scope, was uniquely effective. What they were not doing was pioneering the British Empire, laying the foundations for Nelson's Navy, inventing the line of battle, or any of the other anachronistic programmes which later historians have wished upon the Elizabethans.[91] English naval men of the seventeenth century were to make a start on all these, but to do so they had to leave behind the warship designs and the tactics which had been developed in the mid-sixteenth century to defeat the galley.

SEVENTEEN

The Council of the Marine

Administration 1509–1574

England under Henry VIII had not had a permanent navy for the best part of five hundred years. It was at the end of his reign that the crown first established a standing fleet of ships intended, and increasingly designed, for war. From this point the modern Royal Navy of Britain can trace a continuous history. The *scipfyrd* of late Anglo-Saxon England, the galley squadrons of Richard I, the great carracks of Henry V, all may be claimed as predecessors of the modern Navy, but they cannot accurately be described as ancestors. Henry VIII was not a naval visionary who foresaw and provided for future greatness, but his policies and ambitions caused a crisis which called into being a larger fleet than any English king had personally possessed since the Conquest. What really distinguished this fleet from its predecessors, however, was not size but permanence, and what made it permanent was an administration to support it. Ships, especially warships, have always been large, complex and costly structures, expensive to build and maintain, requiring heavy investment in yards, bases, stores, equipment and technical resources of all kinds. The sixteenth century, when a first-class warship could be valued at £1,500,[1] may seem to the modern reader a world of elegant simplicity, but it was as true then as it is now that 'your ships are a charge intolerable', best left to merchants and princes.[2] The reason why Henry VIII's navy did not go the way of Henry V's on his death is partly because of the mortal dangers to England which Henry VIII left as his legacy, but also because an administrative and logistical structure had been created which was capable of maintaining a permanent navy. Nothing like it had ever existed in England before, and nothing like it then existed in any other country outside the Mediterranean (except perhaps Portugal). The creation of this naval administration is the single most important achievement of sixteenth-century England in relation to sea power. Impressive fleets had come and gone with their creators, in England, Scotland and many other countries, but the English naval administration provided the essential continuity which made possible a permanent navy. Without it there could have been no standing force; with it it was possible for a navy to grow and develop. We shall see that sixteenth-century England's answer to the requirement for sea power was in many ways a provisional one which was to prove unsatisfactory in the long run, but it was able to change in the face of the new challenges of another century thanks to the administrative structure which sustained it. Continuity, long-term planning and investment, have always been keys to a successful navy. The more the English navy was obliged to change, the more it depended on institutional memory and support.

The failure of Henry VIII to establish any sort of administrative structure for the fleet he rapidly built up is one of the many reasons for doubting that he had any sophisticated concept of the value of sea power. On the contrary, English naval administration remained rudimentary for the great part of his reign. Though the ancient office of Clerk of the King's Ships existed, it remained as it had always been, one of a number of informal channels through which naval business might be transacted. Robert Brigandine remained in office until his retirement in 1523 and accounted for some parts of the naval administration, mainly at Portsmouth, but he had no central role. His successor in office seems to have been simply the dockmaster at Portsmouth. Other more important naval responsibilities were distributed to whomever happened to be available. The Bishop of Winchester and the Southampton Customs officers victualled the 1513 campaign. The paymaster for the building of the *Henry Grace à Dieu* was William Bond, later Clerk of the Poultry in the royal household, while the overseer was one of the Gentleman of the Chapel Royal, William Crane, who in due course graduated from shipbuilding to become Master of the Choristers.[3]

The real germ of a future naval administration seems to have sprung from storekeeping. During and just after the war of 1512–13 new storehouses were built at Erith and Deptford to support Henry's growing fleet. Erith seems to have been used as an advanced base for routine maintenance, to save the time taken to go up the Thames to Deptford, but it had disadvantages. The anchorage was a lee shore in north-westerlies, and the sills of the storehouse doors had to be raised two feet in 1521, 'for the keeping out of the high tides, for at every tide afore there was two foot deep of water in the said storehouse.'[4] Nevertheless Erith seems to have been the centre of activity of naval administration from 1514 into the 1540s. John Hopton, appointed 'Clerk Controller' in 1512 to act jointly with Brigandine, became in addition Keeper of the Storehouses (of Erith and Deptford) in 1514, and rapidly became the most prominent figure in naval administration. By the time Brigandine retired, Hopton was responsible for the bulk of naval expenditure, but there was still no administrative structure, no permanent officials except Brigandine and Hopton, and no budget.[5]

When Hopton died in 1524 his two offices were separated, Thomas Spert becoming Clerk Controller and William Gonson Keeper of the Storehouses. Both of them were merchants, shipowners and sea-captains (Spert was a former master both of the *Mary Rose* and of the *Great Harry*), and Gonson was in addition an official of the Exchequer, a judge in the Admiralty Court, Vice-Admiral of Norfolk and Suffolk, and one of the wealthiest citizens of London. During the later 1520s and 1530s he increasingly dominated the naval administration. The Lord Admiral of England from 1525 was a child, the king's bastard son the Duke of Richmond, but his household was a vehicle for the influence of Cardinal Wolsey, the Lord Chancellor, to whom Gonson reported. This meant that naval administration was under the eye of the king's most powerful minister; and after Wolsey's fall, his successor Thomas Cromwell continued to take a close interest in it. Both of them preferred to manage through an informal group of trusted subordinates without creating any structures which might take on an authority of their own, and the efficient Gonson was the man they needed. Spert (Sir Thomas in 1535) continued to serve until shortly before his death in 1541, but his responsibilities were more limited. In 1539 Gonson received for the first time a payment of £500 'to be by him employed about his Highness' affairs upon the sea'; which is to say that he was being trusted to manage a small budget on his own responsibility. By the time of his suicide in 1544, Gonson was being called, what he had for some time been in reality, the Paymaster of the Navy.[6]

Besides the storehouses at Deptford, Woolwich and Erith, the naval resources included 'docks' at Portsmouth, Woolwich, Limehouse, Erith and Barking Creek. Most of these were evidently more or less elaborate examples of the traditional mud dock, used for building and long repairs, but the dock at Erith, which accepted no fewer than thirteen ships in four months over the winter of 1512–13, was perhaps more in the nature of a graving place. At Portsmouth a second dock was built in 1522–3, though the reference to 'vices, or capstans ... for winding the ships aground', leaves open the possibility that in this case the 'dock' was something like a slip.[7] The major innovation of this period was the building in 1517 of the Deptford Pond – if it was an innovation, for it resembles a reduced version of James IV's docks at the Pools of Airth, built six years before. There there were three basins covering eight acres, deep enough to float the 1000-ton *Michael*.

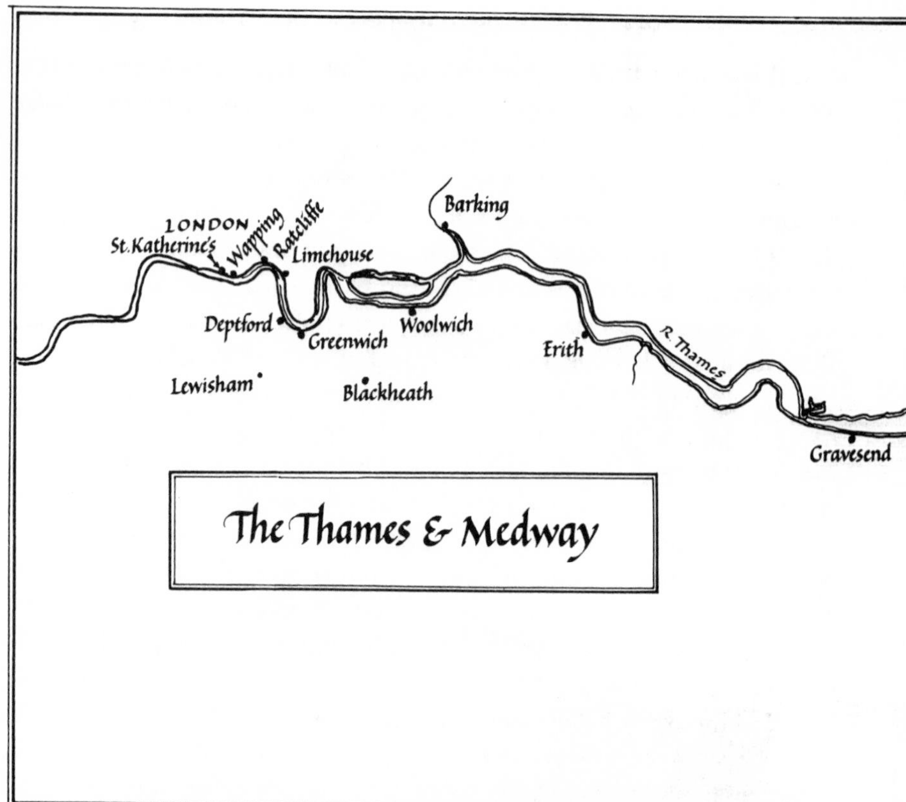

Hopton contracted to construct at Deptford, 'in a meadow next adjoining unto the storehouse . . . a good and able pond wherein shall ride at all times and float these ships ensuing, that is to say the *Great Galley*, the *Mary Rose*, the *Peter Pomegranate*, the *Great Bark* and the *Lesser Bark*'. There was to be 'a good able and sufficient head', and sluices to admit the tide at both springs and neaps. Evidently this was a large wet dock or basin in which these ships could lie in reserve, afloat at all states of the tide, but the head presumably had to be dug out to allow them in or out, in the usual fashion of a dock. Perhaps this was too laborious to be useful in practice, for later in the century it seems to have been used mainly to store masts.[8]

The sudden death of Gonson in the middle of war left the naval administration in crisis, and it may have been this which prompted developments of great importance. His son Benjamin was appointed temporarily to succeed him, but the young man of course lacked his father's experience and standing. A memorandum of January 1545 names the three existing positions in the naval administration and adds four more: the Lieutenant of the Admiralty, the Treasurer, the Surveyor and Rigger of the Ships, and the Master of Naval Ordnance. Next year these offices were formally created and united into a

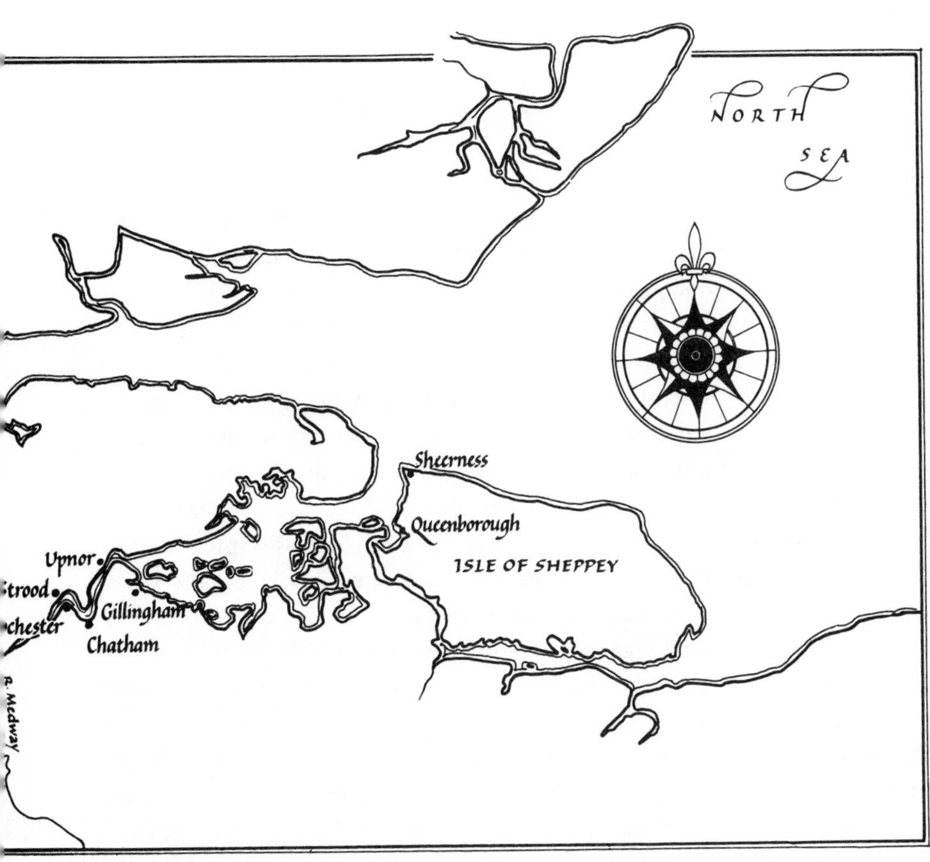

corporate body which is usually known to history by its later title of the Navy Board, but which at the time was more often called the 'Council of the Marine' or 'the Chief Officers of the Admiralty'. It is not clear who was behind this development, nor what exactly they had in mind. Boards were in fashion (the Navy Board followed shortly after the very similar Ordnance Board, Board of Works, and Council of Calais), and Cromwell's successors were trying to impose some order on his legacy of personal connections. However the officers' only truly collective function, specified in their patent, was to sign one another's accounts. The board as a collective body existed formally as a court of audit.[9]

In practice the 'Officers of the Navy' (to give another form of their title) were each individually responsible for a particular aspect of naval administration, but they met together regularly. On these occasions the Lieutenant of the Admiralty (otherwise known as the Vice-Admiral of England) presided as the Lord Admiral's deputy, and the board acted as an all-purpose committee advising the Lord Admiral, the King or the Privy Council. The Master of Naval Ordnance was also a member of the Ordnance Board, and acted as a link between the two boards, to each of which he was responsible for the safe keeping and issue of naval guns. In practice he contracted independently for small arms, but drew heavy guns from the Ordnance Board's central store.[10] The importance of this new structure is difficult to exaggerate. For the first time it gave the English navy a permanent administration with clear lines of command, supervised by well-paid officials. Almost at once they acquired what no settled organization can do without: 'a new house builded at Deptford Strand for the officers' clerks of the Admiralty to write therein.'[11]

Moreover the first appointees were men of standing and ability. Sir William Woodhouse the first Master of Naval Ordnance, then in 1552 Lieutenant of the Admiralty, was a sea commander of long experience. He came, too, of a Norfolk family close to that of the Lord Admiral, William, Lord Howard of Effingham.[12] Many of his colleagues also had close family connections with naval administration. Richard Howlett, the new Clerk of the King's Ships, was godson to William Gonson's widow. Sir Thomas Clere the first Lieutenant, and Robert Legge the Treasurer were merchants and shipmasters; Legge had been over thirty years involved in the Iceland fishery and was a leading London fish-merchant. These men knew as much as anyone about the management of ships in port and at sea. In August 1545 three members of the new board, the Lieutenant, the Controller William Broke and the Surveyor Benjamin Gonson were commanding ships or squadrons at sea.[13]

This was to be the characteristic pattern of sixteenth-century English naval administration. It was run by men of proven competence who knew about ships – but that was only another way of saying that it was run by private interests. These men did not cease to be shipowners and merchants when they became royal officials, and inevitably their work involved numerous cases of what the twentieth century calls conflicts of interest and the sixteenth century regarded as legitimate opportunities. The new naval administration created at the close of Henry VIII's reign was strikingly more efficient and 'modern' than that of any other European state of the day (Venice and perhaps Portugal excepted), but it was not 'modern' at all in the way in which it integrated public and private business. The crown co-opted expertise without which it could not have maintained an efficient navy, but private interests gained considerable control over the king's ships. They could, and did, charter them for private voyages, and sell the navy stores and equipment on their private accounts, appearing alternately if not simultaneously as royal captains, admirals and Officers of the Admiralty, or as private merchants, shipowners, and shipmasters, not to say privateers and pirates. This alliance of interests distinguishes English naval affairs in the sixteenth century, both from earlier and later periods, and from the practice of other countries at the time. It was very different, in itself and in its consequences, from the sort of royal impositions laid on the merchant fleet which had done so much damage to English merchant shipping in the fourteenth century, and was to have just as destructive an effect on Spanish shipping in the sixteenth. It was more in the nature of an informal partnership, not of equals but of parties neither of whom could do without the other, and each of whom could exploit the arrangement to his own advantage. For good and ill, it shaped the distinct character of English naval warfare in the sixteenth century, and especially of the Elizabethan naval war against Spain.[14]

Much the same duality marked the office of Lord Admiral of England. For much of Henry's reign the office was held, sometimes by active sea commanders like Sir Edward Howard and his brother Lord Thomas (later Earl of Surrey, and eventually Duke of Norfolk); at other times by former sea officers like the Earl of Southampton and his successor Lord John Russell (1536–43); and for eleven years by the boy Duke of Richmond. As with so many other aspects of naval affairs, it was only right at the end of Henry's reign that a clear policy suddenly emerges, in this case with the appointment in 1543 of John Dudley, Viscount Lisle. Lisle had been a vice-admiral and squadron commander for several years, and was an intelligent student of naval tactics. Unlike any recent Lord Admiral, he concerned himself with administration ashore as well as command at sea, working closely with William Gonson. He may well be the real originator of the Navy Board of 1546.[15] The trend was continued by Lord Clinton, Lord Admiral from 1550 to 1554 and again 1558 to 1585 – over thirty years in office during which he worked closely with the Navy Board.[16] In some ways the Lord Admiral's relationship with the Officers of the Admiralty was that of an executive head to his departmental managers, though the 'managers' also met together as his advisory council. However it is well not to lean too much on modern analogies to explain sixteenth-century administration. The Lord Admiral was interested in naval administration and involved in it at a certain level of generality, but he was by no means the sole or even principal head of it. His real function was command at sea rather than administration ashore. The Officers of the Admiralty, separately and together, looked at least as much to the Privy Council, the all-purpose central authority of Tudor government, which in all important decisions either advised the sovereign or acted itself, and whose formal or informal committees superintended every aspect of government. In wartime important strategic decisions always came before the Council, usually to the committee known in Queen Elizabeth's time as the Council of War.[17]

In the event, the original structure of the Navy Board lasted little more than ten years. The political turmoil and warfare of Edward VI's reign left naval administration very little time to settle down. The Treasurer was handling larger and larger sums of money on general warrants, which left him free to spend it according to his judgement. However honestly and carefully the money was spent, any central administration was bound to wonder who was in control. Moreover, Queen Mary and her husband were dissatisfied with the performance of a navy which was not able to ready twelve ships to escort the Emperor down the Channel in 1555,[18] and suspicious of the tangled web of *ad hoc* administrative arrangements left by Henry VIII's and Edward VI's ministers. The Marquess of Winchester, Lord Treasurer from 1550 to his death in 1572, was tightening up the efficiency of the Exchequer and reforming its accounts. Over the winter of 1556–7 the Privy Council ordered a series of unannounced musters and checks on different aspects of naval administration.

This is the background to the reforms of 1557, which effectively placed the Navy Board under the supervision of the Lord Treasurer, with the Treasurer of the Navy as his deputy on the spot. The central feature of the new system was the formal adoption in 1557 of an 'Ordinary' or standing naval budget. Ostensibly this was simply to spare Queen Mary trouble, 'where heretofore the Queen's Majesty hath been sundry times troubled with the often signing of warrants for money to be defrayed about the necessary charges of her Highness's navy'. The crucial point is that Winchester took personal responsibility for 'the sum of £14,000 by year to be advanced half yearly to Benjamin Gonson, Treasurer of the Admiralty, to be by him defrayed in such sort as shall be prescribed unto him by the said Lord Treasurer, with the advice of the Lord Admiral'.[19] For this sum Winchester undertook to get the navy into a state of full repair and readiness, after which he believed that £10,000 a year would suffice. The Officers of the Admiralty continued to act as an advisory body for the Lord Admiral, but neither he nor they any longer had any real power to spend money without the Lord Treasurer's approval. English naval administration was now, and remained into the 1590s, firmly under Treasury control.[20]

The immediate result was a large programme of building and rebuilding. Winchester had made it clear that in his view the navy needed much money to restore it to efficiency, and he proceeded to spend. In the two calendar years 1557 and 1558 at least £157,638 was spent on the dockyards and naval victualling. Admittedly it was wartime, but expenditure five and a half times the budget certainly demonstrated one advantage of Treasury control. When Elizabeth succeeded her sister in November 1558 she at once set on foot a commission to survey the state of the navy, and ordered the stockpiling of guns and stores. Her first Parliament was asked for money 'for the continual maintenance of the English Navy to be ever in readiness against all evil happs; the strongest wall and defence that can be against the enemies of this island.'[21] Between January 1559 and January 1561 seven new ships were built for the navy. It was then proposed to keep up the fleet on an Ordinary of £12,000 a year, but by the end of 1561 the actual expenditure for the year had risen to £28,381. By the end of 1564, fourteen new ships had been built in less than six years.[22]

Though naval expenditure then declined, there was much more to this than a panic reaction to a passing crisis. It seems to be clear that Winchester and his colleague Sir William Cecil, the Secretary of State (subsequently Lord Burghley, and in 1572 Winchester's successor as Lord Treasurer), were keenly interested in long-term naval policy and planning. The 1558 commission produced the 'Book of Sea Causes',[23] which surveyed the existing fleet of thirty-four ships,[24] and classified eleven great ships (200 tons and upwards), ten barks and pinnaces and one brigantine as 'meet to be kept', while the remaining twelve, including the two galleys, were to be cast off as 'of no continuance and not worth repair.' In addition to the queen's ships, the report noted the existence of forty-five 'merchant ships which may be put in fashion for war', and twenty more fit to serve as victuallers. They gave detailed consideration to the manning of this potential fleet, and reported that it could be mobilized in two months, given 'ready money for the doing thereof.' They recommended that 'the Queen's Majesty's Navy' (we may now use the capital letter, for it is from about this date that contemporaries generally distinguished the Navy Royal from the mass of shipping of the realm) be laid up in the Medway, in Gillingham Water below Rochester Bridge, with Portsmouth used as an advanced base in the summer months only. Most interesting of all, the report establishes a proper size for the Navy: twenty-four ships in sizes between 200 and 800 tons, four barks of 60–80 tons, and two pinnaces of 40 tons. This proposed fleet of thirty sail differed from that actually in existence chiefly in adding to the middle sizes, between 300 and 600 tons, and it seems very likely that these new ships were meant to be of the new galleon type. William Winter, already Surveyor and lately appointed Master of Naval Ordnance, was a principal author of the report and the ablest sea officer of the younger generation; he had much sea experience with the 1545 galleasses, and his advice was very likely decisive in shaping the proposed programme. It was not immediately followed, either in numbers or design: the new ships built in the early 1560s included the 1,200-ton *Triumph* and the 1,000-ton *White Bear*, while the 800-ton *Victory* was bought from merchant owners. Several old ships recommended for disposal were kept in service, and even so the number of great ships available in 1565 was only seventeen rather than twenty-four. Nevertheless, the report marks an epoch in being the first attempt in England to plan naval requirements on first principles: the first piece of naval staff-work. It also undoubtedly marks the maturity of a naval administration which had been working for fifteen years, and was backed by a considerable weight of experience.[25]

In the same year, 1558, detailed orders were issued regulating the business of the Navy Board, the 'Office of the Admiralty and Marine Affairs' as it is named. The Board was to meet at least weekly to report to the Lord Admiral, or in his absence the Vice-Admiral. The Treasurer was in addition to report monthly and account quarterly, while the Master of Naval Ordnance also made a quarterly report of his department. The precise duties of the Surveyor, the Controller, the Clerk of the Ships and the Clerk of Stores were defined, and they were charged with having twelve to sixteen ships always ready to be mobilized at a fortnight's notice. All these numerous reports were to be made to the Lord Admiral, who in fact figures far more prominently in these orders than in the original 1546 patent of the Navy Board. Nevertheless, the real power remained with the authority to spend money, firmly in the Lord Treasurer's hands. The system ashore was quite capable of functioning without a Lord Admiral.[26]

By the early 1560s, 'the regulation and government of the office of Admiralty and Marine Affairs, the Navy being the chief defence of the Realm', was solidly established.[27] The Navy Board with its office at Deptford was by then responsible for a substantial infrastructure of stores and dockyards with salaried staff, almost all of which had grown up over the past twenty years. Initially the Crown's naval establishments were almost all stores, and building was done elsewhere – Smallhythe in the case of the *Great Bark* and *Lesser Bark* of 1515, and the *Grand Mistress* of 1545. When the *Great Harry* was built in a dock at Woolwich in 1514, shipwrights were impressed in the standard medieval style from all over southern England. The first salaried Master Shipwright was James Baker, who received 4d a day in 1538 and 8d in 1544, when his colleagues John Smyth, Robert Holborn and Richard Bull were also given 4d a day 'in consideration of their long and good service and that

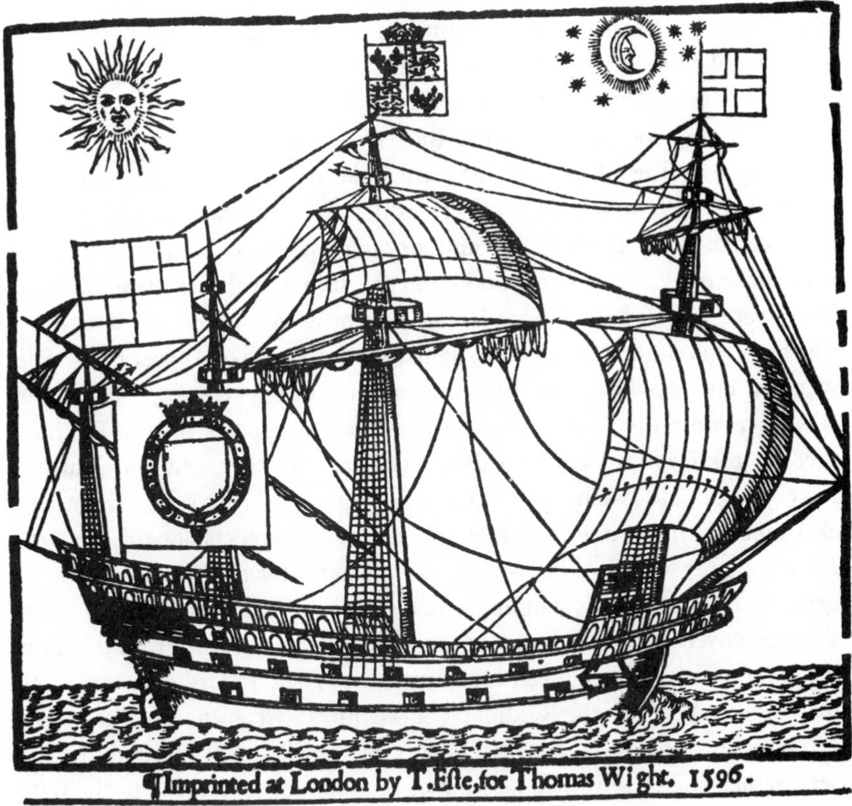

Clinton's flagship, from the title page of William Bourne's *A Regiment for The Sea* (first published 1576). The ship is not named, but must be one of the older 'high-charged' ships of the 1560s, perhaps the *Victory* or *Triumph*, certainly not one of the new galleons.

they should instruct others in their feats.'[28] By 1548 at least thirty-seven shipkeepers, watermen, clerks, storemen, victuallers and purveyors were in 'ordinary wages' (that is, on established salaries) at Deptford, Woolwich, Harwich, Portsmouth and Gillingham. Deptford seems to have been the most important yard at this date, and about 1550 the Treasurer of the Navy paid £88 to pave Deptford High Street, which was 'so noisesome and full of filth that the King's Majesty might not pass to and fro to see the building of his Highness's ships.'[29] The level of payments for wages implies that between 1548 and 1551 there were on average about a hundred shipwrights employed in total. Ten years later, in the first quarter of 1559, 520 shipwrights and nearly 100 labourers were working at Deptford, Woolwich and Portsmouth together. To put this in perspective, the largest private enterprise in

London at the end of the fifteenth century was a master pewterer employing seven journeymen and eleven apprentices, while the largest private industrial concern called for a capital of about £20.[30]

The Master Shipwrights were rapidly becoming the most important figures in the dockyards, though they were not in any formal sense in authority over the whole establishment. Like many sixteenth-century state employees, they were paid retainers rather than full salaries and charged their own daily wages on the account for each building or repair job, together with those of everyone else working on the ship and all the materials used. They were not disbarred from doing private work outside the dockyards. The best-paid of the master shipwrights was the Venetian Augustino Levello, who was employed for over forty years to look after two galleys which were laid up almost the whole time. In 1562 Levello appears on the Ordinary account for Deptford at 16d a day, together with Peter Pett and Matthew Baker at 12d, and twenty-four other shipwrights at lower rates. There were also nine mariners, one grommet and a boy, shipkeepers aboard the *Great Bark*, together with her boatswain, purser and steward. This is one of the earliest appearances of 'standing officers', meaning warrant officers of the ship employed on the Ordinary of the yard to maintain her. From this came the seventeenth- and eighteenth-century naval term 'in Ordinary' for a ship in reserve. Also on the Ordinary at Deptford were the Keeper of the Timberyard, the Messenger, the Keeper of the Plug ('daily attending and serving her Highness in safe keeping of the plug for letting out of the water for the dry keeping of the dock'), and expenses for victualling and lodging, under which head Joan King, Alice Barry, Elizabeth Frances, Joan Rock and eighteen other landladies of Deptford, Greenwich, Lewisham and thereabouts were paid 'for the lodging of 170 of the aforementioned shipwrights, caulkers, sawyers, smiths, topmakers, boatmakers and others working upon her Grace's said new ships, in 98 feather beds . . .'[31] The fact that most of the shipwrights were lodged and victualled by the Crown shows that they were still temporary workers taken on to build a particular ship, but the organization as a whole is strikingly sophisticated. In 1562 the monthly and annual maintenance charges for the queen's ships was carefully calculated. A plan of about 1565 lays out a mooring and an establishment of shipkeepers for each one. Most of them by this time were kept in the new anchorage in the Medway, and the four 'Masters of the Navy', who were the masters of the biggest ships, took it in turn to be in charge of the whole 'Ordinary' afloat as a 'Master of Attendance'.[32]

Parallel with the growth of the Navy Board and the dockyards was the rise of the Ordnance Board, upon which the Navy Board may have been modelled. Certainly the relationship of the Master of the Ordnance, a great officer at court, to the Lieutenant of the Ordnance and the other officers was very similar to that of the Lord Admiral to the Lieutenant and his colleagues. As a Board, the Ordnance Board was only slightly older than the Navy Board, but as an organization it went well back into the fifteenth century. It was responsible for obtaining all sorts of weapons and warlike stores, and supplying them to the Navy, forts, and whatever field army might from time to time be raised. It handled everything from armour, bows, arrows and small arms to the heaviest guns, and all equipment associated with them. It provided ships not only with their guns, but with gun carriages, tackle and all gunners stores, down to cartridge paper. Ships' guns were the particular responsibility of the Master of Naval Ordnance, who kept a separate store at Woolwich. He, for example, arranged to unload ships' guns when they were grounded for repairs. William Winter as Master of Naval Ordnance accounted in 1558 for 264 brass and 48 iron guns afloat in various ships. By 1562 he had forty-seven carpenters, smiths, wheelwrights and sawyers working at Woolwich, though apparently not all full-time. The Ordnance Board manufactured arms only in small quantities, but nurtured relationships with private contractors such as we have already described in the case of gunfounders. Some of them had formal titles and were paid retainers, much like the Master Shipwrights; such an investment in their skill implied for the Crown a privileged but not exclusive claim on their services. These contractors were in business on a big scale. Walter Handy the King's Fletcher, for example, supplied 10,000 sheaves of arrows in 1511, and 180,000 arrowheads in 1513. The Board also retained a number of skilled artificers at its headquarters in the Tower of London who worked on repair and maintenance. By 1571 there were at least twelve of these patented artificers in a total workforce of between 87 and 140. The new office of Surveyor was created in 1537 to oversee the inspection of new heavy guns. The Master Gunner of England was especially responsible for training. As early as 1516 there were twenty-six gunners in training, and by 1552 he had up to two hundred 'scholars sworn to the shooting of great ordnance' at any one time. The Board took an active interest in the design as well as manufacture of heavy guns, experimenting continually with new patterns. By the early 1570s, and probably well before, it was moving to standardize gun calibres.[33]

The Navy and Ordnance Boards both represented a remarkable and sudden advance in the efficiency and sophistication of administration. Though the Ordnance Board had long roots, the naval administration was still largely improvised well into the 1530s. Both Boards then advanced with precocious speed, and in less than twenty years had large, settled and complex organizations. There was, however, another administrative requirement, equally demanding of skill and technology, without which no fleet could undertake any lengthy warlike operations; victualling. Amongst the many weaknesses of Henry VIII's large fleets, its victualling arrangements had always been conspicuous, and it was the one area of naval business from which the Navy Board was excluded. Until 1550 there was no permanent organization. Officials, often either bishops or officers of the royal household, were appointed for every campaign, and dealt directly with the pursers of ships who bought supplies from them. Bishop Gardiner complained in 1544 that all he got in return for his labours as a victualler was the nickname 'Simon Stockfish'.[34]

In 1513 Sir Edward Howard was acutely hampered by failures of supply. Having struggled against foul winds as far west as Plymouth, he begged for food to be sent after him, 'or else we shall be driven to come again into the Downs and let the Frenchmen take their pleasure, and God knoweth when we shall get us up so high westward again.'[35] Having left their pursers in London to speed their victuals, they had no paperwork and no information of what stocks were actually on board. The rash attack on the French galleys in which Howard lost his life was driven partly by the knowledge that there were no supplies to keep the fleet any longer on station. What he did receive was short in quality and quantity: 'they that received their proportion for two months' flesh cannot bring about for five weeks, for the barrels are full of salt, and when the pieces keepeth the number, where they should be penny pieces they be scant halfpenny pieces, and where two pieces should make a mess, three will do but serve.'[36] This became something like a pattern for constant complaints from naval commanders, and indeed from the army as well. In thirteen months from September 1544 to October 1545 the Boulogne garrison received £26,000-worth of food, of which £11,000 had to be written off as worthless. In August 1545 Suffolk and Lisle reported sickness in the ships at Portsmouth, 'which we think groweth by the great heat, and the corruption of their victual, by reason of the disorder in the provision, and strait and warm lying in the ships.'[37]

Part of the problem was the inherent weakness of an improvised administration run by amateurs, or at least men without much experience of the particular problems of victualling ships. By the time the Navy Board had had a chance to establish itself the advantages of a settled administration must have been obvious, and in 1550 Edward Baeshe was appointed 'General

Surveyor of the Victuals for the Seas'. Though he drew his money from the Treasurer of the Navy and was regarded as a member of the Navy Board, he ran a distinct administration and kept separate accounts. Instead of selling victuals to the pursers, he assumed financial responsibility. Baeshe was an experienced (if cantankerous) official long involved in victualling, and he was able to provide the essential knowledge and continuity which the system had lacked. He had agents and officials in each of the yards and in every county. About 1560 the former abbey of St Mary Graces on Tower Hill was bought and fitted out as his headquarters and central stores, in addition to which storage was rented at Ratcliffe, St Katherine's and Rochester.[38]

In 1565 the victualling system was put on a new basis when Baeshe agreed to assume responsibility as a contractor for the whole process, accounting separately from the rest of the naval administration. In return for 4½d a day for every man serving in harbour, and 5d for every man at sea, Baeshe agreed to provide a standard ration, according to what was already the traditional naval pattern. Each man had a gallon of beer and a pound of bread daily (fresh bread in port, biscuit at sea). On four 'flesh days' a week the men received either 2lbs fresh beef, ½lb salt beef, or ½lb bacon. On the three fish days (Wednesday, Friday and Saturday) they had either a quarter of a stockfish or four herrings, plus 4 ounces of butter and ½lb cheese. So long as the quality was acceptable, this was a fully adequate diet (yielding approximately 4,257 calories a day) and we know that it was unofficially supplemented with things like fruit and vegetables. Baeshe also took over provision of 'purser's necessaries' (firewood, candles and the like), and paid the rent on the storehouses and the wages of his staff. He agreed to have victuals for one thousand men for a month always ready, and not to use 'purveyance' (the royal right to buy at fixed prices) unless he had to victual at least 2,000 men at short notice.[39]

The contract was Baeshe's proposal, but the Crown had driven a hard bargain, perhaps harder than it realized, for in assuming a fixed-price contract in an age when price inflation was beginning to rise, Baeshe soon ran into difficulties. In 1573 the rates he received were increased by a penny a day, and in 1587 by another penny, by which time Baeshe, certainly elderly and on his own account heavily in debt, was in the process of handing over to his successor. Baeshe was undoubtedly honest and efficient. His record, both in the quality and the quantity of what he provided, was markedly better than that of his predecessors, and indeed successors, but he had the good fortune to work largely in a period of peace.[40]

What he could not change was the nature of the agricultural market and the technology of food preservation. London was the only town in England whose population exceeded the size of a wartime squadron, and the only port able to victual any considerable number of ships. Even then, Baeshe needed long notice to warn his agents in the shires to obtain the supplies he would need. If squadrons had to operate from other ports, they normally depended on victuals sent from London, and if the 'other ports' were down Channel (Portsmouth, say, or Plymouth) the transports would in all probability have to beat up against the prevailing winds, with the inevitable result of long and unpredictable delays. Drying, drysalting and packing in salt pickle were the only available methods of food preservation. Both the packing of salt beef and the brewing of beer could only be done safely in the winter months, and it seems that even then the results could not be relied on for more than a few months, especially in warm weather. The quality of the casks in which the victuals were packed was crucial, but both casks and coopers were often in short supply when fleets were fitting out. Moreover one man's victuals for a 28-day month took a quarter or three-eighths of a ton of stowage (beer alone required about six tuns a month for every fifty men),[41] and wartime complements, of the queen's ships and of privateers, averaged one man for every 1½ or 2 tons burthen. With their fine lines, heavy armaments and constricted hulls, English warships could not generally stow victuals for more than three or four months. For all these reasons victualling remained a major weakness of English fleets throughout the sixteenth century and for long afterwards. Any voyages to distant seas, any prolonged operations in nearby waters, were almost bound to run against the limitations of contemporary markets and technology. No other single weakness accounts for so many of the English failures to match naval performance to aspirations. If there was one single factor which allowed the fleets of the eighteenth century to keep the seas for long periods and voyage far from home, it was the steady, unspectacular improvement over three hundred years in the quality of victualling.[42]

To build, arm and maintain ships, to feed and pay their crews, three things above all were necessary, in the words of a well-known sixteenth-century cliché: money, money, and yet more money. The smaller and poorer the state, the more heavily the burden of a navy bore. James IV by the time of his death was spending about one-fifth of his entire income simply paying the crew of the *Michael*.[43] His income was £30–40,000 a year in Scots currency, or £7,500–10,000 sterling. Henry VIII spent nearly £700,000 in the year 1513. In the critical years of the 1540s, recklessly consuming the proceeds of dissolving the monasteries, he was spending £650,000 a year on revenues of £250,000. He was not the only Renaissance monarch doing the same, but he was much less able to afford it than Charles V or Francis I. Henry spent £1,300,000 in 1544–5, and in the five years from 1542 to his death the Navy cost a total of £265,000.[44]

The result was that Queen Mary inherited an empty treasury and heavy debts abroad. She managed her affairs with great prudence, and still spent £21,000 a year on the Navy,[45] the pattern which Elizabeth followed. Having spent £246,380 on the Havre expedition with nothing to show for it, she reverted to the prudent husbanding of scant resources.[46] In the ten years from 1565 to 1574 she spent on average just under £16,000 a year on her Navy, or about 6.5 per cent of her income.[47] It was a modest share of a modest total, and it might seem unlikely that any English fleet sustained by such slender resources could hope to confront the superpower of the age. Yet the Elizabethan naval war was to show that in many essential respects English sea power was actually superior to Spanish. This would have been extraordinary in any area of national life; in naval warfare, which has always been the domain of high technology and high expenditure, it was doubly remarkable.

EIGHTEEN

The Spanish War

Operations 1572–1587

Though peace and trade with Spain were restored in 1572, the peaceful years of the 1560s did not return. The rebellion in Flanders against Spanish rule, virtually extinguished by Alba's savage repression, survived by then only in exile. Notable among these exiled Protestant rebels were the pirate group known as the 'Sea Beggars', who operated under English toleration out of Dover. With the improvement in Anglo-Spanish relations they were ordered to leave the country. The result was no comfort to Spain, and perhaps was not meant to be. On 1 April 1572 the Sea Beggars seized the small Dutch port of Brielle, which was the base of the Spanish North Sea squadron. One week later they took Flushing, the only true deep-water port on the Dutch coast. At a stroke, Spanish sea power in the north was virtually eliminated, and the rebellion broke out anew in Zealand and Holland. Within a few months only Middelburg on the island of Walcheren and the port of Amsterdam in Holland remained in Spanish hands.[1] When Alba's relief the Duke of Medinaceli arrived in May aboard a large convoy commanded by the Basque admiral Don Martín Jímenez de Bertendona, he found no major port open to receive him.[2] Over the next two years, three successive Spanish squadrons were defeated in inshore waters; off Flushing in November, in the Zuider Zee in October 1573 and in the eastern Scheldt in January 1574. In February Middelburg capitulated after a two-year siege, and in May of that year the last Spanish inshore squadron was eliminated. The result was that the rebels controlled the inshore waterways of Holland and Zealand, making it very difficult for the mighty Spanish army to get to grips with them.[3] That same year a large fleet assembled in Spain under the command of the veteran admiral Don Pero Menéndez de Avilés, who intended to cruise in the Western Approaches, using Scilly or Irish ports, and thus control the trade of England and Flanders. This bold plan might have turned the tables on both Dutch and English if he could have made it work, but in the event his fleet was completely disabled by influenza, which killed him and prevented it from sailing at all. With his death, sea communications between Spain and Flanders were more than ever dependent on English goodwill.[4]

Meanwhile, far away across the Atlantic, English raiders were beginning to make a modest impact on the Spanish empire. As yet they were very much the junior partners of the Huguenots and Scots, who had been raiding in the West Indies since the 1520s. As early as 1537 Jean d'Ango of Dieppe had taken nine ships out of a Spanish convoy. French ships took Cartagena in 1543 and 1559, Santiago in 1553, and Havana in 1555. Scottish ships were involved by 1547 at latest, and in 1567 a Franco-Scots force sacked Burburata.[5] In 1562 the French founded a colony in Florida, directly on the route of the Spanish convoys homeward bound through the Florida Channel. This grave threat aroused the Spaniards to decisive action. Menéndez de Avilés organized an expedition which took the settlement in 1565 and massacred all the settlers.[6] This was the movement in which the English began to participate in the 1570s. The trades to Africa, South America and the Caribbean which the Hawkins family and their associates had explored tended in these years to become less profitable or more dangerous, but in their place came a different sort of enterprise. John Hawkins was the most respectable of pirates; he acted with at least the tacit approval of his sovereign, and his piracy was an adjunct to trade rather than a replacement for it. The young Francis Drake and his contemporaries who now began to make their mark in the Caribbean were there for plunder alone.

By the 1570s Spanish rule was established throughout the Caribbean basin, in Central America, and along the Caribbean and Pacific coasts of South America, while the Portuguese were settled on the coast of Brazil. Everywhere the Spanish and Portuguese settlements were scattered, mostly small and ill-defended, and the biggest of the Spanish towns tended to be inland. Economically the Spanish empire was relatively poor and unproductive; its only significant exports were hides and pearls, though the Portuguese in Brazil were already exporting sugar in large quantities. There was, however, one overwhelming economic asset: gold and silver. By the 1570s gold production was declining, but the output of the silver mines, above all the great mine at Potosí in the Andes, was rapidly increasing.

The whole system of sea communications which bound the Spanish empire together was designed essentially to distribute this silver. First it was carried north along the Pacific coast to the city of Panama. Thence it crossed the isthmus by mule-train through the jungles to the settlement of Nombre de Dios on the Caribbean coast. This unhealthy little place was largely empty

San Agustín
FLORIDA
GULF OF MEXICO
Havana
C. CORRIENTES
ISLE OF PINES
Vera Cruz
San Juan de Ulúa
Puerto de Caballos
HONDURAS
PACIFIC OCEAN
OLD PROVIDENCE ISLAND
Porto Bello

The Caribbean

except for the few busy weeks each year when the silver was carried across to meet the annual convoy, the *flota*, from Spain. The Spanish Atlantic trade system, the *Carrera de Indias* or 'Indies Trade', was a legal monopoly of the port of Seville, controlled by a merchant guild called the *Casa de Contratación*, which each year organized two convoys to the Caribbean. The trade had sailed in convoy since 1526, and under compulsory escort since 1543. These escorts were armed merchantmen provided by the *Casa de Contratación* from the proceeds of a tax (the *avería*) laid on the trade. The system by the 1560s was for two convoys to sail each year from Seville. One departed in early spring and divided on entering the Caribbean, part going direct to winter at San Juan de Ulúa (the port for Vera Cruz) where it collected the produce of the Central American mines, while other ships called either in Honduras or (until 1581) at Santo Domingo, the original capital of Spanish America. A later convoy collected the Peruvian silver from Nombre de Dios, wintered in Cartagena, and united with the other convoy in Havana in the early summer of the following year. Well before the autumn hurricane season, if all went well, the combined convoy left the Caribbean northward through the Florida Straits and back across the Atlantic, usually calling in the Azores on the way, and making its final landfall at Cape St Vincent. The whole system was designed to protect the bullion shipments, one-fifth of which went to the Spanish crown, and only incidentally to ship essential supplies to Spanish America or provide the colonials with opportunities to export their produce. Ports off the regular convoy routes had few opportunities of trade, and very little protection beyond what they could provide for themselves.[7]

The dream of both the French and the English had always been to capture the fabulous wealth of a *flota*, and this became a dominant, perhaps the dominant theme in English naval strategy not only in the sixteenth century but well into the eighteenth. They never succeeded. In its primary aim of safeguarding the bullion shipments, the Spanish convoy system was an outstanding success. Between 1540 and 1650 the convoys lost about 2.6 per cent of their ships a year, only 0.5 per cent to enemy action. Once only in three hundred years was a complete *flota* captured, by the Dutch West India Company in 1628.[8] But in the 1570s the French and English raiders were especially interested in the possibility of cutting the silver route at what seemed to be its most vulnerable point, the crossing of the Panama isthmus. This was the target of Francis Drake in 1571. His initial night attack on Nombre de Dios miscarried, and was in any case made too late in the year, after the silver had been shipped away. Most pirates would have departed in search of other prey, but Drake was at his best in adversity. He lay up on the coast, suffering heavy losses from yellow fever but making contact with the *cimarrones*, escaped slaves who had established themselves in the jungle and waged a guerrilla war on the Spaniards. With their help, and that of the French raider Guillaume le Testu, Drake mounted a successful raid on a mule train of silver in February 1573. Le Testu was killed and much of the silver recaptured, but Drake returned with enough to make himself wealthy and famous: 'and so arrived at Plymouth on Sunday about sermon time August 9, 1573. At what time the news of our captain's return . . . did so speedily pass over all the church . . . that very few or none remained with the preacher . . .' His takings amounted to no more than 5 per cent of the silver shipments of that year, but the moral effect of his success was enormous, both in England and Spain.[9]

The Spaniards particularly feared that with the help of the *cimarrones* their isthmian trade route would be cut for good, but in the event their counter-measures were effective. Drake's companion John Oxenham, who crossed the isthmus to attack Panama in 1576, was defeated and captured, while in 1579 the Spaniards eventually subdued the *cimarrones*. Possibly the Huguenot leader Coligny, Admiral of France, might have supplied the leadership and state backing needed for so ambitious an enterprise, but he was killed in the massacre of St Bartholomew on 24 August 1572.[10] Though other raiders, English and French, followed into the Caribbean in the 1570s, their efforts and their successes were on a small scale, and did not seriously undermine the improvement in Anglo-Spanish relations. Other projects for large overseas expeditions were disapproved by the government. These included one sponsored by Sir Richard Grenville in 1574–5, which was probably meant to found a colony in the southern part of South America, beyond the limits of Spanish and Portuguese settlement.[11] Drake meanwhile found it prudent to find work in distant waters: in 1575 he was briefly hired by the Earl of Essex to support his efforts to settle Ulster by patrolling the North Channel. He landed the troops who massacred a large number of women and children who had taken refuge on Rathlin Island, though he was not himself involved in the killing.[12]

He was soon back in England, planning a venture much more daring even than attacking Nombre de Dios. The origins of his 1577 voyage are obscure, and it is not at all clear that he and his backers had the same objectives in mind, but it seems likely that the germ of the voyage lay in Grenville's earlier proposal, expanded to cover an armed reconnaissance into the Pacific. All but the most naïve would have expected Drake to make the voyage pay by piracy. The plan's sponsors were Sir Francis Walsingham the Secretary of State, Sir Christopher Hatton, the Earls of Leicester and Lincoln – the group of aggressive, Protestant-minded courtiers who consistently argued for overseas expansion at Spanish expense. The Lord Treasurer Sir William Cecil (now Lord Burghley), always more cautious and peaceable, certainly did not approve and probably was not informed. The queen was allowed into the secret, and invested some money, but gave no formal commission.[13]

On 15 November 1577 Drake sailed from Plymouth, with the small but well-armed galleon *Pelican* (later renamed *Golden Hind*). In September 1578 he passed through the Straits of Magellan into the Pacific. Magellan himself, fifty-seven years earlier, was the only European who had ever passed before through that cold, deep and dangerous channel, and when the *Golden Hind* appeared on the coast of Peru in December she entered a tranquil world which had never known an enemy. At Tarapaza, 'being landed, we found by the sea side a Spaniard lying asleep, who had lying by him 13 bars of silver, which weighed 4000 ducats Spanish; we took the silver, and left the man.'[14] Further north, on the coast of what is now Ecuador, Drake took the *Nuestra Señora de la Concepción* laden, among other things, with twenty-six tons of silver. Eluding all pursuit, he refitted his ship, crossed the Pacific, picked up a part-cargo of spices in the Moluccas, and in September 1580 was back in Plymouth.[15]

So familiar has this voyage become that it is hard in the twentieth century to realize the sensation it caused. Simply as a feat of navigation it was extraordinary. Only one ship, Magellan's, had ever circumnavigated the world before, and the great Portuguese explorer had not lived to complete the passage. If anyone was to repeat his voyage, it would surely have been another Portuguese, a Spaniard, or at least a Frenchman, for these were the recognized experts in oceanic navigation. For the English (though not the Scots), deep-sea voyaging was a novelty. The first recorded occasion when an English ship passed south of the Equator was in 1555: 'they overtook the course of the sun, that they had it north from them at noon'.[16] In 1558 there was probably not one Englishman capable unaided of navigating a ship to the West Indies, and in 1568, only one.[17] Yet within ten years Drake had brought off a feat which aroused the unfeigned admiration of the greatest navigators alive.[18] In political terms, his triumph demonstrated in the most forceful possible manner the wealth and vulnerability of the Spanish empire. His success, 'inflameth the whole country with a desire to adventure unto the seas'. His officially-declared booty was worth £307,000; the true total

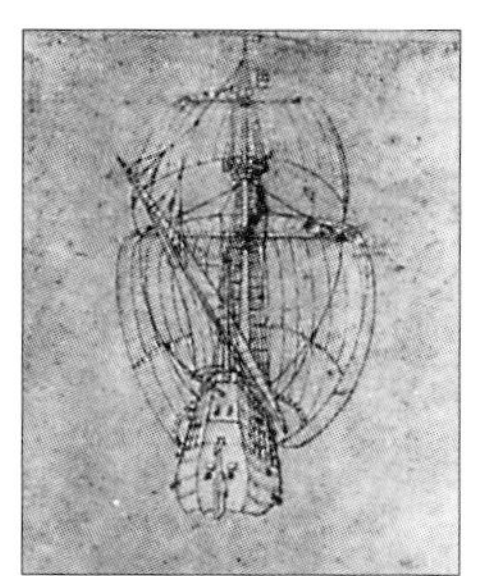

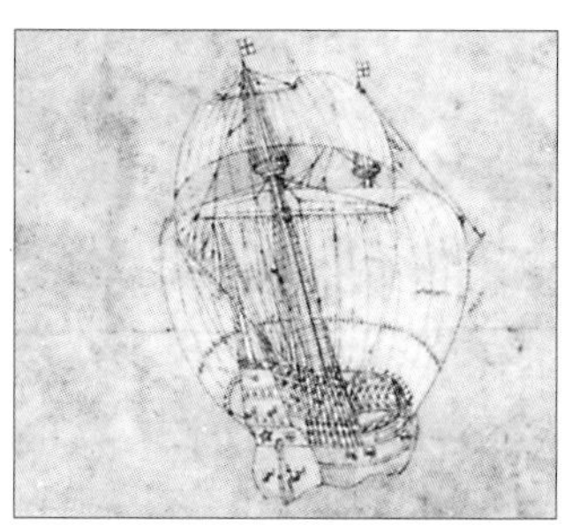
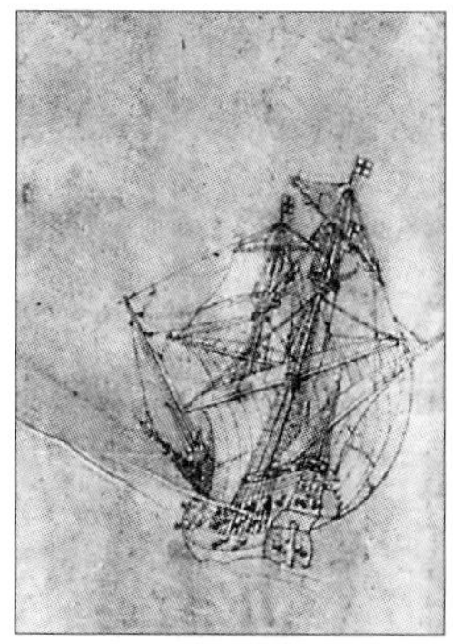
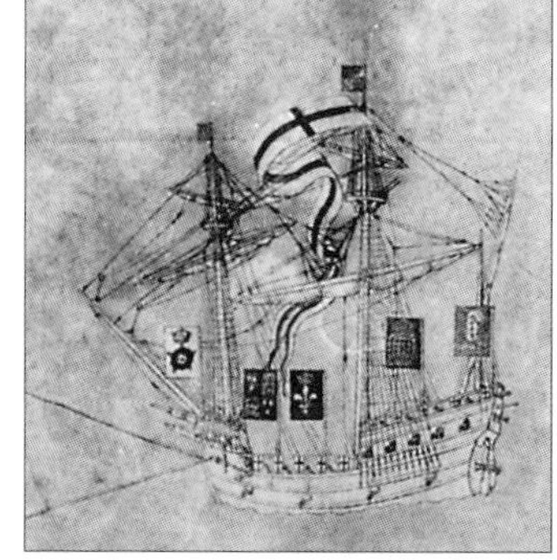
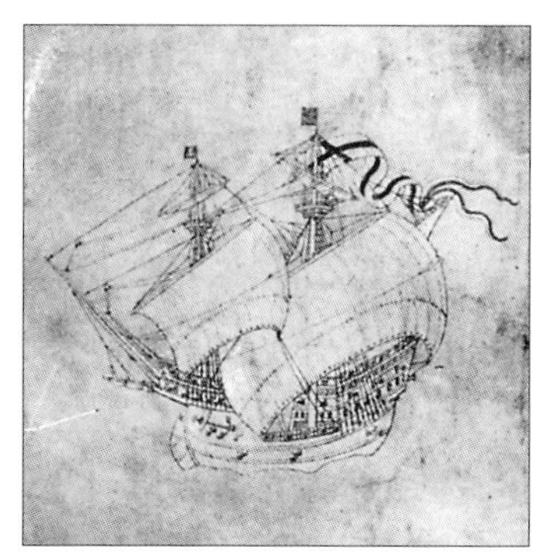

18. *Above* Ships from a panorama of Calais Roads drawn by Thomas Pettyt about 1540 (though the ships are perhaps rather earlier).

19. *Left* A modern model of the *Mary Rose* as she was at the time of her loss. The detail of bow and stern is conjectural.

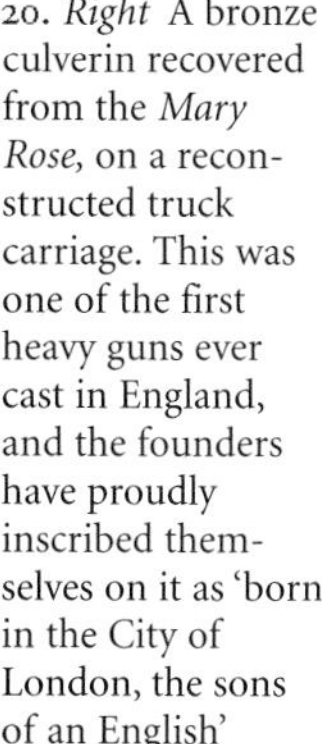

20. *Right* A bronze culverin recovered from the *Mary Rose,* on a reconstructed truck carriage. This was one of the first heavy guns ever cast in England, and the founders have proudly inscribed themselves on it as 'born in the City of London, the sons of an English'

21. The French attack on Brighton, 1545, showing galleys in a typical amphibious operation, bows-on to the beach to land troops and lay down fire support if necessary. This was the galley's pre-eminent rôle; the big ships anchored offshore were ill-adapted to assist.

23. *Left* The rowbarge *Flower de Luce*, from the Anthony Roll.

24. *Below* An English 'Mediterranean-style' galley, the *Galley Subtle* of 1543, from the Anthony Roll.

25. *Left* The galleass *Tiger*, as originally built, from the Anthony Roll. Her oars are shipped, but the oar ports are visible below the broadside guns. The quarter view, conventional in this period, partly conceals her heavy bow chase guns.

26. *Below* The *Jesus of Lubeck*, from the Anthony Roll. She was a Baltic hulk, another 'high-charged' merchant ship type like the carrack.

22. *Opposite* The 'Cowdray Engraving' of the Spithead action of 19th July 1545; an eighteenth-century version of a lost contemporary painting. The French fleet is out of view on the left; the galleys advanced skirmishing with the *Henry Grace à Dieu*. The *Mary Rose* has just foundered off Southsea Castle in the foreground; her mastheads are still visible.

27. Edward Fiennes, Lord Clinton, as Lord Admiral of England, by Hans Eworth, 1562. His whistle of command is round his neck.

28. *Right* One of the new galleons with their characteristic crescent profile, possibly the *Swiftsure* of 1573. Note how the broadside guns are 'bowed' to fire as nearly forward as possible.

29. *Below* A merchant ship of about 1560, from the elder Breughel's *The Fall of Icarus*. This is probably a Flemish or Spanish carrack, typical of the many merchantmen which formed the bulk of the Spanish Armada of 1588.

30. *Above* A galleon bow, from Matthew Baker's notebook, later entitled by Samuel Pepys, 'Fragments of Ancient English Shipwrightry'. The galley-style beakhead, the heavy battery of chase guns, the 'bowing' of the broadside guns, and the English truck carriages are all visible.

31. *Above* An English shipwright, probably Matthew Baker himself, at work in his drawing-office with his assistant, about 1586. The technique of designing a ship on paper was then new and extremely secret.

32. *Left* The sheer and rigging plan of a galleon from Baker's notebook. The hull is a galleon of about 1586, and has been variously identified; the spars and rigging were probably added somewhat later. Note the 'bowing' of the broadside guns.

33. *Below* A large pinnace or small galleon, from Baker's notebook. The gun-deck has a 'fall' aft. Her broadside guns are 'bowed' and 'quartered'. The elaborate sums written beside the sketch show the difficulties of using mathematics in ship design in an era when the most sophisticated calculation available was long division; the next generation invented logarithms to help with such problems.

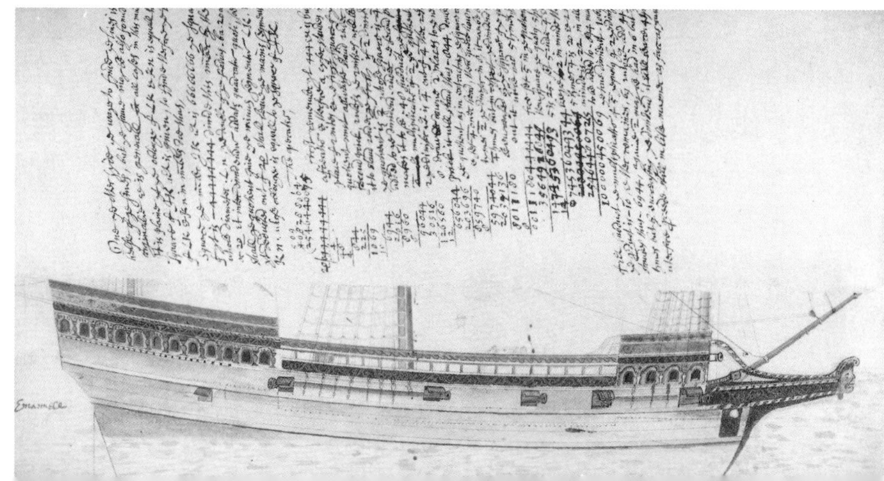

34. Sir William Winter's squadron at Smerwick in 1580, probably drawn by his son William, captain of the *Achates*. The ships include the *Revenge*, the *Swiftsure* and the rebuilt *Tiger*. The big ships have anchored off while the smaller come in to deliver repeated 'charges' at the fort, but all of them are using their main armament, either bow or stern chasers, in preference to their broadsides. The four small ships at the bottom of the bay are 'victuallers'; the West Coast of Ireland was too far away from its bases for the Elizabethan Navy to operate without supply ships.

35. *Below* The *Black Pinnace* bringing home the body of Sir Philip Sidney in 1586. She is cleared for action, with waist-cloths, yardarm pendants and anti-boarding nets rigged.

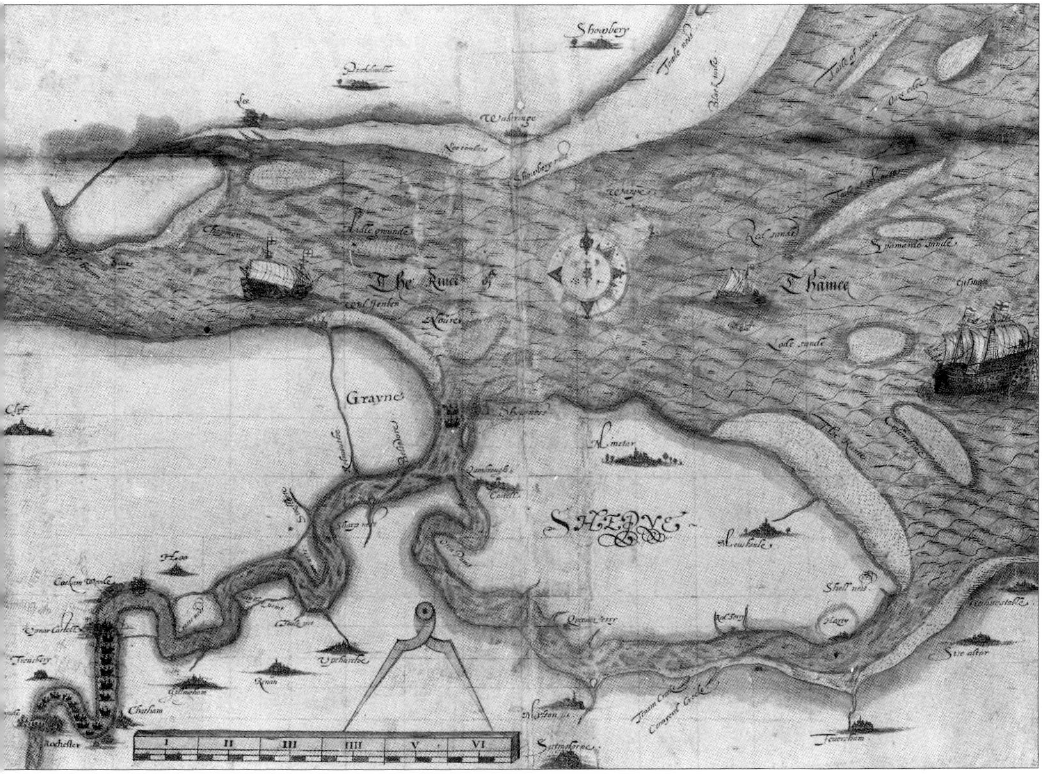

36. A chart of the Thames and Medway about 1580. The Queen's ships can be seen lying (bottom left) at their moorings below Rochester, protected by Upnor Castle and the two pinnaces anchored off Sheerness Fort at the mouth of the Medway.

37. *Left* Detail of a similar chart, showing the Queen's ships at their moorings in the Medway, and the beginnings of the naval yard at Chatham.

38. The 'Chatham Portrait' of Sir John Hawkins, painted in 1581 when he was 44.

was probably at least £600,000. The investors made a 4,700 per cent return on the £5,000 it had cost to fit out the expedition. The queen's share was £300,000, more than an entire year's ordinary income. With this she paid off her whole foreign debt, and still had £42,000 to invest in the new Levant Company.[19]

Here was a potent temptation, but it was not only money which persuaded the queen to tolerate Drake's open piracy, keep her share of the money, and knight 'the master thief of the unknown world' on his own deck.[20] By 1580 the threat of Spanish power was inexorably growing, and growing ever closer to England. In 1578 the Catholic party in France, led by the Guise family, had accepted Spanish money; the other great power in Europe was again disabled by internal strife from acting in its usual role as Spain's natural counterweight. In Flanders the new commander-in-chief of the Spanish army was the Duke of Parma, by common consent the best general of the age, and under his leadership the famous Spanish infantry were steadily crushing the Dutch rebellion. In 1580 the last king of Portugal died without heirs, and Philip II as his nearest relative promptly occupied the kingdom. The wealth of the Portuguese empire was now added to Spain's. Only in the Azores was the authority of the Portuguese pretender Dom Antonio accepted. Commissions issued by him were now added to those of the Prince of Orange (leader of the Dutch rebels) and the Huguenots as a convenient cover for pirates, many of them English.[21] At the same time English rule in Ireland was threatened by Desmond's rebellion. In August 1579 Sir James Perrott took a squadron of five ships to the remote south-west coast, where the rebel James Fitzmaurice had landed in Dingle Bay. In March 1580 Sir William Winter returned to patrol the same waters, until early September when his victuals expired. A few days later a Spanish squadron commanded by Don Juan Martínez de Recalde landed a small force of troops at Smerwick. Hastily re-victualling, Winter returned to bombard the landing force, which surrendered after twenty-four hours and was immediately massacred.[22]

In these circumstances, Queen Elizabeth had reason to feel that her situation was becoming steadily more dangerous, and that the danger came chiefly from Spain. Her own Navy Royal was virtually her only safeguard, and adventurers like Drake her only means of offensive action at a distance. Tolerating Drake's voyage round the world was meant to warn Philip II that England was not powerless to retaliate. Whether the warning was well judged is more difficult to say. Spectacular as Drake's achievement was, there were only a handful of English pirates, and a handful of English ships, capable of long-distance cruising. In 1582 the entire English merchant fleet contained only twenty ships as large as two hundred tons.[23] Only ten Spanish ships at most were taken by English pirates in the whole world in the three years 1578 to 1581.[24] Compared to the vast extent of the Spanish empire and its trade, this was a trivial achievement. Moreover Edward Fenton's expedition of 1582, intended to do in the East Indies what Drake had done in the Pacific, disintegrated through poor leadership and achieved nothing.[25] Drake had done enough damage to make himself famous, and Philip II angry, but neither he nor all the pirates in England were yet able to do much to undermine Spanish power. We know now that it was Drake's voyage which first turned Philip's thoughts to the possibility of striking directly against England.

Meanwhile Spanish sea power was deployed nearer home. The occupation of Portugal in 1580 had been carried out partly by amphibious forces.[26] Now Spain's greatest admiral the Marquis of Santa Cruz was put in charge of a fleet to conquer the Azores from Dom Antonio. The Portuguese leader attempted to raise a fleet in England in return for a base in the Azores, and Drake among others was interested in taking up the offer, but in the end Elizabeth was not willing to go so far, and the fleet which faced Santa Cruz in 1582 was largely made up of French ships.[27] Although the Portuguese-French fleet was larger and much better armed with heavy guns, Santa Cruz won a crushing victory on 26 July.[28] He completed the campaign the following year with the conquest of Terceira, the last island in Dom Antonio's hands – an operation which involved another naval victory followed by an assault landing under heavy fire after a passage of 900 miles across the open Atlantic.[29] These operations taught everyone some important lessons. Whoever had thought that Spanish naval (as distinct from maritime and imperial) power was confined to the Mediterranean could now see how mistaken they had been. A galley admiral, with a fleet partly composed of galleys, using the classic galley tactics of the line abreast, had operated successfully in the open Atlantic and decisively defeated a fleet of gun-armed sailing ships. The message for the English was obvious and unpleasant; for the Spaniards, it was a triumph promising further successes. Santa Cruz urged Philip II to keep his fleet together and send it at once to deal with the pirate queen.[30]

Elsewhere Spanish forces were equally successful. In the Netherlands Parma took the ports of Dunkirk and Nieupoort in 1583, allowing the re-establishment of a Spanish squadron in the North Sea and permitting ships of up to 200 tons to voyage from Spain.[31] The death of the Duke of Anjou on 31 May 1584 left the Huguenot Henry of Navarre as heir to the throne of France, making further civil war almost certain, and neutralizing France's capacity to thwart Spanish plans. Moreover, though the English did not yet know it, by a secret treaty the Guise party, who controlled much of the Channel coast, had become Spanish clients. In July William of Orange was assassinated, leaving the Dutch rebellion leaderless and its final extinction apparently imminent. 'The best soldiers at this day in Christendom' would then be available for further service, and the discovery of another plot (the 'Throckmorton Plot') against Elizabeth's life, in which the Spanish ambassador was deeply implicated, left little doubt where they might be sent.[32]

The queen and her ministers now faced an agonizing dilemma. On the evidence available to them, it seemed clear that the jaws of Spanish power were slowly but inexorably closing on England. Sooner or later Elizabeth would have to fight for her throne; the only choice seemed to be whether to take arms now, when she still had some freedom of manoeuvre, or to wait until the Dutch had been crushed, and fight alone.[33] Even the cautious Burghley was convinced:

> Although her Majesty should thereby enter into a war presently, yet were she better able to do it now, while she may make the same out of her realm, having the help of the people of Holland and before the King of Spain should have consummated his conquests in these countries . . . and shall be so strong by sea and so free from all other actions and quarrels . . . as that her Majesty shall no wise be able with her own power, nor with the aid of any other, neither by sea nor land, to withstand his attempts, but shall be forced to give place to his insatiable malice.[34]

But it was a fearful risk to oppose Spain in any circumstances, and only the most foolhardy would not have hesitated before it. Drake, never a man to rate himself too lowly, might boast over dinner of taking on the King of Spain, but sober heads judged that Philip was 'the greatest monarch on earth, who was strong enough to wage war on all the world united.'[35] His 'empire of empires'[36] embraced not only Spain, Portugal, the Low Countries, and much of Italy, but all the Americas and all the parts of the Far East settled by Europeans. Germany and most of Central Europe was ruled by his Habsburg cousin Rudolph II. The only country in Christendom capable of opposing Spain was France, which was disabled by civil war. Spain's only formidable enemy was Turkey, still the ultimate menace to Christian Europe, still slowly advancing at sea in the Mediterranean even after the failure to capture Malta in 1565 and the defeat of Lepanto in 1571. It was to protect the western Mediterranean against the Turks and their North African dependencies that Spain maintained the great fleet which in the early 1570s reached its maximum strength of over 140 galleys and sixty or seventy ships.[37]

All this depended on financial resources which no Christian monarch could match. Between 1571 and 1580 Philip II received twelve million ducats (about £3,300,000 at the then exchange rate of 5s 6d to the ducat) in silver from the Americas. In the next ten years the figure was 18.7 million, and between 1591 and 1600 it was over 25 million. The two Caribbean convoys of 1587 alone brought 12.6 million ducats, of which nearly five million was for the king. Whereas in 1575 the monarchy's burdens had forced it into 'bankruptcy' (or more accurately, a forced renegotiation of its debts), by the mid-1580s Spain's resources were again growing rapidly. Philip's total income, which was 8.7 million ducats in 1577, was nearly thirteen million when he died in 1598. Moreover, American silver was merely an additional revenue to an empire which drew most of its resources from internal taxation; two-thirds of Philip's income came from Castile.[38] By comparison, Queen Elizabeth's ordinary annual income in 1585 was about £300,000, not more than a tenth of Philip II's. After ten years of frugal management, by 1585 she had accumulated a reserve of another £300,000.[39] Elizabeth did not know exactly the size of Philip II's revenues (nor in fact did he), but the English were well aware of the disparity of force. The decision which faced the queen and her ministers in the autumn of 1584 was whether to risk war with the wealthiest monarch in the world.

Convinced (reasonably, from what she knew, but almost certainly wrongly) that Philip II had already committed himself to attacking England, the queen decided that she had no choice. In the autumn of 1584 she offered aid to the Dutch rebels, and in August 1585, by the Treaty of Nonsuch, Elizabeth bound herself to provide 4,000 infantry and 400 cavalry to save the besieged city of Antwerp, to pay 600,000 florins a year, and send a naval expedition to the West Indies. Though they were too late to save Antwerp, there were no fewer than 8,000 English troops in the Netherlands by December 1585 when the Earl of Leicester arrived to command them.[40] At the same time the English government turned to the plans of the Hawkins–Drake circle. In July 1584 John Hawkins had proposed a scheme for privateering under Dom Antonio's flag from 'a certain port' (meaning Plymouth) under 'a certain leader' (meaning himself). In November this had developed into a plan for an expedition, possibly to South America, to be commanded by Drake and backed by the queen, Hawkins, and the usual circle of court investors.[41] This plan lay ready to hand when the decision was taken to risk war with Spain. Then, on 26 May 1585, the Spanish government seized northern shipping in Spanish ports under authority of a royal proclamation which announced that the ships were embargoed to serve the Spanish crown on a forthcoming expedition. One of these foreign ships was the *Primrose* of London, which managed to escape from Portugalete with the official who had tried to arrest her and his proclamation. The English at once assumed that the expedition referred to was an invasion of England, and used the Spanish embargo to justify Drake's expedition. It is usually said that the expedition sailed as a consequence of, and in retaliation for, the Spanish embargo, but it is certain that it had been planned well before Philip acted. It seems likely that the embargo was not in fact directed primarily against England (most of the ships arrested were Dutch) and it was certainly lifted very soon, but not before it had done Spain some essential harm.[42] Abroad, it served to justify English attacks. In England it damaged and enraged the large and wealthy community of London merchants engaged in trade with Spain, and converted them overnight from advocates of peace and accommodation, to ardent proponents of a naval war. These men knew the languages and the trade of Spain and its empire, and owned most of the few big ships in the English merchant fleet; they were to become essential supports of the English naval war effort.[43]

Drake sailed from Plymouth on 14 September with twenty-nine ships, including the queen's *Elizabeth Bonaventure* and *Aid*, the earl's *Galleon Leicester*, and some powerful London ships, one of which was the *Primrose*; they carried a landing force of 2,300 infantry. The squadron touched first at Vigo and the Cape Verde Islands, getting food, water and booty, and then rested over Christmas on St Christopher's in the Windward Islands. On the last day of the year they approached Santo Domingo, the oldest Spanish city in the New World. Landing their troops by night through heavy surf on a coast the Spaniards believed impossible, the English took the city in twenty-four hours. After a month's stay they sailed for Cartagena. This bigger and more important city was likewise taken in spite of an alert defence led by professional soldiers and two galleys, the English troops rushing the defences in a night attack. The squadron sailed from Cartagena on 4 April, laden with booty, ransom money and provisions for the homeward voyage. Sickness had by this time so reduced the force that further major landings were impossible, but on their way home they destroyed the Spanish fort of San Agustín in Florida, and took off the starving and disheartened colonists from Roanoke Island.[44]

Drake's squadron was formed by the same process of private investment, and much the same syndicate of investors, as had backed Hawkins's

Caribbean voyages, Drake's round the world, and Fenton's unhappy attempt of 1582. The queen contributed two warships, but what made this squadron essentially different was that Drake carried her commission. Though composed of the same mixture of public and private interests as earlier naval expeditions, this one was unequivocally a public operation of war, undertaken in the queen's name. This did not mean that the expedition was a purely strategic exercise. All the investors, particularly the queen, were in it for the money, which she needed to honour her obligations to the Dutch. All of them had their eyes fixed on the wealth of the Indies, the only support of Spanish power, and most of them had very high expectations of how much could be achieved. Drake certainly hoped to take and hold Panama and use Havana as a permanent English naval base.[45] Modern historians are inclined to pour cold water on this 'heroical design of invading and possessing America',[46] seeing it as example of Drake's vaunting ambition and lack of strategic judgement.[47] Certainly we can see with hindsight that the effects of the tropical climate were bound to make sustained operations impossible and that maintaining a permanent base so far away would have been beyond English resources. Nevertheless Drake came within a few hours of intercepting the homeward-bound *flota*, carrying silver worth over £700,000.[48] Moreover the Spaniards did not underestimate what the English might do. They fully expected that the English could and would take and hold virtually any coastal city in the Indies they chose.[49] The Marquis of Santa Cruz informed King Philip that he required not less than thirty-five large and twenty-eight smaller ships, twelve galleys and at least 10,000 infantry for the fleet he was ordered to take in pursuit of Drake.[50]

The psychological shock to the Spanish system was profound. Nothing so greatly sustained a prince as his reputation; no prince had, and needed, so formidable a reputation as Philip II. Now an impudent pirate from a minor power on the margins of Europe had demonstrated how few clothes the emperor really possessed. The conclusion drawn in Madrid was not only that the defences of the Indies must be strengthened, but that so dangerous an example must be punished at source lest the fabric of the whole empire be shaken. It was at this point that Philip ordered serious planning to begin for the invasion of England. Elizabeth's attempt to deter war had instead provoked it.[51]

Both sides now regarded themselves as being officially at war, but in the short term neither was able to do much about it. The Spanish government began planning, but was a long way from being able to act. The English government authorized privateering against Spanish shipping, and sharply increased expenditure on shipbuilding, but there was not much more it could do immediately. Drake's expedition did not pay its way financially, and by the time he returned to England in June 1586 it was too late to send him anywhere else that year. A strong patrol was maintained in the Narrow Seas, and John Hawkins was sent to sea with a squadron of twenty ships, five of them the queen's and the rest of them in her pay. With them he cruised off the Portuguese coast from August to October, taking four prizes but missing the homeward-bound silver convoys. This was not a spectacular operation, but it showed that English ships could stay at sea for three months, on the enemy coast six hundred miles from their base, an achievement which would have astonished Henry VIII and did alarm Philip II.[52]

The following year Drake was at sea again with four of the queen's galleons and seventeen other ships, several of them of some size and power. By this time it was obvious that an invasion was preparing in Spain, and Drake's task was to interfere with it. His force incorporated a powerful squadron of London ships commanded by Captain Robert Flicke which had been preparing a cruise off Lisbon to intercept the Portuguese carracks from the East Indies; thus the pre-war Iberian trade powerfully contributed to the naval war. Drake sailed on 2 April, meeting the London ships at sea, and pushed southward with a screen of pinnaces intercepting any passing vessel which might give warning of his presence. On the 19th they appeared off Cadiz and sailed straight into the bay. Coming without warning, wearing no admiral's flags, they achieved complete surprise. They remained three days in the harbour, repelling the efforts of six galleys[53] to dislodge them, and left having destroyed twenty-four ships, some of them large and valuable, one of them a galleon belonging to Santa Cruz himself. Drake then moved to Cape Sagres, a headland near Cape St Vincent where all inward-bound shipping from the West and East Indies sought their landfall, and which all coastal shipping between Lisbon and the Andalusian ports and the Mediterranean had to round. There Drake captured the castle and lay under the Cape waiting for whatever might swim into his jaws. Cape St Vincent was a notorious place for pirates: Spanish sailors called it the 'cape of surprises',[54] but there had never been so unpleasant a surprise as this. In this position Drake effectively threatened all inward-bound shipping from both the West and East Indies, and stopped the preparations of the Armada at Lisbon. He also aroused counter-measures which would eventually have threatened overwhelming attack if the storms of autumn had not first driven him from his open anchorage. In the event, however, he did not wait for either, but sailed on 31 May, intending to intercept the *flota* and the Portuguese carracks

BAY OF BISCAY
C. Ortegal
Ferrol
Corunna
C. Finisterre
GALICIA
Vigo
Santander
Portugalete
Guetaria
Fuenterrabia
San Sebastián
NAVARRE
CASTILLE
ARAGON
Madrid
PORTUGAL
EXTREMADURA
Peniche
R. Tagus
Lisbon
Cezimbra
ANDALUSIA
R. Guadalquivir
Seville
C. St. Vincent
C. Sagres
Sanlúcar de Barrameda
Cadiz
Malaga
Cartagena
Gibraltar
STRAITS OF GIBRALTAR
MEDITERRANEAN SEA
Iberia

in the Azores. His departure, no one knew whither, caused even more consternation than his presence in so crucial a position had done. Fortunately for the Spaniards, his ships were scattered by a storm, but unfortunately for the Portuguese, he captured the carrack *São Phelipe*, and returned to Plymouth in triumph on 7 July. The carrack's cargo was officially valued at £140,000 after heavy looting.[55] Five days after Drake returned, Santa Cruz got to sea from Lisbon with thirty-seven ships, followed by Juan Martínez de Recalde with his squadron. For three months they searched in vain, returning in October with their ships exhausted, sickly and weatherbeaten (though they did see the returning *flota* safe into port).[56]

In terms of material damage, Drake's raid had achieved relatively little, though the preparations for the Armada had been severely delayed and disrupted. (His claim to have destroyed hoops and pipestaves sufficient for 25–30,000 tuns, often cited as the cause of the Armada's subsequent problems with victuals and water, does not seem to be borne out by Spanish documents.[57]) In psychological terms, however, it had a devastating effect. The English had gained fabulous wealth from the chance capture of a tiny fraction of the seaborne trade of Philip II's empire. All those who argued for a systematic blockade to cut off Philip from the sources of his wealth drew support from Drake's success. In Spain the shock and horror aroused by the capture of Santo Domingo and Cartagena were multiplied by this violation of one of the chief seaports of Spain herself.

> With this corsair at sea in such strength, we cannot protect any island or coast, nor predict where he may attack, so it is not clear what we can do to stop him.[58]

Everywhere in Europe Spain's enemies took heart, Spain's rivals took pleasure, and Spain's friends took fright. But Drake himself, though an inveterate boaster, was well aware that he had done no more than 'singe the King of Spain's beard': he had infuriated and humiliated Philip II, but he had scarcely weakened him at all.[59] 'I dare not almost write unto your Honour of the great forces we hear the King of Spain hath out . . . Prepare in England strongly, and most by sea. Stop him now, and stop him ever.'[60]

NINETEEN

The Advantage of Time and Place

Operations 1588

Miscalculation on both sides brought Spain and England to a war which neither of them desired. For Philip II, England was a natural and necessary ally which he would never have attacked if his own interests had not seemed mortally threatened. Strongly as he felt about the defence of the Catholic faith, he had hitherto resisted all attempts by Catholic exiles or by the Pope to manoeuvre him into action, and would certainly have continued to do so if Spain had not been attacked.[1] Elizabeth, for her part, would never have provoked so powerful an enemy if she could have preserved the peace, and did not give up hope of restoring it even after Drake's raid on Cadiz. Her war aims were limited: not total victory over Spain, which would have been the merest fantasy, but some compromise settlement which would keep Spanish armies out of the Low Countries and preserve her life and throne without unduly assisting a future revival of France.[2] Some of her more aggressive courtiers and admirals, those who thought naturally in terms of a great Catholic conspiracy to enslave Protestants, argued, as Ralegh later put it, that 'if the late Queen would have believed her men of war as she did her scribes, we had in her time beaten that great empire in pieces and made their kings kings of figs and oranges as in old times',[3] but such an objective was neither possible nor desirable for the queen. On both sides, the war was not only unwanted but unexpected. Since there was of course no land frontier between England and any part of the Spanish empire, it was perforce a naval war, the first in modern times outside the Mediterranean or the Baltic. Neither the English nor the Spaniards had ever undertaken such a war, and neither had very clear ideas how to do it. The English had some relevant experience from the Scottish wars, and the Spaniards were acknowledged experts in large-scale amphibious operations, which they had frequently mounted in the Mediterranean and lately in the Atlantic. Spanish success in the Azores, and English at Cadiz, inclined each side to optimism, but no one really knew what to expect.

Neither side was well equipped to strike at the other. Queen Elizabeth, as we have seen, possessed a small but formidable fleet largely composed of new galleons, and supplemented by a number of large merchantmen of similar design: perhaps forty big ships in all. This was a powerful defensive force, but not well suited to offensive operations at long range. Philip II had several large galley fleets in the Mediterranean and one in the Atlantic. His subjects owned by far the largest merchant fleet in the world; Spanish and Portuguese shipping all but monopolized oceanic trade. Unfortunately he had very little in the way of a regular navy in Atlantic waters. Of course he could assemble very large fleets by requisitioning merchant ships, which could be or were already armed. The ships of the *Guarda de Indias*, the 'Guard of the Indies', which the *Casa de Contratación* provided to escort the *flotas*, were by Spanish standards particularly well armed. Further well-armed ships were built in Cantabrian shipyards in the 1580s. However the only ships which could be regarded as true warships in the English style were the galleons of the Portuguese royal fleet, captured in 1580. There had been twelve of these of varying sizes, but not all in good repair, and in the event only three were left to sail with the fleet in 1588. Otherwise there was no navy, no dockyard, and no naval administration.[4] Enormous maritime and military resources were available, but they were largely dispersed, under local rather than central control. There was no Spanish equivalent of the Navy Board, the Ordnance Board, or even the Privy Council. All chains of command and responsibility met in the person of the 'bureaucrat king' himself.[5] Immured in his tiny office in the Escorial, assisted only by a handful of secretaries, Philip II controlled his vast empire by a ceaseless exchange of paper.[6]

The king was remarkably well informed and proverbially cautious, but he had no specialized knowledge of military or naval affairs and he did not take kindly to unwelcome advice or disagreeable facts. He was apt to suspect the loyalty of those who pointed out difficulties, however exalted their rank and distinguished their service. He did not welcome initiative, even when it succeeded, and he never excused failure to carry out his orders, even when they were impossible. 'Kings use men like oranges', the Duke of Alba said from bitter experience,'they squeeze out the juice and then throw them away'.[7]

There were essentially two different strategies proposed to King Philip for an invasion of England. Santa Cruz argued for an expanded version of his successful Azores campaign. Like many Spanish sea officers, especially those with knowledge of the Channel, he wanted to seize a port in the West Country or Ireland from which communication could be kept up with Spain.[8] Experienced commander that he was, he presented his plan (in February 1586) in great detail, meticulously costed. He called for a total of 510 sailing ships and 86 oared vessels of all sizes, manned with 16,512 men, and carrying a landing force of 55,000 infantry and 1,200 cavalry. All this would cost 2,589,519 ducats 140 maravedís – and there was the problem, for the king at once concluded that he could never find so much money, nor so many ships and men.[9] Soon after reading Santa Cruz's proposal, Philip received a letter from Parma in Flanders suggesting that he could prepare a landing force in great secrecy and disembark, without the benefit of a fleet, before English defences were alerted.[10] It has been doubted whether so experienced a general really thought he could prepare a great expedition in total secrecy, and he must have been aware that the English kept a standing squadron in the Narrow Seas winter and summer, but for the moment his project greatly encouraged King Philip.[11] A third voice in the planning was that of the Duke of Medina Sidonia, one of Spain's most experienced naval administrators, long involved with everything to do with the Andalusian ports and the *Carrera de Indias* in particular. In 1586 he revived Menéndez de Avilés's plan for a Spanish fleet to command the Channel,[12] but he remained one of the most eminent of the many experienced voices warning the king of the risks of invasion:

> All that I have heard from the experts is that the great strength of the English is at sea, so that your Majesty's fleet will have to be much stronger than what they can gather in those waters.[13]

In addition to the strategic choices he was presented with, Philip II had to consider the political and diplomatic factors. To avoid uniting Protestant princes against him, he needed to present the operation as an affair of state rather than a religious crusade. To rally the Catholic world behind him, he needed to do the opposite. The Pope, whose financial support was essential and whose moral support was very desirable, would not give them to another piece of Spanish aggrandizement, and insisted that the landing be commanded by a non-Spaniard of independent standing, the Duke of Parma. Parma was Philip's nephew, and served him with unswerving loyalty; but he was a foreigner, a sovereign prince in his own right, and obliged by his situation to run a semi-independent foreign policy. He also had a good dynastic claim on the throne of England, and his son had an excellent one on the throne of Portugal. Philip was forced to name him commander-in-chief, but he was not forced to trust him, and he had every intention of returning England to the Spanish empire whatever Sixtus V thought.[14]

From all these elements Philip assembled a compromise plan. Initially he intended two distinct but simultaneous landings: by Santa Cruz in the West Country or Ireland, and by Parma in England. After Drake's raid, the two were amalgamated. In its final form of September 1587, the plan envisaged that a fleet under Santa Cruz would gather at Lisbon and proceed to the English Channel, where Parma would assemble the bulk of his army with suitable landing craft. The English would either run away or fight and be defeated, whereupon Parma's troops would disembark in Kent. A good deal of thought was given to the campaign after landing, and vast administrative efforts were put into assembling both fleet and army, but neither at this nor any subsequent stage did Philip closely study how and where the fleet and army were to join. He was certainly encouraged in the summer of 1587 by the news that Parma had taken the port of Sluys, which he may have thought capable of receiving a large fleet, but Santa Cruz was not ordered to go there.[15] Instead, he was to 'proceed directly up the English Channel to the Cape of Margate in order to join hands with my nephew the Duke of Parma, and cover his crossing.'[16]

Presently the plan ran into difficulties. In Lisbon Santa Cruz struggled to assemble his huge fleet from ships and supplies slowly arriving from all over the empire, his preparations greatly disrupted by Drake's activities and he himself much hurt to discover that he was not to command the eventual landing. Throughout the autumn of 1587 he had to fend off a stream of orders from the king to sail at once regardless of the state of his ships and supplies. At this stage Philip hoped that an initial squadron might sail to cover Parma's crossing, followed later by reinforcements, but in December 1587 he was forced to abandon the plan on news of English mobilization.[17]

Meanwhile in Flanders Parma soon lost whatever enthusiasm he may ever have had for a surprise attack, and warned Philip in increasingly blunt terms that he was not ready to embark, never would be ready if he did not receive more money and support, and that when he was, nothing could be achieved without complete naval victory.[18] In March 1588 he advised that,

> At present there could be nothing better nor more honourable, nothing which would more please your subjects and curb those who envy your Majesty's greatness (especially the heretics who fear you most), than to settle a good and honourable peace and avoid all the risks of disaster which might otherwise ensue.[19]

He had already opened secret negotiations with the English, which Philip regarded as a blind; but Parma now pursued them with increasing urgency as an escape from the disaster he foresaw.[20]

By the end of 1587 the Armada was slipping rapidly into chaos, and the whole project was in crisis. The victualling arrangements were beset by corruption and incompetence and there was an acute shortage of cask. In January 1588 the fleet began taking in what was supposed to be eight months' supply of biscuit. By April they had enough for five months, and they sailed in May with four months' stocks. By then the fleet had consumed 150 per cent of its original stores. To check desertion the troops had to remain aboard ship, where an epidemic of typhus carried off increasing numbers. Some of the ships were so leaky that they threatened to sink in harbour, and a gale in November caused further damage. There was an acute shortage of guns, powder, shot, small arms and warlike stores of all kinds. Naval stores, cheese and other imports from the Baltic were wanting because Hansa ships, which had suffered in the 1585 embargo, declined to risk the same again. All the while the fleet was costing 700,000 ducats a month, or about four-fifths of the entire revenues of the Spanish crown.[21] Informed observers (notably the Pope, who had a sneaking admiration for Queen Elizabeth and resented being treated as a Spanish puppet) openly mocked Spain and predicted that the fleet would never sail. The queen's distaff, Sixtus was reported to have remarked after the Cadiz raid, seemed to be worth more than the king's sword.[22] In Paris the wits were giving six to one against the Armada ever reaching the Channel.[23] Philip reacted as usual to these difficulties: he accused Santa Cruz of disloyalty. Secret enquiries were set on foot, and in January 1588 the Count of Fuentes, a tough young soldier with no naval experience, was sent to Lisbon as a royal inspector. He arrived to find the elderly hero ill in bed, and addressed him in openly contemptuous terms. Ten days later, the marquis was dead.[24] There was no one left to blame and the Armada was in chaos.

In this desperate situation, with the future strategy and present reputation of the Spanish empire in the balance, the most urgent requirement was administrative skill. Someone was needed of mature judgement and extensive experience in organizing fleets, a man of unequalled rank, credit and influence, who could make up in his own person for the weaknesses of Spanish government. There was never any doubt who it must be, and the Duke of Medina Sidonia had already been warned to expect the summons even before Santa Cruz's death, but it was none the less unwelcome. The duke pleaded ill-health and poverty, but all in vain.[25] Two days later he wrote in much stronger terms, setting out exactly why, in his view, the Armada was bound to fail and should be abandoned forthwith. Horrified, the royal secretaries suppressed the letter, warning the duke that if it became known that he had used that sort of language to the king, he would lose 'his reputation in the eyes of the world for courage and judgement.'[26] Faced with virtual blackmail, the duke unwillingly set out for Lisbon.[27]

There his energy and experience achieved what many had thought impossible. On 18 May the whole fleet was finally at sea – a grand total of 141 ships and vessels of all sorts, manned by 7,667 seamen, and carrying 20,459 troops.[28] Almost at once Medina Sidonia began to receive reports of spoilt provisions and leaky casks. Many of the victuals had been on board up to nine months already, and the duke soon decided that he would have to put into port to replace them. On 9 June he entered Corunna, ahead of the bulk of his fleet, which was scattered by a gale that night. Five days later, as he laboured to collect and provision his ships, he made a last attempt to persuade Philip II to abandon the whole enterprise. In his usual style, the king assured Medina Sidonia that under so experienced a commander, with the undoubted help of God, the Armada could not fail.[29] The duke certainly did not agree, nor did any of his experienced sea officers. A few months before, Martín de Bertendona had reported to the king a conversation with the dying Santa Cruz in which they had agreed on the risks of entering the Channel with no deep-water port available: 'but since it is your Majesty who has decided everything, we must believe that it is God's will'. Just before the Armada sailed, an unnamed senior officer, very likely Bertendona again, confided his private opinion to a papal diplomat:

> It is well known that we fight in God's cause. So, when we meet the English, God will surely arrange matters so that we can grapple and board them, either by sending some strange freak of weather or, more likely, just by depriving the English of their wits. If we can come to close quarters, Spanish valour and Spanish steel (and the great masses of soldiers we shall have on board) will make our victory certain. But unless God helps us by a miracle the English, who have faster and handier ships than ours, and many more long-range guns, and who know their advantage just as well as we do, will never close with us at all, but stand aloof and knock us to pieces with their culverins, without our being able to do them any serious hurt. So we are sailing against England in the confident hope of a miracle.[30]

The sixteenth century was an age of faith, and we must not read modern cynicism into either remark, but one can hardly avoid hearing irony. When the Armada finally got under way again from Corunna on 11 July, restored and revictualled as far as the duke's administrative genius could manage, neither he nor any of his admirals looked forward to the forthcoming campaign.

In England the situation was quite different. For two years the English government had watched Spanish preparations with intense anxiety, but apart from sending Drake's squadron to raid Cadiz, it had done virtually nothing in response. No huge administrative effort had been set in train, no vast fleet was slowly assembling in any English port. Instead there was a deceptive calm which undoubtedly encouraged Philip II to hope that the Armada would meet no serious opposition at sea. The lack of activity in England was based on two factors. The first was an experienced naval administration with a sophisticated mobilization system which in principle allowed England's entire strength to be got to sea at very short notice. The second was a complete absence of money. Philip had to borrow heavily to build up his Armada, especially as he had been forced to take the ships of the *Guarda de Indias* to strengthen it and suspend the silver fleets for 1588 – but he could negotiate loans against the credit of the most powerful monarchy in the world and the silver of the Americas. Queen Elizabeth could not borrow at all, except small sums for short periods. Her wartime income was increased by parliamentary grants worth about £72,000 a year, and at the beginning of 1588 she still had £154,000 left in her reserves.[31] That would not go far against pre-war estimates that even a partial naval mobilization would cost over £15,000 a month, especially when she had paid £160,000 to the Dutch in the first year of the alliance.[32] Elizabeth could not afford to send the bulk of her ships to sea until the last moment. The English system was in its way much more efficient and sophisticated than the Spanish, but with so little money to back it, it was extremely fragile.

Consequently the English maintained only small patrols at sea throughout 1587, and when Drake's squadron returned from Cadiz most of the ships were paid off. There were also pinnaces scouting on the enemy coast, one of which actually went up the Tagus by night to count the enemy fleet.[33] During that year, while the Armada was costing Philip nearly £200,000 a month, Elizabeth spent only £73,547 on her fleet, all but £7,000 of which went on Drake's expedition.[34] Mobilization was not ordered until the end of November, on intelligence that Santa Cruz had been ordered to sea; it was the news of this mobilization which caused Philip to abandon his plan to send a small advanced squadron to cover Parma's landing. The English fleet was at sea before Christmas, in less than a month from the first order to mobilize, and by the middle of January most of it had been reduced again to semi-readiness with half crews. The latest intelligence indicated further delay, if not cancellation, of the Spanish preparations, and the English could not afford to keep their fleet long at sea. Furthermore, cruising in wintertime would certainly mean sickness among the crews, and damage which would take time to repair. Drake was sent to Plymouth with a small squadron 'to ply up and down between the realm of Ireland and the west part of this our realm', and Sir Henry Palmer lay in the Narrow Seas with another. The rest of the queen's ships were taken in hand to have their bottoms cleaned, ready to mobilize again in March.[35] Lord Howard of Effingham, the Lord Admiral of England, agreed with the necessity of remaining in port, but fretted at the inactivity: 'If it were not for her Majesty's presence I had rather live in the company of these noble ships than in any place. And yet would I be glad there were something to do . . .'[36]

Meanwhile there was a lot to think about, for it was not at all clear how and where to fight the Spaniards. There were two schools of thought: the orthodox, defensive strategy implied waiting for the Armada to come; the bolder, offensive strategy of which Drake was the leading spokesman, wanted to sail to Portugal and attack first. In each case there were many questions to answer. Should the fleet stand on the defensive in the Narrow Seas, opposite Parma's army, or to the westward, to cover the South Coast, or even at sea, to cover Ireland? Should it be divided or united? If the offensive strategy was adopted, was the object to catch the Armada at sea or in port? Perhaps the Armada had already been abandoned, in which case should the fleet cruise to intercept the silver convoys? The queen's ministers and officers debated these problems with virtually no experience to guide them, with scanty intelligence, and with no margin for error.

In Howard's orders of 20 December, he was to concentrate on Parma, while Drake covered the Western Approaches. If 'you shall receive any certain advertisements that the navy of Spain shall repair into these parts with such forces and strength as the ships committed to the conduction of our servant Drake shall not be able to make head against them', Howard was at his discretion either to reinforce Drake, or recall him to concentrate in the Narrow Seas. With two mortal threats, widely separated, there seemed to Burghley and the defensive strategists to be no alternative to splitting the fleet.[37] For Drake and his colleagues, however, most of them West Country men and all of them seamen who had made their careers cruising in the open sea, it seemed imperative to concentrate as far to the westward, and consequently windward, as possible; they were backed by Leicester, Walsingham and others of the aggressive, Protestant-minded group at court.[38] If the English allowed themselves to be bottled up at the leeward end of the Channel watching Parma, the Armada could land anywhere to the westward without opposition; 'but if there may be such a stay or stop made by any means of this fleet in Spain, that they may not come though the seas as conquerors – which I assure myself they think to do – then shall the Prince of Parma have such a check thereby as were meet.'[39] Above all, they longed to strike at the Spanish fleet while it was still assembling, while they knew exactly where to find it:

> I would to God we had been now upon that coast; the impediments would have been great unto their army gathering together, more than I dare presume to write, in my poor opinion. We rest here, a great number of valiant men, and a great charge unto my gracious mistress, and a great grief of mind to spend her Majesty's treasure and do nothing upon the enemy.[40]

'The advantage of time and place in all martial actions is half a victory', Drake wrote on 13 April, begging to be allowed to attack, and avoiding the queen's very pertinent question how he was going to get at a fleet lying in the heavily defended port of Lisbon.[41] By this time Drake had converted Howard to his views, and Howard had the Council's agreement to take the bulk of the fleet westward. On 21 May he sailed for Plymouth, leaving Lord Henry Seymour with a squadron in the Downs. Howard now added his voice to those asking to be allowed to attack the Armada before it sailed.[42] Running through all these pleas to be allowed to sail is the victualling problem. In sixteenth-century conditions, supplying any large fleet with food was bound to be difficult. Doing it at short notice, and sending the victuals to a port far to windward of London, was acutely difficult. The local market in Devon ('a narrow corner of the realm, where a man would think that neither victuals were to be had, nor cask to put it in') was quite unable to supply so many ships.[43] Throughout 1588 the English fleet seldom had more than a few weeks' supplies to hand, and sometimes only a few days. Contemporaries blamed the queen's 'parsimony', as modern historians have generally done, but in truth no amount of money (supposing she had had it) could have overcome all the problems. Drake and Howard wanted to attack the Armada first partly because they suspected the Spaniards of playing a waiting game, delaying until the English were forced to lay up their fleet.[44] Three times that spring they sailed, on 30 May, 19 and 23 June, and three times they were blown back into port by hard gales, the last time having almost sighted the Spanish coast. On 12 July the whole fleet was back once more in Plymouth.[45]

One week later, Lord Burghley in London drew up a gloomy statement of the kingdom's desperate shortage of money: 'a man would wish, if peace cannot be had, that the enemy would no longer delay, but prove (as I trust) his evil fortune'.[46] His wish was about to be granted. That same afternoon, 19 July by English reckoning, the pinnace *Golden Hind* came into Plymouth with the news that she had sighted the Armada off the Lizard. Possibly Drake may have been playing bowls on Plymouth Hoe, but he certainly would not have lingered after hearing the news, for the enemy was only a few hours away, many of the English ships were not yet revictualled for sea, and there was a grave risk of their being trapped in port by just such a surprise attack as they had planned to deliver themselves. Undoubtedly the rest of the day was spent in furious activity. As soon as the ebb started to run, after dark that evening, the English ships began to warp out of the Cattewater and down the Sound, towing behind their boats into the teeth of the wind.[47]

The last clause of Lord Howard's instructions runs as follows:

> Lastly, forasmuch as there may fall out many accidents that may move you to take any other course than by these our instructions you are directed, we therefore think it most expedient to refer you therein to your own judgement and discretion, to do that thing you may think may best tend to the advancement of our service.[48]

The queen has sometimes been accused of interfering with her admirals, but few commanders-in-chief in so critical a situation have ever been trusted with such complete discretion – and few have had so little as the unfortunate Duke of Medina Sidonia. His sailing orders were the same as those originally drafted for Santa Cruz the previous autumn, intended to forbid the old admiral to make a landing, or do anything whatever on his own initiative, except to proceed to the Downs and make contact with Parma.[49] The English need not have worried about a surprise attack on Plymouth. The Spaniards certainly considered it, but the duke could not vary his master's orders.

The actual strength of the Spanish fleet at this juncture was probably 127 ships of all sorts and sizes. Of these about twenty were warships or armed merchantmen of some size and force, including four galleasses (hybrid oared galleons or 'super-galleys' which had made a great reputation for themselves at Lepanto, not the English type of the 1540s), and the rest were transports and small craft. Four galleys and one other ship had already parted company through stress of weather. The biggest ships on both sides were about a thousand tons, but the average size of the Spanish fleet was greater than that of the English, because of its many large transports. In fighting strength, on the other hand, there could be no comparison. Howard had with him no more than about eighty ships of all sizes, but the core of his force was composed of fast, heavily armed galleons which were greatly superior to any ship in the Spanish fleet, and overall his ships carried at least twice the gun armament of their enemies. Furthermore the English officers, in marked contrast to their Spanish counterparts, felt a pride and confidence in their ships which shines out of their correspondence: 'Our ships doth show themselves like gallants here', wrote Sir William Winter, 'I assure you it would do a man's heart good to behold them.' Lord Howard felt the same: 'I have been aboard of every ship that goeth out with me and in every place where any may creep, and I thank God that they be in the estate they be in, and there is never a one of them that knows what a leak means . . .' [50] A few days later he warmed to the same theme:

> I think there were never in any place in the world worthier ships than these are, for so many. And few as we are, if the King of Spain's forces be not hundreds, we will make good sport with them. And I pray you tell her Majesty from me that her money was well given for the *Ark Ralegh*,[51] for I think her the odd ship in the world for all conditions; and truly I think there can no great ship make me change and go out of her. We can see no sail, great nor small, but how far soever they be off, we fetch them and speak with them.[52]

The only factor in which the Spanish fleet was superior was infantry, and 12,000 of the 18,000 embarked were new recruits who had never been in action before.[53]

These infantrymen could only be deployed, of course, if the fleets came to fighting hand to hand, and it seems clear that this is what Philip anticipated. Whether it was Drake's squadron at Plymouth, or Howard's main fleet (which he still expected to be in the Straits of Dover), the enemy must either stand and await the Spanish attack, or run away. However formidable the English gunnery (of which the king was perfectly well informed), they could not avoid this choice.[54] Probably Santa Cruz had encouraged the hope, for this was what had happened at Terceira, but it is very unlikely that Medina Sidonia and his experienced admirals were fooled. Tough Basque seamen like Recalde, Bertendona and Miguel de Oquendo (aged 62, 49 and 59 respectively in 1588), who had been commanding ships and fleets all their adult lives,[55] were extremely familiar with the gunnery tactics which had long been established among all seafaring nations. The faster and more weatherly ships seized the weather gage and the opportunity to attack. The slower and more leewardly had perforce to endure it – and none of the Spanish officers were under the slightest illusion about which position they were going to be in. The new English galleons with their powerful bow chasers could attack so much the more effectively as they ran down on their enemy, but they certainly would not run alongside to board.

What the Spaniards had to expect was repeated attacks from the windward by a succession of ships each of which would discharge a heavy volume of fire before hauling off to windward to reload. There is some doubt exactly what reloading techniques were used by both English and Spanish ships in 1588, but hardly any doubt that no one was accustomed to reload in action. The attacking ship 'gave the charge' from the windward, coming down with all her guns run out, and probably secured to fire 'non-recoil'. The English used compact 'truck' gun carriages designed to allow their guns to be canted round ('bowed' or 'quartered' in the terminology of the time) to fire as nearly forward or aft as possible. Each broadside gun was trained on its own, fixed bearing, and fired as it came to bear on the order of the master gunner, who conned the ship into action. The bow chasers were followed by the lee broadside guns, one by one, as the attacker drew abeam of the target, then the stern chasers as she luffed up to go about, and the other broadside as she paid off onto the other tack. She then withdrew to windward to reload, while another ship came in to attack. If there were sufficient ships to keep up a continuous attack, the defending ship to leeward would have no opportunity at all to reload her heavy guns.[56]

On the early afternoon of 20 July, when the two fleets first sighted one another in thick, drizzly weather, the Armada was proceeding down Channel in accordance with its orders. Its initial formation was the standard line abreast, with the main fighting strength, as it seems, in the centre, and the two wings trailing to form the characteristic crescent shape of a galley fleet in battle order (and of the *flotas* with their escorts on either beam).[57] Howard with the bulk of the English fleet had cleared Plymouth Sound during the night, crossed the front of the Armada, and was beating up to windward on their seaward flank. A smaller and later group of English ships, probably under Drake, was also beating up, but still between the Armada and the land. Presently the English gained the weather gage, and Howard started the battle with a gesture out of the traditions of chivalry, sending his pinnace the *Disdain* to fire a single shot, by way of a 'defiance' or challenge. Then he led his squadron to attack the seaward wing of the Armada, while Drake attacked the other.[58]

The pattern established that afternoon was to endure for a week of fighting down Channel. The Spaniards with their famous military discipline and their long experience of convoy warfare, preserved 'excellent good order'.[59] Attacking from the windward, astern, the English could not risk penetrating between the two trailing 'horns' or wings of the Spanish formation to get at the mass of transports in the centre, for they could easily have been trapped. They therefore confined their attacks to the two wings, where the best Spanish fighting ships were stationed. The attack was in the classic style, apparently at a range at which the Spanish light guns were ineffective. With a succession of ships attacking the handful of Spanish ships on each wing, they had little opportunity to reload their heavy guns. Both sides had greatly exaggerated expectations of the effectiveness of heavy gunnery. The Spaniards feared, and the English confidently expected, that they really would knock the enemy to pieces. By the end of the first day's fighting, it was becoming clear that this was not going to happen soon. The Spaniards had experienced the intense frustration of being attacked without being able to reply effectively, but they had received no mortal damage.

It was after this day's fighting, by accident, that they suffered their only serious losses. The *Nuestra Señora del Rosario* lost her bowsprit and foremast in a series of collisions, and the *San Salvador* was badly damaged by a powder explosion. Having failed to tow the *Rosario*, Medina Sidonia left her behind. No attempt was made to take off Don Pedro de Valdés whose flagship she was, nor any of her ship's company, nor even a pay-chest containing 50,000 ducats.

That night Howard had ordered the English fleet to follow the stern lantern of Drake's flagship the *Revenge*. During the night the lantern went out, and the following morning Howard found himself dangerously close to the enemy, with most of his own fleet nowhere in sight. Drake's own account was that he had sighted sails to the southward heading down Channel, and gone to investigate in case they were Spanish ships trying to regain the weather gage. It may have been true, for there is some evidence that the sails really existed (they were Hansa merchantmen),[60] but contemporaries suspected that the instincts of a lifetime of piracy had overcome the respectable admiral in Drake. What is certain is that next morning the *Revenge* was close to the *Rosario*. Drake called Valdés to his ship and offered him 'fair wars' (meaning quarter) if he would surrender; it was unnecessary to spell out what he was being offered if he chose to fight it out. 'Whereupon the said Don Pedro paused a little while with himself, and afterwards yielded'.[61] It was not a transaction he would have wished to be reported in Madrid.[62] Drake gained a valuable prize and the furious jealousy of some of his colleagues, notably Martin Frobisher. As a result of the disorder of the English fleet, there was no fighting that day, though later they took possession of the abandoned wreck of the *San Salvador*.

The following morning, Tuesday 21st, both fleets were off Portland Bill when the wind backed south-east, giving the Spaniards the weather gage. Throughout the morning the English attempted to work round the Armada's flanks to regain it, and at one point the Spanish galleasses tried to trap Frobisher, whose flagship the *Triumph* was the biggest and possibly the slowest of all the English ships, against the land of Portland Bill. In the course of this manoeuvre the galleasses seem to have got into Portland Race, which must have given them more than enough to think about without worrying about the enemy. At all events the Spaniards failed to force the close action they so much desired, and when the wind veered south-westerly again that evening the situation was much as before.

For the next three days, Wednesday to Friday, the two fleets moved slowly up the Channel before very light breezes, each side looking for opportunity to force action on their own terms. On Wednesday morning the English surrounded a Spanish straggler, the *Gran Grifón*, until other Spanish ships put back to relieve her. That afternoon the wind fell away completely, and Howard took the opportunity to call a council of war. Hitherto the English seem to have fought virtually without any order, beyond some tendency for Howard, Drake and other senior officers to lead into the attack. Contemporary illustrations suggest a very rough line abreast, which is what one would naturally expect as the traditional fleet formation, and the only one adapted to deploy galleons' heavy ahead-firing armament. On the other hand it was very ill-adapted for any sort of concentration or mutual support. Howard therefore reorganized his fleet into four divisions, commanded by himself, Drake, Frobisher and Hawkins. This must have been intended to assist the squadrons to go into action in line ahead, each ship in turn firing all her guns at whatever target was under attack, then withdrawing to give place to her next astern.

Next morning both fleets were off the Isle of Wight, where in light and shifting airs there was further heavy fighting. The moment seemed to be critical, for both Spaniards and English had identified the Solent as one of the few places on the South Coast where a large fleet could lie in safety and make a landing. Medina Sidonia was authorized to do so – but only if he had first tried and failed to make contact with Parma. He had decided to compromise: the fleet would anchor at Spithead without landing, and there await precise instructions from the Duke of Parma where and how to meet. This intention was frustrated by an attack that afternoon on the seaward wing of the fleet, almost certainly by Drake and his squadron, which tended to drive the Armada towards the shoals known as the Owers which stretch out from Selsey Bill. In order to avoid this threat, the Spaniards were forced to abandon the idea of entering the Solent and altered course to seaward.

This was a great relief for the English, who had achieved their minimum aim 'so to course the enemy as they shall have no leisure to land',[63] but for the moment it was all they could do. 'Forasmuch as our powder and shot was well wasted, the Lord Admiral thought it was not good in policy to assail them any more until their coming near unto Dover.'[64] On Friday morning Howard knighted Hawkins, Frobisher and several of his captains, but no one thought they had won any victory. As the undefeated and unbroken Armada approached the Duke of Parma's army, the crisis of the campaign was upon them.

For Medina Sidonia, the situation was equally critical. In spite of numerous messages, he had no answer from Parma to suggest when the troops would be ready nor where they should meet. His orders were to go to the 'Cape of Margate', presumably meaning the North Foreland, which Recalde understood to mean the Downs. In this anchorage the Armada could at least have ridden secure – if it could enter without local pilots and remain in the teeth of shore batteries (this was where Henry VIII had concentrated his forts) and the English fleet. But perhaps now the duke had faced up to the critical gap in Philip's plans, a gap of only thirty miles or so but one which was quite unbridgeable. Even if the Armada could somehow control the deep water between the Goodwin Sands and the Flanders Banks, that still left ten miles of shoal water where big ships could not go. Before Parma's largely defenceless barges could cross the Flanders Banks, the Dutch would have time to sink them several times over. The only answer would have been for the Armada to bring shallow-draught warships of its own to make up for the lost North Sea squadron which Parma was only just beginning to reconstruct. Spain had a large fleet of vessels ideal for such operations – galleys – and Santa Cruz had insisted all along that they would be essential. But Philip II had refused to release more than four, all of which fell out crossing the Bay of Biscay. So there was no means of escorting Parma's army from the Flanders shore to the Downs. Philip II's inflexible orders to make no independent landing but to embark Parma's troops condemned the 1588 Armada to certain failure. Without sufficient shallow-draft warships to protect the landing craft from the Dutch the operation as planned was impossible, and would have been impossible even if the English Navy had not been present in force. Perhaps it was for this reason that Medina Sidonia abandoned his orders for the first time, and on Saturday 27th anchored off Calais.

It was an open and dangerous road, but it was on the right shore and not far from Parma.[65]

The English anchored close to windward, joined late that evening by Seymour's squadron from the Downs, bringing the English forces to their maximimum strength of about 140 sail. (A total of 197 English ships of all sizes were subsequently listed, victuallers included, from the giant *Triumph* to the 20-ton pinnaces *Black Dog*, *Katherine*, *Pippin* and *Little John*, but they were not all present at the same time.)[66] At the same time Medina Sidonia received the unpleasant news that Parma's troops would not be embarked and assembled until Friday. Instead of immediately attempting, somehow, to join with the embarkation force, he now faced six days in an exposed anchorage with the enemy directly to windward and the shoal water of the Flanders banks directly to leeward. Though Parma had often and clearly explained that it would take time to move troops from their billets, to embark on their barges and prepare for sea; though he had equally plainly pointed out that he had too few armed vessels to face the Dutch, who would certainly massacre his troops in their unprotected barges as soon as they left harbour; yet it still seems to have been believed in the Armada that as soon as they drew near to the Flanders coast, Parma's famous infantry would immediately join them.[67]

The same thing was believed in the English fleet. Parma was only thirty miles away at Dunkirk; whether he came by land or sea, he would doubtless come soon, and something had to be done at once to stop him. It was obvious enough what. From the smaller ships of the fleet eight fireships were improvised, and late on Sunday night, with a freshening wind and the spring tide behind them, they were loosed on the Spanish fleet. Medina Sidonia had foreseen such a well-known form of attack, and his screen of boats managed to grapple and tow aside two of the fireships. The rest were avoided by the Spanish fleet, which cut and slipped their cables and stood out to sea as ordered. In the process they lost their cohesion, and only a few anchored again with the duke as ordered.

Next morning the English saw what they had done and at once weighed anchor to attack. Only Medina Sidonia with five big ships were in sight, plus one damaged galleass inshore which the Lord Admiral took for himself, leaving the other four divisions of his fleet to tackle the galleons. This was a mistake, for he did not rejoin the main action until the afternoon. Medina Sidonia and his small group of ships formed the rearguard, attempting with great courage to cover the bulk of the fleet as they slowly reformed to leeward. Now for the first time the English closed to fight at effective range:

half musket-shot (about 50 yards) was one estimate, close enough for ships to hail one another. Possibly they had learnt from studying the armament of the captured *Rosario*; undoubtedly they had learnt from experience. Many Spanish ships were now running out of shot for their light guns and small arms, while still carrying great quantities of shot for heavy guns which they were unable to fire because the English gave them no respite to reload.[68] What evidence we have suggests that English rates of fire were of the order of one or one and a half rounds an hour per gun; Spanish about the same *per day*.[69] In these circumstances, and at these ranges, English gunnery began to tell. At least one ship was sunk, two more driven on to the shoals and taken by the Dutch. Many others were damaged more or less seriously, while the English received negligible damage themselves. Even so, Spanish courage and military discipline gradually restored a fighting formation – but by afternoon the weather was rapidly worsening and the Armada was being driven inexorably to leeward towards the Zealand Banks.

All that night the English followed the Spaniards as they drove into shoal water, waiting for their inevitable destruction. From this peril the battered Spanish fleet was saved, as they believed, by a miracle. At the last possible moment, soon after dawn on Tuesday 30th, the wind backed suddenly to the southward, allowing the Armada to haul off the northward and once more restore their formation. By this time the English were virtually out of ammunition and could not renew the action. So they followed the Spaniards into the North Sea, 'setting on a brag countenance' and hoping their bluff would not be called before they received fresh powder and shot.[70] No one believed the fighting was over. 'I will not write unto her Majesty before more be done', wrote Howard to Walsingham on the evening of the 29th. 'Their force is wonderful great and strong; and yet we pluck their feathers by little and little. I pray to God that the forces on the land be strong enough to answer so puissant a force.'[71] The English speculated anxiously in which friendly port the Armada would take refuge; Hamburg, Denmark, Norway and Scotland all offered possibilities.[72]

It is something of a mystery why Medina Sidonia was not thinking in the same terms, for that was the only way he could have returned to renew his attempts to make contact with Parma. It is true the Armada lacked charts or pilots for the North Sea,[73] whereas the route about the north of Scotland would have been familiar to both German and Spanish seamen who had kept up Spain's Baltic trade that way. It was equally obvious that to go northward was to abandon the mission, and that the Armada's food and water supplies were already failing and could not sustain so long a passage.

Nevertheless that was Medina Sidonia's decision. The Armada held on northwards. On 2 August, past the latitude of the Firth of Forth, the English turned back, leaving some pinnaces to shadow the enemy. Meanwhile the Armada faced the long voyage home. Many of them damaged, with heavy casualties, all of them already reduced to one-third allowance of food and water, exhausted by days of fighting and demoralized by the consciousness of defeat, they struggled westwards into the autumn gales of the North Atlantic. The duke's orders were to keep company and not to turn southward for Spain until the ships had reached far out into the Atlantic, 'and take great heed lest you fall upon the island of Ireland'.[74] All those who were able to keep up the duke brought home to Spain: sixty-seven ships in all, including most of the best warships.[75] Many of the ships were badly damaged, a high proportion of the men were dead or dying from disease and thirst. At least one-third of the total manpower of the Armada did not return.[76] Those ships which lost company and sought water and shelter on the coast of Ireland were virtually all lost, their companies drowned or killed by the Irish or English. Only Recalde brought a small group of ships into the same waters where he had landed eight years before, and got away to tell the tale.[77]

Like his colleague Oquendo, Recalde returned to Spain only to die in evident despair within a few weeks.[78] Though the campaign had been a major disappointment for the English, who had hoped for so much from their new galleons and culverins, it is absurd to suggest (as some modern historians have done)[79] that Spain did not really need and had not really meant to win, that merely to parade down the Channel was sufficient to frighten the English into conceding Spain's war aims, and that in some sense this would have been a drawn battle or even a Spanish triumph but for some unlucky bad weather.[80] Nobody at the time imagined anything of the kind. It was a catastrophe which plunged all Spain in mourning, which went far to shatter the myth of invincibility which Spanish armies had built up, which put fresh heart into Spain's enemies everywhere. England was not frightened into conceding anything whatever, but emboldened to fresh attacks on Spain. Looking back, 1588 was seen as the moment when the tide of Spanish expansion began to turn.[81]

TWENTY

The Method of Jason

Operations 1589–1603

So much does the 1588 Armada dominate the general view of the Spanish War that it is hard to remember that it was only the first major campaign in a war which still had fifteen years to run. For the English it was a deliverance by a narrow margin. Even as the Spanish ships were passing about the north of Scotland, the English fleet was running out of all the things it needed to remain effective. Powder and shot had gone already, victuals were scarce, a number of ships were crippled by severe outbreaks of illness and, above all, there were no more funds to keep the fleet at sea. Though no English ship had suffered any serious damage,[1] all of them needed routine maintenance after the wear and tear of six months at sea: 'utterly unfitted and unmeet to follow any enterprise from hence without a thorough new trimming, refreshing, and new furnishing with provisions, grounding, and fresh men'.[2] For these reasons, the idea of intercepting the Armada in the Western Approaches as it struggled homeward had to be abandoned. Expert opinion, including Drake's, still concentrated on the nearer and greater danger: 'we ought much more to have regard unto the Duke of Parma and his soldiers than to the Duke of Sidonia and his ships.'[3] Early in September Parma's army moved inland to besiege Bergen-op-Zoom, but by then it was too late to attempt further naval operations before the autumn gales. Long before the remains of the Armada were back in Spanish ports, the queen's ships were once again lying to their moorings in the Medway.[4]

The English were full of the euphoria of victory, but at the same time perplexed what to do next. The failure of their new weapons to achieve the devastating effects they had expected was worrying. The same strategic dilemma faced them as before: should they stand on the defensive in home waters, concentrating on the threat from Parma's army, or should they go on the offensive in Spanish waters and cut off 'the Spanish sinews of war, his money from the West Indies'?[5] Spain's power did not appear to be fundamentally diminished, and we know now that Philip's revenues were still growing fast. It looked as though the opportunity opened by victory over the 1588 Armada would not last long, but the resources to mount a swift counter-attack were very hard to find.

Out of these considerations grew the English expedition of 1589. Because the queen could not finance a major expedition out of her own pocket alone, it was floated by the familiar mechanism of the joint-stock enterprise, with private investors contributing a large part of the ships and men. In this case the investors were led by Drake, who took command of the fleet while his old comrade-in-arms Sir John Norris led the troops. Unfortunately the joint-stock organization did nothing to resolve a basic confusion about the objects of the expedition. There were three things it might have done. The first was to destroy the survivors of the 1588 Armada, including virtually all the ships of any force which Spain possessed, which were lying defenceless in Santander and San Sebastián. The second was to intercept the 1589 silver *flotas*, believed to be especially valuable, and especially vulnerable, because those of 1588 had been stopped to spare the 'Guard of the Indies' for the Armada. The last and most ambitious of all was to land in Portugal, excite a popular uprising in favour of Dom Antonio, and restore him to his throne. The queen's orders were absolute that nothing was to be attempted until the warships were destroyed. Drake and Norris promised to obey, but it seems clear that they never intended to do so. The Spanish warships lay in ports deep in the Bay of Biscay to leeward. However easy they might be to destroy, it would take weeks for a fleet to beat out of the Bay again afterwards, leaving little enough time to make a return on anyone's investment. A *flota*, on the other hand, would repay any outlay, and restoring Dom Antonio would be even better, for he had promised to open the fabulous wealth of the East Indies to English merchants if only they would restore him to power.

So Drake and Norris made no attempt to go after the warships beyond visiting Corunna (which is on the direct route southward), where they destroyed three Armada survivors, easily captured the lower town with quantities of victuals, and wasted time failing to take the well-defended upper town. Then they pushed on southward, and landed their troops on the coast of Portugal. Norris marched forty-five miles to the gates of Lisbon, meeting no Spanish resistance and no Portuguese enthusiasm. Having failed to break into the city, he then had to retreat, his men falling sick as he did so. Drake meanwhile waited to force the heavily-defended narrows of the Tagus until Norris could take the batteries in the rear; when he returned in no state to do so, the troops were re-embarked. Calms and foul winds frustrated their attempts to reach the Azores, and in the end the expedition came home devastated by sickness, with virtually nothing achieved beyond the satisfaction (and considerable political value) of having made three separate landings on Spanish or Portuguese soil without meeting ships or troops which could face them in battle. £100,000 and the lives of between eight and eleven thousand men had been thrown away for almost nothing.[6]

The queen was justifiably angry. The chance had been lost of crushing Spanish sea power – just at the point, as it soon appeared, when Spain was making vigorous efforts to create a modern navy.

> If Sir Francis had gone to Santander as he went to the Groyne, he had done such service as never subject had done. For with 12 sail of his ships he might have destroyed all the forces which the Spaniards had there, which was the whole strength of the country by sea. There they did ride all unrigged and their ordnance on the shore and some 20 men only in a ship to keep them. It was far overseen that he had not gone thither first.[7]

Such an opportunity might not, and in fact did not, ever occur again. Besides leaving Drake in disgrace, the débâcle left the queen convinced that it was useless risking her ships and money in the hands of the offensive strategists. At the same time the strategic situation was changing rapidly.

In August 1589 Henry III of France was murdered, leaving the kingdom to his Huguenot cousin Henry of Navarre. Henry IV at once sought English help against his Guise enemies of the 'Holy League', and 4,000 English troops campaigned with him in the autumn of 1589, helping to prepare for his great victory at Ivry in March 1590.[8] This was satisfactory for England, but on the Flanders frontier another threat was gathering. Philip had promised to help his Guise allies if Henry of Navarre became king, and in September 1589 Parma was ordered to do so. Illness, mutiny, want of money and reluctance to abandon a victorious campaign all delayed him, but in the summer of 1590 he campaigned in northern France, saving Paris (held by the League) from Henry IV. Though he returned to Flanders for the winter, most of the Channel ports were now firmly in the hands of the League. In October a Spanish squadron landed 3,000 troops at the fine harbour of Blavet on the south coast of Brittany, where they at once began to construct a fortified base. Spain was now within reach of controlling the whole southern coast of the Channel from Flanders to Brittany, with a naval base directly to windward of Britain.[9]

In the face of this threat Elizabeth mounted two major expeditions. Three thousand men under Sir John Norris landed in Brittany in May 1591, while soon after another force under the queen's favourite the Earl of Essex went to help Henry IV besiege Rouen. By August not less than 14,000 English troops were on the Continent: 3,000 in Brittany, 4,000 in Normandy, and 7,000 with the Dutch. The results were frustrating and disappointing for the English. In April 1592 Parma in person relieved Rouen, while in May the French royalist army in Brittany (including Norriss's force) was heavily defeated.[10] The English navy was scarcely involved in all these large and expensive operations except for covering transports, though four pinnaces operated in the Seine in support of the Normandy campaign over the winter of 1591–2.[11]

By the summer of 1593 it was clear that so long as he remained a Protestant, Henry IV could no longer sustain his campaign, let alone reconcile the majority of his countrymen to his rule. His conversion to Catholicism was, paradoxically, a gain for England, for Spain's partisans in France were now an isolated minority, and Henry IV continued the war against them. That autumn Elizabeth withdrew her troops from Normandy, but the Spanish presence in Brittany remained a serious threat.[12] It became much more serious in March 1594 when Spanish troops from Blavet established themselves on the rocky headland of Roscanvel (the modern Pointe des Espagnols) near Crozon and began to build a fort there. When finished it commanded the Goulet, the narrow channel between the inner and outer roads of Brest, and effectively controlled that port. 'I think', Norris wrote,

> there never happened a more dangerous enterprise for the state of your Majesty's country than this of the Spanish to possess Brittany, which (under humble correction) I dare presume to say will prove as prejudicial for England as if they had possessed Ireland. It is very late for your Majesty to help it, but it is truly said better too late than never.[13]

In the face of this threat the queen reluctantly agreed to reinforce Norris's little force. That autumn his troops combined with the French royalists and a squadron under Sir Martin Frobisher to attack the new fort. The position was extremely strong and bad weather favoured the besieged, but on 7 November the French and English stormed the fort and massacred its garrison. Frobisher was wounded in the assult and died later. This forgotten victory was in its way as decisive as that of 1588. It largely dispelled English fears of Spanish expeditions to England, Ireland or Scotland, and allowed the remaining English troops to be withdrawn. Though a Spanish garrison remained at Blavet with a squadron of galleys, they were too far away to pose a threat except to the West Country.[14] The following summer there was a sensational raid by four galleys from Blavet, which landed men and

NEWFOUNDLAND
Quebec
NOVA SCOTIA
ATLANTIC OCEAN
VIRGINIA
ROANOKE IS.
CARIBBEAN SEA
WINDWARD IS.
BRAZIL

The North Atlantic
ICELAND
SHETLAND
ORKNEY
GREAT BRITAIN
IRELAND
USHANT
C. Finisterre
PORTUGAL
Lisbon
Seville
Cape St Vincent
Sallee
MOROCCO
NSET
MADEIRA
CANARIES
TENERIFFE
S.
ANTIAGO
GUINEA
CORVO
Ponta Delgada
FLORES
STA CRUZ
TERCEIRA
Angra do Terceira
FAYAL
PICO
SAO MIGUEL
SANTA MARIA

burnt Penzance, Newlyn and Mousehole, exciting much public alarm in England.[15]

When Norris's troops returned in February 1595 a phase of the war ended which had been largely concerned with the struggle to keep Spain from controlling France, and especially the Channel ports. In retrospect it can be seen that Philip threw away an imminent victory (not for the first or last time) by diverting Parma's forces to open a new front in France, but at the time Elizabeth's government had reason to think that this was a mortal threat to her survival, and that by comparison purely naval operations were a diversion if not a frivolity. For five years after the failure of Drake and Norris had discredited grand expeditions, English efforts by sea remained on a small scale, and the queen's participation in them limited. The bulk of the English naval activity outside home waters was in the eastern Atlantic, roughly in the triangle bounded by the Scillies, the Azores and Gibraltar, and the basic object was always to make war according to the 'method of Jason by fetching away his golden fleece', in Fulke Greville's words, meaning to make the war pay for itself by prizes.[16] In the autumn of 1589 both Frobisher and the Earl of Cumberland were cruising for the *flotas*, unusually vulnerable for want of their escorts, but just as elusive as ever. Both made a profit from other prizes, but missed their main objective. The basic difficulty was that convoys, in the sixteenth century even more than the twentieth, were virtually impossible to detect in the vastness of the ocean. Only at straits and landfalls where they had to pass was there any reasonable chance of interception, and only then if ships could remain on station for some time. In the case of the *flotas*, this meant the Florida Straits, the Azores and Cape St Vincent. The early Virginia colonies were intended to provide a base adjacent to the Florida Straits, but they did not succeed until after this war. The Azores were nearer home, and there was only one well-fortified port (Angra do Terceira) to watch, but English ships tended to spend much of their time looking for food and water when they should have been cruising to the westward – which is what Cumberland was doing when the storm-damaged *flota* slipped into Angra.[17]

There it landed five million ducats. The following February Sir John Hawkins was about to sail in the hope of intercepting that money on its way home when a false rumour of another Spanish invasion caused his sailing to be cancelled. Not until June were two squadrons allowed to sail, Frobisher to the Azores and Hawkins to lie off Finisterre to guard against the movement of Spanish fleets. All this was in vain; the main *flotas* were held at Havana that year, while the silver was brought home by a new scheme devised by the Duke of

Medina Sidonia in fast frigates or *gallizabras* which made the Atlantic crossing unescorted, without touching at the Azores.[18] Hawkins, who had long held relatively sophisticated ideas of mounting a permanent blockade on the Spanish coast,[19] behaved in a very unsophisticated way, abandoning his blockading station to go off to the Azores after non-existent *flotas*. This allowed a Spanish force to sail unmolested to occupy Blavet, while another fleet put to sea to pursue Hawkins, until it was scattered by gales.[20]

Moreover in these years when Queen Elizabeth's attention was concentrated on the war in France, King Philip was making real efforts to remedy the lack of sea power which had been shown up in 1588. 'Clearly', he was advised, 'it is necessary for your Majesty to have a fleet on the high seas, since it seems that not having one has resulted in all that has befallen until now.'[21] Twelve warships, the 'Twelve Apostles' were ordered to be built at the king's expense. In 1590 the Ragusan shipowner Pedro de Ivella (Ivelja Ohmučević Grgurić in Croat) contracted to provide another twelve new ships of 700 tons. In the ten years after 1588 sixty or seventy ships of all sizes were built for the Crown. By 1593 the 'Armada of the Ocean Sea'[22] had three squadrons; its main force at Ferrol, the Portuguese squadron at Lisbon, and the *Guarda de Indias* (now one-third paid for by the Crown) at Cadiz. Between them they amounted to between forty and sixty ships of all types, though fewer than half actually belonged to the Crown. The next year a nascent 'Admiralty Board', the *Junta de Armadas*, was created.[23]

All this tended to make the eastern Atlantic more dangerous for the English than it had been. In 1591 Lord Thomas Howard took a squadron to the Azores. It was known that the previous years' *flotas* had been cancelled, so there was a prospect of a particularly rich prize. Not until after he had sailed did the English government get intelligence that the *flota* was to be heavily escorted, and that Don Alonso de Bazán (brother of the late Marquis of Santa Cruz) was to meet it in the Azores with another squadron. Though reinforcements for Howard were organized, they did not arrive until too late. At the end of August he had with him only seven warships, six of them the queen's: the large *Defiance*, *Revenge*, *Elizabeth Bonaventure* and *Lion*, with the smaller *Foresight* and *Crane*, and the *Galleon Ralegh*. Unlike Cumberland the previous year, he was in the right place at the right time, at Flores, the westernmost of the Azores and the natural landfall for the incoming *flota*; but he had not been warned of Bazán's fleet. He was lucky that the Earl of Cumberland, privateering on the Spanish coast, sighted the Spanish ships and sent his pinnace the *Moonshine* to warn Howard, but she arrived only just in time, early on the morning of 30 August.[24]

Howard's ships were watering at Ponta Delgada, at the northern end of the island, and at that moment Bazán's fleet was approaching from the south in two groups, one each side of the island, inshore so that the high land would hide their approach. The English had sick ashore while they 'rummaged' or cleaned the ships internally, a process which included landing the ballast, and they had only a few hours' warning to prepare for sea. Nevertheless they got to sea just in time to escape the jaws of Bazán's trap. Only the *Revenge*, flagship of Lord Thomas's second Sir Richard Grenville, failed to get away. Perhaps it was because he would not abandon a foraging party (as his cousin Sir Walter Ralegh claimed in his famous account of the battle), but Grenville was not noted for concern for his men: 'his own people hated him for his fierceness, and spake very hardly of him'.[25] His contemporaries were sure that it was the arrogance of an old-fashioned gentleman with limited sea experience who would not be seen to run away, 'a man very unquiet in his mind, and greatly affected to war', and they condemned him for it, 'in that he suffered the height of his spirit to transport him both beyond his discretion and charity.'[26] Furthermore he fought his ship in the old way long abandoned by English seamen. Having fired her heavy guns with devastating effect in the opening stages of the action, the *Revenge* fought on largely with small arms for fifteen hours. When her officers forced the dying Grenville to surrender rather than incur useless bloodshed by blowing the ship up, only eight out of 78 barrels of powder had been expended.[27] Grenville died cursing the anonymous heroes, his men who had spent 'their lives and limbs in this service for the good of our native country of England'.[28] His folly cost the queen one of her best ships, what the Spaniards reported as the finest battery of brass guns afloat, and a needless boost to Spanish morale. That autumn, far away in his prison overlooking the Tagus, a young English officer,

> beheld a great galleon of the King's turning up the river in her fighting sails, being sumptuously bedecked with ancients, streamers and pendants, with all other ornaments, to shew her bravery. She let fly all her ordnance in a triumphant manner for the taking of Sir Richard Grenville in the *Revenge* . . .[29]

It was some compensation for what was otherwise a bad year for Spain at sea. Worm-eaten after two seasons in the Caribbean, the *flota* suffered disastrously from storms on the passage homeward, though the silver was safely brought in by the frigates. More than sixty ships foundered or were wrecked, besides thirteen taken by English privateers in the West Indies and four picked up by a London squadron which arrived too late to reinforce Howard. Bazán's fleet also suffered, and among the wrecks was the captured *Revenge*.[30]

The experience of this year gave the queen additional reasons not to risk her ships far away. In 1592 the privateering leaders at court, led by Ralegh and the Howards, planned an expedition to the West Indies, where Bazán's squadron from Ferrol would be unlikely to interfere, but in the event they got no further than the Azores and the Spanish coast, where various groups, including two of the queen's ships, cruised during the summer. Off the Azores one group narrowly missed a Portuguese carrack, but after a prolonged fight took another, the *Madre de Deus*. Unlike the Spaniards, whose Atlantic trade was handled by ships not over 500 tons (the limit for crossing the Guadalquivir Bar to go up to Seville), the Portuguese *Carrera da India* (or East Indies trade) was carried in huge carracks of fifteen hundred tons or more. Though not very well armed, they were heavily manned and extremely difficult to board. In this case it took ten English ships led by Sir John Burgh in the queen's *Roebuck*, with the *Foresight* and Hawkins's *Dainty*, nearly a whole day to take the carrack. This was the biggest and richest prize yet taken in the war. After the ruthless looting of virtually everything portable, including jewels, ambergris, musk and other valuables estimated to be worth £100,000, her remaining cargo was officially valued (certainly under-valued) at £141,120. Sir Robert Cecil, meeting the sailors streaming away from Plymouth, claimed he 'could well smell them almost, such has been the spoils of amber and musk among them.' The small proportion of loot recovered included 847 diamonds, 1,027 rubies, 880 pearls and a quantity of gold and jewellery. The queen made £80,000 from selling the cargo of pepper alone.[31]

Yet even a sum equal to a quarter or even a third of her annual revenue did not tempt Elizabeth to take up the naval war again. Her eyes remained firmly concentrated on France, and she left cruising largely to her subjects. The most ambitious scheme was that of Sir John Hawkins's younger son Richard, who sailed in June 1593 to emulate Drake by passing through the Straits of Magellan into the Pacific. Fifteen years after Drake, and eight years after Thomas Cavendish had gone the same way, the coast was still largely undefended, and he succeeded where several other navigators had failed in getting through the Straits. But Hawkins, one of the most civilized and attractive of the Elizabethan privateers, was on his own admission too easygoing for a wartime captain and, allowing his men to overrule his better judgement, was captured by warships from Callao.[32]

In 1595 the nature of the war changed again. The conversion of Henry IV, the collapse of the League which had been the Spanish party in the French civil war, and the expulsion of the Spaniards themselves from most of Brittany, allowed Queen Elizabeth to withdraw English troops from everywhere on the Continent except the Netherlands. There too the respite provided by Philip II diverting his armies to France had been put to good use; the rebels had established a secure frontier based on the great rivers, the Maas and the Waal, which put them beyond the reach of any short-term threat. At the same time events revived the naval war. Spanish sea power was once again able – indeed, more able than in 1588 – to mount direct attacks on the British Isles, and the outbreak of the Earl of Tyrone's rebellion in Ireland provided an obvious opportunity. Wales, still partly Catholic and possessed of the remote and capacious harbour of Milford Haven, was another possibility of which Spain was aware.[33] In England the political situation was changing. The older generation of political leaders who had served the queen since her accession were dying. For nearly forty years the aggressive, expansionist voices of Walsingham, Leicester and their friends had been balanced by the caution of Lord Burghley. Leicester died in 1588, Walsingham in 1590, leaving only Burghley to represent the old order until his death in 1598, and only an elderly queen without heirs to preserve the security of the kingdom. Now the political scene was increasingly dominated by the brilliant, unstable, headstrong figure of the Earl of Essex, a backer of aggressive schemes, and one determined to win himself glory by leading them in person.[34]

Essex was not just a gilded youth with money and ambition, advanced by the queen's favour to a height which threatened the tranquillity if not the stability of the state. He was also an intelligent strategist with coherent ideas on the conduct of naval war and the chance to put them into practice. His starting-point was the obvious commonplace; as Cumberland put it, 'All the world knoweth that knows anything of the Spanish greatness that it groweth merely from the wealth the East and West Indies yield'.[35] So far the English had been unable to deploy naval strength sufficient to intercept this wealth at a distance, and their efforts at blockade had degenerated into what Essex called 'idle wanderings upon the sea'. What was needed, he argued, was to take and hold a base close enough to the Spanish trade routes to permit an effective blockade.[36]

From these considerations grew the West Indies expedition of 1595. Rehabilitated under Essex's patronage, Drake was once again allowed to try his ideas and talents in the waters where he had won his early fame, 'that kingdom from whence he [Philip II] hath feathers to fly to the top of his high desires'.[37] But English flights were hampered by the same limitations as before. This expedition like its predecessors had to be financed on a joint-stock basis, with the senior officers representing, as they usually did, the interests of the major investors. The queen paid two-thirds of the cost (£33,266 13s 4d); the major private backers were Drake and Hawkins, and old Sir John may have been included as joint commander-in-chief as a prudent check on the headstrong Drake. If so the result was an unfortunate combination of the worst of each. The expedition sailed on 29 August 1595, well-found and victualled, with twenty-seven ships (six of them the queen's). The usual problems of supplying a large force led them to divert first to the Canaries, then Dominica, and finally Guadaloupe. It is possible that the original objective had been to cross the isthmus and take Panama, but under pressure from the queen they had settled for the much easier and nearer target of San Juan, Puerto Rico, where a disabled ship laden with silver was reported to have taken refuge. However lapses of security and their slow advance (much slowed by Hawkins's caution) had given the Spaniards time to send warning ahead, and after heavy fighting the attack was narrowly repulsed. The same day, 12 November, Sir John Hawkins died at sea.[38]

Drake now reverted to the original plan and crossed the Caribbean, raiding Rio de la Hacha and Santa Marta and taking Nombre de Dios, where the troops under their commander Sir Thomas Baskerville were landed to march across the isthmus. Conditions on the jungle track were appalling, and the Spaniards, forewarned, had fortified the pass over the mountains. The assault was beaten back, and on 2 January the survivors re-embarked. So far the expedition had failed on a large scale in somewhat the same way as Drake himself had failed twenty-three years before, and it looks as though his reaction was the same; to keep his nerve, lie low for a while, and try again when the Spanish defenders had been stood down. He must have known that no garrison could be kept permanently in the jungle, and he might have succeeded at the second attempt,[39] but as the fleet approached Porto Bello on 28 January, Drake died of dysentery. He had many epitaphs, but perhaps none better than the comment of Don Alonso de Sotomayor, the officer who had organized the defence of the isthmus:

> one of the most famous men of his profession that have existed in the world, very courteous and honourable with those who have surrendered, of great humanity and gentleness, virtues which must be praised even in an enemy.[40]

Baskerville now took command of the fleet, which on its way home was intercepted on 1 March off the Isle of Pines, at the north-west end of Cuba, by a Spanish fleet under Don Bernardino Delgadillo de Avellaneda which had been sent in pursuit. This was the only occasion in eighteen years of war (apart from 1588) when English and Spanish fleets met in action, and it would be good to have clearer accounts of what happened. The English had the weather gage, but were trapped against the land and forced to attack the Spanish and drive through to leeward in order to round Cape Corrientes. This they achieved, it seems with little damage, though the Spaniards followed them for some time without renewing the action.[41]

The failure of this expedition showed that Spanish defences in the West Indies were more alert than before, but Avellaneda's performance does not suggest that Spain was yet a great sea power.[42] Bad luck and bad judgement on the English side explain much, but in addition the expedition clearly shows how difficult it was in sixteenth-century conditions for even the most careful preparation to keep a large force healthy and properly victualled for nine months in tropical waters. Moreover it must be extremely doubtful if a local base such as San Juan, supposing it to have been taken, could in fact have been supplied and held against counter-attack, so far from home. The West Indies were simply beyond the effective operational range of an Elizabethan expeditionary force.

Well before Baskerville and his ships came home in May 1596, another and larger expedition was preparing for a nearer target. This was not a joint-stock operation but a royal expedition, entirely paid for by the queen, commanded by the Lord Admiral and ordered,

> . . . by burning of ships of war in his havens before they should come forth to the seas, and therewith also destroying his magazines of victuals and his munitions for the arming of his navy, to provide that neither the rebels in Ireland should be aided and strengthened, nor yet the king be able, of long time, to have any great navy in readiness to offend us.[43]

The object was a pre-emptive strike against warships, and only secondarily silver fleets. The background was growing anxiety about Spanish naval preparations.

Howard's fleet sailed from Plymouth on 1 June.[44] He had no fewer than seventeen of the queen's ships, and for the first time a Dutch squadron under Johan van Duivenvoorde participated in the operation.[45] The whole force was at least a hundred sail including transports. In contrast to the proceedings of Drake and Hawkins the previous year, Howard's security was tight and his movements swift. Sealed orders were distributed off Cape Ortegal, but few of the officers were aware of the expedition's target until they arrived. The fleet sailed south well out of sight of land, a screen of pinnaces snapping up any passing vessel which might have given the alarm. The first warning the Spaniards received was when the fleet was sighted rounding Cape St Vincent on the 19th. The next day they anchored off Cadiz, and at high water, dawn the following morning, they attacked. The Spanish warships in the bay were taken or destroyed, Essex and the troops were landed, and the city carried by storm in a few hours. Jealousy and poor co-ordination between Essex, Howard and their subordinates lost what should have been the crowning success, for a large outward-bound *flota* with rich cargoes was lying in the inner bay, and could probably have been taken by boats had they moved faster. As it was the ships were set on fire, apparently by their own crews to conceal their looting. Nevertheless the operation was an outstanding success. The good discipline of the English troops and their humane treatment of the inhabitants of the city were noteworthy. The local civil and military authorities proved cowardly and incompetent; only the bishop displayed any powers of leadership. No effective defence was organized until the Duke of Medina Sidonia arrived the day after the city had fallen, while for a fortnight the English 'lived in great tranquillity and ease as if we had been in Cheapside'.[46] Howard wrote to the duke in elegant Latin proposing an exchange of prisoners: 'As I was entrusted with the command by my lady the Queen's Majesty in the year 1588, I suppose I may not be unknown to you . . .'[47]

Having taken Cadiz, the question was what to do with it. Howard's orders were clear, and holding Cadiz permanently was no part of them. But Essex's strategy was to capture and hold a port in Spain or Portugal from which the trade from both West and East Indies could be completely stopped, 'whereby we shall cut his sinews and make war upon him with his own money'. Then Elizabeth could truly rule the seas, 'which is what the queen of an island should aspire to'.[48] Duivenvoorde supported him, but they were overruled by the council of war and the expedition returned, bringing with it two new Spanish warships, 1,200 pieces of ordnance, and booty worth (on the Spanish estimate) twenty million ducats.[49] Of this only £12,838 in coin and plate, with some quantities of pearls, quicksilver, silks, sugar, hides, bells and other commodities were subsequently recovered by the crown.[50] The attackers left the fortifications and public buildings of Cadiz destroyed, thirteen warships, eleven Indies ships and a large number of smaller vessels burnt.[51] Many members of the expedition profited handsomely by it, and the cause of reformed religion was not forgotten. Edward Doughtie, the Lord Admiral's chaplain, stole seventeen works of theology from the library of the Jesuit college, and subsequently presented them to Hereford Cathedral, where they remain today as a testimony to his piety.[52] Essex, not to be outdone, took the entire library of the Bishop of Faro and gave it to Sir Thomas Bodley's new foundation in Oxford.[53]

For Spain, the loss of Cadiz was a material and political catastrophe. The silver fleets from 1595 and 1596 were completely disrupted, and that autumn the Spanish crown was again driven to repudiate its debts.[54] The capture of a mainland Spanish town was a disgrace and humiliation.

> It is not so much that in six hours we have lost so famous a city and port, with a fleet of war and a flota and the standard of Xeres and 600 horses, as the prestige that is destroyed, in that the enemy have seen that even in Andalusia, the most populous and fertile province in Spain, we could not in a fortnight gather forces enough about Cadiz to turn them out of the city . . . and though we are so near that the smoke is driving in our eyes, we know, with what feelings your Majesty may imagine, that we cannot stir a finger to save it.[55]

Philip's reaction was to order his fleet to mount an immediate counter-attack. It is a measure of the improvement in Spanish naval administration that in only three months Don Pedro de Zubiaur was able to take to sea a fleet of 126 sail, including about sixty which might be considered warships, half of them the king's. The English had only short warning, too short for the queen's ships which were refitting at Chatham to get to the West Country or Ireland. Had the blow fallen there would have been only local defences to meet it; but on 18 October the Armada was caught on a lee shore on the Galician coast by a south-westerly gale, losing more than thirty large ships and driving the rest into port.[56]

The 1596 campaign shows that the English navy, like the Spanish, was learning lessons from the war and becoming more efficient as it did so. Howard's skilful and confident management of a difficult combined operation shows high professional competence in him and his captains. The evidence suggests that the English were handling their heavy guns less tentatively (perhaps also with more efficient reloading procedures) than they had in 1588. Most of the bigger warships fired a large part of their ammunition; 400 or 500 rounds in only one or two days' action, which represented an unprecedented volume of fire.[57]

Queen Elizabeth composed a prayer for the expedition before it sailed:

> Thou that by this foresight dost truly discern how no malice of revenge nor quittance of injury, nor desire of bloodshed nor greediness of lucre, hath bred the resolution of our now set out army, but a heedful care and weary watch . . .[58]

It is hardly fair to describe her style as 'a ghastly premonition of Mr George Meredith',[59] but it has to be said that greediness of lucre was extremely high among her personal priorities, and she was formidably angry when the triumphant fleet returned with plenty of booty for its officers and men and very little for her. The crown recovered £8,359, in place of the £3,500,000 (ten years' ordinary revenues of the English crown) reported to have been burnt with the outward-bound West India fleet and the £4,000,000 of the incoming *flota*.[60] She was therefore receptive to Essex's proposals that he be allowed to try out his strategy of seizing a Spanish port and paralysing Spanish trade. At the same time the abortive Spanish invasion was a serious worry. Though English intelligence was good, communications were slow, and if Spain could now put a fleet to sea in three months there could be no guarantee that the English fleet could mobilize in time, especially to meet a threat to Ireland or the West Country. Permanent mobilization was financially impossible, and next time here might be no lucky gale.

So a plan was born for an attack on the 'Armada of the Ocean Sea' in its main base, Ferrol. The difficulty was that Ferrol lies deep in an inlet with a narrow entrance surrounded by high ground – a much tougher proposition than Cadiz, on an island with open water on three sides. In the end Essex was entrusted with 5,000 men and seventeen of the queen's ships, including one of her two galleys, and the two Spanish prizes from Cadiz which were to be expended in the attack. A gale in the Bay of Biscay on 15 July damaged and scattered the fleet; the slow and leewardly Spanish prizes ('two great carts', Essex called them), and the ships commanded by Essex and his military followers like Sir Walter Ralegh, suffered notably worse than those of Lord Thomas Howard and the sea officers. Sailing a second time, the fleet was again scattered by leaks and mishaps. They reassembled off Lisbon, now missing the forces essential to attack Ferrol, and Essex decided instead to blockade the Portuguese coast between Lisbon and Cape St Vincent. This reasonable plan was presently abandoned on the flimsiest grounds in favour of going to the Azores after the *flota*. It was just such an 'idle wandering upon the sea' as Essex had deplored, and more idle than most, for Essex the brilliant armchair strategist proved to be a feeble and vacillating leader in practice. The fleet dispersed about the islands, and entirely failed to intercept the *flota* when it appeared.[61]

The 'Islands Voyage' was worse than another missed opportunity, for it was entirely wishful thinking which had persuaded Essex that the Ferrol fleet would not put to sea that year. While he took the bulk of the queen's ships to the Azores, the Spanish fleet was preparing another major operation. On 9 October Don Martín de Padilla[62] sailed with 136 ships carrying 9,000 troops, to be joined by the galleys from Blavet with further men, the plan being to intercept Essex's fleet on its return and establish a Spanish base at Falmouth. This was a feasible plan, and thanks to Essex there was nothing to stop it, but the season of the equinoctial gales was a bad time to undertake it. Padilla was within thirty miles of the Lizard on 12 October when his fleet was struck by a severe storm which sank twenty-eight of his ships. Several others were driven into English ports; one came into St Ives, whose master had spent the previous three years scouting English waters to prepare for invasion.[63]

The news of Padilla's fleet burst on an unsuspecting court on 26 October, soon after Lord Howard of Effingham had been invested as Earl of Nottingham. Essex's fleet was scattered by the same gale; he himself arrived at Plymouth the same day, unaware of the peril that he and the country had been in. He was received very coldly by the queen, and reacted petulantly.[64] He was never given another chance to prove his strategic ideas, not just because he had demonstrated his incompetence as a sea commander, but because the strategic situation was changing again. Peace between France and Spain was under discussion, and was concluded in the spring of 1598. As part of this settlement the Spaniards evacuated their base at Blavet, and Henry IV published the Edict of Nantes giving the Protestant towns of France a large measure of self-government.[65]

Spain was left without a valuable base, but also free of a major distraction, and ready to try once more to strike at England. We can see now that Spanish sea power was past its peak, with Philip II dying and the finances of Spain collapsing. Richard Hawkins, a prisoner in Spain, described the situation well enough:

> If Spain make a navy, three years is needful to join shipping and those to be bought, embargoed, or hired from Flemings, Venetians, Genoese, or Argoteses. For Spain is utterly without shipping of regard. Of men, there is no kingdom that at this day is so poor . . . Of mariners and gunners there is not a ship which is not partly furnished with Flemish and English.[66]

But the English government was determined not to be caught by surprise again. Possibly because a Dutch squadron was operating on the Spanish coast that summer, Elizabeth decided that it was not necessary for her to mount a major offensive, but the government remained alert. In July 1599 rumours of a Spanish fleet assembling at Corunna caused a serious alarm. Ten ships were mobilized in a month (marginally slower than in 1588, but still a respectable performance) and troops assembled around London in case the Spanish army in Flanders attempted anything. In the event this 'Invisible Armada' was diverted southward in pursuit of the Dutch and never came near England, but it generated alarm and preparations almost on the scale of 1588, with a main fleet at Plymouth under Lord Thomas Howard ('prettily strong and in good plight, for so short warning'), and a Channel Guard under Sir Richard Leveson.[67]

Meanwhile England was increasingly caught up with an overseas campaign of her own, in Ireland. English rule there had long been precarious, and Tyrone's rebellion in Ulster threatened to end it completely. Ulster was remote from the centre of English power in the Pale around Dublin, and the galleys of the MacDonalds of the Isles kept up free communication with their McDonnell cousins which were of great value to Tyrone. In these waters a tiny squadron of the queen's smallest ships had for thirty years been struggling to keep open communications across the Irish Sea to Dublin, and to interfere with those across the North Channel. In 1565 Captain George Thornton, part-time pirate and senior naval officer in these waters for thirty-five years, had the 60-ton pinnace *Saker*, the 40-ton bark *Hare*, and two small galleys, the brigantines *Makeshift* and *Post* built in 1562 to operate in the Seine. He was not able to achieve much against the Highland galleys, and by 1568 the squadron had been withdrawn. Thornton was back in 1576 with the 90-ton *Handmaid*, succeeded in 1587 by the *Popinjay*, and finally in 1601 by the *Tramontana*. These ships were the first English royal warships ever to be based overseas.[68] Some galleys were intercepted, but Thornton's success was limited. In 1582 Angus MacDonald of Islay was chased without success, though he suffered losses in a storm, while three years later Sorley Boy McDonnell of Antrim brought two thousand men from Islay in twenty-four galleys, again eluding the English.[69] Elizabeth's main hope in these waters rested on an alliance with Sir Lachlan Mór Maclean of Duart,[70] the enemy of the MacDonalds, but diplomacy achieved even less than English sea power and the MacDonalds murdered Maclean in 1598.[71] The only real gain of the connection came in 1588, when the Ragusan ship *Santa Maria della Grazie e San Giovanni Battista*, a refugee of the Armada, arrived in

Tobermory Bay, and was presently blown up, probably by an English agent and no doubt with Maclean's connivance.[72] Meanwhile Ruari Og MacNeill of Barra[73] made a career of piracy which would have done credit to a vice-admiral of Devon. Throughout Elizabeth's reign the 'Galleys of Kisimul' (still celebrated in Gaelic folksong) raided the length the Irish Sea as far south as the Bristol Channel; in 1580 they took cargo worth £1,200 out of the *White Hart* of Bridgewater. The queen, perhaps remembering the *Mary Willoughby*, limited her response to diplomatic protests to James VI of Scots, but the next MacNeill, Ruari 'the Tatar', was still adding to his fleet some time after James had succeeded her on the English throne.[74]

In 1599 Essex was sent to Ireland to suppress the rebellion. For him personally this was an opportunity to redeem his reputation, but for both him and the queen it was a situation full of risk. The Queen was sixty-six and had no direct heir: Essex was popular, ambitious, discontented, and now despatched on an unwelcome and unpromising campaign. He had longstanding connections with James VI of Scots, a leading claimant to succeed Elizabeth, and one perhaps willing to speed his prospects by promoting a coup d'état. Whether Essex succeeded or failed in Ireland, he was a source of intense anxiety to the English government.[75] He realized that the key to success against Tyrone lay in naval supremacy, for it was only by command of the waters around Ulster that the Irish could be isolated and attacked in the rear, but he was denied the naval support he wanted, partly because of the mobilization against Spain, partly perhaps because Elizabeth's ministers were unwilling to give him control of the waters between England, Scotland and Ireland lest he use it for an improper purpose. Essex avoided serious campaigning, those of his subordinates who tried to attack were defeated, and his negotiations with Tyrone strengthened rather than weakened the rebels. By the end of the year the English held little more than Dublin.[76]

Meanwhile the English suffered further alarms at sea. By 1599 English seamen had had repeated successes against galleys, notably at Cadiz in 1587 and 1596, and no longer held them in as much awe as before. In Spain too they were out of fashion, but there remained at least one true believer with the energy, courage and wealth to back his faith: Federico Spinola, a son of the Genoese banking house which did so much to finance the Spanish empire. His preparations were masked by those of the Corunna squadron, and his appearance in the Channel came as a complete surprise. On 1 September, the same day that Howard paid off the main fleet, Spinola's six galleys passed the Straits of Dover. With a calm sea and a stiff wind, perfect conditions for galleys, they could outsail anything afloat, and Spinola got successfully into Dunkirk without being intercepted by either English or Dutch.[77] The shallow waters of the Flanders coast were ideal for galleys, and under Spinola's bold leadership his squadron had an effect out of all proportion to its numbers. The galley recovered much of its former status, and in both England and the Netherlands galley-building programmes were hastily set on foot.[78]

Elsewhere there was little major naval activity during 1600, if only because neither Philip III of Spain nor Queen Elizabeth could afford it. Leveson took a small squadron on a fruitless cruise in search of carracks that summer,[79] but otherwise English efforts were concentrated in Ireland. There the new English general Lord Mountjoy was putting into practice the naval campaign against Tyrone. The key to his strategy was a garrison landed at Lough Foyle in the rear of Tyrone's position, maintained by sea with the support of a small squadron of the queen's ships led by the *Tramontana*. She achieved an unusual success in taking a large galley belonging to the Irish chieftain Grace (or Grainne) O'Malley of Clare Island, who had long exercised local naval control on the West Coast.[80]

During 1601 Mountjoy's noose closed in on Tyrone. At the same time there was some intelligence suggesting that after many years of fair words and small assistance, Spain might be preparing real support for the Irish. It was obvious that Spain might 'at very little cost achieve the same effect as the Queen does by aiding the [Dutch] rebels . . .', as the Spanish Council of State advised Philip III in June 1600.[81] However a Spanish fleet might equally be intended to run relief through to the army in Flanders, whose usual supply route, the 'Spanish Road' overland from northern Italy, was blocked by war between France and Savoy.[82] In the end when Don Diego de Brochero did land three thousand men at Kinsale on 23 September they took everyone by surprise. Instead of landing in Ulster early in 1600, when there was everything to hope for, they arrived eighteen months too late, too few, and in the wrong corner of Ireland. Moreover Brochero's ships were victualled only for a fortnight and had to return at once, allowing Mountjoy to seize the forts commanding the mouth of Kinsale Harbour and blockade the Spanish troops. Meanwhile Leveson, commanding the Channel Guard, hastily embarked 2,000 men in his warships and sailed westward, landing them at Kinsale on 15 November. Soon afterwards Spanish reinforcements under Zubiaur arrived on the coast and entered Castlehaven, where Leveson attacked them on 6 December. He was able to force his way into the harbour and sink or drive ashore most of the Spanish ships, but without a landing force he could do no more against the troops dug in ashore. Meanwhile, to meet the Spaniards Tyrone was obliged to march the length of Ireland through a devastated, starving winter land. On Christmas Eve outside Kinsale his army was totally defeated, and on 6 January the Spaniards surrendered.[83]

Before the news of this decisive victory reached England, when the issue still seemed completely uncertain, Sir Robert Cecil the new Secretary of State wrote to Mountjoy bluntly refusing his request that warships should be stationed on the Irish coast to guard against Spanish reinforcements:

> For the fleet to continue, Sir, we cannot allow it, neither do we hold it the way to restrain Spanish succours to keep Irish harbours, whereof there be more than the Queen hath ships. To Spain therefore we send and for the rest you must take your chance.[84]

Experience had once again driven the queen's ministers back to an offensive strategy as the only way of countering Spanish sea power with England's limited resources. 'It is much more honourable for the Queen and safe for the State to maintain a fleet upon the coast of Spain than to stand upon the defensive at home.'[85] However many times they had failed to make it work, there seemed to be no alternative, and the hope of co-operating with the growing naval strength of the Dutch gave new impetus to their plans. Their dilemma was that without more money they could not keep large forces on station for any length of time six hundred miles away on the coast of Portugal; but without such a regular blockade they could not take the prizes which would pay for the campaign. Ingenious schemes were proposed to surmount this difficulty, but none was made to work.[86]

In 1602 Leveson was again sent out with a squadron to cruise on the coast of Spain. For the only time in this war, he achieved the English dream of intercepting a *flota*, but with six of the queen's ships he was outnumbered three or four to one, and was obliged to disengage. However he and his second Sir William Monson had the compensation of cutting out the Portuguese carrack *São Valentinho* from Cezimbra Roads, in the teeth of both galleys and shore batteries. Her cargo fetched £44,000, almost enough to pay for the summer's campaign. After they had brought her home Monson went out again, and on 26 September fell in with Brochero's ships returning from Kinsale. He had no difficulty avoiding trouble, but with only two ships against twenty-four that was all he could do.[87]

The eight galleys which Leveson and Monson met at Cezimbra (of which they sank two) had been assembled by the indefatigable Spinola to reinforce his Flanders squadron. This time he was not so lucky; conditions were again ideal ('Galleys will outsail all ships in such a loom gale of wind and smooth sea as we had that night'),[88] but his enemies were forewarned and waiting for him in the Straits of Dover. The English squadron under Sir Robert Mansell intercepted some of the galleys and forced the rest into the hands of the Dutch. Only Spinola's own galley and one other escaped. He continued his campaign with what remained to him, but the Dutch increasingly had his measure, and in May 1603 he was killed in action with Joos de Moor, Vice-Admiral of Zealand.[89]

By this time Queen Elizabeth was dead, James VI of Scots had succeeded to the English throne, and peace negotiations with Spain had been opened. Even before the queen's death Cecil had concluded that with Ireland secure, France reunited, the Dutch established behind defensible frontiers, and Spain evidently exhausted, England had achieved all she had any need to fight for or any hope of winning. She had survived, and more than survived. Though neither Spain nor England had been able to injure one another mortally over a range of six hundred miles, in 1603 the English Navy Royal was in most respects stronger and more capable than it had been on the outbreak of the war twenty years before, while Spanish sea power, after a precocious growth in the 1590s, was already decaying fast.[90]

Nor was this all, for the war years had wrought an extraordinary transformation in the English merchant fleet – if 'merchant fleet' is the right term for privately-owned men-of-war which spent the war years pursuing profit by other means than peaceful trade.[91] Empire-building, in the opinion of the Jesuit missionary Francis Xavier, was no more than 'to conjugate the verb to rob in all its moods and tenses'.[92] In this sense, if not in any other, the Elizabethan English were the purest of imperialists. Drawing on their long pirate tradition (especially in the West Country) and their apprenticeship with the Huguenots of La Rochelle, English seamen and shipowners threw themselves into the war against Spain as soon as it broke out, and in many cases before. The government was tolerant towards past and present piracies; 'her Majesty shall not need to espy the faults of those that will venture their own to do her service'.[93] The experience of those like Hawkins who had traded illegally in the Spanish and Portuguese empires before the war, and of the merchants whose legal trade with Spain had been wrecked by the 1585 embargo, added to the effectiveness of the attack.

Contemporaries, and until recently historians, tended to take most notice of those noblemen and gentlemen who involved themselves in private war. By far the most prominent of these was the Earl of Cumberland, who in 1598 triumphed where Drake had failed in taking San Juan, Puerto Rico,[94] but his large and expensive enterprises were financially ruinous (in his own words, he 'threw his lands into the sea').[95] Cumberland commanded his squadrons in person, with more skill than luck, but most men of his rank were investors rather than sea commanders. Gentlemen like Sir Richard Grenville, whose well-armed galleon the *Castle of Comfort* was raiding under French colours ten years before the war broke out,[96] were joined in the 1580s by great London merchants, many of whom moved from buying Spanish colonial goods before the war to capturing them during it – with such success that by the 1590s imports were sometimes cheaper in London than in Seville.[97] The capture of the *Madre de Deus* in 1592 flooded a hundred tons of quicksilver onto a market which normally took five tons a year.[98] As the war continued an extensive alliance of privateer owners and investors developed. At its head stood the Lord Admiral, himself a large investor in privateering, as were many of the great men at court. Money and management was added by the London merchants, while the ships were fitted out and commanded by a growing corps of experienced seamen, mainly from Plymouth, the south coast ports and London. At every level the men, their expertise and money, their guns and equipment were freely interchanged with the queen's ships. An operation like the 1596 Cadiz expedition, at one level an affair of state, was just as much a foregathering of all the leading personalities in the privateering war.

That war was run for profit, by professionals who knew what they were after and did not allow nice scruples to stand in their way. For every one of the gentlemen 'whose funerals were all made in the bottomless sea, and their lands consumed and turned into the element of water,'[99] there were probably several merchants or mariners who made modest or immodest fortunes at sea during the war. It has been estimated that prize goods worth £1–200,000 a year were being brought into England, equal to 10–15 per cent of all legal imports, and providing a massive injection of capital into English trade.[100] Much of this was invested in new ships. In 1582 there were twenty merchant ships in the country of 200 tons or more. In the next fifteen years seventy-two more were built, and the shipbuilding boom continued to the end of the war. By 1600 the merchant fleet was estimated to be twenty times the size of the queen's. [101]

The great bulk of the privateering effort was concentrated in the eastern Atlantic and around the British Isles. Attacks on Dutch, Danish, Hansard, Scottish, Polish, Swedish and other neutral ships and cargoes bringing Spain the Baltic commodities (grain, timber, copper, naval stores) on which she depended did England much diplomatic damage – which she could ill afford when England too needed Baltic imports, when most of her cloth exports now went to Hansa ports, and when Elizabeth's likely heir James VI of Scots had married a Danish princess.[102] The damage to Spain, however, was infinitely greater. In the first three months of the war the English took at least twenty-seven Spanish ships, valued at 294,500 ducats; over the whole war, the total was at least one thousand.[103] Twenty years of incessant losses to the English, and ruthless demands by the Spanish Crown, bled white the merchant fleet of Spain, and above all the Basque and Cantabrian ports where most of the ships and seamen came from. Three hundred years later it had not recovered its strength of the 1570s.[104]

Only a minority of English privateers operated as far away as the Caribbean and, with the exception of Cumberland's Puerto Rico expedition, none of them was on a scale sufficient to take a major port, still less a *flota*. But these smaller forces could more easily be victualled and maintained for a season in the West Indies, and their cumulative effect on Spanish trade and settlements away from the major cities was literally devastating. There were at least 150 English privateering voyages to these waters during the war.[105] Those who had the capital to invest in this, the costliest and riskiest area of privateering, and the professional skills and luck to make a success of it, could reap large rewards. The great London merchant John Watts admitted in 1591 to having made £32,000; the following year one-armed Captain Christopher Newport sacked four towns and took nineteen prizes.[106] In 1595 Sir Anthony Sherley described Puerto de Caballos on the Honduras coast as 'the most poor and miserable place of all India'; he spoke with authority, as he was the sixth person to have destroyed it in five years, and by no means the last.[107] In 1603 Newport occupied it for eighteen days, took the flagship and vice-flagship of the *flota* of New Spain, and departed with great booty.[108] In 1602 William Parker took Porto Bello in spite of the expensive fortifications which had recently been installed.[109] By the end of the war much of the Spanish Caribbean outside the big cities was ruined and depopulated. What local trade still existed was in English, French or Dutch hands.[110] In the Mediterranean, where English privateers appeared in great numbers in the 1590s, hardly any distinction was made between enemies like Spain and neutrals like Venice, whose Levant commerce suffered severely.[111]

The legacy of the privateering war was a transformation of the English merchant fleet, and of the London merchant class who owned so large a share of it. The same war which ruined Spanish shipping served to create the first English merchant fleet capable of long-distance trade, and to back that fleet with capital, skills and ambitions none of which had existed before.

The aggressive mentality of a small minority had spread throughout the nobility, gentry and mercantile classes, and a conviction had widely taken root that wealth and glory were to be won by war at sea. England was still 'little in territory, not extraordinarily rich and defended only by itself,'[112] but twenty years of warfare had transformed her outlook. Where previously the queen herself had owned an impressive, but almost isolated fleet, now naval and maritime strength was genuinely a national endeavour. A generation before it had been taken for granted that the country's prosperity was bound up with the cloth trade to Antwerp: now it seemed equally obvious that England's future lay across the open oceans. Perceptive observers had realized since the 1540s that, 'Our shipping and sea service is our best and safest defence as being the only fortification and rampart of England.'[113] Now Englishmen had learnt to see the sea as something more than a defence against a hostile world; it had become the means 'to seek new worlds, for gold, for praise, for glory.'[114]

TWENTY-ONE

The Path to Fame

Social History: Officers 1509–1603

The ship's companies of English ships in Henry VIII's time seem to have been made up much as they had been in the previous century. The same officers are present: captain, master, boatswain, carpenter, master gunner, purser and surgeon. Of these the master, boatswain, carpenter and gunner usually had a mate each, and in big ships there were further subordinates. The *Henry Grace à Dieu* when new had not only a boatswain's mate but a coxswain, coxswain's mate, two yeomen of the 'strikes'[1] and two yeomen of the ports, all four with a mate each. Similarly, the purser's subordinates included three stewards, three cooks and their mates; while the carpenter had not only a mate but an under-carpenter and two caulkers.[2] In 1513 Lord Ferrers, commanding the *Sovereign*, had four captains and four 'petty captains' under him, but it is not clear if they were all in the same ship.[3] Smaller ships taken up from trade also had a substantial hierarchy of officers. The *Elizabeth* in 1512–13 had a captain (Lewis Sotheran, her peace-time master), master, master's mate, four quartermasters and two mates, boatswain and gunner each with their mates, purser, steward and clerk, and a carpenter.[4] Later in the century the shipboard hierarchy became more complex. On Fenton's 1582 expedition, intended for the East Indies, the companies of the *Galleon Leicester* and *Edward Bonaventure* included not only a full set of officers and petty officers, but trumpeters and musicians, stewards, cooks, smiths, bakers, tailors, shoemakers, a 'garbler', a 'plat-drawer', jeweller, apothecary, and distiller.[5] Even the little *Crescent* which Dartmouth fitted out against the Armada in 1588, had a captain, a master and two mates, a pilot, four quartermasters and three mates, the boatswain, gunner and carpenter each with their mates, four quarter gunners, a steward, cook, surgeon, swabber, cooper, corporal and lieutenant – all to command thirty-eight seamen and three boys. Her consort the *Hart* had eighteen officers and petty officers for twelve seamen and two boys.[6] The high proportion of officers to men is an indication of the quality and wide variety of skill which was needed afloat. Already a warship's company, very unlike a company of troops, was a team uniting many talents and professions.

At the summit of this hierarchy stood the Lord Admiral of England (or Scotland), when he was present commanding at sea.[7] Several Lords Admiral were, as we have seen, too old or young to command, and the dignity of the office confined it to the largest seagoing fleets. The Lieutenant of the Admiralty or Vice-Admiral might deputize for the Admiral at sea, as he did at the Navy Board, but the office declined in significance after the Lord Treasurer took over the Navy Board, and disappeared at Sir William Woodhouse's death in 1565.[8] Most seagoing flag officers were 'admirals' in a different sense. The word in fact had at least four meanings. There was the Lord Admiral of England or some other country. There was the Admiral of the Narrow Seas or of some other fleet, sometimes called Vice-Admiral to indicate that he was junior to the Lord Admiral. These were formal offices appointed by the crown, but in addition, by common parlance, any senior officer in any warlike context was an 'admiral', regardless of who owned the ships or how many of them were present. If two merchantmen traded together in dangerous waters one would become the admiral and the other the vice-admiral; if a convoy chose one of their number to command, he became the admiral for the voyage. Moreover, so did his ship, for 'admiral' referred to the flagship as well as the flag officer, and so likewise did 'vice-admiral'. A vice-admiral was the deputy of an admiral in any of the possible senses, and some others besides. In every maritime county the Lord Admiral had a deputy called the Vice-Admiral who claimed his legal and financial rights, and sometimes convened a local Vice-Admiralty Court. These Vice-Admirals of Counties were not sea commanders at all, except by coincidence. To cover all these ambiguities, Elizabethan English used the word 'general' roughly in the sense of the modern 'commander-in-chief'. A general might command either a fleet or an army, sometimes both together, and the term usually implied formal appointment by the crown, with a commission under the Great Seal and the authority to invoke martial law.[9] Thus Edward Fenton, general of the abortive 1582 expedition, had 'absolute power and auctority . . . to order, rule, govern, correct and punish by imprisonment and violent means and by death'.[10] Lord Howard had the authority, not normal even for a Lord Admiral, to make knights in the queen's name.[11]

A general commanding a large fleet would normally have a vice-admiral as his second, and if necessary a rear-admiral as well. In the 'joint-stock' expeditions of the Spanish War, these officers often represented both the interests of different investors and the constituent parts of a force made up from different sources. At Cadiz in 1587, Drake was general, William Borough vice-admiral, and Robert Flicke rear-admiral; but in another sense Drake represented the Plymouth squadron and West Country investors, Borough (Clerk of the Ships and the most senior member of the Navy Board) represented the Navy Royal, and Flicke (appropriately in the *Merchant Royal*) represented the London merchants.[12] In the spring of 1588 Drake as vice-admiral commanding at Plymouth seems to have been regarded as an independent general on the same footing as the Vice-Admiral of the Narrow Seas. When Lord Howard took the main fleet westward to join him there was a formal transfer of command, by which Drake ceased to be a general but became Howard's vice-admiral, in effect Vice-Admiral of England, so that a loss of independence was balanced by a gain in status.[13] When Howard divided his fleet during the Armada campaign, he informally created four squadrons each with its own flag officer. In the Cadiz expedition of 1596 this scheme was taken a stage further, with each squadron wearing its own distinctive ensigns. The Lord Admiral himself commanded one with crimson colours, Essex (also joint general) the orange-tawny squadron, Lord Thomas Howard, vice-admiral of the fleet, took the blue squadron, and Sir Walter Ralegh the rear-admiral had the white, with the Dutch forming a fifth squadron. Each of the four English flag officers was admiral of his own squadron in addition to his title in the force as a whole, with a vice-admiral and rear-admiral of the squadron under him. The admirals of each squadron flew their flags at the maintop, the vice-admirals at the foretop and the rear-admirals at the mizzentop, in the fashion that was to become standard in future centuries, but the Lord Admiral as the queen's representative flew the royal standard at the main.[14]

In command of all but the smallest warships, whether owned by the queen or private citizens, was the captain. We have seen that the traditional picture of the gentleman-soldier coming to take command from the plebeian mariner is untrue, and it continued to be untrue throughout the sixteenth century, but it is true that captains were usually of higher social standing than masters. Large royal warships were always commanded by knights or gentlemen, men of the rank which the age expected in such important commands. 'There is no doubt but that a sea captain, having the charge of one of his Majesty's royal ships, hath as enlarged a commission and of as high a consequence committed unto him, and of as high a nature as any colonel at land.'[15] Many of these captains, however, were the same people as the peacetime masters, or had risen from shipmasters and shipowners. Men like William Gonson or Sir William Woodhouse under Henry VIII,

Drake, Hawkins, Winter and many others under Elizabeth, had used the sea to rise to a social rank to which they could not otherwise have aspired. Other captains, born into a higher social rank, spent enough of their careers commanding at sea to become experienced, even in some sense professional sea officers.[16] For smaller ships the supply of gentlemen might not suffice; in 1545 Lisle proposed:

> As concerning the mean ships I know none other way (I mean those that come out of the West parts and such of London as were victuallers that want captains) but to place them with mean men to be their captains, as serving men and yeomen that be most meet for the purpose.[17]

As part of its mobilization plans, the English government drew up in 1586 a list of seventy-six potential captains, arranged in social rank. It begins with the Lord Admiral himself, followed by four noblemen, eight knights, eighteen esquires, twenty-eight gentlemen, and seventeen others. The knights include a mixture of soldiers, courtiers and country gentlemen with limited sea experience, like Sir Walter Ralegh, Sir John Perrott and Sir Richard Grenville; with mariners like Sir William Winter and Sir Francis Drake who had risen by their service at sea. The same mixture occurs among the esquires, but among the gentlemen, who were of varied social origins, there is nobody without considerable sea experience, and the others are clearly all professional seamen.[18]

Taken as a whole, this list shows several social trends. Service at sea, even on a semi-professional basis, was clearly respectable for men of high (in the case of the Earl of Cumberland, almost the highest) social rank. Equally it could be the means of advancing men from modest origins. Few were born in real poverty, like Drake, but many were the sons of shipowners and small merchants in provincial ports who could not otherwise have expected to rise to knights or esquires.[19] At a higher social level, the Navy Royal's status as an honourable service of great importance to the state is shown by the participation of noblemen who were more or less amateurs. Prominent among them in the 1590s were the relatives of the Lord Admiral: Lord Henry Seymour his brother-in-law, Lord Thomas Howard his cousin, Lord Sheffield his nephew, and Sir Richard Leveson his son-in-law. But they were not just noble amateurs. All of them, from Lord Howard downwards, made real efforts to become familiar with the sea; Thomas Howard and Leveson were the outstanding admirals of the closing years of the war. Lord Howard's handling of the fleet at Cadiz in 1596 showed considerable professional talent. Other men of his rank were also making great efforts to master the advanced and demanding skills of the mariner. Robert Dudley, son of the Earl of Leicester,

> determined at any cost to enter the marine army, on which at that time the reputation and greatness of England depended. He had also a desire to discover new countries. Therefore, from the age of seventeen, he gave himself to the study of navigation, and of marine discipline and war.[20]

He was probably the first English navigator ever to plot a great-circle course, 'the which how difficult a thing it is . . . let those who have been seamen all [the] days of their lives judge.'[21] Many young men, not nobly born but of good family, tried their fortunes the same way. 'I like the sea and the sea life, and the company at sea, as well as any that ever I lived withal. The place is good and healthful to a willing mind.'[22] Some of them, like the sixteen-year-old William Monson, ran away to sea, 'led thereunto by the wildness of my youth'.[23]

The common feature in all these sea careers is that naval warfare was an opportunity for men to better themselves, socially in many cases, financially in almost all.[24] Lord Howard himself was 'as goodly a gentleman as the times had any, if Nature had not been more attentive to complete his person, than Fortune to make him rich . . .'[25] Other noblemen like Cumberland were at sea to repair their fortunes – though like him, they did not all succeed. At every level of society, the eldest son inherited what there was to inherit, leaving the younger with 'that which the cat left on the malt heap.'[26] That had always been true, but the Elizabethan age was the first in which it became acceptable for young gentlemen to seek their fortunes at sea.

The presence of men of good birth provoked tensions in a shipboard society in which everything depended on teamwork, and in which the safety and prosperity of all depended on the professional skill of each. Noblemen and gentlemen were the unquestioned leaders of society for reasons which had nothing to do with professional skill, except to some extent in the use of arms. Until the sixteenth century they had intruded into the mariner's world only briefly and in defined circumstances. As soon as men of high rank began to make something like a career at sea, their presence effectively posed the question of what conferred authority on shipboard. Was it the master's skill, operating as it traditionally had through the consent of the ship's company, who might be persuaded but could not be driven? Or was the imperative claim of rank, backed perhaps by royal authority, to override all mechanical abilities? In the face of disobedience all a master could do was 'repeatedly order, request, even implore'.[27] Was this sufficient when the safety of the state might hang on obedience to orders? Shortly before she foundered, the captain of the *Mary Rose* hailed that he had 'a sort of knaves I cannot rule':[28] it seemed to be an awful example of the perils of indiscipline, and if a gentleman had so much difficulty, how much the harder would it be for one who had himself risen from a common mariner.

Drake was always noted for the strict discipline which he maintained.[29] 'He treats them [his men] with affection, and they treat him with respect.'[30] But this was written only after he had surmounted an acute crisis of authority on his voyage round the world. Himself a man despised for 'the baseness of his birth and education, his ostentation and vain-glorious boasting',[31] he had with him a number of gentlemen of high birth and good connections, just those whom his contemporaries would expect to be in command. Thomas Doughty was one of them; a courtier with powerful connections, a gentleman of polish and learning who saw himself, and was seen by others, as the natural leader of the expedition. In the face of disaffection centred around Doughty, Drake acted ruthlessly, dramatically and illegally.[32] After a show trial (which Drake had no power to conduct), Doughty was executed. Drake then made a famous speech:

> Here is such controversy between the sailors and the gentlemen and such stomaching between the gentlemen and sailors, that it doth even make me mad to hear it. But, my masters, I must have it left. For I must have the gentleman to haul and draw with the mariner and the mariner with the gentleman. What! Let us show ourselves to be all of a company and let us not give occasion to the enemy to rejoice at our decay and overthrow. I would know him that would refuse to set his hand to a rope, but I know there is not any such here. And as gentlemen are very necessary for government's sake in the voyage, so have I shipped them to that, and to some further intent; and yet though I know sailors to be the most envious people in the world, and so unruly without government, yet may I not be without them.[33]

This speech is a favourite among naval officers today. What they do not realize is that it is preserved thanks to a bitter enemy of Drake, who quoted it in order to ruin him. These are the words of a base-born mariner bent on upsetting the God-given order of society, and had he not returned rich and triumphant, they might well have done him the damage intended.[34]

What is striking is that this thoroughly subversive principle was followed by Lord Howard and other nobleman officers who made a point of being seen to haul and draw with the mariners. Howard made himself familiar with the seaman's work, 'namely sheet, halliard, bowline, tack and helm'; he could handle navigational instruments and lay a gun himself.[35] He well knew that 'men kindly handled will bear want and run through the fire and water';[36] he cared

> specially for the poor toiling and continual labouring mariner, himself daily making enquiry how they did, and calling to them by name to know in what case they stood, and what they did lack . . .[37]

Other noblemen did the same. Seymour excused himself in 1588 for writing by the hand of his secretary, because 'I have strained my hand with hauling of a rope.'[38] Weighing anchor in a hurry with the wind rising, Cumberland took his place at the capstan with his men.[39] This was not the kind of behaviour which came naturally to an English nobleman in the sixteenth century; it must be conscious policy by officers who appreciated the value of such gestures in moulding a united ship's company, transcending social divisions, however wide.

Equally striking is the easy, indeed familiar tone in which the Lord Admiral dealt with his captains. These orders, for example, were sent in August 1599 to Captain George Fenner, to intercept Spinola's galleys in the Channel:

> G. Fenner, you are a wise man and have experienced how to use stratagems. It will not be amiss, if you think good, to lay a bait for them in this sort; that some league before you some bark may be sent, and take in her ordnance as though she were no man-of-war, which peradventure may entice them from the shore to come off and take her; but this we do but remember unto you, leaving all things to your discretion. Expedition is now all, and resolution . . .[40]

It is hard to think of another context in which a sixteenth-century earl would have addressed the younger son of a provincial shipowner in such words as these: 'Tarry not, good George, but do the best you can, for we would be very glad these baggages might be catched or canvassed . . .'[41]

It seems in fact that by the closing years of the Spanish War relations between the queen, the Lord Admiral and seagoing commanders were much improved. With relatively small squadrons entirely in the queen's pay, the tensions of the joint-stock arrangement were avoided, and there was a large degree of mutual confidence between Nottingham and the senior officers (most of them his kinsmen). Unlike the admirals of Henry VIII's time, they were trusted to use their discretion: 'leaving many particular things to your own discreet judgements, whose experience we know needs not more remembrances.'[42]

For the admiral at sea, it was traditional though not obligatory to call a council of war before major decisions. For the late Victorian naval historians, writing at a time when the Royal Navy firmly resisted the idea of staff-work, the council of war was nothing but an expression of indecision, but in the circumstances of the time, with no means of communicating effectively between ships but by personal visit, it served as the equivalent of a naval staff and a briefing meeting. It was the opportunity to bring collective expertise to bear, to assemble intelligence, and to distribute orders.

> The admiral shall not take in hand any exploit to land or enter into any harbour enemy with the King's ships, but he shall call a council and make the captains privy to his device and the best masters in the fleet or pilots, known to be skilful men on that coast or place where he intendeth to do his exploit, and by good advice. Otherwise the fault ought to be laid on the admiral if anything should happen but well.[43]

When Drake led straight into Cadiz Bay in 1587 without consulting anyone, his vice-admiral William Borough, probably the most experienced navigator of the day, was appalled at the risks he had run. His protest against landing at Sagres without consultation, followed by the mutiny of his flagship in which he was suspected to be complicit, led to Drake holding a court martial on him for mutiny and condemning him to death. (This is usually held to be the first court martial in British naval history.[44]) Drake did have the queen's commission of martial law, and the trial was technically legal, but the return of the expedition saved Borough from sharing Doughty's fate.[45] The episode demonstrates both the strengths and weaknesses of Drake's style of command. His boldness and judgement were at their best in an unexpected emergency, but he was not a team player. Lord Howard, by contrast, was tactful and conciliatory (notably with Drake himself in 1588), generously acknowledging the expertise of his subordinates while stilling their quarrels and directing their energies.[46]

Though masters could and often did become captains of men-of-war, the arrival of gentlemen captains, increasingly numerous and increasingly skilled, inevitably provoked tensions. At the same time masters themselves in the course of the century acquired new and greater skills. Until the 1550s English masters remained essentially coastal pilots. A minority of them were accustomed to voyage out of sight of land to Iceland or Spain, but there were probably few English navigators capable of fixing a ship's position by the sun or stars.[47] John Borough, master of the *Michael* of Barnstaple in 1533 and a follower of Lord Lisle, owned some simple instruments including a cross-staff, and pilot books in Spanish and Portuguese, which indicates where he must have learnt skills which must have been almost if not completely unique in England.[48] The Iceland fishery, and even more the Newfoundland fishery which Bristol opened up in the early sixteenth (possibly late fifteenth) century, were fine schools of seamanship, but not of oceanic navigation.[49]

Up to the 1550s at least, Scottish seamen were well in advance of the English. They regularly made long open sea passages, while the English remained tied to coastal waters. There were close Scottish links with Dieppe and Le Havre, where in the 1530s and 1540s a brilliant school of Huguenot navigators, explorers and pirates flourished. Many Scots were among them, and Scottish ships and seamen participated in their raids to the Caribbean. In 1540 the Scottish pilot Alexander Lindsay piloted James V through the Pentland Firth to the Western Isles, compiling a sophisticated 'rutter' or pilot-book of the coasts of Scotland. Charts and pilots from this Franco-Scottish school were one of the keys to English successes in Scottish waters in 1544, and one of Somerset's major blunders was to lose the services of these pilots, who returned to France to guide Strozzi's galleys to St Andrew's. The result was that for some years French ships had a great advantage in these waters, even galleys passing through the Pentland Firth where no English ship is known to have gone.[50]

Prince Philip, anxious to improve the capabilities of his wife's subjects, sent Stephen Borough in 1558 to study at the navigation school maintained by the Casa de Contratación in Seville. He brought back the standard Spanish textbook, Martín Cortés's *Arte de Navegar*, which was at once translated into English.[51] From this date the competence of English navigators grew rapidly, forced first by the new long-distance trades, and then by piracy and privateering. In the Guinea trade in the 1560s we meet young masters, poor but well-educated, treasuring charts, astrolabes and cross-staffs among their meagre possessions.[52] The Spanish war produced a large class of literate, even learned navigators, skilled in the arts which the Portuguese and Spaniards had pioneered.[53] By the 1590s English scholars were themselves making important original advances in mathematics and navigation. In one generation they had passed from pupils of the Spaniards to teachers of the Dutch.[54]

This was a remarkable improvement, but navigation remained a very inexact science. In the absence of any method of fixing longitude, all easting and westing had to be estimated by dead reckoning. Latitude in principle was easily observed, but in 1596 Lord Howard found the masters of his fleet differed widely in their reckoning after only a few days at sea.[55] Returning from the South Atlantic in 1583, Captain Luke Ward and the officers of the *Edward Bonaventure* could not agree if they had sighted Ushant or the Pointe du Raz; it turned out to be the Scilly Isles, so that they were 100 miles of longitude and nearly 120 miles of latitude out of their reckoning.[56] Luck and judgement continued to play as large a part as science and mathematics in any successful voyage. The weather was forecast from the behaviour of porpoises and seabirds, to say nothing of pigs and cockroaches.[57] Masters were often supplemented by pilots. Sometimes these were local or coasting pilots of the modern kind, familiar with a particular port or coast, but there were also deep-sea pilots, specialized ocean navigators who provided skills which many masters had not yet acquired.[58]

Other officers were essentially landmen whose particular skills were needed afloat. 'The wings of man's life are plumed with the feathers of death',[59] and seamen took comfort from the presence of doctors. The 1513 fleet had four master surgeons and 'divers other petty surgeons', while by the time of the 1545 campaign there was some established organization for providing surgeons and even physicians for warships.[60] Surgeons were also carried on trading voyages into distant waters.[61] During the Spanish war, surgeons often went to sea, and sometimes physicians accompanied important expeditions.[62] In 1588 the Barber-Surgeons' Company impressed surgeons, and the Privy Council ordered physicians to join Howard's fleet. In both 1596 and 1597 the queen sent her personal physicians to sea.[63] This in its way is as striking a witness to the new respectability of seafaring as the presence of noblemen, for physicians were the gentlemen of the medical world, men of learning who never soiled their hands by touching a patient. Surgeons, by contrast, were regarded as artisans: barbers, surgeons or tooth-drawers as occasion required.[64]

The purser kept the ship's books, and in a merchantman was the owner's representative. He was responsible for victualling the ship, and mustered the company. He might also take responsibility for repairs, and indeed for any business which involved handling money or keeping accounts.[65] By 1588 an admiral's secretary was recognized as an official position in the Navy.[66]

In Queen Elizabeth's time both her ships and privateers often took chaplains. Thirteen served in 1588,[67] and there were nine on the 1596 Cadiz expedition, all in the retinue of Howard, Essex or other great men. One of them preached at an Anglican liturgy in Cadiz cathedral on Sunday 27 June.[68] The position of a chaplain in a privateer, especially before the outbreak of open war in 1585, could be awkward. Shakespeare's 'sanctimonious pirate, that went to sea with the Ten Commandments, but scraped one out of the table' was not an invention.[69] John Oxenham for one did precisely that, and the chaplains of Fenton's expedition made themselves very unpopular by preaching that armed robbery might not always be warranted by scripture.[70] Drake in 1577 went further, excommunicating his chaplain Francis Fletcher, probably for implying that the *Golden Hind*'s grounding in the Moluccas was God's punishment for the murder of Doughty. Fletcher was a seaman of experience who stood watches, and his quarrel with Drake was later made up.[71] As an investor as well as participant in the voyage,[72] he evidently did not disapprove of plunder, and nor did another of Drake's chaplains, Philip Nichols, who in 1587 assured him 'that he might lawfully recover in value of the King of Spain, and repair his losses upon him anywhere else. The case was clear in sea-divinity . . .'[73] So it was in the minds of most of those involved in this sort of war, 'affirming that we could not do God better service than to spoil the Spaniard both of life and goods, but indeed under colour of religion all their shot is at men's money'.[74] The great London privateer-owner Thomas Middleton ended his accounts of the voyage of the *Vineyard* to the West Indies in 1603 with this prayer:

> . . . beseeching Allmighty God to bless and preserve the said ship with her pinnace, and all the company in them and send them safely to return into England with all their lading, to God's glory and our comfort – I say my part is [£]1568.19.9.[75]

The duties of chaplains were to preach, which they frequently did at sea; and to celebrate Communion, which seems to have been done largely if not entirely on shore. Fenton was ordered to

> have an especial care to see that reverence and respect be had to the ministers appointed to accompany you in this voyage, as appertaineth to their place and calling, and to see such good orders as by them shall be set down for reformation of life and manners, duly obeyed and performed.[76]

Prayers might be read once or twice a day, but not necessarily by the chaplain even if present; Hawkins and Drake always did it themselves.[77] In the 1596 fleet the standing orders issued by Howard and Essex do not mention chaplains, but enjoined captains to 'take especial care to serve God by using of common prayer twice every day', and stop the men quarrelling about religion, 'for it is not fit that unlearned men should argue of so high and mystical matters'.[78] Opinions clearly varied a good deal. There were vigorous Puritans like Francis Fletcher, sufficiently outraged by the sight of a cross erected on a headland to take a boat and go ashore to destroy it – 'but with great dislike as well to some of our own company'.[79] There were those like Cavendish and Oxenham who counted time well spent in killing priests and desecrating churches,[80] but officers commanding royal forces generally forbade the destruction of churches,[81] while most privateers concentrated on business rather than pleasure. There were also English chaplains who acted charitably towards their enemies: John Walker, one of the chaplains of Fenton's expedition, with some difficulty persuaded his shipmates not to harm a boatload of Spanish friars whom they met on the coast of Brazil.[82] Drake, though an ardent Puritan, was notably tolerant towards his prisoners, permitting them to absent themselves from daily prayers to say the rosary, and even ordering fish to be served in Lent to a captured priest.[83]

Perhaps the least educated, but certainly not the least important of a warship's officers were the master gunner, carpenter and boatswain. Master gunners, whose skill was scarce and in demand everywhere, often had very varied service.[84] One Garland, killed in action in 1602 after serving in various English ships throughout the war, had been master gunner of the flagship of the papal galleys at the battle of Lepanto in 1571.[85] Theirs was an art mingled with some elements of science and mathematics; the market for books on gunnery, like those on navigation, was growing fast in the last years of the century.[86] The master gunner had to

> know the names of his pieces, their bores or height, their weight, the weight of the shot, the weight of the powder, the goodness of powder, and how far every piece will carry, both at random and at point blank...[87]

He had to keep the breechings and tackles in good order, and be ready to haul in the lower deck guns and caulk the ports if it became necessary 'by the sudden growing and working of the sea'.[88] Gunners had entire charge, not only of their guns, but of ammunition, magazines and their equipment. Their handling of these was not notoriously honest: 'their deceits in powder and shot, and other things under their charge, are intolerable . . .'; 'such like gunners used to sell powder by the barrel to maintain their idle lascivious expenses.'[89] They were responsible for the lavish salutes, always fired with shotted guns and often causing accidents, which seem to have been the only form of gunnery drill ever carried out on shipboard.[90] Thus ships parted from their admiral only 'after they had done those reverences accustomed at sea to his Lordship . . . with vollies of great and small shot of all parties...'[91]

Carpenters were, or at least could be, highly skilled men on whom the survival of a ship in distant waters might depend.[92] The carpenters of warships, at least, were probably men who had learnt their craft by regular apprenticeship, either on shipboard or in a shipyard. Boatswains, on the other hand, were invariably former seamen who had risen by experience. Only six of the boatswains of the queen's ships who rendered reports of the state of their masts and rigging after the 1588 campaign could sign their names, against eleven who made only a mark.[93] The boatswain's responsibilities included,

> the charge of all the cordage, tackling, sails, fids and marline spikes, needles, twine, sailcloth, and rigging the ship. His mates have the command of the long boat, putting out the anchor and fetching it home, wafting, towing, and mooring . . . As the master is to be abaft the mast so the boatswain, and all the common sailors under his command, are to be afore the mast . . . As the master commands the tacking of the ship, the hoisting or striking the yard, the taking in or putting forth the sails, upon the winding of the master's whistle the boatswain takes it with his, and sets the sailors with courage to do their work, every one of them knowing by their whistle what they are to do. The boatswain is to see the shrouds and other ropes set taut, the deep sea line and plummet in readiness against their coming into soundings, and tallowed . . . In a fight he must see the yards slung, top-armours and waist cloths, the flag and pendants put forth, and call up every man to his labour and office . . . And to conclude, his and his mate's work is never at an end, for it is impossible to repeat all the offices that are put upon them.[94]

He was responsible for clearing the ship for action ('to stow down in hold all trunks, chests and other things aloft, making the decks afore and aft fair platforms clear of any pestering or impediments'),[95] stowing the ballast and cargo, laying in cordage and boatswain's stores, managing lighters and cranes. Boatswains usually stood watches at sea, and were often on their way to become masters.[96]

Two other officers should be mentioned last, because they were usually listed last and were not full members of a ship's company: the lieutenant and his deputy the corporal. They first appear in the 1580s as the officers commanding troops embarked as small-arms men to strengthen a ship's company in action (as distinct from troops intended to form a landing force).[97] Corporals also acted as musketry instructors.[98] In 1588 the queen's biggest ships had a lieutenant and four corporals each, and the smaller a lieutenant and two corporals; but there were only 26 lieutenants in the entire fleet, as against 126 captains.[99] Very soon it was realized that a gentleman officer might be of more general assistance to the captain, and by the end of the war lieutenants were coming to be thought of as assistant or trainee captains.[100] This was another symptom of the rising social standing of sea service, and it easily became a source of 'heart-burning between the lieutenant and the master.'[101]

These tensions arose because naval warfare was becoming a national preoccupation, and an honourable occupation for men of much higher social class than ever would have gone to sea for a living before. The wars of the sixteenth century, and especially Queen Elizabeth's naval war against Spain, established the sea war, and to a limited extent the Queen's Navy, as a symbol of national pride and a point of national identity. Though England's survival had at least as much to do with land campaigns in Flanders, France and Ireland, the sea service came to have a unique place in the English national imagination. As a matter of historical fact, Scotland owed more to sea power than England, certainly up to the 1580s, but it does not seem that the sea ever gained that social status which it had in England by the 1590s, a status which drew noblemen and gentlemen to share the hardships of the sea with the common mariner. In Drake's words,

> Who seeks by worthy deeds to gain renown for hire,
> Whose heart, whose hand, whose purse is pressed, to purchase his
> desire,
> If any such there be that thirsteth after Fame,
> Lo, here a means to win himself an everlasting name...
> So that, for each degree, this treatise doth unfold,
> The path to Fame, the proof of zeal, and way to purchase gold.[102]

TWENTY-TWO

Sailors for my Money[1]

Social History: Men 1509–1603

'No kind of men of any profession in the common wealth pass their years in so great and continual hazard . . . and . . . of so many so few grow to grey hairs.'[2] So wrote Richard Hakluyt in 1598 of the seamen of his day, and for the historian who seeks to know something of the daily life of the sixteenth-century seafarer, what is striking is not only these vivid words themselves, but the fact that they were written at all. In this century, and especially in the last years of the century during England's naval war against Spain, the sea and seamen entered the national consciousness in a way they had not done in England for over five hundred years. It would be impossible to imagine such a man as the younger Hakluyt making a career a century before as a publicist of *The Principal Navigations Voyages Traffiques & Discoveries of the English Nation*, to take the title of his famous compilation. Though the deeds and sufferings of the common sailor remained remote from the attention of great men ashore, ships and the sea were rapidly becoming subjects of absorbing interest, and symbols of national identity. Many literate and even learned men went to sea themselves, while the literacy of the professional seamen (not only the élite of navigators) was itself improving very rapidly. For these reasons a flood of light can be cast for the first time on the seafarers of the sixteenth century, and especially of the Elizabethan age.

Moreover this was an age when the English language itself was written with an incomparable freshness and vigour which suffuses the most workaday contexts. We hear it in one senior officer's daily orders: 'Serve God daily, love one another, preserve your victuals, beware of fire, and keep good company';[3] and in another's report of proceedings: 'Myself, with the rest of her Majesty's fleet, do here wait for a wind that may give us liberty to go look upon these bravoes, and then I doubt not but to make them wish themselves at home in an ill harbour.'[4] We hear it in one chaplain's private diary: 'The 3rd being Whitsunday I preached of concord and the coming of the Holy Ghost, and the same day was sea-sick . . .';[5] and in another's notes on the wonders of Creation: 'This good and excellent creature of God, I mean the flying fish, is of the length and bigness of a reasonable pilchard . . .'[6] We hear it in the triumphs of life: 'Thus we departed from them, passing hard by Carthagena, in the sight of all the fleet, with a flag of Saint George in the maintop of our frigate, with silk streamers and ancients down to the water, sailing forward with a large wind . . .';[7] and in the bald reports of death: 'We took a view of his things and prised them, and heaved him overboard, and shot a piece for his knell.'[8] For the first time we can see and know a multitude of seamen as individuals; men like the pirate Captain Luke Ward, who commanded the *Edward Bonaventure* on Fenton's 1582 voyage: 'great in words and sufficiently crafty, bold as well as hard-working, irascible, inexorable, grasping.'[9]

In the early years of the century ship's companies were still recruited as indentured retinues. The entire fleet in 1512–13 was technically the personal retinue of Sir Edward Howard, who indented to raise, pay, feed and clothe it himself, 'sub-contracting' the retinues of other noblemen and gentlemen, just as his ancestor Lord Howard had done forty years before.[10] This arrangement suited the essentially medieval nature of the ships' companies, in which soldiers outnumbered seamen by at least two to one (three to one in the case of the Scottish *Michael*).[11] A quarter bill for the *Henry Grace à Dieu* at some unknown date gives the action stations of 516 men – apparently seamen, as far as their work can be identified, but it is difficult to believe that even the clumsiest rig really required one man to every two tons of burthen (double the usual medieval ratio) simply to handle the sails: some of them must be soldiers.[12] Another document tells us that in 1513 the *Great Harry* had 400 soldiers, 260 seamen and 40 gunners; her armament included 2,000 longbows, 1,500 bills and 1,500 morris pikes. The 400-ton *Great Bark* had 150 soldiers, 88 seamen and twelve gunners.[13] Apart from the gunners, there was nothing in this pattern of manning and armament which would have surprised Henry V, or even Edward III. In this as in virtually all other aspects of naval warfare, the decisive changes start not at the accession of Henry VIII, but near the end of his reign, in the 1540s. In the Anthony Roll of 1546 the *Great Harry* has 349 soldiers, 301 mariners and 50 gunners; the same total of 700, but not in the same proportions as thirty years before. Similarly, the *Great Bark* now had 136 soldiers, 138 mariners, and 26 gunners.[14] Three years later she was in commission with exactly the same complement, but in 1557 it had changed again, to 50 'hacbutters or arquebusiers', 80 soldiers, 190 mariners and 30 gunners. No other ship in the squadron had even as many soldiers as this in proportion to seamen.[15]

A considerable change had happened over forty years. Part of it was clearly the decline of the longbow and the introduction of firearms in its place. By 1575 English warships carried four or five times as many arquebuses as bows.[16] Possibly the lesser number of soldiers also reflects a reduced expectation of hand-to-hand fighting, but it would be very rash to assume that some 'big-gun revolution' had taken place when the number of gunners remained at about one for each heavy gun. Having risen in the early years of the century to about 20 per cent of a ship's company, the proportion of gunners tended to fall somewhat thereafter.[17] According to one rule from early in the Spanish War, gunners should form one-seventh of a wartime ship's company calculated at three men for five tons: twenty-eight gunners for a 500-ton ship, which would have carried at least that many heavy guns.[18] In the light of the experience of 1588, one commentator argued for a large increase, sufficient 'to traverse, run out and haul in the guns', but his idea was not adopted.[19]

Opinions differed on how many men in total a warship should carry. John Hawkins learnt from long voyages in tropical waters to man lightly, in the ratio of about one to every six tons, in the hope of keeping his ships healthy (and, no doubt, his costs down), but for fighting purposes this was not enough.[20] In 1585 he and Sir William Winter persuaded the Privy Council to base their mobilization plans on the figure of two tons a man rather than one and a half.[21] Three tons to the man plus the same number of soldiers for a landing force, which Drake took to the Caribbean in 1585, was not excessive.[22] Modern historians have tended to criticize the Elizabethans for overmanning their ships, for reasons of prestige and tradition, when fewer would have been healthier;[23] some contemporaries were aware of the danger,[24] but the experience of the Spanish War persuaded most that they needed more men, particularly to work the guns, if only they could have stowed enough victuals to feed them.[25] English fighting tactics of the late sixteenth century emphasized a superiority of speed, handiness and weatherliness. They had to fight under full sail, tacking or wearing repeatedly. The best explanation for the changing complements of warships is not so much that the English felt they needed fewer soldiers, as that they needed more seamen as they moved towards a style of fighting based on speed and manoeuvre. Such experience in turn suggested that they needed more men to the guns to develop a higher rate of fire, but at the end of the Spanish War they were still some way from achieving this.[26]

Changing tactics, and operations at longer range, called for more seamen at a time, in the middle years of the century, when the national population of seamen was, if anything, decreasing. This may have been part of the reason for the abandonment of recruitment by indentured retinue, a system particularly unsuitable for a mobile population like seamen. It is certain that by the 1540s the manning of the fleet had become entirely a responsibility of the state. Though wages were raised, the competition from privateers licensed by the 1544 proclamation affected the king's ships.[27] It was reported from Devon and Dorset in 1545 that men were so scarce that women were crewing the fishing boats.[28] In 1548 it was estimated that five thousand men would be needed, 'which will be some difficulty', and the following year still more were called for. The crown's reponse was to press the necessary seamen. This of course was an ancient and normal method of manning, not a new response to scarcity. It remained, as it had always been, impossible to gather a large body of men, especially skilled men, by the natural mechanisms of a labour market which only operated at a local level. The authority of the crown had to be invoked to recruit on a national scale, particularly if there were any need of haste. It is significant, however, that it is in the 1540s that the phenomenon of individual desertion first appears, and by the 1560s naval wages had probably fallen behind those which a deep-sea sailor could earn elsewhere.[29] Nevertheless, when men were pressed for the Navy in the 1560s, it was not thought necessary to escort them from wherever they had been recruited. They were simply ordered, as one party from Ipswich were in 1568, 'that you do immediately repair to Chatham in Kent, where as her Highness's ships now be, and there to present yourselves before the officers of her Highness's ships, who will place you as it shall seem good unto them'.[30]

From about this time, the efforts of Elizabeth's government to plan for naval mobilization begin to provide us with good estimates of the seafaring population of the country, and the requirement of the queen's ships. In 1575 it was estimated that the whole Navy Royal needed 5,450 men, out of a total of 16,255 seamen in the whole country counted in 1583.[31] As soon as the Spanish War broke out, privateers began to use a large number of seamen. In 1586 inland counties were ordered to be ready to send men to help the maritime counties.[32] By the 1590s the drain of seamen was worrying the government, and leading to shortages of fish.[33]. Men impressed for the 1596 expedition ran away, as Sir Walter Ralegh complained: 'the pursuivant found me in a country village, a mile from Gravesend, hunting after runaway mariners, and dragging in the mire from ale-house to ale-house . . .'[34] Next year Essex was complaining of 'men utterly unsufficient and unserviceable taken up by the pressmasters, in mariners' clothes but shall not know any one rope in the ship . . .'[35] By 1599 the queen's ships were in real difficulty:

in the *Nonpareil*, 'there lacketh 60, and of them there be not any men to make a master's mate, pilot, quarter's master, or above 50 that knoweth their labour.'[36] By this time the queen's officers were convinced that privateers were to blame for their shortage:

> The chief maim of all our presses is the great licence of small men-on-war in these parts, for, though we have strict order for their stay till her Majesty's ships were set out, they forbear not in this very port to steal and carry away our pressed men . . .[37]

There are two views on the manning difficulties of the late Elizabethan Navy Royal. Some modern historians blame it all on the officers.[38] Contemporary officers blamed it all on the 'unruly mariners, who be as well void of reason as of obedience.'[39]

> We find it in daily experience that all discourse of magnanimity, of national virtue, of religion, of liberty, and whatsoever else hath wont to move and encourage virtuous men, hath no force at all with the common soldier in comparison of spoil and riches.[40]

Ralegh omitted to mention that gentlemen like himself were not unaware of the possibilities of spoil and riches. Seamen, in the view of most Elizabethan gentlemen, were fickle and ungovernable, their skills of little account, their way of life disgraceful.

> For when to serve the Queen you should,
> You seek all shifts you may:
> If counterfeit excuses fail,
> You hide your selves away . . .
> You live at sea a lawless life,
> For murther and piracy,
> Which on the land you do consume,
> On whores and jollity.[41]

Notwithstanding the queen's generosity,

> their minds are but little reformed of their abuses towards her Majesty's service, but daily run away, making no more difference between receiving her Majesty's prest than an ordinary private action in a man-of-war; for it is an incredible thing to inform you of the number of sailors that are run away since our coming home.[42]

The truth is perhaps more complex than either view. It seems that the inflation of the late sixteenth century eroded the value of seamen's wages more in the Navy Royal than in merchant ships, but this was not easy for contemporaries to perceive. It was, and is still, difficult to calculate the true rate of pay in merchant ships, which varied greatly between different ports, trades and seasons, and came in a bewildering mixture of cash, credit, allowances and perquisites.[43] The age was used to fluctuating prices, but had no acquaintance with long-term inflation. If impressment failed to produce the quantity and quality of men desired, contemporaries inclined to blame the system. In particular they accused the pressmasters of accepting bribes to let the best men go and delivering the worst instead.[44] No doubt they did, but we may doubt if the most rigorous honesty would have supplied enough men in an age when demand for seamen was rising so rapidly. Nor can inadequate wages alone account for the Navy's manning difficulties, for privateers successfully competed for men without paying wages at all.[45] A privateering voyage was a lottery, but many men were ready to gamble.[46] Admittedly they were not all seamen, for the prospect of riches drew many landmen into privateering.[47] In the 1570s the lure of pirates operating from the Isle of Wight was such that the Hampshire farmers,

> came to me making their moan that they could not be sure certain of any servant they had for five nobles or forty shillings a year and might make their share at sea within one week four or five pound . . .[48]

What made all manning problems worse was that ships not only employed seamen but consumed them.[49] Sixteenth-century armies reckoned to lose one-third of their strength a year on campaign, to disease and desertion,[50] and the figure for ships was probably as bad. Any large gathering of men, ashore or afloat, could expect to be affected by disease, and many fleets and armies were crippled by it. In 1545 Lisle lost more than a quarter of his 12,000 men to plague in a fortnight.[51] Clinton's 1558 Channel campaign was abruptly halted by sickness so sudden 'that I think the like was never seen, for there were many ships that half the men were thrown down sick at once.'[52] Thirty years later at the end of the Armada campaign, parts of Lord Howard's fleet were badly affected.

> Sickness and mortality begins wonderfully to grow amongst us . . . the *Elizabeth Jonas*, which hath done as well as ever any ship did in any service, hath had a great infection in her from the beginning, so as of the 500 men which she carried out, by the time we had been in Plymouth three weeks or a month there were dead of them 200 and above, so as I was driven to set all the rest of her men ashore, to take out her ballast and to make fires in her of wet broom three or four days together, and so hoped thereby to have cleansed her of her infection, and thereupon got new men, very tall and able as ever I saw, and put them into her.

> Now the infection is broken out in greater extremity than ever it did before, and [they] die and sicken faster than ever they did, so as I am driven of force to send her to Chatham.[53]

The 1589 expedition suffered worse; perhaps as many as 8,000 soldiers and sailors were lost. The *Dreadnought* had 114 dead out of a ship's company of 300, with only eighteen men left on their feet to work the ship into Plymouth.[54]

In the face of sickness, sixteenth-century Englishmen were guided by two principles. One was the already ancient medical belief that foul air caused or transmitted disease. Infection was therefore to be prevented by keeping the air as clean and sweet as possible, which meant cleaning and disinfecting the ships in the fashion described by Lord Howard.[55] For this reason John Hawkins advocated increasing seamen's pay in 1585, so that 'her Majesty's ships would be furnished with able men such as can make shift for themselves, keep themselves clean without vermin and noisesomeness, which breedeth sickness and mortality.'[56] In the same vein Howard's standing orders of 1596 instructed captains that 'you shall give order that your ship may be kept clean daily and sometimes washed, which (with God's help) shall preserve you from sickness, and avoid many other inconveniences.'[57] This attention to cleanliness distinguished English ships from Spanish: 'their ships are kept foul and beastly, like hog-sties and sheep-cots in comparison with ours,' whereas an English captain 'overlooks the ship once or twice a day that she be kept sweet and clean, for avoiding sickness, which comes principally by slothfulness and disorders.'[58]

The other conviction was that nothing much could possibly go wrong with an Englishman supplied with plenty of good beef and beer, and that consequently illness was most likely to arise from bad victuals: 'in the late Queen's time many thousands did miscarry by the corruption as well of drink as of meat.'[59] Thus in 1599 Lord Thomas Howard reported

> that both our drink, fish and beef is so corrupt as it will destroy all the men we have, and if they feed on it but a few days, in very truth we should not be able to keep the seas, what necessity soever did require the same, unless some new provision be made, for as the companies in general refuse to feed on it, so we cannot in reason or conscience constrain them . . .[60]

At the same time there were many intelligent and curious men at sea, some of them surgeons or physicians, making observations which might have advanced medical knowledge considerably if they had not subsequently been submerged by the greater prestige of learned fashions. In 1572 a merchant familiar with Vera Cruz noted that 'this town is inclined to many kinds of diseases by reason of the great heat, and a certain gnat or fly which they call a "mosquito", which biteth both men and women in their sleep ... this mosquito or gnat doth most follow such as are newly come into the country. Many there are which die of this annoyance.'[61] This was the first generation of English seamen to encounter scurvy, and their ideas about it, though confused, were much nearer the mark than those of later generations.[62] Several of them noted the use of oranges and lemons: 'This is a wonderful secret of the power and wisdom of God,' Sir Richard Hawkins wrote, 'that hath hidden so great and unknown virtue in this fruit, to be a certain remedy for this infirmity.'[63]

The basic diet of English seamen continued to revolve around the same short list of foods which were capable of being preserved: biscuit, beer, salt beef and pork, pease and dried cod. In the Navy, as we have seen, there was a set allowance of these; in privateers much depended on the honesty of the investors, whom the men might have reason to accuse of skimping on quality or quantity. Frobisher had a bad reputation for just this.[64] At home or in foreign ports, men bought fresh bread, vegetables, fruit, cheese, hens, bacon and the like to supplement their rations, and at sea they caught themselves fish.[65] In the Caribbean, they hunted 'fish, fowl, hogs, deer, conies, etc, whereof there is great plenty'.[66] Longer voyages, and the necessity of revictualling in foreign parts, exposed the Elizabethans to all sorts of novelties. In the Magellan Straits, on Drake's voyage round the world,

> we found great store of strange birds which could not fly at all, nor yet run so fast as that they could escape us with their lives ... their feeding and provision to live on is in the sea, where they swim in such sort, as nature may seem to have granted them no small prerogative in swiftness ... they are a very good and wholesome victual.[67]

In 1587 Cavendish revictualled in the Azores with

> corn as much as we would have, and as many hogs as we had salt to powder them withall, and great store of hens, with a number of bogs of potato roots, and about 500 dried dog fishes and Guinea Wheat which is called maize.[68]

English seamen seem not to have been so conservative in their tastes as they later became, and we hear of no complaints at these foreign exotica. On the contrary, 'these potatoes be the most delicate roots that may be eaten, and do far exceed our parsnips or carrots.'[69] The last voyage of Drake and Hawkins was even supplied with a small amount of 'a certain victual in the form of hollow pipes . . . called by the name of *macaroni* among the Italians.'[70]

If there is one quality which distinguished the sixteenth-century seamen it was youth. His was a hard lot: 'but to endure and suffer, as a hard cabin, cold and salt meat, broken sleeps, mouldy bread, dead beer, wet clothes, want of fire, all these are within board'.[71] It was a trade for young men, for the young and ambitious, with little to lose and much to hope for. Whenever we find information about the age of a ship's company (at least of a ship making long voyages), the men are overwhelmingly young and unmarried. Many of them had no homes but lodgings in port.[72] When Drake sailed for the West Indies in 1572, the eldest of the 73 men aboard was 52, and none of the rest was over 30.[73] On the ill-fated Fenton expedition of 1582, there were not ten mariners over 30 among the 180 men of the *Galleon Leicester*.[74] There were older men at sea, especially in the coasting and short-sea trades, but the great majority were under 40.[75] On voyages to West Africa in the 1560s, about a quarter of the ship's company (mainly the officers) were married, most of them recently, to judge by the absence of children.[76]

Young as they were, these were not an undifferentiated mass of common seamen, but a little society divided by experience and trade. At its head were the mates, the deputies and natural successors of the master, master gunner, carpenter and boatswain, whose skills they were learning.[77] Below them were various petty officers, whose exact status and duties are not always clear. Quartermasters seem to have had approximately the same status and pay as the mates (and in big ships had mates of their own), but were particularly associated with the ship's fighting organization.[78] Originally it seems that the ship's company in action was divided into four quarters, each with a quartermaster, so that 'quarters' (in the modern sense of action stations) were literally that.[79] Already at the end of the fifteenth century, however, Philip of Cleves was recommending a fifth quarter below decks, 'with some mariners, carpenters, caulkers and other craftsmen, under a captain of the hold', to function, in the modern terminology, as a damage-control party.[80] John Griffin of Erith, quartermaster of the *Barbara* in 1540, had a silver whistle and chain worth no less than 46s 8d, besides £5 in ready money, a sword, a handgun, and a substantial wardrobe including a cap with 'my Lord Lisle's badge in the silver thereon'.[81] He was clearly an officer of substance, and the admiral's badge indicates a personal connection. His whistle (the modern 'boatswain's call') was an emblem of authority also carried by boatswains, masters, captains, the Lord Admiral and even King Henry VIII himself when he wanted to dress up as an admiral.[82] Below quartermasters came the coxswain (who commanded the longboat); and in big ships a yeoman of the sheets and another of the jeers, who presumably took charge of the men hauling on the falls of the running rigging on deck.[83]

Although the words 'mariner' and 'sailor' are occasionally used as though they had distinct meanings, and the term 'grommet' (Spanish *grumete*, apprentice, trainee seaman) was sometimes used, sixteenth-century seamen were seldom divided according to skill.[84] Most ships had one or two boys, but not more.[85] In 1513 there was only one boy in the entire fleet.[86] Later in the century the number tends to rise somewhat. Drake had three on his voyage round the world, in 1582 the *Galleon Leicester* and *Edward Bonaventure* had five each, and in 1588 Dartmouth's two small ships had five boys among only one hundred officers and men.[87] There is not much evidence of what they did, apart from learning the ropes, but Richard Hawkins refers to the wisdom of having 'younkers in the top continually' as lookouts, and their duties included standing anchor watch in port while the rest of the crew were ashore enjoying themselves.[88]

Besides the seamen, every warship carried craftsmen and specialists such as cooks, stewards, coopers and smiths.[89] An essential 'officer' (in the Elizabethan sense of one who held a particular office, not necessarily of authority) was the swabber, responsible for the ship's cleanliness within board. Another was the liar:

> He that is first taken with a lie upon a Monday morning is proclaimed at the main mast with a general cry, 'A liar, a liar, a liar'; and for that week he is under the swabber, and meddles not with making clean the ship within board, but without.[90]

His job was to clean the ship's head, beneath the beakhead which served as the crew's latrine.

Musicians were a distinctive part of a large warship's company. Trumpets were both an emblem of authority and a practical means of conveying orders; there were three trumpeters in 1513, 'appointed to attend upon my Lord Admiral ... by the King's most honourable Council'.[91] In the 1582 mobilization scheme, each of the queen's ships, even down to the pinnaces, was allowed a 'drum and fife' and at least one trumpeter; in the biggest ships a 'noise' of three or four.[92] The trumpeter, we are told,

> should have a silver trumpet, and himself and his noise to have banners of silk of the admiral's colours. His place is to keep the poop, to attend the general's going ashore and coming aboard, and all other strangers or boats, and to sound as an entertainment to them, as also when they hail a ship, or when they charge, board or enter her ...[93]

On their last voyage in 1595 Drake and Hawkins took 'sundry instruments of music for eight musicians and nine trumpeters.'[94] Even trading voyages to Guinea justified a fife and drum, trumpeters and a minstrel.[95] When the Levant Company's *Centurion* was attacked in the Straits of Gibraltar in 1591,

> there was a sore and deadly fight on both sides, in which the trumpet of the *Centurion* sounded forth the deadly points of war, and encouraged them to fight manfully against their adversaries. On the contrary part, there was no warlike music in the Spanish galleys, but only their whistles of silver, which they sounded forth to their own contentment.[96]

Trumpeters were not necessarily only musicians, especially in a small ship. On Drake's voyage round the world, it was the trumpeter and the chaplain who were standing watch together in the *Golden Hind* in the desperate gale off Cape Horn in which the little *Marigold* foundered.[97] Drake's Spanish prisoners were greatly impressed that he sat down to dine to the music of shawm and trumpet,[98] as Grenville's were: 'he seemed to be a man of quality, for he was served elaborately on silver and gold plate, by servants. Many musical instruments were played when he dined . . .'[99] Trumpets also served for practical purposes in signalling. Meeting strange sails in the Channel in 1594, Robert Dudley 'hailing them with his noise of trumpets made them know their duty unto our English colours by vailing their topsails.'[100]

It was not so easy, however, to make Englishmen know their duty. When the queen had so much difficulty in getting her admirals to obey their orders (especially on the joint-stock expeditions of the first part of the war), it is no surprise that the admirals in turn had difficulty with their captains, and the captains with their officers and men. 'To govern and command the dissolute mariner from his riot' taxed all powers of command.[101] Drunkenness, brawls and violence were commonplace, especially in privateers, 'where no discipline is used, nor authority obeyed'.[102] A privateer captain,

> though he be styled the captain yet do they not use to obey him so strictly as him that has power from a General . . . for they receive no pay whereby to oblige them but every one goes upon his own adventure.[103]

The division of booty often caused quarrels and mutinies.[104] When a prize was brought into port, the men pillaged and stole, while the owners cheated the men of pay and prize money: 'all these sea goods are mixed with birdlime; for no man can lay his hand of them, but is limed, and must bring away somewhat. Watch and look ever so narrowly, they will steal and pilfer.'[105] Of the prizes brought back by the 1589 expedition,

> two-third parts of all the lading were spoiled and embezzled by the men of war and mariners at the sea before they were brought into Plymouth and . . . one-half of that third remaining was purloined and scattered since the arrival of the ships in that haven, so that nothing was left aboard the ships but that which was too cumbersome or heavy to carry away . . .'[106]

Heirs of a tradition of rule by consensus, seamen expected their voices to be heard and mutinied if they were not, especially in privateers where they regarded themselves as being in some sense shareholders in the voyage. On Fenton's 1582 voyage, the men refused to weigh anchor without what they regarded as sufficient navigators; 'saying they ventured for the thirds and would not therefore go without the pilots.'[107] At sea, 'mariners are like to a stiff-necked horse, which taking the bridle betwixt his teeth, forceth his rider to what him list mauger his will . . .'[108] What they demanded was usually plunder. 'As to the business of pillage, there is nothing wherein they promise to themselves so loudly nor delight in more mainly.'[109] 'All sailors of late are fallen into such vile order that they shame not to say that they go to sea to rob all nations, and unless the captain consent thereto, he is not fit for this time':[110] if officers made difficulties about piracy or showed scruples about plundering neutrals, English seamen could be relied upon to remind them that they had not come to sea for pleasure, but for 'some little comfortable dew from heaven,' as Drake put it.[111] John Walker, one of Fenton's chaplains in 1582, was horrified to find himself shipped with a crew of unashamed pirates: the pilot 'rejoiced in things stark naughty, bragging in his sundry piracies.'[112] The Navy Royal was unpopular firstly because 'the common seamen are more narrowly looked unto, and cannot so well shark and carve for themselves as in private ships, where they live under less command.'[113]

In the queen's ships it was possible to maintain greater discipline, and to punish crimes against shipmates. Thieves were either whipped at the capstan or ducked from the yard-arm.[114] Other punishments included putting men in irons and stopping their rations. Keel-hauling was mentioned as a possibility, and several orders threatened death for striking a captain, master or lieutenant, but it is not clear that either punishment was ever applied in practice.[115] The death penalty was in fact very rare, though Cumberland hanged a man for rape, and Drake another for buggery.[116] The list of picturesque punishments, which included a murderer being bound to the body of his victim and thrown overboard, one who drew a knife losing his right hand, and a man found four times asleep on watch being left to starve in a basket hung on the bowsprit, though often cited by naval histories of this period,[117] appears to have been an antiquarian revival of a code allegedly issued by Richard I to his Mediterranean fleet in 1190, rather than anything actually enforced in the sixteenth century.[118]

By the end of the century, as we have seen, desertion was a problem, but it was mainly a problem of men avoiding or escaping impressment.[119] Most major operations consisted of a single cruise of some months, during which there was little chance to desert, and after which the ships paid off for refit. There could be no question of men being retained for long periods in the queen's service, for the endurance of the ships did not permit unlimited operations. For the same reasons leave was mainly an issue in port before setting sail. It seems to have been assumed that men could and would go ashore, and there are references to a special flag to recall libertymen to their ships,[120] but naturally they did not all return, and experience convinced some officers,

> that it is neither good that sailors should be suffered to go on shore when they lie in harbour, neither that strong drink should be suffered in haven towns, for through liberty on the one side and temptation on the other side many a good wind and tide is forslood, and much disorder both in ship and town committed and more charges both to owner and sailor than is needful.[121]

The problem was not confined to the queen's ships. Richard Hawkins, and no doubt even more other privateer captains whose families did not dominate their home ports, had the same experience:

> And so began to gather my company abroad, which occupied my good friends and the justices of the town two days, and forced us to search all lodgings, taverns and ale houses. For some would ever be taking their leave and never depart; some drink themselves so drunk, that except they were carried aboard, they of themselves were not able to go one step; others, knowing the necessity of the time, feigned themselves sick; others, to be indebted to their hosts, and forced me to ransom them, one his chest, another his sword, another his shirts, another his card and instruments for sea; and others, to benefit themselves of the imprest given them, absented themselves, making a lewd living in deceiving all whose money they could lay hold of . . .[122]

In this and many other contexts, the impossibility of keeping Englishmen sober ashore was a constant source of complaint. It was the great weakness of sixteenth-century English infantrymen, whose performance when sober was admired even by the Spaniards.[123]

Already it was true, as it was to be for centuries, that many saw and despised the drunken sailor ashore, but few knew and admired him at his work afloat. The mariner was seen as a man without religion or morality; to take his evidence under oath but 'lost labour and offence to God.'[124] Yet 'how slightly soever many esteem sailors all the work to save ship, goods and lives must lie upon them.'[125] Seamen were certainly capable of cruelty, and sometimes tortured their prisoners for information,[126] but they were highly skilled in their profession and by no means ignorant brutes.[127] A surprising number seem to have been literate (some, as we have seen, to a high degree), and even the illiterate majority were accustomed to use written documents for legal and other purposes. Since seamen were never paid (advances excepted) before the end of a voyage, the shipboard economy with its extensive trade in clothes, food and personal belongings, was based entirely on debts, which were recorded with care.[128] Though seldom rich, seamen were not destitute, and often possessed sea chests containing a reasonable wardrobe. The seamen's clothes were adapted versions of those common ashore, with short jerkins or 'petticoats' worn over stockings and loose 'slops' or breeches. Most men had several shirts. Gowns, cassocks and capes were worn in foul weather. Many seamen owned mattresses and bedding (including from the 1590s the new-fangled 'Brazil beds' or hammocks), and there are references to hats and caps, boots and shoes.[129] In Henry VIII's reign seamen in the king's ships were sometimes clothed in livery coats, in the late medieval fashion, but as fleets grew larger and senior officers ceased to recruit their own retinues this was abandoned.[130] Occasionally clothes were supplied (and charged to wages) when men were away from home for long periods. In 1580 clothes were sent to the Irish squadron, and Hawkins took some for his men in 1595.[131] Otherwise seamen were expected to find sufficient clothes to go to sea. Men impressed in 1602 were ordered to come not 'unarmed and naked without any convenient clothes', as had happened in the past, but properly dressed with daggers, at their expense or that of their 'parents, masters or friends'.[132]

In its nature the seafarer's life was hard and dangerous, but there was time to relax in harbour and even at sea, off-watch and in fair weather. Men took dice and various board games, they had musical instruments to dance and sing to.[133] Camping in the Gulf of Darien in 1572, Drake's men enjoyed themselves ashore:

> Our archers made themselves butts to shoot at, because we had many that delighted in that exercise, and wanted not a fletcher to keep our

> bows and arrows in good order. The rest of the company, every one as he liked best, made his disport at bowls, quoits, keels, &c. For our captain allowed one half of their company to pass their time thus, every other day interchangeably, the other half being enjoined to the necessary works about our ship and pinnaces, and the providing of fresh victual . . .[134]

Shanties were used to aid the labour of heaving and hauling, indeed were probably already ancient. [135] Seamen went swimming, keeping a good look-out for sharks, for 'it hath chanced that a younker casting himself into the sea to swim, hath had his leg bitten off above the knee by one of them'.[136] Becalmed in the lee of Tenerife on Christmas Day 1595, Dudley's men 'swimming from ship to ship made great cheer each to other'.[137] The literate minority, mainly officers, might read the Bible. Drake whiled away his time colouring in the pictures in Foxe's *Book of Martyrs*, a work which one of his Spanish prisoners understood him to say, 'is to them what the Bible is to us'.[138] Richard Hawkins,

> Devised to keep my people occupied, as well to continue them in health (for that too much ease in hot countries is neither profitable nor healthful), as also to divert them from remembrance of their home, and from play, which breedeth many inconveniences, and other bad thoughts and works which idleness is cause of. And so, shifting my company, as the custom is, into starboard and larboard men, the half to watch and work whilst the others slept and take rest, I limited the three days of the week which appertaineth to each to be employed in this manner: the one for the use and cleansing of their arms; the other for rummaging, making of sails, nettings, decking and defences for our ships; and the third for cleansing of their bodies, mending and making their apparel and necessaries . . .[139]

Our most vivid descriptions of incidents at sea come, as in every age, from passengers unfamiliar with the shipboard world, and ready to take note of what was commonplace to the professionals. Dr Roger Marbecke, the physician who sailed with the 1596 Cadiz expedition, thus describes the ceremony of cheering ship:

> They presently man the ship and place every one of their companies both upon the upper and middle deck and also upon the waist and shrouds and elsewhere to the most advantage they can make the bravest show and appear the greatest number. Then the masters and mates of the ships immediately upon the sounding of their whistles in a pretty loud tunable manner, all the whole company shaking their hands, hats and caps, giving a marvellous loud shout, consisting of so many loud,

> strong and variable voices, maketh such a sounding echo and pleasant report in the air, as delighteth very much. And this ceremony is done three times by them, and three times interchangeably answered.[140]

The world of the Elizabethan seamen was in many respects a young one. There had always been English seamen, and at its lowest ebb the English merchant fleet had contained many ships and men familiar with coasting voyages in English waters and nearby. But the English came late to deep-sea voyaging; later than the Scots and French, much later than the Portuguese and Spaniards. In this the men who mounted the cruises and expeditions of the Elizabethan naval war were not the heirs of an ancient seafaring tradition, but the first generation of their countrymen ever to venture across the great oceans. This was a new frontier for Elizabethan England, and like frontiers everywhere it was lawless and violent, offering great opportunities for the lucky and unscrupulous. It was a brawling and vigorous world, where men lived by their wits; where many sought their fortunes and many lost their lives.

TWENTY-THREE

The Undertakings of a Maiden Queen[1]

Administration 1574–1603

Sea power cannot be improvised. In every age and in every circumstance, the successful navies have been those which rested on long years of steady investment in the infrastructure essential to keep running the complex and delicate machinery of a seagoing fleet. Though it takes much longer to build a squadron than it does to raise an army, shipbuilding itself is relatively quick and simple compared to the slow nurturing of the manifold resources and skills on which all successful naval operations must be based. This is a truth not universally understood in the twentieth century and hardly demonstrated at all in the sixteenth, yet it was precisely in this that the precocious strength of the Elizabethan Navy rested.

From the beginning of the queen's reign her ministers were involved in forward planning. Throughout the 1560s and 1570s, when relatively little money was being spent on ships and the fleet remained small – no more than twenty or twenty-five ships fit to go to sea – Lord Burghley and his colleagues in government were giving sustained attention to mobilization. The 1559 'Book of Sea Causes' was followed in 1560 by the first of many surveys of merchant shipping, and in 1562 by a new Act of Parliament 'touching certain politic constitutions made for the maintenance of the navy', which offered encouragement to merchant shipping.[2] At the same time Parliament was asked to 'let the old course of fishing be maintained by the straightest observation of fish days, for policy sake; so the sea coasts shall be strong with men and habitations and the fleet flourish more than ever.'[3] The 1569 rebellion in the north, during which the rebels seized Hartlepool and looked for Spanish support by sea, inspired a survey of the shipping and seamen of the country the following year. This in turn was succeeded by a much fuller survey in 1572, listing all ships of 100 tons or more in England, with their names, home ports and masters' names, together with the numbers of ships down to ten tons. The total was 1,383 merchant ships between 6 and 240 tons. Further papers compiled during the 1570s considered the men, munitions and equipment needed to fit out the Navy Royal, surveyed the ports of England, enumerated foundries and furnaces able to cast guns or shot, listed all the shipmasters living along the Thames, and proposed names of captains for the queen's ships.[4] In 1576 a commission surveyed the effect of the legislation requiring Englishmen to eat fish on Wednesday as well as Friday, and reported that if the act lapsed, 'whensoever the Queen's Majesty should have any occasion to send her Highness's ships to the seas, there would not be found seafaring men to man the same.'[5] In February 1580 a paper considered, 'how all her Majesty's ships are to be set in order . . . to be in a readiness for all attempts of any foreign power.' Significantly, it did not really plan against 'any foreign power' but one particularly, for it proposed that the fleet should be stationed 'in such place in the West Country or upon the sea as the Council shall appoint'; ready, that is, for an attack from the Atlantic, which could only mean from Spain.[6] In the autumn of 1580 a detailed mobilization plan was drawn up and costed for the Navy Royal and twenty-two selected merchantmen.[7] Meanwhile mobilization had been practised more than once. In July 1570 alarm at the Spanish ships preparing to escort Anne of Austria down Channel led to a partial mobilization. Another was ordered, but subsequently cancelled, in 1574 in response to the fleet of Menéndez de Avilés.[8]

As tension with Spain rose, the English planning effort intensified. In 1582 Clinton, the Lord Admiral, organized a new and more detailed survey listing every seagoing merchant ship, together with the names of the shipmasters and the numbers of mariners, fishermen and watermen available in every parish in England. Consequently the government now knew that there were 143 masters dwelling in London, and along the Thames from London Bridge to Gravesend there were 991 mariners, 957 wherrymen and 195 fishermen; in Boston there were 5 masters and 32 mariners, and so on throughout the kingdom.[9] Not only did Burghley and his colleagues have more information available about their country's fundamental naval resources than any contemporary government,[10] they had fuller knowledge than any subsequent English government before the twentieth century.[11] With this information Burghley produced in February 1584 a detailed war plan, envisaging the fleet divided into three squadrons, stationed at Scilly, the Isle of Wight and the Downs or Harwich, to meet a simultaneous threat from Spain and the Netherlands. 'Generally', he noted, 'if the Q[ueen's] Navy be strong upon the sea, neither Portsmouth, Sheppey nor Harwich have need of strength; otherwise surely these three places will be in danger.'[12]

All these plans were tested in 1587 and 1588. It has been explained that the extreme fragility of English finances made it impossible to keep the English fleet mobilized for any length of time. In sixteenth-century conditions, no large force could expect to remain healthy and efficient indefinitely, and the English did not have the money to try, but, thanks to long planning and preparation, they did not have to. The initial mobilization of September to December 1587 took less than three months, while the Armada took three years. The English ships were then paid off for the worst of the winter, in the knowledge that they could be swiftly mobilized again in the spring. Though England's resources were a small fraction of Spain's, they could be concentrated exactly where and when they were needed.[13] This capacity to mobilize quickly remained the key to English defences for the rest of the war. Though several times badly frightened by Spanish attacks, or rumoured attacks, of which no warning had reached England, Queen Elizabeth's government had no choice, since it was impossible to keep the bulk of the fleet in continuous commission.

As war planning intensified in the 1570s, a new programme of shipbuilding for the Navy Royal got under way. In 1570 the 300-ton ship *Foresight* was built, and the old galleasses *Bull* and *Tiger* rebuilt. (These 'rebuilds', it should be explained, were more or less new ships incorporating the reusable timbers from the old.) It seems probable that this is the date at which the English Navy definitely adopted the galleon type, if it had not done so already. Traditionally the change has been ascribed to the genius of John Hawkins, and dated either about this time (on the argument that he was already influential behind the scenes) or to 1577, the year he became Treasurer of the Navy.[14] We now have reason to believe, however, that he had reservations about the new ships built in this decade.[15] We can say that illustrations of various ships (not all identifiable) built in the 1570s and early 1580s all show the characteristic crescent shape of the galleon. These new ships were the *Dreadnought* and *Swiftsure* with the smaller *Achates* and *Handmaid*, all of 1573; the *Revenge* and *Scout* of 1577; the *Swallow*, *Elizabeth Bonaventure*, *Antelope* and *Lion*, rebuilt in 1580–1; and the *Nonpareil* of 1584.[16] In broad terms, the building of the 1560s had produced a handful of very big ships (the *Victory*, *Triumph*, *White Bear* and the original *Elizabeth Bonaventure*) with some galleys. In the 1570s and early 1580s new construction concentrated on small to medium-sized ships, probably galleons. Three more were built in 1586, two of which (the *Vanguard* and *Rainbow*) were of a shallow-draught design intended for the Narrow Seas;[17] at the same time the *Victory* was 'altered into the form of a galleon'[18] and the Navy's weakness in small vessels for scouting was addressed by building nine pinnaces. With the addition of the large galleon *Ark Royal*, bought new from Sir Walter Ralegh in 1587, this was the fleet which fought the Spaniards in 1588.[19] Eight ships of various sizes (one of them a rebuild) were added to the Navy Royal in 1589–90, and nine more (including five rebuilt) in the 1590s. Some of these ships probably carried their guns on two (or at least one and a half) decks;[20] in action against Spinola's galleys in the Straits of Dover in 1602, Sir Robert Mansell in the *Hope* 'discharged about thirty pieces of ordnance of my upper and lower tier at her.'[21] With a number of prizes, smaller vessels, and the four galleys built to match Spinola in 1601, this made up the building effort of the Elizabethan Navy during the Spanish War. The design of the 1590 ships was settled by a committee presided over by the Lord Admiral, including most of the Navy Board, Drake, Edward Fenton, and the master shipwrights Richard Chapman and Matthew and Christopher Baker; this seems to have been only a more formal version of the regular procedure.[22]

The Tudor tradition was to paint the upperworks of ships in bright colours and geometric patterns. In 1502 the *Mary Fortune* was painted with gold, vermilion, russet, white lead, brown, Spanish white and verdigris.[23] The queen's *Bear* was painted red, the *Elizabeth Bonaventure* black and white, the *Revenge* and *Scout* green, and the *Lion*, 'timber colour'. These colours were towards the end of the reign supplemented with gold and silver foil, at least in the bigger ships.[24] Most big ships had some carved work, including a figurehead: the *Nonpareil*, *Adventure*, *Dreadnought* and *Hope* had dragons; the *Defiance*, *Rainbow*, *Repulse*, *Garland* and the pinnace *Charles* lions; the *Mary Rose* a unicorn, and the *Swiftsure* a tiger. 'The hull is very handsome,' a visitor to Rochester remarked in 1599, 'the body above the water being painted in diverse colours, and often at the stern the device from which the ship takes her name is artistically carved or painted.'[25] When the *Elizabeth Jonas* was rebuilt in 1598, £180 was spent on,

> New painting and gilding with fine gold her beakhead on both sides with her Majesty's whole arms and supporters; for painting the forecastle, the cubbridge heads on the waist, the outsides from stem to stern; for like painting and new gilding of both the galleries with her Majesty's arms and supporters on both sides, the stern new-painted with divers devices and beasts gilt with fine gold; for new painting the captain's cabin, the summer-deck as well overhead as on the sides, the barbican, the dining room and the study.[26]

This was part of a trend to use warships as emblems of royal power, emphasized by costly decoration. For this reason tourists, especially influential foreigners, were encouraged to visit and marvel at the queen's ships. At

Flushing in March 1588, the Lord Admiral recorded five thousand visitors a day.[27] When the Duke of Stettin visited Chatham in 1602, he was deeply impressed by the 'cabins decorated with costly paintings and most beautiful carvings.'[28]

The Navy Board continued throughout Elizabeth's reign in what was by then its established course. The Treasurer of the Navy presided at the Board's collective meetings, as the representative of the Lord Treasurer. The Controller was mainly responsible for buying timber and naval stores, the Storekeeper for storing them, and the Surveyor for shipbuilding and repairs. The Clerk of the Ships acted as secretary to the Board. The position of Master of Naval Ordnance, vacant on the death of Sir William Woodhouse, was revived with the appointment of William Winter on the outbreak of war in 1557. From 1569 to 1583 he relinquished control of the naval ordnance stores at Deptford, Woolwich and Portsmouth, and remained simply a liaison officer between the Ordnance and Navy Boards, but when the war broke out again the old arrangement was restored. On Winter's death in 1589 it lapsed for good, and from then until 1855 the Ordnance Board was solely responsible for naval guns.[29]

In practice, the lines of responsibility between members of the Navy Board were vague and often crossed, especially when one or more of the officers were at sea.[30] Like the Ordnance Board, the Navy Board nurtured relationships with favoured contractors, of whom one of the most important was the queen's 'Baltic Merchant', who negotiated with the Hansa merchants for masts, cordage and other naval stores. William Watson the first holder actually lived in Danzig, an exposed position at a time of diplomatic tension with the Hansa, as he discovered in 1542 when he was 'cast into a vile stinking prison amongst a sort of vile persons, vagabonds and whores'.[31] His successors Thomas Allen (appointed 1561) and Robert Savage appeared to have stayed in London, but still did their business with effect. Savage reported in 1598 that 'last year I disappointed the King of Spain's factors of 24 great masts that were in Danzig, 18 of which I brought hither to Her Majesty . . .'[32]

The most important change in the Navy Board's structure in these years came with the appointment of John Hawkins to succeed his father-in-law Benjamin Gonson as Treasurer of the Navy in November 1577. From then until his death he was the dominant figure in English naval administration. He was a man of long experience, strong character and clear ideas – but so were many of his colleagues, notably William Winter, and the result was intermittent quarrels and mutual accusations of corruption. This was normal in all areas of Elizabethan administration, and useful in an age which had very few mechanisms to detect dishonesty. 'As I desire comfort at God's hands', Winter wrote of his colleague's management, 'there is nothing in it but cunning and craft to maintain his pride and ambition and for the better filling of his purse, and to keep back from discovering the faults that are left in her Majesty's ships at this day . . .'[33]

It is a mistake, however, to see the work of Hawkins and his colleagues too much in terms of honesty and corruption. There seems little doubt that Hawkins was notably honest and efficient, but 'corruption' was then, and has been until recently for many historians, the all-purpose explanation for anything which did not work satisfactorily. It is always simpler to blame individual wickedness rather than explore the obscure weaknesses of complex systems, and it suited the outlook of the nineteenth-century historians who have shaped our view of English naval history. For them, history was, in Carlyle's words, 'but the biography of great men', and morality was the foundation of efficiency. But Hawkins lived in an age when officials like himself were not salaried civil servants so much as privileged contractors with an ill-regulated business relationship with the crown. They were expected to make a profit for themselves while doing a good job for the queen, preferably at less cost than their predecessors. Accusations of corruption were usually just a bid to take over a contract from a rival. Dealings certainly took place which the sixteenth century regarded as corrupt, but nobody seriously suggested that it was illegal or improper to make a profit from office, so long as the Navy did not suffer. 'Corruption' was then in many cases just a pejorative term, and is now in many cases just an anachronistic term, for inefficiency or misfortune. Contemporaries took it for granted that officials would make money from their positions; what they wanted to know was whether the crown was getting value for that money.[34]

This is the background to the controversy which surrounded Hawkins's service as Treasurer of the Navy. He gained the office by mounting charges against Winter and his colleagues of having built and repaired ships at excessive cost with poor materials. Perhaps Burghley was convinced that Winter was 'corrupt', but Winter continued in his important and responsible offices of Controller and Master of Naval Ordnance until he died in 1589. More likely Burghley simply considered that Hawkins was the best man for this job, and he continued to support him against his rivals throughout his seventeen years in office.[35] In 1579, Hawkins proposed and the government accepted a major change in his responsibilities. Like Baeshe with the victualling, Hawkins offered by his first 'Bargain' or 'Reformation' to contract for the routine maintenance of the Navy. Since 1567 the Ordinary had remained at £5,714 a year, which provided for the maintenance of the queen's ships in port and the staff of the dockyards. Victualling had been separately accounted for since 1565, while naval operations, new shipbuilding and major repairs were paid for by 'extraordinary' warrants. Total naval expenditure in the 1570s averaged about £10,000 a year. Hawkins's first Bargain consisted essentially of two contracts: he himself undertook to maintain the fleet moorings at Chatham for £1,200 a year, while the master shipwrights Matthew Baker and Peter Pett would regularly ground and caulk the ships for a further £1,000. There was no suggestion of reducing the Ordinary; the implicit advantage to the crown was that better maintenance would reduce Extraordinary warrants for repairs. Apparently Hawkins suggested that he could save £4,000 a year.[36]

Hawkins's Bargain naturally generated controversy, and in 1583 the queen appointed a commission under the chairmanship of Lord Howard of Effingham, then the Lord Chamberlain, to investigate. With Howard sat Lord Burghley, the then Lord Admiral the Earl of Lincoln, and the two Secretaries of State Sir Walter Mildmay and Sir Francis Walsingham. They were assisted by a panel of nautical experts, including sea commanders like Drake and the master shipwrights Matthew Baker, Peter Pett and Richard Chapman. A version of the commission's report has recently come to light which plainly exonerates Hawkins and repeats his charges against his predecessors. It seems, however, that he himself was the author of this paper, which naturally did not convince his rivals. The evidence suggests that he did indeed reduce the Ordinary to about £4,000, but it is hard to say how much, if any of this was a real saving, and how much was simply shifted onto the Extraordinary expenditure undertaken during these years for new building and squadrons sent to Ireland. It was, and is, extremely difficult to define such terms as 'repair' and 'maintenance' in sufficiently watertight terms.[37]

Burghley, however, continued to support Hawkins, who in 1585 proposed a new and more radical Bargain. By the terms of this contract Hawkins undertook to keep the Ordinary at £4,000 a year, and to allocate the savings of £1,714 'every year to do such reparations as shall be needful, either in the making of a new ship, repairing in dry-dock, or any otherwise that shall be needful.'[38] This seems to mean a rolling programme of building or rebuilding one ship each year.[39] Since there were about twenty-five major ships in the Navy, this implied that with routine maintenance a ship should remain in service that number of years, and in fact the average life-span of the sixteen ships rebuilt in Elizabeth's reign was twenty-four years.[40] Hawkins's programme shows him to have been a man with a long-term vision and a capacity for planning well matched with Burghley's. The second bargain, however, was never effectively implemented, because war with Spain broke out as soon as it was signed, and Hawkins's orderly plans were overtaken by extensive new building and repairs under extraordinary warrants. By the summer of 1587 he was trying to cancel a contract which had become unworkable.[41]

When the fleet mobilized that autumn there was therefore a background of controversy over the state of the queen's ships. Lord Howard was unequivocal in backing Hawkins against his critics: 'her Majesty may be sure, what false and villainous reports soever have been made of them, she hath the strongest ships that any prince in Christendom hath'.[42] In March 1588 the *Elizabeth Bonaventure* grounded off Flushing and lay two tides pounding on the sand before she was got off:

> . . . and in all this time there came never a spoonful of water into her well. My Lord, except a ship had been made of iron, it were to be thought unpossible to do as she hath done; and it may be well and truly said there never was nor is in the world a stronger ship than she is, and there is no more to be perceived or known any ways of her being aground than if she were new made. She is 27 years old . . . and for that which Sir William Winter and I have seen now, we will take upon us that the good ship the *Elizabeth Bonaventure* shall serve her Majesty these 12 years . . .[43]

After 1588, the criticisms of Hawkins died away, perhaps because his Bargain lapsed, but certainly also because the good condition of the queen's ships spoke for itself. Hawkins was a rich man when he took office as Treasurer, and not less rich when he died. He certainly did not live on nothing but his official salary of £220 18s 4d less expenses, but the evidence suggests that we may believe what he wrote to Burghley in November 1587:

> For mine own part I have lived in a very mean estate since I came to be an Officer, neither have I vainly or superfluously consumed her Majesty's treasure, or mine own substance, but ever been diligently and carefully occupied to prepare for the danger to come.[44]

We know Hawkins deducted 3d in the pound (1.25 per cent) from suppliers' bills – but in return he paid them promptly, using his own credit to cover the delay and uncertainty in payments from the Exchequer, so they did not object.[45] Long after his death, when much greater difficulties had overtaken naval administration, men looked back on his time as a golden age of efficiency and honesty.[46]

The references to dry-docks in Hawkins's second bargain and many other documents make it clear that they continued to be reserved for building, rebuilding and major repairs, as well as for laying-up ships in reserve. Though Deptford and Woolwich each had a permanent dock with timbered sides, it seems that up to the 1580s, the dockhead still had to be excavated to pass a ship in and out, in the fashion of the medieval mud dock. The dockyard accounts regularly mention 'labourers, marshmen and others' excavating the dockhead whenever a new or rebuilt ship was launched.[47] It took six men a fortnight to dig out the *Elizabeth Jonas* at Woolwich in 1578.[48] Routine maintenance was carried out by graving or grounding the ships on a firm beach to work on their hulls at low water. The disadvantages of this were obvious. It was difficult and dangerous to ground a ship without a flat bottom; with only a few hours between tides, the hull below the waterline could not be opened up for repairs; and the process imposed considerable strains on the hull. 'The strength of the ships generally is well tried,' as Hawkins wrote in 1588, 'for they stick not to ground often to tallow, to wash, or any such small cause, which is a most sure trial of the goodness of the ships, when they are able to abide the ground.'[49] As an alternative to graving, the Navy increasingly adopted in the 1590s the Mediterranean practice of careening, or heeling the ship afloat to work on one side of the hull at a time.[50] This could even be done at sea in exceptionally calm weather,[51] but it was hard to get at the keel and garboard strakes, and it might strain the hull as much or more than grounding.

The solution to this problem seems to have been approached by gradual evolution rather than any sudden discovery. The details remain obscure, but in 1578 the considerable sum of £150 was paid to build a pair of gates for the Deptford dock, and in the early 1580s the yard accounts cease to record payments to the marshmen for digging out the dockhead whenever a ship was launched.[52] The obvious implication is that the dock now had watertight gates which could be opened and closed at will; it is not irrelevant that the first pound lock in England had recently been built on the Exeter ship canal.[53] Early in the next century the Woolwich dock had gates which had to be shored and caulked when shut, and could only be rebuilt behind a coffer dam, all of which must mean that they normally took the pressure of the sea at high water without the help of earthworks.[54] By 1625, when the new dock at Chatham was graving five ships on every spring tide (say over two or three days), it must have been possible to open and shut the gates without difficulty.[55] So long as the Spanish War lasted, the Elizabethan Navy seems to have continued to regard dry docks as suitable only for major works taking many months (as late as 1602 a 'grounding place' was made at Saltash, 'to serve the Queen's great ships for ever'),[56] but the installation of dock gates, which marks the invention of the true dry dock, was a very important development. It was to become one of the key technical achievements underpinning English sea power. Not until 1666, when Colbert ordered the building of a dry dock 'à l'anglaise' at his new dockyard at Rochefort, did any foreign naval power acquire a true dry dock, and by then the English had a lead which they never lost.[57]

Woolwich and Deptford were in Queen Elizabeth's reign the only dockyards for the Navy Royal, for they had the only working docks, but as proposed in 1559, 'Gillingham Water' became its main anchorage. There, along the Medway between Rochester Bridge and the new fort at Upnor, there was sufficient deep water for the whole Navy Royal to ride in security, whereas the Thames at Deptford and Woolwich was narrow, shallow, heavily used, and too far from the open sea. Initially there was no shore establishment on the Medway, but the convenience, indeed necessity, of routine maintenance on the spot soon led to stores being kept locally. In 1570 up to sixty shipwrights were working there, on the rebuilding of the *Bull* and *Tiger* among other things, though the permanent shore staff still consisted only of the gunners at Upnor, a clerk, a purveyor and the rat-catcher. A house was rented 'wherein the officers of her Majesty's ships do meet and confer from time to time touching her Highness's weighty affairs.'[58] By 1578 Chatham, as it was now often called, had several storehouses and a mast-pond; two years later a new wharf was built, 378 feet long and 40 feet broad. On the outbreak of war in 1585 the river was blocked by a chain at Upnor, with a battery at Sheerness at the mouth of the river, and two pinnaces stationed to patrol.[59]

Portsmouth remained a forward anchorage with only a minor naval establishment. Most of the work recorded in the 1570s was maintenance of the galley *Eleanor*, stationed there for local defence, and it does not appear that the old docks were much in use, but small sums were spent on keeping them in repair, and by 1587 the galley was laid up in one of them.[60]

The senior staff of each naval yard was headed by the master shipwright and the storekeeper. The storekeepers were as near permanent officials as the sixteenth century could approach, but the master shipwrights remained more like privileged contractors, who had work outside the royal yards, and built most though not all of the queen's ships under contract. Matthew Baker, for example, in 1590 built the 690-ton *Merhonour* under contract for £3,600 and the 223-ton sister ships *Quittance* and *Answer* for £1,400 each.

Four years later he built the *Adventure* at day wages, and according to Baker at much greater cost to the crown, but of course he was a highly partisan witness.[61] Ordinary shipwrights in 1588 were paid between 1s and 1s 5d a day, according to their skill, together with free lodging, three meals a day, and as much beer 'as shall suffice them'. From All Hallows to Candlemas (1 November to 2 February) they worked from dawn to dusk, and for the rest of the year from five o'clock in the morning to seven at night (six on Saturdays). They had an hour for dinner at noon, marked by the ringing of a bell.[62]

The victualling organization was taken over on Baeshe's death in 1587 by James Quarles and Marmaduke Darrell. It was perhaps unfortunate that Baeshe's long experience was lost in the crisis of 1588, but his successors as officials of the royal household were familiar with feeding the only organization which equalled the size of even a small seagoing squadron, and they seem to have approached their task methodically. They spent the winter of 1586–7 taking inventories of stocks and calculating requirements; on 14 September a warrant was issued to victual ten thousand men for three months and all was delivered by mid-November, well before the fleet was ready to go to sea.[63] At this stage most of the ships were still in the Thames. The real victualling problems started when the bulk of the fleet was unexpectedly ordered westward in the spring. Though Burghley had occasion to complain of weaknesses in Darrell's paperwork, and though more money would certainly have helped, the shortage of victuals arose very largely from the inherent difficulties of feeding so large a force so far to windward of its victualling base.[64] Considering the technical limitations it faced, the English victualling system seems remarkably efficient by the standards of its age. Since it was run by contract, Quarles as Surveyor-General took the risk of rising prices or unexpected difficulties. The other side of this coin was that he could not make an adequate return if he lavished too much on his purchases, and as his organization did not itself pack or manufacture foodstuffs, he was at the mercy of his suppliers.[65] In the long run, experience was to teach that only a government victualling organization responsible for every stage of packing and manufacture could furnish the quality and quantity which the Navy needed – but it is unlikely that the sixteenth century's resources of administrative competence and honesty could have sustained such a thing.

Furthermore, it seems clear that the efficiency and honesty of English government were declining in the 1590s, though historians debate why it happened and how far it went. Most aspects of naval administration seem to have been less efficient in, say, 1598 than they had been ten years earlier.

The queen herself lamented in 1601 that 'now the wit of the fox is everywhere on foot so as hardly a faithful or virtuous man may be found'.[66] Two years later Captain John Norris wrote,

> if I should enter into discourse of whatsoever is wastefully spent or out of necessity stolen, the packet would be over great to be easily carried. For to say the truth the whole body is so corrupted as there is no sound part almost from the head to the foot. The great ones feed on the less and enforce them to steal both for themselves and their commanders.[67]

Lord Burghley had died in 1598; his son and successor Sir Robert Cecil was more dishonest in his private conduct than his father had been, and less rigorous as a bulwark against other men's dishonesty. By the 1590s court politics were no longer balanced between factions, always ready to denounce one another's real or imagined misdeeds, but increasingly dominated, first by Essex, then by Cecil and the Howard family.[68] The privateer *Truelove*, paid for out of Cecil's secret service money and jointly owned by Cecil and Lord Howard, sailed on the Cadiz expedition victualled at the crown's expense as a ship of the Navy Royal, and at double the number of men she actually bore. She then parted company for a lucrative cruise on her owners' account.[69] Together they invested in piratical voyages to the Mediterranean, discreetly putting pressure on the judge of the High Court of Admiralty to favour their interests in the resulting lawsuits:

> Mr Caesar, I pray you note a friendly care tomorrow in our case before you. Mr Secretary is far interested in it. If it speed well you are sure he will requite it in anything that shall concern you.[70]

Hawkins was not replaced as Treasurer of the Navy for three years, during which his former clerk Roger Langford acted as Paymaster of the Navy, making payments but not providing the leadership his master had given.[71] The new Treasurer was Fulke Greville, a courtier with some sea experience but very little knowledge of administration. Greville was honest and did his best, but he was contending with a situation which was beyond his control.

> Many have been asked, why they should rob from so good a princess that pays them their wages every quarter. The answer was made that all that they have is her Majesty's at command, and that we may better take from her than from any other, and the substantious reason that they have is, it comes from the commonwealth.[72]

In the dockyards the master shipwrights put in incompetent deputies, men were appointed by 'mere favour without respect of merit', gunpowder was adulterated with sand, the musters padded with fictitious names. In the house at Chatham of Sir John Trevor, the Controller,

> The chamber was repaired, new wainscotted, new windows, tables, presses, and all other necessaries belonging to carpentry, joiners', or masons' work made at the Queen's charge; and for the furnishing thereof with bed, stools, chairs, and such like provisions £30 was delivered.[73]

Greville was warned

> that the courses you take to husband things for the Queen are found too straight by those which seek to draw the power and profit of all into one, and that therefore they lie in wait for all advantages to make you pliant perforce to that you mislike.[74]

There was ample opportunity to apply pressure on him, for the Treasurer could not pass his accounts without the signature of at least two members of the Navy Board:

> So long as the Treasurer's account is thus subject to the officers and they withal permitted to make provisions for the Navy, either the Treasurer shall not pass his account or else shall be forced if the rest be corrupt to conspire with them to make prey of the Queen as they have done heretofore.[75]

The Navy Board itself had fallen into disorder: 'there is neither place, time, order, nor means appointed for their meetings and counsels, nor any distinction made of their several offices.'[76] After Hawkins's death the condition of the queen's ships seems to have noticeably deteriorated. The six year-old *Merhonour* almost sank from a leak on the Cadiz expedition.[77] On the 'Islands Voyage' the following year, Essex in the new *Repulse*

> beat it up till my ship was falling asunder, having a leak that we pumped 80 tons of water a day out of her, her main and fore masts cracked, and most of her beams broken and rent, besides the opening of all her seams. Now I have been almost as long time at sea as I was first victualled for, and the supply of a month's victual is not come to me: but I will, by God's grace, yet live at sea till I see winter come in, if my month's victual come to me . . .[78]

As for the victualling, in 1599 Fulke Greville in the Channel complained that 'Our drink, fish and beef is so corrupt as it will destroy all the men we have, and if they feed on it but a few days, in very truth we should not be able to keep the seas.'[79]

In the Ordnance Office, which was riven by violent quarrels, the Lieutenant-General Sir George Carew complained in 1592 of 'this troublesome place where I have at no time found either profit or ease; . . . and, which is worse, my fellows in office so corrupt and of such malicious spirits as but in hell I think their matches can hardly be found.'[80] Wearied by dishonesty and discord, the virtuous Carew went off on the Cadiz expedition in 1596, where he was accused of looting 44,000 ducats in gold, and thence to Ireland as Lord President of Munster, where he gained £150,000 in eight years by fraud and speculation. Sir Thomas Sherley, Treasurer at War in the Netherlands, was said to be making £16,000 a year more than his salary.[81] The war was regarded at every level of administration as a fleeting opportunity to make a fortune. The Navy and Ordnance with their established and relatively sophisticated administrations suffered much less than the army in France, Flanders and Ireland.[82]

The relative efficiency of England's permanent naval administration, moreover, contrasted with heroic improvisation in Spain. One illustration must serve. In 1588 Don Juan de Acuña Vela, lately appointed Captain-General of Artillery, inherited on paper an established administration with four provincial departments, depots and accountants – but in practice he lacked virtually everything he needed to arm the fleet at Lisbon. In the whole of Spain there was only one gun foundry, at Malaga, and one shot foundry, which had been out of action for many years. In all Iberia there were five gunfounders, one of whom was blind. Though iron, copper, sulphur and saltpetre were abundant in Spain, virtually all of them had to be imported. Copper came from Hungary, lead and tin from England, sulphur from Italy. Guns, armour and shot were manufactured in Italy and Flanders. Powder was inadequate in quantity and quality, and in 1587 all the mills had stopped working for want of money. [83] Virtually alone apart from his secretary, with little time and less money, Acuña Vela had to improvise everything. He personally boarded the ships as they arrived at Lisbon, inspected and listed their guns. He ransacked the fortresses of Spain and Portugal for artillery, he negotiated with gunfounders all over Europe, he searched the woods of Extremadura for timber to make gun-carriages. He let contracts with gunsmiths and powdermakers, he sent to Flanders and Germany in search of gunners. He negotiated with the recalcitrant local authorities of Lisbon for a site for a foundry, supervised its building, scrounged the metal and cast the guns.[84] The English Ordnance Board may have been corrupt and slothful by modern standards, but with its staff of over 150, its large stocks of powder (55 lasts in 1578, equivalent to eight months' Spanish production at that date) and shot (51,500 rounds in 1578, 87,000 in 1595), its network of skilled gunfounders casting 700–800 tons of iron guns a year, its strategic reserve of bronze gunmetal, its extensive resources of expertise and experience, it makes a striking contrast to the situation in Spain.[85]

English administration, moreover, was a model of honesty as well as organization compared to the situation in Spain.[86] The rising corruption of late Elizabethan government was in many ways an early and mild symptom of a general problem, affecting most European states as they struggled to meet the costs and demands of modern war with political and constitutional structures inherited from the medieval world. Everywhere the wartime expenditure of government far outran its revenues, its employment and consumption far exceeded its capacity to pay staff or suppliers, and corruption filled some of the gap. Spanish government was a mass of competing and overlapping jurisdictions.[87] Spanish garrison troops were seldom paid, and tended to be away earning a living when their fortresses were attacked. Those who could not, literally starved, or hanged themselves, or sold themselves into slavery. More than a thousand galleymen, unpaid for five years, clad only in sacking, with twenty-four days' rations for three and a half months, perished of hunger and cold over the winter of 1595–6. Even the captains of Spanish warships went shoeless, their children begging for bread in the streets of Ferrol.[88] Meanwhile the crown's unpaid debts mounted at 14 per cent compound interest, and the royal accounts were so confused that it was impossible to establish income or expenditure. When Philip II died in September 1598, he owed one hundred million ducats, and interest payments were consuming two-thirds of his revenues.[89]

Queen Elizabeth's management of her war effort was by comparison highly conservative. She could not borrow to any great extent, and did not chose to debase the coinage.[90] In addition to her peacetime income of about £300,000 a year, she received parliamentary grants of £72,000 a year in 1586–93, £150–160,000 in 1594–5, and £104,000 in 1596. In 1588 she spent £420,000. Over the next six years she sent £100,000 a year to the Netherlands. In all £370,000 went to help Henry IV of France, and Tyrone's rebellion cost nearly £2,000,000 to suppress.[91] By 1590 her savings had all gone, and only in easy years could she save enough money to float a naval expedition. Nevertheless in the course of the war the Navy received over £1,500,000 (plus the naval share of Ordnance expenditure), which was about one-third of total government spending.[92] Over the whole war Elizabeth spent about £4,500,000, of which £2,700,000 came from taxation, £5–600,000 from land sales, £98,000 was owing in 1603, and the rest came from ordinary income. In the 1590s

English taxpayers were paying about £90,000 a year, and the falling yield of the taxes suggests that the limit of what was politically possible had been reached.[93] But in real terms Queen Elizabeth spent less on seventeen years of war against Spain than her father had done in ten years against France and Scotland, and she spent mostly out of income, rather than capital.[94] In 1545 Henry VIII was spending 8–9 per cent of national income, but by 1588 his daughter had only about 2 per cent, which was worth less in real terms than the income of Edward III or Henry V had been.[95] By the end of the war, as spending in Ireland rose to its peak, English government finances were under acute strain, and new methods were under discussion of getting the people to contribute to the war effort.

One of these was ship money. For many centuries English kings had levied shipping, and sometimes money in lieu, from coastal towns. Elizabeth did the same, especially in 1588, where by cajolery and pressure most of the seaports were persuaded to send ships at their expense to join Howard's fleet; even the Cinque Ports made a token contribution.[96] Once this crisis was past, however, the ports became notably reluctant to assist the war effort in any way which did not profit themselves, and several flatly refused. Demands on the basis of royal prerogative for their unpaid service were made in 1591, 1594–6, 1599 and 1601–3. In 1596 the coastal counties were assessed in addition, the total demand being twenty-six ships plus five from London, and the result seventeen plus twelve Londoners.[97] But these demands were unsatisfactory as well as unpopular. London's big and well-armed ships excepted, the contributions were of little value to major operations. At the same time trade had to fend for itself, for the queen's ships were too few and too busy for escort work. From these considerations grew the 1603 scheme for a second Navy for the protection of trade, distinct from the Navy Royal, to be financed by a voluntary levy on all counties, inland as well as coastal.

> Although this matter most concerneth the safety of foreign commerce, who is it that dwells so far within the land, that shall not feel sure effects of such an interruption when the wealth and strength of this kingdom hath so much dependency upon maintenance of trade and navigation, which being overthrown and that the home commodities shall not be vented, what can be looked for, but poverty and confusion as well upon the inland as the maritime?[98]

Although the contributions were supposed to be voluntary, the reluctance of inland parts to pay led the Privy Council to lay compulsory levies on them, while the preference of many seaports for offering money rather than ships also made this 'voluntary' scheme look very like a new tax. In the event the queen died soon after it was introduced, and the scheme was abandoned – but the problem it addressed remained to vex a future generation.[99]

In her policy of using sea power to preserve her life and independence from the great powers, the queen was necessarily dependent on that small group of merchants, shipowners, sea commanders and investors who had been closely involved in the management of the Navy Royal since her father's day, and whose private ventures in trade and piracy were often hard to distinguish from activities of the crown. In her situation, it was impossible to run a naval or foreign policy unaffected by their private affairs. She might not be personally concerned with slaving on the Guinea Coast in defiance of the monopoly claimed by Portugal, in illegal trade with Spanish America, in piracy all over the eastern Atlantic – but her Navy was managed by and dependent on men who were. It was not so much an instrument of state policy as an alliance of royal and private interests which the queen could not completely control.[100] This uniquely Elizabethan hybrid war effort, which made up for some of the weakness of royal finances by invoking private investment, was partly based on the long-standing pirate traditions of England in general, and the West Country in particular. The crown co-opted and to some extent diverted the energies of its best, indeed almost its only seamen capable of oceanic naval warfare – but the more it encouraged and depended on them, the less it controlled them. In peacetime, the crown frequently regarded piracy as a local problem for shipowners to sort out for themselves. In wartime, the patriotic pirate who only attacked foreigners could be sure of having public opinion on his side, whatever the diplomatic damage done by plundering neutrals.[101] Captain Diggory Piper, whose name is still familiar to musicians from the delightful dance called 'Captain Diggory Piper's Galliard', took out letters of reprisal in 1586 to cruise in his ship the *Sweepstake* against the Spaniards and Portuguese. He started with some Flemings, continued with two French ships, and then took a Dane.[102] The worst such a man had to fear in the Admiralty Court was pressure to compound; that is, to clear himself at law by paying back some proportion of his booty. Piracy was usually treated as a civil dispute, and murder, wounding or torture were of no concern to the court.[103] Very rarely did foreign victims get any diplomatic redress, though the redoutable Mrs Agnes Cowty of Dundee, owner of the *Grace of God* which was taken off Dungeness in 1582, succeeded where the Admiral of France had failed in shaming the English government into paying compensation.[104]

The government had never had a very effective means of dealing with pirates in the West Country and Wales where the local gentry were on their side, for the gentry were the crown's only local agents.[105] In South Wales, as the local justices explained, 'it was common policy as the world went now' to favour pirates.[106] In 1578 one of the queen's own ships was plundered by pirates at Newport.[107] Sir John Perrott, Vice-Admiral of Pembrokeshire until his disgrace in 1592, actively encouraged pirates to bring their business into local ports. 'Pirates (it is commonly reported) are furnished, victualled, aided, received and succoured – and their goods openly sold in Cardiff.'[108] Perrott's neighbour Sir John Wogan did the same, and no doubt would have gone on doing so, had the two families not fallen out and denounced one another.[109] Sir George Carey, Captain of the Isle of Wight, sent his own ships on pirate cruises and encouraged other pirates to bring their spoils to the island, covering his activities by a close relationship with the judge of the Admiralty Court, and with his kinsman Lord Howard.[110] In Dorset at least forty prizes were brought into Studland Bay in three years in the early 1580s. There in the Isle of Purbeck the pirates were favoured by local gentlemen like Sir Richard Rogers, who maintained a base at Lulworth Cove: 'the place of their repair is here', a local official admitted, 'where in truth they are my masters'. Some pirates had even more influential friends: Captain John Piers, a Cornishman based at Studland who blockaded the port of Rye in the summer of 1581, was reputed to be aided by the black arts of his mother, the witch of Padstow.[111]

In Devon, 'the keeping in of the men of war, which is the principal trade of this whole coast, is to interdict them fire and water.'[112] Sir Walter Ralegh's father had never allowed his position as Vice-Admiral of Devon to interfere with his piracy, and nor did his successors. Sir Richard Grenville and William Hawkins were both involved.[113] In the 1570s, Gilbert Peppitt, Sergeant of the Vice-Admiralty Court of Devon, was receiving the booty of Captain John Challis of the *Cost-me-Nought*, a notorious pirate who was steadily favoured by the gentry of England and Wales. Occasionally when his activities grew too embarrassing he would buy a pardon and take up some 'legitimate' activity, usually in the service of his friends the Fenners of Chichester, cruising with a commission 'to suppress piracy', with predictable results. In the course of a career of thirty years Challis took ships of Portugal, Spain, France, Brittany, Scotland, Pomerania, Lübeck, Denmark, Hamburg, Flanders and various Italian ports. He was never effectually punished, and died in his bed in 1587.[114] Sir John Killigrew of Arwennack, Captain of Pendennis Castle and a close connection of the Cecils, was head of the

Commission of Piracy for Cornwall – and none was better qualified, for he was the most notorious pirate in Cornwall himself. His grandfather and his father ('as proud as Ammon, as covetous as Ahab and as cruel as Nero'), had been pirates before him and his wife, though a gentlewoman who permitted only the most respectable pirates to stay at Arwennack, was not above leading a cutting-out party herself.[115] There were pirates even within a few miles of London. In 1586 a hoy going down to Queenborough was boarded: 'five or six persons in a wherry laid the hoy aboard below Woolwich, near the halfway tree, with swords drawn, and robbed the hoy.'[116] The hoy *James* of Manningtree was attacked in the Orwell by a pirate boat with fourteen men.[117] On the East Coast the Lord Admiral's servants established a pirate base at Ingoldmells in Lincolnshire. The Suffolk squire Edward Glemham cruised in the Mediterranean, though his pawning some of his men into slavery in Algiers was regarded as bad form.[118]

It is fashionable among historians to speak of piracy as an activity of marginal, outcast communities, excluded from profitable trade.[119] In sixteenth-century England, on the contrary, it was often an activity of the wealthy and well-connected, privately and sometimes publicly backed by the queen and her ministers.[120] Some Hamburg merchants were robbed by a ship called the *Henry Seckforde*, 'whereof is owner one Henry Seckforde esquire, one of the gentlemen of your Majesty's Privy Chamber.' Naturally their petition got nowhere.[121] As Lord Admiral, Lord Howard's attitude towards the pirates was equivocal. It was his duty to suppress them, but their activities generated numerous suits in the Admiralty Court, from which he profited directly, and in practice he tended to 'suppress' them by granting pardons in return for a fine or composition – which was equivalent to taxing their activities. He treated the judge of the High Court of Admiralty as the manager of his franchise, and intervened as necessary to ensure that his interests were safeguarded. During the war he freely issued retrospective letters of reprisal for a fee, so many sailed without any legal authority and bought themselves a cheap legality on return. His own ships, often fitted at royal expense, engaged in piracy under the flimsy cover of suppressing it.[122]

This was not the romantic world of the gallant Elizabethan sea-dogs which an older generation of writers loved to conjure up. It was a business of greed and cruelty at sea, deceit and betrayal ashore. Victims were tortured and killed, partners double-crossed and crews cheated.[123] It was inherently disorderly, beyond effective control by government. Certainly it generated ships and seamen which immeasurably strengthened England's maritime power, but it also made it difficult to deploy that power in a coherent military form. It worked in the Spanish War partly because the very great power of Spain could not be brought to bear for want of an effective navy. Against foreign powers nearer to England and better able to put warships to sea, the Elizabethan system of a small professional Navy Royal surrounded by a chaotic swarm of privateers and pirates would not have been adequate. Her successors faced just such threats, and were forced to try to develop new forms of seapower to meet them. When the old queen died and peace was made with Spain, her legacy was an enduring conviction among Englishmen that their true and patriotic way of warfare was at sea, and that naval war in the English style was easy, glorious and profitable. In the long term, the experience of naval warfare as a unifying national enterprise was to set England on a distinctive path not followed by any other country – but events were to show that the idea that it was easy to defeat a superpower at sea, and make one's fortune in the process, was not a very helpful guide to the future.

TWENTY-FOUR

No More Drakes

Operations 1603–1630

The accession of James VI of Scots to the throne of England in 1603, and the peace with Spain which followed soon after, left England and the English Navy more securely at peace than they had been for nearly a century. ('English Navy' seems to be the correct usage: King James favoured the term 'Great Britain', but his two kingdoms were constitutionally quite independent, the Scottish fleet had disappeared in the civil wars of the mid-century, and the Navy Royal was entirely financed from English revenue.) No great power menaced England or Scotland. Spain was still fully occupied with her many other enemies, France was barely recovering from the civil wars, Scotland's ally Denmark protected the Baltic trades. The new king was himself a man of peace; his upbringing in a weak and unstable kingdom had taught him the risks of war and men of war, at home and abroad. James was a learned and in many ways an intelligent man, keenly interested in politics, and much better informed about foreign affairs than most of his English subjects, but not interested in administrative detail.

James's peaceful accession was managed by the Cecil–Howard interest which now dominated English politics. This at once introduced a tension, for King James disliked pirates as much as any other men of violence, but Sir Robert Cecil discreetly, and Lord Nottingham openly in his official capacity of Lord Admiral, were the effective heads of the privateering interest which had grown and gained so much during the war. The great merchants of London redirected their peacetime energies into the armed trading for which their ships and their experience were so suitable: in the Mediterranean, as the Levant Company, in the East, as the new East India Company, and everywhere in Europe where neutral merchantmen able to defend themselves stood to capture trade from the belligerents. In many minor ports, however, especially in the West Country, men had no alternative trade to take up, but continued in their accustomed ways. The private enterprises of the Elizabethan naval system, sometimes an embarrassment even in wartime, were distinctly unwelcome to a soverign committed to peaceful coexistence. As a legacy of war the government faced a serious problem of piracy everywhere around the British Isles, even in the Thames. A Dutch ship, aground at low water at Gravesend, was robbed by pirates who took off their shoes and stockings and waded out to her – and it was not only obscure merchantmen which suffered.[1] In 1603 the Venetian ambassador was robbed by English pirates on his way to England; in 1614 King James's brother-in-law Christian IV of Denmark suffered likewise.[2] Nottingham as Lord Admiral, though only once caught taking bribes to favour piracy, was deeply ambiguous towards it.[3] 'Your lordship shall see there shall be no fault in me, but I do not look to see England or France free of pirates; they are relieved in some ports or creeks, and what mine officers can do they shall.'[4] But many of them did not. Sir Richard Hawkins as Vice-Admiral of Devon sold blank pardons to pirates. Hannibal Vivian, Vice-Admiral of South Cornwall, and William Restarrock, his colleague on the north coast, permitted captured pirates to buy their freedom. [5] Lundy in the Bristol Channel, Bardsey Island, Pwllheli and Milford Haven in Wales were all notorious haunts of pirates.[6] As late as 1634 the Vice-Admiral of North Wales was warned that,

> It will be in vain for his Majesty to set forth ships to sea to apprehend pirates, if they on the coast through the connivance of Vice Admirals find so easy a way to sell their stolen goods and to supply themselves with provisions to support their lewd course of life.[7]

Many pirates, like Henry Mainwaring, were commissioned by Nottingham under pretence of making reprisals 'beyond the line', within the Spanish imperial monopoly.[8] At least one went as far as the East Indies.[9]

If pirates were taken, the common seamen were usually pardoned and often the leaders as well.[10] The general pardon of 1612, intended as an amnesty to encourage pirates to abandon their trade, allowed them to keep their loot, and hardly restrained them from restarting their careers.[11] The notorious Scots pirate Captain Herriot, having cruised in the Channel for years, was finally captured by a Dutch admiral in the Helford River in 1624, but the reaction of the Vice-Admiral towards the pirates was that 'if his Majesty's mercy give them life they may prove able and honest subjects.'[12] Two years later the Lord Deputy of Ireland recommended pardon for another as 'a spirit of action and experience both of seas and foreign countries [who may be of] valuable service in these stirring times.'[13] Robert Walsingham stepped directly from his pirate ship to the command of one of the king's, while Henry Mainwaring finished his career as an admiral and a knight.[14] Captains of warships enjoyed ambiguous relations with pirates, if not actually engaging in piracy themselves.[15]

The most successful of the Jacobean pirates were based in overseas ports, usually Mamora or Sallee in Morocco in wintertime, and Munster in the summer. Pirate leaders like Mainwaring and Peter Easton commanded powerful squadrons with nothing to fear from the English Navy. In 1609 Richard Bishop, vice-admiral to Captain John Ward (then based at Tunis), arrived in Irish waters with a squadron of ten or eleven ships carrying a thousand men; Easton had at least twenty ships.[16] He declined to take advantage of the 1612 pardon with the disdainful remark, 'I am, in a way, a king myself.'[17] The years 1608 to 1614 were the heyday of these English and Dutch pirates, and the north Atlantic was their cruising ground, from Iceland to the Canaries, and from the Newfoundland Banks to the Channel.[18]

This long-range and large-scale piracy changed attitudes in Britain. Justices and vice-admirals who had been happy to support local enterprise grew alarmed at these more formidable fleets, and the government found it easier to enlist their support.[19] Though local expeditions against pirates were sometimes just another cover for piracy themselves, some modestly effective efforts were made.[20] The Piracy Commissions established in 1608 led to the dismissal of Sir Richard Hawkins and chastened others, at the same time as the 1609 truce between Spain and the Netherlands tended to reduce the possibilities of piracy in the Channel.[21] Only in Ireland, and especially among the English settlers of the Munster plantation, did the old attitudes persist. Lord Nottingham was his own Vice-Admiral for Munster, and his deputies were deeply committed to piracy. Baltimore and Crookhaven were the great pirate bases, where all the justices and indeed all the population were involved. The men went to sea with the pirates, sold them victuals or bought their booty; the women of Baltimore were reported to be all the wives or mistresses of pirates.[22]

The government of James VI & I had no answer to piracy on this scale, and it is not altogether clear why it declined. The Spanish capture of Mamora and the Dutch attack on Crookhaven, both in 1614, undoubtedly did damage.[23] Some of the most eminent pirates retired: Mainwaring joined the Royal Navy; Easton became a Savoyard nobleman, married an heiress, converted to Catholicism and died in the odour of wealth and sanctity.[24] Perhaps more important was competition from the 'Barbary pirates' of Algiers and Tunis. Whereas the English pirates operating out of Moroccan ports were allowed freedom to pursue their own policies, those like Ward who were based in one of the 'Regencies' found themselves circumscribed by a strong local government with its own long-standing interests in piracy. For a few years the European Barbary pirates had a devastating effect, especially on the trade of Venice. Ward's capture in 1607 of the *Reniera e Soderina*, valued at £100,000, caused a sensation.[25] But very soon the Algerines and Tunisians learnt for themselves how to handle European rigs and heavy guns, and needed Englishmen or Dutchmen purely as subordinates. Algiers above all rapidly swept the Western Mediterranean of all but the most heavily armed Christian merchantmen and moved into the Atlantic, copying the English and Dutch pirates. In 1616 they reached Iceland, in 1617 they attacked Madeira, by the 1620s they were off Nova Scotia and Newfoundland. With a hundred warships, sixty of them from 24 to 30 guns, Algiers had by far the largest fleet in Europe. Between 1613 and 1621 the Algerines brought in 447 Dutch, 193 French, 120 Spanish, 60 English and 56 German prizes, not counting those sunk. Another source suggests that they took not less than 446 English ships between 1609 and 1616.[26]

The arrival of the Barbary pirates radically changed English attitudes. Instead of patriotic pirates plundering foreign cargoes and bringing them home to enrich their countrymen, the 'Turks' were in the usual Mediterranean business of slave-raiding – and now the English were the victims.[27] The West Country men suffered the heaviest, and did not appreciate the irony. The Newfoundland fishery, dominated by Devon ports, lost at least twenty ships in 1611 alone, taken either in the Atlantic or in the Mediterranean, where they were accustomed to sell their fish. Heavily manned for a summer season fishing from small boats, the Newfoundlandmen were perfect targets for slavers.[28]

Naturally these losses generated an outcry, but it was not at all clear what could be done about them. It had never been customary for the Navy Royal to protect merchantmen against piracy, nor if it tried could it have matched the strength of the Algerines. In any case the Navy was largely demobilized in peacetime. The most considerable operation of these years was the 1614 expedition to the Western Isles to suppress the MacDonalds of Islay, in the course of which some galleys were destroyed and Dunivaig Castle taken.[29] Otherwise the customary small squadron in the Narrow Seas transported ambassadors and dignitaries to and fro and cruised in the Channel.[30] There it attempted, with the usual English arrogance, to enforce the 'salute to the flag' which the English believed to be their immemorial right. In 1603 a French vice-admiral transporting the French ambassador Sully was forced to strike his colours; three years later King Christian IV of Denmark, visiting England with part of his own large fleet, suffered the same indignity.[31]

The practice generated ill-feeling, but caused no serious trouble so long as it was regarded as a mere gesture without legal significance. The French were as yet too weak to show resentment, and the Dutch and Spaniards, so long as they were at war, had each strong reasons to cultivate English friendship.[32]

James VI & I, however, introduced significant innovations. In his reign, for the first time, the English attempted to define the limits of the 'Narrow Seas' within which they claimed the right to be saluted. Scots law, unlike English, had a concept of what would now be called territorial waters, in theory within a 'land-kenning' of the shore, in practice within the deep firths and lochs of the Scottish coast, where Scots kings for centuries had charged foreign boats for licences to fish.[33] The main English deep-sea fisheries had traditionally been in distant waters off Iceland, claimed as 'territorial' seas by the King of Denmark, while the Flemings' rights to the North Sea fisheries had been confirmed by numerous treaties. So by tradition the English had stood for free seas. Now the case was altered: Denmark was an ally, and the Dutch had built up their North Sea herring fishery, the 'Great Fishery', to a level which excited the awe and envy of every nation in Europe. Sober modern calculations suggest that it earned a million pounds a year and directly or indirectly employed half a million people, one fifth of the population of the Netherlands; English estimates greatly inflated those figures. This was the 'Dutch Indies', from which they drew their silver as surely as the Spaniards did from America.[34] Initially James was concerned to safeguard English neutrality by defining coastal waters, the 'King's Chambers', within which the belligerents were supposed not to fight. Not until the 1609 truce did he make the first tentative moves to tax the Dutch offshore fisheries. For diplomatic and other reasons nothing ensued at this stage but mutual annoyance and lengthy negotiations.[35]

The same was true of another irritant to Anglo-Dutch relations during James VI & I's reign. Except during the Twelve Years' Truce (1609–21) between Spain and the Netherlands, the greatest threat to Dutch shipping was the Spanish squadron at Dunkirk, the revived 'Armada of Flanders'. A large Dutch force was maintained for much of the year to blockade Dunkirk, a task nearly impossible even at odds of four to one because of the numerous sands which guard the port and the extraordinary speed of the Dunkirkers' ships. 'In spite of all our measures', complained the Dutch admiral Jan Gerbrandtszoon in 1603, 'the Dunkirkers still get outside the sands.'[36] On the renewal of war in 1621 the Dunkirk squadron was rebuilt in greater strength.[37] England was a neutral power, but Sir Robert Cecil the Secretary of State, Lord Nottingham, Lord Admiral to 1618, and Sir William Monson,

Admiral of the Narrow Seas 1604–16, were all in receipt of secret Spanish pensions, and there was money to be made in convoy fees by 'wafting' Spanish ships into Dunkirk.[38]

Such opportunism naturally bred bad feelings between the erstwhile allies, without teaching the English and Spaniards to trust one another very much. It also complicated the already very difficult problem of Algerine piracy. The political pressure was such that the Navy had to do something against Algiers, but to operate so far away help from the Spaniards was essential and from the Dutch very desirable. Money was equally necessary, and James VI & I, like Queen Elizabeth, was forced to raise contributions from shipowners by a combination of persuasion and compulsion. The resulting squadron was commanded by Sir Robert Mansell, who had the best fighting record of any of the Elizabethan admirals still young enough to serve, with Sir Richard Hawkins as his second.

Mansell sailed in September 1620 with six of the king's ships and twelve armed merchantmen. His orders were to co-operate with both Spaniards and Dutch, which was hardly easy when they were sliding towards a renewal of war with each other. On 27 November Mansell arrived before Algiers. His position there was unenviable. Though the Algerines could not match his biggest ships and did not attempt to fight, the coast was a lee shore throughout the year, its few harbours fortified and inaccessible, and it was virtually impossible to blockade under sail two hundred miles from the nearest friendly port. Still less could Mansell attack the formidable defences of Algiers, a city as large as London; in fact he was forbidden to try, if only to avoid offending the city's nominal overlord the Turkish Sultan. Some time was wasted in futile diplomacy before Mansell was obliged to retire to Alicante for the winter. In May he returned, and on the night of the 24th an unsuccessful attempt was made to attack Algiers harbour with fireships. The fleet stayed another ten days, by which time it was clear that they could not prevent ships slipping in and out of the harbour by night, and then returned to Spain. Mansell still hoped to mount another operation with the help of Spanish galleys which could work close inshore, but he was recalled before his negotiations with the Spanish authorities got anywhere.[39]

Mansell did his best in the teeth of acute logistical difficulties, but it is doubtful if in any circumstances he could have achieved much. The very able Dutch admiral Lambrecht Hendricksz. Verhouven had had an equally frustrating experience in 1617–18.[40] The northern powers generally had yet to learn that the North African Regencies were virtually invulnerable to any pressure they could bring to bear. The best that even a powerful squadron could achieve was a few weeks of oriental diplomacy, leading to the ransoming (at or above the market price) of some slaves. The main effect of Mansell's operations was to make things much more difficult for English merchantmen in the Mediterranean: 'the estate of the poor merchant is most miserable, and I will be bold to say, much the worse since our late unhappy, imperfect attempt; for they are enraged dogs and protest a bloody revenge upon this nation.'[41] There were loud complaints from the 'many English which, since the stirring of this wasps' nest, have been stung.'[42]

Mansell was ordered home partly because there were more serious problems looming even than Barbary piracy. King James's daughter Princess Elizabeth had married Frederick V, Elector Palatine, one of the leading Protestant princes in Germany, where tension between Catholic and Protestant states was intense. In 1619 Prince Frederick was elected King of Bohemia in defiance of the Catholic majority of the Holy Roman Empire, a move which unleashed what became known as the Thirty Years War. The 'Winter King' lasted only a few months before being driven from both his new and his old thrones. James now had powerful motives of personal honour and political prestige for intervention to restore his son-in-law to the Palatinate, but it was not at all clear how to do so. The Navy Royal was his only significant diplomatic or military asset, and there was not much it could do in the Rhineland.

The dilemma was all the sharper because of the wide difference of perception between the king and his ministers, and Parliament, without whose grants of taxation no war could possibly be mounted. Many (though not all) in Parliament, especially in the Commons, saw the situation in religious terms as the struggle of Protestantism against the Antichrist, in which England had no choice but to league with the Netherlands, Denmark, Sweden and the rest against the Catholic powers of Spain and the Empire. Such a war, they believed, would be fought by England chiefly at sea against Spanish trade, where victory would be easy and vastly profitable. James and his advisers, however, could see no way of restoring Prince Frederick but by earning the help of Spain (whose army had occupied the Palatinate). Moreover they tended to see the European situation in political rather than religious terms, and were beginning to perceive that Spain was no longer the major threat she had been. Declining in power, still far away, Spain needed English help to keep open the sea route up the Channel to Flanders. It was the rapidly growing power of France just across the Channel which was the long-term worry, and particularly far-sighted observers were beginning to be concerned about the extraordinary growth of Dutch economic and

NORTH ATLANTIC OCEAN
CLARE ISLAND
CONNAUGHT
ULS
LEI
R. Shannon
Bonratty
Limerick
MUNSTER
Smerwick
DINGLE BAY
Duncannon
Waterford
Cork
Youghal
Kinsale
Castlehaven
Crookhaven
Baltimore

SCOTLAND
NORTH CHANNEL
RATHLIN IS.
ANTRIM
Larne
Carrickfergus
GALLOWAY
Kirkcudbright
SOLWAY FIRTH
Carlisle
CUMBERLAND
ENGLAND
ISLE OF MAN
Carlingford Lough
IRISH SEA
Ireland
Dublin
Wexford
ST GEORGE'S CHANNEL
WALES

commercial strength. So James looked to the possibility of a Spanish alliance which many of his people regarded with horror.[43]

The initial plan was to marry James's heir Prince Charles to Philip IV's eldest daughter, but she and her family would not contemplate marriage to a heretic, and it was unthinkable in England that Prince Charles should become Catholic or offer any toleration to English Catholics. In an endeavour to resolve this impasse Charles voyaged 'incognito' to Spain in the spring of 1623 to woo the Infanta in person. With him went his close friend and the king's favourite the Duke of Buckingham, now Lord Admiral of England and effective foreign minister. The trip produced nothing but embarrassment, and in October Charles and Buckingham returned full of anger with Spain and ready to yield to popular pressure for war against her. Buckingham now tried to make a marriage alliance with France against Spain, but here too the religious issue bedevilled negotiations. Louis XIII also demanded concessions for English Catholics, while English opinion worried about the position of his Protestant subjects the Huguenots. In December 1624, Princess Henrietta Maria was betrothed to Prince Charles, but Louis's new chief minister Cardinal Richelieu still avoided committing France to war.[44] At this juncture the Huguenot Prince Soubise rebelled, seizing much of the nascent French royal fleet at Blavet. Since Soubise was unauthorized by his co-religionists, and threatened to wreck Buckingham's plans, the duke agreed to lend English warships to France to suppress the rising. By the time they arrived, however, the Huguenot rebellion had become general. Buckingham ordered the English admiral Sir John Pennington to do all he could, even to secretly encouraging mutiny, to prevent his ships serving against their fellow Protestants, but he was effectively outwitted by Richelieu, and they did participate in the battle in which Soubise was defeated in August 1625.[45]

All this confirmed the suspicions of many in Parliament that Buckingham was an agent of international Catholic conspiracy. The Parliament of 1624, called upon to vote money for the war against Spain which they had repeatedly demanded, was deeply reluctant to give anything to so untrustworthy a minister. Moreover, few members of the Commons had any conception of the cost of modern war; most believed that war against Spain would pay for itself without taxation, or that fresh burdens laid on the English Catholics would provide all that was needed. 'Spain is rich,' Sir John Elliott declared, 'Let her be our Indies, our storehouse of treasure.'[46] 'We are the last monarchy in Christendom that retain our original rights and constitutions,' cried Sir Robert Phelips, opposing a grant of money to support the war. 'Let them not perish now. Let not posterity complain that we have done for them worse than our fathers did for us.'[47] They tended to regard tax grants, not as a necessary preparation for war, but as a reward for success in a godly cause.

This was not a uniquely English problem. Everywhere in Europe, parliaments inherited from the Middle Ages strove to protect traditional liberties, above all the right of the well-to-do not to pay taxes, and insisted that war and foreign policy was the business of kings. Sovereigns, faced with the inexorable demands of modern war for money and resources on an unprecedented scale, everywhere found themselves driven to try to avoid or crush these traditional liberties. Some succeeded, and in the process created the new 'absolute', centralized monarchies with their powerful standing armies which were to dominate Europe for three hundred years. Many failed, were conquered and absorbed. None of this was yet clear to most Englishmen in 1624; they were committed to the idea that the ancient constitution would answer all their requirements, that victory could be had without compromising liberty.[48]

So Buckingham prepared to go to war against Spain in 1625 with very little money. It was nearly thirty years since England had organized a major overseas expedition. Because of the acute shortage of money, the force took far too long to prepare. Only when the victuals had been provided did the Ordnance Board begin to get money, so that food was consumed or decayed while the ships waited for powder and shot.[49] The fleet of approximately one hundred sail (of which thirteen were the king's and twenty Dutch) finally sailed on 8 October:

> That month and day had been fitter . . . to have sought England after a voyage, winter approaching, than to have put themselves and ships to the fortune of a merciless sea, that yields nothing but boisterous and cruel storms, uncomfortable and long nights, toil and travail to the endless labour of the poor mariners.[50]

The fleet was poorly found in many essentials, and immediately ran into an equinoctial gale. Old, leaky ships overloaded with guns laboured badly. Spars and rigging were rotten; the captain of the *St George* even claimed that his second suit of sails had been worn by the *Triumph* against the Armada in 1588.[51] Of the admirals, Pennington and Sir Henry Palmer were employed elsewhere, Mansell was in disgrace as an opponent of Buckingham, and Monson because his Spanish pension had been discovered. Buckingham initially intended to command in person, but in the event the expedition sailed under the command of Sir Edward Cecil, created Viscount Wimbledon, a professional soldier with many years of service in the Dutch army. Virtually all his senior officers were either soldiers or noblemen with no fighting experience.[52]

Wimbledon himself adopted the position of a detached observer, powerless to influence the course of events.

> I dare say that no Navy, in the most stirring time, so full of wants and defects was ever made more ready at so short a warning, than this, which is the first undertaking fleet after twenty years' peace . . . The time of the year for war should be made in summer, especially at sea; our enemy hath all the intelligence that he can wish and we have spared him a whole summer to fortify against us; we have no rendezvous but must be forced to beat it out at sea (for all our enemies) these long winter nights, where we shall be in danger to lose most of our long boats, and so we lose the best means we have for landing of our men; and, which is worst, the fleet is threatened by storms to be dispersed, so that all of us are not likely to meet again; our men will fall sick through the illness of the weather, being raw men and by nature more sickly, even in summer, than any nation of the world.[53]

As an observer, his comments were shrewd; as a commander-in-chief, 'Viscount Sitstill' (as the seamen called him) lacked all force of character, taking refuge from every difficulty in innumerable councils of war. He did not even issue orders to his ships until captains began to enquire what they were meant be doing. His most original contribution to the expedition was an intelligent attempt to apply the principles of military discipline to naval tactics, which had no practical result since there was no fleet action.[54]

Buckingham's plan was the same as Essex's had been in 1597, to seize and hold a Spanish port as a base from which to mount a blockade. The choice of Cadiz was made at the last moment, and when Cecil's fleet entered the bay he lost his chance of surprise in prolonged consultations, in spite of which the attack was made in complete disorder. The merchantmen refused to fight, most of the king's ships waited for orders, and only Lord Essex and the Dutch showed any initiative. The defenders were able to remove their merchant shipping to safety, and run supplies into the city by galley across the bay. The troops were eventually landed, but without food, 'by reason of the uncertain course which was yet holden touching their victualling and the not delivery and misdelivery of their provisions.' Presently they found some wine, with predictable results: 'the whole army, except only the commanders, was all drunken and in one common confusion, some of them shooting at one another amongst themselves'.[55] They were lucky to re-embark without serious loss.[56]

On the return journey Wimbledon held six councils of war in a fortnight without resolving one issue of importance. Disease spread among the cold and overcrowded ships, and the victuals were now long past their expected life. The meat 'so stinks that I presume hath been the cause of the death and sickness which is amongst us; no dog of Paris [*parrish*] Garden I think will eat it.'[57] The fleet was scattered and several of the ships almost sank. Wimbledon's flagship the *Anne Royal* (rebuilt from the *Ark Royal* of 1587) 'took in so much water as all the mariners were forced to work in water up to their knees.'[58] She barely got into Kinsale on 11 December, with six feet of water in her hold and only fifteen men to a watch left on their feet.[59]

Public opinion blamed Buckingham for the disaster of Cadiz. What was worse for him, it came close on the heels of the Soubise affair which had convinced many that the duke was a secret enemy of Protestantism. Buckingham himself was enraged by Richelieu's failure to fulfil any of the promises to act against Spain and to favour the Huguenots, with which he had bought English assistance, and the Franco-Spanish treaty of February 1626 was the last straw. So far from supporting the war effort, Parliament concentrated on impeachment proceedings against Buckingham: it was constitutionally impossible to blame the new king, and naturally unthinkable to blame themselves, so he was the obvious target of their frustration. His only escape was a victory, but for that money was totally lacking, and there was serious fear of a Spanish invasion, either from Flanders or Spain.[60]

In order to raise money, Sir John Pennington was sent to cruise in the Channel in February, bringing in valuable ships and cargoes worth £50,000. In September, Lord Willoughby brought in some French prizes, further damaging relations with France, and leading to the arrest of the English wine convoy (two hundred sail). For defence against invasion, London was asked to contribute a squadron of twenty ships. After endless complaint and resistance, they finally appeared in October, 'very mean things and such as are not fit for men-of-war, neither in respect of their going or force . . .', as Pennington complained.[61]

> The ships themselves are not capable to do service, for the most of them have ill ordnance and ill conditioned ships and goes basely . . . I think they could not have picked up so many more base ships in the river of Thames. And for men, a great part of them were rogues taken up in the streets, that hath neither clothes nor knows anything.[62]

With these ships Pennington was sent to attack Le Havre. At the same time another squadron under Willoughby put to sea in the hope of intercepting a *flota*, but was scattered by gales in the Bay of Biscay.[63]

By this time relations with France, so recently cemented by the marriage of King Charles I to Henrietta Maria, were sliding rapidly towards war. Richelieu had cheated Buckingham, making him look a fool in the eyes of the world and a traitor in the eyes of Parliament. The rapidly increasing French fleet seemed to be intended

> for the usurping of an absolute or equal dominion with His Majesty upon the British Ocean, to the great prejudice of his Majesty's regality and the ancient inheritance of his imperial crown. [64]

Not everyone was so alarmist,[65] but Buckingham concluded that a pre-emptive strike was essential, before France became too strong. To retrieve his political position, he had to help the Huguenots of La Rochelle, and as there was a real possibility of another Spanish Armada, the fleet had to stay between Spain and England. Thus was born the 1627 expedition. The intention was to cause the overthrow of Richelieu, detach France from alliance with Spain, and satisfy Parliament. Desperate as it was to make war on France as well as Spain, for 'no man that knoweth their estates and ours will conceive that we are equal to either, and much less to both', there seemed to be no alternative.[66]

Though Pennington brought in some more prizes early in 1627, the new expedition was prepared amidst an even more desperate shortage of money than before. Buckingham took command himself, and his energy and private purse did much to complete it. He sailed on 27 June 1627 with one hundred ships, sixty of them transports carrying a total of seven thousand troops. The Huguenots of La Rochelle did not wish to be identified as enemies of the state while there was still a chance of reconciliation with their sovereign, and initially refused to accept Buckingham's help, so instead he landed on the island of Ré, which dominates the approaches to the port, and besieged the citadel of St Martin. By the time the Huguenots had changed their mind, the French royal army (commanded by Richelieu in person) had blocked the mouth of the harbour with a barrage. The siege of St Martin's narrowly failed, and Buckingham was forced to withdraw his troops, losing heavily in a re-embarkation under fire. Buckingham behaved throughout with energy and great gallantry and failed by a narrow margin, but he failed totally. When he returned to England in November, the political and military situation was worse than ever.[67]

So was the situation of the besieged Huguenots in La Rochelle. The duke now bent his energies to organizing a relief fleet under the Earl of Denbigh. Money, food and men were again in acutely short supply. Though France and Spain together were threatening invasion, Parliament refused to vote money. Denbigh arrived in May 1628, but found the blockade tighter than ever, and pushed his attack with more prudence than gallantry.[68] Buckingham, desperate to keep La Rochelle alive while Franco-Spanish relations worsened, laboured to equip another expedition with 'explosion vessels' to destroy the French barricades. Lord Lindsey's fleet arrived on 18 September, but his attack was faintly supported ('our fireships played the beast worse than before') and achieved nothing. It was too late, both for La Rochelle and for Buckingham. He was murdered on 23 August, and the starving city surrendered on 18 October.[69] The last of Denbigh's squadron returned to Portsmouth on 12 November. A fortnight later the triumphant fleet of the Dutch West India Company anchored in Falmouth on their way home with an entire Spanish silver *flota*. Piet Hein had succeeded where Drake had failed.[70]

The privateering war, which in Queen Elizabeth's day had provided the English with so many spectacular successes to set against the failure of great expeditions, was a shadow of its former self. Buckingham, like Nottingham before him, allowed unlimited 'reprisals', and as before privateering rapidly engendered a revival of piracy on a large scale; the Isle of Wight was described as 'another Argier'. At least 737 prizes, possibly as many as a thousand, were taken between 1626 and 1630. Most of them, however, were small and of little value. Three-fifths were French, mostly coasters or fishing boats, one-fifth Spanish or Portuguese, and 15 per cent belonged to neutral or friendly powers which, as always, England could ill afford to alienate.[71] Buckingham cared little for neutral rights, and favoured the piratical activities of his connections; men like Sir John Hippisley, Lieutenant of Dover Castle, whose policy is aptly indicated by the names of his ships, the *Have at All*, *Sweepstake*, *John & Fortune* and *Revenge*.[72] The Lord Admiral of Scotland was also licensing privateers.[73] But the privateers' freedom was more circumscribed than before. Sir Henry Martin, Judge of the High Court of Admiralty, was considerably less pliable than Sir Julius Caesar had been, and rebuffed Buckingham's efforts to influence him.[74] Above all the English suffered more than their enemies from privateering, added to piracy and the slave-raids of the Barbary corsairs.[75] The French, and for the first time the Spaniards, sent out privateers of their own. The Cornishmen complained that 'Egypt was never more infested with caterpillars than the Land's End is with Biscayners.'[76] In fact, though there were Basque privateers at sea, they seldom ventured as far north as the Channel, and only seven English ships in all were taken by privateers from Spanish ports during the war.[77] The real damage was done by the Dunkirkers, which in five years took at least 300 ships, possibly one-fifth of the English merchant fleet.[78]

In this war only the Earl of Warwick played the parts which had once been played by Leicester as a promoter of aggressive Protestantism and Cumberland as a leader of privateering expeditions. Warwick's 1627 Atlantic voyage was mounted on a substantial scale, with a squadron of ten including three large warships, but achieved nothing. He received a royal commission, with powers of martial law and the adjudication of prizes.[79] Much more successful was Sir Kenelm Digby's Mediterranean voyage the following year. Digby was a Catholic courtier, son of one of the executed conspirators of the 1605 Gunpowder Plot, and accounted 'the most accomplished cavalier of his time'. Poet, lover, connoisseur, alchemist and duellist, he was an extravagant figure in public and private life, but his small squadron was considerably better disciplined and handled than Warwick's. He appears to have at least recovered his costs, but the Levant Company paid the price as the Turkish government exacted reprisals for his piracy.[80] Digby's expedition, like its leader, was unique, but Warwick's was part of a long-term policy which continued after the war. Warwick, with a circle of friends and investors, was a patron of colonization and privateering in the Elizabethan mould and, like Leicester, his ideas were strongly coloured by religion. Before the war he had invested in piracy in the East Indies and slaving to Africa and Virginia. In the process he split the Virginia Company and nearly wrecked the East India Company's trade. After the war he and his friends founded the Providence Island Company to establish a privateering base in the Caribbean, where they waged a private war in the name of Protestantism and profit in the true Elizabethan style.[81]

Some may have taken comfort from his activities, but for most Englishmen the wars of 1625–30 were a profoundly depressing experience. So soon after their triumphs over Spain had made England the admiration of Europe, the country had become a laughing-stock. In Queen Elizabeth's time, men concluded, nobility, gentry and merchants,

> did apply themselves much to sea affairs ... but we have no such shipping nor such affection to sea affairs; neither have we such seamen to put in execution, and few that know the right way to perform any royal service.[82]

The self-confidence of a generation before gave way to depression. 'The truth is, more might have been done,' admitted an officer who had been at Cadiz, 'But the action is too great for our abilities, of which I am so much ashamed that I wish I may never live to see my sovereign nor Your Excellency's face again.'[83] In the Navy Royal 'as it is now, there is neither order or command, and it seemeth never hath been before . . .'[84] 'More ignorant captains and officers can hardly be found, and men more careless of his Majesty's honour and profit; there might have been much more done.'[85] In 1627 it was worse: 'Such a rotten, miserable fleet, set out to sea, no man ever saw. Our enemies seeing it may scoff at our nation.'[86] And so they did. By 1630, with Europe embroiled in a general war, England aroused amusement and contempt rather than respect.[87] Well might men say that 'there were now no more Drakes in England, all were hens'.[88]

TWENTY-FIVE

The Inward Cause of All Disorders

Administration 1603–1630

It was obvious to contemporaries that much of what had gone wrong since Queen Elizabeth's day must be in the naval administration. Corruption and inefficiency were already sapping the Navy's operations in the 1590s, and with the coming of peace things rapidly got worse. This was not an aspect of administration which particularly concerned Nottingham, but he was extremely careful to keep all patronage in his own hands and to put his own relations and connections into important posts.

> The Lord Admiral hath drawn into his hands not only the appointments of captains and commanders but of all clerks of the cheque, masters, boatswains, pursers, stewards, cooks, smiths, joiners, carpenters, sail-makers, and all manner of workmen.[1]

All these positions were sold, and all the purchasers looked to recoup their investment: 'without recovery of some part of those means by filching, which they laid out for the purchases at large, they should famish both themselves and their families.'[2] Boatswains paid about £20 for their places, cooks £30, and pursers £100 or more. Robert Hooker bought the pursership of the *Repulse* for £120, and sold it for £120 and a cow.[3]

At the head of the pyramid stood Nottingham's Welsh kinsmen Sir Robert Mansell, Treasurer of the Navy from 1604, and Sir John Trevor the Surveyor. Sir Henry Palmer, Controller of the Navy since 1598, was no match for his more forceful colleagues. Together Mansell and Trevor supplied the Navy with stores at double the prices they had paid for them. Demands and receipts were signed with the quantities left blank. Mansell bought masts and timber from the king's 'Eastland Merchant' Hildebrand Pruson (Trevor's relative by marriage), and sold them on, over-measured and at a higher rate, splitting the profit with Pruson. Pruson supplied ratline at 26s 8d the hundredweight against a usual price of 23s, marline at 32s 8d (usually 20s), twine at 9d a pound (usually 6½d), 30-fathom sounding lines for 3s (instead of 1s 8d), tarred line at 32s 8d the hundredweight (usually 27s), and canvas at 28s a bolt (instead of 26s 6d).[4]

> This gain is not so much loss to the King as that the providers, finding sweetness by it, do ordinarily find means to thrust into the store such quantities as the fleet cannot orderly expend, but that the same are sold again in the country and much of it comes back again to be sold at London.[5]

Money was spent on 'bad and superfluous provisions . . . when for want of necessary materials and monies the ships decayed, the works stood still and men's wages ran on.'[6] Mansell's clerk John Wells, 'the trusty Roger in all these jugglings', erased and altered dates and sums on bills, or tore out inconvenient pages from the imprest book.[7] When injured or wounded men applied to the Chatham Chest, the charitable fund established in 1590 by Drake and Hawkins, Mansell

> falls presently into raging passions and pangs . . . that which should sustain only the poor and impotent and no other, is perverted (by a partial kind of lending) to the support of the rich and sufficient. It is lent by those that have no authority and borrowed by those that have no need . . . hungry officers that care not though the poor souls that have spent their youth or wasted their ability or lost their limbs consume and pine, so as their own turns may be served and their hunger satisfied.[8]

In 1605 Mansell, Trevor and Phineas Pett, the master shipwright at Woolwich, improving on the precedent of the *Truelove* of 1596, together built the *Resistance*. She was built with the king's timber and labour, manned and stored at the king's expense, chartered to the king as a transport supporting the new embassy to Spain, but freighted with a private cargo which was sold together with the king's guns and stores. A 'lucky ship', Pett called her.[9]

The example of Mansell and Trevor was followed by their subordinates. Boatswains cut off the bitter ends of cables, which left the stores ninety fathoms long and returned fifty or sixty fathoms. Worn mooring cables were sold privately instead of being turned into oakum, so that for want of good oakum the ships' caulking fell out. Every sort of ship's stores were sold by the officers in charge of them. Ships' musters were padded with fictitious men, and captains, pursers and victuallers shared the profit.[10]

> Being asked who these six or seven men men were who were always absent as aforesaid, he sayeth that there were four men named though there was no such men in truth. And one Evestead, another who was

> a man but never came aboard, and for the other two there were neither names, nor men.[11]

Captain Thomas Button's ship the *Answer* in 1605 had seventy men aboard for every hundred on her muster. Thirty fictitious men were worth 17s 6d a month in victuals, of which the purser took 4s, Button 6s, and the victuallers 7s 6d. This they thought too little, so the purser was forced to victual for 5½d a day instead of 7½d.[12] Shipbuilders and timber-merchants arranged to 'borrow' boards from the dockyards, 'which they have not restored again, nor meant to restore again until they were called for, which they make account will never be.'[13] In four years, 1605–8, it was reckoned that fraud had consumed £39,094.[14]

All this took no account of new and needless offices, inflated salaries and padded expense accounts. Nottingham's last sea command was to carry the newly wed Prince Frederick and Princess Elizabeth across the Channel in 1613. For this arduous service he allowed himself £4 a day for expenses, in addition to pensions totalling £2,700 a year; he had fought the Spanish Armada in 1588 for £3 6s 8d a day in all. Admittedly, entertaining royalty was expensive, but that did not explain why more money was spent on pilotage for the five ships on this voyage to Flushing (a port well-known to most English seamen) than the whole Navy Royal had spent on pilots in the last five years of the war.[15] Ships which were supposed to be at sea, it was reported,

> now do nothing else but waste the King's cordage with riding out all weathers in the Downs, or else thrust into some harbour where the companies run ashore and scatter, and yet charge his Majesty with wages and victuals as if they were fed and in service: and the captains, receiving not only their large wages upon the sea books but also double and never-heard-of allowances out of the Exchequer, spend all at London, or at home, or elsewhere at their pleasure.[16]

'Every one practiseth to accomplish his own end of profit, not caring how he hath it so he can come by it'.[17]

Much of this fell squarely into the definition of corruption as contemporaries understood it. Forging false receipts and delivery notes for goods never purchased, selling stores and recording them as issues, re-using warrants for issues, under-accounting returns, overcharging for purchases; all these were corruptions, 'damnable and infinite'.[18] But the legal definitions of fraud and embezzlement were extremely narrow. The Controller's oath of office bound him to act 'directly to his Majesty's best advantage, and no way particular to your own profit by his Majesty's loss' – which was as much as to say that he was free to profit wherever he judged that it was no loss to the king.[19] In an age when the sale of office was virtually universal, when salaries fell far behind inflation, and when the crown paid its servants and suppliers partially, tardily, seldom, or not at all, no one doubted that officials must and would profit from their offices.[20] Sir Thomas Button was one of the most shamelessly corrupt of all Jacobean admirals – but in 1625 the crown still owed him £3,615 13s 4d for services done in Queen Elizabeth's reign.[21] Anyone who waited patiently for the crown to pay its debts would have starved. Sir Alan Apsley had to bribe the Lord Treasurer, Lord Suffolk, £600 a year to get his accounts as Surveyor of Marine Victuals paid.[22] This Earl of Suffolk was that excellent Elizabethan admiral Lord Thomas Howard, who presumably would not have accepted that he was damaging the efficiency of the Navy or the welfare of seamen. The difference between a fee and a bribe was very hard to define, and fees were a universal feature of administration. Officials who supported themselves by taking fees from the public, when the king could not afford to pay them properly, in effect increased the king's tax revenue – by a third or even a half, it has been calculated. What was happening in the naval administration in England, moreover, was happening in all administrations everywhere, sometimes to a greater extent.[23]

The expenditure of public money was a matter of politics as much as administration. It was an essential function of royalty that it should be the fount of wealth and honour at which all loyal servants might drink. Mansell and Trevor were clients of Nottingham, to be rewarded for the service he had done in putting James on the throne of England. Those who accused them of corruption sought to take their places, of course, but they also sought to force themselves on the king. To attack his choices was to attack his prerogative – and many of those who attacked corruption in Parliament were the same common lawyers who attacked the royal prerogative courts from motives of professional rivalry as well as constitutional principle.[24]

All this helps to explain the fate of the 1608 royal commission on the management of the Navy. It was mounted at the instigation of yet another Howard, the Earl of Northampton, who had fallen out with his kinsmen and taken up the mantle of 'reformer' as the obvious weapon with which to attack Nottingham and his clients. The commission went about its work thoroughly and took evidence which made very clear the extent of the depredations made by Mansell, Trevor and their followers. It found that Mansell alone had made £12,000 from naval stores and embezzled £1,000 in wages in a single year. But King James was not much interested in naval administration, there was no imminent risk of war, he was habitually extravagant in his spending himself, and he chose to see these sums as examples of his own generosity towards the followers of his son Prince Henry, the Prince of Wales. So Mansell and Trevor were let off with a lecture on the merits of honesty, and continued just as before. In the middle of the enquiry, which was looking in particular at waste and fraud by Phineas Pett in his building of a new great ship, the king went down in person to name her the *Prince Royal*. The symbolism was clear: Nottingham's men were being defended because the attack on them was indirectly an attack on royal authority, on the king's and the prince's right to choose their servants and reward them as they pleased.[25]

Northampton's next effort, in 1613, fared even less well.[26] It was not until 1618, when he was dead and the political landscape had changed, that the cause of naval reform was taken up more effectually. Prince Henry had died in 1612 and a new eminence was rising at court, the king's favourite and Prince Charles's best friend the young Marquess of Buckingham. To achieve real power he needed to displace the Howard connection, and once again the management of the Navy was their vulnerable flank. The moment was auspicious in other ways. James's extravagance had brought on a crisis in the royal finances, and a new minister, Lionel Cranfield, was leading a royal commission to reform and retrench the royal household. With the addition of some naval experts (notably Greville's former deputy John Coke) this commission was reformed to deal with the Navy.[27] What it found only confirmed and amplified what the 1608 commission had reported ten years before: 'very great and intolerable abuses, deceits, frauds, corruptions, negligences, misdemeanours and offences.'[28]

> We find the chief and inward causes of all disorders to be the multitude of officers and poverty of wages, and that the chief officers commit all the trust and business to their inferiors and clerks, whereof some have part of their maintenance from the merchants that deliver in the provision that they are trusted to receive. And these men are governed by the chief officers' verbal directions, which the directors will not give under their hands when it is required. And which of all is the most inconvenient, they are the warrants and vouchers for the issuing of all his Majesty's monies and stores, who are most interested in the greatness of his expense; and therefore the business ever was and is still so carried, that neither due survey is taken of ought that cometh in, nor orderly warrant given for most that goeth out, nor any particular account made nor now possible to be made of any one main work or service that is done.[29]

'The annual charge to decay the Navy' was £53,000, and the results in some cases worse than if no money had been spent at all:

> as that when ships were to be brought up from Woolwich or Deptford to be repaired, it had been better for his Majesty to have given them away at Chatham, and £300 or £400 in money, to any that would have taken them.[30]

The commission went beyond the exposure of misdeeds to recommend future naval policy. Surveying the strength of the Navy as far back as Henry VIII's reign, it proposed a fleet of thirty ships: four 'ships royal' of 900–1,200 tons, fourteen 'great ships' of 600–800 tons, six 'middling ships' of 450 tons, two 'small ships' of 350 tons, and four pinnaces, one of them as large as 250 tons. To achieve this with honest administration would require £30,000 a year for five years, and £20,000 a year thereafter.[31] 'This Navy', as the commission pointed out,

> will contain at least 3,050 tons more than the Navy of Queen Elizabeth when it was greatest and flourished most . . . This Navy and no less will for greatness and state of ships, force of men and munition and all manner of service exceed the navies of all our former kings, and under God's protection be sufficient with the ships of his Majesty's subjects without foreign aid, to encounter the sea forces of any prince or state whatsoever.[32]

The commissioners also argued that the structure of the Navy Board itself had disintegrated. Once each member had had his particular duties:

> the Treasurer for the monies, the Surveyors, one for the ships, another for the victuals; the Clerk of the Navy for the works and provisions and the Controller for all their accounts . . . [now] They have changed their proper ministerial duties into general duties of governors or commissioners-at-large, all interesting themselves in all things of advantage or pre-eminence but none submitting himself to any thing of service or account.[33]

This had all been true in 1608, and indeed long before.[34] The difference this time was that James was ready to accept change, and the commission had the powerful backing of the new favourite. Even so, the king treated the delinquents mildly. Nottingham retired with due honour and was replaced by Buckingham. Mansell was allowed to sell his office (and was next year appointed to command the Algiers expedition), while Sir Richard Bingley and Sir Guildford Slingsby (who had succeeded Trevor and Palmer respectively in 1611) were suspended on full pay. The result of the report was not just their removal, but the replacement of the Navy Board itself by the new commission. Royal commissions were flexible instruments, and there were many standing commissions, hardly distinguishable from committees of the Privy Council, charged with particular tasks. The new Navy Commission, dominated by John Coke, now took over the work of the former Navy Board, in conjunction with the new Treasurer Sir William Russell, a wealthy City merchant and shipowner. His function under the new scheme was essentially to act as the Navy's banker. The new regime, like the old, was symbolized by the naming of two new ships, in this case by Buckingham: the *Happy Entrance* and the *Constant Reformation*.[35]

Happily entered upon its task, the new Commission seems to have had considerable success with its 'constant reformation' of naval administration: 'for the business of the Navy, we follow it daily, where we find all things to succeed better than we could hope.'[36] With the all-important political backing of Buckingham and Cranfield (who became Lord Treasurer in 1621), and the diligence of Coke, 'the soul of the Commission', it made steady progress with its programme. Its success can certainly be judged by the resentment of those whose activities it had curtailed, among them Slingsby, who threatened to murder Coke in 1624 if he were not restored to office. The Commission concentrated shipbuilding at Deptford, where one of its members, William Burrell, was master shipwright, leaving Pett at Woolwich with fewer opportunities to misuse. However some of the Commission's members were not completely free of suspicion of corruption themselves, and its improvements depended heavily on more regular support from the Exchequer than the Nottingham regime had had.[37]

Arguably it was too successful for its own good. As the international situation worsened, and the condition of the Navy improved, Buckingham and King James were tempted to use it. But the improvements which had been wrought in peacetime, with the Navy demobilized, could only be translated into warlike operations with sufficient money, which meant with the support of Parliament.[38] The voyage of Buckingham and Prince Charles to Spain in 1623 cost £20,719, equivalent to a whole year's planned expenditure. To bring Queen Henrietta Maria across the Channel in 1625 cost £35,986.[39] The Cadiz expedition the same year cost half a million pounds, and still sailed unprovided with many essentials.[40] The response of the 1624 Parliament was to provide grants amounting to £300,000 under careful restrictions.[41] The Parliament of 1625 voted £140,000 before hurriedly disbanding to avoid an outbreak of plague. They did not make the customary grant of Tunnage and Poundage for the new king's lifetime, and their willingness to trust

Buckingham and Charles I with larger sums was badly shaken by the disasters of 1625.[42] In 1626 relations between Parliament and ministers broke down altogether, with a Spanish invasion seemingly imminent and Parliament preferring to impeach Buckingham rather than vote any money. Coke informed the Commons that no less than £1,067,221 was required for the war effort, including £313,000 still owed from the Cadiz expedition; but they were prepared to vote less than a quarter of this, on conditions which Charles regarded as unacceptable. Even as the Commons demanded that the Navy protect shipping against piracy, they rejected Tunnage and Poundage, until Charles finally dissolved Parliament.[43]

In 1627 the constitutional crisis deepened as the king resorted to a 'forced loan' of dubious legality, and the financial situation grew yet more desperate. Willoughby's brief voyage in the autumn of 1626 cost £90,382.[44] The expedition to the Île de Ré cost half a million and left a debt of £100,000. In February 1628, with the international situation more threatening still, the government announced an unprecedented national levy to pay for the Navy, but before it could be put into effect it was abandoned. Russell negotiated a loan of £95,000, which temporarily tided the Navy over, and instead Parliament was summoned again.[45] This Parliament offered limited funding in return for the constitutional guarantees embodied in the 'Petition of Right'. When Tunnage and Poundage was again refused in 1629 Charles I felt he had exhausted the possibilities of co-operation with Parliament. For the next eleven years he ruled without it.[46]

By the peace of 1630 five years of war had cost £2,560,000, at least equal to the ordinary revenues of England over that period.[47] It had brought military disaster and prolonged constitutional crisis, which was postponed rather than resolved by abandoning both Parliament and the war. It had cost Buckingham his life, and once again wrecked the naval administration established in 1618. The duke himself, unhappy at the Navy Commission's failure to equip Willoughby's fleet sufficiently to face a winter gale, had instituted another commission of enquiry in 1626. This in turn was abandoned in the crisis of 1627, and the Navy Board was restored in February 1628. Buckingham lived just long enough to regret the move, but not to do anything about it.[48]

The same turmoil and instability marked the Admiralty during the war years. Buckingham presided at the Navy Commission, treating it as an advisory as well as administrative board, much as it had been in its early years.[49] But its, and his, relationship with the Privy Council was not clear, and it became less so with the reconstitution of the Council of War in 1624. This was a Council committee specifically intended to consider wartime policy and grand strategy, but it was also seen by some in the House of Commons as a potential instrument of greater control over the course of the war.[50] Coke (especially sensitive because his old enemy Mansell was a member) warned Buckingham not to allow the Council to usurp his authority:

> I have received a letter written to your Grace by some of the Council of War and therewith certain articles for an exact account to be given of all particulars concerning the Navy. I must first inform you they usurp upon your office and put the King's service out of course ... The duty and trust of the Council of War is to advise the King, only by proposition. As for examination, provision and execution, they are peculiarly yours and every other great officer's in their own orbs. And to this you must reduce them if you will not come under their lee.[51]

In 1626 Buckingham and Coke joined the Council at War, which received wider powers, but in practice it remained an advisory body which disappeared after the war.[52] Further changes followed from the appointment of Sir John Coke (as he now was) as Secretary of State in 1625. He remained the effective head of the Navy Commission, and continued to devote detailed attention to the Navy, acting sometimes as Buckingham's deputy, sometimes as the king's minister.[53]

Buckingham's murder again threw the whole system into confusion. As an interim measure Charles I put the office of Lord Admiral in commission. At the same time, on the advice of Buckingham's secretary Edward Nicholas, and Sir Henry Martin the Judge of the High Court of Admiralty, the judicial and naval functions of the Admiralty were separated. The court was now independent of the new Admiralty Board, and its profits went to the crown. The Board was in effect another Privy Council committee, and explicitly subordinate to the Council. Moreover Charles I was much more interested in his Navy than his father had been, and after Buckingham's death he himself took major decisions, sending his orders by Coke as Secretary of State.[54]

By the peace of 1630 naval administration had passed through three distinct phases since Queen Elizabeth's death: fifteen years of neglect and decay, six years of retrenchment and reform, and a further six of desperate wartime improvisation and deepening crisis. Every part of the naval administration was marked by these changes. In the victualling, for example, Sir Marmaduke Darrell was joined in 1603 by Sir Thomas Bludder, whose ruthless exploitation of the office fills the pages of the 1608 commission's evidence, and who was alleged to have made £9,951 by fraud in the years 1604–8,

39. An English galleon fighting a Spanish galley, bow to bow, from Baptista Boazio's engraving 'The Famous West Indian Voyage,' published to accompany the *Summary and True Discourse* describing the expedition of 1584-5. Since the galleon is flying the Royal Standard, she is presumably Drake's flagship the *Elizabeth Bonaventure*.

40. *Right* Sir Francis Drake by Nicholas Hilliard, painted in 1581 when he was 42.

41. Drake's forces attack Santiago, Cape Verde Islands, in 1585. Some of the squadron are distracting the town batteries while the troops are landed out of sight to the right and march across the mountains to take the town in the rear. In the final scene on the left the English pursue the fleeing enemy. Note the standard Elizabethan infantry regiment in formation, pikemen in the centre surrounded by the 'small shot' with their arquebuses. The striped flags were often used by English troops and ships.

Scale
Cadiz
A. The great and first fort in cadiz
B. The Second fort
C. The Towne gate, ordnance vppon it,
d. The gallies at our comming in
E Caruayles and smal Barkes.
F. Ships. Aragozia. Biscayns. frensh. hulkes, &c.
G. Roaders at pointal
h. a Ship of the Marques of Sta crus
J. Ships and gallies by port Rial
k. gallies to haue stayd the lions passadge that way
3 Admirals { o for the Bonauenter / o for the lyon / o marchant Rial
l. The gallies dreuen back by ye lyon
columbe de serailes
m. The pece that hit ye lion
n. a pece planted for G
Jsla de Cadiz
Sta pedro
Puente de Suaca
puental
las puen
dian
Sta katarina
el puerto de Sta maria
Rio Guadelette
Portal
Puerto Rial
a. The Bonauenter
b. The lyon
c. The marchant Rial
A. the rest of the fleete
At her first Ankor
d. the Bonauenter at her second Ankoring
e. The Bonauenter at her third Ankoring
f. The leon at second Ankoring
G. The rest of the fleet at Second Ankoring
h. the Edward Bonauenter a ground
J. the lion at third Ankoring
M. our fleet at Anker vppon a Brauado
W. Borough
26

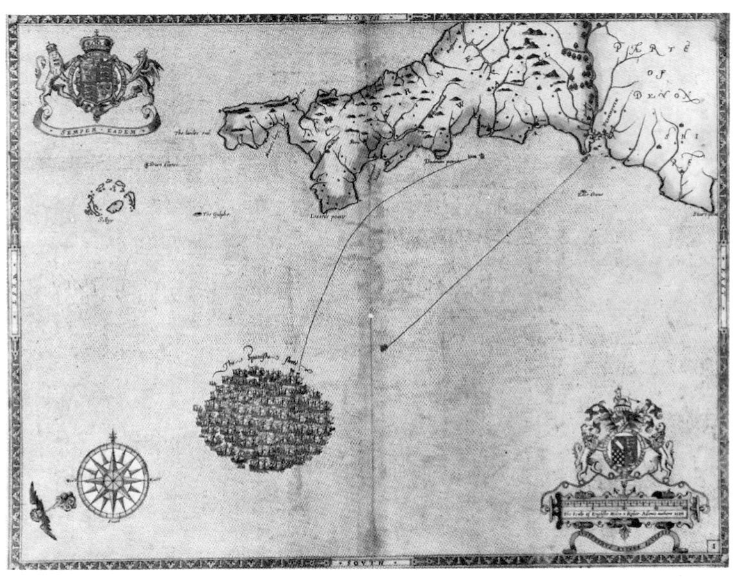

43. The first of the series of charts of the Armada campaign drawn by Augustine Ryther for the Lord Admiral. The Spanish fleet is in the mouth of the Channel; a caravel has been sent ahead to capture a Cornish fishing boat in search of intelligence, while the English pinnace *Golden Hind* runs for Plymouth with news of sighting the enemy.

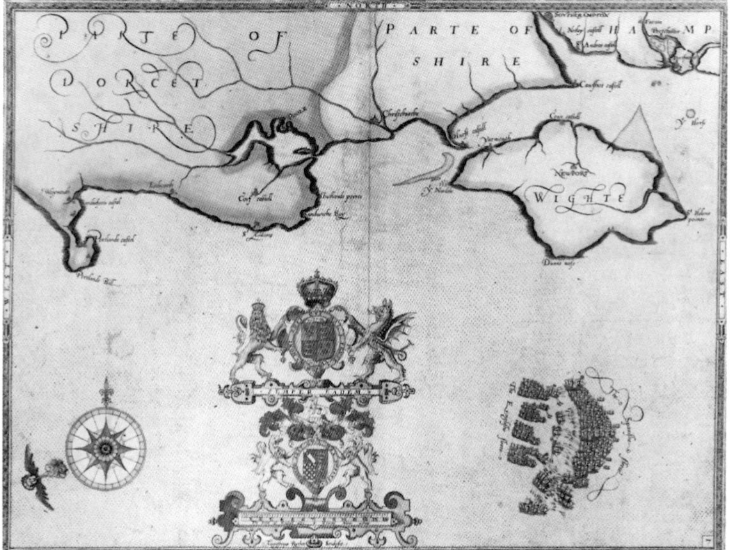

44. *Left* Another of Ryther's charts, showing the action off the Isle of Wight on 23rd July. The English fleet has now been re-organised into four squadrons, but the ships are still attacking individually or in ones and twos, more or less in line abreast.

45. *Below* An eighteenth-century engraving of one of the lost Armada tapestries made for Lord Howard. This shows the first engagement off Plymouth: the Lord Admiral's pinnace the *Disdain* fires the first shot, and the *Ark Royal* bears up astern of her to lead the attack.

42. *Opposite* William Borough's plan of the raid on Cadiz, 1587. His exact knowledge of the shoals, no less than his fluent Spanish and elegant Italic handwriting (very different from the usual English hands of the day), reveal his training as a navigator in the *Casa de Contratación* at Seville.

46. *Above* A scene from Hendrik Vroom's painting of the battle of Gravelines. In the foreground Medina Sidonia's flagship the *San Martín* is attacked by Drake's flagship the *Revenge,* which has already gone about to fire her other broadside, while beyond them is Howard's flagship the *Ark Royal.* Note that the English ships are attacking bows-on in no particular order. The scene is imaginary (for Drake's squadron and Howard's were nowhere near one another at this point), but the tactics are authentic.

47. *Centre* The Battle of Gravelines, with a Spanish galleass in the foreground, as depicted in the the anonymous 'Armada Cartoon'.

48. Another engraving from the Pine series, showing the battle of Gravelines. In the foreground the boats of Howard's squadron are attacking the grounded galleass, while the rest of the Spanish fleet retreats to leeward in the background.

49. *Above* An engraving of the 1602 action against Spinola's galleys.

50. *Right* A miniature of Charles, Lord Howard of Effingham by Nicholas Hilliard, painted in 1605 when he was 69.

51. *Below* A sketch with sailing directions for part of the coast of 'Terra Firma,' the 'Spanish Main' (in this case part of modern Panama). 'This morning when the description noted or taken of this land, being the 28th of January 1595 [1596], being Wednesday in the morning, Sir Francis Drake died of the bloody flux right off the islands de Buena Ventura some 6 leagues at sea, whom now resteth with the Lord'.

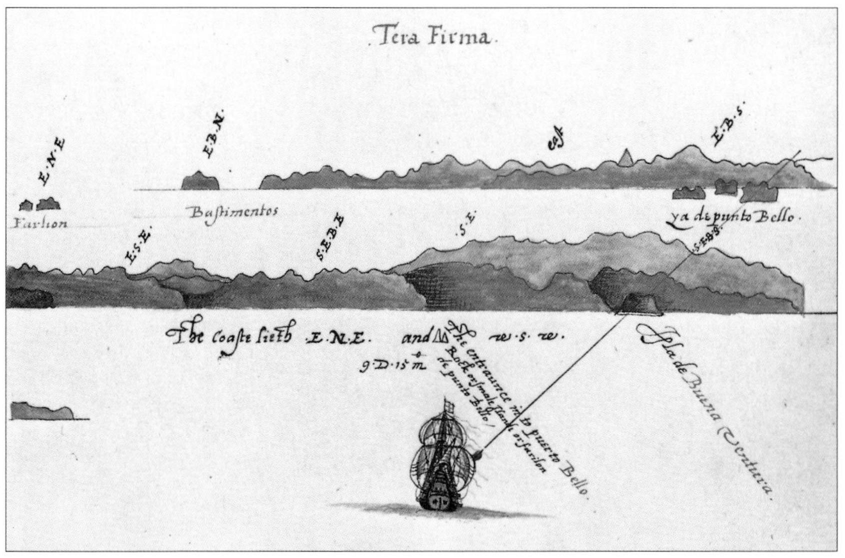

52. *Left* The *Prince Royal* arriving at Flushing in 1613 with the newly-wed Princess Elizabeth and Prince Frederick, painted by Hendrik Vroom. Note the arrangement of the ports, showing the falls in her gundecks.

53. *Below left* Buckingham's 'manifesto,' the *Constant Reformation* of 1619, drawn by the elder Van de Velde in 1648, the year she led the squadron which went over the royalists.

54. *Below* The English squadron entering Portsmouth Harbour in 1623, the *Prince Royal* leading, bringing Prince Charles and Buckingham home from their abortive voyage to Spain. The ships are in their winter rig with topgallants sent down, which gives them a dumpy appearance. The painting is attributed to Hendrik Vroom.

55. Detail of an engraving showing bird's eye views of the stages of the Ile de Ré expedition. In this scene the English fleet is shown landing the troops; the smaller ships are lying inshore providing covering fire.

56. A carving of a wounded seaman, from St. Bartholomew's Hospital.

57. Rainsborough's squadron blockading Sallee, 1637.

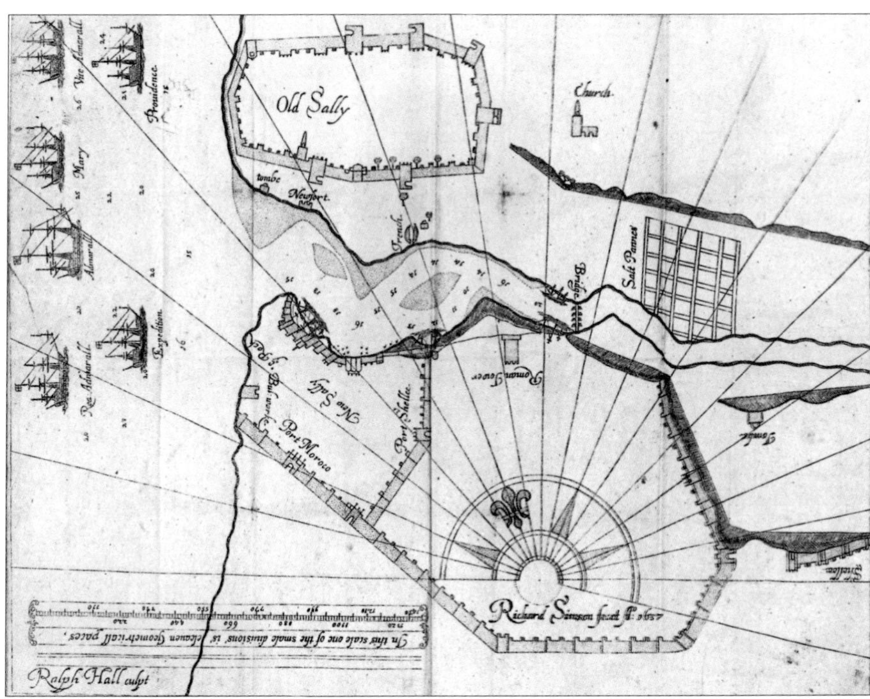

58. 'The true portraiture of his Majesty's royal ship the *Sovereign of the Seas*,' engraved by J. Payne.

59. Gunners loading outboard, sketched by Willem Van de Velde the younger about 1664.

about one-sixth of all victualling expenditure.[55] Pieces of beef which were supposed to weigh 2lbs actually weighed as little as 10 ozs, and 'the beef and pork for the most part is ill-salted and stinketh, and . . . the beer is always put into oil cask (which is always short guage) which is enough to poison any man.'[56] Bludder was replaced in 1613 by Sir Alan Apsley, who remained the active partner in the victualling until 1630, latterly in partnership with Darrell's son Sampson. Apsley and Darrell took over the contract at the new rate of 7½d a man a day in harbour and 8d at sea, in return for which they took the risk of waste or loss, 'except the ships perish by wracks, be taken by the enemy, or fire happen them or the storehouses, which God forbid.'[57] Some of the practical difficulties of his task Apsley explained in 1623:

> I know your Lordship's judgement and experience will believe oxen and porks cannot be bought until the next market day. They must be cooled before they be slaughtered, after that cooled again before they be quartered and weighed, then after that cut out and weighed again into 2lb pieces, then salted and remain a time in standards to drain out the blood, then repacked and returned again into hogsheads, then proportioned and marked forth for each several ship, then laden in carts and delivered into the transporters by the contents of pieces and number. And each of these have a space of days, as the wheat to be bought, ground, bolted, bracked, made in cakes, baked, cooled, culled, bagged, weighed; and after all this fair weather and the tide must be attended in the embarking or all will be corrupt and lost and like in the rest of the provisions.[58]

This was in peacetime, with only a small squadron at sea. In April 1625 Apsley had to victual a major expedition and needed £35–45,000 at once:

> But to prepare the value thereof in divers sorts of lasting sea victuals, that will ask time to provide which can be neither suddenly nor easily performed. And yet if the flesh be not killed and the beer brewed by the middle of next month (which cannot be done without present money), to make any such provisions afterwards will not only hazard the loss of the victuals, and the lives of men, but the overthrow of the whole voyage . . .[59]

In the event he did not get the money in time, beer had to be brewed and meat packed in the warm months, and then the expedition did not sail until its victuals were past their reasonable life.[60] By December Coke was desperate:

> For God's sake (my good lord) let us first see how possibly we can raise money to discharge this unfortunate fleet and army that cometh

> home before there be any debate or mention of increasing more charge.[61]

In 1626 things were yet worse. Sir Henry Palmer commanding the Channel Guard had 'of late suffered more trouble and affliction to keep those men under my charge from dangerous mutinies, for want of victual and clothes, than I have ever been acquainted with'.[62] Pennington begged Buckingham 'to take some speedy course for our supply; otherwise we must be constrained to discharge our men and let the ships ride destitute, for without victuals we cannot keep them.'[63] The 1627 expedition was only victualled at all because Apsley stretched his private credit to the limit; by the end of the year the crown owed him £41,000, and when he died in 1630 it was £100,000, which Charles I refused to repay his heirs on the grounds of incomplete accounts.[64] Such was the common experience of senior officials during the war years. Buckingham died £70,000 in debt, mostly to the crown; he and Sir William Russell between them found £70,000 of their own for the Ré expedition. Captains, admirals, pursers and yard officers paid expenses, sometimes hundreds of pounds, out of their own pockets.[65] In 1629 one ship had 'not any beer but what the captain procureth from day to day where he can get it, and his credit is at the farthest stretch, and want hath put his company into a mutiny.'[66] This was the context of many irregularities which contemporaries (and historians) have been content to classify as simple corruption.

> The boatswains, masters, carpenters, gunners, and the mariners themselves, though they have had no money in ten months, yet they come ashore and want not money to spend in the alehouse; and this they get by no way but stealing of the King's stores of all sorts.[67]

Sir James Bagg, 'Bottomless Bagg' as his enemies called him, was Vice-Admiral of Devon and deputy victualler at Plymouth, in which capacities he was certainly guilty of careless accounting, if not worse; but by 1630 he had spent over £51,000 on the crown's behalf, and was still owed more than half of it.[68] Undoubtedly there were numerous corrupt practices during the war years, but to equate, say, Bagg's conduct with Bludder's, is to confuse what were practically and morally two completely different situations.

The Ordnance Board passed through the same phases as the rest of the naval administration. In the years up to 1618 it well earned a reputation for corruption and inefficiency. In 1618 and again in 1620 it was investigated by commissions of reform, but the good they did was undermined as soon as war broke out by the general shortage of money.[69] Protocol required that the Lord Admiral's warrants to arm ships be directed to the Master-General rather than to the Ordnance officers directly; but in 1625 the seventy-year-old Lord Totnes suffered a stroke, and declared that during his convalescence, 'I mean not to overcharge my spirits with public affairs,' so there were long delays in forwarding letters.[70] Confusion of responsibility did not help: the same year Wimbledon evaded the question of 'how the soldiers and land service might be supplied with powder and shot' (one which an experienced general might have thought relevant to his command), as being the business of Lord Valentia, named Master of Ordnance for the expedition.[71] The Ordnance Board always came last in the queue for what was available, and to add to its difficulties the Master-General, the Lieutenant-General and the Master Gunner all either went to Portsmouth or actually sailed on the 1627 expedition.[72] Nevertheless, the Board's performance in 1627 has been defended in the most recent study.[73]

The dockyards were the largest and most complex parts of the naval administration, and by far the largest industrial establishments in the country. The discipline of timekeeping was by now well established. Chatham in 1603 acquired 'a vane to give certain notice of the wind', and two 'dials of brass to give knowledge of the time of the day'; by the 1630s it had a clock. Something of the yards' administrative sophistication is revealed by the fact that in 1604 Chatham alone spent £22 on paper, ink, wax, sand, quills and counters for the clerks to write and reckon with. This compares with £5 for re-thatching one side of the storehouse, and £4 to Henry Strickland, 'ratkiller, for so much by him laid out in making of banes to destroy vermin in his Majesty's ships and storehouses for the better preserving of the sails and other provisions.'[74] The yards shared fully in the laxity and dishonesty of the first fifteen years of King James's reign. Master shipwrights inflated their costs and diverted timber and materials to their private yards.[75] Pett in particular exploited to the full his position as the favourite shipbuilder of the Nottingham regime. He built the *Prince Royal* out of substandard and unseasoned timber. In 1621, when she was only eleven years old, she was so weak that £500

> will but make her ride afloat and be able to go to sea upon our own coast rather for show than for service, and that to make her a strong and perfect ship will require at least £6,000 charge . . . This we write to your Honour with grief and some just indignation, seeing a ship which so lately cost his Majesty near £20,000, and was boasted to be of force to fight for a kingdom so suddenly perish.[76]

The clerks of the cheque who took the yard musters tolerated widespread absenteeism.[77] The shipwrights' perquisite of 'chips' (offcuts of timber) was extensively abused: 'in their . . . bags of chips they oftentimes carry away bolts of iron, spikes, nails, night-lights etc so as I verily believe £200 or £300 per annum is lost by these abuses.'[78]

There was a particular problem with the 'standing officers' (boatswains, gunners and carpenters) and shipkeepers who were supposed to maintain the ships in reserve. The 1608 commission waxed eloquent about their deficiencies:

> The Navy is for the greatest part manned with aged, impotent, vagrant, lewd and disorderly companions. It is become a ragged regiment of tapsters, tinkers, cobblers, and many common rogues which will never prove good seamen, and yet in respect of their number have in effect the safety of the ships in their power . . . Of these the [Principal] Officers place some as their creatures, being better pleased that they should live upon the King's purse than their own; the clerk of the cheque at Chatham placeth many, some out of his own humour, some to the use of his wife, his men and maids . . . Thus stand the ships in great peril by the base condition and bad qualities of the riff-raff company; the country thereabouts is vexed by their bad rule, and the commonwealth pestered with a swarm of filthy beggars . . .[79]

The standing officers neglected their duty to train the men. The commission proposed 'a present discharge of that rabble of loose people now harboured in them, and intend to prepare for a yearly supply of the ablest young men about the Thames who we would have trained to discharge both great ordnance and muskets and to make sails and cordage,'[80] but it did not work. Of 93 shipkeepers at Chatham interviewed in 1625 by Captain Joshua Downing, not ten 'could say either their belief, the Lord's Prayer or Ten Commandments, nor so much as their compass.'

> I rowed up and down the river from the dock to the barracado and back to Rochester bridge, and found but one boatswain on board, and never a gunner but in the two smaller pinnaces; the watch at the barracado I found drunk aboard of another ship and no watch kept there; and from thence to the bridge a man might have rowed on board all the ships (as I did) and, except three of them, might have gone on board and done what mischief he would without being discovered.[81]

Musters of the Ordinary were only possible at dinner-time, 'for no longer than they are tied by the teeth are they to be kept on board.'[82]

Meanwhile, however, the yards were growing and changing. A great deal of money was being spent on capital improvements. The Deptford Pond was apparently back in use at this period; in 1615 a visiting Icelander was most impressed by the ships in reserve: 'A little way below the city of London, in a closed harbour, within barriers, lay King James's ships of war, huge and majestic', though three years later the Venetian ambassador was more dismissive about the king's ships, 'shut up in a ditch of stagnant water, disarmed and abandoned'.[83] It must have been during James's reign that the Navy began to use dry docks as the ordinary means of cleaning ships' bottoms, which presumably explains the large number which were built. Sir Henry Mainwaring's 'Seaman's Dictionary', written in the early 1620s, defines a dry dock as one 'made with flood gates to keep out the tide, in which we build ships and repair them.'[84] The old dock at Woolwich was 'made double' some time before 1606, lengthened to take two of the biggest ships in 1615, and rebuilt again in 1626. Around 1620 the yard was greatly increased in size, with a large amount of levelling and excavation.[85] At Deptford the dock was enlarged in 1610, a new dock was built in 1620, and another authorized in 1623.[86] Chatham already had at least one dry dock by 1611, when the Master Housecarpenter rebuilt and rehung its gates and constructed a mast pond. In 1618 two docks at Chatham were lengthened and a third constructed. That year a further seventy or eighty acres of land were leased, and between 1619 and 1626 the Navy Commission added a double dock, which admitted its first ship on 4 October 1624, officers' houses, stores and a ropehouse.[87] In 1623 the old great dock at Portsmouth, long disused and evidently poorly situated, was filled up and its mouth rammed with stones 'for the better preserving of the yard against the violence of the sea'. In 1627 a new dry dock and wharf were authorized at Buckingham's urging, but opinions differed on the value of Portsmouth as a naval base, and the dock was apparently not built.[88] It is difficult to disentangle an exact total from the overlapping references to various sorts of dock built and rebuilt, but it looks as though from two true dry docks with gates in 1603, the yards had grown to have as many as three double and three single docks by 1626, a fourfold expansion, almost all the work of the 1618 Navy Commission.

In these and other ways the early Stuart Navy was not merely a decayed and corrupted version of the Elizabethan Navy, but a force attempting to respond to a new threat. Certainly it was under acute strain from human and administrative failings, but it is not sufficient to explain the Navy's weakness simply in moral terms. If every Jacobean administrator had been another John Hawkins, the Navy would still have struggled to adapt to a new and more dangerous strategic situation. More honest naval administration in the years before 1618 would undoubtedly have better prepared for the war years of 1625–30, but the basic problem would have remained, unless the political system had been able to supply an income sufficient to sustain a modern war. Many of the Navy's difficulties were not unique to it, but were symptoms of strains that were falling on government and society in general, in England and abroad. Everywhere there was real corruption, as contemporaries understood it, but it was as much an effect as a cause of administrative crisis. The historian's rhetoric of 'corruption' and 'reform' has obscured many developments which might be equally well thought of as growing pains. The question in 1630 was whether the Navy, and the English constitution, could grow and change fast enough.

TWENTY-SIX

A Diamond in his Crown

Operations and Administration 1630–1639; Ships 1603–1639

At the end of the wars against Spain and France in 1630, Charles I had surmounted a series of political and military crises, but faced a threatening and uncertain future. Parliament was dissolved, but it remained to be discovered if the king could govern without it. Peace had been regained, but a peace with little honour and less security. Prince Frederick was as far away as ever from recovering the Palatinate. The great powers of Europe were deeply embroiled in the Thirty Years War, deploying forces by land which vastly exceeded any army which England might contemplate. The English Navy had thrown away all the reputation it had won in Queen Elizabeth's reign, and there were at least three navies, those of Spain, Algiers and the Netherlands, which certainly outnumbered and possibly outmatched it. The Spanish fleet had very recently been maturing serious plans for invasion, and for a Habsburg Baltic fleet which would cut off the Dutch and English from the source of so much of their wealth and naval strength.[1] Across the Channel France was applying revenues of which Charles could only dream (a naval budget in the 1630s of between 1,500,000 and 4,500,000 *livres*, or £125,000–412,000) to the rapid growth of a fleet which was openly aimed against England.[2] 'Whoever is master of the sea', Richelieu was advised, 'has a great power over the land.'[3] A navy which had effectively not existed in 1625 had thirty-nine ships of 200 tons or more in 1631, against twenty-eight in the English fleet.[4]

In the face of these threats, Charles urgently needed to restore the battered reputation of the English Navy. He could not afford to go to war, but if he was to preserve his independence and neutrality amongst the far wealthier states fighting all around him, he had to make the Navy once more a force to be reckoned with. 'Reputation' was essential to any seventeenth-century monarch, but it was especially vital to Charles I because he had to deter attack without provoking war. 'A monarchy which has lost its reputation,' as a Spanish statesman put it, 'even if it has lost no territory, is a sky without light, a sun without its rays, a body without a soul.'[5]

Charles's weapon for the restoration of his naval reputation was a renewal of English claims to the 'sovereignty of the seas', a title to 'sparkle like a diamond in his crown.'[6] In the form in which it was now stated, this was an almost complete novelty, based on antiquarian fantasy without legal precedent. All English, Scottish or foreign ships were to strike their colours and their topsails to any of the king's ships within the limits of the 'British Seas'. What those limits might be was less than clear.[7] When Monson as Vice-Admiral in 1635 asked for a definition, he was unhelpfully informed by Coke that 'his Majesty's seas are all about his dominions and to the largest extent of [those] seas.'[8] In practice English ships enforced the salute wherever and whenever they could, but especially in the Channel.[9] Even in foreign ports English ships did not scruple to open fire if the salute was refused. 'This summer', reported Captain Richard Plumleigh of the *Antelope* in 1631, 'I was at the Texel in Holland where come in divers Frenchmen, and though the Hollanders bade me domineer at home in England, yet I forebore not to fetch down their flags with my ordnance.'[10] The next year Plumleigh forced French ships in Calais Roads to strike their colours, 'at which they repined heavily'.[11] He took exactly the same attitude in home ports. Ordered by the Landguard Fort outside Harwich to salute,

> I told them that without an order from the Council or the Commissioners of the Admiralty, I durst do no such obeisance; they answered that if I refused they would sink me, and that they had warrant from my lord of Warwick so to do. I slighted that authority and replied that I thought myself as able to beat their paper fort to pieces with my ordnance as they to sink me, and bid them take heed how they made the first shot. Upon this we fell to worse words, and at length to some blows, in which they had nothing the better.[12]

For the moment this arrogant approach provoked nothing worse than resentment abroad, and it was English and Scots ships which most frequently neglected the salute.[13]

Historians have tended to condemn Charles's approach. 'Images attracted Charles I', it has been said, 'reality repelled or bored him.'[14] His great battleship the *Sovereign of the Seas* has been dismissed as a costly irrelevance: 'Charles I was probably always more interested in what she represented than in what she might achieve'.[15] But this contrast between fantasy and reality is not a helpful way of understanding Charles's situation. Deterrence has always been, and is still, a matter of persuasion, of creating an image, and in the seventeenth century gilded magnificence was the image of power.[16] 'Superpowers in any age function much on strategic credit. Their writ, that is, runs much more on the basis of their reputation for effective coercion than on the actual exercise of power.'[17] England was not a superpower, but a reputation for effective coercion was exactly what Charles I needed, and what the assertion of 'sovereignty of the seas' was supposed to achieve.[18] Diplomats were well aware of the impression made by a powerful fleet: 'Although my lord of Lindsey do no more than sail up and down, yet the very setting of our last fleet out to sea is the greatest service that I believe hath been done the king these many years'.[19]

But to set out a fleet required much money, and Charles I was governing without the benefit of parliamentary taxation. To restore the English Navy to an effective deterrent it was essential to find a copious new source of revenue. For thirty years the English government had been looking for a better way to finance the Navy; there had been Queen Elizabeth's abortive ship money scheme of 1603, the 'voluntary' payments for Mansell's Mediterranean expedition, and the 1626 shipping levy to which London contributed so reluctantly and other ports not at all. In 1627 there had been a proposal, abandoned in the face of parliamentary opposition, to finance convoys for the East Coast coal trade with a special levy on the colliers. That year a small Scottish navy was refounded using Scottish revenues, but they proved inadequate to keep it going. Then there was the 1628 project, abandoned at a late stage in favour of another appeal to Parliament. At a local level ports such as Yarmouth and Lynn obtained naval protection for their fishermen by contributing victuals and men.[20] In 1633 the idea of another expedition against the Barbary pirates was floated, but sank in the face of reluctance among shipowners to pay for it.[21]

None of these was a very hopeful precedent to guide Charles's ministers towards a source of the very large sums needed to finance a powerful fleet. Nevertheless there was a long tradition of drawing on the shipping and seaports of the country, directly or indirectly, to finance naval defence, and there were some precedents for extending the obligation to inland parts. Historical research into these precedents, and into the legal basis of English sovereignty of the seas, were combined in the scheme from which Ship Money was born in 1634. It was assessed on the maritime counties, notionally in the form of ships, but with the intention of getting money instead. It yielded £79,586 of the predicted £80,069, in addition to some actual ships furnished by London.[22] So successful was Ship Money that it was decided to extend it in 1635 to the inland counties, and to alter the mechanism of collection, giving local authorities some freedom to arrange the assessment of their own counties. This proved to be a mistake which generated inconsistency, injustice and anger, but the new levy was nevertheless a notable success. By the end of 1636 95 per cent of the sum assessed in 1635 had been paid, with no serious national protest. Ship Money was officially treated as a payment in lieu of service, rather than a tax, and paid directly to the Treasurer of the Navy instead of into the Exchequer (which Nicholas, now Secretary of the Admiralty Board, hoped would in time make the Navy independent of Treasury control). The Ship Money fleet was kept financially distinct from the rest of the Navy. At the same time as Ship Money was extended in 1635, the government issued John Selden's book *Mare Clausum*, a learned defence of the doctrine of sovereignty of the seas in terms of international law. The two were explicitly linked, for the justification of Ship Money was the 'many depredations, violence, and hostile acts committed daily on the Narrow Seas, and even within his Majesty's ports . . . to the dishonour of his Majesty's sovereignty in those seas . . . amd the infinite disturbance and prejudice of trade.' [23] After the success of 1635, Ship Money became a regular annual levy. Between 1634 and 1640 it raised a total of £800,000, compared with only £600,000 from parliamentary taxation in the whole of Charles I's reign. Over 80 per cent of the assessments, and 90 per cent of those up to 1639, were paid within the year.[24]

Ship Money allowed Charles I to put to sea a series of impressive summer fleets. The first, with nineteen of the king's ships and five armed merchantmen, was commanded by Lord Lindsey in 1635. Lindsey's instructions for the first time required him not only to enforce the salute, but to prevent belligerents fighting one another within 'his Majesty's seas', which in practice meant that his ships were to help any vessel which sought their protection from an enemy.[25] The following summer the Earl of Northumberland commanded a larger Ship Money fleet, of twenty-seven king's and three merchant ships, which cruised in the Channel without meeting the French, before proceeding into the North Sea.[26] Northumberland found the experience of a summer's cruise frustrating, and in 1637 it was worse.

> We are extremely idle . . . to ride at this place [the Downs] at anchor a whole summer together without hope of action, to see daily disorders in the fleet and not to have the means to remedy them, and to be in an employment where a man can neither do service to the state, gain honour to himself nor do courtesies for his friends, is a condition that I think nobody will be ambitious of.[27]

But however tedious the admiral found his summer's cruise, the Ship Money fleets were not wasting their time. In 1635 Lindsey had fifteen king's ships of real force; the next year Northumberland had seventeen.[28] Neither the ships nor the fleets of Queen Elizabeth had been so formidable. These fleets were effacing the memory of Cadiz and the Île de Ré, and restoring England's reputation as an ally worth gaining and an enemy worth appeasing.

Charles's new and ambitious legal claims were not merely intended to assert English sovereignty and sea power in an impartial and abstract fashion. His foreign policy, like his father's and for much the same reasons, leaned towards Spain as a counter to the growing power and alliance of France and the Netherlands, and as the only power which could restore the Palatinate to his brother-in-law. Though Charles was chary of entering the war, and at a tactical level was prepared to sell his favours to the highest bidder, it was primarily French and Dutch pretensions against which the Ship Money fleets were directed. A secret Anglo-Spanish treaty of 1634 provided for joint convoys in the Channel, to escort Spanish ships into Flemish ports. Spanish troops and money were landed in West Country ports, transported overland to Dover, and carried across to Dunkirk in English ships, through the Dutch blockade.[29] This being the diplomatic context, Spanish and Dunkirker ships made few difficulties about saluting the English flag, but trouble with the French and Dutch was expected, indeed courted. However it did not immediately come, for the French and Dutch could see quite clearly why, and in whose interest, the English were acting so provocatively. Richelieu ordered French warships to keep out of the way of the Ship Money fleets, while the States-General instructed their officers to yield the salute to the English flag on the explicit understanding that it was a matter of courtesy rather than the acknowledgement of a legal jurisdiction.[30]

Where the Dutch would not yield, however, was on the question of fishing licences. Emboldened by his formidable fleet, Charles decided to employ it in a manner which would effectively demonstrate its power, deter the Dutch, and gain some useful fraction of the vast income which the Dutch drew from the North Sea fisheries, by reviving his father's attempts to charge Dutch fishermen for licences. This was Northumberland's mission in the North Sea in 1636. The result was a limited success: the English fleet arrived late in the season and encountered only a few of the Dutch fishermen, but they successfully issued about two hundred licences. The mutual prudence of Northumberland and Philips van Dorp, the Dutch admiral, avoided any incident. The result was not financially impressive – £501 15s 2d in a mixture of currencies for fishing licences, and £999 in convoy fees from Spanish ships escorted into Dunkirk, to set against the £188,529 4s 10d it had cost to put the fleet to sea – but the precedent was encouraging.[31] For the Dutch, however, it was disastrous, for this was an issue so economically vital to them and so politically sensitive that they could not afford to compromise. Van Dorp was relieved of his command for failing to protect the fishermen against both the Dunkirkers and the English, and in 1637 the fishing fleets were strongly escorted. When an English warship attempted to take licence fees from Dutch fishermen off the coast of Scotland, she was warned off by the Dutch escorts. There were Dutch fishermen, and Dutch statesmen, who would have been prepared to pay for licences if the English fleet had been able and willing to protect them from the Dunkirk privateers in return.[32] Unfortunately the Ship Money fleets, for all their impressive power, were no more able (and much less willing) to protect Dutch shipping against this sort of threat than they were to protect English shipping.

Here lay the source of part of King Charles's domestic difficulties, for while he was building up an impressive, and in the diplomatic world effective fleet, the shipping and fishing of his subjects, especially in the West Country, continued to suffer from the slave raids of the Barbary pirates. In 1625 the 'Turks' took prizes in Plymouth Harbour; the mayor claimed that in a year they had taken a thousand seamen:

> the pitiful lamentations that are made by wives and children ... is so grievous that we know if your lordships heard it as we do, we are assured that it would move the same passion and grief in your noble hearts as it does in us.[33]

The single Cornish fishing village of East Looe lost eighty men in ten days in 1626, and sixty-nine ten years later. The fishermen who survived refused to go to sea in the face of such losses, and it was the same with deep-sea shipping, especially in the vulnerable Newfoundland trade. Between 1631 and 1640 fourteen Cornish ships were brought into Algiers alone (out of eighty-four owned in the county in 1626). Between 1616 and 1642, 350 to 400 English ships and 6,500 to 7,000 prisoners were taken, half of them from the West Country.[34] The average price to redeem a slave was £45, and the English were notoriously reluctant to subscribe to this sort of charity, nor did a proposal to exchange the captives for 'harlots and the idle and lascivious portion of the female sect [*sic*]' meet with any success.[35] The most spectacular of all the slave raids was the attack on Baltimore in 1631, when the Dutch renegade Murat Reis (otherwise Jan Jansz. of Haarlem) took 109 men, women and children.[36]

In the 1630s things became worse as the Moroccan port of Sallee was again active in Atlantic raiding; the Dutch pirate Claes Geritsz. Compaen alone was supposed to have taken over 350 prizes in two years based there.[37] Sallee inspired the only effective measure against Barbary raids undertaken in Charles's reign, the expedition of 1637. This was unique among Charles I's fleets in being commanded by a commoner, Captain William Rainsborough, lately Northumberland's flag-captain and for many years master of ships in the Levant trade. Rainsborough's squadron resembled one of the better-found Elizabethan privateering forces: compact, well-equipped, led and organized by commanders with naval connections but not exactly of the Navy. There were two of the king's ships, two merchant ships, and two specially-built pinnaces of high speed and shallow draught. Rainsborough's vice-admiral Sir George Carteret was a naval gentleman captain who in effect represented the Navy Royal; the others were all men of similar origins to Rainsborough himself. His force was nicely judged: just big enough for the job but not too big to be victualled for a distant operation, with the all-important pinnaces for inshore work which Mansell had lacked. Arriving off the port in March, Rainsborough set up and maintained a tight blockade for five months until the New Town surrendered, freeing 340 English captives. To blockade a port facing onto the open Atlantic for five months was a remarkable feat, but even so Rainsborough could never have succeeded had he not intelligently exploited the political struggle between Old Sallee, the pirate port of New Sallee (the modern Rabat, on the opposite bank of the river), and their mutual overlord the Emperor of Morocco.[38]

Rainsborough's expedition was an almost unqualified success, demonstrating the efficiency of Charles I's Navy, and meeting the demands of the public for naval protection against piracy. Unfortunately for the king, it was too little to offset the general impression of a monarch and his court intent on personal prestige and indifferent to the sufferings of his people. Though the Sallee rovers were eliminated for the moment, the activities of the Algerines more than made up. The Irish Sea was so dangerous that it became acutely difficult to send money to Dublin to pay the King's little squadron there. In 1640 the Algerines took the English ship *Rebecca* with £260,000 in Spanish silver aboard, badly damaging the English reputation as well-armed and reliable carriers in a dangerous world.[39] Many ships were taken in the English Channel and Irish Sea; William Okeley was taken off the Isle of Wight in 1639, and in the following year the Irish clergyman Devereux Spratt was taken crossing from Cork to Bristol.[40] Where the Barbary raids were least felt, on the East Coast, the Dunkirk privateers and the Armada of Flanders were most active. Colliers and fishermen were robbed or seized, even in sight of royal warships. The seas over which Charles I claimed sovereignty were violated by the belligerents on both sides. The Dunkirkers took Dutch fishing boats from their summer bases in the Shetlands, and the Dutch cut out Dunkirk privateers from the Downs.[41]

All this was possible because Charles I's new Ship Money fleets, formidable in themselves and for a time effective as a deterrent, were neither designed nor suitable for the protection of trade. The trend of English naval architecture since the 1590s had been towards larger and more powerful battleships. The big ships of the late Elizabethan fleet aroused numerous complaints, especially in the 1620s. They were of course old by then, but it seems clear that they were also overloaded with heavy guns, especially heavy chase guns which their fine hull lines could not support properly.[42] The natural result was that they worked and pitched badly in a seaway. The *Lion* and others on Mansell's expedition were reported by Hawkins as

> very unfit for these seas being very laboursome and unable to carry out their lower tier of ordnance in any gale of winds ... the *Lion* is weak about the bows and in any foul weather labours much.[43]

Likewise Wimbledon's experience in the *Anne Royal* in 1625 persuaded him that,

> such great ships, and especially the old ones, that are so over-loaden with ordnance, are not for an offensive war, but more fit for a defensive at home; for when she was rolling and working in the Spanish seas in foul weather ... her own burden did her more harm than anything else, and had we not put much of the ordnance into the hold, the ship had sunk in the sea, she proved so leaky.[44]

Another common complaint against them was that 'this ship [the *Anne Royal*] is very unfit by reason her lower deck lieth so low as the water comes in'.[45]

In reaction against these faults, English shipwrights began to build ships with fuller lines underwater, better able to support their weight of armament. Phineas Pett's *Prince Royal* of 55 guns, completed in 1610, was the most impressive symbol of this trend. It has hitherto been something of a mystery how an ill-qualified novice shipwright managed to design this great ship, which carried an unprecedented armament on two full gun decks with a third battery of lighter pieces on the upper deck. We now know, however, that the *Prince Royal* was not an original creation of Pett's, but a more or less exact copy of the *Tre Kroner*, flagship of the Danish fleet which carried Christian IV to London in 1606. The technical credit belongs to David Balfour, the young Scots shipwright who built her. This raises some interesting questions in itself, for Balfour was only twenty-three when he arrived in Denmark in 1597, having left his native St Andrews at an early age to train 'abroad'. Since he used the distinctive English 'whole-moulding' design technique, which was quite unlike the methods used elsewhere, 'abroad' must have been in England, notwithstanding the jealousy with which English shipwrights guarded their secrets from foreigners. To carry the *Tre Kroner*'s great weight of guns, however, Balfour adopted a very different and much fuller hull form, and this was what Pett copied. The older generation of naval architects like Matthew Baker criticized the *Prince Royal*'s full lines. They were right that she would be incapable of the nimble manoeuvres necessary for Elizabethan gunnery tactics, and right too that Pett's dishonest dealings over timber would limit her life, but they failed to see that the fine hull forms of late Elizabethan warships were overloaded with their existing guns, and could not support any growth in armament.[46]

Balfour's achievement was not negligible, as we may see by comparing the *Tre Kroner* and *Prince Royal* with some other early two-deckers, such as the Swedish *Vasa* of 1628, which capsized and sank within half an hour of sailing on her maiden voyage.[47] Similar problems occurred on a smaller scale with the English *Unicorn* of 1633.

> She stooped so much that she laid the upper edge of the ports of her lower tier in the water. But before I put her to it, I caused all my ordnance to be hauled in, and the ports to be caulked up, otherwise we had sunk downright . . . the poor man that built her (who is now much dejected) hath performed his work very well, for she is as well contrived as a ship may be, only she wants two or three foot of breadth, which he sayeth was none of his fault, for the dimensions were delivered him, and he gave her twenty inches more than he had order for.[48]

The design had been certified by Trinity House and the Shipwrights' Company, which did nothing to improve the reputation of professional seamen at Charles's court.[49] The *Unicorn*'s problem was, however, treatable: the most serious weakness of the new generation of English warships was that they still did not carry their lower deck of guns high enough out of the water to be usable in a seaway. The *Happy Entrance* and *Constant Reformation* of 1618, 'have their lowest ordnance laid so low that they are altogether un-useful at sea; so they are but half ships';[50] with three months' provisions stowed, the *Charles* of 1633 carried her midships ports only 3ft 2in above the waterline.[51]

Nevertheless the techniques of naval architecture continued to advance rapidly. Plans on paper were now standard: Coke instructed the master shipwrights that 'before any ship be new built they are to give unto the

Officers a plot of the ship, containing the length, breadth and depth of the ship, which is to be delivered unto the Lord Admiral by the Principal Officers.'[52] Dockyard officers were involved in developing the new logarithms, which allowed mathematical techniques to save the errors (and waste of timber) consequent on geometrical scaling-up from small plans.[53] It was now possible (though not at all common) to calculate displacement.[54] The standard ship rig of all large warships continued to develop. Abolishing the bonaventure mizzen simplified handling, while the spritsail topsail forward and the mizzen topsail aft added canvas to manoeuvre the ship more easily, and the general adoption of topgallants above the topsails gave more power to drive her.[55]

By far the most obvious difference to the landman between the big ships of the sixteenth century and those of the seventeenth was their decoration. The carved and gilded embellishment of late Elizabethan men-of-war was carried much further in the big ships which embodied royal grandeur in its most impressive form. The *Prince Royal* was the first to be heavily gilt; her carving cost £441, painting and gilding at least £868 more.[56] It was no doubt because of her status as a symbol of majesty that Charles I insisted on rebuilding her (at a cost of £17,450) when the Navy Board wanted to scrap her and build afresh.[57] In magnificence and size, however, she was far surpassed by the remarkable *Sovereign of the Seas* of 1637. This ship, also built by Pett, carried 100 guns and was the first true three-decker. Ignoring Trinity House's expert opinion that 'the art or wit of man cannot build a ship fit for service with three tier of ordnance', Charles I personally ordered that she carry 102 guns instead of the 90 Pett had planned. He also ordered that she be armed throughout with bronze pieces, each with the royal arms cast and chased.[58] Then and for at least twenty years after, she was easily the most powerful ship in the world. (Her nearest rival, the French *Couronne*, was slightly bigger but carried only 88 guns.)[59] Contemporaries were deeply impressed by her, and when she went into action for the first time during the First Dutch War, her fighting power was just as devastating as her appearance. The 'golden devil', the Dutch called her, for she was entirely black and gold, with no colour at all. From the royal arms on the taffrail to the figurehead of King Edgar trampling seven kings, she was covered with an elaborate programme of carvings mixing classical, heraldic, mythological and historical themes all emphasizing Charles's sovereignty of the seas. She cost the staggering sum of £65,586 16s 9½d; the carving and gilding alone, at £6,691, was equal to the normal hull cost of a two-decker.[60] 'A glorious vessel of burden, defense and rich ornament, doubtless one of the most admirable naval fabrics that ever spread cloth before the wind', John Evelyn called her.[61] The English traveller Peter Mundy described

> Her head, waist, quarter and stern so largely enriched with carved work overlaid with gold that it appears most glorious even from afar, especially her spacious lofty stately stern, wheron is expressed all that art and cost can do in carving and gilding.

Having seen the wonders of many lands, Mundy thought there were three things in which the English excelled every nation: the *Sovereign of the Seas*, St Paul's Cathedral and 'our sweet and artificial ringing of tuneable bells'.[62]

The *Sovereign* could not have carried so many guns but for continued advances in English gunfounding and gun design. Although she was armed in bronze for reasons of prestige, by the 1630s the Ordnance Board's Master Gunfounder William Brown claimed to be able to cast iron guns lighter than bronze to stand double proof. At the same time Thomas Pitt, head of another famous gunfounding family, was reducing the weight of bronze guns: in 1626 he claimed to have brought down the weight of a full 'cannon of seven' from 7,000lbs to 4,100; a demi-cannon from 5,300lbs to 3,300; and a culverin from 3,800lbs to 2,200. Unfortunately for him, bronze guns still cost at least four times as much as iron and demand for them was naturally weak.[63] The reduced weight of guns was partly a matter of improved casting techniques and partly of better design, eliminating unnecessary length to give shorter guns which were more easily handled. At the same time charges were reduced, giving lower muzzle velocity and in part reproducing the smashing effect of stone shot (now almost vanished from English service), where Elizabethan guns had often shot straight through the enemy, leaving only a small hole which could easily be plugged. The *Sovereign* was entirely armed with these short, light guns, called 'drakes', and could not possibly have carried so many guns of the older and heavier patterns. Being lighter, they must have recoiled more violently (for a given charge), and being shorter, they could more easily be run inboard, so it seems probable that recoil firing on the broadside became general by the 1630s if it had not already been adopted.[64] For the same reason the 'traversing' of guns must have fallen out of use. It is also clear now, and was perceived then, that big ships with the great majority of their guns on the broadside could not possibly be fought in the Elizabethan style, firing off the whole armament in turn before withdrawing to reload. How they should be handled was still to be discovered.[65]

While the English were advancing in the design of battleships (to adopt a term for which there was no contemporary English equivalent), others took the lead with smaller and faster vessels. It is not certain exactly where and when the small galley-type known as a frigate was first adapted to carry square rig, but the English several times during the 1590s encountered such vessels. Richard Hawkins vainly chased one in 1593: 'she was long and snug, and spread a large clew.'[66] In 1599 a Spanish frigate was reported from Dover,

> of so fine a shape, and having 30 oars in her, that she is so swift of sail as that she can hardly be overtaken by any of our ships, considering how she always new talloweth and trimmeth herself the tide before she purposeth to go out to the sea, and the Queen's ships are commonly very green and foul . . .[67]

However it was certainly at Dunkirk in the early years of the seventeenth century that the new frigates first became well known.[68] Very long, with fine shallow hulls and a great spread of sail (including such novelties as studding sails), they carried a light armament mostly amidships. Though poor sea-boats, and lightly built with short working lives, they were by a large margin faster and more weatherly than any English ship.[69] They were soon adopted by cruisers, privateers and pirates everywhere, so that English captains reported in the 1620s that Dutch ships literally ran rings round them.[70]

It was obvious that the English would have to build similar vessels if they wanted to compete, but in practice other priorities and financial crises intervened. Four fast but very small pinnaces were built in 1626.[71] In February 1628 Buckingham ordered the building of ten fast pinnaces to catch the Dunkirkers.[72] These became the ten *Lion's Whelps*, which have some claim to be the first English ships ever 'built to a class'. They enjoyed some initial success, but were never as fast as frigates, and were soon overloaded with guns.[73] Their inability to stow much provisions made them unsuitable for cruising; 'for they spend as they take in victuals and consequently are obliged to hang about the port's mouth for fear of starving.'[74] Nevertheless they were for ten years the Navy's only small cruising warships, and were heavily used for all their deficiencies. They were sometimes disguised as merchantmen in the hope of entrapping the frigates which they could not catch.[75] After Buckingham's death the problem of frigates was neglected. The capture of the Flushing pirate *Swan* in 1635 revived some interest and led to the building by Pett of the *Greyhound* and *Roebuck*, but in the usual English style they proved to be strongly-built, well-armed, but slow. Other frigates were occasionally captured, but the only successful English designs were the two pinnaces of Rainsborough's Sallee expedition.[76] They showed that English builders could produce fast ships, if only the Navy called for them. Unfortunately the priorities of Charles I's Navy were elsewhere.

The ten years from the peace of 1630, the years of Charles I's 'personal government', were for the Navy a period of reconstruction and growth. Though money was never plentiful, the devastating financial crises of the war years were over. Ship Money paid only for the actual operations of the summer fleets, and for the two pinnaces built for the Sallee expedition. All other shipbuilding (including the *Sovereign*), the dockyards, routine maintenance and the Ordnance Board were still paid for by the Exchequer out of the crown's general income (£620,000 in 1635).[77]

The Admiralty Board which succeeded Buckingham continued for ten years to be responsible for the Navy, and worked to improve its administration. Charles I, who took a close interest in his Navy, decided to retain the Board after visiting the dockyards in 1631 and judging that they had been sufficiently reformed.[78] It was replaced in 1638 when the Earl of Northumberland was appointed Lord High Admiral during the infancy of the king's younger son Prince James, who was named Lord Admiral for his lifetime.[79] Northumberland may have been installed as a result of complaints he had made in 1636 about aspects of naval administration, leading to a commission of enquiry.[80] The Navy Board, as restored in 1628, was weakened by a quarrel over precedence between the Surveyor Sir Thomas Aylesbury and his colleagues the Treasurer and the Controller, Aylesbury claiming to preside at the Board (although the Surveyor normally ranked third) because Russell was a junior baronet, and Slingsby only a knight bachelor. However Slingsby died and Aylesbury was bought out in 1632, the corrupt Treasurer Sir Sackville Crowe was pressured into resigning, and the Admiralty was able to appoint a number of able and reasonably honest men to the Navy Board, including Kenrick Edisbury, as Surveyor, and Sir Kenelm Digby, appointed 1630 in effect as Coke's representative on the Navy Board.[81] Sir William Russell as Treasurer of the Navy 1618–27 and 1629–42 took poundage, as Hawkins had done, and like Hawkins extended his own credit, sometimes as much as £50,000, to cover the shortfalls of the Exchequer. He was well rewarded for bearing high costs and risks.[82] The Surveyors of Marine Victuals continued to act as contractors, likewise carrying the risks themselves. Sir Sampson Darrell suffered from poor harvests and consequent high prices, but died in 1635 in debt to the crown. His successor John Crane, another official of the royal household, was heavily in debt by 1640 and was never repaid at least £3,825.[83] At least one knowledgeable visitor to Chatham dockyard in the 1630s was impressed by the good order of the stores:

> Everything is admirably organised, so that all the requisite apparatus is always in readiness, carefully guarded and deposited . . . divided into several compartments, each one containing everything necessary for arming a ship. The arms or device of the name of each ship is placed on the door of these apartements, and thus distinguishes what belongs to them.[84]

These examples suggest that the quality of naval administration had greatly improved since James I's reign, but it must not be thought that all officials were suddenly incorruptible and disinterested.[85] Sir Sackville Crowe, Treasurer for two years 1627–9 when Russell was apparently ill, took poundage and gave nothing in return. On the contrary, he 'borrowed' £3,005 from the Chatham Chest and never repaid it, in spite of being sued for the money.[86] As before, officials' wages were often long in arrears. The master shipwright Henry Goddard, for example, in 1641 had been paid only up to 1635, which made it difficult to take a strict view of his misdemeanours.[87]

> What is the reason that in thirteen years' experience of the Navy I never knew any man suffer as an officer for any kind of delinquency in his place, though he hath been convicted of direct stealths, burglaries etc? – but only the discretion of the Officers, or rather their charity, in smothering those offences with sharp reproofs and admonitions only, because they knew they could not live without them by the King's pay.[88]

Shipkeepers were as always the subject of colourful complaints. In 1634 Edisbury reported that

> now the whole Navy almost consists of masters and servants, for of 330 men borne on the harbour there are but 42 men that are properly termed the King's own men and most of them old and married, not very apt for employment at sea, because of the long time they have wrought in the yard, which I confess is as beneficial for his Majesty, but those whom they now usually take to be their servants are for the most part raw youths which they hire for small wages for their particular profit.[89]

In 1639 another naval administrator described them as

> altogether ignorant of that kind of labour, being some gardners, tailors, glovers, coachmen, smiths etc., or incapable of labour of all kinds, being either old serving-men, decayed citizens, alehouse-keepers, horse-grooms, or at least servants to servants that serve the King's servants.[90]

It was the same story in 1640: 'His Majesty's ships have been made receptacles for aged and decrepit persons or else for persons of all callings that have had broken and decayed fortunes'.[91] The Ordnance Office was described as a 'very chaos' in 1630, and in 1639 it was claimed that 'the accountant nor other officers keep no books, and the ancient officers and clerks are adverse to all new propositions which meet their inveterate frauds and defects.'[92]

All this shows that English naval administration had not escaped the normal limitations of public life in the seventeenth century, but it does not explain the crisis which was about to unfold. The standard of administration was slowly improving. Naval finance seemed at last to be on a sound long-term footing. Some delays, but no more, were caused in 1638 by the famous lawsuit brought against the legality of Ship Money by John Hampden, and won by the crown only by a narrow margin and a good deal of pressure on the court.[93] More worrying for the future was the fact that Hampden was not an isolated individual, but put up by the Earl of Warwick and his associates of the Providence Island Company, of which he was a director.[94]

The real fragility of Charles I's Navy, and his regime, lay in the unresolved issues exposed by the wars of the 1620s. The world around Britain was becoming daily more threatening, and the threats called for a naval response – or rather, they called for two different naval responses; and herein lay the problem. The king and his ministers had built up a powerful fleet in response to a genuine and unavoidable need to deter aggression and defend the country. But they had largely failed to build the sort of Navy which a growing sector of public opinion demanded, a Navy of cruisers and escorts to defend shipping, fishermen and coast-dwellers everywhere; also a Navy which might have been capable of asserting the sovereignty of the seas and collecting fishing licences. Buckingham, and perhaps only he, had tried to provide for such a force, but it is doubtful if money could have been found for it even if war had not swept away all his plans.[95] Though in principle most men active in public life accepted the need for a strong English Navy, and already regarded it as being in some sense the true and natural expression of English warlike endeavour, there was no agreement at all on what sort of Navy was required. Though neither side in this debate was clearly aware of it, both were in fact arguing for something new, a replacement for the old Elizabethan hybrid seapower. The king wanted a powerful fleet as an instrument of deterrence and influence abroad, and not least as a symbol of his own majesty. In the face of major fleets in neighbouring waters which had not existed thirty years before, something much stronger than Queen Elizabeth's Navy was essential. His enemies were inclined to regard this fleet as an expensive personal indulgence. They wanted a Navy to do what no English Navy had done before, at least without payment; to protect the shipping of private citizens. The one was a navy for foreign policy, the other a navy for domestic politics.[96]

There was no money, even in peacetime, to build both fleets. What was worse, there was no constitutionally proper or politically acceptable mechanism by which to raise enough money to put any fleet whatever on a war footing. In a Europe in which the staggering cost of the 'military revolution' was rapidly sorting nations into the few fitted to survive because they had developed efficient taxation systems, and the many doomed to disappear because they could not cope with modern war, England was one of the failures.[97] Her only hope was to avoid being drawn into the general European war, and in this Charles's fleet was successful up to 1639. How long the Navy could have continued to deter foreigners after the humiliations of that autumn is an open question, but before it could be answered the Navy and the country were facing civil war.

TWENTY-SEVEN

One and All

Social History 1603–1639

English warships of the Elizabethan era were predominantly officered and manned by experts. Though the prestige of the war at sea (and the chance of making a fortune) attracted gentlemen and even noblemen, they understood the need of skill in this most complex and least forgiving of all professions. With limited exceptions in 1588 and at Cadiz in 1596, there were very few serving at sea who were not fairly experienced either as seamen or soldiers. With the coming of peace this began to change. The Navy of James I was a great institution of the state and a great opportunity for personal profit, with which many were anxious to be connected, and in peacetime the question of professional abilities was more or less dormant. The old queen had never had more than three admirals at once; by 1617 there were three admirals and four vice-admirals in commission, one for each ship then at sea.[1] Not that they were at sea:

> These admirals and vice-admirals with their 20 shillings and 10s per diem, together with the allowance of their retinue and other advantages are raised to a condition that enables them to live so contentedly at land that they cannot brook the seas and therefore they begin to get captains under them in their ships to govern their companies as lieutenants in their absence . . . Every ship in a while will have an admiral on shore and a captain at sea.[2]

Contemporaries were sure that many gentlemen became captains purely to make money: 'being for the most part poor gentlemen, [they] did mend their fortunes by combinings with the pursers for weekly or monthly allowances.'[3] Inexperienced when present aboard their ships, these gentleman officers were frequently absent:

> His Majesty's ships are very often so ill manned that they might be made ready prizes to any pirate or other that durst assail them; but the true cause hereof is not this limitation of the men, but that the captains and commanders do almost never come on board, which is a disorder

> that no state but ours would endure, nor did ours in former times.[4]

The result was that at the outbreak of war with Spain in 1624, there was an acute shortage of good officers. Few of the Elizabethan admirals and captains were still available to serve; on the 1623 voyage to Spain Sir Henry Mainwaring went as flag-captain to guide Lord Rutland, but in 1625 many of the captains were as incompetent as the admirals.[5] The flagship nearly lost her mainmast because her shrouds were not set up taut, two heavy guns broke adrift in a gale, and on the return voyage they had trouble making a landfall on the English coast because no one had thought to send lookouts aloft.[6] The fleet was divided into no fewer than five divisions, each with a full complement of flag officers:[7]

> I never heard nor saw in my life that any fleet was divided into more then three squadrons save only this . . . these five divisions were rather invented to give content to such as could not endure to live without the title of admiralship, than in any respect to good order or conveniency.[8]

These flag officers passed their time in quarrelling over precedence. Lords Cromwell and Valentia, both vice-admirals, argued that as Irish viscounts they took precedence over Rear-Admiral Lord Delaware as an English baron. Delaware disagreed, because he was senior to Cromwell in the English baronage, and 'this was an English and not an Irish action, and the colours contended for the flag of St. George and not of St. Patrick'. Wimbledon was incapable either of making up his mind or of imposing his authority, so the issue was never settled, and the fleet returned with different admirals flying the same flag and disputing each other's orders.[9]

Although he complained about the disobedience of his captains, Wimbledon did nothing about it.[10] When Valentia, who had no sea experience, tried to give orders to the master of his flagship, John Grant, he refused, 'telling his Lordship in direct terms that the ship was in the master's charge and not in his Lordship's, and that therefore he would not hoist sail when his Lordship commanded.' Raleigh Gilbert the flag-captain, one of the few professional seamen commanding a ship, supported his master. Wimbledon as usual evaded a decision, suggesting that a nobleman be regarded as 'chief commander' of his ship, but give orders sparingly: 'But this he did not by way of order or resolution of the Council but only by delivery of his own opinion.'[11]

Wimbledon was ineffably feeble, but this was a genuinely difficult issue which might have puzzled the most masterful character, for no concept of permanent military rank existed and it was not obvious how to reconcile ordinary social rank with the practical necessity of professional skill. On land it was still possible to proceed on the traditional assumption that the hereditary military virtues of the nobility were the first (if not the only) qualification for command, but only the utterly inexperienced believed that idea would work at sea. The more the sea service rose in prestige and attracted men of high birth, the more difficult it became to find an acceptable basis of authority. Both Raleigh in 1617 and Wimbledon in 1625, assuming a gentleman-captain of limited experience, attempted to follow the Spanish system of limiting the master's authority to the seamen, and the captain's to the soldiers.[12] This of course evaded the crucial question of who was in command of the ship. 'These latter times have advanced captains who only take upon them that name, holding it a maxim that they need not experience but refer themselves to the direction of a master.'[13] The consequence was both practical confusion and social tension, as seamen in general and masters in particular resented the presence of ignorant gentlemen put over them.

This was a problem generated by social change and not specific to the Navy; the same thing occurred in privateers like Warwick's *Hector*.[14] Abroad, other navies faced the same difficulty. Richelieu could not decide whether he wanted 'persons of quality' to go to sea, or whether he preferred 'coarse bold mariners, bred to the sea and the bottle.'[15] The Dutch squadron in 1625 was commanded by the nephew of the Dutch Captain-General Prince Frederick Henry of Nassau, a young nobleman with some military experience who had never been to sea. His vice-admiral was the former governor of the Dutch East Indies (and brother of the secretary of the Amsterdam Admiralty), a diplomat, poet, scholar, scientist, linguist and theologian of eminence. The rear-admiral was an experienced sea-captain.[16] All three brought qualities and experience to high command which the age, with some reason, regarded as valuable. The difficulty, in the absence of any professional sea service, was to combine them in one person.

The new generation of amateur gentleman officers was even more ruthless than the old in their exploitation of their position. Wimbledon was appalled by their greed and incompetence:

> More ignorant captains and officers can hardly be found, and men more careless of his Majesty's honour and profit, as if they were rather enemies then servants, studying their own ease and commodity more than anything else, which had they not done there might have been much more done; and officers are so set upon cozenage and thievery that they rather combine with the mariners then correct them, their own faults are so great and the cause of all.[17]

His captains ignored all orders not to pilfer prizes; 'a thing of such custom at sea, that without more wages, and a more particular oath of true service, I cannot see how it will be remedied.'[18]

The principal sufferers from ignorant and dishonest officers were the common seamen. When many names on the books were fictitious, the remainder had to do the work of two or three men each. On board Button's *Adventure*, 'it was a great discouragement to those few sufficient men that laboured in the said ship, that so great work lay upon so few men's hands, which made some of them (through the extremity of weariness) to leave the ship and run away and lose their wages.'[19] In the *Bonaventure* in 1623 there were only seventy working men out of a complement of 160, and 'when they are at the best there is not 20 helm men and but three that can heave a lead', besides which many were sick, and some 'as mad as any in Bedlam'.[20]

The natural result was that recruitment was difficult. 'That which we find most difficult in this service,' it was reported from Devon in 1618,

> is the taking up of seafaring men, who are both infinitely decayed in these parts for want of employment and wonderful loath to enter into his Majesty's service, for that they fear to be long detained in these employments, and doubt they shall be forced willingly to leave the service without their pay at the last, to the loss both of their time and means, whereby those that are married men and have families are brought to great distresses and poverty, the which makes as many as hears of any press either to fly the country or to hazard the course of justice.[21]

Impressment remained the normal method of recruiting for the Navy, and in spite of the difficulties of the 1590s, contemporaries still did not expect that seamen would refuse to enter. Pressed men were still normally told to make their own way to port, and given a shilling 'prest money' (as an 'imprest', or advance on wages, hence they were properly 'imprest' rather than 'impressed' men).[22] Naturally not all impressed men appeared at their destination; in 1628 it was reported that one-sixth had gone missing.[23] The Navy Board's lavish distribution of protections from impressment created further difficulties.[24] Only occasionally were men impressed at sea, particularly but not only Englishmen in foreign ships.[25] To the disgust of sea officers, watermen (whose seamanlike skill went no further than rowing) were heavily drawn on.[26]In 1627 it was suggested that 15–20 per cent of a ship's company might be made up of landmen, to 'serve for musketeers in their first voyage and help to do all heavy labour upon the decks', but this novel idea was not adopted.[27] Contemporary references to 'landmen' usually mean soldiers:

Wimbledon expected that they be taught 'the names and places of the ropes, that they may assist the sailors in their labours upon the decks, though they cannot go up to the tops and yards,' but the experience of at least one captain was that they were so seasick that they had to be beaten to work in an emergency.[28]

Recruiting had to be done during the winter, 'for if seamen be not taken at the beginning of March, by the middle thereof they are gone upon their voyages, and all England will not be able to furnish so many men as will man his Majesty's ships.'[29] Impressment was carried out by press-masters who were usually former warrant or petty officers, and in some cases by the vice-admirals of the maritime counties (each of whom was given a quota by the Privy Council).[30] Otherwise captains sent their own officers out to recruit, or at least to apply to the local authorities. Sir John Pennington in 1627,

> presently sent my lieutenant and master away to Dartmouth to get me what men they could . . . they returned from Dartmouth but brought me never a man, notwithstanding I had formerly sent warrants to Sir John Drake, Vice-Admiral of Devon, as also to the Mayor of Dartmouth for the pressing 160 men for us, but their answer is they can find none. But I know there be men and good men, which do absent themselves and [are] winked at.[31]

The next year Captain Philip Hill of the *Fellowship* had the same experience in another part of Devon.

> We repaired to Stonehouse on the 16th March last past and demanded the aid of the High Constable of that hundred, who was denied to be at home, but we had notice of the contrary, and by importunity spake with him, who told us he had friends to supper and could not assist us . . .[32]

For obvious reasons Kent tended to be the first to be called on for men: 'Those who do often attend the Navy do abide at Rochester, Chatham, or near thereabouts, and his Majesty expecteth not that others, who dwell further off, should look for the freedom of being exempted.'[33] Next was the West Country, from which the 1625 fleet was largely manned[34] – and not well manned, if we are to believe the complaints of the officers. In the *Lion* Sir Francis Stewart,

> found men enough aboard her, but most of them such as . . . there could not be picked 40 good men amongst them all that know how to find or handle a rope aright . . . some of them tailors, some shoemakers,

> weavers, combers of wool, blacksmiths, turners, tinkers, husbandmen and the like.[35]

Press-masters had a uniformly bad reputation for taking up 'loose, unskilful and base people', some of which was undoubtedly deserved.[36]

> Those peoples knows not whom they press, nor where their dwellings are, nor indeed whether they be sea or land men, but they take up a rabble of poor rogues of all occupations, that knows nothing when they come aboard, and that hath neither clothes to shift themselves, or bodies or minds to perform the service. And if they meet with any able men that have money to give them, those are dismissed.[37]

It was proverbial that 'the mustermasters do carry away the best and ablest men in their purses.'[38] William Rainsborough, pressing in Dorset in 1625, 'made them serve, and I was extraordinarily railed at because I would not clear men for money.'[39] In their defence it must be said that the press-masters had few legal and practical powers, and could only act with the help of local authorities whose highest priority was not usually the good manning of the Navy.[40] They were also the natural scapegoats for the false mustering and incompetence of captains:

> Business of this nature hath few friends and less tongues to speak well of the actor's care or service. Such men as we take were of the best, only let me advise that their own reports carry no credit, for they will, in hope to avoid the service, disparage themselves for this business. I have not spared my friends nor burdened those that least affected me more than my nearest acquaintance. I and my people are free of bribery and corruption . . .[41]

Moreover the distinction between seamen and landmen was blurred in many parts of the country. A press-master at Dartmouth in 1623 acknowledged taking 'mechanical men and husbandmen', because 'very few mariners in these parts but . . . in the winter time employ themselves in the divers labours of the country.'[42]

Buckingham revived the Elizabethan precedent of surveying the maritime population as a basis for planning and recruitment.[43] In 1634 there was a scheme for local authorities to register the seafaring population and send up quotas as required, but in the face of local hostility it did not go ahead.[44] Rainsborough's 1637 proposal to transfer all impressment to local authorities foundered on the same rock.[45] Impressment was used not only for seamen but for all sorts of specialists, including officers. Trinity House impressed masters and pilots for the Navy.[46] The Barber-Surgeons' Company impressed surgeons.[47] Lord Lindsey even pressed fiddlers for the 1635 Ship Money fleet.[48]

All pre-war manning problems were insignificant compared to those of the war years between 1625 and 1629. Men had suffered from corrupt officers in peacetime when there were few ships in commission, but they suffered far more in wartime when money was acutely short. The natural consequence was mutiny and desertion. From the beginning of the war, 'the confidence which many mariners and seafaring men have taken of late in disobeying his Majesty's prests, running from his ships, and serving foreign power, is notoriously known.'[49] The crews of the ships on the Cadiz expedition,

> were the worst that ever were seen, and it is so confessed by the most experienced seamen that have been with us; for they are so out of order and command and so stupified, that punish them or beat them, they will scarce stir, doing their duties so unwillingly as if they had neither heart nor mind to do any service, their ordinary talk being that his Majesty presseth them, and giveth them so little means that they are not able to live on it, and that it were better to be hanged or serve the King of Spain, or the Turk, then his Majesty.[50]

When the expedition returned, the scale of its problems overwhelmed the available resources. 'I wish you were a spectator a little', Pennington wrote to Buckingham from Plymouth, 'to hear their cries and exclamations; here die eight or ten daily.'[51] The crew of the *Swiftsure* mutinied and deserted in a body. Pennington persuaded them to return, but

> their cases are so lamentable that they are not much to be blamed, for when men have endured misery at sea and cannot be relieved at home in their own country, what a misery of miseries it is! . . . It would grieve any man's heart to hear their lamentations, to see their wants and nakedness, and not to be able to help them.[52]

In 1626 it was worse. Mutinous seamen attacked and wrecked Buckingham's coach, and disrupted the meetings of the Navy Commissioners. Sir William Russell, with £3,000 in hand to pay £50,000 arrears of wages, was attacked in his house.[53] At Portsmouth in July,

> There came on shore into the dockyard very early the greatest part of all the ordinary seamen in the fleet, utterly refusing to receive any pay at all except they might have the full of their wages, both old and new. Such of them as had served in the former voyage pretended want of means (without their full pay) to relieve their wives and children, and those of the new imprest, want of clothes to enable them for a winter service, generally protesting that if they might now receive the full of their wages they would not foresake the service, otherwise they must

> take their course for London and petition his Majesty; wherein, we not being able to give them satisfaction, they presently cried 'away, away', and so are gone towards London to the number of about 500, neither could we possibly discover the leaders of that disorder, because they generally answered 'one and all, one and all.'[54]

These men were turned back before they reached London, but in November three hundred from Chatham rioted in London and were paid to get rid of them, which of course encouraged others to do the same.[55]

The following year Sir Sackville Trevor of the *Assurance* lost sixty men who deserted from leave. Leave was stopped, but desertion was not. Seamen were forbidden to appeal to the Navy Commission, 'under pretext of want of wages or provisions', and threatened with the penalties of treason if they did. The Lords Lieutenant were given powers of martial law to deal with rioters and deserters, though they were reluctant to use them.[56] At the return of the fleet to Plymouth from the Île de Ré there were scenes of horror: 'I vow to God', Sir Henry Mervyn wrote, 'I cannot deliver it in words.'[57]

> I have in the *Vanguard* above 40 men fallen down since I wrote my last letters, and the rest of the ships all in like proportion; many of our men for want of clothes are so naked that, exposed to the weather in doing their duties, their toes and feet miserably rot and fall away piecemeal, being mortified with extreme cold. I beseech your Grace once more that some clothes may be speedily sent down and also 500 hammacoes, for most lodge on the bare decks . . .[58]

'They say they are used like dogs,' Sir Ferdinando Gorges reported,

> forced to keep aboard without being suffered to come ashore to refresh themselves. They have not means to put clothes on their backs to defend them from cold, or to keep them in health, much less to releive their poor wives and children. When they happen to fall sick, they have not any allowance of fresh victuals to comfort them, or medicines to help to recover them. Some of their sick fellows being put ashore in houses erected for them, are suffered to perish for want of being looked unto, their toes and feet rotting from their bodies, and so smelling that none are able to come into the rooms where they are. Some provisions put aboard them is neither fit nor wholesome for men to live on. They had as lief be hanged as to be dealt with all as they are.[59]

In March 1628 three men were killed in fighting following a major mutiny at Plymouth.[60] In June Sir John Coke wrote from Portsmouth,

> We have already had two mutinies, one aboard the *Norfolk*: and another on Monday last of all the ships in the harbour: out of which 150 men

> at least, refusing to weigh anchor at the Admiral's command, went on shore with a flag towards there to call to them the rest of the fleet.[61]

It is not surprising that Denbigh had difficulties manning his squadron.

> The want of seamen in this fleet is very great. Our number grows every day less and less, partly by sickness and partly by runagates, from which there is no possible means to restrain them. When any ships go to sea, we are constrained to man them out of such as stay behind, which breeds much discontent among seamen . . .[62]

He sailed 42 per cent undermanned.[63]

Denbigh's was the last major expedition of the war, but for those ships still at sea, 1629 was little better. Mervyn, commanding in the Narrow Seas, wrote of

> the state of six ships here in the Downs, two of which, the *Dreadnought* and *Third Whelp*, have neither meat nor drink. The *Tenth Whelp* hath drunk water these three days . . . Now with what confidence can punishment be inflicted on men who mutiny in these wants? . . . These neglects be the cause why mariners fly to the service of foreign nations to avoid his Majesty's . . . His Majesty will lose the honour of his seas, the love and loyalty of his sailors, and his Royal Navy will droop.[64]

It is not surprising that these years saw the first examples of the round robin, and the classic cry of the mutineer, 'one and all'.[65]

The principal cause of all the wartime problems was unquestionably want of money, but in addition, the level of naval pay, which had been ten shillings for a twenty-eight-day month since 1585, was falling behind the wages in merchantmen, even if it had been paid promptly. At the urging of Wimbledon, among others, the ordinary seaman's pay was raised in January 1626 to 15s, but it is doubtful if even then it equalled what a good mariner could earn elsewhere[66] – or would have equalled had it been paid. The proportion of seamen's wages for the war years which was eventually paid has been variously calculated as not more than a third and over half.[67]

So horrifying, and memorable, were the sufferings of the seamen during the war years, that their experience has been freely invoked to explain the Navy's adherence to Parliament during the Civil War.[68] It is unlikely, however, that there were many men in the Navy of 1642 who had personal memories of Cadiz or the Île de Ré, and the experience of serving in the 1630s was different. The discipline and social life of the Ship Money fleets show a growing professionalism and stability, in which we can see the germ of a regular naval service.

This was particularly true of the gentleman officers. In 1630 Mervyn was complaining about captains 'who know neither how to command, nor how to obey', and asking for John Mennes, 'that he might once more have some captains that had passed their ABC.'[69] But more and more of them had – not least because the 'ABCs', the 'seaman's dictionaries', were being written and published to educate the literate and enquiring minds of the new generation of gentleman officer.[70] They understood that 'the seamen are stubborn or perverse when they perceive their commander is ignorant of the discipline of the sea, and cannot speak to them in their own language.'[71] There were still inexperienced courtiers at sea, but for the most part as passengers. Viscount Conway, for example, experienced a storm aboard the *Triumph* in 1636, in which they could,

> neither sleep nor eat quietly ... we were one night sitting down to supper, when a tumble of the ship flung all the dishes on the ground. Dowse let go the hold of a post to take up a shoulder of mutton, but his unsteady footing made him sit down on the sauce of one dish, with his foot in the buttered meat of the other.[72]

Later he complained that 'we are like to have a sad journey, for my Lord of Northumberland hath discharged the fiddlers.'[73] But Conway was not a sea officer. The captains of the 1630s belonged to a new breed of gentlemen who were making their careers in the Navy, most of them good seamen and capable commanders.[74] Their leading representative was Sir John Pennington, the mainstay of every fleet in those years; loyal, dependable, a fine seaman resolute in the face of endless frustrations. Asking for leave in 1636, Pennington explained that

> he had been at sea all the winter months without sleeping one night ashore. So he should be glad to solace himself with a summer on land otherwise he fears he shall change his nature from flesh to fish, and his mind to believe that there is no content or happiness in this world ... but he is a household servant of the King and therefore must and will obey whatever he commands.[75]

It is noteworthy that Pennington understood and followed the seafarer's tradition of consensus and consultation. In October 1631, for example, his flagship the *Convertine* was lying in the Elbe.

> My captain doubting whether we might ride safely here before Ritzebüttel [*Rickebottle*] without endangering his Majesty's ship by reason of the ice that was likely to come down the river if the frost continued, called the officers of the ship together to hear their opinion, viz. the

> lieutenant, the master and his two mates, the pilot, the gunner and boatswain, who all affirmed we might safely ride here so long as the wind continued southerly.[76]

This is as far removed as could be from the conduct of Lord Valentia in 1625. Pennington even seems to have regarded the officers as having a sort of collective authority, next after his own. In March 1638,

> Having received warrant from the Lords Commissioners for the Admiralty for my coming to London, I left the command of my ship unto Doctor Daniel Ambrose, chaplain, Mr Robert Fox, lieutenant, and Mr Peter White, master of her.[77]

Pennington, and doubtless other professional gentleman officers like him, had their followers, seamen who chose to serve with them, and 'if they should be put with anyone else they would all run away.'[78] When problems occurred with victuals in the 1630s, as they sometimes did, the machinery of inspection by ships' officers seems to have worked properly; the inedible was condemned and thrown overboard, and replaced at the victuallers' expense.[79]

The Navy of the 1630s gives the impression, for the first time, of a settled service developing a sense of itself as distinct from merchant shipping and privateers. The complexity of shipboard society continued to develop with the creation of new positions. The first offical establishments both of chaplains and of surgeons were made by Buckingham in 1626, which was also the year the first dockyard chaplain was appointed.[80] The fact that Pennington entrusted his ship to the chaplain, lieutenant and master (in that order) suggests the standing that a good chaplain could enjoy, though Dr Ambrose's colleague Willoughby Dixon of the *Assurance* was described as as 'a deboshed man of ill quality'.[81] The duty in action of John Pothan, chaplain of the pinnace *Nicodemus*, was literally to praise the Lord and pass the ammunition, and thanks to him we have a rare piece of evidence of the rate of fire of English ships (about three rounds an hour in this case, but from very small guns).[82] Surgeons were scarce during the war years, and not of the best quality: 'careless and commonly debauched fellows', whom Coke could not extract from the Portsmouth taverns.[83] The surgeon of the *St James* in 1627 was discovered to be 'by profession an armourer'.[84] Still more unlikely was the qualification of Philip Ward, appointed first purser of the *Sovereign of the Seas* because his 'judgement in the art of painting' qualified him to look after her internal decorations.[85] John Glanville was named as Wimbledon's secretary over his own protests that 'he is a mere lawyer, unqualified for the employment of a secretary: his handwriting is so bad that hardly any but his own clerk can read it.'[86] The trumpeter was still a person of importance, and one watch-bill suggests he should be responsible for the seamen handling the mizzen sails (from the poop, his traditional station), with the master taking the main and the boatswain the foresails.[87] Midshipman was now an occasional rating of a working petty officer in big ships.[88]

The discipline of men-of-war seems to have followed tradition. Buckingham's orders in 1625 were that 'companies live together orderly and peaceably together, without swearing, gaming, pilfering, or quarrelling amongst themselves or with strangers', which were certainly among the commonest vices of seamen.[89] The punishments listed by Pennington in 1627 were 24 hours in irons for missing a watch, gambling, lighting candles after the watch had been set for the night, or overstaying leave; and three buckets of water poured over the head for sleeping on watch three times. For striking or fighting another man the offender was to be ducked three times and discharged without pay; a thief received five lashes from each man in the ship and was likewise discharged without pay.[90] All of these seem to have been more or less standard penalties.[91] A thief in Digby's squadron was ducked 'and then towed at my boat's stern to every one of my ships'; a deserter was ducked; and a boatswain who led a mutiny, ducked and discharged.[92] Drunkards were usually put in irons.[93] Shore leave was regarded as normal, indeed essential, though the 'extravagant lewdness' and 'dissolute wildness' of seamen ashore was something that even the best disciplinarians could not control.[94]

Outside the desperate conditions of the war years, however, mutiny and gross indiscipline does not seem to have been a great problem in the Navy.[95] Some contemporaries, indeed, thought naval discipline was much too lax.[96] The death penalty, though theoretically possible, was in practice unknown.[97] Whipping in the Navy still seems to have been more or less confined to thieves,[98] and the severest common punishment was ducking, which meant being dropped into the sea from the yardarm. Discipline in privateers was usually worse, and perhaps as a consequence, punishments more savage.[99] It was aboard one of Warwick's privateers in 1627 that a court martial condemned two men to die for raising a mutiny over being served cheese instead of butter, though the sentence was commuted to keel-hauling (something also unknown in the Navy). On this occasion a master's mate on the jury was disrated to common seaman for refusing to convict.[100] The master of this ship described his men as 'a contentious, turbulent, troublesome, unruly, inhuman company ... Newgate not yielding worse, nor Tyburn enjoying the like'.[101] The legal authority of the master of a merchantman to 'correct or chastise' was not disputed, and the boatswain likewise 'has power to beat any under his command on a just cause, this being the custom of the sea.'[102] It was the master of an East Indiaman who flogged his men for mutiny, describing them as 'this intolerable scum of rascals, whom the land hath ejected for their wicked lives and ungodly behaviour'.[103]

Standing orders invariably required prayers to be said at morning and noon (in the dockyard Ordinary as well as at sea), with a psalm at the setting of the watch in the evening, but even ships with chaplains aboard seldom seem to have gone further.[104] Wimbledon and his officers went to Communion at five in the morning before landing at Cadiz, which was a rare if not unique case of a Communion service afloat, though Buckingham and the captains of the 1627 fleet took Communion together before sailing.[105] The religious feeling of the common seamen, as far as it is recorded, was chiefly displayed in a vigorous hatred of Catholics.[106] Though Digby maintained good discipline in spite of his religion, there was trouble in Rutland's squadron in 1623 when it was rumoured (apparently wrongly) that he had brought Catholic officers with him:

> there hath been great disorder and miscarriage aboard the fleet, by the Popish insolent gentlemen, in so grievous manner interrupting prayers and singing of psalms, that the mariners could scarce be stayed from throwing them overboard to feed haddocks.[107]

The daily life of a man-of-war had perhaps become more orderly and organized than it had been, or than it still was in merchantmen, but there was still a great deal of incompetence and disorder. The firing of extravagant salutes on the most trifling occasions, often with shotted guns, caused death and injury, wasted prodigious quantities of powder, and concealed the gunners' thefts of more.[108] Saluting was an admitted weakness of the English, 'who herein are the vainest of all nations, even more than the Dutch, who use it only when they are drunk.'[109] Not that so much practice necessarily taught English gunners to handle powder with respect. The *Seventh Whelp* blew up in action in 1630 when the gunner's mate entered the magazine with a lighted candle.[110] Tactics in action, according to contemporary authorities, still followed the Elizabethan practice of getting the weather gage and 'giving the prow', but in practice the bigger ships of the early Stuart Navy were incapable of being handled in this fashion, and the broadside was more and more often referred to as the ship's main armament, though the tactical consequences of this were yet to be worked out.[111] The number of men assigned to each gun had risen to three or even four by the 1630s, which was probably enough to allow one broadside to be fought continuously, at a slow rate of fire. By then soldiers were no longer taken to sea as part of a warship's complement, but as many as a fifth of the seamen were posted as small-arms men.[112]

The catastrophic illness, almost certainly typhus, which overtook the fleets of 1625 and 1627 was the natural, perhaps in the seventeenth century inevitable, consequence of large bodies of men remaining crowded together for long periods, especially ill-fed and ill-clad in cold weather.[113] The only answer known was to clean and disinfect the ships, as Sir Henry Mervyn did the *Vanguard*; she was washed every other day and with vinegar twice weekly, 'perfumed with tar burnt and frankincense ... aired twixt decks with pans of charcoal', the hammocks and bedding aired on shore.[114] This was more or less standard practice.[115] Slops (seamen's clothes) were first issued in 1623 'to avoid nasty beastliness by continual wearing of one suit of clothes, and thereby bodily diseases and unwholesome ill smells in every ship.'[116] The disadvantage of the practice became evident in 1625: 'it was not intended to clothe the mariners in harbour to make them handsome to run away.'[117] Moreover the slops were bad, expensive, and consequently unpopular among the men.[118] Simpler, but less effective as a preservative of health amidst 'the prodigious scents, smells and savours ... betwixt the decks where our men lodged', was to chew garlic.[119] When men fell sick and were sent ashore, there were no hospitals to receive them, and little or no charity. Greville at the end of Elizabeth's reign had started the practice of taking money to sea so that the sick could be discharged with their wages, and pay for their own treatment, but it was not revived.[120]

Epidemic disease was a largely problem of wartime expeditions, but the Navy of the 1630s still had many faults. Corruption was commonplace, as it was everywhere in the seventeenth century, especially where salaries were long in arrears.[121] The pursers petitioned in 1639 that their pay 'cannot afford maintenance in a very mean quality without the continuance of what has ever been tolerated, or else the grant of a competent salary.'[122] The 1631 raid on Baltimore went unopposed in spite of the *Fifth Whelp* being nearby at Kinsale partly because the little Irish squadron, of which she formed half, was immobilized by a quarrel over victualling between her captain and its admiral, Sir Thomas Button, commanding from his house near Cardiff and determined to monopolize the profit himself.[123] The Irish Squadron was unusual in not being victualled by the Surveyors, whose performance in the 1630s seems generally to have been satisfactory, but things were not always perfect in the main fleets. Lindsey had to ask for 'better ordering of the victuals, which now is so bad for quality, and small for quantity, that it doth much discourage our seamen.'[124] Masters, bred to the sea, were just as willing to exploit their positions as needy gentlemen. Some of them bought the places of boatswains of their own ships, the better to certify their own expenses.[125] The management of the Chatham Chest was a matter of public scandal.[126] Manning in general remained a problem, and in 1636 it was said that 'no terror of punishment will restrain mariners from abandoning his Majesty's service.'[127]

Weighing all these factors, we may still say that the Navy of the 1630s was an increasingly coherent and professional force. By the standards of the age, its administrative weaknesses were not crippling. What was more significant was the social division within the Navy, and between the Navy and merchant shipping. Gentleman captains like Pennington were making their careers in the Navy, and in the 1630s, with the experience of the war years, the position of lieutenant emerged as the first stage in such a career.[128] Its function was now understood to be 'to breed young gentlemen for the sea service.'[129]

> The reason why there are not now so many able sea captains as there is use of is because there hath not been formerly allowances for lieutenants whereby gentlemen of worth and quality might be encouraged to go to sea; and if peace had held a little longer the old sea captains would have been so worn out as that the state must have relied wholly on mechanic men that have been bred up from swabbers to be masters of ships and would be captains, and (though some few of such men deserve the honour to be captains yet) to make many of them would cause sea service in time to be despised by gentlemen of worth who will refuse ever to serve at sea under such captains.[130]

A career structure was being established for 'gentleman of worth and quality', but it was being curtailed for 'tarpaulin' officers who had come up from the lower deck. Masters naturally resented the new lieutenants, even more than they resented the gentleman captains, for usurping their opportunities to rise to command. They were 'much discouraged, of late times, by preferring of young, needy, and inexperienced gentlemen captains over them in their own ships. As also by placing lieutenants above the masters in the King's ships, which have never been accustomed by the English till of late years.'[131]

It was this which made the choice of Rainsborough and his captains in 1637, and the fact that they succeeded where many gentlemen had failed, so significant. Traditional, indeed extremely old-fashioned in itself, the choice of 'tarpaulin' officers pointed up what had become a social fault-line.[132] It seems to have run, not so much between gentleman captains and their men, as between gentleman captains and masters of other ships. 'No ships are more stubborn and unwilling to give his Majesty's ships respect than our own merchants,' wrote Captain Henry Stradling in 1632, 'They hate all gentlemen, especially such as serve his Majesty at sea.'[133]

> Our merchants like not to have any gentlemen commanders in any of their ships, but leave the command to the masters only. And this hath produced this common ill-effect, that these masters being blown up on this fashion of late, undergo the command of a captain over them with a great deal of grudging and sullenness, even in his Majesty's own ships.[134]

The problem was not that 'a landman being commander at sea has never the love of his company',[135] for there were few if any 'landmen' still in command, and it was the masters rather than the ship's company at large who felt the most acute grievance.

Considering the Navy in isolation, this social tension was probably not insoluble. The real problem was that it mirrored on a small scale the political fault-line which divided the country. Gentleman captains were part of the Royal Navy as shaped by Charles I to serve royal purposes, to support the dignity of the Crown and overawe foreign princes. 'Tarpaulin' masters belonged naturally to a different social and political system. They represented the trade which the Navy did not protect, the parliamentary politics which the king had suppressed, and the anti-Catholic foreign policy which he had rejected. Worst of all was the fact that this social and political division was also a religious schism. The king personally stood for an 'Arminian', High Church Anglicanism which for many of his subjects was indistinguishable from popery. Among shipmasters and shipowners Presbyterianism and various strains of Puritan independence were strong. The Navy therefore reflected and shared in the profound divisions of English society, and its future depended on their resolution.

TWENTY-EIGHT

The Fall of Three Kingdoms

1640–1649

For all Charles I's evident political, diplomatic and financial weaknesses in the late 1630s, he might very well have overcome them all in time if only he had been able to keep his three kingdoms at peace within themselves and neutral in the European war raging all around them. But to maintain internal peace in the seventeenth century without religious uniformity was exceptionally rare and difficult, and Charles I was divided from many of his Protestant subjects by his Arminian principles, widely perceived as no more than diluted or disguised popery. The hatred and fear which English and Scots Protestants felt for Catholics was beyond any other motive in guiding their political consciousness (and it is a motive which modern historians find especially difficult to understand). It not only made them suspicious of their own sovereign, it divided his kingdoms, for in most of Ireland and parts of Wales the common people remained largely, and the nobility and gentry partly, Catholic. Moreover, as events were to show, religion divided Protestants amongst themselves almost as violently as it divided them from Catholics. Most political activity was expressed in a religious context, using religious language, and to an extent particular doctrinal positions tended to correspond with particular political principles. What was most dangerous for the king was that the defence of true religion was morally legitimate, indeed obligatory, in the eyes of very many subjects who would never otherwise have claimed the right of rebellion against an anointed sovereign. It was the coincidence of religious and political divisions which finally shattered the stability of Charles I's government.

The crisis came with the king's attempts to impose a new Prayer Book and an episcopalian system on the Church of Scotland, which aroused riots in Edinburgh in July 1637 and led to the circulation of the 'National Covenant', whose signatories pledged to defend the existing Presbyterian order of the Church of Scotland. Charles's reaction was to plan English punitive expeditions to Scotland. One royal army was to march across the border, while an amphibious force landed in the Firth of Forth and the royal army crossed from Ireland to land on the west coast. The use even of Protestant troops from Ireland was sensitive, and much more so was the king's interest in a proposed attack by the Catholic Randall McDonnell, Earl of Antrim, on the West Highland territories lost by his MacDonald kinsmen. There in the Western Isles the ancient feud continued between the MacDonalds, once Lords of the Isles, and their mainland rivals, now led by the Protestant and Covenanter Campbells. The MacDonalds were on the king's side, but the Campbells had the troops and galleys with which to continue a ruthless private war, and the Navy Royal did not attempt to interfere so far from its bases.[1] Charles I had acute difficulty in raising forces even in England, and the united opposition of the Scots left him on the defensive, losing all the major royal fortresses in Scotland, and barely saving Berwick and Carlisle. Two armies of approximately equal size met on the border, but after only a few skirmishes the 'Pacification of Berwick' in June 1639 brought an end to the first 'Bishops' War'.[2] The bulk of the Ship Money fleet, under the Earl of Hamilton, cruised in the Forth, but it lacked small cruisers and had barely begun to mount an effective blockade.[3]

The truce agreed at Berwick settled nothing. The Covenanters had made good their defence and the king's authority was severely damaged. Abroad, too, Charles faced new challenges. At sea both the French and the Dutch were growing more convinced of the hollowness of his claims to sovereignty of the seas, and more confident in their own ability to confront him. The 1638 Ship Money fleet had had difficulty in defending English 'sovereignty'.[4] Away from the Channel, French ships began to force English ships to strike their colours.[5] In 1639 for the first time the Dutch stopped English ships carrying Spanish troops through their blockade of Dunkirk and removed the men. While continuing to salute English warships, they paid no heed to them, but searched both English and foreign ships even in English ports.[6] Charles ordered Sir John Pennington to enforce English 'sovereignty' with whatever force was needed. But Pennington was quite clear in his own mind that the Dutch were exercising legitimate belligerent rights in the face of very un-neutral English conduct, and in any case his squadron was completely outmatched. Only the mutual forbearance and good sense of Pennington and the Dutch admiral Maarten Harpertszoon Tromp prevented violence. 'My advice was', Tromp reported, 'that no-one could command at sea further than his guns could reach.'[7]

In the autumn the crisis at length arrived. In a final, desperate gambler's throw, Spain had assembled a huge fleet under Don Antonio de Oquendo to bring succour to her forces in Flanders. Harried by Tromp's smaller squadron, Oquendo took refuge in the Downs on 8 September and Tromp anchored to windward to await reinforcements. Pennington lay nearby, with orders to enforce the neutrality of an English anchorage on two fleets each of which was far larger than his own. When the Dutch were ready, on 11 October, they attacked, destroying Oquendo's fleet and contemptuously ignoring Pennington's shot. By the end of that day a new naval power had arisen to dominate the waters of northern Europe and two once great navies had been humiliated. Charles I, unlike Philip IV, still had his ships and men, but he had lost his reputation. It was now clear to everyone that the sovereign of the seas was an emperor with no clothes.[8]

At home, the calling and subsequent dismissal of the English Parliament in the spring of 1640 provided a focus for opposition, but no money for a war. Charles's second attempt to impose his religious settlement on Scotland further undermined royal prestige. His plan in 1640 was similar to that of the previous year, but it was still further from fulfilment when General Leslie's Covenanter army crossed the border and marched south. Within a fortnight Leslie had defeated the English, occupied Newcastle and won the second 'Bishops' War'.[9] Political turmoil and collapsing royal authority made the collecting of Ship Money very difficult, but the English fleet briefly mounted an effective blockade of the Forth. By October, however, the fleet was back in the Downs, the Scots army was occupying Durham, and an English Parliament had been summoned again. When the Long Parliament met in November, almost its first act was to vote Ship Money illegal, and its next was to demand that the Navy act against the Algerines who were again raiding Cornwall.[10]

It is not necessary here to follow in detail the political crisis as it unfolded during 1641. The tension in England was heightened by the outbreak in October of a widespread rebellion in Ireland, led predominantly by Catholic noblemen and clan chiefs. The rebels were believed in England and Scotland to have massacred settlers of the new Ulster Plantation.[11] The English Parliamentary leaders insisted that the forces sent to suppress it be under their control and not the king's, intending that if necessary they should be available for use against Charles rather than against themselves. Since the first requirement was the relief of isolated garrisons which could only be reached by sea, Parliamentary committees were quickly made aware of the difficulty of operating ships without adequate money. To meet it, the Parliamentary leader John Pym, long an associate of the Earl of Warwick in the privateering activities of the Providence Island Company, imitated its structure by floating an Elizabethan-style joint-stock company to wage war in Ireland, the investors to be rewarded by grants of Irish land taken from the rebels. It was specifically intended not merely to dispossess the Irish lords, but to drive their tenantry from the land and replace them with English settlers. A few investors had misgivings about leaving women and children to starve, but it was not a fashionable sentiment among English Protestants. While this scheme was developing in the spring of 1642, Scottish troops under General Monro occupied the McDonnell lands in Antrim (essentially in the Campbell interest, for the Earl of Antrim was not in rebellion) and protected the (mainly Scottish) settlers in Ulster.[12]

Meanwhile the English crisis came to a head. In January 1642, having failed to arrest the leaders of the Parliamentary opposition, the king left London, effectively abandoning to Parliament the control of the city and with it the Navy and the Ordnance Board. A large part in defending the Parliamentary leaders was played by two thousand seamen led by the Earl of Warwick.[13] The list of officers proposed for the 1642 fleet was now vetted by a Parliamentary committee. The Earl of Northumberland, the Lord Admiral, desired only to avoid having to take sides; when the Commons objected to Pennington as his vice-admiral and seagoing deputy, he consented to the appointment of Warwick instead. With Pennington, Parliament removed many of the gentleman captains of the Ship Money fleets and replaced them with 'tarpaulins'. The key figure was William Rainsborough; virtually all the 1642 captains were his friends and associates, none of them had been naval captains for long, and only one had been a lieutenant. Many of them were masters of Levant or East India Company ships, and a considerable proportion had been privateers in the 1620s. This social and political revolution, begun in the spring, was completed in July when Charles's attempt to regain control of the fleet failed. Warwick ignored the king's letter dismissing him, Pennington failed to seize command, and the remaining royalist captains were removed. With the single exception of Sir George Ayscue, the gentleman officers of the 1630s remained loyal to the king and refused to serve without his approval.[14]

The loss of the fleet he had so painfully built up was 'of unspeakable ill consequence to the King's affairs.'[15] To understand the importance of the Navy in the civil war now unfolding we need to stand back and look at the strategic situation. It can most simply be understood as a series of zones arranged in concentric circles centred on London. Here was the focus of the rebellion, the city whose financial and economic support sustained the Parliamentary war effort. Around it the Home Counties and East Anglia were almost entirely under Parliamentary control. Beyond them was a broad zone of mixed allegiance running from the North Sea across the English Midlands to the Channel, with individual towns and even country houses disputed between Royalists and Parliamentarians. Beyond that again the north, Wales and the West Country were more or less solidly for the king. Further out still lay Scotland and Ireland, to which each side in the English Civil War was to appeal. Scotland was neutral and at peace, having already gained what she wished to fight for. Ireland was involved in her own civil war, with the rebels of the Confederation of Kilkenny already controlling most of the country; but the English government still held Cork, Dublin, various inland garrisons and parts of the east coast, and Monro's Scots remained in Antrim.

The use of the sea was economically and militarily indispensable to both sides in the civil war, though neither party was able to command the sea and deny it to the enemy. The overseas trade of London, which provided 70 per cent of the customs revenue of the kingdom, was the economic engine which drove the entire Parliamentary war effort. Had the king controlled the Navy, he could have blockaded the Thames and forced the immediate collapse of the rebellion. Parliament did attempt to blockade ports in royal hands, but they were too numerous and too distant to be effectively closed. If Charles's friends overseas, particularly in Denmark and Holland, had yielded the help he had some reason to hope for, it is unlikely that the Navy could have stopped it coming.[16] The king also taxed the export of coal from Newcastle and tin from Cornwall to pay for munitions, virtually all of which he had to import.[17] Parliament, the king and the Irish rebels all commissioned privateers, which involved the English civil war with the general European war as privateers took commissions from their friends abroad to justify attacking neutrals. Many of the 'Irish' privateers were Spanish subjects from Flanders, happy to escape the Franco-Dutch blockade of Dunkirk by moving to Waterford or Wexford.[18] Warwick and his friends who now ran the Navy were the lineal descendants of the Elizabethan privateering interest, ready to continue the same sort of war, against the same enemy. Even in the midst of civil war in England, Warwick sent out powerful expeditions to raid the Spanish Caribbean. Captain William Jackson, who sailed in September 1642 with a squadron of seven ships, achieved spectacular success in the Caribbean, temporarily capturing Jamaica.[19]

Strategically, the possession of the Navy gave Parliament its only effective means of attacking the flank and rear of the royalist areas in the north and west, and its only means of invoking or denying the participation of Ireland

and Scotland. Without the Navy no effective Parliamentary campaigns could have been mounted beyond the English Midlands. But the Navy could not act without bases, and the opening moves of the civil war were directed by both sides against the key seaports around the coasts of England and Wales. In August the king's attempt to seize Hull was foiled by the arrival of Parliamentary warships, and Portsmouth, which had declared for the king, was captured in September. By the end of the year Parliament held Hull, Yarmouth, Dover, Portsmouth, Dartmouth, Plymouth and Bristol, allowing it to operate ships on all the coasts of England and Wales.[20] On land, the royal advance on London that autumn was pushed back. Only in Ireland, where the forces under Lord Forbes operated with a mixture of brutality and incompetence, was the Parliamentary war effort going badly.[21]

In 1643 the position of the Royalists improved, largely because of Parliament's neglect of the Navy. The Parliamentarians, whose ignorance of the requirements of modern war had wrecked the war effort twenty years before, were only slowly educated by the responsibility of power. Having voted Tunnage and Poundage to support the Navy in August 1642, they were not quickly persuaded that anything more was needed. In November they voted to keep the summer fleet in commission as a 'Winter Guard' in order to avoid finding money to pay the ships off. For the next two months naval operations were paralysed by a quarrel between the Lords and Commons, the peers wanting to re-appoint the lukewarm Northumberland as commander-in-chief as a gesture to promote negotiations with the king, while the Commons demanded Warwick. In February 1643 they won their point, and at the same time seamen's wages were raised. However there was no money to pay the increase, so the fleet was continued in commission again, disgusting the men and leaving the ships foul and leaky after twelve months' continuous service.[22]

In February Queen Henrietta Maria, who had been abroad collecting support, landed at Bridlington with a convoy escorted by Dutch warships and laden with essential munitions. The same month Plymouth withstood a Royalist siege with the help of supplies brought in by sea, but during June and July the Royalists took both Exeter and Bristol.[23] The fall of Bristol not only gave Charles I a major port with shipping and Customs revenue, but went far to deny Parliament the use of the Irish Sea and immediately affected the course of the Irish civil war. The Irish rebels had been doing well even before the loss of Bristol forced the Parliamentary squadron under Captain Richard Swanley to hasten back to protect its only remaining port, Milford Haven. There Swanley was fully occupied throughout the autumn in a struggle to retain this isolated foothold, with no port available for victualling or repairs nearer than Portsmouth. In November his ships withdrew in search of victuals. By the autumn, with Bristol, Chester, Exeter and Dartmouth in the king's hands, and Hull and Plymouth under siege, the Royalists had gone a long way to denying the Parliamentary Navy the use of the seas to the east and west.[24]

On 1 August the Earl of Ormonde, Charles's lieutenant in Ireland, mounted a royalist coup d'état in Dublin, and the following month he negotiated an armistice with the rebel Confederation of Kilkenny. With the Parliamentary Navy removed from the Irish Sea, there was now nothing but an acute shortage of ships and money to stop Ormonde bringing his army across to England, and in November and December four thousand men landed near Chester. At the same time the rebel privateers of Wexford and elsewhere now extended their operations from Cornish and Breton ports, cruising everywhere from the Bay of Biscay to the Baltic, and causing heavy losses to Parliamentary shipping.[25] Though warships succeeded in relieving Hull and Plymouth, there was no disguising the fact that the Parliamentary cause faced a grave strategic crisis in the autumn of 1643, and that naval weakness was partly responsible. It seemed all the graver because most people on the Parliamentary side were convinced that the object of the armistice in Ireland was not simply to release Ormonde's army to intervene in England, but to bring over the Catholic forces of the Confederation to impose the bloody tyranny inseparable from popery. Warwick warned Parliament that he could not save their cause without more ships and money, and that unpaid seamen would desert to Royalist privateers.

> If my Lords will have their business done as I desire thoroughly, they must be pleased to send me means to do it, by more shipping; else, if your enemies get a considerable fleet out, it will be hard restraining them again; and if the mariners again taste the pillaging of your merchants, they will have mariners enough, and you few enough: for it is easy to give content out of other men's goods.[26]

Pym now strengthened naval administration, and reduced Parliamentary interference, by getting Warwick appointed as Lord Admiral (rather than just commander-in-chief under Parliamentary orders, as he had been since 1642). In November Parliament imposed the most hated and unconstitutional of all taxes, a duty on food, the 'Excise on Salt and Flesh', for the support of the Navy.[27] At the same time it set about obtaining the alliance of the Scots to counterbalance the king's appeal to Ireland. To this end the English

Parliament undertook to abolish bishops and bring the Church of England to a Presbyterian form. In addition the 'Solemn League and Covenant' between the Parliaments of the two kingdoms required the English Navy to provide squadrons on both East and West Coasts to cover the lines of communication of a Scottish army in England, and created a joint 'Committee of Both Kingdoms' to conduct the war effort.[28]

But all this took time to put into effect, and meanwhile the course of the war turned on two obscure amphibious campaigns, in North and South Wales. Ormonde's troops were carried across from Dublin to the Dee, and the Royalist squadron based at Dublin under Captain Thomas Bartlett was much superior to the handful of Parliamentary ships at Liverpool. But Bartlett does not seem to have appreciated the importance of striking while he had the chance, and he was certainly hampered by acute shortages of money and supplies; his men mutinying for their pay. 'In short,' Ormonde wrote in December,

> without ships I know not how that which is left of this kingdom to his Majesty can be preserved, much less be of any use to him; nor is it possible here to provide anything towards the defraying of the charge of them, as the case stands.[29]

In January 1644 the formidable Captain Swanley returned to Milford Haven, and in two months had driven the Royalists out of that corner of Pembrokeshire, made his base secure, and sent ships north to interfere with the Royalist communications from Dublin. Selecting seventy Irishmen and two women from the surrendered garrison of Carmarthen, he bound them back to back and threw them into the sea, 'to wash them to death from the blood of the Protestants that was upon them'.[30] He must have known that the men were soldiers of Ormonde's army, until lately fighting to preserve the Protestant ascendancy in Ireland against the Catholic rebels, but English public opinion made little distinction and his action was loudly applauded. In October a Parliamentary ordinance officially ordered the killing of all Irishmen (irrespective of faith or politics) taken in arms against the Parliament, and meanwhile Swanley had been thanked by the Commons and decorated with a chain of gold (possibly the first English naval decoration) for his services to the godly cause.[31] It is fair to add that Swanley had been known for brutality long before the war, and not all Parliamentary officers followed his example.[32] While Swanley was receiving his gold chain in London in June, and his ships were receiving much-needed stores and repairs, the Royalists of South Wales retook most of Pembrokeshire.[33]

The Scottish army marched into England in January, but the English squadron which should have protected it on the West Coast was not there. Swanley's little squadron, fully occupied on the coast of Wales, was all the naval strength Parliament could provide in the Irish Sea. The way was therefore open that summer for Royalist shipping collected in Waterford and Wexford to sail up the west coast of Ireland to embark a thousand men recruited among the McDonnells in Ulster and land them in the West Highlands. These men formed the core of the Royalist army of Highlanders under the Earl of Montrose, whose brilliant campaign in 1645 and 1646 eventually forced the Scottish army to withdraw from England. Once again sea power, or the lack of it, permitted Ireland and Scotland to tip the balance of the English civil war.[34]

Long before this, in July 1644, the Scottish army (and the availability of Hull as a northern supply base) had helped Parliament to the great victory of Marston Moor, which effectively ended the Royalist cause in the north. Meanwhile, however, the main Parliamentary army under the Earl of Essex had pushed far into the West Country. His advance was delayed in order to lift the Royalist siege of Lyme, a virtually indefensible and strategically insignificant town which, with the help of Warwick's squadron and the gallant leadership of an obscure army officer named Robert Blake, had held out for over two months. But Essex pushed too far west, and too far inland, to be supported by the Navy, and on 2 September his army was surrounded and forced to surrender in Cornwall.[35]

Essex's unfortunate strategy, fully backed by Warwick, was based on political as well as military considerations. Like most of the moderate men who had led the Parliamentary cause since 1642, they were still fighting to force the king to a peace acceptable to their essentially conservative ideas. Alarmed by the political and religious radicalism of other Parliamentry officers, Essex hoped to win his sort of victory before they grew any more powerful. He also wanted to establish himself in the west to make contact with the Earl of Inchiquin in Munster, a Protestant lord so unhappy at Ormonde's dealings with the rebels that he was contemplating going over to the Parliamentary side. In August, after the news of Marston Moor and before Essex's débâcle, Inchiquin declared for Parliament. This gave Parliament the ports of Cork, Youghal and Kinsale, with the opportunity of opening a second front against the king in Ireland – but only if there were ships to exploit it. At this point Swanley was still in London, and his second-in-command Captain Robert Moulton was fully occupied trying to secure his base in Milford Haven from the Royalists. Presently Essex's surrender put Plymouth in great danger. Fortunately for Moulton the Royalists of Pembrokeshire were withdrawn to face the Parliamentary troops advancing south after Marston Moor, allowing him to spare ships and troops for Ireland. Another squadron under Warwick's deputy William Batten restored the supplies and morale of the Plymouth garrison, and by the end of September Parliament had the makings of a second front in Ireland.[36]

After these successes it might be thought that Parliament would have reinforced its successful naval commanders and exploited the opportunities they had opened up. In fact in the crucial waters to the westward the Parliamentary Navy remained largely on the defensive for the next nine months, struggling to retain each end of the axis connecting Milford Haven with the southern Irish ports. This was partly because of the inherent difficulties of operating so far from the Navy's main bases, in the home waters of a Royalist privateer force which was estimated by Warwick to have as many as 250 ships, and probably had 40 or 50 in reality.[37] In addition, the Navy's political base was weakening. John Pym was dead, Warwick was associated with Essex's disastrous strategy, and the influence of radical army officers like Oliver Cromwell was rising as Parliament's New Model Army began to take the field. The result was the Self-Denying Ordinance of April 1645, forbidding members of either House of Parliament to hold commands in the army or navy. This measure was intended to strengthen the control of the Parliamentary radicals by eliminating moderate (and incompetent) leaders like Essex, but it also forced Warwick to resign as Lord Admiral. Batten, the new commander-in-chief, was an able officer, but he was closely tied to the authority of Parliamentary committees which had political and personal interests to distract them from sea operations.[38]

From January to March 1645 the Parliamentary squadron in the west was heavily committed to the defence of Duncannon, a small port commanding the entrance of the river going up to Waterford which was besieged and eventually taken by the Confederacy. Then in May the Royalists of Pembrokeshire returned and almost completely drove the Parliamentary forces out. Swanley was for a time reduced to a precarious shelter in Angle Bay at the mouth of Milford Haven.[39] In July the squadron was again defending an Irish port under attack by the Catholic forces, this time Youghal, which was successfully held. During these operations a young sea officer named William Penn distinguished himself as acting vice-admiral of the squadron.[40] Meanwhile the Parliamentary forces were winning decisive victories in England, culminating in the New Model Army's great triumph of Naseby on 14 June. In September Parliament retook Bristol, and in November

Chester was besieged. These successes came just in time, for now Charles really was negotiating with the Confederates of Kilkenny for the assistance of a Catholic Irish army, but the loss of his ports, and the effective extinction of the Royalist Irish squadron with the capture of the *Swan* in November, made it impossible for him to call Ireland to his aid in England.[41]

The English civil war was now nearly over. In May 1646 Charles I surrendered to the Scottish army at Newark, and with the fall of Pendennis Castle outside Falmouth in August, and of the Isles of Scilly the next month, the Parliamentary cause was finally triumphant. In Scotland Montrose had been beaten by the Covenanters. Only in Ireland were the enemies of Parliament still undefeated. There Penn was involved in another operation from May to July 1646 at Bonratty Castle on the Shannon, where the Protestant Earl of Thomond had admitted a Parliamentary garrison. The place offered the possibility of blocking the privateering port of Limerick (as Duncannon had Waterford), but it was too far from deep water to be defended by ships alone, and in July it was taken.[42]

With military victory in England, the future of the English Navy was bound up with the political settlement, or unsettlement, of the Parliamentary regime. To understand this we need to go back to the outbreak of the civil war to examine how and why Parliament organized its naval administration. In a physical sense, Parliament gained control of the king's fleet in 1642, but in a political and strategic sense it replaced that 'foreign policy' Navy of big ships, with the 'home policy' Navy of smaller ships for the defence of trade and the coast, which Charles I had not chosen to build. The biggest ships of the Royal Navy were laid up (the *Sovereign* immediately, the *Prince* in 1643), while the remainder were supplemented by a large number of chartered merchantmen suitable for the business of convoy escort, transport and amphibious operations which formed the bulk of the Navy's work. In organization and policy, the Navy reverted to the Elizabethan model of which Warwick, Pym and their friends of the Providence Island Company were the last exponents. Once more the Navy was run by a group of men who combined public office with private business as shipowners, shipmasters, privateers and naval contractors.

Instead of the Lord Admiral and the Navy Board, the Navy was controlled by an interlocking web of Parliamentary committees. The first of these was the Navy and Customs Committee, established in 1641 to control and allocate revenue. In September 1642 the Navy Board was replaced by a Navy Commission, combining professional members with Parliamentary representatives. Operational command remained with Warwick, as commander-in-chief so long as Northumberland remained nominally Lord Admiral, while his functions were discharged by an Admiralty Commission. From February 1643 until April 1645 Warwick was Lord Admiral himself, and when he was forced to resign by the Self-Denying Ordinance he became working chairman of the revived Parliamentary Admiralty Commission.

The active members of the Navy and Customs Committee, the distinct Customs Commission of 1643, the two Admiralty Commissions of 1642 and 1645, the Prize Commission of 1644, and the Parliamentary representatives on the Navy Commission, were virtually the same. Giles Grene, John Rolle, the brothers Alexander and Squire Bence, and Samuel Vassall their brother-in-law, were members of the Navy and Customs Committee, the Navy Commission, and both Admiralty Commissions. Sir Henry Vane the younger, Treasurer of the Navy, was also a member of the Navy Commission and both Admiralty Commissions. Richard Cranley was a shipmaster, a shipowner, a Navy Commissioner and a Prize Commissioner. Thomas Smith was Secretary of the Admiralty, privateer owner and Collector of Prize Goods. William Batten, a naval captain and shipowner, was Surveyor of the Navy, continued as a member of the Navy Commission in 1642, and in 1645 was simultaneously acting as Surveyor and commander-in-chief.[43] The names of these different committees were used loosely, they shared secretaries and clerks, their meetings often followed one another in the same rooms, their records were intermingled then, and have been inextricably confused by subsequent archivists.[44]

There is no doubt of the energy and devotion of these men who had committed their lives and fortunes to the Parliamentary cause. The earliest and still the most influential study of naval administration in this era praises them as 'prompt, capable, honest and energetic, sparing themselves neither in purse nor person.'[45] This judgement has to be qualified. Undoubtedly the Parliamentary naval administration was not technically corrupt, in that monies were voted, spent, received and audited by the proper persons – only those persons were all the same, or friends, relatives and business associates of one another.

> At the first of the war it was accounted an high character of a well-affected man to accomodate the service with ships for their money . . . but I must tell my reader and them that their zeal burnt as hot in another chimney as the state's interest . . . when the same man shall be an owner, a commissioner, a committee man, nay, a chairman of that committee, and in these capacities hire to the state (as a signal service) his or their ships by order from themselves to a third man . . .[46]

The principal reason for the dissolution of the mixed Navy Commission in November 1643 was the suspicion that it had abused its position to enrich its members, but the removal of the Parliamentary members did not cure the problem. Between 1643 and 1645 the Navy Commission accounted for 124 merchantmen with 9,486 men chartered for a total of £250,184, compared with £451,917 spent on the Navy Royal proper; 'a vast, expensive and eating charge to the state', greatly exceeding the cost of the Ship Money fleets. The famous privateer *Constant Warwick*, jointly owned by Warwick, Swanley, Batten and Moulton, was continuously chartered from her building, earning £12,051 between 1645 and 1647. In sixteen months the Navy Committee paid over £8,000 in respect of ships owned by the Bences and Vassall; Vassall's *Mayflower* alone earned £6,475 in fourteen months.[47] It was the same story with contracts for naval stores.

> That the same man should at the same time be both clerk of the cheque, clerk of the stores, merchant or factor to buy and pay for all provisions, treasurer to pay all moneys, muster-master, victualler &c, is one of the monsters of the Navy; but that this same man that is all these and more, should be one of the Commissioners of the Navy, or worse, one of the Commissioners of the Admiralty, is the wonder of wonders.[48]

The Prize Commissioners sold prizes and cargoes in their public capacities and bought them as private merchants. Between March 1644 and April 1649 prizes to the value of £123,202 18s 2d were sold, but instead of one-third each, the crews got only 11¾ per cent, and the state 22 per cent.[49] As Treasurer of the Navy, Sir Henry Vane was tireless and ruthless, an equal master of administrative procedure and political intrigue. A dominant figure when he chose, he absented himself from the committees at convenient moments and ignored inconvenient resolutions. Although he promoted the Self-Denying Ordnance, he got himself excepted from it. He was confirmed as Treasurer in 1645 on condition of paying back half his profits from poundage, but failed to do so, presenting incomplete accounts to the Revenue Committee, whose chairman happily chanced to be his father.[50] In the centre of this web of interlocking committees sat the amphibious figure of Giles Grene, chairman of the Navy Committee, one 'that could easily help a lame dog over the stile.'[51] Those who fell foul of him found mysterious delays attending the payment of their accounts.[52]

It is certain that Parliamentary naval administration benefited from the services of experienced and devoted men, but it (and they) benefited even more from political support and copious revenue. The taxes refused to

Charles I, the liberties of Englishmen – all the sacred cows which Parliament had fought so zealously to preserve were slaughtered to feed the war effort.[53] The single county of Kent was paying £35,000 a week in taxes during the civil war, eight or nine times its annual assessment for Ship Money. Members of Parliament like Samuel Vassall who had been imprisoned for refusing to pay Tunnage and Poundage without Parliamentary consent, now imposed it without royal assent. Between 1642 and 1647 the Navy received a total of £1,186,879 10s 5½d, of which £923,864 2s 10½d came from the Customs and £145,471 17s 7d from the Excise of Flesh and Salt.[54]

The civil war had broken the constitutional stalemate and provided the means to finance a modern navy and army. What the Parliamentary victory had not done was create a lasting constitutional settlement, and the end of the war was immediately followed by a political crisis. Crudely simplifying a complicated situation, we may say that there were two main parties, whose politics were identified by their religious views. The Presbyterians represented the moderate peers, politicians and merchants who had fought and won the war to bring the king to acceptable terms. They and their allies the Scots hoped for a restored Parliament, a monarchy with limited powers, Anglicanism without bishops, and sea power without a standing army (except in Ireland). But to win the war they had created the New Model Army, many of whose officers and men were Independents in religion and radicals in politics. The political crisis of 1647 was in part a struggle between Parliament and army, but the Navy was equally involved, for the 'New Merchants' (the smaller independent merchants, privateers and interlopers of pre-war days, not members of the great trading companies like the East India or Levant Companies) who dominated naval administration were a key element of the Presbyterian party, so that the army and navy were in effect on opposite sides.[55] Moreover the regime was in growing financial difficulties. The naval debt was £130,000 at the beginning of 1646, and £220,000 a year later, shortly before the abolition of the Excise on Salt and Flesh made the situation much worse. By the summer of 1647 Royalist privateers from Ireland and Jersey were operating in squadrons which the reduced Parliamentary fleet could scarcely challenge.[56]

This was a great moment of opportunity for Ireland. Nearly united and independent for the first time in recorded history, and provided with effective sea power, the country might have taken control of its own destiny. In principle the ships available to the Confederation of Kilkenny were sufficient to control Irish waters and put such pressure on English trade as might have brought any English government to terms. The number of prizes brought into Irish ports between 1642 and 1650 may have been as many as the 1,900 claimed by an informed contemporary. The Irish weakness, as so often in Irish history, was political rather than military. The Confederation was less than united, it had no effective naval administration, and its ships were primarily in the service of private profit rather than any coherent strategy. England's political chaos gave Ireland a brief opportunity, but the Confederation did not, or could not, exploit it.[57]

The English political crisis came to a head in the summer of 1647, when the army seized Charles I and occupied London. They ejected most of the Presbyterians from naval administration, which was now dominated by Vane, Sir Henry Mildmay, and Colonel Thomas Rainsborough, son of Captain William. They forced the resignation of Batten as commander-in-chief, and replaced him with Rainsborough: 'another, such another thrust in to be my successor, as, till then, I never imagined would be Vice-Admiral of a Navy'.[58] As a Leveller, Rainsborough stood for political views which were too radical even for the army commanders, and he was exiled to the fleet partly to get him out of the way. In the Navy he was regarded as the army's tool; his religious and political views, and his 'insufferable pride, ignorance and insolency' were deeply unpopular. The seamen complained of 'no settled form of divine worship, no communions, little or no preaching on board but by illiterate and mechanic persons.' They objected also to references to 'the Parliament's' instead of 'his Majesty's' ships: they had 'fought all this time to fetch the King to his Parliament, yet now it is made treason to offer to bring him hither . . .'[59]

In January 1648 the Independents dissolved the Committee of Both Kingdoms (thus breaking the alliance with Scotland) and replaced it with the 'Derby House Committee', dominated by themselves. At the same time Rainsborough was ordered to purge the Navy of Presbyterian officers. In the spring of 1648 unpaid garrisons in South Wales mutinied, followed by a widespread rebellion in Kent against the army's rule. Though not exactly Royalist, the rebels wanted negotiations with the king. The officers and men of the main fleet lying in the Downs agreed, and when Rainsborough tried to board his flagship on 27 May he was informed by a boatswain's mate that 'the case was altered, that they had concurred with the Kentish gentlemen, and that there was no admittance for him'. The seamen demanded the return of their old commander the Earl of Warwick, and the Independents reluctantly agreed to restore him as Lord Admiral, as the only alternative to driving the whole fleet into the hands of the Royalists.[60]

In this they succeeded only partially. Twelve ships under Batten now declared openly for the king and mounted a blockade of the Thames, which in less than a fortnight reduced the 1647 Customs receipts for the port of London by a quarter.[61] Had the Kentish rebels captured Chatham or held a suitable anchorage for long enough (both of which they narrowly failed to do) the naval mutiny might have decided the fate of the Parliamentary cause, but without a base Batten had to withdraw to Holland. Warwick retained a fleet of about the same number but heavier armament, while another squadron at Portsmouth also remained loyal to Parliament.[62] Warwick and Batten narrowly missed one another at sea off Shoeburyness on 30 July, and on 19 September Warwick anchored off the port of Helvoetsluis, kept apart from the Royalist ships by Dutch warships. He remained for two months, but with little support from home, where the naval administration was acutely short of money and its leaders deeply suspicious of him, was unable to keep up the blockade over the winter. The Royalist fleet had even less money, but the energy and determination of its new commander Prince Rupert kept a core of warships operational. On 1 January 1649 he sailed for Ireland with a squadron of seven ships, flying his flag in the *Constant Reformation*.[63]

Warwick had done his best, but between unpaid and unfed seamen on one hand and his political enemies on the other, his position was impossible, especially as his brother Lord Holland was executed as a royalist conspirator.[64] The Independents now moved to consolidate their grip on power. On 6 December 1648 in the military coup known as 'Pride's Purge', moderates and Presbyterians were expelled from Parliament, leaving the 'Rump' of Independents in control. In January the military regime set up a Committee for the Regulation of the Navy and Customs, to remove from both the administration and the sea service everyone not of their party, which in both cases meant the majority. On 30 January King Charles was executed.[65]

England was now ruled by a military dictatorship supported only by a minority of religious fanatics. Abroad it had no friends: Scotland and Ireland were open enemies, all Christendom was aghast at the murder of the king. The foreign trade on which London and the regime depended was exposed to heavy attack from Royalist privateers. That part of the Navy which remained in the Rump's control was demoralized, disorganized, short of money, and stripped of most of its experienced officers. Whatever other verdict might have been passed on England by a dispassionate observer early in 1649, it must have seemed that over a century's efforts to establish a permanent Navy, supported by an effective and durable political, financial and administrative system, had ended in disappointment if not outright failure.

Conclusion

So ended a thousand years of naval history in the British Isles, with the future relationship and future independence of the three kingdoms as doubtful as they had ever been. This is a history of the British Isles rather than of England not simply in the sense that it tries to avoid being crudely anglocentric. Part of its argument is certainly that Scotland, Wales and Ireland have naval histories worth knowing about; but beyond that, the very existence and shape of the three kingdoms and one principality which historically make up the nations of the British Isles is itself the product of the successes and failures of sea power. There never was any inevitable reason why these nations, all of which were in origin politically and racially divided, had to coalesce in the forms they did, and seaborne warfare had a great deal to do with the making of the British Isles into the political and national entities we know today. What is more it had much to do with the relations between the nations of the British Isles. In the tenth century, and again for a while in the eleventh, the sea power of newly-united England was well advanced in establishing an informal maritime empire over most or all of the British Isles. This empire vanished with the English navy after 1066, the date which marks the dissolution of the English empire and the partition of the British Isles. Henceforward the relations of the English with their Celtic neighbours were military rather than naval: they turned on intermittent warfare, raid, settlement and conquest. The pattern involved the domination, subjugation and eventual destruction of political and social systems which were perceived as being hostile and racially inferior.

The consequences are with us yet, but they were never inevitable. In the relations of Æthelstan or Edgar with the Celtic princes, insofar as our evidence allows us to know them, we seem to see the same sort of imperial overlordship and protection as distinguished the British empire of the nineteenth century. It is instructive to consider the case of Hywel Dda ('the Good'), prince of Gwynedd in the first part of the tenth century. He figures in Welsh history as the great lawgiver, whose long and peaceful reign stands in sharp contrast to the turbulent and bloody histories of his successors. It is no coincidence that this Hywel is the same 'Howell the Subking' who occupied an honoured place at Æthelstan's court and witnessed the English king's charters next after the Archbishop of Canterbury and before any of the English noblemen; nor that after his death and the decline of English sea power his successors suffered repeated attacks from Ireland and Man. Wales had three open flanks, on the north, west and south; it was vulnerable to seaborne attack, and sufficiently protected only by the mountains along the English border. An English alliance backed by annual fleets cruising in the Irish Sea protected Hywel against rivals at home and abroad. At the cost of notional dependence, he gained real security.[1] This sort of maritime empire gave Æthelstan and Edgar allies, dependencies or buffer states at little or no cost beyond that of the fleet which they needed in any case for their own protection. For the Celtic princes who accepted English overlordship, the discreet pressure of sea power was a conservative force, sustaining their authority against internal and external enemies and supporting their social system against outside disruption.

In all this there are obvious parallels with the way in which the nineteenth-century British Empire co-opted friendly native rulers all over the world, incorporating their authority and their social systems into an empire which was racially and socially very diverse. Only in the more empty lands without established native governments was there widespread English settlement.[2] We might compare Hywel Dda with the late nineteenth-century rulers of Fiji and Tonga who sought and obtained British overlordship in order to protect themselves against outside pressures which threatened to destroy their societies. The consequence today is that these islands are independent states, ruled by descendants of those who negotiated with the British authorities a century before. Though not of course unaffected by the passage of time and contact with the outside world, their culture and language remain thoroughly Polynesian. Other island groups like Tahiti and Hawaii fell into the hands of imperialists of a different kind and were incorporated into the imperial state. As a result their people are prosperous, but their independence and their culture are gone for ever.

It is not unreasonable to wonder, in the light of these examples, what would have happened in the British Isles if English sea power had not been destroyed by the Normans, and Celtic rulers in Wales, Ireland and Highland Scotland had continued to be part of an informal English maritime empire. Certainly the greater wealth and more advanced economy of a united England, especially one which included Lowland Scotland, as in such circumstances it probably would have done, would have influenced Celtic societies. But Celtic rulers like Hywel Dda, like the princes who rowed Edgar's ship down the Dee, would have enjoyed English support against political and social disruption. In the event they lost that possibility with the collapse of English sea power, and the pattern of English domination was set by Henry II's expedition to Ireland, by Edward I's campaigns in Wales, and by innumerable English expeditions, public and private, aimed at conquest and dispossession.

In this way the political and social formation of the British Isles was indelibly marked by the loss of sea power, and it continued to be affected by the lack of naval power in its relations with the outside world. Though everyone has heard of the Viking invasions, a facile idea is current among modern historians that after 1066 England was in some sense 'invasion-proof' because it was surrounded by the sea.[3] Nothing could be further from the truth. The sea certainly offered an obstacle of sorts, and it is easy to find examples of would-be invasions which were dispersed by gales, or (more often) which failed to surmount the considerable logistical difficulties of a seaborne attack. But the sea is a highway as much as a barrier, and in the Middle Ages it was a much better highway than most of those on land. Compared to a respectable mountain range like the Alps, the Pyrenees or even the Cheviots, the English Channel and the North Sea were trivial obstacles. The result was that England and Scotland were repeatedly invaded by sea. English governments have been overthrown by seaborne invasions at least nine times since the Norman Conquest: in 1139, 1153,[4] 1326, 1399, 1460, 1470, 1471, 1485 and 1688; to which should be added the 1332 invasion of Scotland, and at least seven other successful landings of major forces in England (in 1069, 1101, 1215, 1405, 1462, 1469 and 1487, plus one in Scotland in 1708) which went on to campaign but did not overthrow the regime. These figures take no account of lesser raids and landings, or of seaborne assistance against England sent to Wales, Scotland or to English rebels; they ignore all expeditions which did not succeed in putting troops ashore, and they do not include landings of any kind in Ireland. The sea is no safeguard at all to those who are not capable of using it for their own defence.

Part of the theme of this book is the slow process by which the peoples of the British Isles learnt, relearnt, or did not learn at all how to use the sea for their own defence. After many centuries of fumbling and incompetence, it was the English in the sixteenth century who first achieved a reasonably permanent and effective form of sea power, including the core of a standing state navy. It could be said that the sea was really a safeguard for Queen Elizabeth, as it had not been for any length of time to any of her predecessors since the Conquest. The facts of geography had not changed, but the English had learnt to exploit them. They were fortunate, too, in the sixteenth century, that their nearest and most dangerous rivals were eliminated. France and Scotland were both in advance of England in naval technology and in the use of the open ocean, before civil wars in the mid-century knocked them out of the naval race. Denmark, whose fleet was larger than England's in 1558, was first distracted by war against Sweden in the 1560s and then for twenty years by internal troubles.[5]

The process of learning to use the sea was not just a matter of growing understanding. It was above all a process of growing capability. War has always been a supreme test of individuals and societies, and naval warfare has always been the most costly and demanding of all forms of war. We have seen that there were many ways of organizing, or not organizing, to use the sea in warfare, most of which were tried at one time or another in the course of a thousand years of the history of the British Isles. Only in the sixteenth century did Scotland, briefly, and then England more durably, reach the last and most difficult stage of all with a standing state navy. Unquestionably this was, and is, the most formidable method of making war at sea, but it was also the most expensive and burdensome. Warships were and still are the most complex and advanced of all artefacts. To build and operate them requires a mass of technical, industrial and professional skills, ashore and afloat, and a sophisticated system of management to mould them into an effective whole. Above all it requires long-term commitment, for sea power cannot be improvised. Ships can be constructed relatively quickly, but the skills and capabilities which make up an effective navy can only be built up with long years of investment. Elizabethan England was the first state in the British Isles, and one of the first in Europe, to reach this level of political commitment and administrative sophistication.

This raises an important historical question. It is almost a commonplace among historians now that the growth of powerful absolutist states in the sixteenth and seventeenth centuries was closely connected with the sharply increased demands of modern warfare consequent on the 'military revolution'.[6] In its simplest form the argument is that the new armies and new styles of land warfare, especially bastioned fortifications and the long sieges necessary to defeat them, imposed enormous costs on states. Some were able to meet the challenge by eliminating or emasculating their medieval representative institutions, increasing the power and wealth of the state at the expense of traditional liberties, creating powerful, centralized 'absolute' monarchies large and strong enough to support the new armies. Others, more numerous, failed the test and were conquered or absorbed. England was quite clearly one of the failures, spared from conquest only because of being supposedly 'invasion-proof',[7] or because the great powers of the 1640s were too busy in Germany.

The weakness in this argument is obvious. New and bigger armies certainly cost a lot of money, and in some few aspects (mainly the artillery trains) they made novel technical and industrial demands, but by comparison with navies, armies were, and indeed still are, cheap and simple. The prime requirement for an army in the early modern period was a large number of unemployed peasants to make soldiers, and a lesser number of unemployed noblemen to make officers. From time to time they had to be fed and paid, if they were not living off somebody else's country by the 'contributions' system,[8] but the burden on the state was greater than before chiefly because the armies were bigger, not because they were different. Clearly an army of 100,000 in 1600 cost more than one of 5,000 in 1400 – but it is highly unlikely to have cost as much as a navy of even 20,000 men. In any case, money was the easiest essential of sea power to find, much easier than the necessary technical and practical skills and resources. The new armies represented an increased burden largely in quantitive terms, the navies in qualitative terms as well. The case of 1588 shows clearly that the resources which were sufficient to make Spain the greatest military power in Europe, resources which included the largest merchant fleet and seafaring population in the world as well as unequalled financial strength, were completely inadequate to supply a navy equal to the English. Spain had ten times the money, but she did not have the skill. The problem was not just that Spain was over-committed elsewhere: no amount of money could have created an efficient Spanish fleet in two or three years. There were plenty of experienced seamen in Spain, but much more was needed to make a navy than ships and seamen. Armies could be improvised, indeed had to be, for wastage on campaign was so high that no force would remain operational for any length of time without constant recruitment. Navies demanded long-term planning and commitment.

The reader of this book will be in no doubt that a sixteenth-century 'naval revolution' did take place, and that a modern navy of the kind created in England made unique demands on state and society. If it was the demands of the 'military revolution' which created the absolutist monarchies (Spain, France, Sweden, later Prussia, Austria and Russia), it should logically follow that the much greater demands of the sixteenth-century 'naval revolution' would have propelled the leading naval powers (England and the Dutch Republic) into the forefront of the autocratic monarchies. Instead they were the two large states which conspicuously retained their medieval constitutions, complete with what seemed to be archaic and ineffectual representative institutions. It will not do to shuffle past this problem with a few embarrassed remarks to the effect that navies did not matter, or did not cost much, or did not exist until later.[9]

Considering the 'military revolution' and the 'naval revolution' together suggests that absolutist monarchy was essentially a system of government for mobilizing manpower rather than money. More efficient in its way than the medieval constitutions it replaced, it was poorly adapted to meet the much greater strains imposed on state and society by a modern navy. For that, it may be suggested, what was needed was a system of government which involved the maximum participation by those interest groups whose money and skills were indispensable to sea power – not just the nobility and peasantry whom absolutism set to work, but the shipowners and seafarers, the urban merchants and financiers, the industrial investors and managers, the skilled craftsmen; all the classes, in short, which absolutist government least represented and least favoured. The demands of sea power were not only greater in themselves, but fell upon a much wider cross-section of society, and required a much greater degree of social, political and administrative integration than armies did. A military regime could sustain itself by force, but a navy had to earn public support. Autocracy was adequate for an army, but navies needed consensus. This, we may suggest, is why Spain failed the naval test in the sixteenth century, just as France failed it in the eighteenth, Germany and Russia in the twentieth.

It has been powerfully argued that the successful naval powers were those whose navies were backed by the largest and most influential coalition of 'interest groups'.[10] It was of limited use if the friends and backers of naval strength held power for a while, only to lose it to others with other ideas, for without continuity of policy there could be no well-founded naval strength. That was where England failed in the seventeenth century. Elizabethan government had created a consensus in favour of its unique hybrid form of sea power. It was an uneasy consensus covering constant tension between the queen's defensive strategic priorities, and the offensive ambitions of her naval men: the queen again and again redeploying her scanty resources to face successive mortal dangers (almost all of them nearby), while the 'men-of-war' mounted bold expeditions to distant waters in pursuit of expansive visions of private profit and national aggrandizement. In its day it worked, but it did not evolve, and in the next century its constituent elements parted company. The Stuarts were unable to assemble a coalition to support the more ambitious fleet they built to face the new and more serious threats of the era of the Thirty Years War.

Part of the problem was that Queen Elizabeth's Navy Royal largely preceded the growth of English merchant shipping. In her time it was Spain which had the great merchant fleet; English sea power was a hybrid made up of the defensive royal fleet and the offensive, predatory privateer fleet. The Stuarts tried to build a Navy for the same purposes of national defence and deterrence for which Elizabeth had planned, but the threats they faced were nearer and greater, and they also had to respond to demands for protection from a large and politically powerful merchant shipping interest. Considered as an organization in isolation, the Royal Navy of the 1630s was as successful as Elizabeth's rather different Navy Royal had been. Its administration, its discipline and professional skills, its ships and weapons were probably still a match for anything in Europe. But its political and constitutional foundations were unsound; it was not rooted in the broad national support needed to sustain so complex and costly a force. Charles I's attempt to build a navy without consensus helped to fracture the country and lead to civil war and the collapse of the regime. What was needed for successful sea power was a broadly based coalition of 'interest groups' of one mind not only on the need for a navy, but on the size and type of navy which was needed. Early Stuart England probably already had a consensus in favour of a navy, but it had no agreement on the nature of the fleet and how it might be financed. In real terms, the government of Charles I enjoyed roughly the same share of national income (2 per cent in peacetime, 3–4 per cent in wartime) as his predecessors as kings of England had done for three hundred years. Only Henry VIII, recklessly spending the capital confiscated from the monasteries, had briefly raised that figure to 9 or 10 per cent.[11] To establish the navy he wanted, Charles would have had to increase significantly the crown's historic share of national income, and to do that he would have had to create a political coalition in favour of naval expenditure. His attempt to go ahead without national consensus led to a civil war in which the king and his Navy both perished. Parliament won its war by greatly increasing its share of national revenue, but the navy on which it spent part of that money, and the regime which inherited it, were further away than ever from enjoying broad national support.

So a thousand years of naval endeavour in the British Isles seemed to have ended in failure. Promising experiments by Edgar and Æthelstan, by Edward the Confessor and Richard the Lionheart, by Henry V and Henry VIII, by James IV, Elizabeth I and Charles I, had all in their way demonstrated the possibilities of sea power and the difficulties of making it last. Again and again monarchs had seen the need of an effective navy, and discovered the extreme difficulty of establishing it permanently. Much had been learnt, forgotten and relearnt about the sea as the only reliable safeguard of the three kingdoms against external invasion, and the essential guarantee of any settlement of their own affairs. Internal and external peace could never be assured without naval power, but in 1649 it was as hard as it had been at any time in a thousand years to guess where it might be found and how it might be secured. Still small and relatively weak, disunited, unstable and surrounded by powerful enemies, England did not look like a great power, still less a great naval power about to spring fully armed from the sterile soil of military dictatorship.

Only with hindsight is it possible to see how many of the foundations of sea power had been laid. The myths as much as the reality of the Elizabethan naval war had persuaded Englishmen that their future hopes somehow lay at sea and overseas. Success at sea had become a mark of national pride, and failure at sea a symbol of national humiliation. The governing classes of England, both the Parliamentarians in control and the Royalists in exile, had learnt by hard experience the high cost of modern war; and the still higher cost of lacking an effective navy. In this way the groundwork had been laid for a national consensus to sustain permanent sea power. The merchant fleet and the overseas trade it carried had grown enormously in size and wealth, and with it the seafaring population had expanded manyfold. Above all an extensive and sophisticated naval administration had grown up over more than a century, with docks and slips, stores and offices, smithies and ropewalks, foundries and powder mills; with a numerous staff of long experience, backed by advanced and prosperous private industry. The materials lay ready for an astonishing transformation, which within five years of the death of Charles I was to see the victorious fleets of the English Republic dictating terms of peace to Spain and the Netherlands, and within fifty had restored England to the ranks of the great powers: 'I see in my mind a noble and puissant nation rousing herself like a strong man after sleep, and shaking her invincible locks. Methinks I see her as an eagle mewing her mighty youth, and kindling her undazzled eyes at the full midday beam.'[12]

APPENDIX I

CHRONOLOGY

This is a summary of known naval operations, mainly but not only English, together with related military, political and diplomatic events. Sources are given only for those incidents not mentioned in the main text; much of the background is drawn from Storey's *Chronology of the Medieval World* and Williams' *Chronology of the Expanding World.*

684
King Ecgfrith of Northumbria raids Ireland.

685
Ecgfrith killed by the Picts at the Battle of Nechtansmere.

719
First recorded sea battle in the British Isles, in the Western Isles.

789
Viking raid on Portland.

793
Vikings destroy Lindisfarne Abbey.

836
King Egbert of Wessex defeated by Vikings at Carhampton.

851
Vikings' first winter in England. London and Canterbury stormed. Kentish ships fight Danish raiders at Sandwich.

860
A Viking army takes Winchester.

865
The Danish 'Great Army' invades England.

866
November 1: The Great Army takes York.

871
Alfred succeeds as King of Wessex. The Danes occupy London.

875
Alfred fights a small Danish squadron.

878
May: By the Peace of Wedmore, the Danish leader Guthrum accepts baptism and withdraws to East Anglia.

882
Alfred fights a small Danish squadron.

885
Naval actions against Danish ships in the Stour.

886
Alfred recaptures London from the Danes. A treaty defines the frontier of the Danelaw.

892
Alfred campaigns against Danish forces landing in Kent.

895
Alfred campaigns against Danish forces in Essex.

896
Alfred builds large warships of a new design.

927
July: Kings of Scots and Strathclyde acknowledge Æthelstan's overlordship.

934
Æthelstan's fleet sails to Caithness.

937
Æthelstan's victory over a Norse–Scots invasion at Brunanburh.

939
English fleet helps Brittany against Vikings in the Loire, and intervenes on behalf of Henry the Fowler of Germany.[1]

972
Godfrey Haraldsson of Man temporarily captures Anglesey.[2]

973
King Edgar's coronation ceremony on the Dee.

991
Olaf Tryggvason defeats Ealdorman Brytnoth of East Anglia at the Battle of Maldon. First payment of Danegeld.

992
Æthelred II orders ships to assemble at London.

1000
Æthelred leads a naval expedition to Man and Cumberland.

1008
Æthelred orders a national shipbuilding programme.

1009
English fleet assembles at Sandwich, but is broken up by storm and mutiny. The Danish fleet of Thorkell the Tall lands in Kent.

1013
King Swein Forkbeard of Denmark accepted as King of England; Æthelred II exiled.

1014
Death of Swein Forkbeard and restoration of Æthelred II.

1016
April 23: Death of Æthelred II of England.
November 30: Death of King Edmund Ironside of England. Cnut the Great of Denmark is accepted as King of England.

1028
King Cnut conquers Norway with an Anglo-Danish fleet.[3]

1042
June 8: Edward the Confessor becomes King of England.

1045
Large English fleet assembles in face of a threatened invasion.

1048
Earl Godwin commands an English fleet assembled in the Solent.

1049
Large English fleet assembled to intervene in Flanders. Norse–Irish force comes up the Severn to raid the Midlands.

1051
English succession crisis; Earl Godwin driven into exile in Flanders.

1052
English succession crisis: Earl Godwin lands in Sussex, rival fleets in the Thames, civil war narrowly averted.

1054
English military and naval expedition to Scotland in support of Malcolm Canmore.

1058
Norwegian–Welsh attack on England.

1063
Earl Harold Godwinsson leads an English naval expedition against Gruffydd ap Llywelyn of Gwynedd.

1066
January: Death of King Edward. Harold Godwinsson seizes the throne.
May ?: English fleet assembles in the Solent.
September: Norwegian fleet comes up the Ouse and captures York.
September 8: English fleet sails for the Thames.
September 12: Norman fleet sails from Dives, but is driven into St Valéry.
September 25: Battle of Stamford Bridge; King Harald of Norway killed.
September 29th: Duke William of Normandy lands in England.
October 14: Battle of Hastings.

1068
Harold's sons raid Somerset from Dublin.

1069
Harold's sons land in Devon but are defeated. Danish fleet captures York.

1070
Danes blockade the Thames, until William I buys them off with Danegeld.

1071
Rebellion of Earl Morcar: naval blockade of Ely.

1072
English expedition to and naval blockade of Scotland.[4]

1075
Danish fleet raids York. Gruffydd ap Cynan attacks Gwynedd with fleets from Dublin.

1081
Gruffydd ap Cynan recovers throne of Gwynedd with naval expedition from Dublin, but is displaced by Norman attack.

1085
Threatened Danish invasion inspires 'scorched earth' policy in England.

1088
Rebellion of Odo of Bayeux; blockade of Pevensey Castle.

1091
Malcolm of Scots attacks England. English fleet wrecked in gale.[5]

1094
Gruffydd ap Cynan again recovers Gwynedd with naval forces from Dublin.

1098
Earl Hugh of Chester killed in Anglesey by the Norwegian fleet.

1099
Gruffydd ap Cynan's fifth and ultimately successful invasion of Gwynedd.

1101
June: Duke Robert Curthose avoids Henry I's ships and lands at Portsmouth to dispute the throne of England.

1102
Rebellion of Arnulf de Montgomery of Pembroke.

1136
King Stephen blockades Baldwin de Redvers in the Isle of Wight.

1137
Diarmit Mac Murchada of Leinster attacks Waterford with 200 Dublin ships.[6]

1138
Danish fleet raids the East Coast.

1139
September 30. The Empress Matilda lands in England to campaign against King Stephen.

1141
March 3: The victorious Matilda is proclaimed Queen of England (but the civil war with Stephen is soon resumed).

1144
Count Geoffrey of Anjou conquers Normandy.

1147
October: Anglo-Flemish expedition captures Lisbon from the Saracens.

1153
January: Count Henry of Anjou lands in England to capture the throne from King Stephen, who makes peace by recognising Henry as his heir.

1154
October 25: Death of King Stephen of England and accession of Henry II.

1157
Henry II campaigns in North Wales.

1165
Henry II raises a Norse–Irish fleet in Dublin to support his campaign in Wales.

1171
Henry II's expedition to Ireland.

1177
John de Courcy with the Manx fleet conquers part of Ulster.

1190
Richard I sails on Crusade.

1194
Richard I released from captivity and returns to England.

1203
Battle of Les Andelys (R. Seine); a Norman squadron under Trenchemer fails to break through to lift the siege of Château Gaillard.

1212
August: English galleys under Geoffrey de Lucy raid the Welsh coast.[7]

1213
May 31–June 1: Battle of Damme; a French invasion fleet in port is partly destroyed by the English under Salisbury. He lands and is repulsed, but the French burn their own remaining ships.

1214
July 27: Battle of Bouvines; French victory over King John's Flemish allies destroys his hopes of regaining his empire.
Autumn: English recapture Sark.[8]

1215
Summer: Folkestone raided by Eustace the Monk.[9]
December: French troops sent to assist baronial rebels against King John.

1216
January 7: Further French reinforcements land at London.
May 2: English fleet dispersed by a gale.
May 20: Prince Louis of France lands in Kent and takes Sandwich.

1217
May 16: Dover Straits; P. d'Aubigny disperses a French squadron bringing reinforcements.
August 24: Battle of Dover; an English squadron under Hubert de Burgh defeats the French under Eustace the Monk, who is killed.

1223
Summer: Pembroke retakes Cardigan, Carmarthen and Kidwelly from Llywelyn ap Iorwerth with the help of Irish troops.
August: An expedition to recover Normandy is summoned, then abandoned.

1224
French overrun Poitou and take La Rochelle.
Pembroke suppresses Lacy's rebellion in Ulster.

1225
March: Expedition under Cornwall sails to Gascony.

1226
June: Reinforcements sent to Gascony.

1229
An expedition for Poitou is prepared.

1230
May: Henry III lands in Brittany and campaigns ineffectually in Poitou.

1233
August: Pembroke rebels in S. Wales and his ships blockade various royal castles, until the king's galleys break the siege in November.

1242
May: Revolt in Poitou against French; Henry III mounts an expedition in support, but is defeated in July and withdraws to Bordeaux.
October: Bayonne galleys attempt a blockade of La Rochelle with little success.

1244
Unsuccessful English campaign in Wales, supported by ships from Ireland.

1253
June: Expedition to Gascony.

1254
April: Expedition to Gascony.

1256
Prince Edward campaigns ineffectually in Wales.

1257
Henry III advances along the coast of N. Wales, but is forced to retreat for want of supplies from Ireland.

1263
October 3: Battle of Largs; Alexander III of Scots defeats Håkon IV of Norway.

1264
August: Montfort summons fleet to Sandwich to guard against invasion by Queen Eleanor.[10]

1266
July 2: By the Treaty of Perth, Norway cedes the Isle of Man and the Hebrides to Scotland.

1275
Scots ships suppress a Manx rebellion.

1277
June: 1st Welsh War; Edward I invades N. Wales by the coastal route. Naval forces occupy Anglesey.

1282
August: 2nd Welsh War; English invasion of N. Wales. Naval forces occupy Anglesey.
November 6: English attack from Anglesey over pontoon bridge is defeated.

1290
Summer: Isle of Man taken by the English.[11]

1293
May 15: Battle of St Matthew between Normans and Anglo-Gascon fleet, followed by the sack of La Rochelle.

1294
October: Reinforcements sail for Gascony, enter the Gironde and recapture Bourg and Blaye.
December: Edward I marches into N. Wales to suppress Welsh revolt, while ships supply isolated castles.

1295
April: Fleet ordered to assemble against French invasion threat.[12]
April: Invasion of Anglesey.[13]
August 2: French raid Dover but are repulsed at Winchelsea.
August: A small squadron sent north up the East Coast.[14]
September: Ships over 40 tons arrested for an expedition to Gascony.[15]

1296
January 15: Lancaster's fleet sails for Gascony.
March: Edward I invades Scotland and takes Berwick.
April 27: Scots defeated at Dunbar.

1297
March–April: Fleet summoned for the expedition to Flanders.[16]
May: William Wallace leads Scots rebellion.
August 24: Edward I sails for Flanders; Yarmouth and Cinque Ports ships fight in the Swyn.
October: Truce in Gascony lifts the sieges of Bourg and Blaye.
November: English fleet ordered to concentrate against French invasion threat.[17]

1298
February: Ships summoned to Sluys to bring Edward I home.[18]
July 22: Scots defeated at Falkirk, but English army has to retreat for want of supplies.

1299
August: Cinque Ports ships summoned to Carlisle.[19]
December: Transports summoned to Berwick.[20]

1300
Summer: English campaign in Galloway and capture Caerlaverock Castle, with support from ships and supplies from Ireland; Scots capture Stirling Castle.

1301
Summer: English campaign in Scotland on both coasts, but Scots avoid battle.

1302
July 11: The French defeated by the Flemings at Courtrai.

1303
May: Edward I advances up E. Coast, crosses the Forth and winters in Dunfermline. An Irish army in English service lands in the Clyde.
May 20: All Gascony restored to England by the Treaty of Paris.

1304
July 14: Gravelines surrenders to French fleet which includes 20 English ships.[21]
July 20: Surrender of Stirling Castle marks English conquest of Scotland.

1306
February: Robert Bruce raises rebellion, but is defeated and driven into the Isles.
September: English ships looking for Bruce take Dunaverty Castle.

1307
January: Ships from Ireland ordered to join the hunt for Bruce in the Western Isles.
August: After the death of his father, Edward II campaigns briefly in Scotland.

1308
October: 20 ships ordered to the defence of Berwick.[22]

1309
October: 2 ships ordered to the defence of Perth.[23]

1310
June: Ships ordered to relieve Perth.[24]

1311
May: Fleet ordered to assemble at Larne at end of June.[25]
September: Edward II campaigns ineffectually in Scotland.

1313
January 13: Perth captured by the Scots.
Summer: The Scots recover the Isle of Man.[26]
July: Fleet ordered to muster at Sandwich and Winchelsea by the end of August.[27]

1314
April: Fleet to assemble at Conwy then move to Dublin.[28]
June 24: Battle of Bannockburn; the Scots defeat Edward II and force his withdrawal from Scotland.
July: 30 ships urgently demanded to go to Hull.[29]

1315
January 14: Scots surprise night attack on Berwick fails.[30]
February: Eoin MacDougall of Lorne retakes Man for the English.[31]
March: Yarmouth ships ordered to intercept Scots cogs at Sluys.[32]
May: Edward Bruce invades Ireland.[33]
July: English fleet assembled in the Irish Sea.[34]

1317
February: Robert Bruce campaigns in Ireland. The Scots retake Man.[35]
February–March: English fleet assembled at Haverford to carry reinforcements to Ireland and then cruise in Irish Sea.[36]
Summer–autumn: John of Athy, English admiral in the Irish Sea, captures and kills the Scots commander Thomas Dun.[37]

1318
April 8: Berwick taken by the Scots.[38]
May: Scots raid into Yorkshire, exacting tribute.
October 14: Edward Bruce defeated and killed by English forces in Ireland.

1319
August: English besiege Berwick.
September 20: English defeated by a Scottish army in Swaledale; siege of Berwick abandoned.

1322
August: Ineffectual English campaign in Scotland, followed by Scots raids into England.
October 14: Bruce defeats English at Byland.

1324
May: Fleet summoned to Plymouth for an expedition to Gascony.[39]
July: Fleet against the French summoned to Sandwich and Dover.[40]
August: French invade Gascony, opening the War of St Sardos.

1326
May: The English attack Norman shipping.[41]
August: Southern and western fleet to assemble at Portsmouth.[42]
September: Northern fleet to assemble at Orwell; other ships from E. Coast ports ordered on local patrol.[43] The English burn Cherbourg.[44]
September 26: Isabella and Mortimer land in Suffolk; they take control of the government, imprison Edward II and proclaim his son Edward III.

1327
January: The Scots break the truce and attack Norham Castle.[45]
March 31: War of St Sardos ended and Gascony restored to the English.
April: Robert I of Scotland lands in Ireland.[46]
May: Squadrons summoned to Carlisle and Yarmouth against threatened Scots invasion.[47]
June: An English squadron briefly operates from Yarmouth. The English army in Durham is outmanoeuvred and humiliated by the Scots.[48]

1328
April–May: Robert I campaigns in northern England and exacts tribute; Edward III recognizes him as King of Scots.[49]

1330
May: A fleet is summoned for Gascony.[50]

1332
August 12: Edward Balliol and 'the Disinherited' land in Fife and defeat the Regent of Scotland at Dupplin Muir.
September: A proposed English expedition to Ireland is cancelled.[51]
December 12: Edward Balliol defeated and escapes to England.[52]

1333
April: E. Coast fleet assembled at Newcastle.[53]
May: The English besiege Berwick.[54]
June: The English occupy Man.[55]
July 19: An English victory at Halidon Hill leads to the surrender of Berwick.

1334
June 12: Edward Balliol, restored to the throne of Scotland by English arms, cedes most of the Lowlands to England.
September: Balliol forced to flee by a renewed Scottish rebellion.
November: The English army musters at Newcastle.[56]
December: All ships over 40 tons summoned for the war in Scotland.[57]

1335
February: Edward III abandons his winter campaign at Roxburgh.[58] The English fleet is dismissed except for cruisers sent against ships carrying supplies to the Scots.[59]

April–May: Irish and English ships ordered to muster at various ports.[60]
July: Edward III campaigns in Scotland to little effect. Ships from Ireland unsuccessfully attack Rothesay.[61]
July–August: Ships arrested everywhere to resist expected Scots invasion.

1336
February: All shipping to be arrested against an imminent Scots invasion.
Summer: The French assemble an invasion fleet.[62]
July: Edward III campaigns in the Highlands.
August: French and Scottish cruisers take ships off the Isle of Wight and Suffolk.[63]
October: An English fleet gathers in the Downs to resist invasion.[64]
December: Shipping ordered to Portsmouth for an expedition to Gascony.[65]

1337
March: Shipping ordered to assemble at Portsmouth and Orwell.[66]
May: Philip VI of France announces the confiscation of Gascony.
October: Edward III claims the throne of France.

1338
February: All seagoing ships ordered to the Orwell.[67]
March 24: Portsmouth burnt by French galleys and Jersey raided.
July: Edward sails to Antwerp.
August 23: Castilian galleys take 2 prizes from an English convoy off the Gironde.
September: Genoese galleys capture Guernsey. The French and Genoese capture five prizes including two of Edward III's ships at Middelburg. All armed English ships are ordered to sea against the enemy galleys.[68]
October 5: Genoese and French galleys burn Southampton. Reinforced English fleet ordered to stay at sea; coast defences are prepared.[69]

1339
March: A Franco-Genoese squadron reinforces Guernsey, attacks Jersey without success, and escorts a convoy to La Rochelle.
April: They enter the Gironde and capture Bourg and Blaye. Another Genoese galley squadron raids Harwich. English and Franco-Genoese convoys meet and fight off Sluys. Scots barges harass the English garrisons of Perth, Stirling and Cupar.
May: Genoese burn Hastings and attack Plymouth.
July: A French raid on the Cinque Ports repulsed. Genoese galleys in French service mutiny for want of pay and return home, engendering a popular revolt in Genoa. Franco-Scots blockade of the Tay enforces the surrender of Cupar and Perth.
September: Simon Boccanegra installed as Doge of Genoa by a popular rising, upsetting French plans to obtain Genoese galleys.

October: Indecisive campaign in Picardy between Edward III and Philip VI. Franco-Genoese squadron sails from Sluys to attack the Yarmouth herring fishery, but is dispersed by storms.

1340

January: Cinque Ports raid Boulogne and burn 18 French galleys. Dieppe is also raided.
May: Tréport is raided by the English.
June 24: Battle of Sluys.
July 26: French galleys take 30 prizes out of a wool convoy.
August: French galleys raid the Isles of Wight and Portland, burn Teignmouth but are driven off from Plymouth. English fleet ordered to sea to search for them.[70]
September 25: Truce of Espléchin between England and France.

1341

April: The death of Duke John III of Brittany precipitates the Breton War of Succession.
May: All ships of 60 tons to be at Sandwich by the end of May; later altered to Winchelsea and Yarmouth in August.[71]
June: English garrison expelled from Edinburgh; David II of Scots returns from France.
June: An English fleet ordered to sea against enemy galleys.[72]
Summer: French, Castilian and Portuguese galleys operate in the Bay against English convoys to Gascony.

1342

January: Ineffectual English campaign in Scotland.
March: The Scots capture Roxburgh. An English fleet summoned to Orwell too carry Mauny to Brittany.[73]
April: Franco-Genoese squadron caught in Quimperlé river by Mauny's expedition and destroyed.
June: English expedition under Mauny relieves the siege of Hennebont.
August: Northampton's expedition to Brittany sails from Southampton. French galleys burn Portsmouth. Naval battle off Guernsey.
September 30: English forces in Brittany defeat French at Morlaix.
October: Edward III lands in Brittany.
November: English ships unsuccessfully attack Castilian galleys in the Bay of Bourgneuf.

1343

January: Truce of Malestroit between England and France.
February: Fleet for Brittany countermanded.[74]
December: 24 ships levied to carry reliefs to castles in Brittany.[75]

1344
March: All ships over 30 tons to be arrested.[76]

1345
June: All ships over 30 tons to be ready for the king's passage to France.[77]
August: Bayonne galleys retake Guernsey.
October: Another fleet to assemble at Portsmouth.[78]
October 21: Lancaster defeats the French in Gascony.

1346
April: The siege of Aiguillon in Gascony, with much river fighting.[79] After numerous delays a fleet assembles at Portsmouth.[80]
July: Edward III lands at St Vaast-la-Hougue and invades Normandy.
August 26: The French defeated at Crécy.
September: Edward III begins the siege of Calais. Genoese galleys capture 25 ships of the blockading fleet.
October 17: David II of Scots defeated and captured at Neville's Cross.

1347
March: A French convoy gets through to Calais. Tunnage & Poundage granted to maintain 120 ships.[81]
April 2: Another French convoy enters Calais.
June 25: The English destroy the last French relief convoy at Le Crotoy.
August 4: Surrender of Calais.
September: Anglo-French truce.

1348
August: Victuallers ordered to supply the English army in Scotland.[82]

1349
April–July: A fleet assembled for Gascony.[83]

1350
August 29: Battle of Winchelsea.

1352
March: A fleet for Gascony summoned to Southampton.[84]
September: Ships arrested for the king's passage to Brittany.[85]

1353
June: Shipping for Gascony to assemble.[86]
September: Bordeaux trade to sail under convoy.[87]

1355
June: Shipping summoned to Southampton to carry the Black Prince to Gascony.[88]
September: Shipping summoned to Sandwich to carry the king to France.[89]
November: Edward III campaigns briefly in Picardy; the Black Prince raids

Southern France: the Scots take Berwick.[90]
December: A fleet ordered to the east coast of Scotland.[91]

1356
January: Edward III retakes Berwick and raids as far as Edinburgh.
June: Lancaster lands in Normandy.
September: The Black Prince raids into France from Gascony and wins the battle of Poitiers, capturing John II of France.

1357
March: Truce of Bordeaux between England and France.
October: Truce of Berwick between England and Scotland; David II released.

1359
April: Shipping summoned to Sandwich for the king's passage.[92]
July–August: Further shipping summoned to Sandwich.[93]
December: Edward III besieges Rheims.

1360
March 15: French forces sack Winchelsea. All large ships mobilized, the rest to be hauled up out of harm's way.[94]
May: After further English campaigns in France, the Treaty of Brétigny makes peace between the two. Edward III recovers the Angevin empire.

1361
August: Irish ships summoned to bring over Prince Lionel; Bristol ships to carry Stafford to Gascony.[95]

1362
July: Shipping arrested for Ireland and Gascony.[96]

1363
March: Smaller ships to be at Bristol for passage to Ireland.[97]
April: Larger ships to be at Plymouth for Gascony.[98]

1364
January: W. Coast ships to Liverpool to carry troops to Ireland.[99]
July–August: Further shipping ordered to Liverpool to take Clarence to Ireland.[100]
September 29: Battle of Auray; defeat and death of Charles de Blois, the French claimant to the throne of Brittany.

1365
March: France recognizes John de Montfort as Duke of Brittany.

1366
March: Henry of Trastámara expells Pedro the Cruel and seizes the throne of Castile.
Summer: The Danish fleet raids East Anglia.[101]

1367

April 3: The Black Prince defeats Henry of Trastámara at Nájera and briefly restores Pedro the Cruel.

1369

January: A rebellion against English rule in Gascony.
February: Southern fleet ordered to assemble.[102]
March: Henry of Trastámara defeats and kills Pedro the Cruel and again is king of Castile.
April: French overrun Ponthieu.
May: Anglo-French war formally resumes.
June: Northern fleet ordered to assemble.[103]
September: Lancaster raids northern France from Calais to Harfleur. French burn Portsmouth.
December: Owain ap Thomas sails from Harfleur, but his squadron is scattered by a storm.

1370

January: All large ships summoned to Winchelsea and Plymouth.[104]
May: The whole fleet to assemble in the Orwell.[105]
June 10: French galleys burn Gosport.
July: Knolles raids northern France.
September: The Black Prince raids southern France and sacks Limoges.
November: Warning of imminent French invasion.[106]

1371

January: A fleet to assemble at Lynn.[107]
August 1: A Flemish fleet captured by the English in the Bay of Bourgneuf.[108]

1372

April: Ships arrested for the king's passage.[109]
June: Owain ap Thomas raids Guernsey.[110]
June 23: Battle of La Rochelle; Castilians defeat an English squadron and capture the Earl of Pembroke. Castilian galleys blockade Poitou.
August: Ships arrested to carry Neville to Brittany.[111]
August 15: The French capture La Rochelle.
August 23: Owain ap Thomas's galleys capture the Captal de Buch.
August 31: An English relief fleet sails from Portsmouth, but is forced back by gales.
December: The French complete the reconquest of Poitou.

1373

March: A royal squadron ordered to escort shipping to Gascony.[112]
April: Pro-French revolt in Brittany drives out Duke John IV and leaves only Brest in English hands.

Salisbury relieves Brest and burns St Malo.
August: Lancaster marches from Calais on an expedition through Champagne and Burgundy.

1374
September: Shipping ordered to Dartmouth and Plymouth to take Cambridge to Brittany.[113]

1375
June: Truce of Bruges between England and France.
August 10: Castilian galleys take 39 prizes out of an English Bay fleet.

1376
March: A fleet to assemble at Sandwich and Hamble to await orders.[114]

1377
March: A fleet to assemble in the Thames.[115]
June 29: French galleys burn Rye.
July: French galleys raid Rottingdean, Lewes, Folkestone, Portsmouth, Dartmouth and Plymouth. Beacons ordered in Kent and Essex to warn of enemy ships in the Thames.[116]
August: They attack the Isle of Wight, burn Hastings and part of Poole, but fail before Southampton, Winchelsea and Dover.
September: Boulogne barges raid the Yarmouth herring fishery.
October: An English squadron based at Calais raids Boulogne and burns 28 ships. Buckingham sails from London to intercept a Castilian fleet detained in Sluys, but his squadron is dispersed by storm and mutiny.
November: Part of this squadron under Percy takes 22 ships out of the Castilian convoy. Parliament agrees to a national programme of balinger-building.

1378
January: Buckingham relieves Brest.
Spring: Philpot's private squadron cruises against Mercer's Scots force.[117]
May: Lancaster's fleet assembles at Southampton.[118]
June: Charles II of Navarre grants the English Cherbourg. An English fleet fails to break through the French besiegers of the Navarrese garrison of Pont-Audemer (action of La Bressolière on the Risle, with Grimaldi's galleys).
August: Franco-Castilian galleys raid Cornwall.
September: An English fleet fails to take St Malo.
October: English squadron returning from installing the garrison of Cherbourg is defeated by the French and Genoese, who blockade the place.

1379
March: E. Coast ships to assemble at Kirkely.[119]
August: Duke John IV recovers Brittany from the French party.
December: Arundel's expedition to Brittany destroyed in a gale.

1380

June 10: Castilian fleet defeated by the English at Kinsale.
July: Buckingham leaves Calais to raid central France.
August: Castilian galleys burn Gravesend.

1381

June: The Peasants' Revolt occupies London but is suppressed. The Castilian galleys defeat the Portuguese and blockade the Tagus, trapping an English fleet until December.

1382

January: Bordeaux and Bayonne to provide a fleet to carry the King of Navarre to England.[120]
Autumn: Castilian galleys under Cabeza de Vaca operating in the Channel.

1383

April: All ships to be arrested for the Flanders expedition.[121]
May: The Bishop of Norwich's unsuccessful expedition to Flanders.
July: Philpot blockades the Seine.[122]

1384

February: The Scots raid Cumberland.
April: An English army reaches Edinburgh.
September: All shipping for Gascony to sail in convoy.[123]

1385

January: Shipping arrested for an expedition to Portugal.[124]
May: French blockaded in Sluys by squadron of Percy and Radyngton.[125]
July: A Franco-Scottish force raids Northumberland.
August: Richard II sacks Edinburgh.
August 14: Battle of Aljubarrota; John I of Castile is heavily defeated by the Portuguese, with English help.
October: Gascon trade ordered to sail under convoy.[126]

1386

May: Ten Portuguese galleys chartered. Lancaster's fleet ordered to assemble at Plymouth.[127]
July: Lancaster sails from Plymouth under Anglo-Portuguese escort to Corunna (failing to raise the siege of Brest en route), to invade Castile, which throne he claims. After his ships return home, the Castilian galleys blockade Corunna.[128]
Summer: The French assemble an invasion fleet in Flanders, but abandon their plan.
August: Coastal districts warned of imminent invasion. Gascon trade to sail under convoy.[129]
December: Flanders wool trade to sail under convoy.[130]

1387
March 25: Arundel intercepts a Flemish convoy in the Straits of Dover and takes 70 prizes.
May: An English squadron patrolling the Norman coast is defeated off Dieppe.
May: Treaty of Troncoso between Lancaster and Castile.
October: Gascon trade to sail under convoy.[131]

1388
February: The baronial opposition to Richard II, the 'Lords Appellant', take control of the government.
June: Arundel's expedition to sail.[132]
August 5: Douglas killed winning the Scots' victory at Otterburn.
August: Ships sent to Bordeaux to bring Lancaster back.[133]

1389
May: Richard II resumes personal rule.

1394
January 21: The English hand over Cherbourg for a payment of 25,000 *livres*.[134]
June: Shipping to assemble for king's passage to Ireland.[135]
October: Richard II lands at Waterford.

1395
April: Shipping taken up to bring the king back from Ireland.[136]
May: Richard II sails from Dublin to England.
Bordeaux convoy action and the loss of the *Christopher*.[137]

1396
March: Truce between England and France.
August: Cinque Ports ships summoned to report at Dover.[138]

1397
June: The English garrison of Brest is withdrawn by treaty with Brittany.

1398
May: Various ships licensed to cruise against pirates.[139]
August: Shipping arrested for Surrey's passage to Ireland and Dorset's to Aquitaine.[140]

1399
April: All shipping to be arrested for the king's Irish expedition.[141]
June: Richard II's second Irish expedition.
July: Lancaster lands at Ravenspur and raises rebellion; Richard returns from Ireland.
September: Richard II deposed; Lancaster becomes Henry IV.

1400

June–July: The Cinque Ports summoned to support Henry IV's Scottish campaign.[142]
August: Further shipping summoned to support the campaign in Scotland.[143]
October: Henry campaigns in N. Wales.

1401

January: Henry IV orders balingers and barges to be built.
April: Welsh rebels take Conwy Castle.
June: Shipping arrested to guard the seas.[144]
July: Shipping arrested to carry Rutland's expedition to Gascony.[145]
October: Henry's second Welsh campaign fails to crush the revolt.

1402

March: Shipping summoned to keep the sea, and to carry princesses to and from the Continent.[146]
June: Owain Glyndŵr captures Edmund Mortimer.
August: Northumberland defeats a Scottish force invading England.
September: Henry campaigns ineffectually in Wales.

1403

April: £10,000 worth of English goods confiscated at Sluys in reprisals for English piracy.[147] Enquiries into English piracies are mounted.[148]
July: Defeat and death of Henry 'Hotspur' ends his revolt. Glyndŵr captures Carmarthen Castle.
September: Carmarthen retaken by the English. Gascon fleet ordered to the Isle of Wight.[149]
November: Warning of an intended French naval raid on Bordeaux and England.[150]
December: Glyndŵr takes Cardiff. Unsuccessful French raid on the Isle of Wight.

1404

March: All shipping ordered to be arrested for unspecified service.[151]
March–April: The Welsh capture Criccieth, Harlech and Aberystwth.
April 15: Unsuccessful Breton attack on Dartmouth.[152]
June: The English raid Brittany and unsuccessfully attack Brest.[153]
July: Franco-Welsh and Franco-Castilian alliances.

1405

March: Glyndŵr defeated at Grosmont.
May: Glyndŵr defeated at Usk. Scrope's rebellion collapses.
July: Troops arrayed to resist French invasion.[154]
August: A French expedition lands at Milford Haven; Glyndŵr takes Carmarthen with French help.[155]
September: Henry retakes Carmarthen but otherwise achieves little.

December: The fleet assembled to carry the king to Gascony is ordered to wait still longer.[156]

1406

February: The French blockade the Thames.[157]
March: Prince James of Scotland (James I in April) captured at sea by a ship of Cley-next-the-Sea.[158]
May: The merchants to keep the sea for 17 months.[159]
Summer: The English capture 8 prizes from a French squadron bringing reinforcements to Wales and force the rest to retreat.[160]
October: French invasion of Gascony. Collapse of the arrangement for 'merchant-seakeeping' following numerous complaints of piracy.[161]

1407

January: The French abandon the siege of Bourg and withdraw from Gascony after their supply convoy from La Rochelle is defeated in the Gironde.[162]

1408

February: The exiled Northumberland, invading from Scotland, is defeated and killed.

1409

January: The Welsh surrender Harlech Castle.
October: Shipping for Calais embargoed for fear of French interception.[163]

1411

September: Shipping assembled for the king's passage to Gascony.[164]

1412

June: Cinque Ports summoned for an intended expedition.[165]

1413

March: All shipping embargoed.[166]
August: Ships for Gascony ordered to sail in convoy.[167]

1414

May: Anglo-Burgundian alliance.

1415

May: All shipping summoned for an expedition.[168]
August: English invasion of France. Warnings of Scottish seaborne attacks.[169]
September 22: Capture of Harfleur.
October 25: Battle of Agincourt.

1416

July: A fleet ordered to Southampton.[170]
August 15: Battle of the Seine: Bedford defeats a Franco-Genoese fleet blockading Harfleur.

1417
March–May: Ships ordered to assemble at Southampton.[171]
July 25: Huntingdon's victory in the Bay of Seine.
August 1: Henry V lands at Trouville to invade Normany.
September 20: Henry takes Caen.

1418
July: Henry V begins the siege of Rouen.

1419
January: The fall of Rouen marks the English conquest of Normandy.
February: Warning of an imminent Castilian raid on Southampton.
March: Huntingdon is ordered to blockade the Seine.[172]
June: The Franco-Castilian Treaty of Segovia promises the Armagnacs the help of 40 large ships.
July: Intelligence received of Castilian plans to besiege Bayonne, and convey Scots troops to France.
December 30: The Castilians defeat an English-Hansa fleet near La Rochelle.

1421
May: The Cinque Ports summoned for service.[173]

1423
June: Shipping taken up to carry reinforcements to France and Gascony.[174]

1424
February: Shipping summoned to Winchelsea.[175]
March: James I of Scots released and makes a seven-year truce with England.

1425
June: Suffolk's squadron blockading Mont St Michel is defeated.[176]

1426
August: Shipping taken up for reinforcements for France.[177]

1427
February: Shipping mustered at Sandwich to carry reinforcements to France.[178]
June: Shipping ordered to carry reinforcements to Ireland.[179]

1428
March: Shipping assembled to carry reinforcements to France and Ireland.[180]

1429
June: A fleet summoned to carry reinforcements to France.[181]

1430
A fleet mustered from Western ports.[182]
April: Shipping of E. and S. Coast ports to assemble at Sandwich.[183]

1431
April: A fleet ordered to Sandwich to embark reinforcements for France.[184]
June: Further shipping assembled to carry reinforcements from Sandwich to France, from Plymouth to Bordeaux, and from Lancaster to Ireland.[185]

1432
August: A fleet summoned to Winchelsea to carry the king and his army to France.[186]

1433
April: Shipping ordered to carry reinforcements to France.[187]

1435
June: All ships to assemble at Sandwich.[188]
September: At the Congress of Arras, the Burgundians change sides.
October: The French capture Dieppe.

1436
March: All ships over 16 tons to assemble at Winchelsea.[189] A Burgundian convoy from La Rochelle is attacked in the Trade.[190]
April: The French capture Paris.
August: The Burgundian siege of Calais and the Scots siege of Roxburgh are abandoned. Gloucester raids Flanders.[191]

1439
October: Shipping arrested for a fleet.[192]
September: A truce between England and Burgundy.

1440
January: A fleet to assemble at Poole to carry Somerset to Normandy.[193]
Courtenay and Bonville take a squadron to sea. Speke's squadron at the siege of Harfleur.[194]

1442
April: A fleet ordered to Winchelsea to carry Talbot to Normandy.[195]
August: The fleet assembles at Winchelsea.[196]
September: The Parliamentary fleet assembles at Southampton.[197]

1443
August: Somerset lands at Cherbourg and marches south.
December: Somerset retreats from Anjou to Normandy.

1448
May: Anglo-Scottish war breaks out.

1449
May 23: Winnington captures the Hansa salt fleet returning from the Bay of Bourgneuf.

October: Rouen taken by the French.

1450

April: Shipping assembled for Suffolk's voyage to France.[198]
May: having been impeached and sentenced to exile, Suffolk is murdered on shipboard leaving the country.
July: 'Jack Cade's' rebellion at its height.
August: The fall of Cherbourg completes the French reconquest of Normandy.
September: Rivers' fleet assembles at Plymouth for Gascony.[199]

1451

June: Bordeaux surrenders to the French. Rivers' expedition is abandoned after a prolonged wait.[200]
August: E. Coast ships summoned to Sandwich.[201] The fall of Bayonne completes the French conquest of Gascony.

1452

February: A fleet summoned to Sandwich to defend Calais and the Straits; it is later diverted to Bordeaux.[202]
October: Bordeaux rebels against the French and restores English rule.

1453

July: Shrewsbury defeated and killed at the Battle of Châtillon.
October: Bordeaux surrenders to the French again.

1454

March: York elected Protector of England during the insanity of Henry VI: he proposes a scheme for keeping the sea.[203]
Summer: The Archbishop of Dublin is captured by Scots pirates in Dublin Bay.[204]
December: York dismissed on Henry recovering his sanity.

1455

May: York and the Nevilles attack the court at St Albans, capturing Henry VI and starting the Wars of the Roses.

1457

August 28: The French sack Sandwich.

1458

May 29: Warwick defeats a Castilian fleet in the Channel.
July 29: Warwick seizes part of the Hansa Bay fleet.

1459

Summer: Warwick captures Genoese and other neutrals.

1460

May: The royal fleet under Exeter meets Warwick at sea but avoids action.
June: Warwick occupies Sandwich, capturing the royal fleet and its commanders.

August: The Scots take Roxburgh, but James II is accidentally killed.

1461

March: Edward of York assumes the English throne as Edward IV.
April: Henry VI, in exile in Scotland, cedes Berwick to the Scots.
The French take Mt Orgeuil Castle, Jersey.

1462

Treaty of Ardtornish between Edward IV and John II, Lord of the Isles.
May–June: All available ships arrested for the king's fleet.[205]
September: Warwick raids Le Conquet and the Île de Ré.
November: Queen Margaret lands from France and captures Alnwick; Yorkist ships and troops based on Newcastle counter-attack.[206]

1463

August: English ships patrol the east coast to stop French aid reaching the Lancastrians.[207]

1468

March: The Orkneys and Shetlands are pledged in dower to Scotland on the marriage of Princess Margaret of Denmark.
June: The Danes capture an English fleet in the Sound.[208]
Summer: A small English force sent to Jersey.
October: Scales cruises for 6 weeks in the Channel.

1469

Spring: Warwick at sea, possibly in the Bay.
July: Warwick lands at Sandwich to intervene again in the civil wars, but is obliged to withdraw to France.

1470

April 14: Warwick and Clarence sail from Exeter, fail to seize the *Trinity* at Southampton, and are refused entry to Calais.[209]
April 20: Warwick takes a Flemish convoy in the Straits of Dover.[210]
Summer: A small English squadron campaigns against the Hansa.[211]
September: Warwick invades England.
October: Warwick restores Henry VI. Edward IV escapes from Lynn.

1471

March 11: Edward IV sails from Flushing in a fleet raised with Burgundian aid, and lands at Ravenspur.
April: Edward IV defeats and kills Warwick and regains the English throne.
May: Fauconberg lands in Kent and attacks London with the help of ships from the Cinque Ports, but is defeated by the Londoners.
July 19: English ships defeat Hansa privateers on the Flanders coast.[212]

1473
February: Edward IV agrees to provide regular convoys to Calais.

1474
February: Besieged Lancastrians in St Michael's Mount surrender.
December: Selected ships over 16 tons arrested to serve in the invasion force.[213]

1475
Summer: Squadrons patrol the Channel and Straits to protect the invasion force and suppress piracy.[214]
July: Edward IV lands at Calais to begin the reconquest of France.
August: Edward IV is bought off by the Treaty of Picquigny.

1476
July: John MacDonald, Lord of the Isles, submits to James III of Scots.

1481
Summer: English squadrons operate against Scotland on both coasts, and in the Straits of Dover against France. At the battle of Bloody Bay Angus Og MacDonald defeats his father and becomes effective Lord of the Isles.

1482
June: English invasion of Scotland, supported by a fleet.
August: The English recapture Berwick.

1483
December: An English squadron under Wentworth sent against Brittany.[215]

1484
February: Iceland trade ordered to sail under convoy.[216]
September: Convoys to Calais are organized.[217]

1485
August 1: Henry Tudor, Earl of Richmond, sails from Harfleur to invade England.
August 22: Richmond defeats and kills Richard III at Bosworth and becomes King Henry VII.

1487
March: A squadron is ordered to sea.[218]
June: The forces of the pretender Lambert Simnel invade England from Ireland but are defeated.

1489
February: The Anglo-Imperial Treaty of Dordrecht aims to guarantee the independence of Brittany against France; ships are mustered and English troops are sent there.[219]

1490
Sir Andrew Wood defeats an English squadron off May Island.

1491
December: Duchess Anne of Brittany marries Charles VIII of France.

1492
Summer: A squadron under Sir Edward Poynings assists Imperial forces to recapture Sluys from the rebel Count of Ravenstein.[220]
October: Henry VII invades France from Calais but is soon bought off by the Treaty of Etaples.

1493
July: Trade between England and Flanders is stopped because the pretender Perkin Warbeck is received at the Burgundian court.

1494
Summer: Scots ships briefly capture MacDonald of Dunivaig's castle at Dunaverty.
October: A Yorkist conspiracy broken up; in Ireland the new Lord Deputy Sir Edward Poynings suppresses Yorkist rebellion.

1495
May: James IV leads an expedition to the Western Isles.
July: Warbeck fails to land at Deal or take Waterford.

1496
February: The 'Magnus Intercursus' treaty ends England's dispute with Burgundy.
July: England joins the 'Holy League' against France.
September: James IV of Scots with Warbeck raids Northumberland.

1497
June: Cornish rebels defeated by Henry VII at Blackheath. The English raid Scotland by land and sea.
August: The Scots besiege Norham Castle. Warbeck sails to Cork but fails to raise a rebellion.
September: The Anglo-Scottish Truce of Ayton, to last for seven years. Warbeck lands in Cornwall from Ireland.
October: Final defeat of the Western rebellion and surrender of Warbeck.

1502
January: Peace between England and Scotland.
May–July: Unsuccessful Scots expedition to help Denmark against the Norwegian–Swedish rebels.[221]

1503
August: James IV of Scots marries Princess Margaret of England.

1504
April: Scots expedition against Donald Dubh MacDonald.

1506
Summer: Stornoway Castle falls to the King of Scots; Donald Dubh later captured.

1511
August: Sir Edward Howard defeats and kills the Scottish pirate Andrew Barton.
November: Henry VIII joins 'Holy League' against France.

1512
June: Dorset's army lands at Fuentarrabia, meaning to invade France.
August 10: Battle with French fleet off Brest: the *Regent* and *Cordelière* burnt.

1513
March: English fleet sails for Brittany and blockades Brest.
April 25: Sir Edward Howard killed attacking French galleys near Brest.
June: Henry VIII lands at Calais and invades France.
August 16: Battle of the Spurs, followed by surrender of Thérouanne and Tournai.
September 9: James IV defeated and killed at Flodden.

1522
May: England declares war on France. Sabyn's squadron attacks the Firth of Forth.
June 13: Surrey raids Cherbourg.[222]
July 1: Surrey sacks Morlaix.
August: Surrey invades northern France, but achieves little.

1523
August: Sir William FitzWilliam cruises in the Channel and burns Tréport. The Duke of Albany with 3,000 troops sails from France to Scotland.
September: Suffolk invades France from Calais, but again withdraws.

1525
August: Peace with France.

1532
March: Scottish warships off the Start interrupt Channel trade.[223]

1533
February–April: Scottish blockade of the East Coast.[224]
April: The *Mary Willoughby* taken by the Macleans of Duart.

1536
August: James V sails from Kirkaldy to Dieppe to marry Princess Madeleine of France.[225]

1540
May–June: James V circumnavigates Scotland and cruises in the Western Isles.[226]

1542
October: Henry VIII declares war on Scotland. Norfolk's advance into Scotland disintegrates for want of supplies, and naval blockade fails.
November 25: Scots defeat at Solway Moss.
December 14: James V dies and is succeeded by the week-old Princess Mary.

1543
June: French convoy brings money and supplies to Scotland.[227]
July: Brief peace between England and Scotland.

1544
May: English landing near Leith, followed by capture of Edinburgh.
September 14: English army takes Boulogne.
November: Sir Thomas Seymour's squadron in the Channel is dispersed by gales.
December: English proclamation allows unrestricted privateering against France and Scotland.

1545
February: Scots victory at Ancrum Moor.
March 1: Robert Reneger takes the *San Salvador* off Cape St Vincent.
July 3: French ships land 3,500 troops in Clyde.
July 19: Spithead action; *Mary Rose* lost but French withdraw.
August 15: Action off Shoreham.
September 2: Lisle lands and burns Tréport.

1546
May 18: The *Galley Blanchard* taken from the French off Boulogne.
June 7: England makes peace with France.

1547
January 28: Henry VIII dies.
March 7: Scottish ships *Lion*, *Lioness* and *Marie-Galante* taken off Yarmouth.
May 29: Scots Protestant rebels murder Cardinal Beaton and seize St Andrews Castle.
July 30: French galleys under Leo Strozzi retake St Andrews Castle.
September: Somerset invades Scotland and defeats Scots at Pinkie outside Edinburgh. English garrisons left behind at Inchcolm, Inchkeith and Broughty.
December: English occupy Dundee and Arbroath.

1548
January: French ships land supplies at Dumbarton.

February: English garrison Dumfries.
April: English garrison Haddington.
June: 22 French galleys land 6,000 French troops at Leith.
August: Arrival of Mary Queen of Scots in France marks union of crowns of France and Scotland. Shrewsbury relieves garrison of Haddington.

1549

July: French galleys seize and fortify the Isle of Sark.
August: France declares war on England and attacks Boulogne. English garrison of Haddington evacuated. French galleys defeated off Guernsey.

1550

February 6: Evacuation of Broughty, last English garrison in Scotland.
March: England makes peace with France and surrenders Boulogne.

1553

July: Death of Edward VI and failure of Northumberland's attempt to put Lady Jane Grey on throne.

1554

January: Wyatt's rebellion.
July 25: Marriage of Queen Mary and Philip of Spain.

1557

April: Thomas Stafford lands from France and seizes Scarborough Castle.
June: England at war with France. Cherbourg sacked.
August 12: Sir John Clere killed attempting a landing in Orkney.

1558

January: Calais taken by surprise attack.
July 13: English ships assist the Imperial army to defeat the French at Gravelines.
July 31: An English expedition lands in Brittany, burning Le Conquet but having no success against Brest.
September 19: Sir Thomas Cotton lands in Kintyre.
November 17: Death of Queen Mary and accession of Queen Elizabeth.

1559

April 2: Peace of Câteau-Cambrésis.
May: Protestant rebellion in Scotland seeks English support.
July 10: Accession of Francis II of France; personal union of France and Scotland.
August: 1,000 French troops land at Leith.
December: Further French troops arrive at Leith. William Winter ordered to attack French ships going to Scotland.

1560

January: French reinforcements under Elboeuf dispersed by a gale in the North Sea. Winter arrives in the Forth and blockades the French in Leith.

April: Anglo-Scottish army besieges the French in Leith.
July 6: By Treaty of Edinburgh the French agree to withdraw from Scotland.
December 5: Death of Francis II and dissolution of the Franco-Scottish union.

1562
October: Le Havre is given to England by the Huguenots as surety for English help.

1563
July 28: The English garrison surrenders Le Havre.
September 28: Anglo-French skirmish off La Rochelle.

1567
Franco-Scots force sacks Burburata.

1568
September 17: John Hawkins' ships attacked in San Juan de Ulua.
October: Huguenot squadron from La Rochelle takes refuge in Plymouth.
November: Spanish ships carrying money for Alba's army in the Low Countries are driven into English ports and seized.

1569
November: Revolt of the Northern Earls: Captain John Henshaw with three ships blockades Hartlepool.[228]

1570
July: Partial mobilization of English Navy.
Summer: William Borough, commanding a Russia Company convoy to Narva, defeats a Polish squadron.[229]

1572
April 1: Dutch rebels take Brielle.
July 22: Drake attacks Nombre de Dios.
August 24: Admiral Coligny and other Huguenot leaders killed in the Massacre of St Bartholomew.
November 5: Spanish squadron defeated by the Dutch off Flushing.

1573
February: Drake captures a mule-train of silver near Panama.
October: Spanish squadron defeated on the Zuider Zee.

1574
January 29: Spanish squadron defeated off Bergen-op-Zoom.
May 30: Spanish Flanders squadron defeated by the Dutch at Lillo.

1577
November 15: Drake sails from Plymouth for the Pacific.

1579
February 28: Drake captures the *Nuestra Señora del Rosario.*

1580
January 31: King Henry of Portugal dies, and Philip II of Spain occupies the country.
September 26: Drake returns to Plymouth having circumnavigated the world.
November 9: Spanish troops at Smerwick surrender.

1582
July 26: Spanish victory over Dom Antonio's French–Portuguese fleet in the Azores.
September 23: Fenton's squadron fights Spanish ships on the coast of Brazil.

1583
July: Final Spanish conquest of Terceira.

1585
August 10: Treaty of Nonsuch, offering English help to the Dutch rebels.

1586
January 1: Drake takes Santo Domingo.
February 10: Drake takes Cartagena.

1587
April 19: Drake attacks Cadiz.
June: Drake's squadron takes the Portuguese carrack *São Phelipe* off the Azores.
July 26: Parma takes the English-garrisoned port of Ostend.
August 5: Parma takes Sluys.
November 4: Cavendish captures the *Santa Ana* off Baja California.[230]

1588
May 18: Spanish Armada sails from Lisbon.
July 11: Armada sails from Corunna.
July 19: Armada sights the Lizard.
July 20: Spanish and English fleets meet off Plymouth.
July 27: The Armada anchors off Calais.
July 29: Battle of Gravelines.

1589
April 24: Drake and Norris land at Corunna.
May 16: English troops land at Peniche to march on Lisbon.
August–October: Cumberland cruising in the Azores.

1590
April 24: Levant Company convoy beats off Spanish galleys in the Straits.[231]
October: Spanish forces fortify a base at Blavet.

1591
September 1: The *Revenge* taken by Spanish ships off Flores.

1592
August 3: Capture of the Portuguese carrack *Madre de Deus* off the Azores.

1593
April 14: English ships in the Gironde defeated by a Spanish squadron under Pedro de Zubiaur.[232]

1594
March: Spanish troops build fort at Roscanvel.
June 19: The *Dainty* captured by Spanish ships on the Pacific coast of South America.
November 7: English ships and troops take the Spanish fort of Roscanvel and eliminate the threat to Brest.

1595
July 24: Spanish galleys burn Penzance.
August 28: Drake and Hawkins sail for the Caribbean.
November 12: English attack on San Juan, Puerto Rico repulsed. Hawkins dies.
December 31: English advance on Panama beaten back.

1596
January 28: Drake dies off Porto Bello.
March 1: English and Spanish squadrons fight off the Isle of Pines.
June 21: Anglo-Dutch squadron attacks and takes Cadiz.
October 18: Spanish invasion fleet wrecked by gales near Cape Finisterre.

1597
July 10: Essex's fleet sails to attack Ferrol, but is dispersed by a gale.
August 17: Essex's fleet sails for the second time on the 'Islands Voyage'.
October 12: Spanish invasion fleet scattered in the approaches to the Channel.

1598
April 22: Peace of Vervins between France and Spain.
June 6: Cumberland takes San Juan, Puerto Rico.

1599
September 1: Spinola's galleys pass the Straits of Dover.

1600
May 15: Sir Henry Docwra lands at the head of Lough Foyle and establishes himself at Derry.

1601
January 7: Rebellion (and subsequent execution) of Essex.
September 23: Spanish troops land at Kinsale.

December 6: Leveson attacks Spanish ships at Castlehaven.
December 24: Mountjoy defeats Tyrone outside Kinsale.

1602

January 2: Spanish troops at Kinsale surrender.
February 6: William Parker captures Porto Bello.
June 3: Leveson and Monson cut out the carrack *São Valentinho* from Cezimbra Road.
September 23: Spinola's galleys intercepted in the Straits of Dover by English and Dutch ships.

1603

March 24: Death of Queen Elizabeth and accession of James VI of Scots.
March 30: Submission of Tyrone.

1604

August 18: Peace between England and Spain.

1612

October 12: English East Indiamen defeat the Portuguese off Surat.[233]

1614

March: Dutch attack on English pirates in Crookhaven.
August: The Spanish capture of Mamora deprives English pirates of a base.
December: The *Phoenix* assists in the siege of Dunivaig Castle.

1615

January 20: English East Indiamen again defeat Portuguese off Surat.[234]
July: The English pirate Henry Mainwaring defeats a Spanish squadron off Cadiz.[235]

1617

March 17: Sir Walter Ralegh sails for Guiana.

1618

May: A Protestant rebellion in Bohemia against the Empire begins the Thirty Years War.

1619

January 28: The Earl of Buckingham becomes Lord High Admiral of England.
August: James I's son-in-law Frederick V, Elector Palatine, is elected King of Bohemia by the Protestant rebels.

1620

October 29: Battle of the White Mountain (near Prague); Frederick V defeated and loses both Bohemia and the Palatinate.
November 27: Mansell's squadron arrives off Algiers.

1621
May 24: Mansell unsuccessfully attacks Algiers.

1622
April 23: The Portuguese surrender Ormuz to an Anglo-Persian force.[236]

1623
March 7: The Prince of Wales and the Duke of Buckingham arrive in Madrid to negotiate a marriage with the Infanta.

1624
March 10: England declares war on Spain.

1625
January: Huguenot revolt of the Comte de Soubise, who seizes French royal ships at Blavet. Buckingham agrees to lend English ships to suppress it.
February 1–3 and 14: Anglo-Dutch actions with the Portuguese off Gombroon.[237]
March 27: Charles I succeeds his father James VI and I.
August 26: French ships with English and Spanish help defeat Soubise.
October 8: Lord Wimbledon's fleet sails for Cadiz.
October 23: Anglo-Dutch force unsuccessfully attacks Cadiz.
October: English East Indiamen fight the Portuguese off Surat.[238]
November 8: English East Indiaman *Lion* taken by the Portuguese off Gombroon.[239]

1626
February: Pennington cruises off Portugal.
September: Willoughby cruises in the Channel.
October: Willoughby's squadron dispersed by gales in the Bay of Biscay.

1627
January: Outbreak of war with France.
July 15: English troops landed on the Île de Ré.
October: *St Esprit* taken in Texel Road.[240]
October 28: English troops evacuated from the Île de Ré.

1628
May: Denbigh's squadron fails to relieve La Rochelle.
August 23: Murder of the Duke of Buckingham.
September 23: Lindsey's fleet fails to relieve La Rochelle.
October 28: Fall of La Rochelle.

1629
July 10: Scots captain David Kirke takes Quebec.[241]
August 30: Scottish settlement of Fort Ochiltree in Nova Scotia taken by the French.[242]

1630
November 5: Treaty of Madrid ends the war with Spain.

1631
June 30: Murat Reis raids Baltimore.
July: Anglo-Spanish naval treaty.

1634
October 20: First Ship Money writs are issued.

1637
July 27: The Old Town of Sallee surrenders to the Emperor of Morocco, marking the success of Rainsborough's expedition.

1638
August 12: Spanish fleet disastrously defeated by the French at Guetaría.
December 7: Imperialist surrender of Breisach cuts the Spanish Road.

1639
February: Outbreak of the First Bishops' War between England and Scotland.
June 18: Pacification of Berwick ends the First Bishops' War.
October 11: Battle of the Downs: Dutch fleet under Tromp defeats the Spaniards under Oquendo.

1640
May 5: Short Parliament dissolved on refusing to vote money.
August 20: Scottish invasion of England starts the Second Bishops' War.
October: By the Treaty of Ripon Charles I buys a temporary peace with Scotland.
November 3: Long Parliament meets.

1641
May 2: Princess Mary marries William of Orange, son of the Statholder.
August 20th: Definitive peace between England and Scotland.
October 23: Rebellion breaks out in Ireland.

1642
January: Charles I fails to arrest Parliamentary leaders and leaves London. Parliament takes control of the Navy.
July 2: Sir John Pennington fails to regain the fleet for Charles I.
July 6: Parliamentary ships save Hull from Royalist attack.
July 21: Tromp arrests English ships breaking the blockade of Dunkirk.
August: English Civil War begins.
September 7: Parliamentary forces take Portsmouth.
October 23: Battle of Edgehill, followed by Royalist advance on London.

1643
February 21: Tromp lands Queen Henrietta Maria with supplies at Bridlington.

Royalist siege of Plymouth abandoned.
March 25: Parliamentary privateer Captain William Jackson takes Jamaica.
July 26: Royalists take Bristol.
August 1: Royalist coup in Dublin.
September 15: Ormonde signs a truce with the Confederation of Kilkenny.
October 11: Warships again save Hull from Royalist attack.
November: English adoption of Presbyterianism seals alliance between the English and Scottish Parliaments. Parliamentary warships relieve Plymouth. Royal troops from Ireland landed in North Wales.

1644

January 19: Scottish army invades England.
January 23: Swanley's squadron returns to Milford Haven.
June 14: Royalist siege of Lyme abandoned.
July 2: Royalist defeat at Marston Moor.
August: Earl of Montrose raises Royalist rebellion in Scotland with troops from Ulster. Earl of Inchiquin defects from the Confederation of Kilkenny to Parliament.
September 2: Essex's army surrenders to the Royalists near Fowey.
September 9: Plymouth repels Royalist attack.
October 22: The Scots capture Newcastle-upon-Tyne.

1645

February 2: Montrose defeats Covenanters at Inverlochy.
March 17: Duncannon taken by Irish rebels.
May: Royalists again recover Pembrokeshire.
June 14: Parliamentary New Model Army wins a decisive victory at Naseby.
August: Rebel siege of Youghal lifted.
September 10: Parliamentary forces retake Bristol.
November 6: Capture of the *Swan* off Dublin effectively ends the Royalist squadron in the Irish Sea.

1646

May 5: Charles I surrenders to the Scottish army at Newark.
July: Bonratty Castle taken by Irish rebels from Parliament.
August: Pendennis Castle surrenders to Parliament.
September: Isles of Scilly taken by Parliament.
October: French take Dunkirk, leading to many Spanish/Royalist privateers moving to Wexford or Kinsale.

1647

January: Scots sell Charles I to Parliament.
May 1: Swedish warships forced to salute the English flag.[243]
August: having seized Charles I, the army under Oliver Cromwell occupies London and takes power.

December: Charles I makes secret treaty with Scots to accept Presbyterianism in return for their help to restore him to the throne.

1648

March: Unpaid garrisons in South Wales mutiny and declare for Charles I.
May 1: Scots invasion starts the Second Civil War.
May 27: Main fleet in the Downs mutinies and joins the Kentish rebellion.
June 10: Rebel fleet sails to join the Royalists in Holland.
July 30: Warwick meets the Prince of Wales's squadron off Shoeburyness but declines action.
August 17: Scottish army defeated at Preston.
October 14: Peace of Westphalia ends the Thirty Years War.
December 6: Pride's Purge reinforces army control of Parliament.

1649

January 1: Prince Rupert with the Royalist fleet sails from Holland for Ireland.
January 16: Independent/Radical purge of the Navy and dockyards.
January 30: Charles I executed.

APPENDIX II

SHIPS

This appendix provides information about the size and number of warships available to the English crown at various dates.

1. Building Programmes, 1200–1500

This is a summary of the known occasions when ships were ordered by the English crown to be built for military purposes. Until the fifteenth century most of them were oared vessels (galleys, balingers or barges). In some cases it is doubtful if all, or even any, of the ships ordered were actually built. The great majority of ships used for war were of course modified or unmodified merchantmen. Some of them belonged to the crown, but few of them were built at royal order, and the distinction between the king's ships (in the modern sense) and those available to the crown by requisition or charter is of relatively little significance. Large oared vessels, and in the fifteenth century large carracks, were the only ones which might be described in the modern sense as warships, and were the only classes many of which were actually built at the order of the crown. Shipbuilding for the crown was infrequent, and it is no indicator at all of the number of ships available for war, but it is a good indicator of the occasions when naval warfare assumed a high priority.

1206–12
At least 20 galleys built in various ports and more than 30 ships assembled.[1]

1222
Irish ports ordered to build at least 5 galleys.[2]

1232
Two galleys built at Winchelsea.[3]

1234
Irish ports ordered to build 6 galleys (2 of 60 oars, 4 of 40 oars).[4]

1241
Irish ports ordered to build 5 galleys, the Channel Isles 2, and Bristol 1.[5]

1242
Four fast barges to be built at Dover.[6]

1244
Galleys to be built in Jersey and Guernsey.[7]

1257
Four galleys and 4 barges built at Winchelsea, Dunwich and Yarmouth.[8]

1294–95
Twenty large galleys ordered, but only 8 built.[9]

1298–99
Two barges built at Hull and Ravenspur.[10]

1303–04
Galleys built at Ipswich, Yarmouth and possibly elsewhere.[11]

1335
The *Cog Edward* built at Southampton.[12]

1336–37
The galley *Philippa* and a barge built at Lynn, 2 galleys at Hull and Winchelsea.[13]

1354
At least 6 ships and a barge built at Ipswich, Ratcliffe, Sandwich, Dover and Exeter.[14]

1356
At least 6 'floats' built at Yarmouth, London, Lynn and Ratcliffe.[15]

1358
Ships *St Mary* and *Christopher* built at Southampton.[16]

1373
At least 70 barges of 40–50 oars ordered.[17]

1378
Thirty-two balingers built.[18]

1401–02
Thirty-six balingers and 18 barges ordered; it is uncertain how many were completed.[19]

1408
A galley built at Drogheda.[20]

1409
A Mediterranean 'great galley', the *Jesus Maria*, is built or acquired.[21]

1413
The *Trinity Royal* rebuilt.[22] Building of the balingers/barges *Paul*, *Peter* and *Swan*.[23]

1414–16
The carrack *Jesus* (1,000 tons) built at Winchelsea; the *Holy Ghost* rebuilt from the Spanish prize *Santa Clara.*[24] Building of the balingers/barges *James* and *Anne.*[25]

1416–18
The *Grace Dieu* (1,400 tons) built at Southampton.[26] Building of the balingers/barges *Valentine, Falcon, George* and *Nicholas.*[27]

1419
An unnamed carrack of great size under construction at Bayonne.[28]

1449
The *Grace Dieu* of Holdernesse built at Hull.[29]

1464
Building of the carvel *Edward* for the king and Lord Howard.[30]

1473
The *Grace Dieu* rebuilt.[31]

1483
The *Mary Ash* rebuilt.[32]

1485
The *Governor* built.[33]

1487
The carracks *Regent* and *Sovereign* built.[34]

1497
The *Sweepstake* and *Mary Fortune* built.[35]

2. Shipbuilding for the English Crown, 1500–1648

This is a list of ships of 100 tons or more known to have been built, rebuilt or purchased for the English Navy Royal from 1500. The information is in many cases approximate or uncertain, especially tonnage, number of guns, and the dates at which the ships ceased to be operational. Where the dimensions are known a range of tonnages can be given, representing acceptable variations in measurement practice. 'Rebuilds' were new ships, following roughly the dimensions of the old and sometimes re-using hull timbers from them, but the distinction between substantial repair and rebuilding is often unclear. Alternative names are in brackets.

Abbreviations:

A = bought	G = given away	R = rebuilt
B = built (i.e. completed for service)	L = lost	RN = renamed
BU = broken up	LM = last mentioned	S = sold
E = embargoed or requisitioned	P = prize	

Name	Type/ No. of Guns	Date	Comments	Tonnage	Fate
Mary Rose		B 1510		5–600	R 1536
Peter Pomegranate		B 1510		450	R 1536
Lion		P 1511	Scottish	120	S 1513
Mary and John (Carvel of Ewe)		R 1512	after fire damage	180–260	LM 1528
Gabriel Royal	carrack ?	A 1512	Genoese	700–1,000	LM 1526
Katherine Fortileza	carrack ?	A 1512	Genoese	700	LM 1521
Maria de Loreto	carrack ?	E 1514	Genoese	800	Released 1514
John Baptist		A 1512		400	L *c.* 1534
Great Nicholas		A 1512		400	LM 1521
Christ		A 1512		300	L 1515 (taken by Barbary pirates)
Great Bark		B 1512		200–400	S *c.* 1531
Mary James		A 1512		260–300	LM *c.* 1529
Mary George		A 1512		240–300	LM 1526
Less Bark		? 1512		160–240	R 1536
Anne Gallant (Anne of Greenwich)		? 1512		140–160	L 1518
Barbara of Greenwich (Little Barbara)		? 1512		140–160	LM 1514
Lizard		B 1512		120	LM 1522
Dragon		B 1512		100	LM 1514
Great Barbara		A 1513	ex *Mawdelyn*	400	LM 1524
Henry of Hampton		A 1513		120	LM 1521
Mary Imperial		? 1513		90–120	LM 1525
Henry Grace à Dieu		B 1514		1500	R 1539
Great Elizabeth	Hulk	A 1514	ex *Salvator* of Lübeck	900	L 1514

Name	Type/ No. of Guns	Date	Comments	Tonnage	Fate
Great Galley		B 1515		800	R *c.* 1538
Mary Gloria		A 1517		300	LM 1522
Katherine Pleasaunce (Katherine Bark)		B 1518		100	LM 1525
Spaniard		1522	Gift from the Emperor	large	LM 1523
Mawdelyn of Deptford		A 1522		120	LM 1525
Minion		B 1523		180	R 1536
Primrose		B 1523		160	R *c.* 1538
Mary Guildford		B 1524		160	LM 1539
Trinity Henry		B 1530		250	S 1566
Sweepstake		B 1535		300	LM 1559
Mary Willoughby		B 1532		160	L 1533 (taken by Scots)
Lion		B 1536		140	LM 1559
Minion		R 1536	Chartered 1550–56	300	S 1570
Mary Rose		R 1536		700	L 1545
Peter Pomegranate		R 1536		600	LM 1558
Less Bark		R 1536		400	LM 1553
Great Galley (Great Galleass)		R 1538		500–600	R 1564
Primrose		R 1538		240	LM 1545
Jennet		B 1538		160–180	R 1559
Henry Grace à Dieu		R 1540	RN *Edward* 1547	1000	L 1553 (burnt)
Dragon		B 1542		120–140	LM 1553
Pansy (Pauncey)		B 1543		450	LM 1557
New Bark		B 1543		200	LM 1566
Lartigue		P 1543	ex French *Feronière*	140	S 1547
Mary James		P 1543	French ?	120	LM 1546
Mary Thomas		P 1543	French ?	100	LM 1546
Galley Subtle (Red Galley)	Galley	B 1544		200–300	LM 1559
Salamander		P 1544	Scots, ex French	300	LM 1559

Name	Type/ No. of Guns	Date	Comments	Tonnage	Fate
Unicorn		P 1544	Scots	240	S 1555
Swallow		B 1544		300	R 1559
Jesus of Lubeck	Hulk	A 1545		600–700	L 1568
Struse of Dawske	Hulk	A 1545	ex Danzig	400	S 1553
Mary Hamboro	Hulk	A 1545	ex Hamburg	400	S 1555
Christopher	Hulk	A 1545	ex Bremen	400–500	S 1555
Grand Mistress		B 1545		420	S 1555
Anne Gallant		B 1545		450	LM 1559
Morian	Hulk	A 1545	ex Danzig	500	S 1551
Greyhound	*Hulk*	A 1545		160–200	L 1563
Matthew (Matthew Gonson)		A 1545?		600	LM 1554
Antelope	Galleass	B 1546		300	R 1558
Hart	Galleass	B 1546		300	L 1563
Tiger	Galleass	B 1546		200	R 1570
Bull	Galleass	B 1546		200	R 1570
Galley Blanchard	Galley	P 1546	French (same as *Mermaid* ?)	200	LM 1562
Mary Willoughby		P 1547	Scots, ex English	160	R 1551
Galley Mermaid (Black Galley)	Galley	P 1548	French	200	LM 1562
Gerfalcon		? 1550		140	S 1562
Primrose		B 1551		300	S 1554
Mary Willoughby		R 1551	see 1547	200	S 1573
Sacrett		P 1556	French	160	LM 1562
Philip and Mary		B 1556		500	R 1584
Mary Rose		B 1557		600	R 1589
Lion		B 1557		500	R 1582
Falcon		R 1558	built 1545 as 80 tons	100	S 1575
Jennet		R 1559	see 1538	300	Made a lighter 1580
Elizabeth Jonas	64	B 1559		800	R 1598
Swallow		R 1559	see 1544	300	R 1580
Hope	33	B 1560		500	R 1603

Name	Type/ No. of Guns	Date	Comments	Tonnage	Fate
Speedwell	Galley	P 1560	French	200	LM 1580
Tryright	Galley	P 1560	French	200	LM 1580
Christopher		A 1560		800	LM 1563
Primrose		A 1560	1551 ship re-possessed	300	S 1575
Triumph	58	B 1562		1000	R 1596
Victory	52	B 1562		800	BU 1606
Aid	30	B 1562		250	LM 1599
Eleanor	Galley	A 1563	given in pledge by Huguenots	200	R 1584
Bear (White Bear)	60	R 1564	*Great Bark* of 1538	900	R 1599
Eliazabeth Bonaventure		A 1567		600	R 1581
Foresight	Galleon ? 28	B 1570		300	LM 1604
Bull	Galleon ? 21	R 1570	see 1546	200	LM 1594
Tiger	Galleon ? 24	R 1570	see 1546	200	exchanged 1584
Dreadnought	Galleon ? 34	B 1573		400	R 1592
Swiftsure	Galleon, 34	B 1573		400	R 1592
Achates	Galleon, 28	B 1573		100	hulked 1600
Revenge	Galleon, 40	B 1577		500	L 1591
Scout	Galleon, 20	B 1577		120	hulked 1600
Swallow	Galleon ? 30	R 1580	see 1559	300	LM 1603
Elizabeth Bonaventure	40–47	R 1580	see 1567	600	LM 1611
Antelope	Galleon ? 28–38	R 1581	see 1546	300	R 1618
Lion (Golden Lion)	Galleon, 40–60	R 1582	see 1557	500	R 1609
Nonpareil	Galleon, 40–50	R 1584	*Philip & Mary* of 1556	500	R 1603
Bonavoglia	Galley	R 1584	*Eleanor* of 1563	200	LM 1603
Tiger		A 1584	*Sea-Dragon* exchanged	200	hulked 1600
Rainbow	Galleon, 36	B 1586		500	R 1617
Vanguard	Galleon, 36	B 1586		500	R 1615
Tramontana	Galleon, 21	B 1586		140	LM 1618
Ark Royal	Galleon, 55	A 1587	ex *Ark Ralegh*	800	R 1603

Name	Type/ No. of Guns	Date	Comments	Tonnage	Fate
Mary Rose	Galleon, 39	R 1589	see 1555	475–495	wharf 1618
Merhonour	Galleon, 41	B 1590		690–860	R 1615
Garland	Galleon, 45	B 1590		530–670	wharf 1618
Defiance	Galleon, 46	B 1590		470–590	R 1615
Answer	Galleon, 21	B 1590		210–260	R 1604
Quittance	Galleon, 25	B 1590		210–260	LM 1618
Crane	Galleon, 24	B 1590		200–250	LM 1624
Advantage	Galleon, 18	B 1590		140–180	L 1614 (burnt)
Eagle	Hulk	A 1592	ex Lübeck	890	hulked, L 1683
Dreadnought	Galleon, 41	R 1592	see 1573	360–450	R 1612
Swiftsure	Galleon, 41	R 1592	see 1573	330–420	R 1607
Adventure	Galleon, 26	B 1594		270–340	S 1645
St Andrew		P 1596	Spanish *San Andreas*	1300	G 1604
St Mathew		P 1596	Spanish *San Mateo*	1300	G 1604
Triumph	Galleon, 68	R 1596	see 1562	760–950	S 1618
Repulse (Due Repulse)	Galleon, 50	B 1596		620–780	R 1610
Warspite	Galleon, 29	B 1596		520–650	hulked 1635
Elizabeth Jonas	Galleon, 56	R 1598	see 1559	680–850	S 1618
Bear (White Bear)	Galleon, 40	R 1599	see 1564	730–910	S 1629
Vanguard	Galleon, 31	R 1599	see 1586	450–560	R 1615
George	Hoy	B 1601	or B 1588	100	LM 1603
Advantagia	Galley	B 1601		100	S 1629
Superlativa	Galley	B 1601		100	S 1629
Gallarita	Galley	B 1601		100	S 1629
Volatillia	Galley	B 1601		100	S 1629
Moon	Pinnace	R 1602	1586, 70–85 tons	100	LM 1626
Nonsuch	Galleon, 38	R 1603	ex *Nonpareil*, 1584	460–620	S 1645
Assurance	Galleon, 34	R 1603	ex *Hope*, 1559 (rebuilt since ?)	450–600	S 1645
Answer		R 1604	see 1590	200	S 1629
Speedwell		R 1607	ex *Swiftsure*, 1592	400	L 1624

Name	Type/ No. of Guns	Date	Comments	Tonnage	Fate
Anne Royal	44	R 1608	ex *Ark Royal*, 1587	620–820	L 1636
Lion (Red Lion)	38	R 1609	see 1582	520–700	R 1640
Prince Royal	55	B 1610		890–1190	R 1641
Repulse	40	R 1610	see 1596	570–760	BU 1645
Dreadnought	30	R 1613	see 1592	410–550	BU 1648
Phoenix	20	B 1613		180–250	LM 1624
Merhonour	40	R 1615	see 1590	710–950	S 1650
Defiance	38	R 1615	see 1590	660–870	S 1650
Vanguard	40	R 1615	see 1599	500–660	R 1631
Seven Stars	14	B 1615		110–140	LM 1624
Convertine	34	E 1616	ex Sir W. Ralegh's *Destiny*	470–620	Royalist 1648, S 1650
Rainbow	40	R 1617	see 1586	550–730	breakwater 1680
Antelope	34	R 1618	see 1581	380–510	Royalist 1648, L 1649
Happy Entrance	30	B 1619		400–540	L 1658
Constant Reformation	40	B 1619		560–740	Royalist 1648, L 1651
Victory	40	B 1620		540–720	R 1666
Garland	34	B 1620		420–570	L 1652
Swiftsure	44	B 1621		560–750	R 1653
Bonaventure	32	B 1621		420–560	L 1653
St Andrew	42	B 1622		590–780	L 1666
St George	42	B 1622		590–790	hulked 1687
Triumph	44	B 1623		580–780	S 1688
Mary Rose	26	B 1623		240–320	L 1650
Charles	14	B 1623		140	LM 1627
St Denis	38	P 1625	French	400–530	S 1645
St Claude		P 1625	French	300	G 1632
St Anne		P 1626		350	S 1630
Saint Esprit		P 1627	French	800	LM 1628
Fortune		P 1627		300	LM 1635
First Whelp	14	B 1628		140–190	hulked 1642
Second Whelp	14	B 1628		140–190	hulked 1642
Third Whelp	14	B 1628		130–170	S 1642
Fourth Whelp	14	B 1628		140–190	L 1636

Name	Type/ No. of Guns	Date	Comments	Tonnage	Fate
Fifth Whelp	14	B 1628		140–190	L 1637
Sixth Whelp	14	B 1628		140–190	L 1628
Seventh Whelp	14	B 1628		140–190	L 1630
Eighth Whelp	14	B 1628		120–160	S 1645
Ninth Whelp	14	B 1628		140–190	G 1639
Tenth Whelp	14	B 1628		140–190	S 1655
Vanguard	40	R 1631	see 1615	560–750	L 1667
Charles	44	B 1633	RN *Liberty* 1650	610–810	L 1650
Henrietta Maria	42	P 1633	RN *Paragon* 1650	590–790	L 1655
James	48	B 1634		660–870	S 1682
Unicorn	46	B 1634		570–770	S 1688
Swallow	34	B 1634		360–480	Royalist 1648, S 1653
Leopard	34	B 1635		390–520	P 1653
Greyhound	12	B 1636		90–130	L 1656
Nicodemus	6	P 1636	Dunkirker	90–120	S 1657
Providence	30	B 1637		230–300	L 1668
Expedition	30	B 1637		230–300	S 1667
Sovereign of the Seas	100	B 1637		1140–1520	R 1660
Lion	42	R 1640	see 1609	470–630	R 1658
Prince Royal	64	R 1641	see 1610	890–1190	R 1663
Swan	12–20	B 1641		200	Royalist 1642, taken 1645, S 1654
Crescent	12	A 1642		120–170	Royalist 1648, L 1649
Robert	8	P 1642	Royalist	100–130	P 1649 (Irish)
Fellowship	28	P 1643	Royalist	300–390	hulked 1651
Hector	22	P 1643	Royalist	200–270	S 1656
Warwick	frigate ? 22	A 1643	Dunkirker	190–250	BU 1660
Cygnet	frigate ? 18	A 1643	Dunkirker	160–210	S 1654
Hind	13	A 1643		140–200	Royalist 1648, LM 1651
Star	frigate ? 12	A 1643	Dunkirker	130–200	LM 1652
Sampson	20	P 1644		300	exchanged 1646

Name	Type/ No. of Guns	Date	Comments	Tonnage	Fate
Globe	24	P 1644		250–330	S 1648
Welcome	pink, 14	P 1645		100–130	seized by French, 1647
Weymouth	12	P 1645	ex Royalist *Cavendish*	120–160	S 1662
Increase	12	P 1645		100–130	L 1650
John	28	A 1646		270–370	L 1652
Peter	10	P 1646		100–133	LM 1647
Nonsuch	34	B 1646		390–520	L 1664
Adventure	32	B 1646		380–510	S 1688
Assurance	32	B 1646		340–560	S 1698
Satisfaction	26	P 1646		220–290	Royalist 1648, L 1662
President	26	A 1646	exchange for *Sampson* of 1644	220	fireship 1656
Roebuck	14	P 1646	Dunkirker	110	Royalist 1648, S 1651
Tiger	32	B 1647		440–610	R 1681
Elizabeth	32	B 1647		470–640	L 1667
Phoenix	32	B 1647		410–560	L 1664
Dragon	32	B 1647		410–560	R 1690
Recovery	20	P 1647	Flushinger	300	S 1655
Pelican	10	? 1647		100–133	Royalist 1648, LM 1648
Constant Warwick	26	A 1648	ex privateer built 1645		Royalist 1648, R 1666

Sources: Anderson, *English Men-of-War*; Glasgow, 'List of Ships'; Boulind, 'Ships of Private Origin'.

3. Operational Strength

A list of ships in the chronological order in which they were built or acquired gives an idea of effort over time. It is much harder to establish how many ships were actually available for service at any one time. In practice, especially with wooden ships, a fleet's effective strength is not capable of being exactly defined, but is a function of the time and resources available to get ships into repair. Generally the shorter the notice and the less the preparations, the smaller the proportion of the ships which can be made operational. Even with information as complete as it was possible to collect, the results of a mobilization effort were difficult for contemporaries to predict with certainty. It is virtually impossible for the historian to say with confidence exactly what proportion the active fleet bore at any one moment to the theoretical total. In practice, however, the measure which matters is the number of ships actually in service, which can be given with rather more confidence, so long as it is well understood that never (1588 perhaps excepted) did any one fleet represent a supreme effort of total mobilization. The following tables give the actual operational strength of English fleets on various campaigns. Note how the proportion of merchantmen to H.M. ships falls steadily over time, to virtually nothing in 1636, only to rise sharply again in the Parliamentary fleets of 1643.

August 1512: English fleet off Brest

Regent, *Mary Rose*, *Peter Pomegranate*, *Mary John* (240 tons), *Anne of Greenwich*, *Mary George*, *John Baptist*, *Nicholas Reed* (400 tons), *George* of Falmouth (140 tons), *Peter* of Fowey (120 tons), *Henry Katherine* of Hampton (120 tons), *Christopher Davy* (160 tons), *Sabyn* (120 tons), *Barbara of Greenwich*, *Dragon*, *Jennet Purwyn* (70 tons), *Martinet* (180 tons), *Nicholas* of Hampton (200 tons), two victuallers, two rowbarges.

[Spont, *War with France*, pp. 4–12, 34].

April 1513: English fleet in the Trade

King's Ships: *Sovereign*, *Gabriel Royal*, *Maria de Loreto*, *Katherine Fortileza*, *Mary Rose*, *Peter Pomegranate*, *John Baptist*, *Nicholas Reed*, *Mary George*, *Mary James*, *Christ*, *Great Bark*, *Less Bark*, *Lizard*, *Jennet Purwyn*, *Barbara of Greenwich*, *Anne Gallant*, *Henry Katherine* of Hampton, *Sweepstake*, *Swallow*, three barks.

Chartered ships, 70–230 tons: *Nicholas* of Hampton, *Trinity* of Bristol, *Christopher Davy*, *Nicholas Draper*, *Elizabeth* of Newcastle, *Erasmus* of London, *Matthew Cradock*, *Jermaine*, *Sabyn*, *Margaret* of Topsham, *Baptist* of Calais, *Mary of Walsingham*, *Mary* of Brixham, 'Gibb's ship', *Julian* of Dartmouth, *Margaret Bonaventure*, *Christopher* of Dartmouth, *James* of Dartmouth, *Margaret Bonaventure*, *Christopher* of Dartmouth *Thomas* of Hull, *Baptist* of Harwich, seven Genoese and Spanish ships identified by patrons' names only.

[Spont, *War with France*, pp. 87–8]

July 1545: English fleet at Portsmouth

Order of Battle issued by Lord Lisle:

Vanguard, 1st Rank: *Great Argosy*, *Samson* of Lübeck, *Johannes* of Lübeck, *Trinity* of Danzig, *Mary* of Hamburg, *Pelican*, *Morion* of Danzig, *Sepiar* of Danzig.

Vanguard, 2nd Rank: *Henry Grace à Dieu*, the 'Venetian', *Peter Pomegranate*, *Matthew Gonson*, *Pansy*, *Great Galley*, *Sweepstake*, *Minion*, *Swallow*, *New Bark*, *Saul Galley*.

Vanguard, 3rd Rank: *'Berste Denar'*, *Falcon Lively*, *Henry* of Bristol, *Trinity Smith*, *Margaret* of Bristol, *Trinity Reneger*, *Mary James*, *Pilgrim* of Dartmouth, *Mary George* of Rye, *Thomas Tipkins*, *Gorges Brigges*, *Anne Lively*, *John Evangelist*, *Thomas Modell*, *Lartigo*, *Christopher Bennet*, *Mary Fortune*, *Mary Martin*, *Trinity* of Bristol.

Right Wing: *Grand Mistress*, *Salamander*, *Jennet*, *Lion*, *Greyhound*, *Thomas of Greenwich*, *Less Pinnace*, *Hind*, *Harry*, *Galley Subtle*, 'two boats of Rye'.

Left Wing: *Anne Gallant*, *Unicorn*, *Falcon*, *Dragon*, *Saker*, *Merlin*, *Roe*, *Reneger* pinnace, 'the foist', two boats of Rye.

[Corbett, *Fighting Instructions*, pp. 20–2]

June 1557: Lord Howard of Effingham's Squadron in the Channel

Great Bark, *Jesus* of Lübeck, *Trinity*, *Swallow*, *Salamander*, *Hart*, *Antelope*, *Anne Gallant*, *New Bark*, *Mary Willoughby*, *Bull*, *Tiger*, *Greyhound*, *Jerfalcon*, *George*, six pinnaces.

[Derrick, *Memoirs*, p. 19]

April 1587: Drake's squadron at Cadiz

Queen's Ships: *Elizabeth Bonaventure*, *Lion*, *Rainbow*, *Dreadnought*, *Spy* and *Cygnet* (pinnaces).

London merchants: *Merchant Royal* (400 tons), *Susan* (350 tons), *Edward Bonaventure* (300 tons), *Margaret & John* (210 tons), *Solomon* (200 tons), *George Bonaventure* (150 tons), *Thomas Bonaventure* (150 tons).

Private men-of-war: *White Lion* (150 tons, Lord Howard), *Minion* (200 tons, Sir W. Winter), *Thomas* (200 tons, Sir F. Drake), *Bark Hawkins* (130 tons, Sir J. Hawkins), *Drake* and *Elizabeth* (Sir F. Drake, pinnaces), *Makeshift*, *Speedwell*, *Little John*, *Post* (pinnaces).

[Corbett, *Spanish War*, pp. 99–100]

July 1588: Lord Howard's fleet in the Channel

Queen's Ships: *Ark Royal, Elizabeth Bonaventure, Rainbow, Lion, Bear, Vanguard, Revenge, Elizabeth Jonas, Victory, Antelope, Triumph, Dreadnought, Mary Rose, Nonpareil, Hope,* Galley *Bonavolia, Swiftsure, Swallow, Foresight, Aid, Bull, Tiger, Tramontana, Scout, Achates; Charles, Moon, Advice, Merlin, Spy, Sun, Cygnet* (pinnaces), *Brigandine, George* hoy.

'Merchant ships appointed to serve westwards under Sir F. Drake': *Galleon Leicester, Merchant Royal* (400 tons), *Edward Bonaventure, Roebuck* (300 tons), *Golden Noble, Galleon Dudley* (250 tons), *Griffin, Minion, Bark Talbot, Thomas Drake, Spark, Hopewell, Virgin God Save Her, Hope Hawkins* (200 tons), *Bark St Leger, Bark Mannington* (160 tons), *Bark Bond, Bark Bonner, Bark Hawkins* (150 tons), *Bear Yonge* (140 tons), *Unity, Elizabeth Drake, Bark Buggins, Elizabeth Founes, Heartsease, Golden Hind, Makeshift, Diamond* of Dartmouth, *Speedwell, Chance, Delight, Nightingale* (pinnaces), Flyboat *Yonge*, 'the small caravel'.

'Set forth and paid upon the charge of the City of London': *Hercules* (300 tons), *Toby Centurion* (250 tons), *Mayflower, Minion, Ascension, Primrose, Margaret & John, Tiger, Red Lion* (200 tons), *Gift of God* (180 tons), *Royal Defence, Brave, Bark Burr* (160 tons), *Golden Lion, Thomas Bonaventure* (140 tons), *George Noble, Antelope, Prudence, Toby* (120 tons), *Salamander, Jewel, Dolphin* (110 tons), *Anthony, Rose Lion, Pansy* (100 tons), *Diana, Passport, Moonshine, Release* (pinnaces).

Merchant ships and barks in the Queen's pay: *Susan Parnell, Violet* (220 tons), *George Bonaventure* (200 tons), *Edward* of Maldon (186 tons), *Anne Frances* (180 tons), *Solomon* (170 tons), *Vineyard, Nightingale* (160 tons), *Samuel, White Lion* (140 tons), *Jane Bonaventure* (100 tons); *Disdain, Lark, Fancy, Marigold, Black Dog, Katherine, Pippin* (barks and pinnaces).

Coasters under the Lord Admiral, paid by the Queen: *Minion* of Bristol (230 tons), *Bark Potts* (180 tons), *John Trelawny* (150 tons), *Crescent* of Dartmouth (140 tons), *Bartholomew* of Topsham, *Unicorn* of Bristol (130 tons), *Rose* of Topsham (110 tons), galleon of Weymouth (100 tons), *Jacob* of Lyme, *Bark Webb, Handmaid* of Bristol, *John* of Chichester, *Katherine* of Weymouth, *Hart* of Dartmouth, *Revenge* of Lyme, *Hearty Anne, Aid* of Bristol, *Little John, Gift* of Topsham (90–25 tons).

Coasters under Lord Henry Seymour, most paid by the seaports: *Daniel* (160 tons), *Galleon Hutchins, Bark Lamb, Grace* of Yarmouth, *Mayflower, Marigold* (150 tons), *William* of Ipswich (140 tons), *Katherine* of Ipswich (125 tons), *Primrose* of Harwich, *Elizabeth* of Dover (120 tons), *Robin* of Sandwich (110 tons), *William* of Colchester (100 tons), *William* of Rye, *Handmaid, Griffin, Fancy, Anne Bonaventure, John Young, Little Hare, Grace of God, Susan, Hazard* of Feversham, *Matthew* (80–35 tons).

'Voluntary ships that came into the fleet after the coming of the Spanish forces upon our coast': *Sampson* (300 tons), *Samaritan* of Dartmouth (250 tons), *Frances* of Fowey (140 tons), *Golden Ryall* of Weymouth, *William* of Plymouth (120 tons), *Grace* of Topsham (100 tons), *Elizabeth* of Lowestoft, *Rat* of Wight, *Unicorn* of Dartmouth, *Bark Sutton* of Weymouth, *Heathen* of Weymouth, *Bark Halse*, *Thomas Bonaventure*, 'the flyboat', *Margaret*, *Carouse*, *Elizabeth*, *Raphael*, *Gallego* of Plymouth, *John* of Barnstaple, *Greyhound* of Aldborough, *Jonas* of Aldborough, *Fortune* of Aldborough (90–30 tons and unknown).

Total: 182 ships and 15 victuallers.

[*DSA* II,324–331]

August 1595: Drake and Hawkins sail for the Caribbean

Queen's Ships: *Defence*, *Garland*, *Hope*, *Elizabeth Bonaventure*, *Adventure*, *Foresight*.

London ships: *Concord* (330 tons), *Susan Bonaventure* (alias *Susan & Parnell*) (250 tons), *Salomon*, *Saker*, *Desire* (246 tons), *Amity*, *John Bonaventure* (200 tons), *Elizabeth* (194 tons), *Jewel* (130 tons), *Little John* (100 tons), *Pegasus*, *Phoenix* (80 tons), *Help* (caravel), *Richard* (victualler).

Others: *John Trelawney* (alias *Pulpit*) of Plymouth (150 tons), *Exchange* of Bristol (140 tons), *Delight* of Hamton, *Elizabeth Constant* of Bridgewater (pinnaces), *Francis* of Greenwich (35 tons), *Nannycock*, *Blessing* (Ramsgate ketches).

[Andrews, *Drake's Last Voyage*, pp. 36–39]

June 1596: Howard and Essex take Cadiz

Lord Admiral's Squadron: Queen's Ships *Ark Royal* (admiral), *Lion* (vice-admiral), *Dreadnought* (rear-admiral) *Truelove*, *Lion's Whelp* (pinnace); *Darling* of London, *Delight* of London, *Swan* of London (pinnace); nineteen victuallers and transports.

Earl of Essex's Squadron: Queen's Ships *Repulse* (admiral), *Rainbow* (vice-admiral), *Vanguard* (rear-admiral), *Tramontana*, *Charles* (pinnace); *Lioness* & *Chameleon* (both of London); twenty-one victuallers and transports.

Lord T. Howard's Squadron: Queen's Ships *Merhonour* (admiral), *Nonpareil* (vice-admiral), *Crane* (rear-admiral), *Moon* (pinnace); *Violet*, *Golden Dragon*, *Reuben* (or *Ruby*), *Alcedo* (all of London); seventeen victuallers and transports.

Sir W. Ralegh's Squadron: Queen's Ships *Warspite* (admiral), *Swiftsure* (vice-admiral), *Quittance* (rear-admiral), *Mary Rose*; *Roebuck* & *Centurion* (of London); seventeen victuallers and transports.

Dutch Squadron: *Neptunus* (admiral), *Leeuw* (vice-admiral), *Aal* (rear-admiral), fifteen men-of-war and six victuallers.

[Corbett, 'Slyngisbie's Relation', pp. 46–50. *MNT* I,358–361. De Jonge, *Nederlandsche Zeewesen* I,143]

August 1599: An Emergency Mobilization

Main fleet, Lord T. Howard: *Elizabeth Jonas, Ark Royal, Triumph, Merhonour, Garland, Mary Rose, Hope, Bonaventure, Nonpareil, Defiance, Foresight, Repulse, Rainbow, Lion*; *Mercury* & *Merlin* (pinnaces); merchant ships *Rebecca* (310 tons), *Flying Dragon* (290 tons), *Triumph* (255 tons), *Swallow* (250 tons), *Rose Lion* (200 tons), 12 London ships (details unknown).

Cruising off Ushant, Captain G. Fenner: *Dreadnought, Swiftsure, Advice.*

Irish Sea squadron, Sir R. Mansell: *Antelope, Adventure*; *Charles, Moon* & *Popinjay* (pinnaces); 2 hired ships.

Channel Guard, Sir R. Leveson: *Crane, Quittance, Answer, Advantage, Tramontana*; *Spy* (pinnace); four others transferred to Lord T. Howard.

Thames & Medway Guard, Sir H. Palmer: *Foresight, Advantage, Achates*; *Sun* (pinnace).

[*MNT* II,87–90]

October 1625: Wimbledon's fleet at Cadiz

Admiral's Squadron: *Anne Royal* (admiral), *St Andrew* (vice-admiral), *Convertine* (rear-admiral); twenty-seven transports and victuallers.

Earl of Essex's Squadron: *Swiftsure* (admiral), *St George* (vice-admiral), *Constant Reformation* (rear-admiral); twenty-six transports.

Sir Francis Stewart's Squadron: *Lion* (admiral), *Rainbow* (vice-admiral), *Elizabeth Bonaventure* (rear-admiral); twenty-seven transports.

Additional: *Assurance, Dreadnought, Mary Rose, Mercury* (pinnace).

Dutch Squadron: Approximately twenty ships.

[Clowes, *Royal Navy* I,60–61. Winkel-Rauws, *Nederlansch-Engelsche Samenwerking*]

1636 Ship-Money Fleet

Triumph (admiral), *St Andrew* (vice-admiral, replacing the damaged *Anne Royal*), *James* (rear-admiral), *Repulse, Victory, Unicorn, Defiance, Charles, Henrietta Maria, Nonsuch, Convertine, Assurance, Garland, Bonaventure, Happy Entrance, Adventure, Mary Rose*; *Second, Third, Fourth, Fifth* & *Tenth Whelps*; *Black George, Jonas, Great* & *Lesser Pinnace, Great Neptune.*

[Clowes, *Royal Navy* II,74; *MNT* III,252 gives a slightly different list]

1643 Summer Guard

Main Fleet, H.M. Ships, 1st–5th Rates: *Prince Royal* (admiral), *St Andrew* (vice-admiral), *St George* (rear-admiral), *Swiftsure, James, Rainbow, Victory, Charles, Convertine, Antelope, Happy Entrance, Leopard, Swallow, Dreadnought, Mary Rose, Eight* & *Tenth Whelps*; five 6th Rates, four ketches, 2 others.

Main Fleet, Merchant Ships: *Martin, Hercules, Mayflower, Scipio, Golden Lion, Golden Angel, Prosperous,* (400–532 tons); *Hopeful Luke, Maidenhead, Anne & Jonas, Leopard, Friendship, Speedwell, Providence, John & Barbary, Exchange, Blessing* (350 tons, T. Ashmore master), *Blessing* (200 tons, T. Shaftoe master) (200–399 tons); *Elizabeth & Anne, George* of Dover, *James* of Youghal, *Charity, Jocelyn* (88–199 tons).

Colliers: *Recovery, Edward & Elizabeth, Dragon, Hector* (260–360 tons).
Fire Ships: *Swan, Sarah, Andrew & John, Lion* of London (200–250 tons).

Irish Guard, H.M. Ships: *Bonaventure* (admiral), *Lion* (vice-admiral), *Expedition* (rear-admiral), *Providence*; four 6th Rates.
Irish Guard, Merchant Ships: *Employment, Ruth, Peter* (81–132 tons).

'Merchant Ships on the Coast of Ireland': *Zante Merchant, Good Hope, Achilles, George Bonaventure, Mary Bonaventure, Hopewell, Katherine, Pennington, Dolphin, Peter* (135–390 tons).

[*DCW* pp. 69–72]

APPENDIX III

MEDIEVAL FLEETS

These lists are examples of very many generated by medieval naval administration, most of which have never been printed. As a rule they list merchant ships available, or notionally available, for royal service. In some cases they may represent an attempt at a complete list of ships over a certain size, but they are never to be understood as a complete 'merchant navy list'. They do however give a good general impression of the distribution of merchant ships (and in a few cases, warships) available to the crown. Unless otherwise stated the lists are arranged in geographical order, proceeding clockwise around the coasts of England and Wales from Berwick, and Ireland from Malin Head. Unidentified places are inserted where the order of the original document suggests, but as the documents seldom follow an exact order, and sometimes list places quite at random, this should not be taken as more than a rough indication of where they may have been.

In many cases the obligation to pay for and provide a ship or ships was laid on a 'syndicate' of seaports. In principle all were really ports with access to navigable water, though in practice it is difficult to believe that ships actually lay (though they may have been owned) in some of these places. Since it is difficult or impossible to tell how these grouped ports really compared in prosperity and shipowning, I have divided the obligation equally among them. Figures (many of them fractional) resulting from such calculations are in square brackets. Note that medieval administrative convention sometimes grouped the ports of an estuary together under a single name. I have treated these as 'syndicates', thus:

Goseford	Woodbridge (& the Deben Estuary)
Orwell	Harwich & Ipswich
Exemouth	Exeter, Topsham & Starcross[1]
Portlemouth	Salcombe & Kingsbridge
River Severn	Berkeley & Gloucester

1. The modern town of Exmouth was founded in the eighteenth century

1. Disposition of Royal Galleys, 1206 and 1235

	1206	1235
Lynn	5	
Yarmouth	3	
Dunwich	5	2
Ipswich	2	
London	5	
Thames at 'Newebree'		2
Sandwich	3	
Romney	4	3
Rye	3	
Winchelsea	2	2
Newhaven [*Neueiheiam*]	2	
Shoreham	5	2
Portsmouth		4
Southampton	2	1
Exeter	2	
Bristol	3	2
Gloucester	1	
Ireland	5	6

[Sources: *RLC* I,33 & *CCR* 1234–37 p. 163, printed by Brooks, *English Naval Forces*, pp. 138 and 150–151. The Portsmouth figure (of 1228) from *CLR* I,68 and 108; by 1233 there were only two there: *CPR* 1232–47 pp. 27–28; *CCR* 1231–34 p. 329.]

2. Requisitioned Fleets *c.*1297, 1301, 1303, 1311, 1326, 1340, 1343, 1347 and 1372

The first list is of about 1297, and probably represents a fleet summoned for the relief of Gascony; it includes not less than 100 ships of Bayonne. The list is partly illegible, and hence incomplete. It includes four galleys (one each from Yarmouth, Sandwich, Hythe and Dover) but excludes 20 packet-boats from Dover and two barges of Yarmouth.

The next column represents medieval staff-work: it is an estimate made by the barons of the Cinque Ports of the ships which Edward I might be able to raise for the Scottish war 'without great complaint' (*saunz graunt grevaunts*). It may be compared with the number he then summoned in the third column. This is the original list; a later revision struck out the ships from Yarmouth and St Helen's, Chepstow, and one of those from London.

The next three are lists of ships summoned for service; they did not necessarily all appear as ordered. In 1301 two lists of ships were ordered to be at Berwick by Midsummer's Day, on 14 February and 27 March. They appear to be duplicates, except that Swine appears only in the second list, and the demand from Saltfleet, Wainfleet and Lynn was lower the second time. On 27 March the ships of the Cinque Ports were ordered to be at Dublin on the octave of Trinity Sunday, and 17 ships of the earlier list were diverted thither. In 1303 the ports listed were to have their ships at Newton-on-Ayr by Ascension Day, and 50 ships from unspecified East Coast ports were to be at Berwick by Whitsunday. The 1311 squadron was to operate off the West Coast of Scotland.

The 1326 summons was not against Scotland but against the threatened invasion of Queen Isabella and Prince Edward. In spite of this large force, the Queen landed successfully and overthrew the government of her estranged husband Edward II, who was soon after murdered. This list represents the actual fleet of ships of at least 50 tons assembled at Portsmouth in September. Ports from the Thames northwards were to have all ships of 30 tons and over in the Orwell by 21 September, but no list of them has been found. The only E. Coast ships listed below are some squadrons for local defence in addition to the main fleets.

The 1340 list is of ships actually in service for at least some part of that year, most of which probably fought at the battle of Sluys.

The 1343 list is of ships accused of having deserted or evaded the king's service during the previous year.

The 1347 list is of the fleet assembled to support the siege of Calais.

The 1372 list is a survey of ships and barges supposedly available in southern ports.

	1297	1301	1301	1303	1311	1326	1340	1343	1347	1372
Fenwick								1		
Bamburgh									1	
Newcastle upon Tyne			2				1	7	17	
Walwick									1	
Hartlepool									5	
Whitby			1							
Scarborough			2						1	
Bridlington								1		

	1297	1301	1301	1303	1311	1326	1340	1346	1347	1372
Withernsea							2			
Sternthorp								1		
Ravenspur			1				5	3	1	
Hedon			1							
Swine [*Swynhumbre*]			1				5		1	
Hull			1				13	15	16	
York									1	
Newland								1		
Snaith								1		
Thorne							1			
Swinefleet							2	1	1	
Stockwith									1	
Nottingham							1			
Barton-on-Humber								1	5	
Grimsby			1				2	6	11	
Grainthorpe								4		
Saltfleet			[1½]				1	1	2	
Surfleet							1			
Wainfleet			[1½]				1		2	
Wrangle									1	
Boston			1				6	8	17	
Spalding						2				
[King's] Lynn			3				9	9	19	
Wiggenhall							1			
Denver									1	
Snettisham						2				
Hunstanton						2				
Heacham			[½]							
'Flychene'			[½]							
Holme-next-the-Sea			[½]			2	1			
Thornham			[½]							
Brancaster [*Skottemuth*]			[½]							
Burnham			[½]							
Stiffkey [*Stokenhuth*]							1			
Blakeney			2			2	3	3	2	
Cromer							2			
Great Yarmouth	61		6				60	24	43	
Little Yarmouth								4		
'Milleflet'								1		
Dunwich	30		1				9	3	6	

	1297	1301	1301	1303	1311	1326	1340	1343	1347	1372
Orford			1				6	1	3	
Woodbridge			2				15	11	13	
Ipswich	16		2			[6]	9	11	12	
Harwich			1			[6]	1	9	13	
Whitlowness								1	1	
Brightlingsea							4		6	
Colchester							7	3	5	
Mersea							2	1	1	
Salcott								1		
Maldon								2	2	
Hadleigh							1			
Broad Hope									2	
London		3	2			3	10	15	25	
Greenwich							1	1		
Northfleet		1	1							
Cliffe		1	1			[4/5]				
Hoo									2	
Strood						[4/5]	1	1		
New Hythe									5	
Aylesford									2	
Maidstone						[4/5]	2	1	2	
Mote									2	
Rochester						[4/5]				
Gillingham		1	1			[4/5]				
Faversham	[2 1/2]					1+1	1	1	2	
Margate								2	15	
[Cinque Ports]		12	12							
Sandwich	12?					8	10	3	22	
Dover	[2 1/2]					2		1	16	
Hythe	12					1+2	4	1	6	
Romney	7					1	1	1	4	
Rye	18					3	2	2	9	
Smallhythe							1			
Winchelsea	?					18	16	8	21	
Hastings				1		2	3		5	
Eastbourne [*Burn*]				[1/2]				2		
Seaford	3	1	1	[1/2]		1		2	5	[1]
Lewes										[1]
Aldrington	[3 1/3]	[2/3]	2	[1/4]						
Brighton		[2/3]	[1/3]	[1/4]						
Hove	[3 1/3]			[1/4]						

	1297	1301	1301	1303	1311	1326	1340	1343	1347	1372
Shoreham	[3 1/3]	[2/3]	[1/3]	[1/4]	2	2	1	2	20	3
'Newmouth'									2	
Cudlow								2		
Ford										[1]
Wittering										2
Chichester										2
Portsmouth		1	[1/3]	[1/2]	1	2				1
Portchester								2		
Gosport				[1/2]						
Hamble-Rice						2		3	7	[3]
Hamble-Hook				[1/2]		4	6	8	11	[3]
Southampton		2	2	2	3	13	10	3	21	5
Millbrook								1	1	
Calshot								1		
Lymington				[1/2]	[1 1/2]	2	4	2	9	1
[Isle of Wight]									13	
Yarmouth, I.o.W.		[1/2]		[1/2]		2				
Newport, I.o.W.						2				
Quarr							1			
St Helen's		[1/2]		[1/2]				4		
Freshwater								1		
Christchurch				1						
Branksome	[2]			[2/3]						
Poole	15	1	1	[2/3]	[1 1/2]	6	6	3	4	3
Ower	[2]									
Wareham	[2]			[2/3]	1		1		3	
Studland	[2]									
'Durfeldyn'							1			
Melcombe	2					3	3			
Weymouth	20	2	1	1	2	2	6	2	15	4
Lyme [Regis]	10	2	1	1	2	5	5	1	4	
Seaton				[1/2]	[1]		1	2	2	
Sidmouth				[1/2]	[1]	3	3	3	3	
Ottermouth								1		1
Topsham	[3 1/4]	[1/3]	[1/3]			[2]	[3/5]	[2 1/3]	[3 1/3]	
Exeter	[3 1/4]	[1/3]	[1/3]	1	2	[2]	[3/5]	[2 1/3]	[3 1/3]	2
Starcross	[3 1/4]	[1/3]	[1/3]			[2	[3/5]	[2 1/3]	[3 1/3]	
Dawlish				[1/2]						
Teignmouth	[3 1/4]	1	1	[1/2]	2	8	6	1	7	2
'Weseworth'							1			
Brixham										2

	1297	1301	1301	1303	1311	1326	1340	1343	1347	1372
Dartmouth	20	3	2	[¼]	3	10	9	10	31	12
Kingsbridge				[¼]				[1]	[2½]	[6]
Salcombe				[¼]				[1]	[2½]	[6]
Bigbury [*Berry*]				[¼]						
'Seaham'										1
R. Yealm				[⅓]					2	
Plympton				[⅓]						
Plymouth	2	1	1	[⅓]	1	3	6	9	26	10
Sutton						2				
Saltash				[⅓]						2
Porthpean				[⅓]						
Looe		1	1	[⅓]	[1]	4	3	7	20	1
Polruan				[¼]			1	5	1	[2]
Lostwithiel				[¼]						[2]
Bodmin				[¼]						
Fowey		1	1	[¼]	[1]	2	6	9	47	[2]
Falmouth							1	2	2	2
Padstow	1								2	1
Barnstaple	1			[½]	[1]				2	11
Ilfracombe				[½]	[1]				6	1
Dunster										1
Combwich										4
Bridgewater	3	1	1	1	[1]				1	?
Bristol	20	3	2	2	3	6	9	10	22	16
Berkeley	[7½]									2
Gloucester	[7½]									
Hereford		1								
Chepstow	2	1			1					
Cardiff									1	
Swansea [*Syneseye*]							1		1	
Carmarthen									1	
Tenby					2					
Pembroke	2									
Haverford [West]	3		1		[1]					
Cardigan					[1]					
Conway					1					
Chester					2		1			
'Caylesworth'							1		1	
'Wadworth'									1	

	1297	1301	1301	1303	1311	1326	1340	1343	1347	1372
Coleraine					[1]					
Carrickfergus					[1]					
Drogheda		1	1		3					
Dublin		1	1		3		1			
Wexford					2					
New Ross		2	2		3		1			
Waterford		1	1		3					
Youghal		3	3		3		1			
Cork		2	2		3					

Notes on Place-Names:

Swine: The documents suggest that the royal clerks were sometimes confused about Swine and Swinefleet, and the distinction between the two should not be regarded as certain.

Nottingham: Printed thus by Lyon, but possibly a mis-reading; this edition shows a shaky grasp of English geography.

Little Yarmouth: Often included under Great Yarmouth.

Hastings: 'Battle Abbey' in 1303.

Hamble: Hamble-le-Rice is the modern village of Hamble; Hamble-in-the-Hook lay on the opposite bank, near the modern Warsash.

Exeter: 'Exeter & Exemouth' in 1303.

Sources:

1297: PRO: E 101/684/54/4.

1301: PRO: SC 1/16 No.37.

1301: *CCR* 1296–1302 pp. 482–483 and 486–487. *CPR* 1297–1301 pp. 583–584.

1303: *CCR* 1296–1302 p. 612. *CPR* 1301–07 pp. 75–76.

1311: *CPR* 1307–13 pp. 352–353.

1326: *CCR* 1323–27 pp. 608–613 and 641–642. *CPR* 1324–27 pp. 315–316

1340: Lyon, *Wardrobe Book*, pp. 365–384, with some identifications supplied.

1343: *CCR* 1343–46 pp. 128–134.

1347: Charnock, *Marine Architecture* I,xxxviii–xliii, printing a 'MS of the Dean and Chapter of Canterbury', collated with BL: Cotton MSS Titus F.3 ff.265–266 (a Tudor transcript of part of Walter of Wetwang's accounts, 1344–47), and BL: Harleian MSS 782 ff.62–67 (a transcript of the same MS made in 1604 by the herald Rafe Brooke). None of the three is satisfactory, but to an extent they correct one another. The original is not in PRO: E 101, where many of the surviving Wardrobe accounts are to be found, and has not been traced elsewhere. Oppenheim discusses other surviving transcripts in *MNT* III,193–199. The list has also been printed, from either the Cotton or Harleian transcript, by: *PN* I,297–299; *A Collection of Ordinances and Regulations for the Government of the Royal Household* ... (Soc. of Antiquaries, London, 1790) pp. 6–8; and John Topham, 'A Description of an ancient Picture at Windsor Castle ...', *Archaeologia* VI (1782) pp. 213–215. Nicolas, *Royal Navy* II,507–510 and others, reprint from one or other of these.

1372: PRO: C 47/2/46 No.15.

APPENDIX IV

RATES OF PAY

The first 'naval personnel' whose rate of pay we have any means of calculating were the 'lithsmen' of Cnut and Edward the Confessor. It seems that each man (or possibly each soldier) received £4 to £6 a year, 2½d to 4d a day, a rate of pay considerably greater than that of the paid knights in the household of the early Norman kings.[1] A century after the Conquest, when our evidence again allows us to catch a glimpse of English seamen in royal service, there seems to have been a standard rate of 1d a day for a sailor and 2d for the steersman.[2] On occasion, however ships were paid more: two Colchester ships operating against the rebel Cinque Ports in 1172 were paid 1½d a man and 3d for the steersmen (though ships from other ports at the same time received the usual rate), and next year a squadron taking reinforcements to Pembroke was also paid 3d and 1½d a day.[3] When Prince John sailed to Ireland in 1184 the two masters and forty seamen of his personal *esnecca* received 5d and 2d a day respectively,[4] and in Richard I's crusading fleet in the 1190s a 'boatswain' was paid 4d a day and a seaman 2d.[5] Possibly the higher pay reflected warlike or distant voyages, but there does not seem to be any close relationship.

From 1204 or thereabouts[6] the standard rate of pay was invariably 1½d a day for boys, 3d for seamen, and 6d for masters and constables, later also clerks and carpenters.[7] Archers and men-at-arms were usually paid the same as seamen, but occasionally 4d.[8] The Black Death of 1349, which killed a third or even more of the population of England, made labour scarce and forced wages up. In 1370 the seaman's wage was raised to 4d, but by 1379 the House of Commons was complaining that it was not enough.[9] In indentures of retinue, which were then becoming common, the 'accustomed wages of war'[10] were 6d a day for archers and 12d for men-at-arms. A knight received two 'pays' (meaning twice a man-at-arms' wage, or 2s), and a banneret in command, four pays. An admiral was paid as a banneret, baron (6s 8d) or earl (8s 4d) according to his rank.[11] Moreover inflation had forced the addition of a bounty or victualling allowance (*regard* in French), of 6d a week for seamen.[12] When the king's ship the *Trinity of the Tower* went to Bordeaux for wine in 1395–96, her seamen were paid 3d a day plus 4s for the voyage, a total of about 36s for 131 days' service.[13] The 'king's mariners' sometimes received permanent salaries. John Mayhew, master of the *Trinity of the Tower*, was granted 10 marks a year in 1389, increased to 15 marks in 1395, 40 marks in 1399, and finally the extraordinary sum of £40 later the same year, when the new monarch Henry IV was clearly trying to buy the loyalty of a key person.[14] Next year William Usher, master carpenter of the same ship, was allowed 1s a day for life.[15] Henry V provided a regular annual salary of from five to ten marks, according to the size of their ships, for each of 28 of his masters.[16]

There is some suggestion that by this time wages may have fallen again. In Henry V's ships men were receiving the old rates of 6d, 3d and 1½d a day, with sometimes 6d a week 'regard',[17] and in 1440 men serving in an indentured retinue were paid 1s 6d a week with the same for victualling.[18] The abortive 1442 Parliamentary scheme for keeping the seas offered the men half the prize money but only 2s a month wages, plus 2d a day for victualling.[19] In Lord Howard's squadron the seamen were paid 15d a week and victualled at the crown's expense for 12½d a week.[20] The same rate of pay was expressed as one 'share' of 5s a (lunar) month, with masters and quartermasters taking two each.[21] In the 1490s a master received 10s a (lunar) month, a mate 8s, and seamen 6s 8d, 5s or 3s 4d according to their skill and experience (which implies that something like the later ratings of petty officer, able and ordinary seaman already existed).[22] By this date sea and harbour pay were distinct, with seamen getting 1s in port and 1s 3d at sea, boys 6d and 9d. In the *Sovereign* in 1496 the master received 3s 4d a week or 13s 4d a month (presumably reflecting his status as master of the king's biggest ship), boatswain and purser 1s 8d to 2s, the master gunner 1s 3d to 1s 10½d, quartermasters 1s 4d to 1s 6d, the steward and cook 1s 3d to 1s 6d.[23] As late as the 1500s English seamen in merchantmen were still receiving the old standard rates of pay of 6d a day for the master, 3d for seamen and 1½d for boys.[24] A Scots seaman aboard one of James IV's ships at the end of the century earned 35s a month in Scots currency, or about 8s 9d sterling.[25]

Under the terms of Sir Edward Howard's indenture the soldiers, mariners and gunners of the 1512 and 1513 fleets were paid 5s a (28-day) month for wages, and the same for victuals. Boys had 2s 6d. 'Deadshares' or extra pays were distributed among the officers: in the *Sovereign*, for example, the master had seven shares in addition to his basic pay, his mate two, the boatswain two and his mate one.[26] The seaman's basic pay was raised in the 1540s to 6s 8d a month,[27] but the 'deadshare' system continued until the new pay scale of 1582, the first to specify pay for each rank or rating, and to grade the officers' pay according to the size of ship they served in. For administrative purposes naval pay was sometimes expressed as a 'medium' or average figure arrived at by dividing the total wage bill by the number of officers and men; in the 1550s the figure was 9s 4d.[28] Some confusion has been generated from time to time by historians misreading this as an actual rate of pay.[29]

1582 Scale of Sea Pay and Complement

By the 28-day month	1st Rates				2nd Rates				3rd Rates				4th Rates				5th Rates				6th Rates			
	£	s	d	No	£	s	d	No	£	s	d	No	£	s	d	No	£	s	d	No	£	s	d	No
Master	2	1	8	1	2	0	0	1	1	16	8	1	1	11	8	1	1	6	8	1	1	1	8	1
Master's Mate	1	1	8	2	0	16	8	2	0	16	8	1	0	11	8	1	0	11	8	1	0	11	8	1
Boastwain	1	1	8	1	0	16	8	1	0	11	8	1	0	11	8	1	0	11	8	1	0	11	8	1
Boatswain's Mate	0	11	8	2	0	11	8	1	0	9	2	1	0	9	2	1	0	9	2	1		–		
Quartermaster	0	16	8	4	0	11	8	4	0	11	8	4	0	11	8	4	0	11	8	4	0	11	8	2
Quartermaster's Mate	0	11	8	4	0	9	2	4	0	9	2	4	0	9	2	4	0	9	2	4		–		
Yeoman of the Tacks	0	11	8	1	0	11	8	1		–				–				–				–		
Coxswain	0	11	8	1	0	11	8	1	0	9	2	1		–				–				–		
Coxswain's Mate	0	9	2	1	0	9	2	1		–				–				–				–		
Yeoman of the Jeers	0	11	8	1	0	11	8	1		–				–				–				–		
Yeoman's Mate	0	9	2	1		–				–				–				–				–		
Purser	0	16	8	1	0	11	8	1	0	11	8	1	0	11	8	1	0	11	8	1	0	9	2	1
Cook	0	11	8	1	0	11	8	1	0	11	8	1	0	11	8	1	0	8	11	1	0	9	2	1
Cook's Mate	0	9	2	2		–				–				–				–				–		
Steward	0	11	8	1	0	11	8	1	0	11	8	1	0	11	8	1	0	11	8	1	0	9	2	1
Steward's Mate	0	9	2	2	0	9	2	2	0	9	2	2	0	9	2	2		–				–		
Master Carpenter	0	16	8	1	0	16	8	1	0	11	8	1	0	11	8	1	0	11	8	1	0	11	8	1
Carpenter's Mate	0	11	8	2	0	11	8	1	0	9	2	1	0	9	2	1	0	9	2	1		–		
Swabber	0	9	2	1	0	9	2	1	0	9	2	1	0	7	6	1			– –					
Master Gunner	0	10	0	1	0	10	0	1	0	10	0	1	0	10	0	1	0	10	0	1	0	10	0	1
Gunner's Mate	0	7	6	2	0	7	6	2	0	7	6	1	0	7	6	1	0	7	6	1	0	7	6	1
Quarter Gunner [Gunner's 'Quartermaster']	0	7	6	4	0	7	6	4	0	7	6	4	0	7	6	4	0	7	6	2		–		
Quarter Gunner's Mate	0	7	6	4	0	7	6	4	0	7	6	4	0	7	6	4	0	7	6	2		–		
Surgeon	0	15	0	1	0	15	0	1	0	15	0	1	0	15	0	1	0	15	0	1		–		
Surgeon's Man	0	6	8	2	0	6	8	1	0	6	8	1		–				–				–		
Trumpeter	0	15	0	4	0	15	0	2	0	15	0	1	0	15	0	1	0	15	0	1	0	15	0	1
Drum & Fife	0	10	0	1	0	10	0	1	0	10	0	1	0	10	0	1	0	10	0	1	0	10	0	1
Pilot	1	0	0	1	1	0	0	1	0	16	8	1	0	16	8	1	0	15	0	1		–		
Seaman	0	10	0		0	10	0		0	10	0		0	10	0		0	10	0		0	10	0	

By the 28-day month	1st Rates				2nd Rates				3rd Rates				4th Rates				5th Rates				6th Rates			
	£	s	d	No	£	s	d	No	£	s	d	No	£	s	d	No	£	s	d	No	£	s	d	No
The following were added in 1588:																								
Preachers [total of five]	2	0	0		2	0	0																	
Lieutenant	2	10	0	1	2	10	0	1	2	10	0	1			–				–					
Corporal	0	17	6	4	0	17	6	4	0	17	6	2	0	17	6	2			–	–				
Also one Lord Admiral's chaplain at £3-0-0d, two admirals' secretaries at £1-10-0d.																								

The 'classes' or rates were as follows:
1st: *Elizabeth Jonas, Triumph, Bear, Victory* [800 tons and above]
2nd: *Mary Rose, Elizabeth Bonaventure, Lion, Philip & Mary, Hope, Revenge* [500–800 tons]
3rd: *Dreadnought, Swiftsure, Antelope, Swallow, Foresight* [300–500 tons]
4th: *Aid, Bull, Tiger* [200–300 tons]
5th: *Scout, Handmaid, Achates* [100–200 tons]
6th: *Merlin* pinnace.

[Sources: Corbett, *Spanish War*, pp. 258–262; *ARN* p. 153; *DSA* II,231.]

Many of the officers' rates of pay were raised in 1618,[30] but the seaman's pay remained at 10s until the new scale of 1626.[31]

1626 Scale of Sea Pay and Complement

By the 28-day month	1st Rates				2nd Rates				3rd Rates				4th Rates				5th Rates				6th Rates			
	£	s	d	No	£	s	d	No	£	s	d	No	£	s	d	No	£	s	d	No	£	s	d	No
Captain	14	0	0	1	11	4	0	1	9	6	8	1	7	0	0	1	6	12	0	1	4	13	4	1
Lieutenant	3	10	0	1	3	10	0	1	3	10	0	1			–				–				–	
Master	4	13	9	1	4	10	0	1	3	15	0	1	3	7	6	1	3	0	0	1	2	6	8	1
Pilot	2	5	0	1	2	0	0	1	1	17	6	1	1	13	9	1	1	10	0	1	1	3	4	1
Master's Mate	2	5	0	3	2	0	0	2	1	17	6	1	1	13	9	1	1	10	0	1	1	3	4	1
Boatswain	2	5	0	1	2	0	0	1	1	13	4	1	1	10	0	1	1	6	8	1	1	3	4	1
Boatswain's Mate	1	6	3	2	1	5	0	2	1	0	8	1	1	0	8	1	1	0	8	1	1	0	8	1
Quartermaster	1	10	0	4	1	5	0	4	1	5	0	4	1	5	0	4	1	5	0	2	1	0	0	2
Quartermaster's Mate	1	5	0	4	1	0	8	4	1	0	8	2	1	0	8	2	1	0	8	2	0	17	6	2

By the 28-day month	1st Rates				2nd Rates				3rd Rates				4th Rates				5th Rates				6th Rates			
	£	s	d	No	£	s	d	No	£	s	d	No	£	s	d	No	£	s	d	No	£	s	d	No
Yeomen of the Halliards, Sheets, Tacks and Jeers	1	5	0	4	1	1	0	4	1	1	0	2	1	1	0	2			–				–	
Corporal	1	10	0	1	1	8	0	1	1	5	8	1	1	3	4	1	1	0	0	1	0	18	8	1
Master Carpenter	1	17	6	1	1	17	6	1	1	10	0	1	1	6	8	1	1	3	4	1	1	1	0	1
Carpenter's Mate	1	5	0	1	1	4	3	1	1	3	4	1	1	1	6	1	0	19	2	1	0	18	8	1
Other Carpenters and Caulkers	1	0	8	9	1	0	0	6	1	0	0	4	1	0	0	3			–				–	
Purser	2	0	0	1	1	16	8	1	1	10	0	1	1	3	8	1	1	3	4	1	1	3	4	1
Steward	1	5	0	1	1	5	0	1	1	5	0	1	1	3	4	1	1	3	4	1	1	3	4	1
Cook	1	5	0	1	1	5	0	1	1	5	0	1	1	3	4	1	1	3	4	1	1	3	4	1
Surgeon	1	10	0	1	1	10	0	1	1	10	0	1	1	10	0	1	1	10	0	1	1	10	0	1
Surgeon's Mate	1	0	0	1	1	0	0	1	1	0	0	1			–				–				–	
Master Trumpeter	1	8	0	1	1	6	8	1	1	5	0	1	1	5	0	1	1	5	0	1	1	10	0	1
Other Trumpeters	1	3	4	4	1	3	4	3			–				–				–				–	
Drum and Fife	1	0	0	1	1	0	0	1	1	0	0	1	1	0	0	1			–				–	
Coxswain	1	5	0	1	1	5	0	1	1	3		1	1	0	0	1			–				–	
Coxswain's Mate	1	0	8	1	1	0	8	1	0	19	2	1			–				–				–	
Skiffswain	1	0	0	1			–				–				–				–				–	
Skiffswain's Mate	0	17	6	1			–				–				–				– –					
Swabber	1	0	8	2	1	0	0	1	0	18	6	1	0	17	8	1	0	17	6	1			–	
Swabber's Mate			–		0	17	10	1	0	16	8	1			–				–				–	
Armourer	1	1	0	1	1	1	0	1	1	1	0	1	1	1	0	1			–				–	
Master Gunner	2	0	0	1	1	16	8	1	1	10	0	1	1	6	8	1	1	3	4	1	1	3	4	1
Gunner's Mate	1	2	6	2	1	1	0	2	1	0	0	1	1	0	0	1	1	0	0	1	0	18	8	1
Quarter Gunner	1	0	0	4	0	18	8	4	0	18	8	1	0	18	8	1	0	17	6	1	0	17	6	1
Quarter Gunner's Mate	0	18	8	4	0	17	6	4			–				–				–				–	
Yeoman of the Powder Room	1	0	0	1	0	18	8	1	0	18	8	1	0	18	8	1			–				–	
Master Cooper	0	16	8	1	0	16	8	1	0	16	8	1	0	16	8	1			–				–	
Common [Sea]men	0	15	0	367	0	15	0	204	0	15	0	146	0	15	0	65	0	15	0	41	0	15	0	23
Grommet	0	11	3	6	0	11	3	5	0	11	3	4	0	11	3	3	0	11	3	2	0	11	3	1
Boy	0	7	6	5	0	7	6	4	0	7	6	3	0	7	6	3	0	7	6	2	0	7	6	1
Gunmaker	1	1	0	1	1	0	0	1			–				–				–				–	

The rates were as follows: 1st, 400–500 men; 2nd, 250–300 men; 3rd, 160–200 men; 4th, 100–120 men; 5th, 60–80 men; 6th, 40–50 men.

[Source: *MNT* III,185–186.]

On 3rd february 1643 Parliament raised seamen's pay from 15s to 19s a month, but apparently the officers' rates were not formally changed until 1647.[32]

1647 Scale of Sea Pay

By the 28-day month	1st Rates	2nd Rates	3rd Rates	4th Rates	5th Rates	6th Rates
	£ s d	£ s d	£ s d	£ s d	£ s d	£ s d
Captain	21 0 0	16 16 0	14 0 0[33]	10 10 0	8 8 0	7 0 0
Lieutenant	4 4 0	4 4 0	3 10 0	–	–	–
Master	7 0 0	6 6 0	4 13 4	4 4 0	3 14 8	Captain & Master
Master's Mate	3 14 8[34]	2 16 0	2 16 0	2 6 8	2 2 0	2 2 0
Pilot	3 14 8[35]	2 16 0	2 16 0	2 6 8	2 2 0	2 2 0
Boatswain	3 10 0	2 16 0	2 9 0	2 4 4	2 2 0	1 12 8
Master Carpenter	3 3 0	3 3 0	2 6 8	1 19 8	1 19 8	1 15 0
Master Gunner	3 3 0	3 3 0	2 6 8	1 19 8	1 19 8	1 15 0
Boatswain's Mate	1 10 4	1 10 4	1 10 4	1 8 0	1 8 0	1 8 0
Carpenter's Mate	1 8 0	1 10 4[36]	1 8 0	1 5 8	1 5 8	1 5 8
Gunner's Mate	1 8 0	1 8 0	1 5 8	1 5 8	1 5 8	1 3 4[37]
Quartermaster	1 15 0	1 8 0	1 8 0	1 8 0	1 8 0	1 8 0
Quartermaster's Mate	1 8 0	1 5 8	1 5 8	1 5 8	1 5 8	1 3 4[38]
Quarter Gunner	1 3 4	1 1 0	1 1 0	1 1 0	1 1 0	1 1 0
Seaman	0 19 0	0 19 0	0 19 0	0 19 0	0 19 0	0 19 0

Sources: Bodleian Library: Rawlinson MS A.224 f.101, and BL: Add.MSS 18772 f.12v. Both MSS give rates by the day, which I have converted; Rawlinson A.224 also gives the 'old' (i.e. 1626) rates, with slight differences from the table above. Both of these sources look like careless copies, and Rawlinson A.224 is written in a slapdash mixture of roman and arabic numerals.

APPENDIX V

ADMIRALS AND OFFICIALS

These are lists of English admirals and other key officials. No complete list of the Admirals of Scotland appears to exist, but some information is in McMillan, 'Admiral of Scotland'.

1. English Admirals, 1295–1408

'Admirals' or 'Captains and Admirals' of particular fleets, thus: N = Northern (i.e. East Coast), S = Southern (otherwise 'Western', i.e. Channel), W = Irish Sea. The appointments were for a single year. I have omitted some initial nominations which were cancelled before the opening of the campaigns, and taken appointments in November or December to refer to the following year. Dates in parenthesis thus [1350] refer to the same man's earlier or later periods of office.

1295 Sir William Leyburn [1297], Sir John de Botetourt [1315]

1297 Sir W. Leyburn [1295]

1300 Gervase Alard [1304] (Cinque Ports)

1304 G. Alard [1300] (Cinque Ports, S & W)

1306 Edward Charles (N)

1310 Sir Simon Montagu

1311 'Sir John of Argyll' (i.e. Eoin MacDougall of Lorne) [1314] (W)

1314 Sir John Sturmy [1324], Peter Bard (N); E. MacDougall [1311] (W)

1315 Sir William Cray (W); John Lord Botetourt [1295] (N)

1318 Sir John Athy (W)

1319 Sir Simon Driby (W ?)

1322 John Perbroun [1323] (N); Robert Bataill [1323] (Cinque Ports); Sir Robert Leyburn [1326] (W)

1323 Robert Bataill [1322] (W ?); John Perbroun [1322, 1327] (N)

1324 John Lord Cromwell (Gascony); Sir J. Sturmy [1314] (N); Sir Robert Bendyn and Stephen Alard (W)

1325 Sir Nicholas Kyriel (S)

1326 Sir R. Leyburn [1322] (N)

1327 J. Perbroun [1323, 1333] (N); Sir Waresius de Valognes (S)

1333 J. Perbroun [1327] and Henry Randolf (N ?); William Lord Clinton [1340] (S)

1335 Sir John Howard [1347] (N); Sir Roger of Higham (S); Sir Richard Holand (W)

1336 Sir John Norwich (N); Geoffrey Lord Say (S); Sir John Ufford (Newcastle)

1337 John Lord Ross and Robert Ufford, 1st Earl of Suffolk [1344]; later Sir Walter Mauny [1348] (N); William Montagu, 1st Earl of Salisbury; later Bartholomew Lord Burghersh (S)

1338 Sir Thomas Drayton (N); Peter Bard (S)

1339 Robert Lord Morley [1341] (N); Sir William Trussell [1343] (S)

1340 William Clinton, 1st Earl of Huntingdon [1333, 1341] (Thames to Portsmouth); Richard FitzAlan, 3rd Earl of Arundel [1345] (Portsmouth westward); Lord Morley (N)

1341 Lord Morley [1339, 1342] (N); Earl of Huntingdon [1340] (S)

1342 Lord Morley [1341, 1348] (N); Sir John Montgomery [1347] (S)

1343 Sir W. Trussell [1339] (N); Sir Robert Beaupel (S)

1344 Earl of Suffolk [1337] (N); Sir Reginald Cobham [1348] (S)

1345 Earl of Arundel [1340] (S)

1347 Sir J. Howard [1335] (N); Sir J. Montgomery [1342] (S)

1348 Walter Lord Mauny [1337], then Lord Morley [1342, 1350] (N); Reginald Lord Cobham [1344] (S)

1349 John Lord Beauchamp of Warwick [1350]

1350 Lord Morley [1342, 1355] (N); Lord Beauchamp [1349, 1355] (S)

1351 William Bohun, 1st Earl of Northampton (N); Henry of Grosmont, Duke of Lancaster (S)

1353 Thomas Beauchamp, 3rd Earl of Warwick (S)

1354 John Gibbon (Earl of Lancaster's expedition to France)

1355 Lord Morley [1350] (N); Lord Beauchamp [1350, 1360] (S)

1356 Guy Lord Brian [1370] (S)

1360 Lord Beauchamp [1355] (N, S and W)

1361 Sir Robert Herle (N, S and W)

1364 Sir Ralph Spigurnell (N, S and W)

1369 Sir Nicholas Tamworth (N); Sir Robert Ashton [1371] (S)

1370 John Lord Nevill (N); Lord Brian [1356] (S); Sir Ralph Ferrers [1371] (Sir Robert Knolles's expedition to France)

1371 Sir R. Ferrers [1370] (N); Sir R. Ashton [1369] (S)

1372 Sir William Nevill (N); Sir Philip Courtenay [1380] (S)

1376 William Ufford, 2nd Earl of Suffolk (N); William Montagu, 2nd Earl of Salisbury (S)

1377 Sir Michael de la Pole (N); Sir Robert Hales, Prior of the Hospitallers in England (S)

1378 Thomas Beauchamp, 4th Earl of Warwick (N); Richard FitzAlan, 4th Earl of Arundel [1387], later Sir Hugh Calveley (S)

1379 Sir Thomas Percy [1385] (N)

1380 Sir William Elmham (N); Sir P. Courtney [1372] (S)

1382 Walter Lord FitzWalter (N); Sir John de Roches (S)

1384 Henry Percy, 1st Earl of Northumberland (N); Edward Courtenay, 3rd Earl of Devon (S)

1385 Sir T. Percy [1379, 1399] (N); Sir John Raddington, Prior of the Hospitallers in England (S)

1386 Philip Lord Darcy (N); Sir Thomas Trivet (S)

1387 Earl of Arundel [1378, 1388] (N and S)

1388 Earl of Arundel [1387] (N and S)

1389 John Lord Beaumont (N); John Holand, 1st Earl of Huntingdon (S); Sir J. de Roches (W ?)

1391 Edward of York, Earl of Rutland [1392] (N)

1392 Earl of Rutland [1391] (N and S)

1398 John Beaufort, 1st Marquis of Dorset [1407] (N and S)

1399 Thomas Percy, 1st Earl of Worcester [1385] (N and S)

1400 Earl of Worcester [1399] (N and S)

1401 Richard Lord Grey of Codnor (N); Sir Thomas Rempston (S)

1403 Thomas Lord Berkeley (S)

1404 Sir Thomas Beaufort [1408]

1405 Thomas Plantagenet, later Duke of Clarence ('King's Admiral')

1406 Nicholas Blackburn (N); Richard Clitheroe (S)[1]

1407 John Beaufort, 1st Earl of Somerset [1398]; later Edmund Holand, Earl of Kent (N and S)

[Adapted with permission from *Handbook of British Chronology* ed. E. B. Fryde *et al.* (Royal Historical Society, 3rd edn 1986), pp. 134–140]

1. Parliamentary nominees.

2. Admirals of England

The office was now national and permanent, each Admiral holding office from shortly after the death or dismissal of his predecessor. The common form of the title became first 'Lord Admiral' in the sixteenth century, then 'Lord High Admiral' in the seventeenth.

1408, 21 Sep:	Sir T. Beaufort, 1st Earl of Dorset 1412, 1st Duke of Exeter 1416 [1404]
1426, 26 Jul:	John, 1st Duke of Bedford
1435, 2 Oct:	John Holand, 2nd Earl of Huntingdon, 1st Duke of Exeter 1444
1447, 9 Aug:	William de la Pole, 1st Marquis of Suffolk
1450, 23 Jul:	Henry Holand, 2nd Duke of Exeter
1462, 30 Jul:	William Nevill, 1st Earl of Kent
1462, 12 Oct:	Richard Plantagenet, 1st Duke of Gloucester (later King Richard III) [1471]
1471, 2 Jan:	Richard Nevill, Earl of Warwick
1471, Apr:	Duke of Gloucester [1462]
1483, 25 Jul:	John Howard, 1st Duke of Norfolk
1485, 21 Sep:	John de Vere, 13th Earl of Oxford
1513, Mar 17:	Sir Edward Howard
1513, 4 May:	Lord Thomas Howard, Earl of Surrey 1514, 3rd Duke of Norfolk 1524
1525, 16 Jul:	Henry Fitzroy, 1st Duke of Richmond
1536, 16 Aug:	William Fitzwilliam, 1st Earl of Southampton 1537
1540, 28 Jul:	John Lord Russell, 1st Earl of Bedford 1550
1542, Dec:	Edward Seymour, 1st Earl of Hertford
1543, 26 Jan:	John Dudley, Viscount Lisle, 1st Earl of Warwick 1547 [1549]
1547, 17 Feb:	Thomas Lord Seymour
1549, 28 Oct:	Earl of Warwick [1543]
1550, 14 May:	Edward Fiennes, Lord Clinton, 1st Earl of Lincoln 1572 [1558]
1554, 20 Mar:	William Howard, 1st Lord Howard of Effingham 1554
1558, 10 Feb:	Lord Clinton [1550]
1585, 8 Jul:	Charles, 2nd Lord Howard of Effingham, 1st Earl of Nottingham 1597
1619, 28 Jan:	George Villiers, 1st Marquis of Buckingham, 1st Duke of Buckingham 1623

[Fryde, *Handbook of British Chronology*, pp. 141–142. Rodger, *Admiralty*, pp. 1–2]

3. Admirals and Admiralty Boards, 1628–1649

1628, 20 Sep:	Richard Weston, 1st Lord Weston, 1st Earl of Portland 1633, Lord Treasurer and 1st Lord of the Admiralty
1635, 10 Apr:	Robert Bertie, 1st Earl of Lindsey, Lord Chamberlain and 1st Lord of the Admiralty
1636, 16 Mar:	William Juxon, Bishop of London, Lord Treasurer and 1st Lord of the Admiralty
1638, 13 Apr:	Algernon Percy, 4th Earl of Northumberland, acting Lord High Admiral during the minority of the Duke of York.[2]
1642, 19 Oct:	Earl of Northumberland, senior Commissioner of the Admiralty
1643, 7 Dec:	Robert Rich, 2nd Earl of Warwick, Lord High Admiral
1645, 19 Apr:	Earl of Northumberland, senior member of the Parliamentary Admiralty Committee (but Warwick was its effective chairman)
1648, 29 May:	Earl of Warwick, Lord High Admiral
1649, 23 Feb:	The Lord Admiral's powers transferred to the Council of State

[Fryde, *Handbook of British Chronology*, pp. 141–142. Rodger, *Admiralty*, pp. 1–2]

4. Treasurers of the Navy, 1546–1649

'Treasurer of Marine Causes' as established 1546.

1546, 24 Apr:	Robert Legge (died 1548)
1549, 8 Jul:	Benjamin Gonson (died 1577)
1578, 1 Jan:	(Sir) John Hawkins (died 1595)
1598, 22 Dec:	Fulke Greville, later 1st Lord Brooke
1604, 26 Apr:	Sir Robert Mansell
1618, 10 May:	Sir William Russell
1627, 5 Apr:	Sir Sackville Crowe
1630, 21 Jan:	Sir William Russell (jointly with Sir Henry Vane the younger, 12 Jan 1639 to Dec 1641)
1642, 5 Aug:	Sir Henry Vane

[*ARN* pp. 85, 104, 144–145, 149, 189, 195 and 281. Rowe, *Vane*, pp. 120, 124]

2. Commission revoked by Charles I on 25 June 1642, but continued to act. In December 1643 the King appointed Francis, 1st Lord Cottington as Lord Admiral, but having no access to the fleet, he could not exercise the office.

5. Controllers of the Navy, 1546–1649

Originally 'Controller of the King's Ships'.

1546, 24 Apr:	William Broke (died 1561)
1561, 12 Dec:	William Holstock
1589:	William Borough
1598, 20 Dec:	Sir Henry Palmer (the father; died 1611)
1611, 7 May:	Sir Guildford Slingsby (suspended 1618)
1619, 12 Feb:	(Navy Commission: Sir John Coke was its leading member)
1628, Feb:	Slingsby reinstated (died 1632)
1632:	Sir Henry Palmer (the son)
1639, 11 Dec:	Sir George Carteret jointly with Palmer
1641, Nov:	Carteret sole Controller
1642, Sep:	(No member of the Navy Commission acted particularly as Controller)

[*ARN* p. 85, 149, 189, 195 and 282. Baumber, 'Navy during the Civil Wars', p. 47. Clayton, 'Naval Administration', p. 10. John, 'Principal Officers', p. 48]

6. Surveyors of the Navy, 1546–1649

Originally 'Surveyor of the King's Ships'.

1546, 24 Apr:	Benjamin Gonson
1549, 8 Jul:	(Sir) William Winter (also Master of Naval Ordnance from 1557. Died 1589)
1589, 11 Jul:	Sir Henry Palmer
1598, 20 Dec:	(Sir) John Trevor
1611, 7 May:	Sir Richard Bingley
1616, 16 Feb:	Sir Thomas Aylesbury (suspended 1618)
1619, 12 Feb:	(Navy Commission: Thomas Norris acted as Surveyor, died 1625)
1625:	(Joshua Downing acting as Surveyor)
1628, Feb:	Sir Thomas Aylesbury reinstated
1632, 19 Dec:	Kenrick Edisbury (died 1638)
1638, 26 Sep:	William Batten (continued as a member of the Navy Commission, Sep 1642–1648, but much of the time actually at sea)

[*ARN* pp. 85, 104, 111, 149, 189, 195 and 281. Clayton, 'Naval Administration', p. 10. John, 'Principal Officers', p. 49]

REFERENCES

Foreword

1 James Boswell, *Life of Dr Johnson*, ed. R. W. Chapman (Oxford, 3rd edn, 1970), p. 301.

Introduction

1 *EHD*, I, 853; cf. M. K. Lawson, 'Archbishop Wulfstan and the homilectic element in the laws of Æthelred II and Cnut', *EHR* CVII (1992), pp. 565–86, at p. 571 n.3.
2 I mean complete on a large scale; there have been many single-volume histories.
3 *The Oxford Illustrated History of the Royal Navy*, ed. J. R. Hill (Oxford, 1995).
4 Another recent example is Friel, *The Good Ship*, p. 12: 'England often had a strong navy between the thirteenth and sixteenth century . . .'
5 John Ehrman, *The Navy in the War of William III, 1689–1697: Its State and Direction* (Cambridge, 1953), p.xxii.

1 The Three Seas

1 Campbell, *Anglo-Saxons*, p. 64.
2 Campbell, *Anglo-Saxons*, p. 61. Loyn, *Anglo-Saxon England*, p. 149.
3 Campbell, *Anglo-Saxons* p. 61. Loyn, *Anglo-Saxon England*, p. 149. Lewis, *Northern Seas*, pp. 428–9. For gifts of warships see: Loyn, *Vikings in Britain*, p. 66 (Harald Fairhair of Norway to Æthelstan); Hooper, 'Observations on the Navy', p. 205 (Earl Godwin to Harthacnut); Whitelock, *Anglo-Saxon Wills*, pp. 52–3, 161–2 (Archbishop Ælfric and Bishop Ælfwold, both to Æthelred II).
4 Haywood, *Dark Age Naval Power*, p. 37. Abels, *Lordship and Military Obligation*, pp. 117–19.
5 Mollat, 'Les marines et la guerre sur mer', p. 1009.
6 Haywood, *Dark Age Naval Power*, p. 120.
7 Musset, 'Problèmes militaires' p. 257.
8 Haywood, *Dark Age Naval Power*, p. 37.
9 So named in Bede's *History of the English Church and People*, but it is uncertain if they were really three distinct peoples.
10 The old argument, based on an absence of archaeological evidence, that the Anglo-Saxons (and Vikings) did not know the use of sail before the 8th or even 9th centuries, has been weakening for some time (e.g. Bruce-Mitford, *Sutton Hoo*, I, 422–3), and is altogether demolished by Haywood, *Dark Age Naval Power*, but Christensen, *Earliest Ships*, pp. 78–83, still puts it as late as the 7th century. See also Hope, *Shipping*, pp. 28–9.
11 Bannerman, *Dalriada*, p. 153; but the document survives only in a much later copy, and both its dating and its interpretation could be disputed.
12 Bannerman, *Dalriada*, pp. 152–3. Haywood, *Dark Age Naval Power*, p. 174 n.83.
13 Haywood, *Dark Age Naval Power*, pp. 43, 61.
14 Bannerman, *Dalriada*, p. 143. Bernard S. Bachrach, 'Logistics in Pre-Crusade Europe', in Lynn, *Feeding Mars*, pp. 57–78, at pp. 68–70. Note that the English territorial 'hundred' was a Latin short hundred of five score, though the

English otherwise counted by the northern long hundred of six score.

15 Haywood, *Dark Age Naval Power*, p. 61. D. P. Kirby, *The Earliest English Kings* (London, 1991), p. 85.

16 Haywood, *Dark Age Naval Power*, p. 61. *ASC*, p. 23.

17 Hill, *Atlas of Anglo-Saxon England*, p. 75. Margaret Gelling, 'The Place Name Burton and Variants', in Hawkes, *Weapons and Warfare*, pp. 145–53.

18 Abels, *Lordship and Military Obligation*, pp. 52–3. Brooks, 'Military Obligations'.

19 Campbell, *Anglo-Saxons*, pp. 118–22. Loyn, *Anglo-Saxon England*, p. 41.

20 Brooks, 'Military Obligations'. Abels, *Lordship and Military Obligation*, pp. 52–6.

21 But not all historians interpret it as a true defensive work, intended to be held against serious attack.

22 Abels, *Lordship and Military Obligation*, p. 54. Brooks, 'Military Obligations', p. 79.

23 *ASC*, p. 43.

24 Sawyer, *Kings and Vikings*, pp. 100–11. Loyn, *Vikings in Britain*, pp. 103–5.

25 *ASC*, pp. 35–6.

26 *EHD*, I, 776.

27 *ASC*, p. 41.

28 *ASC*, p. 41.

29 *ASC*, p. 42. *SCP*, I, 62.

30 Sawyer, *Kings and Vikings*, pp. 85–6. Haywood, *Dark Age Naval Power*, pp. 122–4, 134–5.

31 *ASC*, pp. 42–3.

32 'Mycel scip here': *ASC*, p. 45. *SCP*, I, 67.

33 Campbell, *Anglo-Saxons*, p. 145. Smyth, *King Alfred*, p. 63.

34 The outline of Alfred's reign can be followed in *ASC*, and in such standard histories as Stenton, *Anglo-Saxon England*; Sawyer, *Kings and Vikings*; Keynes & Lapidge, *Alfred the Great*, Loyn, *Vikings in Britain*, and now Smyth, *King Alfred*.

35 *ASC*, p. 48. *SCP*, I, 74. The word *sciphere* does not necessarily mean a large force.

36 *ASC*, pp. 50–1.

37 Campbell, *Anglo-Saxons*, p. 147. Smyth, *King Alfred*, p. 110.

38 Not implausible, if one imagines a fleet sheltering in Swanage Bay from a S.W. gale which then backed S.E.

39 *ASC*, p. 48.

40 Hill, *Atlas of Anglo-Saxon England*, pp. 65–71, Maps 108–129, shows vividly the high mobility of Danish forces during the campaigns of 980–1016.

41 Brooks, 'England in the Ninth Century', pp. 17–19.

42 *ASC*, p. 54.

43 Abels, *Lordship and Military Obligation*, p. 73.

44 Kuhn, *Altnordische Seekriegswesen*, p. 40, argues that Alfred was inspired by the Norwegian naval victory of Hafrsfjord in 870: he surely had more persuasive reasons much closer to hand.

45 *ASC*, p. 57.

46 Æthelstan, sub-king of Kent, eldest son of King Æthelwulf of Wessex. Æthelstan died before his father, who was succeeded by four younger sons in turn, of whom Alfred was the youngest.

47 Morcken, *Langskip, knarr og kogge*, p. 174. *KLNM*, XII, 253, sv. *Naust*. Ellmers, *Frühmittelalterliche Handelsschifffahrt*, p. 147.

48 Possibly coined by King Alfred (see below p. 15), and probably taken from the Latin: Simek, *Schiffsnamen*, p. 164.

49 ON *snekkja*, OE *snæcc*. Alternative etymologies are possible, mostly indicating something sharp or thin: Simek, *Schiffsnamen*, pp. 174–5. Schnepper, *Die Namen der Schiffe*, pp. 18, 36. Kuhn, *Altnordische Seekriegswesen*, p. 42 offers a meaning of 'snail'!

50 Simek, *Schiffsnamen*, is the best guide.

51 Brøgger & Shetelig, *Viking Ships*, on which see Christensen, 'Viking Age Ships' p. 22. Christensen's *Earliest Ships* deals only briefly with Viking ships. For a later period we now have Hutchinson, *Medieval Ships and Shipping*, and Friel, *The Good Ship*.

52 Brøgger & Shetelig, *Viking Ships*, pp. 169–71.

53 Binns, 'Ships of the Vikings', pp. 289–90. Crumlin-Pedersen, 'Viking Shipbuilding and Seamanship', p. 284.

54 Olsen & Crumlin-Pedersen, 'Skuldelev Ships (II)', p. 118. Crumlin-Pedersen,

'Viking Ships of Roskilde', p. 9. Crumlin-Pedersen, 'Ship Types and Sizes', n.1. A reconstruction of her is printed on p. 13.

55 Crumlin-Pedersen,"Viking Shipbuilding and Seamanship', pp. 274–6. Unger, *Ship in the Mediaeval Economy*, pp. 58–61. Hutchinson, *Medieval Ships and Shipping*, pp. 10–20.

56 ON *rými* & *sessan*; equivalents existed in all the Scandinavian languages, and probably in English too.

57 Evans, 'Sutton Hoo Ship'.

58 ON *tvítugsessa*.

59 Simek, *Schiffsnamen*, pp. 147–50. Crumlin-Pedersen,'Viking Shipbuilding and Seamanship', p. 279. Musset, 'Problèmes militaires', p. 255. Brøgger & Shetelig, *Viking Ships*, pp. 173–4.

60 Rodger, 'Cnut's Geld', pp. 400–1.

61 Musset, 'Problèmes militaires', p. 255. Brøgger & Shetelig, *Viking Ships*, pp. 187–90. Simek, *Schiffsnamen*, p. 34. To allow the rowers space to move, each 'room' needs to be at least three feet long, and 25–30% must be added for the ends to give an overall length for the ship.

62 Morcken, *Langskip, knarr og kogge*, pp. 29–35.

63 Marcus, 'Evolution of the Knörr', p. 120. *SCP*, I, 109. Simek, *Schiffsnamen*, pp. 36–7.

64 Roberta Frank, 'King Cnut in the verse of his Skalds', in Rumble, *Reign of Cnut*, pp. 106–24.

65 Brøgger & Shetelig, *Viking Ships*, pp. 187–90. Laurence M. Larson, *The Earliest Norwegian Laws, being the Gulathing Law and the Frostathing Law* (New York, 1935), p. 200. *KLNM*, X, 435, s.v. *Leidang*. Crumlin-Pedersen,'Viking Shipbuilding and Seamanship', p. 279. Simek, *Schiffsnamen*, pp. 174–5. Kuhn, *Altnordische Seekriegswesen*, pp. 62–71.

66 Brøgger & Shetelig, *Viking Ships*, pp. 181, 192. Simek, *Schiffsnamen*, pp. 35, 90–2. Kuhn, *Altnordische Seekriegswesen*, p. 43.

67 Rodger, 'Cnut's Geld', pp. 392–3. Simek, *Schiffsnamen*, p. 35.

68 Bannerman, *Dalriada*, pp. 152–4.

69 Morcken, *Langskip, knarr og kogge*, pp. 28, 36–7, 59. *KLNM*, X, 435, s.v. *Leidang*. Brøgger & Shetelig, *Viking Ships*, pp. 72, 203, 207, 210. Kuhn, *Altnordische Seekriegswesen*, pp. 44–5.

70 Or possibly 1064.

71 *EHD*, II, Pl.IV–VI, XXVII.

72 Marcus, 'Evolution of the Knörr', p. 117.

73 *ASC*, p. 57. *SCP*, I, 90.

74 *EHD*, I, 32, 293, 917–18. Keynes & Lapidge, *Alfred the Great*, pp. 140, 142.

75 Simek, *Schiffsnamen*, pp. 58–9, Schnepper, *Die Namen der Schiffe*, pp. 18, 37–8, and Kuhn, *Altnordische Seekriegswesen*, p. 37, sum up what little is known about the *æsc*.

76 Keynes & Lapidge, *Alfred the Great*, p. 289. Crumlin-Pedersen, 'Vikings and the Hanseatic merchants'. Ellmers, 'Cog as Cargo Carrier', pp. 33–6. Hutchinson, *Medieval Ships and Shipping*, pp. 10–20.

77 Since ships never fought under sail, I take the reference to be to speed under oars, but in either case fineness of hull form would be the critical factor.

78 Brøgger & Shetelig, *Viking Ships*, pp. 72, 106. Morcken, *Langskip, knarr og kogge*, pp. 36–7, 40.

79 *ASC*, pp. 57–8. Keynes & Lapidge, *Alfred the Great*, p. 291, perceive a difficulty in that the Danish ships must have beached on the top of the tide and ought not to have floated off first: but we do not know the respective draught of Danish and English ships, and we do know that quite large warships could with sufficient manpower be hauled in and out of the water. Perhaps the Danes were on a shelving beach some way up the river, giving a footing to manhandle the ships, while the English had grounded on mudflats at the mouth.

80 Smyth, *King Alfred*, pp. 112–13, argues that they were a failure and soon forgotten. That may be, but it contradicts his own view that the *Chronicle* is Alfredian propaganda which omits everything to the King's discredit.

2 The First English Empires

1 *ASC*, p. 61.
2 *EHD*, I, 278.
3 *ASC*, p. 69. *SCP*, I, 109.
4 *EHD*, I, 38, 279. Florence of Worcester claims they landed in the Humber, but the English poem which is our main source for the battle describes the defeated enemy retreating to Dublin; their commanders were Constantine, King of Scots, and Anlaf, probably chief of the Dublin Vikings.
5 Loyn, 'Wales and England'. Dumville, *Wessex and England*, p. 153. *ASC*, p. 69.
6 Stenton, *Anglo-Saxon England*, p. 347.
7 Campbell, *Anglo-Saxons*, p. 160. Lewis, *Northern Seas*, p. 324. Stafford, *Unification and Conquest*, p. 115.
8 Loyn, *Vikings in Britain*, pp. 66, 73–4.
9 John, *Land Tenure*, pp. 113–24. Campbell, *Anglo-Saxons*, p. 173. John, 'War and Society', pp. 176–81. *ASMI*, pp. 111–13.
10 *ASMI*, pp. 76–7.
11 Whitelock, *Anglo-Saxon Wills*, pp. 32–3, 52–3.
12 'Folces fyrdscip'. Loyn, *Anglo-Saxon England*, p. 164. Harmer, *Anglo-Saxon Writs*, pp. 80–1.
13 *ASC*, pp. 82, 84–6.
14 *ASMI*, p. 124. *EHD*, I, 45. John, *Land Tenure*, pp. 119–20. Loyn, *Anglo-Saxon England*, pp. 85, 99. *ASC*, p. 77. Hill, *Atlas of Anglo-Saxon England*, pp. 61–2. Dumville, *Wessex and England*, p. 145. Campbell, *Anglo-Saxons*, p. 173. Stubbs, *Memorials of St. Dunstan*, p. 423. Thorpe, *Chronicon ex Chronicis*, I, 143–4.
15 *ASC*, p. 77. *EHD*, I, 853. Hill, *Atlas of Anglo-Saxon England*, pp. 61–2. The identification is in some cases uncertain, but they were certainly all Celtic princes from around the shores of the Irish Sea. Stafford, *Unification and Conquest*, p. 126, interprets this as a conference to discuss common measures against the Viking threat; a sort of 10th-century NATO.
16 Dumville, *Wessex and England*, p. 145.
17 R. R. Davies, 'The Peoples of Britain and Ireland, 1100–1400, Identities', *TRHS* 6th S. IV (1994), pp. 1–20, at pp. 11–12, quoting the twelfth-century Anglo-Norman writer Geoffrey Gaimar.
18 M. K. Lawson, 'Archbishop Wulfstan and the homilectic element in the laws of Æthelred II and Cnut', *EHR* CVII (1992) pp. 565–586, at p. 571 n.2.
19 'Þa scipu þe ahtes wæron': *SCP*, I, 127; *ASC*, p. 82.
20 Lewis, *Northern Seas*, p. 399. Abels, 'Tactics, Strategy and Military Organization', pp. 144–5.
21 *ASC*, p. 85. Hill, *Atlas of Anglo-Saxon England*, pp. 63–6. Keynes, 'Battle of Maldon', p. 85. Lawson, *Cnut*, p. 23.
22 John, 'War and Society', pp. 184–90.
23 Sawyer, *Kings and Vikings*, p. 145.
24 Campbell, *Anglo-Saxons*, p. 198.
25 *ASC*, pp. 85–6.
26 *ASC*, p. 88. Loyn, *Anglo-Saxon England*, p. 164. *ASMI*, pp. 41, 109–10. Abels, *Lordship and Military Obligation*, p. 93.
27 Lawson, 'Those Stories Look True', pp. 393–4. *ASC*, p. 89.
28 *ASC*, p. 89.
29 Abels, 'Tactics, Strategy and Military Organization', pp. 144–5. Hooper, 'Observations on the Navy', pp. 205–6.
30 Campbell, *Anglo-Saxons*, pp. 189–93. John, 'War and Society'.
31 Lawson, *Cnut*, pp. 39–44.
32 Lawson, 'Those Stories Look True', pp. 396–7, discusses the size of Swein's forces; cf. Kuhn, *Altnordische Seekriegswesen*, pp. 54, 73.
33 *ASMI* gives the older view; Abels, *Lordship and Military Obligation*, is the most recent.
34 *ASMI*, pp. 76–7. Hawkes, *Weapons and Warfare*. John, *Land Tenure*, pp. 122–4. Abels, *Lordship and Military Obligation*, p. 65.
35 *ASMI*, pp. 104–15.
36 Keynes & Lapidge, *Alfred the Great*, p. 211. Schnepper, *Die Namen der Schiffe*, p. 33, deals with the word 'scip-hlæst'.
37 *ASMI*, pp. 96, 105.
38 Uwe Schnall, 'Early Shiphandling and Navigation in Northern Europe', in Christensen, *Earliest Ships*, pp. 120–8.
39 Hill, *Atlas of Anglo-Saxon England*, p. 93,

Maps 165, 166. Taylor, 'Military Obligations of the See of London'.

40 *DB* Worcester, pp. 173c, 174c; Norfolk, p. 199b; Bedford, p. 217c. Domesday records landholding rather than residence, but in the case of men with one smallish holding each I assume they lived on their estates.

41 Hooper, 'Observations on the Navy', p. 212.

42 *ASC*, p. 57. Hooper, 'Observations on the Navy, p. 204.

43 *DB* Sussex, p. 26a.

44 *DB* Warwick, p. 238a; Malmesbury, p. 64c.

45 The first element is apparently *buza*, a type of ship; Simek, *Schiffsnamen*, pp. 78–9.

46 *ASMI*, pp. 108–12.

47 Napier & Stevenson, *Crawford Charters*, pp. 23, 126–8. I know no source for the statement of Brøgger & Shetelig (*Viking Ships*, p. 179) that Æthelred built ships of 43 rooms, which appears to be quite impossible.

48 Rodger, 'Cnut's Geld', pp. 401–2. Lawson, 'Danegeld and Heregeld', pp. 737–8. Roberta Frank, 'King Cnut in the verse of his Skalds', in Rumble, *Reign of Cnut*, pp. 106–24. Simek, *Schiffsnamen*, p. 35. Stenton, *Anglo-Saxon England*, p. 413, refers to Cnut possessing a *drekkar* of 120 oars: the figure is incredible, and one naturally suspects a confusion between men and oars. Unfortunately he gives no authority, and nor do any of the historians who have copied the story from one another, according to R. C. Anderson who attempted to trace it to its source: 'The Oars of Northern Long-Ships', *MM* XXIX (1943), pp. 190–5, at p. 192.

49 *ASMI*, pp. 85–6. Hooper, 'Anglo-Saxons at War', p. 195.

50 Hooper, 'Anglo-Saxons at War', pp. 192–3. Hooper, 'Observations on the Navy', p. 209.

51 Morcken, *Langskip, knarr og kogge*, pp. 28, 42. *KLNM*, XII, 252–3, sv. *Naust*. Ellmers, *Frühmittelalterliche Handelsschifffahrt*, pp. 134–5.

52 The archaeologists have found none, but this proves very little as they have not been looking for such structures, nor digging in the likely places: see P. Marsden, 'Early shipping and the waterfronts of London', in Milne & Hobley, *Waterfront Archaeology*, pp. 10–16; and *Ships of the Port of London, First to eleventh centuries AD* (London, 1994), pp. 138ff. D. M. Goodburn, 'Anglo-Saxon Boat Finds from London, Are they English?', in Westerdahl, *Crossroads in Ancient Shipbuilding*, pp. 97–104, records (p. 103) fragments of an 11th-century longship from the Thames.

53 *ASC*, pp. 114, 123. Le Patourel, *Norman Empire*, p. 172. Peter Marsden, *Ships of the Port of London, First to eleventh centuries AD* (London, 1994), p. 136.

54 McGrail, *Ancient Boats*, p. 273. Ellmers, *Frühmittelalterliche Handelsschifffahrt*, pp. 155–63.

55 McGrail, *Ancient Boats*, pp. 232–9. Roberts, 'Viking Sailing Performance'. Gillmer, 'Single Square Sail Rig'. Christensen, 'Viking Age Rigging'. Hutchinson, *Medieval Ships and Shipping*, p. 59. Ole Crumlin-Pedersen, 'Problems of Reconstruction and the Estimation of Performance' in Christensen, *Earliest Ships*, pp. 110–19.

56 Abels, *Lordship and Military Obligation*, pp. 117–19. *EHD*, I, 566. Hill, *Atlas of Anglo-Saxon England*, p. 92.

57 *ASMI*, p. 125. Hooper, 'Anglo-Saxons at War', p. 192–3. Hill, *Atlas of Anglo-Saxon England*, p. 14.

58 *ASMI*, pp. 110, 124.

59 Barlow, *Edward the Confessor*, pp. 95, 174.

60 'Landes manna scipa': *ASC*, pp. 112–13. *SCP*, I, 168.

61 *ASMI*, p. 123.

62 Lawson, 'Danegeld and Heregeld'. Campbell, *Anglo-Saxons*, pp. 203–5. Loyn, *Anglo-Saxon England*, p. 121. Metcalf, 'Large Danegelds'. Campbell, 'Agents and Agencies', p. 205. Hooper, 'Military Developments'.

63 One group of 62 (some sources say 60) and another of 32, but the *Chronicle*

could be read as meaning that the 32 were part of the 62, continued in pay for a further period. *ASC*, p. 105. Lawson, 'Danegeld and Heregeld', pp. 737–8. Lawson, *Cnut*, p. 190.

64 Loyn, *Anglo-Saxon England*, p. 121. Lewis, *Northern Seas*, p. 461. Hooper, 'Military Developments', p. 98.

65 Campbell, 'English Government', p. 156.

66 Hooper, 'Observations on the Navy', pp. 206–7.

67 Murray, *Constitutional History*.

68 *DB* Kent, p. 1a. *ASMI*, pp. 116–22.

69 *ASMI*, pp. 115–16.

70 *ASC*, p. 122. See also Rodger, 'Cinque Ports', pp. 649–50. The translation of 'snaca' as 'small boats' is questionable (see Simek, *Schiffsnamen*, pp. 174–5), but they cannot have been large unless they carried more than 21 men.

71 Kuhn, *Altnordische Seekriegswesen*, pp. 54–87. *ASMI*, p. 113. Randsborg, *Viking Age in Denmark*, p. 32. Musset, 'Problèmes militaires', pp. 279–84.

72 Kuhn, *Altnordische Seekriegswesen*, pp. 62–71. Loyn, *Vikings in Britain*, pp. 73–4. Jones, *Vikings*, pp. 93, 120–1.

73 Campbell, 'Anglo-Norman State', p. 186. Roesdahl, *Viking Age Denmark*, p. 157. Lund, 'Armies of Swein Forkbeard and Cnut'. Kuhn, *Altnordische Seekriegswesen*, p. 71 suggests the Danish system derived from Norway rather than directly from England.

74 Loyn, *Vikings in Britain*, pp. 143–4. Marwick, 'Naval Defence in Norse Scotland'. Bannerman, *Dalriada*, pp. 140–1.

75 *ASC*, p. 100. Campbell, *Anglo-Saxons*, p. 214.

76 Stenton, *Anglo-Saxon England*, pp. 429–30. Barlow, *Edward the Confessor*, p. 59. *ASMI*, p. 126. *EHD*, II, 205.

77 Hudson, 'Cnut and the Scottish Kings'. Lawson, *Cnut*, p. 106.

78 *ASC*, pp. 108–12. *EHD*, II, 205. Barlow, *Edward the Confessor*, p. 59.

79 Maund, *Ireland Wales and England*, pp. 130–3.

80 Maund, *Ireland Wales and England*, p. 166.

81 Maund, *Ireland Wales and England*, p. 124.

82 *ASC*, p. 129. Barlow, *Edward the Confessor*, p. 68. Abels, *Lordship and Military Obligation*, p. 169. Hooper, 'Anglo-Saxons at War', p. 198.

83 *ASC*, pp. 130–1. *EHD*, II, 210.

84 Campbell, *Anglo-Saxons*, p. 222. Loyn, *Vikings in Britain*, pp. 103–4.

85 Barlow, *Feudal Kingdoms of England*, p. 71.

86 Hooper, 'Anglo-Saxons at War', p. 198. *EHD*, II, 211. Hill, *Atlas of Anglo-Saxon England*, p. 72.

87 *ASMI*, p. 124.

88 E.g. *ASC*, pp. 112–13, and *SCP*, I, 168, referring to the 1048 fleet commanded by Earl Godwin and his sons Harold and Tosti.

89 Campbell, *Anglo-Saxons*, p. 212. Barlow, *Feudal Kingdom of England*, pp. 61–6.

90 Campbell, *Anglo-Saxons*, p. 220.

91 Campbell, *Anglo-Saxons*, pp. 224–5. Hooper, 'Military Developments', p. 98.

92 Campbell, *Anglo-Saxons*, pp. 224–5. *EHD*, II, 206–8.

93 *EHD*, II, 208–9. Stenton, *Anglo-Saxon England*, pp. 566–9. Barlow, *Feudal Kingdom of England*, pp. 63–6. *ASC*, pp. 120–3.

3 The Partition of Britain

1 Barlow, *Feudal Kingdom of England*, pp. 68–9, 74–9. Brown, *Normans and the Norman Conquest*, pp. 147–8.

2 *EHD*, II, 212–13.

3 *DB* Essex, p. 14b. *ASC*, pp. 140–1. Loyn, *Norman Conquest*, p. 90.

4 Loyn, *Norman Conquest*, pp. 89–90.

5 *EHD*, II, 220, quoting William of Poitiers, one of William's court chaplains.

6 Campbell, *Anglo-Saxons*, p. 216. Lawson, *Cnut*, pp. 110–12. Laporte, 'Les opérations navales', p. 6, refers to an expedition in 1029.

7 Van Houts, 'Ship List of William the Conqueror', for the size of the fleet. Gillmor, 'Naval Logistics', pp. 116–21, and Laporte, 'Les opérations navales', p. 9, on assembling it.

8 Davis, *Medieval Warhorse*, pp. 78–9.
9 G. A. Furse, *Military Expeditions beyond the Seas* (London, 1897, 2 vols), I, 220–1, 273–5. M. H. Hayes, *Horses aboard Ship, A Guide to their Management* (London, 1902), pp. 95–6, 208–11. Pryor, 'Transportation of Horses', p. 21. Waley, 'Combined Operations', p. 121.
10 Davis, 'Warhorses of the Normans', p. 79; and *Medieval Warhorse*, p. 25.
11 Brown, *Normans and the Norman Conquest*, p. 150. Bachrach, 'Some observations', pp. 3–5.
12 Hooper, 'Anglo-Saxons at War', p. 195. *ASC*, p. 142. *EHD*, II, 213.
13 Brown, *Normans and the Norman Conquest*, pp. 152–3.
14 Gillmor, 'Naval Logistics', p. 124. Bachrach, 'Some observations', pp. 8–9. Howarth, *1066*, p. 124n.
15 *EHD*, II, Pl.xliii-xlvi. Roberts, 'Descendants of Viking Boats', p. 19. Modern replica Viking ships can make good a course better than 6 points off the wind: Hutchinson, *Medieval Ships and Shipping*, p. 59.
16 Howarth, *1066*, p. 146.
17 *EHD*, II, 220 (quoting William of Poitiers). Barlow, '*Carmen de Hastingae Proelio*', p. 203. Howarth, *1066*, p. 125. Laporte, 'Les opérations navales', p. 30. This St Valéry (in Ponthieu, therefore foreign territory) is not to be confused with St Valéry-en-Caux in Normandy.
18 *EHD*, II, 221.
19 Neumann, 'Hydrographic and Ship-Hydrodynamic Aspects', and Grainge & Grainge, 'Pevensey Expedition', have ingenious calculations on the passage. To clear the Somme and make Pevensey requires a wind between south and east.
20 Howarth, *1066*, p. 152. Beeler, *Warfare in England*, pp. 13–14.
21 Beeler, *Warfare in England*, pp. 14–17.
22 Glover, 'English Warfare in 1066', p. 3, refers to William's 'supine loitering'; it seems more likely that he was unable to move for want of riding horses.
23 William of Poitiers, *Gesta Guillelmi ducis Normannorum et regis Anglorum*, ed. Raymonde Foreville (Paris, 1952), p. 180. *EHD*, II, 221. Barlow, '*Carmen de Hastingae Proelio*', p. 206.
24 Bachrach, 'Some observations', p. 23. Glover, 'English Warfare in 1066', p. 3, interprets them as being intended to cover a re-embarkation in the event of defeat, which I do not find plausible.
25 Morillo, *Anglo-Norman Kings*, p. 164.
26 *ASC*, pp. 148–9. Maund, *Ireland Wales and England*, p. 167. Benjamin Hudson, 'William the Conqueror and Ireland', *IHS* XXIX (1994), pp. 145–158.
27 Flanagan, *Irish Society, Anglo-Norman Settlers*, pp. 62–7. Maund, *Ireland, Wales and England*, pp. 179–81. Lucas, 'Irish-Norse Relations', pp. 68–71. Holm, 'Slave Trade', pp. 338–42.
28 *ASC*, p. 175. Barlow, *Feudal Kingdom of England*, pp. 164–5. Loyn, *Vikings in Britain*, p. 105. Beeler, *Warfare in England*, pp. 214–7. Maund, *Ireland Wales and England*, pp. 168–9, 179.
29 *ASC*, pp. 148–52, 169. Lewis, *Northern Seas*, p. 462. Binns, 'Towards a North Sea Kingdom', pp. 55–8. Beeler, *Warfare in England*, p. 48. Lawson, *Cnut*, p. 212.
30 *ASC*, p. 161. Barlow, *Feudal Kingdom of England*, p. 97. Lewis, *Northern Seas*, p. 462.
31 Hooper, 'Observations on the Navy', pp. 206–7.
32 Hollister, *Military Organization of Norman England*, pp. 248–51. *ASC*, p. 154. Beeler, *Warfare in England*, p. 46.
33 There is an irony here, since the Domesday survey was inspired by the Danish naval threat.
34 *DB* Lincoln, p. 336b.
35 *ASC*, p. 154. *ASMI*, p. 122. Hollister, *Military Organization of Norman England*, p. 30.
36 Beeler, *Warfare in England*, p. 62. Hollister, *Military Organization of Norman England*, p. 251. Morillo, *Anglo-Norman Kings*, pp. 174–6.
37 Barlow, *Feudal Kingdom of England*, pp. 96–7.
38 *ASC*, p. 169. Barlow, *Feudal Kingdom of England*, p. 156. Hollister, *Military Organization of Norman England*, p. 121. Beeler, *Warfare in England*, p. 65.

39 Contamine, *War in the Middle Ages*, p. 55.
40 As implied by van Houts, 'Ship List of William the Conqueror', p. 172.
41 G. W. S. Barrow, *The Anglo-Norman Era in Scottish History* (Oxford, 1980), p. 139. Robertson, 'Rise of a Scottish Navy', p. 8.
42 Brooks, *English Naval Forces*, p. 162. *CChR*, II, 352.
43 Prestwich, 'War and Finance'.
44 There are numerous references in the Pipe Rolls of Henry II's and Richard I's reigns under 'Hampshire' and 'Southampton'. See also Hardy, *Rotuli Normanniae*, pp. 27, 28, 58, 63.
45 Le Patourel, *Norman Empire*, pp. 163–4.
46 John Le Patourel, 'Le gouvernment de Henri II Plantagenêt et la mer de la Manche', in *Recueil d'Etudes offert au Doyen M. de Bouärd* (*Annales de Normandie* extra No., Caen, 1982), II, 323–33, at pp. 324–6.
47 E.g. *PR 21 Hen.II*, p. 187; *PR 22 Hen.II*, p. 199.
48 *PR 24 Hen.II*, p. 112. Other ships were owned by Ralph Calf the younger and William Calf, no doubt his sons: *PR 23 Hen.II*, p. 177.
49 *PR 30 Hen.II*, p. 58. *PR 31 Hen.II*, p. 216. *PR 33 Hen.II*, pp. 23, 203.
50 *PR 5 Ric.I*, p. 150. *PR 7 Ric.I*, p. 113.
51 *PR 30 Hen.II*, pp. 86–7. *Chancellor's Roll 8 Ric.I*, ed. D. M. Stenton (PRS NS 7, 1930), p. 20.
52 *PR 8 Ric.I*, p. 20.
53 *MF*, I, 300–1.
54 *ASC*, p. 177. Barlow, *Feudal Kingdom of England*, pp. 175–6, 181. Beeler, *Warfare in England*, pp. 72–4.
55 Beeler, *Warfare in England*, pp. 83, 99.
56 Flanagan, *Irish Society, Anglo-Norman Settlers*, p. 67.
57 Barlow, *Feudal Kingdom of England*, p. 287. Beeler, *Warfare in England*, pp. 242–3. *EHD*, II, 325.
58 Beeler, *Warfare in England*, pp. 249–51. *EHD*, II, 333. Flanagan, *Irish Society, Anglo-Norman Settlers*, p. 144.
59 Beeler, *Warfare in England*, p. 262.
60 Paul Latimer, 'Henry II's campaign against the Welsh in 1165', *Welsh History Review* XIV (1988–9), pp. 523–52, at p. 528.
61 Flanagan, 'Anglo-Norman Intervention'. Lydon, 'Lordship and Crown'. Duffy, 'Bruce Brothers', p. 60. Lucas, 'Irish-Norse Relations', p. 68.
62 Seán Duffy, 'The First Ulster Plantation: John de Courcy and the Men of Cumbria', in *Colony and Frontier in Medieval Ireland: Essays presented to J. F. Lydon* ed. T. B. Barry, Robin Frame & Katharine Simms (London, 1995), pp. 1–27 (which reference I owe to the kindness of John G. Gillingham). Flanagan, 'Anglo-Norman Intervention', pp. 72–3. Flanagan, *Irish Society, Anglo-Norman Settlers*, p. 259.
63 John Gillingham, 'The English Invasion of Ireland', in *Representing Ireland: Literature and the Origins of Conflict, 1534–1660*, ed. B. Bradshaw, A. Hadfield & W.Maley (Cambridge, 1993), pp. 24–42; and 'The Beginnings of English Imperialism', *Journal of Historical Sociology* V (1992), pp. 392–409. I am very grateful to Professor Gillingham for drawing my attention to these papers.
64 Barlow, *Feudal Kingdom of England*, p. 166.
65 Graboïs, 'Anglo-Norman England' pp. 136–8. The biography of this remarkable man is Reginald of Durham, *Libellus de vita et miraculis S. Godrici...* ed. Joseph Stevenson (Surtees Society Vol.20, 1847).
66 Lewis, 'Northern European Sea Power', pp. 140–5.
67 Lewis, 'Northern European Sea Power', pp. 145–51.
68 Barlow, *Feudal Kingdom of England*, p. 224.
69 At least 44 ships were purchased for the expedition: *PR 2 Ric.I*, pp. 8–9.
70 Barlow, *Feudal Kingdom of England*, pp. 355–60. Nicolas, *Royal Navy*, I, 106–14.
71 Nicolas, *Royal Navy*, I, 119–24, 424–7. *MF*, I, 145–7. Pryor, *Geography, Technology and War*, pp. 120–1.
72 Barlow, *Feudal Kingdom of England*,

pp. 358–60. Pryor, *Geography, Technology and War*, pp. 127–30.

73 Gillingham, 'Richard I, Galley-Warfare and Portsmouth'.

74 *Oeuvres de Rigord et de Guillaume le Breton*, ed. H. F. Delaborde (Paris, 1882), II, 183, 186, discussed in Gillingham, 'Richard I, Galley-Warfare and Portsmouth'. I am indebted to Professor Gillingham for this reference and much helpful discussion of the question.

75 Gillingham, 'Richard I, Galley-Warfare and Portsmouth'. Sarah Quail, *The Origins of Portsmouth and the First Charter* (Portsmouth, 1994), pp. 14–15.

76 Simek, *Schiffsnamen*, pp. 174–5. Schnepper, *Die Namen der Schiffe*, p. 36.

77 Le Patourel, *Norman Empire*, pp. 166, 177–8.

78 See the Pipe Rolls *passim* from the mid-1160s; the ship was paid a standard rate of £7 10s for fifteen days at 2d a day for the steersman and 1d for the men. *PR 2 Ric.I*, p. 8 credits her with 61 men in 1189, which in a financial context I read as 59 plus the steersman.

79 Lindemann, 'English *Esnecca*', p. 77.

80 *PR 5 Ric.I*, p. 150; *PR 7 Ric.I*, p. 113. It seems plausible to assume that the ship of 1193 was one of the three 'longships' of 1195; in 1194 he is described as crossing the Channel in his 'longship': *Chronica Magistri Rogeri de Houedene*, ed. William Stubbs (London, 1868–71, 4 vols), III, 251.

81 *LQCG*, pp. 275–9. In 1230 a ship called the *Snake* belonged to Seaford: *CPR 1225–32*, p. 414.

82 *Chancellor's Roll 8 Ric.I*, 1196, ed D. M. Stenton (PRS NS 7, 1930), p. 20.

83 *PR 17 Hen.II*, p. 139. *PR 30 Hen.II*, pp. 80, 86–7. *PR 34 Hen.II*, pp. 14, 179.

84 *PR 24 Hen.II*, p. 112.

85 In Latin usually *gubernator*.

86 John Gillingham, *The Angevin Empire* (London, 1984), pp. 43–6; cf. *Magni Rotuli Scaccarii Normanniæ sub Regibus Angliæ*, ed. Thomas Stapleton (London, 1840–4, 2 vols), II, xliv.

87 Loyn, 'Wales and England in the Tenth Century', p. 289. Stafford, *Unification and Conquest*, p. 114.

88 Hill, *Atlas of Anglo-Saxon England*, p. 72.

89 Maund, *Ireland, Wales and England*, p. 168. Loyn, *Vikings in Britain*, pp. 103–4. Holm, 'Slave Trade', pp. 338–42.

90 Campbell, 'Observations on English Government'; and 'Agents and Agencies', p. 218.

4 The Fall of the House of Anjou

1 'Den n'en deuz tremenet ar Raz, Hep n'en defe bet aon pe c'hlaz'; Bernard, *Navires et Gens de Mer*, I, 445. The Raz de Sein is one of the channels into Brest Roads.

2 Bernard, *Navires et Gens de Mer*, I, 427–8.

3 Adapting a remark of Fowler, *Hundred Years War*, p. 5.

4 *MF*, I, 300–1.

5 *PR 10 John*, p. 171. *PR 11 John*, p. 66. Nicolas, *Royal Navy*, I, 142.

6 Nicolas, *Royal Navy*, I, 259–60. *MF*, I, 302–5.

7 *PR 6 John*, pp. 85, 125. *PR 9 John*, pp. 168, 179. *PR 10 John*, pp. 9, 63, 171. *PR 11 John*, pp. 124, 145. *PR 12 John*, p. 163. *PR 16 John*, p.xiv.

8 Gillingham, *Richard the Lionheart*, p. 22.

9 Stacey, *Politics, Policy and Finance*, pp. 161–4.

10 Appendix III. The 'squadrons' were probably administrative rather than operational units.

11 *PR 14 John*, p.xix. Brooks, 'King's Ships and Galleys', p. 26, credits him with 50 galleys.

12 Gillingham, *Richard the Lionheart*, pp. 278–9.

13 *PR 30 Hen.II*, pp. 145–6. *PR 31 Hen.II*, p. 226.

14 Brooks, 'William de Wrotham'. *Idem*, 'Naval Administration', pp. 361–7.

15 See the Pipe Rolls (as printed by PRS) *passim*, especially 9–16 John (1207–14).

16 Powell, 'Navy and the Stannaries', p. 186. *PR 14 John*, p.xix, calculates at least £3,816 spent on ships in 1212. In July 500 marks was sent to pay seamen at Portsmouth: *Documents illustrative of*

English History in the Thirteenth and Fourteenth Centuries, ed. Henry Cole (London, 1844), p. 235.

17 Brooks, 'William de Wrotham'. Powell, 'Navy and the Stannaries'.

18 Clayton, 'Naval Administration', p. 278.

19 *BND* No.29. PRO: C 54/5 m.9, printed *RLC*, I, 117. *PR 11 John*, p. 145. *PR 16 John*, pp. 126, 163.

20 Hutchinson, *Medieval Ships and Shipping*, pp. 110–11. P. Marsden, 'Early Shipping and the Waterfronts of London', in Milne & Hobley, *Waterfront Archaeology*, pp. 14–16. Friel, 'Maritime Technology', p. 7. A large tidal basin was built at Harfleur in 1391–6: *MF*, II, 153.

21 Brooks, 'King's Ships and Galleys', p. 25.

22 Brooks, 'Battle of Damme', p. 265.

23 Nicolas, *Royal Navy*, I, 168–9.

24 *MF*, I, 306–8. Nicolas, *Royal Navy*, I, 168–9. Brooks, 'Battle of Damme'. Mollat, *La vie quotidienne*, p. 161. Mollat, 'L'Etat Capétien', p. 108.

25 Brooks, *English Naval Forces*, pp. 142–6, 209–10; and 'King's Ships and Galleys', pp. 31–3. Murray, *Constitutional History*, pp. 34–5. *MF*, I, 309.

26 Carpenter, *Minority of Henry III*, pp. 1, 113–14.

27 Carpenter, *Minority of Henry III*, pp. 113–14.

28 Brooks, *English Naval Forces*, pp. 146, 213–15. *MF*, I, 311.

29 *BND* No.9.

30 In particular the word 'loof': see *BND* No.9.

31 *EHD*, III, 92. Carpenter, *Minority of Henry III*, p. 43. Nicolas, *Royal Navy*, I, 176–81, 427–30. Brooks, *English Naval Forces*, pp. 217–19.

32 Carpenter, *Minority of Henry III*, pp. 307–11, 344, 370–1. Lydon, 'Ireland's Participation', p. 102. *CPR* 1216–25, pp. 465, 484, 503, 514–15.

33 Brooks, 'King's Ships and Galleys', p. 37.

34 Brooks, 'King's Ships and Galleys', p. 37; and 'Naval Administration', pp. 376–7. Nicolas, *Royal Navy*, I, 187–9. *BND* No.10. Carpenter, *Minority of Henry III*, pp. 374–8. *CPR* 1225–32, pp. 11, 14–15, 34, 36, 41, 49, 53, 130. *RLC*, II, 150, 205.

35 Stacey, *Politics, Policy and Finance*, pp. 169–73. *CLR*, I, 136–7, 140. *CCR* 1227–31, pp. 245, 276. *CPR* 1225–32, p. 259.

36 Brooks, *English Naval Forces*, pp. 155–7. Gruffydd, 'Sea Power and the Anglo-Welsh Wars' pp. 30–1. *CPR* 1232–47, pp. 13, 27–8, 35, 318–19, 322. *CCR* 1231–34, pp. 497, 543–4. For de Burgh's rescue: Marvin L. Colker, 'The "Margam Chronicle" in a Dublin Manuscript', *Haskins Society Journal* IV (1992), pp. 123–48, at pp. 136–8 (which reference I owe to the kindness of Dr Martin Brett).

37 Stacey, *Politics, Policy and Finance*, pp. 184–99. Brooks, *English Naval Forces*, pp. 220–3. Weir, 'English Naval Activities'. Bémont, 'La campagne de Poitou'. *CPR* 1232–47, pp. 310, 337. *CCR*, 1237–42 pp. 456, 499; 1242–47, pp. 1, 8, 13–14, 35, 68–9. *RFR*, I, 246–7. *CLR*, II, 182, 189.

38 Carpenter, *Minority of Henry III*, p. 372; at p. 381 he puts Henry's revenue at £16,500 in 1225.

39 Carpenter, *Minority of Henry III*, p. 376.

40 Stacey, *Politics, Policy and Finance*, pp. 199, 208; his income by then was £27–31,000 p.a.

41 *CPR* 1247–58, pp. 230, 238, 363. *CLR*, IV, 134; V, 26. *CCR* 1251–53, pp. 364, 471; 1253–54, pp. 110, 121, 124, 128. Prestwich, *Edward I*, p. 10.

42 Lydon, 'Ireland's Participation', pp. 137, 147. Prestwich, *Edward I*, pp. 18–19. *CCR* 1242–47, p. 318. Gruffydd, 'Sea Power and the Anglo-Welsh Wars', p. 35.

43 Brooks, *English Naval Forces*, pp. 223–5. *EHD*, III, 181. Rodger, 'Cinque Ports', p. 650. *CCR* 1261–64, pp. 356, 384; 1264–68, p. 80. *CPR* 1258–66, pp. 345, 349, 351, 547, 551, 652–5. Murray, *Constitutional History*, pp. 39–40.

44 Allmand, *Hundred Years War*, pp. 82–3. Mollat, 'L'Etat Capétien', p. 110.

5 Ships of War

1 Burwash, *English Merchant Shipping*, p. 102, identifies 43 types mentioned in late 15th-century documents alone.

2 Unger, *Ship in the Mediaeval Economy*, pp. 37–52. Pryor, 'Mediterranean Round Ship', pp. 59–66. Hutchinson, *Medieval Ships and Shipping*, p. 36. Steffy, *Wooden Ship Building*, pp. 77–91.

3 Pryor, 'Mediterranean Round Ship', pp. 67–8, 71. Friel, 'Carrack', p. 78. Phillips, 'Caravel and Galleon', p. 93. Morrison, *Age of the Galley*, pp. 152–4, 204.

4 Hutchinson, *Medieval Ships and Shipping*, pp. 5–10. Steffy, *Wooden Ship Building*, pp. 100–13.

5 Friel, 'Maritime technology', p. 106. Hutchinson, *Medieval Ships and Shipping*, pp. 50–5. Plate 4 depicts the 1200 seal of Ipswich, the first to show clearly a ship with a stern rudder.

6 Crumlin-Pedersen,'Viking Shipbuilding and Seamanship', p. 280. Brøgger & Shetelig, *Viking Ships*, pp. 192–207. Morcken, *Langskip, knarr og kogge*, pp. 28, 40, 42.

7 Friel, 'Maritime technology', pp. 62–74. *MEST*, I, 85. Bill, 'Ship Construction', pp. 152–4.

8 McGrail, *Ancient Boats*, p. 200. Crumlin-Pedersen, 'Vikings and the Hanseatic merchants', pp. 190–1. Ellmers, *Frühmittelalterliche Handelsschifffahrt*, pp. 63–75, 150–69. Ellmers, 'Cog as Cargo Carrier'. Hutchinson, *Medieval Ships and Shipping*, pp. 15–20. Steffy, *Wooden Ship Building*, pp. 114–24. *MGN*, I, 115–21.

9 Unger, *Ship in the Mediaeval Economy*, pp. 138–47. Friel, 'Maritime technology', p. 110. Richon, 'Le navire de la cathédrale de Bayonne'. *MEST*, I, 185. Ellmers, 'Cog as Cargo Carrier', p. 43. Bernard, *Navires et Gens de Mer*, I, 281. Hutchinson, *Medieval Ships and Shipping*, p. 153. Ewe, *Schiffe aus Siegeln*, has many illustrations of castles.

10 Crumlin-Pedersen, 'Vikings and the Hanseatic merchants', pp. 186–7. Ellmers, *Frühmittelalterliche Handelsschifffahrt*, pp. 59–63. Hutchinson, *Medieval Ships and Shipping*, pp. 10–15. *MGN*, I, 121–7.

11 Christensen, 'Medieval ship model'. Ellmers, 'Cog as Cargo Carrier', pp. 45–6. Hutchinson, *Medieval Ships and Shipping*, p. 27.

12 Tinniswood, 'English Galleys', pp. 301–3. Ellmers, 'Cog as Cargo Carrier', p. 38. Roberts, 'Descendants of Viking Boats', pp. 20–1 interprets the sails as squarer.

13 Friel, 'Maritime technology', pp. 153–4; and *The Good Ship*, pp. 87–8.

14 Friel, 'Maritime technology', p. 154.

15 PRO: E 404/75/3 No.3.

16 Friel, 'Carrack', p. 83.

17 Friel, 'Maritime technology', pp. 327–8. Roberts, 'Descendants of Viking Boats', p. 21. Ellmers, 'Cog as Cargo Carrier', p. 41. Hutchinson, *Medieval Ships and Shipping*, pp. 47–8. Howard, *Ships of War*, pp. 24–5.

18 E.g. *PR 34 Hen.II*, p. 197.

19 Friel, 'Maritime technology', pp. 170–3; and 'Winds of Change', p. 184. *MEST*, II, 24–7, 53–62; III, 12–15.

20 *MEST*, III, 30–5, 70–8. Roberts, 'Descendants of Viking Boats', pp. 21–2.

21 Pryor, *Geography, Technology and War*, pp. 71–2. Lane, *Venetian Ships and Shipbuilders*, p. 13. Hoheisel, 'Hanse Cog of 1380'. Baykowski, 'Kieler Hanse-Cog'.

22 Roberts, 'Descendants of Viking Boats', p. 15.

23 Hutchinson, *Medieval Ships and Shipping*, pp. 61–4.

24 The replica cog, however, as tried in ballast, is handy under sail, stays easily and points high, but is so leewardly that she is effectively incapable of winning ground to windward: Baykowski, 'Kieler Hanse-Cog'; Hoheisel, 'Hanse Cog of 1380'. Deep-laden, one would expect her to be less leewardly but more unhandy; bigger ships would undoubtedly be clumsier in any circumstances.

25 E.g. *CIM*, IV, 88 (1378); *EHD*, IV, 1217 (*c*.1450).

26 Russell, *English Intervention*, pp. 229–31. Villain-Gandossi, *Le Navire Médiéval*, p. 28. Mott, 'Ships of the 13th-century

Catalan Navy'. Pryor, *Geography, Technology and War*, pp. 59–66. Fourquin, 'Galères du Moyen-Age'. Dotson, 'Galley Design'. Foerster Laures, 'Warships of the Kings of Aragón'. Morrison, *Age of the Galley*, pp. 101–16. Guilmartin, *Gunpowder and Galleys*, p. 72. Rodgers, *Naval Warfare*, p. 232.

27 E.g. Nicolas, *Royal Navy*, I, 424–9 (Geoffrey de Vinsauf and Matthew Paris). It does not help that the Latin *rostrum*, 'ram', can also be used of a spur, and the French *éperon* is completely ambiguous.

28 Runyan, 'Ships and Fleets', and 'Cog as Warship', p. 56. Kuhn, *Altnordische Seekriegswesen*, p. 45. Morillo, *Warfare under the Anglo-Norman Kings*, p. 176.

29 Probably from the Byzantine Greek γαλεος, a swordfish: Fourquin, 'Galères du Moyen-Age', p. 67. Simek, *Schiffsnamen*, p. 109. Matthew Bennett, 'Norman Naval Activity in the Mediterranean c.1060–c.1108', *ANS* XV (1992), pp. 41–58, at p. 49, offers another etymology.

30 Guilmartin, *Gunpowder and Galleys*, pp. 68–71. Rodgers, *Naval Warfare*, pp. 231–2.

31 Morrison, *Age of the Galley*, pp. 127–8, 201–4. Guilmartin, *Gunpowder and Galleys*, pp. 62–3, 68–71. Olesa Muñido, *La galera*, I, 207–9.

32 Russell, *English Intervention*, p. 233. Coates, 'Power and Speed of Oared Ships'. Morrison, *Age of the Galley*, p. 213.

33 Lane, *Venetian Ships and Shipbuilders*, p. 16.

34 Pryor, *Geography, Technology and War*, pp. 71–85. Morrison, *Age of the Galley*, pp. 130, 194, 208, 210, 218–22; at pp. 218–20 John E. Dotson implies the effective radius of Venetian galleys was about 100 miles.

35 Morrison, *Age of the Galley*, pp. 208–10.

36 Verbruggen, *Het Leger en de Vloot*, pp. 140–1. Friel, 'Winds of Change', p. 191.

37 Martínez Valverde, 'La note marinera', pp. 35–7. *BND* No.17.

38 Nicolas, *Royal Navy*, I, 285. Russell, *English Intervention*, pp. 232–5. Allmand, *Hundred Years War*, p. 89.

39 Pryor, *Geography, Technology and War*, pp. 69–72. Morrison, *Age of the Galley*, p. 204.

40 Unger, *Ship in the Mediaeval Economy*, p. 176. Lewis, 'Northern European seapower'. Lane, *Venetian Ships and Shipbuilders*, pp. 13–26. Dotson, 'Galley Design'. Morrison, *Age of the Galley*, pp. 117–18, 123–6, 213. Hutchinson, *Medieval Ships and Shipping*, p. 84. Villain-Gandossi, *Le Navire Médiéval*, Pl.87–8 shows great galleys under sail.

41 Morrison, *Age of the Galley*, p. 124.

42 Lewis, 'Northern European seapower', p. 158.

43 Lane, *Venetian Ships and Shipbuilders*, pp. 13–14. Alban, 'National Defence', p. 277.

44 Lewis, 'Northern European seapower', p. 139.

45 Friel, 'Maritime Technology', pp. 125, 353–4.

46 Paviot, *La politique navale*, pp. 294–300. De Vries, 'Shipboard Artillery'. Bernard, *Navires et Gens de Mer*, I, 242–5; but the Basque shipwrights built clinker-fashion; Friel, 'Winds of Change', p. 183.

47 *RLP*, p. 15 (of 1202) is apparently the first reference to an English (or in this case possibly Norman) 'galley'; I owe it to John G. Gillingham.

48 Anderson, *Oared Fighting Ships*, pp. 43–4, 49. Tinniswood, 'English Galleys'.

49 PRO: E 372/78 rot.16d. Tinniswood, 'English Galleys', pp. 286–7. *MEST*, I, 51. Crumlin-Pedersen, 'Vikings and the Hanseatic Merchants', p. 188.

50 Gelsinger, 'Some Unusual Ships', pp. 177–8.

51 Whitwell & Johnson, 'Newcastle Galley', p. 147. Tinniswood, 'English Galleys', pp. 293–6. Hutchinson, *Medieval Ships and Shipping*, pp. 151–2, reconstructs a plausible scheme; Friel, *The Good Ship*, pp. 112–13, has an apparently impossible one.

52 Both the London and Southampton galleys of 1295 were built by a Bayonnais

shipwright: Johnson, 'London Shipbuilding', p. 425; Platt, *Medieval Southampton*, p. 61. Richmond, 'War at Sea', p. 102, suggests that they were adopted as a response to the Castilian galleys, but balingers appeared in English waters long before the Castilians.

53 Friel, 'Maritime technology', p. 106. Bernard, *Navires et Gens de Mer*, I, 247–52. Paviot, *La politique navale*, pp. 284–5.

54 Tinniswood, 'English Galleys', p. 299.

55 Paviot, *La politique navale*, pp. 285–6.

56 60% of known English pirates were barges or balingers: Meehan, 'English Piracy', p. 87.

57 Unger, *Ship in the Mediaeval Economy*, pp. 172, 204. Tinniswood, 'English Galleys', p. 279. Burwash, *English Merchant Shipping*, pp. 103–8. Sherborne, 'English Barges and Ballingers'. Friel, 'Archaeological sources', p. 55; and *The Good Ship*, pp. 113–14.

58 PRO: E 101/3/26 m.2.

59 *LQCG*, pp. 272–9. Tinniswood, 'English Galleys', p. 279.

60 Steer & Bannerman, *Monumental Sculpture*, pp. 97–8, 180–3. MacInnes, 'West Highland Sea-Power'. A. W. Farrell, 'The Use of Iconographic Material in Medieval Ship Archaeology', in McGrail, *Medieval Ships and Harbours*, pp. 227–46, at p. 231. O'Neill, *Merchants and Mariners*, p. 127. Many Highland galleys are reproduced from grave-slabs in Lord Archibald Campbell, *Argyllshire Galleys* (London, 1906).

61 Appendix II, assuming all those ordered were built.

62 Prestwich, *War, Politics and Finance*, p. 138. Friel, 'Lyme Galley'. Whitwell & Johnson, 'Newcastle Galley'. Johnson, 'London Shipbuilding'. Tinniswood, 'English Galleys', p. 277. PRO: E 101/5/8. Platt, *Medieval Southampton*, pp. 61–2. Anderson, 'English Galleys in 1295'.

63 Appendix II.

64 Appendix II.

65 Sherborne, 'Hundred Years' War', p. 169. Alban, 'National Defence', pp. 279–80. Friel, 'Maritime Technology', pp. 81–3. Moore, 'Barge of Edward III'. *RFR*, III, ii, 998–9; IV, 28. *CCR* 1377–81, pp. 32–3, 43–4, 46–7, 51–2, 55, 57, 114, 120, 181–2.

66 *BND* No.32. PRO: E 101/42/39 & 43/6. Friel, 'Maritime Technology', p. 6. *RP*, III, 458. *CCR* 1399–1402, pp. 238–40. *RFO*, VIII, 172.

67 Friel, 'Maritime technology', p. 350; 'Carrack', *passim*; and *The Good Ship*, pp. 158–60. Bellabarba, 'Square-rigged Ship'. Hutchinson, *Medieval Ships and Shipping*, pp. 41–3, 85. Howard, *Ships of War*, pp. 16–27.

68 Friel, 'Maritime technology', p. 352; and 'Carrack', p. 80.

69 Appendix III. The only exception was the *Cog Edward* built at Southampton by Edward III in 1335: Prince, 'Army and Navy', p. 378.

70 Listed by Rose, *Navy of the Lancastrian Kings*, pp. 250–3.

71 Rose, *Navy of the Lancastrian Kings*, pp. 34, 247.

72 Turner, 'Southampton' p. 40. Rose, *Navy of the Lancastrian Kings*, p. 247. Friel, 'Maritime technology', pp. 30–3.

73 Turner, 'The *Holy Ghost of the Tower*'. Turner, 'Southampton', p. 42. Rose, *Navy of the Lancastrian Kings*, p. 247.

74 Turner, 'The *Gracedieu*'. Turner, 'Southampton', pp. 43–4. Rose, *Navy of the Lancastrian Kings*, p. 37. PRO: E 364/61 rot.E. Friel, 'Henry V's *Grace Dieu*'.

75 Prynne, 'Henry V's *Grace Dieu*'.

76 Laughton, 'Great Ship of 1419'. Ellis, *Original Letters*, II, i, 69–70 (also *EHD*, IV, 222–3).

77 Rose, 'Henry V's *Grace Dieu*'; and *Navy of the Lancastrian Kings*, pp. 50–1.

78 Clarke, 'R. Hamble wreck'. Hutchinson, *Medieval Ships and Shipping*, pp. 30–1; and 'Henry V's Warship Grace Dieu', in Bound, *Archaeology of Ships of War*, I, 22–5.

79 Morrison, *Age of the Galley*, pp. 115, 132, 223.

80 Bernard, *Navires et Gens de Mer*, I, 252.

81 Colvin, *King's Works*, II, 988 n.7.

82 *CPR* 1232–47, pp. 27–8. *CCR* 1231–34, p. 206.

83 *CLR*, I, 279.

84 *CLR*, II, 201. *BND* No.31. *CCR* 1242–47, p. 176.

85 *CLR*, I, 481; IV, 48–9; V, 25; but in these cases the Latin *cooperire* is ambiguous, and might mean that the galleys were housed-over or covered in some less substantial fashion than a permanent house.

86 *CLR*, IV, 466. *CCR* 1259–61, p. 60.

87 Friel, 'Maritime technology', p. 37.

88 Built in 1256: *CLR*, IV, 332.

89 Tout, *Administrative History*, IV, 445–70.

90 Prince, 'Army and Navy', p. 377. Rose, *Navy of the Lancastrian Kings*, p. 31. Tout, *Administrative History*, IV, 294, is mistaken in thinking that there was a naval establishment at Rotherhithe: see PRO: E 372/210 rot.53; E 101/391/20 m.1; Colvin, *King's Works*, II, 993.

91 Rose, *Navy of the Lancastrian Kings*, p. 39. Richmond, 'War at Sea', p. 113. Turner, 'Building of the *Gracedieu*', p. 61.

92 Turner, 'Southampton', pp. 43ff. Rose, *Navy of the Lancastrian Kings*, pp. 52–5. Friel, 'Maritime technology', p. 35.

93 The English word is always used, even in French and Latin documents.

94 Friel, 'Maritime technology', pp. 32–7, 360–1; and *The Good Ship*, pp. 53–5. José P. Merino, 'Graving Docks in France and Spain before 1800', *MM* LXXI (1985), pp. 35–58, at p. 35. Mud docks of this sort were used into the twentieth century by British gunboats wintering on the North China rivers.

95 Tanner, 'Henry VII's Expedition', p. 16. Colvin, *King's Works*, IV, 491.

96 Friel, 'Maritime technology', pp. 39–40. Goldingham, 'Navy under Henry VII', pp. 480–1. Harrison, 'Maritime Activity under Henry VII', pp. 108, 120–1. *ARN*, pp. 39–40. Oppenheim, *Accounts & Inventories*, pp. 143–61, prints Brigandine's accounts for rebuilding the dock.

97 Friel, 'Maritime technology', pp. 335–40; 'Henry V's *Grace Dieu*', p. 6; and *The Good Ship*, pp. 128–9. Hutchinson, *Medieval Ships and Shipping*, p. 49. Howard, *Ships of War*, p. 25.

98 Turner, 'Southampton', p. 46. Richmond, 'Royal Administration', p. 61.

99 Friel, 'Three-masted Ship'. Hutchinson, *Medieval Ships and Shipping*, pp. 43–4. Howard, *Ships of War*, pp. 28–31. Unger, *Ship in the Medieval Economy*, pp. 216–21.

100 Friel, 'Maritime technology', pp. 146–50, 382–3; 'Carracks', p. 80; 'Winds of Change', p. 192; and *The Good Ship*, pp. 158–60. *MEST*, II, 73–8. Roberts, 'Descendants of Viking Boats', p. 24. Hutchinson, *Medieval Ships and Shipping*, p. 61.

101 Hutchinson, *Medieval Ships and Shipping*, pp. 61–4. Howard, *Ships of War*, pp. 28–30.

102 Ratlines are mentioned from the mid-14th century: Friel, 'Maritime technology', p. 241; but see also *MEST*, III, 80–4. A carving of an English cog dated to the early 14th century shows boys working on the yard without footropes: Richon, 'Le navire de la cathédrale de Bayonne', p. 38; cf. Roberts, 'Descendants of Viking Boats', p. 22. Brails (i.e. bunt-lines) are mentioned as early as the 12th century, but it is not clear how the sail was brailed up: *MEST*, II, 28–9.

103 Friel, 'Carrack', p. 81. Hutchinson, *Medieval Ships and Shipping*, p. 64. Unger, *Ship in the Medieval Economy*, pp. 227–8.

104 Friel, 'Maritime technology', pp. 146–50.

105 Edwards, 'Fifteenth-Century Iberian Vessels'. Phillips, 'Caravel and Galleon'. Elbl, 'Portuguese Caravel'. Pedro Castiñeiras Muñoz, 'La época de los descubrimientos geograficos', in Manera Regueyra, *El buque*, pp. 63–86, at pp. 76–84. Unger, *Ship in the Mediaeval Economy*, pp. 212–14. Roger C. Smith, *Vanguard of Empire: Ships of Exploration in the Age of Columbus* (Oxford, 1993), pp. 31–46. *MGN*, I, 127–34.

106 Phillips, 'Caravel and Galleon'. Henri Touchard, *Le commerce maritime breton à la fin du Moyen Age* (Paris, 1967),

pp. 316–19. Mollat, *La vie quotidienne*, pp. 141–2. Friel, 'Maritime technology', pp. 368–72. Rieth, 'La construction navale à franc-bord'. Bernard, *Navires et Gens de Mer*, I, 359–61. Unger, *Ship in the Medieval Economy*, pp. 222–5, 231.

107 Phillips, 'Caravel and Galleon', p. 96. Hutchinson, *Medieval Ships and Shipping*, pp. 44–6.

108 PRO: E 404/71/4 No.38 (Genoese carracks in English service, 1460). Horrox & Hammond, *Harleian Manuscript 433*, I, 255; II, 190–1 (purchase of Genoese carrack, 1485).

6 The Northern Wars

1 *EHD*, III, 306–7.

2 Davies, 'In Praise of British History', pp. 16–17. MacInnes, 'West Highland Sea-Power', p. 230. Frame, 'Political Configuration'.

3 Duffy, 'Bruce Brothers', p. 79. Gruffydd, 'Sea Power and the Anglo-Welsh Wars', p. 35, quoting Matthew Paris on the Welsh galleys.

4 Brøgger & Shetelig, *Viking Ships*, pp. 192–207; at p. 192 they list 8 Norwegian ships of 30 rooms or more built between 1206 and 1263. Morcken, *Langskip, knarre og kogge*, pp. 36–7, 40.

5 Gelsinger, 'Some Unusual Ships', p. 176.

6 Lydon, 'Lordship and Crown', p. 59. Duffy, 'Bruce Brothers', p. 69. Grant, 'Scotland's "Celtic Fringe"', p. 123.

7 Holm, 'Slave Trade', p. 342.

8 Barrow, *Kingdom of the Scots*, p. 383.

9 Eames, 'Sea Power and Welsh History', pp. 28–9.

10 Prestwich, *War, Politics and Finance*, p. 137; and *Edward I*, pp. 177–82. Morris, *Welsh Wars*, pp. 106–8.

11 Prestwich, *War, Politics and Finance*, p. 137; and *Edward I*, pp. 189–200. Morris, *Welsh Wars*, pp. 173–80. Powicke, *Thirteenth Century*, pp. 422–7. Vale, *Angevin Legacy*, p. 19. PRO: E 101/3/26.

12 They are described by A. J. Taylor in Colvin, *King's Works*, I, 293–408.

13 Matthew Strickland, 'Securing the North: Invasion and the Strategy of Defence in Twelfth-Century Anglo-Scottish Warfare', *ANS* XII (1989), pp. 177–98

14 Prestwich, *Edward I*, p. 231. Llanbadarn (Aberystwyth) had some value as the western end of a route through the Welsh mountains, but the route was seldom practicable against serious opposition.

15 Morris, *Welsh Wars*, p. 108.

16 Fryde, *Book of Prests*, pp.xxxiv–xxxv. Morris, *Welsh Wars*, pp. 259–60. Gruffydd, 'Sea Power and the Anglo-Welsh Wars', p. 46. Lydon, 'Ireland's Participation', pp. 173–7.

17 Prestwich, *Edward I*, p. 220.

18 Fryde, *Book of Prests*, pp.xxxix–xl.

19 Prestwich, *Edward I*, pp. 220–2. Fryde, *Book of Prests*, pp.xxviii–xl, l–lii. Morris, *Welsh Wars*, pp. 259–60. Gruffydd, 'Sea Power and the Anglo-Welsh Wars', p. 46. Lydon, 'Ireland's Participation', pp. 173–7.

20 Richmond, 'English Naval Power', p. 2.

21 Prestwich, *Edward I*, p. 231.

22 PRO: C 47/29/3 No.7, printed (very inaccurately) in *Lettres des Rois, Reines et autres personnages des Cours de France et de l'Angleterre ... 1162–1515*, ed. A. Champollion-Figéac (Paris, 1839–47, 2 vols), I, 396–7; also (wrongly dated) in Marsden, *Law and Custom*, I, 50–6, and partly translated in *BND* No.11. Vale, *Angevin Legacy*, pp. 183–4.

23 'Du temps qil ny ad memoire du contraire, averoient este en paisible possession de la sovereigne seigneuries de la meer Dengeleterre et des isles esteans en ycele': Chaplais, *Diplomatic Practice*, I, 206. Nicolas, *Royal Navy*, I, 308–14, and Fulton, *Sovereignty*, pp. 43–51, 741–4 discuss this text, a favourite of Selden and other seventeenth-century English writers on the sovereignty of the sea.

24 Chaplais, 'Règlement des conflits'. Krieger, *Rôles d'Oléron*, pp. 43–7.

25 'En aperte oppression et apoverissement et peril de desheritance ... mesmement pur ce qils sont enclos de la grant mer

en la marche de toutes nacions': Chaplais, *Diplomatic Practice*, I, 207.

26 'Une reale frountier et forte ville de guerre': Saul, 'Great Yarmouth', p. 106 n.15.

27 Marsden, *Select Pleas*, I, xv–xix.

28 But Runyan, 'Naval Logistics', p. 81, is mistaken in referring to a 1322 letter from the French king [*RFO*, II, 475] as acknowledging English sovereignty; in fact it makes no mention of it.

29 'Il est seigneur de la mer et la dite roberie fut fait sur la mer dans son poer'; Marsden, *Select Pleas*, I, xxii. The scene of the crime was actually the Breton port of Crozon.

30 Fulton, *Sovereignty*, pp. 54–6. Nicolas, *Royal Navy*, I, 387–9.

31 Carpenter, *Minority of Henry III*, p. 378. A few Gascon vineyards still make 'clairette', but most Bordeaux wine today is matured in the heavier style needed to survive a voyage to England.

32 Sumption, *Hundred Years War*, pp. 69–70. Lewis & Runyan, *Naval and Maritime History*, p. 135.

33 Fowler, *Hundred Years War*, p. 4.

34 Sumption, *Hundred Years War*, p. 72.

35 Vale, *English Gascony*, p. 14. Fowler, *Hundred Years War*, p. 4. There are numerous licences to export foodstuffs to Gascony in the English records, e.g.: *CPR* 1345–48, pp. 281–3 [1347]; PRO: C 61/64 mm.7–9 [1352].

36 Fowler, *Hundred Years War*, pp. 4, 13.

37 Vale, *Angevin Legacy*, pp. 149–50, 194; and 'Edward I and the French', p. 170. Bernard, *Navires et Gens de Mer*, II, 491.

38 Prestwich, *Edward I*, pp. 377–9. Vale, 'Edward I and the French', p. 170. La Roncière, 'Le Blocus Continentale', pp. 402–7. Nicolas, *Royal Navy*, I, 267–70. *CPR* 1292–1301, p. 16. *CCR* 1288–96, p. 284.

39 Sumption, *Hundred Years War*, pp. 81–2.

40 Prestwich, *War, Politics and Finance*, p. 173. Sumption, *Hundred Years War*, p. 35. Lyon, *Wardrobe Book*, pp.vi–vii.

41 A remarkable performance; the modern expert M. H. Hayes (*Horses aboard Ship: A Guide to their Management* [London, 1902], pp. 208–11) reckoned cavalry horses needed three months' rest to recover from a one-month voyage.

42 Prestwich, *Edward I*, pp. 381–6. Nicolas, *Royal Navy*, I, 272.

43 Vale, *Angevin Legacy*, pp. 204–9.

44 Vale, *Angevin Legacy*, pp. 209–10.

45 Merlin-Chazelas, *Clos des Gallées*, I, 27.

46 Those who believe the Clos had a basin include *MF*, I, 404–7, Mollat, 'L'Etat Capétien', pp. 116–17, and Richmond, 'War at Sea', pp. 104–5. Merlin-Chazelas, *Clos des Gallées*, I, 29–32, is more cautious.

47 Prestwich, *Edward I*, p. 383. Fryde, *Book of Prests*, p.xlvii. Freeman, 'Moat Defensive', pp. 445–6. *MF*, I, 333–47.

48 Powicke, *Thirteenth Century*, p. 613. Freeman, 'Moat Defensive', p. 442. La Roncière, 'Le Blocus Continentale', p. 423. Mollat, 'L'Etat Capétien', p. 115.

49 Anderson, 'English Galleys in 1295'.

50 Prestwich, *War, Politics and Finance*, p. 143; and *Crisis of 1297–98*, p. 32, and No.134. PRO: E 163/2/8 lists the casualties.

51 Prestwich, *Edward I*, p. 400.

52 Prestwich, *War, Politics and Finance*, p. 175. Fryde, *Book of Prests*, pp.l–lii.

53 Prestwich, *War, Politics and Finance*, p. 141.

54 Prestwich, *Edward I*, pp. 401–2.

55 Prestwich, *Edward I*, pp. 387–400; and *War, Politics and Finance*, p. 142.

56 Verbruggen, *Het Leger en de Vloot*, pp. 141–5. Nicolas, *Royal Navy*, I, 373–80. *MF*, I, 364–74. Mollat, 'L'Etat Capétien', p. 120.

57 *CCR* 1302–07, p. 205. Mollat, 'L'Etat Capétien', p. 120. PRO: E 101/10/21 m.8 (a writ ordering ships to assist the French invasion of Flanders).

58 Prestwich, *Edward I*, pp. 415–35, 470–6. *EHD*, III, 209.

59 Prestwich, *Edward I*, pp. 476–82.

60 *EHD*, III, 278. *CPR* 1292–1301, pp. 249, 372. Some medieval English maps show open water from Forth to Clyde.

61 Prestwich, *Edward I*, pp. 484–7. *CCR* 1296–1302, pp. 348, 401–2.

62 *CPR* 1297–1301, p. 588, empowering the

Barons of the Cinque Ports to appoint their own admiral, subject to the approval of various named Highland chiefs. On the MacRuaris see Barrow, *Kingdom of the Scots*, p. 382.

63 Prestwich, *Edward I*, pp. 483–7. *LQCG*, pp. 271–9. *CCR* 1296–1302, pp. 307, 348, 401–2, 486–7. *CPR* 1292–1301, pp. 455, 583–584, 588, 596. O'Neill, *Merchants and Mariners*, p. 113. Appendix III lists the ships summoned in 1301.

64 *BND* No.24. PRO: E 101/11/4. *The Making of King's Lynn, A Documentary Survey*, ed. Dorothy M. Owen (London, 1984), Nos.483, 484.

65 Prestwich, *Edward I*, pp. 498–502; and *War, Politics and Finance*, p. 146. O'Neill, *Merchants and Mariners*, p. 113. Lydon, 'Edward I, Ireland and the War in Scotland'. Reid, 'Sea-Power in the Anglo-Scottish War', pp. 7–12.

66 *CPR* 1301–07, pp. 75–6, 121, 128, 131, 203. *CCR* 1296–1302, p. 612; 1302–07, pp. 76, 120–1.

67 Reid, 'Sea-Power in the Anglo-Scottish War', p. 13. Duffy, 'Bruce Brothers', pp. 72–75. O'Neill, *Merchants and Mariners*, p. 120. Grant, 'Scotland's' "Celtic Fringe"', p. 123.

68 Prestwich, *Edward I*, p. 507. Duffy, 'Bruce Brothers', pp. 64–6. Lydon, 'Ireland's Participation', p. 274. *CCR* 1302–07, p. 482.

69 I follow McKisack, *Fourteenth Century*, for the general narrative.

70 Reid, 'Sea-Power in the Anglo-Scottish War', p. 17 n.2.

71 McKisack, *Fourteenth Century*, pp. 33–4. Reid, 'Sea-Power and the Anglo-Scottish War', pp. 18–21. *CPR* 1313–17, pp. 8–9, 447, 509; 1317–21, p. 141. *RS*, I, 129. *RFR*, II, 265. *CCW*, pp. 414, 424, 427, 432.

72 Duffy, 'Bruce Brothers', pp. 55–9, 71–7. Duncan, 'Scots' Invasion of Ireland'. O'Neill, *Merchants and Mariners*, pp. 119–20. Gruffydd, 'Sea Power and the Anglo-Welsh Wars', p. 43. Nicholson, *Edward III and the Scots*, pp. 43, 53–4. *RS*, I, 107, 116–17, 125, 144, 174. *RFR*, II, 246, 313. *CCR* 1313–18, pp. 183, 333. *TR*, I, 540–2. *CCW*, pp. 424, 584. *CPR* 1313–17, pp. 574–5, 603, 632, 696; 1317–21, pp. 164–5, 195, 313.

73 McKisack, *Fourteenth Century*, pp. 45–75. *CPR* 1321–24, p. 12. *CCR* 1318–23, pp. 462–3.

74 McKisack, *Fourteenth Century*, pp. 79–83. *CCR* 1323–27, pp. 412–13, 420–2, 467–8, 471–2, 484, 564, 566, 608–13, 641–7. *CPR* 1324–27, pp. 208–12, 278–9, 315–16.

75 Nicholson, *Edward III and the Scots*, pp. 76–145. *EHD*, IV, 54–9.

76 Nicholson, *Edward III and the Scots*, pp. 164–222.

77 *MF*, I, 393. Sumption, *Hundred Years War*, p. 158.

78 Alban, 'National defence', pp. 3–5. Nicolas, *Royal Navy*, II, 8. PRO: C 71/15–16 *passim*. *CCR* 1333–37, pp. 431, 439, 544, 572–3. *RS*, I, 363, 366, 368, 402. *RFR*, II, ii, 915, 919.

79 Nicolas, *Royal Navy*, II, 41. *BND* No.13.

7 Edward III at Sea

1 *MF*, I, 383–4.

2 Hewitt, *Black Prince's Expedition*, p. 13. Cf. Richmond, 'English Naval Power', p. 4: 'In the naval warfare of that century there was never much at stake' – a statement contradicted by everything he has written.

3 '[La] guerre sans feu ne valoit rien, non plus que andouilles sans moustarde': Gillingham, 'Richard I and the Science of War', p. 85, quoting the chronicler Jean Juvenal des Ursins. Prestwich, *Three Edwards*, p. 199.

4 PRO: C 71/15 m.24; C 71/16 m.33, two of many orders to set up beacons to warn of Scots ships (1335–6). Alban, 'National Defence', pp. 190–202. More beacons were erected in the 1370s and 1440s: *CCR* 1377–81, p. 77; *CPR* 1446–52, pp. 316–17.

5 Hewitt, *Organization of War*, pp. 7–15. Sumption, *Hundred Years War*, p. 227. Freeman, 'Moat Defensive', describes its predecessors.

6 *CCR* 1237–42, pp. 467, 40; 1261–64, p. 401. *CPR* 1292–1301, p. 291; 1324–27,

p. 162. Alban, 'National Defence', p. 273.

7 Alban, 'National Defence', pp. 259–60. Nicolas, *Royal Navy*, II, 39.

8 Prestwich, *Three Edwards*, p. 271. Hewitt, 'Organisation of War', p. 78. Runyan, 'Organization of Royal Fleets', pp. 46–8.

9 Lyon, *Wardrobe Book*, p.lii.

10 Pryor, *Geography, Technology and War*, p. 127.

11 Verbruggen, *Art of Warfare*, pp. 257, 261, paraphrasing Adam's *De modo Sarracenis extirpandi*. Scammell, *World Encompassed*, pp. 163, 174.

12 Barnie, *War in Mediaeval Society*, p. 93, quoting Grey's *Scalachronica*.

13 Terrier de Loray, *Jean de Vienne*, pp. 82–3.

14 Sumption, *Hundred Years War*, p. 228.

15 Russell, *English Intervention*, pp. 229–30. At various times in the fourteenth century Benedetto Zaccaria, Ambrogio and Egidio Boccanegra were Admirals of Castile, Carlo Grimaldi Admiral of France, Manuel Pessagno and his son Lanzarotto Admirals of Portugal, and Niccolò Usodimare Vice-Admiral of Gascony.

16 Russell, *English Intervention*, p. 229. Pérez Embid, 'La Marina Real Castellana'.

17 Vale, 'Edward I and the French', p. 172. Pryor, 'Roger of Lauria', p. 200.

18 La Roncière, 'Le Blocus Continentale', p. 422.

19 Russell, *English Intervention*, pp. 5–6.

20 Pérez Embid, 'La Marina Real Castellana'.

21 Alban, 'National Defence', p. 277. *RFO*, VII, 520. *CSL*, 514. Sumption, *Hundred Years War*, p. 381. *MF*, II, 51. Richmond, 'War at Sea', p. 103. Suárez Fernández, *Navigación y Comercio*, pp. 19–20; and 'House of Trastámara', pp. 58–65.

22 Sumption, *Hundred Years War*, pp. 156–67. *MF*, I, 393, 411–12. Richmond, 'War at Sea', p. 96. Nicolas, *Royal Navy*, II, 20.

23 Oppenheim, *VCH Sussex*, II, 138.

24 Sumption, *Hundred Years War*, pp. 226–49. Richmond, 'The War at Sea', p. 96. *MF*, I, 413–19. Alban, 'National Defence', pp. 1, 10. Nicolas, *Royal Navy*, II, 27. *TR*, II, 490. Platt, *Medieval Southampton*, pp. 109–11. Hughes, 'Fourteenth-Century French Raids', pp. 124–5.

25 'De portu ad portum et loco ad locum per costeram terre maritime dicti regni, ubi naves existunt et poterunt inveniri, divertere se proponunt ad navigium ejusdem regni accendendum, capiendum et destruendum et subsequenter portus et alias villas supra mare et maris brachia situatas aggrediendos, invadendos, depredandos et comburendos, aliaqua mala irreperabilia pro viribus perpetranda': *TR*, II, 617.

26 Sumption, *Hundred Years War*, pp. 260–3, 273–6. Alban, 'National Defence', pp. 7–14. *MF*, I, 428–30.

27 Sumption, *Hundred Years War*, pp. 264–6, 320–1. *MF*, I, 432–6 (at I, 432 he dates the Boulogne raid to August 1339).

28 Sumption, *Hundred Years War*, pp. 321–4.

29 There are many chronicle accounts, of which the most useful are: Adam Murimuth, *Continuatio Chronicarum*, and Robert of Avesbury, *De Gestis Mirabilibus Regis Edwardi Tertii*, ed. E. M. Thompson (London, 1889), pp. 105–6, 312; Geoffrey le Baker, *Chronicon*, ed. E. M. Thompson (London, 1889), pp. 68–9 [in English in *EHD*, IV, 68–9]; Henry Knighton, *Chronicle*, ed. J. R. Lumby (London, 1889–95, 2 vols), II, 17–18; *Chroniques de London*, ed. G. J. Aungier (Camden Soc. 39, 1844), p. 76; *Chronographia Regum Francorum*, ed. H. Moranvillé (Soc. de l'Histoire de France, Paris, 1891–97, 3 vols), II, 121; *Chroniques de J. Froissart*, ed. Siméon Luce *et al.* (Soc. de l'Histoire de France, Paris, 1869–1975, 15 vols), II, 34–5, 219, 221; *Les Grandes Chroniques de France*, ed. Jules Viard (Soc. de l'Histoire de France, Paris, 1920–53, 10 vols), IX, 183.

30 M.Cornaert, *Knokke en het Zwin* (Tielt, 1974), pp. 350–3. I owe this reference to the kindness of Mr A. D. A. Rodger.

31 *EHD*, IV, 68–9. Sumption, *Hundred Years War*, pp. 324–7, has a vivid

account, but his map is incorrect and I interpret the English fleet's movements differently.

32 Foerster Laures, 'Warships of the Kings of Aragón', p. 26. Foote & Wilson, *Viking Achievement*, pp. 282–3.

33 Sumption, *Hundred Years War*, pp. 324–8. Richmond, 'War at Sea', pp. 97–8. *MF*, I, 443–54. Nicolas, *Royal Navy*, II, 48–68, 501–2. *BND* No.14.

34 Fulton, *Sovereignty*, pp. 36–8.

35 Lyon, *Wardrobe Book*, pp.vi–vii, xlviii–liii. Fowler, *Hundred Years War*, p. 7. Richmond, 'War at Sea', pp. 97–9. Kepler, 'Battle of Sluys'.

36 Sumption, *Hundred Years War*, pp. 346–7, 381. Alban, 'National Defence', p. 18. Hughes, 'Fourteenth-Century French Raids', pp. 125–6.

37 Jones, 'Edward III's Captains'.

38 Allmand, *Hundred Years War*, p. 85. Sumption, *Hundred Years War*, pp. 34–5. Jones, *Ducal Brittany*, pp. 143–4.

39 Kerherve, *L'état breton*, II, 675–85.

40 Alban, 'National Defence' p. 18. Jones, *Ducal Brittany*, pp. 143–4.

41 Jones, 'Edward III's Captains'. Fernández Duro, *La Marina de Castilla*, pp. 71–4. Sumption, *Hundred Years War*, pp. 386–408. Hall, 'Naval Forces', pp. 134–7. *MF*, I, 464–7. Nicolas, *Royal Navy*, II, 73, 80–1. Hughes, 'Fourteenth-Century French Raids', p. 216. *RFR*, III, i, 57. José Cervera Pery, *El Poder Naval en los Reinos Hispanicos (La Mariña de la Edad Media)* (Madrid, 1992), p. 153.

42 Sumption, *Hundred Years War*, pp. 483–500. *EHD*, IV, 77–8, 498. Wrottesley, *Crecy and Calais*, p. 11. Hall, 'Naval Forces', pp. 146–7. Vale, *Angevin Legacy*, p. 201.

43 Clifford J. Rogers, 'Edward III and the Dialetics of Strategy', *TRHS* 6th S. IV (1994), pp. 83–102, argues that he did, but assumes that he planned from the beginning to land in Normandy.

44 Sumption, *Hundred Years War*, pp. 501–10. Wrottesley, *Crecy and Calais*, pp. 13, 204.

45 Sumption, *Hundred Years War*, pp. 537, 559–77. Barber, *Edward Prince of Wales*, pp. 74–5. *EHD*, IV, 87–8. Hall, 'Naval Forces', pp. 151–5. *MF*, I, 476–94. Nicolas, *Royal Navy*, II, 95–6.

46 Barber, *Edward Prince of Wales*, pp. 99–100. *BND* No.15. Richmond, 'War at Sea', pp. 100–1. Fernández Duro, *La Marina de Castilla*, pp. 63–4, 100, 419–25. *MF*, I, 497. Nicolas, *Royal Navy*, II, 102–13. Cerezo Martínez, *La proyección marítima de España*, p. 81. Prestwich, *Three Edwards*, p. 179, is incorrect to describe it as 'an unprovoked attack on a Castilian merchant fleet'.

47 Appendix I.

48 *MF*, I, 516. Alban, 'National Defence', pp.xviii, 27–8. Nicolas, *Royal Navy*, II, 125.

49 'Omnes naves . . . ad terram longe a mari distantem pro securiori salvacione earundem traheri facitis': Alban, 'National Defence', p. 422, quoting PRO: C 54/198 m.39v. Ships as large as 200 tons actually were hauled out in response to this order: *CIM*, III, 421.

50 Platt, *Medieval Southampton*, p. 113. Alban, 'National Defence', pp. 289–303.

51 Alban, 'National Defence', pp. 289–303.

52 Mirot, 'Une tentative d'invasion', p. 441 n.6. David Crook, 'The Confession of a Spy, 1380', *BIHR* LXII (1989), pp. 346–50. Paviot, *La politique navale*, p. 72.

53 Nicolas, *Royal Navy*, I, 165. *CPR* 1324–27, pp. 208–12.

54 *CCR* 1323–27, pp. 471–2.

55 Alban, 'National Defence', p. 190.

56 Richmond, 'War at Sea', p. 97. Lyon, *Wardrobe Book*, p. 215. *EHD*, IV, 68–9. Sumption, *Hundred Years War*, pp. 323–4. Nicolas, *Royal Navy*, II, 47–68. *MF*, I, 445.

57 Sumption, *Hundred Years War*, p. 226.

58 Lyon, *Wardrobe Book*, p. 213. Sumption, *Hundred Years War*, pp. 246–7.

59 Horrox & Hammond, *Harleian Manuscript 433*, II, 65.

60 Richmond, 'War at Sea', p. 97.

61 Gillingham, 'Richard I and the Science of War', pp. 81–3.

62 Bernard, *Navires et Gens de Mer*, I, 407.

63 'Societas Navium Baionensium'; Vale, *Angevin Legacy*, p. 150.
64 *PR 24 Hen.II*, p. 112. *BND* No.10. *CPR* 1225–32, pp. 11, 14–15. PRO: C 66/34 m.8.
65 *LQCG*, p. 274. Reid, 'Sea-Power in the Anglo-Scottish War'.
66 John E. Dotson, 'Naval Strategy in the First Genoese-Venetian War, 1257–1270', *AN* XLVI (1986), pp. 84–90.
67 *CCW*, p. 427. *CPR* 1321–24, p. 12. *CCR* 1318–23, p. 708.
68 *RP*, II, 105.
69 *RFR*, II, ii, 950–1. *RS*, I, 467–8. *CPR* 1340–43, pp. 567–70. Nicolas, *Royal Navy*, II, 114.
70 E.g. *CPR* 1350–54, p. 486; *CPR* 1381–85, p. 302; *CCR* 1381–85, pp. 480–1; *CCR* 1385–89, pp. 12–13, 257, 293.
71 *RFR*, III, i, 187–8. *CPR* 1348–50, p. 556. *CCR* 1377–81, p. 267.
72 Nicolas, *Royal Navy*, II, 414–15. *RP*, IV, 85–6.
73 Alban, 'National Defence', pp. 281, 284.
74 PRO: E 372/183 rot.51. *RS*, I, 485. Nicolas, *Royal Navy*, II, 26.
75 E.g. Nicolas, *Royal Navy*, I, 201; *RS*, I, 320, 322; *CCR* 1333–37, p. 414; *RFR*, II, i, 265; ii, 943;
76 *RS*, I, 485.
77 *RS*, I, 498.
78 'Pur greuer nos enemis auantditz e lenuaismes depiezca': *TR*, I, 540–2.

8 Decline and Fall

1 Suárez Fernández, *Navigación y Comercio*, pp. 19–20; and 'House of Trastámara', pp. 58–60. Russell, *English Intervention*, pp.xxi–xxii. *MF*, II, 2.
2 Alban, 'National Defence', pp. 34–5. The chronicler John of Reading is the only authority for the 1366 raid.
3 Alban, 'National Defence', p. 36; these measures were taken in 1363.
4 *MF*, II, 5–11. Hall, 'Naval Forces', p. 165. Carr, *Owen of Wales*, pp. 23–4.
5 *CCR* 1369–74, pp. 158, 202–3.
6 Ambrogio Boccanegra, mentioned by Fernández Duro (*La Marina de Castilla*, pp. 130–4) and others as commanding the Castilian galleys, was the Admiral of Castile, but apparently not present at the battle.
7 Sherborne, 'Battle of La Rochelle'. Russell, *English Intervention*, pp. 193–4. Fernández Duro, *La Marina de Castilla*, pp. 130–4, 432–9. Suárez Fernández, 'House of Trastámara', p. 60. *MF*, II, 15–19. Nicolas, *Royal Navy*, II, 141–6.
8 Sherborne, 'Battle of La Rochelle', pp. 23–4; and 'Hundred Years' War', p. 171. Suárez Fernández, 'House of Trastámara', p. 60. Carr, *Owen of Wales*, p. 37.
9 Carr, *Owen of Wales*, p. 35.
10 Sherborne, 'Battle of La Rochelle', pp. 25–8. Suárez Fernández, 'House of Trastámara', p. 62. *MF*, II, 31. Nicolas, *Royal Navy*, II, 153, 510–13.
11 Terrier de Loray, *Jean de Vienne*. Mollat, 'Les enjeux maritimes', p. 164.
12 *MF*, II, 51–7. Alban, 'National Defence', pp. 49–50. Richmond, 'War at Sea', p. 105. Russell, *English Intervention*, pp. 238–40. Terrier de Loray, *Jean de Vienne*, pp. 104–15. Suárez Fernández, *Navigación y Comercio*, pp. 39–40; and 'House of Trastámara', p. 62.
13 *MF*, II, 57. *CIM*, IV, 88. *CCR* 1377–81, p. 21. Richmond, 'War at Sea', p. 105.
14 They were the dowry of his French queen, Charles V's sister, who died in 1378, when Navarre turned to England for help against Castile.
15 *MF*, II, 57–9. Russell, *English Intervention*, p. 242. Terrier de Loray, *Jean de Vienne*, pp. 118–25.
16 *MF*, II, 61. Russell, *English Intervention*, p. 242. Terrier de Loray, *Jean de Vienne*, p. 126.
17 Russell, *English Intervention*, p. 243.
18 Sherborne, 'Indentured Retinues', p. 731.
19 *MF*, II, 67–8. Nicolas, *Royal Navy*, II, 285. Sherborne, 'Indentured Retinues', p. 731. Suárez Fernández, *Navigación y Comercio*, pp. 47–8; and 'House of Trastámara', p. 63. Oppenheim, *VCH Sussex*, II, 140.
20 Appendix II.
21 Sherborne, 'Hundred Years' War', p. 167. The suggestion of Lewis & Runyan, *Naval and Maritime History*, p. 126, that

Edward III built ninety king's ships between 1340 and 1377 is fantastic; these were undoubtedly merchant ships arrested for naval service, neither built nor owned by the crown.

22 Oppenheim, *VCH Dorset*, II, 187–8.

23 Nicolas, *Royal Navy*, II, 271. Robertson, 'Rise of a Scottish Navy', p. 4.

24 Richmond, 'War at Sea', pp. 105, 107. Suárez Fernández, *Navigación y Comercio*, pp. 50–1; and 'House of Trastámara', pp. 63–5. *MF*, II, 71.

25 Templeman, 'Two French Attempts', pp. 225–31. Terrier de Loray, *Jean de Vienne*, pp. 187–205. Alban, 'National Defence', pp. 65–9. Mirot, 'Une tentative d'invasion', p. 254. *MF*, II, 80–1. Suárez Fernández, *Navigacióan y Comercio*, p. 63. Paviot, *La politique navale*, pp. 43–4.

26 Templeman, 'Two French attempts', pp. 232–4. Fowler, *Hundred Years War*, p. 7. Terrier de Loray, *Jean de Vienne*, pp. 207–14. Alban, 'National Defence', pp. 69–76. Mirot, 'Une tentative d'invasion'. *MF*, II, 90–3. Mollat, 'Les enjeux maritimes', p. 166. Paviot, *La politique navale*, pp. 44–50.

27 Terrier de Loray, *Jean de Vienne*, pp. 221–4. Mollat, 'Les enjeux maritimes', p. 167.

28 *MF*, II, 94. Nicolas, *Royal Navy*, II, 318–321. *EHD*, IV, 153. Suárez Fernández, *Navigación y Comercio*, pp. 66–7; and 'House of Trastámara', p. 65. Paviot, *La politique navale*, pp. 47–50.

29 Suárez Fernández, *Navigación y Comercio*, p. 87; and 'House of Trastámara', p. 66.

30 'Tous les pays tenoient et appelloient nostre avandit seignour le Roi de la mier'; *RP*, II, 311.

31 Alban, 'National Defence', pp. 45–53.

32 'Defaut de bone Governance sur la Meere': *RP*, III, 138.

33 According to the English chronicler Thomas Walsingham (*EHD*, IV, 196) the French lost almost all their horses on passage from lack of water; this is plausible, as a warhorse would need 5–10 gals. a day (Morrison, *Age of the Galley*, p. 116), but it must reflect incompetence born of lack of experience in organising seaborne expeditions, for English fleets of the period took horses on considerably longer passages.

34 Gruffydd, 'Sea Power and the Anglo-Welsh Wars', pp. 47–52. *MF*, II, 177–85. *EHD*, IV, 196. Alban, 'National Defence', pp. 57–9.

35 Richmond, 'War at Sea', p. 111. Pistono, 'Henry IV and the English Privateers'; and 'Henry IV and John Hawley'. Ford, 'Piracy or Policy'. Suárez Fernández, *Navigación y Comercio*, pp. 87–8; and 'House of Trastámara', p. 70. *BND* Nos.16, 17. Martínez Valverde, 'La nota marinera'. Cerezo Martínez, *La proyección marítima de España*, p. 85.

36 *EHD*, IV, 194–5.

37 Hewitt, *Organization of War*, p. 22. Meehan, 'English Piracy', pp. 19–20. Appleby, 'Devon Privateering', p. 91. Mollat, '"Être roi sur la mer"', pp. 282–3.

38 *CPR* 1216–25, pp. 2, 8. *CCW*, p. 449. *CIM*, II, 300. *RFR*, II, ii, 1082. *CCR* 1337–39, pp. 206, 236. Appleby, 'Devon Privateering', p. 91.

39 Nicolas, *Royal Navy*, I, 359.

40 Nicolas, *Royal Navy*, II, 20.

41 Sumption, *Hundred Years War*, p. 264. Lyon, *Wardrobe Book*, pp.cxii, 213. *CPR* 1338–40, pp. 143, 149, 491–2. Marsden, *Select Pleas*, I, xxxv, claims that Edward III chose this moment to revive his claim to 'sovereignty of the sea', which seems most unlikely; after 1340 he could do so with some credibility.

42 *CPR* 1340–43, pp. 319, 358, 469, the last of which gives the sum as £12,000.

43 Marsden, *Law and Custom*, I, 31, 74. *CPR* 1343–45, p. 218.

44 *CPR* 1385–89, pp. 147, 255.

45 Pistono, 'Henry IV and the English Privateers', p. 323.

46 *CPR* 1408–13, p. 323.

47 Ford, 'Piracy or Policy', modifies the argument of Pistono, 'Henry IV and the English Privateers' and 'Henry IV and John Hawley'.

9 The Chief Support of the Kingdom

1 *CCR* 1402–05, p. 193.
2 'La dit Naveye est la greindre substance du bien, profit, & prosperitee du vostre dit Roialme': *RP*, IV, 79.
3 Richmond, 'Keeping of the Seas', pp. 463–4.
4 'Of Westminster' *c.*1305–25; 'of the Tower' *c.*1340–1420.
5 *BND* No.3.
6 Turner, 'Southampton', p. 39.
7 This last was the arrangement of the 1377 balinger programme: Sherborne, 'Hundred Years' War', p. 169.
8 Lyon, *Wardrobe Book*, p. 363.
9 Lyon, *Wardrobe Book*, p.ciii.
10 Brooks, *English Naval Forces*, p. 189. Powicke, *Thirteenth Century* p. 95, quotes 230.
11 Prestwich, *War, Politics and Finance*, p. 142; and *Edward I*, p. 392.
12 Sumption, *Hundred Years War*, p. 398.
13 Prestwich, *The Three Edwards*, p. 197. Sumption, *Hundred Years War*, pp. 492, 497.
14 Wrottesley, *Crecy and Calais*, p. 204 (also *EHD*, IV, 498). Nicolas, *Royal Navy*, II, 507–10.
15 *CPR* 1334–38, p. 566. *CCR* 1354–60, p. 10. The compulsory purchase of a cargo of fruit and spices in 1243, and a sail for a royal galley in 1252, was presumably justified by the royal household's right of 'purveyance': *CCR* 1242–47, p. 140; 1251–53, p. 260.
16 Eugene H. Byrne, *Genoese Shipping in the Twelfth and Thirteenth Centuries* (Cambridge, Mass., 1930), pp. 23–4. Scammell, *World Encompassed*, p. 97.
17 Platt, *Medieval Southampton*, p. 130. Bernard, *Navires et Gens de Mer*, II, 591, 603. Russell R. Menard, 'Transport costs and long-range trade, 1300–1800: Was there a European""transport revolution" in the early modern era?', in Tracy, *Political Economy of Merchant Empires*, pp. 228–5, at pp. 241–2.
18 By the fifteenth century tonnage 'by calculation' (*per estimacionem*) was already distinct from capacity in actual tuns of wine, but the calculation seems to have been quite accurate: Friel, 'Archaeological sources', pp. 54–5. On tonnage see Bernard, *Navires et Gens de Mer*, I, 221–3.
19 Depending on what figure one allows for wages and operating costs.
20 Two to four round voyages from London to Bordeaux could be made in a year: Bernard, *Navires et Gens de Mer*, I, 399.
21 There are very numerous examples in *CCR* and *CPR*.
22 *CPR* 1348–50, p. 281.
23 *BND* No.22.
24 *CCR* 1237–42, pp. 401, 429, 431, 432.
25 *CCR* 1253–54, p. 124.
26 *Naves guerrinas, niefs del Tour, naves de guerra, nefs defensables* etc: *CCR* 1333–37, pp. 22, 414, 431.
27 'Sex naves guerrinas de maioribus & fortioribus navibus': PRO: E 372/180 rot.44 m.2; cf. C 71/15 m.29.
28 Oppenheim, *VCH Kent*, II, 267.
29 E.g. *CPR* 1422–29, pp. 192, 402–3, 493, 552 (20–200 tons, 1423; 20–140 tons, 1427; 20–100 tons, 1428; 20–90 tons, 1429).
30 Nicolas, *Royal Navy*, I, 129–30.
31 PRO: C 47/2/16 Nos.16–20 inc. returns from Glamorgan, Essex and London. PRO: E 101/684/54/4 may belong to this year.
32 *RS*, I, 146–7.
33 *CPR* 1350–54, pp. 376, 420.
34 Devon, *Issue Roll*, pp. 180, 245. Hall, 'Naval Forces' p. 165.
35 PRO: C 47/2/46 Nos.11 & 12 (Ipswich, 1372).
36 Ewe, *Schiffe aus Siegeln*, provides a gallery of ship-portraits, many of them English.
37 E.g. Fryde, *Book of Prests*, pp. 87–8; Devon, *Issue Roll*, pp. 180, 198; Prestwich, *Crisis of 1297–98*, No.105.
38 Hewitt, 'Organisation of War', p. 84. The earliest order mentioning brows and hurdles which I have seen is 1170: *PR 17 Hen.II*, p. 2.
39 Devon, *Issue Roll*, p. 269.
40 Hewitt, *The Black Prince's Expedition*, p. 35. *CCR* 1242–47, p. 67.
41 E.g. Thomas Alard of Winchelsea

accompanying the royal clerk William of Thorncroft in 1295: Fryde, *Book of Prests*, p. 96.

42 Prince, 'Army and Navy', pp. 381–2. Hewitt, 'Organisation of War', p. 85. Hall, 'Naval Forces' pp. 66–7, 72.

43 *CPR* 1343–45, p. 533.

44 Kepler, 'Battle of Sluys', pp. 72–3. Sumption, *Hundred Years War*, p. 177.

45 Wrottesley, *Crecy and Calais*, pp. 58, 62, 65, 66.

46 Sherborne, 'Hundred Years' War', p. 166.

47 *CCR* 1337–39, p. 197.

48 Gardiner, *West Country Shipping* No.8. *CPR* 1401–05, p. 356 gives other examples from this year.

49 *CLR*, I, 169. Byerly, *Wardrobe and Household* II, No.857. Lydon, 'Edward I, Ireland and the War in Scotland', p. 49.

50 Sherborne, 'Hundred Years' War', p. 165. Runyan, 'Merchantmen to Men-of-War', p. 34, claims MS authority for the suggestion that in 1301 shipowners were paid 7s a ton freight.

51 *BND* No.3.

52 PRO: C 47/2/15 No.8. Jones, 'Two Exeter Ship Agreements'.

53 *CCR* 1288–96, pp. 458–60; 1296–1302, p. 348.

54 *CPR* 1350–54, pp. 68–9.

55 *CCR* 1288–96, pp. 497–8; 1296–1302, p. 26.

56 *CPR* 1345–48, p. 260.

57 PRO: E 368/99 rot.34, abstracted in *CMR* 1326–27, p. 123.

58 Or perhaps repay it; her invasion force had landed not far from Dunwich the previous year.

59 *CPR* 1385–89, pp. 73, 364.

60 *CLR*, II, 158–9.

61 Lyon, *Wardrobe Book*, p.lxxxvii. Runyan, 'Ships and Mariners', p. 11, claims £1,000 was paid for 45 ships lost or damaged on the 1342 Brittany expedition; in 'Merchantmen to Men-of-War', p. 35, he claims fewer than 100 cases of compensation for damage during the fourteenth century, and none at all for loss; both figures are also in his 'Naval Logistics', p. 82.

62 PRO: C 61/64 m.6.

63 *CPR* 1358–61, p. 27.

64 *CPR* 1313–17, p. 509.

65 *CCR* 1302–07, p. 76; 1339–41, p. 196. *CPR* 1301–07, p. 131. *CDS*, V, 561, 565.

66 PRO: E 368/99 rot.34. *RS*, I, 192.

67 *CPR* 1324–27, pp. 315–16. *CCR* 1323–27, pp. 608–12.

68 Sumption, *Hundred Years War*, p. 178.

69 *CPR* 1334–38, p. 407.

70 *TR*, II, 617. *RFR*, II, ii, 1061.

71 *CPR* 1338–40, p. 252.

72 Nicolas, *Royal Navy*, II, 45. Sumption, *Hundred Years War*, p. 319.

73 E.g. *BND* Nos.25, 26. PRO: SC 1/33 No.123, Dartmouth to Edward II, 30 Mar 1324. *CDS*, V, 557–65. *CIM*, II, 1500.

74 PRO: C 47/2/28.

75 *CCR* 1251–53, p. 167; 1253–54, p. 121.

76 E.g. *CPR* 1301–07, pp. 121, 203; *CCR* 1302–07, p. 76 (all 1303); *CPR* 1334–38 p. 580 (1337); PRO: C 47/2/30; *CPR* 1338–40, p. 71; *TR*, II, 715; *CCR* 1341–43, pp. 624–5, 629–30, 700–1 (all 1338).

77 *CPR* 1348–50, p. 322. Runyan, 'Ships and Mariners', p. 16.

78 'Une grande criee de gentz de la vile qui diseyent que il ne poeynt le service le roy aprester pur grant duresce que on leur fist . . . [tallies] briserent saunz fere a eux bref ou allowance ou autre chose qui valer leur peuft . . . il sunt mout angussez': PRO: SC 1/47 No.172, R. of Burgersh [*Borgerssche*] to John of Droxford [*Drokenesford*] [1300–7].

79 *CPR* 1301–07, pp. 52–3, 61, 121, 203. *CCR* 1302–07, p. 76.

80 *CPR* 1334–38, p. 215.

81 *CCR* 1333–37, p. 593.

82 *CPR* 1334–38, p. 329.

83 Sumption, *Hundred Years War*, p. 236.

84 Hall, 'Naval Forces', p. 118. Sumption, *Hundred Years War*, p. 392.

85 Hall, 'Naval Forces', pp. 134–6. Sumption, *Hundred Years War*, pp. 403–7. *CPR* 1343–45, p. 92. *CCR* 1343–46, pp. 128–34. *CFR*, V, 343. Appendix III.

86 *CPR* 1343–45, p. 404.

87 Hewitt, *Organization of War*, pp. 77, 92. Vale, *English Gascony*, p. 220. Sherborne, 'Hundred Years' War'.

88 Saul, 'Great Yarmouth', pp. 108–9.

89 *CIM*, III, 14.
90 *BND* No.3; but this was special pleading, not to be taken literally.
91 PRO: C 64/8 mm.24d-26d. Hardy, *Rotuli Normanniae*, pp. 320–9.
92 Alban, 'National Defence' pp. 269–70. Sumption, *Hundred Years War*, p. 49.
93 Rodger, 'Cinque Ports', p. 644. Nicolas, *Royal Navy*, I, 284.
94 Prestwich, *Edward I*, p. 438–50. McKisack, *Parliamentary Representation*, pp.ix–xi, 131–2. W. M. Ormrod, 'Political Theory in Practice: the Forced Loan on English Overseas Trade of 1317–18', *HR* LXIV (1991), pp. 204–15.
95 PRO: E 352/120 rot.49. *CCR* 1323–27, p. 566.
96 Sumption, *Hundred Years War*, p. 178.
97 Oppenheim, *VCH Kent*, II, 267.
98 *CCR* 1341–43, p. 519.
99 *BND* No.1. *RFR*, III, i, 4.
100 Sumption, *Hundred Years War*, p. 568. *RFR*, III, i, 105–6.
101 *CCR* 1369–74, pp. 109–10. *RFR*, III, ii, 880.
102 McKisack, *Parliamentary Representation*, p. 25.
103 *RFR*, III, ii, 1002.
104 Richmond, 'War at Sea', p. 109. *BND* Nos.2, 3. PRO: C 65/5 m.2 No.9; C 65/33 m.3 No.67. *RP*, II, 307, 311, 320; III, 66, 74, 138, 212, 223, 458. Nicolas, *Royal Navy*, II,294.
105 *RP*, II, 307, 311. *BND* No.2.
106 *CPR* 1345–48, p. 264. *ARN*, pp. 10, 17, implies that it was not granted by Parliament until 1373, which seems to be wrong: see PRO: E 101/25/23 m.1.
107 PRO: E 101/25/23 m.1. Sumption, *Hundred Years War*, p. 568. Other examples: PRO: E 404/24 No.38 and Richmond, 'Royal Administration', p. 175 (1406).
108 Richmond, 'Royal Administration', pp. 218–27.
109 *CChR*, V, 3. There was a further grant in 1390: *CPR* 1388–92, p. 338.
110 Devon, *Issue Roll*, pp. 247, 249–50, 259–66. Hall, 'Naval Forces', p. 82.
111 *RP*, II, 320.
112 *RP*, III, 86, 212, 223.
113 Sherborne, 'Hundred Years' War', p. 165. Richmond, 'War at Sea', p. 108, implies that 3s 4d was paid every year from 1380, and 2s from 1385, which I have not seen evidence to confirm.
114 Bernard, *Navires et Gens de Mer*, I, 399; II, 683.
115 Goldingham, 'Navy under Henry VII', p. 476. Bernard, *Navires et Gens de Mer*, II, 603, gives 15th-century freight rates.
116 Though in 1244 four ships were chartered locally at Newcastle to act as a floating wine-cellar for the royal household: *CCR* 1242–47, p. 260.
117 Rodger, 'Cinque Ports', pp. 644–6.
118 Nicolas, *Royal Navy*, I, 265. *CPR* 1225–32, p. 53. Bernard, *Navires et Gens de Mer*, I, 245. Vale, *Angevin Legacy*, pp. 149–50.
119 *RS*, I, 432. *RFR*, II, ii, 943. *TR*, II, 622.
120 Murray, *Constitutional History*, p. 39.
121 Platt, *Medieval Southampton*, p. 107.
122 Rodger, 'Cinque Ports', argues this case in detail. See also Oppenheim, *VCH Kent*, II, 259–62.
123 Sumption, *Hundred Years War*, p. 15.
124 Sumption, *Hundred Years War*, pp. 24, 46, 72.
125 Kepler, 'Battle of Sluys', p. 71.
126 Sherborne, 'Cost of English Warfare', p. 149.
127 But the *livre tournois* was falling rapidly in value at this time: see Spufford, *Medieval Exchange*, pp. 174, 209.
128 Verbruggen, *Art of War*, pp. 278–9.
129 Mollat, 'Les enjeux maritimes', p. 166.
130 Sumption, *Hundred Years War*, p. 174.
131 Richmond, 'War at Sea', p. 102. At this date there were about 5½ *livres* to the pound sterling.
132 *CPR* 1313–17, p. 603.
133 *CCR* 1337–39, p. 366.
134 Richmond, 'War at Sea', p. 102.
135 *RFO*, VII, 520.
136 *PR 16 John*, p. 144. Nicolas, *Royal Navy*, I, 238–9. Marsden, *Law and Custom*, I,5, 8.
137 Fermoy, 'Maritime Indenture', p. 557. Marsden, *Law and Custom*, I, 1. Oppenheim, *VCH Suffolk*, II, 201.
138 Marsden, 'Early Prize Jurisdiction', p. 675.

139 Marsden, *Law and Custom*, I, 35.
140 Marsden, 'Early Prize Jurisdiction', p. 675; but there is an Irish case of 1295: *CCR* 1288–96, p. 428. The Cinque Ports in the Welsh War in 1277 were allowed all their booty and prisoners, but this apparently means in warfare ashore, and the Welsh had few or no ships: *CPR* 1272–81, p. 225.
141 *BBA*, I, 21–3. *CCR* 1323–27, pp. 412–13.
142 Marsden, 'Early Prize Jurisdiction', p. 676.
143 *BND* No.3.
144 *CPR* 1399–1401, p. 350.
145 Richmond, 'Keeping of the Seas', pp. 230–1, 237–8, 242.
146 Richmond, 'Keeping of the Seas', p. 217.
147 Richmond, 'Keeping of the Seas', pp. 93–113, 167. Meehan, 'English Piracy', pp. 19–20.
148 Marsden, 'Early Prize Jurisdiction', p. 682. Marsden, *Law and Custom*, I, 19. Nicolas, *Royal Navy*, I, 275–6. *CPR* 1232–47, p. 328.
149 Gardiner, *West Country Shipping*, p.xv; and 'Belligerent rights'. Chavarot, 'Lettres de marque'. Chaplais, 'Règlement des conflits'. Mas Latrie, 'Du droit de marque'. Alban, 'National Defence', p. 272. Hall, 'Naval Forces', pp. 35–6. Nicolas, *Royal Navy*, I, 358–62. Marsden, *Law and Custom*, I, 119–24. *CPR* 1313–17, pp. 8–9. Mollat, '"Être roi sur la mer"', pp. 282–3.
150 *Custos maris*, or *custos marinae*, 'keeper of the coast'.
151 Brooks, 'Naval Administration', pp. 374–88. Powicke's remark (*Thirteenth Century*, p. 95) that the 1230 mobilization was organized by officials with duties 'equivalent to those of a modern Board of Admiralty', suggests he was not very familiar with the modern Admiralty.
152 E.g. *CCR* 1231–34, pp. 26, 497; 1247–51, pp. 148–9, 197, 334, 495.
153 E.g. Runyan, 'Naval Logistics', p. 81.
154 Prince, 'Army and Navy', pp. 381–3. PRO: E 101/391/20, mm.1, 3. Runyan, 'Ships and Mariners', p. 6.
155 PRO: E 101/391/20 m.1.
156 Lyon, *Wardrobe Book*, pp.xx–xxi.
157 *PR 14 John*, p.xx. Tout, *Administrative History*, I, 233–8.
158 Tout, *Administrative History*, IV, 294–480. Lyon, *Wardrobe Book*, pp.xxiv–xlvii.
159 Tout, *Administrative History*, IV, 469–70.
160 Tout, *Administrative History*, IV, 294. *EHD*, IV, 374.
161 PRO: E 101/391/20 (accounts for 1348–50).
162 Tout, *Administrative History*, IV, 459. PRO: E 101/400/10.
163 Lyon, *Wardrobe Book*, pp.xxxi–xlvi.
164 Lyon, *Wardrobe Book*, p.xlvii. Rose, *Navy of the Lancastrian Kings*, p. 35. PRO: E 403/624 gives 15th-century examples.
165 *CPR* 1391–96, p. 489.
166 *CPR* 1396–99, p. 476.
167 No formal accounts were rendered by a Clerk of Ships between 1386 and 1404, though rough accounts survive of some naval work under Chamberleyn: *MEST*, I, 212–15.
168 *CFR*, XIII, 40.
169 *CFR*, XIII, 168. Moore, 'John Starlyng'.
170 Rose, *Navy of the Lancastrian Kings*, pp. 30–6. Turner, 'Southampton', p. 40. Turner, 'The *Gracedieu*', p. 57. PRO: E 403/624 (Issue Roll 4 Henry V, 1416) illustrates the wide variety of officials making payments for naval purposes.
171 Rose, *Navy of the Lancastrian Kings*, pp. 35–9.
172 Richmond, 'War at Sea', p. 113.

10 Captains and Admirals

1 *CPR* 1292–1301, p. 81.
2 *LQCG*, p. 278.
3 *CCR* 1288–96, p. 407.
4 Appendix IV: 'amiraux de nostre navie Dengleterre'. Marsden, *Law and Custom*, I, 38. Vale, *Angevin Legacy*, pp. 19, 204. In 1290 Robert Bendyn had apparently been described as 'king's admiral' at Dartmouth: Arthur Bending, 'Sir Robert Bendyn, the King's Admiral', *Devon and Cornwall Notes and Queries* XXXV (1982–6), pp. 386–9.

5 Via Bayonne, according to Vale, *Angevin Legacy*, p. 19.

6 Powicke, *Thirteenth Century*, pp. 655–6. Hewitt, 'Organisation of War', p. 85. Murray, *Constitutional History*, p. 211. Nicolas, *Royal Navy*, II, 193–202, 484–501. *BBA*, I, 1–7.

7 'Omnes naves & marinaros quacumque portum nostrum in unum locum quem ad defensionem eiusdam regnum nostrum & classis seu flote inimice impugnacionem & resistenciam videritis aptiorem congregari sine diffugio faciatur': PRO: E 159/68 rot.80.

8 Devon, *Issue Roll*, pp. 206–7.

9 PRO: C 32/19 mm.2, 3, 10. Nicolas, *Royal Navy*, I, 279.

10 Ford, 'Piracy or Policy', p. 65.

11 PRO: E 101/5/8 m.12. Nicolas, *Royal Navy*, II, 181–2, 445–7. *RFR*, III, i, 116.

12 PRO: E 372/149 rot.3.

13 Powicke, *Thirteenth Century*, p. 655. Gardiner, *West Country Shipping*, p. 27. Mirot, 'Une tentative d'invasion', pp. 448–50.

14 Mirot, 'Une tentative d'invasion', p. 454. Nicolas, *Royal Navy*, II, 434–5, 446–7.

15 *CDS*, V, 618.

16 *BND* No.11. Marsden, *Law and Custom*, I, 50–6. Nicolas, *Royal Navy*, II, 181–2. The measurements are at least 6ft by 90ft.

17 *MF*, I, 423–5. *BBA*, I, 1–29. Mollat, *La vie quotidienne*, p. 171.

18 *BBA*, I, 16–19. Nicolas, *Royal Navy*, I, 238; II, 208.

19 *BBA*, I, 18–21. Martínez Valverde, 'La note marinera', p. 35. Jongkees, 'Armement et action', p. 310.

20 *BBA*, I, 26–7.

21 *CDS*, V, 492 (xiv).

22 Richmond, 'English Naval Power', p. 2.

23 Sumption, *Hundred Years War*, pp. 486–8, 495–7. Nicolas, *Royal Navy*, II, 93.

24 *MF*, II, 205–6.

25 *MF*, II, 59.

26 *CLR*, V, 253, 289; VII, 269.

27 PRO: E 364/8 rot.F; E 101/31/31.

28 Jones, 'Edward III's Captains'.

29 Sherborne, 'Indentured Retinues', p. 741.

30 'Duos magistros rectores ad eas regendas, et duos alios qui superiorem curam inde habeant': *RLP*, p. 52.

31 *BND* No.13. *CCR* 1337–39, p. 366.

32 *RFR*, III, ii, 965.

33 Brooks, 'Cinque Ports' Feud with Yarmouth', at p. 47. *RS*, I, 432. *RFR*, II, ii, 943. *TR*, II, 622.

34 Appendix IV.

35 'Versus partes boriales percostera maris': Fryde, *Book of Prests*, p. 88.

36 PRO: E 101/68/8 No.181 (of 1379); but these were Spanish knights, who may have felt the issue of status more keenly.

37 'Secundum legem maritimam': PRO: C 61/64 m.8.

38 *CFR*, VIII, 207–8.

39 'Solont lusage de meer . . . por la garnisement des ditz niefs': PRO: C 81/1656 No.4. This Hankin was almost certainly one of the well-known Harwich seafaring family, possibly the one who had distinguished himself in the battle of Winchelsea in 1350: Oppenheim, *VCH Essex*, II, 264.

40 Hall, 'Naval Forces', p. 72.

41 'Per forciblement estuffer trois Barges queux sont ordeignez daler a dertemuth': PRO: C 81/1759 No.11.

42 Sherborne, 'Indentured Retinues'. Michael Powicke, *Military Obligation in Medieval England: A Study in Liberty and Duty* (Oxford, 1962), p. 166–70.

43 E.g. *RFR*, III, ii, 971, and Nicolas, *Royal Navy*, II, 149–50 (1372). *RFR*, III, ii, 971, and PRO: E 101/68/5 No.95 (1373), E 101/68/8 No.181 (1379).

44 PRO: E 403/624 m.6.

45 PRO: E 101/70/3 No.640.

46 *CPR*, 1292–1301, pp. 147, 149, 152, 157, 169.

47 Hewitt, 'Organisation of War', pp. 76–7.

48 *CPR*, 1292–1301, p. 149.

49 Alban, 'National Defence', p. 286.

50 Marsden, 'Vice-Admirals of the Coast'. Hall, 'Naval Forces', pp. 66–7. *BBA*, I, 1–7. *CPR* 1345–48, p. 473 (1346), is the first formal appointment I have noted of an admiral's 'lieutenant'.

51 *RP*, II, 119. *CPR* 1350–54, p. 125.

52 The 1359 expedition and the abortive 1372 expedition both involved 12–13,000 men: Sherborne, 'Indentured Retinues',

p. 735, and 'Hundred Years' War', p. 171.
53 PRO: E 372/184 rot.38d m.1, accounts of Geoffrey de Say for victuals supplied in 1338–9. *BND* No.23.
54 'Potus sive breuvagium'; Bernard, *Navires et Gens de Mer*, II, 623–4.
55 *BND* No.28.
56 *CCR* 1369–74, pp. 179–81.
57 *CPR* 1350–54, p. 125. *CCR* 1402–05, pp. 456–7.
58 Bernard, *Navires et Gens de Mer*, II, 623.
59 Mollat, *La vie quotidienne*, p. 145.
60 *CPR* 1350–54, p. 125.
61 Bernard, *Navires et Gens de Mer*, II, 624.
62 Crawford, *Howard Household Books*, II, 79. *RP*, I, 119. Rose, *Navy of the Lancastrian Kings*, p. 47.
63 PRO: E 372/184 rot.38d m.1. *BND* No.23. Crawford, *Howard Household Books*, I, 488; II, 79. Goldingham, 'Navy under Henry VII', pp. 487–8. Burwash, *English Merchant Shipping*, pp. 72–6.
64 Nicolas, *Royal Navy*, I, 292.
65 Jongkees, 'Armement et action', p. 310.
66 *PR 9 John*, p. 168.
67 In Latin, *rector* or *magister* replaces *gubernator*.
68 PRO: C 81/1759 No.28, undated.
69 *CPR* 1313–17, p. 334.
70 *PR 21 Hen.II*, p. 187.
71 The term applied to Jeremy, master of Henry III's flagship the *Cardinal*, in 1227 (*CLR*, I, 17, 26, 59–60, 108); William Marchant in 1294 (*CPR* 1292–1301, p. 99); Thomas Springet in 1326 (*CCW*, p. 580); Adam Cogger in 1340 (Lyon, *Wardrobe Book*, p. 436); and Simon Springet in 1343 (*CPR* 1343–45, p. 20).
72 *CLR*, I, 122 (of 1229). *RS*, I, 115–16 (of 1314). *CPR* 1324–27, pp. 7, 278–9 (of 1324 and 1326). *CCW*, p. 580 (of 1326). *TR*, II, 602, 877–8 (of 1338). PRO: E 101/391/20 mm.1–2 (of 1348–50). *CPR* 1385–89, p. 344 (of 1387). *CPR* 1396–99, pp. 102, 223 (of 1397). PRO: E 404/76/4 Nos.134–6 (of 1478). E 404/77/1 No.33 (of 1480). *CPR* 1476–85, p. 402 (of 1484). Hall, 'Naval Forces', pp. 58–9.
73 *CPR* 1292–1301, p. 99.
74 *CCW*, p. 580.
75 *CPR* 1334–38, p. 564.
76 Van Houts, 'Ship List of William the Conqueror', p. 173. Musset, 'Un empire à cheval', p. 418. Le Patourel, *Norman Empire*, pp. 177–8. *EHD*, II, 297.
77 Devon, *Issues of the Exchequer*, pp. 6–7. *CLR*, I, 173.
78 *PR 19 Hen.II*, p. 51. *PR 20 Hen.II*, pp. 132, 134. *PR 21 Hen.II*, p. 187. *PR 23 Hen.II*, p. 177.
79 Lyon, *Wardrobe Book*, pp. 363–4. *BND* No.35. *TR*, II, 602, 877–8. *CPR* 1343–45, p. 20.
80 Lyon, *Wardrobe Book*, pp. 363–4. *TR*, II, 602, 877–8.
81 *CCR* 1251–53, p. 510 (of 1253), is the first mention of a constable afloat I have noted.
82 PRO: E 101/3/26 mm.1–2.
83 PRO: E 101/3/26 m.2; E 101/5/8 m.14 (the York galley in 1295).
84 Platt, *Medieval Southampton*, p. 61.
85 PRO: E 352/120 rot.49.
86 PRO: E 315/317 f.22v. Burwash, *English Merchant Shipping*, p. 36. *CPR* 1476–85, p. 402.
87 PRO: C 81/1759 No.20.
88 PRO: E 101/15/4 (probably 1315) mentions unnamed merchantmen with a 'porfmayster' and a 'mestre de la bourse'.
89 PRO: E 101/5/8 m.14.
90 Prestwich, *Crisis of 1297–98*, p. 32. *BND* No.35 (of 1315).
91 Lyon, *Wardrobe Book*, p. 363.
92 Prince, 'Army and Navy', p. 383.
93 PRO: E 101/5/8 m.14.
94 PRO: E 101/7/25.
95 Lyon, *Wardrobe Book*, p. 363.
96 *CPR* 1391–96, p. 710.
97 Newhall, *Conquest of Normandy*, p. 32 n.159. Allmand, *Henry V*, pp. 228–9.
98 Sumption, *Hundred Years War*, pp. 323–4.
99 Latin *supersalientes*.
100 Nicolas, *Royal Navy*, I, 285.
101 *BND* No.27. Nicolas, *Royal Navy*, I, 285.
102 *CPR* 1317–21, p. 195 (1318). *CPR* 1324–27, pp. 7, 278–9 (1324 and 1326). *RS*, I, 351, printing PRO: C 71/15 m.27 (1335). *BND* No.36 (1335). *TR*, II, 602, 877–8 (1338). PRO: E 101/391/20 m.2 (1348–50). C 61/64 m.6 (1352); C 81/1759

No.28 (*c.*1370). *CCR* 1374–77, p. 7 (1374). PRO: C 81/1656 No.7 (1401). Horrox & Hammond, *Harleian Manuscript 433*, II, 72, 123 (1483–4).

103 *CPR* 1358–61, p. 351. I interpret the common name *Rodecog* as referring to the Holy Rood (i.e. Cross), though sometimes *Red Cog* may be meant.

104 *CPR* 1396–99, p. 439.

105 PRO: C 47/2/25 No.9, names of men chosen to serve in the *Saint Mary Cog* and *Cog John* of Carmarthen (1335?). PRO: C 47/2/46 Nos.11 & 12, lists of Ipswich seamen present, absent or already serving (1372).

106 *CIM*, II, 2034.

107 *CPR* 1348–50, p. 456; 1370–74, pp. 240, 493–4.

108 *BND* No.35.

109 *CPR* 1350–54, p. 386. *CPR* 1354–58, pp. 203, 446–7. *CPR* 1358–61, p. 38. *CPR* 1391–96, pp. 489, 710. Turner, 'Building of the *Gracedieu*', p. 65.

110 *CPR* 1385–89, p. 344.

111 *CPR* 1354–58, p. 275. *CPR* 1396–99, p. 80. *CPR* 1494–1509, p. 92.

112 *CPR* 1396–99, p. 102.

113 *CPR* 1396–99, p. 511; this was in Ireland.

114 Davies, 'Supply Services', pp. 75–6.

115 *CPR* 1385–89, p. 188.

116 Nicholson, *Edward III and the Scots*, p. 209. Brooks, *English Naval Forces*, p. 42. PRO: E 372/195 rot.44 (1350).

117 Lyon, *Wardrobe Book*, p. 363.

118 Crawford, *Howard Household Books*, I, 213. The *Margaret Cely* in 1487 had only one boy: Burwash, *English Merchant Shipping*, p. 35.

119 Crawford, *Howard Household Books*, II, 3, 63, 111–12.

120 Richon, 'Le navire de la cathédrale de Bayonne', p. 38. *EHD*, IV, 1217. Ellmers, 'Cog as Cargo Carrier', p. 41.

121 Baykowski, 'Kieler Hanse-Cog', pp. 261–2. Bernard, *Navires et Gens de Mer*, I, 392. Firth, *Songs and Ballads*, p. 5, quotes a 15th-century ballad which seems to be describing this process.

122 Ewe, *Schiffe aus Siegeln*, pp. 77, 124, 138, 180, 186.

123 Krieger, *Rôles d'Oléron*.

124 *BBA*, I, 133–47.

125 *BBA*, I, 33. The references to the admiral show that this is a 14th-century text.

126 'Et si le maistre enserge ung de ses compaignons de la nef il lui doit attendre la premiere collee comme de poing ou painne. Et si le mariner fiert de plus il se doit deffendre': *BBA*, I, 104, correcting this corrupt 18th-century transcript.

127 Burwash, *English Merchant Shipping*, pp. 63–5.

128 Burwash, *English Merchant Shipping*, pp. 61–2. *BBA*, I, 89–94. Bernard, *Navires et Gens de Mer*, II, 638–9, 646.

129 Bernard, *Navires et Gens de Mer*, II, 642–3.

130 *BBA*, I, 94–7.

131 'Si no y havia sino un clau de que s'pogues pagar se deu pagar': Burwash, *English Merchant Shipping*, p. 56.

132 Notably Fowey church, whose tower was erected in the mid-fifteenth century by the Treffrys with money inherited from the famous pirate Mark Mixtow; *ex inf.* Mr David Treffry. In 1430 a Dartmouth pirate hung up in St Petrox chapel the flag of a Dundee merchantman he had taken: Gardiner, *West Country Shipping*, p. 27.

133 Burwash, *English Merchant Shipping*, pp. 71–2. Nicolas, *Royal Navy*, I, 295.

134 Mollat, 'French Maritime Community', p. 119.

11 The End of the Empire

1 Allmand, *Henry V*, p. 222. Richmond, 'War at Sea', p. 112. Rose, *Navy of the Lancastrian Kings*, pp. 247–52, lists and describes all Henry V's ships. Richmond, 'Keeping of the Seas', p. 30, gives the size of the royal fleet for each year 1398–1422.

2 Richmond, 'War at Sea', pp. 112–15; and 'Royal Administration', p. 30. Allmand, *Henry V*, pp. 222–31.

3 Newhall, *Conquest of Normandy*, pp. 22, 29–33. PRO: C 64/8 mm.24d–26d (printed by Hardy, *Rotuli Normanniae*, pp. 320–9); E 403/624 m.6. Richmond, 'Royal Administration', p. 26. *BND*

No.18. *EHD*, IV, 219. *CSL* No.787. Nicolas, *Royal Navy*, II, 419–25. Rose, *Navy of the Lancastrian Kings*, p. 49.

4 Nicolas, *Royal Navy*, II, 431–4. *BND* No.19. Stansfield, 'John Holland', p. 107. Walker, 'John Holand'. *MF*, II, 227. Some of these authorities date the battle 29 June.

5 Newhall, *Conquest of Normandy*, pp. 58–9; cf. Paviot, *La politique navale*, p. 47. The French verb 'escumer' is roughly equivalent to the modern naval verb to 'sweep'; it was often used of pirates.

6 Richmond, 'War at Sea', p. 115.

7 *MF*, II, 235–9. Suárez Fernández, 'House of Trastámara', pp. 71–2. *CSL* No.856. *RFO*, IX, 783, 791.

8 Allmand, *Henry V*, p. 231.

9 PRO: E 101/70/3 No.640.

10 Vale, *Angevin Legacy*, p. 201.

11 Prestwich, *Three Edwards*, p. 176. Barber, *Edward Prince of Wales*, p. 47. Sumption, *Hundred Years War*, pp. 493–4, 497–500. *EHD*, IV, 77–8.

12 Richmond, 'War at Sea', pp. 112, 115. Allmand, *Hundred Years War*, pp. 83–4.

13 Richmond, 'War at Sea', p. 99; and 'English Naval Power', p. 1.

14 Friel, *The Good Ship*, p. 29.

15 Nicolas, *Royal Navy*, II, 406–7.

16 Allmand, *Hundred Years War*, p. 84. Paviot, *La politique navale*, pp. 69–83.

17 *EHD*, IV, 516–22. *RP*, IV, 433–8.

18 *EHD*, IV, 376–7.

19 *CPR* 1343–45, p. 555; 1377–81, p. 405; 1385–89, p. 339.

20 *CPR* 1429–36, pp. 510–5.

21 Richmond, 'Royal Administration', pp. 177–90.

22 Richmond, 'Royal Administration', pp. 206–12; and 'Keeping of the Seas'.

23 'Except Poair roiall des Enemys': *RP*, III, 569–70. *CCR* 1405–09, pp. 46, 61, 156–7.

24 Richmond, 'Royal Administration', p. 175. *RP*, III, 602–3.

25 Richmond, 'Royal Administration', pp. 213–27. *RP*, V, 59–60. *BND* No.5. *EHD*, IV, 466–7. Marsden, *Law and Custom* I, 130–2. PRO: E 364/77. Manwaring, 'The Safeguard of the Sea, 1442'.

26 Richmond, 'Royal Administration', pp. 240–5. PRO: C 65/102 m.10. *BND* No.6.

27 O'Neill, *Merchants and Mariners*, p. 125.

28 Ellis, *Original Letters*, III, i, 72–4, printing PRO: C 81/1364 Nos.34, 35.

29 Richmond, 'Royal Administration', p. 105.

30 Friel, 'Maritime technology', pp. 369–70.

31 Richmond, 'Royal Administration', pp. 93–113. PRO: C 47/6/4, proceedings for piracy against J. Hawley the elder, 1393–4. *EHD*, IV, 1228–33, proceedings against Fowey and other pirates, 1450–60. Gardiner, *West Country Shipping*, *passim*, and 'John Hawley'. *CPR* 1385–89, p. 372; 1388–92, p. 159; 1401–05, pp. 276–7, 363, 428. *CIM*, VII, 227. Mollat, *Le commerce maritime normand*, p. 76. Appleby, 'Devon Privateering', p. 91.

32 Richmond, 'Royal Administration', pp. 126–54. Meehan, 'English Piracy', pp. 145–82. Kingsford, *Prejudice and Promise*, pp. 78–106. Appleby, 'Devon Privateering', p. 91.

33 Gardiner, *West Country Shipping*, pp. 29–30.

34 Richmond, 'Royal Administration', p. 141. Gardiner, *West Country Shipping*, pp. 80–4.

35 Marsden, 'Early Prize Jurisdiction', p. 680; and *Select Pleas*, I, xli–xlii, though the officer in this case was not strictly an admiral. *RS*, I, 351. Nicolas, *Royal Navy*, I, 441–56, prints early admirals' commissions.

36 Leyburn was told to settle a dispute over a prize as early as 1297: *CCR* 1296–1302, pp. 33–4. *EHD*, IV, 482, prints an Admiralty case of 1361.

37 Marsden, 'Early Prize Jurisdiction', p. 683.

38 Appendix V. The Lord Admiral of Scotland appears at almost the same time as in England, with very similar powers and duties: McMillan, 'Admiral of Scotland'.

39 *BND* No.20. Richmond, 'Royal Administration', pp. 93–167. Meehan, 'English Piracy', pp. 6, 56–8.

40 Richmond, 'Keeping of the Seas', p. 296;

and 'Royal Administration', pp. 197–200. *BND* No.20 (quoted). Meehan, 'English Piracy', pp. 4–5. Scammell, *World Encompassed*, pp. 58–9. Hutchinson, *Medieval Ships and Shipping*, pp. 73–4. Paviot, *La politique navale*, pp. 203–4. Ellmers, 'Cog as Cargo Carrier', pp. 37–40, conveniently summarizes the rise of the Hansa.

41 Dollinger, *German Hansa*, pp. 303–4. Lloyd, *England and the German Hanse*, pp. 180–2.

42 *MF*, II, 271.

43 Richmond, 'Royal Administration', p. 25.

44 *RP*, V, 180.

45 *EHD*, IV, 1030.

46 Richmond, 'Royal Administration', p. 458. *EHD*, IV, 1041.

47 *CChR*, VI,40, 121, 128, 131, 149, 181, 194, records grants to places on the coast from Sussex to Yorkshire attacked or exposed to attack, 1444–68.

48 Oppenheim, *VCH Somerset*, II, 251.

49 Richmond, 'Royal Administration', p. 6, quoting Warwick's 1469 manifesto from Warkworth's Chronicle. 'Defence of' means defence against. Fulton, *Sovereignty*, p. 31 n.3, gives other examples of usage.

50 Richmond, 'Keeping of the Seas', p. 10.

51 *RP*, V, 59, printing PRO: C 65/96 m.4 No.30; cf. *BND* No.5. Candlemas and Martinmas are 2 February and 11 November respectively.

52 Sir John Fortescue, *The Governance of England*, ed. C. Plummer (Oxford, 1885), pp. 122–3. *BND* No.8. Allmand, *Hundred Years War*, p. 89.

53 Richmond, 'Keeping of the Seas', p. 230.

54 Horrox & Hammond, *Harleian Manuscript 433*, III, 23.

55 PRO: E 404/72/4 No.43, referring to Howard's carvel the *Edward* in 1464.

56 E.g. *CCR* 1261–64, p. 356. PRO: E 159/68 rot.80. *CDS*, V, 178. *TR*, II, 622. *RFR*, II, ii, 1133.

57 *RP*, V, 254. 'Convenable' = suitable, 'puissance' = strength.

58 *CCW*, p. 427.

59 'Supra mare proficiscamini, dictas galeas exploraturi, insequituri, expugnaturi et destructuri, prout melius, auxiliante Domino, videritis expediri': *TR*, II, 844–5.

60 Warner, *Libelle of Englyshe Polycye*, p. 1. 'Libel' here means a pamphlet.

61 Holmes, 'Libel of English Policy'. Richmond, 'Keeping of the Seas', pp. 283–5.

62 Sumption, *Hundred Years War*, pp. 228–32.

12 Change and Decay

1 Richmond, 'Royal Administration', pp. 256–88, quoted at pp. 268, 287. *BND* No.21. Meehan, 'English Piracy', pp. 72–6. Lloyd, *England and the German Hanse*, p. 195.

2 Richmond, 'Royal Administration', pp. 281–5. Meehan, 'English Piracy', pp. 72–6. Scofield, *Edward IV*, I, 51. The best modern sources for the 15th-century civil wars are John Gillingham, *The Wars of the Roses: Peace and Conflict in Fifteenth-Century England* (London, 1981) and A. Goodman, *The Wars of the Roses: Military Activity and English Society* (London, 1981).

3 Ross, *Edward IV*, pp. 145–50. Richmond, 'Royal Administration', pp. 308–44. Crawford, *Howard Household Books*, pp.xxiii–xxiv. Paviot, *La politique navale*, pp. 162–74.

4 Ross, *Edward IV*, pp. 160–1, 173–4. *EHD*, IV, 315–16. Naval guns are dealt with in Chapter 13.

5 PRO: E 404/72/4 No.43.

6 Richmond, 'Royal Administration', pp. 171, 389–408.

7 Richmond, 'Royal Administration', pp. 353–4, 398–9. PRO: E 101/71/5 No.954.

8 PRO: E 404/77/1 No.33. He commanded another convoy in 1474: Richmond, 'Royal Administration', p. 399.

9 John Fudge, 'Anglo-Baltic Trade and Hanseatic Commercial Systems in the Late Fifteenth Century', in *Britain and the Northern Seas: Some Essays*, ed. Walter Minchinton (Pontefract, 1988), pp. 11–19, at pp. 11–12. Lloyd, *England and the German Hanse*, pp. 206–36.

Dollinger, *German Hansa*, pp. 306–9.
10 Richmond, 'Royal Administration', pp. 343–59. *MF*, II, 365–6.
11 Richmond, 'Royal Administration', pp. 361–7. Crawford, *Howard Household Books*, pp.xxiv, II *passim*. MacDougall, *James IV*, p. 225. *CPR* 1476–85, p. 240.
12 Richmond, 'English Naval Power', p. 11.
13 Connell-Smith, *Forerunners of Drake*, p. 31.
14 *RFO*, XII, 23. The sum is £10–12,000 if the 'crown' is the French *écu à la couronne*.
15 Richmond, 'Royal Administration', pp. 508–10. Horrox & Hammond, *Harleian Manuscript 433*, II, 126.
16 Richmond, 'Royal Administration', pp. 501–2. Horrox & Hammond, *Harleian Manuscript 433*, II, 190–2, 196.
17 Laughton, 'Square-Tuck Stern', pp. 101–2.
18 MacDougall, *James IV*, p. 226. Robertson, 'Rise of a Scottish Navy', pp. 46–8.
19 Harding, *Sailing Navy*, p. 10.
20 Tanner, 'Henry VII's Expedition'.
21 Robertson, 'Rise of a Scottish Navy', pp. 57–9. *CPR* 1494–1509, p. 91.
22 *WBA*, pp. 27–44.
23 Appendix II, observing that the *Grace Dieu* of 1449 was not originally built for the Crown, though much used and later acquired by it.
24 Newhall, *Conquest of Normandy*, p. 30.
25 *CCR* 1402–05, p. 250; 1413–19, pp. 94–5; 1435–41, p. 194.
26 Loades, 'King's Ships', p. 103.
27 *EHD*, IV, 1028.
28 Richmond, 'Royal Administration', pp. 303–5.
29 Mollat, 'French Maritime Community', p. 118. Paviot, *La politique navale*, pp. 206–12.
30 Richmond, 'Royal Administration', pp. 306–7. Meehan, 'English Piracy', p. 78. Harrison, 'Maritime Activity', p. 176.
31 Richmond, 'Royal Administration', p. 506. Horrox & Hammond, *Harleian Manuscript 433*, II, 106–7. Lloyd, *England and the German Hanse*, pp. 201, 238–9. Dollinger, *German Hansa*, pp. 306–7.
32 Horrox & Hammond, *Harleian Manuscript 433*, II, 146.
33 PRO: C 60/174 m.24, printed Marsden, *Law and Custom*, I, 92–4. *CFR*, VIII, 207–8.
34 *CPR* 1381–85, p. 302; 1388–92, p. 12.
35 Crawford, *Howard Household Books*, p.xxxv.
36 Richmond, 'Royal Administration', p. 298. Horrox & Hammond, *Harleian Manuscript 433*, I, 219. Harrison, 'Maritime Activity', pp. 181–2.
37 Richmond, 'Royal Administration', p. 507.
38 Harrison, 'Maritime Activity', p. 173.
39 Nicolas, *Royal Navy*, II, 448–51, 517–23.
40 Horrox & Hammond, *Harleian Manuscript 433*, II,63. 'Recounter' = encounter.
41 Crawford, *Howard Household Books*, pp.xxiv, II, 9–10.
42 Crawford, *Howard Household Books*, II, 9; the 'landmen' here are soldiers. Note that Howard was an admiral in the modern sense, but not yet Lord Admiral of England.
43 Crawford, *Howard Household Books*, II, 9–10.
44 Rose, *Navy of the Lancastrian Kings*, p. 55. Richmond, 'Royal Administration', pp. 80–4.
45 Harrison, 'Maritime Activity'.
46 Horrox & Hammond, *Harleian Manuscript 433*, I, xviii. *EHD*, IV, 381–2.
47 Richmond, 'English Naval Power', p. 10; and 'Royal Administration', pp. 361, 375, 426–7.
48 PRO: E 404/77/3 No.83.
49 Richmond, 'Royal Administration', p. 440. Horrox & Hammond, *Harleian Manuscript 433*, I, 182, 272; II, 81; III, 10–11.
50 Richmond, 'English Naval Power', pp. 11–12. Goldingham, 'Navy under Henry VII', p. 477.
51 Harrison, 'Maritime Activity', p. 25.
52 Richmond, 'English Naval Power', pp. 11–12. *CPR* 1494–1509, p. 91.
53 Goldingham, 'Navy under Henry VII', p. 477.
54 Crawford, *Howard Household Books*, pp.xiv, II, 3–4. The same rate is given

by *ARN*, p. 34, and *EHD*, IV, 1028, printing PRO: E 101/55/8.

55 Goldingham, 'Navy under Henry VII', p. 488.

56 Horrox & Hammond, *Harleian Manuscript 433*, II, 92–93.

57 Crawford, *Howard Household Books*, p.xxii. Scofield, *Edward IV*, I, 404–18. Scammell, 'Shipowning in England *circa* 1450–1550', pp. 119–21. Richmond, 'Royal Administration', pp. 250–5, lists at least 42 noble shipowners in the period 1422–85.

58 Childs, 'Devon's Overseas Trade', p. 85. Appleby, 'Devon Privateering', p. 92.

59 Harrison, 'Maritime Activity', pp. 103–16. *CCR* 1485–1500 No.1236. *CPR* 1494–1509, pp. 81, 280, 402, 432, 549. Henry III 'bareboat' chartered his big ship the *Queen* for 50 marks a year in 1232: Nicolas, *Royal Navy*, I, 221; *CCR* 1231–34, p. 28.

60 MacDougall, *James IV*, p. 234. Robertson, 'Rise of a Scottish Navy', p. 52.

61 *CPR* 1494–1509, p. 588.

62 Harrison, 'Maritime Activity', p. 105. Cf. Scammell, 'Shipowning in England *circa* 1450–1550', pp. 109–13, and 'Shipowning in . . . Early Modern England', p. 406.

63 Lewis, *Sea-Officers*, p. 26.

64 Goldingham, 'Navy under Henry VII', p. 487.

65 Horrox & Hammond, *Harleian Manuscript 433*, II, 146.

66 *CPR* 1485–94, p. 296. But the Bayonne balinger *Aygla* had both in 1415: Bernard, *Navires et Gens de Mer*, II, 632 n.193.

67 Horrox & Hammond, *Harleian Manuscript 433*, I,182.

68 *CPR* 1494–1509, p. 92.

69 Crawford, *Howard Household Books*, II, 9–10 (where the 'landmen' are soldiers).

70 Bernard, *Navires et Gens de Mer*, II, 631.

71 PRO: E 404/76/4 Nos.134–6.

72 Crawford, *Howard Household Books*, II, 80.

73 Goldingham, 'Navy under Henry VII', p. 487. Burwash, *English Merchant Shipping*, pp. 35–8.

74 *CSL* No.291.

75 Crawford, *Howard Household Books*, II, 47, 54, 61.

76 Goldingham, 'Navy under Henry VII', p. 487.

77 Richmond, 'Royal Administration', p. 358. *ARN*, p. 41.

78 Jongkees, 'Armement et action', p. 313. Mollat, 'French Maritime Community', p. 122.

79 Brooks, *English Naval Forces*, p. 42.

80 Crawford, *Howard Household Books*, II, 6.

81 Crawford, *Howard Household Books.*, II, 275–7.

82 Nicolas, *Royal Navy*, I, 222. Friel, 'Maritime technology', p. 116; and *The Good Ship*, pp. 117–18. Burwash, *English Merchant Shipping*, p. 74.

83 *BBA*, I, 111.

84 Ellmers, 'Cog as Cargo Carrier', p. 40. Hutchinson, *Medieval Ships and Shipping*, pp. 165–9.

85 *The Canterbury Tales*, General Prologue, ll.401–9. 'Lodemenage' = coastal pilotage, 'Carthage' is probably Cartagena.

86 Ellmers, 'Cog as Cargo Carrier', p. 40.

87 Hutchinson, *Medieval Ships and Shipping*, pp. 171–4, with a map of medieval lights around the British Isles. Bernard, *Navires et Gens de Mer*, II, endpapers, has excellent maps of the shipping routes of the Bay of Biscay.

88 Bernard, *Navires et Gens de Mer*, I, 413. Hutchinson, *Medieval Ships and Shipping*, p. 98.

89 Martínez Valverde, 'La note marinera', p. 29.

90 Rose, *Navy of the Lancastrian Kings*, p. 47. G. B. P. Naish, 'The "Dyoll" and the Bearing-Dial', *Journal of the Institute of Navigation* VII (1954), pp. 205–8.

91 Warner, *Libelle of Englyshe Polycye*, p. 41. Hutchinson, *Medieval Ships and Shipping*, pp. 177–8. Waters, *Navigation*, p. 22, refers to the first English compasses in 1410–12.

92 Hope, *Shipping*, pp. 64–6.

93 PRO: E 404/72/2 No.17; E 364/77 rot.Pd. Friel, 'Carrack', p. 87. Hutchinson, *Medieval Ships and Shipping*, p. 156.

94 Brooks, *English Naval Forces*, p. 65.

95 Brooks, 'Naval Armament', p. 125. *CDS*, V, 562. Sumption, *Hundred Years War*, p. 167. Brooks, *English Naval Forces*, pp. 60–4. *RLC*, p. 51. *CLR*, II, 145. *CCR* 1237–42, pp. 480–1; 1251–53 pp. 508–9.
96 Platt, *Medieval Southampton*, p. 62.
97 *BND* No.17. Prestwich, *Edward I*, p. 382. Martínez Valverde, 'La note marinera', p. 21. Hutchinson, *Medieval Ships and Shipping*, p. 163.
98 Friel, 'Winds of Change', p. 186, quoting PRO: E 101/20/27. Smith, 'Artillery and the Hundred Years War', p. 145.
99 Tout, *Administrative History*, IV, 470–2. *BND* No.17. Hutchinson, *Medieval Ships and Shipping*, p. 163. Kenyon, 'Coastal Artillery Fortifications', p. 149. The English fortress of Cherbourg had in 1379 one gun firing 7.6in stone shot, and three of 4.8in calibre: Tout, 'Firearms in England', p. 686 (giving circumference, which I have converted to diameter).
100 Van Oosten & Bosscher, 'Het Zeilschip', p. 867.
101 PRO: E 403/624 mm.3–4; E 364/77 rot.Pd; E 404/72/1 No.17. DeVries, 'Shipboard artillery'. Hutchinson, *Medieval Ships and Shipping*, pp. 156–8. Friel, 'Winds of Change', p. 186. Howard, *Ships of War*, pp. 38–9.
102 PRO: E 315/317 f.13. Oppenheim, *Accounts and Inventories*, pp. 194–5, 204–5, 261, 264, 274. Friel, 'Carrack', pp. 88–9. Smith, 'Swivel-guns', classifies this sort of weapon.
103 PRO: E 36/8 ff.91, 97 & 101v.
104 A. D. Saunders, *Dartmouth Castle* (London, 3rd edn, 1991), pp. 21–5; and *Fortress Britain*, pp. 26–7. Kenyon, 'Coastal Artillery Fortifications'. R. A. Erskine, 'The Military Coast Defences of Devon, 1500–1956', in *Maritime History of Devon*, ed. Duffy, I, 119–29, at p. 120.
105 Villain-Gandossi, *Le Navire Médiéval*, Pl.76. Rieth, 'La construction navale à franc-bord', p. 17. Howard, *Ships of War*, pp. 12, 26–7.
106 Cipolla, *Guns and Sails*, pp. 80–1.
107 Ewe, *Schiffe aus Siegeln*, p. 71.
108 Konstam, 'Naval Artillery', pp. 99–102.
109 Paviot, *La politique navale*, pp. 294–9. DeVries, 'Shipboard artillery'.
110 Guilmartin, *Gunpowder and Galleys*, pp. 210–11.

13 Departed Dreams

1 Gunn, 'French Wars', pp. 35–47.
2 MacDougall, *James IV*, p. 257. Gunn, 'French Wars', pp. 28–32. *WBA*, pp. 82–4. Cruikshank, *Invasion of France*, pp. 1–4.
3 *WBA*, p. 84.
4 Cruikshank, *Invasion of France*. *WBA*, pp. 85–7.
5 *ARN*, p. 49.
6 MacDougall, *James IV*, p. 223. Robertson, 'Rise of a Scottish Navy', p. 11.
7 MacDougall, *James IV*, p. 223.
8 MacDougall, *James IV*, pp. 224–7, 238–42. Robertson, 'Rise of a Scottish Navy', pp. 18–49, 80–1, 112–14. Ditchburn, 'Piracy and War at Sea'.
9 Grant, 'Scotland's "Celtic Fringe"', p. 131. The Gaelic title is 'rí nan eileanan', 'King of the Isles'.
10 Nicholson, *Scotland: The Later Middle Ages*, p. 481. Steer & Bannerman, *Monumental Sculpture*, pp. 207–10. Grant, 'Scotland's "Celtic Fringe"'.
11 Nicholson, *Scotland: The Later Middle Ages*, pp. 482, 541–4. Robertson, 'Rise of a Scottish Navy', pp. 53–4, 64–6. MacDougall, *James IV*, pp. 228–9.
12 Konstam, 'Naval Artillery', p. 87.
13 Nicholson, *Scotland: The Later Middle Ages*, p. 564. Robertson, 'Rise of a Scottish Navy', pp. 69–72. MacDougall, 'James IV's *Great Michael*', p. 41.
14 Queen Margaret of Scots and Princess Mary were respectively Henry VIII's elder and younger sister.
15 MacDougall, *James IV*, pp. 233–8. Robertson, 'Rise of a Scottish Navy', pp. 97–100. MacDougall, 'James IV's *Great Michael*', pp. 36–41. *ARN*, p. 47. *ERS*, IV, lxxiv, 451–507.
16 Barfod, 'Den danske orlogsflåde', pp. 263–5. Davies, 'Supply Services', pp. 64–7.

17 MacDougall, *James IV*, pp. 239–42. Robertson, 'Rise of a Scottish Navy', pp. 112–14.
18 MacDougall, *James IV*, p. 259.
19 Webb, 'William Sabyn', p. 211, quoting Hall's Chronicle.
20 *TN*, pp. 57–62. *MF*, III, 92–102. Spont, *War with France*, pp.xi–xxvii, 47–50, 77–88. Clowes, *Royal Navy*, I, 451.
21 'Elle luy fera ung merveilleux proffit, et si donnera à penser au roy d'Angleterre': Duc de La Trémoille to M. d'Aumont. 10 June 1512, in Spont, *War with France*, p. 21.
22 *TN*, pp. 62–3. *MF*, III, 104–6. Spont, *War with France*, pp. 121–33. Scammell, 'War at Sea', pp. 77–8.
23 Lord T. Howard to T. Wolsey, 7 May 1513, in Spont, *War with France*, p. 159.
24 J. D. Alsop, 'Lord Admiral William FitzWilliam', *MM* LXV (1979), p. 242, quoting an anonymous 17th-century life of Howard. Spont, *War with France*, p.xxxviii.
25 Edward Echyngham to T. Wolsey, 5 May 1513, in Spont, *War with France*, p. 148.
26 *TN*, pp. 63–4. Spont, *War with France*, pp. 132–61. *MF*, III, 107–10. Webb, 'William Sabyn', p. 213. Scammell, 'War at Sea', pp. 79–80.
27 Spont, *War with France*, pp.xl–xlii. Ronald Pollitt, 'Devon in the French and Spanish Wars', in Duffy, *Maritime History of Devon*, I, 108–14, at p. 114.
28 *MF*, III, 112–13. *TN*, pp. 65–6. MacDougall, *James IV*, pp. 268–9. Robertson, 'Rise of a Scottish Navy', pp. 147–58, 160–1. Spont, *War with France*, pp. 171–84. Macdougall, 'James IV's *Great Michael*', pp. 45–56.
29 *MF*, III, 114–15. Spont, *War with France*, pp.xlv–xlvi, 197–210. *WBA*, p. 88.
30 Elton, 'War and the English', p. 16, quoting Thomas Cromwell.
31 MacDougall, *James IV*, p. 266. Robertson, 'Rise of a Scottish Navy', pp. 145–6. Macdougall, 'James IV's *Great Michael*', pp. 52–6.
32 Spont, *War with France*, p.xlvi, 104–6, 127–8, 157–8. Davies, 'Supply Services', pp. 213–19.
33 *WBA*, p. 88.
34 Elton, 'War and the English', p. 16.
35 *WBA*, p. 89. Gunn, 'French Wars', pp. 35–6.
36 Webb, 'William Sabyn', pp. 214–15.
37 *MF*, III, 168–9, 174–5.
38 *ARN*, pp. 66–8.
39 *WBA*, pp. 94–100.
40 The Lord Thomas Howard of the previous war, whose father, the victor of Flodden, had since been restored as Duke of Norfolk
41 *TN*, pp. 104–5. Davies, 'Supply Services', pp. 226–7. *MF*, III, 171, 177. Webb, 'William Sabyn', p. 217.
42 *WBA*, p. 102.
43 Davies, 'Supply Services', p. 224. Webb, 'William Sabyn', p. 216. Scammell, 'War at Sea', p. 82. *TN*, p. 105.
44 Ditchburn, 'Piracy and War at Sea', p. 40. Scammell, 'War at Sea', pp. 83–4. *MF*, III, 180.
45 *TN*, pp. 107–11. *MF*, III, 181.
46 S. J. Gunn, 'The Duke of Suffolk's March on Paris in 1523', *EHR* CI (1986), pp. 596–634. *WBA*, pp. 102–5, quoting (at p. 105) Roper's *Life of Sir Thomas More*. *TN*, p. 107.
47 *WBA*, pp. 106–10. *TN*, p. 109.

14 Precarious Isolation

1 Professor Loades's *Tudor Navy* has lately lent the argument renewed authority.
2 Edward, Lord Herbert of Cherbury, *The Reign of Henry VIII* (London, 1649), p. 18, quoting unnamed royal councillors.
3 *WBA*, pp. 111–21.
4 *WBA*, pp. 122–41.
5 Fowler, *English Sea Power*, p. 30.
6 Saunders, *Fortress Britain*, pp. 34–52. Gunn, 'French Wars', p. 30.
7 Hale, *War and Society*, p. 234; and 'Armies, Navies and the Art of War', pp. 552–3.
8 Frank Kitchen, 'The Defence of the Coast of Cornwall during the Reign of Henry VIII', *Cornwall Association of Local Historians Journal* No.22 (1991), pp. 4–8, quoting Hall's Chronicle at p. 4. Cf. M. Brayshay, 'Plymouth's

Coastal Defences in the Year of the Spanish Armada', *TDA* CXIX (1987), pp. 169–96, at p. 172.

9 *WBA*, pp. 143–4. *TN*, p. 121.

10 *ARN*, p. 95. *LPH8*, V, 424; VI,67, 75, 84, 93, 175. Loades, 'King's Ships', p. 30. *The Hamilton Papers*, ed. Joseph Bain (Edinburgh, 2 vols, 1890–2), I, 404–5.

11 Robertson, 'Rise of a Scottish Navy', p. 165. *Accounts of the Lord High Treasurer of Scotland*, ed. T. Dickson, Sir J. B. Paul *et al.* (Edinburgh, 1877–1978, 13 vols), VI, 134. *ERS*, XVI, 566. Boulind, 'Ships of Private Origin', pp. 393–5. *LPH8*, XI, 163, 251; XXXI, ii, 249.

12 Boulind, 'Ships of Private Origin', p. 394. Scammell, 'War at Sea', p. 183.

13 Davies, 'Supply Services', pp. 250–2; and 'Provisions for Armies', p. 244.

14 Scammell, 'War at Sea', pp. 85–6.

15 Scammell, 'War at Sea', pp. 87–92. *WBA*, pp. 152–6.

16 *TN*, pp. 126–7. Davies, 'Supply Services', pp. 254–7, 270–1; and 'Provisions for Armies', p. 245. Boulind, 'Ships of Private Origin', pp. 391–2. Scammell, 'War at Sea', pp. 92–3. *WBA*, p. 157.

17 *TN*, p. 128. *WBA*, p. 158.

18 *TN*, pp. 135–6. Andrews, *Trade, Plunder and Settlement*, pp. 61–2. Connell-Smith, *Forerunners of Drake*, pp. 133–5. Williamson, *Hawkins of Plymouth*, p. 35. Andrews, *Drake's Voyages*, pp. 15–16. *WBA*, pp. 158–9.

19 Connell-Smith, *Forerunners of Drake*, pp. 136–47, 152–5, 163, 175.

20 *MF*, III, 414–19. *WBA*, pp. 159–60. Hale, 'Armies, Navies and the Art of War', p. 564.

21 Henry Ellis, 'An Account of two ancient drawings . . .', *Archaeologia* XXIV (1832), pp. 292–8. *MF*, III, 419. L. G. C. Laughton, 'The Burning of Brighton by the French', *TRHS* 3rd S. X (1916), pp. 167–73.

22 *MF*, III, 419–24. *WBA*, p. 160. Rowse, *Grenville*, p. 39. Williamson, *Maritime Enterprise*, pp. 391–5. Corbett, *Drake*, I, 49–55. M. de Brossard, 'The French and English Versions of the Loss of the *Mary Rose* in 1545', *MM* LXX (1984), p. 387.

23 *MF*, III, 425–8. Williamson, *Maritime Enterprise*, pp. 395–9. Corbett, *Drake*, I, 56–8.Clowes, *Royal Navy*, I, 464–5.

24 *MF*, III, 430. Boulind, 'Ships of Private Origin', p. 403. Oliveira, *A arte da guerra do mar*, p. 117, was present on this occasion.

25 *MF*, III, 412. MacInnes, 'West Highland Sea-Power', p. 530. *WBA*, p. 162.

26 Scammell, 'War at Sea', pp. 94–6.

27 *WBA*, p. 162. Pollitt, 'Elizabethan Navy Board', p. 29.

28 *WBA*, p. 162.

29 *TN*, pp. 141–2. *MF*, III, 432–4. *WBA*, p. 163–9. Bonner, 'Recovery of St. Andrews'.

30 *WBA*, pp. 169–70. *TN*, pp. 141–2. Davies, 'Supply Services', pp. 258–9; and 'Provisions for Armies', p. 245. Boulind, 'Ships of Private Origin', pp. 393–5.

31 Connell-Smith, *Forerunners of Drake*, p. 134. 'Colmsinch' = Inchcolm.

32 *WBA*, pp. 170–3. *TN*, pp. 143–6. Davies, 'Supply Services', p. 260. Saunders, *Fortress Britain*, pp. 57–61.

33 *TN*, pp. 143–6. *MF*, III, 434–42.

34 *TN*, pp. 143–146. *MF*, III, 434, 437, 441. *WBA*, pp. 173–4.

35 *TN*, pp. 147–8. Davies, 'Supply Services', pp. 260–62. *WBA*, pp. 174–6.

36 *TN*, p. 148. Glasgow, 'Oared Vessels', p. 371; and 'Philip and Mary's War', p. 327. Appleby, 'Neutrality, Trade and Privateering', p. 63. H. Bourde de la Rogerie, 'Occupation de Serk par les Français en 1549', *Transactions of the Société Guernsiaise* XIII, 2 (1938), pp. 178–85. The account of Strozzi's action in *MF*, III, 444–51 (based at this point on chronicles rather than MSS), is not borne out by English sources.

37 *WBA*, pp. 174–8.

38 Davies, 'Supply Services', p. 242.

39 *ARN*, p. 94. Glasgow, 'Philip and Mary's War', p. 327.

40 Dietz, *English Government Finance*, p. 437.

41 'Considéré que l'une des principalles choses dignes de nostre grandeur . . . c'est d'estre fort et grossement équippé par la mer': *MF*, III, 455.

42 *MF*, III, 453–9.

43 *TN*, p. 136. Connell-Smith, *Forerunners of Drake*, pp. 134–84.

44 *WBA*, pp. 179–90. Stone, 'State Control', p. 107. *Tudor Economic Documents*, ed. R. H. Tawney & Eileen Power (London, 1924, 3 vols), II, 125, quoting notes by Lord Burghley, *c.*1581.

45 Davies, 'Supply Services', p. 64, quoting PRO: SP 1/9 p. 614.

46 Davies, 'Supply Services', pp. 26–9, 34–9, 43–6, 51–63. Stone, 'State Control', p. 112.

15 The Flower of England's Garland

1 *WBA*, pp. 193–204.

2 *WBA*, pp. 204–6. *TN*, pp. 155–6.

3 *WBA*, pp. 205–7.

4 *WBA*, pp. 208–17, 221–3.

5 *TN*, pp. 164–5. Glasgow, 'Philip and Mary's War', p. 324.

6 *WBA*, pp. 217–31. *TN*, pp. 162–3. Glasgow, 'Philip and Mary's War', pp. 328–9. Davies, 'England and the French War', pp. 160–1.

7 When Charles V abdicated in 1556 and divided his empire between his brother Ferdinand and his son Philip, the Low Countries went to Philip and thus became 'Spanish'.

8 *TN*, pp. 170–1. Glasgow, 'Philip and Mary's War', pp. 330–2. Davies, 'England and the French War', pp. 164–6.

9 Davies, 'England and the French War', pp. 168–78. *TN*, pp. 172–3. Glasgow, 'Philip and Mary's War', p. 333.

10 *TN*, p. 174. Glasgow, 'Philip and Mary's War', p. 336. Davies, 'England and the French War', p. 181. Tenison, *Elizabethan England*, I, 120–5.

11 *TN*, pp. 174–5. Glasgow, 'Philip and Mary's War', pp. 336–7. Davies, 'England and the French War', pp. 180–1.

12 *TN*, pp. 174–5. Glasgow, 'Philip and Mary's War', pp. 337–9. Davies, 'England and the French War', p. 179. Corbett, *Spanish War*, p. 295.

13 Corbett, *Drake*, I, 132. Glasgow, 'Philip and Mary's War', pp. 322–3. and 'Naval Administration', pp. 3–6.

14 *BND*, pp. 100–1.

15 *TN*, p. 170. Corbett, *Drake*, I, 132. Glasgow, 'Philip and Mary's War', pp. 322–3; and 'Naval Administration', pp. 3–6. Davies, 'England and the French War', p. 164. Rodríguez-Salgado, *Armada*, pp. 41–2.

16 '. . . defensionem Regni Angliae in hoc consistere quod naves semper sint prompte et in bone ordine ut possint servire tuitioni Regni ab omni invasione': PRO: SP 11/6 fo.26 (a copy of which I owe to the courtesy of Professor Geoffrey Parker); cf. P. F. Tytler, *England under the Reigns of Edward VI and Mary* (London, 1839, 2 vols), II, 485–6.

17 *WBA*, pp. 225–8. Glasgow, 'Philip and Mary's War', pp. 327, 332. *ARN*, p. 114. Davies, 'England and the French War', p. 163. Andrews, *Drake's Voyages*, pp. 12–15. J. C. Appleby, 'The *Anne* of Dublin: a sixteenth-century man-of-war', *Irish Sword* XVII (1987), pp. 74–80.

18 *WBA*, p. 229, quoting SP 12/8 No.52.

19 *WBA*, pp. 235–45. *TN*, p. 209.

20 *WBA*, p. 279 and *MNT*, I, 7, quoting Sir Nicholas Throckmorton.

21 Glete, *Navies and Nations*, I, 118. *ARN*, pp. 115–18, gives the older judgement on Elizabeth's naval policy.

22 Glasgow, 'Elizabethan Undeclared War', p. 26.

23 *TN*, pp. 209–12. *MF*, IV, 26–9. Glasgow, 'Undeclared War', pp. 23–36; and 'Oared Vessels', p. 371. *WBA*, pp. 251–8. *EWP*, p. 553. Cruikshank, *Elizabeth's Army*, p. 213.

24 Glasgow, 'Le Havre Expedition', pp. 281–8; and 'Oared Vessels', p. 373. 'English Royal Ships lost at Caudebec, 1562', *MM* LI (1965), p. 356; and 'The Wreck of the Greyhound – 1563', *MM* LII (1966), p. 78. *WBA*, pp. 265–7. *TN*, p. 214. *MF*, IV, 36–7.

25 Glasgow, 'Le Havre Expedition', pp. 290–3. *MF*, IV, 39–3.

26 *MF*, IV, 44–5.

27 Glasgow, 'Le Havre Expedition' p. 289. *TN*, p. 215. Appleby, 'Devon Privateering'. Michael J. G. Stanford,

'The Raleighs take to the Sea', *MM* XLVIII (1962), pp. 18–35. French, 'Privateering'. *WBA*, p. 281

28 Mas Latrie, 'Du droit de marque'. Chaplais, 'Règlement des conflits'. Kendall, *Private Men-of-War*, pp. 3–4. Tenison, *Elizabethan England*, VIII, 200. Powell, *Bristol Privateers*, p.xvi.

29 'Our soverane lord and lordis of consale ar sickirlie informit that ane certane [number] of his liegis, maisteris, awnaris and marinaris of schippis [dwell]and in Leith is to depart in weirefare, and be thar rubrys and spulzeis maid upon frenndis thai have causit our soverane lord and his liegis to have mony inymyis quhilkis war frenndis before, and presuponis that thai sall do siclik in tyme tocum . . .': *Acts of the Lords of Council in Public Affairs 1501–1554*, ed. R. K. Hannay (Edinburgh, 1932), pp. 219–20. 'Sickirlie' = certainly, 'quhilkis' = which, 'presuponis' = assumes, 'siclik' = likewise.

30 *Acta Curiae Admirallatus Scotiae 1557–1562*, ed. T. C. Wade (Stair Soc. Vol.2, 1937), pp. 194–203. MacDougall, *James IV*, p. 239.

31 The 'lines of amity' ran west of the Azores and south of the Canaries, so the Atlantic islands were open to foreign trade.

32 Davis, *Commercial Revolution*, pp. 3, 6. Croft, 'English Commerce with Spain', pp. 236–7. Scammell, 'Atlantic Islands', pp. 297–300.

33 *WBA*, pp. 290–2. Wernham, 'Elizabethan War Aims', pp. 343–4.

34 Andrews, *Drake's Voyages*, pp. 16–29; and *Trade Plunder and Settlement*, pp. 116–28. Williamson, *Hawkins of Plymouth*, pp. 57–146; and *Drake*, pp. 52–90. Wright, *English Voyages*, pp. 7–26. Corbett, *Drake*, I, 397–9. *TN*, pp. 221–2. *BMO*, I, 4–5.

35 *MF*, IV, 102–18. Dietz, 'Huguenot and English Corsairs'. Williamson, *Hawkins of Plymouth*, pp. 165–70.

36 Conyers Read, 'Queen Elizabeth's Seizure of the Duke of Alva's Pay-Ships', *JMH* V (1933), pp. 443–64. *TN*, p. 218. *BMO*, I, 6–34.

37 Pollitt, 'Mobilization of English Resources', p. 19.

38 *WBA*, pp. 299–308.

39 Williamson, *Hawkins of Plymouth*, pp. 173–7.

16 The Galley and the Galleon

1 Salisbury, 'Woolwich Ship'.

2 Anderson, *English Men-of-War*, pp. 5–6. Davies, 'Supply Services', p. 21.

3 'La plus triomphante chose que jamaiz marinier vit': *MF*, III, 176. 'Smisurata grandezza tal che si stima dover esse innavigabile': Braudel, *Mediterranean*, I, 298. Mollat, "'Être roi sur la mer"', p. 296. K. G. Davies, *The North Atlantic World in the Seventeenth Century* (Minneapolis, 1974), p. 32.

4 Rodger, 'Broadside Gunnery'.

5 Cleves, *Toutes manieres de guerroyer*, pp. 125–44. Conflans, 'Le livre des "faiz de la Marine"', pp. 25–7, 40–4. Weber, *De seinboken*, pp. 23–7. Extracts from the *Espejo de Navegantes* of Alonso de Chaves, printed by Fernández Duro, *Armada Española*, I, 379–91, and translated by Corbett, *Fighting Instructions*, pp. 6–13; Bytharne, 'Book of War'. The English orders wrongly attributed to Thomas Audley, printed by Corbett, *Fighting Instructions*, pp. 14–17, and discussed by C. S. L. Davies, 'Naval Discipline in the Early Sixteenth Century', *MM* XLVIII (1962), pp. 223–4. De Jonge, *Nederlandsche Zeewesen*, I, 736–46. Oliveira, *A arte da guerra do mar*.

6 Tenison, *Elizabethan England*, IV, 191, gives an example of a man killed by the concussion of gunfire.

7 Digby, *Journal*, p. 100.

8 Konstam, 'Naval Artillery', pp. 99–114. Laughton, 'Early Tudor Ship Guns'. Howard, 'Early Ship Guns'. Caruana, *Sea Ordnance*, pp. 5–22. Kenyon, 'Ordnance and the king's fleet'. Guilmartin, 'Guns and Gunnery', pp. 145–6.

9 Nance, 'Ship of the Renaissance', p. 291. Laughton, 'Early Tudor Ship Guns',

pp. 251–4. Konstam, 'Naval Artillery', p. 144. Howard, *Ships of War*, p. 45. Anderson, 'The *Mary Gonson*'.

10 'Auz deux costes du gouvernail, à chacun un [*scil.* canon de fonte, ou de fer], affustez comme ils doibvent estre en tel cas. Et doibvent avoir les portes qui se lievent à cordes, quand on veult, pour tirer desdicts bastons, quand le temps le peult porter': Cleves, *Toutes manieres de guerroyer*, p. 128.

11 Mollat, '"Être roi sur la mer"', p. 291. Laughton, 'Early Tudor Ship Guns', pp. 250–1. Howard, 'Early Ship Guns', p. 440.

12 Rule & Dobbs, 'Tudor Warship', pp. 27–8.

13 This is the figure suggested by calculation from the surviving hull of the ship.

14 Glasgow, 'Elizabethan Navy in Ireland', p. 306.

15 Laughton, 'Early Tudor Ship Guns', pp. 250–6. Howard, *Ships of War*, pp. 46–9.

16 Laughton, 'Early Tudor Ship Guns', pp. 259, 264–6, 275–8.

17 *BND*, pp. 120–1. Scammell, 'War at Sea', p. 187.

18 Guilmartin, *Gunpowder and Galleys*, pp. 210–11. J. R. Hale, 'Men and Weapons: the Fighting Potential of Sixteenth Century Venetian Galleys', in *Renaissance War Studies* (London, 1983), pp. 309–31 (originally in *War and Society* I [1975], pp. 1–23).

19 The best general treatments of galleys are Olesa Muñido, *La galera*, and Guilmartin, *Gunpowder and Galleys*. See also Guilmartin, 'Artillery Armament'; Olesa Muñido, *La organización naval*, I, 313–14; Lane, *Venetian Ships and Shipbuilders*, pp. 9–33; Boyer, 'Artillerie et tactique navale'; Fernández Duro, *Armada Española*, I, 323–4; Padfield, *Guns at Sea*, p. 19; Mollat, '"Être roi sur la mer"', pp. 294–5.

20 Glete, *Navies and Nations*, I, 140.

21 Cleves, *Toutes manieres de guerroyer*, pp. 128–9. In Vroom's painting of the Armada of 1588 (Pl. 47) in the Tiroler Landesmuseum Ferdinandeum, Innsbruck, the *San Martín* has a pair of guns mounted thus.

22 Rodger, 'Broadside Gunnery', develops this argument in more detail.

23 Elton, 'War and the English', p. 11. Oliveira, *A arte da guerra do mar*, p. 67.

24 Anderson, *English Men-of-War*, p. 6. Anderson, 'Henry VIII's "Great Galley"'. *TN*, p. 71.

25 Anderson, 'Armaments in 1540'.

26 Glasgow, 'Naval Administration', p. 4. *ARN*, p. 109. Oliveira, *A arte da guerra do mar*, pp. 66–7.

27 *MF*, III, 458–9; IV, 449, 552. Casada Soto, *Los barcos españoles*, p. 192. Rotz, *Idrography*, p. 17.

28 Martine Acerra, 'Observations de Nicolas Nicolay d'Arfeuille, cosmographe du roi, touchant la diversité des navires (Paris, 1582)', in *La France et la mer*, ed. Masson & Vergé-Franceschi, pp. 339–52, at p. 345. Corbett, *Drake*, I, 34–7, 52. Glasgow, 'Oared Vessels', p. 374. *MF*, III, 422, 458–45.

29 I.e. the Italian *galea sottile*, a light or war galley.

30 Etienne Taillemite, 'Les ordonnances de marine au XVIe siècle', in *La France et la mer*, ed. Masson & Vergé-Franceschi, pp. 55–68, at p. 57. Bennell, 'English Oared Vessels', pp. 180–2. The 'Bank' is the South Bank in Southwark, still a haunt of common players and evil-disposed persons to-day.

31 Bennell, 'English Oared Vessels', pp. 180–5. *ARN*, p. 125. Corbett, *Drake*, I, 383–5. Glasgow, 'Oared Vessels'. Boulind, 'Ships of Private Origin', pp. 403–7. Davies, 'Supply Services', p. 16. Adair, 'English Galleys', pp. 508–11.

32 *ARN*, pp. 58–60. Corbett, *Drake*, pp. 25–32.

33 Corbett, *Drake*, I, 57–8, quoting Lisle.

34 Glasgow, 'Oared Vessels', p. 376.

35 Ashley, 'Office of Ordnance', p. 123. Kirsch, *Galleon*, p. 14, suggests that he may have been the brother of the painter and chartmaker Cornelis Anthoniszoon (for whom see *MGN*, I, 241–3). It is remarkable and deplorable

that the information on the 'Anthony Roll' has never been fully printed.

36 Glasgow, 'H.M.S. Tiger'; and 'Oared Vessels', p. 376. *TN*, pp. 95, 195. Howard, *Ships of War*, pp. 81–3. Kirsch, *Galleon*, pp. 11–12.

37 The significant exception is Dutch, in which *galjoen* refers not to the ship, but to her characteristic feature, the beakhead.

38 Scammell, 'War at Sea', p. 180.

39 Rodríguez-Salgado, *Armada*, pp. 162–3. *ARN*, p. 126. Bjorn Landström, *The Royal Warship Vasa*, trans. Jeremy Franks (Stockholm, 1988), pp. 9–10. Phillips, *Six Galleons*, pp. 44, 230; and 'Caravel and Galleon', pp. 98–106, 114. Nance, 'Ship of the Renaissance', p. 294. Kirsch, *Galleon*, pp. 3–14. Casada Soto, *Los barcos españoles*, p. 193. Niels M. Probst, 'The Introduction of Flushed-Planked Skin in Northern Europe – and the Elsinore Wreck', in Westerdahl, *Crossroads in Ancient Shipbuilding*, pp. 143–52. Olesa Muñido, *La organización naval*, I, 265. Corbett, *Successors of Drake*, pp. 417 n.3, 421. Martin, 'Ships of the Spanish Armada', pp. 45–8. Lane, *Venetian Ships and Shipbuilders*, pp. 50–1. Barfod, 'Den danske orlogsflåde', p. 267. Corbett, *Drake*, I,24–33, and *Spanish War*, pp. 337–9, now requires some modification.

40 Konstam, 'Naval Artillery', p. 87. Davies, 'Supply Services', p. 88.

41 Bull, 'The Furie of the Ordnance', pp. 48–52. Konstam, 'Naval Artillery', pp. 74–5. Guilmartin, *Gunpowder and Galleys*, pp. 284–91.

42 Rule, *Mary Rose*, p. 165.

43 Davies, 'Supply Services', pp. 34–41.

44 Davies, 'Supply Services', pp. 43, 89. Bull, 'The Furie of the Ordnance', pp. 35–6. Konstam, 'Naval Artillery', p. 83. Schubert, *Iron and Steel Industry*, pp. 171–2. Howard L. Blackmore, 'The Boxted Bombard', *Antiquaries' Journal* LXXVII (1987), pp. 86–96.

45 Guilmartin, '*Santíssimo Sacramento*', p. 567.

46 The Ordnance Board paid £40–60/ton for bronze ordnance (*ARN*, p. 159); captured Spanish guns were priced for scrap in 1586 at £6 13s 4d/ton cast iron, £60/ton brass (Corbett, *Spanish War*, p. 90). In practice the differential varied a good deal with the price of copper.

47 *ARN*, p. 159.

48 Bull, 'The Furie of the Ordnance', p. 37. Cleere & Crossley, *Iron Industry*, pp. 117–30. Schubert, *Iron and Steel Industry*, pp. 249–53. Goring, 'Wealden Ironmasters'. For the Ordnance Board, see below pp. 232–3.

49 Cleere & Crossley, *Iron Industry*, pp. 170–2. Goring, 'Wealden Ironmasters', pp. 217–18. Schubert, *Iron and Steel Industry*, p. 253. PRO: E 101/64/18, E 134/45 Elizabeth/Hil/19.

50 These serpentines, bases, slings, murderers etc are described by Smith, 'Swivel guns'.

51 Davies, 'Supply Services', p. 33.

52 Bull, 'The Furie of the Ordnance', p. 37.

53 See Lewis, 'Armada Guns' and *Spanish Armada*; Mattingley, *Spanish Armada*; Thompson, 'Spanish Armada Guns'; Martin & Parker, *Spanish Armada*.

54 Corbett, *Spanish War*, pp. 315–36. *MNT*, IV, 36–42.

55 Guilmartin, 'Guns and Gunnery'; and '*Santíssimo Sacramento*'. Caruana, *Sea Ordnance*, pp.xiii, xviii.

56 Caruana, *Sea Ordnance*, pp. 8–9. Rodger, 'Elizabethan Naval Gunnery'.

57 Bull, 'The Furie of the Ordnance', pp. 168–72.

58 Hawkins, *Observations*, p. 130.

59 *MNT*, IV, 43.

60 Andrews, *Last Voyage of Drake & Hawkins*, pp. 104–5, quoting Thomas Maynarde; cf. Maynarde, *Sir Francis Drake his Voyage, 1595*, ed. W. D. Cooley (HS Vol.4, 1849), p. 23.

61 Caruana, *Sea Ordnance*, p.xvii. See below, p. 265 and Rodger, 'Elizabethan Naval Gunnery', for firing and loading drill.

62 Guilmartin, '*Santíssimo Sacramento*', p. 563.

63 Ashley, 'Office of Ordnance', p. 53. A. J. Marsh, 'The Taking of Goree, 1758', *MM* LI (1965), pp. 117–30, at p. 118.

64 Caruana, *Sea Ordnance*, pp. 184–9. Guilmartin, 'Guns and Gunnery', pp. 139–41.

65 Cerezo Martínez, *Las Armadas de Felipe II*, pp. 177–9. Andrews, *Spanish Caribbean*, pp. 102, 145, 164; and *English Privateering Voyages*, pp. 278–9. Wright, *English Voyages*, p. 203. *BMO*, I, 314, 532; III, 241–2, 257. Richard Boulind, 'Shipwreck and Mutiny in Spain's Galleys on the Santo Domingo Station, 1583', *MM* LVIII (1972), pp. 297–330, at pp. 298–9. Hoffman, *Defense of the Caribbean*, p. 174.

66 *MNT*, II, 163; cf. Corbett, *Successors of Drake*, pp. 369–77, and HMC *Salisbury*, XII, 183–4.

67 HMC *Salisbury*, XII, 162.

68 Mainwaring, *Works*, II, 131.

69 Lewis, 'Armada Guns', XXVIII, 273.

70 Wright, *Further English Voyages*, p. 44.

71 Goodman, *Power and Penury*, p. 108. *ARN*, p. 156.

72 Mainwaring, *Works*, II, 184.

73 Butler, *Dialogues*, p. 259. Nathaniel Butler was an early Stuart voyager and colonial governor.

74 Smith, *Sea Grammar*, p. 72, drawing on Mainwaring. This is Captain John Smith, first governor of Virginia.

75 Oliveira, *A arte da guerra do mar*, p. 127.

76 Phillips, *Los Tres Reyes*, p. 8.

77 '... porque a la yda es necesario embiarlas, según comen los ingleses, cargadas de vitualla, y a la vuelta, quando tuviesen el comercio seguro, han de dexar la mitad de la nao vazía para ellos, siendo tan largo el viaje': Don Bernardino de Mendoza to Philip II, 16 July 1583, in *BMO*, I,393. Dyer, 'Elizabethan Sailorman', p. 136.

78 Phillips, 'Caravel and Galleon', p. 106. Andrews, *Trade, Plunder and Settlement*, p. 25; and 'Elizabethan Seaman', p. 246. Rodger, 'Guns and Sails'.

79 Wright, *English Voyages*, p. 254, quoting *Sir Francis Drake Reviv'd* of 1628.

80 Corbett, *Spanish War*, pp. 339–41; and *Drake*, I, 33–4, 138. Glasgow, 'Oared Vessels', pp. 373–5. Andrews, *Elizabethan Privateering*, pp. 35–6; and *English Privateering Voyages*, p. 19.

81 Donno, *Madox Diary*, p. 114. Richard Madox was her chaplain on Fenton's expedition.

82 Barker, '"Many may peruse us"'; and 'Design in the Dockyards'. Dotson, 'Treatises on Shipbuilding'. Probst, 'Nordeuropæisk spanteopslagning', pp. 7–11.

83 Howard, *Ships of War*, pp. 82–3.

84 Barker, '"Many may peruse us"', p. 539 n.2, quoting John Davis's *The Seaman's Secrets* of 1594.

85 Waters, *Navigation*, p. 168, quoting the chronicler Holinshed.

86 *ARN*, p. 132, quoting James Montgomery.

87 Probst, 'Nordeuropæisk spanteopslagning', pp. 7–10.

88 Cerezo Martínez, *Las Armadas de Felipe II*, pp. 181–2. Pérez-Mallaína Bueno & Torres Ramírez, *La Armada del Mar del Sur*, pp. 112, 119, 252–3.

89 'Quasi scherzando' (the reporter was a Venetian): Braudel, *Mediterranean*, I, 230.

90 Corbett, *Successors of Drake*, p. 190.

91 I echo a theme of many of K. R. Andrews's writings. See also Rodger, 'Broadside Gunnery'.

17 The Council of the Marine

1 The (rather low) valuation of the ten year-old *Galleon Leicester* when the Earl her owner died in 1588: Stone, *Crisis of the Aristocracy*, p. 364. The Queen had just bought the new and slightly bigger *Ark Ralegh* for £5,000.

2 Stone, *Crisis of the Aristocracy*, p. 366.

3 *TN*, pp. 50–2, 74. Davies, 'Administration', p. 270; and 'Supply Services', pp. 103–5.

4 Oppenheim, *VCH Kent*, II, 339. *ARN*, p. 71.

5 Davies, 'Administration', p. 271. Johns, 'Principal Officers', p. 35. *TN*, pp. 68–72. Davies, 'Supply Services', pp. 106–7.

6 *TN*, pp. 75–80. *ARN*, pp. 83–4. Davies, 'Supply Services', pp. 107–10, 146. Harris, *Trinity House*, pp. 24–5.

7 Colvin, *King's Works*, IV, 492.
8 *TN*, pp. 69–70, 80, 89–90. *ARN*, pp. 68–72. Oppenheim, *VCH Kent*, II, 340. MacDougall, *James IV*, pp. 235–6. *ERS*, IV, xlviii–xlix. Frederic Hendry, 'James IV and the Scottish Navy', *Aberdeen University Review* VII (1919–20), pp. 46–8. Charnock, *Marine Architecture*, II, 106–7. Hopton's contract is printed in *BND*, pp. 121–2.
9 *TN*, pp. 81–4. *ARN*, pp. 85–7. Davies, 'Administration', pp. 272–4; and 'Supply Services', pp. 112–15, 141–3. Johns, 'Principal Officers', p. 41. Pollitt, 'Elizabethan Navy Board', pp. 27–31. *BND*, pp. 95–6. Guy, *Tudor England*, p. 189.
10 Davies, 'Supply Services', p. 115.
11 Davies, 'Supply Services', p. 118, quoting PRO: E 351/2194.
12 Glasgow, 'Philip and Mary's War', p. 325; and 'Vice Admiral Woodhouse', pp. 254–5.
13 Davies, 'Supply Services', pp. 148–50.
14 Andrews, *Drake's Voyages*, pp. 9–13; and 'Cecil and Mediterranean Plunder', pp. 531–2.
15 *TN*, p. 77. Davies, 'Administration', pp. 269–70.
16 Pollitt, 'Elizabethan Navy Board', pp. 107–17.
17 *EWP*, pp. 25–9. Pollitt, 'Elizabethan Navy Board', pp. 43–52. Kenny, *Elizabeth's Admiral*, pp. 49, 60. *MNT*, II, 267–86.
18 Glasgow, 'Philip and Mary's War', p. 322.
19 *ARN*, p. 112.
20 *TN*, pp. 4, 166–8. Glasgow, 'Naval Administration', pp. 3–8. *ARN*, pp. 112–13. *BND*, pp. 70–1.
21 Pollitt, 'Elizabethan Navy Board', p. 203.
22 *ARN*, pp. 113–14. Pollitt, 'Elizabethan Navy Board', pp. 203–9.
23 Printed *BND*, pp. 62–70.
24 Two fewer than the Danish fleet in the same year; Barfod, 'Den danske orlogsflåde', p. 269.
25 Corbett, *Drake*, I, 133–42. Glasgow, 'Philip and Mary's War', pp. 326–7; and 'Naval Administration', pp. 11–15. *TN*, pp. 179–82.
26 Corbett, *Drake*, I, 138–41. Pollitt, 'Elizabethan Navy Board', pp. 221–2.
27 Pollitt, 'Rationality and Expedience', pp. 72–5; and 'Elizabethan Navy Board', p. 221. Corbett, *Drake*, I, 139–40. De Beer, 'Lord High Admiral', prints the 1560 instructions.
28 *ARN*, p. 73. Pett, *Autobiography*, pp.xx–xxv.
29 *ARN*, p. 103.
30 *ARN*., pp. 73–4. Davies, 'Administration', p. 277; and 'Supply Services', pp. 74–83. *BND*, pp. 98–9.
31 *BND*, pp. 122–6.
32 *ARN*, pp. 128, 150–2. Glasgow, 'Vice Admiral Woodhouse'; and 'Naval Administration', p. 10. Pollitt, 'Elizabethan Navy Board', p. 219.
33 Davies, 'Administration', pp. 286–8; and 'Supply Services', pp. 119–36. Ashley, 'Office of Ordnance', pp. 10–81. Caruana, *Sea Ordnance*, pp. 13–32. Bull, 'The Furie of the Ordnance', pp. 149–57. Rodger, 'Elizabethan Naval Gunnery'. PRO: E 101/64/31 (Accounts of Winter as 'Master of Ordnance for Sea Causes', 1561–63). *BND*, pp. 118–20.
34 *TN*, pp. 84–5. Davies, 'Supply Services', pp. 172–6.
35 To T. Wolsey, 5 April 1513: Spont, *War with France*, p. 105.
36 To T. Wolsey, 5 April 1513: Spont, *War with France*, pp. 104–6 (quoted pp. 104–5), 126–9, 154–61.
37 Davies, 'Supply Services', p. 280, quoting PRO: SP 10/1 p. 799.
38 *ARN*, pp. 103–4. *TN*, pp. 86, 151, 203. Davies, 'Administration', p. 176.
39 *TN*, pp. 203–4. *ARN*, pp. 140–1. *BND*, pp. 102–3. HMC *Salisbury*, I, 293. C. S. L. Davies, 'Les rations alimentaires de l'armée et de la marine anglaise au XVIe siècle', *Annales* XVIII (1963), pp. 139–41.
40 *TN*, pp. 204–6. *ARN*, pp. 141–2. Pollitt, 'Elizabethan Navy Board', pp. 232–3.
41 Corbett, *Spanish War*, p. 263. HMC *Salisbury*, X, 405, which however assumes rather small tuns; with a standard 36-gal. barrel it should be just under 5 tuns.
42 *TN*, p. 207. *BND*, pp. 103–6. Andrews,

Elizabethan Privateering, pp. 39–40. Scammell, 'Sinews of War', pp. 365–6. Phillips, 'Caravel and Galleon', p. 106. Andrews, 'Elizabethan Seaman', p. 246. The whole subject of victualling technology needs research.

43 MacDougall, 'James IV's *Great Michael*', p. 43.

44 *ARN*, pp. 93–4. Pollitt, 'Elizabethan Navy Board', p. 29. *BND*, pp. 96–8. Hale, *War and Society*, p. 233.

45 *WBA*, p. 184. Dietz, *English Government Finance*, p. 202. Loades, 'King's Ships', p. 35.

46 Glasgow, 'Le Havre Expedition', p. 293.

47 *ARN*, p. 161.

18 The Spanish War

1 P. J. Blok, 'De Watergeuzen in Engeland (1568–1572)', *Bijdragen voor Vaterlandsche Geschiedenis en Oudheidkunde* 3rd S. IX (1896), pp. 226–63. J. C. A. de Meij, *De Watergeuzen en de Nederlanden 1568–1572* (Amsterdam, 1972). J. B. Black, 'Queen Elizabeth, the Sea Beggars and the Capture of Brille, 1572', *EHR* XLVI (1931), pp. 30–47. French, 'Privateering'. Parker, *Dutch Revolt*, pp. 126–42. Riaño Lozano, *Los medios navales*, pp. 59–60. Cerezo Martínez, *Las Armadas de Felipe II*, pp. 165, 242. Gómez-Centurión Jiménez, *Felipe II*, pp. 108–13.

2 Pi Corrales, *Felipe II*, pp. 144–51. Gómez-Centurión Jiménez, *Felipe II*, p. 111. Fernández Duro, *Armada Española*, II, 266–74. Casada Soto, *Los barcos españoles*, p. 40.

3 Riaño Lozano, *Los medios navales*, pp. 71–87. Pi Corrales, *Felipe II*, pp. 132–3. Fernández Duro, *Armada Española*, II, 269–70, 277–85.

4 Pi Corrales, *La Otra Invencible*. *BMO*, I, 92–6.

5 Quinn & Ryan, *England's Sea Empire*, pp. 79–81. Davies, *North Atlantic World*, p. 25. Boulind, 'Spanish Control', pp. 234, 242, 247. Scammell, *World Encompassed*, p. 438. Aydelotte, 'Elizabethan Seamen', p. 2.

6 Andrews, *Spanish Caribbean*, p. 86, 91–2. Scammell, *World Encompassed*, p. 439.

7 Andrews, *Elizabethan Privateering*, pp. 161–2. Casada Soto, *Los barcos españoles*, pp. 27–34. Cerezo Martínez, *Las Armadas de Felipe II*, pp. 83, 126, 174–5. Hoffman, *Defense of the Caribbean*, *passim*. Phillips, *Six Galleons*, pp. 9–15.

8 Chaunu, *Séville et l'Atlantique*, VI, ii, 876–80. Cerezo Martínez, *Las Armadas de Felipe II*, pp. 174–75. *BMO*, II, xxv.

9 Corbett, *Drake*, I, 144–89, quoting (at p. 189) *Sir Francis Drake Reviv'd* of 1628. Andrews, *Spanish Caribbean*, p. 139. Chaunu, *Séville et l'Atlantique*, VIII, ii, 514. Wright, *English Voyages*, pp. 245–326.

10 Andrews, *Spanish Caribbean*, pp. 140–5. Wright, *English Voyages*, pp.xlviii–lxiii, 327–31. *PN*, X, 77–81. Andrews, *Drake's Voyages*, pp. 33–9.

11 Rowse, *Grenville*, pp. 89–110. Andrews, *Drake's Voyages*, pp. 47–59. Chope, 'Grenville'.

12 Corbett, *Drake*, I, 199–200. Sugden, *Drake*, pp. 81–6.

13 Andrews, 'Aims of Drake's Expedition'; and *Drake's Voyages*, pp. 50–7. Taylor, 'More Light on Drake'. Spate, *Spanish Lake*, pp. 238–42. MacCaffrey, *Making of Policy*, p. 332.

14 *PN*, XI, 114–15, printing 'The Famous Voyage of Sir Francis Drake'.

15 Drake, *World Encompassed*. Andrews, *Drake's Voyages*, pp. 58–81. Corbett, *Drake*, I, 216–310. *BMO*, I, 143–64. Nuttall, *New Light on Drake*.

16 Waters, *Navigation*, p. 92, quoting the narrative of Lok's second Guinea voyage from Richard Eden's *Decades of the Newe World*; but English ships with French pilots had been visiting 'Brazil' (i.e. the northern parts of South America) for some years, and may have crossed the Equator: Marsden, 'Voyage of the *Barbara*', pp. 3–4.

17 Waters, *Navigation*, pp. 79–80, 101.

18 Richard Boulind, 'Drake's Navigational Skills', *MM* LIV (1968), pp. 349–71, depreciates his skill on the ground that it

was based on the use of captured charts and pilots; one could argue that assembling the best sources of information was part of the navigator's skills rather than a reproach to them.

19 Andrews, *Drake's Voyages*, pp. 81–3; and *Elizabethan Privateering*, p. 4 (quoting John Hooker). Spate, *Spanish Lake*, pp. 263–4.

20 Andrews, *Drake's Voyages*, p. 81, quoting Stow's *Annals*.

21 Andrews, *Drake's Voyages*, p. 85.

22 Glasgow, 'Elizabethan Navy in Ireland', pp. 295–8. Sir Charles Petrie, 'The Hispano-Papal Landing at Smerwick', *Irish Sword* IX (1969–70), pp. 82–94. Glasgow & Salisbury, 'Smerwick Map'. Rebholz, *Greville*, pp. 42–5.

23 *ARN*, p. 175. Andrews, *Ships, Money and Politics*, pp. 204–5. *BND*, pp. 107–9.

24 *BMO*, I, 319–20.

25 Taylor, *Fenton's Voyage*. Donno, *Madox Diary*.

26 Casada Soto, *Los barcos españoles*, p. 45.

27 Read, *Walsingham*, II, 51–2. Donno, *Madox Diary*, p. 18. Andrews, *Drake's Voyages*, p. 88. *WBA*, p. 362.

28 Although fought between S. Miguel and Sta Maria, this is usually called the battle of Terceira (from the Spanish 'Las Terceras' = the Azores).

29 Pi Corrales, *Felipe II*, pp. 214–63. Ricardo Cerezo Martínez, 'La conquista de la isla Tercera (1583)', *RHN* I (1983), No.3 pp. 5–45; and *Las Armadas de Felipe II*, pp. 292–304. Casada Soto, *Los barcos españoles*, pp. 47–50. Tenison, *Elizabethan England*, IV, 167–215. *MF*, IV, 183–92.

30 *TN*, p. 262. Casada Soto, *Los barcos españoles*, p. 51. *BMO*, I, 395.

31 Cerezo Martínez, *Las Armadas de Felipe II*, p. 166. *BMO*, I, 412–13. Stradling, *Armada of Flanders*, p. 7. Parker, *Dutch Revolt*, p. 213.

32 Parker, *Dutch Revolt*, pp. 216–17, quoting the Earl of Leicester. *WBA*, pp. 367–8. Read, *Walsingham*, II, 116–17.

33 Adams, 'Outbreak of the Elizabethan Naval War', p. 52. *WBA*, p. 370. *EWP*, pp. 74–6.

34 Read, *Walsingham*, III, 82–3.

35 Corbett, *Drake*, I, 319, quoting the Earl of Sussex from *CSPS*, III, 307.

36 Stradling, *Decline of Spain*, p. 30: Philip ruled the Aragonese, Portuguese, Burgundian, Aztec and Inca empires in addition to his ancestral kingdom of Castile.

37 Thompson, 'Naval Warfare', pp. 70–2.

38 Parker, *Army of Flanders*, pp. 233–41. *BMO*, III, 1134–5. Morineau, *Incroyables gazettes*, pp. 81–2. Thompson, *War and Government*, pp. 68–9. Davis, *Atlantic Economies*, p. 68.

39 Andrews, *Elizabethan Privateering*, p. 10. Dietz, *English Public Finance*, p. 55. Wernham, 'Elizabethan War Aims', p. 355. *EWP*, p. 64.

40 Parker, *Dutch Revolt*, pp. 217–18.

41 Andrews, *Drake's Voyages*, pp. 92–3.

42 Adams, 'Outbreak of the Elizabethan Naval War', pp. 45–52. *TN*, pp. 234–5. *BMO*, I, 482–6. Andrews, *Spanish Caribbean*, p. 148. Loades, 'King's Ships', p. 44.

43 Andrews, *Drake's Voyages*, p. 94.

44 The narratives and documents of this voyage are printed in Keeler, *Drake's West Indian Voyage*, Wright, *Further English Voyages*, and Corbett, *Spanish War*. Corbett, *Drake*, II, 1–59 is still worth reading.

45 Keeler, *Drake's West Indian Voyage*, pp. 9–23. Quinn & Ryan, *England's Sea Empire*, pp. 78–9. Wernham, 'Elizabethan War Aims', p. 362. Andrews, *Spanish Caribbean*, pp. 147–9.

46 Rebholz, *Greville*, p. 73, quoting Fulke Greville.

47 Andrews, *Spanish Caribbean*, pp. 150–2.

48 Wright, *Further English Voyages*, p.xxxii n.4. This was the official, registered cargo, to which a substantial percentage should be added for smuggled, unregistered bullion.

49 Andrews, *Trade, Plunder and Settlement*, p. 281; and *Elizabethan Privateering*, p. 162. Wright, *Further English Voyages*, pp.lxv—lxvi.

50 *BMO*, II, 94–6.

51 Parker, *Dutch Revolt*, pp. 218–19. Andrews, *Trade, Plunder and Settlement*, p. 229. *EWP*, p. 564.

52 *MNT*, I, 134–5. *TN*, p. 237 (cf. comments by G. Parker reviewing this book in *Sixteenth Century Journal* XXIV [1993], p. 1022).

53 *BMO*, III, 283; Drake claimed twelve.

54 'Cabo de las sorpresas': Chaunu, *Séville et l'Atlantique*, VIII, i, 267.

55 Corbett, *Spanish War*, pp. 97–206; and *Drake* II, 66–107. *TN*, pp. 239–41. Ribas Bensusan, *Asaltos a Cádiz*, pp. 40–59. Maura Gamazo, *El Designio de Felipe II*, pp. 181–203. Casada Soto, *Los barcos españoles*, p. 163. *BMO*, III, xxx–xxxiv, 241–57, 412, 425–8, 460. Robert Leng, 'Sir Francis Drake's memorable Service done against the Spaniards in 1587' ed. Clarence Hopper, in *Camden Miscellany V* (CS Vol.87, 1864).

56 Martin & Parker, *Spanish Armada*, pp. 131–2, 136. *BMO*, III, 1251–2, 1261–2, 1307–21.

57 Corbett, *Spanish War*, p. 131, often quoted by both English and Spanish historians, but not supported by any document in *BMO*. There was a serious shortage of cask, but it was nowhere attributed to destruction by Drake.

58 'Hallándose este corsario en la mar con el poder que trae, no se puede tener seguridad de ningunas yslas y costas maritimas, ni entenderse las probinçias que a de acometer; y asi es ynçierto el remedio que se puede prevenir': Bernardino de Escalante to Philip II, 2 May 1587, in Herrera Oria, *Felipe II*, p. 98; also *BMO*, III, 251, with minor variations.

59 *TN*, p. 242. Corbett, *Drake*, II, 108. Ribas Bensusan, *Asaltos a Cádiz*, pp. 60–2. Rodríguez-Salgado, 'Anglo-Spanish War', p. 20; and *Armada*, pp. 22–3. Cerezo Martínez, *Las Armadas de Felipe II*, p. 314. Herrera Oria, *Felipe II*, p. 21. *BMO*, III, xxxv. Chaunu, *Séville et l'Atlantique*, VIII, ii, 759.

60 To Sir F. Walsingham, 27 April 1587, in Corbett, *Spanish War*, p. 109.

19 The Advantage of Time and Place

1 Rodríguez-Salgado, 'Anglo-Spanish War', pp. 2–8.

2 Wernham, 'Elizabethan War Aims'. Andrews, *Trade, Plunder and Settlement*, pp. 226–9.

3 Wernham, 'Elizabethan War Aims', p. 340.

4 Cerezo Martínez, *Las Armadas de Felipe II*. Glete, *Navies and Nations*, I, 150–1. Casada Soto, *Los barcos españoles*, pp. 118–53. Thompson, 'Spanish Armada', pp. 70–3. Adams, 'Gran Armada', p. 245.

5 'El rey papelero': Braudel, *Mediterranean*, I, 372.

6 Thompson, 'Spanish Armada', p. 76; and *War and Government*, p. 33.

7 Koenigsberger, 'Western Europe', pp. 240–4, quoted p. 244. Pi Corrales, *Felipe II*, p. 271. There are numerous examples of Philip's approach in his correspondence with Santa Cruz and Parma, e.g. *BMO*, II, xxiv; III, lxxxv–lxxxix, 961, 1006–7; Herrera Oria, *La Armada Invencible*, p. 117; Fernández Duro, *La Armada Invencible*, I, 495.

8 There was similar advice from others, e.g. Bernadino de Escalante (Herrera Oria, *Felipe II*, pp. 86–7, and *La Armada Invencible*, pp. 371–8), Antonio de Guevara (*BMO*, III, 1750), and Juan Martínez de Recalde (Rodríguez Salgado, 'Pilots, Navigation and Strategy', p. 138).

9 *BMO*, I, 564; II, x, 45–74. Herrera Oria, *Felipe II*, p. 10. Casada Soto, *Los barcos españoles*, pp. 158–60.

10 *BMO*, II, 110–11. Pi Corrales, *Felipe II*, pp. 290–4.

11 O'Donnell, *Los sucesos de Flandes*, pp. 79–80. Cerezo Martínez, *Las Armadas de Felipe II*, p. 321 n.43.

12 Kraus, *Drake*, p. 129. In July 1587 the Consejo de Guerra made a similar proposal: *BMO*, III, 718–19.

13 'Y así, por lo que siempre he entendido de personas muy prácticas, es que la mayor fuerza que los ingleses han de poner, ha de ser en la mar, por cuyo respecto debe ir la Armada de S.M. muy superior a cualquiera de la que se junta en aquellas partes . . .': to Philip's secretary, Don Juan de Idiáquez, 5 March 1587 NS, in Maura Gamazo, *El Designio de Felipe II*, p. 169.

14 Rodríguez-Salgado, *Armada*, pp. 16–21.

15 *BMO*, III, lvii, 1006–7. Fernández Duro, *La Armada Invencible*, II, 7–10. Adams, *Armada Campaign*, pp. 12–13. Fernández-Armesto, *Spanish Armada*, pp. 82–8, 117–24. Adams, 'Battle that never was', pp. 176–7. Martin & Parker, *Spanish Armada*, pp. 112–19, 133–40. Rodríguez-Salgado, *Armada*, pp. 24–5.

16 'Iréys derecho al Canal de Inglaterra subiendo por él arriba hasta el cabo de Margat, para daros allí la mano con el Duque de Parma, mi sobrino, y allanar y asegurar el paso para su tránsito . . .': *BMO*, III, 106.

17 Herrera Oria, *Felipe II*, pp. 37–58; and *La Armada Invencible* pp. 88, 117. *BMO* III, lxxxv–lxxxviii, 1274, 1662–3. Rodríguez-Salgado, *Armada*, p. 27.

18 *BMO*, III, 951, 1083–5, 1238, 1830, 1834. Rodríguez-Salgado, *Armada*, pp. 25–26. O'Donnell, *Los sucesos de Flandes*, pp. 80–95.

19 'No le pueda al presente suceder mejor ni más honrosa suerte, ni hacer cosa que más gusto pueda dar a estos sus vasallos y más refrenados pueda tener a los émulos de la grandeza de Va. Ma. y a los herejes en particular que son los que más la temen, que establecer una buena y honrosa paz y evitarse del riesgo que se corre de los desastres que pueden acontecer . . .': to Philip II, 20 March 1588 NS, in Riaño Lozano, *Los medios navales*, p. 245.

20 Francisco Fernández Segado, 'Alejandro Farnesio en las Negociaciones de Paz entre España e Inglaterra (1586–1588)', *Hispania* XLV, p. 513. O'Donnell, 'Requirements of the Duke of Parma', p. 91.

21 *BMO*, III, lxii–lxxxv, 1195–1201, 1211, 1251–2, 1261–2, 1279–88, 1317–21, 1435–40, 1555. Thompson, 'Naval Warfare', pp. 81–2. Rodríguez-Salgado, *Armada*, pp. 29–30.

22 *BMO*, III, 734. Braudel, *Mediterranean*, I, 373 (and in the original French edn) spoils the point of the jibe by mistranslating it.

23 Martin & Parker, *Spanish Armada*, p. 156.

24 *BMO* III, lxxxix–xci, 1757. Martin & Parker, *Spanish Armada*, pp. 142–3. Herrera Oria, *La Armada Invencible*, p. 88.

25 *BMO*, I, xv; III, 1923. The well-known reference to sea-sickness in this letter as printed by Fernández Duro, *La Armada Invencible*, I, 415, is a misreading.

26 'La reputacion y opininion q[ue] el mundo oy tiene de su valor y prudencia': from Don Cristobal de Moura and Don J. de Idiáquez, 22 Jan 1588 NS, in Herrera Oria, *La Armada Invencible*, p. 152; cf. Martin & Parker, *Spanish Armada*, p. 148.

27 Thompson, 'Medina Sidonia', pp. 204–11. Pierson, 'Commander for the Armada' and *Commander of the Armada*, pp. 80–7. Kraus, *Drake*, pp. 132–3. Martin & Parker, *Spanish Armada*, pp. 146–7. Naish, 'Spanish Armada', pp. 11–13.

28 Casada Soto, *Los barcos españoles*, pp. 178–226, analyses the fleet in exhaustive detail.

29 Naish, 'Spanish Armada', pp. 22–5. Martin & Parker, *Spanish Armada*, pp. 158–63.

30 Martin & Parker, *Spanish Armada*, pp. 152–3. Mattingly, *Spanish Armada*, pp. 191–2.

31 Dietz, *English Public Finance*, p. 55. Wernham, 'Elizabethan War Aims', p. 355. *EWP*, pp. 64–7, 565–6.

32 PRO: SP 12/143 No.20. Corbett, *Spanish War*, p. 280. *WBA*, pp. 377–8.

33 *MNT*, I, 161.

34 Parker, '*Dreadnought* Revolution', p. 289.

35 Corbett, *Drake*, II, 113–15, 119–24. *DSA*, I, 51. HMC *Foljambe MSS* (15th R.App.V), pp. 109–10; quotation from Howard's orders of 20 December 1587, in the Karpeles Manuscript Library, Santa Barbara, California. (I am indebted to Professor Geoffrey Parker for a copy of this document.)

36 To Sir F. Walsingham, 28 Jan 1588: *DSA*, I, 51.

37 Howard's orders, in the Karpeles MS library; Corbett, *Drake*, II, 130. W. F. Tilton, 'Lord Burghley on the Spanish Invasion, 1588', *AHR* II (1896–97), pp. 93–8.

38 Read, *Walsingham*, III, 301.

39 Drake to the Privy Council, 30 March 1588, in *DSA*, I, 124.

40 Thomas Fenner to Sir F. Walsingham, 3 March 1588, in *DSA*, I, 92.

41 *DSA*, I, 148.

42 Corbett, *Drake*, II, 140–1.

43 Howard to Sir F. Walsingham. 13 June 1588, in *DSA*, I, 199; cf. *MNT*, IV, 198.

44 *DSA*, I, 137, 187, 197–205, 216, 220, 234–43.

45 Adams, *Armada Campaign*, p. 16. Corbett, *Drake* II, 158–73.

46 *DSA*, I, 285.

47 Corbett, *Drake*, II, 176.

48 Howard's orders of 20 December, in the Karpeles MS Library.

49 Rodríguez-Salgado, *Armada*, p. 27.

50 Sir W. Winter to the Navy Board, 28 Feb, and Howard to Burghley, 21 Feb 1588, in *DSA*, I, 81, 79. Howard's letter (PRO: SP 12/208 No.79) is misdated by Laughton.

51 The *Ark Royal*, his flagship, lately bought from Sir Walter Ralegh.

52 To Burghley, 29 Feb 1588, in *DSA*, I, 85–6.

53 Corbett, *Drake*, II, 178. Casada Soto, *Los barcos españoles*, pp. 178–228. Thompson, 'Naval Warfare', pp. 82–6; 'Gun Procurement'; and 'Spanish Armada Guns'. Adams, 'Gran Armada', p. 246.

54 O'Donnell, *Los sucesos de Flandes*, p. 145. Herrera Oria, *Felipe II*, p. 73. Fernández Duro, *La Armada Invencible*, II, 9–10. Fernández-Armesto, *Spanish Armada*, p. 124.

55 *BMO*, I, 83–4. Martin & Parker, *Spanish Armada*, pp. 23–6. Pierson, *Commander of the Armada*, p. 88. F. F. Olesa Muñido, 'Algunas consideraciones en torno a la Gran Armada', *RHN* I (1983) No.1, pp. 31–93, at pp. 83–4.

56 Rodger, 'Broadside Gunnery'.

57 Martin & Parker, *Spanish Armada*, 163–4, 285. Olesa Muñido, *La galera*, II, 107–19. Cerezo Martínez, 'La táctica naval'; and *Las Armadas de Felipe II*, pp. 141–4. Pierson, *Commander of the Armada*, p. 137. Older histories (e.g. Lewis, *Spanish Armada*, p. 117) wasted much time trying to arrange the Armada's squadrons into a plausible fighting order, not realizing that they were purely administrative units.

58 The events of the week's fighting are well-known and I have confined my notes for what follows to disputed points and quotations. Contemporary English narratives of the Armada campaign are printed by *DSA*, and Naish, 'Spanish Armada'. Spanish narratives are in Fernández Duro, *La Armada Invencible*, Herrera Oria, *La Armada Invencible* and *Felipe II*, Maura Gamazo, *El Designio de Felipe II*, and eventually *BMO*. The best modern account of the campaign is Martin & Parker, *Spanish Armada*, but Corbett, *Drake*, II, 173–285, is still the most detailed. Parker, '*Dreadnought* Revolution', adds some new evidence. Pierson, *Commander of the Armada*, has highly detailed battle plans, which, however, go well beyond reliable evidence and largely ignore winds, tides and shoals.

59 Nicholas Oseley (aboard the *Revenge*) to Sir F. Walsingham, 23 July 1588, in *DSA*, I, 302.

60 Sugden, *Drake*, p. 242 n.1. A very similar incident had happened in 1585, but in this case by day, when Drake was able to shift his flag to another ship as 'guide of the fleet' while he went off in pursuit of a strange sail: Keeler, *Drake's West Indian Voyage*, p. 91.

61 PRO: E 134/3 James I/Mich/19, quoting Drake's servant James Baron, who was present at the interview.

62 Fernández-Armesto, *Spanish Armada*, pp. 174–5.

63 Howard to Sussex, 22 July 1588, in *DSA*, I, 299.

64 Ubaldino's 'Relation of Proceedings', in *DSA*, I, 14.

65 Adams, 'The Battle that never was', pp. 187–91. Maura Gamazo, *El Designio de Felipe II*, p. 172. *BMO*, I, 400; II, 48, 290; III, lxxviii, 1549, 1793, 1799, 1872. Fernández Duro, *La Armada Invencible*, I, 417, 445.

66 *DSA*, II, 324–31 and Appendix II.

67 Martin & Parker, *Spanish Armada*, p. 181–5.
68 *Spanish Armada*, pp. 199–200, 203–4. Parker, '*Dreadnought* Revolution', pp. 278–82.
69 Rodger, 'Broadside Gunnery', pp. 310–14.
70 Howard to Sir F. Walsingham, 7 Aug 1588, in *DSA*, II, 54.
71 *DSA*, I, 341, corrected from the original, PRO: SP 12/213 No.64.
72 *DSA*, I, 343, 350, 361; II, 59, 68, 97–9. Rodríguez-Salgado, 'Pilots, Navigation and Strategy', p. 171 n.100.
73 Herrera Oria, *La Armada Invencible*, pp. 156–80. Rodríguez Salgado, 'Pilots, Navigation and Strategy'. Goodman, *Power and Penury*, p. 80.
74 *DSA*, II, 240.
75 Casada Soto, *Los barcos españoles*, pp. 245–9, gives a total of 92 survivors, including 19 small vessels and some which fell out before the Channel fighting.
76 Gracia Rivas, 'Medical Services', p. 212.
77 Fallon, *Armada in Ireland*, is a thorough guide. See also Martin, *Full Fathom Five*; and D. Higueras Rodríguez & M. P. San Pío Aladrén, 'Irish Wrecks of the Great Armada: the Testimony of the Survivors', in *God's Obvious Design*, ed. Gallagher & Cruikshank, pp. 143–66.
78 Herrera Oria, *Felipe II*, p. 169 prints Recalde's last letter.
79 Thompson, 'Medina Sidonia', pp. 200–1. Fernández-Armesto, *Spanish Armada*, pp. 208–9, 236.
80 Historians of meteorology do not agree on whether the weather was exceptionally bad that autumn; see K. S. Douglas, H. H. Lamb & C. Loader, *A Meteorological Study of July to October 1588: The Spanish Armada Storms* (University of East Anglia Climatic Research Unit Report No.6, Norwich, 1978), with supplement: K. S. Douglas & H. H. Lamb, *Weather Observations and a Tentative Meteorological Analysis of the Period May to July 1588* (1979); J. L. Anderson, 'Climatic Change, Sea-Power and Historical Discontinuity: the Spanish Armada and the Glorious Revolution of 1688', *The Great Circle* V (1983), pp. 13–23, at p. 16; S. Daultrey, 'The Weather of Northwest Europe during the Summer and Autumn of 1588', in *God's Obvious Design*, ed. Gallagher & Cruikshank, pp. 113–41.
81 Parker, *Dutch Revolt*, pp. 221–2. Martin & Parker, *Spanish Armada*, pp. 255–61.

20 The Method of Jason

1 *DSA*, II, 241–9. Parker, '*Dreadnought* Revolution', p. 280.
2 Sir J. Hawkins to Burghley, 4 Sep 1588, in *DSA*, II, 212–13.
3 To Sir F. Walsingham, 23 Aug 1588, in *DSA*, II, 148.
4 *WAA*, pp. 1–11.
5 Boulind, 'Spanish Control', p. 756, quoting Fuller's *Worthies* (Yorks, p. 203) on Cumberland.
6 Wernham, *Drake-Norris Expedition* and 'Portugal Expedition'; cf. *WAA*, pp. 16–133; *EWP*, pp. 86–94; Corbett, *Drake*, II, 294–333.
7 Edmund Palmer (English agent at St Jean-de-Luz), to Sir F. Walsingham, 25 July 1589 NS, in Wernham, *Drake-Norris Expedition*, p. 217. 'The Groyne' = Corunna.
8 Wernham, 'Elizabethan War Aims', pp. 352–3. *WAA*, pp. 137–80.
9 *WAA*, pp. 181–91.
10 *WAA*, pp. 268–420. *WRA*, p. 2. *EWP*, pp. 152–70.
11 *WAA*, pp. 364, 371, 390. *MF*, IV, 224–5.
12 *WAA*, pp. 488–513.
13 *WAA*, p. 528.
14 *WAA*, pp. 522–51. *EWP*, pp. 182–91. Nolan, 'Operations around Brest'.
15 Dickinson, 'Spanish Raid'. Cerezo Martínez, *Las Armadas de Felipe II*, pp. 400–1. Corbett, *Drake*, II, 380–1.
16 *WAA*, p. 236.
17 *WAA*, pp. 235–7. *MNT*, I, 236–9.
18 Cerezo Martínez, *Las Armadas de Felipe II*, p. 113. Phillips, *Six Galleons*, p. 29. Corbett, *Drake*, II, 340. *WAA*, pp. 243, 346. Wright, *Further English Voyages*, pp.lxxi–lxxxi. Pierson, *Commander of the*

Armada, p. 66. Andrews, *Spanish Caribbean*, p. 153.

19 *DSA*, I, 59–60. Wernham, 'Elizabethan War Aims', p. 358. Andrews, *Drake's Voyages*, pp. 149–51. Williamson, *Age of Drake*, p. 377.

20 *WAA*, pp. 239–45. Howell A. Lloyd, 'Sir John Hawkins's Instructions, 1590', *BIHR* XLIV (1971), pp. 125–8.

21 Thompson, *War and Government*, p. 32, quoting Don Guillén de Causas, former governor of Yucatán.

22 'La Armada del Mar Oceáno'. 'Armada' = armed [fleet]; the 'Ocean Sea' is the Atlantic, as distinct from 'the Sea', the Mediterranean.

23 Thompson, *War and Government*, pp. 33, 40, 192–3. Pierson, *Commander of the Armada*, p. 194.

24 Earle, *Revenge*, gives the most detailed account of this campaign, with new evidence. See also *WAA*, pp. 297–341.

25 *PN*, VII, 82, quoting the Dutch traveller Jan van Linschoten, who was in the Azores at the time. Earle, *Revenge*, p. 113. Ralegh's account is in *PN*, VII, 38–53, supported by Hawkins, *Observations*, p. 16; Tennyson's reference to delaying for the sick is pure embroidery.

26 *PN*, VII, 81. Butler, *Dialogues*, p. 303.

27 Earle, *Revenge*, p. 124. Parker, '*Dreadnought* Revolution', n.19.

28 Earle, *Revenge*, p. 137, but I cannot trace his reference.

29 The future Sir William Monson, in *MNT*, V, 172.

30 Wright, *Further English Voyages*, pp.lxxxv–lxxxvi. *WAA*, pp. 345–6. Earle, *Revenge*, pp. 149–61.

31 Kingsford, 'Taking of the Madre de Dios'. E. W. Bovill, 'The *Madre de Dios*', *MM* LIV (1968), pp. 129–52. C. R. Boxer, 'The Taking of the *Madre de Deus*, 1592', *MM* LXVII (1981), pp. 82–4. Williamson, *Cumberland*, pp. 91–100. W. R. Drake, 'Notes on the Capture of the "Great Carrack" in 1592', *Archaeologia* XXII (1829), pp. 209–40. *WAA*, pp. 446–8. Andrews, *Elizabethan Privateering*, p. 73. *MNT*, I, 292 (quoting Cecil).

32 Hawkins, *Observations*, pp. Spate, *Spanish Lake*, pp. 286–9. Pérez-Mallaína Bueno & Torres Ramírez, *La Armada del Mar del Sur*, pp. 252–3. Gerhard, *West Coast of New Spain*, pp. 79–80, 95.

33 Herrera Oria, *Felipe II*, pp. 86–7; and *La Armada Invencible*, pp. 371–8. *BMO*, II, 270; III, 1114. J. M. Cleary, 'Dr. Morys Clynnog's Invasion Projects of 1575–1576', *Recusant History* VIII (1966), pp. 300–22.

34 *WRA*, pp. 3–5. *EWP*, pp. 9–13, 453–91.

35 Williamson, *Cumberland*, p. 220.

36 *WRA*, pp. 126–9.

37 Andrews, *Last Voyage of Drake & Hawkins*, p. 86, quoting Thomas Maynarde.

38 Andrews, *Last Voyage of Drake & Hawkins*, prints all important documents on this expedition. See also *WRA*, pp. 25–7, 45–9; *MNT*, I, 312–40; Andrews, *Drake's Voyages*, pp. 159–77.

39 Jameson, 'New Spanish Documents', pp. 25–8.

40 Jameson, 'New Spanish Documents', p. 29.

41 Andrews, *Last Voyage of Drake & Hawkins*, pp. 237–49. *PN*, X, 226–65.

42 As argued by Corbett, *Drake*, II, 402–37; cf. Andrews, *Last Voyage of Drake & Hawkins*, pp. 7–9.

43 *TN*, pp. 263–4.

44 General narratives of the expedition are in *WRA*, pp. 55–106; *EWP*, pp. 114–121; Corbett, *Successors of Drake*, pp. 56–115; Pierson, *Commander of the Armada*, pp. 195–211; Kenny, *Elizabeth's Admiral*, pp. 167–96; Ribas Bensusan, *Asaltos a Cádiz*. Usherwood, *Counter-Armada*, and Corbett, 'Slyngisbie's Relation', print documents on the expedition.

45 Bruijn, *Dutch Navy*, p. 21. De Jonge, *Nederlandsche Zeewesen*, I, 142–5.

46 Usherwood, *Counter-Armada*, p. 151, quoting the journal of Sir George Carew, captain of the *Mary Rose*.

47 'Et quoniam in anno Domini 1588 id nobis tunc muneris assignatum erat a serenissima nostra Regina domina mea . . . idcirco non opinamur vobis ignotum esse . . .': *PN*, IV, 263; cf. HMC *Salisbury*, VI, 241–2. The Latin is by Dr Roger Marbeck, the queen's physician, who took part in the expedition.

48 *EWP*, pp. 118–19, quoting Essex. Hammer, 'Capture of Cadiz'.
49 Ribas Bensusan, *Asaltos a Cádiz*, p. 67; but the figure is hard to swallow.
50 S. R. Meyrick, 'Report of the Commissioners appointed to enquire into the amount of booty taken at Cadiz in 1596 . . .', *Archaeologia* XXII (1829), pp. 172–89, at pp. 175–8; *WRA*, p. 120, gives a lower figure.
51 *WRA*, pp. 108–12.
52 Curry, 'English Sea-Chaplains', p. 131. Usherwood, *Counter-Armada*, p. 112.
53 *MNT*, II, 7–8. P. S. Allen, 'Books brought from Cadiz in 1596', *EHR* XXXI (1916), pp. 606–10. Hammer, 'Capture of Cadiz'.
54 Chaunu, *Séville et l'Atlantique*, VIII, ii, 1017.
55 Don Luis de Fajardo to Philip II, in Corbett, *Successors of Drake*, p. 116.
56 *WRA*, pp. 132–40. Corbett, *Successors of Drake*, pp. 139–51.
57 PRO: WO 55/1627; cf. Parker, '*Dreadnought* Revolution'., pp. 274–7.
58 *PN*, IV, 239.
59 The opinion of Oppenheim, in *MNT*, II, 48 n.26.
60 *WRA*, pp. 116–21. *EWP*, p. 120. Hammer, 'Capture of Cadiz'.
61 *WRA*, pp. 143–78. *EWP*, pp. 126–9. Corbett, *Successors of Drake*, pp. 170–211. *MNT*, II, 24–83.
62 Don Martín de Padilla Manrique, also Count of Buendía, Count of Santa Gadea, and hereditary *Adelantado Mayor* of Castile; to the confusion of subsequent historians, he is referred to by all three titles as well as his name.
63 *WRA*, pp. 184–90. Corbett, *Successors of Drake*, pp. 212–27. Albert J. Loomie, 'An Armada Pilot's Survey of the English Coastline, October 1597', *MM* XLIX (1963), pp. 288–300.
64 *WRA*, pp. 186–94. Corbett, *Successors of Drake*, pp. 219–25, gives slightly different dates.
65 *WRA*, pp. 233–45.
66 HMC *Salisbury*, VIII, 209; cf. *WRA*, p. 251, and *MNT*, II, 94. 'Argoteses' = Ragusans.
67 *WRA*, pp. 259–72. *EWP*, pp. 525–6. Kenny, *Elizabeth's Admiral*, pp. 223–9, quoted p. 229. Corbett, *Successors of Drake*, pp. 258–77. *MNT*, II, 86–108.
68 Glasgow, 'Elizabethan Navy in Ireland'. Andrews, *Trade, Plunder and Settlement*, p. 186. Corbett, *Drake*, I, 199–200. Sugden, *Drake*, pp. 81–6.
69 MacInnes, 'West Highland Sea-Power', pp. 530–8. Glasgow, 'Elizabethan Navy in Ireland', p. 299.
70 Lachlan *Mór* = Lachlan the Great.
71 *EWP*, pp. 324–6.
72 Kostič, 'Ragusa and the Spanish Armada', p. 217.
73 Ruari *Og* = Young Rory.
74 MacInnes, 'West Highland Sea-Power', pp. 527, 539, 544. Powell, *Blake*, p. 11. Kisimul Castle was (and still is) the stronghold of the MacNeills of Barra.
75 *EWP*, pp. 520–6, 535–6.
76 *WRA*, pp. 283–318. *EWP*, p. 419. C. Falls, Elizabeth's Irish Wars (London, 1950) pp. 230–46.
77 Gray, 'Spinola's Galleys', pp. 71–6. *WRA*, pp. 267–71. Corbett, *Successors of Drake*, pp. 278–88.
78 L. Th. Lehmann, *Galleys in the Netherlands* (Amsterdam, 1984), pp. 12–14, 50–86; and 'Dutch Galleys', *MM* LXV (1979), p. 63. Glasgow, 'Oared Vessels', p. 372. Corbett, *Successors of Drake*, pp. 301–2.
79 *WRA*, pp. 332–3. Corbett, *Successors of Drake*, pp. 295–8. *MNT*, II, 114.
80 *WRA*, pp. 337–8. *EWP*, pp. 431–3. Corbett, *Successors of Drake*, pp. 309–10. Glasgow, 'Elizabethan Navy in Ireland', p. 302. Fallon, *Armada in Ireland*, pp. 45–6.
81 'Hazer el mesmo effecto que la reyna haze por la de los rebeldes a muy poca cosa': Silke, *Kinsale*, p. 5.
82 *WRA*, pp. 372–3. Parker, *Army of Flanders*, pp. 68–70.
83 *WRA*, pp. 377–87. Glasgow, 'Elizabethan Navy in Ireland', pp. 303–5. Corbett, *Successors of Drake*, pp. 323–54. Silke, *Kinsale*, pp. 92–139. *MNT*, II, 124, 145. J. J. N. McGurk, 'Rochester and the Irish Levy of October 1601', *MM* LXXIV (1988), pp. 57–66.
84 *WRA*, p. 393.
85 Sir R. Leveson to Salisbury, *c.* 15 March 1601, in HMC *Salisbury*, XI, 129.

86 *WRA*, p. 375. Corbett, *Successors of Drake*, pp. 396–97. *MNT*, V, 49–56.
87 *WRA*, pp. 394–400. Corbett, *Successors of Drake*, pp. 366–85. *MNT*, II, 154–64. HMC *Salisbury*, XII, 133, 183–4.
88 Maunsell & Statham, *Maunsell*, I, 372, quoting Mansell's *True Report of the Service done upon certaine Gallies...* (London, 1602).
89 *WRA*, pp. 400–1. Corbett, *Successors of Drake*, pp. 386–97. HMC *Salisbury*, XII, 335. Gray, 'Spinola's Galleys', pp. 78–82.
90 *WRA*, p. 414. Adams, 'Spain or the Netherlands?', p. 93. Thompson, *War and Government*, pp. 223–7.
91 What follows is based, as all discussion of the Elizabethan privateering war must be, on Andrews, *Elizabethan Privateering*.
92 Scammell, *First Imperial Age*, p. 92.
93 Andrews, *Elizabethan Privateering*, p. 3, quoting Sir George Carey.
94 Spence, *Privateering Earl*, pp. 157–75. *WRA*, pp. 252–6. Corbett, *Successors of Drake*, pp. 239–52.
95 Andrews, *Elizabethan Privateering*, pp. 70–9 (quoted p. 79).
96 Rowse, *Grenville*, pp. 117–21.
97 Andrews, *Spanish Caribbean*, p. 187.
98 Boulind, 'Spanish Control', p. 312.
99 Sir W. Monson, in *MNT*, II, 297.
100 Andrews, *Elizabethan Privateering*, p. 128.
101 Andrews, *Trade, Plunder and Settlement*, pp. 252–3; and *Elizabethan Privateering*, pp. 230–1. Thomas Wilson, 'The State of England anno dom. 1600', ed. F. J. Fisher, *Camden Miscellany XVI* (CS 3rd S. Vol.52, 1936), pp. 36–7.
102 *WAA*, pp. 246–59. Chaunu, *Séville et l'Atlantique*, VIII, ii, 971–2. *MNT*, I, 273–75.
103 *BMO*, I, 527. Scammell, *First Imperial Age*, p. 241.
104 Chaunu, *Séville et l'Atlantique*, I, 209; VI, 866; VIII, i, 255–7; VIII, ii, 969. Casada Soto, *Los barcos españoles*, pp. 27, 117–18. Gómez-Centurión Jiménez, *Felipe II*, pp. 125–33, 249. Silke, *Kinsale*, p. 148. Pi Corrales, *Felipe II*, pp. 97–8.
105 Andrews, *Spanish Caribbean*, p. 156; cf. his 'English Voyages to the Caribbean'.
106 Andrews, *Spanish Caribbean*, p. 163.
107 Andrews, *English Privateering Voyages*, p. 308.
108 Andrews, *Spanish Caribbean*, p. 166.
109 Andrews, *Elizabethan Privateering*, pp. 178–80.
110 Andrews, *Spanish Caribbean*, pp. 165–92; *Elizabethan Privateering*, pp. 182–4; and 'Caribbean Rivalry and the Anglo-Spanish Peace of 1604', *History* LIX (1974), pp. 1–17. Engel Sluiter, 'Dutch-Spanish Rivalry in the Caribbean Area, 1594–1609', *Hispanic American Historical Review* XXVIII (1948), pp. 165–96.
111 Andrews, 'Cecil and Mediterranean Plunder'. Tenenti, *Piracy*, pp. 56–71.
112 Essex in *EWP*, p. 6.
113 Sir William Knollys (1596) in Corbett, *Successors of Drake*, p. 147.
114 Sir Walter Ralegh, in Lee, *Son of Leicester*, p. 61.

21 The Path to Fame

1 'Strike-ropes' were apparently some sort of brail: see *MEST*, III, 108–9.
2 *ARN*, p. 75.
3 Spont, *War with France*, p. 119.
4 Scammell, 'War at Sea', pp. 193–4.
5 Donno, *Madox Diary*, pp. 121–7; also Taylor, *Fenton's Voyage*, pp. 157–60. A 'garbler' sifts or sorts spices; a 'platdrawer' draws plots or charts.
6 Windeatt, 'Fitting Out', pp. 317–20.
7 Christopher Lloyd, 'The Title of Lord High Admiral', *MM* XL (1954), pp. 236–7, deals with the forms of the title.
8 Glasgow, 'Maturing of Naval Administration', p. 20. Pollitt, 'Elizabethan Navy Board', p. 63.
9 *MNT*, III, 438; IV, 1–2.
10 Donno, *Madox Diary*, p. 29.
11 HMC *Foljambe*, pp. 118–20.
12 Corbett, *Drake*, II, 66–8.
13 *DSA*, I, 202. Corbett, *Drake*, II, 143–7.
14 *WRA*, p. 84. Corbett, 'Slyngisbie's Relation', pp. 29, 44–50. 'Orange-tawny' is the heraldic tincture *tenné*, a reddish brown.
15 Butler, *Dialogues*, p. 33. (Written in

Charles I's time, when 'royal ship' = capital ship.)

16 *TN*, pp. 101–2. Scammell, 'War at Sea', pp. 190–3.

17 *ARN*, p. 78. 'Mean' = middling, indifferent.

18 Corbett, *Spanish War*, pp. 291–9.

19 Corbett, *Successors of Drake*, p. 257. Richard Boulind, 'Tudor Captains: The Beestons and the Tyrrells', *MM* LIX (1973), pp. 171–8. Scammell, 'Sinews of War', pp. 361–2.

20 Lee, *Son of Leicester*, p. 54.

21 Warner, *Dudley's Voyage*, p. 21, quoting Wyatt's narrative of Dudley's 1594 voyage. Lee, *Son of Leicester*, p. 64. Waters, *Navigation*, pp. 77, 201 n.3.

22 Rowse, *Grenville*, pp. 298–9, quoting Philip Gawdy.

23 *MNT*, III, 43.

24 Andrews, *English Privateering Voyages*, p. 22.

25 Sir Robert Naunton, in Kenny, *Elizabeth's Admiral*, p. 36.

26 Thomas Wilson, 'The State of England anno dom. 1600' ed. F. J. Fisher, *Camden Miscellany XVI* (CS 3rd S. Vol.52, 1936), p. 24.

27 'Sepius monitus et requisitus, ymmo rogatus': Bernard, *Návires et Gens de Mer*, II, 647, quoting PRO: HCA 24/2 No.28 (of 1536).

28 *ARN*, p. 80.

29 *BMO* I, 148, 153–5. Nuttall, *New Light on Drake*, p. 171. Wright, *Further English Voyages*, pp. 45, 225.

30 Drake's former prisoner Don Francisco de Zárate to Don Martín Enríquez, Viceroy of New Spain, 16 April 1579, in Nuttall, *New Light on Drake*, p. 207; the original Spanish in *BMO*, I, 155.

31 Sir W. Monson, in *MNT*, IV, 271.

32 Senior, *Naval History in the Law Courts*, pp. 1–8.

33 Drake, *World Encompassed*, p. 164; also Corbett, *Drake*, I, 249.

34 Andrews, *Drake's Voyages*, pp. 63–7. Spate, *Spanish Lake*, pp. 242–4. Drake, *World Encompassed*, p. 125.

35 D. W. Waters, 'Lord Howard as Seaman, 1578', *MM* XLI (1955), pp. 336–7. Corbett, *Successors of Drake*, p. 443.

36 Howard to Sir F. Walsingham, 13 June 1588, in *DSA*, I, 198.

37 Keevil, *Medicine and the Navy*, I, 80, quoting Roger Marbecke's 'Brief and True Discourse' of the 1596 Cadiz expedition.

38 *DSA*, I, 224.

39 *PN*, VII, 11.

40 HMC *Salisbury*, IX, 332; these are Privy Council orders signed by Nottingham, Lord Hunsdon and Sir Robert Cecil, but undoubtedly written by the Lord Admiral.

41 HMC *Salisbury*, IX, 332.

42 Nottingham & Sir R. Cecil to Lord T. Howard, 28 Aug 1599: HMC *Salisbury*, IX, 327–8.

43 Corbett, *Fighting Instructions*, pp. 17–18; the fractured syntax printed thus.

44 *ARN*, pp. 382–91. Marsden, *Select Pleas*, II, xvi. Corbett, *Drake*, II, 100–1.

45 Corbett, *Spanish War*, pp. 123–30, 149–85. Corbett, *Drake*, II, 73–4, 88–9, 106–7.

46 Kenny, *Elizabeth's Admiral*, pp. 142–4. *DSA*, I, 202. Corbett, *Drake*, II, 143–7.

47 Waters, *Navigation*, pp. 78–9.

48 Waters, *Navigation*, p. 79 n.1. Hope, *Shipping*, p. 89. Taylor, *Haven-Finding Art*, pp. 193–5. John may be the father of Stephen and William Borough, who certainly came from north Devon.

49 Hope, *Shipping*, pp. 84–5.

50 Bonner, 'Recovery of St. Andrews', pp. 578–85. Rotz, *Idrography*, pp. 3–7. Waters, *Navigation*, pp. 14–16. Riis, *Auld Acquaintance*, I, 40–2. Lindsay, *Rutter of the Scottish Seas*, pp. 9, 13, 19, 30–1.

51 *The Arte of Navigation...* (London, 1561), trans. Richard Eden from *Breve Compendio de la Sphera y de la Arte de Navegar* (Seville, 1551).

52 Hair & Alsop, *Seamen and Traders*, pp. 132–3.

53 Andrews, 'Elizabethan Seaman', p. 260.

54 Waters, *Navigation*, pp. 203–32. Thomas R. Adams, 'The Beginnings of Maritime Publishing in England, 1528–1640', *The Library* 6th S. XIV (1992), pp. 207–20.

55 *WRA*, p. 94.

56 Taylor, *Haven-Finding Art*, p. 216.

57 Scammell, 'European Seamanship', pp. 357–8.

58 *MNT*, IV, 30–1. Butler, *Dialogues*, pp. 25–8. Scammell, 'English Merchant Service', pp. 151–2.

59 Keevil, *Medicine and the Navy*, I, 76, quoting 'an old sea-captain' from PRO: SP 12/118 No.12 of 1577.

60 Spont, *War with France*, p. 118. James Watt, 'Surgeons of the *Mary Rose*: The Practice of Surgery in Tudor England', *MM* LXIX (1983), pp. 3–19.

61 Hair & Alsop, *Seamen and Traders*, p. 33.

62 Donno, *Madox Diary*, p. 27.

63 Keevil, *Medicine and the Navy*, I, 69, 80–1, 128, 140. Pollitt, 'Bureaucracy and the Armada', p. 125.

64 Keevil, *Medicine and the Navy*, I, 123–44.

65 Scammell, 'English Merchant Service', pp. 152–3. Hair & Alsop, *Seamen and Traders*, p. 89. Spont, *War with France*, p. 119. *MNT*, IV, 55–7.

66 *DSA*, II, 231.

67 *DSA*, II, 231. *ARN*, p. 164.

68 Scott, 'Naval Chaplain', p. 9. Curry, 'English Sea-Chaplains', pp. 47–8.

69 *Measure for Measure*, I, ii, 7–9.

70 Wright, *English Voyages*, pp. 117–22. Donno, *Madox Diary*, p. 30.

71 Taylor, *Sea Chaplains*, pp. 29–34, 47. Drake, *World Encompassed*, p. 133.

72 Dyer, 'Elizabethan Sailorman', p. 141.

73 Taylor, *Sea Chaplains*, p. 40, quoting Thomas Fuller's *The Holy and the Profane State*.

74 Donno, *Madox Diary*, p. 144.

75 Andrews, *English Privateering Voyages*, p. 339 n.4.

76 Taylor, *Fenton's Voyage*, p. 58.

77 Nuttall, *New Light on Drake*, p. 325. Williamson, *Hawkins of Plymouth*, p. 71.

78 Corbett, 'Slyngisbie's Relation', p. 51.

79 Drake, *World Encompassed*, p. 97.

80 Gerhard, *West Coast of New Spain*, p. 93. Spate, *Spanish Lake*, p. 281. Wright, *English Voyages*, pp. 117–22.

81 *PN*, VII, 8. *MNT*, II, 213. Williamson, *Hawkins of Plymouth*, p. 120.

82 Taylor, *Fenton's Voyage*, pp. 211–15.

83 Nuttall, *New Light on Drake*, pp.xxii–xxiii, 348.

84 Scammell, 'English Merchant Service', p. 151.

85 *MNT*, II, 181; V, 179.

86 Adams & Waters, *English Maritime Books*, p. 314.

87 *MNT*, IV, 35.

88 Hawkins, *Observations*, p. 129. *MNT*, IV, 91. Bourne, *Arte of Shooting*, pp. 52, 57. Mainwaring, *Works*, II, 110. Smith, *Sea Grammar*, p. 85.

89 Monson, in *MNT*, II, 242; IV, 229.

90 *MNT*, II, 243; IV, 132–7. Scammell, 'European Seamanship', p. 365.

91 R. Marbecke, in Andrews, *English Privateering Voyages*, p. 243.

92 Scammell, 'English Merchant Service', p. 151.

93 *DSA*, II, 241; other reports were not subscribed at all.

94 Monson, in *MNT*, IV, 32–3.

95 Warner, *Dudley's Voyage*, p. 59.

96 Scammell, 'English Merchant Service', pp. 149–50.

97 Corbett, *Spanish War*, p. 24. Windeatt, 'Fitting Out', pp. 319–20.

98 Butler, *Dialogues*, p. 32.

99 *DSA*, II, 231. *ARN*, p. 163.

100 Powell, 'Early Naval Lieutenant', pp. 358–9. Butler, *Dialogues*, p. 32.

101 Monson, in *MNT*, IV, 16.

102 Poem, supposedly by Drake, prefaced to Sir George Peckham's *A True Report of the Late Discoveries...* (London, 1583; reprinted without the prefatory poem in *PN*, VIII, 89–131).

22 Sailors for my Money

1 The title of a famous ballad from the 1630s by Martin Parker, better known today in the form reworked by Thomas Campbell in the eighteenth century as 'Ye Mariners of England': Firth, *Songs and Ballads*, p.xxvi.

2 Scammell, 'English Merchant Service', p. 131.

3 Hawkins's in 1564, in Williamson, *Hawkins of Plymouth*, p. 71.

4 Lord T. Howard to Sir R. Cecil, 27 Aug 1599; HMC *Salisbury*, IX, 327.

5 Taylor, *Fenton's Voyage*, p. 199, quoting John Walker.

6 Drake, *World Encompassed*, p. 104, quoting Francis Fletcher.
7 Wright, *English Voyages*, p. 323, quoting the narrative of Drake's 1572 voyage in *Sir Francis Drake Reviv'd* of 1628.
8 *PN*, XI, 198, quoting Luke Ward's narrative of Fenton's 1582 voyage; 'prised' = appraised, valued.
9 Donno, *Madox Diary*, p. 52.
10 *TN*, p. 99. *ARN*, p. 74.
11 MacDougall, 'James IV's *Great Michael*', p. 41.
12 *TN*, p. 101. *ARN*, p. 80. *The Oxford Illustrated History of the Royal Navy*, ed. J. R. Hill (Oxford, 1995), pp. 36–7.
13 *TN*, p. 97. *ARN*, p. 56.
14 Derrick, *Memoirs*, p. 303. It is extraordinary that this second-hand note remains the nearest thing we have in print to a complete text of the Anthony Roll, though Caruana, *English Sea Ordnance*, pp. 18–21, abstracts the gunnery information.
15 Derrick, *Memoirs*, pp. 14, 19.
16 *BND*, pp. 103–6.
17 Scammell, 'War at Sea', p. 195. *BND*, pp. 103–6. Corbett, *Spanish War*, pp. 270–2. Derrick, *Memoirs*, pp. 14–15, 19, 25, 303–6.
18 Corbett, *Spanish War*, p. 265.
19 Corbett, *Drake*, II, 288–9. *DSA*, II, 324–5 gives complements in 1588.
20 Williamson, *Hawkins of Plymouth*, p. 70.
21 Pollitt, 'Elizabethan Navy Board', p. 185. Williamson, *Hawkins of Plymouth*, p. 280. *BND*, pp. 103–6. Corbett, *Spanish War*, p. 265.
22 Andrews, *Drake's Voyages*, p. 102.
23 Andrews, 'Elizabethan Seaman', p. 246. Scammell, 'Sinews of War', pp. 351–2.
24 Butler, *Dialogues*, p. 61.
25 *MNT*, II, 243; IV, 224. Butler, *Dialogues*, pp. 49–52.
26 Rodger, 'Broadside Gunnery', pp. 313–4.
27 *TN*, p. 98. *ARN*, p. 74.
28 Oppenheim, *VCH Dorset*, II, 197.
29 *BND*, pp. 132–3. Hair & Alsop, *Seamen and Traders*, p. 123. *TN*, p. 99.
30 *BND*, p. 102.
31 *BND*, pp. 103–6, 129.
32 Pollitt, 'Elizabethan Navy Board', p. 253.
33 *WAA*, pp. 416–17.
34 Corbett, *Successors of Drake*, p. 47.
35 *MNT*, II, 40.
36 An anonymous note, in HMC *Salisbury*, IX, 427.
37 F. Greville & Sir R. Leveson to Nottingham & Sir R. Cecil, 19 July 1602: HMC *Salisbury*, XII, 237.
38 Andrews, 'Elizabethan Seaman', p. 248.
39 H. Oughtred to Leicester, 1 May 1582: Taylor, *Fenton's Voyage*, p. 46.
40 Lloyd, *British Seaman*, p. 38, quoting Sir W. Ralegh. 'Soldier' here means any fighting man.
41 [Capt T. Wye], *A briefe discourse . . . betwene Baldwyne & a Sayler...* (London, 1580), sigg. A.vii, B.ii.
42 Sir W. Monson to Nottingham, 16 Aug 1602: HMC *Salisbury*, XII, 304.
43 Andrews, 'Elizabethan Seaman', pp. 255–6. Burwash, *English Merchant Shipping*, pp. 43–52. Brooks, 'Wage Scale'.
44 *MNT*, IV, 228. Scammell, 'Sinews of War', p. 358.
45 Andrews, 'Elizabethan Seaman', p. 252, explicitly argues that low pay made it impossible for the Navy to compete with privateers, which paid no wages at all: there may be some inconsistency here.
46 Andrews, *English Privateering Voyages*, pp. 20–34.
47 Andrews, *Elizabethan Privateering*, p. 44.
48 Sir Henry Radclyffe, Governor of Portsmouth, in French, 'Privateering', p. 179.
49 Scammell, 'Sinews of War', pp. 351–3.
50 Thompson, *War and Government*, p. 103. Parker, *Military Revolution*, p. 56. *EWP*, p. 46.
51 *ARN*, p. 77. Keevil, *Medicine and the Navy*, I, 61–3.
52 *ARN*, p. 114, quoting Clinton.
53 Howard to Burghley, 10 Aug 1588: *DSA*, II, 96. *ARN*, p. 137, has the usual slapdash transcription.
54 Wernham, *Drake-Norris Expedition*, pp.lxiv–lxv, 194–5.
55 Keevil, *Medicine and the Navy*, I, 25.
56 Keevil, *Medicine and the Navy*, I, 100.
57 Corbett, 'Slyngisbie's Relation', p. 52.
58 Sir W. Monson, in *MNT*, IV, 63–4. Martin & Parker, *Spanish Armada*, pp. 56–7. Butler, *Dialogues*, p. 62.

59 *ARN*, p. 136, quoting 'a 17th-century writer'. Keevil, *Medicine and the Navy*, I, 71–6, follows the Elizabethans in attributing the 1588 sickness to food-poisoning.
60 HMC *Salisbury*, IX, 336.
61 *PN*, IX, 379, quoting Henry Hawks.
62 For later medical ideas about scurvy see N. A. M. Rodger, 'Medicine, Administration and Society in the Eighteenth-Century Royal Navy', in *IX Deutsch-Französisches Symposium zur Geschichte der Schiffahrts- und Marinemedizin*, ed. Hans Schadewaldt & Karl-Heinz Leven (Düsseldorf, 1988), pp. 126–32.
63 Hawkins, *Observations*, p. 56. Keevil, *Medicine and the Navy*, I, 111–12. Waters, *Navigation*, p. 293. Donno, *Madox Diary*, p. 305. Purchas, *Pilgrimes*, II, 396. Carpenter, *Scurvy*, pp. 13–18.
64 Donno, *Madox Diary*, pp. 55, 185. Taylor, *Fenton's Voyage*, p. 49.
65 Rule, *Mary Rose*, p. 197. Hair & Alsop, *Seamen and Traders*, pp. 138–9. Keeler, *Drake's West Indian Voyage*, p. 96.
66 Wright, *English Voyages*, p. 275, quoting *Sir Francis Drake Reviv'd*.
67 Drake, *World Encompassed*, pp. 27–8. These were of course penguins.
68 Dyer, 'Elizabethan Sailorman', p. 137, quoting Purchas.
69 Williamson, *Hawkins of Plymouth*, p. 76, quoting John Sparke's narrative of Hawkins's 1564 voyage.
70 Keevil, *Medicine and the Navy*, I, 108. Andrews, *Last Voyage of Drake & Hawkins*, p. 60.
71 Dyer, 'Elizabethan Sailorman', p. 134, quoting Luke 'North-West' Fox the Arctic explorer.
72 Hair & Alsop, *Seamen and Traders*, pp. 109–14.
73 Wright, *English Voyages*, p. 254.
74 Taylor, *Fenton's Voyage*, p. 234.
75 Scammell, 'English Merchant Service', p. 138.
76 Hair & Alsop, *Seamen and Traders*, pp. 110–11.
77 Scammell, 'English Merchant Service', pp. 148–51.
78 *ARN*, p. 75. Moore, 'Complaynt of Scotlande', p. 81.
79 Scammell, 'English Merchant Service', p. 150. Paviot, *La Politique navale*, p. 309.
80 'Avec aucuns maronniers, charpentiers, calfateurs, & autre gents de mestier, au capitaine de dessoubs': *Toutes manieres de guerroyer*, pp. 134, 136.
81 Marsden, 'Voyage of the *Barbara*', pp. 7–8.
82 Peter Whitlock, 'The Boatswain's Call – an Updating', *MM* LXXI (1985), pp. 167–8. Hair & Alsop, *Seamen and Traders*, p. 346. For Henry VIII's and Sir Edward Howard's whistles of command, see pp. 171, 210 above. James IV had one earlier: MacDougall, *James IV*, p. 233.
83 Corbett, *Spanish War*, pp. 258–62.
84 Phillips, *Six Galleons*, p. 140.
85 Hair & Alsop, *Seamen and Traders*, pp. 105–7.
86 Spont, *War with France*, pp. 109–21.
87 Nuttall, *New Light on Drake*, p. 186. Donno, *Madox Diary*, pp. 121–7. Windeatt, 'Fitting Out', pp. 317–18.
88 Hawkins, *Observations*, p. 32. Davis, *English Shipping Industry*, p. 113.
89 *MNT*, IV, 59–62. Nuttall, *New Light on Drake*, p. 186.
90 Sir W. Monson, in *MNT*, IV, 60.
91 Spont, *War with France*, p. 118.
92 Corbett, *Spanish War*, pp. 258–62.
93 Sir W. Monson, in *MNT*, IV, 57.
94 Andrews, *Last Voyage of Drake & Hawkins*, p. 55.
95 Hair & Alsop, *Seamen and Traders*, pp. 106–7.
96 Anonymous narrative, in *PN*, VII, 36.
97 Drake, *World Encompassed*, pp. 132–3.
98 Nuttall, *New Light on Drake*, p. 171, and *BMO*, I, 148, correcting the translation of *chirimías*.
99 Wright, *Further English Voyages*, p. 15, quoting a statement by the Spanish prisoner Enrique Lopez, Nov 1585.
100 Warner, *Dudley's Voyage*, p. 4. To 'vail' = to dip, in token of salute.
101 F. Greville & Sir R. Leveson to Nottingham & Sir R. Cecil, 8 July 1602: in HMC *Salisbury*, XII, 217.
102 Andrews, *English Privateering Voyages*,

pp. 24–6. Scammell, 'Sinews of War', pp. 359–60. *MNT*, I, 267; II, 237, quoting Sir W. Monson.

103 Sir W. Monson, in *MNT*, IV, 17.

104 Andrews, *English Privateering Voyages*, pp. 24–6; and *Elizabethan Privateering*, p. 41. *PN*, XI, 326.

105 Sir G. Carey to Sir F. Walsingham, 29 Aug 1588: *DSA*, II, 187. Andrews, *Elizabethan Privateering*, pp. 42–3. Hawkins, *Observations*, pp. 110–13.

106 Admiralty Court judges to the Privy Council, 16 Feb 1594: Wernham, *Drake-Norris Expedition*, p. 315.

107 Donno, *Madox Diary*, p. 141.

108 Hawkins, *Observations*, p. 12.

109 Butler, *Dialogues*, p. 37.

110 Joseph May to Lord Cecil, 8 June 1603: HMC *Salisbury*, XV, 127.

111 Wernham, *Drake–Norris Expedition*, p. 179 (quoted). *MNT*, II, 247–8. Taylor, *Fenton's Voyage*, p. 78. Hawkins, *Observations*, pp. 101, 125.

112 Taylor, *Fenton's Voyage*, p. 202.

113 Butler, *Dialogues*, p. 40.

114 Donno, *Madox Diary*, pp. 144, 157, 321. Usherwood, *Counter-Armada*, pp. 63, 129.

115 *MNT*, III, 436; IV, 199. Corbett, 'Slyngisbie's Relation', p. 57.

116 *MNT*, II, 213. Corbett, *Spanish War*, p. 10. Keeler, *Drake's West Indian Voyage*, p. 148.

117 *TN*, p. 100. *ARN*, p. 79. Kemp, *British Sailor*, pp. 12–13. The source is a collection of naval documents made in 1568 by the London fishmonger James Humfrey, now MCC: Pepys MS 1266.

118 Not the Laws of Oleron, as suggested by *TN*, p. 100, though Humphreys copied them also into his collection. Nicolas, *Royal Navy*, I, 89.

119 Scammell, 'Sinews of War', pp. 356–8.

120 *MNT*, IV, 199.

121 Donno, *Madox Diary*, p. 105. 'Forslood' = lost through sloth.

122 Hawkins, *Observations*, p. 20.

123 *BMO*, I, 153–5; III, 412. Usherwood, *Counter-Armada*, p. 145. Corbett, *Successors of Drake*, pp. 90, 104. *WBA*, p. 400.

124 *MNT*, I, 293, quoting the commissioners who investigated the plundering of the *Madre de Deus* in 1592.

125 Andrews, 'Elizabethan Seaman', p. 260, quoting Captain John Smith.

126 Connell-Smith, *Forerunners of Drake*, pp. 170–1. Andrews, *Elizabethan Privateering*, p. 210. Gerhard, *West Coast of New Spain*, p. 83. *The Last Voyage of Thomas Cavendish 1591–1592*, ed. D. B. Quinn (Chicago, 1975), p. 34. *PN*, XI, 309. Corbett, *Spanish War*, p. 10. Wright, *English Voyages*, pp.xxxv, lvi, 98. Ewen, 'Organized Piracy', p. 37.

127 Scammell, 'Sinews of War', pp. 360–1.

128 Scammell, 'English Merchant Service', p. 136. Hair & Alsop, *Seamen and Traders*, pp. 2, 33–5, 88, 119, 127–36.

129 Burwash, *English Merchant Shipping*, pp. 78–9. Hair & Alsop, *Seamen and Traders*, pp. 129–36, 342–55. Marsden, 'Voyage of the *Barbara*', pp. 7–8. Andrews, *Last Voyage of Drake & Hawkins*, p. 64.

130 *ARN*, pp. 76, 113.

131 *ARN*, p. 139.

132 McGurk, 'A Levy of Seamen', p. 139.

133 Rule, *Mary Rose*, p. 198. Aydelotte, 'Elizabethan Seamen', p. 16 n.1.

134 Wright, *English Voyages*, p. 275, quoting *Sir Francis Drake Reviv'd*. 'Keels' = skittles.

135 Burwash, *English Merchant Shipping*, pp. 79–81. Moore, 'Complaynt of Scotlande', pp. 76, 79.

136 Hawkins, *Observations*, pp. 47–8.

137 Warner, *Dudley's Voyage*, p. 11.

138 Scammell, *World Encompassed*, p. 466. Kraus, *Drake*, p. 106. Nuttall, *New Light on Drake*, pp. 19, 326, 348 (quoted), 354–7.

139 Hawkins, *Observations*, p. 32.

140 Corbett, *Successors of Drake*, p. 443.

23 The Undertakings of a Maiden Queen

1

How brave, advantageous an instrument
A well-framed navy is to entertain . . .
Not only in surprising of the main
But in possessing land and cities too,

By undertakings of a maiden Queen
May, as in models to the world, be seen.
Fulke Greville, *A Treatise of Monarchy*

2 Quinn & Ryan, *England's Sea Empire*, p. 55. *ARN*, pp. 167, 172.
3 Pollitt, 'Elizabethan Navy Board', p. 206.
4 Pollitt, 'Contingency Planning', pp. 26–8; and 'English Resources', pp. 22–3. *ARN*, pp. 172–3.
5 Pollitt, 'Contingency Planning', p. 29; cf. *ARN*, p. 167.
6 Pollitt, 'Contingency Planning', p. 29.
7 PRO: SP 12/143 No.20.
8 Pollitt, 'English Resources', p. 19. Corbett, *Drake*, I, 351. See pp. 238–9 above.
9 Pollitt, 'Contingency Planning', p. 30. *ARN*, pp. 174–7. *TN*, p. 192. *BND*, pp. 107–9. Andrews, *Ships, Money and Politics*, pp. 204–5, 221–3.
10 Cf. the primitive Spanish surveys in *BMO*, I, 83–4, 119–22.
11 But these were surveys for a specific purpose rather than a general census, and probably understate the total seafaring population: Andrews, 'Elizabethan Seaman', p. 253.
12 Pollitt, 'Contingency Planning', p. 31, quoting Burghley's 'Memorial 1584 of sundry things to be executed within the realm to withstand perils'; Pollitt 'Bureaucracy and the Armada', pp. 120–1. Corbett, *Spanish War*, pp. 270–80.
13 Parker, 'If the Armada had landed', p. 365. Pollitt, 'Elizabethan Navy Board', pp. 243–9, 265–6. Kenny, *Elizabeth's Admiral*, pp. 126–37.
14 Williamson, *Hawkins of Plymouth*, pp. 249–50. Corbett, *Drake*, I, 348–50. Pollitt, 'Elizabethan Navy Board', pp. 224–5. Quinn & Ryan, *England's Sea Empire*, p. 65. Lewis, *Hawkins Dynasty*, pp. 140–2.
15 Adams, 'The "Reformation" of John Hawkins', p. 106.
16 Parker, '*Dreadnought* Revolution', p. 270–3.
17 Adams, 'Battle that never was', p. 189.
18 *ARN*, p. 129.
19 Glasgow, 'Ships that defeated the Spanish Armada'. Anderson, *English Men-of-War*, pp. 13–15.
20 Corbett, *Successors of Drake*, pp. 425–9.
21 Gray, 'Spinola's Galleys', p. 81, apparently quoting Mansell's *True Report of the Service done upon Certain Galleys.* The *Hope* was an old ship, built 1559 and rebuilt 1603 as the *Assurance.* One suspects she had already been reconstructed if she had two gun-decks; she was certainly reported as needing dry-docking in 1588 (*DSA*, II, 251).
22 Anderson, *English Men-of-War*, pp. 15–16. *ARN*, p. 129. Kenny, *Elizabeth's Admiral*, p. 113. Rodríguez-Salgado, *Armada*, pp. 152–3. McGowan, *Jacobean Commissions*, p. 234.
23 PRO: E 315/317 f.22v.
24 *ARN*, pp. 130–1. PRO: E 134/6 Jas I/Hil/19, depositions of H. Diamond and D. Hollyman.
25 Young, 'Emblematic Decoration', p. 65, quoting Thomas Platter.
26 *ARN*, p. 130. 'Summer-deck' = poop.
27 *DSA*, I, 100.
28 'Die Stuben waren mit köstlischen Gemählden und auch sehr schönen emblematibus gezieret': Young, 'Emblematic Decoration', p. 65.
29 Ashley, 'Office of Ordnance', pp. 81–4. Pollitt, 'Elizabethan Navy Board', p. 74. Glasgow, 'Naval Administration', p. 21.
30 Pollitt, 'Elizabethan Navy Board', pp. 74–84. Glasgow, 'Naval Administration', pp. 15–16. *A Collection of Ordinances and Regulations for the Government of the Royal Household...* (Soc. of Antiquaries, London, 1790), pp. 253–4.
31 Davies, 'Supply Services', p. 69, quoting PRO: STAC 2/30 No.2.
32 Boulind, 'Spanish Control', p. 738.
33 Corbett, *Spanish War*, p. 207.
34 *ARN*, pp. 392–7, discusses Hawkins's honesty from Oppenheim's standpoint.
35 Williamson, *Hawkins of Plymouth*, pp. 251–4. *ARN*, pp. 144–8.
36 Adams, 'The "Reformation" of John Hawkins', pp. 98–101, which supersedes Williamson, *Hawkins of Plymouth*, pp. 251–77, and other older accounts of Hawkins's Bargains. Many documents

are printed by Corbett, *Spanish War*, pp. 207–57, and *DSA*, I, 34–44, 87–90, II, 266–8; cf. J. P. Collier, 'On the charge of the Ordinary and Extraordinary Service of the English Navy . . .', *Archaeologia* XXXIII (1849), pp. 191–4.

37 Adams, 'The "Reformation" of John Hawkins', pp. 101–4, 107–11. Kenny, *Elizabeth's Admiral*, pp. 28–9. Corbett, *Drake*, I, 343. *TN*, pp. 183–5.

38 *DSA*, I, 35.

39 Adams, 'The "Reformation" of John Hawkins', pp. 105–106.

40 Anderson, *English Men-of-War*, pp. 12–17; this is life-span from first building to rebuilding.

41 Adams, 'The "Reformation" of John Hawkins', p. 106.

42 To Sir F. Walsingham, 14 June 1588, in *DSA*, I, 201; cf. I, 274, and p. 264 above.

43 Howard to Burghley, 9 March 1588: *DSA*, I, 97. She was in fact twenty-one years old, but had been rebuilt in 1581, and lasted until she was broken up in 1611; her total service was fourteen years before and thirty after reconstruction.

44 Corbett, *Spanish War*, p. 234.

45 McGowan, *Jacobean Commissions*, pp. 173, 180–1, 217.

46 *ARN*, p. 397. *MNT*, IV, 141.

47 *BND*, p. 122, referring to Deptford in 1562.

48 *TN*, p. 189.

49 To Burghley, 17 July 1588: *DSA*, I, 275.

50 Richard Barker, 'Careening: Art and Anecdote', *Mare Liberum* 2 (Lisbon, 1991), pp. 177–207. *MNT*, II, 117–18. HMC *Salisbury*, XII, 36.

51 Bard, 'Warwick's Voyage', p. 59, gives an example from 1627.

52 *ARN*, p. 150. Oppenheim, *VCH Kent*, II, 341. *TN*, p. 189.

53 Joyce Youings & Peter W. Cornford, 'Seafaring and Maritime Trade in Sixteenth-Century Devon', in Duffy, *Maritime History of Devon*, I, 98–107, at p. 99.

54 Pett, *Autobiography*, pp. 30, 34, 94–5, 142.

55 HMC *Cowper*, I, 189.

56 F. Greville & Sir R. Leveson to Nottingham & Sir R. Cecil, 19 July 1602: HMC *Salisbury*, XII, 238.

57 Merino, 'Graving Docks', pp. 36–7. This dock still exists.

58 *TN*, p. 187. This was at Tower Hill, apparently not the site of the modern Hill House but on the opposite side of the river near Upnor.

59 *TN*, pp. 185–91. Glasgow, 'Naval Administration', pp. 11–14. *ARN*, pp. 149–51.

60 *TN*, pp. 189–90. *ARN*, p. 150. Corbett, *Spanish War*, p. 230.

61 McGowan, *Jacobean Commissions*, pp. 232–3.

62 *ARN*, p. 151.

63 Pollitt, 'Elizabethan Navy Board', pp. 261–5. *DSA*, I, 52–4. *BND*, pp. 109–12.

64 *DSA*, I, 216, 252–3, 268–71; II, 109–12. Pollitt, 'Bureaucracy and the Armada', pp. 126–9. Brian Pearce, 'Elizabethan Food Policy and the Armed Forces', *EcHR* XII (1942), pp. 39–46.

65 Scammell, 'Sinews of War', p. 366.

66 Hurstfield, 'Political Corruption', p. 16.

67 To J. Coke, 12 Oct 1603: HMC *Cowper*, I, 45.

68 *EWP*, pp. 453–9. *TN*, pp. 272–3. Andrews, *Elizabethan Privateering*, pp. 237–8.

69 Lawrence Stone, 'The Fruits of Office: the Case of Robert Cecil, First Earl of Salisbury, 1596–1612', in *Essays in the Economic and Social History of Tudor England in Honour of R. H. Tawney*, ed. F. J. Fisher (Cambridge, 1961), pp. 89–116.

70 Andrews, 'Cecil and Mediterranean Plunder', quoting (p. 530 n.8) Nottingham to Julius Caesar.

71 Lloyd, 'Sir John Trevor', p. 86.

72 Clayton, 'Naval Administration', pp. 3–4.

73 Young, *Servility and Service*, p. 19, quoting J. Coke.

74 From J. Coke, Aug 1600: Rebholz, *Greville*, p. 167.

75 Anonymous advice to F. Greville, in HMC *Cowper*, I, 27; cf. Rebholz, *Greville*, p. 165.

76 Young, *Servility and Service*, p. 22, quoting J. Coke.
77 Usherwood, *Counter-Armada*, p. 158.
78 Essex to E. Reynolds, 13 Aug 1597: HMC *Salisbury*, VIII, 351.
79 Lord T. Howard, Sir W. Ralegh & F. Greville to Nottingham & Sir R. Cecil, 31 Aug 1599: HMC *Salisbury*, IX, 335–6.
80 HMC *Salisbury*, IV, 555.
81 Ashley, 'War in the Ordnance Office'. Prestwich, *Cranfield*, p. 4. Guy, *Tudor England*, p. 396.
82 *EWP*, pp. 41, 54–7. C. G. Cruikshank, *Elizabeth's Army* (Oxford, 2nd edn 1966), p. 281.
83 Thompson, *War and Government*, pp. 36, 235–7, 241–3, 247–8.
84 *BMO*, II and III *passim* for Acuña Vela's correspondence.
85 Ashley, 'Office of Ordnance', pp. 11, 101–4. Bull, 'Furie of the Ordnance', p. 106. *Ordinances and Regulations for the Government of the Royal Household*, p. 272. Thompson, *War and Government*, p. 36, giving Spanish consumption as 2,000 quintals in 1577. Olesa Muñido, *La organización naval*, II, 918–20, 931–5.
86 Thompson, *War and Government*, pp. 47–78 and *passim*.
87 Thompson, *War and Government*, pp. 38–62.
88 Thompson, *War and Government*, pp. 35, 74–5, 179, 227.
89 Thompson, *War and Government*, pp. 77–8. Koenigsberger, 'Western Europe', p. 312.
90 *EWP*, p. 565.
91 Wernham, 'Elizabethan War Aims', pp. 355–6.
92 Parker, '*Dreadnought* Revolution', pp. 284–5, 289.
93 *EWP*, pp. 64–8. Dietz, *English Public Finance*, p. 55. Prestwich, *Cranfield*, p. 7.
94 Stone, 'State Control', p. 111 n.1. Hale, *War and Society*, p. 233.
95 O'Brien & Hunt, 'Fiscal State', pp. 149–52, 160, 174.
96 Murray, *Constitutional History*, p. 207. Lewis, *Elizabethan Ship Money*, pp. 10–11. Mayhew, 'Rye', pp. 117–19.
97 Lewis, *Elizabethan Ship Money*, pp. 18–26, 62–98.
98 Lewis, *Elizabethan Ship Money*, p. 33, quoting the Privy Council circular announcing the scheme. 'Vented' = sold.
99 Lewis, *Elizabethan Ship Money*, pp. 34–44. Corbett, *Successors of Drake*, pp. 396–7.
100 Andrews, *Drake's Voyages*, pp. 13–15.
101 Andrews, *Drake's Voyages*, pp. 30–3, 183–5. *BND*, pp. 71–3. *ARN*, pp. 177–9.
102 *ARN*, p. 180.
103 Ewen, *Golden Chalice*, p. 14.
104 Florence E. Dyer, 'A Woman Shipowner', *MM* XXXVI (1950), pp. 134–43. Ewen, 'Organized Piracy', p. 37. Dyer, 'Reprisals', pp. 191–7. *ARN*, pp. 178–80.
105 Appleby, 'Devon Privateering'.
106 Hughes, 'Wales and Piracy', p. 90.
107 Mathew, 'Cornish and Welsh Pirates', p. 338.
108 Hughes, 'Wales and Piracy', p. 213, quoting PRO: SP 12/111 No.16.
109 Hughes, 'Wales and Piracy', pp. 106–93, 214–19. Mathew, 'Cornish and Welsh Pirates', p. 346.
110 Andrews, *English Privateering Voyages*, pp. 87, 105.
111 Ewen, 'Organized Piracy'. Rowse, *Grenville*, p. 162. Mathew, 'Cornish and Welsh Pirates', p. 346. Chope, 'Grenville', p. 249. Oppenheim, *VCH Dorset*, II, 201.
112 F. Greville & Sir R. Leveson to Nottingham & Sir R. Cecil, 8 July 1602: HMC *Salisbury*, XII, 217.
113 Michael J. G. Stanford, 'The Raleighs take to the Sea', *MM* XLVIII (1962), pp. 18–35. *ARN*, p. 178.
114 Ewen, *Golden Chalice*.
115 Rowse, *Grenville*, pp. 164–8. Mathew, 'Cornish and Welsh Pirates', pp. 340–1. Alwyn A. Ruddock, 'The Earliest Records of the High Court of Admiralty (1515–1558)', *BIHR* XXII (1949), pp. 139–51, at p. 145. Oppenheim, *VCH Cornwall*, I, 487–90.
116 Andrews, 'Elizabethan Seaman', p. 249.
117 John Webb, 'Elizabethan Piracy: The Evidence of the Ipswich Deposition Books', *Suffolk Review* II (1959–64), pp. 59–65.
118 Mathew, 'Cornish and Welsh Pirates',

pp. 345–7. Oppenheim, in *VCH Suffolk*, II, 215.
119 Hale, *War and Society*, pp. 81–2. Anne Pérotin-Dumon, 'The pirate and the emperor: power and the law on the seas, 1450–1850', in Tracy, *Political Economy of Merchant Empires*, pp. 196–227.
120 Andrews, *Drake's Voyages*, pp. 181–5. Dyer, 'Reprisals'.
121 *ARN*, p. 180. Susan Maxwell, 'Henry Seckford: Sixteenth-Century Merchant, Courtier and Privateer', *MM* LXXXII (1996), pp. 387–97.
122 Kenny, *Elizabeth's Admiral*, pp. 42–5, 63–8, 75–6, 265. Andrews, *Elizabethan Privateering*, pp. 22–30, 89, 235–8. *English Privateering Voyages*, pp. 3–12; and 'Cecil and Mediterranean Plunder', pp. 524–9.
123 Appleby, 'Devon Privateering', pp. 94–5; Andrews, 'Elizabethan Privateering'.

24 No More Drakes

1 Senior, *Nation of Pirates*, p. 110.
2 Fisher, *Barbary Legend*, p. 142.
3 Kenny, *Elizabeth's Admiral*, pp. 267–71.
4 Nottingham to the Privy Council, 6 Aug 1604: HMC *Salisbury*, XVI, 203.
5 Senior, *Nation of Pirates*, pp. 127–33.
6 Eames, 'Sea Power and Welsh History', p. 102.
7 Hughes, 'Wales and Piracy', pp. 316–17, quoting PRO: SP 16/267 No.68.
8 Mainwaring, *Works*, I, 11. Senior, *Nation of Pirates*, p. 45.
9 Calvin F. Senning, 'Piracy, Politics and Plunder under James I: The Voyage of the Pearl and its Aftermath, 1611–1615', *Huntingdon Library Quarterly* XLVI (1983), pp. 187–222.
10 Mainwaring, *Works*, II, 18–19.
11 Senior, *Nation of Pirates*, pp. 40–1, 71.
12 Sir J. Bagge to Buckingham, 21 Aug 1624: HMC *Cowper*, I, 123; cf. J. C. Appleby, 'Neutrality, Trade and Privateering, 1500–1689', in Jamieson, *People of the Sea*, pp. 59–105, at p. 64.
13 Appleby, 'English Privateering', p. 16.
14 Senior, *Nation of Pirates*, pp. 73–4; and 'Robert Walsingham: A Jacobean Pirate', *MM* LX (1974), pp. 141–2.
15 Appleby, 'Nursery of Pirates', p. 25. Shilton & Holworthy, *High Court of Admiralty*, p. 70. McGowan, *Jacobean Commissions*, pp. 64–5.
16 Ewen, *Captain John Ward*, p. 10. Appleby, 'Nursery of Pirates', p. 7.
17 Lloyd, *English Corsairs*, p. 66.
18 Senior, *Nation of Pirates*, pp. 60–75. Hughes, 'Wales and Piracy', p. 72. Corbett, *England in the Mediterranean*, I, 51–2. Mainwaring, *Works*, I, 11–13. *ARN*, pp. 198–9. Weber, *De Beveiliging van de Zee*, pp. 38–47.
19 Hughes, 'Wales and Piracy', p. 73.
20 Senior, *Nation of Pirates*, pp. 140–1. Richard W. Cotton, 'An expedition against Pirates', *TDA* XVIII (1886), pp. 184–196.
21 Senior, *Nation of Pirates*, pp. 134–8.
22 Appleby, 'Nursery of Pirates'. Senior, *Nation of Pirates*, pp. 56–8. Appleby & O'Dowd, 'Irish Admiralty', pp. 307–8, 322–3.
23 Senior, *Nation of Pirates*, pp. 76–7. Appleby, 'Nursery of Pirates', p. 25.
24 Senior, *Nation of Pirates*, p. 72.
25 Tenenti, *Piracy*, pp. 61–85. Ewen, *Captain John Ward*, p. 5.
26 Braudel, *Mediterranean*, II, 870–2, 884–5. Earle, *Corsairs*, p. 45. J. de Courcy Ireland, 'The Corsairs of North Africa', *MM* LXII (1976), pp. 271–83. Harris, *Trinity House*, p. 232. De Jonge, *Nederlandsche Zeewesen*, I, 231.
27 Hebb, *Piracy*, pp. 11–20. Earle, *Corsairs*, pp. 11–18. Senior, *Nation of Pirates*, pp. 148–9.
28 Gray, 'Turkish Piracy', p. 161.
29 Donald Woodward, 'Sir Thomas Button, the Phoenix and the Defence of the Irish Coast 1614–1622', *MM* LIX (1973), pp. 343–4. Milford, 'Navy at Peace', p. 31.
30 Milford, 'Navy at Peace', pp. 29–30.
31 Lacour-Gayet, *La marine militaire*, pp. 2–3. *MF*, IV, 364. *MNT*, III, 45–55. R. C. Anderson, *Naval Wars in the Baltic during the Sailing Ship Epoch, 1522–1850* (London, 1910), p. 28.

32 Fulton, *Sovereignty*, pp. 9–15, 204–8.

33 Fulton, *Sovereignty*, pp. 59, 75–85. A land-kenning is the range at which the land can be seen from the seaward; the lawyers defined it as 14 miles.

34 Fulton, *Sovereignty*, pp. 86–112, 124–36. Wilson, *Profit and Power*, p. 34. Scammell, *World Encompassed*, p. 379. Edmundson, *Anglo-Dutch Rivalry*, pp. 19–25. *MGN*, II, 289–94.

35 Fulton, *Sovereignty*, pp. 118–24, 146–201. Edmundson, *Anglo-Dutch Rivalry*, pp. 28–90. Howat, *Foreign Policy*, pp. 54–9. Riis, *Auld Acquaintance*, I, 131.

36 'Omdanks alle genomen maatregelen komen de Duinkerkers nog steeds buitengaats': Pollentier, *De Admiraliteit*, p. 113.

37 Pollentier, *De Admiraliteit*, pp. 113–14. Stradling, *Armada of Flanders*, pp. 31–43.

38 Milford, 'Navy at Peace', p. 26. Guy, *Tudor England*, p. 396. *MNT*, I, xxi–xxxi.

39 Hebb, *Piracy*, pp. 21–134 is the fullest account of this expedition, superseding Corbett, *England in the Mediterranean*, I, 86–116.

40 Bruijn, *Dutch Navy*, pp. 23–4. This is the officer better known as 'Moy ('Handsome') Lambert'.

41 Strachan, *Roe*, pp. 137–8, quoting Sir Thomas Roe, the English ambassador at Constantinople.

42 Purchas, *Pilgrimes*, VI, 145.

43 Adams, 'Foreign Policy', pp. 139–52; and 'Spain or the Netherlands?', pp. 87–92. Howat, *Foreign Policy*, pp. 26–9. Elliott, *Olivares*, pp. 211–14. N. M. Sutherland, 'The Origins of the Thirty Years War and the Structure of European Politics', *EHR* CVII (1992), pp. 587–625.

44 Elliott, *Olivares*, pp. 207–8. Adams, 'Foreign Policy', pp. 151–7. Howat, *Foreign Policy*, pp. 29–32. Cogswell, 'Prelude to Ré', pp. 1–9.

45 Lockyer, *Buckingham*, pp. 230–54, 291–2. Cogswell, 'Foreign Policy and Parliament', pp. 250–61; and 'Prelude to Ré', p. 7. Lacour-Gayet, *La marine militaire*, pp. 67–70. *MF*, IV, 467, 479. Gardiner, *History of England*, V, 375–91; and *Impeachment of Buckingham*, pp.vii–ix, 139–302. Young, *Servility and Service*, pp. 138–140. Nicholas, *Nicholas*, pp. 44–6.

46 Harold Hulme, *The Life of Sir John Eliot, 1592–1632: Struggle for Parliamentary Freedom* (New York, 1957), p. 52.

47 Lockyer, *Buckingham*, p. 266.

48 Russell, *Parliaments and English Politics*; and 'Monarchies, Wars and Estates', *passim*. See also Adams, 'Spain or the Netherlands?', p. 80; Lockyer, *Buckingham*, pp. 244, 250, 363, 427–8, 467–74; Gardiner, *History of England*, VI, 191.

49 Thrush, 'Navy under Charles I', pp. 297–8.

50 Sir W. Monson, in *MNT*, III, 150.

51 Dalton, *Wimbledon*, II, 226. This absurd story has frequently been repeated from *ARN*, p. 220 (where the reference is faulty). Whether Geere (whom Wimbledon thought very poorly of: *MNT*, III,168, and HMC *Cowper*, I, 259) actually believed it, or was trying to make mischief, is not clear.

52 *ARN*, pp. 219–20. Clayton, 'Naval Administration', pp. 435–48, 452–3. Richard W. Stewart, 'Arms and Expeditions: the Ordnance Office and the assaults on Cadiz (1625) and the Isle of Rhé (1627)', in Fissel, *War and Government*, pp. 112–32.

53 To Charles I, 4 Oct 1625: Dalton, *Wimbledon*, II, 143.

54 Dalton, *Wimbledon*, II, 249 n.1. *Two Original Journals of Sir Richard Granville...* (London, 1724), pp. 3–4. Glanville, *Voyage to Cadiz*, pp.xl–xliii, 5–19. Corbett, *Fighting Instructions*, pp. 63–72.

55 Glanville, *Voyage to Cadiz*, p. 60.

56 Glanville, *Voyage to Cadiz*, pp. 33–44. Stearns, 'Caroline Military System', pp. 33, 45. Clayton, 'Naval Administration', pp. 456–63. Glanville, *Voyage to Cadiz*, pp. 36–62. Ribas Bensusan, *Asaltos a Cádiz*, pp. 116–29. Elliott, *Olivares*, p. 240.

57 Sir Michael Geere to W. Geere, 11 Dec 1625: Dalton, *Wimbledon*, II, 226. Paris Garden was near Covent Garden.

58 Sir E. Cecil to Sir J. Coke, 8 Nov 1625: HMC *Cowper*, I, 224.
59 Glanville, *Voyage to Cadiz*, pp.xliv, 90–113.
60 Lockyer, *Buckingham*, pp. 277–8, 300, 339. Gardiner, *Impeachment of Buckingham*.
61 Wren, 'London and the Twenty Ships', p. 333.
62 Lockyer, *Buckingham*, p. 360, quoting Sir J. Pennington.
63 Lockyer, *Buckingham*, pp. 303, 339, 344, 368. Wren, 'London and the Twenty Ships'.
64 Lockyer, *Buckingham*, pp. 345–6, quoting the 1626 naval commission.
65 E.g. Secretary Conway, in *BND*, p. 148.
66 Lockyer, *Buckingham*, pp. 346–52, 371. Cogswell, 'Prelude to Ré'. Herbert, *Isle of Rhe*, pp. 15–16. *BND*, p. 147, quoting 'Considerations touching France' by Lord Conway (Secretary of State), 6 Oct 1626.
67 Lockyer, *Buckingham*, pp. 368–403. *MF*, IV, 507–30. Herbert, *Isle of Rhe*. Pierre Castagnos, *Richelieu face à la mer* (Rennes, 1989), pp. 28–42. Josiah Burchett, *A Complete History of the Most Remarkable Transactions at Sea* (London, 1720), pp. 371–8.
68 Lockyer, *Buckingham*, pp. 420–37. *MF*, IV, 537–47. Young, *Servility and Service*, pp. 195–200. *BND*, pp. 156–7.
69 Lockyer, *Buckingham*, pp. 444–60. *MF*, IV, 550–4. *BND*, pp. 157–8. Ingram, *Three Sea Journals*, pp. 6–16, quoting (p. 11) the journal of Captain D. Cooper of the *Pelican* pink.
70 Penn, *Navy under the Early Stuarts*, p. 218.
71 Appleby, 'English Privateering', *passim*.
72 Appleby, 'Pathway out of Debt'.
73 Digby, *Journal*, p. 5.
74 Appleby, 'English Privateering', pp. 79, 87; and 'Pathway out of Debt', pp. 253–6.
75 Kepler, 'Ships gained and lost'. Andrews, *Ships, Money and Politics*, pp. 16–34, argues that the West Country and smaller ships suffered disproportionately, but other sectors did better out of the war. See also Powell, *Bristol Privateers*, pp. 70–85.
76 Gray, 'Turkish Piracy', p. 160.
77 Enrique Otero Lana, *Los corsarios españoles durante la decadencia de los Austrias: El corso español del Atlántico peninsular en el siglo XVII (1621–1697)* (Madrid, 1992), pp. 224–7.
78 Stradling, *Armada of Flanders*, p. 59. Kepler, 'Ships gained and lost'.
79 Bard, 'Warwick's Voyage'. Craven, 'Earl of Warwick', pp. 467–8.
80 Andrews, *Ships, Money and Politics*, pp. 106–127. Digby, *Journal*, is Sir Kenelm's own account.
81 Craven, 'Earl of Warwick'.
82 Andrews, *Ships, Money and Politics*, p. 1, quoting Captain Richard Gifford.
83 Lockyer, *Buckingham*, p. 283, quoting Sir William St Leger.
84 Wimbledon, in Glanville, *Voyage to Cadiz*, p.xliii.
85 Sir E. Cecil to Sir J. Coke, 27 Feb 1626: HMC *Cowper*, I, 258.
86 J. Ashburnham to E. Nicholas, 26 Oct 1627: Penn, *Navy under the Early Stuarts*, p. 134.
87 Penn, *Navy under the Early Stuarts*, p. 223.
88 Andrews, *Ships, Money and Politics*, p. 1.

25 The Inward Cause of All Disorders

1 Young, *Servility and Service*, p. 20, quoting J. Coke.
2 Peck, *Court Patronage*, p. 118, quoting Lord Northampton.
3 *ARN*, p. 194. McGowan, *Jacobean Commissions*, p. 201.
4 McGowan, *Jacobean Commissions*, pp. 36–48, 57–9, 79–83, 93–8, 241–2, 267–9. Clayton, 'Naval Administration', pp. 151–70.
5 Clayton, 'Naval Administration', p. 170, quoting MCC: Pepys MS 2878, p. 267.
6 Clayton, 'Naval Administration', p. 171, quoting PRO: SP 14/112 No.101.
7 Clayton, 'Naval Administration', p. 150.
8 Clayton, 'Naval Administration', pp. 220–1, 550–2, quoting BL: Eg.MSS 2975 f.47.
9 McGowan, *Jacobean Commissions*, pp. 11–22. Pett, *Autobiography*,

pp.lviii–lxi. Clayton, 'Naval Administration', pp. 258–9.

10 McGowan, *Jacobean Commissions*, pp. 22–34, 59–68.

11 Evidence of Robert Hooker, purser of the *Acquittance*, before the 1608 Commission: McGowan, *Jacobean Commissions*, p. 81.

12 McGowan, *Jacobean Commissions*, p. 60.

13 Evidence of Thomas Nash to the 1608 Commisssion: McGowan, *Jacobean Commissions*, p. 100.

14 Clayton, 'Naval Administration', p. 106.

15 Kenny, *Elizabeth's Admiral*, p. 315. *DSA*, II, 314. *ARN*, pp. 190–1. Clayton, 'Naval Administration', p. 205.

16 Navy Commission to Buckingham (draft by J. Coke), March 1619: HMC *Cowper*, I, 105.

17 Clayton, 'Naval Administration', p. 225, quoting T. Norris from the Coke MSS.

18 Bull, 'Furie of the Ordnance', p. 206. Young, *Servility and Service*, p. 21. Peck, *Northampton*, quoted p. 147.

19 Peck, *Court Patronage*, p. 108.

20 Hurstfield, 'Political Corruption'. Lloyd, 'Sir John Trevor', pp. 87–90.

21 Thrush, 'Navy under Charles I', pp. 154–6.

22 Prestwich, *Cranfield*, p. 160.

23 Aylmer, 'Administrative Reform', pp. 229–30; and 'Office Holding', p. 234. Linda Levy Peck, 'Problems in Jacobean Administration: Was Henry Howard, Earl of Northampton, a Reformer', *HJ* XIX (1976), pp. 831–58.

24 Prestwich, *Cranfield*, pp. 17–27. Hurstfield, 'Political Morality'. Peck, *Court Patronage*, p. 1. Lloyd, 'Sir John Trevor', pp. 90–100.

25 Prestwich, *Cranfield*, p. 212. Peck, *Court Patronage*, p. 106; and *Northampton*, pp. 153–5. Lloyd, 'Sir John Trevor', pp. 90–100. McGowan, *Jacobean Commissions*, pp. 1–255, prints much of the evidence of the commission.

26 Aylmer, 'Administrative Reform', p. 234. Kenny, *Elizabeth's Admiral*, pp. 316–8. Prestwich, *Cranfield*, p. 212.

27 Prestwich, *Cranfield*, pp. 210–13.

28 McGowan, *Jacobean Commissions*, p.xx.

29 Report of the 1618 Commisssion: McGowan, *Jacobean Commissions*, pp. 273–4.

30 Prestwich, *Cranfield*, pp. 212, 214, quoting Cranfield.

31 Prestwich, *Cranfield*, pp. 214–15.

32 McGowan, *Jacobean Commissions*, pp. 286–8.

33 McGowan, *Jacobean Commissions*, pp. 296–7.

34 Young, *Servility and Service*, p. 22.

35 Prestwich, *Cranfield*, pp. 212–17. Quinn & Ryan, *England's Sea Empire*, pp. 220–4. Young, *Servility and Service*, pp. 42–51. Aylmer, *King's Servants*, pp. 21–2; and 'Buckingham as Administrative Reformer?', *EHR* CV (1990), pp. 355–62, at p. 362.

36 Cranfield to Buckingham, 17 Nov 1618: Alexander, *Charles I's Lord Treasurer*, p. 7.

37 Pett, *Autobiography*, p.lxxxiii. Thrush, 'Navy under Charles I', p. 189. Clayton, 'Naval Administration', pp. 27–8. *BND*, pp. 164–5.

38 Young, *Servility and Service*, pp. 79–80.

39 Peck, *Court Patronage*, pp. 125–126.

40 Andrews, *Ships, Money and Politics*, p. 8. Lockyer, *Buckingham*, p. 273.

41 Adams, 'Foreign Policy', p. 121. Clayton, 'Naval Administration', p. 91. Young, 'Buckingham, War, and Parliament', pp. 50–1; and *Servility and Service*, p. 122.

42 Russell, *Parliaments and English Politics*, pp. 219–29. Young, *Servility and Service*, pp. 141–5. Cogswell, 'Foreign Policy and Parliament', p. 247.

43 Lockyer, *Buckingham*, p. 339. Russell, *Parliaments and English Politics*, pp. 284–5, 290. Young, *Servility and Service*, p. 164.

44 Peck, *Court Patronage*, p. 126.

45 Swales, 'Ship Money', pp. 168–72. Lockyer, *Buckingham*, p. 424. Thrush, 'Navy under Charles I', p. 143.

46 Russell, *Parliaments and English Politics*, pp. 78–83. Young, 'Buckingham, War, and Parliament', p. 61. Sharpe, *Charles I*, p. 98.

47 Stearns, 'Caroline Military System', pp. 314–15.

48 Clayton, 'Naval Administration',

pp. 75–84. Lockyer, *Buckingham*, pp. 345, 367, 447. Peck, *Court Patronage*, p. 129. Mainwaring, *Works*, I, 146–150. McGowan, 'Navy under Buckingham', pp. 265–75. Young, *Servility and Service*, p. 201.

49 James & Shaw, 'Admiralty Administration', pp. 10–11, 172. *RFO*, XVII, 124. Perrin, 'Lord Admiral', p. 129.

50 Stearns, 'Caroline Military System', pp. 133–5. Aylmer, *King's Servants*, p. 22. Young, *Servility and Service*, p. 133.

51 HMC *Cowper*, I, 164.

52 Stearns, 'Caroline Military System', pp. 140–150. Lockyer, *Buckingham*, p. 422.

53 Clayton, 'Naval Administration', pp. 39–40.

54 James & Shaw, 'Admiralty Administration', pp. 173–6. *ARN*, p. 279. Thrush, 'Navy under Charles I', pp. 28–33. Perrin, 'Lord Admiral', pp. 124–9.

55 Clayton, 'Naval Administration', pp. 177, 195.

56 Evidence of Edward Willis, quartermaster of the *Acquittance*, to the 1608 Commission: McGowan, *Jacobean Commissions*, pp. 228–9. Oil followed wine measure, so an oil barrel contained at least 12 per cent less than a beer barrel.

57 Clayton, 'Naval Administration', p. 182. McGowan, 'Navy under Buckingham', pp. 239–41.

58 To Middlesex, 11 Aug 1623: *BND*, pp. 163–4.

59 Sir A. Apsley to Sir J. Ley, 20 April 1625: *BND*, p. 165.

60 Thrush, 'Navy under Charles I', pp. 279–80, 294–7.

61 To Conway, 14 Dec 1625: Young, *Servility and Service*, p. 189.

62 To Buckingham, July 1626: Lockyer, *Buckingham*, p. 302.

63 Lockyer, *Buckingham*, p. 303.

64 Lockyer, *Buckingham*, p. 341. Peck, *Court Patronage*, p. 115. Thrush, 'Navy under Charles I', pp. 139, 178.

65 Lockyer, *Buckingham*, p. 460. Thrush, 'Navy under Charles I', pp. 140–3.

66 Thrush, 'Navy under Charles I', p. 249, quoting PRO: SP 16/149 No.90.

67 Young, *Servility and Service*, p. 199, quoting Coke's diary.

68 Thrush, 'Navy under Charles I', pp. 145–6, 260–72; also 'The Bottomless Bagg? Sir James Bagg and the Navy, 1623–8', in Duffy, *Maritime History of Devon*, I, 115–16.

69 Bull, 'Furie of the Ordnance', p. 212. Prestwich, *Cranfield*, p. 218. Young, *Servility and Service*, p. 87.

70 Thrush, 'Ordnance Office', p. 344. This Totnes was the former Sir George Carew.

71 Stewart, 'Arms and Expeditions', p. 119.

72 Bull, 'Furie of the Ordnance', pp. 213, 251–4.

73 Thrush, 'Ordnance Office', pp. 339–40.

74 Clayton, 'Naval Administration', pp. 267, 142, quoting PRO: E 351/2241–2242. Thrush, 'Navy under Charles I', p. 110.

75 Hollond, *Discourses*, pp. 27–30. McGowan, *Jacobean Commissions*, pp. 231–4.

76 Navy Commission to Buckingham (draft by J. Coke), 1621: HMC *Cowper*, I, 114–15.

77 Hollond, *Discourses*, pp. 30–31.

78 Thrush, 'Navy under Charles I', p. 119, quoting Captain Joshua Downing from PRO: SP 14/182 No.29.

79 Powell, '"Shipkeepers" and Minor Officers', pp. 157–8; cf. *ARN*, p. 188, with defective text and reference.

80 J. Coke to Buckingham, 7 Nov 1618: HMC *Cowper*, I, 99–100.

81 Clayton, 'Naval Administration', p. 263, quoting PRO: SP 14/182 No.29. Cf. Powell, '"Shipkeepers" and Minor Officers', pp. 160–1. 'Their belief' = the Creed; 'say their compass' = box the compass; the 'barracado' is the boom at Upnor.

82 Powell, '"Shipkeepers" and Minor Officers', p. 162.

83 *The Life of the Icelander Jón Ólafsson...* ed. Bertha S. Phillpotts (HS 2nd S. Vols. 53 and 68, 1923–31), I, 32. Penn, *Navy under the Early Stuarts*, p. 46.

84 Mainwaring, *Works*, II, 141.

85 Clayton, 'Naval Administration', pp. 148,

276. Pett, *Autobiography*, pp. 30, 34, 94–5, 115, 142. Oppenheim, *VCH Kent*, II, 343. Courtney, 'Excavations at Woolwich'.

86 HMC *Cowper*, I, 109. McGowan, 'Navy under Buckingham', p. 209. *ARN*, p. 209.

87 Clayton, 'Naval Administration', pp. 147–8, 267–78. *ARN*, pp. 210, 295–7. HMC *Cowper*, I, 166, 173. McGowan, *Jacobean Commissions*, pp. 294–5. Oppenheim, *VCH Kent*, II, 344. Jonathan Coad, *The Royal Dockyards 1690–1850: Architecture and Engineering Works of the Sailing Navy* (Aldershot, 1989), p. 5.

88 Clayton, 'Naval Administration', pp. 278–80. *ARN*, pp. 209–10, 295–7. Lockyer, *Buckingham*, p. 366. Sharpe, *Charles I*, p. 99. *BND*, pp. 151. Mainwaring, *Works*, I, 140–2.

26 A Diamond in his Crown

1 Alcalá-Zamora, *España, Flandes y el Mar del Norte*, pp. 225–8. Elliott, *Olivares*, pp. 219, 272, 329–35, 352, 361. K. R. H. Frick, *Vergessene Flotten: Flotten und Flottenbaupläne im Heiligen Römischen Reich deutscher Nation vom 15. Jahrhundert bis 1632* (Graz, 1990), pp. 96–114.

2 *MF*, IV, 588.

3 'Quiconque est maistre de la mer, a ung grand pouvoyr sur la terre': *MF*, IV, 490, quoting Isaac de Razilly. Cf. Hubert Granier, 'La pensée navale française dans la première moitié du XVIIe siècle (1600–1661)', in *L'évolution de la pensée navale*, ed. Hervé Coutau-Bégarie (Paris, 1990–95, 5 vols), II, 37–53.

4 *ARN*, p. 265. Thrush, 'Naval Finance', p. 135.

5 Elliott, *Olivares*, p. 58, quoting Don Baltasar de Zuñíga.

6 Quintrell, 'Charles I and his Navy', p. 160.

7 Fulton, *Sovereignty*, pp. 15–20, 209–12.

8 Quintrell, 'Charles I and his Navy', p. 169.

9 *MF*, IV, 627–8.

10 To Sir J. Coke, 23 Sep 1631: HMC *Cowper*, I, 443.

11 Fulton, *Sovereignty*, p. 280.

12 Oppenheim, *VCH Suffolk*, II, 226. Warwick was Lord Lieutenant of Suffolk.

13 *MNT*, IV, 119–27. Fulton, *Sovereignty*, pp. 276–85. HMC *Muncaster*, pp. 277, 281–2, 286–7.

14 Richard Ollard, *The Image of the King: Charles I and Charles II* (London, 1979), p. 33.

15 Quintrell, 'Charles I and his Navy', p. 172. Cf. Kennedy, 'Common Seamen', p. 171.

16 Young, *His Majesty's Royal Ship*, pp.xvii, xx–xxi.

17 Colin S. Gray, *The Leverage of Sea Power: The Strategic Advantage of Navies in War* (New York, 1992), p. 142.

18 Sharpe, *Charles I*, pp. 102–3. Andrews, *Ships, Money & Politics*, p. 10. Quintrell, 'Charles I and his Navy', pp. 164–5. Hebb, *Piracy*, pp. 219–21.

19 Thrush, 'Navy under Charles I', p. 12, quoting Sir Kenelm Digby (English ambassador in Paris) from BL: Add.MSS 64910.

20 Thrush, 'Naval Finance', pp. 142–7; and 'Navy under Charles I', pp. 61–3. Harris, *Trinity House Transactions*, pp. 68, 89–90.

21 Hebb, *Piracy*, p. 217.

22 Sharpe, *Charles I*, pp. 549–54. Thrush, 'Naval Finance', p. 145. Bonsey & Jenkins, *Ship Money Papers*, pp.x–xii. Alexander, *Charles I's Lord Treasurer*, pp. 209–12.

23 Sharpe, *Charles I*, pp. 555–86. Alexander, *Charles I's Lord Treasurer*, quoted p. 209. Thrush, 'Navy under Charles I', pp. 49–50. Dietz, *English Public Finance*, p. 267. Bonsey & Jenkins, *Ship Money Papers*, p.xii. Russell, *Fall of the British Monarchies*, pp. 7–8.

24 Sharpe, *Charles I*, pp. 588–93. Dietz, *English Public Finance*, pp. 279–80.

25 Quintrell, 'Charles I and his Navy', pp. 164–9. Fulton, *Sovereignty*, pp. 259–75. Mainwaring, *Works*, I, 228–33.

26 Fulton, *Sovereignty*, pp. 286–92. Mainwaring, *Works*, I, 234–5.

27 Quintrell, 'Charles I and his Navy', pp. 172–3.
28 *MNT*, III, 223–4. Appendix II.
29 Alcalá-Zamora, *España, Flandes y el Mar del Norte*, pp. 347–56, 510–12. Edmundson, *Anglo-Dutch Rivalry*, pp. 106–19. Elliott, *Olivares*, pp. 507–8, 535. Adams, 'Spain or the Netherlands?', pp. 84–5. Alexander, *Charles I's Lord Treasurer*, pp. 215–17. Harland Taylor, 'Trade, Neutrality, and the "English Road", 1630–1648', *EcHR* 2nd S. XXV (1972), pp. 236–60. Havran, *Caroline Courtier*, p. 103.
30 Fulton, *Sovereignty*, pp. 265, 276–85. Sharpe, *Charles I*, pp. 103–4. The States-General was the parliament of the Dutch Republic.
31 Fulton, *Sovereignty*, pp. 293–301, 307–11. Quintrell, 'Charles I and his Navy', p. 171. Sharpe, *Charles I*, pp. 545–7. Dyer, 'Ship-Money Fleet'.
32 Fulton, *Sovereignty*, pp. 313–21. De Jonge, *Nederlandsche Zeewesen*, I, 236–7.
33 *ARN*, p. 275, quoting 'some of the Navy Commissioners' in 1626.
34 Gray, 'Turks, Moors and Cornish Fishermen'; and 'Turkish Piracy'.
35 Gray, 'Turkish Piracy', quoted p. 166. Hebb, *Piracy*, pp. 138–46. Fisher, *Barbary Legend*, p. 165.
36 Barnby, 'Attack on Baltimore'. Hebb, *Piracy*, pp. 149–50. For Jansz see Coindreau, *Les corsaires de Salé*, pp. 67–70, and Lloyd, *English Corsairs*, pp. 98–9.
37 Hebb, *Piracy*, pp. 212–16. Coindreau, *Les corsaires de Salé*, p. 57 n.1.
38 Andrews, *Ships, Money & Politics*, pp. 165–83. Hebb, *Piracy*, pp. 237–63. Coindreau, *Les corsaires de Salé*, pp. 30–45. *MF*, IV, 691–2. Thrush, 'In Pursuit of the Frigate', p. 44. Chaplin, 'William Rainsborough'. *The Barbary Voyage of 1638 . . . of Sir George Carteret*, ed. Boies Penrose (Philadelphia, 1929).
39 Thrush, 'Navy under Charles I', p. 128. Hebb, *Piracy*, pp. 266–70, 273–5. Davis, 'England and the Mediterranean', pp. 127–30.
40 Lloyd, *English Corsairs*, p. 119. *The Autobiography of the Reverend Devereux Spratt*, ed. T. A. B. Spratt (London, 1886).
41 *ARN*, pp. 275–6. Stradling, 'Spanish Dunkirkers'; and *Armada of Flanders*, pp. 59, 83–4. R. Baetens, 'The Organization and Effects of Flemish Privateering in the Seventeenth Century', *Acta Historiae Neerlandicae* IX (1976), pp. 48–75.
42 *ARN*, p. 212.
43 Sir R. Hawkins to Buckingham, 8 Feb 1621: Hebb, *Piracy*, p. 129.
44 Sir E. Cecil to Sir J. Coke, 27 Feb 1626: HMC *Cowper*, I, 259; cf. Glanville, *Voyage to Cadiz*, p.xliii.
45 Captain T. Love to Sir J. Coke, 2 Nov 1625: HMC *Cowper*, I, 222.
46 McGowan, *Jacobean Commissions*, pp. 230–2. Anderson, 'The *Prince Royal*'. Pett, *Autobiography*, pp.lxvii–lxxxii. Salisbury, 'Jacobean Three Decker'. Probst, 'Nordeuropæisk spanteopslagning', pp. 12–21. Riis, *Auld Acquaintance*, I, 108; II, 54.
47 Anders Franzén, 'Därför kantrada "Vasa"', *Svensk Sjöfarts Tidning* 46 (16 Nov 1984), pp. 10–11.
48 Sir J. Pennington to Charles I, 8 May 1634: *BND*, pp. 176–7; cf. HMC *Muncaster*, p. 283.
49 *ARN*, pp. 257–8. Harris, *Trinity House*, pp. 223–5; and *Trinity House Transactions*, pp. 123–4.
50 Clayton, 'Naval Administration', p. 288, quoting the Coke MSS.
51 HMC *Muncaster*, p. 284.
52 Clayton, 'Naval Administration', p. 231, quoting the Coke MSS. Cf. Pett, *Autobiography*, pp. 136, 157.
53 Barker, 'Design in the Dockyards', p. 64.
54 *BND*, pp. 179–80.
55 *BND*, pp. 175–6. Moore, 'Rigging in the Seventeenth Century'; Alan Villiers, *Give me a Ship to Sail* (London, 1958), p. 253.
56 Clayton, 'Naval Administration', p. 298. Clowes, *Royal Navy*, II, 5.
57 Thrush, 'Navy under Charles I', p. 182.
58 Young, *His Majesty's Royal Ship*, pp.xiv–xvi.
59 *MF*, IV, 594–7.
60 Young, *His Majesty's Royal Ship*. Anderson, 'The *Royal Sovereign*'. Pett,

Autobiography, pp.xci–xcviii, 207–10. *ARN*, pp. 260–2. Van Oosten & Bosscher, 'Het Zeilschip', p. 1015.

61 *The Diary of John Evelyn*, ed. E. S. de Beer (Oxford, 1965, 6 vols), I, 22.

62 *The Travels of Peter Mundy*, ed. Sir R. C. Temple (HS 2nd S. 17, 35, 45, 46 & 55 [4 vols in 5], 1905–25), IV, 35, 48–9.

63 Bull, 'Furie of the Ordnance', pp. 47, 73–8, 482–7. Cleere & Crossley, *Iron Industry*, pp. 176–7.

64 Caruana, *Sea Ordnance*, pp. 50–66.

65 Rodger, 'Broadside Gunnery', p. 309, 317.

66 Hawkins, *Observations*, p. 29.

67 Sir Thomas Fane to Lord Cobham, 23 March 1599: HMC *Salisbury*, IX, 114.

68 Enrique Otero Lana, 'Un avance en la construcción naval: las fragatas construidas en La Habana hacia 1600', *RHN* IX (1991), pp. 87–94. Johan E. Elias, *De Vlootbouw in Nederland in de eerste Helft der 17e Eeuw, 1596–1655* (Amsterdam, 1933), pp. 40–58. Stradling, *Armada of Flanders*, pp. 165–73. *MGN*, II, 56–61. Van Oosten & Bosscher, 'Het Zeilschip', p. 1007.

69 Thrush, 'In Pursuit of the Frigate'. Clayton, 'Naval Administration', p. 492.

70 *ARN*, pp. 252–3.

71 Thrush, 'In Pursuit of the Frigate', p. 38.

72 Lockyer, *Buckingham*, p. 423.

73 Thrush, 'In Pursuit of the Frigate', pp. 40–1. Howard, *Ships of War*, pp. 152–3. *ARN*, p. 256. Hebb, *Piracy*, p. 206. John Wassell, 'The Lion's Whelps', *MM* LXIII (1977), pp. 368–9.

74 Eames, 'Sea Power and Welsh History', p. 129, quoting R. Plumleigh from PRO: SP 16/223 No.6.

75 HMC *Muncaster*, p. 283.

76 Thrush, 'In Pursuit of the Frigate', pp. 42–4. Hebb, *Piracy*, pp. 241–2.

77 Thrush, 'Naval Finance', pp. 149–52; and 'Navy under Charles I', pp. 171–3. *ARN*, pp. 293–4. Aylmer, *King's Servants*, pp. 64–8. Alexander, *Charles I's Lord Treasurer*, p. 220.

78 Thrush, 'Navy under Charles I', pp. 34–6, 90–1, 103–9.

79 Aylmer, 'Administrative Reform', p. 238. Perrin, 'Lord Admiral', p. 132. Thrush, 'Navy under Charles I', pp. 25, 95–102. Sharpe, *Charles I*, p. 599.

80 Thrush, 'Navy under Charles I', pp. 95–102. Mainwaring, *Works*, I, 246–50. Aylmer, 'Administrative Reform', pp. 237–9.

81 Young, *Servility and Service*, pp. 207–8. Thrush, 'Navy under Charles I', pp. 34–6, 76–8, 86–91. Aylmer, *King's Servants*, pp. 77–8.

82 Thrush, 'Navy under Charles I', pp. 132–5. Ashton, 'Disbursing Official', pp. 163–5.

83 Thrush, 'Navy under Charles I', pp. 131–2, 254–6. L. C. Martin, 'John Crane (1576–1660) of Loughton, Bucks: Surveyor-General of all Victuals for Ships, 1635–42', *MM* LXX (1984), pp. 143–8.

84 Thrush, 'Navy under Charles I', p. 102, quoting the Venetian ambassador from *CSPV* 1632–6, p. 365.

85 Aylmer, *King's Servants*, p. 350. Pett, *Autobiography*, pp.lxxxix–xc.

86 Thrush, 'Navy under Charles I', pp. 132–5. McGowan, 'Navy under Buckingham', pp. 154–5. Ashton, 'Disbursing official', p. 165.

87 Thrush, 'Navy under Charles I', pp. 136, 188.

88 Hollond, *Discourses*, p. 102.

89 Powell, '"Shipkeepers" and Minor Officers', pp. 162–3.

90 Hollond, *Discourses*, p. 14.

91 Powell, '"Shipkeepers" and Minor Officers', p. 163.

92 Aylmer, 'Administrative Reform', p. 244. *ARN*, p. 290.

93 Sharpe, *Charles I*, p. 588. Ian Ferrier, 'Ship Money Reconsidered', *British Tax Review* V (1984), pp. 227–36; Russell, *Fall of the British Monarchies*, p. 11.

94 Nelson P. Bard, 'The Ship Money Case and William Fiennes, Viscount Saye and Sele', *BIHR* L (1977), pp. 177–84.

95 Hebb, *Piracy*, pp. 203–9. Thrush, 'In Pursuit of the Frigate', pp. 29–42. Lockyer, *Buckingham*, p. 364.

96 Andrews, *Ships, Money & Politics*, pp. 131–8.

97 This is a major theme of Russell, *Fall of*

the *British Monarchies*, and 'Monarchies, Wars and Estates'.

27 One and All

1 Clayton, 'Naval Administration', p. 205.
2 Peck, *Court Patronage*, pp. 119–120, quoting the 1618 Navy Commission.
3 Evidence of Captain Thomas Norris to the 1608 Commission, in McGowan, *Jacobean Commissions*, p. 69.
4 Clayton, 'Naval Administration', pp. 29–30, quoting the 1618 Navy Commission.
5 Clayton, 'Naval Administration', pp. 389, 452–3.
6 Glanville, *Voyage to Cadiz*, pp. 24, 118.
7 *MNT*, IV, 1. Glanville, *Voyage to Cadiz*, p. 5.
8 Clayton, 'Naval Administration', p. 492, quoting J. Waymouth from BL: Add.MSS 26,051 f.11b.
9 Glanville, *Voyage to Cadiz*, pp. 83–8.
10 *MNT*, III, 168.
11 Glanville, *Voyage to Cadiz*, pp. 28–9. Dalton, *Wimbledon*, II, 156–7.
12 Corbett, *Fighting Instructions*, pp. 37, 53.
13 Sir W. Monson, in *MNT*, IV, 14.
14 Bard, 'Warwick's Voyage', p. 65.
15 '... de gros mariniers vaillans, nourris dans l'eau et la bouteille': *MF*, IV, 491, 599.
16 Winkel-Rauws, *Nederlansch-Engelsche Samenwerking*, pp. 14–17, 48–62.
17 Glanville, *Voyage to Cadiz*, p.xxxvii.
18 HMC *Cowper*, I, 224. Glanville, *Voyage to Cadiz*, p.xxxv, and Dalton, *Wimbledon*, II, 217.
19 Evidence of William Ward, boatswain of the *Answer*, to the 1608 Commission: McGowan, McGowan, *Jacobean Commissions*, p. 64.
20 Clayton, 'Naval Administration', p. 309.
21 Clayton, 'Naval Administration', p. 317, quoting Sir F. Gorges from PRO: SP 14/103 No.66.
22 McGowan, 'Navy under Buckingham', p. 130. According to McCaughey, 'Politics and Administration', pp. 18–19, the legal penalties for resisting impressment were abolished in 1623.
23 Thrush, 'Navy under Charles I', p. 233.
24 Thrush, 'Navy under Charles I', pp. 222–3.
25 HMC *Muncaster*, p. 285. McGowan, 'Navy under Buckingham', p. 132. Thrush, 'Navy under Charles I', p. 216. Shilton & Holworthy, *High Court of Admiralty*, p. 15.
26 Thrush, 'Navy under Charles I', pp. 225–6.
27 Thrush, 'Navy under Charles I', p. 227, quoting Sir John Watts.
28 Corbett, *Fighting Instructions*, p. 56. Glanville, *Voyage to Cadiz*, p. 5. Ingram, *Three Sea Journals*, p. 19.
29 Sir W. Monson, in *MNT*, III, 381.
30 Clayton, 'Naval Administration', p. 395. Thrush, 'Navy under Charles I', p. 230.
31 Gray, *Early-Stuart Mariners*, p.xiii.
32 To Lord Denbigh, 1 April 1628: *BND*, pp. 167–8. The hundred is Roborough Hundred.
33 Clayton, 'Naval Administration', quoting Sir J. Coke from PRO: SP 16/116 No.53.
34 Pollitt, 'Devon in the French and Spanish Wars', p. 113.
35 Thrush, 'Navy under Charles I', pp. 215–16, quoting BL: Add.MSS 64883 fo.108.
36 Clayton, 'Naval Administration', quoted p. 318. *MNT*, III, 381; IV, 149–51. Hollond, *Discourses*, pp. 49–51.
37 HMC *Muncaster*, p. 292, quoting Sir J. Pennington's journal.
38 Kennedy, 'Parliament and the Navy', p. 34.
39 Thrush, 'Navy under Charles I', p. 228, quoting PRO: SP 16/337 No.1.
40 Thrush, 'Navy under Charles I', pp. 235–7.
41 Sir J. Bagg to the Navy Commission, 6 May 1625: HMC *Cowper*, I, 193.
42 Thrush, 'Navy under Charles I', p. 229, quoting Hugh Watkin.
43 Gray, *Early-Stuart Mariners*, pp.xiv–xv. Clayton, 'Naval Administration', pp. 360–1. *ARN*, p. 244. *ARN*, pp. 270–1 and Andrews, *Ships, Money & Politics*, pp. 206–9, give the associated shipping surveys.
44 McCaughey, 'Politics and

Administration', pp. 19–21. Kennedy, 'Parliament and the Navy', p. 33.

45 Thrush, 'Navy under Charles I', pp. 230–2.

46 Harris, *Trinity House*, pp. 219–20.

47 Keevil, *Medicine and the Navy*, I, 179, 186.

48 *MNT*, III, 367.

49 Clayton, 'Naval Administration', p. 395, quoting a Privy Council circular.

50 Sir E. Cecil to Sir J. Coke, 27 Feb 1626: Glanville, *Voyage to Cadiz*, p.xlii, and HMC *Cowper*, I, 258.

51 *ARN*, p. 223.

52 *ARN*, p. 224.

53 Lockyer, *Buckingham*, pp. 339–43. *ARN*, pp. 226–9.

54 Denis Fleming & J. Downing to Sir J. Coke, 18 July 1626: *BND*, pp. 181–2; the version in HMC *Cowper*, I, 274, is not complete.

55 McGowan, 'Navy under Buckingham', pp. 113–15.

56 Thrush, 'Navy under Charles I', pp. 239–240. Kennedy, 'Common Seamen', p. 174. Lockyer, *Buckingham*, p. 362.

57 Keevil, *Medicine and the Navy*, I, 183.

58 Clayton, 'Naval Administration', p. 501, quoting PRO: SP 16/90 No.38; cf. *ARN*, p. 232. 'Hammacoes' = hammocks.

59 Clayton, 'Naval Administration', pp. 503–4: I have chosen his version in preference to *ARN*, p. 233.

60 Kennedy, 'Parliament and the Navy', p. 39.

61 Kennedy, 'Parliament and the Navy', pp. 41–2, quoting PRO: SP 16/108 No.18.

62 Denbigh to Buckingham, 22 June 1628: Clayton, 'Naval Administration', pp. 509–10, quoting PRO: SP 16/107 No.101. 'Runagates' = renegades, deserters.

63 Thrush, 'Navy under Charles I', p. 203.

64 *ARN*, p. 235, and Kennedy, 'Common Seamen', p. 173.

65 Wren, 'London and the Twenty Ships', p. 335. Butler, *Dialogues*, p. 44. Andrews, *Ships, Money & Politics*, pp. 63–4.

66 *ARN*, pp. 225–6. HMC *Cowper*, I, 258. Glanville, *Voyage to Cadiz*, p.xlii. Lockyer, *Buckingham*, p. 298. Thrush, 'Navy under Charles I', p. 213. Kennedy, 'Parliament and the Navy', pp. 22–4.

67 Young, *Servility and Service*, p. 192. McGowan, 'Navy under Buckingham', pp. 118, 121.

68 Notably by *ARN*, followed by others since.

69 Mainwaring, *Works*, II, 281.

70 Mainwaring's 'Seaman's Dictionary' (*Works*, Vol.II), Smith's *Sea Grammar*, Monson's *Naval Tracts*, Butler's *Dialogues*, Hollond's *Discourses* etc. Cf. Waters, *Navigation*, pp. 462–3.

71 Sir W. Monson, in *MNT*, III, 434.

72 Conway to George Garrard, 28 June 1636: HMC *Portland*, III, 35.

73 Conway to George Garrard, 13 Sep 1636: HMC *Portland*, III, 40.

74 Kennedy, 'Parliament and the Navy', p. 83.

75 Dyer, 'Ship-Money Fleet', pp. 198–9.

76 HMC *Muncaster*, p. 279, quoting Pennington's journal.

77 HMC *Muncaster*, p. 296, quoting Pennington's journal.

78 Dyer, 'Ship-Money Fleet', p. 199.

79 Mainwaring, *Works*, I, 249–50.

80 Scott, 'Naval Chaplain', pp. 14, 27–8. McGowan, 'Navy under Buckingham', pp. 172, 188–9.

81 K. Edisbury, in Scott, 'Naval Chaplain', p. 25. 'Deboshed' = debauched.

82 Shilton & Holworthy, *High Court of Admiralty*, p. 279.

83 Kennedy, 'Parliament and the Navy', p. 46. Keevil, *Medicine and the Navy*, I, 202.

84 Keevil, *Medicine and the Navy*, I, 179.

85 Young, *His Majesty's Royal Ship*, p.xx.

86 Glanville, *Voyage to Cadiz*, p.vi.

87 McGowan, 'Navy under Buckingham', p. 142.

88 Powell, '"Shipkeepers" and Minor Officers', p. 172. Butler, *Dialogues*, p. 299. McGowan, 'Navy under Buckingham', p. 140.

89 Clayton, 'Naval Administration', p. 310; his 1628 orders are on p. 512.

90 McGowan, 'Navy under Buckingham', p. 128.

91 *BND*, pp. 182–4. *MNT*, III, 436. Mainwaring, *Works*, I, 105. Appleby,

'English Privateering', p. 236. Digby, *Journal*, p. 60.

92 Digby, *Journal*, p. 62. HMC *Muncaster*, p. 291. McGowan, 'Navy under Buckingham', p. 127.

93 Mainwaring, *Works*, I, 105.

94 *MNT*, III, 258–9, 386–7. *BND*, p. 184. Butler, *Dialogues*, pp. 42–4. Digby, *Journal*, pp. 56, 60.

95 But Andrews, *Ships, Money & Politics*, pp. 62–83, argues that mutiny became much commoner after 1625 and remained so for a century and a half.

96 Andrews, *Ships, Money & Politics*, pp. 62–3.

97 McGowan, 'Navy under Buckingham', p. 136.

98 Bard, 'Warwick's Voyage', p. 36, has a privateersman whipped for attacking a boatswain's mate.

99 Appleby, 'English Privateering', p. 119. Digby, *Journal*, p. 85. Shilton & Holworthy, *High Court of Admiralty*, p. 286.

100 Bard, 'Warwick's Voyage', pp. 28, 35, 49–50. *MNT*, III, 436, mentions keel-hauling as a 'sea punishment'. Shilton & Holworthy, *High Court of Admiralty*, p. 225, have it being threatened in a merchantman, but I do not know any case of it being used in the Navy.

101 Bard, 'Warwick's Voyage', p. 67, quoting William Ball's private journal.

102 Shilton & Holworthy, *High Court of Admiralty*, pp. 15, 137.

103 Powell, *Bristol Privateers*, p. 61, quoting Captain Martin Pring of the *James Royal*. Hope, *Shipping*, pp. 179–80, gives another instance of flogging for mutiny in a merchantman.

104 *BND*, p. 182. Corbett, *Fighting Instructions*, pp. 36, 52. Bard, 'Warwick's Voyage', p. 84. *MNT*, IV, 3. Scott, 'Naval Chaplain', p. 14.

105 Glanville, *Voyage to Cadiz*, p. 44. McGowan, 'Navy under Buckingham', p. 109.

106 Kennedy, 'Common Seamen', p. 175.

107 John Chamberlain to Revd Joseph Mead, 20 June 1623: [Thomas Birch], *The Court & Times of James the First* (London, 1848, 2 vols), II, 407. Scott, 'Naval Chaplain', p. 12.

108 Hebb, *Piracy*, p. 95. McGowan, *Jacobean Commissions*, p. 66. *MNT*, III, 383.

109 Clayton, 'Naval Administration', p. 490, quoting J. Waymouth from BL: Add.MSS 26,051 f.1.

110 HMC *Cowper*, I, 411–12.

111 Rodger, 'Broadside Gunnery', pp. 309, 316–17.

112 *ARN*, p. 214. *MNT*, IV, 91. Mainwaring, *Works*, I, 54–5. John Brand, 'The Names of his Majesties Shipps . . .', *Archaeologia* XV (1806), pp. 53–8. Harris, *Trinity House Transactions*, pp. 115–16. Thrush, 'Navy under Charles I', p. 226.

113 Keevil, *Medicine and the Navy*, I, 164–73. Thrush, 'Navy under Charles I', pp. 250.

114 Keevil, *Medicine and the Navy*, I, 183.

115 Clayton, 'Naval Administration', p. 513. *BND*, p. 183. Butler, *Dialogues*, p. 62.

116 Kemp, *British Sailor*, p. 27.

117 Sir J. Coke to Buckingham, 25 Aug 1625: Gardiner, *Impeachment of Buckingham*, p. 15.

118 Lloyd, *British Seaman*, p. 64.

119 Bard, 'Warwick's Voyage', p. 52, quoting W. Ball's journal.

120 Mainwaring, *Works*, I, 250. *MNT*, IV, 148.

121 *ARN*, p. 287; but this violent opponent of Charles I produces only a thin catalogue, with no references at all.

122 Kemp, *British Sailor*, p. 25.

123 Barnby, 'Attack on Baltimore', pp. 28–9. Thrush, 'Navy under Charles I', pp. 263–4.

124 HMC *Muncaster*, p. 291. McCaughey, 'Politics and Administration', pp. 31–2.

125 HMC *Cowper*. I, 188.

126 Mainwaring, *Works*, I, 247. *ARN*, pp. 247–8. Keevil, *Medicine and the Navy*, I, 193–6.

127 Sharpe, *Charles I*, p. 100 (quoted). Mainwaring, *Works*, II, 248–9. Thrush, 'Navy under Charles I', pp. 204–12. *BND*, pp. 184–5.

128 Powell, 'Early Naval Lieutenant'. Kennedy, 'Naval Captains', pp. 182–92.

129 *ARN*, p. 226.
130 McCaughey, 'Politics and Administration', p. 16; cf. *ARN*, p. 226, where the reference is defective.
131 Sir W. Monson, in *MNT*, III, 435.
132 Andrews, *Ships, Money & Politics*, p. 80.
133 Andrews, *Ships, Money & Politics*, p. 78.
134 Butler, *Dialogues*, p. 31.
135 Kennedy, 'Common Seamen', p. 170, quoting Nathaniel Knott's 'Device of a Seaman'.

28 The Fall of Three Kingdoms

1 Ohlmeyer, *Civil War and Restoration*, pp. 93–4.
2 Fissel, *Bishops' Wars*, pp. 3–39. Ohlmeyer, *Civil War and Restoration*, pp. 77–92.
3 Powell, *Civil War*, p. 4. Russell, *Fall of the British Monarchies*, p. 77. Mainwaring, *Works*, I, 267–75. Sharpe, *Charles I*, p. 805.
4 Fulton, *Sovereignty*, pp. 327–8. Mainwaring, *Works*, I, 254–63.
5 Fulton, *Sovereignty*, p. 327. HMC *Muncaster*, p. 290.
6 Fulton, *Sovereignty*, pp. 327–30.
7 'Mijn advijs was, dat niemandt vorder in zee conde commanderen dan sijn canon conde reycken': De Boer, *Tromp*, p. 132. Boxer, *Tromp's Journal*, pp. 25–34, 52–3, 117–18. Johanna K. Oudendijk, *Maerten Harpertszoon Tromp* (2nd edn, The Hague, 1952), p. 70. Stradling, *Armada of Flanders*, p. 106. C. R. Boxer, 'M. H. Tromp, 1598–1653', *MM* XL (1954), pp. 33–54, at pp. 49–50. Andrews, *Ships, Money & Politics*, pp. 156–8. Elliott, *Olivares*, p. 548.
8 Boxer, *Tromp's Journal*, pp. 48–68. M. G. De Boer, *Tromp en de Armada van 1639* (Amsterdam, 1941). Fulton, *Sovereignty*, pp. 328–37. De Jonge, *Nederlandsche Zeewesen*, I, 351–70. Mainwaring, *Works*, I, 283–5. Elliott, *Olivares*, pp. 549–50. Groenveld, *Verlopend Getij*, pp. 139–40. Alcalá-Zamora, *España, Flandes y el Mar del Norte*, pp. 403–43.
9 Fissel, *Bishops' Wars*, pp. 50–61.
10 Mainwaring, *Works*, I, 286–91. Sharpe, *Charles I*, pp. 834–7. Russell, *Fall of the British Monarchies*, p. 231.
11 The bloodshed was certainly exaggerated, but not altogether invented: see Ohlmeyer, *Civil War and Restoration*, pp. 108–10.
12 Baumber, 'Civil War in Ireland 1641–1643', pp. 385–90; and 'Navy during the Civil Wars', pp. 2–14. Russell, *Fall of the British Monarchies*, pp. 242–3. Ohlmeyer, *Civil War and Restoration*, pp. 111–14. MacCormack, 'Irish Adventurers'. Sharpe, *Charles I*, p. 922. Andrews, *Ships, Money & Politics*, pp. 195–7.
13 Baumber, 'Navy during the Civil Wars', p. 9. Powell, *Civil War*, p. 3.
14 Andrews, *Ships, Money & Politics*, pp. 185–7. Baumber, 'Navy during the Civil Wars', pp. 19–31, 54–7, and 'Parliamentary Naval Politics', p. 399. *DCW*, pp. 13–24. Kennedy, 'Naval Captains'; and 'Parliament and the Navy', pp. 83–93. Junge, *Flottenpolitik*, pp. 49–52. Stephen J. Greenberg, 'Seizing the Fleet in 1642: Parliament, the Navy, and the Printing Press', *MM* LXXVII (1991), pp. 227–34.
15 Clarendon, *History*, II, 224.
16 Groenveld, *Verlopend Getij*, pp. 90–110; and 'English Civil Wars', pp. 543–7. Powell, *Civil War*, pp. 12, 25. Baumber, 'Navy during the Civil Wars', pp. 25, 109–110. McCaughey, 'Politics and Administration', p. 73.
17 Baumber, 'Navy during the Civil Wars', p. 15. Powell, *Civil War*, pp. 27–8, 35.
18 Ohlmeyer, 'Irish Privateers', pp. 120–2.
19 Andrews, *Ships, Money & Politics*, pp. 36–7. Brenner, *Merchants and Revolution*, pp. 433–4; and 'Civil War Politics', pp. 68–78. Johns, 'The *Constant Warwick*', pp. 254–9. Groenveld, 'English Civil Wars', pp. 550–1. Craven, 'Earl of Warwick', pp. 468–77. 'The Voyages of Captain William Jackson (1642–1645)', ed. V. T. Harlow, in *Camden Miscellany* XIII (*CS* 3rd S. XXXIV, 1924).
20 Baumber, 'Navy during the Civil Wars',

pp. 41–4. Powell, *Civil War*, pp. 22–5.

21 Baumber, 'Navy during the Civil Wars', pp. 37–9.

22 McCaughey, 'Politics and Administration', p. 65. Baumber, 'Navy during the Civil Wars', pp. 51–4.

23 Baumber, 'Navy during the Civil Wars', pp. 60–1. Powell, *Civil War*, pp. 33–43. *DCW*, p. 61.

24 Baumber, 'Civil War in Ireland 1641–1643', pp. 393–5; and 'Navy during the Civil Wars', p. 66. Powell, *Civil War*, pp. 44–5. Eames, 'Sea Power and Welsh History', pp. 158–63.

25 Baumber, 'Civil War in Ireland 1641–1643', pp. 99, 396–7; and 'Civil War in Ireland, 1643–46', pp. 255–6. Powell, *Civil War*, pp. 49–52. Ohlmeyer, 'Irish Privateers', pp. 124–5.

26 Warwick to Northumberland, 22 Nov 1634: *DCW*, p. 105.

27 Baumber, 'Navy during the Civil Wars', pp. 76–87, and 'Parliamentary Naval Politics', pp. 400–1. Powell, *Civil War*, pp. 53–5.

28 Baumber, 'Navy during the Civil Wars', pp. 126–7; and 'Civil War in Ireland, 1643–46', p. 259.

29 Eames, 'Sea Power and Welsh History', pp. 188–99, quoted p. 199; and 'The King's Pinnace, the *Swan*', *MM* XLVII (1961), pp. 49–55. Baumber, 'Navy during the Civil Wars', pp. 99–100; and 'Civil War in Ireland, 1643–46', p. 256. *DCW*, pp. 105–6.

30 *DCW*, p. 136, quoting a Parliamentary newsletter.

31 Baumber, 'Navy during the Civil Wars', pp. 100–7; and 'Civil War in Ireland, 1643–46', pp. 257–8. Powell, *Civil War*, pp. 56–61, 71. McCaughey, 'Politics and Administration', p. 101. *DCW*, pp. 136, 138, 141, 149. Firth & Rait, *Acts & Ordinances*, I, 554–5.

32 M. L. Baumber, 'An East India Captain', *MM* LIII (1967), pp. 265–79. Eames, 'Sea Power and Caernarvonshire', p. 38, gives another example of prisoners drowned.

33 Baumber, 'Navy during the Civil Wars', pp. 122–3; and 'Civil War in Ireland, 1643–46', p. 260. Powell, *Civil War*, p. 71.

34 Baumber, 'Civil War in Ireland, 1643–46', pp. 259–60.

35 Baumber, 'Navy during the Civil Wars', pp. 117–19; and 'Civil War in Ireland, 1643–46', pp. 263–4. *DCW*, pp. 141–55. Powell, *Civil War*, pp. 63–70, 73, 74–6; 'Blake and the Defence of Lyme Regis', *MM* XX (1934), pp. 448–74; and *Blake*, pp. 33–45.

36 Powell, *Civil War*, pp. 75–7. Baumber, 'Civil War in Ireland, 1643–46', pp. 261–4.

37 Powell, *Civil War*, pp. 62, 92. Ohlmeyer, 'Irish Privateers'; and '"The Dunkirk of Ireland"'. Loeber & Parker, 'Military Revolution', p. 86.

38 Powell, *Civil War*, pp. 81, 91. Baumber, 'Navy during the Civil Wars', pp. 140–3; and 'Parliamentary Naval Politics', pp. 402–3.

39 Powell, *Civil War*, pp. 86–9, 93; and 'Siege of Duncannon'. Baumber, 'Civil War in Ireland, 1643–46', pp. 264–5; and 'Navy during the Civil Wars', pp. 145–6.

40 Penn, *Penn*, I, 123–32. Powell, *Civil War*, pp. 96–104; and 'Penn's Attempt to relieve Youghal'. Baumber, 'Civil War in Ireland, 1643–46', pp. 265–6.

41 Baumber, 'Civil War in Ireland, 1643–46', pp. 266–7. Eames, 'Sea Power and Caernarvonshire', pp. 36–7.

42 Powell, *Civil War*, pp. 111–22; and 'Penn's Expedition to Bonratty'. Baumber, 'Civil War in Ireland, 1643–46', pp. 266–7.

43 Dewar, 'Naval Administration', pp. 406–8. Andrews, *Ships, Money & Politics*, pp. 44–9, 188–90. Baumber, 'Navy during the Civil Wars', pp. 5–7, 46–7, 88–90, 378–80, and 'Parliamentary Naval Politics', pp. 400–4. Kennedy, 'Parliament's Admiralty', pp. 275–9; and 'Parliament and the Navy', pp. 149–66. Rowe, *Vane*, pp. 120–7. McCaughey, 'Politics and Administration', pp. 60–2. Cogar, 'Naval Administration', pp. 10–19. Johns, 'The *Constant Warwick*', pp. 254–5. Brenner, *Merchants and Revolution*, pp. 432–4.

44 Many of the records are now in the BL and the Bodleian: those which remain in

the PRO are listed in chronological order regardless of content, and misleadingly described. The editors of the CSPD consistently conflated the Navy Commission with the Navy & Customs Committee, and both of them with the Admiralty Commission.

45 *ARN*, p. 306.

46 Hollond, *Discourses*, pp. 265–6.

47 Andrews, *Ships, Money & Politics*, pp. 191–5. Baumber, 'Navy during the Civil Wars', pp. 162–3, and 'Parliamentary Naval Politics', p. 401. McCaughey, 'Politics and Administration', pp. 162–180, 280–6. Brenner, *Merchants and Revolution*, pp. 432–4. Kennedy, 'Parliament and the Navy', pp. 158–70.

48 Hollond, *Discourses*, p. 303.

49 Andrews, *Ships, Money & Politics*, p. 198. McCaughey, 'Politics and Administration', pp. 158–60. Kennedy, 'Parliament and the Navy', pp. 182–190.

50 Rowe, *Vane*, pp. 58, 94–5, 114–15, 128–31, 135, 260.

51 Hollond, *Discourses*, p. 139.

52 Kennedy, 'Parliament and the Navy', p. 172.

53 J. S. Morrill, 'The Army Revolt of 1647', in *Britain and the Netherlands* VI, ed. A. C. Duke & C. A. Tamse (The Hague, 1977), pp. 54–78, at p. 54.

54 Morrill, 'Army Revolt of 1647', p. 54. Sharpe, *Charles I*, p. 927. McCaughey, 'Politics and Administration', pp. 55–65. Kennedy, 'Parliament and the Navy', p. 154.

55 Powell, *Civil War*, pp. 127–33. McCaughey, 'Politics and Administration', p. 191. Brenner, 'Civil War Politics', pp. 61–88. *DCW*, pp. 264, 287. Baumber. 'Parliamentary Naval Politics'. p. 404.

56 Baumber, 'Navy during the Civil Wars', pp. 194, 197, 201. Powell, *Civil War*, pp. 144–6.

57 Ohlmeyer, 'Irish Privateers'; and '"The Dunkirk of Ireland"'. Loeber & Parker, 'Military Revolution', p. 86.

58 Baumber, 'Navy during the Civil Wars', pp. 201–4, and 'Parliamentary Naval Politics', pp. 201–4. Powell, *Civil War*, pp. 137–9. Kennedy, 'Naval Revolt', pp. 247–8. Rowe, *Vane*, pp. 114–5. Junge, *Flottenpolitik*, quoted p. 86.

59 *DCW*, pp. 334, 354–5. Kennedy, 'Naval Revolt'; and 'Parliament and the Navy', pp. 234–83. Capp, *Cromwell's Navy*, pp. 15–18.

60 Kennedy, 'Naval Revolt' (quoted); and 'Parliament and the Navy', pp. 255–68. *DCW*, pp. 330–55. Baumber, 'Navy during the Civil Wars', pp. 206–19, and 'Parliamentary Naval Politics', pp. 405–7. Powell, *Civil War*, pp. 140–57. Junge, *Flottenpolitik*, pp. 84–107. Capp, *Cromwell's Navy*, pp. 18–22.

61 McCaughey, 'Politics and Administration', pp. 7–8.

62 *DCW*, p. 306, lists the three squadrons.

63 Capp, *Cromwell's Navy*, pp. 23–41. Baumber, 'Navy during the Civil Wars', pp. 240–1. Powell, *Civil War*, pp. 157–86.

64 Baumber, 'Parliamentary Naval Politics'. pp. 405–7. The last Admiralty Committee minute signed by Warwick was on 3 Feb 1649 (Bodleian MS Rawlinson A.224 f.10); the Council of State assumed the duties of the Admiralty on 23 Feb.

65 Powell, *Civil War*, pp. 184–6. Capp, *Cromwell's Navy*, pp. 41–6. Baumber, 'Navy during the Civil Wars', pp. 278–83. Brenner, *Merchants and Revolution*, pp. 552–5. Firth & Rait, *Acts & Ordinances*, I, 1257–60. Rowe, *Vane*, p. 152.

Conclusion

1 Loyn, 'Wales and England'; and *Vikings in Britain*, pp. 103-4.

2 But New Zealand is a partial exception.

3 Hale, *War and Society*, p. 19.

4 Perhaps 'seriously undermined' would describe these two occasions better than 'overthrown'.

5 Barfod, 'Den danske orlogsflåde', p. 269. Riis, *Auld Acquaintance*, I, 20–35. Glete, *Navies and Nations*, II, 596, gives a somewhat lower figure for the Danish fleet.

6 The literature on this subject is enormous. Good introductions are: *The Military Revolution Debate: Readings in the Military Transformation of Early Modern Europe*, ed. Clifford Rogers (Boulder, Colorado, 1995); Parker, *Military Revolution*; Paul Kennedy, *The Rise and Fall of the Great Powers: Economic Change and Military Conflict from 1500 to 2000* (London, 1988), pp. 44–58; André Corvisier, 'Armées, état et administration dans les temps modernes', in *Les hommes, la guerre et la mort* (Paris, 1985), pp. 23–37.

7 *The Medieval Military Revolution: State, Society and Military Change in Medieval and Early Modern Europe*, ed. Andrew Ayton & J. L. Price (London, 1995), p. 6.

8 Parker, *Military Revolution*, pp. 66–7.

9 Brian M. Downing, *The Military Revolution and Political Change: Origins of Democracy and Autocracy in Early Modern Europe* (Princeton, 1992), pp. 72–3, 165, 224, who has the merit of admitting the problem. Others, e.g. Frank Tallett, *War and Society in Early-Modern Europe, 1495–1715* (London, 1992), p.vii, simply ignore the existence of navies altogether.

10 Glete, *Navies and Nations*, I, 158–61.

11 O'Brien & Hunt, 'Fiscal State', pp. 155–61.

12 John Milton, *Areopagitica*, in *Complete Prose Works of John Milton: Vol. II. 1643–38*, ed. Ernest Sirluck (London, 1959), pp. 557–8.

Appendix I Chronology

1 Lewis, *Northern Seas*, p. 323. Stenton, *Anglo-Saxon England*, p. 347.

2 Loyn, *Vikings in Britain*, pp. 103–4.

3 Campbell, *Anglo-Saxons*, p. 214. *ASC*, p. 100.

4 *ASC*, p. 154. *SCP*, I, 208.

5 *ASC*, p. 169. *SCP*, I, 226.

6 Flanagan, *Irish Society, Anglo-Norman Settlers*, p. 75.

7 *PR 14 John*, ed. P. M. Barnes (PRS NS 30, 1955), p.xix. *RLC*, I, 121.

8 *MF*, I, 308.

9 *MF*, I, 308.

10 *CCR* 1261–64, p. 356.

11 Duffy, 'Bruce Brothers', p. 62.

12 PRO: E 159/68 rot.80.

13 Fryde, *Book of Prests*, pp.xxxix–xl.

14 Fryde, *Book of Prests*, p. 88.

15 *CPR* 1292–1301, pp. 146, 149–150.

16 *CCR* 1296–1302, pp. 99–102. *CPR* 1292–1301, p. 301.

17 *CDS*, V, 178.

18 *CPR* 1292–1301, pp. 328, 331.

19 *CCR* 1296–1302, p. 307.

20 *CPR* 1292–1301, p. 455.

21 Mollat, 'L'Etat Capétien', p. 120.

22 *RS*, I, 58.

23 *RS*, I, 78.

24 *RS*, 1, 78. *RFR*, II, 108.

25 *CPR* 1307–13, pp. 352–3.

26 Reid, 'Sea-Power in the Anglo-Scottish War', p. 17. Duncan, 'Scots' Invasion of Ireland', p. 102.

27 *CPR* 1313–17, p. 6.

28 *RS*, I, 116–17, 125–6.

29 *RS*, I, 129.

30 *EHD*, III, 267, quoting the Lanercost Chronicle.

31 Reid, 'Sea-Power in the Anglo-Scottish War', p. 19. Duncan, 'Scots' Invasion of Ireland', p. 103.

32 *RFR*, II, 265.

33 *EHD*, III, 267, quoting the Lanercost Chronicle.

34 *RS*, 1, 144. *CPR* 1313–17, pp. 333–4. *CCR* 1313–18, p. 183. *TR*, I, 540–2. *CCW*, p. 424.

35 Reid, 'Sea-Power in the Anglo-Scottish War'.

36 *RFR*, II, 305. *CPR* 1313–17, pp. 574–5, 632, 696.

37 O'Neill, *Merchants and Mariners*, p. 120.

38 Reid, 'Sea-Power in the Anglo-Scottish War', p. 21. *EHD*, III, 269, quoting the Lanercost Chronicle.

39 *CPR* 1321–24, p. 413. *RFR*, II, 552, 562.

40 *RFR*, II, 562.

41 *MF*, I, 383.

42 *CCR* 1323–27, pp. 608–12, 641–4.

43 *CCR*, pp. 612–13, 643–4. *CPR* 1324–27, pp. 315–16.

44 *MF*, I, 384.

45 Nicholson, *Edward III and the Scots*, p. 15.

46 Duffy, 'Bruce Brothers', p. 85. Nicholson, *Edward III and the Scots*, p. 17.
47 *CCR* 1327–30, p. 118. *RS*, I, 209–11.
48 Nicholson, *Edward III and the Scots*, pp. 19–43.
49 Nicholson, *Edward III and the Scots*, pp. 45–8.
50 *CCR* 1330–33, pp. 16, 28, 36.
51 *CCR*, p. 581.
52 Nicholson, *Edward III and the Scots*, p. 104.
53 *CCR* 1333–37, pp. 22, 25, 37. *RS*, I, 228, 231–5.
54 Nicholson, *Edward III and the Scots*, pp. 119–21.
55 Nicholson, *Edward III and the Scots*, p. 123.
56 Nicholson, *Edward III and the Scots*, p. 174.
57 *RS*, I, 305–9.
58 Nicholson, *Edward III and the Scots*, pp. 182–8.
59 *RS*, I, 320, 322, 324.
60 *RS*, 1, 337. *CCR* 1333–37, p. 397.
61 Nicholson, *Edward III and the Scots*, pp. 195–222.
62 Fowler, *Hundred Years War*, p. 6. Richmond, 'War at Sea', p. 96. Sumption, *Hundred Years War*, p. 156.
63 Sumption, *Hundred Years War*, pp. 154.
64 Sumption, *Hundred Years War*, p. 167.
65 *RFR*, II, ii, 950–1. *RS*, I, 467–8, 470.
66 *RS*, 1, 477–8, 482. *CCR* 1337–39, p. 18. *CPR* 1334–38, p. 39. *RFR*, II, ii, 963, 965.
67 *TR*, II, 149, 152, 477–8. *RFR*, II, ii, 1008.
68 *TR*, II, 844–5.
69 *TR*, II, 617, 619–22. *RFR*, II, ii, 1061–2.
70 *RFR*, II, ii, 1133.
71 *RFR*, II, ii, 1150, 1173. *CCR* 1339–41, pp. 59, 263; 1341–43 p. 208. *CPR* 1340–43, pp. 252, 272.
72 Alban, 'National Defence', p. 20.
73 *RFR*, II, ii, 1189.
74 *CCR* 1341–43, pp. 629–30; 1343–46, pp. 1, 33. *RFR*, II, ii, 1219.
75 *RFR*, II, ii, 1242.
76 *RFR*, III, i, 10–11.
77 *CCR* 1343–46, p. 492. *CPR* 1343–45, p. 517. *RFR* III, i, 10–11.
78 *RFR*, III, i, 57. Wrottesley, *Crecy and Calais*, p. 58.
79 Sumption, *Hundred Years War*, pp. 486–8, 495–7. Nicolas, *Royal Navy*, II, 93.
80 *CPR* 1343–45, p. 514. *RFR*, III, i, 66, 68, 70–1, 78. Wrottesley, *Crecy and Calais*, pp. 65–70.
81 *CPR* 1345–48, p. 264. *CCR* 1346–49, pp. 307, 394.
82 *RS*, I, 700.
83 *CPR* 1348–50, pp. 281, 322, 386.
84 *RFR*, III, i, 238. PRO: C61/64 m.8.
85 *CPR* 1350–54, p. 343.
86 *CPR* 1350–54, pp. 420, 425, 515.
87 *CPR* 1350–54, p. 486.
88 *RFR*, III, i, 298.
89 *RFR*, III, i, 313.
90 Hewitt, *Black Prince's Expedition*.
91 *RS*, I, 784.
92 *RFR*, III, i, 412.
93 *RFR*, III, i, 427–8. *CCR* 1354–60, p. 574.
94 *RFR*, III, i, 471–2, 475–6, 478. *CPR* 1358–61, p. 350. *CCR* 1360–4, p. 101.
95 *CCR* 1360–64, p. 187. *CPR* 1361–4, pp. 33–4.
96 *CPR* 1361–64, pp. 203–4, 215. *CCR* 1360–64, p. 420.
97 *CPR* 1361–64, p. 317.
98 *CPR* 1361–64, p. 317.
99 *CPR* 1361–64, p. 415.
100 *CPR* 1361–64, p. 518; 1364–67, p. 12.
101 Alban, 'National Defence', p. 34.
102 *RFR*, III, ii, 861.
103 *RFR*, III, ii, 871.
104 *RFR*, III, ii, 885. *CCR* 1369–74, p. 65.
105 *CCR* 1369–74, p. 177. *RFR*, III, ii, 889.
106 *CCR* 1369–74 pp. 158, 202–203.
107 *RFR*, III, ii,,909.
108 *MF*, II, 13.
109 *RFR*, III, ii, 938, 940.
110 *MF*, II, 13–14. Carr, *Owen of Wales* pp. 29–30.
111 *RFR*, III, ii, 961.
112 *CFR*, VIII, 207–8.
113 *RFR*, III, ii, 1006, 1017.
114 *RFR*, III, ii, 1046. *CCR* 1374–77, pp. 290, 302.
115 *RFR*, III, ii, 1072, 1076–7.
116 *CCR* 1377–81, p. 77.
117 Nicolas, *Royal Navy*, II, 271.
118 *RFR*, IV, 41.
119 *CCR* 1377–81, pp. 181–2. *RFR*, IV, 57.

120 *RFR*, IV, 59.
121 *RFO*, VII, 391.
122 *MF*, II, 76.
123 *CCR* 1381–85, pp. 480–1.
124 *RFO*, VII, 453.
125 *MF*, II, 80. Alban, 'National Defence', p. 284.
126 *CCR* 1385–89, p. 2.
127 *RFO*, VII, 500, 504, 520.
128 *MF*, II, 89. Suárez Fernández, *Navigación y Comercio*, p. 64.
129 *CCR* 1385–89, pp. 253, 257.
130 *CCR* 1385–89, p. 293.
131 *CCR* 1385–89, p. 435.
132 *CCR* 1385–89, p. 488.
133 *CPR* 1388–90, p. 140.
134 Suárez Fernández, *Navigación y Comercio*, p. 74.
135 *CPR* 1391–96, p. 518.
136 *CPR* 1391–96, p. 590.
137 Fernández Duro, *La Marina de Castilla*, pp. 154–5. Nicolas, *Royal Navy*, II, 414–15.
138 *CCR* 1392–96, pp. 468–9.
139 *CPR* 1396–99, pp. 366–7.
140 *CPR* 1396–99, pp. 432, 438. *CCR* 1396–99, p. 327.
141 *CPR* 1396–99, p. 511. *CCR* 1396–99, p. 446.
142 *CCR* 1399–1402, pp. 158, 170.
143 *CCR* 1399–1402, pp. 168–9. *CPR* 1399–1401, p. 350.
144 *CCR* 1399–1402, p. 334. *CSL*, 38.
145 *CPR* 1399–1401, p. 551.
146 *CPR* 1401–05, p. 71. *CCR* 1399–1402, p. 468.
147 Pistono, 'Henry IV and the English Privateers', p. 323.
148 *CPR* 1401–05, pp. 276–7.
149 *CCR* 1401–05, pp. 185–6.
150 *CCR* 1402–05, p. 222.
151 *CCR* 1402–05, pp. 263, 268, 329.
152 Pistono, 'Henry IV and John Hawley', p. 153.
153 *MF*, II, 178. *EHD*, IV, 89, quoting Walsingham's *Annales Henrici Quarti*.
154 *RFO*, VIII, 403.
155 *EHD*, IV, 196, quoting Walsingham's *Historia Anglicana*.
156 *CSL*, 514.
157 *CCR* 1405–09, pp. 93–4.
158 *EHD*, IV, 199, quoting Walsingham's *Annales Henrici Quinti* and Fordun's *Scottichronicon*.
159 *CCR* 1405–09, pp. 46, 61.
160 *EHD*, IV, 196, quoting Walsingham's *Historia Anglicana*.
161 *CCR* 1405–09, pp. 156–7.
162 *MF*, II, 205–6.
163 *CCR* 1409–13, p. 3.
164 *CCR* 1409–13, p. 166. *RFO*, VIII, 700.
165 *CCR* 1409–13, pp. 273–4.
166 *CCR* 1413–19, p. 5.
167 *CCR* 1413–19, pp. 94–5.
168 *RFO*, IX, 215, 218. *CCR* 1413–19, p. 162. *CPR* 1413–16, pp. 342–3.
169 *CCR* 1413–19, p. 278.
170 *RFO*, IX, 370.
171 *CCR* 1413–19, pp. 336, 339, 343, 391.
172 PRO: E 101/70/3 No.640.
173 *CCR* 1419–22, pp. 141–2.
174 *CPR* 1422–29, p. 124.
175 *CPR* 1422–29, p. 192.
176 Richmond, 'Royal Administration', p. 205.
177 *CPR* 1422–29, p. 362.
178 *CPR* 1422–29, pp. 402–3.
179 *CPR* 1422–29, p. 424.
180 *CPR* 1422–29, pp. 469, 493.
181 *CPR* 1422–29, p. 552.
182 Richmond, 'Royal Administration', p. 172.
183 *CPR* 1429–36, p. 71.
184 *CPR* 1429–36, p. 130.
185 *CPR* 1429–36, pp. 133, 152–3.
186 *CPR* 1429–36, p. 202.
187 *CPR* 1429–36, p. 277.
188 *CPR* 1429–36, p. 474.
189 *CPR* 1429–36, pp. 533–5.
190 Paviot, *La politique navale*, p. 70.
191 Richmond, 'Royal Administration', p. 182. Paviot, *La politique navale*, pp. 74–81.
192 Richmond, 'Royal Administration', p. 173.
193 *CPR* 1436–41, p. 372.
194 Richmond, 'Royal Administration', pp. 173, 209–12.
195 *CPR* 1441–46, p. 79.
196 *CPR* 1441–46, pp. 105–6.
197 Richmond, 'Royal Administration', pp. 213–27.
198 *CPR* 1446–52, p. 380.

199 Richmond, 'Royal Administration', p. 229.
200 Richmond, 'Royal Administration', p. 229. *CPR* 1446–52, p. 462.
201 *CPR* 1446–52, p. 446.
202 Richmond, 'Royal Administration', pp. 230–2.
203 Richmond, 'Royal Administration', pp. 240–4.
204 O'Neill, *Merchants and Mariners,* p. 124.
205 *CPR* 1461–67, pp. 203–4.
206 Crawford, *Howard Household Books,* p.xxiii.
207 Crawford, *Howard Household Books,* p.xxiii.
208 Richmond, 'Royal Administration', p. 336. Lloyd, *England and the German Hanse,* p. 201.
209 Ross, *Edward IV,* p. 145.
210 Ross, *Edward IV,* p. 146.
211 Crawford, *Howard Household Books,* p.xxiv.
212 Lloyd, *England and the German Hanse,* p. 208.
213 Ross, *Edward IV,* p. 218.
214 Richmond, 'Royal Administration', pp. 355–9. Ross, *Edward IV,* p. 219.
215 Horrox & Hammond, *Harleian MS 433,* II, 63, 65.
216 Horrox & Hammond, *Harleian MS 433,* II, 106–7, 146.
217 Horrox & Hammond, *Harleian MS 433,* II, 161.
218 *CPR* 1485–94, p. 164.
219 *CPR* 1485–94, p. 277.
220 Clowes, *Royal Navy,* I, 445.
221 MacDougall, *James IV,* pp. 231–2.
222 Clowes, *Royal Navy,* I, 458.
223 *LPH8,* V, 424.
224 *LPH8,* VI,67, 75, 84, 93, 175.
225 *LPH8,* XI, 163, 251.
226 Lindsay, *Rutter of the Scottish Seas,* pp. 9–13.
227 *WBA,* p. 156.
228 Pollitt, 'Contingency Planning', p. 26; and 'Mobilization of English Resources', pp. 16–18.
229 Scammell, *Chartered Trading Companies,* p. 23.
230 *BMO,* III, 1684, 1775. *PN,* XI, 324–5.
231 Clowes, *Royal Navy,* I, 494.
232 *WAA,* pp. 476–80. Hawkins, *Observations,* p. 15.
233 Clowes, *Royal Navy,* II, 34.
234 Clowes, *Royal Navy,* II, 35–6.
235 Mainwaring, *Works,* I, 26.
236 Clowes, *Royal Navy,* II, 37.
237 Clowes, *Royal Navy,* II, 41–4.
238 Clowes, *Royal Navy,* II, 44–5.
239 Clowes, *Royal Navy,* II, 45.
240 Clowes, *Royal Navy,* II, 70.
241 *MF,* IV, 630–4.
242 *MF,* IV, 636.
243 *DCW,* pp. 277–80.

Appendix II Ships

1 *PR 14 John, 1212,* ed. P. M. Barnes (PRS NS 30, 1955), p.xix.
2 *CPR* 1216–25, p. 337.
3 PRO: E 372/78 rot.16d. *CLR,* VII, 2254.
4 O'Neill, *Merchants and Mariners,* p. 112. Lydon, 'Ireland's Participation', p. 21. *CPR* 1232–47, pp. 28, 35.
5 O'Neill, *Merchants and Mariners,* p. 112. *CLR,* II, 84–5, 108.
6 *CLR,* II, 139.
7 *CLR,* II, 239.
8 *CCR* 1256–59, pp. 155–6, 231, 242–3. *CLR,* IV, 399–400, 418, 465.
9 Prestwich, *War, Politics and Finance,* p. 138. Friel, 'Lyme Galley'. Whitwell & Johnson, 'Newcastle Galley'. Johnson, 'London Shipbuilding'. Tinniswood, 'English Galleys', p. 277. PRO: E 101/5/8. Platt, *Medieval Southampton,* pp. 61–2. Anderson, 'English Galleys in 1295'.
10 PRO: E 101/7/25.
11 Saul, 'Great Yarmouth' p. 111. PRO: E 372/149 rot.3.
12 Prince, 'Army and Navy', p. 378.
13 Sumption, *Hundred Years War,* p. 249. *CPR* 1334–38, pp. 379, 388, 1340–43, p. 383. *RFR,* II, ii, 958.
14 *CPR* 1354–58, pp. 12, 117, 203, 212, 221.
15 *CPR,* pp. 362–3, 406, 446–7.
16 *CPR* 1358–61, p. 38. *CPR* 1361–64, p. 21 may refer to the same ships, still building 3 years later, or to others.
17 PRO: C 47/2/46, Nos.16, 17. Alban, 'National Defence', p. 278. *RFR,* III, ii, 998–9.

18 Sherborne, 'Hundred Years' War', p. 169. Alban, 'National Defence', p. 279. Friel, 'Maritime Technology', pp. 81–3. *RP*, III, 42. Moore, 'A Barge of Edward III'. *CCR* 1377–81, pp. 32–3, 43–4, 46–7, 51–2, 55, 57, 114, 120, 181–2. *RFR*, IV, 28. *CIM*, IV, 55.

19 *BND* No.32. PRO: E 101/42/39, 43/6. Friel, 'Maritime Technology', p. 6. *RP*, III, 458. *CCR* 1399–1402, pp. 238–40. *RFO*, VIII, 172.

20 O'Neill, *Merchants and Mariners*, p. 121.

21 Friel, 'Maritime Technology', p. 125. Rose, *Navy of the Lancastrian Kings*, p. 252.

22 Rose, *Navy of the Lancastrian Kings*, p. 247.

23 *ARN*, p. 12. Rose, *Navy of the Lancastrian Kings*, pp. 251–2.

24 Turner, 'Southampton' pp. 40–3. Turner, 'The *Holy Ghost of the Tower*'. Rose, *Navy of the Lancastrian Kings*, p. 247.

25 *ARN*, p. 12. Rose, *Navy of the Lancastrian Kings*, pp. 251–2.

26 Rose, *Navy of the Lancastrian Kings*, p. 247. PRO: E 364/61 rot.E. Turner, 'Building of the *Gracedieu*'.

27 *ARN*, p. 12. Rose, *Navy of the Lancastrian Kings*, pp. 251–2. Turner, 'Building of the *Gracedieu*'.

28 *EHD*, IV, 222–3.

29 Richmond, 'Keeping of the Seas', pp. 84–8. Anderson, 'The *Grace de Dieu* of 1446–86'.

30 PRO: E 404/72/4 No.43. Crawford, *Howard Household Books*, pp.xxi, I, 197–214.

31 Anderson, 'The *Grace de Dieu* of 1446–86'.

32 PRO: E 404/77/3 No.83.

33 Goldingham, 'Navy under Henry VII', pp. 474–5.

34 Goldingham, 'Navy under Henry VII', pp. 474–5. Harrison, 'Maritime Activity', pp. 71–2.

35 Goldingham, 'Navy under Henry VII', pp. 474–5.

Appendix IV Rates of Pay

1 Lawson, 'Danegeld and Heregeld'. Campbell, 'Agents and Agencies', p. 205. Rodger, 'Cnut's Geld', pp. 398–402.

2 This can be calculated from numerous entries in the Pipe Rolls, eg: *PR 17 Hen.II*, pp. 12, 19, 82, 89, 96, 113 etc (all relating to the Irish expedition).

3 *PR 19 Hen.II*, p. 31. *PR 19 Hen.II*, p. 143.

4 *PR 31 Hen.II*, p. 154.

5 *ASMI*, pp. 64, 106.

6 *PR 9 John*, p. 168. *PR 10 John*, p. 171.

7 *CLR*, I, 59, 108; IV, 177. Prestwich, *War, Politics and Finance*, p. 143. PRO: E 352/120 rot.49; E 372/195 rot.44; E 101/5/8 m.14; E 101/3/26 m.2. Lyon, *Wardrobe Book*, pp.cii, 363. *CCR* 1323–27, pp. 608–12. Bernard, *Navires et Gens de Mer*, II, 591.

8 PRO: E 372/183 rot.51; E 372/195 rot.44; E 101/3/26 m.2. Nicholson, *Edward III and the Scots*, p. 209.

9 *RP*, III, 66. Nicolas, *Royal Navy*, II, 177. Saul, 'Great Yarmouth', p. 114. *BBA*, I, 13, perhaps referring to the 1370s, quotes 3½d a day and 6d a week 'regard' for seamen.

10 'Gages de guerre acustumez': PRO: E 101/68/5 No.95 (of 1373, using what was already the standard wording).

11 PRO: E 101/70/3 No.640. Nicolas, *Royal Navy*, II, 193.

12 PRO: E 101/68/5 No.95. Nicolas, *Royal Navy*, II, 194, 451.

13 Bernard, *Navires et Gens de Mer*, II, 591.

14 *CPR* 1396–99, p. 573; 1399–1401, p. 33.

15 *CCR* 1399–1402, p. 78.

16 Ellis, *Original Letters*, III, i, 72-4.

17 Rose, *Navy of the Lancastrian Kings*, p. 47.

18 *ARN*, p. 25.

19 Richmond, 'Royal Administration', p. 217.

20 Crawford, *Howard Household Books*, pp.xliv, II, 4, 9.

21 Crawford, *Howard Household Books*, II, 80.

22 PRO: E 315/317 f.22v.

23 Goldingham, 'Navy under Henry VII', pp. 486-7.

24 Bernard, *Navires et Gens de Mer*, II, 591.

25 MacDougall, 'James IV's *Great Michael*', p. 43; taking £1 = S£4. The rate about this time varied from Scots 72s to 90s = £1: Spufford, *Medieval Exchange*, p. 212.

26 Spont, *War with France*, pp.xiii, 3–13. *TN*, p. 99. *ARN*, p. 75.

27 *ARN*, p. 134. Hair & Alsop, *Seamen and Traders*, p. 123.

28 *ARN*, p. 113.

29 E.g. *ARN*, p. 225, and *MNT*, III, 185, where the 'temporary rise to 14s' in 1625 is the medium of the 1582 scale.

30 McGowan, *Jacobean Commissions*, pp. 276–8. Clayton, 'Naval Administration', p. 212.

31 The 1626 rates were somewhat below those proposed by Trinity House: Harris, *Trinity House Transactions*, pp. 67–70.

32 Firth & Rait, *Acts & Ordinances*, I, 73–4.

33 £16 16s in Rawlinson A.224.

34 £3 5s 4d in Add.MSS 18772.

35 £3 5s 4d in Add.MSS 18772.

36 *Sic* in both sources.

37 £1 9s 4d in Add.MSS 18772.

38 £1 5s 8d in Add.MSS 18772.

GLOSSARY

Historical and nautical terms are covered only in the senses in which they occur in this book; the glossary is not meant to be in any way exhaustive.

abaft, see **aft**.
abeam, adj. In the direction at right angles to the ship's centre line.
admiral, sb. 1. The officer commanding a squadron of ships. 2. The Lord (High) Admiral, an officer of the crown with jurisdiction over Admiralty and naval affairs. 3. A flagship (16–17th century).
afore, see **fore**.
aft, abaft, adj. Towards the stern or after part of the ship.
aftercastle, sb. A tower or fighting platform built at the stern of the ship (13th–14th century).
aloft, adj. 1. Relating to the masts and rigging, upwards. 2. On deck.
amidship(s), adj. Along or relating to the middle or centreline of the ship.
ancient, sb. 1. An ensign or standard. 2. An ensign or standard-bearer.
ashore, adj., adv. Towards or on the shore.
astern, adj. Behind a ship, in the direction from which she is moving.
astrolabe, sb. A navigational instrument used for measuring the altitude of heavenly bodies, and hence the ship's latitude.

back, vb. 1. To trim sails so that they catch the wind from ahead and check the ship's way. 2. (Of the wind) to change in an anti-clockwise direction.
backstay, sb. A stay supporting a mast from aft.
balinger, sb. An oared sailing vessel used for war and trade (14th–16th century).
ballast, sb. Stones, gravel or other weight stowed low in a ship to improve her stability.
ballot, vb. (Of shot) to rebound from side to side of the bore of a gun.
banneret, knight banneret, sb. The officer commanding a squadron of knights.
bar, sb. A shoal across the mouth of a tidal estuary.
barbican, sb. An outwork defending the gate of a castle.
bareboat, adj. (Of a ship) chartered for a long period, the charterer manning and fitting out the ship.
barge, sb. An oared sailing vessel used for war and trade (14th–16th century).

bark, sb. Any small seagoing vessel (16th century).

barrel, sb. 1. A cask of specified capacity, usually 30–34 gallons. 2. The tube forming the principal part of a gun.

basilisk, sb. A type of long heavy gun, usually breech-loading (15th–16th century).

basin, sb. An enclosed body of water impounded so that ships may lie afloat regardless of the state of tide.

battery, sb. 1. The broadside guns mounted on one deck, or one side of the ship. 2. A group of guns mounted ashore to fire on ships.

beach, vb. To run a ship aground or ashore.

beakhead, sb. A horizontal projection of the ship's stem above water.

beam, sb. 1. The width of the ship. 2. The direction at right angles to the centre line. 3. A timber running from side to side of a ship to support a deck.

bear, vb. 1. To enter names in the ship's books as part of the ship's complement. 2. To lie or point in a particular direction. 3. **—away**, to bear up, to turn downwind. 4. **—room**, to bear up (16–17th century). 5. **—up**, to turn downwind.

beat, vb. (Of a ship) to work to windward by successive tacks.

birlin, sb. A type of warship in the West Highlands of Scotland, similar to a galley but smaller.

bitter end, sb. The inboard end of the anchor cable, which is made fast to the bitts.

bitts, riding bitts, sb. A pair of heavy timber heads to which a ship's anchor cables are made fast.

block, sb. A pulley.

blockship, sb. A ship deliberately sunk to block a channel.

boatswain, sb. 1. A ship's officer responsible for sails, rigging and ground tackle. 2. **—'s mate**. A petty officer assisting the boatswain.

bolt, sb. A short arrow fired from a crossbow.

bombard, sb. A type of heavy gun (14–15th century).

bonaventure mizzen, see **mizzen**.

boom, sb. 1. A light running spar, particularly one extending the foot of a sail. 2. A floating barrier protecting a harbour.

bound, adj. Intended for a specified destination.

bow, sb. Either side of the foremost part of the ship's hull, as it widens from the stem.

bow, vb. To cant a broadside gun to fire as far forward as possible (16th century).

bowline, sb. A line or tackle led forward from the leach or clew of a square sail to haul the weather leach taut when beating to windward.

bowsprit, sb. A spar projecting over the bows, spreading various items of rigging and one or more sails.

box, see **compass**.

brail, sb. 1. A line rove through an eye in the leach of a fore-and-aft sail, thence to the mast and down to the deck, serving to gather the sail against the mast. 2. A bunt-line (11th–13th century).

breech, sb. The inner or rear end of a gun.

breeching, sb. A rope attaching the breech of the gun to the ship's side, to restrain the recoil or movement of the gun.

breech-loader, sb. A gun loaded by the breech.

brigantine, sb. A type of small oared warship of the Mediterranean galley family (16th century).

broadside, sb. 1. The side of the ship. 2. The number of guns mounted or bearing on one side. 3. The simultaneous fire of these guns. 4. **—on**, adj. Of a ship showing her broadside at right angles to the observer's line of sight, or to a named point of reference.

brow, sb. A portable bridge for crossing from quayside to ship, or ship to ship.

bunt, sb. 1. The middle or belly of a square sail. 2. **—line**, A line rove through an eye in the foot of a square sail, thence to the yard and down to the deck, serving to gather the sail to the yard.

buoy, sb. A float, anchored as a navigational marker or as a means of mooring ships.

burthen, burden, sb. The internal volume or cargo capacity of a ship.

buss, sb. A type of small two-masted sailing vessel, principally used for fishing (15th–18th century).

cable, sb. 1. A large rope or hawser, particularly the anchor cable. 2. A measure of distance, 120, later 100 fathoms or one-tenth of a nautical mile.

cable-laid, adj. Of rope made up by twisting some number (usually three or four) smaller ropes ('strands') together.

caisson, sb. A watertight chest or float, used to seal the mouth of a dry dock.

calibre, sb. The bore or internal diameter of a gun.

caltrap, sb. A device of interlinked spikes so arranged that one always points upward however it falls; a weapon against cavalry.

camber, sb. 1. A slope of deck causing water to run off from the centre line to either side. 2. A harbour or anchorage.

cannon, sb. 1. A type of muzzle-loading gun, distinguished by heavy metal in relation to calibre. 2. A full cannon, a cannon firing a shot of 30–50 lbs. (16–17th century).

cant, vb. (Of a ship, gun etc) to turn, to change the heading or direction. **—frame**, see **frame**.

cape, vb. To navigate coastwise by setting course from one headland to another.

capstan, sb. A mechanical device for hauling in cables, consisting of a vertical revolving drum turned by bars inserted in its rim.

caravel, sb. A small seagoing lateen-rigged vessel (15–16th century).

careen, vb. To heel a ship over to expose one side of her underwater hull for cleaning or repairs.

carrack, sb. A large ocean-going merchantman distinguished by high superstructure fore and aft (15–16th century).

carry away, vb. To break off, fall off, be blown away.

cartridge, sb., A cloth or paper bag containing the propellant charge of a gun.

carvel, adj. Of the 'skeleton-first' method of ship construction, in which a frame of timbers is clad with planking laid edge to edge.

cast, vb. 1. To throw. 2.—**loose**, to weigh anchor, to set a sail. 3. —**off**, to release or let go a mooring.

castle, sb. 1. A structure erected forward, aft or on the mast to provide a fighting platform (12–15th century). 2. **after**—, see **aftercastle**. 3. **fore**—, see **forecastle**. 4. **top**—, see **topcastle**.

caulk, vb. To make seams watertight.

caulking, sb. Material for caulking, usually oakum and pitch.

chamber, sb. 1. A detachable breech containing the propellant charge of a gun (15–16th century). 2. The inner end of the bore of a muzzle-loading gun, bored to a smaller diameter than the rest to accept a reduced charge.

charge, sb. 1. The explosive propellant to fire a gun. 2. The attack of one ship on another, usually bows-on from the windward.

chase, sb. 1. The pursuit of one ship or squadron by another. 2. The ship pursued. 3. The outer portion of the barrel of a gun. 4. —**gun, piece**, A gun mounted to fire ahead or astern

chaser, see **chase gun**

check, cheque, sb. 1. A tick set against a man's name in a muster to denote absence with leave. 2. **clerk of the** —, see **clerk**.

check, cheque, vb. 1. To check or tick a man's name. 2. To stop.

chips, sb. Offcuts of wood, supposedly waste, taken as a perquisite by dockyard shipwrights.

clean, vb. To clean weed and barnacles from a ship's bottom.

clear for action, vb. To prepare the ship for action by removing loose fittings etc.

clench, see **clinker**.

clerk, sb. 1. An administrative official. 2. —**of the Acts**, one of the Principal Officers of the Navy, the secretary of the Navy Board. 3. —**of the cheque**, the senior financial official of a dockyard. 4. —**of the King's Ships**, a royal official involved in naval administration (14th–15th century).

clew, sb. The lower corner of a square sail.

clinker, clench, adj. Of the system of ship construction in which the hull is made of overlapping strakes of planking built up from the keel, with light frames inserted later for stiffening.

close-fights, sb. Bulkheads forward and aft of the waist, closing off the spaces under quarter-deck and forecastle and allowing a ship to be defended against boarding (16th–17th century).

close-hauled, adj., adv. Steering as nearly towards the wind as possible.

cocha, sb. A type of ship, intermediate between cog and carrack (14th–15th century).

coffer dam, sb. A temporary dam excluding water from an excavation.

cog, sb. A type of merchant ship with a flat bottom and high freeboard, rigged with a single mast and sail (13–15th century).

compass, sb. 1. An instrument permitting a constant course to be held by reference to a magnetic needle or card pointing to north. 2. **Box the —**, vb. to recite the thirty-two points of the compass in order.

complement, sb. The total number of the ship's company.

con, vb. To steer or pilot a ship.

constable, sb. 1. A junior military officer (13–16th century). 2. A parish official responsible for law and order (13–19th century). 3. **high —**, An official responsible for law and order in a hundred (13–19th century).

convoy, sb. 1. A body of merchant ships under escort. 2. The warships providing the escort (15–18th century).

convoy, vb. To protect a body of merchant ships.

cooper, sb. 1. An artificer skilled in making and repairing casks. 2. A rating employed to assist the purser to dispense beer and other liquids.

cordage, sb. Rope or rigging.

corporal, sb. A junior officer, assistant to the lieutenant (16th century).

course, sb. 1. The direction of a ship's movement. 2. The foresail or mainsail, the lowest square sails.

court martial, sb. A court held under naval or military law.

coxswain, sb. A petty officer in charge of a boat's crew.

crew, sb. The group of men required to man a ship, boat, gun etc.

cross-staff, sb. An instrument for observing the altitude of sun or star in order to fix the observer's latitude.

cubbridge head, sb. A heavy bulkhead constructed of clinker planking, closing off the space under the forecastle from the waist and allowing it to be defended against boarders.

culverin, sb. 1. A type of muzzle-loading gun, longer in the chase and of heavier metal than a cannon. 2. A full culverin; a culverin firing a shot of about 18 lbs. (16–17th century). 3. **demi—**, see **demi-culverin**.

Danegeld, sb. A tax levied in late Anglo-Saxon and early Norman England, the product of which was intended to buy off Viking raiders.

deck, sb. 1. A floor or platform within a ship. 2. **—head**, the underside of the deck above. 3. **cage** —, a light spar deck over the waist (16th century). 4. **gun** —, the deck carrying the main battery (16–19th century). 5. **half** —, the after end of the main deck, below the quarter deck. 6. **main** —, the highest deck running the whole length of the ship. 7. **quarter** —, a deck above the main deck over the after part of the ship. 8. **spar** —, a lighter framework supporting spare spars. 9. **weather** —, the uppermost deck, exposed to the weather.

demi-culverin, sb. A gun of the culverin type, firing a shot of about 9 lbs.

demurrage, sb. A payment made by a shipper to the shipowner in compensation for unreasonably detaining the ship on her voyage.

dice shot, see **shot**.

disembark, vb. To land or be landed from a ship.

dock, sb. 1. An excavation or basin for ships. 2. —**head**, the wall or gate keeping the water out of a dock. 3. —**yard**, see **yard**. 4. **double** —, a dry dock long enough to take two ships at once. 5. **dry** —, a dock with gates, capable of being drained of water to expose the underwater hull of ships within it. 6. **graving** —, a dry dock. 7. **mud** —, a temporary excavation by way of a dock. 8. **wet** —, a basin impounding the water so that ships may lie afloat at all states of the tide.

drake, sb. A short gun of the culverin type (17th century).

draught, sb. 1. The depth of water required to float a ship. 2. A plan or chart. 3. The drawings showing the design of a ship.

draw, vb. 1. To haul. 2. (Of a sail) to be filled with wind, to pull. 3. (Of a ship) to require a specified depth of water to float her.

drekki (pl. *drekkar*) [ON], sb. A 'dragon', a particularly large warship.

drift, sb. The distance by which a ship is driven off her course by wind or current.

dromon, sb. A large oared warship of the Byzantine navy.

dub, vb. To trim or smooth timber, especially with an adze.

ealdorman, sb. An English nobleman or provinicial governor (9–11th century).

easting, sb. Distance run or made good to the eastward.

ebb, sb. The falling tide.

embargo, sb. An order forbidding merchant ships to sail.

embark, vb. To board or be loaded on board a ship.

eneke, ***esnecca***, see ***snacca***.

fall, sb. 1. A step or change of level of a deck. 2. (pl) The hauling part of a purchase, part of the running rigging led down to the deck.

fast, adj. 1. Secure. 2. **make** —, vb., to tie up.

fetch, vb. To catch, reach, attain.

feudal, adj. Antiquarian term for the early medieval system of landholding by military tenure.

fid, sb. A bar or spike, particularly the bar driven through holes in the head of the lower mast and the heel of the topmast to secure them together.

flag, sb. An admiral's distinguishing flag. 2. **—captain**, the captain of a flagship. 3. **—ship**, the admiral's ship.

flat, sb. An internal space in a ship, especially one off which other compartments open.

flood, sb. The rising tide.

floor, sb. The bottom of the hold, the ship's bottom.

foot, sb. The lower edge of a sail.

footrope, sb. A rope suspended beneath a yard for men to stand on while working on the yard.

fore, **afore**, adj. Towards the bow of the ship.

fore-and-aft, adj. Of a type of rig in which sails of various shapes move about positions parallel to the ship's centre line.

forecastle, sb. 1. A castle or fighting platform forward (12–15th century). 2. A deck built over the forward end of the main deck (16–18th century).

foremast, see **mast.**

foresail, see **sail.**

forestage, sb. The projecting forecastle of a carrack.

forestay, sb. A stay supporting the foremast from ahead.

form, hull —, sb. The shape of the underwater hull.

foretop, see **top**

forward, adj., adv. Relating to the fore part of ship, or motion towards the bow.

foul, adj. 1. (Of rope etc) obstructed, tangled. 2. (Of the weather) stormy. 3. (Of a ship's hull) weed-grown, in need of cleaning.

founder, vb. To sink.

fowler, sb. A light breech-loading anti-personnel gun (16th–17th century).

frame, sb. 1. A pair of timbers erected on the keel to support the ship's sides, in the manner of a pair of ribs. 2. The assembly of keel and frames, the ship's skeleton. 3. **cant —**, a frame at bow or stern set at an angle to the keel to accommodate the curve of the hull.

freeboard, sb. The minimum height of the ship's side above the waterline.

frigate, sb. 1. A small type of Mediterranean galley (16th century). 2. A small sailing warship of fine form and high speed (17th century).

fyrd, sb. [OE], 1. The English national army. 2. ***scip–***, the ***fyrd*** when serving afloat.

gage, see **weather gage.**

galleass, sb. One of several types of hybrid oared sailing warships (16th century).

galleon, sb. A sailing warship of fine lines, with a high upperworks aft and a galley bow with a heavy battery of chasers (16th century).

gallery, sb. A walkway or balcony projecting from the stern or quarters of a ship.

galley, sb. 1. A type of warship propelled primarily by oars. 2. The kitchen or cook-room of a ship.

galliot, sb. A small galley.

gallizabra, sb. A type of Spanish sailing warship, small, fast and equipped with oars (16th century).

garboard strake, see **strake**.

gear, sb. Rigging or equipment.

general, sb. A commander-in-chief (16–17th century).

grapple, vb. To make fast to another ship with hooks etc.

grave, vb. To ground a ship in order to work on her underwater hull at low tide.

great-circle, adj. Of the shortest possible course between two points on the globe.

grommet, sb. An apprentice seaman, an older boy (16–17th century).

ground, sb. 1. The beach or seabed. 2. **—tackle**, see **tackle**.

ground, vb. 1. To run aground. 2. To beach a ship in order to work on her underwater hull at low tide.

gun, sb. 1. A piece of artillery. 2. The firing of a gun. 3. **—deck**, see **deck**. 4. **—room**, a space at the after end of the main or lower deck. 5. **—shot**, the range of a gun. 6. **chase —**, see **chase**. 7. **great —**, a heavy gun, a carriage gun.

gunner, sb. 1. The Master Gunner, an officer responsible for the ship's heavy guns. 2. A subordinate assisting the Master Gunner (16th century).

gunwale, sb. A heavy timber forming the top of the ship's side and of the bulwarks.

hail shot, see **shot**.

half-deck, see **deck**.

halyard, sb. A rope or tackle used to hoist a yard or sail.

hammock, sb. A canvas bed slung from beneath the deckhead.

handy, adj. Handling easily, manoeuvrable.

hatch, **hatchway**, sb. An opening in a deck.

haul, vb. 1. To pull on a rope. 2. **—one's wind**, to alter course into the wind, to be close-hauled. 3. **—up close**, see **close-hauled**.

hawser, sb. A large rope or cable.

head, sb. 1. The foremost part of the ship's hull, projecting outwards and forward of the stem, ending in the beakhead and partly supporting the bowsprit. 2. The ship's heading, the direction in which she points. 3. The top of a cask. 4. **cubbridge —**, see **cubbridge.**

heave, vb. 1. To haul a rope. 2. (Of a ship) to rise and fall in a swell. 3. **—down**, to careen. 4. **—to**, (of a ship) to stop or lie to by backing some of the sails. 5. **—the lead**, to take soundings with a lead.

height, sb. The bore or calibre of a gun (16th century).

helm, sb. 1. The tiller. 2. The means of steering a ship. 3. **—sman**, the man steering the ship, a seaman qualified to steer.

hoy, sb. A type of sailing barge, square rigged on a single mast.

hulk, sb. 1. A type of merchant vessel, developed from the cog (15–17th century).

hull, sb. The body or main structure of a ship or vessel.

hundred, sb. An administrative division of a county (7th–19th century).

impress, press, vb. 1. To recruit men, often by force. 2. To imprest.

imprest, prest, vb. 1. To issue an advance against future expenses. 2. To make a first payment of wages by way of establishing a contract of employment.

imprest, sb. An advance payment.

inboard, adj., adv. In, into the ship.

inshore, adj., adv. Near, towards the shore.

jeers, sb. A heavy tackle used to hoist the lower yards.

karfi (pl. *karfar*), sb. [ON] A type of small ship used in coastal waters.

keel, sb. 1. The timber lying centrally along the length of the bottom of the ship, forming a spine upon which other parts of her frame are erected.

keel-haul, vb. To haul a man with ropes under the bottom of a ship from one side to the other.

kenning, sb. [Scottish] The distance at which the land can be seen from the seaward; conventionally reckoned as 14 miles.

knarr (pl. *knarrar*), sb. [ON] A type of merchant vessel.

labour, vb. To pitch and roll heavily in a seaway.

lading, loading, sb. The ship's cargo.

lateen, adj. Of a type of fore-and-aft rig in which large triangular sails are bent to yards which are set so that the foot is made fast on deck and the middle hoisted to the masthead.

latitude, sb. A position lying on a line around the earth parallel to the Equator, hence fixed in a north-south direction.

leach, sb. 1. One of the vertical edges of a square sail. 2. The after or leeward edge of a fore-and-aft sail.

lead, sb. A weight on a marked line, used for sounding.

league, sb. A measure of distance, three miles.

lee, sb. 1. The direction towards which the wind is blowing. 2. The water sheltered from the wind by land or by a ship. 3. **—shore**, a coastline towards which the wind is blowing.

leeward, adj. Relating to the direction towards which the wind is blowing.

leewardly, adv. (Of a ship) tending to drift rapidly to leeward when trying to sail close-hauled.

lieutenant, sb. 1. An officer commanding troops serving afloat (16th century). 2. The captain's deputy or second-in-command (17th century).

lighter, sb. A type of barge used for moving cargo in harbour.

linstock, sb. A short staff with a grip for holding slowmatch, used to fire a gun.

line, sb. 1. **ahead**, A navigational or fighting formation in which one or more ships follow a leader, imitating his movements. 2. **—of battle**, a fighting formation in which the ships of a fleet form a straight line in a predetermined order. 3. **centre —**, a line down the middle of the ship from bow to stern. 4. **deep-sea —**, a sounding line of extra length for sounding in deep water. 5. **water—**, see **waterline**.

longboat, sb. The largest of the ship's boats.

longitude, sb. A position lying on a straight line drawn around the earth's surface from one pole to the other, hence fixed in an east-west direction.

longship, sb. English or Norse term for a warship (10–12th century).

loof, sb. A spar serving to boom out the tack of a square sail when beating to windward (10th–13th century).

luff, sb. 1. The broadest part of the ship's hull just abaft the bows (16–17th century). 2. The windward edge of a fore-and-aft sail.

lymphad, sb. A type of Highland galley.

magazine, sb. 1. A storehouse. 2. A storehouse for explosives. 3. A compartment in the ship for storing powder.

mainmast, see **mast**.

mainsail, see **sail**.

maintop, see **top**.

marline, sb. Light line or small rope of two strands.

marlinespike, sb. A rigger's tool consisting of a pointed spike used to break apart the strands of rope in order to splice them.

marshman, sb. A digger of trenches and excavations (16th century).

mast, sb. 1. A vertical spar or spars supporting sails, rigging and other spars. 2. **fore—**, the foremost mast. 3. **lower —**, the lowest and principal element of fore, main or mizzen mast, on which the topmast is stepped. 4. **made —**, a mast made up of more than one tree assembled together. 5. **main—**, the tallest (usually second) mast. 6. **mizzen—**, see **mizzen**. 7. **topgallant —**, **top—**, see **topgallantmast**, **topmast**.

mast-pond, see **pond.**

master, sb. 1. The commanding officer of a merchant ship. 2. An officer responsible for the navigation and pilotage of a warship (16–19th century). 3. **—'s mate**, a petty officer assisting the master. 4. **quarter—**, see **quartermaster**. 5. **—shipwright**, see **shipwright.**

match, sb. 1. A type of small rope treated with an inflammable composition. 2. **quick —**, fast-burning match, used to ignite explosives etc. 3. **slow —**, slow-burning match, used to fire guns and as a delayed-action detonator of explosives.

mate, sb. A petty officer assisting a warrant officer or more senior petty officer; usually used in compound form: **boatswain's —**, **master's —**, **quartermaster's —** etc.

mess, sb. A unit of some number of men, a division of the ship's company for the distribution of victuals.

midship(s), see **amidship(s).**

midshipman, sb. An inferior or petty officer (17–18th century).

mizzen, sb. 1. The aftermost mast of a ship. 2. **bonaventure —**, the fourth and aftermost mast of a great ship (16th century).

mizzentop, see **top.**

moor, vb. To secure a ship by anchoring or making fast to a buoy.

mooring, moorings, sb. 1. The ground tackle by which a ship or buoy rides. 2. A mooring buoy and its ground tackle considered as a whole.

mould, sb. 1. Hull form (16–17th century). 2. A template for shaping the ship's frames.

mould, vb. To design a ship (16th century).

musket, sb. A type of light breech-loading gun in a swivel mounting (16th century).

muster, sb. 1. A record of the names of the ship's company or dockyard workforce. 2. An assembly held to compile or check the muster. 3. **—master**, an official responsible for mustering ships' companies and recruits.

muster, vb. To assemble people in order to take a muster.

muzzle, sb. The mouth of a gun.

muzzle-loader, sb. A gun loaded by the muzzle.

oakum, sb. Rope fibres made by breaking up old rope, used for caulking.

oar-port, sb. A small hole cut in a ship's hull to accept an oar pulled from within the hull.

observation, sb. A measurement of the position of sun, moon or star for the purpose of calculating latitude or longitude.

officer, sb. 1. A person holding a specified office (15–17th century). 2. A person having rank and authority in the Navy (17–20th century). 3. **—of**

the Navy, one of the Principal Officers of the Navy, a member of the Navy Board (16–17th century). 4. **petty** —, a senior rating. 5. **standing** —, one of the four warrant officers (Purser, Boatswain, Gunner and Carpenter) appointed permanently to a ship whether in or out of commission (17–18th century).

offing, sb. The open sea, as viewed from on shore or inshore.

onshore, adj., adv. Towards or on the shore.

Ordinary, sb. 1. A fixed annual budget (16–17th century). 2. A part of the Navy Estimates, in theory to support routine activities (17–19th century). 3. Ships in reserve, and the staff to maintain them (17–19th century).

outboard, adj., adv. Relating to, towards, the outside of the ship.

overlop, orlop, sb. An internal deck (16th century).

patent, letters patent, sb. A document under the Great Seal appointing persons to office under the Crown.

patron, sb. The commanding officer of a Mediterranean galley.

pavisade, sb. A portable shield or breastwork (13–15th century).

pay, vb. 1. To coat the hull with pitch. 2. —**off**, a) to discharge a ship's company with their whole wages; to place a ship out of commission; b) (of a ship in stays) to fall off onto one or other tack.

pendant, pennant, sb. A narrow flag or streamer.

perier, sb. A type of gun of large calibre but light metal, firing stone shot with small charges at low velocity (16th century).

pilot, sb. 1. A mariner with local knowledge employed to guide a ship through hazardous waters. 2. A deep-sea navigator (16th century).

pinnace, sb. 1. A small cruising warship of the galleon type. 2. A large ship's boat.

pipe sb. 1. A whistle, used by the boatswain to pass orders. 2. An order given by pipe. 3. A cask, equivalent to the butt, containing half a tun or two hogsheads. 4. —**stave**, see **stave**.

pitch, vb. To dip head and stern alternately into the waves.

plot, sb. A map or chart.

plummet, sb. A sounding lead.

point, sb. 1. A point of the compass, one of the thirty-two divisions of the compass card. 2. The interval between two points, an arc of 11¼°. 3. A point of sailing, one of the directions relative to the wind in which a vessel may sail.

point, vb. 1. (Of a ship) To head in a particular direction. 2. (Of a gun) to be laid on some particular target. 3. —**high** (of a ship) to lie particularly close to the wind when close-hauled.

point-blank, sb. A range at which the line of flight of the falling shot cuts the 'line of metal', the gunner's line of sight from base-ring to muzzle.

pond, sb. 1. An enclosed basin for ships or masts to lie afloat in. 2. **mast —**, a basin for storing masts under water.

poop, sb. 1. A short deck built over the after end of the quarter deck.

port, sb. 1. A hole cut in the ship's side either to load cargo, or to allow a gun mounted below decks to fire. 2. **—piece**, sb. A small breech-loading iron gun mounted in a swivel (16th century).

portage, sb. 1. The act of hauling or carrying a boat or vessel across land. 2. The burthen of a ship (16th century).

press, prest, sb. 1. see **impress, imprest**. 2. **—warrant**, an order empowering a named officer to impress seamen.

press-master, sb. An official employed in recruiting men.

prow, sb. The bows or stem of the ship. 2. **give the —**, vb., to attack bows-on.

purchase, sb. An arrangement of rope led through pulleys in order to haul at a mechanical advantage.

purser, sb. An officer responsible for victuals.

purveyance, sb. The sovereign's right to obtain supplies for the royal household at a fixed price.

purveyor, sb. An official employed to purchase supplies, especially of timber, for a dockyard (16–18th century).

quarrel, sb. The bolt or dart fired from a crossbow.

quarter, sb. 1. The sides of the ship's stern. 2. (pl.) a) Each man's post or station in action; b) accommodation ashore. 3. The outer part of a yard. 4. Mercy, safety on surrender. 5. **—bill**, A list allocating each man his station in action. 6. **—deck**, see **deck**. 7. **—master**, sb. A petty officer assisting the master to handle the ship.

quarter, vb. 1. To appoint men to their action stations. 2. To cant a gun to fire as far aft as possible.

quay, sb. A harbour wall at which ships may lie.

race, tiderace, sb. A channel through which the tide floods or ebbs at speed.

rake, sb. An angle from the vertical.

ransack, vb. To search thoroughly (16th–17th century).

ratline, sb. 1. A light line seized across the shrouds like the rung of a ladder, permitting men to go aloft. 2. Rope of the thickness used to make ratlines.

reach, vb. To sail with the wind abeam.

rear-admiral, sb. 1. An admiral third in command of a fleet (16–17th century). 2. The flag officer commanding the rear division of a fleet. 3. A rear-admiral's flagship.

reckoning, sb. 1. A calculation of the ship's position. 2. **dead —**, an estimation of the ship's position without benefit of observations, by calculating course, speed and drift from a known point of departure.

reef, sb. 1. A tuck taken in a sail to reduce its area. 2. A line of submerged rocks.

reef, vb. To shorten sail by bundling part of the sail against yard or boom.

reeve, vb. To run or lead a piece of running rigging through a block, eye etc.

relief, sb. A ship or person ordered to take the place of another.

ride, vb. To lie at anchor.

rider, sb. An additional beam laid over the internal planking of the hold.

rig, sb. 1. The style or arrangement of a ship's masts and sails. 2. **ship** —, see **ship** 2.

rig, vb. To prepare or set up something, particularly a ship's masts and rigging.

rigger, sb. One who rigs ships, a seaman employed in a dockyard.

rigging, sb. 1. The ropes supporting and controlling the masts and spars. 2. **running** —, rigging controlling the movement of sails and moveable spars. 3. **standing** —, rigging supporting the masts.

rivet, sb. A clench-nail, a sort of unthreaded bolt of which the tail is hammered over a rove or washer.

road, **roadstead**, sb. An anchorage.

roll, vb. (Of a ship) to heel from one side to the other under the pressure of the waves.

room, sb. 1. The space between two adjacent frames. 2. The number of rooms, used as a measure of the size of a ship (8th–12th century).

round robin, sb. A collective letter or petition of which the signatures are arranged as the radii of a circle, making it impossible to identify who signed first.

round to, vb. to turn to windward, to come up into the wind.

rowbarge, sb. A type of small oared warship (16th century).

rudder, sb. 1. A paddle or blade turned to steer the ship. 2. **quarter** —, a rudder mounted on the quarter and pivoted on a point above the waterline. 3. **stern** —, a rudder hinged on the sternpost.

rummage, vb. To search thoroughly, especially to search the cargo of a ship.

run, vb. 1. To sail downwind, in the direction towards which the wind is blowing. 2. To desert from a ship or convoy.

sail, sb. 1. A piece of cloth spread aloft by masts and rigging to catch the wind and propel a ship. 2. Some number of ships. 3. **fore**—, the fore course, the lowest square sail set on the foremast. 4. **head** —, a sail set forward of the foremast. 5. **main**—, the main course, the lowest square sail set on the mainmast. 6. **studding** —, a light sail temporarily spread outboard of course or topsail in light airs. 7. **top—**, a square sail hoisted on the topmast, above the course.

sail, vb. 1. (Of any sort of ship) to move, to proceed. 2. **make** —, to hoist, spread sail. 3. **shorten** —, to reduce, take in sail.

saker, sb. A small gun of the culverin class.

scantlings, sb. The structure of the ship's hull.

scuttle, vb. 1. To cut a hole in the ship's deck or side. 2. To sink a ship deliberately.

sea, sb. 1. A wave or waves. 2. **—board**, sb. the coast. 3. **—way**, the open sea with a swell running. 4. **head** —, a wave or waves coming at the ship from ahead.

seam, sb. The joint between two strakes of planking.

secure, vb. To make fast, fix, restrain, set in order.

serpentine, sb. 1. A light breech-loading gun (15–16th century). 2. A type of gunpowder.

shallop, sb. 1. A small cruising warship. 2. A type of ship's boat (16–17th century).

sharp, adj. (Of a ship's hull) with fine bows, narrow forward.

sheer, sb. 1. The curve of the ship's hull along her length, as bow and stern rise from the horizontal. 2. **—plan**, a draught of the ship seen from the side.

sheer, sheer up, vb. 1. To alter course sharply. 2. **—off,** to alter course away from something.

sheet, sb. A rope or tackle controlling the clew of a sail.

shift, vb. 1. To exchange or replace. 2. To calculate (especially in the phrase 'to shift tides').

ship, sb. 1. A seagoing vessel. 2. A vessel square-rigged on three or more masts (16–20th century). 3. **—keeper**, a seaman employed to look after a ship inactive in harbour. 4. **—'s husband**, the managing partner or agent of a merchant ship, responsible for her maintenance. 5. **royal** —, a warship of the largest class (early 17th century).

ship, vb. 1. To bring inboard, to stow. 2. **—water**, to take in water through stress of weather.

shipwright, sb. 1. A carpenter skilled in shipbuilding. 2. **Master** —, the yard officer responsible for all building and repairs.

shoal, adj. Shallow.

shoal, sb. A sandbank or shallow place.

shot, sb. 1. A bullet or (non-explosive) projectile fired from a great gun. 2. **chain** —, hollow shot formed in two halves containing and linked by a length of chain, designed to damage rigging. 3. **dice** —, shot formed of small jagged pieces of iron. 4. **random** —, the extreme range of a gun. 5. **small** —, musketeers, small-arms men (16–17th century).

shroud, sb. A stay supporting a mast from the side.

sling, sb. 1. A type of small gun (16th century). 2. A bight or loop of rope used to lift heavy articles. 3. (pl). The chains securing a standing yard to the masthead. 4. (pl.) The middle portion of a yard, where the slings are made fast.

sling, vb. 1. To lift or hoist something. 2. To secure a standing yard with slings.

slip, sb. An inclined plane running into the water, on which a ship is built, or one up which vessels may be hauled for repairs.

slip, vb. 1. To haul a small vessel up a slip for repairs. 2. To cast off a rope, especially to cast off (and buoy) the cable, in order to sail without waiting to weigh anchor.

slops, sb. Naval-issue clothes or cloth.

snacca [OE], *snekkja* [ON], *eneke* [Norman French], *esnecca* [Latin], sb. A 'snake', a term for a warship, presumably but not certainly the same in the different languages (9–13th century).

snug, adj. (Of a ship) low, compact.

soke, sb. 1. A local government area. 2. **ship—**, a soke obliged to provide a ship for the fleet (8–11th century).

sound, vb. To take a sounding, to measure the depth of water beneath a ship.

sounding, sb. A measurement of the depth of water.

spar, sb. 1. A mast, pole or boom. 2. **—deck**, see **deck**.

speak, vb. To speak with another ship.

splice, vb. To marry two rope's ends, or two parts of the same rope, by parting the strands and weaving them into one another.

spread, sb. The breadth of a sail or length of a yard.

spread, vb. To stretch, extend, keep apart.

spring, see **tide.**

spring, vb. (Of a mast or spar) to split along the grain.

springald, sb. A type of heavy crossbow on a mounting.

spritsail, sb. 1. A sail set on a yard below the bowsprit. 2. **—topsail**, a sail set on a small mast stepped on the end of the bowsprit.

square, adj. 1. (Of sails) broad in proportion to height. 2. At right angles. 3. **—rig**, a rig in which quadrangular sails are bent to yards lying horizontal to the masts on which they are set, and move about positions at right angles to the ship's centre line.

staple, sb. An organization in a port having the monopoly of a particular trade or commodity, especially the English wool staple at Calais, later Antwerp.

staunch, adj. (Of a ship) structurally sound, tight, not leaky.

stave, sb. A plank tapered at each end, forming part of the shell of a cask.

stave in, vb. (part. **stove**) To break a hole in a cask or ship's side.

stay, sb. 1. A piece of rigging supporting a mast from ahead or astern. 2. **back—**, see backstay. 3. **fore—**, see **forestay**.

stay, vb. 1. To tack. 2. **in stays**, adj. of a ship pointing into the wind while in the process of going about. 3. **miss stays**, vb., in tacking, to fail to turn into the wind and to fall back onto the original tack.

stem, **stempost**, sb. 1. A timber rising in a curve from the keel and forming the centrepiece of the bows. 2. **—head**, the top of the stem or sternpost, projecting above the hull; a feature of ships built in the Viking tradition.

stern, sb. 1. The after end of the ship. 2. **—post**, a straight timber erected on the after end of the keel, supporting both the rudder and the structure of the stern.

steward, sb. A rating responsible for serving or managing victuals.

stockfish, sb. Dried cod.

stoop, vb. To heel (16–17th century).

stow, vb. To put away.

strake, sb. 1. A line of planking from stem to stern. 2. **garboard —**, the first strake of planking either side of the keel.

strand, vb. To run aground.

strand, sb. One of the constituent elements of cable-laid rope.

stream, sb. The tide or current

strike, vb. 1. To lower a mast, sail etc. 2. To strike colours, to surrender. 3. To run aground.

supercargo, sb. A merchant travelling aboard ship as business manager of the ship or agent for the shippers, to sell and buy cargo.

swabber, sb. A rating employed to keep the ship clean.

tabard, sb. A surcoat bearing the coat of arms of the wearer or his lord.

tack, sb. 1. A rope or tackle serving to haul down the clew of a square sail. 2. The course held by a ship beating to windward.

tack, vb. 1. To shift tacks, to go about, to turn into the wind and so onto the opposite tack. 2. To beat to windward by successive tacks.

tackle, sb. 1. A purchase formed of cordage and two or more blocks. 2. rigging or gear in general. 3. **ground —**, anchors and their cables. 4. **gun—**, a purchase used to handle a carriage gun.

tally, sb. An accounting device consisting of a notched stick or note recording a sum of money owed.

tarpaulin, sb. 1. A waterproof canvas cloth used for hatch-covers, coats etc. 2. An officer brought up in merchant ships, a person of low birth (17th century).

taunt, adj. (Of a mast) tall in proportion to the spread of the yards or the size of the ship.

thick, adj. (Of the weather) misty, hazy.

thwart, sb. A bench or seat spanning a pair of frames in an open boat.

tide, sb. 1. The diurnal rise and fall of sea-level. 2. **—race**, see **race**. 3. **spring —**, the highest and lowest tides which occur twice a month.

tier, sb. The broadside guns mounted on one deck.

tight, adj. Not leaky.

top, sb. 1. A platform built at the head of the lower mast, serving to spread the shrouds of the topmast. 2. **—armour**, A screen of canvas or other cloth (often decorated) fitted around the top. 3. **—castle**, sb. A fighting platform on the mast (13–16th century). 4. **—gallant**, see **topgallant**. 5. **—mast**, a mast fitted to the top of the lower mast and extending it. 6. **—sail**, see **sail**. 7. **fore—**, **main—**, **mizzen** — a) The platform built at the head of the foremast, mainmast, mizzenmast; b) The fore, main or mizzen topmast head, the head of the topmast or topgallant mast.

topgallant, sb. 1. A square sail set on the topgallant mast, above the topsail. 2. **—mast**, a mast fitted to the top of the topmast and extending it.

topmast, see **top**.

train, vb. To alter the direction in which a gun is pointing.

train, sb. 1. The tail of a land gun-carriage. 2. An artillery train, a battery of siege guns.

transom, sb. 1. One of the timbers crossing the sternpost and forming the structure of the stern. 2. **—stern**, a flat stern built up on transoms.

traverse, vb. To cant or train a gun.

trebuchet, sb. A type of siege engine with a swinging arm worked by a counterweight.

treenail, **trenail**, sb. A wooden peg or pin used to fasten together the parts of the hull of a wooden ship.

trim, vb. To adjust the set of the sails.

truck, sb. The wheel of a gun carriage.

van, sb. The leading one of three divisions of a fleet.

vane, sb. 1. A short pennant. 2. A weather-vane.

vanguard, **vanward**, sb. The van.

veer, vb. 1. To pay out a cable. 2. To alter course sharply. 3. To wear. 4. (Of wind) to change in a clockwise direction.

vice-admiral, sb. 1. An officer second in command of a squadron (14–17th century). 2. The flag officer commanding the van division of a fleet. 3. The deputy of the Lord Admiral in one of the maritime counties or colonies. 4. A vice-admiral's flagship.

victual, vb. To supply victuals.

victualler, sb. 1. A victualling contractor or agent. 2. A ship transporting victuals.

victuals, sb. Foodstuffs.

waft, vb. To protect or convoy merchant ships (16–17th century).

wafter, sb. A convoy escort.

waist, sb. 1. That part of the main deck amidships not covered by forecastle or quarter deck. 2. The level of the main deck (17th century). 3. **—cloth,** A canvas screen above the waist bulwarks.

wake, sb. 1. The track of the ship's passage through the water astern. 2. **In — of**, see **way**.

wale, sb. A strake of extra heavy hull planking.

warp, sb. A heavy cable, especially for towing.

warp, vb. 1. To tow a ship with boats. 2. To move a ship by hauling on warps made fast to the shore or to buoys.

watch, sb. 1. One of the seven divisions of the nautical day. 2. One of the two or three divisions of the ship's company, taking turns to be on duty. 3. The length of one watch, a spell of duty on deck.

waterline, sb. 1. The line of the water surface against the ship's hull.

way, sb. 1. The movement of a ship though the water. 2. **in —of**, adj., in a line with, adjacent to. 3. **steerage —**, movement at a speed sufficient to allow the ship to be controlled by the helm. 4. (pl.) Pairs of heavy timbers laid as rails on a launching slip or graving place to support the weight of a ship.

wear, vb. 1. To alter course from one tack to the other by turning before the wind. 2. To fly a particular flag or carry some distinguishing mark.

weather, adj. 1. Relating to the direction from which the wind is blowing.

weather, sb., 1. **—deck**, see **deck.** 2. **—gage**, the windward position in relation to another ship or fleet.

weather, vb. To get to windward of something.

weatherly, adv. (Of a ship) tending to drift little to leeward when close-hauled.

weigh, vb. To raise something (most often an anchor) from the seabed.

westing, sb. Distance run or made good to the westward.

wharf, sb. A quay, a harbour wall at which ships may lie.

wherry, sb. A type of rowing boat used to carry passengers on the Thames.

wind, sb. 1. The direction from which the wind blows. 2. The windward position, the weather gage. 3. **—'s eye**, straight into the wind, in a line directly to windward. 4. **fair —**, a wind favourable for a ship's intended course. 5. **leading —**, a wind blowing straight up or down a channel. 6. **off the —**, adv., sailing with the wind abaft the beam. 7. **on the —**, adv., sailing close-hauled.

windlass, sb. A mechanical device for hauling in cable, consisting of a horizontal drum turned by bars inserted in holes.

windward, adj. Relating to the direction from which the wind is blowing.

wing, sb. A flanking squadron, often of galleys (15–16th century).

work, vb. 1. To beat to windward (16–18th century). 2. To flex or move under the strain of the waves. 3. To handle a ship.

works, sb. 1. Parts of the ship's structure. 2. **upper—**, parts of the ship's structure above the main deck, not part of the hull structure.

yard, sb. 1. A spar hung horizontally from a mast to spread the head or foot of a square sail. 2. An establishment to build, repair and supply warships. 3. **—arm**, the extreme ends of a yard. 4. **dock—**, a naval yard with one or more dry docks.

yare, adj. Brisk, smart, handy.

ABBREVIATIONS

AHR	*American Historical Review*
AN	*American Neptune*
ANS	*Anglo-Norman Studies*
ARN	Oppenheim, *Administration of the Royal Navy*
ASC	Whitelock, *Anglo-Saxon Chronicle*
ASMI	Hollister, *Anglo-Saxon Military Institutions*
BBA	Twiss, *Black Book of the Admiralty*
BIHR	*Bulletin of the Institute of Historical Research*
BL	British Library
BMO	Calvar Gross, *La Batalla del Mar Océano*
BND	Hattendorf, *British Naval Documents*
CChR	*Calendar of Charter Rolls*
CCR	*Calendar of Close Rolls*
CCW	*Calendar of Chancery Warrants*
CDS	*Calendar of Documents relating to Scotland*
CFR	*Calendar of Fine Rolls*
CIM	*Calendar of Inquisitions Miscellaneous*
CLR	*Calendar of Liberate Rolls*
CMR	*Calendar of Memoranda Rolls*
CPR	*Calendar of Patent Rolls*
CS	Camden Society
CSL	*Calendar of Signet Letters*
CSPD	*Calendar of State Papers Domestic*
CSPS	*Calendar of State Papers Spanish*
CSPV	*Calendar of State Papers Venetian*
DB	*Domesday Book*
DCW	Powell & Timings, *Documents relating to the Civil War*
DSA	Laughton, *Defeat of the Spanish Armada*
EcHR	*Economic History Review*
EHD	*English Historical Documents*

EHR	*English Historical Review*
ERS	*Exchequer Rolls of Scotland*
EWP	MacCaffrey, *Elizabeth I, War and Politics*
HJ	*Historical Journal*
HMC	Historical Manuscripts Commission
HR	*Historical Research*
HS	Hakluyt Society
IHS	*Irish Historical Studies*
IJMH	*International Journal of Maritime History*
IJNA	*International Journal of Nautical Archaeology*
JMH	*Journal of Modern History*
KLNM	*Kulturhistorisk Leksikon for Nordisk Middelalder*
LPH8	*Calender of Letters and Papers Henry VIII*
LQCG	*Liber Quotidianus Contrarotulatoris Garderobae*
MCC	Magdalene College, Cambridge
MEST	Sandahl, *Middle English Sea Terms*
MF	La Roncière, *Marine Française*
MGN	*Maritieme Geschiedenis der Nederlanden*
MM	*Mariner's Mirror*
MNT	Monson, *Naval Tracts*
NMM	National Maritime Museum
NRS	Navy Records Society
NS	New Series, New Style
OE	Old English
ON	Old Norse
PN	Hakluyt, *Principal Navigations*
PR	Pipe Roll (as printed by the PRS)
PRO	Public Record Office
PRS	Pipe Roll Society
RFO	Rymer, *Foedera* (original edn)
RFR	Rymer, *Foedera* (Record Commission edn)
RHN	*Revista de Historia Naval*
RLC	*Rotuli Litterarum Clausarum*
RLP	*Rotuli Litterarum Patentium*
RP	*Rotuli Parliamentorum*
RS	*Rotuli Scotiae*
SCP	Plummer & Earle, *Two of the Saxon Chronicles Parallel*
SHR	*Scottish Historical Review*

TDA	*Transactions of the Devonshire Association*
TN	Loades, *Tudor Navy*
TR	*Treaty Rolls*
TRHS	*Transactions of the Royal Historical Society*
VCH	*Victoria County Histories*
WAA	Wernham, *After the Armada*
WBA	Wernham, *Before the Armada*
WRA	Wernham, *Return of the Armadas*

BIBLIOGRAPHY

This is a select list of the works most useful in writing this book, not a comprehensive bibliography of British naval history. I have cited English translations in preference to original works in other languages where there are acceptable versions available. In references to journals, roman numerals refer to annual volumes, and arabic to individual parts or numbers.

Abels, Richard P., *Lordship and Military Obligation in Anglo-Saxon England* (Berkeley, 1988). The latest major study of this subject.

— 'English Tactics, Strategy and Military Organization in the Late Tenth Century', in Scragg, *Battle of Maldon*, pp. 143–55.

Adair, E. R., 'English Galleys in the Sixteenth Century', *EHR* XXXV (1920), pp. 497–512. Now rather outdated but still useful for details.

Adams, Simon, *The Armada Campaign of 1588* (Historical Association, 1988).

— 'Foreign Policy and the Parliaments of 1621 and 1624', in *Factions and Parliament: Essays on Early Stuart History*, ed. Kevin Sharpe (Oxford, 1978), pp. 139–71.

— 'Spain or the Netherlands? The Dilemmas of Early Stuart Foreign Policy', in *Before the English Civil War: Essays on Early Stuart Politics and Government*, ed. Howard Tomlinson (London, 1983), pp. 79–101. Surveys England's strategic situation.

— 'The Battle that never was: the Downs and the Armada Campaign', in Rodríguez-Salgado & Adams, *England, Spain and the Gran Armada*, pp. 173–96 (also in Spanish in *RHN* VI [1988] No.23, pp. 73–88). One of the best discussions of Philip II's intentions.

— 'The Outbreak of the Elizabethan Naval War against the Spanish Empire: The Embargo of May 1585 and Sir Francis Drake's West Indies Voyage', in Rodríguez-Salgado & Adams, *England, Spain and the Gran Armada*, pp. 45–69. Deals with the still disputed question of who provoked whom to war.

— 'The Gran Armada: 1988 and After', *History* LXXVI (1991), pp. 238–49. A review article.

— 'New Light on the "Reformation" of John Hawkins: the Ellesmere Naval Survey of January 1584', *EHR* CV (1990), pp. 96–111. An important article which revises previous views of Hawkins's naval administration.

Adams, Thomas R., & David W. Waters, *English Maritime Books printed before 1801, relating to Ships, their Construction and their Operation at Sea* (Providence R.I. & Greenwich, 1995). An essential bibliographic reference.

Alban, J. R., 'National Defence in England, 1337–89' (Liverpool Ph.D. thesis, 1976). A useful thesis with some treatment of naval warfare.

Alcalá-Zamora y Queipo de Llano, José, *España, Flandes y el Mar del Norte (1618–1639): La última ofensiva europea de los Austrias Madrileños* (Barcelona, 1975). Admirable study of Spanish naval strategy in northern waters.

Alexander, Michael Van Cleave, *Charles I's Lord Treasurer: Sir Richard Weston Earl of Portland (1577–1635)* (London, 1975). A leading member of the 1628 Admiralty Board.

Allmand, Christopher, *Henry V* (London, 1992).

— *The Hundred Years War: England and France at War c.1300–c.1450* (Cambridge, 1988).

Anderson, R. C., *Oared Fighting Ships, From Classical times to the coming of steam* (London, 1962). A characteristically austere piece of scholarship, still valuable in spite of recent researches.

— 'The *Royal Sovereign* of 1637', *MM* III (1913) pp. 109–12, 168–70, 208–11.

— 'The *Prince Royal* and other Ships of James I', *MM* III (1913), pp. 272–5, 305–7, 341–2.

— 'The *Grace de Dieu* of 1446–86', *EHR* XXXIV (1919), pp. 584–6.

— 'Henry VIII's *Great Galley*', *MM* VI (1920), pp. 274–81.

— 'Armaments in 1540', *MM* VI (1920), p. 281.

— 'English Galleys in 1295', *MM* XIV (1928), pp. 220–41.

— *List of English Men-of-War 1509–1649* (Society for Nautical Research Occasional Publication No.7, 1959). An essential work of reference; see Glasgow's amendments.

— 'The *Mary Gonson*', *MM* XLVI (1960), pp. 199–204.

Andrews, K. R., *Elizabethan Privateering* (Cambridge, 1964). A classic study, the first of many by the leading authority on the subject.

— ed., *English Privateering Voyages to the West Indies 1588–1595* (HS 2nd S. Vol.111, 1959)

— *Drake's Voyages: A Re-assessment of their place in Elizabethan Maritime Expansion* (London, 1967). Concerned to debunk the Victorian Drake.

— ed., *The Last Voyage of Drake and Hawkins* (HS 2nd.S. Vol.142, 1972).

— *The Spanish Caribbean: Trade and Plunder 1530–1630* (New Haven, 1978).

— *Trade, Plunder and Settlement: Maritime Enterprise and the Genesis of the British Empire, 1480–1630* (Cambridge, 1984).

— *Ships, Money and Politics: Seafaring and Naval Enterprise in the Reign of Charles I* (Cambridge, 1991). Various studies rather than a complete history.

— 'The Aims of Drake's Expedition of 1577–1580', *AHR* LXXIII (1967–68), pp. 724–41.

— 'Sir Robert Cecil and Mediterranean Plunder', *EHR* LXXXVII (1972), pp. 513–32. Reveals the extent of Cecil's involvement in piracy.

— 'English Voyages to the Caribbean, 1596 to 1604: An Annotated List', *William and Mary Quarterly* 3rd S. XXXI (1974), pp. 243–54.

— 'Caribbean Rivalry and the Anglo-Spanish Peace of 1604', *History* LIX (1974), pp. 1–17.

— 'Beyond the Equinoctial: England and South America in the Sixteenth Century', *Journal of Imperial and Commonwealth History* X (1981), pp. 4–24. Bears on the origins of Drake's voyage round the world.

— 'The Elizabethan Seaman', *MM* LXVIII (1982), pp. 245–62. An admirable introduction to the social history which has still not been thoroughly covered in print.

— 'Elizabethan Privateering', in *Raleigh in Exeter 1985: Privateering and Colonisation in the Reign of Elizabeth I*, ed. Joyce Youings (Exeter, 1985), pp. 1–20.

Appleby, J. C., 'English Privateering during the Spanish and French Wars, 1625–1630' (Hull Ph.D. thesis, 1983). A good thesis from a limited range of sources.

— 'Devon Privateering from Early Times to 1688', in Duffy, *New Maritime History of Devon*, I, 90–7.

— 'Neutrality, Trade and Privateering, 1500–1689', in *A People of the Sea: The Maritime History of the Channel Islands* ed. A. G. Jamieson (London, 1986), pp. 59–105.

— 'A Pathway out of Debt: The Privateering Activities of Sir John Hippisley during the Early Stuart Wars with Spain and France, 1625–30', *AN* XLIX (1989), pp. 251–61.

— 'A Nursery of Pirates: The English Pirate Community in Ireland in the Early Seventeenth Century', *IJMH* II (1990) No.1, pp. 1–27.

— & Mary O'Dowd, 'The Irish Admiralty: Its Organisation and Development, c.1570–1640', *IHS* XXIV (1985), pp. 299–326.

Ashley, Roger, 'The Organisation and Administration of the Tudor Office of Ordnance' (Oxford B.Litt. thesis, 1972).

— 'War in the Ordnance Office: the Essex connection and Sir John Davis', *HR* LXVII (1994), pp. 337–45.

Ashton, R., 'The disbursing official under the early Stuarts: the cases of Sir

William Russell and Philip Burlamachi', *BIHR* XXX (1957), pp. 162–74. Russell was Treasurer of the Navy.

Aydelotte, Frank, 'Elizabethan Seamen in Mexico', *AHR* XLVIII (1942–43), pp. 1–19. Inquisition records about the men abandoned by Hawkins in 1568.

Aylmer, G. E., *The King's Servants: The Civil Service of Charles I* (London, 2nd edn 1974). Very important for the structure of government and society.

— 'Attempts at administrative reform, 1625–1640', *EHR* LXXII (1957), pp. 229–59.

— 'Office Holding as a Factor in English History, 1625–42', *History* XLIV (1959), pp. 228–40.

— 'Buckingham as Administrative Reformer?', *EHR* CV (1990), pp. 355–62.

Bachrach, Bernard S. 'On the Origins of William the Conqueror's Horse Transports', *Technology and Culture* XXVI (1985), pp. 505–31.

— 'Some observations on the military administration of the Norman Conquest', *ANS* VIII (1985), pp. 1–25. Learned comments by a scholar painfully ignorant of the sea.

Bannerman, John, *Studies in the History of Dalriada* (Edinburgh, 1974).

Barber, Richard, *Edward, Prince of Wales and Aquitaine: A Biography of the Black Prince* (London, 1978).

Bard, Nelson P., ed., 'The Earl of Warwick's Voyage of 1627', in *The Naval Miscellany* V, ed. N. A. M. Rodger (NRS Vol.125, 1984), pp. 15–93. Prints a narrative by the master of Warwick's flagship.

Barfod, Jørgen H., 'Den danske orlogsflåde før 1560', *Historisk Tidsskrift* XCIV (1994), pp. 261–70.

Barker, Richard, '"Many may peruse us": Ribbands, Moulds and Models in the Dockyards', *Revista de Universidade da Coimbra* XXXIV (1987), pp. 539–59.

— 'Design in the Dockyards, about 1600', in *Carvel Construction Technique: skeleton-first, shell-first; 5th international symposium on boat and ship archaeology, Amsterdam, 1988*, ed. Reinder Reinders & Paul Kees (Oxford, 1991), pp. 61–9. Valuable articles on the obscure but important subject of naval architecture.

Barlow, Frank, *The Feudal Kingdom of England 1042–1216* (London, 2nd edn 1961).

— 'The *Carmen de Hastingae Proelio*', in *The Norman Conquest and Beyond* (London, 1983), pp. 189–222 (originally in *Studies in International History: Essays presented to W. Norton Medlicott*, ed. K. Bourne & D. C. Watt [London, 1967], pp. 35–67).

— *Edward the Confessor* (London, 1970).

Barnby, Henry, 'The Algerian Attack on Baltimore 1631', *MM* LVI (1970), pp. 27–31. Useful detail, but not entirely accurate.

Barnie, John, *War in Mediaeval Society: Social Values and the Hundred Years War 1337–99* (London, 1974). Not much about naval war.

Barrow, G. W. S., *The Kingdom of the Scots: Government, Church and Society from the eleventh to the fourteenth century* (London, 1973).

Baumber, M. L., 'The Navy during the Civil Wars and the Commonwealth, 1642–1651' (Manchester MA thesis, 1967). An excellent thesis; quoted by permission of the John Rylands University Library.

— 'The Navy and the Civil War in Ireland 1641–1643', *MM* LVII (1971), pp. 385–97.

— 'The Navy and the Civil War in Ireland, 1643–46', *MM* LXXV (1989), pp. 255–68.

— 'Parliamentary Naval Politics 1641–49', *MM* LXXXII (1996), pp. 398–408.

Baykowski, Uwe, 'The Kieler Hanse-Cog – A Replica of the Bremen Cog', in Westerdahl, *Crossroads in Ancient Shipbuilding*, pp. 261–4. Brief description of sea-trials.

Beeler, John, *Warfare in England, 1066–1189* (Ithaca, NY, 1966).

Bellabarba, Sergio, 'The Square-rigged Ship of the *Fabrica de Galere* Manuscript' *MM* LXXIV (1988), pp. 113–30, 225–39. Deals with the development of the *cocha.*

Bémont, Charles, 'La campagne de Poitou 1242–1243', *Annales du Midi* V (1893), pp. 289–314.

Bernard, Jacques, *Navires et Gens de Mer à Bordeaux (vers 1400–vers 1550)* (Paris, 1968, 3 vols). A richly detailed study, much of it of English shipping.

Bill, Jan, 'Ship Construction: Tools and Techniques', in Unger, *Cogs, Caravels and Galleons*, pp. 151–9.

Binns, Alan, 'The Ships of the Vikings, were they "Viking Ships"?', in *Proceedings of the Eighth Viking Congress*, ed. Hans Bekker-Nielsen, Peter Foote & Olaf Olsen (Odense, 1981), pp. 287–94.

— 'Towards a North Sea Kingdom? Viking Age Incursions and later Attempts to Establish Scandinavian Rule "West over the Sea"', in *The North Sea: A Highway of Economic and Cultural Exchange; Character –History*, ed. Arne Bang-Andersen, Basil Greenhill & Egil Harald Grude (Stavanger, 1985), pp. 49–62.

Bonner, Elizabeth, 'The Recovery of St. Andrews Castle in 1547: French Naval Policy and Diplomacy in the British Isles', *EHR* CXI (1996), pp. 578–98.

Bono, Salvatore, *I Corsari Barbareschi* (Turin, 1964). A useful general study, dealing only with the Mediterranean Regencies.

Bonsey, Carol G., & J. G. Jenkins, eds., *Ship Money Papers and Richard Grenville's Note-Book* (Buckinghamshire Record Society Vol.13, 1965). The practicalities of collecting Ship Money in the shires.

Boulind, Richard, 'The Strength and Weakness of Spanish Control of the Caribbean, 1520–1650: The Case for the *Armada de Barlovento*' (Cambridge Ph.D. thesis, 1965). A valuable but eccentric thesis; in spite of its title, it is largely confined to the sixteenth century, and has virtually nothing to say about the *Armada de Barlovento.*

— 'Ships of Private Origin in the Mid-Tudor Navy: the *Lartigue*, the *Salamander*, the *Mary Willoughby*, the *Bark Aucher* and the *Galley Blanchard*', *MM* LIX (1973), pp. 385–408.

Bound, Mensun, ed., *The Archaeology of Ships of War* (Oswestry, 1995–, one vol. to date). Conference papers, some of them useful.

Bourne, William, *The Arte of Shooting in Great Ordnance* (London, 1587). A gunner's manual.

Boxer, C. R., trans. & ed., *The Journal of Maarten Harpertszoon Tromp, Anno 1639* (Cambridge, 1930). Indispensable for the Downs campaign. The original Dutch text is printed by S. P. L'Honoré-Naber in the *Bijdragen en Mededelingen van het Historisch Genootschap* LII (1931).

Boyer, Pierre, 'Artillerie et tactique navale en Méditeranée au XVIe siècle', *Revue Historique des Armées* 174 (1989), pp. 110–21. Galley artillery tactics.

Braudel, Fernand, *The Mediterranean and the Mediterranean World in the Age of Philip II*, trans. Siân Reynolds (London, 1972, 2 vols; originally *La Méditerranée et le Monde Méditerranéan à l'Epoque de Philippe II*, Paris, 1949, 1966). One of the great works of modern history, though relatively less well-informed about the English and other northerners.

Brenner, Robert, *Merchants and Revolution: Commercial Change, Political Conflict, and London's Overseas Traders, 1550–1653* (Cambridge, 1993). Important for the connections betrween politics, merchant shipping and the Navy.

— 'The Civil War Politics of London's Merchant Community', *Past and Present* 58 (1973), pp. 53–107.

Brøgger, A. W., & Haakon Shetelig, *The Viking Ships, their Ancestry and Evolution*, trans. Katherine John (Oslo, 1953; originally *Vikingskipene: deres forgjengere og etterfølgere*, Oslo, 1950). Ageing but still unreplaced general study.

Brooks, F. W. *The English Naval Forces, 1199–1272* (London, 1932). Scholarly and valuable, though narrow in focus.

— 'William de Wrotham and the Office of Keeper of the King's Ports and Galleys', *EHR* XL (1925), pp. 570–9.

— 'Naval Armament in the Thirteenth Century', *MM* XIV (1928), pp. 115–31.

— 'The King's Ships and Galleys, mainly under John and Henry III', *MM* XV (1929), pp. 15–48.

— 'The Cinque Ports', *MM* XV (1929), pp. 142–91.

— 'Naval Administration and the Raising of Fleets under John and Henry III', *MM* XV (1929), pp. 351–90.

— 'The Battle of Damme – 1213', *MM* XVI (1930), pp. 263–71.

— 'The Cinque Ports' Feud with Yarmouth in the Thirteenth Century', *MM* XIX (1933), pp. 27–51.

— 'A Wage Scale for Seamen, 1546', *EHR* LX (1945), pp. 234–46. Illustrates the appalling complexity of merchant seamen's wages.

Brooks, N. P., 'England in the Ninth Century: the Crucible of Defeat', *TRHS* 5th S. XXIX (1979), pp. 1–20.

— 'The Development of Military Obligations in eighth- and ninth-century England', in *England before the Conquest: Studies in Primary Sources presented to Dorothy Whitelock* (Cambridge, 1971), pp. 69–84.

Brown, R. Allen, *The Normans and the Norman Conquest* (London, 1969).

Bruce-Mitford, Rupert, *The Sutton Hoo Ship-Burial* (British Museum, 1975–84, 3 vols in 4).

Bruijn, Jaap R., *The Dutch Navy of the Seventeenth and Eighteenth Centuries* (Columbia, S.C., 1993). An admirable introduction.

Bull, S. B., 'The Furie of the Ordnance: England's Guns and Gunners by Land 1600–1650' (Wales Ph.D. thesis, 1988). A thorough and valuable study.

Burwash, Dorothy, *English Merchant Shipping 1460–1540* (Toronto, 1947). A short but rich study.

[Butler, Nathaniel] *Boteler's Dialogues*, ed. W. G. Perrin (NRS Vol.65, 1929). Writings of an early Stuart voyager; the editor preserved the spelling of the author's name under which the Dialogues were first printed, rather than that which Butler himself always used.

Byerly, Benjamin F., & Catherine R., eds., *Records of the Wardrobe and Household 1285–1286* and *Records of the Wardrobe and Household 1286–1289* (London, 1977, 1985). Include much of military and naval interest; I have treated them as two volumes of a single work.

Bytharne, Jehan, 'Book of War by Sea and Land, Anno 1543', in Laughton, *Naval Miscellany I*, pp. 1–21. Guidance for a naval commander.

Calendar of Chancery Warrants, 1230–1326 (London, 1927). These are warrants, chiefly under the signet or privy seal, to issue instruments largely under the Great Seal. They include items omitted from the Chancery rolls, and give more detail.

Calendar of Charter Rolls (London, 1903–27, 6 vols). Charters 1226–1516, many of them printed more or less complete.

[Calendar of] Close Rolls; i.e. *Close Rolls Henry III* (London, 1902–38, 14 vols) and *Calendar of Close Rolls* (London, 1892–1963, 47 vols). Royal letters 'Close' (sealed and directed to named individuals) on all aspects of government business, transcribed in full for 1227–72, and calendared for 1272–1509. For convenience I have treated them as a single series.

Calendar of Documents Relating to Scotland, ed. Joseph Bain (Edinburgh, 1881–8, 4 vols, with supp. vol ed. G. G. Simpson & J. D. Galbraith, 1986). English documents, many of them bearing on the Anglo-Scottish wars. Vol.V is usable as a means of reference to the *Rotuli Scotiae.*

Calendar of Fine Rolls (London, 1911–49, 20 vols). Records of payments in money or kind for all sorts of grants and privileges, 1272–1471.

Calendar of Inquisitions Miscellaneous (London, 1916–68, 7 vols). Judicial enquiries, 1219–1422, in connection with disputes, lawsuits, alleged crimes etc. A number have to do with shipping.

Calendar of Letters and Papers . . . Henry VIII, ed. J. S. Brewer *et al.* (London, 1862–1932, 21 vols in 44 plus 2 vols Addenda). Covers the principal classes of Public Records and many other archives.

Calendar of Liberate Rolls (London, 1917–64, 5 vols). Writs (1226–72) ordering expenditure from the Exchequer, or allowing sums already expended against accounts to be audited there. They cover the whole range of royal business.

Calendar of Memoranda Rolls (Exchequer) . . . 1326–1327, ed. R. E. Latham (London, 1968). Covers a wide range of government business.

[Calendar of] Patent Rolls (i.e. *Patent Rolls 1–16 Henry III* (London, 2 vols, 1901–3), and *Calendar of Patent Rolls* (London, 1891–16, 52 vols). The full text (1216–32) and calendar (1232–1509) of royal letters 'Patent' (unsealed and addressed to the public at large). I have treated transcripts and calendars as a single series.

Calendar of Signet Letters of Henry IV and Henry V (1399–1422), ed. J.L. Kirby (London, 1978). Mainly Chancery warrants similar to those in *CCW.*

Calendar of State Papers Domestic (London, 1856–97, 35 volumes to 1649). Calendars of varying completeness of the domestic (including military and naval) papers of the Secretaries of State from 1547.

Calendar of State Papers Spanish (i.e. *Calendar of Letters and State Papers relating to English Affairs . . . in the archives of Simancas*), ed. M. A. S. Hume (London, 1892–99, 4 vols). Covers the reign of Elizabeth. As far as naval documents go, it is being progressively replaced by Calvar Gross, *La Batalla del Mar Océano.*

Calendar of State Papers Venetian (i.e. *Calendar of State Papers and*

Manuscripts relating to English Affairs existing in ... Venice) ed. R. Brown *et al.* (London, 1864–1940, 38 vols in 40). Includes the invaluable reports, full, frequent and well-informed, of Venetian diplomats abroad.

Calvar Gross, Jorge, *et al.*, eds., *La Batalla del Mar Océano: Corpus Documental de las hostilidades entre España e Inglaterra (1568–1604)* (Madrid, 1988ff., 3 vols to date). A massive documentary collection, planned to print all significant documents in Spanish archives on the naval war; so far it has reached February 1588.

Campbell, James, 'Observations on English Government from the Tenth to the Twelfth Century', in *Essays in Anglo-Saxon History* (London, 1986), pp. 155–70 (originally in *TRHS* 5th S. XXV [1975], pp. 39–54).

— 'The Significance of the Anglo-Norman State in Administrative History', *ibid.*, pp. 171–188 (originally in *Histoire comparée de l'Administration [IVe–XVIIIe Siècles]* [Actes du XIV Colloque Historique Franco-Allemand, Tours, 1977], ed. W. Paravicini & K. F. Werner [Munich, 1980], pp. 117–34).

— 'Some Agents and Agencies of the Late Anglo-Saxon State', in *Domesday Studies*, ed. J. C. Holt (Woodbridge, 1987), pp. 201–18. Three penetrating and influential studies.

— Eric John, & Patrick Wormald, *The Anglo-Saxons* (Oxford, 1982). One of the best general surveys.

Capp, Bernard, *Cromwell's Navy: The Fleet and the English Revolution, 1648–1660* (Oxford, 1989). A social and political study of the State's Navy.

Carpenter, D. A. *The Minority of Henry III* (London, 1990).

Carpenter, Kenneth J., *The History of Scurvy and Vitamin C* (Cambridge, 1986). Dispels many tenacious myths.

Carr, A. D., *Owen of Wales: The End of the House of Gwynedd* (Cardiff, 1991). A life of the Welsh admiral and soldier of fortune Owain Llawgoch ap Thomas ap Rhodri.

Caruana, Adrian B., *The History of English Sea Ordnance 1523–1875: Volume 1, The Age of Evolution, 1523–1715* (Rotherfield, Sussex, 1994). The latest work on an important and neglected subject.

Casada Soto, José Luis, *Los barcos españoles del siglo XVI y la Gran Armada de 1588* (Madrid, 1988). Thorough and scholarly. See also his 'Atlantic Shipping in Sixteenth-Century Spain and the 1588 Armada', in Rodríguez-Salgado & Adams, *England, Spain and the Gran Armada*, pp. 95–132.

Cerezo Martínez, Ricardo, *Las Armadas de Felipe II* (Madrid, 1988). A useful general survey of Spanish seapower.

— *La proyección marítima de España en la época de los Reyes Católicos*

(Madrid, 1991). Somewhat cursory survey of Spain's strategic situation in the early 16th century.

— 'La táctica naval en el siglo XVI', *RHN* I (1983) No.2, pp. 29–6. Helpful introduction to a neglected subject.

Chaplais, Pierre, *English Medieval Diplomatic Practice* (London, 2 vols in 3, 1975–82). Diplomatic documents and their interpretation. See also *Treaty Rolls*.

— 'Règlement des conflits internationaux franco-anglais au XIVe siècle (1293–1377)', *Le Moyen Age* LVII (1951), pp. 259–302. Bears on the origin of letters of reprisal.

Chaplin, W. R., 'William Rainsborough (1587–1642) and his Associates of the Trinity House', *MM* XXXI (1945), pp. 178–97.

Charnock, John, *History of Marine Architecture* (London, 1801, 3 vols). Prints documents.

Chaunu, Huguette & Pierre, *Séville et l'Atlantique (1504–1650)* (Paris, 1955–9, 8 vols in 11). Massive and essential survey of Spanish Atlantic trade.

Chavarot, Marie-Claire, 'La pratique des lettres de marque d'après les arrêts du Parlement (XIIIe–debut XVe siècle)', *Bibliothèque de l'Ecole des Chartes* CXLIX (1981), pp. 51–89. The origin of letters of reprisal.

Chazelas, see Merlin-Chazelas

Childs, Wendy R., 'Devon's Overseas Trade in the Late Middle Ages', in Duffy, *New Maritime History of Devon*, I, 79–89.

Chope, R. Pearse, 'New Light on Sir Richard Grenville', *TDA* XLIX (1917), pp. 210–82. Prints documents on Grenville's projected voyage of 1574.

Christensen, Arne Emil, ed., *The Earliest Ships: The Evolution of Boats into Ships* (London, 1996).

— 'Viking Age Rigging: A Survey of Sources and Theories', in McGrail, *Medieval Ships and Harbours*, pp. 183–93.

— 'Viking Age Ships and Shipbuilding', *Norwegian Archaeological Review* XV (1982), pp. 19–28. A brief survey of recent work.

— 'Boat finds from Bryggen', in *The Bryggen Papers, Main Series* I (Bergen, 1985), ed. Asbjørn E. Herteig, pp. 47–278.

— 'A medieval ship model', *IJNA* XVI (1987), pp. 69–70.

Cipolla, Carlo M., *Guns and Sails in the Early Phase of European Expansion 1400–1700* (London, 1965). An influential book, explaining European success by the superiority of their ships and weapons.

Clarendon, Edward Hyde, Earl of, *The History of the Rebellion and Civil Wars in England*, ed. W. D. Macray (Oxford, 1888, 6 vols).

Clarke, Richard, *et al.*, 'Recent work on the R. Hamble wreck near Bursledon,

Hampshire', *IJNA* XXII (1993), pp. 21–2. The wreck of Henry V's *Grace Dieu.*

Clayton, Norman, 'Naval Administration, 1603–1628' (Leeds Ph.D. thesis, 1935). A helpful thesis. The pagination of the Brotherton Library's copy is added in pencil, defective and partly invisible.

Cleere, Henry, & David Crossley, *The Iron Industry of the Weald* (Leicester, 1985). Important for gunfounding.

Cleves, Philip of Ravenstein, Duke of, *Instruction de Toutes Manieres de guerroyer, tant par terre que par mer, & des choses y servantes* (Paris, 1558). An influential treatise dealing with naval tactics among other things. It was written *c.*1505 and reflects late 15th-century practice.

Clowes, William Laird, *The Royal Navy: A History from the Earliest Times to the Present* (London, 1897–1903, 7 vols). Still the only complete history, though by now almost entirely outdated.

Coates, John, 'Power and Speed of Oared Ships', in Westerdahl, *Crossroads in Ancient Shipbuilding*, pp. 249–55. A technical discussion by the naval architect who designed the trireme replica *Olympias.*

Cogar, W. B., 'The Politics of Naval Administration, 1649–1660' (Oxford D.Phil. thesis, 1983).

Cogswell, Thomas, 'Foreign Policy and Parliament: the case of La Rochelle', *EHR* XCIX (1984), pp. 241–67.

— 'Prelude to Ré: The Anglo-French Struggle over La Rochelle, 1624–1627', *History* LXXI (1986), pp. 1–21.

Coindreau, Roger, *Les corsaires de Salé* (Paris, 1948). A sober work on the Sallee rovers.

Colvin, H. M., *et al.*, *The History of the King's Works* (London, 1963–73, 6 vols). They include coastal fortifications and a handful of naval works.

Conflans, Antoine de, 'Le livre des "faiz de la Marine et navigages"', ed. Michel Mollat du Jourdin & Florence Chillaud-Toutée, *107e Congrès nationale des Sociétés savantes, Collection d'histoire maritime* (Brest, 1982) pp. 9–44. A naval treatise.

Connell-Smith, Gordon, *Forerunners of Drake: A Study of English trade with Spain in the early Tudor period* (London, 1954). A study of piracy as much as trade.

Contamine, Philippe, *War in the Middle Ages*, trans. Michael Jones (Oxford, 1984; originally *La guerre au moyen âge*, Paris, 1980). An egregious example of a common approach; the distinguished author blandly announces that he proposes to ignore naval warfare altogether 'as a matter of maintaining internal balance', because it is too complicated.

Corbett, Julian S., ed., *Papers relating to the Navy during the Spanish War 1585–1587* (NRS Vol.11, 1898).

— *Drake and the Tudor Navy* (London, 2nd edn 1899, 2 vols). One of the first and still one of the greatest of naval historians, whose interpretations continue to set the tone of debate today.

— *The Successors of Drake* (London, 1900).

— ed., *Fighting Instructions 1530–1816*, (NRS Vol.29, 1905).

— *England in the Mediterranean: A Study of the Rise and Influence of British Power within the Straits 1603–1713* (London, 2nd edn 1917, 2 vols).

— ed., 'Sir William Slyngisbie's Relation of the Voyage to Cadiz, 1596', in Laughton, *Naval Miscellany I*, pp. 23–92.

— *Some Principles of Maritime Strategy* (London, 1911).

Courcy Ireland, J. de, 'Ragusa and the Spanish Armada of 1588', *MM* LXIV (1978), pp. 251–62. An Irishman comments on the controversy between Novak and Kostić. See also Peter Pierson, 'Ragusa and the Spanish Armada', *MM* LXVII (1981), pp. 91–2.

Courtney, T. W., 'Excavations at the Royal Dockyard, Woolwich, 1972–1973', *Post-Medieval Archaeology* VIII (1974), pp. 1–28, and IX (1975), pp. 42–102.

Craven, W. Frank, 'The Earl of Warwick, a Speculator in Piracy', *Hispanic American Historical Review* X (1930), pp. 457–79. The Providence Island Company.

Crawford, Anne, ed., *The Household Books of John Howard, Duke of Norfolk, 1462–1471, 1481–1483* (Stroud, 1992). A reprint with new matter of parts of *Manners and Household Expenses of England in the Thirteenth and Fifteenth Centuries*, ed. Beriah Botfield (Roxburghe Club, 1841), and *Household Books of John, Duke of Norfolk and Thomas, Earl of Surrey, 1481–1490*, ed. J.Payne Collier (Roxburghe Club, 1844). Norfolk was Lord Admiral and his accounts have much to do with ships.

Croft, Pauline, 'English Commerce with Spain and the Armada War, 1558–1603', in Rodríguez-Salgado & Adams, *England, Spain and the Gran Armada*, pp. 236–63. See also her 'Englishmen and the Spanish Inquisition 1558–1625', *EHR* LXXXVII (1972), pp. 249–68, and 'English Mariners trading to Spain and Portugal, 1558–1625', *MM* LXIX (1983), pp. 251–66.

Cruikshank, C. G., *Elizabeth's Army* (Oxford, 2nd edn 1966).

— *Henry VIII and the Invasion of France* (Stroud, 1990).

Crumlin-Pedersen, Ole, 'The Viking Ships of Roskilde', in *Aspects of the History of Wooden Shipbuilding* (NMM, 1970), pp. 7–23.

— 'The Vikings and the Hanseatic merchants: 900–1450', in *A History of Seafaring based on Underwater Archaeology*, ed. George F. Bass (London, 1972), pp. 181–204.

— 'Viking Shipbuilding and Seamanship', in *Proceedings of the Eighth Viking Congress* ed. Hans Bekker-Nielsen, Peter Foote & Olaf Olsen (Odense, 1981), pp. 271–86.

— 'Experimental Boat Archaeology in Denmark', in McGrail, *Maritime Archaeology and Ethnography*, pp. 97–121.

— 'Ship Types and Sizes AD 800–1400', in *Aspects of Maritime Scandinavia AD 200–1200*, ed. Crumlin-Pedersen (Roskilde, 1991), pp. 69–82.

Curry, Anne, & Michael Hughes, eds., *Arms, Armies and Fortifications in the Hundred Years War* (Woodbridge, 1994).

Curry, J., 'English Sea-Chaplains in the Royal Navy (1577–1684)' (Bristol MA thesis, 1956). Not entirely reliable.

Davies, C. S. L., 'Supply Services of the English Armed Forces, 1509–50' (Oxford D.Phil. thesis, 1963). A most valuable piece of research.

— 'Provisions for Armies, 1509–60: A Study in the Effectiveness of Early Tudor Government', *EcHR* 2nd S. XVII (1964), pp. 234–48.

— 'The administration of the Royal Navy under Henry VIII: the origins of the Navy Board', *EHR* LXXX (1965), pp. 268–88.

— 'Sixteenth Century Administration', *MM* LV (1969), p. 310.

— 'England and the French War, 1557–9', in *The Mid-Tudor Polity c.1540–1560*, ed. Jennifer Loach & Robert Tittler (London, 1980), pp. 159–85.

Davies, K. G., *The North Atlantic World in the Seventeenth Century* (Minneapolis, 1974).

Davies, R. R., ed., *The British Isles 1100–1500: Comparisons, Contrasts and Connections* (Edinburgh, 1988).

— 'In Praise of British History', in Davies, *The British Isles*, pp. 9–26.

Davis, Ralph, *The Rise of the English Shipping Industry in the Seventeenth and Eighteenth Centuries* (Newton Abbot, 2nd edn 1971). A study of fundamental importance.

— *A Commercial Revolution: English Overseas Trade in the Seventeenth and Eighteenth Centuries* (Historical Association, London, 1967).

— *The Rise of the Atlantic Economies* (London, 1973).

— 'England and the Mediterranean, 1570–1670', in *Essays in the Economic and Social History of Tudor England in Honour of R. H. Tawney*, ed. F. J. Fisher (Cambridge, 1961), pp. 117–37.

Davis, R. H. C., *The Medieval Warhorse: Origin, Development and Redevelopment* (London, 1989).

— 'The Warhorses of the Normans', *ANS* X (1987), pp. 67–82.

De Beer, E. S., 'The Lord High Admiral and the Administration of the Navy', *MM* XIII (1927), pp. 45–50. Mainly in the 1560s.

De Boer, M. G., *Het Proefjaar van Maarten Harpertsz. Tromp, 1637–1639* (Amsterdam, 1946). Covers his skilful and tactful dealings with English warships, culminating in the Downs campaign.

De Jonge, J. C., *Geschiedenis van het Nederlandsche Zeewesen* (Haarlem, 2nd edn 1858–62, 5 vols). An irreplaceable work based on documents since lost.

Derrick, Charles, *Memoirs of the Rise and Progress of the Royal Navy* (London, 1806). A collection of lists and tables of ships compiled by a Navy Office clerk.

Devon, Frederick, ed., *Issue Roll of Thomas de Brantingham...* (London, 1835). Accounts from 1370 with much naval and military expenditure.

— ed., *Issues of the Exchequer...* (London, 1837). Accounts of various dates.

DeVries, Kelly R., 'A 1445 reference to shipboard artillery', *Technology and Culture* XXXI (1990), pp. 818–29. Early galley-mounted heavy guns.

Dewar, A. C., 'The naval administration of the Interregnum, 1641–59', *MM* XII (1926), pp. 406–30. From printed sources; useful but not entirely accurate.

Dickinson, Robert, 'The Spanish Raid on Mount's Bay in 1595', *Journal of the Royal Institution of Cornwall* NS X (1987–90), pp. 178–86.

Dietz, B., 'The Huguenot and English Corsairs during the Third Civil War in France, 1568 to 1570', *Proceedings of the Huguenot Society* XIX (1952–58), pp. 278–94.

Dietz, Frederick C., *English Government Finance 1485–1558* (Urbana, Ill., 1921).

— *English Public Finance 1558–1641* (New York, 1932).

Digby, Sir Kenelm, *Journal of a Voyage into the Mediterranean . . . A.D. 1628*, ed. John Bruce (CS Vol.96, 1868).

Ditchburn, David, 'Piracy and War at Sea in Late Medieval Scotland', in *Scotland and the Sea*, ed. T. C. Smout (Edinburgh, 1992), pp. 35–58.

Dollinger, Philippe, *The German Hansa*, trans. & ed. D. S. Ault & S. H. Steinberg (London, 1970; originally *La Hanse*, Paris, 1964).

Domesday Book, ed. A. Farley & H. Ellis (London, 1783–1816, 4 vols). This edn is reproduced with facing translation in the county volumes published by Phillimore, which are the most accessible for the ordinary reader nowadays.

Donno, Elizabeth S., ed., *An Elizabethan in 1582: The Diary of Richard Madox, Fellow of All Souls* (HS 2nd S.146, 1976). An intelligent and open-minded layman at sea commenting on things which seamen took for granted and most landmen knew nothing about.

Dotson, John E., 'Merchant and Naval Influences on Galley Design at Venice and Genoa in the Fourteenth Century', in *New Aspects of Naval History*, ed. Craig L. Symonds (Annapolis, Md., 1981), pp. 20–32. Gives dimensions and plans of light and great galleys.

— 'Treatises on Shipbuilding before 1650', in Unger, *Cogs, Caravels and Galleons*, pp. 160–8. The development of designing on paper.

Drake, Sir Francis, *The World Encompassed and analagous contemporary documents concerning Sir Francis Drake's Circumnavigation of the World*, ed. N. M. Penzer (London, 1926). Drake's voyage round the world, published by his nephew (also Sir Francis) from the notes of participants.

Duffy, Michael, *et al.*, eds., *The New Maritime History of Devon*, (London & Exeter, 1992–4, 2 vols). A wide-ranging collection of studies.

Duffy, Seán, 'The Bruce Brothers and the Irish Sea World, 1306–29', *Cambridge Medieval Celtic Studies* 21 (1991), pp. 55–86.

Dumville, David N., *Wessex and England from Alfred to Edgar: Six Essays on Political, Cultural and Ecclesiastical Revival* (Woodbridge, 1992).

Duncan, A. A. M., 'The Scots' Invasion of Ireland, 1315', in Davies, *The British Isles 1100–1500*, pp. 100–117.

Dyer, Florence E., 'The Elizabethan Sailorman', *MM* X (1924), pp. 133–46.

— 'Reprisals in the Sixteenth Century', *MM* XXI (1935), pp. 187–97.

— 'The Ship-Money Fleet', *MM* XXIII (1937), pp. 198–209. Three older studies still with useful detail.

Eames, Aled, 'Sea Power and Welsh History, 1625–1660' (University of Wales MA thesis, 1954). An excellent thesis, of Ph.D. standard.

— 'Sea Power and Caernarvonshire, 1642–1660', *Transactions of the Caernarvonshire Historical Society* XVI (1955), pp. 29–51.

— 'The King's Pinnace, the *Swan*', *MM* XLVII (1961), pp. 49–55. The English Civil War in the Irish Sea.

Earle, Peter, *Corsairs of Malta and Barbary* (London, 1970). The best study of the Maltese corsairs.

— *The Last Fight of the Revenge* (London, 1992). New evidence on a subject clouded in myth.

Edmundson, George, *Anglo-Dutch Rivalry during the first half of the Seventeenth Century* (Oxford, 1911). Now outdated on diplomacy, but still good on social and cultural history.

Edwards, Clinton R., 'Design and Construction of Fifteenth-Century Iberian Vessels: A Review', *MM* LXXVIII (1992), pp. 419–32. A useful survey, à propos Columbus's ships.

Elbl, Martin Malcolm, 'The Portuguese Caravel and European Shipbuilding: Phases of Development and Diversity', *Revista da Universidade de Coimbra* XXXII (1985), pp. 543–72.

Elliott, J. H., *The Count-Duke of Olivares: The Statesman in an Age of Decline* (New Haven, 1986). Essential for Spanish policy in the period of the Thirty Years War.

Ellis, Henry, ed., *Original Letters Illustrative of English History* (London, 1824–46, 11 vols in 3 series). Documents, mainly from the British Library.

Ellmers, Detlev, *Frühmittelalterliche Handelsschifffahrt in Mittel- und Nordeuropa* (Neumünster, 1972). Deals with warships as well as merchantmen; still very helpful, though in need of updating to take account of recent archaeology.

— 'The Cog as Cargo Carrier', in Unger, *Cogs, Caravels and Galleons*, pp. 29–46.

Elton, Geoffrey, 'War and the English in the Reign of Henry VIII', in *War, Strategy and International Politics: Essays in Honour of Sir Michael Howard*, ed. Lawrence Freedman, Paul Hayes & Robert O'Neill (Oxford, 1992), pp. 1–17.

English Historical Documents: I, c.500–1042 ed. Dorothy Whitelock (London, 2nd edn 1979); *II, 1042–1189* ed. David C. Douglas & George W. Greenaway (London, 1953); *III, 1189–1327* ed. Harry Rothwell (London, 1975); *IV, 1327–1485* ed. A. R. Myers (London, 1969). Invaluable collections of key documents in translation.

Evans, Angela Care, *The Sutton Hoo Ship Burial* (British Museum, 1986).

Ewe, Herbert, *Schiffe aus Siegeln* (Rostock, 1972). An excellent study, drawn mostly from the rich archives of the Hansa ports.

Ewen, C. L'Estrange, *Captain John Ward, 'Arch-Pirate'* (Paignton, 1939).

— *The Golden Chalice: A Documented Narrative of an Elizabethan Pirate* (Paignton, 1939).

— 'Organized Piracy round England in the Sixteenth Century', *MM* XXXV (1949), pp. 29–42.

Exchequer Rolls of Scotland, The (Edinburgh, 1878–98, 18 vols).

Fallon, Niall, *The Armada in Ireland* (London, 1978). A good survey from local knowledge.

Fermoy, B. E. R., 'A Maritime Indenture of 1212', *EHR* XLI (1926), pp. 556–9

Fernández-Armesto, Felipe, *The Spanish Armada: The Experience of War in 1588* (Oxford, 1988). Elsewhere the author writes that 'the study of perceptions is more rewarding than that of events'; his book is certainly more rewarding as a study of perceptions than of events at sea.

Fernández Duro, Cesáreo, *La Armada Invencible* (Madrid, 1884–5, 2 vols). An indispensable collection of documents, but printed from indifferent transcripts; in process of being replaced by *BMO*.

— *La Marina de Castilla desde su origen y pugna con la de Inglaterra hasta la refundacion en la Armada Española* (Madrid, [1894]).

— *Armada Española desde la unión de los Reinos de Castilla y de Aragón* (Madrid, 1895–1903, 9 vols). The great work of the pioneer Spanish naval historian: outdated but unreplaced, printing many important documents.

Firth, C. H., ed., *Naval Songs and Ballads* (NRS Vol.33, 1908). Words without music; valuable for social history.

— & R. S. Rait, eds., *Acts and Ordinances of the Interregnum, 1642–1660* (London, 1911, 3 vols). An essential source.

Fisher, Sir Godfrey, *Barbary Legend: War, Trade and Piracy in North Africa 1415–1830* (Oxford, 1957). An exuberant defence of the Barbary corsairs.

Fissel, Mark Charles, *The Bishops' Wars: Charles I's Campaigns against Scotland, 1638–1640* (Cambridge, 1994). Primarily a study of the English army.

— ed., *War and Government in Britain, 1598–1650* (Manchester, 1991).

Flanagan, Marie Therese, *Irish Society, Anglo-Norman Settlers, Angevin Kingship: Interactions in Ireland in the Late Twelfth Century* (Oxford, 1989).

— 'Strongbow, Henry II and Anglo-Norman intervention in Ireland', in *War and Government in the Middle Ages: Essays in Honour of J. O. Prestwich*, ed. John Gillingham & J. C. Holt (Woodbridge, 1984). pp. 62–77.

Foerster Laures, Federico, 'The warships of the Kings of Aragón and their fighting tactics during the 13th and 14th centuries AD', *IJNA* XVI (1987), pp. 19–29.

Foote, Peter, & David M. Wilson, *The Viking Achievement: The Society and Culture of Early Mediaeval Scandinavia* (London, 1970).

Ford, C. J., 'Piracy or Policy: The Crisis in the Channel, 1400–1403', *TRHS* 5th S. XXIX (1979), pp. 63–78. Argues that Henry IV organized and controlled piracy as an instrument of diplomacy.

Fourquin, Noël, 'Galères du Moyen-Age', in *Quand voguaient les galères* (Paris, Musée de la Marine, 1990), pp. 67–87.

Fowler, Elaine W., *English Sea Power in the Early Tudor Period 1484–1558* (Ithaca, NY, 1965). Now largely outdated.

Fowler, Kenneth, ed., *The Hundred Years War* (London, 1971).

Frame, Robin, 'Aristocracies and the Political Configuration of the British Isles', in Davies, *The British Isles*, pp. 142–59.

Freeman, A. Z., 'A Moat Defensive: The Coast Defense Scheme of 1295', *Speculum* XLII (1967), pp. 442–62.

— 'Wooden Walls: The English Navy in the Reign of Edward I', in R. W. Love, ed., *Changing Interpretations and New Sources in Naval History* (New York, 1980), pp. 58–67.

French, M. J., 'Privateering and the Revolt of the Netherlands: the *Watergeuzen* or Sea Beggars in Portsmouth, Gosport and the Isle of Wight, 1570–71', *Proceedings of the Hampshire Field Club & Archaeological Society* XLVII (1991), pp. 171–80.

Friel, Ian, 'The documentary evidence for maritime technology in later medieval England and Wales' (Keele Ph.D. thesis, 1990). A most important contribution to a neglected subject. A short form of it is now published as *The Good Ship: Ships, Shipbuilding and Technology in England, 1200–1520* (London, 1995).

— 'Archaeological sources and the medieval ship: some aspects of the evidence', *IJNA* XII (1983), pp. 41–62.

— 'The Three-masted Ship and Atlantic Voyages', in *Raleigh in Exeter 1985: Privateering and Colonisation in the Reign of Elizabeth I*, ed. Joyce Youings (Exeter, 1985), pp. 21–37.

— 'The Building of the Lyme Galley, 1294–1296', *Dorset Natural History & Archaeological Society Proceedings* CVIII (1986), pp. 41–4.

— 'Henry V's *Grace Dieu* and the wreck in the R. Hamble near Bursledon, Hampshire', *IJNA* XXII (1993), pp. 3–19.

— 'Winds of Change? Ships and the Hundred Years War', in Curry & Hughes, *Arms, Armies and Fortifications*, pp. 183–93.

— 'The Carrack: The Advent of the Full Rigged Ship', in Unger, *Cogs, Caravels and Galleons*, pp. 77–90.

Fryde, E. B., ed., *Book of Prests for the King's Wardrobe for 1294–5, presented to John Goronwy Edwards* (Oxford, 1962). Accounts of operations in Wales.

Fulton, T. W., *The Sovereignty of the Sea* (Edinburgh, 1911). A thorough and illuminating study of a legal concept and the attempts to put it into practice.

Gallagher, P., & D. W. Cruikshank, eds., *God's Obvious Design: Papers for the Spanish Armada Symposium, Sligo, 1988* (London, 1990). A few useful items.

Gardiner, D. A., 'The History of belligerent rights on the high seas in the fourteenth century', *Law Quarterly Review* XLVIII (1932), pp. 521–46.

Gardiner, Dorothy A., 'John Hawley of Dartmouth', *TDA* XCVIII (1966), pp. 173–205. The notorious pirate, probably Chaucer's Shipman.

— ed., *A Calendar of Early Chancery Proceedings relating to West Country Shipping, 1388–1493* (Devon & Cornwall Record Society NS XXI, 1976)

Gardiner, S. R., *History of England from the Accession of James I to the Outbreak of the Civil War, 1603–1642* (London, 1883–4, 10 vols).

— ed., *Documents illustrating the Impeachment of the Duke of Buckingham in 1626* (CS Vol.45, 1889).

Gelsinger, Bruce E., 'Some Unusual Ships in Thirteenth-Century Norway', *MM* LXVII (1981), pp. 173–80.

Gerhard, Peter, *Pirates on the West Coast of New Spain 1575–1742* (Glendale, Cal., 1960),

Gillingham, John, *Richard the Lionheart* (2nd edn 1989).

— 'Richard I and the Science of War in the Middle Ages', in *War and Government in the Middle Ages: Essays in Honour of J. O. Prestwich*, ed. Gillingham & J. C. Holt (Cambridge, 1984), pp. 78–91.

— 'Richard I, Galley-Warfare and Portsmouth: The Beginnings of a Royal Navy', in *Thirteenth-Century England VI*, ed. Michael Prestwich (Woodbridge, 1997) pp. 1–15. I am indebted to Professor Gillingham for sight of this important article before its publication.

Gillmer, Thomas, 'The Capability of the Single Square Sail Rig: A Technical Assessment', in McGrail, *Medieval Ships and Harbours*, pp. 167–81.

Gillmor, C. M., 'Naval Logistics of the Cross-Channel Operation, 1066', *ANS* VII (1985), pp. 105–31.

Glanville, John, *The Voyage to Cadiz in 1625, being a Journal written by John Glanville*, ed. Alexander B. Grosart (CS NS Vol.32, 1883). Glanville was Wimbledon's secretary.

Glasgow, Tom, Jr., 'The Shape of the Ships that defeated the Spanish Armada', *MM* XLIX (1963), pp. 177–98. The first of a learned series, important for ship design and naval operations.

— 'The Elizabethan Navy in Ireland', *Irish Sword* VII (1965–6), pp. 291–307.

— 'The Royal Navy at the Start of the Reign of Elizabeth I', *MM* LI (1965), pp. 73–6.

— 'Oared Vessels in the Elizabethan Navy', *MM* LII (1966), pp. 371–7.

— 'H.M.S. Tiger', *North Carolina Historical Review* XLIII (1966), pp. 115–21.

— 'The Navy in Philip and Mary's War, 1557–1558', *MM* LIII (1967), pp. 321–42.

— 'The Navy in the first Elizabethan Undeclared War, 1559–1560', *MM* LIV (1968), pp. 23–37.

— 'The Navy in the Le Havre Expedition, 1562–1564' *MM* LIV (1968), pp. 281–96.

— 'Maturing of Naval Administration 1556–1564', *MM* LVI (1970), pp. 3–26.

— 'List of Ships in the Royal Navy from 1539 to 1588 – The Navy from its Infancy to the Defeat of the Spanish Armada', *MM* LVI (1970), pp. 299–307 (also a note in *MM* LXI (1975) pp. 352–3). Corrections to Anderson's lists.

— 'Gorgas' *SeaFight*', *MM* LIX (1973), pp. 179–85.

— 'Vice Admiral Woodhouse and Shipkeeping in the Tudor Navy', *MM* LXIII (1977), pp. 253–63.

— & W. Salisbury, 'Elizabethan Ships pictured on the Smerwick Map, 1580', *MM* LII (1966), pp. 157–65.

Glete, Jan, *Navies and Nations: Warships, Navies and State Building in Europe and America, 1500–1860* (Stockholm, 1993, 2 vols). A work of the first importance. His tables for the first time allow the size of different navies to be compared over time; note for comparison with this book that his figures are estimated displacement in metric tons.

Glover, Richard, 'English Warfare in 1066', *EHR* LXVII (1952), pp. 1–18.

Goldingham, C. S. 'The Navy under Henry VII' *EHR* XXXIII (1918), pp. 472–88.

Gómez-Centurión Jiménez, Carlos, *Felipe II, la Empresa de Inglaterra y el comercio septentrional (1566–1609)* (Madrid, 1988). An important study of Spanish northern trade and grand strategy.

Goodman, David, *Power and Penury: Government, Technology and Science in Philip II's Spain* (Cambridge, 1988).

Goring, J. J., 'Wealden Ironmasters in the Age of Elizabeth', in *Wealth and Power in Tudor England: Essays presented to S. T. Bindoff*, ed. E. W. Ives, R. J. Knecht & J. J. Scarisbrick (London, 1978), pp. 204–27.

Graboïs, A., 'Anglo-Norman England and the Holy Land', *ANS* VII (1985), pp. 132–41.

Gracia Rivas, Manuel, 'The Medical Services of the *Gran Armada*', in Rodríguez-Salgado & Adams, *England, Spain and the Gran Armada*, pp. 197–215. Summarizes his *La sanidad en la jornada de Inglaterra (1587–8)* (Madrid, 1988).

Grainge, Christine & Gerald, 'The Pevensey expedition: brilliantly executed plan or near disaster?', *MM* LXXIX (1993), pp. 261–73. The yachtsman's view of the Norman Conquest.

Grant, Alexander, 'Scotland's "Celtic Fringe" in the late middle ages: the Macdonald Lords of the Isles and the Kingdom of Scotland', in Davies, *The British Isles*, pp. 118–41.

Gray, Randal, 'Spinola's Galleys in the Narrow Seas, 1599–1603', *MM* LXIV (1978), pp. 71–83.

Gray, Todd, 'Turkish Piracy and Early Stuart Devon', *TDA* CXXI (1989), pp. 159–71.

— 'Turks, Moors and Cornish Fishermen: Piracy in the early seventeenth Century', *Journal of the Royal Institution of Cornwall* NS X (1987–90), pp. 457–75

— ed., *Early-Stuart Mariners and Shipping: The Maritime Surveys of Devon and Cornwall, 1619–35* (Devon & Cornwall Record Society NS Vol.33, 1990). Cf. his 'The Duke of Buckingham's Survey of South Devon Mariners and Shipping, 1619', in Duffy, *New Maritime History of Devon*, I, 117–18.

Groenveld, Simon, *Verlopend Getij: De Nederlandse Republiek en de Engelse Burgeroorlog 1640–1646* (Dieren, 1984). More about the impact of the English Civil War on Dutch politics than the reverse.

— 'The English Civil Wars as a Cause of the First Anglo-Dutch War, 1640–1652', *HJ* XXX (1987), pp. 541–66.

Gruffydd, K. Lloyd, 'Sea Power and the Anglo-Welsh Wars, 1210–1410', *Maritime Wales* 11 (1987), pp. 28–53.

Guilmartin, John F., *Gunpowder and Galleys: Changing Technology and Mediterranean Warfare at Sea in the Sixteenth Century* (Cambridge, 1974). A book of great importance and influence, demonstrating that traditional naval history does not fit galley warfare, but in the process reinforcing some stereotypes of naval warfare under sail which equally deserve to be dislodged.

— 'The Early Provision of Artillery Armament on Mediterranean War Galleys', *MM* LIX (1973), pp. 257–80.

— 'The Guns of the *Santissímo Sacramento*', *Technology and Culture* XXIV (1983), pp. 559–601. The crucial and generally misunderstood ballistics of smooth-bore guns firing black powder.

— 'Guns and Gunnery', in Unger, *Cogs, Caravels and Galleons*, pp. 139–150.

— 'Ballistics in the Black Powder Era', in Smith, *British Naval Armaments*, pp. 73–98.

Gunn, Steven, 'The French Wars of Henry VIII', in *The Origins of War in Early Modern Europe*, ed. Jeremy Black (Edinburgh, 1987), pp. 28–51.

Guy, John, *Tudor England* (Oxford, 1988).

Hair, P. E. H. & J. D. Alsop, eds., *English Seamen and Traders in Guinea 1553–1565: The New Evidence of their Wills* (Lampeter, 1992). Important for the social history of mid-16th-century seamen.

Hakluyt, Richard, *The Principal Navigations Voyages Traffiques & Discoveries of the English Nation* (2nd edn of 1599–1600, as printed Glasgow, 1903–05, 12 vols). The great Elizabethan collection, without which we would know very much less about the Elizabethans at sea.

Hale, J. R., *War and Society in Renaissance Europe 1450–1620* (Leicester, 1985).

— 'International Relations in the West: Diplomacy and War', in the *New Cambridge Modern History*, I, 259–91.

— 'Armies, Navies and the Art of War', *ibid.* (2nd edn), II, 540–69.

— 'Armies, Navies and the Art of War', *ibid.*, III, 171–208.

Hall, Adrian T., 'The Employment of Naval Forces in the Reign of Edward III' (Leeds MA thesis, 1955).

Hammer, Paul E. J., '"Myth-making": Politics, Propaganda and the Capture of Cadiz in 1596', *HJ* XL (1997) pp. 621–642. I am indebted to Dr Hammer for allowing me to see this article before its publication.

Harding, Richard, *The Evolution of the Sailing Navy, 1509–1815* (Basingstoke, 1995). An excellent new textbook.

Hardy, Thomas Duffus: see *Rotuli Litterarum Clausarum*, *Rotuli Litterarum Patentium*, *Rotuli Normanniae.*

Harmer, F. E., *Anglo-Saxon Writs* (Manchester, 1952).

Harris, G. G., *The Trinity House of Deptford, 1514–1660* (London, 1969).

— ed., *Trinity House of Deptford Transactions, 1609–35* (London Record Society Vol.19, 1983).

Harrison, W. E. C., 'Maritime Activity under Henry VII' (London MA thesis, 1931).

Hattendorf, John B., *et al.*, eds., *British Naval Documents 1204–1960* (NRS Vol.131, 1993). A collection of key documents for naval history.

Havran, Martin J., *Caroline Courtier: The Life of Lord Cottington* (London, 1973).

Hawkes, Sonia Chadwick, ed., *Weapons and Warfare in Anglo-Saxon England* (Oxford University Committee for Archaeology Monograph No.21, 1989).

[Hawkins, Sir Richard] *The Observations of Sir Richard Hawkins*, ed. James A. Williamson (London, 1933). The mildest and most civilized of the English pirates.

Haywood, John, *Dark Age Naval Power: A Re-assessment of Frankish and Anglo-Saxon seafaring activity* (London, 1991). An important study, revising many accepted views.

Hebb, D. D., *Piracy and the English Government, 1616–1642* (Aldershot, 1994). Barbary rather than English piracy, and its political impact on the Ship Money issue.

Herbert, Edward, Lord Herbert of Cherbury, *The Expedition to the Isle of Rhe* ed. Lord Powis (Philobiblion Soc., London, 1860; written in English but first published as *Expeditio in Ream Insulam*, trans. T. Baldwin, London, 1656). A defence of Buckingham by a friend.

Herrera Oria, Enrique, ed., *La Armada Invencible: Documentes Procedentes del Archivo General de Simancas* (Valladolid, 1929).

— *Felipe II y el Marqués de Santa Cruz en la Empresa de Inglaterra* (Madrid, 1946). Two important collections of documents. Since Fr Herrera makes much of the inaccuracy of other people's transcripts, it should be noted that his own quotations often differ in detail from the same texts as given in his appendices, and both of them from *BMO.*

Hewitt, H. J., *The Black Prince's Expedition of 1355–1357* (Manchester, 1958).

— 'The Organisation of War', in Fowler, *The Hundred Years War*, pp. 75–95.

— *The Organization of War under Edward III, 1338–62* (Manchester, 1966).

Hill, David, *An Atlas of Anglo-Saxon England* (Oxford, 1981).

Historical Manuscripts Commission

No.9, *Manuscripts of the Most Hon. the Marquis of Salisbury* (24 vols, 1883–1976). The most important collection of documents outside the PRO and the BL for all aspects of Elizabethan and early Stuart government.

No.13, *Manuscripts of the Earl of Westmorland . . . Lord Muncaster and others* (10th Report App.IV, 1885). The Muncaster MSS include Pennington's journals (the originals of which are now in the NMM).

No.23, *Manuscripts of Earl Cowper* (12th Report App.I–III, 1888–89). Prints many of Sir John Coke's naval papers.

No.29, *Manuscripts of His Grace the Duke of Portland* (13th Report App.I–II, 14th R.App.II, 15th R.App.IV, 1891–97). Some letters relating to the Ship Money fleets.

No.41, *Manuscripts of the Rt. Hon. F. J. Savile Foljambe* (15th Report App.V, 1897). Includes a few papers relating to the 1588 Armada.

Hoffman, Paul E. *The Spanish Crown and the Defense of the Caribbean, 1535–1585: Precedent, Patrimonialism and Royal Parsimony* (Baton Rouge, LA, 1980) By 'patrimonialism' the author means paternalism.

Hoheisel, Wolf-Dieter, 'A Full-Scale Replica of the Hanse Cog of 1380', in Westerdahl, *Crossroads in Ancient Shipbuilding*, pp. 257–60. Sea-trials of the replica cog.

Hollister, C. Warren, *Anglo-Saxon Military Institutions on the eve of the Norman Conquest* (Oxford, 1962). An excellent study, now dated.

— *The Military Organization of Norman England* (Oxford, 1965).

Hollond, John, *Two Discourses of the Navy, 1638 and 1659*, ed. J. R. Tanner (NRS Vol.7, 1896). A naval administrator enlarges on the malpractices of his colleagues and superiors.

Holm, Poul, 'The Slave Trade of Dublin, Ninth to Twelfth Centuries', *Peritia* V (1986), pp. 317–45. The fleets of the Irish Vikings.

Holmes, G. A., 'The "Libel of English Policy"', *EHR* LXXVI (1961), pp. 193–216. Corrects some serious misconceptions.

Hooper, Nicholas, 'Anglo-Saxon Warfare on the eve of the Conquest: a brief survey', *ANS* I (1978), pp. 84–93.

— 'Some Observations on the Navy in Late Anglo-Saxon England', in *Studies in Medieval History presented to R. Allen Brown*, ed. Christopher

Harper-Bill, Christopher J. Holdsworth & Janet L.Nelson (Woodbridge, 1989), pp. 203–13.

— 'The Anglo-Saxons at War', in Hawkes, *Weapons and Warfare in Anglo-Saxon England*, pp. 191–202.

— 'Military Developments in the reign of Cnut', in Rumble, *Reign of Cnut*, pp. 89–100.

Hope, Ronald, *A New History of British Shipping* (London, 1990).

Horrox, Rosemary, & P. W. Hammond, eds., *British Library Harleian Manuscript 433* (Richard III Soc., 1979–83, 4 vols). A unique survivng Signet Register, giving a detailed view of Richard III's government at work.

Howard, Frank, *Sailing Ships of War 1400–1860* (London, 1979). A pioneering study of a subject little studied then, and not studied enough yet.

— 'Early Ship Guns', *MM* LXXII (1986), pp. 439–53, and LXXIII (1987), pp. 49–55.

Howarth, David, *1066, The Year of the Conquest* (London, 1977). More aware than most historians of the realities of wind, weather and navigation.

Howat, G. M. D., *Stuart and Cromwellian Foreign Policy* (London, 1974).

Hudson, Benjamin T., 'Cnut and the Scottish Kings', *EHR* CVII (1992), pp. 350–60.

Hughes, C. E., 'Wales and Piracy, a Study in Tudor Administration, 1500–1640' (U.C. Swansea MA thesis, 1937).

Hughes, Michael, 'The Fourteenth-Century French Raids on Hampshire and the Isle of Wight', in Curry & Hughes, *Arms, Armies and Fortifications*, pp. 121–43.

Hurstfield, Joel, 'Political Corruption in Modern England: the historian's problem', in *Freedom, Corruption and Government in Elizabethan England* (London, 1973), pp. 137–62 (originally in *History* LII (1967), pp. 16–34).

— 'The Political Morality of Early Stuart Statesmen', *ibid.*, pp. 183–96 (originally *History* LVI (1971), pp. 235–43).

Hutchinson, Gillian, *Medieval Ships and Shipping* (London, 1994). An excellent summary of current knowledge, much of it new.

Ingram, Bruce S., ed., *Three Sea Journals of Stuart Times* (London, 1936). Includes the journal of Dawtrey Cooper, captain of the *Pelican* pink at La Rochelle, 1628.

James, G. F., & J. J. S. Shaw, 'Admiralty administration and personnel, 1619–1714', *BIHR* XIV, pp. 10–24, 166–83.

Jameson, A. K., 'Some New Spanish Documents dealing with Drake', *EHR* XLIX (1934), pp. 14–31.

John, Eric, *Land Tenure in Early England: A Discussion of some Problems* (Leicester, 1960). Including ship-sokes.

— 'War and Society in the Tenth Century: the Maldon Campaign', *TRHS* 5th S. XXVII (1977), pp. 173–95.

Johns, A. W., 'The Principal Officers of the Navy', *MM* XIV (1928), pp. 32–54.

— 'The *Constant Warwick*', *MM* XVIII (1932), pp. 254–66.

Johnson, Charles, 'London Shipbuilding, A.D. 1295', *Antiquaries Journal* VII (1927), pp. 424–37.

Jones, Gwyn, *A History of the Vikings* (London, 1968).

Jones, Michael, *Ducal Brittany 1364–1399: Relations with England and France during the Reign of Duke John IV* (London, 1970).

— 'Two Exeter Ship agreements of 1303 and 1310', *MM* LIII (1967), pp. 315–19.

— 'Edward III's Captains in Brittany', in *England in the Fourteenth century: Proceedings of the 1985 Harlaxton Symposium*, ed. W. M. Ormrod (Woodbridge, 1986), pp. 99–118.

Jongkees, A. G., 'Armement et action d'une flotte de guerre: la contribution des comtés maritimes a l'armée générale des "pays de par deçà" en 1477', in *Burgundica et Varia* (Hilversum, 1990), pp. 302–18. The Burgundian fleet.

Junge, Hans-Christoph, *Flottenpolitik und Revolution: Die Enstehung der englischen Seemacht während der Herrschaft Cromwells* (Stuttgart, 1980).

Keeler, M. F., ed., *Sir Francis Drake's West Indian Voyage 1585–86* (HS 2nd S. Vol.148, 1981). Prints the most important documents and narratives.

Keevil, J. J., C. C. Lloyd & J. L. S. Coulter, *Medicine and the Navy, 1200–1900* (Edinburgh, 1957–63, 4 vols). A massive but unsystemmatic and uncritical collection of material. Vol.I (ed. Keevil) runs to 1649.

Kemp, Peter, *The British Sailor, A Social History of the Lower Deck* (London, 1970). Undemanding and now rather dated social history.

Kendall, C. W., *Private Men-of-War* (London, 1931). A useful survey of English privateering.

Kennedy, D. E., 'Parliament and the Navy, 1642–1648: A Political History of the Navy during the Civil War' (Cambridge Ph.D. thesis, 1959)

— 'Naval Captains at the Outbreak of the English Civil War', *MM* XLVI (1960), pp. 181–98.

— 'The Establishment and Settlement of Parliament's Admiralty, 1642–1648', *MM* XLVIII (1962), pp. 276–91.

— 'The English Naval Revolt of 1648', *EHR* LXXVII (1962), pp. 247–56.

— 'The Crown and the Common Seamen in Early Stuart England', *Historical Studies Australia and New Zealand* XI (1963–5), pp. 170–7.

Kennedy, Paul M., *The Rise and Fall of British Naval Mastery* (2nd edn 1983). A now classic history, stressing the economic underpinnings of sea power.

Kenny, Robert W., *Elizabeth's Admiral: The Political Career of Charles Howard Earl of Nottingham 1536–1624* (Baltimore, 1970). Not strong on his naval career.

Kenyon, John R., 'Coastal Artillery Fortifications in England in the Late Fourteenth and Early Fifteenth Centuries', in Curry & Hughes, *Arms, Armies and Fortifications*, pp. 145–9.

— 'Ordnance and the king's fleet in 1548', *IJNA* XII (1983), pp. 63–5.

Kepler, J. S., 'The Effects of the Battle of Sluys upon the Administration of English Naval Impressment, 1340–1343', *Speculum* XLVIII (1973), pp. 70–7.

— 'The Value of Ships gained and lost by the English Shipping Industry during the Wars with Spain and France, 1624–1630', *MM* LIX (1973), pp. 218–21. Concludes that losses much outweighed gains.

Kerherve, Jean, *L'état breton aux 14e et 15e siècles: les ducs, l'argent et les hommes* (Paris, 1987, 1 vol in 2).

Keynes, Simon, *The Diplomas of King Ethelred 'the Unready' 978–1016: A Study in their use as Historical Evidence* (Cambridge, 1980). Technical but important.

— 'The Historical Context of the Battle of Maldon', in Scragg, *Battle of Maldon*, pp. 81–113.

— & Michael Lapidge, ed. & trans., *Alfred the Great: Asser's Life of King Alfred and other contemporary sources* (Harmondsworth, 1983).

Kingsford, C. L., *Prejudice and Promise in XVth Century England* (Oxford, 1925). English piracy.

— ed., 'The Taking of the *Madre de Dios*, anno 1592', in Laughton, *Naval Miscellany II*, pp. 85–121.

Koenigsberger, H. G., 'Western Europe and the Power of Spain', in the *New Cambridge Modern History*, III, 234–318.

Konstam, R. A., 'Naval Artillery to 1550: Its Design, Evolution and Employment' (St Andrews M.Litt. thesis, 1987). One of the few serious contributions to a neglected subject.

Kostić, Veselin, 'Ragusa and the Spanish Armada', *Balcanica* III (1972), pp. 195–235. A Serbian scholar debunks the Croat Novak's extravagant claims; de Courcy Ireland (q.v.) arbitrates.

Kraus, Hans P., *Sir Francis Drake, a Pictorial Biography* (Amsterdam, 1970).

An illustrated catalogue of Kraus's collection, including some important documents not accessible to scholars, with an introduction by D. W. Waters & R. Boulind.

Krieger, Karl-Friedrich, *Ursprung und Wurzeln der Rôles d'Oléron* (Cologne, 1970). The latest, but not the last word on this subject.

Kuhn, Hans, *Das altnordische Seekriegswesen*, ed. Sigrid Engeler & Dietrich Hofmann (Heidelberg, 1991). A sweeping, eccentric and unreliable posthumous work, full of good and bad ideas.

Kulturhistorisk Leksikon for Nordisk Middelalder (Copenhagen etc, 1956–78, 22 vols). A historical encyclopedia of the Viking age; excellent for basic reference.

Lacour-Gayet, G., *La Marine Militaire de la France sous les règnes de Louis XIII et de Louis XIV: I, Richelieu, Mazarin 1624–1661* (Paris, 1911). Scholarly and still useful; Vol.II never appeared.

Lane, Frederick C., *Venetian Ships and Shipbuilders of the Renaissance* (Baltimore, 1934). A classic history; the 2nd edition appeared only in French: *Navires et constructeurs à Venise pendant la Renaissance* (Paris, 1965). See also his *Venice, A Maritime Republic* (Baltimore, 1973).

Laporte, Jean, 'Les opérations navales en Manche et Mer du Nord pendant l'année 1066', *Annales de Normandie* XVII (1967), pp. 3–46. Useful local knowledge of the Norman coast.

La Roncière, Charles de, *Histoire de la Marine Française* (Paris, 1899–1932, 6 vols). A great monument to 19th-century scholarship, still irreplaceable.

— 'Le Blocus Continentale de l'Angleterre sous Philippe le Bel', *Revue des Questions Historiques* NS XVI (1896), pp. 402–41. Not a 'Continental Blockade' in any sense, but a series of invasion projects.

Laughton, J. K., ed., *State Papers relating to the Defeat of the Spanish Armada, anno 1588* (NRS Vols.1 & 2, 1894). A founding work by a founding father of scientific naval history; rather surprisingly, no more English documents on the Armada have been printed since.

— ed., *The Naval Miscellany I & II* (NRS Vols.20 & 40, 1902, 1912).

Laughton, L. G. Carr, 'The Burning of Brighton by the French', *TRHS* 3rd S. X (1916), pp. 167–73.

— 'The Great Ship of 1419', *MM* IX (1923), pp. 83–7. Henry V's last great ship, building at Bayonne.

— 'Gunnery, Frigates and the Line of Battle', *MM* XIV (1928), pp. 339–63.

— 'The Square-Tuck Stern and the Gun-Deck', *MM* XLVII (1961), pp. 100–5.

— 'Early Tudor Ship-Guns', ed. Michael Lewis, *MM* XLVI (1960), pp. 242–85.

Lawson, M. K., *Cnut: The Danes in England in the early eleventh century* (London, 1993).

— 'The collection of Danegeld and Heregeld in the reigns of Aethelred II and Cnut', *EHR* XCIX (1984), pp. 721–38. Taxation as evidence for the wealth and power of Anglo-Saxon England.

— '"Those Stories Look True": levels of taxation in the reigns of Aethelred II and Cnut', *EHR* CIV (1989), pp. 385–406. Part of a debate with John Gillingham inspired by the above article.

Lee, Arthur Gould, *The Son of Leicester: The Story of Sir Robert Dudley* (London, 1964). Biography of a talented English naval exile; drawn mostly from John Temple-Leader, *Life of Sir Robert Dudley* (Florence, 1895), and Anon., *The Italian Biography of Sir Robert Dudley...* (Oxford, n.d.).

Le Patourel, John, *The Norman Empire* (Oxford, 1976).

Lewis, Ada Haeseler, *A Study of Elizabethan Ship Money 1588–1603* (Philadelphia, 1928).

Lewis, Archibald R., *The Northern Seas. Shipping and Commerce in Northern Europe A.D. 300–1100* (Princeton, 1958). A fine sweeping survey, now dated in parts.

— 'Northern European Sea Power and the Straits of Gibraltar, 1031–1350 A.D.', in *Order and Innovation in the Middle Ages: Essays in Honour of Joseph R. Strayer*, ed William C. Jordan, Bruce McNab & Teofilo F. Ruiz (Princeton, 1976), pp. 139–64.

— & Timothy J. Runyan, *European Naval and Maritime History, 300–1500* (Bloomington, Indiana, 1985). A textbook, unfortunately not altogether reliable.

Lewis, Michael, *England's Sea-Officers: The Story of the Naval Profession* (London, 1939). A classic of its day, parts of it still usable with caution.

— 'The Guns of the *Jesus of Lubeck*', *MM* XXII (1936), pp. 324–45.

— 'Armada Guns. A Comparative Study of English and Spanish Armaments', *MM* XXVIII (1942), pp. 41–73, 104–47, 231–45, 259–90; XXIX (1943), pp. 3–39, 100–21, 163–78, 203–31. Formerly very influential articles, building a grand edifice (since largely demolished) on a narrow foundation.

— *The Spanish Armada* (London, 1960). Based on 'Armada Guns', and now almost completely outdated.

— *The Hawkins Dynasty: Three Generations of a Tudor Family* (London, 1969).

Liber Quotidianus Contrarotulatoris Garderobae... ed. J.Topham (London, 1787). Wardrobe accounts, 1299–1300.

Lindemann, Richard H. F., 'The English *Esnecca* in Northern European Sources', *MM* LXXIV (1988), pp. 75–82.

Lindsay, Alexander, *A Rutter of the Scottish Seas*, ed. A. B. Taylor, I. H. Adams & G. Fortune (NMM, 1980). The Franco-Scottish school of navigators and their part in the Anglo-Scottish wars of the 1540s.

Lloyd, Christopher, *English Corsairs on the Barbary Coast* (London, 1981). A good introduction to Mainwaring and his contemporaries.

Lloyd, Howell A., 'Corruption and Sir John Trevor', *Transactions of the Honourable Society of Cymmrodorion* 1974–5, pp. 77–102. One of Lord Nottingham's numerous Welsh relatives, so prominent in naval administration in James I's reign.

Lloyd, T. H., *England and the German Hanse, 1157–1611: A study of their trade and commercial diplomacy* (Cambridge, 1991).

Loades, David, *The Tudor Navy: An administrative, political and military history* (Aldershot, 1992). Now the standard authority.

—'The King's Ships and the Keeping of the Seas; 1413–1480', *Medieval History* I (1990), pp. 93–104.

Lockyer, Roger, *Buckingham: The Life and Political Career of George Villiers, First Duke of Buckingham 1592–1628* (London, 1981). With much on his activities as Lord Admiral.

Loeber, Rolf, & Geoffrey Parker, 'The Military Revolution in seventeenth-century Ireland', in *Ireland from Independence to Occupation 1641–1660*, ed. Jane H. Ohlmeyer (Cambridge, 1995), pp. 66–88. Some information on Irish privateers.

Loyn, H.R., *The Vikings in Britain* (London, 1977).

— *The Norman Conquest* (London, 3rd edn 1982).

— *The Governance of Anglo-Saxon England 500–1087* (London, 1984).

— 'Wales and England in the Tenth Century: The Context of the Athelstan Charters', *Welsh History Review* X (1981), pp. 183–301.

Lucas, A. T., 'Irish-Norse Relations: Time for a Reappraisal?', *Journal of the Cork Historical and Archaeological Society* LXXI (1966), pp. 62–75. Some information on Irish and Norse-Irish fleets.

Lund, Niels, 'The armies of Swein Forkbeard and Cnut: *leding* or *lið*?', *Anglo-Saxon England* XV (1986), pp. 105–18.

Lydon, James F., 'Ireland's Participation in the Military Activities of English Kings in the Thirteenth and Fourteenth Centuries' (London Ph.D. thesis, 1955). Excellent thesis on a then ignored subject.

— 'Edward I, Ireland and the War in Scotland, 1303–1304', in *England and Ireland in the later Middle Ages: Essays in Honour of Jocelyn Otway-Ruthven*, ed. Lydon (Dublin, 1981), pp. 43–61.

— 'Lordship and Crown: Llywelyn of Wales and O'Connor of Connacht', in Davies, *The British Isles*, pp. 48–63.

Lynn, John A., ed., *Feeding Mars: Logistics in Western Warfare from the Middle Ages to the Present* (Boulder, Colo., 1993).

Lyon, Mary, Bryce Lyon & Henry S. Lucas, eds., *The Wardrobe Book of William de Norwell, 12 July 1338 to 27 May 1340* (Brussels, 1983). Military and naval accounts, with an excellent essay on English military and naval administration.

MacCaffrey, Wallace T., *Queen Elizabeth and the Making of Policy, 1572–1588* (Princeton, 1981).

— *Elizabeth I, War and Politics 1588–1603* (Princeton, 1992). Standard detailed scholarly accounts, centred on domestic politics more than the war.

McCaughey, R., 'The English Navy, Politics and Administration, 1640–49' (Ulster D.Phil. thesis, 1983).

MacCormack, J. R., 'The Irish Adventurers and the English Civil War', *IHS* X (1956–7), pp. 21–58. Pym's attempt at a joint-stock war of colonization.

MacDougall, Norman, *James IV* (Edinburgh, 1989). The best modern life, with much attention to his ships.

— '"The greattest scheip that ewer saillit in Ingland or France": James IV's *Great Michael*', in *Scotland and War AD 79–1918* ed. MacDougall (Edinburgh, 1991), pp. 36–60.

McGowan, A. P., ed., *The Jacobean Commissions of Enquiry, 1608 and 1618* (NRS Vol.116, 1971). Detailed evidence of the state of naval administration.

— 'The Royal Navy under the First Duke of Buckingham, Lord High Admiral 1618–1628' (London Ph.D. thesis, 1967).

McGrail, Seán, ed., *Aspects of Maritime Archaeology and Ethnography* (NMM, 1984).

— ed., *The Archaeology of Medieval Ships and Harbours in Northern Europe* (British Archaeological Reports Int.Ser.66, Oxford, 1979).

— *Ancient boats in N.W. Europe: The archaeology of water transport to AD 1500* (London, 1987).

McGurk, J. J. N., 'A Levy of Seamen in the Cinque Ports, 1602', *MM* LXVI (1980), pp. 137–44.

MacInnes, John, 'West Highland Sea-Power in the Middle Ages', *Transactions of the Gaelic Society of Inverness* XLVIII (1972–4), pp. 518–56. One of the few studies of a grossly neglected subject.

McKisack, May, *The Fourteenth Century 1307–1399* (Oxford, 1959).

— *The Parliamentary Representation of the English Boroughs during the*

Middle Ages (London, 1932). Relevant to the relations of the seaports with the crown.

McMillan, A. R. G., 'The Admiral of Scotland', *SHR* XX (1923), pp. 11–18.

[Mainwaring, Sir Henry] *The Life and Works of Sir Henry Mainwaring* ed. G. E. Manwaring & W. G. Perrin (NRS Vols. 54 & 56, 1920–2). The great Jacobean pirate, admiral and lexicographer.

Manera Regueyra, Enrique, ed., *El buque en la Armada Española* (Madrid, 1981). Lavishly illustrated survey, with contributions by several leading scholars.

Manwaring, G. E., 'The Safeguard of the Sea, 1442', *MM* IX (1923), pp. 376–9. Prints the proposal of 1442 from the Parliament Rolls.

Marcus, G. J., 'The Evolution of the Knörr', *MM* XLI (1955), pp. 115–22. A Viking merchant-ship type, studied mainly from literary evidence.

Maritieme Geschiedenis der Nederlande:., ed. G. Asaert *et al.*, (Bussum, 1976–8, 4 vols). Excellent survey of the maritime history of the Low Countries.

Marsden, R. G., ed., *Select Pleas in the Court of Admiralty* (Selden Society, Vols.6 & 11, 1892–7). A legal historian and expert in Admiralty law.

— ed., *Documents relating to Law and Custom of the Sea* (NRS Vols.49 & 50, 1915–16).

— 'The Vice-Admirals of the Coast', *EHR* XXII (1907), pp. 468–77; and XXIII (1908), pp. 736–57.

— 'Early Prize Jurisdiction and Prize Law in England', *EHR* XXIV (1909), pp. 675–97.

— ed., 'Voyage of the *Barbara* to Brazil, Anno 1540', in Laughton, *Naval Miscellany II*, pp. 3–66.

Martin, Colin, *Full Fathom Five: Wrecks of the Spanish Armada* (New York, 1975). Underwater archaeology on Armada wrecks.

— 'The Ships of the Spanish Armada', in Gallagher & Cruikshank, *God's Obvious Design*, pp. 41–68.

— 'A 16th century siege train: the battery ordnance of the 1588 Spanish Armada', *IJNA* XVII (1988), pp. 57–73.

— & Geoffrey Parker, *The Spanish Armada* (London, 1988). The best modern history of the 1588 campaign.

Martin, Paula, *Spanish Armada Prisoners: The Story of the Nuestra Señora del Rosario and her crew, and of other prisoners in England 1587–97* (Exeter, 1988).

Martínez Valverde, Carlos, 'La note marinera en la Cronica de Don Pero Niño', *RHN* III (1985) No.8, pp. 15–43. Chivalrous romance at sea.

Marwick, Hugh, 'Naval Defence in Norse Scotland', *SHR* XXVIII (1949), pp. 1–11.

Mas Latrie, René de, 'Du droit de marque ou droit de représailles au moyen âge', *Bibliothèque de l'École des Chartes* XXVII (1866), pp. 529–77, and XXIX (1868), pp. 294–347, 612–35. The medieval law of reprisals.

Masson, Philippe, & Michel Vergé-Franceschi, eds., *La France et la mer au siècle des grands découvertes* (Paris, 1993).

Mathew, David, 'The Cornish and Welsh Pirates in the Reign of Elizabeth', *EHR* XXXIX (1924). pp. 337–48.

Mattingly, Garrett, *The Defeat of the Spanish Armada* (London, 1959). A brilliant evocation of the diplomatic world, outdated in part but still fine reading. The short section on the defeat of the Spanish Armada was always best omitted.

Maund, K. L., *Ireland, Wales and England in the Eleventh Century* (Woodbridge, 1991).

Maunsell, C. A., & E. P. Statham, *History of the Family of Maunsell...* (London, 1917, 2 vols in 3). Prints many documents about Sir Robert.

Maura Gamazo, Gabriel, Duque de Maura, *El Designio de Felipe II y el episodio de la Armada Invencible* (Madrid, 1957). Based on hitherto unprinted documents in the Medina Sidonia archive.

Mayhew, Graham J., 'Rye and the Defence of the Narrow Seas: A 16th-Century Town at War', *Sussex Archaeological Collections* CXXII (1984), pp. 107–26.

Meehan, M. E., 'English Piracy 1450–1500' (Bristol M.Litt. thesis, 1971).

Merino, José P., 'Graving Docks in France and Spain before 1800', *MM* LXXI (1985), pp. 35–58.

Merlin-Chazelas [Chazelas in Vol.I], Anne, ed., *Documents relatifs au Clos des Galées à Rouen, et aux armées de mer du Roi de France de 1293 à 1418* (Paris, Bibliothèque Nationale, 1977–78, 2 vols).

Metcalf, D. M., 'Large Danegelds in relation to War and Kingship. Their Implications for Monetary History, and Some Numismatic Evidence', in Hawkes, *Weapons and Warfare in Anglo-Saxon England*, pp. 179–89.

Milford, Elizabeth, 'The Navy at Peace. The Activities of the early Jacobean Navy, 1603–1618', *MM* LXXVI (1990), pp. 23–36.

Milne, Gustav, & Brian Hobley, eds., *Waterfront Archaeology in Britain and Northern Europe* (London, 1981).

Mirot, Leon, 'Une tentative d'invasion en Angleterre pendant la Guerre de Cent Ans', *Revue des Etudes Historiques* LXXXI (1915), pp. 249–87, 417–66. The 1385–6 project.

Mollat [du Jourdin], Michel, *Le commerce maritime normand à la fin du Moyen Age* (Paris, 1952).

— 'The French Maritime Community: A Slow Progress up the Social Scale from the Middle Ages to the Sixteenth Century' *MM* LXIX (1983), pp. 115–28.

— *La vie quotidienne des gens de mer en Atlantique (IXe–XVIe siècle)* (Paris, 1983).

— 'Les marines et la guerre sur mer dans le nord et l'ouest de l'Europe (jusqu'au XIIe siècle)', in *Ordinamenti Militari in Occidente nell'alto Medievo* (Spoleto, 1968), pp. 1009–42.

— 'L'État Capétien en quète d'une force navale', in *Histoire Militaire de la France I, Des origines à 1715* ed. Philippe Contamine (Paris, 1992), pp. 107–23.

— 'Les enjeux maritimes de la Guerre de Cent Ans', in Contamine, *Histoire Militaire de la France I*, pp. 153–69.

— '"Être roi sur la mer": Naissance d'une ambition', in *ibid.*, pp. 279–301.

[Monson, Sir William] *The Naval Tracts of Sir William Monson*, ed. M. Oppenheim (NRS Vols.22–3, 43, 45, 47, 1902–14). Voluminous writings of a late Elizabethan admiral, marked throughout by a shrewd understanding and a very bad memory. Oppenheim's editorial matter provides the most detailed history of the naval war yet attempted.

Moore, Alan, 'Rigging in the Seventeenth Century', *MM* II (1912), pp. 267–74, III (1913), pp. 7–13 and IV (1914), pp. 260–5.

— 'Accounts and Inventories of John Starlyng, Clerk of the King's Ships to Henry IV', *MM* IV (1914), pp. 20–6, 167–73.

— 'A Barge of Edward III', *MM* VI (1920), pp. 229–42. This is the *Paul* of 1373.

— 'The Sea Scene from the Complaynt of Scotlande', in *Naval Miscellany II*, ed. Laughton, pp. 67–84. A Scottish ship of 1549.

Morcken, Roald, *Langskip, knarr og kogge: nye synspunkter på sagatidens skipsbygging i Norge og Nordeuropa* (Bergen, 1980). The nearest thing we have to a modern overall study of Viking ships.

Morillo, Stephen, *Warfare under the Anglo-Norman Kings, 1066–1135* (Woodbridge, 1994).

Morineau, Michel, *Incroyables gazettes et fabuleux métaux: les retours des trésors américains d'après les gazettes hollandaises (XVIe–XVIIIe siècles)* (Paris & Cambridge, 1985). An exciting book, of much wider import than the title suggests.

Morris, John E., *The Welsh Wars of Edward I* (Oxford, 1901).

Morrison, John, ed., *The Age of the Galley: Mediterranean Oared Vessels since pre-classical Times* (London, 1995).

Mott, Lawrence V., 'Ships of the 13th-century Catalan Navy', *IJNA* XIX (1990), pp. 101–12.

Murray, K. M. E., *The Constitutional History of the Cinque Ports* (Manchester, 1935).

Murray, Sir Oswyn A. R., 'The Admiralty', *MM* XXIII (1937), pp. 13–35, 129–47, 316–31, XXIV (1938), pp. 101–4, 204–25, 329–52, 458–78, XXV (1939), pp. 89–111, 216–28. An unfinished history of the Admiralty by one of its greatest Secretaries.

Musset, Lucien, 'Problèmes militaires du monde scandinave (VIIe–XIIe siècles)', in *Ordinamenti Militari in Occidente nell'alto Medievo* (Spoleto, 1968), pp. 229–91.

— 'Un empire à cheval sur le mer: les périls de mer dans l'Etat anglo-Normand d'après les chartes, les chroniques et les miracles', in 'Les hommes et la mer dans l'Europe du Nord-Ouest de l'Antiquité à nos jours', ed. Alain Lottin, Jean-Claude Hocquet & Stéphane Lebecq (*Revue du Nord* extra number, 1986) pp. 413–24.

Naish, G. P. B., ed., 'Documents Illustrating the History of the Spanish Armada', in *The Naval Miscellany IV*, ed. Christopher Lloyd (NRS Vol.92, 1952), pp. 1–84. Some Spanish documents in the NMM. The translations are not altogether trustworthy, and the editor was unaware that most of the documents were already in print.

Nance, R. Morton, 'The Ship of the Renaissance', *MM* XLI (1955), pp. 180–92, 281–98.

Napier, A. S., & W. H. Stevenson, eds., *The Crawford Collection of Early Charters and Documents now in the Bodleian Library* (Oxford, 1895). Important Anglo-Saxon documents.

Neumann, J., 'Hydrographic and Ship-Hydrodynamic Aspects of the Norman Invasion, A.D. 1066', *ANS* XI (1989), pp. 221–43.

Newhall, R. A., *The English Conquest of Normandy 1416–1424: A Study in Fifteenth Century Warfare* (New Haven & London, 1924).

Nicholas, Donald, *Mr Secretary Nicholas (1593–1669), His Life and Letters* (London, 1955). Buckingham's secretary, then Secretary of the 1618 Admiralty Board.

Nicholson, Ranald, *Edward III and the Scots: The Formative Years of a Military Career 1327–1335* (London, 1965).

— *Scotland: The later Middle Ages* (Edinburgh, 1974).

Nicolas, Sir Nicholas Harris, *A History of the Royal Navy from the earliest Times to the Wars of the French Revolution* (London, 1847, 2 vols). A great work of pioneering research, still extremely useful. It was completed only to 1422 at the author's death.

Nolan, John S., 'English Operations around Brest, 1594', *MM* LXXXI (1995), pp. 259–74.

Novak, Viktor, 'Učešće Dubrovačke Flote u Španskoj Nepobedivoj Armadi', *Zgodovinski Časopis* VI–VII (1952–3), pp. 604–11. Extravagant claims for Ragusa's share in the Spanish Armada.

Nuttall, Zelia, ed., *New Light on Drake: A Collection of Documents relating to his Voyage of Circumnavigation 1577–1580* (HS 2nd S. Vol.34, 1914). The originals of most of these are now printed by *BMO.*

O'Brien, P. K., & P. A. Hunt, 'The Rise of a Fiscal State in Britain, 1485–1815', *HR* LXVI (1993), pp. 129–76. An article of fundamental importance.

O'Donnell, Hugo, Duque de Estrada, *et al.*, *Los sucesos de Flandes de 1588 en relación con la empresa de Inglaterra* (Madrid, 1988). Parma's campaign and Philip II's plan. See also his 'The Army of Flanders and the Invasion of England 1586–8', in Rodríguez-Salgado & Adams, *England, Spain and the Gran Armada*, pp. 216–35.

— 'The Requirements of the Duke of Parma for the Conquest of England', in Gallagher & Cruikshank, *God's Obvious Design*, pp. 85–99.

Ohlmeyer, Jane H., *Civil War and Restoration in the three Stuart Kingdoms: The Career of Randal MacDonnell, Marquis of Antrim, 1609–1683* (Cambridge, 1993).

— 'Irish Privateers during the Civil War, 1642–50', *MM* LXXVI (1990), pp. 119–31.

— '"The Dunkirk of Ireland": Wexford Privateers during the 1640s', *Journal of the Wexford Historical Society* 12 (1988–9), pp. 23–48.

Olesa Muñido, Francisco-Felipe, *La organización naval de los estados Mediterráneos y en especial de España durante los siglos XVI y XVII* (Madrid, 1968, 2 vols).

— *La galera en la navigación y el combate* (Madrid, 1971, 2 vols). Detailed study of 16th-century Spanish galleys.

Oliveira, Fernando, *A arte da guerra do mar*, ed. Quirino da Fonseca & Botelho de Sousa (Lisbon, 1937, originally Coimbra, 1555). An important theorist as well as one who served in both French and English warships in the 1540s.

Olsen, Olaf, & Ole Crumlin-Pedersen, 'The Skuldelev Ships (II). A Report of the Final Underwater Excavation in 1959 and the Salvaging Operation in 1962', *Acta Archaeologica* [Copenhagen] XXXVIII (1967), pp. 73–174. One of the earliest and still most important pieces of underwater archaeology.

O'Neill, Timothy, *Merchants and Mariners in Medieval Ireland* (Dublin, 1987).

Oppenheim, M., *A History of the Administration of the Royal Navy and of Merchant Shipping in relation to the Navy . . . 1509 to 1660...* (London, 1896). A work of fundamental importance. It is still used so heavily that it is worth pointing out its two chief defects: Oppenheim was extremely prejudiced against royal government and all its works; and his references, quotations and figures are very untrustworthy.

— ed., *Naval Accounts and Inventories of the Reign of Henry VII, 1485–8 and 1495–7* (NRS Vol.8, 1896).

— 'Maritime History'. Oppenheim contributed chapters under this title to the *Victoria County Histories* of Suffolk, Essex, Kent, Sussex, Dorset, Somerset and Cornwall. Another originally written for the *VCH* was eventually published as *The Maritime History of Devon*, ed. W. Minchinton (Exeter, 1968).

Padfield, Peter, *Guns at Sea* (London, 1973). A general history, not overloaded with scholarship.

Parker, Geoffrey, *The Army of Flanders and the Spanish Road 1567–1659* (Cambridge, 1972). A classic study of Spain's army in Flanders and its lines of communication.

— *The Dutch Revolt* (London, 1977).

— *The Military Revolution: Military Innovation and the Rise of the West, 1500–1800* (Cambridge, 1988). Cf. his 'Europe and the wider world, 1500–1750: the military balance', in Tracy, *Political Economy of Merchant Empires*, pp. 161–95.

— 'If the Armada had landed', *History* LXI (1976), pp. 358–68.

— 'The *Dreadnought* Revolution of Tudor England', *MM* LXXXII (1996), pp. 269–300.

Paviot, Jacques, *La politique navale des ducs de Bourgogne, 1384–1482* (Lille, 1995).

Peck, Linda Levy, *Northampton: Patronage and Policy at the Court of James I* (London, 1982). See also her 'Problems in Jacobean Administration: Was Henry Howard, Earl of Northampton, a Reformer', *HJ* XIX (1976), pp. 831–58.

— *Court Patronage and Corruption in early Stuart England* (London, 1991). Has a weak chapter on naval administration.

Penn, C. D., *The Navy under the Early Stuarts* (2nd edn Portsmouth & London, 1920). Still one of the few published works on the period, though quite superseded by various unpublished theses.

Penn, Granville, *Memorials of the Professional Life and Times of Sir William Penn...* (London, 1833, 2 vols). Prints Penn's papers.

Pérez Embid, Florentino, 'La Marina Real Castellana en el siglo XIII', in *Estudios de Historia Marítima* ed. Francisco Morales Padrón (Seville, 1979), pp. 71–127.

Pérez-Mallaína Bueno, Pablo Emilio, & Bibiano Torres Ramírez, *La Armada del Mar del Sur* (Seville, 1987). The Spanish Pacific squadron.

Perrin, W. G., 'The Lord Admiral and the Board of Admiralty', *MM* XII (1926), pp. 117–44.

Petrie, Sir Charles, 'The Hispano-Papal Landing at Smerwick', *Irish Sword* IX (1969–70), pp. 82–94.

Pett, Phineas, *The Autobiography of Phineas Pett*, ed. W. G. Perrin (NRS Vol.51, 1918).

Phillips, Carla Rahn, *Six Galleons for the King of Spain: Imperial Defense in the Seventeenth Century* (Baltimore, 1986). Elegant study of Spanish naval efforts.

— 'The Caravel and the Galleon', in Unger, *Cogs, Caravels and Galleons*, pp. 91–114.

— *Los Tres Reyes: The Short Life of an Unlucky Spanish Galleon* (Minneapolis, 1990).

Pi Corrales, Magdalena de Pazzis, *La Otra Invencible, 1574: España y las potencias nórdicas* (Madrid, 1983). Menéndez's abortive 1574 expedition to Flanders.

— *Felipe II y la Lucha por el Dominio del Mar* (Madrid, 1989). Philip II's wars at sea.

Pierson, Peter, *Commander of the Armada: The Seventh Duke of Medina Sidonia* (New Haven, 1989). A learned but colourless life of the least charismatic of Spanish commanders.

— 'A Commander for the Armada', *MM* LV (1969), pp. 383–400.

Pistono, Stephen P., 'Henry IV and the English Privateers', *EHR* XC (1975), pp. 322–30.

— 'Henry IV and John Hawley, Privateer, 1399–1408', *TDA* CXI (1979), pp. 145–63.

Platt, Colin, *Medieval Southampton, The port and trading community, A.D. 1000–1600* (London, 1973).

Plummer, Charles, & John Earle, eds., *Two of the Saxon Chronicles Parallel* (Oxford, 1892–99, 2 vols). Still the only more-or-less complete edition of the Anglo-Saxon Chronicle, but in process of being superseded.

Pollentier, F., *De Admiraliteit en de oorlog ter zee onder de Aartshertogen (1596–1609)* (Brussels, 1972). The Spanish Flanders squadron and privateers.

Pollitt, Ronald L., 'The Elizabethan Navy Board: A Study in Administrative Evolution' (Northwestern Ph.D. thesis, 1968). Thorough, if somewhat uncritical.

— 'Bureaucracy and the Armada: the Administrator's Battle', *MM* LX (1974), pp. 119–32.

— 'Rationality and Expedience in the Growth of Elizabethan Naval

Administration', in *Changing Interpretations and New Sources in Naval History*, ed. R. W. Love (New York, 1980), pp. 68–79.

— 'Contingency Planning and the Defeat of the Spanish Armada', *AN* XLIV (1984), pp. 25–32.

— 'The Spanish Armada and the Mobilization of English Resources, 1570–85', in *New Interpretations in Naval History: Selected Papers from the Eighth Naval History Symposium*, ed. William B. Cogar (Annapolis, MD, 1989), pp. 14–27.

— 'Devon in the French and Spanish Wars', in Duffy, *New Maritime History of Devon* I, 108–14.

Powell, Isabel G., 'The early Naval Lieutenant', *MM* IX (1923), pp. 358–65.

— '"Shipkeepers" and Minor Officers serving at Sea in the Early Stuart Navy', *MM* X (1924), pp. 156–72.

Powell, J. R., *The Navy in the English Civil War* (London, 1962). The only proper book on the subject.

— *Robert Blake, General-at-Sea* (London, 1972).

— 'Blake and the Defence of Lyme Regis', *MM* XX (1934), pp. 448–74.

— 'Penn's Expedition to Bonratty in 1646', *MM* XL (1954), pp. 4–20.

— 'Operations of the Parliamentary Squadron at the Siege of Duncannon, 1645', *Irish Sword* II (1954–6), pp. 17–21.

— 'Penn's Attempt to relieve Youghal, 1645', *Irish Sword* II (1954–6), pp. 83–7.

— 'The Siege of the Downs Castles in 1648', *MM* LI (1965), pp. 155–71.

— & E. K. Timings, eds., *Documents relating to the Civil War, 1642–1648* (NRS Vol.105, 1963). Essential documents, not well transcribed or edited.

Powell, J. W. D., *Bristol Privateers and Ships of War* (Bristol, 1930).

Powell, W. R., 'The Administration of the Navy and the Stannaries, 1189–1216', *EHR* LXXI (1956), pp. 177–88.

Powicke, Sir Maurice, *The Thirteenth Century, 1216–1307* (Oxford, 1953).

Prestwich, J. O., 'War and Finance in the Anglo-Norman State', *TRHS* 5th Ser. IV (1954), pp. 19–44.

Prestwich, Menna, *Cranfield, Politics and Profits under the Early Stuarts: The Career of Lionel Cranfield, Earl of Middlesex* (Oxford, 1966).

Prestwich, Michael, *War, Politics and Finance under Edward I* (London, 1972).

— *The Three Edwards: War and State in England 1272–1377* (London, 1980).

— *Edward I* (London, 1988).

— ed., *Documents illustrating the Crisis of 1297–98 in England* (CS 4th S. XXIV, 1980).

Prince, Albert E., 'The Army and Navy', in *The English Government at Work,*

1327–1336: Vol.I, Central and Prerogative Administration. ed. James F. Willard & W. A. Morris (Cambridge, Mass., 1940), pp. 332–93.

Probst, Niels, 'Nordeuropæisk spanteopslagning i 1500- og 1600-tallet. Belyst ud fra danske kilder', *Maritim Kontakt* XVI (1993), pp. 7–42. An important article on shipbuilding techniques.

Prynne, M. W., 'Henry V's *Grace Dieu*', *MM* LIV (1968), pp. 115–28.

Pryor, John H., *Geography, Technology and War: Studies in the Maritime History of the Mediterranean 649–1571* (Cambridge, 1988).

— 'Transportation of horses by sea during the era of the Crusades: eighth century to 1285 A.D.', *MM* LXVIII (1982), pp. 9–27, 103–25.

— 'The Naval battles of Roger of Lauria', *Journal of Medieval History* IX (1983), pp. 179–216.

— 'The Mediterranean Round Ship', in Unger, *Cogs, Caravels and Galleons*, pp. 59–76.

Purchas, Samuel, *Hakluytus Posthumus, or Purchas his Pilgrimes* (London, 1625, as printed Glasgow, 1905–07, 20 vols). Hakluyt's continuator.

Quinn, David B., & A. N. Ryan, *England's Sea Empire, 1550–1642* (London, 1983). Excellent introduction to the maritime history of the period.

Quintrell, Brian, 'Charles I and his Navy in the 1630s', *The Seventeenth Century* III (1988), pp. 159–79.

Randsborg, Klavs, *The Viking Age in Denmark: The Formation of a State* (London, 1980).

Rat, Jean-Michel, 'L'éveil de la marine dans l'Angleterre du haut-moyen-âge (du 7ème siècle au 11ème siècle)' (Sorbonne-Paris IV doctoral thesis, 1995). Disappointing.

Read, Conyers, *Mr Secretary Walsingham and the policy of Queen Elizabeth* (Oxford, 1925, 3 vols).

Rebholz, Ronald A., *The Life of Fulke Greville, First Lord Brooke* (Oxford, 1971). Courtier, poet and Treasurer of the Navy.

Reid, W. Stanford, 'Sea-Power in the Anglo-Scottish War, 1296–1328', *MM* XLVI (1960), pp. 7–23.

Riaño Lozano, Fernando, *Los medios navales de Alejandro Farnesio (1587–1588)* (Madrid, 1989). The Duke of Parma's ships.

Ribas Bensusan, Jesús, *Asaltos a Cádiz por los ingleses siglos XVI, XVII y XVIII* (Cadiz, 1974). A competent summary; prints some documents.

Richmond, C. F., 'Royal Administration and the Keeping of the Seas, 1422–1485' (Oxford D.Phil. thesis, 1962). Scholarly and indispensable.

— 'The War at Sea', in Fowler, *The Hundred Years War*, pp. 96–121.

— 'The Keeping of the Seas during the Hundred Years War: 1422–1440', *History* NS XLIX (1964), pp. 283–98.

—'English Naval Power in the Fifteenth Century', *History* NS LII (1967), pp. 1–15.

Richon, Louis, 'Le navire de la cathédrale de Bayonne', *Neptunia* 157 (1985), pp. 37–41. A carving of a cog.

Rieth, Eric, 'La question de la construction navale à franc-bord au Ponant', *Neptunia* 160 (1985) pp. 8–21. The spread of carvel building.

Riis, Thomas, *Should Auld Acquaintance be Forgot . . . Scottish Danish Relations c.1450–1707* (Odense, 1988, 2 vols).

Roberts, Owain, 'Viking Sailing Performance' in McGrail, *Maritime Archaeology and Ethnography*, pp. 123–51.

— 'Descendants of Viking Boats', in Unger, *Cogs, Caravels and Galleons*, pp. 11–28.

Robertson, F. W., 'The Rise of a Scottish Navy, 1460–1513' (Edinburgh Ph.D. thesis, 1934).

Rodger, N. A. M., *The Admiralty* (Lavenham, Suffolk, 1979). A sketchy history.

— 'Elizabethan Naval Gunnery', *MM* LXI (1975), pp. 353–4. Ammunition allowances.

— 'Cnut's Geld and the Size of Danish Ships', *EHR* CX (1995), pp. 392–403.

— 'The Naval Service of the Cinque Ports', *EHR* CXI (1996), pp. 636–51.

— 'The Development of Broadside Gunnery, 1450–1650', *MM* LXXXII (1996), pp. 301–24.

— 'Guns and Sails in the first Phase of English Colonization, 1500–1650', in *The Oxford History of the British Empire* Vol.I, ed. Nicholas Canny (forthcoming).

Rodgers, W. L., *Naval Warfare under Oars, 4th to 16th Centuries: A Study of Strategy, Tactics and Ship Design* (Annapolis, MD,1940). Not entirely out of date.

Rodríguez-Salgado, M. J., *et al.*, *Armada 1588–1988: An International Exhibition to Commemorate the Spanish Armada* (London, 1988).

— 'The Anglo-Spanish War: the final episode in the "Wars of the Roses"?', in Rodríguez-Salgado & Adams, *England, Spain and the Gran Armada*, pp. 1–44.

— 'Pilots, Navigation and Strategy in the *Gran Armada*', in *ibid.*, pp. 134–72.

— & Simon Adams, eds., *England, Spain and the Gran Armada 1585–1604* (Edinburgh, 1991). Important collection of articles.

Roesdahl, Else, *Viking Age Denmark* (London, 1982).

Rose, Susan, *The Navy of the Lancastrian Kings: Accounts and Inventories of*

William Soper, Keeper of the King's Ships, 1422–1427 (NRS Vol.123, 1982).

— 'Henry V's *Grace Dieu* and Mutiny at Sea: Some New Evidence', *MM* LXIII (1977), pp. 3–6.

Ross, Charles, *Edward IV* (London, 1974).

Rotuli Litterarum Clausarum..., ed. Thomas Duffus Hardy (London, 1833–44, 2 vols). The earliest Close Rolls.

Rotuli Litterarum Patentium..., ed. Thomas Duffus Hardy (London, 1835). The earliest Patent Rolls.

Rotuli Normanniae..., ed. Thomas Duffus Hardy (London, 1835). Records of the government of Normandy in the reigns of Richard I, John and Henry V.

Rotuli Parliamentorum... (London, 1783, 6 vols). Surviving proceedings of the English Parliament to 1504.

Rotuli Scotiae... [ed. D. Macpherson *et al.*] (London, 1814–19, 2 vols). English government records concerning the Scottish wars.

Rotz, Jean, *The Boke of Idrography*, ed. Helen Wallis (Oxford, Roxburghe Club, 1981). Otherwise John Ross, one of the leaders of the Franco-Scottish school of navigators.

Rowe, Violet A., *Sir Henry Vane the Younger: A Study in Political and Administrative History* (London, 1970). A dominant figure in Parliamentary naval administration.

Rowse, A. L., *Sir Richard Grenville of the Revenge: An Elizabethan Hero* (London, 1937).

Rule, Margaret, *The Mary Rose: The Excavation and Raising of Henry VIII's Flagship* (London, 1982). Written before the ship was raised, this popular book is still almost all that has been published on her. The 2nd edition, 1983, has a note dated six weeks after the recovery of the ship and an extra chapter on the salvage, but is otherwise unaltered.

— & C. T. C. Dobbs, 'The Tudor Warship Mary Rose: aspects of recent research', in Bound, *Archaeology of Ships of War*, I, 26–9.

Rumble, Alexander R., ed., *The Reign of Cnut: King of England, Denmark and Norway* (Leicester, 1994).

Runyan, Timothy J., 'Ships and Mariners in Later Medieval England', *Journal of British Studies* XVI (1977), pp. 1–17.

— 'Merchantmen to Men-of-War in Medieval England', in *New Aspects of Naval History*, ed. Craig L. Symonds (Annapolis, Md., 1981), pp. 33–40.

— 'Ships and Fleets in Anglo-French Warfare, 1337–1360', *AN* XLVI (1986), pp. 91–9.

— 'The Organization of Royal Fleets in Medieval England', in *Ships,*

Seafaring and Society: Essays in Maritime History, ed. Runyan (Detroit, 1987), pp. 37–52.

— 'Naval Logistics in the Late Middle Ages: The Example of the Hundred Years' War', in Lynn, *Feeding Mars*, pp. 79–100.

— 'The Cog as Warship', in Unger, *Cogs, Caravels and Galleons*, pp. 47–58. Though based on documentary research, these articles are flawed by alarming errors and need to be used with caution.

Russell, Conrad, *Parliaments and English Politics 1621–1629* (Oxford, 1979).

— 'Monarchies, Wars and Estates in England, France and Spain, c.1580–c.1640', *Legislative Studies Quarterly* VII (1982), pp. 205–20,

— *The Fall of the British Monarchies 1637–1642* (Oxford, 1991).

Rymer, Thomas, ed., *Foedera, conventiones, litterae, et cujuscunque generis acta publica*... The great and irreplaceable collection of diplomatic and official documents. My references are either to the original edition (London, 1704–35, 20 vols), or to the better but unfinished Record Commission edition (London, 1816–69, 4 vols in 7).

Salisbury, W., 'A Draught of a Jacobean Three Decker. The *Prince Royal*?', *MM* XLVII (1961), pp. 170–7.

— 'The Woolwich Ship', *MM* XLVII (1961), pp. 81–90. Remains of what was possibly the *Sovereign* of 1488.

Sandahl, Bertil, *Middle English Sea Terms* (Uppsala, 1951–82, 3 vols to date). Indispensable for the study of medieval ships; prints many documents.

Saul, A., 'Great Yarmouth and the Hundred Years War in the fourteenth century', *BIHR* LII (1979), pp. 105–15.

Saunders, Andrew, *Fortress Britain: Artillery Fortifications in the British Isles and Ireland* (Liphook, 1989).

Sawyer, P. H., *Kings and Vikings: Scandinavia and Europe AD 700–1100* (London, 1982).

Scammell, G. V., *The World Encompassed: The First European Maritime Empires, c.800–1650* (London, 1981). A vivid introduction, full of learned enthusiasm.

— *The First Imperial Age: European Overseas Expansion c.1400–1715* (London, 1989).

— *The Engish Chartered Trading Companies and the Sea* (National Maritime Museum, n.d. [1983]).

— 'War at Sea under the Early Tudors: some Newcastle upon Tyne Evidence', *Archaeologia Aeliana* 4th S. XXXVIII (1960), pp. 73–97, and XXXIX (1961), pp. 179–205. Important for the English wars against Scotland under Henry VIII.

— 'English Merchant Shipping at the End of the Middle Ages: Some East Coast Evidence', *EcHR* 2nd S. XIII (1961), pp. 327–41.

— 'Shipowning in England *circa* 1450–1550', *TRHS* 5th S. XII (1962), pp. 105–22.

— 'Manning the English Merchant Service in the Sixteenth Century', *MM* LVI (1970), pp. 131–54.

— 'Shipowning in the Economy and Politics of Early Modern England', *HJ* XV (1972), pp. 385–407.

— 'European Seamanship in the Great Age of Discovery', *MM* LXVIII (1982), pp. 357–76.

— 'The English in the Atlantic Islands c.1450–1650', *MM* LXXII (1986), pp. 295–317.

— 'The Sinews of War: Manning and Provisioning English Fighting Ships c.1550–1650', *MM* LXXIII (1987), pp. 351–67. Important for the social history of English seamen.

Schnepper, Heinrich, *Die Namen der Schiffe und Schiffsteile im Altenglischen* (Kiel, 1908). Useful etymological study.

Schubert, H. R., *History of the British Iron and Steel Industry from c.450 B.C. to A.D. 1775* (London, 1957).

Scofield, Cora L., *The Life and Reign of Edward IV* (London, 1923, 2 vols).

Scott, Walter F., 'The Naval Chaplain in Stuart Times' (Oxford D.Phil. thesis, 1935).

Scragg, Donald, ed., *The Battle of Maldon, AD 991* (Oxford, 1991).

Senior, C. M., *A Nation of Pirates: English Piracy in its Heyday* (Newton Abbot, 1976). The early 17th century.

Senior, William, *Naval History in the Law Courts* (London, 1927).

Sharpe, Kevin, *The Personal Rule of Charles I* (London, 1992).

Sherborne, J. W., 'Indentured Retinues and English Expeditions to France, 1369–1380', *EHR* LXXIX (1964), pp. 718–46.

— 'The Battle of La Rochelle and the War at Sea. 1372–5', *BIHR* XLII (1969), pp. 17–29.

— 'The Hundred Years' War. The English Navy: Shipping and Manpower 1369–1389', *Past and Present* 37 (1967), pp. 163–75.

— 'The Cost of English Warfare with France in the later Fourteenth Century', *BIHR* L (1977), pp. 135–50.

— 'English Barges and Ballingers of the Late Fourteenth Century', *MM* LXIII (1977), pp. 109–14.

Shilton, Dorothy O., & Richard Holworthy, eds., *High Court of Admiralty Examinations 1637–1638* (London, 1932). Valuable for social history.

Silke, John J., *Kinsale: The Spanish Intervention in Ireland at the End of the Elizabethan Wars* (Liverpool, 1970). An excellent study using both Irish and Spanish sources.

Simek, Rudolf, *Die Schiffsnamen, Schiffsbezeichnungen und Schiffskenningar im Altnordischen* (Vienna, 1982). The etymology of ship-names in Old Norse, a subject of wider interest than one might expect.

Smith, John, *A Sea Grammar*, ed. Kermit Goell (London, 1970). An indifferent but accessible edition of Smith's dictionary, first published 1626.

Smith, Robert D., ed., *British Naval Armaments* (Royal Armouries, London, 1989).

— 'Artillery and the Hundred Years War: Myth and Interpretation', in Curry & Hughes, *Arms, Armies and Fortifications*, pp. 151–60.

— 'Wrought-iron swivel guns', in Bound, *Archaeology of Ships of War*, I, 104–13.

Smyth, Alfred P., *King Alfred the Great* (Oxford, 1995). Upsets many established views of the king.

Spate, O. H. K., *The Pacific since Magellan: I, The Spanish Lake* (London, 1979).

Spence, Richard T., *The Privateering Earl* (Stroud, 1995). A life of Cumberland.

Spont, Alfred, ed., *Letters and Papers relating to the War with France, 1512–1513* (NRS Vol.10, 1897).

Spufford, Peter, *Handbook of Medieval Exchange* (Royal Historical Society, 1986). An essential work of reference.

Stacey, Robert, *Politics, Policy and Finance under Henry III, 1216–1245* (Oxford, 1987).

Stafford, Pauline, *Unification and Conquest: A Political and Social History of England in the Tenth and Eleventh Centuries* (London, 1989).

Stansfield, Michael, 'John Holland, Duke of Exeter and Earl of Huntingdon (d.1447) and the Costs of the Hundred Years War', in *Profit, Piety and the Professions in Later Medieval England*, ed. Michael Hicks (Gloucester, 1990), pp. 103–18. Exeter was Admiral of England.

Stearns, Stephen J., 'The Caroline Military System, 1625–1627: The Expeditions to Cadiz and Ré' (California, Berkeley, Ph.D. thesis 1967). Mainly military in the narrow sense.

Steer, K. A., & J. W. M. Bannerman, *Late Medieval Monumental Sculpture in the West Highlands* (Edinburgh, 1977). An important source of evidence for the West Highland galley.

Steffy, J. Richard, *Wooden Ship Building and the Interpretation of Shipwrecks* (College Station, Texas, 1994). A technical handbook of nautical archaeology.

Stenton, F. M., *Anglo-Saxon England* (Oxford, 3rd edn 1971).

Stewart, Richard W., 'Arms and Expeditions: the Ordnance Office and the assaults on Cadiz (1625) and the Isle of Rhé (1627)', in Fissel, *War and Government*, pp. 112–32.

Stone, Lawrence, *The Crisis of the Aristocracy 1558–1641* (Oxford, 1965).

— 'State Control in Sixteenth-century England', *EcHR* XVII (1947), pp. 103–20.

Storey, R. L., *Chronology of the Medieval World, 800–1491* (London, 1973).

Strachan, Michael, *Sir Thomas Roe, 1581–1644: A Life* (Wilton, 1989).

Stradling, R. A., *Europe and the Decline of Spain: A Study of the Spanish System, 1580–1720* (London, 1981).

— *The Armada of Flanders: Spanish Maritime Policy and European War, 1568–1668* (Cambridge, 1992).

—'The Spanish Dunkirkers, 1621–48: a record of plunder and destruction', *Tijdschrift voor Geschiedenis* XCIII (1980), pp. 541–58.

Stubbs, William, ed., *Memorials of Saint Dunstan* (London, 1874).

Suárez Fernández, Luís, *Navigación y comercio en el Golfo de Vizcaya: un estudio sobre la politica marinera de la Casa de Trastámara* (Madrid, 1959). 14th-century Castilian seapower.

— 'The Atlantic and the Mediterranean among the Objectives of the House of Trastámara', in *Spain in the Fifteenth Century 1369–1516*, ed. Roger Highfield, trans. Frances M. López-Morillas (London, 1972), pp. 58–79.

Sugden, John, *Sir Francis Drake* (London, 1990). The latest biography.

Sumption, Jonathan, *The Hundred Years War: I, Trial by Battle* (London, 1990). A lively history, giving due attention to naval warfare.

Swales, R. J. W., 'The Ship Money Levy of 1628', *BIHR* L (1977), pp. 164–76.

Tanner, Ian, 'Henry VII's Expedition to France of 1492: A Study of its Financing, Organisation and Supply' (Keele MA thesis, 1988).

Taylor, E. G. R., ed., *The Troublesome Voyage of Captain Edward Fenton 1582–83* (HS 2nd S. Vol.113, 1959). An Elizabethan naval fiasco.

— 'More Light on Drake, 1577–80', *MM* XVI (1930), pp. 134–51. An interpretation (now generally rejected) of Drake's objectives in 1577.

Taylor, Gordon, *The Sea Chaplains: A History of the Chaplains of the Royal Navy* (Oxford, 1978).

Taylor, Pamela, 'The Endowment and Military Obligations of the See of London: A Reassessment of three Sources', *ANS* XIV (1991), pp. 287–312. Actually the Bishop's naval obligations in late Anglo-Saxon times.

Templeman, G., 'Two French Attempts to invade England during the Hundred Years' War', in *Studies in French Language Literature and History presented to R. L. Graeme Ritchie*, ed. J. J. Milne (Cambridge, 1949), pp. 225–38.

Tenenti, Alberto, *Piracy and the Decline of Venice, 1580–1615* (London, 1967; originally *Venezia e i corsari, 1580–1615*, Bari 1961). Much of this piracy was English.

Tenison, E. M., *Elizabethan England* (Leamington Spa, 1933–60, 12 vols in 14). A massive but undiscriminating collection of documents and illustrations, the latter in many cases little-known.

Terrier de Loray, Henri, Marquis, *Jean de Vienne, Amiral de France 1341–1396* (Paris, 1877). The only full life of one of France's greatest admirals; prints documents.

Thompson, I. A. A., *War and Government in Habsburg Spain 1560–1620* (London, 1976)

— 'The Armada and Administrative Reform: The Spanish Council of War in the Reign of Philip II', *EHR* LXXXII (1967), pp. 698–725.

— 'The Appointment of the Duke of Medina Sidonia to the Command of the Spanish Armada', *HJ* XII (1969), pp. 197–216.

— 'Spanish Armada Guns', *MM* LXI (1976), pp. 355–71.

— 'The Spanish Armada: Naval Warfare between the Mediterranean and the Atlantic', in Rodríguez-Salgado & Adams, *England, Spain and the Gran Armada*, pp. 70–94.

— 'Spanish Armada Gun Procurement and Policy', in Gallagher & Cruikshank, *God's Obvious Design*, pp. 69–84.

Thorpe, Benjamin, ed., *Chronicon ex Chronicis...* (London, 1848–49, 2 vols). The early 12th-century chronicle attributed to Florence of Worcester, drawing on a lost English original.

Thrush, A. D., 'The Navy under Charles I, 1625–40' (London Ph.D. thesis, 1991). Indispensable for this period.

— 'Naval Finance and the Origins and Development of Ship Money', in *War and Government in Britain*, ed. Fissel, pp. 133–62.

— 'The Ordnance Office and the Navy, 1625–40', *MM* LXXVII (1991), pp. 339–54.

— 'In Pursuit of the Frigate, 1603–40', *HR* LXIV (1991), pp. 29–45.

Tinniswood, J. T., 'English Galleys, 1272–1377', *MM* XXXV (1949), pp. 276–315.,

Tout, T. F., *Chapters in the Administrative History of Mediaeval England* (Manchester, 1920–33, 6 vols). Mainly about the Wardrobe, hence military and naval affairs.

— 'Firearms in England in the Fourteenth Century', *EHR* XXVI (1911), pp. 666–702.

Tracy, James D., ed., *The Political Economy of Merchant Empires* (Cambridge, 1991).

Treaty Rolls, ed. Pierre Chaplais *et al.* (London, 1955–72, 2 vols). Diplomatic documents, 1234–1339, many of them omitted by Rymer.

Turner, Barbara C., 'Southampton as a Naval Centre, 1414–1458', in *Collected Essays on Southampton*, ed. J. B. Morgan & Philip Peberdy (Southampton, 1958).

Turner, J. C. W. Carpenter, 'The Building of the *Gracedieu*, *Valentine* and *Falconer* at Southampton, 1416–1420', *MM* XL (1954), pp. 55–72.

— 'The Building of the *Holy Ghost* of the Tower, 1414–1416, and her subsequent History', *MM* XL (1954), pp. 270–81.

Twiss, Sir Travers, ed., *The Black Book of the Admiralty* (London, 1871–76, 4 vols). An important source of medieval legal texts on Admiralty law.

Ubaldini, Petruccio, *La Disfatta della Flotta Spagnola (1588): due 'commentari' inediti*, ed. Anna Maria Crinò (Florence, 1988). The Italian texts of two narratives of the Armada fight by the Florentine journalist; the first representing Howard's views (printed in English in *DSA*, I, 1–18), the second giving more prominence to Drake (printed in English by Naish, q.v.)

Unger, Richard W., *The Ship in the Mediaeval Economy, 600–1600* (London & Montreal, 1980). An excellent textbook.

— ed., *Cogs, Caravels and Galleons: The Sailing Ship 1000 to 1650* (London, 1994).

Usherwood, Stephen & Elizabeth, *The Counter-Armada, 1596: The Journal of the 'Mary Rose'* (London, 1983). Indifferent edition of an interesting narrative of the Cadiz expedition.

Vale, M. G. A., *English Gascony 1399–1453: A Study of War, Government and Politics during the Later Stages of the Hundred Years' War* (Oxford, 1970).

— *The Angevin Legacy and the Hundred Years War, 1250–1340* (Oxford, 1990).

— 'Edward I and the French: Rivalry and Chivalry', in *Thirteenth Century England II: Proceedings of the Newcastle upon Tyne Conference, 1987*, ed. P. R. Coss & S. D. Lloyd (Woodbridge, 1988), pp. 165–76.

Van Houts, Elisabeth M. C., 'The Ship List of William the Conqueror', *ANS* X (1987), pp. 159–83.

Van Oosten, F. C., & Ph. M. Bosscher, 'Het Taktisch Gebruik van het Zeilschip', *Marineblad* LXXX (1970), pp. 997–1035, and LXXXI (1971), pp. 863–889. A useful introduction.

Verbruggen, J. F., *The Art of Warfare in Western Europe during the Middle Ages, from the Eighth Century to 1340* (Amsterdam, 1977). Mainly war on land, as usual.

— *Het Leger en de Vloot van de Graven van Vlaanderen vanaf het ontstaan tot in 1305* (Brussels, 1960). The army and navy of the Counts of Flanders.

Villain-Gandossi, Christiane, *Le Navire Médiéval à Travers les Miniatures* (Paris, 1985). Pictorial evidence for medieval ship-design. See also her 'Illustrations of Ships: Iconography and Interpretation', in Unger, *Cogs, Caravels and Galleons*, pp. 169–74.

— Salvino Busuttil & Paul Adam, eds., *Medieval Ships and the Birth of Technological Societies: Vol.I: Northern Europe* (Malta, 1989).

Waley, D. P., '"Combined Operations" in Sicily, A.D. 1060–78', *Papers of the British School at Rome* XXII (1954), pp. 118–25.

Walker, J. A., 'John Holand, a fifteenth-century Admiral' *MM* LXV (1979), pp. 235–42.

Warner, Sir George, ed., *The Libelle of Englyshe Polycye: A Poem on the Use of Sea-Power, 1436* (Oxford, 1926). The best edition, though its interpretation needs to be corrected by Holmes, q.v.

— ed., *The Voyage of Robert Dudley . . . to the West Indies, 1594–1595* (HS 2nd S. III, 1909).

Waters, David W., *The Art of Navigation in England in Elizabethan and Early Stuart Times* (London, 1958). An essential work of great technical erudition.

— 'The Elizabethan Navy and the Armada of Spain', *MM* XXV (1949), pp. 90–138. A perceptive article, subsequently republished under the same title (NMM, 1975) with the addition of the Spanish documents edited by Naish, q.v.

Webb, John G., 'William Sabyn of Ipswich: An early Tudor Sea-Officer and Merchant', *MM* XLI (1955), pp. 209–21.

Weber, R. E. J., *De Beveiliging van de Zee tegen Europeesche en Barbarische Zeeroovers 1609–1621* (Amsterdam, 1936). Dutch efforts against pirates.

— *De Seinboken voor Nederlandse Oorlogsvloten en Konvoien tot 1690* (Amsterdam 1982). Burgundian, Flemish and Dutch signal books.

Weir, Michael, 'English Naval Activities, 1242–1243', *MM* LVIII (1972), pp. 85–92.

Wernham, R. B., *Before the Armada: The Growth of English Foreign Policy 1485–1588* (London, 1966).

— *After the Armada: Elizabethan England and the Struggle for Western Europe 1588–1595* (Oxford, 1984).

— *The Return of the Armadas: The Last Years of the Elizabethan War against Spain, 1595–1603* (Oxford, 1994). This trilogy gives much the best account of Elizabethan foreign policy and grand strategy.

— ed., *The Expedition of Sir John Norris and Sir Francis Drake to Spain and Portugal, 1589* (NRS Vol.127, 1988).

— 'Queen Elizabeth and the Portugal Expedition of 1589', *EHR* LXVI (1951), pp. 1–26, 194–218.

— 'Elizabethan War Aims and Strategy', in *Elizabethan Government and Society: Essays presented to Sir John Neale*, ed. S. T. Bindoff, J. Hurstfield & C. H. Williams (London, 1961), pp. 340–68.

Westerdahl, Christer, ed., *Crossroads in Ancient Shipbuilding: Proceedings of the Sixth International Symposium on Boat and Ship Archaeology, Roskilde 1991* (Oxford, 1994).

Whitelock, Dorothy, ed., *Anglo-Saxon Wills* (Cambridge, 1930).

— ed., with D. C. Douglas & S. I. Tucker, *The Anglo-Saxon Chronicle* (London, 1961). The best modern translation; also in *EHD* I–II.

Whitwell, R. J., & Charles Johnson, 'The "Newcastle" Galley', *Archaeologia Aeliana* 4th S. II (1926), pp. 142–96. One of the 1294 galley programme.

Williams, Neville, *Chronology of the Expanding World, 1492–1762* (London, 1969).

Williamson, G. C., *George, Third Earl of Cumberland (1558–1605): His Life and his Voyages* (Cambridge, 1920). Essentially a collection of documents with linking passages.

Williamson, James A., *Maritime Enterprise 1485–1558* (Oxford, 1913).

— *Hawkins of Plymouth* (London, 2nd edn 1969). A popular version of his earlier *Sir John Hawkins* (Oxford, 1927), revised to take account of new evidence.

— *The Age of Drake* (London, 3rd edn 1952).

— *The English Channel: A History* (London, 1959).

Wilson, Charles, *Profit and Power: A Study of England and the Dutch Wars* (London, 1957).

Windeatt, Edward, 'The Fitting Out of two Vessels against the Spanish Armada at Dartmouth in 1588', *TDA* XII (1880), pp. 312–21.

Winkel-Rauws, H., *Nederlansch-Engelsche Samenwerking in de Spaansche Wateren 1625–1627* (Amsterdam, 1946). The Anglo-Dutch co-operation was in fact fairly minimal.

Wren, Melvin C., 'London and the Twenty Ships, 1626–1627', *AHR* LV (1949–50), pp. 321–35.

Wright, Irene A., ed., *Documents concerning English Voyages to the Spanish Main 1569–1580* (HS 2nd S. Vol.71, 1932). Follows her *Spanish Documents concerning English Voyages to the Caribbean, 1527–1568* (HS 2nd S. Vol.62, 1928).

— *Further English Voyages to Spanish America 1583–1594* (HS 2nd S. Vol.99, 1951).

Wrottesley, Hon. George, *Crecy and Calais from the Original Records in the*

Public Record Office (London, 1898, reprinted from the *Proceedings of the William Salt Archaeological Society*).

Young, Alan R., 'The Emblematic Decoration of Queen Elizabeth's Warship the *White Bear*', *Emblematica* III (1988), pp. 65–77.

— *His Majesty's Royal Ship: A Critical Edition of Thomas Heywood's A True Description of His Majesties Royall Ship* (New York, 1990). The *Sovereign of the Seas.*

Young, Michael B., *Servility and Service: The Life and Work of Sir John Coke* (Woodbridge, 1986).

— 'Buckingham, War, and Parliament: Revisionism gone too far', *Parliamentary History* IV (1985), pp. 45–69.

INDEX

Dates following ship names are usually those of construction, but when not known they show when the ship was active

THE Famous West Indian voyadge made
by the Englishe fleete of 23 shippes and Barkes
wherin weare gotten the Townes of S. IAGO :
: S. DOMINGO, CARTAGENA and
: S. AVGVSTINES the same beinge begon
from Plimmouth in the Moneth of September
1585 and ended at Portesmouth in Julie
1586 the whole course of the saide Viadge
beinge plainlie described by the pricked line
Newlie come forth
Norumbega
Virginia
Hispaniola
S. Iohns
WEST INDIA
The Ocean commonlie called the South Sea
The Contrye of Peru
Sea Canny
North
East